The Palgrave Handbook of African Colonial and Postcolonial History

Martin S. Shanguhyia · Toyin Falola
Editors

The Palgrave Handbook of African Colonial and Postcolonial History

Volume 1

palgrave
macmillan

Editors
Martin S. Shanguhyia
History Department, Maxwell School of
  Citizenship and Public Affairs
Syracuse University
Syracuse, NY, USA

Toyin Falola
University of Texas at Austin
Austin, TX, USA

ISBN 978-1-137-59425-9   ISBN 978-1-137-59426-6 (eBook)
https://doi.org/10.1057/978-1-137-59426-6

Library of Congress Control Number: 2017950403

© The Editor(s) (if applicable) and The Author(s) 2018
This work is subject to copyright. All rights are solely and exclusively licensed by the Publisher, whether the whole or part of the material is concerned, specifically the rights of translation, reprinting, reuse of illustrations, recitation, broadcasting, reproduction on microfilms or in any other physical way, and transmission or information storage and retrieval, electronic adaptation, computer software, or by similar or dissimilar methodology now known or hereafter developed.
The use of general descriptive names, registered names, trademarks, service marks, etc. in this publication does not imply, even in the absence of a specific statement, that such names are exempt from the relevant protective laws and regulations and therefore free for general use.
The publisher, the authors and the editors are safe to assume that the advice and information in this book are believed to be true and accurate at the date of publication. Neither the publisher nor the authors or the editors give a warranty, express or implied, with respect to the material contained herein or for any errors or omissions that may have been made. The publisher remains neutral with regard to jurisdictional claims in published maps and institutional affiliations.

Cover credit: ilbusca/Getty Images

Printed on acid-free paper

This Palgrave Macmillan imprint is published by Springer Nature
The registered company is Nature America, Inc.
The registered company address is: 1 New York Plaza, New York, NY 10004, U.S.A.

Acknowledgements

This book is the result of unlimited effort from various individuals and institutions. The topics and themes came from an enriching brainstorming and back-and-forth communication and conversation between Toyin Falola and Martin Shanguhyia. Most important, we are grateful to the contributors to this volume who were willing to share some perspectives on how certain topics have been essential to the development of modern African history. They spent their invaluable time making endless revisions to their chapters under time constraints. Our constant communications and conversations were more rewarding than an inconvenience to all involved. We would also like to thank Amy Katherine Burnette, then a Dissertation Fellow at the Humanities Center at Syracuse University, and Thomas Jefferson West III, a doctoral candidate in the Department of Languages, Literatures, and Linguistics, Syracuse University, for the endless hours they spend editing the chapters. Special thanks also to the History Department at Syracuse University for subsidizing funds for editorial services. We also wish to acknowledge Jamie DeAngelo for her expertise in producing the maps.

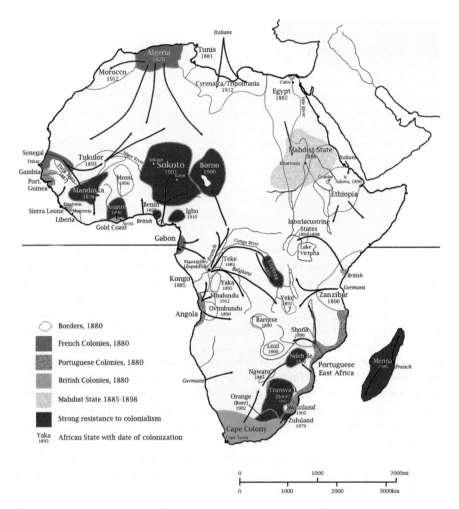

Map 1 Africa on the eve of European scramble and partition, circa 1880

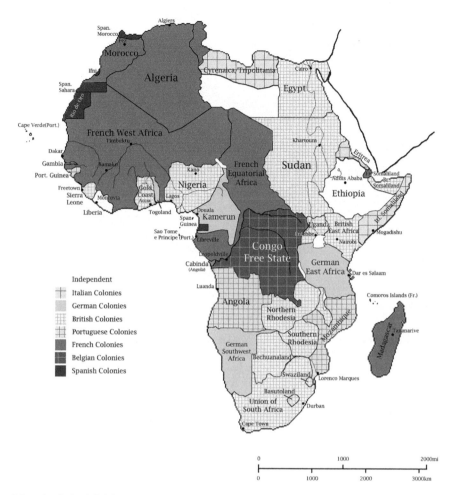

Map 2 Colonial Africa, circa 1914

viii ACKNOWLEDGEMENTS

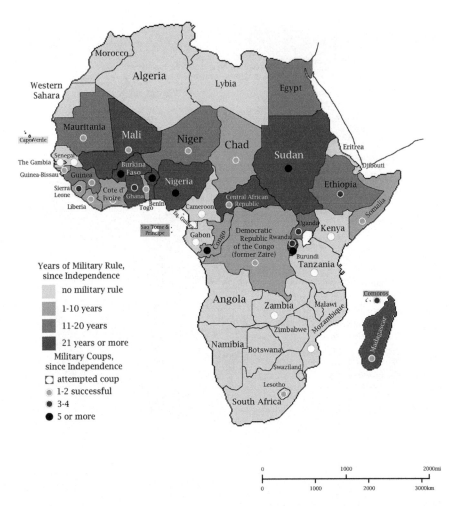

Map 3 Modern Africa: Countries that have experienced military rule

Map 4 Modern Africa: Countries that have experienced political conflict

Contents

1	**Introduction** Martin S. Shanguhyia and Toyin Falola	1

Part I   Colonial Africa

2	**Colonialism and the African Environment** Martin S. Shanguhyia	43
3	**Colonial Administrations and the Africans** Toyin Falola and Chukwuemeka Agbo	81
4	**Slavery in the Colonial State and After** Paul E. Lovejoy	103
5	**Africans and the Colonial Economy** Moses E. Ochonu	123
6	**African Women in Colonial Economies** Judith A. Byfield	145
7	**Colonialism and African Womanhood** Gloria Chuku	171
8	**Administration, Economy, and Society in the Portuguese African Empire (1900–1975)** Philip J. Havik	213

9	Christian Evangelization and Its Legacy Andrew E. Barnes	239
10	Colonial Education Kelly Duke Bryant	281
11	Health and Medicine in Colonial Society Matthew M. Heaton	303
12	African Colonial Urban Experience Uyilawa Usuanlele and Oluwatoyin B. Oduntan	319
13	Africa and the First World War Meshack Owino	339
14	Africa and the Second World War Meshack Owino	355
15	Colonialism and African Migrations Kwabena O. Akurang-Parry and Isaac Indome	373
16	Colonialism and African Childhood Temilola Alanamu, Benedict Carton and Benjamin N. Lawrance	389
17	Literature in Colonial Africa Tanure Ojaide	413
18	Art, African Identities, and Colonialism Sylvester Okwunodu Ogbechie	429
19	Intensification and Attenuation: Colonial Influences on an African Culture Augustine Agwuele	451
20	Youth and Popular Culture in Colonial Africa Jamaine M. Abidogun	479
21	The Horn of Africa and the Black Anticolonial Imaginary (1896–1915) Fikru Negash Gebrekidan	507
22	Colonial Africa and the West Enocent Msindo	535

23	International Law, Colonialism, and the African Ibrahim J. Gassama	551
24	Colonialism and Development in Africa Ruth Rempel	569
25	Nationalism and African Intellectuals Toyin Falola and Chukwuemeka Agbo	621
26	Decolonization Histories Robert M. Maxon	643

Part II Postcolonial Africa

27	Africa and the Cold War Kenneth Kalu	661
28	African Politics Since Independence Ademola Araoye	681
29	Secession and Separatism in Modern Africa Charles G. Thomas	729
30	Postcolonial Africa and the West Enocent Msindo	759
31	The USA and Africa Adebayo Oyebade	785
32	Franco-African Relations: Still Exceptional? Tony Chafer	801
33	Algeria and France: Beyond the Franco-Algerian Lens Natalya Vince	821
34	China and Africa Joshua Eisenman and David H. Shinn	839
35	Africa and Global Financial Institutions John Mukum Mbaku	855

36	Development History and Postcolonial African Experience Ruth Rempel	881
37	African Diasporas and Postcolonial Africa Kwasi Konadu	927
38	Islam in Sub-Saharan Africa Marloes Janson	951
39	The Unfinished Business of Postcolonialism: Theological Perspectives Elias Kifon Bongmba	979
40	South Africa: Apartheid and Post-Apartheid Nancy L. Clark	1005
41	The Pan-African Experience: From the Organization of African Unity to the African Union Horace G. Campbell	1031
42	Africa and Human Rights Edward Kissi	1089
43	Education in Postcolonial Africa Peter Otiato Ojiambo	1109
44	African Women and the Postcolonial State Alicia C. Decker	1137
45	Young People and Public Space in Africa: Past and Present Mamadou Diouf	1155
46	Colonialism and African Sexualities Xavier Livermon	1175
47	Culture, Artifacts, and Independent Africa: The Cultural Politics of Museums and Heritage Sarah Van Beurden	1193
48	Building the African Novel on Quick sand: Politics of Language, Identity, and Ownership Mukoma Wa Ngugi	1213

49	**Music and Postcolonial Africa** Eric Charry	1231
50	**Sports and Politics in Postcolonial Africa** Hikabwa D. Chipande and Davies Banda	1263
51	**Media, Society, and the Postcolonial State** Sharon Adetutu Omotoso	1285
52	**Between Diaspora and Homeland: The Study of Africa and the African Diaspora in the USA** Michael O. West	1305

Index   1323

Editors and Contributors

About the Editors

Martin S. Shanguhyia, Ph.D. is an Associate Professor of African History at the Maxwell School of Citizenship and Public Affairs at Syracuse University, New York. He received his Ph.D. in African history at West Virginia University, Morgantown. He is the author of *Population, Tradition and Environmental Control in Colonial Kenya, 1920–1963* (Rochester, NY: University of Rochester Press, December 2015). His work has also been published in the *International Journal of African Historical Studies* as well as the *Journal of Colonialism and Colonial History* and in several chapters in edited books on themes reflecting the intersection between colonialism, environment, agrarian change, conservation, land, and conflict. His current research focuses on the political economy of state–community and intercommunity relations across Kenya's borderlands with Uganda, South Sudan, and Ethiopia during the colonial period.

Toyin Falola, Ph.D. is the Frances and Sanger Mossiker Chair in the Humanities and University Distinguished Teaching Professor, University of Texas at Austin. He has received various awards and honors, including seven honorary doctorates. He is the author and editor of over 150 books.

Contributors

Jamaine M. Abidogun, is Professor in history, Missouri State University, holds a Ph.D. in curriculum and instruction in secondary education, minor in African and African-American studies, from the University of Kansas. She is a two-time Fulbright Scholar recipient for her work 'Gender Perspectives in Nigeria Secondary Education: A Case Study in Nsukka' (2004–2005) and 'Strengthening Gender Research to Improve Girls' and

Women's Education in Nigeria' (2013–2014). Her co-edited works with Toyin Falola include *Education, Creativity and Economic Empowerment in Africa* (2014) and *Issues in African Political Economies* (2016). Her publications include several chapters and articles in *African and Education Studies*. She is the editor-in-chief of the *African Journal of Teacher Education* (AJOTE), University of Guelph, Ontario and a member of the Fulbright Academy and the Mid-America Alliance for African Studies (MAAAS).

Augustine Agwuele, is an Associate Professor of linguistics in the Department of Anthropology, Texas State University. As an interdisciplinary scholar, he combines the conceptual rigors of theoretical linguistics with ethnographically grounded scholarship in socio-cultural anthropology. With this he studies language, culture, and society, addressing common and habitual practices involved in encoding, transmitting, and decoding messages. He studies closely Yoruba people of Nigeria.

Chukwuemeka Agbo is currently a Ph.D. student in the Department of History, University of Texas at Austin. He is also affiliated to the Department of History and Strategic Studies at the Federal University, Ndufu-Alike, Ikwo (FUNAI), Nigeria. His research focuses on the labor history of Southeastern Nigeria in the nineteenth and twentieth centuries.

Kwabena O. Akurang-Parry, is a Full Sabbatical Professor of Africana studies and world history at the University of Cape Coast, Cape Coast, Ghana. He received his Ph.D. in African history and comparative slavery as well as a Post-Graduate diploma in refugee and migration Studies at York University, Toronto, Canada. Professor Akurang-Parry has authored over 50 peer-reviewed articles in major journals, including *Slavery and Abolition, History in Africa, African Economic History, The International Journal of African Historical Studies, The International Journal of Regional and Local Studies, Left History, Transactions of the Historical Society of Ghana, African Identities,* and *International Working-Class and Labor History.* He is the co-editor of *African Agency and European Colonialism: Latitudes of Negotiation and Containment* (2007). He has held teaching and research positions at: Tulane University, New Orleans, USA; York University, Toronto, Canada; Shippensburg University, Pennsylvania, USA; and the University of Cape Coast, Ghana.

Temilola Alanamu, is a Leverhulme Early Career Fellow at the University of Kent. Her current research focuses on the intersection of gender and the life cycle in Southern Nigeria and encompasses the social experiences of the sexes from birth until death. She has published articles and book reviews in *Africa, Gender and History* and *Church History and Religious Culture* amongst others. She also has other forthcoming projects in *Oxford Bibliographies, Journal of World History* and *The Journal of Colonialism and Colonial History.* She is currently co-editing the *Encyclopaedia of African Religions Beliefs and Practices through History* with Douglas Thomas.

Ademola Araoye, has practiced political analysis, with particular focus on conflict, mediation, and post-conflict reconstruction for over three decades. A former Nigerian diplomat, he was head of the Political, Policy Planning Section of the United Nations Mission in Liberia (UNMIL), and later head of the Peace Consolidation Service of the mission. He is author of *Cote d'Ivoire: The Conundrum of a Still Wretched of the Earth* and *Sources of Conflict in the Post-Colonial Africa State*. He taught part time at the Ibrahim Babaginda Graduate School of the University of Liberia.

Andrew E. Barnes, teaches history at Arizona State University in Tempe, Arizona. He studies the history of Christianity in Africa and Europe. The primary focus of his present research is Christian missions and their interactions with African Christians during the era of European colonialism. He is the author of *Making Headway: The Introduction of Western Civilization in Colonial Northern Nigeria* (2009). His new book, *Industrial Education and the Christian Black Atlantic*, is forthcoming from Baylor University Press.

Davies Banda, is an active researcher in the field of sport and international development and is Deputy Director of the Unit for Child and Youth Studies at York St. John University, UK. His research covers sport-for-development, corporate social responsibility, national sports policies, and social inclusion interventions. He has been engaged as a consultant for the Commonwealth Secretariat, Euroleague Basketball, UK Sport, Laureus Sports for Good Foundation and some charities in Zambia and the United Kingdom.

Judith A. Byfield, is an Associate Professor in the History Department, Cornell University. She is the co-editor of *Africa and World War II* (Cambridge University Press, 2015) and author of *The Bluest Hands: A Social and Economic History of Women Indigo Dyers in Western Nigeria, 1890–1940* (Heinemann, 2002). A former President of the African Studies Association (2010–2011), Byfield has received numerous fellowships including the NEH and Fulbright.

Kelly Duke Bryant, is an Associate Professor of History at Rowan University (New Jersey), where she teaches African history. Her research focuses on colonial education, children and youth, and political change in Senegal. This research has generated several articles and a book, *Education as Politics: Colonial Schooling and Political Debate in Senegal, 1850s–1914* (2015).

Elias Kifon Bongmba, holds the Harry and Hazle Chavanne Chair in Christian theology and is Professor of religion at Rice University, Houston, Texas. His areas of specialization include African religions, theology, and philosophy. His book *The Dialectics of Transformation in Africa* won the Franz Fanon Prize. He has published widely on religion, theology, and is completing a monograph on same-sex relations in Africa.

Nancy L. Clark, is an historian with over 25 years' experience of teaching and research in South African history. She serves as the Jane DeGrummond Professor of history at Louisiana State University where she also served as Dean of the Honors College for over 10 years. Her areas of research have focused on twentieth-century South African history, with special emphasis on the apartheid era. She has published extensively on the impact of segregation and apartheid on the labor force, and most recently published the third edition of *The Rise and Fall of Apartheid,* co-authored with William Worger.

Horace G. Campbell, holds a joint Professorship in the Department of African American Studies and Department of Political Science, Maxwell School-Syracuse University. He has recently published *Global NATO and the Catastrophic Failure in Libya: Lessons for Africa in the Forging of African Unity* (2013) and *Barack Obama and twenty-first Century Politics: A Revolutionary Moment in the USA* (2010). He is also the author of *Reclaiming Zimbabwe: The Exhaustion of the Patriarchal Model of Liberation* (2003), and *Pan Africanism, Pan Africanists and African Liberation in the twenty-first Century* (2006). His most famous book, *Rasta and Resistance: from Marcus Garvey to Walter Rodney* (first published in 1985) is going through its eighth printing. He co-edited (Howard Stein) *Tanzania and the IMF: The Dynamics of* Liberalization (1992). He has published more than 60 journal articles and a dozen monographs as well as chapters in edited books. He was the Kwame Nkrumah Chair of African Studies at the Institute of African Studies, University of Legon, Ghana during 2016–2017.

Benedict Carton, is Robert T. Hawkes Professor of History and Africa Coordinator of African and African American Studies at George Mason University, Fairfax, Virginia. He is the author of *Blood from Your Children: The Colonial Origins of Generational Conflict in South Africa* (University of Virginia Press, 2000) and co-editor of *Zulu Identities: Being Zulu Past and Present* (2008).

Tony Chafer, is a historian specializing in Francophone Africa and French relations with Africa in the late colonial and postcolonial era. He is Director of the Centre for European and International Studies Research at the University of Portsmouth (UK). Recently he has published widely on French military policy in Africa and is currently working on a new edition of his book *The End of Empire in French West Africa: France's Successful Decolonization?*

Eric Charry, is a Professor of Music at Wesleyan University. He has published extensively on music in Africa, including dictionary and encyclopedia entries as well as the books *Mande Music* (2000) and *Hip Hop Africa* (2012).

Hikabwa D. Chipande, is a social historian of twentieth-century Africa. His research work focuses on the relationship between popular culture and politics, particularly football (soccer) and sport. He earned his Ph.D. in African history from Michigan State University in 2015 and is currently teaching at the University of Zambia in Lusaka.

Gloria Chuku, is a historian with over 25 years of teaching and research experience. She is Professor and Chair of Africana Studies, and Affiliate Professor of Gender and Women's Studies, and the Language, Literacy and Culture Ph.D. Program at the University of Maryland, Baltimore County, USA. Her work centers on Nigerian history with particular focus on gender, entrepreneurship, nationalism, ethnonationalisms and conflicts, and Igbo intellectual history. She has published extensively in these areas, including: a monograph, *Igbo Women and Economic Transformation in Southeastern Nigeria, 1900–1960* (2005); two edited volumes, *The Igbo Intellectual Tradition: Creative Conflict in African and African Diasporic Thought* (2013) and *Ethnicities, Nationalities, and Cross-Cultural Representations in Africa and the Diaspora* (2015). She has also publsihed over 50 scholarly articles.

Alicia C. Decker is an Associate Professor of women's, gender, and sexuality studies and African studies at the Pennsylvania State University, where she also co-directs the African Feminist Initiative. Her research and teaching interests include gender and militarism, African women's history, and global feminisms. She is the author of *In Idi Amin's Shadow: Women, Gender, and Militarism in Uganda* (Ohio University Press, 2014), and co-author with Andrea Arrington of *Africanizing Democracies: 1980 to Present* (Oxford University Press, 2014).

Mamadou Diouf, is an historian, and has taught at the Université Cheikh Anata Diop in Dakar (Senegal), and directed the Research and Documentation Department of the Council for the Development of Social Sciences Research. He was the Charles Moody Jr. Professor of History and African and African American Studies at the University of Michigan, Ann Arbor. He is currently the Leitner Family Professor of African studies and history at Columbia University in the City of New York, and a Visiting Professor at Sciences PIO, Paris (France). His research interests have focused on African intellectual and urban histories and youth cultures. His more recent publications include the co-edited book *Tolerance, Democracy and the Sufis in Senegal,* (2014), and co-edited volumes *The Arts of Citizenship in Africa. Spaces of Belonging* (with R. Fredericks), 2015); *Les arts de la citoyenneté au Sénégal. Espaces Contestés et Civilités Urbaines* (with F. Fredericks, 2013); *Rhythms of the Afro-Atlantic: Rituals and Remembrances,* (with I. Nwankwo, 2010) and *New Perspectives on Islam in Senegal: Conversion, Migration, Wealth, Power and Femininity* (with Mara Leichtman, 2009).

Joshua Eisenman, is Assistant Professor at the University of Texas at Austin's LBJ School of Public Affairs and senior fellow for China studies at the American Foreign Policy Council in Washington, DC. His second book, *China and Africa: A Century of Engagement*, co-authored with former US Ambassador to Ethiopia David H. Shinn, was named one of the top three books on Africa in 2012 by *Foreign Affairs* magazine. In 2007, he co-edited *China and the Developing World: Beijing's Strategy for the twenty-first Century*, and wrote the book's chapter on China–Africa relations.

Ibrahim J. Gassama, is the Frank Nash Professor of law at the University of Oregon. His research interests include international humanitarian, human rights, and economic law. His recent international law articles have appeared in the international law journals of Brooklyn (2012), Fordham (2013), Washington (2013), and Wisconsin (2014) Universities. Prior to becoming a law professor, he worked for TransAfrica, the African-American lobby for Africa.

Fikru Negash Gebrekidan, is an Associate Professor of History at St Thomas University in Fredericton, Canada. He regularly teaches courses on African history, world history, and the history of genocide. His major publications have appeared in *Northeast African Studies*, the *International Journal of Ethiopian Studies*, the *Journal of Ethiopian Studies*, *Callaloo*, and the *African Studies Review*. He is the author of *Bond without Blood: A History of Ethiopian and New World Black Relations, 1896–1991* (2005).

Philip J. Havik, is senior researcher at the Instituto de Higiene e Medicina Tropical of the Universidade Nova in Lisbon (IHMT/UNL) where he also teaches the history of medicine. His multidisciplinary research centers upon the study of public health and tropical medicine, state formation and governance, cultural brokerage and entrepreneurship in West Africa, with special emphasis on Lusophone countries, including Guinea Bissau. His most recent publications include (with co-authors Alexander Keese and Maciel Santos) *Administration and Taxation in the former Portuguese Empire, 1900–1945* (2015).

Matthew M. Heaton, is an Associate Professor in the Department of History at Virginia Tech. His research interests are in the history of health and illness, migration, and globalization in Africa with particular emphasis on Nigeria. He is the author of *Black Skin, White Coats: Nigerian Psychiatrists, Decolonization, and the Globalization of Psychiatry* and co-author of *A History of Nigeria*.

Isaac Indome is an M.Phil. History student at the Department of History, University of Cape Coast, Cape Coast, Ghana. He obtained his B.A. (Hons) degree in history from the University of Cape Coast in June 2015 and taught in the same department during the 2015/2016 academic year. His research interests are in migration in colonial Africa, specifically focusing on health and migration in colonial Ghana.

Marloes Janson, is Reader in West African anthropology at SOAS, University of London. Her areas of ethnographic interest include religious reform (both Muslim and Christian), oral history, gender, and youth in the Gambia and Nigeria. She has published extensively in these areas, most recently *Islam, Youth, and Modernity in the Gambia: The Tablighi Jama'at* (Cambridge University Press/International African Institute, 2014). She is the book reviews editor of the *Journal of Religion in Africa*.

Kenneth Kalu, received his Ph.D. from the School of Public Policy and Administration, Carleton University, Ottawa, Canada. He is currently an Assistant Professor at Ted Rogers School of Management, Ryerson University, Toronto, Canada. His research interests revolve around Africa's political economy; with special focus on the nature, evolution, and interactions of economic and political institutions; the political economy of foreign development assistance; and the history of foreign direct investment in Africa. His essays have appeared in several edited volumes, and his article on state–society relations in Africa is forthcoming in *Development Policy Review*. His forthcoming book is on development assistance and the future of Africa. He has held several senior positions in the public and private sectors in Nigeria and Canada.

Edward Kissi, is Associate Professor in the Department of Africana Studies at the University of South Florida. He studies the economic and diplomatic history of Ethiopia and the Horn of Africa, and the comparative history of genocide and human rights, and has published extensively on these subjects. He is the author of 'Obligation to Prevent (O2P): Proposal for a Community Approach to Genocide-prevention in Africa' to be published in *African Security Review*, in September 2016.

Kwasi Konadu, is Professor of history at The City University of New York. Among other books, he is the author of *The Akan Diaspora in the Americas* (2010), *Transatlantic Africa, 1440–1880* (2014), and co-editor of *The Ghana Reader: History, Culture, Politics* (2016). He is also the founding director of the non-profit educational publisher Diasporic Africa Press, Inc.

Benjamin N. Lawrance, is Professor of African History at the University of Arizona, and also the Editor-in-Chief of African Studies Review. His research interests include comparative and contemporary slavery, human trafficking, cuisine and globalization, human rights, refugee issues and asylum policies. Among his books are *Amistad's Orphans: An Atlantic Story of Children, Slavery, and Smuggling* (2014), and *Adjudicating Refugee and Asylum Status: The Role of Witness, Expertise, and Testimony* (2015), with Galya Ruffer; and, *Trafficking in Slavery's Wake: Law and the Experience of Women and Children in Africa* (2012), with Richard L. Roberts.

Xavier Livermon, is an Assistant Professor of African and African diaspora studies at the University of Texas at Austin. He has published widely in the fields of African popular culture and African queer studies. His forthcoming book *Kwaito Futurity* discusses the rise of post-apartheid South African popular culture and its articulation with contemporary politics of race, gender, and sexuality.

Paul E. Lovejoy, is Distinguished Research Professor in the Department of History, York University, Toronto, and holds the Canada Research Chair in African Diaspora History. He is a Fellow of the Royal Society of Canada and was the founding director of the Harriet Tubman Institute for Research on the Global Migrations of African Peoples. His recent publications include *The Transatlantic Slave Trade and Slavery: New Directions in Teaching and Learning* (2013), co-edited with Benjamin Bowser, and *Jihád in West Africa During the Age of Revolutions* (Athens, OH: Ohio University Press, 2016). He has been awarded the Honorary degree of Doctor of the University, by the University of Stirling in 2007, the Distinguished Africanist Award by the University of Texas at Austin in 2010, a Life Time Achievement Award from the Canadian Association of African Studies in 2011, and Faculty of Graduate Studies Teaching Award at York University in 2011. He is General Editor of the Harriet Tubman Series on the African Diaspora, Africa World Press.

Robert M. Maxon, is an historian with more than 45 years of teaching, research and supervision of students at West Virginia University and Moi University. His research interests include East African history, Kenyan political and economic history, the economic history of western Kenya, and Kenya's constitutional history. He has published in these areas, most recently *Kenya's Independence Constitution: Constitution-Making and End of Empire* (2011), *Britain and Kenya's Constitutions 1950–1960* (2011), and *Historical Dictionary of Kenya* (3rd edn, 2014).

John Mukum Mbaku, is an economist, lawyer, and legal scholar with more than 30 years of teaching and research experience. He is currently Brady Presidential Distinguished Professor of economics and John S. Hinckley Fellow at Weber State University (Utah, USA), a Nonresident Senior Fellow at The Brookings Institution (Washington, DC), and an Attorney and Counselor at law (licensed in Utah). His research interests are in constitutional political economy and governance in Africa. He has published extensively in these areas, most recently, *Governing the Nile River Basin: The Search for a New Legal Regime* (2015), with Mwangi S. Kimenyi.

Enocent Msindo, is Associate Professor of History at Rhodes University, South Africa. He has published widely on Africa's social and political history. He is the author of *Ethnicity in Zimbabwe: Transformations in Kalanga and Ndebele Societies* (2012) and is currently completing a monograph on the state, information policy and propaganda in Zimbabwe from 1890 to the present.

Mukoma Wa Ngugi, is an Assistant Professor of English at Cornell University and the author of the novels *Mrs. Shaw* (2015), *Black Star Nairobi* (2013), *Nairobi Heat* (2011), and a book of poetry, *Hurling Words at Consciousness* (2006). *Logotherapy* (poetry) is forthcoming. He is the co-founder of the Mabati–Cornell Kiswahili Prize for African Literature and co-director of the Global South Project—Cornell. The goal of GSP is to facilitate public conversations among writers and scholars from Africa, Latin America, and Asia as well as minority groups in the West. In 2013, *New African* magazine named him one of the 100 most Influential Africans. In 2015 he was a juror for the Writivism Short Story Prize and the Neustadt International Prize for Literature.

Oluwatoyin B. Oduntan, is an Assistant Professor of History at Towson University in Maryland where he teaches courses in world, African and intellectual histories, and historical methods. He focuses his research on elite formation, cultural identity, and modernity in Africa.

Moses E. Ochonu, is Professor of African History at Vanderbilt University. He holds a Ph.D. in African history from the University of Michigan, Ann Arbor, and Graduate Certificate in conflict management from Lipscomb University, Nashville. He is the author of three books: *Africa in Fragments: Essays on Nigeria, Africa, and Global Africanity* (New York: Diasporic Africa Press, 2014); *Colonialism by Proxy: Hausa Imperial Agents and Middle Belt Consciousness in Nigeria* (Indiana University Press, 2014), which was named finalist for the Herskovits Prize; and *Colonial Meltdown: Northern Nigeria in the Great Depression* (Ohio University Press, 2009). Ochonu's articles have been published as book chapters and in several scholarly journals. He is currently working on a book project dealing with a unique form of colonial patronage which saw British colonial authorities sponsor Northern Nigerian emirs and other Muslim aristocrats to London and other metropolitan destinations for sightseeing adventures. Ochonu is two-time recipient of the research fellowship of the American Council of Learned Societies (ACLS). He has also received research grants and fellowships from the Harry Frank Guggenheim Foundation, the Social Science Research Council (SSRC), Rockefeller Foundation, Ford Foundation, National Endowment for the Humanities (NEH), and the British Library.

Sharon Adetutu Omotoso, is a Philosopher (Applied Ethicist) with years of teaching, research and supervision of students, formerly at Lead City University and currently at the Institute of African Studies, University of Ibadan. Her areas of research interest include Applied Ethics, Political Communications, Media & Gender studies, Philosophy of Education, Socio-Political Philosophy, and African Philosophy. She has published significantly in these areas, most recently, a co-edited book: *Political Communication in Africa* (Cham: Springer Publishers, 2017).

Tanure Ojaide, is a writer and scholar, currently The Frank Porter Graham Professor of Africana studies at the University of North Carolina at Charlotte. He has won major awards for his poetry and scholarly works.

Peter Otiato Ojiambo, is an Associate Professor in the Department of African and African-American Studies at the University of Kansas with several years of teaching, research and student supervision experience. His areas of research include: African-centered educational biographies, comparative and international education, educational leadership and non-western educational thoughts. He has written and published extensively on these areas. His recent publication is entitled "Perspectives on Empowering Education", 2014.

Meshack Owino, is an Associate Professor of History at Cleveland State University, Cleveland, Ohio. He earned his B.Ed and M.A at Kenyatta University, Kenya, and an M.A. and Ph.D.. at Rice University, Houston, Texas. Owino's areas of academic interests include the social experience of African soldiers in pre-colonial and colonial wars; and the nature and permutation of the modern African state. Owino has taught African History at several universities, including Egerton University, Kenya and Bloomsburg University, Bloomsburg, Pennsylvania. He has served as a Visiting Professor of African history at Stanford University, Palo Alto, California, and as an Adjunct Professor at Texas Southern University, Houston, Texas.

Adebayo Oyebade, is Professor of history and Chair of the History Department at Tennessee State University at Nashville. He has authored numerous journal articles and book chapters on African and African diasporan history. He is the author, editor, and co-editor of nine books including *United States' Foreign Policy in Africa in the twenty-first Century: Issues and Perspectives* (2014).

Sylvester Okwunodu Ogbechie, is Professor of art history and visual cultures of global Africa at the University of California Santa Barbara. He received his Ph.D. at Northwestern University and is the author of *Ben Enwonwu: The Making of an African Modernist* (2008) which was awarded the 2009 Herskovits Prize of the African Studies Association for best scholarly publication in African studies. He has also authored *Making History: The Femi Akinsanya African Art Collection* (2011), and is editor of *Artists of Nigeria* (2012). Ogbechie is also the founder and editor of *Critical Interventions: Journal of African Art History and Visual Culture*. He is currently a Smithsonian Institution Senior Fellow at the National Museum of African Art.

Ruth Rempel, is a historian in the international development studies program at Canadian Mennonite University. Her research and teaching interests include global and African development history, structural adjustment in Africa, narratives of African development since 1990, and development theory. She has written on these and other topics, and has a forthcoming book on African development history from 1970 to 2010.

David H. Shinn, has been teaching as an Adjunct Professor in the Elliott School of International Affairs at George Washington University since 2001. He previously served for 37 years in the US Foreign Service with assignments at embassies in Lebanon, Kenya, Tanzania, Mauritania, Cameroon, Sudan, and as ambassador to Ethiopia and Burkina Faso. Shinn, who has a Ph.D. from George Washington University, is the co-author of *China and Africa: A Century of Engagement* and the *Historical Dictionary of Ethiopia*, and the author of *Hizmet in Africa: The Activities and Significance of the Gülen Movement*. Shinn has authored numerous journal articles and book chapters on China–Africa issues. He blogs at http://davidshinn.blogspot.com.

Charles G. Thomas, is an Associate Professor of comparative military studies at the Air Command and Staff College. He is the co-editor of *Securing Africa: Local Crises and Foreign Interventions* (2013) and the *Managing Editor of the Journal of African Military History* (Brill Academic Press).

Uyilawa Usuanlele, studied in Nigeria, Sweden, and Canada and majored in African History, Peace, and Conflict Studies. He worked as a researcher with the National Council for Arts and Culture, Nigeria. He was a founding member/Coordinator of Institute for Benin Studies, Benin City, Nigeria. He has contributed articles and chapters to journals and books. He currently teaches African history, as well as peace and conflict Studies at State University of New York (SUNY) Oswego, New York, USA.

Sarah Van Beurden, is an Associate Professor of African studies at the Ohio State University. She received her Ph.D. from University of Pennsylvania, and is the author of *Authentically African: Arts and the Transnational Politics of Congolese Culture* (2015). She has also written several articles and chapters on the colonial and postcolonial history of Congo/Zaire, and cultural heritage and museum politics.

Natalya Vince, is a Lecturer in North African and French Studies at the University of Portsmouth. Her subject area is modern Algerian and French history, and her research interests include oral history, gender studies, and state and nation building in Algeria and France, and more broadly in Europe and Africa. Her monograph *Our Fighting Sisters: Nation, Memory and Gender in Algeria, 1954–2012* was published in 2015.

Michael O. West, is Professor of Sociology, Africana Studies and History at Binghamton University. He has published broadly in the fields of African studies, African diaspora studies, African-American studies, Pan-Africanism, history, and historical sociology. His current research centers on the Black Power movement in global perspectives.

List of Figures

Map 1	Africa on the eve of European scramble and partition, circa 1880	vi
Map 2	Colonial Africa, circa 1914	vii
Map 3	Modern Africa: Countries that have experienced military rule	viii
Map 4	Modern Africa: Countries that have experienced political conflict	ix
Fig. 8.1	Total Revenue (*c*.1949–1972)	224
Fig. 16.1	Staged stick fight, KwaZulu-Natal, South Africa (*c*.1900)	396
Fig. 16.2	Xhosa women practice their martial arts, Eastern Cape, South Africa (1981)	397
Fig. 16.3	Madam and children: Young Zulu servant in his kitchen suit, Natal, South Africa (*c*.1900)	404
Fig. 18.1	Olowe of Ise, *Palace Door*. Wood and pigment, 20th Century (copyright Femi Akinsanya African Art Collection)	434
Fig. 19.1	Masqueraders' family house in Aperin, Ibadan	462

LIST OF TABLES

Table 8.1	Population of Portugal's former African colonies (1926–1970)	222
Table 22.1	Tax revenues in 1934	541
Table 36.1	Trends in social development	889

CHAPTER 1

Introduction

Martin S. Shanguhyia and Toyin Falola

This Handbook was conceived out of the necessity to demonstrate the extent to which African history has expanded in scope, themes, and interpretations since the early 1980s. It focuses on African colonial and postcolonial history, the two eras of the continent's history that seem inseparable, though the extent to which they are similar or different has pervaded scholarly debates for decades and is an aspect that some of the chapters in this volume explore. The book benefits from contributions from established and up-and-coming scholars in African studies, each using the vantage point of their study of Africa and Africans to reveal how we have come to understand the continent's historical trajectory since the professionalization of African history in the 1950s.

The majority of the contributors are historians, while the rest are drawn from diverse fields in African studies, particularly political science, anthropology, art, music, literature, religious studies, education, and international relations. Part of the initiative here is to demonstrate that African history has not evolved in isolation from other disciplines that focus on Africa; rather, in researching and interpreting what they study, historians of Africa have directly and indirectly benefited immensely from other disciplines. One can also argue contrariwise that scholars of African studies have tapped into African history

M.S. Shanguhyia (✉)
History Department, Maxwell School of Citizenship and Public Affairs, Syracuse University, Syracuse, NY, USA

T. Falola
Department of History, The University of Texas at Austin, Austin, TX, USA

to shed light on various aspects of their respective fields. It is fair to argue as well that the production of African history has been, to a certain extent, the result of an interdisciplinary effort.

Work of the nature attempted in this Handbook has been preceded by past initiatives to appraise the state of African historiography, and these fine, early efforts must be applauded. The *Cambridge History of Africa* remains an important starting point for works of this kind. The UNESCO *General History of Africa* volumes published in the early 1980s remain indispensable as they immortalize initiatives of eminent pioneer scholars who virtually laid the foundations of African history as a legitimate professional pursuit. Even before the UNESCO effort, very engaging works reflecting on trends in African history were rolled out in the 1960s and 1970s, a little more than a decade following the historical revisionism that had been launched in the 1950s. Some of these works were concerned with general, broader trends of historical studies that covered Sub-Saharan Africa.[1] Of these, A.D. Roberts's work that focused on colonial Africa is quite relevant to the kind of work partly covered in this volume. Even so, Roberts was mainly concerned with the *earlier* historiography of colonial Africa.[2] Other studies tended toward regional analyses, particularly on East and West Africa.[3]

Later studies on African historiography from the 1980s through the first decade of the twenty-first century build on these earlier efforts, if only to reflect ongoing debates on what direction the interpretation, methods, and scope African history in particular was to take, either as an individual discipline or within the family of African studies. They depict a polarization among historians of the day on interpretation, themes, and value to Africa of African history.[4] We briefly outline this subject below, as various debates contributed to the evolution of the discipline into its present state. The place of Africa in European imperial historiography, particularly that of Britain, has also garnered attention, though many will argue about its validity to a 'true' African history, if such history ever exists, given its strong imperial focus.[5,6]

Since the publication of these earlier works, African colonial and postcolonial histories have experienced expansion in interpretation and thematic focus, the entire breadth of which has not been completely captured in a single volume. Perhaps a more recent effort in this direction is the *Oxford Handbook of Modern African History*, edited by John Parker and Richard Reid. That volume is an excellent analysis of some of the finest works that reflect recent trends in modern African history. Our endeavor in this volume is to present an expanded scope of themes that have formed the cache of African colonial and postcolonial history over the last three or so decades, and to show how those themes, both old and new, have been engaged by various scholars. The themes in the volume illustrate the depth of African modern history, the innovativeness and range of paradigms of its analysis, and the multidisciplinary lens for understanding Africa's past.

Evolution of Colonial and Postcolonial African Historiography

The development of African historiography on the colonial and postcolonial periods has received excellent, detailed attention by several scholars since the 1960s. To avoid redundancy, we have opted only for the key strands of its evolution, but in ways that we hope will help illustrate developments in the discipline in recent decades. The emergence of that historiography has been a product of decades of enriching debates on the nature of the discipline, its methodology, interpretation, ownership of production of historical knowledge, and more importantly, the uses, functions, or value of African history to Africa and Africans. The historiography has also been shaped by debates on the practices and uses of African history in Africa and the West.

In 1965, while reflecting on the importance of periodization of African history, Basil Davidson predicted that 'the larger wisdom of the future' would profit the discipline by engaging, without fear, the interpretation of African history by taking advantage of the increasing 'mass of material'.[7] Certainly, ever since, the growth of African precolonial, colonial, and postcolonial histories has benefited from scholars' access to immense sources of various domains, especially archaeological, linguistic, paleontological, botanical, written and oral sources, among others.[8] Davidson, Terrence O. Ranger, J.D. Fage, Jan Vansina, Anthony G. Hopkins, and an array of indigenous historians of Africa (most notably E.A. Ayandele, Adu Boahen, Jacob Ade Ajayi, Bethwell A. Ogot, Joseph Ki-Zerbo and many others) worked hard to transform the field in its early years of development. They were the pioneer revisionists of African history and had the unenviable task of erasing entrenched, Western, colonial assumptions that Africa and its peoples were devoid of history, and that Africans' historical experience commenced only after intense Western interaction with the continent beginning from the fifteenth century. In other words, African history was an account of European presence in Africa. A proliferation of historical writings about Africa emerged before and during the colonial interface, but most of the analysis lacked objectivity as it served to promote the European intellectual tradition and objectives of the imperial mission. These annals, particularly those produced by colonial states and their agents, became the 'official history' rather than an authentic African history. Its analysis or assessment of Africa and Africans was apologetic to the colonial mission, and rooted in the Enlightenment persuasions of civilizing the non-European world, hence its undisguised emphasis on the administrative practices of colonial states and their benevolence to Africans.[9] This, then, was the background upon which the new generation of scholars of African history at the dawn of independence sought to recover African history. The need to offer a counter-narrative to the colonial presentation of Africa and Africans seemed an urgent mission for those scholars.

Subsequently, historical revisionism in the 1950s and 1960s assumed a nationalist tone, partly acting in tandem with the strong anti-colonial sentiments by Africans that helped bring colonial domination to a close. Above all else, the new nationalist historiography seemed to mellow with the aura of freedom, a feeling of independence and renewal that imbued the new African states and their citizens with a vision to use scholarship to criticize and radically change colonial historiography. There was a need to furnish Africa and Africans with a historiography that gave purpose and meaning to former colonial subjects and their newfound sense of belonging. Freedom, pride, hope, and expectations of visionary leadership inaugurated new 'aggressive self-assertive' political agendas of the decolonized states.[10] The new history was expected to energize and legitimize the status quo.

Therefore, some of the works of history that emerged pointed to Africa's golden past (states, empires, and African economies prior to colonization) to delegitimize the colonial phase and give inspiration to the new Africa. West African indigenous historians of the Ibadan school unearthed the African historical initiative in the years preceding colonial domination, much of it focusing on Nigeria.[11] In East Africa, T.O. Ranger and a vibrant community of historians of the Dar es Salaam school led efforts to recover the African agency in the continent's history. For the Dar es Salaam revisionists, to focus on Africans during the colonial period was to clarify the role of the African not as a victim but as a hero whose achievement lay in fending off colonial invasion and subordination. This nationalist history therefore drew our attention to African resistances against colonialism and colonial oppression across East and Central Africa, themes that lasted into the 1980s.[12] In East and West Africa, the nation-state became hallowed as well by the nationalist historians, whose new studies bore titles after the names of the new states. The contents of the publications reflected aspects of the new ideologies pertaining to nation building.[13]

Pioneer institutions of higher education that had colonial origins, staffed by 'nationalist' African academic scholars with help from Western historians of the liberal persuasion, fronted these recovery efforts. The institutionalization of the discipline was rapid, if not vibrant, in Anglophone Africa. It was also evident, but not as rapid, in other African territories. In Francophone Africa, Senegal seemed to take the lead where the establishment of the Institut Français de l'Afrique Noire (IFAN) in Dakar back in 1937 provided an institutional basis for disseminating African studies in other parts of French-speaking Africa. By 1950, IFAN had branches across many of the French West Africa territories, while the establishment of the University of Dakar in 1957 lent the Institut a permanent intuitional base to promote African studies in Francophone Africa. This revolution also became the cause for liberal scholars of African studies based in a few Western institutions in the USA, France, and especially Britain.[14] Following independence, Senegalese historiography was slow in its growth due to the pedagogical approaches and structures of the university system that had strong French underpinnings—hence a slow pace of Africanization of history. But when Senegalese history took shape by the 1980s, local and foreign scholars were attracted to pre-colonial and early colonial themes, particularly cultural developments, slavery, and Islam.[15] Except for studies that focused on pre-colonial state building and transatlantic connections, works on the colonial (and later, the postcolonial) experience of Lusophone Africa were clearly absent in early revisionist works, both general and specific. These lacunae have been addressed by some of the finest studies that have since been done on Lusophone Africa.[16] Philip Havik's contribution to this book is therefore an excellent effort.

Scholars' quest to tie African authenticity and relevance to nationalism and the new state proved challenging as disappointments of independence crept into the public and political elite. Political practice alienated some, as the moral obligation and levels of tolerance of the nationalist leaders who had ushered their citizens from colonial subjectivity to freedom came under scrutiny. Some critics perceived ironies and distortions in looking to the past, beyond colonialism, to present an authentic African history. Writing in the 1980s, Caroline Neale was lucid on these perceptions:

> That African nationalism has been for many a moving and courageous struggle is in no way disputed; what is of interest ... is the reason for situating its origins far back into the past as possible ... and the distorting effect this had on the representation of African history. As a political movement, nationalism took its force from the colonial situation; but as an idea, it derived its mysterious domination over centuries of African history from the evolutionism which placed Europeans and their political works at the pinnacle of man's development.[17]

Thus, according to Neal's critique, nationalist historians might as well have considered the nationalist triumph of the 1950s and 1960s as the peak of Africa's socio-political progress, victory over an intervening era of history (the colonial period) that had impeded or arrested that progress. Yet aside from the political disappointments of the early years of independence, realities of poverty, inequalities, and other forms of economic and social dilemmas led to the questioning of the nationalist approach to understanding the challenges that faced postcolonial Africa, and how the past was helpful in analyzing and overcoming those challenges. To others, the postcolonial state might as well have been a reincarnation of its colonial counterpart, as they pointed to the nipped public expectations as evidence of their conclusion. Political independence might have effaced Western colonial powers from Africa, and with them 'the illusion of a civilizing Mission and the obvious racial factor'.[18] But antecedents of 'colonial mentality' were perceived to exist in political elites' management of free African states, while their intellectual counterparts (products of the colonial states) slid into social and spatial isolation from the rest of the decolonized society from where they objectified their knowledge. This transformation helped these intellectuals to advance their analysis of Africa from a Western perspective.[19]

Critics also asserted that nationalist scholars overlooked the rupturing effects of colonialism, and treated with hindsight colonial production of social differences in the form of class and gender, or even misconstrued the African peasant, as much as those scholars also ignored the long-standing imperial and global contexts that shaped the continent's historical agency. The emergence in the 1970s of the radical Marxist scholars (the New Dar School) was in direct response to the shortcomings of nationalist scholarship. Poverty and Africa's economic dilemmas, the Marxist scholars argued, were the result of the incorporation of Africa into global capitalism with its domineering tendencies sustained by certain political power structures within and outside Africa, operating in tandem. African economic or developmental history, analyzed within development or underdevelopment theories, was the hallmark of the new scholarship.[20] It epitomized a shift from the optimism of the nationalists to the pessimism of the realities of Africa's stagnation that was measured in terms of economic development and progress.

In fact, for some of these Marxists, the African political elite and members of the African 'petite bourgeoisie' were culpable of the exploitation, oppression, and predicament that African peoples found themselves in at the dawn of independence.[21] The 'bourgeois nationalist' historiography, the label that nationalist, historical analysis had derived,[22] had failed to see through these experiences of the African masses. In Kenya, the national challenges of implementing a sustainable land reform program invited political scientists to provide a critique against the nationalist ideology of independence and socio-economic development. Those challenges also pushed radical nationalists to question whether 'true' independence had been achieved.[23] Perhaps, as Ali Mazrui reminds us, Africa's founding fathers were culpable of promoting postcolonial relations which, dubbed as neo-colonialism, contributed to Africa's persistent dilemmas. Such relations entrenched a 'neo-dependency' status for the continent, with leaders of independent African states cultivating a new role for themselves as 'Client Chief[s]' who, although sovereign, were manipulated by former colonial powers in ways that failed to benefit the Client's peoples.[24] For others, internal social cleavages and tensions within African societies that were driven by materialism (to which nationalists cast a blind eye) could rationally be disentangled and understood through a Marxist lens.[25] Thus, there was a gradual realization that the African historical experience and initiative operated in complex, broader, interconnected relationships with a long history that had to be recognized.

Not every revisionist history within the framework of economic or development history (and its social ramifications) viewed the African as an actor who was completely disadvantaged by the inequalities of the colonial and global orders of the late nineteenth and first half of the twentieth centuries. A liberal approach to this revisionism in the 1970s revealed Africans as rational and innovative actors who, even before formal colonization commenced, were able to navigate the constraints of the global capitalist economy oftentimes to their advantage. It was an initiative that many Africans, particularly in West Africa, continued to sustain through the better part of the colonial period.[26]

During the early years of asserting African historical agency, scholarship by Vansina and Ogot to reclaim African oral traditions as valid sources for writing African history aided in the reconstruction of precolonial histories of Africa. Later on, consultation of the knowledge of the so-called African 'organic intellectuals' or 'encylopaedic informants' helped some historians recover precolonial and colonial historical experiences of such ethnic communities as the Baganda, Yoruba, Kuba, and Luo.[27] The utilization of oral and written sources has since become the custom of the historian of the colonial (and postcolonial) era, and has yielded numerous, interesting works that define the essence of 'local histories', especially within the broader field of social history.[28] Production of biographical histories of African individuals has also immensely benefited from these oral sources.

By the 1960s, South Africa experienced a more divergent historiography; its most dominant aspect emphasized an orthodox orientation produced by white scholars and one that reflected on the developments that stretched back into the nineteenth century. The position of black South Africans was framed within their role as objects of the policies and practices of white South Africans.[29] Though a more liberal scholarship emerged in the 1920s and lasted through the 1950s (in spite of the ascendance of apartheid in 1948), it was trapped into a paradigm of analysis that revolved around the state and its segregated demographic components based on race. For instance, while the *Oxford History of South Africa* captured elements of the African contribution to the making of modern South Africa (more or less in response to the growing interest in African history at Western universities), it left unresolved the roles of structure and power in the configuration of the country's history. It portrayed the African in static and ahistorical terms, and African societies as unchanging and isolated.[30]

South African revisionists of the 1970s, largely of the Marxist school, were enthralled with race, class, development, and materialist accumulation, indicating possible external influence from Africanists and international scholars of the underdevelopment school. They perceived a close connection between the apartheid state and capitalism in the mining and industrial sectors, and with other critical components of that state, most notably migrant labor, the native reserve system, and the aggregated nature of South Africa's rural communities. From the 1980s, the History Workshop Movement inaugurated the focus on popular history of ordinary South Africans, probably the result of wider disaffection across Sub-Saharan Africa with the failure of the political elite to expand avenues of freedom for their citizens. In this tradition, the focus of studies included local protests, social justice movements, and class histories.[31] The transition of South Africa from apartheid to majority rule in 1994 was in itself an historic moment, but has elicited debates on the value of understanding past experiences as a basis for ordering the post-apartheid state. Some scholars have posed the legitimate question of whether South African history has ever been postcolonial despite the end of apartheid.[32]

As regards modern Ethiopia, the typical historiography thrived within the context of Africa's contact with European imperialism. Its key focus was on the intersection between state building, external forces, and indigenous responses to those forces, with the Ethiopian imperial institution providing the framework of analysis. The overthrow of that institution by the 1974 Revolution, while retaining the state as a unit of historical analysis, saw a shift toward a Marxist interpretation of the past, with scholars narrowing down their analysis to structures and processes of the Ethiopian society: social/class relations and social conflict. Periodic episodes of drought and famine in the 1970s and 1980s, and peasant responses to them, hoisted ecology as an important component in the emerging Ethiopian historiography. This prompted scholars to pay attention to questions surrounding the agrarian sector, land relations, and administrative institutions. Conflict with Somalia, the Eritrean movement and foundation of the Eritrean state, and Oromo dissent to the national project led to calls in the 1990s for historians of Ethiopia to rethink the relevance and scope of the existing historiography. Revisionists pointed to the importance of ethnicity and nationalism as the loci for enriching the historical analysis of the modern Ethiopian state.[33] Despite these new developments, ramifications of Adowa have continued to provide some historians with an analytical framework for understanding Ethiopia's influence on historical developments within and outside Africa. Fikru Negash Gebrekidan's chapter in this volume demonstrates this.

Evolution of 'New Histories'

Most of what emerged as 'new histories,' particularly from the 1980s, was the result of criticism against dependency scholarship of the 1970s. Critics faulted dependency scholars for their reliance on Western models of analyzing African experiences, an illustration of just how far the debate had proceeded regarding interpretation and authenticity of methods of analyzing the past. They were also faulted for totalizing the past as a collective, not individual, experience, thereby overlooking the importance of certain sub-categories of Africans whose interaction with the colonial and postcolonial states might have yielded unique experiences. This criticism, common among political economists, was responsible for inaugurating historical analyses that disaggregated African states, communities, and institutions into categories that, though parts of the whole system, could be isolated and analyzed with sufficient depth as to unearth unique historical processes that shaped or were shaped by them. Revisionists of the 1970s saw particular opportunities for growth of social history, as they called for scholars to explore such themes as modes of production and techniques of production, social differentiation and the shifting role of the sexes, relationships between societies and their environment, the experiences of the migrant laborer and urban worker, and creation of popular cultures.[34]

Since the late 1980s and especially in the 1990s, the historical analysis that subscribed to this genre of interpretation yielded a wide range of useful histories which have since endured into the early years of the twenty-first century. Histories focusing on African women and gender and class relations assumed an unparalleled importance.[35] Also important was the paradigm shift from women's to gender history. The latter has allowed historians and other scholars to foreground gender as a set of social and symbolic relations.[36] More broadly, African women histories have largely evolved as part of African social and cultural histories that initially rested on the premise floated by anti-Marxist revisionists that African pre-colonial traditions and institutions would offer a medium for understanding African colonial and postcolonial experiences. In this shift, scholars sought to understand African history from 'below' by making the ordinary man and woman the primary focus of analysis. Consequently, historians, aided by anthropologists, brought to the fore of the discipline aspects of study such as ethnicity, marriage, law, and initiation rites.[37]

This social and cultural orientation of African history also helped scholars reify such concepts as 'masculinity,' 'sexuality', and 'youth' among other things, that continue to be important subjects of study. Some of the chapters in this volume, particularly those by Mamadou Diouf and Xavier Livermon, engage the themes of youth and sexuality, respectively. By extension, works focusing on African social identities in the colonial state have also benefited from this later historiographical revolution.[38] Structures and categories as domains, sites and agents of making African history have thus been helpful in expanding the thematic and analytical scope of the discipline. Several chapters in this book refresh our understanding of these aspects in African history. Given the paucity of works reflecting on the role of women in shaping national politics in postcolonial Africa (from an African historian's perspective), Alicia Decker's contribution to this volume reinforces the importance of gender in crafting modern African history.

Generally, categories such as gender, modernity, coloniality, postcoloniality, and even consumption of material and popular culture have helped enrich African cultural history.[39] These categories have provided scholars of critical African studies with a framework to reassess Africa's position in the current world order. They have also provided a critique of notions of decolonization, subjectivity, and postcolonialism.[40] In fact, though it is yet to have a major impact in African history, postmodernism has provided a few historians and anthropologists focusing on Africa with the methods to unpack political and cultural crises produced in Africa's postcolonial states. Applying this to their social and cultural analysis of national crises in Kenya in the late 1980s and early 1990s, David William Cohen and E.S. Atieno Odhiambo have revealed that local and public discourses at the national and local levels have the propensity to produce knowledge that can be useful to historians of Africa regarding current politics and culture. They argue that the sociologies and politics of knowledge production on 'present concerns and interests' relating to such issues as disease epidemics, refugee crises, civil wars, and environmental dilemmas can yield very authentic histories, if focus is directed on the ordinary African individual and his or her everyday experience.[41]

The quest by a few scholars to construct relations in colonial and postcolonial Africa at global, state, and community levels has prompted the creation of frameworks that apply concepts such as power, hegemony, and resistance to convey the nature and degree of African initiative. Discourses based on these concepts have aided the revision of our earlier understanding of such processes as resistance and production of knowledge and commodities in Africa. Studies focusing on environment, agricultural production, and anti-colonial protests have resulted from this development.[42] Currents of African intellectual history also seem to have tapped into this approach. Long considered the avowed mission of the educated African elite, articulation of anti-colonial protest could equally have been entertained by the African peasant. Steven Feierman's *Peasant Intellectuals* is a masterful revelation of how this category of African society could effectively articulate anti-colonial political discourses and action as did the African educated elite. Peasants did so by harnessing the power that was inherent in the indigenous institutions that governed their moral, productive economy. Aside from being conceived within the broader political economy of colonialism, African medical histories have similarly thrived on discourse analyses, revealing the creation of subjectivity and the category of 'the other'.[43]

The scholarly and public debate on Mau Mau has been more polarizing but enriching than any other theme in postcolonial Kenya, and has spawned studies that fit the description of 'new histories.' In the 1960s and 1970s, this debate provided nationalist radicals who were dissatisfied with the socio-economic and political progress of the new government with an alternative (often a populist) ideology that resonated with a disaffected public.[44] In the years that followed, the debate forced some historians to refocus their energy on depicting the Mau Mau struggle as a 'people's' history: an experience of ordinary men and women, delving deeper into African (rather than imperial) action in the uprising.[45] More recently, the most dominant scholarly threads in this debate have shifted attention to the validity or meaning of freedom for the ordinary citizen, memory, and nationalism, ownership of the struggle for freedom, as well as ethnicity and nation building.[46] These threads have also reminded us of the stigma of colonial repression that postcolonial states inherited at independence. This has in turn inspired studies that urge the need to rethink the legitimacy of imperial trusteeship and responsibility to the former colonial subjects of empire who are now free citizens of postcolonial African states.[47]

The emergence of histories of local, national, and transnational African visual and performance cultures (particularly art, dance, and music) have further defined the varied interests of scholars of Africa's past. Some of these predate the recovery initiatives of the 1960s. For instance, in art history, the African imagination of the West and its colonial modernity was produced by Africans in the Belgian Congo as far back as the 1920s.[48] Current efforts, particularly by a new generation of African scholars, have catapulted African visual arts into African studies. Informed by the historical bearing of African art, works by Aderonke Adesanya among others help us discern gender, leisure, politics, and identity.[49] Overall, such works have promoted an ingenuity that has been at the core of Africa's contribution to civilization, but one that the colonial interlude served to deny. Indeed, Toyin Falola's reflections on the role of works on African art in rehabilitating Africa's past and in restoring the African's innate creative power and dignity, are ideal. He has noted that, in themselves, African artistic expressions are a form of self-definition that enables the rejection of imposed (external) ones, and helps to change the paradigm of negativity to the positive. Above all, works focusing on African art enable us to comprehend how visual and even performance art create a counter-discourse to the hegemonic representations of blackness, thereby allowing blacks to fight back with disdain, anger, and rationalization. More importantly, they provide evidence of civilization in Africa's past, a confirmation of the mission that pioneering works by Du bois and Cheikh Anta Diop sought to promote.[50]

Generally, African history's evolution in scope and analysis, especially since 1980, has expanded in ways that this Introduction cannot capture entirely. Yet, as a new generation of scholars emerges in the field and continues to build on past and recent efforts, and as new paradigms of analysis emerge, the discipline is bound to continue to grow.

A Synthesis

The foregoing analysis reveals that since the 1950s African historiography has been shaped by academic institutions (universities and their intellectual or political ideologies) as well as economic, social, and more recently cultural perspectives that have yielded the existing interpretations of the field. The historiography has also thrived from a multidisciplinary appeal, inviting analyses from history, politics, anthropology, literary studies, visual and performance arts, and even from ecological studies. Generally speaking, debates that have yielded what so far can be credited as African historiography reflect two key components.

The first relates to contested interpretation, which has left scholars divided over the nature of the relationship between Africans and colonialism.[51] Historical analysis of the African past has generally progressed along this divided interpretation, a fact that chapters in this volume reveal. Historians, anthropologists, and literary critics, among others, have contributed to the discourse that makes up the two varied interpretations. There are scholars who view colonialism as a juxtaposition to the 'Other', the African experience, and not a process that produced a hegemonic colonial state that blurred the African place in it. For instance, Jean Comaroff and John Comaroff maintain that colonialism was not a simple exercise in domination and resistance, but was everywhere marked by various forms of complex dialectics, including that which was mediated by social differences and cultural distinctions, yielding 'new frontiers, new signs, and styles', and transformed everyone and everything that came it into contact with.[52] This body of scholarship explores the contradictions that colonialism generated in Africa, and points to the many contestations in the colonial state between Africans, and between colonial officials and Africans over colonial structures, policies, and practices. Therefore, for one to grasp the historical proceedings within the colonial state (and one can make a similar argument for the postcolonial state), this interpretation urges scholars to look beyond the assumed power of such states, and instead peer into the multiple layers of political and social relations and the conflicts and struggles that those relations produced. African cultural and social histories have borrowed from this thread. For instance, using reflections from African gender history, Nancy Hunt contends that:

> colonialism can no longer be viewed as a process of imposition from a European metropole but must be seen as tangled layers of political relations and lines of conflicting projections and domestications that converged in specific local misunderstandings, struggles and misrepresentations ... Social action in colonial and postcolonial Africa cannot be reduced to such polarities as metropole/colony or colonizer/colonized.[53]

Then there are works whose interpretation assumes or perceives an imposing, hegemonic presence of colonialism, which broadly argues that the African historical agency was recognizably directed or influenced by colonial superstructures, however superficial these structures might have been. For instance, African resistance against colonialism was real, directed at certain oppressive state structures that must be accounted for. Teresa A. Barnes is specific on this thinking, and sees colonialism as a period marked by violence, exploitation, deconstruction, improvement, and the tendency to reconsolidate economic, political, and social identities and power. For this reason, to overlook the broader picture in which such dynamism operated while pursuing local structures likely effaces an enriching historical analysis. Where one attempts to understand the dynamic colonial period in a 'deconstructionist mode,' Barnes therefore contends, 'the creative examination of matters ever more local can lead scholars to miss the forest for the trees. Historians may abandon complex narration out of postmodernist scruple, but if narration loses its critical edge, history becomes indistinguishable from soap opera'.[54]

Frederick Cooper has recognized the difficulty that exists in exploring colonial binarism since any attempts to do so unintentionally reproduces 'new variations of the dichotomy' along the lines of modern versus traditional or by a transposition of 'the destructive imperialist versus the sustaining community of the victims'. He particularly notes the difficulty of the African historian in confronting the power that propelled European expansion 'without assuming it was all-determining' of the outcome of the social clashes it unleashed. Cooper seems to proffer a middle-ground approach between the preceding two extremes by urging that historians of Africa consider using binaries of colonizer/colonized, Western/non-Western, or domination/resistance as initial, useful devices for investigating the complex nature of colonialism, particularly questions relating to power. However, as they do so, scholars should not be constrained to search 'for precise ways in which power is deployed and the ways in which power is engaged, contested, deflected, and appropriated'.[55] By using the instance of the connections between the resistance and colonialism, Cooper urges the need to move past superficial, if not simple, analyses that explain that connection in terms of the oppressor/oppressed model. 'Politics in a colony', he argues, 'should not be reduced to anticolonial politics or to nationalism: the "imagined communities" Africans saw were both smaller and larger than the nation, sometimes in creative tension with each other, sometimes in repressive antagonism'.[56]

Aside from producing a divide in interpretation, debates that have produced African historiography over the decades have also rendered the question of epistemological and utilitarian uses of African historical knowledge relevant. To the revisionists of the 1960s, restoring the authenticity of African history implied not only decolonizing its methodology and substance, but also ensuring that the reclaimed historical knowledge, or at least the past, would help reconstruct the African identity and confront postcolonial challenges to African nationhood. The signature of the debate's relevance was the conspicuous adoption of the phrase 'Usable Past'.[57] The crux of the argument in the "usable past" scholarship has been that past knowledge is helpful for the epistemological approach of Africanist scholars to narrow the gap between the paradigm logic applied and the needs and perceptions of the people—and the state. It is a line of argument that was recognizable in the critique against nationalist scholarship in the 1970s. Critics advanced that pride and cultural nationalism that were the core of nationalist scholarship lacked tangible value for the ordinary citizens.

In the mid-1970s, proponents of applying the 'useable past' to achieve meaningful outcomes in the present argued that 'the poor and hungry cannot eat past cultural achievements', and that contemporary African regimes merely manipulated versions of the past and pursued modernist transformations that disregarded African realities.[58] Still dominant at the beginning of the following decade, at which time African scholars of literary criticism plied their professional trade by scrutinizing political malpractices of African governance, the perception that scholarship should inform Africa's plight and its solutions appealed to many African scholars. For Ngugi Wa Thiog'o, neo-colonialism as embraced by African leaders remained a major obstacle to the elimination of economic mismanagement, corruption, political and cultural repression, and the degradation of African culture. In essence, it was a betrayal of the struggle for freedom in Africa.[59] In the mid-1980s, historians of Africa and other Africanists still regarded this question as worth pursuing. In a comprehensive reflection on the debate, Bogumil Jewsiewicki emphasized that the 'Usable Past' ceased to be just 'a matter exclusive academic debate', but a useful lens for reflecting and resolving the paradoxes of postcolonial African states.[60] In this book, a number of scholars revisit these paradoxes as far as postcolonial Africa is concerned.

The 'Usable Past' was thus partly cultivated into existence by a recognition by scholars that Africa faced real political and socioeconomic challenges that academic scholarship was to address. The close of the 1980s witnessed an Africa whose public memory was still ingrained in the uncertainties of the 1960s. Few governments had done much to ignite hope for their citizens, as many political systems exercised repression rather than fostered freedom within the civil society. Many Africans, according to John Lonsdale, saw their governments 'as evils to be evaded rather than as potential instruments of the public good'.[61] Therefore, some historians reasserted the importance of using Africa's past as a way of understanding not only these challenges, but also in projecting the future of Africa. It was important for the historian of Africa to study the past to help them and other political actors (leaders) imagine Africa's future. Lonsdale was lucid on this role while reflecting on the developments of the late 1980s:

> The future is treacherous territory for historians. It is also their continually imagined ideal ... historians cannot help but judge the human successes and failures which they find in their recreation of the past than by the light of their own hopes and fears for the future. Effective political actors in the everyday world of the present require a complimentary feat of the imagination. They can most easily recognize and work for a desired future when they have imagined it, and they are able to portray it to a wider public as a project which builds on the triumphs or avenges the defeats of the living past.[62]

Thus, Africans' acquaintance with their history was supposed to serve the urgent need of promoting free political argument that would in turn aid and formulate alternative societal futures. The past would also inspire African governments to mobilize the public in the pursuit of core values that would help provision a meaningful future.[63]

At the dawn of the twenty-first century, the past has continued to provide historians with a reference framework for social, economic, and political trends in Africa. The aspirations, failures, and fears of early years of independence may be in the distant past, but as Stephen Ellis reminds us, they are still within living memory—so much so that many within and outside Africa have not ceased from making allusions to notions of nation building, liberation, economic development, Pan-Africanism, and freedom from dependency. All these, Ellis contends, are reminiscent of 'the great themes of the independence generation'.[64] Most of these remain only figments of the imagination in Africa because they have not been fully realized. There has been the feeling that historians of Africa have uncritically related the shortcomings of the 1960s to Africa's present experiences, and therefore are to blame for reproducing the status quo, a fact that Ellis makes clear: 'Historians [of Africa] have made their own modest contribution to this unsatisfactory state of affairs by their reluctance to reconsider Africa's contemporary history in terms appropriate to the present state of affairs'.[65]

The 'Usable Past' has also found relevance in efforts to re-image or 're-package' Africa in ways that differ from how the continent and its citizens have been cast by the West in the postcolonial period. Lonsdale juxtaposes the West's optimism for Africa shortly before and after independence with the current, external pessimism and the role to be played by the historian of Africa. African nationalism of the 1950s and 1960s, and the energetic search for the nation by Africans, seem to have cultivated a sympathy, and even an admiration, within the Western public and academic institutions. In those years, as Lonsdale illustrates, 'Press cartoons portrayed Africans, not as starving children or emaciated victims of HIV-AIDS, but as virile nationalist giants, overshadowing puny British politicians'.[66] During those years, African leaders displayed an uncanny energy to take on challenges and opportunities that came with the end of colonialism. But over the years, and particularly by the beginning of the twenty-first century, all this has changed. Ever-increasing global economic and social inequalities, and persistence in political and social dilemmas internal to African states, have complicated any ambitions of positive progress for the continent and its peoples. As a result, Western hopes and optimism for Africa and Africans that was evident in the 1960s have vanished, and has been replaced with perceptions of 'hopelessness'. The West's casting of such perceptions upon postcolonial Africa has in turn cultivated the irony of the 'civilizing mission', whose populist version presents Africans as unable to fend for themselves. The African scholar has therefore been urged to address the arduous task of offering a counter-enlightenment narrative that demonstrates that the realities of the African situation are the result of continued production of Africa as nature and the West as culture.[67]

Thus, Africa as packaged and presented by the West has outlived the end of formal empire. Undeniably, this construction of Africa is still viewed by critics as a cultural construct of imperialism and colonialism, one that, as Achille Mbembe notes, presents Africa as the 'Other'. He presses this interpretation as a reminder that the view that Africa lacks value attributable to human nature, and that the continent excels in elementary and primitive aspects of life that bar its forward progress (relative to the West), have a long history. According to Mbembe, the continued application of this construct long after Africa's independence has allowed the notion of Africa's difference to be stretched to a new level, and served 'the West's desperate desire to assert its difference from the rest of the world'. In this sense, Mbembe, echoing V.Y. Mudimbe, furthers the argument, 'Africa still constitutes one of the metaphors through which the West represents the origin of its own norms and identity'.[68] The enduring role of the West in its definition and casting of Africa, despite the latter's independence, has undoubtedly continued to enrich debates and analysis about Africa's past, present, and future. Questions regarding knowledge production about Africa, producers of that knowledge (scholars of Africa based in or outside the continent), and the authenticity of that knowledge in genuinely confronting challenges unique to Africa, continue to assume importance in scholarship pertaining to Africa. Part of the search for this authenticity in production of knowledge about and for Africa is behind the establishment of the Council for the Development of Social Science Research in Africa (CODESRIA). The Council has provided a platform for the research and publication of some of the most engaging African issues by Africa's finest scholars in history, politics, economics, and other fields. Indeed revision of Africa's past and an engaging analysis of Africa's recent and current experiences from CORDESRIAS's works must be applauded.[69]

The 'Usable Past' has also brought the aspect of audience into the debate. To whom should historians of Africa direct their scholarship? Should historical research address larger, global issues that resonate with the global audience or should those historians narrow down to Africans and localized issues within the continent? Given the everyday life challenges that Africa has continued to experience, some have recently argued that historical focus that deconstructs colonial and postcolonial superstructures is less suited to the audience (ordinary Africans) and historians based in Africa. This is because, critics argue, deconstructionism is an analytical tool rooted in North American rather than African realities. This argument is situated in the current global order in which the marginalization of Africa by global capitalism has tended to sway some analysts to find an explanation within universal models, instead of shifting the focus to localized problems and challenges faced by specific African countries and communities.[70]

Thus far, the foregoing perspectives only proceed to confirm that African historiography is a product of past and ongoing debates and conversations regarding paradigms of analyzing African history and of uses of knowledge that is produced. The diverse debates and their consequences have informed the richness of the field. Development of the discipline has benefited the most from the evolutionary trends in African studies since the 1950s. In his reflection on the prospects of African studies in the twenty-first century, Colin Bundy has concluded: 'Take African history [for instance] … this is a field whose fruits—its scope of enquiry, topics, themes, methodologies, theoretical tools, and links with other disciplines—have for forty years yielded rich harvests. It is a body of work which has increasingly informed debates well beyond Africa; and it has challenged versions of world history that misconstrue or silence African perspectives'.[71]

This volume bears testimony to Bundy's conclusion. While it focuses more on themes and their interpretations, other aspects of African history are also implied, particularly the interdisciplinary approach to production of knowledge in the field. Thematic growth of the discipline over the decades has been tremendous, an indication that there remains a lot to be uncovered. Therefore, not every theme has been captured by the volume, and neither can we argue that the volume is complete and thorough. For instance, themes not accommodated in the volume but which have been important to the field include customary and colonial laws as they related to the African, African technologies, as well as Islam during the colonial era, among others.

The case for a postcolonial African history, reflected in the themes that form the second part of this volume, is validated by major transformations that African countries, generally speaking, have experienced within the last three decades. The ensuing internal changes have occurred not in isolation but partly consonant with Africa's never-ending struggle to adjust to the postcolonial regional and global orders. That struggle has revealed some persistent, old, systemic challenges, but one cannot fail to recognize some positive developments that have occurred during this period. The development challenge continues to ensure that the questions about national debts and foreign aid remain important. Resource-endowment remains Africa's strongest advantage in a world where resource-extraction is critical for development. The extent to which the continent has failed to harness its natural wealth to realize development remains an irony and a vexing question to many Africanists. The education sector has become a point of focus for many African countries and its relevance to modern African needs has led to certain definite developments in that sector. Quality and delivery of knowledge, especially at the tertiary levels, continue to pose challenges.

As regards Africa's postcolonial politics, while some may see secessionism in the emergence of new countries such as Eritrea (1991) and South Sudan (2011), others see nationalism and freedom at work in these political developments. The Rwandan Genocide (1994) still defines how some view Africa's colonial and postcolonial experiences. Mahmood Mamdani's reflections on the latter yield a very engaging perspective as far as comprehending Africa's postcolonial, political challenges: that African nationalists of the conservative order have been part of the problem given their failure to decolonize what he refers to as the native prerogative with regard to the indigenous populations resident in their territories. The political consequences of such colonial legacy proved serious for countries such as Rwanda, Uganda, and Zanzibar, where 'race' (or even ethnicity) became the ultimate standard for defining citizenship, and a major determinant of violence during the political upheavals that rocked these states after independence.[72] It is also undeniable that reflections on ethnicity, identity, and past experiences have provided Rwandans, for example, with a formula for engaging with nation building and dealing with 'Usable Past'. The Biafra War may similarly have defined how modern Nigeria has evolved since the 1960s, at least politically.

On another dimension, the Pan-Africanist project as represented by the African Union has persisted and been reformed to identify itself more with Africa's challenges beyond politics, in spite of external and internal challenges that the project has experienced since its inception. Regional blocs on the continent reflect a new sense of purpose in dealing with systemic political and economic challenges, and an urgency to remedy the divisiveness that hindered meaningful cooperation between African countries in past decades. The African renaissance that some thought was resurging in the 1990s has been evident in these developments, though its intensity remained questionable. Despite the numerous socio-economic challenges, the brightest spot for Africa has been the liberalization of politics in many countries during the 1990s. Civic problems and the slow pace of political accountability may still be evident, but it is gratifying that a few scholars have seized on these developments to revisit constitutional histories of African countries. Accountability and transparency have in turn catapulted into importance the role in public governance of the African media and civil and non-government institutions.

On a macro-scale, decolonization has led to 'reverse migration' whereby postcolonial migrations by Africans into Western countries has become an important 'transnational' challenge for destination countries. Such outmigrations, evident at intra and extra-continental levels, offer development challenges to Africa in the form of brain drains to countries that have historically thrived on Africa's human and natural resources. Some would argue positively about the monetary remittances back to Africa by the continent's intellectual and economic diaspora; but the socio-economic implications of their absence from the continent, and the cultural dislocation they encounter away from home, have had consequences for the individual, country, and continent.[73]

Former colonial powers, notably France, have gradually redefined their relationship with their former colonial territories. The end of the Cold War has inaugurated an era where, strictly speaking, the West has no political stranglehold over the continent. By extension, China's presence in Africa has assumed a degree that is difficult to ignore. Globalization has been responsible for exchange of cultures between Africa and the world, and these have produced categories of identities for Africans in Africa and in the diaspora. All these are developments that chapters focusing on postcolonial Africa consider, reflecting an attempt to embrace the call to scholars of Africa, and of African history in particular, to relate their production of knowledge to Africa's real changes, whether political, social, cultural, or international.

ORGANIZATION OF THE HANDBOOK

This volume is divided into two general parts. Part I is concerned with colonial Africa, while Part II focuses on postcolonial Africa. This division is adopted only for purposes of chronology and flow of themes, and is not an absolute delineation of Africa's historical experience. In fact, as some of the chapters demonstrate, there are certain overlaps and continuities in historical action across the precolonial, colonial, and postcolonial eras. The thematic approach is deliberate, as we endeavored to reflect on the depth of African history by having various scholars engage various themes that have defined the field. We also hope that while doing so, the chapters reveal the paradigms of interpretation that have been used to analyze those themes.

Part I focuses on the African experience in colonial Africa. Martin Shanguhyia contends that Africa's physical environment provided a medium for historical action during the colonial era. This is in no way to state that its environment has determined Africa's history. Rather, by using multiple studies of African environmental history in the colonial period, he attempts to show that the environment offered both colonial states and Africans a platform to express, forge, and preserve their perceptions, notions, meanings, and uses of nature in ways that produced different outcomes and responses. In the next chapter, Toyin Falola and Chukwuemeka Agbo examine relations between Britain and France (the two major European colonial powers in Africa) and their African colonial subjects, as shaped by new administrative structures. The structures are in turn examined within economic, social, and political changes and African response to them. In his chapter, Paul Lovejoy perceives a persistence of slavery during the colonial period in Africa. Instead of disappearing completely (as some have assumed), slavery underwent extensive transformations. For instance, Lovejoy demonstrates, acts of enslavement were undertaken surreptitiously rather than through capture in warfare, judiciously sanctioned punishment, or slave raiding, although kidnapping continued in some places. Although colonial rule was justified as a civilizing mission and slavery was considered an anathema that had to be eliminated, its persistence was a feature of colonial rule, despite policies and development schemes that attempted to redefine social relationships through taxation, migrant labor deployment, Christian practices, redefinition of kinship, and other 'civilizing' mechanisms.

On the colonial economy, Moses E. Ochonu maps the general economic policy trajectories of colonial regimes as well as the active agency of Africans in engaging with these policies, and shows how, in an economy calibrated to serve metropolitan interests, Africans as individuals and groups engaged with the closures and openings presented by colonial land, labor, and agricultural regimes. Women also played fundamental roles in defining and redefining colonial economies, and their place in it. This is the subject of Judith Byfield's chapter. She attempts to move us away from a historiography that privileges men's roles in colonial economies (particularly cash crop production) to strike a consonant with scholars of African women who have identified the numerous direct and indirect ways in which women engaged the colonial economy. She contends that as the scholarship on women continues to expand and explore topics such as artisan production, marriage, and childhood, we have a fuller understanding of the dynamic ways in which women in Africa shaped and were shaped by colonial economies.

More often than not, colonialism brokered into existence ambivalence in pre-existing African indigenous structures and values in ways that redefined the roles of African women and expectations about them by the colonial society. In her chapter, Gloria Chuku reflects on this development by exploring how European colonialism attempted to alter African womanhood (a signifier of responsibility, social etiquette, versatility, independence, hard work and resilience) and expectations of an adult African female in indigenous African societies. Challenges and barriers created by colonialism enhanced, diminished, or placed African women in ambiguous situations as they physically and culturally negotiated the transition from old ways of life to new ones.

Historical works on Anglophone and Francophone Africa often overshadow studies on the colonial experience of Lusophone Africa. Therefore, Philip J. Havick's chapter on the administration, economy, and society in the Portuguese African Empire is a much welcome contribution to this volume. His chapter offers a comparative overview of the Third Portuguese Empire, particularly its economic, political, social, and cultural ramifications and the impact of Portuguese administration upon African societies between 1900 and 1975.

Andrew Barnes revisits the role of Christianity in Africa in an innovative way. In his chapter he shows how the importance of creating and maintaining social welfare institutions (schools, hospitals, and poor houses) for the expansion of Christianity in Europe in turn influenced Christians in Africa to build similar institutions with similar goals. Some European Christian missions in Africa perceived this as a challenge and therefore teamed up with colonial governments to ensure missionary control over evangelization through poor relief. In response, African Christians developed similar but different strategies for evangelizing other Africans. Kelly Duke Bryant offers an overview of the history of colonial education in Africa, particularly the involvement of missionaries and the colonial state, tracing these developments from the early years of colonial rule through the interwar period to the expansion and reform of the postwar era, as well as offering some postcolonial legacies of these developments. She focuses in particular on African responses to and experiences of colonial education, relying on her original research on Senegal. She views this history through the lens of African agency and ambivalence, arguing that although Africans shaped colonial education and the uses to which it could be put, its complicated legacies led colonial education to occupy an ambivalent position in African history.

Health and medicine in colonial Africa have been a growing area of scholarship. Matthew M. Heaton examines health and health care in Africa in the colonial period by analyzing the health consequences of colonial occupation and colonial economies on Africans. He argues that issues of health and medicine should not only be treated in terms of the spread of germs and the provision of health care, but also in terms of the limitations of medical science and the broader social dynamics that affected how both Africans and Europeans thought about the role of health and medicine in colonial Africa. As regards the African experience during the colonial period, Uyilawa Usuanlele and Oluwatoyin B. Oduntan argue that colonial urbanization aimed at achieving financial self-sufficiency of colonies and ensuring the good social (cultural) well-being of European populations. These ideas justified colonial neglect of rural communities and Africans in urban environments. Africans who were affected by these developments resisted, reimagined, and reshaped colonial purposes and designs, and thereby established themselves as co-makers of colonial towns and cities.

Meshack Owino reflects on the African experiences in the First and Second World Wars, each war treated in separate chapters. During the first global war, Africans' contribution was noticeably through provision of supplies and as porters (carriers), but they were also victims of the mayhem that characterized the conflict. Africans' participation in the Second World War was even more remarkable by serving overseas in the main theatres of the conflict. Overall, the wars' specific impact on African soldiers, civilian populations, and the continent is analyzed.

African migration within and out of Africa predates colonialism. However, the inauguration of colonial rule in Africa highly regulated this process, mainly to serve the needs of the various administrations. Kwabena Akurang-Parry and Isaac Indome's chapter demonstrates the extent to which the attritions of colonial rule (wars of conquest and African resistance, conscription of forced labor, taxation, and brutalization of Africans) triggered migrations throughout the colonial period. During the late colonial era, the unintended benefits of colonial rule (such as education, expanding colonial economy, urbanization, and social change) also became inexorable forces of African migrations.

For their part, Benjamin Lawrance, Temilola Alanamu, and Benedict Carton attempt to broach a new ground for agents that have long been neglected in African history. They try to claim the agency of children in African history. They make the pertinent argument that children in Africa have often been marginal to those in power, a fact that, together with the absence of adequate sources, has led to this category of African society being neglected by historians beyond narratives on childhood socialization, labor, education, and play. Their chapter examines how colonialism simplified the complexities of African childhood by having children become workers crucial to capitalist accumulation, perceiving them as malleable minds to be shaped through formal

Western education, and by institutionalizing boys' and girls' expectations in the broader society.

On the subject of literature in colonial Africa, Tanure Ojaide establishes the relationship between African people's culture and literature, and between their history and politics. He maps out the many kinds of literature in colonial Africa which portray history in a non-conventional way as regards social, cultural, economic, political, and psychological consequences of colonialism on Africans. Colonial African literature provides evidence for the suffering, struggle, and resilience of African peoples under colonial rule. On his part, Sylvester Okwunodu Ogbechie reviews the impact of colonialism on African art and identity, especially in the emergent modernity of African artists. He shows how colonial rule impacted the development of new visual languages for modern African art. By examining African artists from different regions of Africa, he maps regional differences in these artists' approach to their practices and their engagement with questions of modernist identity. He reveals that an investigation of discourses of modern art and identity in the colonial era helps us search out points of convergence in how these discourses unfolded in their national spaces and transnational engagements. Augustine Agwuele counters the often presumed view that colonialism radically altered alien cultures. Focusing on Yoruba culture, he argues that colonialism rapidly and radically intensified or attenuated existing practices rather than upended or even radically changed or transformed them. With regard to youth and popular culture in colonial Africa, Jamaine Abidogun's chapter describes how African youths lived through changing times and how they defined popular culture through lived experiences. That culture was the product of negotiated experiences within the realities of European colonization.

Fikru Negash Gebrekidan's chapter reminds us that the practical and symbolic implications of the Battle of Adowa retain value in enriching Ethiopian historiography in ways not captured in previous literature. Gebrekidan explores how Ethiopian victory at Adwa in 1896 helped promote a more far-reaching Pan-African discourse, one in which Ethiopia itself played an important role as a poignant symbol of anti-colonial resistance during the first half of the twentieth century. The chapter is an example of trends in transnational history that have defined African historiography.

Understanding colonial Africa within the 'global' is also evident in Enocent Msindo's analysis of colonial Africa and the West. Msindo views colonialism as an extractive system which legitimized the looting of Africa by Western corporations, safeguarded new markets for Europe's Industrial Revolution, and created Africa's dependency by delegitimizing African indigenous innovations and knowledge systems through incorporation of Africans into Western education and cheap labor regimes. Herein are to be found the roots of poverty on the continent. Western politics and economic power were instrumental in legitimizing this system. Ibrahim J. Gassama critically examines the role of international law and all its manifestations in the lives of Africans during the colonial era and extends the analysis into the present day. He argues that this received law facilitated imperialism and colonialism, and that it remains a manifestation of colonial legacy in modern-day Africa given that few Africans can fully escape its tragic hold on their lives. Aside from implying it in existing historical literature, few historians have explored the deeper connections between colonialism and development in Africa. Ruth Rempel goes into the subterranean connections of colonialism and development in refreshing ways by tracing development as practiced in colonial Africa to its Western roots and other global developments in the first half of the twentieth century. She uses imperial development history in British and French colonies to show how colonial regimes initially used ad hoc development measures in their African colonies before they were pushed to systematize and change them by global war and economic depression, and by persistent African agency. She also examines US involvement in development in Liberia and Ethiopia, and the adoption of a countervailing development project by African nationalists and the United Nations in the 1950s which shared with its imperial rival assumptions about economic growth, planning, and the primary role of the state.

Toyin Falola and Chukwuemeka Agbo offer an engaging analysis of African nationalism since the nineteenth century. They examine the intersection between nationalism and African intellectuals, particularly the quest by African elites to address issues of tradition, change, politics, and power, and to reconstruct a new image for Africa. They are also concerned with the way nationalism shaped the production of knowledge and influenced colonial politics in Africa, leading to the formation of the modern African states. Robert M. Maxon engages African 'Decolonization Histories'. He argues that decolonization was a lengthy process, one that occurred over several decades in the second half of the twentieth century. The lengthy period and varied contexts that marked the change from colonial territories to nation-states as well as differing paths followed means that one narrative does not fit the experience of all. Therefore, Maxon urges that decolonization accounts have to pay attention to the varied forces and factors, paths and actors, timing, and the experiences of former British, French, Belgian, and Portuguese African territories. He particularly demonstrates that African factors were the most significant variable in the continent's decolonization histories.

Chapters in Part II mainly focus on themes in postcolonial Africa. Readers are encouraged to consider the content of this section as overlapping with the previous one, given that topics found in the former have roots in the years preceding independence after 1960. Clear examples include the Cold War, creation of African diasporas, Pan-Africanism, and apartheid. The Cold War emerged as an important external influence on the political trajectories of African states shortly before and after independence. It is one of those themes that transcends any presumed 'boundaries' between colonial and postcolonial Africa. Kenneth Kalu argues that the intrigues of the Cold War shaped Africa's decolonization process in very significant ways, and led to the evolution of extractive and utterly predatory political and economic institutions in postcolonial Africa. Drawing from several cases of foreign interventions in Africa during the Cold War, he demonstrates that the activities of the USA and its allies were not always focused on advancing the interests of Africans, but were more concerned about ensuring that African countries did not imbibe communist ideas. On the other hand, Ademola Araoye navigates post-independence African politics, especially the struggle for partisan and absolute appropriations of state spaces. He notes that different colonial experiences of each individual state, variations in patterns that yielded statehood, the neo-colonial traditions and institutions bequeathed to them by departing powers, and their heterogeneous internal constructions have all influenced African postcolonial politics.

Immediately after independence, African states were often weak and under-representative of their respective ethnic communities, thereby marginalizing significant portions of their population. This contributed to violent struggles by excluded communities for political and economic autonomy from the state. Charles Thomas's chapter charts these developments, and focuses on political dissention that resulted in separatist conflicts, especially civil and secessionist wars. He clearly observes that such conflicts have not occurred without external, usually global, political influences.

Africa's relations with the West following decolonization have been a subject of fruitful debate in African studies literature. Enocent Msindo argues that Africa's postcolonial economic and political transitions have been mainly due to the structural conditions of the new states and the nature of Africa's relationship with the West. Post-independent Africa remained captured by Western capitalist and political enterprises that have dictated Africa's economic and political developments.

For much of the history of the USA's foreign relations, Africa has been a somewhat overlooked entity and sometimes entirely ignored. In his chapter, Adebayo Oyebade provides a lucid analysis of the historic connections and interactions between the USA and Africa. He traces the US-African relationships from the fifteenth century to the postcolonial period and demonstrates the existence of a long-standing connection through which Africa has contributed to the definition of US foreign policy. Franco-African relations after independence in particular have provided interesting scholarly perspectives. In his chapter, Tony Chafer argues that the 'exceptional' nature of these relations span the entire colonial period as successive governments have sought to decolonize, not by preparing the colonies for independence, but by integrating them more closely with France. This aspect of envisioning an African future as part of a Franco-African bloc was challenged during the 1950s, forcing Charles de Gaulle to improvise an 'exit strategy' which involved transferring power to African political leaders while signing an array of cooperation agreements with the newly independent states that tied their futures closely to France. The postcolonial Franco-African special relationship (Françafrique) was born, further perpetuating the notion of French exceptionalism. Franco-Algerian relations have been equally intriguing to scholars. In her analysis, Natalya Vince also challenges the oft-repeated idea that Franco-Algerian relations were 'exceptional' both during the colonial period and into the post-independence era. Although Algeria held a distinct place within the French empire, there were many connections and parallels between Algeria and other parts of the French empire—in terms of people, colonial ideas and policies, the experiences and activism of colonized peoples, and intertwined chains of events. In the post-independence period, a confrontational rhetoric between the two countries has masked pragmatic collaboration. Franco-Algerian 'memory wars' are often more Franco-French and Algero-Algerian than they initially seem. Moreover, rather than being locked in a suffocating embrace, Franco-Algerian relations have always existed and functioned in broader global contexts.

One of the stand-out consequences of the decline of the Cold War has been China's increasing expansion into Africa, to a degree that has forced scholars of Africa to reconsider the importance of the continent to global powers. Consequently, the chapter by Joshua Eisenman and David Shinn is very enlightening. The two scholars explore how China's increasingly proactive foreign policymakers have taken advantage of a void left by an indifferent Russia, a preoccupied USA, and a divided Europe to create fresh opportunities and pursue new bilateral and multilateral dialogues with African countries. In doing so, China has evolved a foreign policy toward Africa designed to secure natural resources, markets, opportunities for its construction firms, and to consolidate its position as leader of the developing world. Beijing has been adept at employing approaches that address African nations' economic, diplomatic, and security needs, while ensuring China's continued ability to influence the political and commercial landscape of the continent.

John Mukum Mbaku provides a critical and rigorous analysis of the often troubled relationship between Africa and global financial institutions. He shows that while African policymakers have looked to these institutions as sources of funds for industrial projects in their respective countries, these institutions' activities in Africa have also imposed significant social, economic, political, and environmental costs on the African peoples. As well as examining the ways in which conditionalities imposed on the African countries by global financial institutions have interfered with public policy in these countries, Mbaku also explores the extent to which these global financial institutions have also impacted political and economic development in the African countries. Ruth Rempel continues with her analysis of Africa and the development experience, but this time focuses on the postcolonial period. She describes African development after independence as a mix of colonial policies and institutions with approaches created in United Nations forums. From advancing national development agendas in the late 1960s, African development aspirations were also guided by the Lagos Plan, a continental development blueprint, during the 1970s. Global economic volatility and the unraveling of nationalist coalitions during that decade undermined earlier state-led development approaches, and opened up avenues for structural adjustment policies in the following decade. She outlines African responses to adjustment and governance reform. She ends by analyzing varied efforts to relaunch a development project in the new millennium, which, like its predecessors, involves the roles of both external and African agencies.

In recent decades, research on a narrowly constituted 'African diaspora' has given way to an increasingly expanded focus on multifarious diasporic communities in Africa, Eurasia, and the Americas. In his chapter, Kwasi Konadu argues that such communities must be understood within the historiography of African diasporas and within the specific contexts that help explain departures and arrivals, sources and destinations. By focusing on two of the most significant trends in diasporic approaches to African history ('Atlantic creoles' and 'Black Atlantic' frameworks), Konadu makes the case for addressing methodological and other shortcomings inherent in those trends, in terms of approaches in the field of African history that can promote an African world perspective and practice in African diaspora studies.

Sub-Saharan Africa is frequently seen as the periphery of the Muslim world, in terms of both geography and religious influence. In her chapter, Marloes Janson demonstrates that Islam has had a presence in Sub-Saharan Africa since the earliest days of its history. She moves away from conventional scholarship that emphasizes 'African Islam' to an approach that helps to capture the fluidity of the different ways of 'being Muslim' in everyday living, thereby challenging ingrained analytical concepts such as an 'African Islam' versus 'Arab Islam,' and an accommodating Sufi Islam versus an orthodox reformist Islam. Christianity and religious philosophy in particular have also shaped postcolonial African politics, social moral fiber, and a platform from which to reflect on postcolonial mentalities and thought processes. This is a subject that Elias Kifon Bongmba engages in his chapter. He unpacks postcolonialism as unfinished business through African theological perspectives.

Reflecting on apartheid and post-apartheid South Africa, Nancy L. Clark offers a comprehensive overview of the incremental elaboration of racial segregation in South Africa, and demonstrates the continuing impact of the past on post-apartheid South Africa. Clark draws attention to the crucial role played by Africans outside the political process in bringing about the end of apartheid through protests, boycotts, and strikes, as well as the growing disenchantment with the African National Congress Government in the post-apartheid period. Using evidence from newly accessed sources, Clark provides a broad picture of how apartheid worked and was defeated, and the current problems facing South Africa.

In what is an in-depth analysis of Pan-Africanism and its connection with the history of the African Union, Horace Campbell explores the ideas and skills of Africans in and outside Africa and their influence on Africa's history of emancipation. Campbell deftly traces the evolution of the global idea of Pan-Africanism and its political and ideological manifestations over the historic period since the transatlantic slave trade. He concludes by calling on scholars and students of Pan-Africanism to break from the traditional and worn-out assumptions of African Reconstruction and embrace the spirit of Ubuntu, which is the new paradigm for Pan-Africanism emanating from victories of a revitalized African people.

In a chapter focusing on human rights in modern Africa, Edward Kissi examines debates over the universal or cultural definitions of human rights, and reveals how human rights have been viewed, used as ideological instruments for contesting and reinforcing oppression, and memorialized in the history of Africa. He concludes that the pursuit of human rights as social policy in Africa has exposed the contradictory embrace of human rights as an organizing principle in African history.

Peter Otiato Ojiambo traces the development of education in postcolonial Africa as part of efforts by governments to address social, political, and economic needs. Many of these reforms have been shaped by varied historical happenings within the African continent. Drawing from his research on development of education in postcolonial Kenya, Ojiambo examines how historical experiences have influenced educational reforms, progress, challenges, and future trends. African women's relationship with the postcolonial state has often been as complex as it had been with the colonial state. Consequently, Alicia C. Decker explores the ways in which African statecraft has created opportunities and challenges for African women. She reveals how state policies and practices have influenced women's lives by examining the political trajectories of several women who got involved in politics and thus became part of the state. Decker considers the role of activism as a tool for engaging the state from the outside, and concludes by returning to the gendering of African statecraft, theorizing how and to what extent African women can make the postcolonial state less patriarchal. As alluded to earlier, this chapter refreshes the gender dimension in African modern history by locating women at the center of modern state politics in Africa.

In his reflection on youth and public space in Africa, Mamadou Diouf reveals how young people are triply positioned in environments of crisis with multiple causes, forms, and consequences. He argues that young people have come to constitute significant actors and resources, as well as the central concern, within the continent that has been shaken by eruptions of violence, social and political movements, and cultural and democratic projects. Young men and women have been both the principal perpetrators and the principal victims of these happenings. Xavier Livermon writes on African sexualities and makes the argument that there is no one 'African sexuality'; instead, African sexualities emerge as discursive and as political formations shaped by Africans themselves as much as by colonial formations. Importantly, the chapter charts new developments in the ways that African sexualities have been reimagined with a particular focus on how scholars and activists have attempted to decolonize this field. Livermon argues that African feminism and African queer studies are sites of contestation toward the production of new directions and alternative histories of African sexualities.

During the colonial period, certain objects from African material cultures were reinvented as art within the context of Western colonial knowledge about cultures and regimes of value. In her chapter, Sarah Van Beurden considers the impact of such reinvention on the development of museum and heritage cultures in postcolonial Africa. For instance, in postcolonial Africa, museums are seen both as subjects of, and tools for, cultural decolonization. Inversely, large collections of what is now considered national heritage in Africa were or are located in the West. Beurden addresses the rising importance of international heritage and conservation regimes supported by organizations such as UNESCO, and their role in the negotiation of restitution claims.

The importance of Mukoma Wa Ngugi's chapter goes beyond the ideal study on Africa's postcolonial literature. Rather, Ngugi provides a novel way in which historians and other scholars of Africa can use literary works to raise and answer questions on decolonization, African languages, 'transnationality', identity, and ownership. He does so by reflecting on early South African Literature (late1800s–early1940s) alongside the literature of decolonization (1950s–1980s) and contemporary transnational literature (1990s–present). He makes a cogent argument: that modern African literary criticism (itself an enriching source of understanding Africa's past and present) can hardly ignore its literary history. This chapter is an excellent complement of Ojaide's contribution in the colonial section of the volume.

In a related thread, Eric Charry outlines how an extraordinary number and diversity of distinct music cultures in Africa is at the root of postcolonial efforts to establish national identities with music and dance ensembles, and forging new multi-ethnic mixes for presentation on the world stage. Charry explores these initiatives within a wide range of issues such as: the influence of colonial education, the role of colonial imports (brass bands and Christian music), regional musical instruments, the stories they tell, and their global reach, Pan-African arts festivals, government audio and video archiving to preserve and stimulate the cultural heritage, the Internet and intellectual property issues, and the rise of independent artists. For their part, Hikabwa D. Chipande and Davies Banda explore the interplay of the complex relationships between sport and postcolonial politics in Africa. They discuss the instrumental role that sport played in nation building and projecting a positive image of the African continent. Since colonial times, communication media have been a vital component of state and society in Africa.

Sharon Omotoso examines this aspect for postcolonial Africa and sees a vertical communication structure of the colonial era as being gradually replaced with a horizontal structure, as new media breeds an enlightened society thereby challenging both conventional media and governance. Within the context of this transformation, Omotoso vouches for an African philosophy of communication, scrutinizes the impacts of media policies on relationships between elites and the grass roots, and, more importantly, examines how media policies in postcolonial Africa have helped bridge communication gaps.

The last chapter, by Michael West, offers incisive perspectives on a theme in African historiography that is increasingly being advocated for: transregional or transnational historical approaches. He rationalizes why African and African diaspora studies in the USA can be enriched by such approaches. West argues that although the end of the Cold War may have resulted in a decline of area studies, it has led to an increased interest in diaspora studies. For him, the defining contribution of the western African diaspora is a worldview that conceives of peoples of African descent not in ethnic, national, imperial, regional, or even continental terms, but in global ones. Consequently, the study of peoples of African descent globally should build on this tradition and eschew particularism, exceptionalism, and national historiography in favor of a transnational, transcontinental, and transoceanic approach.

Notes

1. For instance, T.O. Ranger, ed., *Emerging Themes in African History* (Nairobi: East African Publishing House, 1968); Christopher Fyfe, *African Studies Since 1945* (London: Longman, 1976).
2. A.D. Roberts, "The Earlier Historiography of Colonial Africa," *History in Africa* 5 (1978): 153–67.
3. Examples include Lidwien Kapteijns, *African Historiography Written by Africans, 1955–1973* (Leiden: Afrika-Studiecentrum, 1977); Bethwel Ogot, "Three Decades of Historical Studies in Eastern Africa, 1949–1977," *Kenya Historical Review* 6, nos. 1&2 (1978): 493–510.
4. These works are many, but for key ones, see Arnold Temu and Bonaventure Swai, *Historians and Africanist History: A Critique* (London: Zed Press, 1981); Caroline Neale, *Writing "Independent History": African Historiography 1960–1980* (Westport, CT: Greenwood Press, 1985); Bogumil Jewsiewicki and David Newbury, eds., *African Historiographies: What History for Which Africa?* (Beverley Hills: Sage Publication, 1986); Toyin Falola, ed., *African Historiography* (Harlow: Longman, 1993); and E.S. Atieno-Odhiambo, "From African Historiographies to an African Philosophy of History," in *Africanizing Knowledge: African Studies Across the Disciplines*, ed. Toyin Falola and Christian Jennings (New Brunswick, USA: Transaction Publishers, 2002), 13–63.
5. See, for instance, the chapters by John E. Flint, A.D. Roberts, Toyin Falola, Charles Ambler, and William H. Worger in Robin W. Winks, eds., *The Oxford History of the British Empire* (Oxford: Oxford University Press, 1999).
6. For reasons of concision and common usage, authors throughout have used the terms 'Britain' and 'British' rather than the technically correct 'United Kingdom' and 'UK'.
7. Basil Davidson, *Can We Write African History?* (African Studies Center, Los Angeles: University of California, November, 1965), 6.

8. For a more recent analysis of these sources, see John Edward Philips, *Writing African History* (Rochester: University of Rochester Press, 2006).
9. Though this may be argued across the board for most European empires in Africa, this was undeniably the case with Britain's engagement with the continent as there is enough historical documentation for this assertion. See examples of early colonial literature in British Africa in W.M. Roger Louis, "Introduction," in *The Oxford History of the British Empire: Historiography*, ed. Robin Winks (Oxford: Oxford University Press, 1999), 20–22.
10. Kapteijns, *African Historiography*, 2.
11. These were numerous, and were preceded by K.O. Dike's *Trade and Politics in the Niger Delta* (Oxford: Oxford University Press, 1956); later works included, among many others, Jacob Ade Ajayi's "Nineteenth Century of Nigerian Nationalism," *Journal of the Historical Society of Nigeria* 11, no. 2 (Dec. 1961): 96–105, and *Christian Missions in Nigeria 1841–1891: The Making of a New Elite* (Evanston, IL: Northeastern University Press, 1965), and many other works by E.A. Ayandele, J.C. Anene, A.E. Afigbo, to mention but a few.
12. Terence O. Ranger, *Revolt in Southern Rhodesia, 1896–7: A Study in African Resistance* (Portsmouth: Heinemann, 1967); Terence O. Ranger, *The African Voice in Southern Rhodesia, 1898–1930* (Evanston, IL: Northwestern University Press, 1970); and Gilbert Gwassa and John Iliffe, eds., *Records of the Maji Maji Uprising* (Dar es salaam: East African Publishing House, 1967).
13. Isaria N. Kimambo and Arnold J. Temu, eds., *A History of Tanzania* (Nairobi: East African Publishing House, 1969).
14. Kapteijns, *African Historiography*, 17–19. For a brief but informative account of the development of African historiography in France and Belgium, see Catherine Coquery-Vidrovitch and Bogumil Jewsiewicki, "Africanist Historiography in France and Belgium: Traditions and Trends," in *African Historiographies*, ed. Jewsiewicki and Newbury, 39–164.
15. Mohamed Mbodj and Mamadou Diouf, "Senegalese Historiography: Present Practices and Future Perspectives," in ibid., 207–14; Martin A. Klein, "The Development of Senegalese Historiography," in ibid., 215–23.
16. Allen Isaacman's several works on Mozambique must be recognized in this effort. Linda Heywood's contributions have also been critical, especially *Contested Power in Angola, 1840s to the Present* (Rochester, NY: Rochester University Press, 2000); As regards postcolonial history, see, for instance, Patrick Chabal et al., *A History of Postcolonial Lusophone Africa* (Bloomington, IN: Indiana University Press, 2002).
17. Neale, *Writing "Independent History,"* 10.
18. Bogumil Jewsiewicki, "African Historical Studies Academic Knowledge as 'Usable Past' and Radical Scholarship," *African Studies Review* 32, no. 3 (December 1989), 4, 16.
19. Ibid., 16.
20. The signature publication of the Marxist school was that by Walter Rodney, *How Europe Underdeveloped Africa* (Dar es Salaam: Tanzania Publishing House, 1974). Also Edward A. Alpers, "Rethinking African Economic History: A Contribution to the Discussion of the Roots of Underdevelopment," *Ufahamu* III, no. 3 (1973): 97–129; Edward A. Alpers, *Ivory and Slaves: Changing Pattern of International Trade in East Central Africa to the Later Nineteenth Century* (Berkley: University of California Press, 1975).

21. Neal, *Writing "Independent History,"* 18. "Petite bourgeoisie" or "straddlers" is used here after Gavin Kitching and a few other scholars to refer to African material accumulators who also had access to certain social and economic opportunities that a majority of the African population did not during the colonial period. This placed them on a plane higher in the local social hierarchy. Gavin Kitching, *Class and Economic Change in Kenya* (London: Yale University Press, 1980), 193.
22. Henry Slater, "Dar es Salaam and Postnationalist Historiography in Africa," in *African Historiographies*, ed. Jewsiewicki and Newbury, 254.
23. Oginga Odinga, *Not Yet Uhuru* (London: Heinemann, 1967).
24. Ali Mazrui, *Towards a Pax Africana: A Study of Ideology and Ambition* (Chicago: The University of Chicago Press, 1967), 77.
25. This was the emphasis in Temu and Swai, *Historians and Africanist History*.
26. Anthony G. Hopkins, *An Economic History of West Africa* (Cambridge: University of Cambridge Press, 1973).
27. Atieno-Odhiambo, "From African Historiographies," 34.
28. For instance, Derek R. Peterson, *Ethnic Patriotism and the East African Revival: A History of Dissent, c. 1935–1972* (Cambridge: Cambridge University Press, 2012).
29. Shula Marks, "South African Studies Since World War Two," in *African Studies Since 1945: A Tribute to Basil Davidson*, ed. Christopher Fyfe (London: Longman Group Limited, 1976), 188.
30. Ibid.
31. For an excellent summary on these developments of South African historiography see Atieno-Odhiambo, "From African Historiographies," 28–32.
32. Premesh Lalu, "When was South African History Ever Postcolonial," *Kronos* 34 (November 2008): 267–81.
33. For an overview of these and other issues, as well as key studies in Ethiopian historiography, see Donald Crummey, "State, Society, and Nationalist in the recent Historiography of Ethiopia," *The Journal of African History* 31, no. 1 (1990): 103–19; Bahru Zewde, "A Century of Ethiopian Historiography," *Journal of Ethiopian Studies* 33, no. 2 (November 2000): 1–126; and Donald Crummey, "Ethiopian Historiography in the Latter Half of the Twentieth Century: A North American Perspective," *Journal of Ethiopian Studies* 34, no. 1 (June 2001): 7–24.
34. For instance, T.O. Ranger, "Toward a Usable African Past," in *African Studies Since 1945: A Tribute to Basil Davidson*, ed. Christopher H. Fyfe (London: Longman, 1967), 26–27.
35. These works are many; for examples, see Claire Robertson, *Sharing the Same Bowl: A Socioeconomic History of Women and Class in Accra, Ghana* (University of Michigan Press, 1990); Claire Robertson, *Trouble Showed the Way: Women, Men, and Trade in the Nairobi Area, 1890–1990* (Bloomington: Indiana University Press, 1997); Rose Nancy Hunt, "Domesticity and Colonialism in Belgian Africa: Usumbura's Foyer Social, 1946–1960," *Signs* 15, no. 3 (Spring, 1990): 447–74; See also Nancy Rose Hunt, Tessie P. Liu, and Jean Quataert, eds., *Gendered Colonialisms in African History* (Oxford, UK: Blackwell Publishers, 1997); Luise White, *Comforts of Home: Prostitution in Colonial Nairobi* (Chicago: University of Chicago Press, 1990); Jean Allman, "Adultery

and the State in Asante: Reflections on Gender, Class, and Power from 1800 to 1950," in *The Cloth of Many Colored Silks: Papers on History and Society, Ghanaian and Islamic in Honor of Ivor Wilks*, ed. John Hunwick and Nancy Lawler (Evanston, IL: Northwestern University Press, 1996); Jean Allman and Victoria Tashjian, *I Will Not Eat Stone: A Women's History of Colonial Asante* (Portsmouth, NH: Heinemann, 2000); Jean Allman, Susan Geiger, and Nakanyike Musisi, eds., *Women in African Colonial Histories* (Bloomington: Indiana University Press, 2002). See also Nancy Rose Hunt, Tessie P. Liu, and Jean Quataert, eds., *Gendered Colonialisms in African History* (Oxford, UK: Blackwell Publishers, 1997); Tabitha Kanogo, *African Womanhood in Colonial Kenya 1900–1950* (Athens, OH: Ohio University Press, 2005); and Iris Berger, *Women in Twentieth Century Africa* (Cambridge: Cambridge University Press, 2016).

36. Nancy Rose Hunt, "Introduction," in "Gendered Colonialisms in African History," special issue, *Gender and History* 8, no. 3 (1996): 326; Atieno-Odhiambo, "From African Historiographies," 21.

37. Early works in this category include Margaret Jean Hay and Marcia Wright, *African Women & the Law: Historical Perspectives* (Boston: Boston University, African Studies Center, 1982); Martin Chanock, *Law, Custom, and Social Order: The Colonial Experience in Malawi and Zambia* (Cambridge: Cambridge University Press, 1985); Sally Falk Moore, *Social Facts and Fabrications: "Customary" Law on Kilimanjaro, 1880–1980* (Cambridge: Cambridge University Press, 1986); and Kristin Mann and Richard Roberts, eds., *Law in Colonial Africa* (Portsmouth, NH: Heinemann Educational Books, 1991).

38. For instance, Tim Burke, *Lifebuoy Men, Lux Women: Commodification, Consumption, and Cleanliness in Colonial Zimbabwe* (Durham, NC: Duke University Press, 1996).

39. Atieno-Odhiambo, "From African Historiographies," 21; Hunt, "Introduction," 325. Hunt lists examples of studies that fall in this "lexicon of cultural history" on page 335.

40. For example, Sabelo J. Ndlovu-Gatsheni, *Coloniality of Power in Postcolonial Africa: Myths of Decolonization* (Dakar: CODESRIA, 2013); Sabelo J. Ndlovu-Gatsheni, *Empire, Global Coloniality, and African Subjectivity* (Oxford: Berghahn, 2013).

41. David William Cohen and E.S. Atieno Odhiambo, *The Risks of Knowledge: Investigations into the Death of the Hon. Minister John Robert Ouko in Kenya, 1990* (Athens, OH: Ohio University Press, 2004), 22–23, 27; see also David William Cohen and E.S. Atieno Odhiambo, *Burying "SM": The Politics of Knowledge and the Sociology of Power* (James Currey: London, 1992).

42. Steven Feierman, *Peasant Intellectuals: Anthropology and History in Tanzania* (Madison, WI: The University of Wisconsin Press, 1990); Fiona D. Mackenzie, *Land, Ecology and Resistance in Kenya, 1880–1952* (Portsmouth, NH: Heinemann, 1998); and Jamie Monson, "Relocating Maji Maji: The Politics of Alliance and Authority in the Eastern Highlands of Tanzania, 1870–1918," *Journal of African History* 39 (1998): 95–120.

43. For earlier trends in this historiography, see Maynard W. Swanson, "The Sanitation Syndrome: Bubonic Plague and Urban Native Policy in the Cape Colony, 1900–09," *Journal of African History* 18 (1977): 387–410; for later studies, see Maryinez Lyons, *The Colonial Disease: A Social History of Sleeping Sickness*

in Northern Zaire, 1900–1940 (Cambridge: Cambridge University Press, 1992); Nancy Rose Hunt, *A Colonial Lexicon: of Birth Ritual, Medicalization, and Mobility in the Congo* (Durham, NC: Duke University Press, 1999); Megan Vaughan, *Curing Their Ills: Colonial Power and African Illness* (Stanford: Stanford University Press, 1991). Recent studies also reflect on a few aspects of this interpretation and extend it to the postcolonial period: Emmanuel Akyeampong, Allan G. Hill, and Arthur Kleinman, eds., *The Culture of Mental Illness and Psychiatric Practice in Africa* (Bloomington: Indiana University Press, 2014).

44. Odinga, *Not Yet Uhuru*; on the political polarization of the Mau Mau debate in the 1960s and 1970s, see Daniel Branch, *Defeating Mau Mau, Creating Kenya: Counterinsurgency, Civil War, and Decolonization* (Cambridge: Cambridge University Press, 2009).
45. The literature that is represented under this category is immense and only a few examples can be provided here: Tabitha Kanogo, *Squatters and Roots of Mau Mau* (London: James Currey, 1987); Wunyabari O. Maloba, *Mau Mau and Kenya: An Analysis of a Peasant Revolt* (Oxford: James Currey, 1993); and Greet Kershaw, *Mau Mau from Below* (Athens, OH: Ohio University Press, 1997).
46. E.S. Atieno Odhiambo and John Lonsdale, eds., *Mau Mau & Nationhood: Arms, Authority & Narration* (London: James Currey, 2003).
47. Carol Elkins, *Imperial Reckoning: The Untold Story of Britain's Gulag in Kenya* (New York: Owls Book, 2005); David Anderson, *Histories of the Hanged: The Dirty War in Kenya and the End of Empire* (New York: W.W. Norton, 2005).
48. Bogumil Jewsiewicki, "Painting in Zaire: From the Invention of the West to the Representation of Social Self," in *Africa Explores*, ed. Susan Vogel (New York: The Center for African Art, 1991), 130–75.
49. Aderonke A. Adesanya, *Carving Wood, Making History: The Fakeye Family, Modernity and Yoruba Woodcarving* (Africa Research and Publications, 2011).
50. Toyin Falola, *The African Diaspora: Slavery, Modernity, and Globalization* (Rochester, NY: University of Rochester Press, 2013), 310.
51. For a summary of how historical scholarship on Africa has split historians over the degree of colonial impact or influence on Africans, and one from which the following summary benefits, see Harvey Amani Whitfield and Bonny Ibhawoh, "Problems, Perspectives, and Paradigms: Colonial Africanist Historiography and the Question of Audience," *Canadian Journal of African Studies* 39, no. 3 (2005): 582–600.
52. Jean Comaroff and John Comaroff, *Of Revelation and Revolution: The Dialectics of Modernity on a South African Frontier*, Vol. 2 (Chicago: Chicago University Press, 1997), 28.
53. Hunt, "Introduction," 326. John Lonsdale's analysis of structures and action as essential components of understanding African states also falls into this category of interpretation. John Lonsdale, "States and Social Processes in Africa: A Historiographical Survey," *African Studies Review* 24, nos. 2/3 (June–September 1981): 139–225.
54. Teresa Barnes, *"We Women Worked So Hard": Gender, Urbanization and Social Reproduction in Colonial Harare, Zimbabwe, 1930–1956* (Portsmouth, NH: Heinemann, 1999), xx–xxi.

55. Frederick Cooper, "Conflict and Connection: Rethinking Colonial African History," *American Historical Review* 99, no. 5 (1994): 1517.
56. Ibid., 1519.
57. For instance, Ranger, "Toward a Usable African Past," 17–30; Jewsiewicki, "African Historical Studies," 3.
58. Ranger, "Toward a Usable African Past," 22.
59. Ngugi Wa Thiong'o, *Barrel of a Pen: Resistance to Repression in Neo-Colonial Kenya* (Trenton, NJ: Africa World Press, 1983), 1, 3.
60. Jewsiewicki specifically mentions the confrontations in the 1960s between Cheikh Anta Diop and Leopold Sedar Senghor in Senegal to demonstrate how intellectualism and national politics generated confrontation between scholars who appropriated history as a battlefield to confront the shortcomings of the political practice in Senegal. Jewsiewicki, "African Historical Studies," 3.
61. John Lonsdale, "African Pasts in Africa's Future," *Canadian Journal of African Studies* 23, no. 1 (1989): 127.
62. Ibid.
63. Ibid.
64. Stephen Ellis, "Writing Histories of Contemporary Africa," *The Journal of African History* 43, no. 1 (2002): 6.
65. Ibid., 7.
66. John Lonsdale, "African Studies, Europe & Africa," *Afrika Spectrum* 40 (2005): 378.
67. Ibid., 381–82.
68. Achille Mbembe, *On the Postcolony* (Berkley, CA: University of California Press, 2001), 1–2. This theme is treated in detail by V.Y. Mudimbe, *The Idea of Africa* (Bloomington: Indiana University Press, 1994) and V.Y. Mudimbe, *Invention of Africa* (Bloomington: Indiana University Press, 1988).
69. One of CODESRIA's many works that focuses on African history that stands out is Paul Tiyambe Zeleza, *A Modern Economic History of Africa (Vol. I): The Nineteenth-Century* (Dakar: CODESRIA, 1993).
70. This is the fundamental argument by Whitfield and Ibhawoh, "Problems, Perspectives, and Paradigms," 584–85.
71. Colin Bundy, "Continuing a Conversation: Prospects for African Studies in the 21st Century," *African Affairs* 101, no. 402 (January 2002): 72.
72. Mahmood Mamdani, *When Victims Become Killers: Colonialism, Nativism, and the Genocide in Rwanda* (Princeton: Princeton University Press, 2001).
73. For varied perspectives on the importance of migration and its diasporic implications in and outside Africa, see, for example, Falola, Toyin, *The African Diaspora: Slavery, Modernity, and Globalization* (Rochester, NY: University of Rochester Press, 2013) and Toyin Falola and Adebayo Oyebade, eds., *The New African Diaspora in the United States* (New York, NY: Routledge, 2017).

Bibliography

Adesanya, A. Aderonke. *Carving Wood, Making History: The Fakeye Family, Modernity and Yoruba Woodcarving*. Africa Research and Publications, 2011.

Ajayi, Jacob Ade. "Nineteenth Century of Nigerian Nationalism." *Journal of the Historical Society of Nigeria* 11, no. 2 (December 1961): 96–105.

———. *Christian Missions in Nigeria 1841–1891: The Making of a New Elite*. Evanston, IL: Northeastern University Press, 1965.

Akyeampong, Emmanuel, Allan G. Hill, and Arthur Kleinman, eds. *The Culture of Mental Illness and Psychiatric Practice in Africa*. Bloomington: Indiana University Press, 2014.

Allman, Jean. "Adultery and the State in Asante: Reflections on Gender, Class, and Power from 1800 to 1950." In *The Cloth of Many Colored Silks: Papers on History and Society, Ghanaian and Islamic in Honor of Ivor Wilks*, edited by John Hunwick and Nancy Lawler, 27–65. Evanston, IL: Northwestern University Press, 1996.

Allman, Jean, and Victoria Tashjian. *I Will Not Eat Stone: A Women's History of Colonial Asante*. Portsmouth, NH: Heinemann, 2000.

Allman, Jean, Susan Geiger, and Nakanyike Musisi, eds. *Women in African Colonial Histories*. Bloomington: Indiana University Press, 2002.

Alpers, Edward A. "Rethinking African Economic History: A Contribution to the Discussion of the Roots of Underdevelopment." *Ufahamu* III, no. 3 (1973): 97–129.

———. *Ivory and Slaves: Changing Pattern of International Trade in East Central Africa to the Later Nineteenth Century*. Berkley: University of California Press, 1975.

Amani, Harvey Whitfield, and Bonny Ibhawoh. "Problems, Perspectives, and Paradigms: Colonial Africanist Historiography and the Question of Audience." *Canadian Journal of African Studies* 39, no. 3 (2005): 582–600.

Anderson, David. *Histories of the Hanged: The Dirty War in Kenya and the End of Empire*. New York: W.W. Norton, 2005.

Atieno-Odhiambo, E.S. "From African Historiographies to an African Philosophy of History." In *Africanizing Knowledge: African Studies Across the Disciplines*, edited by Toyin Falola and Christian Jennings, 13–63. New Brunswick, USA: Transaction Publishers, 2002.

Atieno Odhiambo, E.S., and John Lonsdale, eds. *Mau Mau & Nationhood: Arms, Authority & Narration*. London: James Currey, 2003.

Barnes, Teresa. *"We Women Worked So Hard": Gender, Urbanization and Social Reproduction in Colonial Harare, Zimbabwe, 1930–1956*. Portsmouth, NH: Heinemann, 1999.

Berger, Iris. *Women in Twentieth Century Africa*. Cambridge: Cambridge University Press, 2016.

Branch, Daniel. *Defeating Mau Mau, Creating Kenya: Counterinsurgency, Civil War, and Decolonization*. Cambridge: Cambridge University Press, 2009.

Bundy, Colin. "Continuing a Conversation: Prospects for African Studies in the 21st Century." *African Affairs* 101, no. 402 (January 2002): 61–73.

Burke, Tim. *Lifebuoy Men, Lux Women: Commodification, Consumption, and Cleanliness in Colonial Zimbabwe*. Durham, NC: Duke University Press, 1996.

Chabal, Patrick, et al. *A History of Postcolonial Lusophone Africa*. Bloomington, IN: Indiana University Press, 2002.

Chanock, Martin. *Law, Custom, and Social Order: The Colonial Experience in Malawi and Zambia*. Cambridge: Cambridge University Press, 1985.

Cohen, David William, and E.S. Atieno Odhiambo. *Burying 'SM': The Politics of Knowledge and the Sociology of Power*. James Currey: London, 1992.

———. *The Risks of Knowledge: Investigations into the Death of the Hon. Minister John Robert Ouko in Kenya, 1990*. Athens, OH: Ohio University Press, 2004.
Comaroff, Jean, and John Comaroff. *Of Revelation and Revolution: The Dialectics of Modernity on a South African Frontier*, Vol. 2. Chicago: Chicago University Press, 1997.
Cooper, Frederick. "Conflict and Connection: Rethinking Colonial African History." *American Historical Review* 99, no. 5 (1994): 1516–45.
Coquery-Vidrovitch, Catherine, and Bogumil Jewsiewicki. "Africanist Historiography in France and Belgium: Traditions and Trends." In *African Historiographies: What History for Which Africa?* edited by Bogumil Jewsiewiscki and David Newbury, 39–164. Beverley Hills: Sage, 1986.
Crummey, Donald. "State, Society, and Nationalist in the Recent Historiography of Ethiopia." *The Journal of African History* 31, no. 1 (1990): 103–19.
———. "Ethiopian Historiography in the Latter Half of the Twentieth Century: A North American Perspective." *Journal of Ethiopian Studies* 34, no. 1 (June 2001): 7–24.
Davidson, Basil. *Can We Write African History?* Los Angeles: African Studies Center, University of California, November, 1965.
Dike, K.O. *Trade and Politics in the Niger Delta*. Oxford: Oxford University Press, 1956.
Elkins, Carol. *Imperial Reckoning: The Untold Story of Britain's Gulag in Kenya*. New York: Owls Book, 2005.
Ellis, Stephen. "Writing Histories of Contemporary Africa." *The Journal of African History* 43, no. 1 (2002): 1–26.
Falk, Sally Moore. *Social Facts and Fabrications: "Customary" Law on Kilimanjaro, 1880–1980*. Cambridge: Cambridge University Press, 1986.
Falola, Toyin, ed. *African Historiography*. Harlow: Longman, 1993.
———. *The African Diaspora: Slavery, Modernity, and Globalization*. Rochester, NY: University of Rochester Press, 2013.
Falola, Toyin, and Adebayo Oyebade, eds. *The New African Diaspora in the United States*. New York, NY: Routledge, 2017.
Feierman, Steven. *Peasant Intellectuals: Anthropology and History in Tanzania*. Madison, WI: The University of Wisconsin Press, 1990.
Fyfe, Christopher. *African Studies Since 1945*. London: Longman, 1976.
Gwassa, Gilbert, and John Iliffe, eds. *Records of the Maji Maji Uprising*. Dar es salaam: East African Publishing House, 1967.
Heywood, Linda. *Contested Power in Angola, 1840s to the Present*. Rochester, NY: Rochester University Press, 2000.
Hopkins, Anthony G. *An Economic History of West Africa*. Cambridge: University of Cambridge Press, 1973.
Hunt, Rose Nancy. "Domesticity and Colonialism in Belgian Africa: Usumbura's Foyer Social, 1946–1960." *Signs* 15, no. 3 (Spring, 1990): 447–74.
———. "Introduction," in "Gendered Colonialisms in African History." Special issue, *Gender and History* 8, no. 3 (1996): 323–37.
———. *A Colonial Lexicon: of Birth Ritual, Medicalization, and Mobility in the Congo*. Durham, NC: Duke University Press, 1999.
Hunt, Nancy Rose, Tessie P. Liu, and Jean Quataert, eds. *Gendered Colonialisms in African History*. Oxford, UK: Blackwell Publishers, 1997.

Jean, Margaret Hay, and Marcia Wright. *African Women & the Law: Historical Perspectives*. Boston: Boston University, African Studies Center, 1982.

Jewsiewicki, Bogumil. "African Historical Studies Academic Knowledge as 'Usable Past' and Radical Scholarship." *African Studies Review* 32, no. 3 (December 1989): 1–76.

———. "Painting in Zaire: From the Invention of the West to the Representation of Social Self." In *Africa Explores*, edited by Susan Vogel, 130–75. New York: The Center for African Art, 1991.

Jewsiewisckì, Bogumil, and David Newbury, eds. *African Historiographies: What History for Which Africa?* Beverley Hills: Sage, 1986.

Kanogo, Tabitha. *Squatters and Roots of Mau Mau*. London: James Currey, 1987.

———. *African Womanhood in Colonial Kenya 1900–1950*. Athens, OH: Ohio University Press, 2005.

Kapteijns, Lidwien. *African Historiography Written by Africans, 1955–1973*. Leiden: Afrika-Studiecentrum, 1977.

Kershaw, Greet. *Mau Mau from Below*. Athens, OH: Ohio University Press, 1997.

Kimambo, Isaria N., and Arnold J. Temu, eds. *A History of Tanzania*. Nairobi: East African Publishing House, 1969.

Kitching, Gavin. *Class and Economic Change in Kenya*. London: Yale University Press, 1980.

Klein, Martin A. "The Development of Senegalese Historiography." In *African Historiographies: What History for Which Africa?* edited by Bogumil Jewsiewiscki and David Newbury, 215–23. Beverley Hills: Sage, 1986.

Lalu, Premesh. "When was South African History Ever Postcolonial." *Kronos* 34, (November 2008): 267–81.

Lonsdale, John. "States and Social Processes in Africa: A Historiographical Survey." *African Studies Review* 24, nos. 2/3 (June–September 1981): 139–225.

———. "African Pasts in Africa's Future." *Canadian Journal of African Studies* 23, no. 1 (1989): 126–46.

———. "African Studies, Europe & Africa." *Afrika Spectrum* 40 (2005): 377–402.

Lyons, Maryinez. *The Colonial Disease: A Social History of Sleeping Sickness in Northern Zaire, 1900–1940*. Cambridge: Cambridge University Press, 1992.

Mackenzie, Fiona D. *Land, Ecology and Resistance in Kenya, 1880–1952*. Portsmouth, NH: Heinemann, 1998.

Maloba, Wunyabari O. *Mau Mau and Kenya: An Analysis of a Peasant Revolt*. Oxford: James Currey, 1993.

Mamdani, Mahmood. *When Victims Become Killers: Colonialism, Nativism, and the Genocide in Rwanda*. Princeton: Princeton University Press, 2001.

Mann, Kristin, and Richard Roberts, eds. *Law in Colonial Africa*. Portsmouth, NH: Heinemann Educational Books, 1991.

Marks, Shula. "South African Studies Since World War Two." In *African Studies Since 1945: A Tribute to Basil Davidson*, edited by Christopher Fyfe, 186–99. London: Longman Group Limited, 1976.

Mazrui, Ali. *Towards a Pax Africana: A Study of Ideology and Ambition*. Chicago: The University of Chicago Press, 1967.

Mbembe, Achille. *On the Postcolony*. Berkley, CA: University of California Press, 2001.

Mbodj, Mohamed, and Mamadou Diouf. "Senegalese Historiography: Present Practices and Future Perspectives." In *African Historiographies: What History for Which*

Africa? edited by Bogumil Jewsiewiscki and David Newbury, 207–14. Beverley Hills: Sage, 1986.

Monson, Jamie. "Relocating Maji Maji: The Politics of Alliance and Authority in the Eastern Highlands of Tanzania, 1870–1918." *Journal of African History* 39 (1998): 95–120.

Mudimbe, V.Y. *Invention of Africa.* Bloomington: Indiana University Press, 1988.

———. *The Idea of Africa.* Bloomington: Indiana University Press, 1994.

Ndlovu-Gatsheni, Sabelo J. *Coloniality of Power in Postcolonial Africa: Myths of Decolonization.* Dakar: CODESRIA, 2013.

———. *Empire, Global Coloniality, and African Subjectivity.* Oxford: Berghahn, 2013.

Neale, Caroline. *Writing "Independent History": African Historiography 1960–1980.* Westport, CT: Greenwood Press, 1985.

Odinga, Oginga. *Not Yet Uhuru.* London: Heinemann, 1967.

Ogot, Bethwel. "Three Decades of Historical Studies in Eastern Africa, 1949–1977." *Kenya Historical Review* 6, nos. 1&2 (1978): 493–510.

Peterson, Derek R. *Ethnic Patriotism and the East African Revival: A History of Dissent, c. 1935–1972.* Cambridge: Cambridge University Press, 2012.

Philips, John Edward. *Writing African History.* Rochester: University of Rochester Press, 2006.

Ranger, Terence O. *Revolt in Southern Rhodesia, 1896–7: A Study in African Resistance.* Portsmouth: Heinemann, 1967.

———. "Toward a Usable African Past." In *African Studies Since 1945: A Tribute to Basil Davidson,* edited by Christopher H. Fyfe, 17–30. London: Longman, 1967.

———, ed. *Emerging Themes in African History.* Nairobi: East African Publishing House, 1968.

———. *The African Voice in Southern Rhodesia, 1898–1930.* Evanston, IL: Northwestern University Press, 1970.

Roberts, A.D. "The Earlier Historiography of Colonial Africa." *History in Africa* 5 (1978): 153–67.

Robertson, Claire. *Sharing the Same Bowl: A Socioeconomic History of Women and Class in Accra, Ghana.* University of Michigan Press, 1990.

———. *Trouble Showed the Way: Women, Men, and Trade in the Nairobi Area, 1890–1990.* Bloomington: Indiana University Press, 1997.

Rodney, Walter. *How Europe Underdeveloped Africa.* Dar es Salaam: Tanzania Publishing House, 1974.

Slater, Henry. "Dar es Salaam and Postnationalist Historiography in Africa." In *African Historiographies: What History for Which Africa?* edited by Bogumil Jewsiewiscki and David Newbury, 249–60. Beverley Hills: Sage, 1986.

Swanson, W. Maynard. "The Sanitation Syndrome: Bubonic Plague and Urban Native Policy in the Cape Colony, 1900–09." *Journal of African History* 18 (1977): 387–410.

Temu, Arnold, and Bonaventure Swai. *Historians and Africanist History: A Critique.* London: Zed Press, 1981.

Vaughan, Megan. *Curing Their Ills: Colonial Power and African Illness.* Stanford: Stanford University Press, 1991.

Wa Thiong'o, Ngugi. *Barrel of a Pen: Resistance to Repression in Neo-Colonial Kenya.* Trenton, NJ: Africa World Press, 1983.

White, Luise. *Comforts of Home: Prostitution in Colonial Nairobi.* Chicago: University of Chicago Press, 1990.
Winks, Robin W., ed. *The Oxford History of the British Empire.* Oxford: Oxford University Press, 1999.
Zeleza, Paul Tiyambe. *A Modern Economic History of Africa (Vol. I): The Nineteenth-Century.* Dakar: CODESRIA, 1993.
Zewde, Bahru. "A Century of Ethiopian Historiography." *Journal of Ethiopian Studies* 33, no. 2 (November 2000): 1–26.

PART I

Colonial Africa

CHAPTER 2

Colonialism and the African Environment

Martin S. Shanguhyia

African activities and Africa's contacts with foreigners over the centuries have been powerful agents in shaping the continent's history. The African environment in particular provided the medium in which these activities and interactions played out, leaving an indelible mark on Africa's history. The physical environment has been a canvas on which the continent's history has been studied, debated, and written. The nature of that history is evident in the way the environment has impacted on African societies, and the way geographical landscapes and other natural phenomena have been shaped by human and state agencies, or even by forces of nature. This is in no way to state that the environment has determined Africa's history; rather, the environment has played a significant role in the way that history has developed over the centuries. Therefore, any efforts at writing African history at any scale or period with the environment as a major theme is to delve into a complex arena given that such a history not only spans centuries, but also transcends diverse regions and communities, and has to include external (global) elements.

European colonialism was a major external force that has shaped our understanding of African history in general and its environmental dimensions in particular. This chapter provides an overview of the extent to which Africa's encounter with colonialism shaped notions about the African environment and, by extension, how those notions influenced human relations and human–environment relations. It goes further to highlight the way these developments have been perceived or interpreted by scholars whose studies

M.S. Shanguhyia (✉)
History Department, Maxwell School of Citizenship and Public Affairs, Syracuse University, Syracuse, NY, USA

© The Author(s) 2018
M.S. Shanguhyia and T. Falola (eds.),
The Palgrave Handbook of African Colonial and Postcolonial History,
https://doi.org/10.1057/978-1-137-59426-6_2

have focused on that period and how these interpretations have aided our understanding of modern African history. Environmental relations in colonial Africa has enabled scholars to critically examine questions about the nature of colonialism, race, justice, moral economy, culture, identity, power, resistance, social status, belonging, and development, among others. The scope and contents of this chapter are by no means complete, or even comprehensive, given that the environmental theme in African history has been widely captured by many scholars focusing on Africa and the European empires. Neither is this chapter the first to address the meaning, nature, and outcomes of the intersection between European colonialism and the African environments. Prior efforts by a few scholars to highlight this historiography must be applauded.[1] Those efforts provide the starting point for understanding this important aspect of African history.

Historians of Africa and other Africanists have revealed how the 'environmental question' in colonial Africa permeated the politics of the colonial state and defined and was defined by the colonial project. This was true in the colonial pursuit for social control, economic production, demography and settlement patterns, reordering landscapes, confronting human health challenges, regulating built environments, and promoting development, among other aspects. Conflicts of interest emerged on these issues, so much so that ideological and moral arguments characterized conversations about human interactions with the natural environment, the nature of the outcome of those interactions, and about access to, use, and management of natural resources. An analysis of colonial environmental relations precludes any attempts to characterize the colonial experience in Africa as a uniform one. Questions and ideas about the environment were numerous and diverse, reflecting divergent worlds of all those who constituted colonial African states—so much so that, as Jane Carruthers correctly points out, that experience defies mere labeling of 'colonizers' and 'colonized', which is not to say that one should overlook the extent to which colonialism transformed power relations over people and resources with the environment acting as a site of contestation.[2] This then forms the justification for this chapter, which highlights how the colonial phase was significant in shaping these relations in fundamental ways that have helped historians and other scholars understand and write about the African experience under colonialism.

Thus, the roles of colonial states and their African agents in shaping environmental relations have widely informed scholarly analyses. By extension, this scholarship has largely constituted what has emerged as African environmental history, a major sub-field that has served to enrich African historiography, and which has expanded the scope of African history since colonial times. Recently published general academic works by some of the outstanding historians on African environmental history as an emerging sub-field validate this development.[3]

While the introduction of colonialism vastly altered Africa's environment and redefined how Africans interacted with it, some scholars have focused their research on aspects that remind us of the dynamism of the African encounter with nature before the colonial era. Intense human activities and natural forces in precolonial Africa were at play in altering the environment, though the pristine nature of that environment was still evident in many areas.[4] This counters the notions of 'Merrie Africa' or a tropical 'Eden' that were highly held by European colonizers of the twentieth century, whose perceptions of 'Primitive Africa' also served to reinforce scenes of 'uncorrupted' Africans and their environments in the old days.[5] As will be demonstrated later in the chapter, such thinking justified colonial intervention in African modes of production, most notably in sectors such as farming, forestry, and hunting. This intervention was extended into African residential environments, both new and old, that authorities thought were threatened by dangerous insects and infectious diseases. However, colonialism should not be seen as the genesis of transformation of African environments, but rather as a powerful contributing variable to the rhythms that were already shaping their nature, and with it, African inhabitants. It speeded up the process of transformation and left a legacy that continues to elicit historical inquiry and analysis.

AFRICAN ENVIRONMENT AND EUROPEAN IMPERIALISM

Impulses that inaugurated and drove Western imperialism in Africa were to a greater extent shaped by European imagination of the continent's environment. Some scholars of European empires have drawn the link between imperial interests of those powers and geographical knowledge of the colonial world including Africa. For instance, Dane Kennedy observes that European explorers, who were adept at cataloguing their explorations of African (and other) lands and peoples were the vanguard of imperial expansion. Just as Alexander von Humboldt used geographical sceneries of the tropical world in such areas as the West Indies, South America, and the Pacific to construct landscapes (and their inhabitants) that projected notions of difference between these regions and the temperate world, European explorers used the African environment to transpose similar notions. So much so that Kennedy rightly notes, 'By the late nineteenth century, the connection between exploration and empire was often direct and institutionalized'.[6] Even before Victorian and other European explorers' encounters integrated Africa's environments into the imperial quest in the period after 1850, the tropical ecology of some areas of Africa was already under some form of European control. The pristine nature of those environments amazed early Europeans who encountered them. These early colonial encounters were characterized by assumptions that an 'Eden' existed, assumptions that were pronounced by processes that seemed to indicate exhaustion or degradation of some of the continent's natural resources. Cases of environmental dislocation threatened the commercial and therapeutic value of tropical environments to Europeans, a concern that reoccurred with vigor during the colonialism of the twentieth century, a theme that is examined elsewhere in this chapter.

Dreams of an 'Eden' led to scientific experiments to preserve or recreate 'wild' African landscapes by setting up botanical gardens by the British and French in the Cape Colony and Mauritius, respectively. Botanical gardens were miniature versions of grandiose plans that were subsequently implemented to ensure large-scale preservation of the environments in these and other early British, French, as well as Portuguese and Spanish territories in isolated parts of Africa before colonialism expanded to engulf the entire continent during the twentieth century. These developments have been treated within the scholarship that examines global dimensions of the role of the environment in the expansion of mercantile European empires, and especially those focusing on the origin of modern global environmentalism.[7]

Imperial explorers and other European travellers of the nineteenth century expanded the purview within which the West appropriated African environments in the bid to 'recreate' Africa and redefine its people. Even so, it must be emphasized in advance that many of these adventurers may have set upon 'discovery' journeys into Africa not in the service of their European empires; rather, they sought to satisfy their curiosity about the unknown, undertaking adventure for its own sake, or even entertained the humanitarian mission of purging Africa of the carnage of the slave trade and other perceived social evils. Served well by improved channels of communication (especially popular media) and sponsorship from scientific agencies such as the geographical societies, many brought to Europe's knowledge the breathtaking geographical sceneries of Africa, as well as its varieties of plant, animal wildlife, and human communities.

The role of geographical societies in popularizing the use of geography to spur imperialism in Africa is particularly captured in analyses of European empires' origins and expansion. Drawing from a rich source of studies on the historical geography of France, Robin A. Butlin reveals the direct and indirect links, and probable influence, of the Société de Géographie de Paris on the *parti colonial* of French colonial expansion during the nineteenth century. The Société also had connections with numerous other French geographical societies, which for either commercial or cultural reasons may have influenced French colonial acquisition of Tunisia, French West Africa, and Madagascar in the later part of that century. In Portugal, the Africa Committee of the Lisbon Geographical Society, founded in 1875, was tasked with convincing the Portuguese government to consolidate and expand its imperial presence in West Central Africa for economic and cultural reasons. Similar societies in Spain, Belgium, Germany, and Italy had connections to these countries' imperial designs in Africa at the close of the nineteenth century.[8]

The oldest of these, the Royal Geographical Society of London, harnessed scientific and geographical tools and expertise (pertaining to exploration and mapping) to make sense of travellers' accounts and to support geographical expeditions into lesser known parts of Africa. David Livingstone, whose humanitarian journeys across East and South Central Africa were responsible for opening this region to British colonization, and who was the reason for a relief expedition sponsored by the Royal Geographical Society in 1872 to search for him in the deeper parts of the African interior, acknowledged the Society's imperialistic project of using Victorian geography to advance Britain's overseas expansion.[9] Joseph Thompson's memorable expedition across Maasailand in East Africa, too, was a project that the Society embraced and supported.

The economic potential of Africa's resources informed the writings of the likes of Livingstone, Thompson, Henry Morton Stanley, and other explorers who ventured into the continent during the second half of the nineteenth century. Their writings also depicted Africans as 'uncivilized' and in need of the benevolence that flowed forth from European Enlightenment virtues. The two missions to harness the continent's resources and to 'civilize' its inhabitants were hardly inseparable. Later, colonial states strived to accomplish them simultaneously. This external view of the African environment and its inhabitants partly provided the impetus for the 'New Imperialism', creating a foundation upon which European colonial expansion in Africa was justified.

Some historians of Africa have clearly acknowledged this connection in their analyses of these nineteenth-century proceedings. For instance, commenting on Joseph Thompson's writings about his encounters with the Maasai and the East African landscapes in the 1880s, William Beinart and Lotte Hughes emphasize aspects of consumption and expropriation of these landscapes that likely appealed to British power that later dominated this region.[10] This natural and material appeal of African environments in the tales of European explorers resonated with politicians and the general public in Europe. The explorers' links to nineteenth-century imperialism have been aptly summarized by Robert O. Collins and James M. Burns: 'Their tales of adventure and exploration, which emphasized the economic value of Africa's interior and the desperate needs of its peoples, were powerful instruments in the education of the reading public and profoundly shaped its later approval and support for imperialism'.[11]

Aside from the intellectual, cultural, and economic value that African environments offered the West, those environments also presented inherent dangers to imperial expansion. Scholars of empire and of African history have demonstrated how aspects of Africa's natural environment slowed, but did not deter European conquest of the continent. They have focused attention on the African disease ecologies. The African disease ecology is perhaps the most dominant theme in the historiography on this subject. European concerns about Africa's disease and health challenges predate the imperialism of the late nineteenth century. West Africa's coastal areas had posed health problems to

European traders, early adventurers, and troops during the transatlantic slave trade. Reflecting on these processes, historians of African demography (most notably Philip Curtin) and of empire (such as Alfred Crosby, who emphasizes the 'Columbian Exchange' of the transatlantic interactions) have noted the high mortality rates among early Europeans who ventured into the West African coastlands in the days of the slave trade. They attribute this to mosquito-infested environments that bred malaria and yellow fever, a reflection of the dangers for Europeans of being exposed to an unforgiving tropical environment.[12] Africans also suffered high mortality rates but these were much lower than those of Europeans. Africans had coexisted with mosquito ecologies and had developed immunity or a form of tolerance to malaria.

In spite of these health risks, the European push into the continent was relentless, a fact that Curtin attributes to European ignorance of Africa's deadly disease ecologies, at least before 1800. They were also motivated by economic transformation in West Africa following the decline of the slave trade as European profiteers, both in government and private enterprise, began searching for and expanding new avenues in their commercial relations with Africa. This led them to push into Africa's interior, beyond the coastal confines to which they had been condemned for centuries. Imbued with a sense of optimism, Europeans launched a series of explorations into the interior of Africa. Geographical societies and European commercial companies became the handmaidens of these explorations.[13] Thus, the economic imperative remained a powerful lure for European expansion in Africa, even as the disease ecology remained a barrier but not a permanent hindrance to that expansion.

The discovery and use of quinine offered promise against malaria, perhaps the most dangerous of Africa's tropical diseases at the time. It helped Europeans expand their frontiers beyond the coastal areas. From the mid-nineteenth century, traders, missionaries, explorers, and imperial armies moved into deeper parts of the continent equipped with the anti-malarial drug. Malaria remained a threat but could now be checked. Typhoid, cholera, dysentery, and bubonic plague became the major concerns in the West's March to conquer Africa. They resulted from increased global commerce along international sea lanes that connected Africa with other continents.[14] Subsequent medical advances in confronting these diseases also minimized mortality rates among European troops and their African and Indian conscripts.

The historiography on disease ecology in the age of imperial conquest of Africa goes beyond mere improvement in tropical medicine and its role in aiding Western military advances into the continent. Historians of empire have demonstrated that other 'tools of empire' such as steamboats and railroads were important in compressing distances between Africa and the rest of the world, as well as between regions and within the continent. These technologies helped overcome environmental barriers to imperial advances and aided the movement of resources and people.[15] But interconnectedness and closer contact between populations and diverse regions also implied a high incidence of infectious diseases. Compression of time and space ensured that both new and old diseases spread into many parts of Africa in the last decades of the nineteenth century, particularly in West Africa.[16] Thus, while Western technologies helped check Africa's tropical diseases, some of those technologies also served as pathways along which diseases spread in the continent.

Critical historical studies have analyzed how, in the few decades leading to colonization, African communities in Tanzania actively engaged with their production and exchange networks, and interacted with their environments while mastering and shaping (not being constrained by) those environments. This included navigating debilitating human and livestock disease epidemics. Some of these, like rinderpest and the sand flea plague, were linked to global contacts.[17] During this time, local communities in Kenya, Sudan, and Ethiopia devised survival techniques to navigate disease, drought, famine, and other ecological disasters.[18] These examples illustrate the resilience and innovation of African communities in bad times, and seek to depart from narratives that have depicted precolonial Africa as tranquil, undisturbed by the rhythms of nature. Colonial expansion in some of these regions furthered environmental disruptions, rendering weak the coping mechanism that local communities had developed.

THE PURSUIT OF 'HEALTHY' ENVIRONMENTS AND SPACES

Following the pacification of Africa and the establishment of colonial rule, environment-related parasites and diseases remained dangerous to the colonial project. Aside from mosquitoes and malaria, the tsetse fly and trypanosomiasis (sleeping sickness, the disease caused by the fly) proved important. The latter had existed in Africa for centuries, before colonial times. It afflicted Mali, the famed empire of the West African savannahs in the medieval period. During the transatlantic slave trade, European medical observers noted a 'Sleepy Distemper' among African slaves aboard slave ships in the 1700s. By 1850, European hunters and Christian missionaries increasingly encountered the fly in Southern Africa where the Tswana name 'tsetse' was used to refer to the fly.[19] By the end of the nineteenth century, much of Sub-Saharan Africa from Portuguese West Africa (especially in Principe) to the Belgian Congo, Kenya, Uganda, Tanzania, through Southern Africa, the dangers of the tsetse fly and trypanosomiasis to both humans and animals were real.

Colonial initiatives to confront these two problems and their impact on local communities and the natural environment have attracted considerable scholarly attention.[20] Campaigns to combat tsetse and sleeping sickness inaugurated the careers of Western scientific and medical experts in Africa, among them entomologists, parasitologists, medical doctors, and ecologists. Their mission, backed by metropolitan governments and research institutions, was to utilize advances in Western science and technology to study Africa's insects, their ecologies and African relations to them, as an initial step towards understanding causes and solutions to insect-borne diseases. These developments illustrate instances where campaigns against Africa's disease and insect ecologies expanded the scope of Western science in colonizing Africa. Furthermore, knowledge produced from studies carried out by British, German, Swedish, French, and other European scientists working in Africa sharpened the pseudo-scientific notions about Africans and their natural environments. These aspects were the two key subjects of study in natural and medical sciences at the time.[21] Efforts to use Western science to understand Africa's disease environments expanded the cultural lens through which colonizers viewed Africans. Also, since untamed disease ecologies were likely to pose political, economic, and social challenges to colonial states, thereby undermining the position of colonial powers in Africa, official intervention was justified as part of the 'civilizing mission'. Western medical science and technology provided the necessary tools to be used to overcome a problem that 'primitive' communities were unable to eliminate.[22] Such views fit the social analyses of colonial campaigns' search for disease-free environments in Africa.

The social analyses of those campaigns have been inspired by the demographic impact on Africans of those colonial initiatives at eliminating tsetse flies and sleeping sickness. Of interest to historians are the high rates of African mortality resulting from the disease and from some colonial measures to eradicate the flies. For instance, about 300,000 Africans may have perished from the disease in colonial Uganda between 1900 and 1910, without counting hundreds of others who died within the Lake Victoria regions of Tanzania and Kenya.[23] Administrative approaches to the campaigns required relocation of African communities to concentrated settlements that were deemed 'safer' zones, which made it easier for British and German administrations to enforce quarantine measures, administer medical treatments, ensure uninterrupted provision of education, water, agricultural development, and regulate the mobility of African labor.[24]

Belgian anti-tsetse and trypanosomiasis campaigns in the Congo were no different from those enforced in the British and German territories in Eastern Africa. They involved *medicamenteuse* and *biologique* approaches. The former involved medical components such as increasing the number of trained medical staff and establishment of medical clinics and hospitals, all aimed at curing the victims of sleeping sickness. *Biologique* contained a slew of approaches that were pushed by administration and public-health departments, and aimed at preventing the spread of the disease. This involved creating *cordons sanitaires* that separated healthy populations from infected ones, a form of 'social-engineering'.[25] This approach complemented the scientific (biological and chemical) approaches that were directed at the flies and their natural habitats.

All these approaches directly or indirectly disrupted the demographic patterns of African communities by altering preexisting African settlement and migration trends. For instance, in Bunyoro, Uganda, sites to which the Banyoro were relocated were hardly developed to provide for their economic and social needs. Formerly evacuated zones were allowed to revert to bush, which in turn became sanctuary for wildlife and tsetse. This, among other factors related to British colonial conquest, resulted in population decline in Bunyoro.[26] Some scholars have argued that colonial campaigns against tsetse flies in other parts of East Africa may have been ineffective, and could have instead expanded tsetse ecologies. By using evidence from colonial mapping of tsetse-infested areas of colonial Tanzania, Helje Kjekshus has revealed that those areas expanded between 1913 and 1937, in spite of intensive German and British initiatives to control the flies. Kjekshus attributes this to colonial officials' failure to consider African initiatives that had effectively utilized indigenous ecological control measures before colonialism. It would take time, and studies by a few Western experts such as John Ford, to get colonial regimes to integrate African solutions to anti-tsetse fly campaigns and other related environmental problems.[27]

Besides natural environments, urbanization in colonial Africa has offered scholars a window through which to analyze colonial authorities' pursuit of 'healthy environments' and communities. Colonialism led to the emergence of new cities and alteration of old ones. Rapid urbanization attracted many Africans (as well as Asians in East and Southern Africa) into many of these cities. Urban areas offered the migrants economic opportunities but also became sites of contestation between migrant communities and colonial authorities over issues related to environmental health. In the bid to manage urban populations through 'planning', city authorities had to make critical decisions that altered urban relations in the face of emergencies created by disease outbreaks. Plague, cholera, and other epidemics that spread into urban areas at the turn of the nineteenth and early twentieth century led colonial administrations to enforce racial segregation in the affected cities.

As a result, Asians and Africans became targets of strict hygiene measures as part of the health campaign measures to check the outbreak of these diseases. City authorities in Nairobi incinerated Asian buildings on grounds of being a potential source of public-health risk. In Kisumu, western Kenya, the Indian Bazaar was quarantined and merchandise disinfected. In these two urban areas, official British policy insisted on residential zoning along racial lines for public-health reasons.[28] In the South African cities of Cape Town, Durban, and Port Elizabeth, Asians and Africans were also on the receiving end of anti-plague measures in the 1890s and early 1900s. In Durban, Asian living quarters were tagged as 'breeding haunts and nursery grounds for disease' and therefore a source of social discomfort for the European population. Asians were forcefully relocated to zones sited away from European quarters, a move that municipal authorities imagined would help 'cure this our social leprosy'.[29] In Cape Town and Port Elizabeth, Africans and Coloreds were unfairly blamed for infectious disease outbreaks, and just like Asians, they were subjected to racial segregation measures construed by urban authorities as the solution to curbing those epidemics. Labels such as 'undesirable elements' and 'Kafir' gained currency in reference to Africans in their 'filthy' living environments. Consequently, what Maynard Swanson has referred to as the 'sanitation syndrome' came to dominate the minds and actions of administration and health officials in their efforts to confront infectious diseases in Cape Town. They did so by positing infectious disease as a societal metaphor that was used to racialize urban relations, and by promoting discourses on cleanliness, filthiness, overcrowding, slums, and public health that were in turn used to reinforce racial, class, and cultural differences between urban dwellers.[30]

Asians and Africans were not merely passive in these invasive public-health control measures. Concerned that plague control measures would 'fill the "cup of woe"' for Asians as evidenced by vexatious quarantine measures, Mahatma Gandhi passionately engaged colonial authorities in South Africa in defense of the Asian community.[31] In Port Elizabeth, both Asians and Africans did not wait to be relocated into officially designated zones, but on their own accord moved to areas on the city's outskirts that were out of government control. A few Africans purchased plots of land on which they erected their own dwellings. When officials attempted to regulate these new settlements to prevent further disease outbreaks, some refused to relocate without adequate compensation from the government in the form of property.[32] Uitvlugt (Ndabeni), the largest of the relocation sites outside Cape Town, witnessed organized Africans' resistance against the administration for failure to provide basic amenities and assurance of guarantee to permanent property for those settled there by authorities. Their leaders organized train boycotts, petitions, and legal proceedings, forcing authorities to legalize Ndabeni as a permanent African settlement.[33]

These cases of contestations on health and urban environments reveal incidences of race, ethnicity, and class relations regulated by colonial power but contested by the 'victims' (Africans, Asians, and Coloreds) who refused to be labeled as such. They also demonstrate how colonial campaigns for healthy spaces reinforced social identities by creating social constructs such as 'healthy', 'unhealthy', and 'filthy', and applied these to categories of colonial populations in unequal ways. Furthermore, those cases show that economic motives underpinned official involvement in public-health campaigns. Blaming Asians for plague and cholera outbreaks was related to the obvious economic threat that Indians posed to European communities in East and Southern Africa. Those campaigns were also intended to regulate African movements so as to secure rural areas from being afflicted by urban disease epidemics and to ensure healthy reservoirs of African labor.

Generally, scholars of historical epidemiology have linked the emergence of modern disease environments in Africa to rapid urbanization during the colonial period. Gerald Hartwig and K. David Patterson have pointed out that colonialism induced dynamic urbanization developments in Africa that unleashed serious epidemics in cities. The resulting transformation was rapid, as hundreds of migrants flocked to urban areas, leading to overcrowding and poor housing. City authorities were caught unprepared to deal with urban health problems that resulted from inability to cope with sewerage and refuse disposal and the provision of clean water supplies to migrants and other city residents.[34] When these arguments are considered, the 'blame the victim' rationale that colonial authorities adopted when enforcing public-health campaigns in the face of disease epidemics in urban areas begs for a legitimate critique.

COLONIAL ECONOMIES AND THE AFRICAN ENVIRONMENT

Our knowledge of the relationship between colonialism and the African environment also comes from studies focusing on Africa's economic history. Those studies draw a close connection between colonial economies and the African environment. Some of them extrapolate this connection from economic motives of European imperialism, colonial extraction of African resources, and African initiatives in colonial economies. As noted earlier, economic motives were implied in the writings and images about Africa by European explorers and missionaries, and in the annals of European geographical societies that helped drive nineteenth-century imperialism. Following the establishment of colonial rule, colonial powers viewed Africans and Africa's natural resources as playing a vital role in the extractive economies, and in securing the fiscal base, of their respective colonies.

Starting from the early period of formal colonization of the continent, colonial administrators confirmed the wealth of African environments—its dangers notwithstanding. The impact of European settler communities on local African communities is what has garnered the most attention both in general historical works and more specialized studies. The alienation of Africans' land and seizure of their livestock, for which colonial administrations and the settlers offered an economic justification, led to ecological, economic, and social disruption of African systems. French colonization of Algeria after 1830 led to a series of government legislations that resulted in alienation of land from Algerians that was in turn handed over to French *colons*. More land that formerly belonged to the *beylik* and which was inhabited by Arabs and Berbers was forcibly inherited by the French conquest state.[35] Systematic expropriation of rural peasants and nomadic pastoralists by the French led to massive restructuring of traditional society. Many Arabs and Berbers were reduced to supplying hard labor both in towns and rural economies.[36] Earlier colonial pioneers (such as the Dutch, who were propelled by the mercantile imperialism of the sixteenth century) realized how critical African resources were for their survival in what became the Cape Colony in South Africa. These pioneers built their initial colonial fortunes on fertile lands, livestock, and labor, oftentimes forcibly acquired from local African communities in the Cape and beyond. They expanded their settlements by displacing first the Khoikhoi community, and later the Xhosa pastoralists and other local peoples beyond the Cape. British annexation of the Cape Colony after 1806 and their occupation of Natal, and their subsequent expansion from these bases deeper into Southern Africa, led to the loss of land by Africans.[37]

Aside from leading to loss of African land and livestock, Dutch expansion into the Cape Colony and its hinterlands also expanded the human disease ecology, most notably the introduction and spread of smallpox, which ravaged through Khoikhoi society and facilitated the decimation of their culture.[38] Farther north in Kuruman, Nancy Jacobs has illustrated how communities and individuals with power (invested by culture, tradition, or colonialism) manipulated those without it to access and monopolize land and water resources. By using power and racial inclinations, European settlers as well as the twentieth-century South African state and its segregation policies were able to displace Africans from the fertile Kuruman River Valley into the Kalahari. For their part, traditional chiefs seized on these transformations to use their positions to monopolize cattle ownership, thereby creating a mode of dependency that made them patrons to clients without livestock of their own. Thus, in Kuruman, communities and individuals with power used the environment to forge relations that benefited their access to, and use of, resources. The dispossessed negotiated the system by devising certain ways of farming and developing new social relations.[39]

Central and East Africa experienced similar disruptive patterns. In Northern Rhodesia (Zambia), the way the British reorganized settlement patterns so as to access land and African labor for European settlers aided the expansion in tsetse ecology in eastern parts of that colony. Part of this reorganization was to discourage African hunting and emphasize close settlement of African communities, which led to an expansion of bush lands and an increase in wild animals. This in turn led to high incidences of tsetse flies and with them sleeping sickness and *nagana*.[40]

In 1903, Sir Charles Elliot, Kenya's High Commissioner (1900–1904), regarded British acquisition of this territory as 'the greatest philanthropic achievement of the later nineteenth century' partly because of the opportunity this offered Britain to advance its 'civilizing' mission, but most important because 'Europeans can live and thrive not merely in patches of territory here and there, but practically anywhere in the highlands'.[41] Elliot facilitated the origins of the White Highlands that were created from vast stretches of fertile lands and watering areas that were alienated from African communities, most notably the Maasai, Kikuyu, and Kalenjin.[42]

The enforced relocation of the Maasai into the less hospitable Narok Reserve was not without negative ecological impacts on the area, the community, and their livestock. Once resettled in Narok, they no longer had access to their traditional dry weather grazing grounds in Laikipia. Aridity, decline in quality pastures, population pressure, and droughts led to increased ecological deterioration in Narok. East Coast Fever and sleeping sickness took a heavy toll of both the Maasai and their livestock. Whereas colonial officials explained Narok's ecological woes from a Malthusian perspective that reinforced the 'blame-the-victim' narrative, the Maasai, who had all along resisted their relocation into this southern reserve, attributed the area's problems to colonial ignorance of the ecological challenges that existed there. Thus, to the Maasai, the reserve was an unhealthy environment, far from more conducive Laikipia where they had been forced out.[43] If indeed for some historians of Africa an 'Eden' never existed prior to the disruption that colonialism introduced in rural Africa, then the Maasai experience is instructive. In interviews with Maasai elders with knowledge of this colonial debacle, Lotte Hughes has revealed that the Maasai were able to contrast their bitter experiences in Narok with the 'sweetness' (plenty of pasture, water, and disease-free environment), a kind of 'Eden', that was associated with Laikipia.[44]

Some historians of East Africa have revealed how the creation of settler communities closed off frontiers of African access to ecologies that served as 'havens' for survival in times of natural disasters. In this way, settler agricultural economies undermined African environment-based livelihoods. David Anderson has revealed that the Tugen and Ill Chamus of Baringo in Kenya's Rift Valley were precluded from accessing the wetter highlands that were alienated for European settlement. This starved the pastoralists of access to traditional watering and pasture areas. Their attempts to breach physical boundaries that encased those farms to enable them to graze their livestock were criminalized as 'trespassing', leading to imposition of fines and other forms of retribution. Anderson uses the 'Range War' that ensued between colonial administrators and settlers on one hand, and the Tugen and Ill Chamus on the other, to contrast two contested views of land tenure and land use in a settler colonial state. The former viewed land ownership from a Western model—as belonging to the individual, who had sole rights over it. For their part, Africans in Baringo saw land as strictly communal, use of which was open to every member of the community.[45] Excision of indigenous forests in Baringo as Crown or government property, and for private commercial use, had similar effects of undermining local livelihoods. By insulating forests from access by African communities, colonial regimes in Africa dislodged local usage of forest resources. Some communities were unable to acquire wood for fuel and building materials, and were prevented from hunting and gathering food in those forests.[46]

These disruptive trends of colonial expansion into Africa were also evident in territories that did not have European settlers to influence policies on land and other resources. In such territories, colonial administrations and international commercial companies, acting as allies, had particularly strong interests in land resources and collaborated in dispossessing local communities. In the Congo Free State, African lands that were deemed *terres vacantes* (vacant territories) were appropriated by the administration for individual and corporate gain.[47] One of the most extreme, disruptive natures of colonial restructuring and extraction of land-based resources occurred in this territory. The vacant territories were not actually vacant as officials had initially thought; rather; this was land which indigenous Congolese communities used for shifting cultivation, hunting, and gathering. This land was appropriated and divided into Domaines and handed over to international monopolies, and the rest retained by the state. The Domainal system thrived on the extraction of rubber (then in high demand in global markets), ivory, and minerals. This exploitation was aided by forced Congolese labor, with many Africans maimed or killed, leading to human suffering, depopulation, and famine.[48]

Some scholars have opted to direct attention to the ecological transformation of colonial, commercial, agricultural plantations and its impact on Africans. Some cash-crop plantations created regional microclimates that dramatically altered local environments, which in turn affected the health of African migrant farm laborers who worked on those plantations. In German Cameroon, plantations were set up in lowland swampy coastal regions that were hotter, wetter, and vulnerable to malaria and filariasis. African laborers who journeyed seasonally to these plantations from inland savannah areas of Yaounde, Bali, and Fumban suffered high mortality rates from these diseases. Thus, economic developments resulting from changes in man–habitat relationships, coupled with high population mobility and interactions, created 'microenvironmental conditions' that posed health challenges to communities.[49] Elsewhere along the Nile in Egypt, irrigated cotton fields led not only to waterlogging and salinity, but also induced an unhealthy environment that affected peasant communities living there. Malaria, bilharzia, and cholera outbreaks on irrigated farms were frequent occurrences, leading to numerous deaths.[50]

Economic developments in Africa did not always lead to depressing human health conditions and colonial exploitation. Rather, those developments presented some African communities and individuals with opportunities to distinguish themselves as innovative entrepreneurs and important role players in facilitating Africa's integration into the global economy. Their access to land and other natural resources was key to their entrepreneurship. Africans produced and supplied land-based products to regional and global markets even before the commencement of formal colonization, a role that persisted into the colonial period both in non-settler and settler territories. Absence of European settler economies in West African colonies allowed Africans to play a prominent role in resource extraction in those territories. Generally, though, the development of the cash-crop economy in many parts of tropical Africa increased due to the 'second industrial revolution' in Western countries, which stimulated production and export of products such as rubber, palm oil, and groundnuts.[51] The expansion of that economy benefited greatly from legitimate nineteenth-century commerce, which allowed African communities to be innovative in the production of tropical crops as substitutes for slave export.

In West Africa, the active role of African producers was enhanced by the lackluster outcome of early British and French experiments in commercial production of cash crops (cotton, coffee, and groundnuts) in their colonial enclaves here before the 1890s. In West Africa's hinterlands and areas abutting the Atlantic coast, in the area stretching from Senegal, the Gambia, Sierra Leone, through Gold Coast, the Niger Delta, to the Cameroons in the East, enterprising Africans moved into fill the void in supply of products that were required to jumpstart legitimate commerce. They produced and supplied palm oil, palm kernels, cotton, groundnuts, cocoa, timber, rubber, and gold to regional and international markets. Local agricultural and forest products thus largely propelled West Africa's export economy during this period. Reflecting on these developments, economic historian Anthony G. Hopkins sees this role by Africans as evidence of their ability to adjust to global production and market networks by masterfully using natural resources at their disposal. These initiatives led some of them to alter landscapes and settlement patterns by migrating into previously unused lands which they turned into rich productive zones that helped meet the ever increasing demands for tropical products in global markets.[52]

Elements of state coercion in this West African entrepreneurial spirit were rare. But elsewhere in colonial Africa, the pressure of global, capitalist demands fostered by colonialism bore down on African, peasant producers. Cases of colonial regimes enforcing the cultivation of cash crops, particularly cotton, upon African farmers have received scrutiny from historians and other scholars of Africa. In South Sudan during the 1920s and 1930s, the British administration's enforcement of cotton cultivation amongst the Dinka and Shilluk farmers as part of the effort to introduce a cash economy was met with considerable resistance from those communities. Drought and damage from cotton boll weevil did not help local acquiescence with cotton production. The British were interested in 'modernizing' South Sudan's economy through peasant cash-crop production. The Shilluk opposed cotton production as a non-edible crop: for them, planting food crops was the rational insurance against famine which commercial production of cotton did not guarantee.[53] Thus, moral arguments on both sides regarding functional utility of material production from the land ran counter to each other, creating tension in colonial relations.

In German East Africa, African opposition to cotton production that spawned the 1905–1907 Maji Maji Uprising is well documented. Tensions generated by colonial authoritarianism were important causes of the uprising, but the environmental conditions in which communities in Southeastern Tanganyika were forced to produce cotton were equally important. Generally, this opposition was the result of instability, if not uncertainty, caused by forced incorporation of local producers into a rapidly changing global economy. John Iliffe lucidly places the rebellion into these broader developments: 'It took place at the moment of transition from the nineteenth-century economy to the colonial order and it began as a movement of highlanders and frontiersmen resisting incorporation into the colonial economy and reduction to peasant status'.[54]

In colonial Mozambique, peasants weighed returns on their labor expended for cotton cultivation (as demanded by the Portuguese administration) against tending to their own food crops.[55] Food security was imperative to them, a need that was not guaranteed by cultivation of cotton, a non-food crop. Beyond focusing on state authoritarianism and food-security concerns as causes of these African resistances to cash-crop production, Allen Isaacman has stressed the need to consider other factors that shaped this African response. These include the tensions between African peasants and colonial states over rural, labor regimes and differential access to market opportunities and agricultural technologies as determinants of the outcome of relations surrounding cotton economies in colonial Africa.[56]

These cases of community responses to colonial cash-crop economies in rural Africa have been examined as part of African peasant studies that emphasize the principle of rationality as a determining behavior and actions of the peasant producer in a highly state-regulated economy. This view emphasizes the ability of African peasant households to make rational choices in the production process that guarantee the survival and welfare of their members. Rural households that became successful at subsistence and market production during the colonial period did so because they were able to take advantage of market incentives, predict and adapt to market trends, navigate certain strict, state-regulation mechanisms, and innovate ways of overcoming limits imposed on land by population growth and environmental challenges such as soil erosion. Consequently, such households experienced prosperity, and not poverty that resulted from colonial dislocation. Where obstacles to peasant production were overcome, both the colonial state and the farming communities benefited from land-based extractive economies.[57] We have to be cautious about generalizing such stories of success; rural prosperity may also have caused internal social differentiation in farming communities due to differential access to factors of production, most notably land, labor, and technology.

Prosperity for the rural African sometimes brought him into direct conflict with colonial authorities, usually over the question of managing land and other reproductive resources so as to preserve them from physical degradation. Consequently, colonial states enforced resource-conservation programs for much of the colonial period, a subject that has received considerable attention from historians and other scholars of Africa.

ENVIRONMENTAL CONSERVATION IN COLONIAL AFRICA

Conservation (the protection of physical landscapes and natural resources) emerged as an important issue in African colonies following intensified integration of African economies into the global system at the beginning of the twentieth century. Internal developments such as an increase in Africa's rural populations, as well as local and foreign demand for agricultural and other products extracted from the land, facilitated the drive for conservation. From the beginning, colonial conservation efforts were fraught with contradictions because they were marked by the imperative of economic production while requiring that extractive resources be preserved. Achieving such balance proved elusive for colonial regimes, resulting in a tenuous relationship with African communities.

One aspect of the African environment that received early attention in colonial conservation efforts was wildlife. This involved protecting wild animals and their habitats, except where some animals that were regarded as predators to livestock and destructive to crops were methodically eliminated. Hunting became an important aspect of focus for colonial administrations seeking to protect wildlife. Precolonial and colonial hunting practices have provided historians with a lens for analyzing how indigenous communities, European settlers, and colonial regimes perceived or understood wild animals, their social and economic importance, and their habitats. From their studies, we have come to appreciate that before colonial rule, hunting served as an essential source of economic survival for many African communities, as well as possessing political and cultural value beyond the economic imperative. John M. Mackenzie has pointed out that an examination of African hunting has to consider the 'function, technique, the role of animal products in subsistence, crafts and trade, as well as the complex relations associated with the chase'.[58]

The advent of colonialism undermined or redefined the meaning and importance of hunting. Colonial states and settlers commoditized it and used it to draw lines of social distinctions between themselves and Africans, based on new skills and tools of hunting that were very exclusionary, if not discriminatory. In South Africa, the introduction and use of firearms in hunting led to a gradual decline in these resources. Dutch and British expansion from the coastal locations into the interior, the establishment of settlers' agricultural farms, and the resulting upset in African settlement patterns consumed natural habitats for game and altered preexisting African hunting patterns. Colonization of South Africa ensured that more animals were hunted for scientific and commercial purposes.[59]

In East Africa, the global demand for ivory had a long-standing tradition that predated colonialism. This region's early colonial encounters in the late nineteenth and early twentieth centuries increased the economic demand for ivory and other game products, even as hunting transitioned from a fundamental source of African survival to an elite European sport. This transition, and the need to protect certain animal species perceived to be threatened through indiscriminate hunting, marked the development of colonial preservation and conservation in East Africa.[60]

These developments in East and Southern Africa led to decline in certain animals, particularly the hippopotamus, rhinoceros, giraffe, elephant, and springbok. From 1880 onwards, this created urgency within colonial administrations to protect these animals. Besides the fear that indiscriminate hunting led to decline of certain animals, the drive for conservation was also motivated by other factors. Economic motives provided the basis for creating national parks and game reserves as wild-animal sanctuaries for tourism purposes. In these protected areas, licensed hunting for game trophies (that were then sold) was allowed but restricted to Europeans only. Exclusion of Africans from these areas by legislation was deemed necessary on the basis that indigenous hunting techniques were inconsistent with the new conservation ethic. Those who breached such laws were tagged 'poachers', thereby criminalizing African hunting. The emergence of game departments and game warders proceeded out of the need to effect new boundaries that were drawn between Man and wildlife. These restrictions, and the imposition of a British aristocratic hunting ethos, diminished African wildlife knowledge and uses to a state of inferiority which in turn inspired resistances from local communities against exclusionary conservation measures.[61]

In trying to understand the consequences of these developments, historians of Africa have benefited from critical analyses of wildlife conservation from human geographers. By using the case of Mount Meru in Tanzania, Roderick P. Neumann has revealed the limits of state enforcement of wildlife conservation through the creation of animal sanctuaries. By using the case of Mount Meru National Park in Tanzania, Neumann shows how this wildlife sanctuary produced terrains of resistance from local communities opposed to the 'ordering' of nature that resulted in their exclusion from access to and use of enclosed resources.[62]

Sometimes, professionalization of wildlife knowledge through Western sciences was used to exclude or undermine African wildlife knowledge and practices, even when these had the potential to contribute to conservation efforts. This was evident not only in hunting, but also in knowledge regimes pertaining to some types of animals, such as birds. Most recently, Nancy A. Jacobs's seminal study *Birders of Africa* confirms how Africans have managed to fashion a close relationship with their natural environments and wildlife. Focusing on birds and 'birders' (Africans who were knowledgeable about birds), the study reveals that the ability to 'find one's "way to nature" through birds' was not only a preserve of a few European scientists who were categorized as 'ornithologists', but also of 'vernacular birders' of Africa. Because of their vast knowledge about birds, these individuals had an unparalleled ability to 'create productive, healthy, and happy lives' for those who interacted with birds in fields and forests. Such knowledge helped vernacular birders to navigate the hierarchies that European birders (ornithologists) constructed to distinguish both groups along racial lines. Colonial ornithologists in Southern-Central Africa came to depend on local birders such as Jali Makawa (in Nyasaland) to study birds, while the latter used the opportunity to 'mitigate his experience of exclusion'.[63] Here is a classic way in which African local knowledge about nature aided in advancing colonial scientific study of the African environment and animals in ways that helped overcome cultural biases against Africans based on racial stereotypes of the colonial world.

Besides wildlife, other scholars have directed their focus onto colonial conservation of Africa's agrarian landscapes, particularly those that authorities thought were being ruined by African farmers and herders. Farmers and herders relied primarily on land-based resources. In many colonial states, these resources were a major source of the administration's income. Colonial regimes increasingly reached the conclusion that colonial capitalism in the form of crop production for the market could be both a bane and a boon for rural households. This conclusion was aided by trends in African agricultural prosperity in the post-Depression years of the 1930s and in the period following the First World War. This led to increased crop production, made possible by appreciating prices on the market. Colonial administrations in Eastern, Central, and Southern Africa were drawn to serious cases of soil erosion and land degradation in rural areas, which they blamed on African 'overproduction' and inefficient herding practices.

Colonial soil conservation and other land reconditioning measures in colonial Africa have featured prominently in numerous studies. Some of these have focused on colonial arguments on the causes of land degradation. Colonial arguments that African cultivation practices and herding methods were 'wasteful' or 'inefficient', and therefore environmentally unsound as major causes of land degradation, is central to those studies. Others highlight the contradictions that colonial capitalism promoted in rural Africa through agricultural commercialization which led to a strain in household labor as farmers struggled to balance between producing their subsistence and market needs, and satisfying the rigors of conservation demanded by the state. In such cases, rural protests against the colonial state's authoritarianism in conservation were the likely response.[64] These views underpin the economic interpretations of these conservation programs, which argue that colonial administrations unfairly raised the specter of soil erosion and degradation as a reason to undercut Africans' desire to reap the benefits of crop and livestock production.[65] Official claims of African land degradation in settler colonies were also a means to legitimizing settler capitalism in the agricultural sector that thrived on land dispossessed from African communities who were pushed into reserves.[66] Based on this understanding, it is therefore possible to trace the role of colonial capitalism in firstly reorganizing production spaces that differentiated settler farms from African reserves, and, secondly, in using conservation to ensure the permanence of this differentiation. Yet overcrowding in African reserves due to natural increase in population resulted from this territorial reorganization, itself the product of colonial land dispossession and strict regulation of access to public land and forests. This, and the enclosure of alienated farms from encroachment by dispossessed communities, all proved a recipe for environmental degradation.[67]

On the other hand, social interpretations of soil conservation have zeroed in on the opposing ideas, practices, values, and traditions about land use and management held by colonial administrators and experts on one hand, and Africans on the other. This argument has been extended to the argument that African resistances to conservation drew from African spiritual tradition.[68] Others have traced the influence of the gendered structure of social relations of production in precolonial Africa as a factor in rural opposition to colonial enforcement of land reconditioning programs. Focus on gendered aspects has in turn promoted ecofeminist interpretations that acknowledge the value of women's indigenous understanding of nature and resource reproduction. By opposing subjective forms of colonial conservation, African women sought to reassert their environmental and agricultural knowledge in managing their farms.[69]

All these interpretations have directly or indirectly been linked to the anti-colonial sentiments that fuelled African nationalism in the 1950s. They represent an effort to study colonial conservation 'from below', and social interpretations have dominated that approach, and constitute the political interpretations that perceive a close connection between rural resistance and colonial authoritarianism in soil conservation programs with the rise of African nationalism in East Africa in the 1950s.[70]

Scholarly focus on causation and solutions in colonial conservation has exposed a prevailing contrast between Western and indigenous knowledge systems. If colonial castigation of African indigenous cultivation repertoires helped draw that contrast, then the search for solutions to land degradation in general and soil erosion in particular confirmed that contrast. Consequently, colonial imposition of Western environmental solutions to degradation of Africa's rural landscapes has attracted considerable attention from historians and other scholars of Africa. This was true for British colonies in South Africa and East Africa.[71] Those methods proved incompatible with the ecological, economic, and social realities of rural Africa. In South Africa, conservation was devised to cover a broad range of activities beyond soil conservation on African and settler farms. Conservation involved regulation of grass fires, grazing patterns, water and irrigation, an attack on pests and livestock predators, and uprooting of obnoxious weeds.[72] The importance of weeds and management of pastures further raised concerns about 'plant invasions' and their ecological and economic importance in the political economy of rural environments. In these discussions, obnoxious weeds and the Prickly Pear were important.[73]

Colonial emphasis on external ecological solutions reinforced the role of Western experts and science in Africa. Agricultural and livestock experts found place of pride in concerted colonial policies to protect farms from degradation or domesticated animals from being decimated by pests and diseases. The basic motive was to protect and increase the reproductive resources of the agricultural sector.[74] As Diana K. Davies has noted with regard to French colonial territories in North Africa, defining and advancing local environmental crises within Western scientific thinking (such as the declensionist narrative) justified colonial degradation of local preexisting farming knowledge, sanctioned French appropriation of land and social control of the conquered communities, and forcefully articulated local subsistence production into a market-oriented one.[75] Institutionalization of Western knowledge was partly the reason why African knowledge systems and technologies were treated with colonial hindsight. Colonial subjugation of African knowledge and technology systems relating to the use and management of land was evident. This has been analyzed within the poststructuralist paradigm of knowledge–power relations of the colonial state.[76]

Recent revisionist studies have argued that colonial science was not wholly a problematic enterprise that promoted authoritarianism in African colonial states and the privileging of Western knowledge. This view insists that presenting colonial science and technology practices as they relate to the environment as highly subversive renders those components 'as static social artefacts, trapped in the context in which they were generated'.[77] Rather than focus on their coercive elements, revisionists urge us to consider cases where colonial experts and scientific enterprises consciously incorporated African knowledge in dealing with environmental challenges. Helen Tilley has produced perhaps the most convincing study that underscores this interpretation. Citing British development efforts in colonial Africa, Tilley argues that experts in the Africa Research Survey charged with exploring development initiatives hardly ignored local conditions, environmental set-ups, and African needs and knowledge.[78] This approach to colonial initiatives has been cited as the reason for successful rural programs in some colonial states. Indeed, in Uganda, soil conservation measures in Kigezi proceeded unimpeded by the local community because officials integrated land-management techniques that mirrored the traditional *Bakiga* system.[79] Colonial experts and science may thus have allowed for interpenetration of Western and African knowledge systems in ways that earlier studies have overlooked.

Related to this revisionism are recent studies on narratives that are concerned with 'blame-the-victim' in colonial-degradation narratives. They seek to rectify the long-held view of Africans as despoilers of their environments and therefore responsible for deforestation and degradation of landscapes. These studies have instead confirmed cases of African-environment interaction practices that aided the preservation of natural environments. Those practices, often overlooked in official colonial discourses, led to regeneration of vegetation and soils. This perspective was pioneered by Paul Richard's study on West Africa's farming activities that allowed him to conclude

African farmers possessed the ability to utilize their 'ecological knowledge' or 'people's science' to cultivate food crops in ways that promoted environmental sustainability.[80]

Colonial neo-Malthusian arguments of population increase as the cause of degradation have also been overturned by recent research that confirms increases in rural populations in areas such as Machakos and Kenya have actually led to innovation by farmers, which, together with less intrusive state policies and favorable agricultural markets, has led to vegetation regeneration and preservation of the soil since the 1930s.[81] This revelation contradicts colonial narratives that blamed the agricultural and livestock activities of the Kamba community for environmental degradation.

Of all recent 'corrective narratives' on degradation and environmental decline in colonial Africa, the study by Melissa Leach and James Fairhead on colonial forestry in Kissidougou in Guinea, West Africa, has proved the most influential in presenting a shift in paradigms for studying Africa's environmental history. It has also had an influence on modern environmental intervention policies. French colonial experts pointed to open areas in Guinea's savannah grasslands as evidence of human interference that resulted in decline of what they premised as a luxuriant humid forest that existed in the past. Instead, Leach and Fairhead established that traditional settlement patterns in Kissidougou actually led to filling of landscapes with trees, itself evidence that French colonial experts read forest history backwards. Coming from non-historians, these findings have nonetheless provided an analytical framework for some social environmental historians of Africa. Emanuel Kreike's study in southern Angola and northern Namibia is important. Here, Ovambo-speakers experienced decades of resource-based violence, environmental challenges such as famine and rinderpest, followed by colonial displacement. Subsequently displaced as refugees in wilderness spaces, they eventually domesticated their new locations by revegetating the landscape, creating a 'water infrastructure', and keeping livestock. Some of them regenerated fruit trees, thereby creating a sort of 'Eden' in the Ovambo Flood Plain.[82] Ovamboland's case is a classic illustration of the ability of African communities to rehabilitate, use, and preserve environments; one that departs from colonial criticisms of these communities' activities as a major cause of environmental dislocations.

Environment, Colonialism, and Development

Irrespective of the motives and justification that colonial administrations presented for their intervening in Africa's natural resource management and in human relations with the environment, there was always an element of 'development' that was implied. Colonial officials were always convinced that their intervention would help transform every aspect of life in positive ways. The pursuit of 'healthy environments', introduction of cash crops in rural areas, and conservation of wildlife, agricultural, and pastoralist environments were all regarded as development initiatives. This colonial perception began earlier, but became directly implied during the postwar reconstruction agenda after 1945. It has largely been analyzed within the lens of 'colonial developmentalism' initiated during the 'second colonial occupation' after the Second World War.[83] A wide range of European experts and other trained personnel of empire answered a call of duty to help British, Belgian, Portuguese, and French colonies boost their economic potential, and in the process help shore up postwar recovery at home and abroad. In French colonies, these development efforts were implemented through the FIDES and the FERDES.[84] In British colonies, rural development plans were packaged as 'Betterment' programs. They largely targeted the agrarian sector, which was the core of colonial economies, but was perceived as threatened by increased incidences of land degradation after the war. Funded by Colonial Development Corporation and the Overseas Food Corporation, Betterment programs in British colonies sought to improve both the economic and social welfare of rural communities.[85] During the 1940s and 1950s, soil conservation measures may have been the centerpiece of these British programs, but food production, conservation of water, improvement of methods of cultivation and pasturelands, livestock management, afforestation, land resettlement programmed, and large-scale cash-crop initiatives were as important. In French and Portuguese colonies, the mining sector increased in importance.

In many parts of Africa, colonial regimes engaged soil conservation as 'development' which could only be accomplished by recourse to scientific and technological solutions from the USA. This approach was appealing in Southern Africa from the 1920s.[86] It was widely embraced in East Africa, particularly Kenya, from the 1930s through the 1950s. Here, colonial land reconditioning programs in Baringo, Machakos, and Vihiga were patterned after technological solutions imported from the USA and South Africa.[87] Recent studies have revisited these colonial initiatives with the aim of evaluating their success or failure, and as models for configuring policy regarding modern development. For instance, British soil conservation in colonial Kigezi succeeded due to integration of indigenous knowledge and institutions, and has reinforced the calls for modern rural development efforts to consider local conditions in drawing and implementation of policy.[88]

Attempts to define colonial environmental projects as 'development' has also directed some historians' attention to large-scale colonial statist projects. Colonial visions of prosperity and progress in Africa inspired the massive investments of finance and expertise that went into these projects. Such investments were also predicated on the envisioned economic benefits of those projects to the metropolitan powers in terms of export of agricultural products for industrial development back in Europe. Most of these projects failed to take off as planned, or failed to yield the desired economic and social benefits to African communities. This failure illustrated the shortcomings of colonial development plans in Africa in the 1950s. Historians have been interested in the reasons for their failure and lessons that subsequent development can draw from this experience.

Perhaps the most scrutinized of those projects is the East African Groundnut (Peanut) Scheme implemented in central Tanganyika by the British colonial administration in the late 1940s. It proved unsuccessful. This failure has been attributed to poor planning and ignorance of local ecological conditions, these despite the massive financial investments and technical skills that British planners committed to the project.[89] In the French Sudan, the signature project of French colonial developmentalism was the Office du Niger irrigation scheme. The scheme unsuccessfully attempted to transform the Upper Niger delta into a commercial cotton-growing enterprise. French officials were forced by local communities and local geographical conditions to change their development objectives from cotton to rice, a food crop.[90] This outcome points to the possible importance that African communities gave to food security in environments that were considered fragile. But it also confirms the failure of colonial development 'experts' to pay attention to physical environments in which large-scale agricultural projects were sited.

Colonial mega-projects such as damming of water along major rivers for purposes of bringing development to the regions and communities living in riverine locations have also provided opportunities for historical analysis. In Mozambique, the Cahora Bassa Dam involved sophisticated forms of scientific planning by the Portuguese administration aimed at agricultural transformation through irrigation, improvement of transportation in the Zambezi River Valley, flooding control, and electricity supply. For the local African communities, the economic benefits envisioned by the Portuguese colonial (and later, the African) government were outweighed by the social dislocation and absence of services that resulted from the completion of the dam. There was massive population dislocation, exploitation of African labor, violence, and environmental decline, illustrating the contradictions of planned development by modern states.[91] These projects have been subjected to a scholarly framework inspired by James Scott's 'high modernism', a form of modern development pursued by modern states in which scientific planning and the colonial expert and administrator monopolized the vision of development outside the realm of the ideal world of the rural peasant.[92] In northwest Zimbabwe, among the Tonga, the construction of the Kariba Dam in the 1950s ended what Joann McGregor terms as a 'river-focused way of life' that had given cultural and economic sustenance to that community. Damming of water led to their displacement, loss, impoverishment, and exposure to a tsetse environment.[93] Colonial developmentalist projects relating to damming water yielded legacies that have continued to shape not only community–state relations, but also contested access to land in the affected riverine areas. Joost Fontein's recent study on the damming of the Mutirikwi River in Masvingo, southern Zimbabwe, offers an excellent analysis of the impact of external intervention into riverine ecologies with intentions of superimposing elements of modernization by the state. That intervention not only alters community livelihoods, but also, in the long term, reinforces politics of environmental identities and contestations over land in a bid to reassert lineage claims to land.[94]

Conclusion

The outcome of Africa's interaction with colonialism created dynamic environmental relations between colonial states and Africans that have provided scholars of Africa with a rich terrain for studying and writing about Africa's colonial experience. Among the forces that propelled European colonial interests in Africa, the lure of the African natural environment was important. The economic importance of tropical environmental resources to Europe was confirmed following the establishment of colonial rule. Socially, though, nature in Africa afforded colonial interlopers the opportunity to reconstruct images and perceptions about the continent and its peoples, to justify economic imperialism, and to consolidate the politics of the colonial state. The insistence of colonial administrations and their agents on certain environmental ideas, norms, and practices led to two mutually opposed outcomes.

On one hand, it attempted to promote a world of unequal power relations aimed at promoting the notion of 'difference': the difference between the European colonizer and the African subject, one that was partly played out in environmental relations. In doing so, colonizers were aided by advantages offered by 'tools of empire', of which Western science and technology were powerful; so much that the application of new ideas to challenges posed by the African environment (disease, for instance) or to the use and management of natural resources opened avenues for the colonial states to elevate imported knowledge to the service of colonial power. While this subjective role of Western scientific and technical knowledge has dominated studies focusing on colonialism and the environment in Africa, a few scholars have reminded us of the positive value of that knowledge in minimizing, even eliminating, dangers of the environment to human health. No doubt, then, precolonial and colonial efforts to eliminate such diseases as malaria have persisted into the postcolonial era, thereby drawing further interest from some historians.[95]

On the other hand, colonial insistence on an environmental orthodox drew revulsion from Africans who resisted the subjective and marginalizing tendencies of colonial environmental ideas. Sometimes Africans sought to reassert their knowledge in colony–environment relations. Historical analyses of this African response, mostly by peasant communities, have promoted our understanding of Africa's 'subaltern histories' that seek to give agency to these communities in colonial histories. To an extent, the influence of works by subaltern scholars of India has been invaluable in recovering these African histories.[96]

Overall, Africa's encounter with colonialism generated complex environmental issues that have enabled historians to critically evaluate and reexamine diverse themes that emerged from that encounter. The themes include, but are not limited to, imperialism, colonial conquest, health, economy, urbanization, preservation, and management of natural resources. More important, some structural, even abstract, themes have provided an interesting setting for academic study. They include race, ethnicity, identity, power, knowledge, class, gender, language, and culture, among others.

Furthermore, the complexity of the 'environmental question' in colonial Africa has attracted the interest of scholars from multiple disciplines so much that examination of that question has not been limited to the historian. Instead, the historian of Africa has immensely benefited from approaches and findings of multiple disciplines whose scholars have studied Africa's colonial environmental experience. Geography, anthropology, ecology, political science, economics, and development studies have been of particular importance. This has enriched both Africa's environmental history and African historiography. One can conclude emphatically that African environmental history is a blended, interdisciplinary effort. Some of these disciplines (particularly ecology, geography, anthropology, and development studies) have used historical knowledge to shed light on current environmental issues in Africa that are of both local and global significance. These issues (for instance, climate, health, and conservation) are not new to Africa and Africans.

Notes

1. Such key works include William Beinart and JoAnn McGregor, eds., *Social History and African Environments* (Athens: Ohio University Press, 2003); William Beinart and Lotte Hughes, *Environment and Empire* (Oxford: Oxford University Press, 2007); and Gregory Maddox, James Giblin, and Isaria N. Kimambo, *Custodians of the Land: Ecology and Culture in the History of Tanzania* (Athens, OH: Ohio University Press, 1996).
2. Jane Carruthers, "Tracking in Game Trails: Looking Afresh at the Politics of Environmental History in South Africa," *Environmental History* 11, no. 4 (2006): 811.
3. For instance, James McCann, *Green Land, Brown Land, Black Land: An Environmental History of Africa, 1800–1990* (Portsmouth, NH: Heinemann, 1999); Gregory Maddox, *Sub-Saharan Africa: An Environmental History* (Santa Barbara, CA: ABC-CLIO, 2006). More critical studies on African Environmental History include Beinart and McGregor, eds., *Social History*. Other critical works on the relationship between African environmental history and African history, with a larger focus on colonial Africa, include Gregory H. Maddox, "Africa and Environmental History," *Environmental History* 4, no. 2 (1999): 162–67; William Beinart, "African History and Environmental History," in "Centenary Issue: A Hundred Years of Africa," special issue, *African*

Affairs 99, no. 35 (2000): 269–302; and Jane Carruthers, "Africa: Histories, Ecologies and Societies," *Environment and History* 10, no. 4 (2004): 804–29.
4. Among works that give considerable treatment to precolonial African environmental history and the central role of African agency are James C. McCann, *Green Land, Brown London*; James Webb Jr., *Desert Frontier: Ecological and Economic Change Along the Western Sahel, 1600–1850* (Madison: University of Wisconsin Press, 1994); David Schoenburn, *A Green Place, a Good Place: Agrarian Change and Social Identity in the Great Lakes Region to the 15th Century* (Portsmouth, NH: Heinemann, 1998); and Jan Vansina, *Paths in the Rainforest: Toward a History of Political Tradition in Equatorial Africa* (Madison: University of Wisconsin Press, 1990).
5. See a discussion on these perspectives of African historiography in Maddox, Giblin and Kimambo, *Custodians of the Land*, 7–8.
6. Dane Kennedy, "British Exploration in the Nineteenth Century: A Historiographic Survey," *History Compass* 5, no. 6 (2007): 1890.
7. These issues are extensively dealt with in Richard H. Grove, *Green Imperialism: Colonial Expansion, Tropical Island Edens and the Origins of Environmentalism, 1600–1860* (Cambridge: Cambridge University Press, 1996); and Alfred W. Crosby, *Ecological Imperialism: The Biological Expansion of Europe, 900–1900* (Cambridge: Cambridge University Press, 2004).
8. A well-outlined historical role of these societies in Africa is provided by Robin A. Butlin, *Geographies of Empire: European Empires and Colonies c. 1880–1960* (Cambridge: Cambridge University Press, 2009), 275–314.
9. David Livingstone, *The Geographical Tradition: Episodes in the History of a Contested Enterprise* (Oxford: Blackwell, 1992), 167.
10. Beinart and Hughes, *Environment and Empire*, 91–92.
11. Robert O. Collins and James M. Burns, *A History of Sub-Saharan Africa*, 2nd ed. (Cambridge: Cambridge University Press, 2014), 253.
12. Philip Curtin, *Death by Migration: Europe's Encounter with the Tropical World in the Nineteenth Century* (Cambridge: Cambridge University Press, 1989); Crosby, Ecological Imperialism.
13. Philip Curtin, *Disease and Empire: The Health of European Troops in the Conquest of Africa* (Cambridge: Cambridge University Press, 1998), 11–15.
14. Ibid. Curtin details the interface between imperial British and French military campaigns in various parts of Africa during the nineteenth century, and advances in tropical medicine and hygiene by Western countries.
15. On detailed studies on these aspects of technological advances and their relations to imperialism and colonialism, see Daniel R. Headrick, *The Tools of Empire: Technology and European Imperialism in the Nineteenth Century* (New York: Oxford University Press, 1981); and Michael Adas, *Machines as Measures of Men: Science, Technology, and Ideologies of Western Dominance* (Ithaca, NY: Cornell University Press, 1989).
16. For instance, James Brown, "Increased Inter-communication and Epidemic Disease in Early Colonial Ashanti" in *Disease in African History: An Introductory Survey and Case Studies*, ed. Gerald W. Hartwig and K. David Patterson, (Durham, NC: Duke University Press, 1978), 181–206. Also, Myron Echenberg, *Plague Ports* (New York: New York University Press, 2007).

17. Helge Kjekshus, *Ecology Control and Economic Development in East African History* (Athens: Ohio University Press, 1977). For other relevant work on economic production and environment in precolonial and early colonial Tanzania, see James Giblin, *The Politics of Environmental Control in Northeastern Tanzania, 1840–1940* (Philadelphia: University of Philadelphia Press, 1993). Some contributions in *Custodians of the Land*, ed. Maddox, Giblin, and Kimambo also reflect some of these trends.
18. For details, see Douglas Johnson and David Anderson, eds., *The Ecology of Survival: Case Studies from Northeast African History* (London: Croom Helm, 1988).
19. For an excellent outline of the early history of the tsetse fly and its health implications in Africa, see John J. McKelvey Jr., *Man against Tsetse: Struggle for Africa* (Ithaca, NY: Cornell University Press, 1973), chap. 1.
20. The most incisive of these include Helge Kjekshus, *Ecology Control*; John Ford, *The Role of the Trypanosomiases in African Ecology: A Study of the Tsetse Fly Problem* (London: Oxford University Press, 1971); James Giblin, "Trypanosomiasis Control in African History: An Evaded Issue," *Journal of African History* 31 (1990): 59–80; Kirk Hope, *Lords of the Fly: Sleeping Sickness Control in British East Africa, 1900–1960* (Westport, CT: Praeger, 2003); and Maryinez Lyons, *The Colonial Disease: A Social History of Sleeping Sickness in Northern Zaire, 1900–1940* (Cambridge: Cambridge University Press, 1992).
21. McKelvey Jr., *Man against Tsetse* documents these scientific studies and their colonial and intellectual impact in greater detail.
22. Lyons, *The Colonial Disease*, 103.
23. Kjekshus, *Ecology Control*, 165–66; For detailed quantification of these mortality rates, see Hoppe, *Lords of the Fly*. Regarding anti-tsetse fly campaigns in Kenya's Lake Victoria Basin, see George Oduor Ndege, *Health, State, and Society in Kenya* (Rochester: Rochester University Press, 2001), 18–33.
24. Kjekshus, *Ecology Control*, 166, 168–73.
25. Lyons, *The Colonial Disease*, 102–3.
26. Shane Doyle, *Population and Environment in Western Uganda 1860–1955: Crisis and Decline in Bunyoro* (Ohio: Ohio University Press, 2006), 146–50.
27. John Ford, *The Role of Trypanosomiases in African Ecology: A Study of the Tsetse Fly Problem* (London: Oxford University Press, 1971).
28. Beinart and Hughes, *Environment and Empire*, 177; and Ndege, *Health, State, and Society*, 34–40.
29. Maynard W. Swanson, "The Sanitation Syndrome: Bubonic Plague and Urban Native Policy in the Cape Colony, 1900–1909," *Journal of African History* 18 (1977): 390.
30. Swanson, "The Sanitation Syndrome," 387, 394–95, 397; Myron Echenberg, *Plague Ports*, 274–76. For an apt summary of these developments in South Africa, see Beinart and Hughes, *Environment and Empire*, 174–77.
31. Francis Dube, "Public Health and Racial Segregation in South Africa: Mahatma (M.K.) Gandhi Debates Colonial Authorities on Public Health Measures, 1896–1904," *Journal of the Historical Society of Nigeria* 21 (2012): 26–27.
32. Swanson, "The Sanitation Syndrome," 402.
33. Myron Echenberg, *Plague Ports*, 294–97.

34. Gerald Hartwick and K. David Patterson, eds., *Disease in African History: An Introductory Survey and Case Studies* (Durham, NC: Duke University Press, 1978), 15.
35. John Ruedy, *Modern Algeria: The Origins and Development of a Nation*, 2nd ed. (Bloomington, IN: Indiana University Press, 2005), 70–72; and For more details on French colonial land policies in Algeria, see John Ruedy, *Land Policy in Colonial Algeria: Origins of the Rural Public Domain* (Berkeley, CA: University of California Press, 1967).
36. John Ruedy, *Modern Algeria*, 70–72.
37. For an outline of African loss of land and related resources to Dutch (later Afrikaner) and British settlers in South Africa, see Rodney Davenport and Christopher Saunders, *South Africa: A Modern History* (London: Macmillan, 2000), 21–54, 77–125, 129–93.
38. Richard Elphick, *Khoikhoi and the Founding of White South Africa* (Johannesburg: Raven Press, 1985), 234–38.
39. Nancy Jacobs, *Environment, Power, and Injustice: A South African History* (Cambridge: Cambridge University Press, 2003).
40. Leroy Vail, "Ecology and History: The Example of Eastern Zambia," *Journal of South African Studies* 3, no. 2 (1977): 129–55.
41. Report of the H.M. Commissioner on the East Africa Protectorate (1903, cd. 1626), 29–30, as quoted in G.H. Mungeam, *Kenya: Select Historical Documents 1884–1923* (Nairobi: East African Publishing House, Nairobi, 1978), 93.
42. Settler history in Kenya had received much attention with regard to land alienation. For a detailed study on the role of British colonial officials on this development, see G.H. Mungeam, *British Rule in Kenya, 1895–1912* (Oxford: Clarendon Press, 1966); and Lotte Hughes, *Moving the Maasai: A Colonial Misadventure* (New York: Palgrave Macmillan, 2006).
43. For details on these varied views between colonial officials and the Maasai, see Hughes, *Moving the Maasai*, chap. 5, 105–32.
44. Ibid., 105.
45. David M. Anderson, *Eroding the Commons: The Politics of Ecology in Baringo, Kenya 1890–1963* (Oxford: James Currey, 2002).
46. Ibid., 232–66; Jamie Monson, "Canoe-Building Under Colonialism: Forestry and Food Policies in the Inner Kilombero Valley, 1920–1940," in *Custodians of the Land*, ed. Maddox, Giblin, and Kimambo, 200–12; Christopher A. Conte, *Highland Sanctuary: Environmental History in Tanzania's Usambara Mountains* (Athens, OH: Ohio University Press, 2004); and Christopher Conte, "Nature Re-organized: Ecological History in the Plateau Forests of the West Usambara Mountains 1850–1935," in *Custodians of the Land*, ed. Maddox, Giblin, and Kimambo, 96–121.
47. Martin Ewans, *European Atrocity, African Catastrophe: Leopold II, the Congo Free State, and Its Aftermath* (London: Routledge Curtzon, 2002), 157–72.
48. Ibid., 157–65.
49. Mark W. DeLancey, "Health and Disease on the Plantations of Cameroon, 1884–1939," in *Disease in African History*, ed. Hartwick and Patterson, 153–79.

50. Nancy E. Gallagher, *Egypt's Other Wars: Epidemics and the Politics of Public Health* (Syracuse: Syracuse University Press, 1990).
51. Gareth Austin, "Explaining and Evaluating the Cash Crop Revolution in the 'Peasant' Colonies of Tropical Africa, ca. 1890–ca. 1930: Beyond 'Vent for Surplus'," in *Africa's Development in Historical Perspective*, ed. Emmanuel Akyeampong et al. (Cambridge: Cambridge University Press, 2014), 315.
52. A.G. Hopkins, *An Economic History of West Africa* (New York: Columbia University Press, 1973), 124–66. For details on the role of Africans in the production and supply of tropical products to regional and global markets in Gold Coast during this period see Raymond E. Dumett, *Imperialism, Economic Development and Social Change in West Africa* (Durham, NC: Carolina Academic Press, 2013).
53. Robert O. Collins, *Shadow in the Grass: Britain in the Southern Sudan, 1918–1956* (New Haven, CT: Yale University Press, 1983), 306–7. For varied responses by African farmers to colonial cotton production, see Allen Isaacman, *Cotton, Colonialism, and Social History in Sub-Saharan Africa* (Portsmouth, NH: Heinemann, 1995).
54. John Illife, *A Modern History of Tanganyika* (Cambridge: Cambridge University Press, 1979), 168.
55. Allen Isaacman, "Chiefs, Rural Differentiation and Peasant Protest: The Mozambican Forced Cotton Regime 1938–1961," *African Economic History* 14 (1985): 15–56.
56. Allen Isaacman, "Peasants, Work and the Labor Process: Forced Cotton Cultivation in Colonial Mozambique 1938–1961," *Journal of Social History* 25, no. 4 (1992): 815–55; and Allen Isaacman, *Cotton Is the Mother of Poverty: Peasants, Work, and Rural Struggle in Colonial Mozambique, 1938–1961* (Portsmouth, NH: Heinemann, 1995).
57. For instance, Elias Mandala, *Work and Control in a Peasant Economy: A History of the Lower Tchiri Valley in Malawi, 1859–1960* (Madison, WI: University of Wisconsin Press, 1990); Robert Maxon, *Going Their Separate Ways: Agrarian Transformation in Kenya, 1930–1950* (London: Associated University Presses, 2003); Stephen G. Bunker, *Peasants against the State: The Politics of Market Control in Bugisu, Uganda, 1900–1983* (Chicago: University of Chicago Press, 1991); and Gavin Kitching, *Class and Economic Change in Kenya: The Making of an African Petite-Bourgeoisie* (New Haven, CT: Yale University Press, 1980).
58. Mackenzie, *The Empire of Nature*, 56. For an elaborate discussion on the overall importance of hunting and game products in African communities across Central, East, and Southern Africa, see ibid., 54–84. Though a thin line separates "preservation" from "conservation," the former aims at preventing frequent interference, while the latter is more interventionist, aiming at "sustainable" management for the long term. Ibid., 289–90.
59. Ibid.
60. Ibid., 85–165. On details regarding game preservation policies in colonial Kenya, see Thomas P. Ofcansky, *Paradise Lost: A History of Game Preservation in British East Africa, 1895–1963* (Morgantown: West Virginia University Press, 2002).

61. For details on game preservation and conservation in South Africa, see Jane Carruthers, *The Kruger National Park: A Social and Political History* (Pietermaritzburg: University of Natal Press, 1995). As regards Kenya, see Edward I. Steinhart, *Black Poachers, White Hunters: A Social History of Hunting in Kenya* (Athens, OH: Ohio University Press, 2006).
62. Roderick P. Neumann, *Imposing Wilderness: Struggles Over Livelihood and Nature Preservation in Africa* (Berkley, CA: University of California Press, 1998).
63. Nancy J. Jacobs, *Birders of Africa: History of a Network* (Princeton, NJ: Princeton University Press, 2016), 14, 17, 148–79.
64. Maxon, *Going Their Separate Ways*; Mandala, *Work and Control*.
65. Anderson, *Eroding the Commons*; Martin S. Shanguhyia, *Population, Tradition, and Environmental Control in Colonial Kenya* (Rochester, NY: University of Rochester Press, 2015).
66. Anderson, *Eroding the Commons*; Tabitha Kanogo, *Squatters & the Roots of Mau Mau* (Athens, OH: Ohio University Press, 1987).
67. Shanguhyia, *Population, Tradition*; David Anderson, "Depression, Dust Bowl, Demography, and Drought: The Colonial State and Soil Conservation in East Africa during the 1930s," *African Affairs* 83, no. 332 (1984): 321–43.
68. Steven Feierman, *Peasant Intellectuals: Anthropology and History in Tanzania* (Madison, WI: University of Wisconsin Press, 1990).
69. Fiona D. Mackenzie, *Land, Ecology, and Resistance in Kenya, 1880–1952* (Portsmouth, NH: Heinemann, 1998).
70. These studies are many; but for examples, see R.A. Young and H.A. Foosbrooke, *Smoke in the Hills: Political Tension in the Morogoro District of Tanganyika* (Evanston, IL: Northwestern University Press, 1969); Feierman, *Peasant Intellectuals*; David Throup, *Economic and Social Origins of Mau Mau* (Athens, OH: Ohio University Press, 1987); Mackenzie, *Land, Ecology and Resistance*; Mandala, *Work and Control*; John McCracken, "Conservation and Resistance in Colonial Malawi: The 'Dead North' Revisited," in *Social History*, ed. Beinart and McGregor, 155–74; and Pamela A. Maack, "'We Don't Want Terraces': Protest and Identity Under the Uluguru Land Usage Scheme," in *Custodians of the Land*, ed. Maddox, Giblin, and Kimambo, 152–74.
71. William Beinart, *The Rise of Conservation in South Africa: Settlers, Livestock, and the Environment 1770–1950* (New York: Oxford University Press, 2008); and Kate Showers, *Imperial Gullies: Soil Erosion and Conservation in Lesotho* (Athens: Ohio University Press, 2005).
72. Beinart, *The Rise of Conservation*; Lance Van Sittert, "'The Seed Blows About in Every Breeze': Noxious Weed Eradication in the Cape Colony, 1860–1909," *Journal of Southern African Studies* 26, no. 4 (2000): 655–74.
73. Sittert, "The Seed Blows". Regarding the prickly pear, see Karen Middleton, "The Ironies of Plant Transfer: The Case of Prickly Pear in Madagascar," in *Social History*, ed. Beinart and McGregor, 43–59.
74. Karen Brown, "Political Entomology: The Insectile Challenge to Agricultural Development in the Cape Colony, 1895–1910," *Journal of South African Studies* 29, no. 2 (2003): 529–49.

75. Diana K. Davis, *Resurrecting the Granary of Rome: Environmental History and French Colonial Expansion in North Africa* (Athens, OH: Ohio University Press, 2007), xii.
76. Mackenzie, *Land, Ecology, and Resistance*. See Henrietta Moore and Meghan Vaughan, *Cutting Down Trees: Gender, Nutrition, and Agricultural Change in the Northern Province of Zambia, 1890–1990* (Portsmouth, NH: Heinemann, 1993) regarding colonial notions on Bemba land use in colonial Zambia.
77. William Beinart, Karen Brown, and Daniel Gilfoyle, "Experts and Expertise in Colonial Africa Reconsidered: Science and the Interpenetration of Knowledge," *African Affairs* 108, no. 432 (2009): 413–33.
78. Helen Tilley, *Africa as a Living Laboratory: Empire, Development, and the Problem of Scientific Knowledge, 1870–1950* (Chicago: University of Chicago Press, 2011).
79. Grace Carswell, *Cultivating Success in Uganda: Kigezi Farmers and Colonial Policies* (Athens, OH: Ohio University Press, 2007).
80. Paul Richards, *Indigenous Agricultural Revolution: Ecology and Food Production in West Africa* (London: Hutchinson Education, 1985).
81. Mary Tiffen, Michael Motimore, and Francis Gichuki, *More People, Less Erosion: Environmental Recovery* (Chichester: John Wiley, 1994).
82. Emmanuel Kreike, *Re-Creating Eden: Land Use, Environment, and Society in Southern Angola and Northern Namibia* (Portsmouth, NH: Heinemann, 2004); and Emmanuel Kreike, "Hidden Fruits: A Social Ecology of Fruit Trees in Namibia and Angola, 1880s–1990s," in *Social History*, ed. Beinart and McGregor, 27–42.
83. The terms "Colonial Developmentalism" and "Second Colonial Occupation" are used here after Frederick Cooper and D.A. Low and Lonsdale, respectively. See Fredrick Cooper, *Africa since 1940: The Past of the Present* (Cambridge: Cambridge University Press, 2002), 36–37, 59; and D.A. Low and John Lonsdale, "Introduction: Towards the New Order 1945–1963," in *Oxford History of East Africa*, ed. D.A. Low and Alison Smith (Oxford: Oxford University Press, 1976), 12–16.
84. Maddox, Sub-Saharan Africa, 155.
85. Joseph M. Hodge, *Triumph of the Expert: Agrarian Doctrines of Development and the Legacies of British Colonialism* (Athens, OH: Ohio University Press, 2007), especially chap. 7.
86. Soil Erosion, "Conservationism and Ideas about Development: A Southern African Exploration, 1900–1960," *Journal of South African Studies* 11, no. 1 (1984): 52–83.
87. Anderson, *Eroding the Commons*; Shanguhyia, *Population, Tradition, and Environmental Control*.
88. Carswell, *Cultivating Success in Uganda*.
89. The scheme has attracted considerable attention, mostly from scholars of economics and development in the 1950s and in the postcolonial period. For the latter, see, for instance, J.S. Hogendorn and K.M. Scott, "The East African Groundnut Scheme: Lessons of a Large-Scale Agricultural Failure," *African Economic History* 10 (1981): 81–115; and Matteo Rizzo, "What Was Left of the Groundnut Scheme? Development Disaster and Labour Market

in Southern Tanganyika 1946–1952," *Journal of Agrarian Change* 6, no. 2, (2006): 205–38.
90. Monica van Beusekom, *Negotiating Development: African Farmers and Colonial Experts at the Office Du Niger, 1920–1960* (Portsmouth, NH: Heinemann, 2002).
91. Allen Isaacman, *Dams, Displacement, and the Delusion of Development: Cahora Bassa and Its Legacies in Mozambique, 1965–2007* (Athens, OH: Ohio University Press, 2013).
92. James Scott, *Seeing Like the State: How Certain Schemes to Improve the Human Condition Have Failed* (New Haven, CT: Yale University Press, 1998).
93. Joann McGregor, "Living with the River: Landscape and Memory in the Zambezi Valley, Northwest Zimbabwe," in *Social History*, ed. Beinart and McGregor, 87–105.
94. Joost Fontein, *Remaking Mutirikwi: Landscape, Water, and Belonging in Southern Zimbabwe* (London: James Currey, 2015).
95. For instance, James L.A. Webb Jr., *The Long Struggle against Malaria in Tropical Africa* (New York: Cambridge University Press, 2016); and James McCann, *The Historical Ecology of Malaria in Ethiopia: Deposing the Spirits* (Athens, OH: Ohio University Press, 2014).
96. For example, Ranajit Guha, *Elementary Aspects of Peasant Insurgency in Colonial India* (Durham, NC: Duke University Press, 1999); and James C. Scott, *Weapons of the Weak: Everyday Forms of Peasant Resistance* (New Haven, CT: Yale University Press, 1987). However, as Feierman's *Peasant Intellectuals* reveals, frameworks for analyzing the colonial history of African peasants can be centered within local or indigenous experiences.

Bibliography

Adas, Michael. *Machines as Measures of Men: Science, Technology, and Ideologies of Western Dominance*. Ithaca, NY: Cornell University Press, 1989.
Anderson, David M. "Depression, Dust Bowl, Demography, and Drought: The Colonial State and Soil Conservation in East Africa During the 1930s." *African Affairs* 83, no. 332 (1984): 321–43.
———. *Eroding the Commons: The Politics of Ecology in Baringo, Kenya 1890–1963*. Oxford: James Currey, 2002.
Austin, Gareth. "Explaining and Evaluating the Cash Crop Revolution in the 'Peasant' Colonies of Tropical Africa, ca. 1890–ca. 1930: Beyond 'Vent for Surplus'." In *Africa's Development in Historical Perspective*, edited by Emmanuel Akyeampong et al. Cambridge: Cambridge University Press, 2014.
Beinart, William. "Soil Erosion, Conservationism and Ideas about Development: A Southern African Exploration, 1900–1960." *Journal of South African Studies* 11, no. 1 (1984): 52–83.
———. "African History and Environmental History." In "Centenary Issue: A Hundred Years of Africa." Special issue, *African Affairs* 99, no. 35 (2000): 269–302.
———. *The Rise of Conservation in South Africa: Settlers, Livestock, and the Environment 1770–1950*. New York: Oxford University Press, 2008.

Beinart, William, and JoAnn McGregor, eds. *Social History and African Environments*. Athens: Ohio University Press, 2003.
Beinart, William, and Lotte Hughes. *Environment and Empire*. Oxford: Oxford University Press, 2007.
Beinart, William, Karen Brown, and Daniel Gilfoyle. "Experts and Expertise in Colonial Africa Reconsidered: Science and the Interpenetration of Knowledge." *African Affairs* 108, no. 432 (2009): 413–33.
Brown, James. "Increased Inter-communication and Epidemic Disease in Early Colonial Ashanti." In *Disease in African History: An Introductory Survey and Case Studies*, edited by Gerald W. Hartwig and K. David Patterson, 181–206. Durham, NC: Duke University Press, 1978.
Brown, Karen. "Political Entomology: The Insectile Challenge to Agricultural Development in the Cape Colony, 1895–1910." *Journal of South African Studies* 29, no. 2 (2003): 529–49.
Bunker, Stephen G. *Peasants against the State: The Politics of Market Control in Bugisu, Uganda, 1900–1983*. Chicago: University of Chicago Press, 1991.
Butlin, Robin A. *Geographies of Empire: European Empires and Colonies c. 1880–1960*. Cambridge: Cambridge University Press, 2009.
Carruthers, Jane. *The Kruger National Park: A Social and Political History*. Pietermaritzburg: University of Natal Press, 1995.
———. "Africa: Histories, Ecologies and Societies." *Environment and History* 10, no. 4 (2004): 804–29.
———. "Tracking in Game Trails: Looking Afresh at the Politics of Environmental History in South Africa." *Environmental History* 11, no. 4 (2006): 811.
Carswell, Grace. *Cultivating Success in Uganda: Kigezi Farmers and Colonial Policies*. Athens, OH: Ohio University Press, 2007.
Collins, Robert O. *Shadow in the Grass: Britain in the Southern Sudan, 1918–1956*. New Haven, CT: Yale University Press, 1983.
Collins, Robert O., and James M. Burns. *A History of Sub-Saharan Africa*, 2nd ed. Cambridge: Cambridge University Press, 2014.
Conte, Christopher A. *Highland Sanctuary: Environmental History in Tanzania's Usambara Mountains*. Athens, OH: Ohio University Press, 2004.
———. "Nature Re-organized: Ecological History in the Plateau Forests of the West Usambara Mountains 1850–1935." In *Custodians of the Land*, edited by Maddox, Giblin, and Kimambo, 96–121.
Cooper, Fredrick. *Africa since 1940: The Past of the Present*. Cambridge: Cambridge University Press, 2002.
Crosby, Alfred W. *Ecological Imperialism: The Biological Expansion of Europe, 900–1900*. Cambridge: Cambridge University Press, 2004.
Curtin, Philip. *Death by Migration: Europe's Encounter with the Tropical World in the Nineteenth Century*. Cambridge: Cambridge University Press, 1989.
———. *Disease and Empire: The Health of European Troops in the Conquest of Africa*. Cambridge: Cambridge University Press, 1998.
Davenport, Rodney, and Christopher Saunders. *South Africa: A Modern History*. London: Macmillan, 2000.
Davis, Diana K. *Resurrecting the Granary of Rome: Environmental History and French Colonial Expansion in North Africa*. Athens, OH: Ohio University Press, 2007.

DeLancey, Mark W. "Health and Disease on the Plantations of Cameroon, 1884–1939." In *Disease in African History*, edited by Hartwick and Patterson, 153–79.
Doyle, Shane. *Population and Environment in Western Uganda 1860–1955: Crisis and Decline in Bunyoro*. Ohio: Ohio University Press, 2006, 146–50.
Dube, Francis. "Public Health and Racial Segregation in South Africa: Mahatma (M.K.) Gandhi Debates Colonial Authorities on Public Health Measures, 1896–1904." *Journal of the Historical Society of Nigeria* 21 (2012): 26–27.
Dumett, Raymond E. *Imperialism, Economic Development and Social Change in West Africa*. Durham, NC: Carolina Academic Press, 2013.
Echenberg, Myron. *Plague Ports*. New York: New York University Press, 2007.
Elphick, Richard. *Khoikhoi and the Founding of White South Africa*. Johannesburg: Raven Press, 1985, 234–38.
Ewans, Martin. *European Atrocity, African Catastrophe: Leopold II, the Congo Free State, and Its Aftermath*. London: Routledge Curtzon, 2002.
Feierman, Steven. *Peasant Intellectuals: Anthropology and History in Tanzania*. Madison, WI: University of Wisconsin Press, 1990.
Fontein, Joost. *Remaking Mutirikwi: Landscape, Water, and Belonging in Southern Zimbabwe*. London: James Currey, 2015.
Ford, John. *The Role of the Trypanosomiases in African Ecology: A Study of the Tsetse Fly Problem*. London: Oxford University Press, 1971.
Gallagher, Nancy E. *Egypt's Other Wars: Epidemics and the Politics of Public Health*. Syracuse: Syracuse University Press, 1990.
Giblin, James. "Trypanosomiasis Control in African History: An Evaded Issue." *Journal of African History* 31 (1990): 59–80.
———. *The Politics of Environmental Control in Northeastern Tanzania, 1840–1940*. Philadelphia: University of Philadelphia Press, 1993.
Grove, Richard H. *Green Imperialism: Colonial Expansion, Tropical Island Edens and the Origins of Environmentalism, 1600–1860*. Cambridge: Cambridge University Press, 1996.
Guha, Ranajit. *Elementary Aspects of Peasant Insurgency in Colonial India*. Durham, NC: Duke University Press, 1999.
Hartwick, Gerald, and K. David Patterson, eds. *Disease in African History: An Introductory Survey and Case Studies*. Durham, NC: Duke University Press, 1978.
Headrick, Daniel R. *The Tools of Empire: Technology and European Imperialism in the Nineteenth Century*. New York: Oxford University Press, 1981.
Hodge, Joseph M. *Triumph of the Expert: Agrarian Doctrines of Development and the Legacies of British Colonialism*. Athens, OH: Ohio University Press, 2007.
Hogendorn, J.S., and K.M. Scott. "The East African Groundnut Scheme: Lessons of a Large-Scale Agricultural Failure." *African Economic History* 10 (1981): 81–115.
Hope, Kirk. *Lords of the Fly: Sleeping Sickness Control in British East Africa, 1900–1960*. Westport, CT: Praeger, 2003.
Hopkins, A.G. *An Economic History of West Africa*. New York: Columbia University Press, 1973.
Hughes, Lotte. *Moving the Maasai: A Colonial Misadventure*. New York: Palgrave Macmillan, 2006.
Illife, John. *A Modern History of Tanganyika*. Cambridge: Cambridge University Press, 1979, 168.

Isaacman, Allen. "Chiefs, Rural Differentiation and Peasant Protest: The Mozambican Forced Cotton Regime 1938–1961." *African Economic History* 14 (1985): 15–56.

———. "Peasants, Work and the Labor Process: Forced Cotton Cultivation in Colonial Mozambique 1938–1961." *Journal of Social History* 25, no. 4 (1992): 815–55.

———. *Cotton, Colonialism, and Social History in Sub-Saharan Africa.* Portsmouth, NH: Heinemann, 1995.

———. *Cotton is the Mother of Poverty: Peasants, Work, and Rural Struggle in Colonial Mozambique, 1938–1961.* Portsmouth, NH: Heinemann, 1995.

———. *Environment, Power, and Injustice: A South African History.* Cambridge: Cambridge University Press, 2003.

———. *Dams, Displacement, and the Delusion of Development: Cahora Bassa and Its Legacies in Mozambique, 1965–2007.* Athens, OH: Ohio University Press, 2013.

Jacobs, Nancy J. *Birders of Africa: History of a Network.* Princeton, NJ: Princeton University Press, 2016.

Johnson, Douglas, and David Anderson, eds. *The Ecology of Survival: Case Studies from Northeast African History.* London: Croom Helm, 1988.

Kanogo, Tabitha. *Squatters & the Roots of Mau Mau.* Athens, OH: Ohio University Press, 1987.

Kennedy, Dane. "British Exploration in the Nineteenth Century: A Historiographic Survey." *History Compass* 5, no. 6 (2007): 1879–1900.

Kitching, Gavin. *Class and Economic Change in Kenya: The Making of an African Petite-Bourgeoisie.* New Haven, CT: Yale University Press, 1980.

Kjekshus, Helge. *Ecology Control and Economic Development in East African History.* Athens: Ohio University Press, 1977.

Kreike, Emmanuel. *Re-Creating Eden: Land Use, Environment, and Society in Southern Angola and Northern Namibia.* Portsmouth, NH: Heinemann, 2004.

———. "Hidden Fruits: A Social Ecology of Fruit Trees in Namibia and Angola, 1880s–1990s." In *Social History*, edited by Beinart and McGregor, 27–42.

Livingstone, David. *The Geographical Tradition: Episodes in the History of a Contested Enterprise.* Oxford: Blackwell, 1992.

Low, D.A., and John Lonsdale. "Introduction: Towards the New Order 1945–1963." In *Oxford History of East Africa*, edited by D.A. Low and Alison Smith, 12–16. Oxford: Oxford University Press, 1976.

Lyons, Maryinez. *The Colonial Disease: A Social History of Sleeping Sickness in Northern Zaire, 1900–1940.* Cambridge: Cambridge University Press, 1992.

Maack, Pamela A. "'We Don't Want Terraces': Protest and Identity Under the Uluguru Land Usage Scheme." In *Custodians of the Land*, edited by Maddox, Giblin and Kimambo, 152–74.

Mackenzie, Fiona D. *Land, Ecology, and Resistance in Kenya, 1880–1952.* Portsmouth, NH: Heinemann, 1998.

Maddox, Gregory. "Africa and Environmental History." *Environmental History* 4, no. 2 (1999): 162–67.

———. *Sub-Saharan Africa: An Environmental History.* Santa Barbara, CA: ABC-CLIO, 2006.

Maddox, Gregory, James Giblin, and Isaria N. Kimambo. *Custodians of the Land: Ecology and Culture in the History of Tanzania.* Athens, OH: Ohio University Press, 1996.

Mandala, Elias. *Work and Control in a Peasant Economy: A History of the Lower Tchiri Valley in Malawi, 1859–1960.* Madison, WI: University of Wisconsin Press, 1990.
Maxon, Robert. *Going Their Separate Ways: Agrarian Transformation in Kenya, 1930–1950.* London: Associated University Presses, 2003.
McCann, James. *Green Land, Brown Land, Black Land: An Environmental History of Africa, 1800–1990.* Portsmouth, NH: Heinemann, 1999.
———. *The Historical Ecology of Malaria in Ethiopia: Deposing the Spirits.* Athens, OH: Ohio University Press, 2014.
McCracken, John. "Conservation and Resistance in Colonial Malawi: The 'Dead North' Revisited." In *Social History*, edited by Beinart and McGregor, 155–74.
McGregor, Joann. "Living With the River: Landscape and Memory in the Zambezi Valley, Northwest Zimbabwe." In *Social History*, edited by Beinart and McGregor, 87–105.
McKelvey, John J., Jr. *Man against Tsetse: Struggle for Africa.* Ithaca, NY: Cornell University Press, 1973.
Middleton, Karen. "The Ironies of Plant Transfer: The Case of Prickly Pear in Madagascar." In *Social History*, edited by Beinart and McGregor, 43–59.
Monson, Jamie. "Canoe-Building Under Colonialism: Forestry and Food Policies in the Inner Kilombero Valley, 1920–1940." In *Custodians of the Land*, edited by Maddox, Giblin, and Kimambo, 200–12.
Moore, Henrietta, and Meghan Vaughan. *Cutting Down Trees: Gender, Nutrition, and Agricultural Change in the Northern Province of Zambia, 1890–1990.* Portsmouth, NH: Heinemann, 1993.
Mungeam, G.H. *British Rule in Kenya, 1895–1912.* Oxford: Clarendon Press, 1966.
———. *Kenya: Select Historical Documents 1884–1923.* Nairobi: East African Publishing House, Nairobi, 1978.
Neumann, Roderick P. *Imposing Wilderness: Struggles Over Livelihood and Nature Preservation in Africa.* Berkley, CA: University of California Press, 1998.
Oduor, George Ndege. *Health, State, and Society in Kenya.* Rochester: Rochester University Press, 2001.
Ofcansky, Thomas P. *Paradise Lost: A History of Game Preservation in British East Africa, 1895–1963.* Morgantown: West Virginia University Press, 2002.
Richards, Paul. *Indigenous Agricultural Revolution: Ecology and Food Production in West Africa.* London: Hutchinson Education, 1985.
Rizzo, Matteo. "What Was Left of the Groundnut Scheme? Development Disaster and Labour Market in Southern Tanganyika 1946–1952." *Journal of Agrarian Change* 6, no. 2 (2006): 205–38.
Ruedy, John. *Land Policy in Colonial Algeria: Origins of the Rural Public Domain.* Berkeley, CA: University of California Press, 1967.
———. *Modern Algeria: The Origins and Development of a Nation*, 2nd ed. Bloomington, IN: Indiana University Press, 2005.
Schoenburn, David A. *Green Place, a Good Place: Agrarian Change and Social Identity in the Great Lakes Region to the 15th Century.* Portsmouth, NH: Heinemann, 1998.
Scott, James. *Weapons of the Weak: Everyday Forms of Peasant Resistance.* New Haven, CT: Yale University Press, 1987.
———. *Seeing Like the State: How Certain Schemes to Improve the Human Condition Have Failed.* New Haven, CT: Yale University Press, 1998.

Shanguhyia, Martin S. *Population, Tradition, and Environmental Control in Colonial Kenya*. Rochester, NY: University of Rochester Press, 2015.

Showers, Kate. *Imperial Gullies: Soil Erosion and Conservation in Lesotho*. Athens: Ohio University Press, 2005.

Steinhart, Edward I. *Black Poachers, White Hunters: A Social History of Hunting in Kenya*. Athens, OH: Ohio University Press, 2006.

Swanson, Maynard W. "The Sanitation Syndrome: Bubonic Plague and Urban Native Policy in the Cape Colony, 1900–1909." *Journal of African History* 18 (1977).

Throup, David. *Economic and Social Origins of Mau Mau*. Athens, OH: Ohio University Press, 1987.

Tiffen, Mary, Michael Motimore, and Francis Gichuki. *More People, Less Erosion: Environmental Recovery*. Chichester: John Wiley, 1994.

Tilley, Helen. *Africa as a Living Laboratory: Empire, Development, and the Problem of Scientific Knowledge, 1870–1950*. Chicago: University of Chicago Press, 2011.

Vail, Leroy. "Ecology and History: The Example of Eastern Zambia." *Journal of South African Studies* 3, no. 2 (1977): 129–55.

van Beusekom, Monica. *Negotiating Development: African Farmers and Colonial Experts at the Office Du Niger, 1920–1960*. Portsmouth, NH: Heinemann, 2002.

Van Sittert, Lance. "'The Seed Blows About in Every Breeze': Noxious Weed Eradication in the Cape Colony, 1860–1909." *Journal of Southern African Studies* 26, no. 4 (2000): 655–74.

Vansina, Jan. *Paths in the Rainforest: Toward a History of Political Tradition in Equatorial Africa*. Madison: University of Wisconsin Press, 1990.

Webb, James, Jr. *Desert Frontier: Ecological and Economic Change Along the Western Sahel, 1600–1850*. Madison: University of Wisconsin Press, 1994.

———. *The Long Struggle against Malaria in Tropical Africa*. New York: Cambridge University Press, 2016.

Young, R.A., and H.A. Foosbrooke. *Smoke in the Hills: Political Tension in the Morogoro District of Tanganyika*. Evanston, IL: Northwestern University Press, 1969.

CHAPTER 3

Colonial Administrations and the Africans

Toyin Falola and Chukwuemeka Agbo

International relations between Africa and Africans and the outside world, especially Europe, before 1900 were basically trade-related. By the dawn of the twentieth century, however, the interaction had shifted from trade/exchange relations to control and subordination. Conflicts of interests in Europe over African territories and the resultant clashes among European powers led to the convening of the Berlin Conference towards the end of the nineteenth century (1884/1885). The conference, on which sat no African delegation, saw the splitting of Africa among European powers in the pursuit of expansionist and economic advantages in territories outside Europe.

Between 1885 and 1900, most of Africa was taken over as colonies of Europe, a major event that has shaped the course of African history ever since. The long era of free trade and reasonably peaceful relations gave way to one of economic exploitation and political domination. Before the 1880s, very little of Africa was under colonial rule: less than ten percent consisting of small areas along the coast where trade was carried out. The greater part of the African interior was even unknown to Europeans. The few colonies of the British included areas around Freetown in Sierra Leone, forts in the Gambia, Lagos, a protectorate in the southern Gold Coast (now Ghana), and some areas in Southern Africa. The French had control in St Louis and Dakar in

---

Toyin Falola, in his *Key Events in* African history: *A Reference Guide*, has dealt in great detail with this topic. Significant aspects of this chapter are drawn from that study.

T. Falola (✉) · C. Agbo
Department of History, The University of Texas, Austin, TX, USA

© The Author(s) 2018
M.S. Shanguhyia and T. Falola (eds.),
The Palgrave Handbook of African Colonial and Postcolonial History,
https://doi.org/10.1057/978-1-137-59426-6_3

Senegal, Grand Bassam and Assini in Ivory Coast, and a small coastal area in Dahomey (now the Republic of Benin). The Portuguese were established in Mozambique and Angola.

By the 1880s, the long-established Afro-European relations based on trade changed to those of colonial domination. By 1900, with the exception of only Liberia and Ethiopia, imperial administration had been established in Africa. Africa experienced colonial rule during the first half of the twentieth century. By 1914, Europeans had consolidated their hold on the continent. Between then and 1939, they implemented various policies that defined the colonial era. After 1939, a number of reforms were undertaken to respond to African demands for independence.

The colonial era had economic, social, and political impacts. The changes were not only numerous, they were also rapid, and Africans had to learn to deal with them in creative ways. What were the reasons for this change, and what was the process, and how did Africans respond? This chapter answers these three important questions.

European Politics in the Nineteenth Century: Background to the Partition of Africa

We have established that trade relations between Africa and Europe predate the nineteenth century. The Atlantic trade, for instance, as far back as the fifteenth century. With time, the trade expanded to include the Americas and the Caribbean. It was pioneered by Portuguese voyagers who were searching for a sea route to India. By the seventeenth century, slaves had become one of Africa's major exports. African laborers were in high demand in North and South America and in the Caribbean Islands, where they were made to work the sugar, cotton, and tobacco plantations and in mining, too.[1] With the industrialization of Europe, particularly in Britain during the last decades of the eighteenth century, the value of slaves as well as demands for them began to dwindle. After enriching her Treasury with profits from the human traffic, Britain was the first among European states to abolish the slave trade. The slave trade and its abolition prepared the way for the colonization of Africa.

Different arguments have been put forward by scholars for the abolition of the Atlantic slave trade. Our aim is not to dwell on this, but to highlight the key issues raised so as to enhance our understanding of the argument that follows. In 1933, Sir Reginald Coupland published his *British Anti-Slavery Movement* in which he argued that slavery and the slave trade in British dominions were abolished on humanitarian grounds rather than for selfish purposes.[2] The dust raised by Coupland's argument prompted scholars like Eric Williams to respond with a counter-argument. Williams opines that economic self-interest was at the root of the abolition of the slave trade. At the dawn of the nineteenth century, Williams asserts, Britain was already moving from mercantile capitalism to industrial capitalism. The gains of the Industrial Revolution had rendered the slave trade unattractive.[3] As pointed out earlier, it is not our intention to go into any form of detailed analysis of this subject. But, as Njoku and other scholars have asserted, there is no doubt that the abolition movement had a multi-purpose agenda in which could be discerned economic, humanitarian, religious, nationalist, and geo-strategic calculations. The balance of current opinion, however, supports Williams as being nearer to the truth than Coupland. This is to say that without the economic argument, the British government would not have expended so much its public resources in bringing the trade in slaves to an end.[4]

Like the abolition of the slave trade, scholars have proven time and again that the colonization of Africa was primarily an economic project.[5] Njoku, for instance, has observed that the European colonization of Africa was not an end in itself but a means to an end.[6] In pursuit of the objectives of colonization, Njoku further observes that the ultimate economic motive of colonization of Africa would not have been achieved through mechanistic econometrics calculations alone; rather, a combination of other factors needed to be taken into account as vital accessories. For instance, some measures of Western education had to be introduced to enable colonized territories to speak the language of their masters and imbibe their cultural values. Modern means of transportation, a modern portable and standardized currency, and imposition and maintenance of the British system of law and order (the so-called Pax Britannica) were also some preconditions for achieving the colonial project.[7]

From the foregoing, it has been established that African colonies offered great economic opportunities to Europe. The expansion of capitalism and the desire for profits were the principal motives behind the conquest of Africa. Falola summarizes European interest in Africa as follows:

> The contact between Nigeria and Britain predated colonial conquest. From the fifteenth to the nineteenth centuries, Nigeria was involved in both the transatlantic slave trade and the so-called legitimate trade in raw materials. During the late nineteenth century, trade relations gave way to colonial domination. Among the primary objectives of imposing colonial rule were the need to obtain a cheap and constant supply of raw materials for European industries, secure a market for the products of these expanding industries, and create new outlets for investments. The purpose of British rule was thus to initiate a transformation of Nigerian society and its economy in order to meet these objectives.[8]

That the exploitation of Africa by Europe was the principal focus of colonial rule is best exemplified by the statements of two important colonial officials. Emphasizing the principal responsibility of the colonial government in Africa to Britain, Bernard Bourdillon, who served as British colonial governor in Uganda and Nigeria, declared: 'our duty to the British tax payers is to extend the supply of raw materials and the market for the British manufactured goods'.[9] Fredrick Lugard, governor general of Nigeria, expressed a similar opinion. He wrote: 'let it be admitted at the onset that European brains, capital, and energy, have not been and never will they be expended on developing the resources of Africa from the motive of philanthropy; that Europe is in Africa for the mutual benefit of her own industrial classes and of the native races'.[10]

The European merchants who made profits in their business relations with Africa believed that they could make even more profits by pressuring their governments to involve themselves directly in the management of Africa. Profits could be made in two ways: by obtaining cheap raw materials which would be exported to Europe to manufacture various products, and by turning Africa into a huge market to consume imported goods from Europe. As other countries such as Germany, France, and Portugal were catching up with Britain in industrialization, the need for raw materials and markets grew greater than ever before. Excess capital was generated by many industries and merchants, and they wanted to spend their money in making more profits. When gold was discovered in South Africa in the 1880s, Africa was seen as offering great promise as a continent in which to invest for quick rewards. The traders already based in Africa began to pressure their home countries to establish economic monopolies in African countries so that they would gain greater access to raw materials and markets.[11]

The fight for Africa was an extension of the intense competition among the European nations. Various elements in this competition can be seen as the 'political motives' responsible for Africa's partition. The unification of Germany created a major third power in Europe, as well as France and Britain. The three were active in maintaining a balance of power, and were eager to prevent any one of them from gaining too much power. Colonial acquisition was interpreted as evidence of a threat to the balance of power. In 1870, France was defeated by Germany, losing two provinces as a result. One way to overcome the humiliation and gain more territories was to seek them in Africa. By the 1880s, ambitious European nations had no territories left to acquire within Europe, thus forcing them to look elsewhere. Early in the 1880s, Britain established control of Egypt, thereby also controlling the Suez route to the east. The French and the Germans believed that they too had to take parts of Africa in order to minimize the advantages that would accrue to Britain. Nationalism was at stake: the extreme passion of the period supported the possession of a large empire, if only to show other nations that one was a great country and a great power.

Each European country wanted to claim overseas territories to exhibit its military and political strength. The acquisition of a large colony was regarded as evidence of imperial power. Each power wanted to prevent any rival European power from taking an area it was interested in. For instance, the British signed a number of treaties with the chiefs of the Niger Delta in Nigeria in the 1880s, just to prevent the French from encroaching on the area.[12] The European countries believed that they could use acquired territories to build nationalism and prestige. For instance, when Britain acquired the Suez Canal in Egypt in 1882, the French and Germans went elsewhere in Africa to assert themselves, partly to build prestige: the French established claims over the north bank of the River Congo, and Germany established claims over four areas along the African coast, in Togo, Cameroon, Tanganyika (now Tanzania), and South West Africa (now Namibia). King Leopold of Belgium decided to annex territory in Central Africa and created the Congo Free State as his personal estate. The French were interested in possession of the Western Sudan (modern Senegal, Mali, Burkina Faso, and Niger) partly to counteract their humiliation by Germany in the war of 1870–1871. Individual European soldiers and officials in Africa regarded territorial possession as a way to gain glory, attention, and promotion.

Evidence of cultural arrogance can be found in the statements of those who participated in the conquest. A belief that Europeans were superior gave rise to the claim that they had a right to conquer Africa. The belief in white superiority was also used to describe the partition as a 'civilizing mission'– the idea that a superior race had the right to improve the lives of an inferior one, if necessary through force and colonization.[13] The conquest of 'backward races' was even interpreted as a legitimate use of force, as many cited the principle of 'Social Darwinism' (only the most able and superior can survive) based on the idea espoused by Charles Darwin in his 1859 book *The Origin of Species by Means of Natural Selection or the Preservation of Favoured Races in the Struggle for Life*.[14] When this idea was expressed in religious terms, aggressive missionaries claimed that evangelization was a way of uplifting the 'inferior' people.[15] The partition of Africa was seen as an opportunity to do the same.[16]

THE PROCESS

The principal European countries involved in the partition were Britain, Portugal, France, and Germany. The greatest rewards went to Britain and France. The British and the French participated in trade and the spread of Christianity, and maintained control in a few areas before the 1880s. Holland and Denmark withdrew from West Africa and sold their bases to the British. The Germans did not become involved until 1884, but they later annexed the coast of Togoland and the Cameroons. The European countries regarded themselves as competitors and viewed one another with suspicion. In 1876, King Leopold I of Belgium indicated a strong interest in Africa by convening a conference and creating an association to sponsor expeditions to the Congo area. In the same year, Portugal began to send its own expeditions to Africa. France too entered an expansionist phase by exploring some areas in the Congo, participating in a dual control of Egypt with the British, and indicating that it would use force in the Western Sudan. The tensions of the late 1870s and early 1880s, all strongly showing that the European countries were now interested in colonial expansion, led to a major conference to consider the urgency of their aggression and the fate of Africa.

Now known as the Berlin Conference, it was held from 15 November 1884 to 26 February 1885, with Germany as the host. It was agreed that all the European countries were free to participate in the takeover of Africa, that the navigation of the Congo and Niger Rivers was free to all, and that for any country to declare a protectorate over any part of Africa 'effective occupation' of the area was required. When a protectorate was declared by one European country, it must notify the others that it had acquired 'spheres of influence'. The country involved must also give evidence that it would protect certain rights and ensure freedom of trade. The Berlin decisions laid down the rules for partitioning Africa.[17]

After the Berlin Conference, activities aimed at 'possessing' Africa became intense. The leading participants wanted to establish 'effective occupation' in as many areas as possible. As Berlin was unclear whether presence at the coast meant control of the adjoining hinterland, the Europeans challenged one another in areas away from the coastlines. At another conference in 1890 at Brussels, they agreed that the principle of effective occupation also applied to the hinterland. Among the evidence that they used to claim an area as belonging to one of them were the settlement of people or traders from the country, exploration of the area, treaties signed with local chiefs, activities of traders and missionaries, and physical occupation.

After 1885, two strategies were used to acquire colonies. The first was the signing of treaties[18] and the second was direct military attack.[19] Treaties were signed between the representatives of a European power and African chiefs or between one European power and another. In the Euro-African treaties, African leaders signed documents to show that they surrendered their power, and agreed to promote trade and accept other conditions. There is no evidence that many African chiefs understood the contents of the treaties. Treaties among the European powers demarcated boundaries and defined spheres of influence.

Military attacks involved the deliberate use of armies to subdue areas or at least frighten them into surrender. For instance, the French used their army against groups in the Western Sudan, Gabon, and Madagascar. The British attacked many places and peoples as well, including the Yoruba town of Ijebu Ode and the Asante of Ghana. Germany, Italy, and Portugal also used warfare to acquire their colonies.

The Europeans engaged in various disputes, but did not fight many wars among themselves. Their energies were concentrated on sharing Africa among themselves. The British extended their possessions in West Africa and claimed the lucrative and well-populated countries of Nigeria, Ghana, Sierra Leone, and the Gambia. In South Africa, Cecil Rhodes, a private entrepreneur, gained valuable areas for the British. With a fanatical desire to impose

British control from the 'Cape to Cairo', he was ruthless in attacking African nations in areas that later became Botswana and Rhodesia (now Zimbabwe). The British consolidated their hold during the Boer War (1899–1902), which ended in the unification of the Boer republics of the Orange Free State and the Transvaal into the Union of South Africa.[20] British companies in East and Central Africa (the Imperial British East Africa Company and the British South Africa Company) also paved the way to the acquisition of Kenya.

The French invaded the Western Sudan in 1879. Using their existing control of coastal areas, they moved to the hinterland, gaining larger territories and hoping to outflank the British. They moved south from Algeria, northeast from Gabon, and north from Dahomey and Ivory Coast. They also annexed Madagascar and a host of small islands off the coast of East Africa.

With brutal methods, the Congo Free State was expanded. King Leopold treated it as a personal property until 1914 when it was acquired by the Belgian government. The Portuguese and Germans extended their possessions from the coastal areas they controlled prior to 1885. The Italians failed to conquer Ethiopia in 1896, but were able to establish themselves in Eritrea and Somaliland. The Spanish acquired an area on the Guinea Coast (the modern Equatorial Guinea). By the early 1900s, the definitive map of colonial Africa had emerged. Only a few changes followed. Germany lost its colonies at the end of the First World War, as they were transferred to Belgium, France, South Africa, and Britain to manage on behalf of the League of Nations.

African Response

Many African states and leaders were shocked by the European ambition to colonize them. Many struggled to retain their sovereignty and protect their land, their institutions, and their cultures. While many states wanted to maintain friendship with European traders and missionaries, they rejected the attempts to invade and rule them. Indeed, many refused to compromise, preferring even to die in battle. In a mood typical of many leaders, the king of the Mossi in West Africa told a French leader in 1895 that:

> I know the whites wish to kill me in order to take my country, and yet you claim that they will help me to organize my country. But I find my country good just as it is. I have no need of them. I know what is necessary for me and what I want: I have my own merchants: also, consider yourself fortunate that I do not order your head to be cut off. Go away now, and above all, never come back.[21]

Resistance to European conquest was not isolated or restricted to large kingdoms. Eager to portray their conquest in a glowing light, early European accounts exaggerated their welcome by the Africans and criticized their opponents as bloodthirsty tyrants. However, what the African rulers were struggling to retain was their sovereignty. They resorted to various strategies.

In many areas, response took military forms. A state might use its army to fight the European forces, as in the case of the Asante in West Africa or the Zulu in South Africa. Armed resistance could even be prolonged, as in such cases as western Uganda and northern Niger where Africans continued to resist until the 1920s. Samori Touré, the leader of the Mandinka in West Africa, modernized his army and resisted the French for almost seven years.[22]

Resistant Africans were confident of their ability to succeed, trusting their military experience, spiritual forces, and sheer determination to survive. The appeal to religious and magical forces was one way to win the wars, but also a way to seek help from the spiritual realm against the European enemy. Many people and leaders called on ancestors, gods, and spirits for help. Sacrifices were made, in addition to prayers and the use of charms to ward off the 'evil forces' represented by European encroachment.

Diplomacy was yet another option, pursued by forming an alliance or promising to cooperate with the Europeans.[23] Where a group felt threatened by violence, it sought the means to minimize the possibilities of European violence. In situations where a people believed that they could benefit from the European presence, they accepted foreign rule. Among the expected benefits were the introduction of Western education, the spread of Christianity, and expanded opportunities for trade. In expecting positive changes to come with European rule, the Africans misunderstood the objectives of the colonial enterprise.

Religion played an important role. To win wars and build morale, leaders and soldiers used charms. Religious leaders also emerged to lead opposition to Europeans. Religious power could come from indigenous religions, Islam, or Christianity. Religion was used to build unity among people, and to mobilize them for war or disobedience. When the conquest became a reality, religion provided one of the sources of nationalism but also enabled Africans to reconcile themselves to the new situation. Finally, other options were pursued in meeting the challenges of European invasion. Some groups or people took to migration.

Why Europeans Were Successful

In spite of vigorous resistance by a number of African nations and leaders, only Liberia and Ethiopia escaped the imposition of colonial rule. There were a number of reasons for this. To start with, it is misleading to see all of Africa as a single bloc resisting external invasion. Were this the case, it would have been difficult for the European powers to easily take over this huge continent. Not only did the Europeans take on one African nation after another, but there were cases where some African leaders allied with an invading European power against another African people.[24] The European armies included hundreds of Africans, recruited from one group to fight another group.

Other reasons why the Europeans succeeded in imposing colonial rule relate to the power of technology and the availability of resources. Compared to the African nations, the European powers had more resources to use. They had the money to buy arms and pay troops. If they lost a battle, they could regroup, benefiting from the knowledge gained and the resources available. Their armies were professional, devoted to full-time warfare. African nations too had armies, but in many places they were composed of volunteers who had to abandon their farms and other occupations, without the resources to engage in prolonged warfare.

Due to the records supplied by explorers, missionaries, traders, and representatives of governments, the European invaders possessed valuable information about Africa. More Europeans could also go to Africa to serve in the armies and administration. The use of quinine had made it possible to minimize the danger of malaria fever, thus removing the fear of the deadly disease that had frightened off many Europeans in previous years.

The Europeans relied on improved firearms. Africans relied on bows, arrows, and muzzle-loading guns (such as Dane guns) which were slow to load. The European armies in the era of the partition relied on breech loaders, which could fire almost a dozen bullets in a second. Whereas the European armies had adequate modern guns (the Maxim and Gatling), their African rivals lacked access to them. A few nations, such as the Baule of Ivory Coast, had stockpiled large quantities of arms and ammunition, but they were mainly old muskets which were no match for Maxim guns. Where Africans had modern weapons, they did not have access to large quantities of them. The armies of even such large states as the Sokoto Caliphate lacked the tactics to deal with an invading army using machine guns. The tactics of the African armies (cavalry charges, the defense of walled cities, the use of large armies carrying bows and arrows) were ineffective in facing an army equipped with machine guns.

The guns were used to subdue many groups. However, others were forced to surrender because of the threat of violence. When some groups saw the fate of their more powerful neighbors, they chose to give up. In some cases, it could well be that the rulers saw the futility of resistance and wanted to avoid bloodshed. In the end, only Emperor Menelik of Ethiopia was victorious against the mighty European powers. By 1902, the conquest of Africa was almost completed. A new map was created: instead of hundreds of precolonial nations, there were now about forty political units.

Politics and Administration

New countries with new boundaries were created. These boundaries were artificial. Preexisting political units and ethnic groups might be divided into two or more countries. For instance, the empire of Kanem-Borno in the Lake Chad area was divided between Nigeria (a British colony), Cameroon (German), and Niger and Chad (French). In spite of the problems associated with them, the boundaries have since been maintained with only minor changes. The colonial experience also aided the formation of an African identity, with a commitment to national boundaries, a sense of unity based on a common experience of colonial domination, and a desire to liberate the continent from oppression and poverty.

The major colonial policies were determined abroad. Colonies were extensions of Europe, and must reflect changes in Europe rather than the concerns of the African subjects. The officers in Africa regarded themselves as under the control of their governments in Europe. They were expected to carry out the instructions given to them, making them applicable to their local situations. The number of officers (administrators and soldiers) was low, to keep down the cost. Their duties were simple and clearly defined: they must pursue the colonial economic objectives, and they must maintain law and order. What Africans wanted was different: development, so that they could not be exploited; and power, which would threaten the colonial state.

Africans were involved in the administration. The armies and the police were manned by Africans, and many came to believe that they owed their survival and prestige to the colonial state. Educated Africans served in the civil service, mainly in the lower levels of administration. As many of them enjoyed privileges, they began to imitate European ways of life.

African countries were not all governed in the same way, although the broad patterns were clear. After early efforts to administer areas unknown to them, the colonialists evolved administrative systems suited to their objectives and adaptable to the circumstances of conquest. To take just two examples, the British tried a system of indirect rule, and the French a system of assimilation.

THE BRITISH AND INDIRECT RULE

In British colonies, a policy of indirect rule (a method of administering local government) was adopted in many colonies. Indirect rule rested on the assumption that European and African cultures were different, and the best way to govern local communities was through the political system that they had evolved on their own. Above the local government was a central government. Each colony was administered as an autonomous unit, divided into a number of provinces. The governor headed the central administration, aided by executive and legislative councils. The executive councils included only British officers. The legislative councils contained a few Africans, but the power of each council was limited to the colony. The governor was powerful within the colony, but he still obeyed instructions from London. A province was divided into districts, where the system of indirect rule operated.[25]

The British administrator most famous for implementing this idea (in the Sudan and Nigeria) and developing the best manual on it was Lord Lugard, author of *The Dual Mandate in Tropical Africa*.[26] Early in the twentieth century, Lugard faced the task of administering the huge area of Northern Nigeria, formerly part of the extensive Sokoto Caliphate, which had a highly developed political system under a sultan and emirs. The British would have required a large number of people and extensive resources to govern such a huge area. What they chose to do was to control the sultan and emirs, who would in turn control their own people. Indirect rule in Northern Nigeria became a model for other places. The system was later extended to other areas in Nigeria and other colonies such as Gold Coast, Sierra Leone, and the Gambia.

Under indirect rule, existing traditional institutions were modified to meet the needs of the colonial administration. Chiefs, kings, and their officials were used for local administration, to carry out the policies of the colonial government.[27] Indirect rule reduced cost and numbers of foreign personnel, by using Africans to administer themselves. However, many of the Africans involved owed their appointments to the British officers who could also remove them. They were expected to carry out instructions, performing the unpopular duties of collecting taxes and recruiting labor for the government. To return to the example of Northern Nigeria, the British officer, a resident or district officer, supervised and advised the local emir, instructed on how to reform and modernize local institutions, and ensured the collection of taxes. The emir was the head of the Native Administration and appointed district heads, village heads, and tax collectors.

Indirect rule experienced a number of problems and can be criticized on several grounds. Chiefs and kings in many areas actually had more power than before, thus creating tension between them and their people. Indirect rule proved unsuitable to areas that were previously used to powerful kings and their officials. In areas without established centralized institutions or strong kings, as among the Igbo of Nigeria or the Swahili of Tanganyika, powerful chiefs were created for them. Known as 'Warrant Chiefs' among the Igbo, they were given wide powers, they carried out unpopular decisions, and they could be individuals of low social status without much respect in the community.

In the attempt to protect traditional chiefs and institutions, as in Northern Nigeria, the British gave little encouragement to the spread of Christianity and Western education. In some cases, European officers would blame African chiefs for lack of progress, wrongly accusing them of not initiating modernization. In the quest to preserve existing institutions, some officers actually prevented rapid changes, arguing that traditions needed to be preserved at all costs. Finally, where a new African, educated elite emerged, indirect rule excluded them from power. The exclusion of the educated Africans from power created a lingering hostility between them and the Europeans.

THE FRENCH SYSTEM

Proud of their culture, and with a strong belief that they could spread it, the French opted for a policy of assimilation. Their African subjects were expected to become French in culture, and if possible, in citizenship, and the colonies would be run as provinces of France. Not only did the French think that they had attained the highest possible culture, they believed that Africans could acquire the essence of their civilization, as long as the necessary institutions were put in place. Their African subjects should imitate them, and their colonies should become an extension of France.

Senegal in West Africa was the place to experiment with this grandiose project of culture transfer, in the areas known as the 'Four Communes': St Louis, Dakar, Rufisque, and Goree. A French system of local government and schooling was introduced, and the African residents were regarded as French citizens, with the right to elect a representative to the Chamber of Deputies in Paris.[28]

Outside these four areas, the French did not fully assimilate their African subjects. Thus, the colony was divided between the French citizens and 'other Africans'. The French citizens enjoyed wide privileges. Unlike the British colonies, where the Christian missionaries developed the education system, the French government took control of the school system in its colonies. Only a small percentage of Africans had the benefit of Western education, and those who did enjoyed the privileges of citizenship. The non-French did not enjoy freedom of speech, movement, and the press; they could be forced to work to build roads and railways, and they paid direct tax which compelled many of them to take to the production of cash crops in order to raise wages. In a notorious system known as the *indigénat*, a French officer had the power to arrest and jail any non-French African without trial.

Extending the policy of personal assimilation proved difficult, partly because it was difficult to enforce a uniform culture. Cultures and customs varied, and it was hard for the French to impose theirs on all Africans, certainly not on adults who were already set in their ways. There were profound differences between the cultures of the French and the Africans. Aspects of traditional life such as the lineage system, religion (both indigenous and Islamic) and many others were hard to give up. Great differences also existed in terms of laws, rights, and duties which were hard for Africans to abandon. For instance, an African Muslim married to two wives could not become a French citizen since this would violate the law on monogamy. By implication, assimilation would destroy or undermine many aspects of African culture and traditional authorities.

The French side, very early in the twentieth century, began to question the need to extend wide privileges to Africans and make them citizens. There was a fear that over time, the number of Africans who were French citizens would outnumber the European French citizens and could even possibly take over power. Also, the attainment of colonial objectives meant that the French needed millions of Africans to contribute to the colonial economy.[29]

The French, like the British, set up central and local governments. The Ministry of the Colonies in Paris controlled the colonies, preferring to treat many of them as a federation rather than as separate, autonomous countries. For instance, all the French colonies in West Africa (Senegal, Mali, Guinea,

Ivory Coast, Burkina Faso, Niger, Dahomey, and Mauretania) were administered as a single federation under a governor-general based in Dakar.

Power revolved around the governor-general. He represented France in Africa, taking instructions and implementing them. Only the governor-general could transact official business with the ministry in France. He had a large budget, and was financially independent of the separate territories. He controlled appointments to the civil service, while the security forces of the army and police were treated as federal matters. Below him were the governors who headed the component territories. The governors executed the orders sent from Paris through the governor-general.

With respect to the local government, the colonies were divided into *cercles*, units that ignored traditional boundaries and were artificially drawn so as to be similar in size and population. Each cercle was headed by a *commandant de cercle*. A cercle was divided into more manageable units, each administered by the *chef de subdivision* who administered the subdivision. The French used more of their own personnel, who enjoyed a more direct exercise of power. The African chiefs were undermined, left with little or no power, denied judicial power, and reduced to a low status. Many chiefs were removed, and the others became subordinate to French political officers. They were given the most degrading tasks of raising forced labor and collecting tax, two tasks they must carry out to avoid being disgraced or even removed.[30]

If the idea of personal assimilation could not be implemented, it was easier to implement administrative and economic assimilation. In the long run, this had a number of negative consequences: in the case of Algeria, the close links with France made the struggle for independence difficult and violent.

The Economy

The aim of the European powers was to exploit the resources of Africa in various ways: as a supplier of minerals and cash crops, consumer of finished imported products, and provider of revenues to make the colonies financially self-sufficient. Even when important changes were made, they were connected to the colonial economic objectives of generating a massive transfer of wealth from Africa to Europe. The economy rested narrowly on a few products, and was heavily dependent on external demands. New currencies were introduced to replace indigenous ones. Until the dying years of colonial rule, industrialization and economic planning were ignored.

As was the case in British colonies in Africa, the need to attain the colonial objectives meant that new infrastructure had to be built. Roads and railways appeared in areas with exportable resources, in order to facilitate the movement of goods from production centers to port cities, to be transported by ships to Europe. The building of the new roads and railways brought hardships to the Africans who were compelled to perform construction work.

New and efficient for their goal, the communication facilities contributed to the massive expansion of the export economy, the penetration of imported items into cities and villages, the mobility of people, urbanization, and the spread of ideas and religions.

Africans participated in the colonial economy in various ways. The majority were producers, working on their farms. Many others were forced to work for the government or for European ventures. Taxes were imposed, and the need to raise cash in order to pay compelled many people to seek wage incomes, even as laborers.[31] Agriculture was the most important sector of the colonial economy. Among the key products developed and exported were peanuts, cocoa, rubber, coffee, palm oil, and timber. Except in the areas with large numbers of European settlers, agricultural production was mainly in the hands of Africans. Several measures were put in place to ensure production. A common one was the payment of tax in cash which forced millions of people to produce and sell in order to obtain money. In some colonies, people were compelled to work. The perceived benefits of obtaining money to buy luxury items, pay for the education of children, and build houses also served to encourage production.

Foreign firms made considerable profits from the export of agricultural products. In areas and periods when governments became involved in buying crops or regulating prices, they were able to accumulate huge surpluses by underpaying the farmers. Export crops were favored, as the best land was devoted to them. The cultivation of cotton damaged land by reducing its nutrients. The overall consequence of the emphasis on cash crops was to reduce the quantity of food crops available. Mining was developed in areas with gold, tin, coal, diamonds, copper, bauxite, and manganese. The sector was totally dominated by a few foreign companies who made huge profits and paid limited taxes. Africans worked mainly as laborers. Wages were low, and the formation of trade unions was disallowed for a long time.[32]

Direct European involvement in the economy occurred in a few sectors and areas. Where there were large numbers of European settlers, they established plantations, such as the sisal farms in Tanganyika and the large farms of the fertile 'White Highlands' in Kenya. Mining in South Africa, the Belgian Congo, and Northern Rhodesia also witnessed heavy European investments. In Kenya and Rhodesia, where there was a substantial number of European settlers, the foreigners exercised more power than the Africans. They were thus able to award themselves with a number of privileges, including control of trade, access to fertile land, and the use of Africans as domestic and farm workers. This became a source of great tension.

European involvement forced many Africans off their land to work as laborers for European large-scale farmers. Many also migrated to the cities to obtain other kinds of jobs. In some countries, reserves were created to keep the dispossessed Africans in areas where they could be policed. Some Africans were forced to work in European ventures and remunerated with low wages.

African economies were incorporated into the world economic system, with Africans working as producers to supply raw materials to external industries. So important was this role that African areas without raw materials needed for export were regarded as backward, and many of their people could be found as migrant workers elsewhere. To the colonizers, the ability to produce was evidence of progress. This 'progress' became uneven between regions—areas which exported raw materials had better infrastructural provisions and social services. Areas without minerals or exportable raw materials were forced to supply their labor to distant areas, in a 'contribution' which destroyed many rural areas as farmlands and families were abandoned. Countries such as Mali, Basutoland (now Lesotho), Niger, and Chad were regarded as labor reserve areas. When the people were unwilling to work, they could be forced to do so. The requirement that they must pay tax also ensured that they had to seek wage employment in distant areas.

The control of the lucrative export-import trade was in the hands of non-African businesses. European firms enjoyed great advantages, being able to mobilize the capital to control shipping and make huge bulk purchases. Next came the Indian and Lebanese traders who were able to buy raw materials in bulk, sell imported items in retail stores, and advance credit to small producers. African entrepreneurs were pushed to the margins, surviving mainly as small-scale traders in local markets.

Socio-Cultural Changes

There was an increase in the continent's population of about 37.5%. The pace of urbanization increased. New cities were created (e.g. Enugu and Port Harcourt in Nigeria, Abidjan in Ivory Coast and Takoradi in Ghana) and some older ones rapidly expanded, because they served as centers of commerce and administration. Although services tended to be inadequate, the cities enjoyed far better facilities than the rural areas in terms of medical services, leisure facilities, and schools.

Western education spread in many areas, as colonial governments and foreign firms needed clerks and other literate people to work for them. Interest was concentrated on elementary education. Where missionaries were allowed to operate, as in British colonies, they established elementary schools and a few grammar schools. Governments saw the participation of missionaries as saving them money. The missionaries were able to use the school system to convert many Africans to Christianity. The size of the educated elite increased, and they increasingly dominated the economy and politics of the continent. European languages spread among the elite.

Christianity and Islam spread, as missionaries took advantage of the railways and roads to travel to many areas. They were able to reach millions of people in the cities, where new mosques and churches were built. Their spread pushed indigenous religions to the background. Western education,

Christianity, and urbanization had a combined impact on social structure. The traditional elite (chiefs, kings, warriors, blacksmiths, and diviners) lost power and prestige to a new educated class.[33] Africans also became divided along spatial lines between those who lived in cities and those who lived in villages. The cities represented 'civilization' and the villages represented 'backwardness'. Migrations to cities became fairly common, especially among the youth who wanted to learn about new cultures and seek wage employment.

Both the cities and villages were stratified. In the cities, at least three major classes could be found. At the bottom were the 'urban proletariat' comprising artisans and low-income earners. Because of the scarcity of affordable houses and the limited social services, many had to live in shanty areas. Among the poor, prostitution, unemployment, crime, and juvenile delinquency were more common. Above them were the 'sub-elite' comprising primary school teachers, clerks, nurses, and others who had higher incomes than the low-income earners, but lacked power and connections. At the top were the members of the elite (lawyers, politicians, doctors, senior civil servants) who had the resources to enjoy the facilities of the city and participate in politics as leaders. In the villages, there were landowners and landless. In precolonial Africa, everybody had access to land. In colonial Africa, especially in areas with large numbers of European settlers, many were denied land. In Southern and East Africa, large numbers of landless people moved about as migrant workers.

Conclusion

Colonial Administrations in Africa: Positive or Negative Changes?

The evaluation of the comprehensive changes of this period has given rise to three major opinions. First, there are those who see everything as positive. Many missionaries, European officials, and scholars of moderate persuasion regard colonial rule as having been beneficial for the following reasons: peace replaced wars in many areas; Western education and medicine spread; roads and railways were constructed; Africans sold their products abroad for money, and so on. In short, to them, the colonial era brought 'civilization' to a 'dark continent'.[34]

Second, there are those who regard the changes as negative.[35] Rather than development, they see the exploitation and retardation of the continent. Such changes as the building of roads and railways simply provided the infrastructure needed by the colonial powers to take away resources from Africa to Europe. Thus, colonial infrastructures in Africa have best been described as infrastructures of exploitation.[36] To scholars of the 'Dependency School', colonialism destroyed indigenous economies, removed wealth from Africa to Europe, and created the basis for underdevelopment. In the words of Walter Rodney, a famous critic, 'Colonialism had only one hand—it was a one-armed bandit'.³⁷ Other critics of colonial rule do not deny that the era brought positive changes, but they assert that indigenous cultures and environments were damaged in various ways, that women were marginalized in a colonial society dominated by men, that the exploitation of the continent was far greater than the benefits it received, that social services were provided primarily to meet the needs of Europeans and a small number of privileged Africans who lived in the cities, and that racial dominance by Europeans undermined the worth of Africans as a people.

Finally, there are those who see both positive and negative aspects in colonial rule. They agree that some changes had beneficial impacts, such as political stability, the creation of a smaller number of countries with fixed boundaries to replace hundreds of previous states, the creation of a judiciary and civil service, and the creation of conditions that led to African nationalism. On the negative side, they mention, among other things: the end of the sovereignty of African states, the weakening of the traditional basis of power, the creation of small, and land-locked countries, and the rise of ethnicity. With respect to the economy, they praise the creation of new roads and railways and the development of the mineral and agricultural potential of the continent in such a way that wealth was generated by many people whose purchasing power was enhanced. On the negative side, they point to the inadequacies of the communication system, the commercialization of land, the use of forced labor, the acquisition of fertile land by European settlers, the control of lucrative trade by European firms and Lebanese and Indian traders, and other forms of exploitation.

Irrespective of the conclusions of the various analysts, there is no doubt that the colonial era was one of the most significant events in African history. It brought many changes, such as new countries, the spread of European languages and institutions, and the introduction of Western education and health services. Many of these changes have had a lasting impact on the continent.

NOTES

1. See for instance, Onwuka N. Njoku, *Economic History of Nigeria, 19th–21st Centuries* (Nsukka: Great AP Express Publishers, 2014), 163.
2. See Reginald Coupland, *The British Anti-Slavery Movement* (London: Oxford University Press, 1933).
3. See Eric Williams, *Capitalism and Slavery* (The University of North Carolina Press, 1994 ed).
4. Njoku, *Economic History of Nigeria*, 164. See also, David L. Imbua et al., *History, Culture, Diaspora, and Nation Building: The Collected Works of Okon Edet Uya* (Bethesdan: Arbi Press, 2012); David L. Imbua, *Intercourse and Crosscurrents in the Atlantic World: Calabar-British Experience, 17th–20th Centuries* (Durham, North Carolina: Carolina Academic Press, 2012).

5. The following example will suffice, Eric Willaims, *Capitalism and Slavery*; Chinweizu, *The West and the Rest of Us* (New York: Random House, 1975); Walter Rodney, *How Europe Underdeveloped Africa* (Washington, DC: Howard University Press, 1974); Toyin Falola, *Britain and Nigeria: Exploitation or Development* (London: Zed, 1987); and Walter Ofonagoro, *Trade and Imperialism in Southern Nigeria, 1881–1916* (Nok Publishers, 1979).
6. Njoku, *Economic History of Nigeria*, 189.
7. Ibid.
8. Toyin Falola, *Development Planning and Decolonization in Nigeria* (Florida: University of Florida Press, 1996), 2.
9. Bernard Bourdillon, cited in Kehinde Faluyi, "The Response of the People of Oyo Division of Western Nigeria to Cash Crop Development, 1935–1960," *The Nigerian Journal of Economic History* 1: 41.
10. See, Z.A. Konnczacki and J.M. Konczacki, eds., *An Economic History of Tropical Africa*, Vol. II (London: Frank Cass, 1977), 18–19.
11. For more on the economic situation in Europe and the consequent expansionist drive into Africa and ultimately its colonization, see P.J. Cain and A.G. Hopkins, *British Imperialism, 1688–2000* (Essex: Longman, 2002); and A. Boahen, ed., *UNESCO General History of Africa, VII, Africa Under Colonial Domination, 1880–1935*, Abridged ed. (Berkeley: University of California Press, 1990).
12. For details on these treaties, see K.O. Dike, *Trade and Politics in the Niger Delta, 1830–1885: An Introduction to the Economic and Political History of Nigeria* (London: Clarendon Press, 1956).
13. Similar argument to justify the economic explanations for colonizing Africa had been put forward by J.A. Hobson, *Imperialism: A Study* (London: George Allen and Unwin, 1902); and V.I. Lenin, *Imperialism: The Highest Stage of Capitalism* (New York: International Publishers, 1917).
14. Charles Darwin, *The Origin of Species by Means of Natural Selection or the Preservation of Favoured Races in the Struggle for Life* (John Murray, 1859).
15. See for instance E.A. Ayandele, *The Missionary Impact on Modern, 1842–1914: A Political and Social Analysis* (London: Longman, 1966).
16. On the partition of Africa see Richard Reid, *A History of Modern Africa, 1800 to the Present* (Hoboken: John Wiley and Son, 2011); and Deryck Schreuder, *The Scramble for Southern Africa: The Politics of Partition Reappraised* (Cambridge: Cambridge University Press, 1980).
17. See for example Roland Anthony Oliver and Neville Sanderson, *The Cambridge History of Africa, Vol. 6, 1870–1905* (Cambridge: Cambridge University Press, 1985).
18. K.O. Dike, *Trade and Politics in the Niger Delta*.
19. See for example, Toyin Falola, *Nigerian History, Politics, and Affairs: The Collected Essays of Adiele Afigbo* (Trenton, NJ: Africa World Press, 2005), chap. 7.
20. Deryck Schreuder, *The Scramble for Southern Africa*.
21. See Toyin Falola, *Key Events in African History*.
22. For armed reistance against the Europeans, see for example Randy Sparks, *The Two Princes of Calabar* (Massachusetts: Harvard University Press, 2004).
23. Toyin Falola, *Nigerian History, Politics, and Affairs*, chap. 4.
24. Sparks' *The Two Princes of Calabar* serves as one example.

25. For indirect rule in British Africa see Obaro Ikime and Segun Osoba, *Indirect Rule in British Africa* (London: Longman, 1970).
26. Frederick Lugard, *The Dual Mandate in British Tropical Africa* (1922).
27. For indirect rule in Eastern Nigeria see Adiele Afigbo, *The Warrant Chiefs: Indirect Rule in Southeastern Nigeria, 1891–1929* (London: Longman, 1972).
28. A.I. Asiwaju, *West African Transformations: A Comparative Impact of French and British Colonialism* (Ikeja: Malthouse Press, 2001).
29. James Eskridge Genova, *Colonial Ambivalence, Cultural Authenticity, and the Limitations of Mimicry in French-Ruled West Africa, 1914–1956* (New York: Peter Lang, 2004).
30. Lewis H. Gann and Peter Duignan, *Colonialism in Africa, 1870–1960* (London: Cambridge University Press, 1975). For forced labor in colonial French West Africa see Babacar Fall, *Social History in French West Africa: Forced Labor, Labor Market, Women, and Politics* (Amsterdam: SEPHIS, 2002).
31. Ibid.
32. A similar case obtained in British West Africa and the colonialists exploited their colonies as best they could. O.N. Njoku has given considerable attention to the situation in Nigeria in his *Economic History of Nigeria*.
33. Toyin Falola in his *Nationalism and African Intellectuals* (New York: University of Rochester Press, 2001) has dealt with this issue. Also, see Chap. 25 by Toyin Falola and Chukwuemeka Agbo, "Nationalism and African Intellectuals," in this volume.
34. See for instance, J.A. Hobson, *Imperialism: A Study*.
35. The examples of Rodney, Chinweizu, and Ofonagoro, among others, have already been cited earlier.
36. S.A. Olanrewaju, "The Infrastructure of Exploitation: Transport, Monetary Changes, Banking, etc" in Toyin Falola, ed., *Britain and Nigeria: Exploitation or Development*. See also, Njoku, *Economic History of Nigeria*, 213.
37. Walter Rodney, *How Europe Underdeveloped Africa*.

Bibliography

Afigbo, Adiele. *The Warrant Chiefs: Indirect Rule in Southeastern Nigeria, 1891–1929*. London: Longman, 1972.

Asiwaju, A.I. *West African Transformations: A Comparative Impact of French and British Colonialism*. Ikeja: Malthouse Press, 2001.

Ayandele, E.A. *The Missionary Impact on Modern, 1842–1914: A Political and Social Analysis*. London: Longman, 1966.

Boahen, Adu. *African Perspectives on Colonialism*. Baltimore, MD: Johns Hopkins University Press, 1985.

———, ed. *UNESCO General History of Africa, VII, Africa Under Colonial Domination, 1880–1935*, Abridged ed. Berkeley: University of California Press, 1990.

Cain, P.J., and A.G. Hopkins. *British Imperialism, 1688–2000*. Essex: Longman, 2002.

Chinweizu. *The West and the Rest of Us*. New York: Random House, 1975.

Coupland, Reginald. *The British Anti-Slavery Movement*. London: Oxford University Press, 1933.

Darwin, Charles. *The Origin of Species by Means of Natural Selection or the Preservation of Favoured Races in the Struggle for Life*. London: John Murray, 1859.

Davidson, Basil. *Modern Africa: A Social and Political History*, 2nd ed. New York: Longman, 1989.

Dike, K.O. *Trade and Politics in the Niger Delta, 1830–1885: An Introduction to the Economic and Political History of Nigeria*. London: Clarendon Press, 1956.

Fall, Babacar. *Social History in French West Africa: Forced Labor, Labor Market, Women, and Politics*. Amsterdam: SEPHIS, 2002.

Falola, Toyin. *Britain and Nigeria: Exploitation or Development*. London: Zed, 1987.

———. *Development Planning and Decolonization in Nigeria*. Florida: University of Florida Press, 1996.

———. *Nationalism and African Intellectuals*. New York: University of Rochester Press, 2001.

———. *Key Events in African History: A Reference Guide*. Westport: Greenwood Press, 2002.

———. *Nigerian History, Politics, and Affairs: The Collected Essays of Adiele Afigbo*. Trenton, NJ: Africa World Press, 2005.

Faluyi, Kehinde. "The Response of the People of Oyo Division of Western Nigeria to Cash Crop Development, 1935–1960." *The Nigerian Journal of Economic History*, no. 1 (1998): 41.

Gann, Lewis H., and Peter Duignan. *Colonialism in Africa, 1870–1960*. London: Cambridge University Press, 1975.

Genova, James Eskridge. *Colonial Ambivalence, Cultural Authenticity, and the Limitations of Mimicry in French-Ruled West Africa, 1914–1956*. New York: Peter Lang, 2004.

Hobson, J.A. *Imperialism: A Study*. London: George Allen and Unwin, 1902.

Ikime, Obaro, and Segun Osoba. *Indirect Rule in British Africa*. London: Longman, 1970.

Imbua, David L. *History, Culture, Diaspora, and Nation Building: The Collected Works of Okon Edet Uya*. Bethesdan: Arbi Press, 2012.

———. *Intercourse and Crosscurrents in the Atlantic World: Calabar-British Experience, 17th–20th Centuries*. Durham, NC: Carolina Academic Press, 2012.

Konnczacki, Z.A., and J.M. Konnczacki, eds. *An Economic History of Tropical Africa*, Vol. II. London: Frank Cass, 1977.

Lenin, V.I. *Imperialism: The Highest Stage of Capitalism*. New York: International Publishers, 1917.

Lugard, Frederick. *The Dual Mandate in British Tropical Africa*. London: Frank Cass, 1922.

McPhee, Allan. *The Economic Revolution of British West Africa*. New York: Negro Universities Press, 1970.

Njoku, Onwuka. *Economic History of Nigeria, 19th–21st Centuries*. Nsukka: Great AP Express Publishers, 2014.

Ofonagoro, Walter. *Trade and Imperialism in Southern Nigeria, 1881–1916*. New York: Nok Publishers, 1979.

Oliver, Anthony Roland, and Neville Sanderson. *The Cambridge History of Africa, Vol. 6, 1870–1905*. Cambridge: Cambridge University Press, 1985.

Reid, Richard. *A History of Modern Africa, 1800 to the Present*. Hoboken: Wiley, 2011.

Rodney, Walter. *How Europe Underdeveloped Africa*. Washington, DC: Howard University Press, 1974.

Schreuder, Deryck. *The Scramble for Southern Africa: The Politics of Partition Reappraised.* Cambridge: Cambridge University Press, 1980.

Sparks, Randy. *The Two Princes of Calabar.* Cambridge, MA: Harvard University Press, 2004.

Williams, Eric. *Capitalism and Slavery.* Chapel Hill, NC: The University of North Carolina Press, 1994.

CHAPTER 4

Slavery in the Colonial State and After

Paul E. Lovejoy

By the time that colonialism ended in Africa, slavery was hardly something of the past, although its shapes and forms had undergone extensive transformations. It was no longer legal to buy and sell people as slaves, and acts of enslavement were undertaken surreptitiously rather than through capture in warfare, judiciously sanctioned punishment or slave raiding, although kidnapping continued in some places. Slavery had been widespread almost everywhere at the time of the European conquest as an accepted part of the social order. Colonial policies altered official attitudes to slavery primarily because colonial rule was justified as a civilizing mission and slavery was considered an anathema that had been eliminated in European colonies in the Americas and Asia, and indeed in Southern Africa, Sierra Leone, and the French enclaves in West Africa and North Africa. The persistence of slavery nonetheless was a feature of colonial rule, despite a wave of policies and development schemes that attempted to redefine social relationships through taxation, migrant labor deployment, Christian marriage, the invention of 'tribalism' as a method of indirect rule, the redefinition of kinship, and other 'civilizing' mechanisms. Repeatedly, however, slavery surfaced as a reality that dragged the precolonial era into the present. Slavery emerged in court cases, labor unrest, politically inspired disputes over appointments to colonial-sanctioned public office, friction between Christians and Muslims, and even in education. Slavery during the colonial era led some to question whether or not slavery was really an issue any longer, since it became illegal to enslave people let alone buy and sell individuals. Older, preconquest relationships that clearly involved enslavement might be thought to have dissipated, lingering on as

P.E. Lovejoy (✉)
Department of History, York University, Toronto, ON, Canada

vestiges of the past that eventually would disappear with the passing of time, constituting what some officials predicted was the 'slow death of slavery' that would take at least a generation, and in less sanguine predictions, two generations to finish. Despite problems of definition of what constituted slavery, the status of 'slave' clearly continued through the colonial period and resurfaced under the modern conditions of contemporary slavery.

This chapter analyzes slavery during the twentieth century and the implications for understanding why it has continued into the present. In order to do so, several important distinctions are made. First, slavery is understood to mean the status of an individual who was considered to be property, that is someone who could be bought and sold as a person and therefore had a monetary value that was clearly established in local custom and law and was distinct from other forms of servile relationships and methods of exploitation.[1] Moreover, slavery was an inherited status that could not be altered unless individuals or their offspring were emancipated, usually through purchase, death-bed acts of charity, or actions derived from legal proceedings but sometimes through flight, executive order, and in Muslim societies through birth if the father was free. Slavery should therefore be considered to be distinct from forced labor, conscription, debt bondage, pawnship in which individuals were held as collateral for debts, or marriage in which women had no choice. Sometimes, slavery has been confused with other exploitive relationships, which is not to underestimate the degree of coercion during colonial rule but to provide an important analytical distinction that helps to understand the transition that was involved for the institution of slavery as a result of European conquest. As is widely recognized, slavery was extensive in virtually all parts of Africa before the colonial conquest, although the conditions of enslavement, the mechanisms of enslavement, and the extent of the trade in slaves and other means of distribution of those who were enslaved varied considerably across the continent. In most parts of Africa in the period of final European occupation from $c.1885$ to 1900, the proportion of those who were enslaved constituted a substantial population, amounting to more than half the population in many places. Hence the destiny of this considerable population deserves close analysis, regardless of how slavery related to other forms of servility that already existed or that were introduced under colonialism.

Strictly speaking, the nature of slavery became ambiguous under colonial rule. All European powers justified conquest in part on the prevalence of slavery and at least a nominal commitment to its eradication through the self-proclaimed civilizing mission of colonialism.[2] In claiming a moral stance that opposed slavery, European governments made no basic distinction between areas that were Muslim and areas that were not. In reality, however, French and British policies towards slavery reflected extensive and long-standing knowledge of slavery under Islamic rule, the French because they had occupied first Algeria in the 1830s and then subsequently moved inland from the

Senegambian coast by the middle of the nineteenth century, while the British had confronted slavery in Muslim parts of South Asia throughout the nineteenth century. German, Belgian, and Portuguese policies towards slavery readily echoed the common anti-slavery rhetoric but willingly obfuscated distinctions between slavery and other forms of coerced labor that blurred the transition in the conditions of many people who were actually enslaved as opposed to those who were now subjected to colonial dictatorship. In one way or another all colonial regimes instituted laws that prohibited the actual enslavement of individuals through kidnapping, war, and other means for purposes of sale into slavery. They made the trade in human beings illegal, which now became a criminal offence subject to imprisonment, fine or both, and the liberation of the individuals who had been enslaved or were being sold. Nonetheless, no colonial regime actually emancipated the enslaved population at the time of conquest, although provisions for redemption from slavery were often encouraged and strengthened, even when those in slavery faced the same coercive measures of forced labor that all colonial subjects, except the elites, had to endure.

Even the exceptions to where slavery was prevalent are instructive. In British South Africa and Sierra Leone, slavery was formally abolished in 1834 with British emancipation throughout its colonial domains, although the distinction between colonies and protectorates meant that slavery did not end everywhere in the British empire. In British colonies, after a period of apprenticeship that lasted until 1838, the enslaved population was legally free, but in protectorates, which included much of South Asia and also areas of Africa that were conquered at the turn of the twentieth century, the enslaved population was not emancipated, although the legal status of slavery was no longer recognized in British courts, and enslavement and slave trading were legally proscribed and made criminal offences.[3] This fine distinction between emancipation of people who were held as slaves and the change in the legal status of the enslaved population could be confusing, even for colonial administrators who were attempting to understand the difference and act accordingly. For public consumption in Europe, there were supposedly no more slaves with the imposition of the colonial state, but missionaries, some newspaper reporters, and early anthropological inquiry reported otherwise. Moreover, the colonial state allowed coercive measures of labor recruitment that confused the situation over the continuation of slavery even more. Hence it can be argued that the colonial period hardly resolved the issue of slavery in Africa but rather resulted in its obfuscation.

The analysis of slavery during the European colonial occupation of Africa has suffered not only because of confusion over what is meant by slavery but also because of the rhetoric of the era that often failed to make distinctions among the legalisms that were used to describe European occupation and dictatorship. The term 'colonial', for example, once referred to formal settlement of territories by immigrants from the homeland of colonial rule, as in

North America; as distinct from 'empire', which did not necessarily involve European migration and settlement, as in most of Asia. In the twentieth century, Europeans did migrate to some parts of Southern Africa and East Africa where settler regimes eventually emerged that more or less helped shape the policies of European occupation, most especially in South Africa, Kenya, and in Portuguese enclaves in Angola and Mozambique, which complicate the analysis.[4] Forced labor, abusive concessions to European-controlled cartels, and terror allowed the perpetration of measures that allowed the continuation of slavery under terminologies that disguised the abrupt shift from situations in which there was an enslaved population to conditions of colonial servitude. Some of these abuses were exposed, as in André Gide's documentation of the horrors of the Congo Free State (*Voyage au Congo*, 1927). Others were justified on the basis of racist pronouncements of the primitive mentalities of Africans, as described in Dominique-Octave Mannoni's *Prospero and Caliban* (1956). A clear difference marked the continuation and transformation of slavery in areas of European immigration from most of the rest of Africa where European settlement was marginal or non-existent. In all areas, nonetheless, European 'colonial' rule had to allow for existing authority whether through the incorporation of officials of previously independent political states or the cooption of the leadership of acephalous societies and fragmented social structures. In many places, colonial regimes imposed newly created titled officials to facilitate labor recruitment, taxation, and political control who inevitably affected how slavery was perceived and how those who were enslaved were treated.[5] The conquest and the process of stabilization in combination also introduced conditions in which many of those who were enslaved were able to run away, but often to marginal areas to escape detection; and for those who did not flee, there were successful efforts to renegotiate their status and their obligations to their masters.

The division of Africa into European-controlled territories that were called 'colonies' and 'protectorates' changed the context for those who were enslaved and led to dramatic transformations, but not the end of slavery. In the Muslim states of West Africa that were defeated and incorporated into European territories at the end of the nineteenth century, there were more people enslaved than in all of the Americas combined at any time during the era of slavery there.[6] There were also many enslaved people in areas that were not under Muslim governments, such as Asante, the Yoruba states, the interior of the Bight of Biafra and elsewhere, even in stateless societies. In Muslim-controlled areas of East Africa and Christian Ethiopia, slavery continued despite European, particularly British, efforts to end the slave trade in the Indian Ocean and across the Red Sea. Slavery and debt bondage that was often converted into enslavement was common throughout the Bantu-speaking societies and states from the Congo River basin southward to the Zambezi and the Kalahari Desert. The prevalence of slavery was so pervasive in its multifarious forms that some scholars have insisted that there were many types of 'slaveries' that characterized African societies at the beginning of the twentieth century. This situation characterized virtually the whole continent that had been conquered, and even Ethiopia and Liberia that remained independent were no different; it seems that slavery was as widespread as elsewhere.

Even missionary critics of colonial exploitation subscribed to aspects of the ideologies of colonialism, abhorring the supposed backwardness of African populations although insisting that Christian conversion offered the road to civilization and enlightenment. Missionaries were particularly confused on the issue of slavery. On the one hand, the Catholic White Fathers of Cardinal Charles Lavigerie purchased slaves outright, especially children and women, under the pretence that they were freeing them, provided they actually converted to Christianity. This policy was first instituted in Algeria, but was developed to its fullest in the interior regions of East Africa and the Congo River basin.[7] The missionary initiatives that derived from Sierra Leone, including the Church Missionary Society of the Anglican Church and the Methodists, relied on formerly enslaved converts to spread the Gospel and founded enclaves of Christianity on the basis of escaping from slavery, particularly in Yoruba and Igbo regions and in the hinterland of Freetown in Sierra Leone. For many missionaries, including those Africans who had been liberated and now recognized themselves as the vanguard of a new, Pan-African movement of reform and conversion, slavery was only one element of 'heathenism' and was placed alongside such abhorrent practices as the killing of twins, alleged savagery associated with ritualized masquerades, artistic representations in wooden carvings, body scarification, poison ordeals, and other supposedly barbaric practices including nakedness. Human sacrifices at funerals and during public ceremonies were indeed challenging cultural, social, and political obstacles to conversion, not only to Christianity but also to Islam, especially when victims were often those who were enslaved, often acquired specifically for the event. The impact of missionaries extended across Angola through the Belgian Congo to the Great Lakes.[8]

Because slavery was widespread and the ideology of conquest, ironically, was often based in part on opposition to slavery, the military consolidation of European control itself enabled many of the enslaved population to run away during military encounters and the uncertain climate after initial occupation. The slave-holding elites were temporarily without power and therefore could not keep those who wanted to flee from doing so. Hundreds of thousands of the enslaved population in West Africa deserted in the last few years of the nineteenth century and the first years of the twentieth. The new colonial regimes, therefore, had to deal with the issue of slavery, not so much because they used slavery and the slave trade as part of the justification for colonial rule, but because the slave population could seize the opportunity and threaten the establishment of stable colonial regimes. As a result, the colonial governments attempted to make sure that slaves were not immediately emancipated and that slavery was not directly eliminated. The two major colonial regimes that had to confront slavery were British and French; German encounters with slavery ended abruptly with the First World War, while Portuguese and Belgian measures require a separate analysis because the coercive measures that they imposed introduced atrocities that targeted the whole population, not only those who were technically enslaved.

An examination of slavery in the states that had been founded in jihad in West Africa between the late eighteenth century and the nineteenth century demonstrates the scale of the transformation in social relationships that came about as a result of the colonial approach to the slavery issue. These Muslim states stretched from Fuuta Jalon and Fuuta Toro in the Senegambia region through the Umarian empire of al-Hajj 'Umar and the Sokoto caliphate, and indeed dominated the sahel and savannah as far as the Mahdist state in the upper Nile River Valley, reaching the Red Sea by the end of the nineteenth century. Together, these states had a slave population that numbered in the millions. The Sokoto caliphate alone had an enslaved population that surpassed the number of the enslaved in Brazil and Cuba combined. Inevitably, therefore, slavery was a major issue that affected how the British and French brought these Islamic governments under imperial control. How to deal with this situation was a major concern of both British and French officials. In British territories in West Africa, the status of slavery had been ambiguous since the middle of the nineteenth century. Officials debated whether or not they were allowed to provide sanctuary for fugitive slaves, and in an effort to contain the flight of slaves from areas beyond their control, they drafted young males into the evolving forces of the Hausa Constabulary and then the West African Frontier Force, which became the conquering armies of the British advance. Under Frederick Lugard, the newly appointed High Commissioner of the Protectorate of Northern Nigeria, British policy was consolidated under the rubric of 'legal status abolition', following the slavery policy that had been adopted in India and elsewhere.[9] As the leading ideologue and political theorist in British Africa, Lugard had experience in the consolidation of British rule in Uganda and subsequently served in Hong Kong, although his major impact was in Nigeria, first in the region dominated by the Sokoto caliphate and then subsequently after 1913 in all of Nigeria. Lugard was considered the father of 'Indirect Rule' and implemented what was known as the Indian model of slavery policy, which did not emancipate slaves but rather altered the legal status of slavery in the courts. Lugard came to believe that he abolished slavery, or at least his public image required such an interpretation. He played a major role as an anti-slavery expert at the League of Nations in the 1920s and even wrote the entry on slavery in the ninth edition of the *Encyclopedia Britannica* in 1929. The evolution of his impact on slavery policy is best revealed in a remarkable report on the evolution of slavery policies in Northern Nigeria from 1897 through the 1920s that Gordon Lethem, Lieutenant-Governor of Northern Nigeria, assembled, at Lugard's request, in 1931.[10]

In the French sphere, Governor-General E. Roume proclaimed a new judicial system in November 1903 that effectively abolished the legal status of slavery throughout French-controlled territory, a policy which proved to be remarkably similar to the one adopted in British territories. By the terms of administrative decree, both French and indigenous courts and judicial tribunals were no longer permitted to acknowledge the status of slavery in their proceedings and were prohibited from issuing certificates of freedom for those who were seeking emancipation. Because slavery was widespread, several administrators undertook to study the problem, resulting in the official reports of Georges Poulet, Ernest Roume and Georges Dehereme in 1905–1906.[11] Like the British, the French employed fugitive slaves in the military, the *tirailleurs sénégalais*, and placed many fugitives in *villages de liberté* that were stationed along trade routes and the newly constructed railroad into the interior as a dependable labor force.[12] French policy did not prevent the massive desertion of slaves, who left their masters during these years, but it did enable the renegotiation of relationships between the enslaved population which did not flee with their former masters. In the Sahara and the sahel especially, servile and formerly servile people continued to be enmeshed in pseudo and sometimes coercive relationships of dependency for many decades, and in some places lasting until the present.[13]

A major exposé of the enslaved population was undertaken in the 1920s. Initially the concern was the nature of newly imposed policies in the former German territories that the League of Nations placed under mandate to the French and British. It was not clear if policies in adjacent colonies should apply to the mandated territories, and to deflect attention from the problem, the League undertook to investigate the prevalence of slavery and the policies of various governments in its suppression. The League specifically initiated an investigation into the persistence of slavery in Ethiopia in 1922 but soon broadened its mandate. As Suzanne Miers has demonstrated, the League's involvement in the suppression of slavery had rather dubious origins, and in the fifteen years during which the League was concerned with the slavery issue, more was done to protect the interests of colonial governments than to eradicate slavery.[14] Nonetheless, the inquiries of the League indirectly affected colonial policy towards the slavery issue. For public consumption, at least, colonial regimes had to appear to have the slavery situation under control, not only in the mandated territories but throughout their colonial empires.

Lugard surfaced as one of the leading spokesmen in the slavery debate. At the time, he was Britain's appointee to the Permanent Mandates Commission of the League. He was also Vice President of the Abyssinian Corporation, which promoted British commercial interests in Ethiopia. On November 10, 1922, Lord Arthur Balfour, British Foreign Secretary, transmitted a memorandum to the League through Lugard recommending an investigation of slavery in Ethiopia. Lugard assumed the appearance of one who was not directly interested in Ethiopia, despite his connection with the Abyssinian Corporation, but as William Rappard, Director of the Mandates Section of the League, noted at the time, 'the British Government or certain colonial circles were considering the possibility of using the League and Sir Frederick Lugard as a means of intervention in Abyssinia'.[15] Conflict of interest aside, the Anti-Slavery and Aborigines Protection Society, especially through the tireless activities of J.S. Harris, quickly entered the debate over slavery in Ethiopia. The inquiry expanded into an investigation of former German colonies. As Britain's representative on the Mandates Commission, Lugard was well placed to play a role here, too. The Mandates Commission issued reports in 1922, 1923, and 1924, which were forwarded to the International Labour Office. Slavery was visible to anyone who wanted to notice. In December 1923, the Fourth Assembly of the Council of the League adopted a resolution to continue the inquiry into the question of slavery. A Temporary Commission on Slavery was established, with Lugard as Britain's representative. The Commission was instructed to gather information on what legislative and other means were being taken to secure the suppression of slavery. Further, it was to report on the results of the efforts at suppression and whether slavery was completely suppressed or was still dying out. Finally, the Commission was to examine the economic and social impact of anti-slavery measures on former masters, slaves, governments, and the development of territories where slavery was or had been important. The Council wanted replies from the different governments by June 1, 1924.

Lugard drafted the questionnaire to be addressed to governments throughout the world. As might be expected, considering his experience in East Africa, Nigeria, and Hong Kong, the questionnaire was written in terms that were compatible with his commitment to the abolition of the legal status of slavery. The questions addressed slave raiding, slave dealing, domestic or 'praedial' slavery, concubinage and payment for females disguised as dowry, adoption of children through pawnage, and compulsory labor. Lugard convinced the Commission to take a broad perspective 'to enquire into the question of slavery from every point or view', whether or not particular governments wanted to minimize the extent of' slavery in their domains or anti-slavery groups tried to exaggerate the extent of slavery in particular countries. The volume of data that came before the Temporary Commission simply could not be ignored. So much material was submitted that the French delegate, Maurice Delafosse, former official of French West Africa and prominent ethnographer, agreed to summarize the documentation for purposes of discussion.

In preparation for the League's inquiry, the colonial government in Nigeria reviewed existing legislation, only to discover that the Mandated Territories were not fully covered. A circular on November 10, 1922 extended

Northern Nigerian laws to Northern Cameroon, but this circular had questionable legality. Particularly difficult to explain was the practice whereby Islamic courts issued certificates of freedom in situations where individuals had been born free, which was innocently admitted in the report to the Mandates Commission in 1923. In order to repair the damage, the legal status of slavery was formally abolished in the Mandated Territories on February 1, 1924. Confusion continued, nonetheless, because the situation in the Cameroons was similar to that in Northern Nigeria and indeed elsewhere, but it was embarrassing to admit as much. Furthermore, government efforts compounded the problem because the laws of Southern Nigeria were applied to the Mandated Territories, but those laws were based on the Native House Rule Ordinance (1901), which defined all persons living in a single housing compound as members of a 'family,' whether or not they were connected by kinship and in fact might very likely be either pawns or slaves.[16] Unlike the laws of Northern Nigeria, there was no role for the Islamic courts in the Southern Nigeria code, and there was no reference to the freeing of slaves after March 31, 1901, as there was in Northern Nigeria. The Mandates Commission wanted an explanation. The new measures did not actually resolve the sensitive questions being asked at the League, therefore, but confirmed the abolition of the legal status of slavery, declaring that 'all persons heretofore or hereafter born in or brought within the area were free.'[17] This provision made it clear that all children were born free, although it was noted that 'non-recognition by the Administration of the legal status does not imply equal non-recognition in native public opinion'. Hence the pressures brought to bear on Northern Nigeria by the League of Nations resulted in tighter restrictions on slave trading and slavery in the late 1920s.

Lugard introduced a lengthy report on forced labor in July 1925 that led to considerable discussion and deflected attention from Nigeria. In Delafosse's summary of the many reports that had been submitted, he presented his own interpretation of slavery that in turn led to lengthy review. In 1925, Lugard asked officials in Northern Nigeria for comments on Delafosse's memorandum, which allowed the colonial regime to stay abreast of League discussions without drawing attention to Northern Nigeria itself. Lugard made it clear that he disagreed with Delafosse on the approach that should be adopted in dealing with 'slavery in all its forms'. The result of the activities of the Temporary Commission on Slavery was the Slavery Convention, adopted by the League on September 25, 1926, which included twelve articles outlawing slavery and slave trading. As Marjorie Perham, Lugard's biographer, has noted, the Convention was largely based on Lugard's draft. The Slavery Convention recommended the abolition of the legal status of slavery following 'the Indian model'. According to Miers, slavery that no longer had legal status "was now euphemistically called 'permissive' or 'voluntary' slavery since slaves might remain in servitude if they wished'. The similarity to Lugard's policy in Northern Nigeria is obvious. The Temporary Commission was subsequently terminated, its assignment considered to be complete. Thereafter, the League contented itself merely with receiving reports from various governments and made no effort to enforce or otherwise expose slavery practices.

The League, dormant in its campaign to undermine slavery for five years after 1926, once again directed its attention to the slavery issue in 1931. A new Committee of Experts on Slavery was instructed to examine the material that had been submitted by various governments since 1916 and to report on the extent to which slavery was being suppressed throughout the world. Lugard was not only Britain's representative again, but he also served as the Vice Chairman of the Committee. In its report of September 1931, the Committee recommended that a bureau be established to process documentary material and that a permanent commission be appointed 'because the mere existence of such a Commission could enlighten world public opinion in regard to slavery in the world'. The pressure on officials in Northern Nigeria, as elsewhere, was renewed. By this time, Lugard's credentials as an authority on slavery were unsurpassed. It must have come as quite a surprise, therefore, when he was inexplicably not appointed as the British representative to the Advisory Committee of Experts on Slavery, which met from 1934 to 1936. He had to content himself with writing letters to the British newspapers. The Committee of Experts was 'circumscribed' in its duties: because it could only collect information from governments and not from individuals and private organizations. As a result, the Colonial Office apparently wanted someone who had not been connected with the slavery issue, and Lugard's history in Nigeria did not allow him to fill that role. Britain's new champion in the fight against slavery was George Maxwell, who had formerly served as a colonial official in Malaya. Perhaps to everyone's surprise, as Miers has observed, Maxwell turned out to be 'the only truly independent member of the committee'.[18] He raised issues such as why ex-slaves did not leave their masters, and he put a large amount of pressure on the British in particular.

The renewed interest of the League of Nations was anticipated with caution in Northern Nigeria. The establishment of the Permanent Commission of Experts, with Maxwell as the British representative, was not welcomed. The Northern Provinces Advisory Council was already investigating the continuation of concubinage when Lugard requested Lethem to review slavery policy in 1931. Subsequently, lengthy files were compiled, as colonial officials gathered information for its reports to the League, but the purpose was clearly to deflect criticism. In the summer of 1935, Maxwell warned Nigerian officials that the League inquiry into the suppression of slavery was serious. The Slavery Committee would give 'special attention' to the whole issue of 'voluntary slavery' in British and other colonies as well as in the Mandated Territories. Furthermore, the Committee would 'raise the question of the approximate numbers of persons involved,' and hence he requested a census of 'ex-slaves.' The Slavery Committee, in its next report, aimed to show, not merely that slavery was not disappearing, but instead wanted to reveal the manner in which the ex-slaves were being, or had been, absorbed into the normal life of the free population. The League rejected bald statements such as 'slavery has been abolished' or 'slavery is unlawful,' which clearly 'carried little weight' even when supported by circumstantial evidence.

In Northern Nigeria, a census was duly manufactured and forwarded to Maxwell. The census officially reported a population of slaves and ex-slaves and the children of slaves who were still 'living in their previous mode' at 121,005 in 1935–1936.[19] It is amazing that the government of Northern Nigeria was willing to admit publicly to a slave population of this scale. Moreover, problems with the methods that were used to estimate the number of slaves and unaccountable variations in the figures for the provinces raise serious questions as to the accuracy of the census, perhaps not surprisingly. The census deserves closer analysis because it does provide valuable information that suggests that there were something approaching 390,000 or 400,000 slaves, former slaves, and descendants of slaves, rather than the 121,000 who were reported, and these were only the slaves, former slaves, and slave descendants that authorities in Northern Nigeria were willing to confirm.

All the figures are highly suspect. The figure for Sokoto (40,000) was rounded off to the nearest ten thousand, which confirms that no census was actually attempted, or if it was superficially. Officials merely guessed at what they thought would be acceptable to recognize the large slave population that still existed. The figure for Adamawa (11,900) can be compared with an estimate made fourteen years earlier, when the District Officer at the time thought that the number of slaves in *murgu*, that is, who were being allowed to earn wages and otherwise work on their own account in return for cash payments to their masters, was 10% of the total population of Yola, or about 20,000 people. By 1936, presumably, some of the people who had been working under *murgu* arrangements had either died or achieved self-redemption, but others were still under legal restrictions that related to enslavement. In any event, the 1936 estimate was low. The Bauchi figure (14,245) is of the same order but suggests some attempt at actually counting those who were enslaved. Similarly, the figure for Katsina (8430), while low, suggests the existence of a visible slave population, but the estimate is very low, since Katsina certainly had a much larger enslaved population than either Bauchi or Yola. The estimates for Kano (950) and Zaria (650) are so small as to be ridiculous, however. The Emir of Kano alone still had thousands of slaves on his estates, while other officials all had substantial numbers of slaves on the estates that they were still allowed to control. Still, this 'census', despite its clear under-representation and outright fabrication, is an interesting commentary on colonial perceptions of what must have been considered 'acceptable' levels of slavery that they thought could be presented publically to the League. The inquiry clearly made colonial officials nervous, and they had to admit to the presence of slavery on an enormous scale.[20]

When some of the unaccountable differences between provinces and categories are eliminated, the report to the League suggests that perhaps as many as 400,000 people fell into the categories of slavery that had been defined by the League. British officials claimed that only 70,883 slaves had failed to take advantage of the opportunity to ransom themselves before slavery was finally abolished in 1936. Since anyone born after March 1901 was legally free, all these slaves had to be over thirty five years old, moreover. Although the figures for Kano and Zaria are suspiciously low and should be dismissed, the estimates for Bauchi, Adamawa, Niger, Sokoto, and Katsina can be taken more seriously, although still admittedly low. In all cases, there was good reason to underestimate the slave population, and the figures for all provinces are conservative. If adjustments are made to allow for the relative proportions of slaves that were reported in 1916–1919, when 85% of court cases were in the central Hausa emirates, then the total number of slaves aged over thirty five who had not purchased their freedom may well have been as high as 220,000 in those provinces, not 70,883. Similar distortions can be detected in the estimates for the number of slaves who had been ransomed but continued 'in their previous mode of living' and the children of slaves who continued under conditions approximating slavery. Even the more modest estimates of the number of individuals who were still slaves or who were living under modified conditions of slavery were an embarrassment to the British government in London and officials in Nigeria.

The examination undertaken by the League was more detailed than any previous inquiry, and when compared with other information from Nigeria led to the final abolition of slavery in Northern Nigeria through Ordinance No. 19 of 1936. Documentation that was provided to the League revealed that the Yoruba system of pawnship had been abolished, that the Native House Rule Ordinance of Southern Nigeria, which had allowed slavery to continue, had been repealed, and that slavery had been abolished in the Mandated Territories. The question was raised: Why was there still a law in Northern Nigeria that only allowed for the freedom of persons born after March 30, 1901 and if so, why was freedom not conferred on the whole population? In 1936, the Advisory Committee of Experts, with Maxwell in the chair, made it clear that 'voluntary slavery' would not be tolerated as 'a cover for the fact that individuals fear persecution or oppression if they avail themselves of the law'. Governments were instructed to investigate whether or not slaves could gain access to land and 'thereby earn their own living'. The Committee also wanted to know if there were any signs of 'the mental helplessness of a depressed class, especially in Muslim countries, where every attempt should be made to emphasize the liberal attitude of the Koran and tradition (Sunnah) to slavery'. Hence the Slavery Ordinance of 1936 that finally legally abolished slavery was a significant watershed in the history of slavery. Thereafter, slavery truly had no legal status, and all slaves at least in theory were thereby emancipated without further compensation to their masters. While the League continued to focus on Ethiopia and other parts of Africa, particularly Liberia and Bechuanaland (Botswana), the colonial government in Nigeria had to confront a serious critique that undermined its efforts to maintain a low profile on the slavery issue.

The Northern Nigeria case is an important example of the transition in slavery that affected the enslaved population under colonial rule because of the large scale of slavery that had prevailed in the Sokoto caliphate, Borno and indeed throughout the region. The example is also instructive because conditions there were more or less the same as in areas under French control in what became Niger and in the German enclaves in northern Kamerun that had been part of Adamawa. Elsewhere in the Muslim-dominated areas of the western Sudan that were under French rule, in the region of Tchad as well, and in British-controlled Nilotic Sudan the conditions were also the same, which included massive slave desertion for those who were able to leave and decided to do so and the large enslaved population which chose to stay put but somehow renegotiated terms of servitude that resulted in modified forms of slavery. In the Senegal province of French West Africa, for example, the Mourides emerged as the dominant Muslim brotherhood that owed its following to the many former slaves who left their masters and sought sanctuary in the villages where groundnuts became the principal crop grown for export overseas.

This analysis has concentrated on the changes that occurred in those areas that were dominated by Muslim regimes that were formed in the context of jihad. What happened in areas that were not under Muslim control at the time of European conquest? It can be demonstrated that changes were equally profound, although for different reasons, often associated with the presence of Christian missionaries. Colonial strategies towards slavery were complicated for a variety of reasons. First, colonial occupation was often associated with anti-slavery rhetoric, although this does not mean that those who were condemning slavery had anything against exploitative relationships of production. Sometimes, the oppressive relationships of colonialism were worse than the stereotypes of slavery but it is important not to confuse slavery and colonial exploitation. Were individuals being bought and sold? Under forced labor, this was not the operative formulation. Brute force under the guise of supposedly enlightened colonial rule and racist perceptions of African inferiority were analogous to slavery in some ways because of the degree of dehumanization.

The issue of women and slavery is also one that the colonial occupation complicated. Not surprisingly, women were not perceived as anything of importance. They were part of kinship networks, which was a sort of recognition. The civilizing mission abhorred the idea of multiple wives, but in terms of labor, forced or waged, women were usually not conceptualized. When targeted production was enforced, as in rubber extraction, women were implicitly included in the demand for output, but in considering issues of slavery, women were not of particular concern. Migrant labor policy focused on men, not women, who (if they were thought about at all) were generally expected to remain at home, do the child rearing, and farm the land. Men formed the labor force, whether coerced or not. Christian missions enforced monogamy, which undermined existing gerontocracy whereby mature males controlled access to women through polygamy; that is, having more than one spouse at a time, which in fact was polygyny, or males having more than one wife, since it was only males who could have more than one spouse. The practice was gender-specific. Christianity imposed monogamy, if not always fidelity. Nonetheless, the imposed reform limited relationships between genders, since before the insistence on Christian marriage, multiple spouses often meant that second and subsequent wives were not always from respectable families that required negotiated bride prices but could be females being held in pawn or who were slaves. Monogamy inevitably undermined these more complicated and abusive marital relationships.

In Islamic contexts, the continuation of multiple marriages continued, but men could only marry free women, which meant that relationships with the families of wives continued to be important in stabilizing marital relationships. The exception was the legality of concubinage, since Muslim males could legally cohabit with women other than their wife or wives through the practice of concubinage. The problem was that concubines, unlike wives, were supposed to be of slave status. The practice of pressing freeborn girls into concubinage was well established, so much so that British officials were candid in response to an inquiry from the League of Nations, claiming that many women 'prefer to continue in the category of slaves rather than of free persons', particularly 'the daughters of domestic and other slaves [who] frequently prefer to be concubines'. It was admitted that 'many thousands or girls have been ... ransomed who were in fact born free under the Nigerian Ordinance', which was blamed on 'the connivance of their parents'. Concubinage was still common over two decades after the imposition of colonial rule, although British officials predicted its eventual demise. Yet concubinage could be expected to 'operate for a certain limited number of years',[21] in fact, continuing throughout the colonial period to the present.

The issue of pawnship also related to the associated problem of how women were treated under colonialism as a population that was not important and hence classified as dependents and subordinates of men. Individuals who were held as security against debts, that is, pawns, were often female, usually girls. They were not enslaved, and indeed their legal status as pawns usually prevented their enslavement because families were committed to their protection and creditors who held the pawns were bound to uphold both local legal customs and abide by public acknowledgement of personal relationships and guarantees of the safety of those held as pawns. In the colonial mentality, however, pawnship and slavery were linked, both effectively establishing the lack of freedom and hence antithetical to the freedom and civilizing ideology of colonialism, even though the reality of colonial rule was anything but devoted to human rights. The preoccupation of the League of Nations and the colonial regimes was to equate pawnship with slavery, despite the clear distinctions between the two. Pawnship, unpaid dependent labor of kin, and marital relationships converged in social structures and economies that were tied to slavery and hierarchy. As the unpublished reports of the colonial era attest, many officials were acutely aware of the complexities. Nonetheless, the colonial state and the missionary adventure stumbled through policies and actions that confused customary practice and Western interpretations in ways that confused the continuation of slavery with the civilizing mission.

How slavery is remembered and how its legacy and the identification of people with that legacy have prevailed are subjects of considerable reflection. The voices that have emerged in an effort to understand the persistence of slavery as an issue in modern society speak to the contemporary problem. The legacy of slavery affects many people and is reflected in daily experience and social encounters.[22] Moreover, it is claimed that there are more slaves today than ever before.[23] Understanding how the continuation of forms of bondage in which individuals are bought and sold requires careful analysis because there is an important distinction to be made between a time when slavery was legal and clearly defined, and today when it is illegal and not clearly defined. Oppression today does not excuse its existence, but considering contemporary forms of oppression and exploitation 'slavery' does blur the present with history.

Maybe, as has been postulated, it is best to problematize different 'slaveries.' There is the slavery before abolition and emancipation became ideological constructs, and there are contemporary forms of exploitation that are analogous but are not necessarily the same. Even understanding slavery in the past has often been blurred. The initial debate between Marxist-oriented scholars who examined the materialist basis of slavery disagreed with anthropologists and historians who thought about slavery as institutional marginality. Both positions, and the relationship to contemporary discourse, have to be deconstructed. When focusing on former French and British territories and the policies that were adopted in West Africa, it can be seen that the resulting impact on African societies was formative. Despite the legal ending of slavery and the various subterfuges to disguise its continuation, the lives of many individuals, such as those in the sahel and southern Sahara, changed only gradually. When the League of Nations first began its inquiries into the 'question of slavery', it was well understood that there was an enormous problem. Years later UNESCO would undertake its exposé of the 'Slave Route' and the United Nations would declare slavery a 'crime against humanity'. Even after the legal emancipation of slaves and the criminalization of slavery, enslavement has continued, as it has in many parts of the world outside Africa. The links between historic slavery and contemporary forms of human trafficking explain why slavery has persisted as a means of exploitation and human domination.

The distinction between forced labor and bondage in the present is different from historic slavery in the accepted legality of the slavery in the past and the subterfuges to disguise its continuation in various forms. A frequent approach of colonial regimes was to confuse cultural differences for the benefit of exploitation. This conscious manipulation has led some scholars to refer to slavery in a plural form—slaveries. But a plural approach to understanding slavery confuses the issues more. Those who have been forced into labor but who are not actually bought and sold are not slaves, even though they are captives and have virtually no choice in what they do. Forced labor is not a form of slavery, except in a metaphorical sense. Slavery is when individuals are treated as property, not when people can be made to work, although coerced labor might well involve slaves and indeed wage labor might result in the employment of slaves whose wages were confiscated in whole or in part by their masters. Slavery certainly did involve oppressive conditions of labor, but not always. Sometimes, members of the enslaved population, especially males, were allowed to work on their own account in return for specified payments to their masters. Occasionally, individuals were placed in positions of responsibility and rewarded for their loyalty. Forced labor did indeed impose harsh conditions of existence on individuals, but unless people are being bought and sold, or it is possible to do so, it is not slavery. It is forced labor which violates legal proscriptions.

Notes

1. For a definition of slavery, see Paul E. Lovejoy, *Transformations in Slavery: A History of Slavery in Africa*, 3rd ed. (Cambridge: Cambridge University Press, 2011), 1–8.
2. Suzanne Miers, *Britain and the Ending of the Slave Trade* (London: Longman, 1975).
3. For a discussion of "legal status abolition," see Paul E. Lovejoy and Jan Hogendorn, *Slow Death for Slavery: The Course of Abolition in Northern Nigeria, 1897–1936* (Cambridge: Cambridge University Press, 1993).
4. Glyn Stone, "The Foreign Office and Slavery and Forced Labour in Portuguese West Africa, 1894–1914," in *Slavery, Diplomacy, and Empire: Britain and the Suppression of the Slave Trade, 1807–1975*, ed. Keith Hamilton and Patrick Salmon (Brighton: Sussex Academic Press, 2009), 165–95.
5. Frederick Cooper, "Conditions Analogous to Slavery: Imperialism and Free Labor Ideology in Africa," in *Beyond Slavery: Explorations of Race, Labor, and Citizenship in Postemancipation Societies*, ed. Frederick Cooper, Thomas C. Holt, and Rebecca J. Scott (Chapel Hill: University of North Carolina Press, 2000), 107–50.
6. Paul E. Lovejoy, *Jihad in West Africa during the Age of Revolutions* (Athens, OH: Ohio University Press, 2016).

7. Francois Renault, *Lavigerie, l'esclavage Africain et l'Europe* (Paris: E. De Boccard, 1971), 2 vols.
8. David Maxwell, "Freed Slaves, Missionaries, and Respectability: The Expansion of the Christian Frontier from Angola to Belgian Congo," *Journal of African History* 54 (2013): 79–102.
9. Lovejoy and Hogendorn, *Slow Death for Slavery*, 64–65.
10. Lugard asked Lethem to assemble the documents, which became "Early History of Anti-Slavery Legislation," so that Lugard could maintain his stature as anti-slavery crusader. See the discussion in Lovejoy and Hogendorn, *Slow Death for Slavery*, 95.
11. Sydney Kanya-Forstner and Paul E. Lovejoy, *Slavery and its Abolition in French West Africa: The Official Reports of G. Poulet, E. Roume, and G. Deherme* (Madison, WI: African Studies Program, 1994), 7–10.
12. Myron Echenberg, *Colonial Conscripts. The Tirailleurs Sénégalais in French West Africa, 1857–1960* (London: Heinemann, 1991), 8–18. For the background to slavery policy in French West Africa, see Martin A. Klein, *Slavery and Colonial Rule in French West Africa* (Cambridge: Cambridge University Press, 1998).
13. E. Ann MacDougall, "Living the Legacy of Slavery," *Cahiers d études africaines* 45 (2005): 957–86; Marie Rodet, "Escaping Slavery and Building Diasporic Communities in French Soudan and Senegal, ca. 1880–1940," *International Journal of African Historical Studies* 48, no. 2 (2015): 363–86; Bruce S. Hall, "Bellah Histories of Decolonization, Iklan Paths to Freedom: The Meanings of Race and Slavery in the Late-Colonial Niger Bend (Mali), 1944–1960," *International Journal of African Historical Studies* 48, no. 2 (2011): 61–87; and Benedetta Rossi, *From Slavery to Aid: Politics, Labour, and Ecology in the Nigerien Sahel, 1800–2000* (Cambridge: Cambridge University Press, 2015).
14. Suzanne Miers, "Slavery and the Slave Trade as International Issues 1890–1939," *Slavery and Abolition* 19, no. 2 (1998): 16–37; and Miers, "Britain and the Suppression of Slavery in Ethiopia," *Slavery and Abolition* 18, no. 3 (1997): 257–88.
15. As cited in Dogbo Daniel Atchebro, *La Société des Nations et la lute contre l'esclavage, 1922–1938* (Geneva: Institut universitaire de hautes etudes internationals, 1990), 40. Also see Miers, "Britain and the Suppression of Slavery in Ethiopia," 257–88.
16. "The Southern Nigeria Native House Rule Ordinance (1901)," *African Economic History* 40 (2012): 129–36.
17. Summary of Reports to the League of Nations for 1922, 1923, and 1924, submitted to the International Labour Office, October 14, 1925, Nigerian National Archives Ibadan, CSO 26 1/799, Vol. 1. Also see Lovejoy and Hogendorn, *Slow Death for Slavery*, 273.
18. Miers, "Slavery and the Slave Trade," 32–33.
19. The following discussion is based on Lovejoy and Hogendorn, *Slow Death for Slavery*, 278–80. See especially Table 9.3, *Slaves Reported to the League of Nations, 1936*.
20. As discussed in Lovejoy and Hogendorn, *Slow Death for Slavery*, 102–5.

21. Edward J. Arnett's Memorandum to Maurice Delafosse, August 9, 1925, Arnett Papers, Mss. Afr. S.952/2-3, Rhodes and discussion in Lovejoy and Hogendorn, *Slow Death for Slavery*, 251–59.
22. Alice Bellagamba, Sandra E. Greene, and Martin A. Klein, eds., *The Bitter Legacy: African Slavery Past and Present* (Athens, OH: Ohio University Press, 2013); Bellagamba, Greene, and Klein, eds., *African Voices on Slavery and the Slave Trade* (Cambridge: Cambridge University Press, 2013); and Bellagamba, Greene, and Klein, eds., *African Slaves, African Masters: Politics, Memories, Social Life* (Trenton, NJ: Africa World Press, 2017).
23. Kevin Bales, *Disposable People: New Slavery in the Global Economy*, rev. ed. (Berkeley: University of California Press, 2012); and Joel Quirk, *Unfinished Business: A Comparative Study of Historical and Contemporary Slavery* (Paris: UNESCO, 2008).

Bibliography

Akurang-Parry, Kwabena. "The Administration of the Abolition Laws, African Responses, and Post-Proclamation Slavery in the Gold Coast, 1874–1940." *Slavery and Abolition* 19, no. 2 (1998): 149–66.

Allain, Jean. "Slavery and the League of Nations: Ethiopia as a Civilised Nation." *Journal of the History of International Law* 8 (2006): 213–44.

———. *The Slavery Conventions: The Travaux Preparatoires of the 1926 League of Nations and the 1956 United Nations Convention.* Leiden: Martinus Nijhoff, 2008.

Atchebro, Dogbo Daniel. *La Société des Nations et la lute contre l'esclavage, 1922–1938.* Geneva: Institut universitaire de hautes etudes internationals, 1990.

Austin, Gareth. *Labour, Land, and Capital in Ghana: From Slavery to Free Labour in Asante, 1807–1956.* Rochester: University of Rochester Press, 2005.

Bales, Kevin. *Disposable People: New Slavery in the Global Economy*, rev. ed. Berkeley: University of California Press, 2012.

Bellagamba, Alice, Sandra E. Greene, and Martin A. Klein, eds. *The Bitter Legacy: African Slavery Past and Present.* Athens, OH: Ohio University Press, 2013.

———, eds. *African Voices on Slavery and the Slave Trade.* Cambridge: Cambridge University Press, 2013.

———, eds. *African Slaves, African Masters: Politics, Memories, Social Life.* Trenton, NJ: Africa World Press, 2017.

Campbell, Gwyn, ed. *Abolition and Its Aftermath in Indian Ocean Africa and Asia.* London: Routledge, 2005.

Clark, Andrew F. "'The ties that bind': Servility and Dependency among the Fulbe of Bundu (Senegambia), c. 1930s to 1980s." *Slavery and Abolition* 19, no. 2 (1998): 91–108.

Cooper, Frederick. "Conditions Analogous to Slavery: Imperialism and Free Labor Ideology in Africa." In *Beyond Slavery: Explorations of Race, Labor, and Citizenship in Postemancipation Societies,* edited by Frederick Cooper, Thomas C. Holt, and Rebecca J. Scott, 107–50. Chapel Hill: University of North Carolina Press, 2000.

Deutsch, Jan-Georg. *Emancipation without Abolition in German East Africa c. 1884–1914.* Athens, OH: Ohio University Press, 2006.

Echenberg, Myron. *Colonial Conscripts. The Tirailleurs Sénégalais in French West Africa, 1857–1960.* London: Heinemann, 1991.

Eckert, Andreas. "Slavery in Colonial Cameroon, 1880s to 1930s." *Slavery and Abolition* 19, no. 2 (1998): 133–48.

Falola, Toyin. "The End of Slavery among the Yoruba." *Slavery and Abolition* 19, no. 2 (1998): 232–49.

Gyuracz, Veronika. "Comparative Analysis of Contemporary Slavery in West Africa." *European Scientific Journal* (2014): 156–64.

Hahonou, Eric Komlavi. "The Quest for Honor and Citizenship in Post-Slavery Borgu (Benin)." *International Journal of African Historical Studies* 48, no. 2 (2015): 325–44.

Hall, Bruce S. "Bellah Histories of Decolonization, Iklan Paths to Freedom: The Meanings of Race and Slavery in the Late-Colonial Niger Bend (Mali), 1944–1960." *International Journal of African Historical Studies* 48, no. 2 (2011): 61–87.

Hargey, Taj. "Festina Lente: Slavery Policy and Practice in the Anglo-Egyptian Sudan." *Slavery and Abolition* 19, no. 2 (1998): 250–72.

Hillewaert, Sarah. "'Whoever Leaves Their Traditions is a Slave': Contemporary Notions of Servitude in an East African Town." *Africa* 86, no. 3 (2016): 425–46.

Kanya-Forstner, Sydney, and Paul E. Lovejoy. *Slavery and Its Abolition in French West Africa: The Official Reports of G. Poulet, E. Roume, and G. Deherme.* Madison, WI: African Studies Program, 1994.

Klein, Martin A. *Slavery and Colonial Rule in French West Africa.* Cambridge: Cambridge University Press, 1998.

Lecocq, Baz, and Eric Komlavi Hahonou. "Introduction: Exploring Post-Slavery in Contemporary Africa." *International Journal of African Historical Studies* 48, no. 2 (2015): 181–92.

Lovejoy, Paul E., and J.S. Hogendorn. *Slow Death for Slavery: The Course of Abolition in Northern Nigeria, 1897–1936.* Cambridge: Cambridge University Press, 1993.

Lovejoy, Paul E., and Toyin Falola, eds. *Pawnship, Slavery, and Colonialism in Africa.* Trenton, NJ: Africa World Press, 2003.

Lugard, Frederick. "Slavery in All Its Forms." *Africa* 6, no. 1 (1933): 1–14.

MacDougall, E. Ann. "Living the Legacy of Slavery." *Cahiers d études africaines* 45 (2005): 957–86.

Maxwell, David. "Freed Slaves, Missionaries, and Respectability: The Expansion of the Christian Frontier from Angola to Belgian Congo." *Journal of African History* 54 (2013): 79–102.

Miers, Suzanne. *Britain and the Ending of the Slave Trade.* London: Longmans, 1975.

———. "Britain and the Suppression of Slavery in Ethiopia." *Slavery and Abolition* 18, no. 3 (1997): 257–88.

———. "Slavery and the Slave Trade as International Issues 1890–1939." *Slavery and Abolition* 19, no. 2 (1998): 16–37.

———. *Slavery in the Twentieth Century: The Evolution of a Global Problem.* Latham, MD: Altamira Press, 2003.

Miers, Suzanne, and Martin A. Klein, eds. *Slavery and Colonial Rule in Africa.* London: Frank Cass, 1999.

Miers, Suzanne, and Richard Roberts, eds. *The End of Slavery in Africa.* Madison: University of Wisconsin Press, 1988.

Ojo, Olatunji, ed. "The Southern Nigeria Native House Rule Ordinance (1901)." *African Economic History* 40 (2012): 129–36.

Pelckmans, Lotte. "'Having a Road': Social and Spatial Mobility of Persons of Slave and Mixed Descent in Post-Independence Central Mali." *Journal of African History* 53 (2012): 235–55.

———. "Moving Memories of Slavery among West African Migrants in Urban Contexts (Bamako, Paris)." *Revue Européenne des Migrations Internationales* 29, no. 1 (2013): 45–67.

———. "Stereotypes of Past-Slavery and 'Stereo-styles' in Post-Slavery: A Multidimensional, Interactionist Perspective on Contemporary Hierarchies." *International Journal of African Historical Studies* 48, no. 2 (2015): 281–301.

Quirk, Joel. *Unfinished Business: A Comparative Study of Historical and Contemporary Slavery*. Paris: UNESCO, 2008.

Redman, Renee Colette. "The League of Nations and the Right to be Free from Enslavement: The First Human Right to Be Recognized as Customary International Law—Freedom: Beyond the United States." *Chicago-Kent Law Review* 70 (1994): 759–800.

Rodet, Marie. "Escaping Slavery and Building Diasporic Communities in French Soudan and Senegal, ca. 1880–1940." *International Journal of African Historical Studies* 48, no. 2 (2015): 363–86.

Rossi, Benedetta, ed. *Reconfiguring Slavery: West African Trajectories*. Liverpool: Liverpool University Press, 2009.

———. *From Slavery to Aid: Politics, Labour, and Ecology in the Nigerien Sahel, 1800–2000*. Cambridge: Cambridge University Press, 2015.

———. "Dependence, Unfreedom, and Slavery in Africa: Towards an Integrated Analysis." *Africa* 86, no. 3 (2016): 571–90.

Stone, Glyn. "The Foreign Office and Slavery and Forced Labour in Portuguese West Africa, 1894–1914." In *Slavery, Diplomacy, and Empire: Britain and the Suppression of the Slave Trade, 1807–1975*, edited by Keith Hamilton and Patrick Salmon. Brighton: Sussex Academic Press, 2009: 165–95.

Sundiata, Ibrihim K. *From Slavery to Neoslavery: The Bight of Biafra and Fernando Po in the Era of Abolition, 1827–1930*. Madison: University of Wisconsin Press, 1996.

Whyte, Christine. "'Freedom But Nothing Else': The Legacies of Slavery and Abolition in Post-Slavery Sierra Leone, 1928–1956." *International Journal of African Historical Studies* 48, no. 2 (2015): 231–50.

CHAPTER 5

Africans and the Colonial Economy

Moses E. Ochonu

In this chapter, I outline the various ways in which Africans of different vocational inclinations engaged with the colonial economy and with the economic policies and expectations of colonial regimes. How did Africans, as individuals and groups, react to the strictures and opportunities of colonial economics? How did African peasant farmers (producers of export raw materials and consumers of European finished goods) react to colonial schemes to boost agricultural exports? How did African laborers, women, urban traders, and service providers fare in the colonial economy? What specific niches and strictures did colonial agricultural, urbanization, and labor policies wittingly and unwittingly present to Africans? The following analysis answers these questions by surveying the roles and fates of Africans in the colonial economy.

An African colonial proletariat emerged through colonial coercive and appropriative policies and through strategic economic self-repositioning on the part of African workers. African laborers struggled to define and pursue their interests in relation to colonial efforts to maximize labor output while minimizing its cost. Squeezed by colonial pricing, taxation, land, and protectionist policies, African farmers similarly sought to engage with the colonial export economy on their own terms. How do we write the initiatives and self-interested creativity of these Africans into our evaluation of African colonial economies? I provide below some empirical and conceptual roadmaps for understanding the struggles of a wide range of Africans in the expansive orbit of the colonial economy.

M.E. Ochonu (✉)
Department of History, Vanderbilt University, Nashville, TN, USA

© The Author(s) 2018
M.S. Shanguhyia and T. Falola (eds.),
The Palgrave Handbook of African Colonial and Postcolonial History,
https://doi.org/10.1057/978-1-137-59426-6_5

Peasantization and African Initiative

Across Africa's multiple colonial landscapes, a primary goal of colonial economic policy was to encourage export-oriented agricultural production where none had existed and to expand it where it existed prior to colonial conquest. Expanding export production in areas with a tradition of export agriculture was a dicey proposition since it threatened to jeopardize the existing ecological, economic, and social balance of such communities while exposing them to the risk of sacrificing food crops for increased export crop production. Turning African subsistent and semi-subsistent farmers into export-oriented peasants ('peasantization' in the jargon of African economic history) was a difficult, complex, and drawn-out process, requiring multiple mechanisms, some coercive, others persuasive. I begin with a survey of the unfolding of this process, its problems, and the ways in which African initiative and resistance complicated it.

The peasant question (the debate on the extent to which African 'subsistence' producers were turned into peasants and the extent to which they adopted the new export crops preferred by colonial states) has probably loomed larger in colonial African economic history than any other. For dependency theorists, African peasants were sucked into the cash nexus of colonial capitalism and subjected completely to the vagaries of the international market. This perspective has been as controversial as it has been a radical departure from the vent-for-surplus theory of colonial development theorists.[1] Generally, scholars who credit colonial policies with opening up the world economy to African peasants also tend to see precolonial African economies as closed, subsistent or, at best, semi-subsistent agricultural systems. Scholars who view African agriculture at the dawn of colonial conquest as subsistence-based systems of production fall into two categories. Some scholars see 'traditional' or even 'primitive' economies hampered by their mode of production and structure of labor mobilization. Others see subsistence as a pragmatic African response to the absence of markets (or 'vent') for surplus production.[2] Both groups agree that 'subsistent Africans' became peasants through the instrumentality of colonial economic policy.

One question has sustained the debate on African colonial peasantry; that of who, in the context of African colonial economies, is a peasant. Colonial anthropological reports and writings largely cast African producers as crude, subsistence actors in need of market incentives and outlets. This sharp distinction between 'traditional' subsistent production and peasantry (the latter understood as sustained, market-oriented production) reflected colonial understandings of 'backward' African economic practices even though it also sometimes critiqued colonial interventions designed to erase subsistence and semi-subsistence and replace it with market-oriented smallholder production.

This dichotomous perspective was ahistorical. It took hold in spite of evidence from coastal East Africa, Ethiopia, and the Sokoto caliphate of the precolonial existence of agricultural arrangements in which large-scale landholding, rent payment, and market-oriented and surplus production characterized the agricultural system.[3] In Northern Nigeria, the *gandu* system of plantation agriculture provided the basis for transitioning into colonial groundnut export production.[4] In coastal East Africa, especially the Swahili Coast, the messy transformation of a precolonial, export-focused plantation and sharecrop agricultural system into a less successful colonial agricultural system of export cultivation has been documented by Frederick Cooper.[5]

Studies of precolonial, export-oriented agricultural systems in Africa forced a rethink of the reductively simplistic subsistence/peasantry paradigm. Not only were precolonial African peasantries accorded their rightful status; colonial-era African producers, even those who did not explicitly produce for the market, or who only engaged in need-based surplus production, gradually came to be seen as peasant producers. In 1987, when Ralph Austen published his *African Economic History*, his definition of an African peasant clearly reflected this conceptual refinement. African peasants, Austen posited, are 'small-scale agriculture producers occupying their own land'.[6] This conceptual clarification did not answer the question of why some African groups resisted export production because of its risks and uncertainties and remained in subsistent or semi-subsistent production while others embraced export-oriented production with all its instabilities. Different groups of African farmers made different choices in response to colonial export-boosting projects.

African colonial economic history is replete with instances where African producers rejected the strictures and demands (declared and undeclared) of the colonial economy, remained within modes of production that encouraged little if any surplus production, and persisted in smallholder, semi-subsistent cultivation as a matter of strategic choice. This group of African communities became the target of colonial interventions designed to incorporate so-called subsistence producers into the colonial export economy. It is noteworthy that colonial economic policies also sought to expand market production in societies that had traditions of producing for the market or that had willingly embraced the opportunities of the colonial export economy. In other words, colonizers also sought to deepen the integration of societies already connected to the world commodities market.

Mechanisms of Peasantization

Colonial authorities, whether as the political arm of company rule or later as a generic colonial bureaucracy, utilized several mechanisms for expanding African export agriculture production. The provision of transport infrastructure was one incentive of which Africans who wanted to participate in the export economy could take advantage. But this, by itself, proved inadequate for attracting a critical mass of African producers into the colonial export economy. To draw African producers away from semi-subsistence production and to compel market-oriented producers to increase their acreage, colonial economic policymakers deployed multiple tools.

One such measure was the imposition of crop quotas on communities. Quotas were designed in such a way as to hold chiefs and community leaders responsible for achieving them. The incentive for chiefs to compel their subjects to produce the assigned crop quotas was the retention of their positions of privilege in colonial society. The punishment for failure to meet the quota was often dismissal from the position of colonial chief. Another strategy was the seemingly benign distribution of free crop seedlings and the provision of free agricultural extension services. Colonial authorities sometimes adopted this strategy by itself. At other times, they adopted it alternately or simultaneously to crop quota or other coercive measures.

In many colonies, the strategy was to close off alternatives to Africans and compel them to continue their participation in the colonial export economy. Taxation and its strict enforcement made export crop cultivation hard to avoid for many African producers who might have otherwise restricted themselves to the familiar, secure zone of food crop production. In many colonies like Northern Nigeria, European produce buyers and their Levantine, Asian, and African mercantile allies devised a system of advance payment and crop mortgage that kept farmers perpetually indebted to the buyers and ensured that farmers continued to participate in the export economy. Under this system, produce buyers advanced money to farmers to pay their taxes in the dry season before harvest. The farmers in turn mortgaged their harvest against this advance. At harvest, they paid back the 'loan' with all or most of their harvest. They were then forced to obtain yet another advance during the dry season and in the months preceding harvest.[7] The cycle continued, trapping farmers in a conundrum of impoverishment.

In some colonies, authorities adopted forced cultivation, corralling large groups of Africans into plantation-type work gangs on large-scale farms. The Portuguese perfected this brutally coercive method of colonial agricultural production in Angola and Mozambique. In both colonies, they built state-directed colonial economies that came to rest on the forced, large-scale cultivation of cotton and sugarcane for export.[8] Forced cultivation was one extreme in a spectrum of colonial strategies for deepening the participation of African peasants in the colonial export economy. It is worth noting that state-owned agricultural plantations of the Portuguese type were an exception. The British, French, and to a smaller extent the Germans before the First World War tried to establish plantations and to encourage their citizens to set up plantations and settler agricultural communities in several West African colonies with little success. The failure of these early plantation experiments in West Africa reauthorized the strategy of turning African producers into export-oriented peasants and of increasing the production capacity of those Africans who had already embraced export agriculture.[9]

In settler colonies, the strategy of export expansion targeted white farmers, who, by deliberate colonial policy, constituted the basis of colonial export agriculture. In these colonies, colonial authorities sought to ensure the supply of African labor to farms and, more crucially, to prevent Africans who still had access to smallholder plots from competing with settler farmers. Several colonial laws in Kenya prevented African landholders from cultivating coffee, tea, and other crops that the white settler population grew for export.[10] Colonial authorities took similar measures in other East African and Southern African settler colonies. This scenario stands in sharp contrast to the policy adopted in non-settler colonies, where there were no white settler farmers whose interest might provide the overriding impetus for colonial economic management, and where colonial authorities focused, as a result of this absence, on encouraging African producers to restructure their production methods and choices to produce a wide variety of export crops—cocoa, peanut, palm oil, cotton, sesame, and other.

Regardless of whether they were in a settler or non-settler colony, African peasants' economic lots fluctuated wildly during the colonial period. The major catalyst for this economic instability was the fact that the levers of the colonial economy were not in the hands of African producers but in the manipulative grip of colonial authorities as well as in the dynamics of the world economy. African peasants' loss of control over their own economic destinies meant that famines, food shortages, and devastating swings in income levels were common during the colonial period. In many colonies, the biographies of peasants bore out the colonial distortion of rural agricultural life and the cycle of poverty and misery that came to define African peasantry in many colonial territories. In settler colonies, the African peasant was a particular figure of colonial devastation, a stand-in for the instabilities of colonial economic life. Charles van Onselen's biography of Kas Maine, a South African sharecropper, is synecdochical of the colonial transformation of peasantry in Africa.[11]

STRATEGIES OF ECONOMIC CONTROL

The supreme object of colonial economic management was to maintain and reinforce the connection between the economy of the colony and that of the metropolitan country. Keeping the colony's economy dependent on and organically tied to the metropolitan economy entailed strengthening the institutions and practices that increased the demand for and consumption of European manufactured goods and increased the production of exportable crops. Colonial authorities used multiple practices and policy instruments to achieve this goal of tying periphery to metropole economically.

One mechanism was monetization, the introduction of colonial measures of value, mainly currency, and the outlawing of precolonial standards of value and currencies such as manilla, cowrie shells, metal bars, cloth, and others. The introduction of government-issued colonial currencies served several ends. Colonial authorities used it to enforce the payment of taxes in early colonial days when many conquered African groups were struggling to adjust to the unfamiliar routine of taxation. Because tax payment was a compulsory obligation to the colonial government and evasion attracted severe punishment, and because taxes could only be paid in the colonial currency, Africans had no choice but to enter into one or multiple sectors of the colonial economy as a way to earn the colonial currency. The introduction of colonial currencies thus not only minimized the problem of tax evasion; it was also a mechanism for compelling Africans to become laborers on European-owned colonial enterprises, or market-oriented peasant producers.

In addition to monetary connections, African colonial economies had structural ties to the economies of their colonizing countries. The bulk of their exports went to so-called empire markets, markets within the imperial countries' global empire. The bulk of imports also came from within the empire—mostly from metropolitan manufacturers. This reality curtailed the bargaining power of African peasant farmers, reducing the prices of their goods and their income. It also restricted the consumption choices and the range of imported goods available to Africans, compelling them to purchase such goods at uncompetitive high prices. During moments of economic upheaval, colonial authorities escalated this mechanism of protectionist control and regulation, enforcing a policy widely known as Imperial Preference. This was a system of trade tariffs imposed by colonial countries on imports into the colony from countries outside the empire and on exports from the colony to countries outside the empire.

This policy effectively banned the export of African raw materials from British colonies to countries outside the British empire and banned the import of manufactured goods from outside the British empire. Portugal and France used the same instrument to effectively close their African empires to the patronage of countries outside their empires, which were willing to pay more for African exports and sell their imported goods for less. Imperial Preference was used extensively as a system of retaliatory preferential tariffs during the Great Depression and in the brief depression of the 1920s.[12] Preferential imperial tariffs caused the colonies to become cushions for the metropolitan countries in their time of economic distress—at the expense of Africans and their economic aspirations. But even in difficult economic periods, Africans embarked upon ambitious gestures of self-preservation. Many simply exited the formal nodes of the colonial economy; they refused to produce or they reduced their production of colonial cash crops that rendered them vulnerable to colonially mediated vagaries of the world commodities market.

COLONIAL URBANIZATION AND AFRICAN ECONOMIC CREATIVITY

The emergence of colonial towns and cities was a catalyst for an unintended and largely unwelcomed African, urban economy that would become discernibly gendered. Africans made the urban, colonial space the informal entrepreneurial hotbed it became. Colonial towns and cities provided opportunities that Africans seized. Ports, mines, railway stations, and produce-buying stations dotted colonial urban centers, and an urban colonial bureaucratic sprawl, which relied on African low and mid-level labor, served as a magnet for African migration. Urbanization attracted Africans from nearby rural areas and distant hinterlands, but urban opportunities and amenities hardly kept pace with population growth. As a result, urban unemployment rose steadily throughout the colonial period, marked most starkly by the proliferation of urban slums and the ubiquity of economically marginal populations of Africans.

Urbanization also led to the growth of vibrant, informal economies where ingenuity, creativity, and enterprise thrived as unemployed urban dwellers struggled to earn a living on their wits and through petty trading, service provision, and by taking advantage of new niches opened up by the demographic and socioeconomic pressures of colonial urban life. One such niche was sex work. Many single African women, migrants from rural areas who found themselves without formal work in urban centers, and who found few other opportunities in a colonial economy that privileged the labor of men, took to sex work to support themselves.[13] The colonial attitude towards the urban informal economy was ambivalent. On the one hand, colonial authorities feared that unregulated and unbridled urbanization would produce crime and urban squalor, highlight colonial economic problems more sharply, and put pressure on colonial amenities. On the other hand, they recognized that the urban service sector and the services that urban slum dwellers provided were important for replenishing the energy and morale of Africans employed in colonial enterprises. This attitude marked their reaction to sex work, which they condemned in sensational, hyperbolic vocabularies but which they recognized as important to the physical and emotional stability of miners, haulers, railway men, and other African workers in the colonial economy.[14]

AFRICAN WOMEN IN THE COLONIAL ECONOMY

Sex work was not the only arena in which women functioned in the colonial economy. In her book, *African Women: A Modern History*, Catherine Coquery-Vidrovitch documents the numerous ways that African women contributed to the colonial economy and helped sustain their male partners' contributions as laborers or peasant farmers. The Victorian gender ethos of colonial administrators led them to formulate economic policies that marginalized women. Despite the active economic roles that women had played in precolonial societies, colonial authorities saw them only as useful in the domestic realm. Cash crop cultivation, colonial employment, whether in the bureaucracy or in factories, were reserved exclusively for men. The few women who ventured out into the formal workplace were employed only as nannies, wet nurses, and domestic servants for Europeans and, much later, in secretarial jobs considered feminine vocations.[15]

In spite of these strictures, women gradually established themselves as the pivots around which several components of the colonial economy revolved. Women continued to play central roles in the cultivation of cash crops even though colonial authorities took away from them control over the incomes from these crops. In the absence of migrant laborer husbands, women held the family together, cultivating the food crops that their families needed. Given their marginality and unprecedented economic burden during the colonial period, it is a testament to the resilience of African women that they continued to ensure the reproduction of African labor for colonial enterprises.

In the urban sector, women's roles and self-created niches proved particularly important for holding families together and for performing the auxiliary services necessary for urban living.[16] Their petty trading, commercial culinary skills as restaurant owners, their hawking, and their control of the urban leisure and recreation industries gave them a central, indispensable position in the economies of major industrial and urban centers.[17] Thus, despite the marginal roles and positions that colonial economic policymakers imagined for them, African women excelled on many economic fronts, and the actual position of women in the colonial economy was larger and more central than their official status permitted. Some women moved into roles initially reserved for men. Others rebelled against the colonial patriarchal order to create productive economic niches. Yet others thrived in colonial commerce, becoming wealthy and employing many Africans.

The entrepreneurial undertakings of African women in the orbit of colonization, coupled with the vibrant associational platforms that they created for purposes of self-help and economic solidarity, thrust them into prominent economic positions that belied their statutory position in colonial society.[18] Colonial restrictions did not hold back African women. In several respects they regained much of the economic clout they had possessed in many African societies prior to colonization. In some instances, their conditions even bettered their precolonial economic positions, as certain sectors they occupied proved particularly lucrative. The legend of the Nana Benzes, wealthy female traders in colonial and postcolonial West Africa,[19] reflects this paradoxical female economic empowerment in the crevices of the Victorian colonial economy.

Colonial Land Policies and African Livelihoods

In many colonies, settler and non-settler, the land question was the most consequential economic issue. As a result, colonial authorities across the continent often intervened early in the politics of land. Soon after conquest, they acted to regulate and codify land tenure practices and precedents considered favorable to export-oriented agriculture and colonial mining interests. Where land tenure procedures were perceived to be in conflict with colonial agricultural and mining interests, intense interventions in land ensued, unleashing disputes between colonizers and the colonized and among Africans on the maintenance of viable household production and African participation in the colonial export economy.

Several scholars have argued that private property in land was the exception rather than the rule in precolonial Africa and that the codification of land laws by colonial authorities merely legalized a prevailing trend of non-private ownership of land. One of the clearest articulations of this argument comes from political scientist Mahmood Mamdani.[20] Mamdani is correct in calling attention to the prevalence of land tenure practices that depended more on communal control than on individual ownership. He is equally right to assert that colonial 'customary' laws invested indigenous political authorities with despotic powers to regulate access to and transaction in land. But he is only half-right to extrapolate that these 'despotic powers' were actually exercised or that they were always successful in determining land tenure practices on the ground at the colonial grass roots. First, there is now a scholarly consensus on one foundational fact: that with the exception of South Africa, the Rhodesias, and perhaps Kenya (after the colonial conquest), Africa was a 'land-surplus economy', and that the landscape itself was either 'sparsely populated [or] underpopulated'.[21] As a result, there was hardly a struggle over land on a scale that might have necessitated the consistent exercise of juridical powers by local rulers in that respect.

Second, the codification of land tenure by colonial regimes did not preclude the existence of a variety of practices and transactions in land. These land tenure practices evolved in response to colonial realities whose contours were shaped by grass-roots agricultural dynamics rather than colonial logics. Perhaps colonial land policy even led to a proliferation of diverse transactions in land. With regard to Northern Nigeria, for instance, Robert Shenton has shown that a considerable degree of ambivalence characterized British intervention in land matters. It oscillated between attempts by Frederick Lugard, the first governor, to create an indigenous land-owning class and the attempt by his successor, Percy Girouard, to make land a communal possession.[22] Historian Steven Pierce demonstrates that the eventual consensus favoring customary ownership and the symbolic superintendence of chiefs over land foundered because land tenure did not have the valence that the British thought it did, and also because revenue extraction, which was the object of British intervention in land, did not depend on land tenure practices, since the generally high land to labor ratio made land tenure marginal to agriculture.[23] In other words, African peasant farmers often simply ignored colonial land edicts and continued to cultivate agricultural plots over which they had already claimed usage rights. Colonial aims in this domain were therefore doomed to failure.

Land tenure was so porous and was of so little consequence to agricultural production that the British had to move away from land and instead reformed the extant tax system and enacted new tax laws in order to generate much-needed revenue. Adamu Fika notes that the local rulers who, under the land laws of colonial Northern Nigeria, were charged with regulating land tenure, actually resided in provincial capitals, far removed from the centers of production, content with the collection of taxes on grains. This divergence from British teleology attracted reforms aimed at domiciling these local agents of colonialism within the loci of production, but this, too, had little or no impact on land practices.[24]

This trend (the indeterminacy and plurality of rights in land) was more common than outright land ownership systems, in which rights were rigidly defined and understood. These ambivalent regimes of land usage persisted because Africans preferred them to rigid colonial land policies. Sara Berry's findings show that in Southern Ghana and Western Nigeria access to land was controlled by chiefs and lineage groups respectively. But even here, she argues that the increased commercialization of agricultural production of the colonial era brought about a proliferation of rights and claims in land.[25] Similarly, migrant farmers benefited from the delimitation of chiefly territorial jurisdiction in Ghana, as chiefs sought to boost their prestige and revenue base by attracting strangers and granting them favorable sharecropping and land tenure agreements. A similar pattern of increased and liberalized access to land was found in Western Nigeria in the colonial period.[26] African cultivators compelled colonial authorities to come to terms with age-old land usage norms.

In settler colonies, the land question presented a set of new problems for African peasants and settlers alike. Land confiscation to satiate settler hunger for agriculturally viable land produced African victims in the millions. In settler colonies from Kenya to Zimbabwe, land ordinances were the foundations of a racially constituted colonial economy. Like land laws in other settler colonies, South Africa's 1913 land law squeezed out black land-holding farmers from all but a tiny sliver of arable land. In all cases, the colonial politics of land rested on a belief that the economic interests of white settler populations trumped those of blacks and that black land ownership presented a threat to white agricultural profitability and to labor availability. Specifically, colonial authorities, beholden as they were to settler economic interests, feared that black land ownership would produce and nurture a vibrant black peasantry, which in turn would compete with white farmers. Another fear was that black landholding would hurt farm-labor recruitment and jeopardize white settler agriculture.

There was thus an economic logic to land confiscation in settler colonies, a logic that cannot simply be explained by a simplistic invocation of colonial racist ideology. The presence of white settlers determined to use the apparatuses of colonialism to their economic advantage at the expense of the black population predetermined the economic fates of many African groups in settler colonies. This settler economic aggression compounded the economic predicament of many African communities already burdened by the economic obligations of colonial rule. Land was a site to demonstrate white settler privilege, land confiscation a tactic to protect the exclusivity of white export agricultural production. Control over land gave white farmers virtual monopoly over cash crops, and ensured successful labor recruitment from the ranks of displaced and dispossessed African farmers. In Kenya, land confiscation and the conflicts that it triggered between the Kikuyu and the settlers and within Kikuyu society itself produced the Mau Mau anti-colonial uprising.[27]

The contrast between settler and non-settler colonies in the realm of land policy was sharp. In non-settler colonies, African access to land was a crucial plank of colonial economic policy. Here, colonial interventions ranged from attempts to engineer big landholding agriculture to efforts to preserve communal control over land to attempts to encourage secured individual landholding. The goal, however, remained broadly the same: to ensure that Africans had access to cultivable land so they could produce the agricultural raw materials that colonial authorities hungered for. In the settler colonies, by contrast, Africans' continued access to land outside the restrictive purview of state policy stood in the way of colonial economic priorities, and so the goal was to restrict it. In mineral-producing settler colonies like South Africa and Zimbabwe, the hunger for cheap African labor intensified the imperative for restricting African land access.

FORCED LABOR, LABOR MIGRATION, AND 'STABILIZED' LABOR

Another arena in which the colonial economic project is often located, and where it is said to have demonstrated its efficacy, is the use of forced labor and the imposition of other labor regimes on African communities. This happened extensively in different colonial territories in Africa. British colonial authorities used forced labor extensively in railway and road construction.[28] So did the French. The British colonialists used forced labor on a massive scale in South Africa to solve the acute labor problem that developed with the boom in gold and diamond mining.[29]

British colonizers claimed that they did not indulge in forced labor practices after the international labor conference of 1930 banned the practice, and contrasted their labor policies to French labor recruitment methods.[30] But

Frederick Cooper argues that the British, much like the French, who were less pretentious in their reliance on forced labor, continued to rely on coerced labor in periods of economic and political emergencies. A significant period of economic emergency that saw the British plucking African labor by force was the Second World War.[31] Francois Manchuelle has argued that the first wave of migration among the Soninkes of modern Senegal and Gambia in the colonial period took the migrants to the French navy, where they served mostly as sailors but sometimes as ship hands. Known in local parlance as *laptots*, the rank of these migrants had swollen in the 1890s as the French recruited manumitted slaves, and later during the world wars.[32] Later, the *laptot* system birthed a culture of labor migration to French colonial enterprises.

It is important to note, however, that this trend of young Africans taking advantage of participation in colonial enterprises to enhance their personal social and economic worth was greater in some areas than others. For instance, the Southern African colonies, South Africa in particular, provided young African men with few choices to participate in the colonial economy in a transactional framework. In Zambia and Mozambique, where the policy of forced labor, known as *chibaro*, was pursued with a ferocious fervor comparable to that of the French *corvée* system in West Africa, Africans had little space to maneuver.[33] Furthermore, the on-the-job maneuverability of Southern African workers in the South African mines and, to a lesser degree, the Rhodesian gold mines, was curtailed by racist legislation and policies. In South Africa this took the form of pass laws, vagrancy laws, influx control laws, the compound system, and other race-based restrictive legal instruments.

In spite of these stringent conditions, however, Black miners used the practice of flight and mobility to occasionally defeat the restrictive control mechanisms of mines management and colonial authorities. Patrick Harries's work shows how some Mozambican migrants to the South African mines used migration to acquire resources that enabled them to become retailers of consumer goods at home, while others were able to acquire formal Western education and set themselves up in mission and educational work.[34] In Northern Nigeria, labor migration from cash-crop-poor regions to the tin mines on the Jos Plateau became the lifeline for many young men from those regions, enabling them to build modest lives for themselves.[35] These kinds of unforeseen economic consequences should mitigate any reification of colonial hegemonic claims and shift the analysis from colonial intentions and calculations to Africans' strategic use of colonial institutions and policies for their own ends.

As widespread as coerced labor was in colonial Africa, it was never considered an ideal form of labor recruitment, only a crude, desperate method to get colonial work done. In British Africa, forced labor was gradually rolled back. In French and Portuguese colonies, forced labor persisted for a longer period until at least 1930, when the international labor organization took an interest in the matter and banned it. After that, the use of forced labor, even in the French and Portuguese colonial empires, became sporadic. Corvée, the French system of forced labor, persisted in scattered, diminished forms. In much of colonial Africa, a system of migrant labor evolved and replaced forced labor or gradually came to coexist with it. Africans in rural areas were given incentives and compelled by colonial obligations to migrate from rural homelands to mining centers, port cities, and other centers of colonial work. Colonial firms gave the laborers short-term contracts, housed them in hostels, and expected them to return to their rural ancestral homes at the end of their contracts. Colonial authorities supported migrant labor because it was cheap and was technically unforced, saving money and reputation.

Like forced labor, migrant labor had its drawbacks for the colonial economy, which complicated its theoretical advantages. Migrant laborers quickly evolved into a sort of 'floating population'. Migrants, in theory and according to the desire of colonial authorities, should return to their ancestral homelands when their labor contracts ran out. But many did not. The philosophy of mandatory return, as colonial thinkers understood it, was anchored on several problematic assumptions. Many studies conducted by colonial ethnographers and semi-independent anthropologists concluded that young African men (laborers and migrant workers) were tied to their rural homelands by 'tribal' cultural obligations, that the social cohesion of these rural enclaves was worth preserving, and that their return to these rural sites of origin would not only ensure the preservation of rural communities but also enable rural peasant agriculture, the mainstay of many colonial economies, to thrive undisturbed. To these early colonial ethnologists, excessive immersion in colonial institutions and cultures, such as the colonial culture of permanent, disciplined work, would damage 'tribal' African societies.[36]

Colonial policymakers and their anthropological allies counseled that migrant workers from rural hinterlands were not suited to urban life and should not be given permanent employment in urban centers of mining, mechanized agriculture, or seaports. This logic sustained a colonial obsession with migrant labor. Early colonial anthropological studies posited the influential 'target worker' thesis, which held that Africans, unlike European workers, only worked as long as it took them to earn enough to meet a target or need.[37] Once the need was met, it was argued, Africans no longer wanted to work but craved a return to the stability and certainty of their rural homelands. This thesis provided the anthropological and philosophical underpinning for colonial migrant labor practices. It justified short-term contracts as being in line with Africans' cultural predilections. It also justified paying African workers poor wages because of the assumption that, if paid fair wages, African workers would meet their so-called targets quickly, abandon their contracts, and return home to their families. The added advantage of labor migrancy, from the colonial perspective, was that it foreclosed the expenses that come with permanent employment.

Although colonizers swore by its efficacy as a labor recruitment mechanism, migrant labor proved burdensome and became a public relations disaster once the conditions of hostel-housed workers were known to the wider world. The migrant labor system had other problems, too. As determined as they were to maintain migrant labor flows and to control the back and forth movement of workers from rural areas to colonial workplaces, colonial authorities lacked the legal and logistical tools to remove migrant workers who would not return to their ancestral homelands at the end of their contracts. The number of these self-asserting urban laborers and out-of-work young men was increasing. As early as the 1920s, migrant squatter camps and shantytowns began to proliferate around mining, railway, and seaport towns. Along with the development of this unwanted effect of urbanization came crime, prostitution, drunkenness, drug abuse, and other social vices associated with undisciplined urbanization and unbridled rural-urban migration. By the late 1930s, labor migration as a template of colonial labor recruitment was a failure. It began to cost colonial authorities more to remove shantytowns, to fight the crimes that festered in them, and to provide urban amenities than it would cost them to offer permanent labor contracts to African workers.

There was another rather obvious disadvantage to migrant labor: male African migrant workers were not as productive and 'settled' as they could be because they lacked stability, family support, and spousal services that would make them more productive and committed to their work. They were required to leave their wives and children in their rural homelands and were thus deprived of the emotional stability necessary for a productive work life. This disadvantage made a strong economic case for moving away from migrant labor. Together with the other stated unforeseen consequences of rural-urban labor migration, this economic pitfall of labor migration convinced colonial capitalists and colonial administrators that migrant labor was anachronistic and did more socio-economic harm than good. Starting in the late 1930s, colonial authorities embraced the policy of labor stabilization, under which African laborers were given permanent labor contract and encouraged to settle, along with their families, in the urban vicinity of their workplaces—mostly in accommodations provided by their employers.[38]

The transition from migrant labor to stabilized labor also entailed a 'shift from large-scale unskilled labour to a smaller and better-paid skilled force'.[39] Colonial mining companies and other employers saw the potential for training African laborers to become more effective workers, for professionalizing the workforce and thus increasing its productivity. Pioneered by the Union Minière copper mines of Katanga in the Belgian Congo, labor stabilization spread gradually to several other colonies in both British and French Africa. Even the Northern Rhodesia (Zambia) copper mines, which had considered but rejected full labor stabilization, gradually came to treat its migrant laborers as though they were stabilized labor and came to tolerate and recognize the reality that the migrants were no longer guests but settled residents of mine towns.[40]

Labor stabilization solved the problem of labor recruitment and high labor turnover for many colonial employers, but it created new problems. Like migrant laborers, stabilized African workers asserted themselves in ways that challenged colonial expectations. Stabilized labor cost more to maintain and retain. And even though the stabilized laborers were not allowed to organize themselves into unions and were under company control, they had rights and began to act on them. They increasingly became aware of their poor conditions vis-à-vis their rights. This awareness transformed into catalytic labor awakening and activism. From 1939 to 1948, labor agitation spiked across Africa, and paralyzing general strikes rocked Senegal and Nigeria.[41] African workers, stabilized to varying degrees, began to make demands and to picket their workplaces. Some constituted informal unions. Some unions (like those in South Africa and in the colliery of Enugu, Nigeria) became so powerful that mines management had no choice but to recognize and seek dialogue with them.[42]

Frederick Cooper contends persuasively that the labor activism of African workers, especially after the legalization of unions in postwar French and British Africa, snowballed into a full-fledged demand for equal compensation between equivalent white and black workers. This in turn morphed into agitations for decolonization, as labor leaders transformed into nationalist figures and as the labor question was reframed as a nationalist question with expanded demands for autonomy, self-rule, and independence.[43]

Conclusion

The results of colonial economic schemes and policies were mixed, complicated by African maneuverings, resistance, and actions, which were motivated by self-interest and self-preservation. In the four key domains of land tenure, agriculture, urbanization, and labor mobilization, this was particularly true. For the most part, Africans were pushed to the margins of colonial economies, taking their place as producers of agricultural raw materials, laborers, trade middlemen, and operatives in the informal service sector. But Africans, often as a result of their own strategic maneuvering, transcended the roles carved out for them in the colonial economy. They forged new economic paths as innovative urban women, as creative, strategic peasants, and as assertive laborers.

Africans, men and women, rebelled against the strictures of the colonial economy and took advantage of new, mostly unintended opportunities to better themselves to the extent allowed by colonial racism. Some African peasants avoided the colonial export markets altogether, or withheld their crops when prices were low. For their part, African custodians of land subtly resisted colonial tinkering with land usage norms, and those who desired access to land as a way of participating in the colonial export economy insisted on securing access through time-honored and flexible mechanisms, not through rigid, colonially legislated land rights that were frozen in law or in the hands of newly appointed chiefs. African laborers, for their part, resisted colonial attempts to order their existence and work life according to colonial interests or understandings, and when they acquiesced to the work regimes of colonial authorities, they pushed for rights and protections that transgressed the overarching climate of colonial racism.

In settler colonies, the politics of land and labor were particularly charged and intertwined. The two sites were platforms for demonstrating white-settler economic privilege and for displacing Africans from the lucrative loci of the economy. Africans were forcefully removed from their lands in order to turn them into colonial laborers; confiscated land needed to be worked by African laborers in order to generate agricultural profits for settlers and revenues for colonial governments. Often, the success of colonial economic measures, even in settler colonies, depended on the coerced or strategic cooperation of African workers and superintendents of communal land. Africans' cooperation depended on the extent to which they hoped to benefit from the measures and on clear indications that colonial schemes would not adversely affect their economic interests.

African groups had an infinite capacity to render colonial economic policies ineffectual on the ground, regardless of official rhetoric. Colonial archives are full of self-congratulatory claims about European efforts to turn African workers into time-disciplined work machines, and African farmers into agents of export-oriented agricultural raw material production. But the same colonial archives are also full of official frustrations and disappointment at the refusal of Africans to go along with aspects of colonial economic policies and colonial demands that they considered too economically risky or exploitative.

Notes

1. Dependency theory was partly a reaction to the arguments of colonial development theorists. The principal proponent of the vent-for-surplus theory of African colonial economic change is A.G. Hopkins. His book, *Economic History of West Africa* (London: Longman, 1973), argues that colonial authorities provided a vent, a profitable outlet for Africans' latent and idle productive capacity by, among other things, building roads, establishing market relations, and introducing currency.
2. Hopkins, *An Economic History of West Africa*.
3. Paul Tiyambe Zeleza, *A Modern Economic History of Africa, volume 1, the Nineteenth Century* (Dakar: Codesria Book Series, 1993), 8–9.
4. Mohammed Bashir Salau, *The West African Slave Plantation: A Case Study* (New York and London: Palgrave Macmillan, 2011).
5. Frederick Cooper, *From Slaves to Squatters: Plantation Labor and Agriculture in Zanzibar and Coastal Kenya, 1890–1925* (New Haven: Yale University Press, 1981).
6. Ralph Austen, *African Economic History* (London and Portsmouth: Heinemann, 1987), 122.

7. See Robert Shenton, *The Development of Capitalism* (London: James Curry, 1986); Michael Watts, *Silent Violence: Food, Famine, and Peasantry in Northern Nigeria* (Berkeley: University of California Press, 1983); Moses Ochonu, *Colonial Meltdown: Northern Nigeria in the Great Depression* (Athens: Ohio University Press, 2009), chap. 2.
8. Allen Isaacman, *Cotton Is the Mother of Poverty: Peasants, Work, and Rural Struggle in Mozambique 1938–1961* (Portsmouth, NH: Heinemann, 1995); Gervase William Clarence-Smith, *Slaves, Peasants, and Capitalists in Southern Angola, 1840–1926* (Cambridge: Cambridge University Press, 1979).
9. Marion Johnson, "Cotton Imperialism in West Africa," *African Affairs* 73, no. 291 (1974): 178–87; Richard Roberts, *Two Worlds of Cotton: Colonialism and the Economy in French Sudan, 1800–1946* (Stanford: Stanford University Press, 1996); Richard Roberts and Allen Isaacman eds., *Cotton, Colonialism, and Social History in Sub-Saharan Africa* (Portsmouth, NH: Heinemann, 1995).
10. Tabitha Kanogo, *Squatters and the Roots of Mau Mau, 1905–63* (Athens: Ohio University Press, 1987).
11. Charles van Onselen, *The Seed Is Mine: The Life of Kas Maine, a South African Sharecropper, 1894–1985* (New York: Hill and Wang, 1996).
12. Ibid., chap. 1.
13. See Luise White, *The Comforts of Home: Prostitution in Colonial Nairobi* (Chicago: Chicago University Press, 1990); Lynn Thomas, *Politics of the Womb: Women Reproduction, and the State in Kenya* (Berkeley: University of California Press, 2003); Moses Ochonu, "Masculine Anxieties, Cultural Politics, and Debates over Independent Womanhood Among Idoma Male Migrants in Late Colonial Northern Nigeria," *Interventions* 13, no. 2 (2011): 278–98; Catherine Coquery-Vidrovitch, *African Women: A Modern History* (Boulder, CO: Westview Press, 1997).
14. Moses Ochonu, "Masculine Anxieties;" Luise White, *The Comforts of Home*.
15. Jeane Penvenne, *African Workers and Colonial Racism: Mozambican Strategies & Struggles in Lourenco Marques, 1977–1962* (Portsmouth, NH: Heinemann, 1994); Coquery-Vidrovitch, *African Women*.
16. "Women in the Changing African Family," in *African Women South of the Sahara*, ed. Margaret Jean Hay and Sharon Stichter (London and New York: Longman, 1984), 64–67.
17. See Emily Osborne, *Making States: Power, Gender, and Colonial Rule in Kankan-Baté, West Africa, 1650–1920* (Athens: The Ohio University Press, 2011); Coquery-Vidrovitch, *African Women*.
18. Audrey Wipper, "Women's Voluntary Associations," in *African Women South of the Sahara*, ed. Margaret Jean Hay and Sharon Stichter, 69–86.
19. John Heilbrunn, "Commerce, Politics, and Business Associations in Benin and Togo," *Comparative Politics* 29, no. 4 (1997): 473–92.
20. Mamdani, *Citizen and Subject: Contemporary Africa and the Legacies of Late Colonialism* (Princeton: Princeton University Press, 1996), 138–40.
21. See Anthony Hopkins, "The World Bank in Africa: Historical Reflections on the African Present," *World Development* 14, no. 2 (1986): 1479.
22. Robert Shenton, *The Development of Capitalism in Northern Nigeria*, 33–46.
23. Steven Pierce, Looking for the Legal: Land, Law, and Colonialism in Kano Emirate, Nigeria (PhD diss., University of Michigan, 2000).

24. Adamu Fika, *Kano Civil War and British Over-Rule, 1882–1940* (Ibadan: Oxford University Press, 1978).
25. Sara Berry, *No Condition Is Permanent: The Social Dynamics of Agrarian Change in Sub-Saharan Africa* (Madison: University of Wisconsin Press, 1993), 104–8.
26. Ibid., 107–8.
27. Kanogo, *Squatters and the Roots of Mau Mau.*
28. See, for instance, Michael Mason's discussion of extensive use of forced labor in the construction of a railway network in Nigeria. Michael Mason, "Working on the Railway: Forced Labor in Northern Nigeria 1907–1912," in *African Labor History*, ed. Peter Gutkind, Cohen Robin, and Jean Copans (New York: Sage Publications, 1978), 56–79.
29. See Moitsadi Moeti, "The Origins of Forced Labor in the Witwatersrand," *Phylon* 47, no. 4 (1986): 276–84.
30. Frederick Cooper, *Decolonization and African Society: The Labor Question in French and British Africa* (Cambridge: Cambridge University Press, 1996), 28.
31. David Killingray, "Labor Mobilization in British Colonial Africa for the War Effort, 1939–46," in *Africa and the Second World War*, ed. Killingray and Richard (New York: Saint Martin Press, 1986), 68–96, 77.
32. Francois Manchuelle, *Willing Migrants: Soninke Labor Diasporas 1848–1960* (Athens: Ohio University Press, 1997), 130–31.
33. See Charles Van Onselen, *Chibaro: African Mine Labour in Southern Rhodesia 1900–1933* (London: Pluto Press, 1976); Patrick Harries, *Work, Culture, and Identity: Migrant Laborers in Mozambique and South Africa, c.1860–1910* (Portsmouth, London, and Johannesburg: Heinemann, James Curry Ltd., and Witwatersrand University Press, 1994); and Manchuelle, *Willing Migrants.*
34. Harries, *Work, Culture, and Identity*, 83–108.
35. W.M. Freund, "Labour Migration to the Northern Nigerian Tin Mines 1903–1945," *Journal of African History* 22, no. 1 (1981): 73–84.
36. See, for instance, David M. Goodfellow, *Principles of Economic Sociology: The Economics of Primitive Life as Illustrated by the Bantu Peoples of South and East Africa* (London: G. Routledge & Sons, 1939); Max Gluckman, *Custom and Conflict in Africa* (London: The Free Press, 1955); J. Clyde Mitchell, Elizabeth Colson, and Max Gluckman, eds., *Human Problems in British Central Africa: The Rhodes-Livingstone Journal* XIX (1955). The studies conducted by the anthropologists hired and funded by the Rhodes-Livingstone Institute (RLI), which began operations in 1937, proved particularly useful for British colonial authorities in South-Central and Southern Africa. For a critical review of the connections between colonial policies and the works of the Institute, and of how the anthropological studies produced by it shaped colonial economic policies regarding labor and urbanization, see Lynette Schumaker, ""A Tent with a View": Colonial Officers, Anthropologists, and the Making of the Field in Northern Rhodesia, 1937–1960," *Osiris*, 2nd ser., 11 (1996): 237–58. Max Gluckman, who was a director of the Institute, and other anthropologists viewed African cultures and peoples as repositories of "tribal" customs and of functional "tribal" dynamics that excessive colonial intrusions and the inordinate penetration of colonial cultures of work and production into

Africans' lives would destroy. The following passage from the second page of Schumaker's article illustrates the colonial purpose of these early anthropological studies on African peoples, cultures, customs, and needs: "In the 1930s the governor of Northern Rhodesia, keen on the potential uses of anthropology for solving problems of social change in the colony, pushed for the founding of an anthropological institute and garnered support for it from local sources such as the mining companies. After World War II, this institute became part of the British government's postwar colonial development effort and was lavishly funded by the Colonial Social Science Research Council (CSSRC). This enabled the RLI to recruit a team of talented young anthropologists, most of whom were working for their doctorates. The RLI's first directors set out to create a coordinated program of applied anthropology useful for colonial development."

37. David M. Goodfellow, *Principles of Economic Sociology*, 242.
38. Cooper, *Decolonization and African Society*.
39. Ralph Austen, *African Economic History* (London and Portsmouth: Heinemann, 1987), 166.
40. Ibid., 167.
41. Cooper, *Decolonization and African Society*.
42. Keletso Atkins, *The Moon Is Dead! Give Us Our Money! The Cultural Origins of an African Work Ethic, Natal, South Africa, 1843–1900* (Portsmouth, NH: Heinemann, 1993); Caroline Brown, *"We Are All Slaves": African Miners, Culture, and Resistance at the Enugu Government Colliery, Nigeria* (Portsmouth, NH: Heinemann, 2002); Edward Roux, *Time Longer than Rope: A History of the Black Man's Struggle for Freedom in South Africa 2nd edition* (Madison: University of Wisconsin Press, 1967).
43. This is the central thesis of Frederick Cooper's *Decolonization and African Society*.

Bibliography

Atkins, Keletso. *The Moon Is Dead! Give Us Our Money! The Cultural Origins of an African Work Ethic, Natal, South Africa, 1843–1900*. Portsmouth, NH: Heinemann, 1993.
Austen, Ralph. *African Economic History*. London and Portsmouth: Heinemann, 1987.
Berry, Sara. *No Condition Is Permanent: The Social Dynamics of Agrarian Change in Sub-Saharan Africa*. Madison: University of Wisconsin Press, 1993.
Brown, Caroline. *"We Are All Slaves": African Miners, Culture, and Resistance at the Enugu Government Colliery, Nigeria*. Portsmouth, NH: Heinemann, 2002.
Clarence-Smith, Gervase William. *Slaves, Peasants, and Capitalists in Southern Angola, 1840–1926*. Cambridge: Cambridge University Press, 1979.
Cooper, Frederick. *From Slaves to Squatters: Plantation Labor and Agriculture in Zanzibar and Coastal Kenya, 1890–1925*. New Haven: Yale University Press, 1981.
———. *Decolonization and African Society: The Labor Question in French and British Africa*. Cambridge: Cambridge University Press, 1996.
Coquery-Vidrovitch, Catherine. *African Women: A Modern History*. Translated by Beth Gillian Raps. Boulder, CO: Westview Press, 1997.

Fika, Adamu. *Kano Civil War and British Over-Rule, 1882–1940*. Ibadan: Oxford University Press, 1978.
Freund, W.M. "Labour Migration to the Northern Nigerian Tin Mines 1903–1945." *Journal of African History* 22, no. 1 (1981): 73–84.
Gluckman, Max. *Custom and Conflict in Africa*. London: The Free Press, 1955.
Goodfellow, David M. *Principles of Economic Sociology: The Economics of Primitive Life as Illustrated by the Bantu Peoples of South and East Africa*. London: G. Routledge & Sons, 1939.
Harries, Patrick. *Work, Culture, and Identity: Migrant Laborers in Mozambique and South Africa, c.1860–1910*. Portsmouth, London, and Johannesburg: Heinemann, James Curry Ltd., and Witwatersrand University Press, 1994.
Heilbrunn, John. "Commerce, Politics, and Business Associations in Benin and Togo." *Comparative Politics* 29, no. 4 (1997): 473–92.
Hopkins, Anthony. "The World Bank in Africa: Historical Reflections on the African Present." *World Development* 14, no. 2 (1986): 1479.
———. *An Economic History of West Africa*. London: Longman, 1973.
Isaacman, Allen. *Cotton Is the Mother of Poverty: Peasants, Work, and Rural Struggle in Mozambique 1938–1961*. Portsmouth, NH: Heinemann, 1995.
Johnson, Marion. "Cotton Imperialism in West Africa." *African Affairs* 73, no. 291 (1974): 178–87.
Kanogo, Tabitha. *Squatters and the Roots of Mau Mau, 1905–63*. Athens: Ohio University Press, 1987.
Killingray, David. "Labor Mobilization in British Colonial Africa for the War Effort, 1939–46." In *Africa and the Second World War*, edited by Killingray and Richard, 68–96. New York: Saint Martin Press, 1986.
Mamdani, Mahmood. *Citizen and Subject: Contemporary Africa and the Legacies of Late Colonialism*. Princeton: Princeton University Press, 1996.
Manchuelle, Francois. *Willing Migrants: Soninke Labor Diasporas 1848–1960*. Athens: Ohio University Press, 1997.
Mason, Michael. "Working on the Railway: Forced Labor in Northern Nigeria 1907–1912." In *African Labor History*, edited by Peter Gutkind, Cohen Robin, and Jean Copans. New York: Sage, 1978.
Mitchell, Clyde J., Elizabeth Colson, and Max Gluckman, eds. *Human Problems in British Central Africa: The Rhodes-Livingstone Journal* XIX (1955).
Moeti, Moitsadi. "The Origins of Forced Labor in the Witwatersrand." *Phylon* 47, no. 4 (1986): 276–84.
Ochonu, Moses. *Colonial Meltdown: Northern Nigeria in the Great Depression*. Athens: Ohio University Press, 2009.
———. "Masculine Anxieties, Cultural Politics, and Debates over Independent Womanhood Among Idoma Male Migrants in Late Colonial Northern Nigeria." *Interventions* 13, no. 2 (2011): 278–98.
Osborne, Emily. *Making States: Power, Gender, and Colonial Rule in Kankan-Baté, West Africa, 1650–1920*. Athens: The Ohio University Press, 2011.
Pierce, Steven. Looking for the Legal: Land, Law, and Colonialism in Kano Emirate, Nigeria. PhD diss., University of Michigan, 2000.
Roberts, Richards. *Two Worlds of Cotton: Colonialism and the Economy in French Sudan, 1800–1946*. Stanford: Stanford University Press, 1996.

Roberts, Richard, and Allen Isaacman, eds. *Cotton, Colonialism, and Social History in Sub-Saharan Africa*. Portsmouth, NH: Heinemann, 1995.

Roux, Edward. *Time Longer than Rope: A History of the Black Man's Struggle for Freedom in South Africa 2nd edition*. Madison: University of Wisconsin Press, 1967.

Salau, Mohammed Bashir. *The West African Slave Plantation: A Case Study*. New York and London: Palgrave Macmillan, 2011.

Schumaker, Lynette. ""A Tent with a View": Colonial Officers, Anthropologists, and the Making of the Field in Northern Rhodesia, 1937–1960," *Osiris* 11, 2nd ser., (1996): 237–58.

Shenton, Robert. *The Development of Capitalism*. London: James Curry, 1986.

Thomas, Lynn. *Politics of the Womb: Women Reproduction, and the State in Kenya*. Berkeley: University of California Press, 2003.

van Onselen, Charles. *Chibaro: African Mine Labour in Southern Rhodesia 1900–1933*. London: Pluto Press, 1976.

———. *The Seed Is Mine: The Life of Kas Maine, a South African Sharecropper, 1894–1985*. New York: Hill and Wang, 1996.

Watts, Michael. *Silent Violence: Food, Famine, and Peasantry in Northern Nigeria*. Berkeley: University of California Press, 1983.

White, Luise. *The Comforts of Home: Prostitution in Colonial Nairobi*. Chicago: Chicago University Press, 1990.

Wipper, Audrey. "Women's Voluntary Associations." In *African Women South of the Sahara*, edited by Margaret Jean Hay and Sharon Stichter, 69–86. London and New York: Longman, 1984.

Zeleza, Paul Tiyambe. *A Modern Economic History of Africa, volume 1, the Nineteenth Century*. Dakar: Codesria Book Series, 1993.

CHAPTER 6

African Women in Colonial Economies

Judith A. Byfield

African women, as Iris Berger notes, were fully engaged in the economic life of their communities. Whether traders, farmers or craft-makers, women contributed to the production and distribution of goods that sustained village life and urban spaces, local markets, and regional hubs. However, colonial officials were often blind to women's economic contributions and the consequences of their policies on African women.[1] Since the pioneering work of Ester Boserup, Margaret Jean Hay and Claire Robertson, women have been better represented in African economic history and we have a much fuller picture of how colonial economic policies transformed their household responsibilities, workload, and economic opportunities.

Our understanding of African colonial economies is being further enhanced by the recent renaissance in African economic history.[2] The resurgence of interest in African economic history is welcome because scholars are using new technologies to digitize and transcribe vast amounts of data such as the British colonial *Blue Books*, tax censuses, and marriage registers that facilitate research on education, public finance, and population shifts during the colonial period.[3] The new African economic history does not have to reproduce the silences in colonial archives for it is unfolding at an auspicious time in the study of African women and gender. As social historians pay greater attention to topics such as marriage, children, and urbanization they shine a

---

I would like to thank Margot Lovett and James Fenske for their generous comments on an earlier draft of this essay.

J.A. Byfield (✉)
Cornell University, Ithaca, NY, USA

© The Author(s) 2018
M.S. Shanguhyia and T. Falola (eds.),
The Palgrave Handbook of African Colonial and Postcolonial History,
https://doi.org/10.1057/978-1-137-59426-6_6

brighter light on women's economic activities within and beyond the household as well as the ways in which colonial policies shaped these activities.[4] Together, the renewed attention to African economic history and studies on African women and gender refine our understanding of how women contributed to and supported, and in some instances subsidized, the colonial economy even if colonial officials did not always see them.

THE COLONIAL STATE AND ECONOMY

This chapter's main concern is the colonial period; therefore, it is important to begin with some consideration of the colonial state and its policies. Crawford Young argues that all colonial states faced similar imperatives even though the outcomes varied tremendously over time and space. African colonial states at the end of the nineteenth century had to create administrative structures and establish economies that produced revenue for the colonial state as well as resources that integrated these regions into larger imperial networks.[5] Scholars dispute the extent of the reach and administrative capacity of colonial states to control their subjects, with some, like Young, insisting that the colonial state was hegemonic while others argue, like Jeffrey Herbst, that it was weak and unable to broadcast its power.[6] The opposing reflections on the African colonial state do not represent different types of states; rather, Bruce Berman suggests, both qualities existed within the same state. Though the relative strength or weakness of the colonial state varied within each territory and over time, African colonial states straddled two levels of articulation, 'between the metropole and the colony, and, within the latter between introduced forms of capitalist production and the various indigenous modes'.[7] Colonial officials had to help create and protect opportunities for capital accumulation among competing European interests, maintain social and political control over African populations often disrupted by the methods of accumulation, and ensure that the entire enterprise unfolded with little cost to European treasuries. Colonies had to produce revenue quickly to essentially pay for themselves.[8]

In order to better integrate African colonies into their imperial networks that supplied resources or markets to metropolitan industries, colonial officials had to create the infrastructure to facilitate the movement of goods out of and into the colonies. However, just as the reach of colonial power was uneven, so was colonialism's economic geography. Colonies sometimes held multiple forms of economic enterprises: plantations, extractive mining industries, coerced cash-crop production, and dynamic peasant production.[9] Where and how women would be integrated into these enterprises depended on a number of variables including the preexisting economic structures, cultural prescriptions and expectations, and colonial state formation. Periodization was equally important. The early colonial period in many cases opened new opportunities for some women, but many enterprises contracted in the face of the interwar economic depression and the Second World War. The

Depression and the war threatened the colonial economic foundation as income plummeted, leading officials to apply increased pressure on African populations to pay taxes and to increase production of commodities deemed essential to the war effort. In the postwar period, colonial states, partly in response to African political demands, invested in development strategies and increased spending on education. A number of women benefited from this social spending, but it did not radically alter the unequal economic structures created during the early decades of colonial rule.

Constructing the Colonial Economy

Commodities had to be collected and moved toward ports or vice versa; therefore, infrastructure dominated the minds of colonial officials. Large-scale infrastructure projects such as roads and railways dotted the continent. Colonial records often made note of the thousands of men who participated in these projects. In the Congo Free State, the government imported construction workers from British and French territories in West Africa, Hong Kong, Macao, and British Caribbean colonies to begin work on the railway in 1892.[10] In French West Africa, railway construction began in the 1880s and by the first decade of the twentieth century, thousands of miles of railway lines connected Senegal, the Soudan (Mali), French Guinée, Ivory Coast, and Dahomey to ports along the Atlantic Ocean.[11] By the 1890s, Britain also invested in railways connecting the protectorates of Northern and Southern Nigeria in West Africa and in its East African colonies of Kenya and Uganda. Nonetheless, the density of the railways in Africa never matched that of Europe, since they were created for extracting products rather than integrating regions.[12] While railways were vital to the consolidation of the colonial state and economy, the significance of roadways to the colonial project cannot be underestimated, for as Herbst suggests, 'roads ... more than railroads or waterways, brought the most profound changes to African society'.[13] The expanding network of railways and roads, 'reinforce[d] ties with the metropole, [bound] disparate territories together and integrated colonial economies into the world market'.[14] These infrastructure projects also helped determine how state formation would affect different societies and different social groups. Men dominated the work sites of the colonial state. Some were brought in under coercive labor regimes while others were hired as skilled and unskilled labor. In some instances, women were part of forced labor crews even though few traces exist of them in the records.[15] Women's labor became invisible while road construction, railways, and ports became unquestioned male occupational preserves.

Colonial states also required a fiscal infrastructure to bring revenue into their treasuries. In some colonies the bulk of the state's revenue derived from import and export taxes. Colonial governments taxed the main exports: cocoa, cotton, peanuts, palm oil, and rubber. They also taxed items imported for an expanding African consumer base. Leigh Gardner argues that the 'desperate need for revenue along with some colonial officials' desire to bring Africans into the market economy, led most colonial administrations ... to impose direct taxation on Africans from the first years of colonial rule'.[16] Officials created either a flat-rate 'hut tax' on African dwellings or a poll tax paid by African men. These tax systems reflected the idea that the man was the head of the household and responsible for women's head tax, thus reinforcing an idealized notion of women's dependent status. In South Africa, in particular, officials hoped to force men to do 'monetarily productive labor while women concentrated on domestic duties'.[17] Nonetheless, there were exceptions and in Western Nigeria women in several Yoruba communities were taxed independently of men.[18] In some instances, taxes could be paid in kind. In French Guinée in 1896, for example, the military required that districts in the Southern Soudan make tax payments in rubber as part of their effort to dissuade traders from taking their rubber to Sierra Leone.[19] By the end of the First World War, taxes were largely paid in currency, thus accelerating the monetization of colonial economies and forcing tax payers into wage labor, cash-crop production, or other sectors mediated by European currencies.

Women, Cash Crops, and the Colonial Economy

Agricultural production dominated most colonial economies. Although food production for the domestic market remained critical, colonial officials were most concerned with the production of export crops for these were major revenue earners. The main exports included: cocoa, peanuts, cotton, rubber, and palm oil. Production practices varied and created different outcomes for women.

The history of cocoa production in West Africa is a remarkable story of African-led agricultural innovation, but it also illuminates the ways in which women remained largely invisible in the history of this commodity. In 1892, Ghana did not export any cocoa beans, yet by 1911 it had become the world's largest producer of cocoa, exporting 40,000 tons annually. By 1936, Ghana's output surpassed 300,000 tons.[20] The rapid expansion of cocoa production here, and in other parts of West Africa including Nigeria and Ivory Coast, was in part due to technological as well as cultural transformations unfolding in Europe and North America. Cory Ross argues that the real breakthrough began in the 1880s when 'global transport and rising purchasing power in Europe converted cocoa from a luxury article into an item of mass consumption'.[21] Small-holder farmers led the development and rapid expansion of cocoa production in Ghana and other parts of West Africa in the face of colonial doubts about their ability to respond to market demands.

Scholars sought to explain how 'countries like Ghana could very rapidly increase their export production without apparently reducing their existing economic activities, nor benefiting ... from massive immigration'.[22] Building on Hla Myint's vent-for-surplus theory, some scholars argued that these communities had idle hands and idle land and farmers abandoned leisure pursuits in order to invest in cocoa production; or it occurred in local circumstances that had unusually dense populations and less intense labor demands for crops produced for domestic use.[23] However, Gareth Austen demonstrates that these assumptions were faulty and argues instead that cocoa took off because farmers redeployed labor away from less profitable export lines, such as palm products, artisanal gold mining, or the production of inexpensive textiles, and toward cocoa production.[24] Women contributed to the establishment of early cocoa farms. They planted food crops, such as plantain and cocoyams, that provided the shade essential to the growth and protection of young cocoa plants. Moreover, a small group of women featured among the early cocoa entrepreneurs. They tended to be elderly and single, and independent of obligations to lineage elders and husbands.[25]

Asante women's involvement in cocoa production increased; however, for many of them their greater investment in cocoa corresponded to a loss in status. Jean Allman and Victoria Tashjian demonstrate that as new areas were colonized for cocoa farms and households lost access to dependent forms of labor such as pawns after 1908, husbands drew increasingly on the labor of their wives. In addition, families often pawned dependent girls in order to raise capital for cocoa farms. As a result, an increasing number of women entered marriage as pawn-wives in the early twentieth century, and the cultural distinction between free-wife and pawn-wife collapsed.[26]

Women's unremunerated labor was matched by their invisibility in the economic histories of cocoa production in other parts of West Africa as well. In Nigeria, Yoruba women also contributed to cocoa production, especially during the harvest. They spent as much as eight hours daily fetching water, carrying the crops and cooking for all those engaged in farm work, but they did not self-identify as farmers or receive remuneration.[27] It has taken the work of scholars of gender to illuminate women's critical role in the adoption and expansion of cocoa production as well as its social consequences.

The early colonial period also coincided with the tremendous demand for rubber. Rubber played a central role in the engines that supported the Industrial Revolution, the beginning of the automobile industry as well as telecommunications and electrical expansion, for it provided insulation for telegraph, telephone, and electrical wiring.[28] Moreover, rubber products proved vital to leisure culture for it was used in sporting devices, especially bicycles, and shoes. Before the development of synthetic rubber, manufacturers of rubber implements relied on natural rubber derived from trees and vines. Brazil dominated the rubber market. The commercial sale of African rubber only began in the 1850s; however, by the end of the nineteenth century King Leopold's Congo Free State became the second largest rubber exporter after Brazil. Other parts of West Africa and Central Africa (Sierra Leone, Gold Coast, Gabon, Nigeria, Liberia, French Guinée, and Northern Rhodesia) also exported rubber to the international market.[29]

In Africa rubber grew wild and men performed the tasks of locating and tapping rubber vines. In many places individual male entrepreneurs took advantage of the worldwide demand for rubber. In Southern Nigeria, Saros, African returnees from Sierra Leone invested initially in rubber production around Lagos while Christian converts were among those who first participated in rubber extraction as it moved inland.[30] In Benin Province, the Nigerian colonial government established communal plantations to help stem the destructive tapping carried out by tappers from other regions, and both Europeans and Africans established rubber plantations using local and imported plants.[31] In French Guinée men gathered the rubber sap and also dominated the sale and distribution networks that conveyed rubber to Freetown and later Conakry.[32]

Women's role in the rubber economy varied considerably. In French Equatorial Africa, women carried and sold rubber in the markets. Germaine Krull, an avant-garde photographer, captured scenes of African women in markets outside of Brazzaville during the Second World War.[33] In the Congo Free State, where rubber lay at the center of an extraordinarily brutal colonial regime, women played critical though indirect roles in the rubber economy. The concession companies that received control over significant portions of the colony set rubber collection quotas that kept men away for weeks at a time. On average, villages in areas controlled by the Anglo-Belgian India Rubber Company (ABIR) were assigned 'three to four kilos of dried rubber per adult male per fortnight'. This translated into full-time work for the men in those villages, while men in the areas controlled by the Société Anversoise du Commerce au Congo spent about 24 days a month in the forest.[34] Rural women assumed more work in order to try to maintain food production for their households and to meet the company's demands for food. For example, villagers near the ABIR concession had to provide food to feed the soldiers. They were expected to deliver 15 kilos of yams, five pigs, or fifty chickens. While men were away searching for rubber and unable to clear new garden plots, women often replanted crops on nutritionally exhausted fields. As a result, yields declined and famine increased.[35] The agricultural work women performed in maintaining households, farms and villages while men left in search of rubber vines ultimately disappear in narratives constructed primarily around the volume of rubber production or the brutality embedded in the system. In the process, women's contribution to the maintenance of the colonial economy also disappears from the record.

Cotton was an important export crop from many colonies. While rubber and cocoa production developed with colonialism, cotton production had been a long-standing activity and formed the base upon which thriving textile industries existed in different parts of the continent. Scholars believe that cotton was grown, spun, and woven in the region of Nubia between the third century BCE and fourth century CE.[36] Cotton grew wild in the hinterland around Luanda in Angola. Peasants did not cultivate it: however, they collected the wild cotton, spun it into thread, and wove it into cloth for personal use and trade.[37] In West Africa farmers cultivated cotton as early as the tenth century CE. Colleen Kriger notes that West Africans grew cotton from the coast to the Sahel, a substantial region that crossed and connected numerous trade routes and production zones.[38] US and European abolitionists in the nineteenth century became interested in the commercial potential of African cotton for they imagined that it could address several social and economic issues. Thomas Bowen, a US missionary who worked in Yorubaland from 1849 to 1856, argued that commerce and cotton production could end the slave trade as well as revolutionize African households by ending polygyny and domesticating wives.[39]

In the western region of Nigeria, small and large farmers took advantage of missionary efforts to promote cotton production and export to Britain, though it did not lead to the full social transformation missionaries anticipated. Cotton production relied heavily on slave labor locally and did not transform Yoruba women into dependent partners within African households.[40] European industry's continued demand for cheap cotton ensured colonial interest in the commercial potential of African cotton and encouraged what Marion Johnson called cotton imperialism: crush the local weaving industry, export the raw cotton that would have been woven locally, and transform redundant weavers into cotton producers.[41]

The nature of cotton production varied. Among the Baule in Ivory Coast, cotton was a women's crop. After men (husbands, sons) cleared the field, women planted yams and intercropped corn, cassava, and cotton among the yam mounds. Women owned the products of these fields and could dispose of surplus as they saw fit once they had met the family's subsistence needs. In the case of cotton, women carded it and spun it into thread before giving it to male weavers.[42] In Hausa communities in Niger, on the other hand, men controlled the production of cotton; nonetheless, men had an obligation to provide cotton for their wives and other female dependants. Thus, very different social practices gave women control over cotton.[43]

During the colonial period many colonial states invested in efforts to increase the production of cotton for metropolitan factories. In Togo, German officials hired four African Americans from Tuskegee University to train the Togolese to produce cotton for export.[44] In the French Soudan and Egyptian Sudan, officials created large-scale irrigation schemes, the Office du Niger and Gezira, respectively. Both projects relied on forced settlement for their workforce.[45] In the Belgian Congo, colonial officials relied on compulsory production, and rural women in polygynous households shouldered most of the burden of cotton production. Women were heavily involved as well in transporting cotton to trading stations and roads.[46] In Malawi's Tchiri valley, however, the colonial state did not have to resort to compulsory labor. Both men and women in different household formations (monogamous, polygynous, female-headed) integrated cotton production into the existing system of food production. Cotton provided an important avenue of income generation in order to pay taxes. Equally important, Elias Mandala notes that cotton's significance grew because the consolidation of the colonial state and economy narrowed other opportunities to generate cash. The creation of forest reserves, for example, closed opportunities for hunting while the importation of pots and salt contributed to the decline in manufacturing of these items.[47]

Despite women's multifaceted roles in the production of cotton, they are not very visible in colonial narratives of its production. In many societies women derived their access to land through marriage, therefore their hold on land was tenuous especially as land became commoditized. Equally important, colonial officials directed their promotion of cotton production toward men. In the case of the Baule, the French used forced production as well as taxation. Men's need to pay taxes helped to make women's continued role in cotton production invisible.[48] Tax payer, Osumaka Likaka argues, was an administrative category that imposed a colonial, patriarchal worldview. In 1914, Belgian officials passed a decree making the 'healthy adult male' a unit of labor for all industry, labor, and taxation. The category hid women's central role, as well as that of children, in cotton cultivation by suggesting that only the male head of the household grew cotton. This administrative category made husbands and fathers the interface between the colonial state and the household while enhancing male power within the household and over the distribution of cotton money.[49]

While colonial officials did little to note women's contribution to cocoa, rubber, and cotton, women's contribution to palm-oil production was conspicuous, for women processed the palm fruit into palm oil and the inner seed into palm kernel oil. Missionary accounts and later colonial reports acknowledged women's important role in processing the palm fruit. Palm-oil production was usually done within the household and the bulk of the oil produced belonged either to the man who owned the tree or the man who picked the fruit. Women kept what they needed for household use, but they owned the kernels.[50] Men picked the palm fruit; however, 'women carried it to the processing centers, picked the palm seeds from the thorny fruits, fetched water and firewood, boiled and pounded the seeds, extracted oil from the fiber and nuts, separated the fiber from the nuts, and cracked the nuts to produce the palm kernels'.[51] Both items were staples during the era of legitimate trade and remained important commodities into the colonial period. However, as the commercial value of palm products grew, men assumed greater control of palm fruits. Gloria Chuku argues that Igbo men assumed ownership of oil palms, control of palm produce, and new technology, such as palm oil presses and nut-cracking machines, introduced during the colonial era. Women's right to palm kernels remained protected as did their ability to earn cash from the export of palm kernel oil until the expansion of oil mills in the post-Second World War period.[52]

Cash crops did not lead to one outcome for all African women. Some women who were landholders, such as Cãndida da Silva Senna (Dona Cãndida) in Guinea Bissau, took advantage of expanding trade opportunities. Da Silva exercised a monopoly over the trade in rubber, beeswax, and rice in the borderland region between Cacheu and southern Casamance.[53] In Buganda, some women benefited from cotton production and became independent (albeit short-lived) landholders and cotton farmers.[54] Nonetheless, for the great majority of women, cash-crop production relied increasingly on women's uncompensated labor.

Women, Wage Labor, and the Colonial Economy

Taxation played a critical role in expanding African investments in cash crops; it also proved essential to the creation of wage labor. Throughout the colonial period, men dominated wage labor in all sectors: education, trading companies, mines, railways, agriculture, skilled and unskilled government positions. The wages men received were not family wages; they were designed to cover the worker's day-to-day reproduction.[55] As a result, women played a significant role in subsidizing the expansion of wage labor across the continent.

Men dominated mine jobs in the Copperbelt, which extends from the northern part of Northern Rhodesia into the Belgian Congo,[56] the diamond and gold mines in South Africa and the coalmines of Nigeria. In Belgian Congo women were not employed in the mines, but the state relied on women to produce food for mine workers. Women's agricultural labor directly subsidized the cost of social reproduction on the mines. Rural communities, including regions already part of the cotton scheme, were forced to produce food for the mines. Communities were assigned quotas to fulfill and women transported the food to the mines, thus compounding the invisible work they did in support of the mining industry.[57]

Women who lived on the mining compounds as wives of miners also subsidized the mining industry in part by providing a stable home life for their husbands. Although most mining companies resisted the additional costs of providing housing for wives and children, the Copperbelt mines such as Roan Antelope Copper Mine were forced to allow dependants to accompany their husbands, for they were competing for labor with Union Minière in Katanga and Broken Hill Mine in Northern Rhodesia, which allowed miners to bring their families. They also faced competition from the mines in Southern Rhodesia and South Africa that paid higher wages, though they did not allow dependants.[58]

In addition to creating an environment that enabled men to be more productive, married women also supplemented men's salaries through the sale of home-brewed beer. Although the Northern Rhodesian government encouraged mining officials to limit beer brewing so that beer halls could benefit from men's leisure activity, women continued to brew beer.

Mining companies also tried to increase income-generating activities for women. They invited missionary groups into the mine compounds to work with women by teaching them cooking, hygiene, baby care, laundry, as well as handicraft skills that enabled them to stretch their husbands' salaries.[59] Women on the Copperbelt mining compounds helped foster and create the conditions that enhanced productivity and therefore profits.

In Southern Rhodesia wives were not welcome in the mining compounds. Nonetheless, Schmidt revealed the complex ways in which women in Goromonzi District near Salisbury helped build and subsidize the colonial economy. Goromonzi District was distinctive because it was adjacent to a major urban center as well as many mines. The increasing demand for food in the city and at the mines, as well as the outbreak of the South African War which cut off food supplies, helped a thriving African peasantry to develop. As a result, between 1890 and 1912, the bulk of the fresh produce and grain came from African peasants in Southern Rhodesia. Women's customary crops (including green vegetables, potatoes, and groundnuts) added to the miners' diets.[60] African peasants increased the acreage under cultivation and the production of surplus in spite of the migration of men. Schmidt showed that women were largely responsible for the increasing surplus since this was accomplished without the introduction of new technology. Women's customary activities such as beer brewing also became income-generating as women now sold their beer to mine workers. In some instances, women withdrew from agricultural work and hired men to work in their place for beer brewing proved so profitable.

However, by the end of the first decade of the twentieth century, this window of profitable peasant production closed considerably. Colonial officials moved decidedly against African peasant producers in order to bolster settler production. The state took away the most fertile and well-watered land and successive beer laws outlawed the sale of beer in the urban center and on the mine compounds. Miners also expressed a greater desire for ground maize instead of millet, and in order to compete with settler-produced maize, peasants introduced plows which substantially increased women's work. Plows increased the area under cultivation as well as the tasks women and children performed: planting, hoeing, weeding, harvesting, and grinding. Moreover, the peasant economy was greatly affected by the increase in hut taxes, rents, grazing, and dipping fees. By the 1930s, even though peasant production remained high, the value of their crops had declined and male wages became the mainstay of peasant households.[61] The depression also brought about a decline in wages as mines and factories closed. In the face of increasing impoverishment, women entered the workforce as agricultural labor. Some were hired as seasonal workers, but others were hired to perform piecework. Women and children in agricultural work received less payment than men involved in the same tasks. Wage labor in these instances did not replace the unremunerated work women performed on household fields.

Thus, women subsidized the extremely low wages offered to men on multiple fronts simultaneously.[62]

Kikuyu women in Kenya also joined the agricultural wage workforce. Kenya did not have mines; nonetheless, the expansion of settler farms created a significant demand for labor. Some of that demand was satisfied with the creation of the hut tax and through tenant or 'squatter' farmers. The First World War increased labor scarcity as African men were conscripted into the army as porters. In order to fill this vacuum, settlers successfully convinced colonial officials to 'encourage' African women and children to work on coffee plantations. Kikuyu women and children were forced to work on plantations where they often suffered physical and sexual assault. Most of the women and children who worked on the coffee plantations lived in the nearby African reserves to which they returned at night. Working on the coffee plantations did not relieve them of their responsibilities in subsistence farming on the reserves, especially since the coffee harvest coincided with the peak season in peasant agriculture.[63] Overall, our knowledge of women wage earners in the rural workforce awaits greater investigation. John Sender, Carlos Oya, and Christopher Cramer, who examined female wage earners in rural Mozambique in the first decade of the twenty-first century, noted that most scholars still assume rural wage earners are male, even though women (especially single women due to divorce, widowhood, or separation) comprise a significant sector of the workforce. Life histories collected from survey participants reveal that several generations of women had been engaged as casual wage laborers.[64] In addition to working on the farms, some women obtained domestic jobs. In Southern Rhodesia, a small number of African women were employed within settler households as domestic servants. Some remained in Southern Rhodesia, but some ventured into South Africa where they worked on white farms in rural Transvaal close to the Rhodesian border.[65]

Women had few opportunities in the wage labor sectors largely due to European gender prescriptions. Industrial positions in the mines were all male, and very few manufacturing opportunities existed on the continent outside of South Africa. Although women in South Africa participated in industrial work, they were concentrated in certain sectors. Most of them were employed in the textile and garment factories and food-processing industries. Companies initially hired Afrikaner women; however, as they expanded in the 1920s and 1930s, they brought in Colored women. African women would be hired following the postwar expansion of manufacturing.[66] The Second World War proved critical to women's expanding role in manufacturing. During the war new industrial sectors including engineering firms and munitions plants brought in women as emergency workers. Initially restricted to semiskilled jobs, women eventually moved into skilled jobs especially after 1942. However, because they were female their wages were reduced. In 1941, the government went a step further and instituted the practice of paying a lower rate to all women regardless of their job on the basis of their sex: 75% of that of men. South African women in the industrial workforce faced a wage structure that was structured by both race and gender. This wartime contingency had lasting consequences for jobs were reclassified in ways that reflected a deskilling and devaluation of these positions.[67]

The Second World War and postwar development plans stimulated the development of manufacturing in certain colonies. In Ivory Coast, the Gonfreville textile factory actually began production in 1923; however, it was not until 1950 that it began to hire women workers. Entrance into wage labor reflected a radical shift for Baule women who were once producers and owners of cotton and thread. Under colonialism, women became involved in the production of cotton as a cash crop that supplied Gonfreville and ultimately workers in the factory that supplied the cloth they purchased.[68]

A small number of African women held professional positions. African women began to be trained as nurses in Southern Rhodesia in the late 1920s.[69] Those aspiring to professional training did not have to travel to Britain for they could receive it in South Africa.[70] In Nigeria and Ghana, elite African families began sending daughters to London for education in the nineteenth century. Though a small but influential group of women emerged in these colonies and began to organize socially for improved educational opportunities for women, very few were employed either by the state or private firms. In Nigeria, teaching opportunities for women opened slowly in the second decade of the twentieth century. There were 17 female teachers in primary schools in 1912 and by the late 1940s Lagos boasted a total of 260 female primary school teachers in mission-led schools.[71] By the 1920s, Nigerian women began to receive training in Western midwifery and nursing; while many trained in Lagos, some completed British diplomas. These Western-trained nurses could expect to be hired by local authorities, private clinics, or the government hospitals. By the 1930s, women had branched into social work and journalism, but their movement into the civil service and professions like law did not happen until the postwar period.[72]

Limited educational opportunities for girls were essentially repeated across the continent, though the periodization differed. In Uganda, all the schools run by missionary societies as well as the school for the daughters of paramount chiefs stressed domesticity; in other words, preparing girls to be good wives. They were encouraged to be 'diligent mistresses of efficient households ... keep their homes and children clean ... feed their families in nutritious [ways] ... sew and do handicrafts'. In 1928 there were only 26 female elementary school teachers in the country, though the figure would rise to 90 by 1933.[73] In French West Africa, women's access to medical training, specifically midwifery, began relatively early. Blaise Diagne, the first African representative to the French Chamber of Deputies, spearheaded the establishment of the first school of midwifery in Africa in 1918: L'Ecole des sages-femmes.[74] The vast majority of women, however, did not receive Western education and were not literate in the language of the colonial state.

Moreover, the number of educated African women and those engaged in professions deemed appropriate for elite women remained very low throughout the colonial period.

Women Entrepreneurs, Urban Space, and the Colonial Economy

The colonial economy relied on women's labor in agriculture to subsidize cash-crop production and male wage labor. Therefore, policymakers (often at the behest of male authorities) tried to restrict women's movements as well as their ability to live beyond male authority. In Southern Rhodesia, women in Goromonzi District left the rural areas in response to the growing impoverishment of the interwar depression and the intensified demands on their labor. Some fled to towns, mines, and European farms.[75] Framing the young women, often single or in a temporary relationship, as promiscuous and vectors of venereal diseases, the colonial state used public-health policies to try to control their influx. The Public Health Act of 1925, for example, made medical examinations compulsory for African women who were seeking employment, or were already employed or living, in certain areas.[76]

Despite the efforts to contain them in the countryside, women took advantage of migration as economic and social agents, for migration offered more opportunities to earn cash incomes that could help support their families in economically depressed rural areas. Migration also enabled these women to pursue their own strategies for marriage, becoming social adults and creating their own households. Thus, as Karen Jochelson reminds us, women were not passive participants in this exodus from rural locations.[77]

In cities, women found work in the interstices of urban economy: processing and selling food, brewing beer, providing accommodation, and sex services. Most were individual entrepreneurs, though significant economic divisions existed. Some women traders were merchants. They obtained credit from European trading firms, rented stores in the markets, and they hired others to assist them in their business. At the other extreme you had women who barely eked out an existence from their trade. Very often, food sellers were at the bottom of the hierarchy of trade. These women did not have access to credit, relied on assistance from their children or other dependants, and sold on the street because they could not afford the fees to trade in the established markets. Abosede George, Claire Robertson, and Gracia Clarke show that whether we examine the colonial or postcolonial era, for these women, trade was much more about survival than accumulation.[78]

Cultural expectations also shaped the nature of the activities women performed in urban centers. In Uganda, women began to move into cities in the 1920s. They could not get hired for jobs involving manual labor since both British and African men considered these jobs inappropriate for women; in addition, opportunities to sell food and beer were restricted as many migrant women did not have the capital to get started and both British and African men concluded that women should not be involved in the sale of alcohol. Therefore, men were the primary beer brewers in Uganda.[79]

In Nairobi, women had a wider range of opportunities that collectively supported the social reproduction of male workers while providing incomes. Women brewed beer, cooked food, and provided accommodation, for a number of them had invested in property. Many female landlords had been involved in sex work and practiced *malaya*: indoor sex work that often involved domestic services such as meals and laundry.[80] In West Africa, where urbanization had a much longer history, the number of women involved in sex work increased as colonial rule consolidated. In Lagos, a significant number of sex workers migrated to the capital from the immediate hinterland and from parts of Eastern Nigeria like the Cross River Basin. Benedict Naanen attributes the migration of women from Cross River to Lagos and further afield (Cameroon, Gold Coast, Fernando Po) to a number of factors. Though marginal to the colonial economy, this region primarily produced palm oil and women's agricultural burden increased with the imposition of taxes. Migrating for sex work allowed capital accumulation and enabled women to build homes and acquire rents which they used to maintain their dependants. It was not unusual for sex workers to provide the financing to establish their brothers in petty trading. In addition, not all communities saw prostitution as an offence.[81]

A different set of opportunity structures existed for many Yoruba women in Lagos and in the hinterland. In Yoruba society, women as a matter of course were engaged in trade or manufacturing. Yoruba culture required husbands to provide start-up capital for their wives; in addition, since women often pursued the same trade as their mothers, senior women helped them to become established. The introduction of cocoa proved significant to the expansion of trade and manufacturing in some Yoruba towns. In Abeokuta, for example, wealth from cocoa increased the level of consumption, especially of imported items like cloth. In the early decades of the twentieth century, the indigo-dyeing industry flourished as dyers purchased imported cloth and dyed it in highly desired indigo patterns.[82]

Women traders played a significant role in creating colonial cities and expanding the reach of European commodities into African interiors. Robertson notes that women traders and farmers 'were ... key actors in the development of the trading and market gardening system' that fed Nairobi.[83] Women sold dry staples such as maize and beans, vegetables as well as milk, and English potatoes. Some were involved in long-distance trade and others traded daily and returned to their homes at night. Women also traded in imported items such as cloth and soap. The structure of trade was not static, and by the 1930s women became increasingly confined to local trade in the markets, while better-capitalized men traveled around as wholesalers and sold from shops or tea stands.[84]

In many West African societies, women have historically dominated (and still do) the internal markets selling agricultural items, cooked food, as well as a range of imported items from soaps to beauty products to cloth. The textile trade best illustrates the critical role women played in expanding the market for and consumption of European products. Abeokuta's indigo dyers indigenized inexpensive cotton cloth when they created resist-dyed patterns on them. Europeans also had to learn what factors African consumers valued most, such as quality, durability, and price. Moreover, they had to develop an appreciation of African aesthetic values. They introduced patterns drawn from other world regions, as in the case of the Dutch wax prints,[85] they copied the visual effects of African indigo dyeing techniques as well as the geometric patterns on woven raffia.[86] Wax prints, as Paulette Young argues, 'became one of the most lucrative commercial exchanges of the Dutch-Gold Coast'.[87] Women proved central to this commercial relationship because many Dutch merchants married African women, thus benefiting from their social and economic networks. Equally importantly, women named these cloths, thus transposing a foreign import into a product with local meaning and cultural value.[88] Seamstresses further transformed these textiles into clothing that communicated age, status and aspiration within rapidly evolving colonial societies.[89]

The large pool of self-employed women who fall into what scholars call the informal economy played a vital part in the colonial economy. They linked colonial markets and imperial commodities. They were central conduits between rural producers and urban consumers. As significantly, women's agricultural and commercial work subsidized low wages that could not sustain households and dependants. Those subsidies translated into profits for mine owners, settler farmers, European trading companies, as well as tax revenue for the colonial state.

Conclusion

Women played critical roles in colonial economies whether or not they were visible to colonial officials or in colonial records. As this chapter has demonstrated, their contributions were both direct and indirect. West African women traders expanded the markets for European consumer items and processed cash crops for export. In some areas women paid taxes, but where women did not pay taxes directly, they contributed through cash or labor to men's tax payments. Women's greatest contributions to colonial economies may have been in the indirect ways in which they provided maintenance to critical economic sectors. In East and Southern Africa, many women maintained rural economies that prepared new generations of young men for migrant labor systems, and received those too old or infirm to toil in the mines or on the farms. This maintenance, Margaret Jean Hay argues, reflected one way in which women subsidized the colonial economy. In meeting rural food requirements and helping to supply food to labor migrants in town, while colonial officials extracted capital and labor from the rural economy, women in western Kenya subsidized the settler economy.[90] Similarly, women who provided food to miners and soldiers in the Belgian Congo directly subsidized the mining sector.

The nature of the colonial economy as well as European and African gender expectations significantly shaped women's economic activities and their control over resources. In many communities, gender ideals sanctioned men's access to women's labor and the products of that labor. Moreover, the colonial state often intervened to uphold male and generational privileges. However, women were not passive participants. Some women challenged new labor regimes that demanded more of their time or efforts to restrict their mobility. Some pushed back on men's attempts to move into sectors once considered women's spaces, while others created new economic opportunities. In the process, women helped to define and shape colonial economies.

Despite the richer picture we have of African women in colonial economies, many areas require further research. Coumba Mar Gadio and Cathy Rakowski argue, for example, that most scholarship on cash crops focuses on those produced by men for export; few examine cash crops produced for local markets by women.[91] Even where technology is providing new data, gender still shapes the information. Using data culled from *Blue Books*, Ewout Frankema and Marlous van Waijenburg suggest that real wages increased during the colonial period for urban, unskilled African men in many of Britain's African colonies. Moreover, workers would have been able to sustain a nuclear household of five people above subsistence levels. While tantalizing, the authors acknowledge that their assumptions are arbitrary and their comprehension of the purchasing power of African households lacks crucial information, such as the earnings from female and child labor.[92] The lack of data on earnings by women and children also impairs the new studies on taxes. Gardner's study of taxation in the British empire, for example, is insightful on many levels; yet it fails to grapple with the fact that the tax structure was predicated on an assumed male dominance over household resources and dependent labor.[93] Thus, theorizing taxation as an individual male obligation rather than a household obligation involving husbands, wives, and children provides an imperfect understanding of the full consequences of colonial tax policies. In 2009, when Anthony Hopkins drew attention to the renaissance in African economic history, he argued that the turn toward gender and race had been a distraction to scholarship on economic history.[94] While studies on gender and race were not the most compelling reasons for the decline, it is clear that gender as well as race are vital to the work of economic historians if they aspire to document economic history as experienced by historical actors.

Notes

1. Iris Berger, *Women in Twentieth Century Africa* (New York: Cambridge University Press, 2016), 10–11.
2. See: Ester Boserup, *Women's Role in Economic Development* (New York: St. Martin's Press, 1970); Margaret Jean Hay, "Luo Women and Economic

Change During the Colonial Period," in *Women in Africa: Studies in Social and Economic Change,* ed. Nancy Hafkin and Edna Bay (Stanford: Stanford University Press, 1976), 87–110; Claire Robertson, *Sharing the Same Bowl: A Socioeconomic History of Women and Class in Accra, Ghana* (Bloomington: Indiana University Press, 1984). For more on the renaissance in African economic history see: A.G. Hopkins, "The New Economic History of Africa," *Journal of African History* 50, no. 2 (2009); Gareth Austin and Stephen Broadberry, "Introduction: The Renaissance of African Economic History," *Economic History Review* 67, no. 4 (2014): 893–906; James Fenske, "The Causal History of Africa: A Response to Hopkins," *Economic History of Developing Regions* 25, no. 2 (2010): 177–212; A.G. Hopkins, "Causes and Confusions in African History," *Economic History of Developing Regions* 26, no. 2 (2011): 107–10; Daron Acemoglu, Simon Johnson, and James A. Robinson, "The Colonial Origins of Comparative Economic Development: An Empirical Investigation," *The American Economic Review* 91, no. 5 (2001): 1369–401; and Daron Acemoglu, Simon Johnson, and James A. Robinson, "Reversal of Fortune: Geography and Institutions in the Making of the Modern World Income Distribution," *Quarterly Journal of Economics* 117, no. 4 (2002): 1231–94. For important critiques see Gareth Austin, "The 'Reversal of Fortune' Thesis and the Compression of History: Perspectives from African and Comparative Economic History," *Journal of International Development* 20, no. 8 (2008): 996–1027; and Hopkins, "New Economic History," 162–70.
3. Johan Fourie, "The Data Revolution in African Economic History" *Journal of Interdisciplinary History* XLVII, no. 2 (2016): 207.
4. See for example: Saheed Aderinto, *When Sex Threatened the State: Illicit Sexuality, Nationalism, and Politics in Colonial Nigeria, 1900–1958* (Urbana: University of Illinois Press, 2014); Abosede George, *Making Modern Girls: A History of Girlhood, Labor, and Social Development in Colonial Lagos* (Athens: Ohio University Press, 2014); and Emily Osborn, *Our New Husbands Are Here: Households, Gender and Politics in a West African State from the Slave Trade to Colonial Rule* (Athens: Ohio University Press, 2011).
5. Crawford Young, *The African Colonial State in Comparative Perspective* (New Haven: Yale University Press, 1994), 35–42; Bruce Berman and John Lonsdale, "Coping with the Contradictions," in *Unhappy Valley: Conflict in Kenya and Africa.* Eastern African Studies (Athens: Ohio University Press, 1992), 80.
6. For different perspectives on the strength of the colonial state see: Young, *The African Colonial State in Comparative Perspective* (New Haven: Yale University Press, 1994); Mahmood Mamdani, *Citizen and Subject: Contemporary Africa and the Legacy of Late Colonialism* (Princeton: Princeton University Press, 1996); and Jeffrey Herbst, *States and Power in Africa,* 2nd ed. (Princeton: Princeton University Press, 2014), 58–96.
7. Bruce Berman and John Lonsdale, "Crises of Accumulation, Coercion and the Colonial State: The Development of the Labour Control System, 1919–1920," in *Unhappy Valley: Conflict in Kenya and Africa.* Eastern African Studies (Athens: Ohio University Press, 1992), 103–4.
8. Leigh A. Gardner, *Taxing Colonial Africa: The Political Economy of British Imperialism* (Oxford: Oxford University Press, 2012), 23–26.

9. Frederick Cooper, "Conflict and Connection: Rethinking Colonial African History," *American Historical Review* 99, no. 5 (1994): 1529.
10. Adam Hochschild, *King Leopold's Ghost: A Story of Greed, Terror, and Heroism in Colonial Africa* (Boston: Houghton Mifflin, 1999), 170–71.
11. Michael Crowder, *West Africa Under Colonial Rule* (Evanston: Northwestern University Press, 1968), 276.
12. Frederick Cooper, *Africa Since 1940: The Past of the Present* (Cambridge: Cambridge University Press, 2002), 101.
13. Herbst, *States and Power*, 54. See also Elizabeth Wrangham, "An African Road Revolution: The Gold Coast in the Period of the Great War," *Journal of Imperial and Commonwealth History* 32, no. 1 (2004): 1–18.
14. T. W. Roberts, "Republicanism, Railway Imperialism, and the French Empire in Africa, 1879–1889," *Historical Journal* 54, no. 2 (2011): 402. See also David Sunderland, "The Departmental System of Railway Construction in British West Africa, 1895–1906," *Journal of Transport History* 23, no. 2 (2002): 87–112.
15. Judith Byfield, "Taxation, Women and the Colonial State: Egba Women's Tax Revolt," *Meridians* 3, no. 2 (2003): 258.
16. Leigh A. Gardner, "Decentralization and Corruption in Historical Perspective: Evidence from Tax Collection in British Colonial Africa," *Economic History of Developing Regions* 25, no. 2 (2010): 214–15.
17. Mona Etienne, "Women and Men, Cloth and Colonization: The Transformation of Property Relations among the Baule (Ivory Coast)," *Cahiers d'Etudes Africaines* 17, no. 65 (1977): 54. See also Sean Redding, "Legal Minors and Social Children: Rural African Women and Taxation in the Transkei, South Africa," *African Studies Review* 36, no. 3 (1993): 57.
18. Byfield, "Taxation, Women, and the Colonial State"; Marjorie McIntosh, *Yoruba Women, Work, and Social Change* (Bloomington: Indiana University Press, 2009), 226–34; and Nina Mba, *Nigerian Women Mobilized: Women's Political Activity in Southern Nigeria, 1900–1965* (Berkeley: University of California Press, 1983).
19. Emily Lynn Osborn, "'Rubber Fever': Commerce and French Colonial Rule in Upper Guinée, 1890–1913," *Journal of African History* 45, no. 3 (2004): 455.
20. Gareth Austin, "Vent for Surplus or Productivity Breakthrough? The Ghanaian Cocoa Take-off, c. 1890–1936," *Economic History Review* 67, no. 4 (2014): 1035.
21. Corey Ross, "The Plantation Paradigm: Agronomy, African Farmers and the Global Cocoa Boom, 1870s–1940s," *Journal of Global History* 9, no. 1 (2014): 53.
22. Austin, "Vent for Surplus or Productivity Breakthrough?," 1040.
23. Ibid., 1036. See also Anthony Hopkins, *An Economic History of West Africa* (New York: Columbia University Press, 1973).
24. Austen, "Vent for Surplus or Productivity Breakthrough?," 1056–58.
25. Ibid., 1051–52.
26. Victoria Tashjian and Jean Allman, "Marrying and Marriage on a Shifting Terrain: Reconfigurations of Power and Authority in Early Colonial Asante," in *Women in African Colonial Histories*, ed. Jean Allman, Susan Geiger, and

Nakanyike Musisi (Bloomington: Indiana University Press, 2002), 245–49. See also Jean Allman and Victoria Tashjian, *"I Will Not Eat Stone": A Women's History of Colonial Asante* (Portsmouth: Heinemann Press, 2000).
27. Simi Afonja, "Land Control: A Critical Factor in Yoruba Gender Stratification," in *Women and Class in Africa*, ed. Claire Robertson and Iris Berger (New York: Africana Publishing Company, 1986), 86.
28. Hochschild, *King Leopold's Ghost*, 159.
29. Alfred Tembo, "Rubber Production in Northern-Rhodesia During the Second World War, 1942–1946," *African Economic History* 41 (2013): 228–29. Tembo notes that Northern Rhodesia (Zambia) is often excluded from discussion about rubber production, though it began there in the nineteenth century. Olufemi Omosini, "The Rubber Export Trade in Ibadan, 1893–1904: Colonial Innovation or Rubber Economy," *Journal of the Historical Society of Nigeria* 10, no. 1 (1979): 24.
30. Omosini, "The Rubber Export Trade in Ibadan," 33.
31. James Fenske, "'Rubber Will Not Keep This Country': Failed Development in Benin, 1897–1921," *Explorations in Economic History* 50 (2013): 318–26.
32. Osborn, "Rubber Fever," 448.
33. Eric T. Jennings, "Extraction and Labor in Equatorial Africa and Cameroon," in *Africa and World War II*, ed. Judith A. Byfield, Carolyn A. Brown, Timothy Parsons, and Ahmad Sikainga (Cambridge: Cambridge University Press, 2015), 206–7.
34. Hochschild, *King Leopold's Ghost*, 162–63. See also Osumaka Likaka, *Naming Colonialism: History and Collective Memory in the Congo, 1870–1960* (Madison: University of Wisconsin Press, 2009), 33.
35. Hochschild, *King Leopold's Ghost*, 230.
36. Colleen E. Kriger, "Mapping the History of Cotton Textile Production in Precolonial West Africa," *African Economic History* 22 (2005): 91.
37. Ann Pitcher, "Sowing the Seeds of Failure: Early Portuguese Cotton Cultivation in Angola and Mozambique 1820–1926," *Journal of Southern African Studies* 17, no. 1 (1991): 47–48.
38. Colleen Kriger, "Textile Production and Gender in Sokoto Caliphate," *Journal of African History* 34, no. 3 (1993): 368; Kriger, "Mapping the History of Cotton Textile Production in Precolonial West Africa," 96.
39. Judith Byfield, *The Bluest Hands: A Social and Economic History of Women Dyers in Abeokuta (Nigeria), 1890–1940* (Portsmouth: Heinemann Press, 2002), 22.
40. Ibid., 23.
41. Marion Johnson, "Cotton Imperialism in West Africa," *African Affairs*, 73, no. 291 (1974): 182. Johnson's discussion focused specifically on Britain, nonetheless other colonial powers had the same idea.
42. Etienne, "Women and Men, Cloth and Colonization," 47.
43. Barbara Cooper, "Cloth, Commodity Production, and Social Capital: Women In Maradi, Niger 1890–1989," *African Economic History* 21, no. 21 (1993): 55–57.
44. Sven Beckert, "From Tuskegee to Togo: The Problem of Freedom in the Empire of Cotton," *Journal of American History* 92, no. 2 (2005): 498–526. The four men were born to people enslaved in Alabama and all were

connected to Tuskegee. James Calloway was a teacher, while John Robinson, Allen Burks, and Shepherd Lincoln Harris were students at the institution.
45. Jean Filipovich, "Destined to Fail: Forced Settlement at the Office du Niger, 1926–1945," *Journal of African History* 42, no. 2 (2001): 239–60; Victoria Bernal, "Cotton and Colonial Order in Sudan: A Social History with Emphasis on the Gezire Scheme" in *Cotton, Colonialism, and Social History in Sub-Saharan Africa*, ed. Allen Isaacman and Richard Roberts (Portsmouth: Heinemann, 1995).
46. Osumaka Likaka, *Rural Society and Cotton in Colonial Zaire* (Madison: University of Wisconsin Press, 1997), 100–5.
47. Elias Mandala, "Peasant Cotton Agriculture, Gender, and Inter-Generational Relationships: The Lower Tchiri (Shire) Valley of Malawi, 1906–1940," *African Studies Review* 25, no. 2/3 (1982): 30.
48. Etienne, "Women and Men, Cloth and Colonization," 53–54.
49. Likaka, *Rural Society and Cotton in Colonial Zaire*, 27; 107.
50. Susan M. Martin, *Palm Oil and Protest: An Economic History of the Ngwa Region, South Eastern Nigeria, 1800–1980* (Cambridge: Cambridge University Press, 1988), 34, 47.
51. Gloria Chuku, "'Crack Kernels, Crack Hitler': Export Production Drive and Igbo Women During the Second World War," in *Gendering the African Diaspora: Women, Culture, and Historical Change in the Caribbean and Nigerian Hinterland*, ed. Judith A. Byfield, LaRay Denzer, and Anthea Morrison (Bloomington: Indiana University Press, 2009), 224.
52. As the number of mills increased, some men sold the palm fruit directly to the mills, thus circumventing their wives' access to palm kernels. Martin, *Palm Oil and Protest*, 128.
53. Philip Havik, "Gender, Land, and Trade: Women's Agency and Colonial Change in Portuguese Guinea (West Africa)," *African Economic History* 43 (2015): 177.
54. Grace G. Kyomuhendo and Marjorie K. McIntosh, *Women, Work and Domestic Virtue in Uganda, 1900–2003* (Athens: Ohio University Press, 2006), 73.
55. Janet Bujra, "'Urging Women to Redouble Their Efforts …': Class, Gender, and Capitalist Transformation in Africa," in *Women and Class in Africa*, ed. Claire Robertson and Iris Berger (New York: Africana Publishing Company, 1986), 124.
56. Ralph Birchard, "Copper in the Katanga Region of the Belgian Copper," *Economic Geography* 16, no. 4 (1940): 429.
57. Likaka, *Rural Society and Cotton in Colonial Zaire*, 26.
58. Jane L. Parpart, "Class and Gender on the Copperbelt: Women in Northern Rhodesian Copper Mining Communities, 1926–1964," in *Women and Class in Africa*, ed. Claire Robertson and Iris Berger (New York: Africana Publishing Company, 1986), 142–45.
59. Ibid., 146.
60. Elizabeth, Schmidt, *Peasants, Traders, and Wives: Shona Women in the History of Zimbabwe, 1870–1939* (Heinemann, 1992), 55.
61. Ibid., 69, 78.
62. Ibid., 72–73.

63. Cora Presley, "Labor Unrest Among Kikuyu Women in Colonial Kenya," in *Women and Class in Africa*, ed. Claire Robertson and Iris Berger (New York: Africana Publishing Company, 1986), 255–62.
64. John Sender, Carlos Oyo, and Christopher Cramer, "Women Working for Wages: Putting Flesh on the Bones of a Rural Labour Market Survey in Mozambique," *Journal of Southern African Studies* 32, no. 2 (2006): 314, 319. The survey completed by 2626 people (1232 women and 1394 men) was conducted across three provinces in Mozambique in 2002/2003. Single women comprised 40% of those surveyed.
65. Teresa Barnes, "Virgin Territory? Travel and Migration by African Women in Twentieth-Century Southern Africa" in *Women in African Colonial Histories*, ed. Jean Allman, Susan Geiger, and Nakanyike Musisi (Bloomington: Indiana University Press, 2002): 179.
66. Iris Berger, "Sources of Class Consciousness: South African Women in Recent Labor Struggles," in *Women and Class in Africa*, ed. Claire Robertson and Iris Berger (New York: Africana Publishing Company, 1986), 216–19.
67. Nancy Clark, "Gendering Production in Wartime South Africa," *American Historical Review* 106, no. 4 (2001): 1181–213.
68. Etienne, "Women and Men, Cloth and Colonization," 52, 58.
69. Schmidt, *Peasants, Traders, and Wives*, 88.
70. Barnes, "Virgin Territory?," 171.
71. McIntosh, *Yoruba Women, Work, and Social Change*, 176.
72. Ibid., 178–85.
73. Kyomuhendo and McIntosh, *Women, Work, and Domestic Virtue in Uganda*, 54, 60.
74. Jane Turrittin, "Colonial Midwives and Modernizing Childbirth in French West Africa," in *Women in African Colonial Histories*, ed. Jean Allman, Susan Geiger, and Nakanyike Musisi (Bloomington: Indiana University Press, 2002), 71.
75. Schmidt, *Peasants, Traders, and Wives*, 92.
76. Lynette Jackson, "'When in the White Man's Town': Zimbabwean Women Remember Chibeura," in *Women in African Colonial Histories*, ed. Jean Allman, Susan Geiger, and Nakanyike Musisi (Bloomington: Indiana University Press, 2002), 200.
77. Karen Jochelson, "Women, Migrancy, and Morality: A Problem of Perspective," *Journal of Southern African Studies* 21, no. 2 (1995): 326.
78. Abosede George, *Making Modern Girls: A History of Girlhood, Labor, and Social Development in Colonial Lagos* (Athens: Ohio University Press, 2014), 113–41; Claire Robertson, *Sharing the Same Bowl: A Socioeconomic History Women and Class in Accra, Ghana* (Bloomington: Indiana University Press, 1984); and Gracia Clark, *Onions Are My Husband: Survival and Accumulation by West African Market Women* (Urbana: University of Chicago Press, 1994).
79. Kyomuhendo and McIntosh, *Women, Work and Domestic Virtue in Uganda*, 57.
80. Luise White, *The Comforts of Home: Prostitution in Colonial Nairobi* (Urbana: University of Chicago Press, 1990), 158. See also Janet Bujra, 'Women "Entrepreneurs" of Early Nairobi', *Canadian Journal of African Studies* 9, no. 2 (1975): 213–34.

81. Benedict Naanen, "'Itinerant Gold Mines': Prostitution in the Cross River Basin of Nigeria, 1930–1950," *African Studies Review* 34, no. 2 (1991): 69. See also: Saheed Aderinto, *When Sex Threatened the State: Illicit Sexuality, Nationalism, and Politics in Colonial Nigeria, 1900–1958* (Urbana: University of Illinois Press, 2014); Carina Ray, "World War II and the Sex Trade in British West Africa," in *Africa and World War II*, ed. Judith A. Byfield, Carolyn A. Brown, Timothy Parsons, and Ahmad Sikainga (Cambridge: Cambridge University Press, 2015), 339–56.
82. Byfield, *The Bluest Hands*, 87–125.
83. Claire Robertson, *Trouble Showed the Way: Women, Men, and Trade in the Nairobi Area, 1890–1990* (Bloomington: Indiana University Press, 1997), 1.
84. Ibid., 77, 82–86.
85. Paulette Young, "Ghanaian Woman and Dutch Wax Prints: The Counter-Appropriation of the Foreign and the Local Creating a New Visual Voice of Creative Expression," *Journal of Asian and African Studies* 51, no. 3 (2016): 309. The designs on Dutch wax prints were drawn from Javanese batik patterns. Europeans also traded cloth from India in West Africa.
86. Christopher B. Steiner, "Another Image of Africa: Toward an Ethnohistory of European Cloth Market in West Africa, 1873–1960," *Ethnohistory* 32, no. 2 (1985): 94, 99.
87. Young, "Ghanaian Woman and Dutch Wax Prints," 308.
88. Ibid., 313–6. See also Nina Sylvanus, "The Fabric of Africanity: Tracing the Global Threads of Authenticity," *Anthropological Theory* 7, no. 2 (2007): 201–16.
89. McIntosh, *Yoruba Women, Work and Social Change*, 172–73.
90. Hay, "Luo Women and Economic Change During the Colonial Period," 87.
91. Coumba Mar Gadio and Cathy Rakowski, "Farmers' Changing Roles in Thieudeme, Senegal: the Impact of Local and Global Factors on Three Generations of Women," *Gender and Society* 13, no. 6 (1999): 735.
92. Ewout Frankema and Marlous van Waijenburg, "Structural Impediments to African Growth? New Evidence from Real Wages in British Africa, 1880–1965" *Journal of Economic History* 72, no. 4 (2012): 908.
93. Gardner, *Taxing Colonial Africa*, 47.
94. Hopkins, "The New Economic History of Africa," 155–57.

BIBLIOGRAPHY

Acemoglu, Daron, Simon Johnson, and James A. Robinson. "The Colonial Origins of Comparative Economic Development: An Empirical Investigation." *The American Economic Review* 91, no. 5 (2001): 1369–401.

———. "Reversal of Fortune: Geography and Institutions in the Making of the Modern World Income Distribution." *Quarterly Journal of Economics* 117, no. 4 (2002): 1231–94.

Aderinto, Saheed. *When Sex Threatened the State: Illicit Sexuality, Nationalism and Politics in Colonial Nigeria, 1900–1958.* Urbana: University of Illinois Press, 2014.

Afonja, Simi. "Land Control: A Critical Factor in Yoruba Gender Stratification." In *Women and Class in Africa*, edited by Claire Robertson and Iris Berger, 78–91. New York: Africana Publishing Company, 1986.

Allman, Jean, and Victoria Tashjian. *"I Will Not Eat Stone": A Women's History of Colonial Asante*. Portsmouth: Heinemann Press, 2000.

Austin, Gareth. "The 'Reversal of Fortune' Thesis and the Compression of History: Perspectives from African and Comparative Economic History." *Journal of International Development* 20, no. 8 (2008): 996–1027.

———. "Vent for Surplus or Productivity Breakthrough: The Ghanaian Cocoa Take-off, c. 1890–1936." *Economic History Review* 67, no. 4 (2014): 1035–64.

Austin, Gareth, and Stephen Broadberry. "Introduction: The Renaissance of African Economic History." *Economic History Review* 67, no. 4 (2014): 893–906.

Barnes, Teresa. "Virgin Territory? Travel and Migration by African Women in Twentieth-Century Southern Africa." In *Women in African Colonial Histories*, edited by Jean Allman, Susan Geiger, and Nakanyike Musisi, 164–90. Bloomington: Indiana University Press, 2002.

Beckert, Sven. "From Tuskegee to Togo: The Problem of Freedom in the Empire of Cotton." *Journal of American History* 92, no. 2 (2005): 498–526.

Berger, Iris. "Sources of Class Consciousness: South African Women in Recent Labor Struggles." In *Women and Class in Africa*, edited by Claire Robertson and Iris Berger, 216–36. New York: Africana Publishing Company, 1986.

———. *Women in Twentieth Century Africa*. New York: Cambridge University Press, 2016.

Berman, Bruce, and John Lonsdale. "Coping with the Contradictions." In *Unhappy Valley: Conflict in Kenya and Africa*, East African Studies, edited by Bruce Berman and John Lonsdale, 77–100. Athens: Ohio University Press, 1992.

———. "Crises of Accumulation, Coercion & the Colonial State: The Development of the Labour Control System, 1919–20." In *Unhappy Valley: Conflict in Kenya and Africa*, East African Studies, edited by Bruce Berman and John Lonsdale, 101–26. Athens: Ohio University Press, 1992.

Bernal, Victoria. "Cotton and Colonial Order in Sudan: A Social History with Emphasis on the Gezire Scheme." In *Cotton, Colonialism, and Social History in Sub-Saharan Africa*, edited by Allen Isaacman and Richard Roberts, 96–110. Portsmouth: Heinemann, 1995.

Birchard, Ralph. "Copper in the Katanga Region of the Belgian Copper." *Economic Geography* 16, no. 4 (1940): 429–36.

Boserup, Ester. *Women's Role in Economic Development*. New York: St. Martin's Press, 1970.

Bujra, Janet. "Women 'Entrepreneurs' of Early Nairobi." *Canadian Journal of African Studies* 9, no. 2 (1975): 213–34.

———. "'Urging Women to Redouble Their Efforts ...': Class, Gender, and Capitalist Transformation in Africa." In *Women and Class in Africa*, edited by Claire Robertson and Iris Berger, 117–40. New York: Africana Publishing Company, 1986.

Byfield, Judith A. *The Bluest Hands: A Social and Economic History of Women Dyers in Abeokuta (Nigeria), 1890–1940*. Portsmouth: Heinemann Press, 2002.

———. "Taxation, Women and the Colonial State: Egba Women's Tax Revolt." *Meridians* 3, no. 2 (2010): 250–77.

Chuku, Gloria. "'Crack Kernels, Crack Hitler': Export Production Drive and Igbo Women During the Second World War." In *Gendering the African Diaspora: Women, Culture, and Historical Change in the Caribbean and Nigerian*

Hinterland, edited by Judith A. Byfield, LaRay Denzer, and Anthea Morrison, 219–44. Bloomington: Indiana University Press, 2009.

Clark, Gracia. *Onions Are My Husband: Survival and Accumulation by West African Market Women*. Urbana: University of Chicago Press, 1994.

Clark, Nancy Clark. "Gendering Production in Wartime South Africa." *American Historical Review* 106, no. 4 (2001): 1181–213.

Cooper, Barbara. "Cloth, Commodity Production, and Social Capital: Women In Maradi, Niger 1890–1989." *African Economic History* 21, no. 21 (1993): 51–71.

Cooper, Frederick. "Conflict and Connection: Rethinking Colonial African History." *American Historical Review* 99, no. 5 (1994): 1516–45.

———. *Africa Since 1940: The Past of the Present*. Cambridge: Cambridge University Press, 2002.

Crowder, Michael. *West Africa Under Colonial Rule*. Evanston: Northwestern University Press, 1968.

Etienne, Mona. "Women and Men, Cloth and Colonization: The Transformation of Property Relations Among the Baule (Ivory Coast)." *Cahiers d'Etudes Africaines* 17, no. 65 (1977): 41–64.

Fenske, James. "The Causal History of Africa: A Response to Hopkins." *Economic History of Developing Regions* 25, no. 2 (2010): 177–212.

———. "'Rubber Will Not Keep This Country': Failed Development in Benin, 1897–1921." *Explorations in Economic History* 50 (2013): 316–33.

Filipovich, Jean. "Destined to Fail: Forced Settlement at the Office du Niger, 1926–1945." *Journal of African History* 42, no. 2 (2001): 239–60.

Fourie, Johan. "The Data Revolution in African Economic History." *Journal of Interdisciplinary History* 47, no. 2 (2016): 193–212.

Frankema, Ewout and Marlous van Waijenburg. "Structural Impediments to African Growth? New Evidence from Real Wages in British Africa, 1880–1965." *Journal of Economic History* 72, no. 4 (2012): 895–926.

Gadio, Coumba Mar, and Cathy Rakowski. "Farmers' Changing Roles in Thieudeme, Senegal: The Impact of Local and Global Factors on Three Generations of Women." *Gender and Society* 13, no. 6 (1999): 733–57.

Gardner, Leigh A. "Decentralization and Corruption in Historical Perspective: Evidence from Tax Collection in British Colonial Africa." *Economic History of Developing Regions* 25, no. 2 (2010): 231–36.

———. *Taxing Colonial Africa: The Political Economy of British Imperialism*. Oxford: Oxford University Press, 2012.

George, Abosede. *Making Modern Girls: A History of Girlhood, Labor, and Social Development in Colonial Lagos*. Athens: Ohio University Press, 2014.

Havik, Philip. "Gender, Land, and Trade: Women's Agency and Colonial Change in Portuguese Guinea (West Africa)." *African Economic History* 43 (2015): 162–95.

Hay, Margaret Jean. "Luo Women and Economic Change During the Colonial Period." In *Women in Africa: Studies in Social and Economic Change*, edited by Nancy Hafkin and Edna Bay, 87–110. Stanford: Stanford University Press, 1976.

Herbst, Jeffrey. *States and Power in Africa*, 2nd ed. Princeton: Princeton University Press, 2014.

Hochschild, Adam. *King Leopold's Ghost: A Story of Greed, Terror, and Heroism in Colonial Africa*. Boston: Houghton Mifflin, 1999.

Hopkins, Anthony. *An Economic History of West Africa*. New York: Columbia University Press, 1973.

———. "The New Economic History of Africa." *Journal of African History* 50, no. 2 (2009): 155–77.

———. "Causes and Confusions in African History." *Economic History of Developing Regions* 26, no. 2 (2011): 107–10.

Jackson, Lynette. "'When in the White Man's Town': Zimbabwean Women Remember Chibeura." In *Women in African Colonial Histories*, edited by Jean Allman, Susan Geiger, and Nakanyike Musisi, 191–215. Bloomington: Indiana University Press, 2002.

Jennings, Eric T. "Extraction and Labor in Equatorial Africa and Cameroon." In *Africa and World War II*, edited by Judith A. Byfield, Carolyn A. Brown, Timothy Parsons, and Ahmad A. Sikainga, 200–19. Cambridge: Cambridge University Press, 2015.

Jochelson, Karen. "Women, Migrancy, and Morality: A Problem of Perspective." *Journal of Southern African Studies* 21, no. 2 (1995): 323–32.

Johnson, Marion. "Cotton Imperialism in West Africa." *African Affairs* 73, no. 291 (1974): 178–87.

Kriger, Colleen E. "Textile Production and Gender in Sokoto Caliphate." *Journal of African History* 34, no. 3 (1993): 361–401.

———. "Mapping the History of Cotton Textile Production in Precolonial West Africa." *African Economic History* 22 (2005): 87–116.

Kyomuhendo, Grace G., and Marjorie K. McIntosh. *Women, Work and Domestic Virtue in Uganda, 1900–2003*. Athens: Ohio University Press, 2006.

Likaka, Osumaka. *Rural Society and Cotton in Colonial Zaire*. Madison: University of Wisconsin Press, 1997.

———. *Naming Colonialism: History and Collective Memory in the Congo, 1870–1960*. Madison: University of Wisconsin Press, 2009.

Mamdani, Mahmood. *Citizen and Subject: Contemporary Africa and the Legacy of Late Colonialism*. Princeton: Princeton University Press, 2014.

Mandala, Elias. "Peasant Cotton Agriculture, Gender, and Inter-Generational Relationships: The Lower Tchiri (Shire) Valley of Malawi, 1906–1940." *African Studies Review* 25, no. 2/3 (1982): 27–44.

Martin, Susan M. *Palm Oil and Protest: An Economic History of the Ngwa Region, South Eastern Nigeria, 1800–1980*. Cambridge: Cambridge University Press, 1988.

Mba, Nina. *Nigerian Women Mobilized: Women Political Activity in Southern Nigeria, 1900–1965*. Berkeley: University of California Press, 1983.

McIntosh, Marjorie Keniston. *Yoruba Women, Work, and Social Change*. Bloomington: Indiana University Press, 2014.

Naanen, Benedict. "'Itinerant Gold Mines': Prostitution in the Cross River Basin of Nigeria, 1930–1950." *African Studies Review* 34, no. 2 (1991): 57–79.

Omosini, Olufemi. "The Rubber Export Trade in Ibadan, 1893–1904: Colonial Innovation or Rubber Economy." *Journal of the Historical Society of Nigeria* 10, no. 1 (1979): 21–46.

Osborn, Emily Lynn. "'Rubber Fever': Commerce and French Colonial Rule in Upper Guinée, 1890–1913." *Journal of African History* 45, no. 3 (2004): 445–65.

———. *Our new Husbands Are Here: Households, Gender and Politics in a West African State from the Slave Trade to Colonial Rule*. Athens: Ohio University Press, 2011.

Parpart, Jane L. "Class and Gender on the Copperbelt: Women in Northern Rhodesian Copper Mining Communities, 1926–64." In *Women and Class in Africa*, edited by Claire Robertson and Iris Berger, 141–60. New York: Africana Publishing Company, 1986.

Pitcher, M. Ann. "Sowing the Seeds of Failure: Early Portuguese Cotton Cultivation in Angola and Mozambique 1820–1926." *Journal of Southern African Studies* 17, no. 1 (1991): 43–70.

Presley, Cora. "Labor Unrest Among Kikuyu Women in Colonial Kenya." In *Women and Class in Africa*, edited by Claire Robertson and Iris Berger, 255–62. New York: Africana Publishing Company, 1986.

Ray, Carina. "World War II and the Sex Trade in British West Africa." In *Africa and World War II*, edited by Judith A. Byfield, Carolyn A. Brown, Timothy Parsons, and Ahmad A. Sikainga, 339–56. Cambridge: Cambridge University Press, 2015.

Redding, Sean. "Legal Minors and Social Children: Rural African Women and Taxation in the Transkei, South Africa." *African Studies Review* 36, no. 3 (1993): 49–74.

Roberts, T.W. "Republicanism, Railway Imperialism, and the French Empire in Africa, 1879–1889." *Historical Journal* 54, no. 2 (2011): 401–20.

Robertson, Claire. *Sharing the Same Bowl: A Socioeconomic History of Women and Class in Accra, Ghana*. Bloomington: Indiana University Press, 1984.

———. *Trouble Showed the Way: Women, Men, and Trade in the Nairobi Area, 1890–1990*. Bloomington: Indiana University Press, 1997.

Ross, Corey. "The Plantation Paradigm: Agronomy, African Farmers and the Global Cocoa Boom, 1870s–1940s." *Journal of Global History* 9, no. 1 (2014): 49–71.

Schmidt, Elizabeth. *Peasants, Traders, and Wives: Shona Women in the History of Zimbabwe, 1870–1939* (Heinemann, 1992).

Sender, John, Carlos Oyo, and Christopher Cramer. "Women Working for Wages: Putting Flesh on the Bones of a Rural Labour Market Survey in Mozambique." *Journal of Southern African Studies* 32, no. 2 (2006): 313–33.

Steiner, Christopher B. "Another Image of Africa: Toward an Ethnohistory of European Cloth Market in West Africa, 1873–1960." *Ethnohistory* 32, no. 2 (1985): 91–110.

Sunderland, David. "The Departmental System of Railway Construction in British West Africa, 1895–1906." *Journal of Transport History* 23, no. 2 (2002): 87–112.

Sylvanus, Nina. "The Fabric of Africanity: Tracing the Global Threads of Authenticity." *Anthropological Theory* 7, no. 2 (2007): 201–16.

Tashjian, Victoria, and Jean Allman. "Marrying and Marriage on a Shifting Terrain: Reconfigurations of Power and Authority in Early Colonial Asante." In *Women in African Colonial Histories*, edited by Jean Allman, Susan Geiger, and Nakanyike Musisi, 237–59. Bloomington: Indiana University Press, 2002.

Tembo, Alfred. "Rubber Production in Northern-Rhodesia During the Second World War, 1942–1946." *African Economic History* 41 (2013): 223–55.

Turrittin, Jane. "Colonial Midwives and Modernizing Childbirth in French West Africa." In *Women in African Colonial Histories*, edited by Jean Allman, Susan Geiger, and Nakanyike Musisi, 71–91. Bloomington: Indiana University Press, 2002.

White, Luise. *The Comforts of Home: Prostitution in Colonial Nairobi*. Urbana: University of Chicago Press, 1990.

Wrangham, Elizabeth. "An African Road Revolution: The Gold Coast in the Period of the Great War." *Journal of Imperial and Commonwealth History* 32, no. 1 (2004) 1–18.

Young, Crawford. *The African Colonial State in Comparative Perspective*. New Haven: Yale University Press, 1994.

Young, Paulette. "Ghanaian Woman and Dutch Wax Prints: The Counter-appropriation of the Foreign and the Local Creating a New Visual Voice of Creative Expression." *Journal of Asian and African Studies* 51, no. 3 (2016): 305–27.

CHAPTER 7

Colonialism and African Womanhood

Gloria Chuku

In indigenous African society, the concept of 'woman' or 'womanhood' signified: a high level of responsibility; an embodiment of social etiquette; and familial and community expectations of an adult female as a wife, mother, and responsible member of the society. African womanhood embodied versatility, independence, hard work, and resilience of adult females contributing to the socio-economic well-being of their households and communities. However, the presence of European colonial powers (Britain, Belgium, France, Italy, Germany and Portugal) which pursued different but similar political, social, and economic policies in Africa, altered African womanhood by massively transforming African indigenous institutions, worldviews, and livelihoods. The colonial era, for the most part, the period between the 1880s and 1960s, was marked by tumultuous social change and upheaval which had far-reaching ambivalent impact on African women and their societies. The argument here is that colonialism created opportunities, challenges, and barriers as African women physically and culturally negotiated the migration from old ways of life to new ones; and as they carved out new spaces for themselves. Furthermore, through the actions of the colonizers and the colonized, African womanhood was enhanced, diminished, or placed in ambiguous situations. As existing studies have shown, while colonial rule reduced African women's status and leadership positions, decreased their earning power, and increased their workloads, it also offered women opportunities to improve their lives through a number of innovative forces.[1]

G. Chuku (✉)
The University of Maryland, Baltimore County, Baltimore, MD, USA

© The Author(s) 2018
M.S. Shanguhyia and T. Falola (eds.),
The Palgrave Handbook of African Colonial and Postcolonial History,
https://doi.org/10.1057/978-1-137-59426-6_7

African women's colonial historiography has shown not only a historical experience that was marked by both opportunities and limitations, but also women's agency as they negotiated and challenged the normative gender relations engendered by colonialism. Women in both urban and rural areas who conformed to these normative gender relations, and those who acted against the normative ideas of proper female behaviors by challenging African and European male authorities, were all at the forefront of historical change and transformation throughout colonial Africa.[2] This chapter explores the political and socio-cultural structures, institutions, and practices that shaped women's lives in colonial Africa and how African women responded to them. It also examines women's diverse experiences and their heterogeneous modes of resistance, adjustment, and negotiation in defense of African womanhood and agency. These issues are discussed below under the following subheadings: African women's political power and institutions under colonial rule; formal education, transformation, and African women's agency; ambiguities of the colonial legal system and African womanhood; and migration and criminalization of African womanhood.

African Women's Political Power and Institutions Under Colonial Rule

African women have enjoyed a long history of active political engagements in their respective communities, states, and kingdoms. In Asante, Buganda, Lagos, Dahomey, Benin, Swazi, and many other African imperial systems and polities, there were notable female political figures such as regents and queen mothers who not only advised, defended, nurtured, and protected the kings, but also punished and dethroned them. These women built political and military coalitions that brought their sons or relatives to power. Women's age-grade associations, secret societies, and councils in different parts of Africa were involved in governance and maintenance of law and order. Certain women with spiritual powers had led in battles or prepared soldiers for wars, and were also part of the kings' courts, advising and interceding on their behalf and for the good of their polities. With European colonialism, African female political and spiritual figures lost their powers to enthrone or depose kings and to restrain their excesses and actions as new governmental and legal structures and hierarchies were imposed on Africans. The gendered checks and balances of the Buganda political structure as in many other African polities were undermined as the colonial officials dealt directly with Ganda chiefs and male authority figures. In the Dahomey kingdom, where female dependants of the royal court served as soldiers and commanders, ministers of state and counselors, provincial governors, and trade agents, the French colonial rule closed these avenues of power and authority for women. In some wars of resistance against European colonial conquests, some of these women came into direct confrontation with the colonizers. While a number of them were exiled, others were criminalized; and those who remained witnessed a diminished role, power, and influence.³

African colonial historiography has shown that colonialism and its variegated effects created new avenues of power and authority as it foreclosed others. Many of the elite women's precolonial pathways to power (kinship, high spirituality, aptitude in indigenous medicine, military prowess, leadership in women's organizations and secret societies, the marketplace, and the household) were neglected under the masculine terrain of colonial statecraft. As demonstrated by Emily Osborn's study of Kankan (the capital and trading center of the Baté empire in the Milo River Valley of Guinea-Conakry), the Baté state grew out of its households as women went to great lengths to ensure the success of their male relatives. Women used their domestic roles as savvy mothers, respectful wives, and wise and generous sisters to influence social and political processes of Baté. But French colonialism separated the household from the state and depoliticized women's domestic roles as colonial officials treated men as active agents and women as domesticated dependants.⁴ The structures and processes of the colonial state made it impermeable to women's interventions. This explains why African women featured frequently in the precolonial political narratives but less so after colonization. African women's power diminished as colonial officials ignored women and precolonial indigenous institutions that guaranteed their authority and influence. In both the French policy of direct rule and British indirect rule, women had no place in the official corridors of colonial power; but African men served in colonial bureaucracies as chiefs, scribes, tax collectors, policemen, judicial officers and enforcers, interpreters, and other local administrative agents, some of whom often had little or no legitimacy among the people they were to oversee.

An important question here is how African women, especially women political and religious leaders as colonial subjects exercised political authority and how they adjusted and manipulated vectors of power to ensure their continued access to power and resources within the confines of the colonial state. Different processes of unanticipated and uncontrollable interpretations, manipulations and transformations emerged as African male colonial employees attempted to pursue the policies of their employers and also advance their own interests and protect their privileged positions. Among such unanticipated outcomes was the creation of a window of opportunity for a few women to serve in colonial government, a colonial reality that was made apparent by the agency of African womanhood. Examples can be drawn from the Igbo of southeastern Nigeria. The first known example of an Igbo woman serving in the colonial government was that of Madam Okwei (1872–1943), who was appointed a member of the Onitsha Native Court in 1912 in recognition of her political clout, leadership skills, and wealth. The second Igbo woman to occupy important political office during this period was Ahebi Ugbabe, who was appointed the Warrant Chief of Enugu-Ezike Native Court in 1918 and shortly after became the monarch (*eze*) of Ogrute, a position she held until her death in 1948. The appointment was a reward to Ugbabe for assisting the British with vital information that contributed to the conquest of Enugu-Ezike. A few other Igbo women who served as local council members were appointed in 1930 after they demonstrated their leadership during the violent Women's War of 1929: one in the Nguru Mbaise Native Court, another in the Okpuala Native Court, and three out of 30 members of the Umuakpo Native Court.[5]

Other rare exceptions were in such colonies as Sierra Leone, Basutoland, and Dahomey with a history of powerful female political figures in the precolonial period but where the colonial state redefined local governance and provided new avenues for women to maintain and even expand their political authority.[6] While maintaining their traditional roles as queens, wives, and sisters Yoruba-speaking women of Ketu in French Dahomey also served as advisers, treasurers, ritual specialists, and colonial agents.[7] Among the Mende and Sherbro of Sierra Leone, women's political power and prerogatives as paramount chiefs were sustained and even expanded just like their male counterparts by the colonial state. The British indirect rule model left many indigenous political institutions and structures relatively intact. Colonial paramount women chiefs such as Madam Yoko of Kpa Mende, Humonya of Kenema, Maajo of Limeh, and Yaewa of Sendume exercised female agency to maintain their power. Their membership and support by the Poro (male) and Sande (female) societies which maintained social guidelines that empowered both men and women helped these women chiefs transpose their socio-religious powers into political powers. Engagement in military expansion and control of resources (land and labor), serving as mediators in wars and political conflicts, as well as being mothers with many children, senior wives, and female heads of household and female lineage heads were avenues through which Mende and Sherbro women became chiefs and protected their positions under colonialism.[8] In fact, a combination of wealth, military prowess, family ties, and leadership skills guaranteed women political power and authority within the colonial state.

In British Basutoland, women gained more political positions as regents and high chiefs even though the colonial government preferred masculinization of the chieftaincy to its feminization. British officials recommended paying female chiefs two-thirds the salary of their male counterparts. In 1903, the Resident Commissioner chastised the Basutoland National Council for voting to allow women to succeed as chiefs in their own right instead of as regents, even though some British officials admitted that female chiefs often 'ruled with distinction and integrity'.[9] Although the institution of Basotho chieftaincy was predominantly and customarily male, it did open up avenues for women to enter public politics as regents and chiefs. For instance, in 1911, female regents constituted 2% of the total chiefs and 'headmen' but their number increased to 12.5% in 1955. In 1941, Mantsebo Seeiso was elected 'paramount chieftainess' and by 1955, four of the twenty two most senior chiefs (the 'sons' of Moshesh) were women.[10]

The increased visibility of Basotho women in public politics during the colonial period could partly be attributed to colonial conditions in Southern Africa. Migrant male labor created a vacuum and a de facto population that was increasingly female. In order to enhance the 'efficient' flow of Basotho male migrant labor to the mines of South Africa, British officials accommodated the chieftaincy institution where men and women political officeholders cooperated to achieve that goal. But more importantly, it was the support of male chiefs and women's agency that led to the increasing participation of women in government and politics. Male chiefs protected women's political officeholders on the grounds that their positions were 'traditional' even though the British argued for an all-male administration which they saw as being more 'modern'. Women protected their political ambitions through the support of male advisors and relatives, as well as by resorting to the courts and use of violence or its threat. An example was in 1926 when Maletapata of Quthing was accused of inciting a small-scale war in order to seize new lands and expand her political domain. In another example, the widow of Chief Jonathan of Leribe, in her resistance against an unfavorable choice of succession, threatened the Resident Commissioner with a bloodbath in 1929. In the 1940s and 1950s, many women chiefs were accused of and executed for allegedly using 'sorcery' to advance their interests. Another significant point to note is that female chiefs were widely respected by the Basotho people because they were less likely than men to succumb to the temptations of office. Women chiefs advocated women's autonomy and rights. They radically opposed colonial policies that restricted or undermined women's spatial, social, and economic mobility, and their self-worth. These female political officeholders were seen as 'honorary men' by the Basotho people. The women chiefs preferred to be addressed as *Ntate* (Sir).[11]

The above examples of exceptions to the norm notwithstanding, African women generally lost their political powers under European colonialism. However, they were active during the decolonization politics when women collectively and individually struggled to regain their power and authority, an effort they have intensified since independence. A number of studies have been devoted to the role of women in advancing decolonization and claims to independence in the 1950s and 1960s in different parts of Africa.[12] A few examples drawn from French and British colonies are discussed below to illustrate African women's agency and their strategies for meaningful political participation during the decolonization movements.

The French gender ideology was informed by the Napoleonic Code that established the legal framework of women's subordination to their husbands in France. This ideology, that undermined women's status, was exported to the French colonies in Africa under assimilation policy of direct rule. As a result, the French colonial officers ignored African female leaders.

Subsequently, women's right to vote and to political participation and representation in colonial Senegal depended on their status as citizens or subjects. Citizens were Africans who had passed through the French colonial educational system and were literate in French. Africans who became citizens, a tiny minority of the total population of Senegal, came from the Four Communes of Saint Louis, Gorée, Dakar, and Rufisque. A few women from the four communes who went to French schools were considered 'assimilated' but without full citizenship rights. The majority of Senegalese women, particularly those in the countryside, were considered illiterate and colonial subjects. Consequently, while African men obtained the right to vote in 1848, it took their female counterparts a century, with full suffrage in 1946, two years after the same right was granted to French women in metropolitan France. Once the right to vote was granted to French women, Senegalese men campaigned that such right be extended to Senegalese women 'like all women'.[13]

Senegalese men's strong support for women's suffrage in Senegal was not based on their commitment to gender equality but to the electoral threats posed by white and *metis* (mulatto) politicians and the potential power of a politically active female population to neutralize such threats. Subsequently, Senegalese women began playing an active role in urban politics of the 1940s, mobilizing electoral support for men through political rallies where they sang and danced to the praise of their party and its male leadership. As political party auxiliaries, women's massive votes in the 1945 municipal elections (with 21% of the electoral votes in Dakar) ended white political dominance and gave Senegalese men victories and the control of the four communes.[14] Women's huge involvement in the decolonization politics contributed to the election of Senegalese nationalist leaders and the end of colonial rule in 1960.

In French Mali, the political activities of Aoua Keita of Bamako stood out. She was a pioneer product of the School of Midwifery in Dakar (1928–1931) and with strong support from her medical doctor husband M. Diawara, she became politically active. Keita was a trade unionist and a militant member of the Soudanese branch of the Rassemblement Democratique Africain (USRDA) which she joined in 1946. When Malian women became enfranchised in 1956, Keita and Aissata Sow (president of the Soudanese Teachers' Union) became two of the seventeen elected members of the Central Committee of the RDA in 1957. In 1958, Keita organized the women's wing of the USRDA in Bamako, and in December of the same year was appointed to the Constitution Drafting Committee for the proposed Mali Federation. Keita was elected deputy to the Mali Federation in April 1959, and with independence in 1960 she became the first female deputy to the Republic of Mali's national assembly.[15]

By 1946, Africans were regarded as French citizens in Overseas France and had the right to vote for African delegates to the Territorial Assemblies. The period after the Second World War also witnessed an explosion of political parties and mass political mobilization for full self-governance in French

Africa and across the continent. But in Gabon, political activities for independence were muted due largely to the weak political and middle classes and poverty. Only a few educated Gabonese, the 'notable' men (civil servants, ex-soldiers, and assessors in native courts), who constituted 6% of the population could vote in 1946. It was not until 1952 that a restricted group of Gabonese women were allowed to vote, with full suffrage granted in 1956.[16] Muslim women of colonial Algeria were completely disenfranchised. In the two nationalist parties (the Algerian People's Party and Movement for the Triumph of Democratic Liberties [PPA-MTLD] and the Algerian Communist Party [PCA]), women's significant presence was as auxiliaries mobilizing others. Yet when the 1954–1962 war of independence broke out, about 11,000 women joined as fighters, which was 3.1% of all those in active combat; and over 2000 became militants (16% of all militants), dealing with lives of deprivation, hunger, harsh weather, imprisonment, torture, and death. No Algerian woman was a member of the National Liberation Front (FLN) party. They only belonged to the National Union of Algerian Women (UNFA) as auxiliaries of the FLN. Ironically, when independence was achieved, women seemed to have disappeared from the political scene. But with their enfranchisement in 1962, they gained ten seats in the first National Assembly out of 194 members.[17]

Basotho women played active roles in the decolonization politics of the 1950s and 1960s. An important study on the subject has highlighted Basotho women's agency and political activism, including roles as chiefs, politicians, nuns, homemakers, prostitutes, and runaways in the last four decades prior to Lesotho's independence in 1966.[18] In 1960, the British restricted franchise to tax-payers resulted in only 56 women being eligible to vote in the entire Basutoland. The male-dominated Basutoland Congress Party (BCP, former Basutoland African Congress) encouraged women's participation in nationalist politics and also created a platform which fostered the emergence of the first woman leader, Ellen'Maposholi Molapo, in the 1950s. Molapo was a dynamic African National Congress (ANC) activist who organized for the BCP in the Transvaal and was involved in the bitter struggles between the Pan-Africanist Congress and the ANC prior to her expulsion from South Africa. The BCP Women's League played an important role in mobilizing villages and towns in support of the party, and contributed to the party's triumph in 1960. But the party's opposition to the enfranchisement of women and its urban-focused electoral campaigns among other factors led to its narrow defeat in 1965 by Leabua Jonathan's Basotho National Party (BNP).[19] BCP members who testified to the Basutoland Constitutional Commission in 1962 opposed women's enfranchisement on the basis that Basotho women were 'not matured in politics [and] knew nothing about independence'.[20] They also attacked the Catholic Church and the nuns. But Jonathan's BNP campaigned for the protection and emancipation of women, and on a pro-women agenda, including girls' education, health-care centers for women, equal wages for men and women, and guarantee of women's rights. Jonathan praised Basotho nuns and laywomen, referring to the latter as 'bulldozers with breasts'.[21]

Nigerian women participated in the decolonization politics of the 1940s and 1950s with a long history of struggle for political relevance. They were not included in the executive committees or policy-making positions of the early protonationalist parties. They did not enjoy the limited franchise extended to men of the colony. It was out of frustration at being marginalized and excluded in the political process by male nationalists that Oyikan Abayomi founded the Nigerian Women's Party (NWP) in 1944. The NWP was established to demand women's rights: the right to vote and be represented on the Lagos Town Council (LTC) and the Legislative Council for the colony. With limited woman suffrage in 1950, the NWP fielded the first women political candidates of colonial Nigeria. Although the party failed to win the two seats to the LTC that it had contested, its establishment and activities were major achievements in the political history of Nigerian women. Subsequently, more southern women began to play active roles in Nigerian politics. While southern Nigerian women were enfranchised from 1950, their northern Islamic counterparts remained politically powerless and disenfranchised throughout the colonial period. Ironically, as the Islamic emirate governments of the North were suppressing independent women as 'immoral', the same group of women was increasingly vital in political organization and the women's wings of the two major political parties there: the Northern People's Congress (NPC) and the Northern Elements Progressive Union (NEPU). The leader of the NPC Women's Wing was a well-known personality in *karuwanci* (courtesanship). The male leadership of the political parties assumed a paternalistic relationship with the women's wings, with the NPC vehemently opposing women's enfranchisement. But the NEPU under Aminu Kano's leadership advocated female franchise and women's formal education.[22]

Formal Education, Transformation, and African Women's Agency

The ramifications of differential gender-based colonial education (which though transformative and offering African women opportunities for upward social and economic mobility, while at the same time domesticated them) is explored below.[23] Formal education, which was pioneered by the Christian missions, had the greatest transformative impact on young women and girls, offering them opportunities to traverse geographical, cultural, ideological, and social boundaries. Mission and colonial education was a vehicle for vocational training, job acquisition, upward social mobility, and acculturation. Various colonial powers implemented different but similar educational policies in their respective colonies. In all the colonies, both the mission and the government pursued gender-based education that favored men and boys with serious implications for African women and girls. The discussion below draws examples mainly from Belgian, Portuguese, German, British, and French colonial and mission educational policies to demonstrate their differential impacts on African women and girls.

In the early colonial French Africa, Catholic priests and nuns monopolized the education of African children. The first school in Senegal was opened by a Catholic priest in 1816 in Saint Louis. By the 1840s there were four primary schools there: two in Saint Louis and the other two in Goree, with a total enrollment that was under 600. The first schools for girls in Senegal were established in Goree and Saint Louis in the first half of the nineteenth century after colonial officials encouraged the Sisters of Saint Joseph de Cluny to provide instruction to *signares* (mulatto Franco-African women) and their *metis* daughters. With instruction focusing primarily on history, grammar, and geography, the schools witnessed poor attendance by *metis* and African children. But attendance improved after 1852 as the schools started training girls for adult female roles (such as sewing and other housecraft skills) that were socially approved of for African women in the emergent colonial society. For instance, Saint Louis enrollment increased from a couple of dozen girls between 1822 and 1852 to 150 during the 1852–1854 school years, and the Goree school witnessed an enrollment increase in 1853 from 60 to 178 students. In 1873, there were 300 students in both schools, although most of them were Catholic *metisses*. For the first time, a significant minority of Senegalese girls, including a few Muslims, enrolled in the two schools.[24] In 1856, Louis Faidherbe built a school in Saint Louis for the sons of chiefs to train them as intermediaries of the French colonial administration, but there was no similar school for girls.

Following the organization of the colonial administration of French West Africa (AOF) from 1902 to 1904, the government took over the direction of all schools in Senegal, the Soudan, Guinea, Ivory Coast, and Dahomey, and later those in Mauritania, Niger, and Upper Volta. The colonial government stopped funding mission schools and even closed some. Those that remained open called themselves 'workshops', offering students practical skill training. Subsequently, the William Ponty School was established in Saint Louis in 1903 to train the first African primary-school teachers, interpreters, medical personnel, and veterinarians, the products of which became the nucleus of a pioneer African male elite, the so-called Black French. The first *lycée* in AOF was established in 1919 at Saint Louis; it remained the only secondary school serving the whole federation until 1936 when a private school in Dakar began offering secondary courses.[25] In 1938, less than 3% of school-age children in AOF were in full-time education. There were between 56,135 and 68,416 pupils in primary schools, the majority of whom were attending rudimentary semi-schooling, and 717 in *écoles primaires supérieures* (EPSs: higher primary schools after six years of primary education, the equivalent of an American junior high school). The EPSs trained primary-school teachers, low-level clerks, and other local employees of the administration and commerce. In the 1937–1938 academic year, girls comprised only 5892 of the total school enrollments. In French Equatorial Africa (AEF: Chad, Gabon, Congo-Brazzaville, and Ubangi-Shari, later Central African Republic), the poorest and least developed of the colonial federations, there were 9038 African children in 78 primary schools in 1938. Less than 1% of the annual budget was invested in education specifically for the training of a small group of male auxiliaries. There were no public schools or classes for girls; only a tiny number attended the boys' schools. Secondary education was unavailable for African children with the first black African trainee teachers graduating from Ecole Edouard Renard, Brazzaville in early 1939.[26]

Comparatively, the French invested less in the education of Africans compared to the Germans. For instance, the whole Federation of AOF had only 400 primary schools with 22,000 pupils in 1920 compared to 14,000 pupils in German Togo in 1913, and 41,000 in Kamerun, which also had a teacher-training institution, three senior primary schools, and a professional school.[27] Female education in French colonies remained very limited and was worse in Muslim communities. In French North Africa, if male education was limited, girls and women were grossly underrepresented. In Algeria, there were 42,904 Muslim children in primary schools compared to 112,223 European children (with the European population being 20% of the whole) in 1920–1921. Secondary-school bursaries were offered for sons of *qadis* (judges) and junior Muslim functionaries in 1886. In 1914, there were 386 Muslims in lycées, and in 1930 the number increased to 776 (7.7% of the total *lycée* students in Algeria). At the same period in Morocco, restrictions were imposed on African children's access to secondary education; there were no instructions on modern sciences and the humanities.[28] Muslim girls and women were shielded from public spaces such as schools. Only very few of them were enrolled in schools. For example, Senegalese girls' enrollment in public primary schools fluctuated between 200 and 500 in the first three decades of the twentieth century compared to 2500–5000 for boys.[29] Since the French and Islamic ideologies on women were embedded on familial and patriarchal expectations, female education was tailored to reinforce these ideologies and not to alter the fundamental bases of the Muslim family and gender roles. Female education therefore focused on practical training in cooking, childcare, sewing, and other domestic arts.

In both British and French colonies, medicine (training as midwives, nurses, and nursing aids) was one of the first fields that opened for African women an opportunity for post-primary education. But while in British, Belgian Congo and other colonies, these pioneer African midwives were trained in mission institutions,[30] the colonial state took direct responsibility in French West Africa by promoting public health education for African women through the establishment of a school of midwifery in the medical center founded in Dakar, Senegal, in 1918. By 1957, this school had produced over 500 midwives. Before 1938, when teachers' training schools for women were opened in Rufisque, Senegal, and Katibougou in Ivory Coast, colonial midwives were the most highly educated African women in AOF.[31] The *École normale de jeunes filles* (ENJF) for a four-year teacher-training course, and the Dakar School of Medicine and Midwifery (two years of midwifery training) were the only avenues for post-primary advancement for AOF girls and young women. The goal of the ENJF was to produce good housewives and auxiliaries for girls' education. The first class of this elite federal teacher-training college for young women in Rufisque in 1938–1939 comprised seventeen girls from Senegal (mostly from Dakar), nine from Dahomey, eight from Togo, seven from Guinea, four from Ivory Coast, and one from the Soudan. Some 24 of them came from families of government functionaries, eleven from commercial families, seven were daughters of public-work artisans and one was the daughter of a navigator. None of them was the daughter of a traditional elite (chiefs, Islamic clerics, *qadis*, and other leaders). Not only were these girls the daughters of the newly educated African elite, but their fathers provided the strongest encouragement and support for their pursuit of education.[32]

Prior to 1938, women teachers were recruited from those who completed higher primary school in French colonies. At the teacher-training college, their morning classes included French, writing, arithmetic, and the basic sciences, and in the afternoons hygiene, childcare, cooking, sewing, and drawing. Many pioneer graduates of the ENJF later occupied important positions in education, government, and the private sector in Senegal and throughout the AOF where they served as role models especially in the spread of female education. Formal schooling produced African female homemakers, teachers, and professionals. However, both mission and colonial education were lopsided in favor of men and boys. In many colonies, it domesticated African women and girls in ways compatible to European values, gender ideology, and the needs of the colonial state. Formal education, which often was not more than elementary training, was to mold African women and girls into suitable housewives for modern elite men, and ideal mothers and teachers for young children. While boys were trained in literary education (reading, writing, and arithmetic) and to acquire skills and knowledge in literacy, communication, leadership, and other highly skilled artisanal work such as carpentry, building, plumbing, horticulture, and animal husbandry, young women and girls were trained in rudimentary reading, writing, arithmetic, child care and domestic skills. Generally, French education for boys was to train them to perform lower-level bureaucratic services, but female education was to serve as a springboard for the civilizing mission. The expectation was that educated African girls as culturally assimilated young women would foster the reproduction of French colonial society in Africa by becoming pious Catholic wives and mothers instilling French values in future generations of Africans.

Just as in Gabon where 60% of Gabonese pupils and students attended Catholic schools,[33] in the Belgian Congo education in general was entrusted to the Catholic Church.[34] Female education, in particular, which was managed by nuns, was offered to African girls and women with a more conservative gender-based tradition. Boys and men were the first to receive formal education and instruction was in French. Prior to the 1948 educational reform, female education in the Belgian Congo was offered in local languages and it was based on domestic science and home management skills as well as feminine characteristics that were defined by Christian values and convictions. In the first phase of a two-stage primary education, instruction was in local languages. Certain pupils were selected for the second-stage where they were prepared for secondary school and instructed in French. At the secondary level, boys were prepared for careers in public service, private enterprise, and post-secondary education. In the new system, Congolese girls received additional training in household management (cooking, ironing, washing, gardening, home furnishing and decoration, cleanliness and orderliness) and in sewing, arithmetic, religion, French, one's local language, geography, music, singing, drawing, gymnastics, and agriculture. They could pursue a three-year middle school in homemaking, or a four-year teacher training program, or a two-year nursing and midwifery instruction course for nurses, nursing assistants, and midwives, followed by practical training. Much emphasis was placed on practice.

The goal of mission and colonial education in Belgian Congo was to produce male assistant clerks, artisans, and medium-level professionals as female education was oriented toward making perfect wives for the male elite (*les évoluees*), informed mothers of families, household managers, and auxiliary teachers, nurses, and midwives. In 1955, there were twenty three girls' schools for apprenticeship and twenty two teacher-training schools for girls with a combined enrollment of 1600 students compared to 7750 boys enrolled in the same type of institutions. There were only six schools for girls, categorized as 'select' upper primary sections with thirty classes that prepared them for post-primary education. In addition, girls and young women had two professional schools for clothing design and sewing, and seven middle schools for household management. The conservative Christian patriarchal norms of mission education backed by colonial legislation exacerbated the educational disparity between boys and girls, and resulted in a dismal record in female education on the eve of Congo's independence in 1960. For example, in 1960, there were 350,000 girls in primary school out of 1.6 million primary pupils, 10,000 girls were attending post-primary and secondary schools with fewer than 1000 in secondary schools out of 29,000 students; there were no females among several hundred Congolese students in the two universities or in the six post-secondary institutions there. There were no females among the 800 secondary-school graduates. The most educationally advanced Congolese woman was a senior in high school.[35] The result of the educational disparity between boys and girls, men and women was that while the mission and colonial system of education distanced women from salaried work and confined them to 'feminine' work, it prepared men for leadership, technical and professional jobs, and reinforced their patriarchal control. A few women who ventured outside the home were limited to the elementary school, the convent, and hospitals as midwives and nurses' aides; but men were employed in the military, the colonial administration, medical service, trading firms, craft industries, agriculture, construction (such as the railway and buildings), teaching, and mission enterprise.

The British differential application of the indirect rule system in Nigeria, as well as different religious ideologies, and the often antagonistic relationship between the missionaries and colonial officers contributed to the educational imbalance between the Northern and Southern Provinces. Southern Provinces and Lagos had enormous educational advantage over the Northern Provinces because the people embraced the missionaries and formal education earlier and with more enthusiasm than the Muslims in the North. For instance, in the South, between 1846 and 1899, different missions had established over a dozen primary schools, five secondary schools for boys and one post-primary school for girls that started in 1895. The first government primary school was established in Lagos in 1899 for the education of Muslim boys. In 1928 there were 49 government primary schools in the South with 8440 boys and 703 girls. Schools for boys had been established in Northern Nigeria since 1910, but the first two girls' schools here were established in Kano and Katsina in 1930 with 15 and 40 pupils respectively. Until 1933, the two girls' schools were called 'centers' and they primarily taught sewing. But within a few years, the curriculum expanded to include reading and writing, the main purpose being to train urban women to be better, healthier wives and mothers. By 1937, primary-school enrollment in the North was merely 10% and secondary school less than 2% that of the South.[36] Out of a school population of 7,750,000 (under 16 years old) in the mid-1940s, 400,000 were at school, with only 30,000 from the whole of the Northern Provinces.[37]

The gendered educational disparity between the North and South was even worse in secondary and higher education. King's College, Lagos (1909) was the first government secondary school, and Queen's College, Lagos (1927) the first government secondary school for girls. In 1928, there were 16 boys' secondary schools with 612 enrollments, and three girls' secondary schools with 53 students in the South. A Women's Training Center (later in 1942, Women's Training College) was established in Sokoto in 1939 to train Muslim women teachers. It started with 24 students who were daughters of northern Muslim aristocrats, many of whom married soon after graduation and were confined to purdah.[38] Female education in the 1940s revealed 'a very backward situation', with 150 girls at the Queen's College, and 2 domestic centers in the South; and for Moslems in the North there were 4 schools at the junior primary level, 'small in size and mediocre in standard', a good training center in Sokoto, and 4 domestic science centers. It would require up to two decades of serious investment in teacher education alone and commitment by all parties involved to bridge the educational disparity between women in the South and their Muslim counterparts in the North.[39] In 1951, out of 16 million northerners, only one had a full university degree, and a couple of teachers had two-year post-teaching college university training in the United Kingdom. They were all males. In 1952, Aminu Kano, a northern progressive politician, established a school for women in Kano where courses were offered in machine sewing, handicrafts, basic Hausa, and English literacy.

The gendered nature of mission and colonial education in Nigeria privileged boys over girls in terms of access to formal schooling, the breadth of its curriculum, and employment opportunities. In 1955, 70% of males were enrolled in primary school compared to 30% of females.[40] Data on secondary school and post-secondary enrollments were worse than primary-school enrollments for girls. For example, Yaba Higher College, the first post-secondary educational institution established in Nigeria in 1932, had 83 female students out of a total enrollment of 1150 by 1961. The University of Ibadan, a premier institution of higher education established in Nigeria in 1948, had 79 female students out of a total student enrollment of 1116 (excluding non-Nigerians).[41]

Furthermore, in British Kenya, there were no high schools for girls until 1950 when the first high school for African girls (the African Girls High School, later the Alliance Girls High School) was established in Kikuyu territory. The only three girls in high school prior to the opening of the girls' high school were admitted in a boys' school (Alliance Boys' High School) in 1950. Among the three girls was Margaret Kenyatta, the daughter of Kenya's first president who later became the first mayor of Nairobi, the capital city, after independence. In 1950, 61 boys had sat for the school certificate examination (high-school diploma) but no girl had done so; however, in 1963, 1292 boys and 199 girls took the examination. Similarly, Nairobi University College had 40 men and a woman in 1965.[42]

In addition to limited access to formal schooling, colonial education offered boys and young men opportunities to train for leadership and other positions in society while domesticating girls and young women through a curriculum that emphasized wifehood, motherhood, home economics and management, hygiene, needlework, and other related activities. Girls and young women were not taught skills useful for wage employment at the primary schools; they also had limited access to secondary education: two factors that enormously impeded their ability to compete favorably with their male counterparts in the labor market. Only very few Nigerian women, for instance, had the opportunity to pursue and acquire higher education and professional certificates and degrees in the above post-secondary institutions and overseas prior to independence in 1960.[43]

Generally, mission and colonial female education in Africa was domestic-oriented because many missionaries did not see wage work as a desirable career for African women and girls. For example, in 1920s–1930s Southern Rhodesia, girls' and women's education was aimed at producing: farmwomen to take care of rural African communities; wives for African teachers, evangelists, builders, clerks, and interpreters; and mothers to raise elite African children. Part of the expectations was that as literate wives and mothers, African women could help to tie African men and their households to African community without threatening European control of Southern Rhodesia through integration. And by working in European households as servants and retainers, mission-educated African women could help safeguard European women and girls from the constant presence of African male domestic servants, and by so doing secure European families. It is therefore not surprising that female education in this colony focused on agriculture, child care, morality, and domestic service and avoided individualism and careerism.[44]

Similarly, mission education for girls and women in South Africa prior to the 1920s pursued the same ideology of domesticity, focusing on housewifery which included cleaning, cooking, sewing, and how to be 'useful' wives, mothers, and women. Some of the female graduates became nurses, teachers, and church workers.[45] In Zanzibar, where the first government girls' school was established in 1927, the curriculum emphasized marriage and motherhood with instructions on modern hygiene, religion, writing, reading, and arithmetic.[46] This type of education offered girls and women limited opportunities to gain qualifications sufficient for careers in teaching, nursing, midwifery, and secretarial services. For the most part, their education was not for employment but implied domesticity; that is, creation of hardworking virtuous Christian wives for emerging male elite Africans, and caring mothers.

In colonial Mozambique, for example, where few children had access to formal schooling, girls had far fewer opportunities than boys to attend school with a course of study that was oriented toward domestic science skills. While the first schools were established for boys by the Christian missions in the 1850s, a girls' school was opened in the 1890s by Catholic nuns. African parents preferred nuns to teach their daughters for some reason, a practice that impeded the education of girls and young women in Mozambique due to a number of factors, including the scarcity of female teachers which continued into the 1950s. At the rudimentary level, boys and young men were instructed in reading and writing in Portuguese and local languages, basic mathematics, history, science, singing, and drawing. Successful ones were eligible to attend trade schools where they learned moral and civic education, as well as manual skills in agriculture, machinery, carpentry and furniture-making, iron work, tailoring, shoe making, and pottery making (a traditional domain of women). The skills and experiences prepared men for leadership roles and integration into the colonial economy. Girls and young women were taught how to read and write, sing and play piano, draw and paint, cut and sew, crochet, bake, wash and iron clothes, and make better homes for themselves as housewives and mothers. Advanced courses included child care, cooking, literacy, embroidery, household maintenance and budgeting, nursing, and teaching. Yet, as in other colonies in Africa, boys' enrollment outpaced that of girls. For instance, in 1920, there were only 632 girls compared to 5995 boys enrolled in Catholic schools in Mozambique; and in 1940, there were 16,573 (30%) girls out of the total of 56,011 student enrollments throughout the colony.[47]

Low enrollments of girls and young women across colonial Africa was a result of various factors, including cultural inhibitions, household labor needs, early marriage, financial constraints, and parental opposition or lack of support for the education of their daughters. Part of the cultural inhibitions involved the interference of formal schooling in female initiation rites, early marriage, and motherhood. Parental opposition was driven by patriarchal sensibilities, economic factors and religious ideologies. For instance, while African parents saw the education of their sons as an investment, they reasoned that the education of their daughters was a waste of resources since they would be married away and take with them any income they would have earned for their natal families. Yet daughters tended to have more domestic obligations than their brothers, and therefore less time to devote to their studies. They were more likely to be withdrawn from school than their brothers for a number of reasons, including death or sickness or any misfortune in the family. Early and teenage pregnancy also contributed to high dropout rates for girls. Moreover, girls usually started schooling at a later age than their brothers and also spent fewer years in school than boys. As a result, fewer numbers of girls than boys attended school. They were under-represented in school enrollments, particularly in the higher standards or classes. Similarly, their graduation rate was minimally low. For example, in German Duala and Victoria (Kamerun/Cameroon) only three of the twenty five primary graduates in 1900 were girls. All the male graduates were employed as court clerks, sales clerks, teaching aides, customs inspectors or were offered scholarships to study carpentry and teaching.[48]

Gender-based educational imbalance was compounded by the intersection of class and gender. In colonial Africa, particularly in the countryside where the mass of peasants lived, girls and women served as the backbone of subsistence agriculture and rural economies. Here, girls' and women's labor value without formal education was higher than in the cities because they were more active economically in agriculture and trade, two areas vital to their household survival and the sustenance of rural economies. Thus, women's labor value, both in their households and communities, superseded their desire to attend formal schooling. Cost of education, lower quality of girls' schools, long distances to rural schools without adequate and affordable means of transport, and seclusion of Muslim girls at puberty were contributory factors to the low female enrollments in schools and their high dropout rates. Other inhibitive factors were lack of or discrimination in employment opportunities in the public and private sectors for female products of formal education; and the general belief by African parents that the education of their daughters had no benefits to their families since they would be married away.

Often, class played a significant role in determining girls' and young women's access to formal education as children of Western-educated parents and those whose parents were affiliated with the mission or colonial administration or foreign trading companies were more likely than children of rural peasants and pastoralists to attend and graduate from formal schooling. In different parts of colonial Africa, there were many instances of Western-educated fathers demanding that their daughters' education should equip them to become suitably socialized wives for the emergent male elite and future mothers.[49] For example, the education of Senegalese girls only became a major policy discussion after the emergence of a new social class of educated elite males who supported the education of their sons and daughters but with different foci: sons for future leaders and daughters as wives of leaders and future mothers skilled in Western feminine norms, sociability, and accomplishments.

Similarly, in Mozambique, children of the African middle class benefited from the elite status of their parents in many ways. Following the passage of the Missionary Accord in 1940 that transferred the education of African children to the Catholic Church, and the imposition of Portuguese as the language of instruction, many Mozambican children faced restricted access to formal schooling. The Catholic Church imposed school fees, age restrictions, and conversion to Catholicism and baptism of Catholics as conditions for enrollment and promotion to another level. African children were taught in overcrowded classrooms based on rote learning with lack of teaching materials, and were subjected to all kinds of physical violence in the name of discipline for speaking their local languages, engaging in disruptive behaviors, or failing to demonstrate the ability to learn fast. Children of the tiny African middle class, who were fluent in Portuguese because Portuguese was spoken in their homes, had an advantage when entering the colonial education system. Their parents could also afford to pay their school fees. Generally, in their cultural elitism, the Portuguese colonizers who designated African languages as dialects, considered Africans with literacy in African languages as illiterate, and only accepted fluency and literacy in Portuguese as true markers of an educated African eligible for social mobility.[50]

When it came to the decision of whom to send to formal school, African parents for the most part chose their sons over their daughters. Under the colonial system that denied women access to employment opportunities, African parents saw no benefits in girls' education because they were expected to be married away with whatever skills and resources they had acquired. Many parents would argue that a girl did not live by books but in caring for the home and the farm and in engaging in village markets. In many colonies such as the Congo-Brazzaville, daughters were withdrawn from school during peak farming seasons for farm work.[51] In colonial Kenya, formal education was seen as 'a pollutant [that would] affect a wide range of cultural practices and beliefs'; educated females were regarded as 'prostitutes' and 'badly behaved'.[52] Even as late as the 1950s and 1960s, many African men preferred to marry women with little or no literacy skills for fear of their being 'too wise and wayward'. Marrying Western-educated and professional women, referred to as *acada* women by the Igbo of Nigeria (*acada*: a corruption of the English word *academic*), was often considered as taking a bad risk, for such women had passed the age considered normal for marriage and reproduction, and could also be headstrong.[53]

In many parts of colonial Africa, young women and girls generally withdrew from school or abandoned their wage employment, especially when male authority was threatened. In my study of Igbo women of southeastern Nigeria, I documented cases where girls and young women were withdrawn from school and female teachers were forced to abandon their teaching careers for petty trade when they got married because trading offered them the flexibility to carry out their familial responsibilities and expectations.[54] In Southern Rhodesia, the first class of educated African women were hired in the 1920s as infant class teachers or junior teachers until they were married.[55] The resistance against girls' and women's education and wage employment was worse in Muslim communities, where Islam posed a formidable barrier to the expansion of formal education. In Algeria, in 1954, only 4.5% of women could read and write and they had no access to employment except in jobs not demanding professional qualifications. On the eve of independence in 1962, there were no more than six female doctors, 25 secondary-school teachers and no women in higher education. Out of the 500 students at the University of Algiers, only 50 were female.[56] In northern Nigeria there were fewer educated women than among their southern counterparts due to opposition from Muslim men. For example, a 1940 report noted the dearth of women teachers in Nigeria as so worrisome, with only one African graduate in the entire colony, that although European teachers were expensive, it would require 10 more years before an African cadre would be built up in the South, and 25 years in the North.[57]

In Muslim societies such as Zanzibar, parents used puberty as a reason to withdraw their daughters from school, primarily for marriage. To track Zanzibari schoolgirls' physical development and determine their puberty age, medical inspections were introduced in schools in 1913. When medical inspection intensified in the 1930s and 1940s, it became a reason for parents to withdraw their daughters from school. Muslim parents saw marriage as an institution where female sexuality had to be contained, and thus the 'longer a girl spent at school after puberty, the more her respectability came into question'.[58] Breaking the rules of respectability was also why unwed pregnant schoolgirls were expelled from school. Zanzibari schoolgirls were believed to have posed a high risk of disgracing their families and therefore being unmarriageable if they chose academic advancement before marriage.

Generally, in colonial Africa, only a tiny minority of African girls and women, boys and men acquired an education beyond the primary-school grades. For instance, according to a UNESCO publication, 88.5% of African women and 73.4% of men were reported to be illiterate in 1960, and in 1970 the figures were 82.4% for women and 58.3% for men.[59] Some colonies were worse than others, especially Belgian Congo and Portuguese colonies. For example, in 1970 (five years before independence), only 6% of Mozambican women and girls and 12% of boys and men completed primary-school education; and 93% of Mozambican women and 86% of men were considered illiterate in Portuguese.[60] The gender disparity in access to formal education as well as the quality of the content and methods of instruction undercut African women and girls in the labor market. While boys and men were better prepared than women and girls for salaried work, ideologically, they were the ones found ideal to be hired by the government, the military, the mission, and the private sector. The cumulative impact was that fewer African women and girls were gainfully employed in jobs only available to Africans. For example, in Mozambique in 1960, there were 31 female nurses out of 191 African nurses; out of 115 African primary-school teachers, only 4 were women; and there were 14 African women out of a total of 234 African high-school teachers.[61]

Furthermore, the way mission and colonial education domesticated African women and girls distanced them from the labor market, and reinforced male dominance over them. However, female education at all levels was transformative and offered a tiny fraction of African women opportunities for spatial, social, and economic mobility. In spite of the barriers and challenges, African women and girls were able to acquire formal education that prepared them for opportunities outside the household. With their formal education, women and girls in colonial Africa became seamstresses, teachers, secretaries, nurses, midwives, and other professionals, as well as nannies, servants, proprietors of small-scale domestic training centers, catering centers, and businesses, activities which helped them to build independent economic bases. But they were a tiny minority compared to their male counterparts. This group of women became pioneers of a modern, African, female middle class, acquiring new identities and enhanced status in their own right and often refusing to abandon their professions upon marriage, although some succumbed to patriarchal, cultural, and religious pressures. The women successfully negotiated a balance between their family lives, employment, and professional growth. Some of them further enhanced their status through their marriages to members of the new African elite. In addition, many African women and girls took their formal education as a springboard for resistance against patriarchal authorities, including colonial and indigenous ones. Formal education was transformative to this group of women because it equipped them with knowledge of alternative skills, values, and lifestyles to forge new alliances and networks for individual identity and self-esteem as well as for group solidarity and community.

Ambiguities of the Colonial Legal System and African Womanhood

The ambiguities of European colonialism and the nature and range of women's strategic engagements with it were also demonstrated in the legal system. The key question here is: How did women employ colonial legal instruments and strategies to deal with multiple and diverse circumstances, institutions, and authority figures? The colonial dual legal structures of customary/Islamic codes and statutory and common laws ambivalently reinforced patriarchy while at the same time opening new avenues for African women's mobility and self-assertion. They gave African women, individually and collectively, opportunities to challenge with varying degrees of success indigenous social-control institutions, inhibitive practices, and authority figures. The colonial courts were thus battlegrounds where husbands and wives, men and women, fathers and daughters, widows and their in-laws, old and new elites, elders and youths, relatives, neighbors, slaves, and masters, as well as the subordinated and their superiors contested power relations. Sometimes, they presented women with avenues and new opportunities to negotiate autonomy. Studies on the codification of African marriages, bridewealth transfers, divorce proceedings, inheritance, and child custody in public records have demonstrated the ambivalence of such laws in subjecting women to a new dual patriarchy (what Schmidt, in reference to Shona women of Southern Rhodesia, described as being 'beholden to two patriarchies' of African men backed by colonial officials), as well as creating new opportunities for them but within the context of a paternalistic and restrictive colonial state.[62]

The codification and modification of customary marriage laws became imperative in the face of instability in African marriages caused by high divorce rates, exorbitant bridewealth, adultery, and civil and violent conflict between men and women with its negative impact on socio-economic development and population growth. While colonial officials consulted African men and used them to enforce the laws, nobody sought the opinions of African women and girls in the legal matters that affected them, simply because they were seen as minors and dependants of men. In some colonies, the colonial government in collaboration with elite African men reinforced patriarchy by codifying marriage and family laws to enforce senior men's control over women and junior men. The courts had punished adulterous wives and their lovers by imposing fines on them. Runaway wives were also prosecuted and fined. The courts had denied divorces to women on the grounds that their reasons for desiring to end their marriages were insufficient. The male-controlled local courts usually ordered women to return to their husbands or be liable to contempt of court and fined.[63] In this way, they curtailed women's efforts to maintain autonomy over their marital status.

However, African women demonstrated their agency in various ways, including circumventing the laws, or selecting aspects that protected their interests, or negotiating with male authorities to minimize their negative impact. Some of them resorted to divorce, desertion of their husbands, and elopement. Just as in the cases of the Gusii of Kenya and the Yoruba of colonial Lagos, most women stayed in their homes and argued their cases in local African courts presided over by elderly men, or sought justice in colonial courts dominated by Europeans.[64] Yet Zulu women of Natal (now KwaZulu Natal) were active agents in challenging the patriarchal nature and meaning of custom and customary law that attempted to control their bodies and spatial mobility by appearing in colonial courts as litigants and witnesses.[65] The law courts enabled women to strategically negotiate and manipulate the law in their favor and reshape women's expectations in marriage.

African women and girls used the courts to neutralize men's hegemony as they sought for divorce or justified their escape from unsatisfactory marital situations. Women gained some rights, such as those to divorce and certain inheritance. Divorce was always granted to women as long as they transferred back the bridewealth to their husbands and paid for any damages.[66] In Northern Ghana, for example, the colonial courts awarded husbands monetary compensation when their wives abandoned their conjugal homes. The courts granted husbands the right to divorce their wives and claim damages for adultery alone, but wives could divorce their husbands only if the adultery involved crimes such as desertion, incest, rape, cruelty, bestiality, or sodomy. For five decades, women litigated their domestic disputes before the courts, a mark of protracted resistance. But while the courts allowed husbands to assert ownership over their wives, the latter exercised more control outside the courts.[67]

Women contested for inheritance rights and were successful to varying degrees. Widows and heirs of their deceased husbands also contested boundaries of levirate marriage, with the courts granting women the right to make the determination on their marital status. In AOF, Muslim wives of African soldiers turned to French officers for the adjudication of their divorce and inheritance rather than to the Islamic courts, even though the latter allowed the women's families to keep the bridewealth which they had to return in French courts.[68] The French courts as in other colonial legal systems granted legal custody of children to their fathers who had paid bridewealth but maternal care and physical custody for under-aged children. Widows were however granted full custody of their children instead of heirs of the deceased husbands. Moreover, women used both the civil and military courts to sue their husbands for family support or damages from domestic violence.

It is important to note that what the colonial officers codified as customary laws or Islamic laws (sharia) were the males' interpretations, which always protected their status and undermined women's. For example, in the northern Nigerian Kano emirate, women lost their inheritance rights over houses and farms for more than 30 years (1923–1954) as a result of the emirs' interpretation of the sharia on the subject. The British accepted Emir Usman's deliberate misinterpretation of the sharia that women never inherited houses and farms. But the Islamic law guarantees daughters one-half of their brothers' shares of inheritance. Usman used the Islamic law to protect male authority when it was threatened by women's property ownership, capitalizing on women's political powerlessness and the concern that women's property ownership would turn them into prostitutes. However, in 1954, Emir Muhammadu Sanusi restored women's right to inheritance as an ameliorative measure to poverty and destitution of elderly women, citing that the sharia had never prohibited women from inheriting houses and farms.[69]

In spite of gains made in terms of rights to divorce, inheritance, and physical custody of minor children, African women remained undermined by the colonial legal pluralism of common and statutory laws, religious and customary laws which complicated the administration of justice in different colonies. Matters relating to death, divorce, child custody, and inheritance remained under customary law prescribed and enforced by men. With little oversight by European officers, African male elders prescribed and proscribed judgments according to local logic which was guided by discriminatory patriarchal sensibilities and notions of women's appropriate role in social and familial relations. Among all the colonial and customary laws, it was those over land ownership that had the most profound impact on African women because they touched on women's livelihood and economic independence. African women had to learn how to negotiate all the legislative and regulatory measures and prohibitive social conventions imposed on them by colonial officials, the missions, and African men. These new impositions limited African women's choices, their rights, and mobility.

Migration and Criminalization of African Womanhood

Migration of men (especially in East, Central, and Southern Africa to the cities, mines and other sites of employment) and the restriction of women's movement from the countryside to those new sites created by colonialism were other examples of colonial gender discrimination against women. Studies of different colonial settings in Africa have shown how women negotiated their restrictions to migrate to urban areas, where the intersection of African ideologies with European values has been most dramatic and contentious; as well as their criminalization as prostitutes and 'health hazards' for venturing to these centers of employment; and how such discriminatory regulations and invasive medicalization of their bodies circumscribed African women's opportunities, upward mobility, and autonomy.⁷⁰ In many colonies, African women used spatial mobility to new centers (towns, missions, schools, mines, markets, and farms) created by colonialism as a means of neutralizing rural patriarchal control over them and their daughters.

In Basutoland, for example, the British issued the Basutoland Native Women's Restriction Proclamation of 1915, a law which imposed three months' imprisonment on any offender, to institutionalize the control of rural women's spatial mobility. Colonial officials saw urbanized women as fosterers of 'disease, alcoholism and insubordination in naïve young' male miners. But from the 1930s interwar years, Basotho women ignored the law and migrated to towns, mines and to South Africa where they set up shops as brewers and sellers of illicit liquor and sex.⁷¹ In colonial Swaziland, the number of Swazi women engaging in transborder migration to South Africa was curtailed due to the stringent measures, including a pass system, taken by the state, the Church, and local patriarchies to control female spatial mobility.⁷² However, even though old rules and constraints were curtailed in these new centers, African women confronted and devised strategies to deal with new forms of patriarchy with their accompanying challenges and obstacles.

Often the efforts of the colonial state and African local authorities to prevent the urban migration of women which capital and industry had encouraged revealed the complexity and subtlety of a system of alliances and contradictions between the state and capital, women and men, town and countryside, and subsistence and capitalist modes of production, as Chauncey's study of the Zambian Copperbelt and Barnes's account of Southern Rhodesia have demonstrated.⁷³ In both colonies, the state and African local authorities discouraged and worked against the migration of women to mining towns and cities because women were needed for the sustenance of the rural economies. The state, through legislative apparatuses, acknowledged and reinforced African men's claims over women: claims of fathers and husbands over their daughters and wives respectively. In Southern Rhodesia, single women and unemployed men were required to carry passes that authorized them to enter towns, but married women were allowed without passes to join their husbands who were employed. However, the mining companies encouraged the presence of women and families in their compounds and mining towns because women's unpaid labor (all the myriad domestic tasks they performed, including cooking, cleaning, sewing, child rearing, as well as supplementing males' incomes and providing sexual services) were vital for the reproduction of migrant male labor, increased productivity, and the development of colonial capitalism. In spite of the ban, married and single African women managed to migrate to the towns and cities. For example, in Salisbury (Southern Rhodesia) in 1936, there were 150 wives, 150 'respectable' single women, 50 prostitutes, and 450 concubines; and in Bulawayo, there were 200 married women, 300 prostitutes, and 725 concubines.⁷⁴ Many female urban migrants entered into different kinds of relationships with men, including temporary marriages. Such marriages and female entrepreneurship demonstrated the resourcefulness of African women in achieving economic and social independence. Women's independence and the recognition of urban marriages undermined the structural basis upon which elder men controlled the labor of African women and young men in the countryside.

Studies of colonial Africa have shown that African and foreign workingmen in military garrisons, towns, mines, and farms sought 'the comforts of home' exemplified in African female companionship, prepared meals, clean clothing, shelter, and often stable households (where marriage and children were involved).[75] Significantly, even when the power relations between the different actors were largely unequal, agency was not one-sided or limited to one gender. Thus, African women's participation in those relationships was not necessarily as victims but also as actors. African women strategically employed their sexuality for security and mobility. Yet their sexuality was often exploited and criminalized by European colonial officers and their African agents; and demonized by European women. It is not surprising that the control of African women's mobility and sexuality united African men and European men and women in a patriarchal alliance. European women joined the campaign for increased patriarchal control over African women because they wanted to keep African women out of their homes and away from their husbands. They vilified African women and publicized the so-called yellow peril: the miscegenation caused by sexual relations between European men and African women as was the case in Southern Rhodesia.[76]

Furthermore, while the official position of the British Parliament and the colonial authorities was total disapproval of any sexual liaisons between European men and African women, the French pursued an ambivalent policy on the issue. At a certain point, the French government encouraged their officers to take African women as mistresses but at another such practice was discouraged. Although there is evidence that many white men had African mistresses in colonial Nigeria and other British colonies, with some children born out of such liaisons, what guided 'officers' sexual relations across racial boundaries' were discretion and reticence.[77] On the contrary, before racial prejudice overtook French policy in Africa, their officers were allowed and encouraged to take local mistresses. But from the 1880s, African women were banned from military garrisons for allegedly causing the underperformance of French officers, the same period the French encouraged their African soldiers to use kidnapping or raiding of their villages and towns as a means of acquiring 'wives'. In Senegal, French officers blamed African women for all forms of undisciplined behavior by the soldiers, accusing them of having deleterious influence on military conduct and bearing. They called the women 'prostitutes', 'scavengers' and 'parasites', who not only transmitted diseases to the soldiers, but also consumed their earnings and bonuses.[78] The blaming of African women for the transmission and spread of all kinds of diseases, particularly those associated with sexuality, in cities, towns, and around mining centers and military bases led to the invasive medicalization of their bodies across the continent.[79]

Yet despite efforts by the French officers to discourage African soldiers from going after their women, they sought lovers and wives from surrounding villages and vicinities for companionship, food, sexual gratification, and a better shelter the women provided to the soldiers, which was more attractive than the 'stuffy rooms of the barracks or brothels'.[80] Recognizing these important services provided by African women, especially in creating stable family life to the soldiers which helped to increase their morale and reduce desertions, as well as costs of lodging and maintenance, the French colonial military institutionalized the domesticity of their African troops in Senegal from 1880 by encouraging the establishment of families or households in villages near military posts and garrisons. In Congo Brazzaville, the French colonial government established official brothels during the Second World War to cater for the sexual needs of soldiers.[81]

Western Sudan was a region already ravaged by warfare in the 1880s, where most recruits and their women were prisoners-of-war of Al-Hajj Umar and Samori Touré. Recognizing the invaluable services of African women to the colonial military, the French allowed African soldiers (*tirailleurs*) to capture women for marriage. There was, for example, the case of the infamous Voulet-Chanoine expedition of 1898–1899, which adjusted its original plan of occupying Chad to capturing and enslaving more than 600 women from the Bambara and Segun areas. French officers gave these women captives to their African soldiers for marriage as an incentive to gain their loyalty and commitment to service. Within the French colonial circle, these marriages were 'a welcomed liberation from slavery' for the women and the soldiers as well as a great opportunity to establish families and households.[82] But the policy broke marriages in rural villages when some married women abandoned their impoverished husbands for African soldiers who enjoyed economic and social mobility. In Equatorial Africa, while some African soldiers used their allowances for bridewealth, others took in female slaves who had escaped from captivity and sought their protection as wives.

Women in both Western Sudan and Equatorial Africa served as porters and cooks for the military, often following their husbands' or lovers' military columns and pitching their own camps as bands of women and children, cooking and cleaning for their men. On rare occasions, such as at Adrar in Western Sudan in 1905, women fought alongside their husbands who had been ambushed by the Tuareg cavalry.[83] In these areas, wives and female companions served as a bridge between the military and the civilian populations and fostered the colonial government's efforts to harness the resources of the local economy and also save the government money for housing and feeding the African servicemen. Ironically, in spite of the valuable services that African women had rendered to the colonial military, widows were denied their husbands' pensions or any benefits because the French colonial government did not recognize customary marriages. And even though the women served as porters, cooks and servants, they never enjoyed any benefits as their husbands or common-law husbands who were enlisted in the army. In spite of African women's resourcefulness, they were still shortchanged by the colonial state and military through their gender-based policies that were dictated by patriarchal sensibilities and norms.

Conclusion

This chapter has addressed how African women: navigated the many twists and turns of the complex and highly gendered colonial terrains; variously dealt with the tensions and conflicts created as a result of the juxtaposition of indigenous cultural sensibilities and colonial transformative forces and situations; were affected by the encounter with European colonialism and how they responded to colonial conditions in their respective communities. I have argued that African women's diverse experiences and their heterogeneous modes of resistance, adjustment, and negotiation to the changing colonial times and the massively transformed indigenous institutions, worldviews, and livelihoods were in defense of their womanhood and agency, and their households and communities. African women's response to mission and colonial domination and intrusiveness came in various forms, including acceptance, cooperation, compliance, circumvention, migration, outright rejection, violation, boycotts, strikes, sit-ins, protest demonstrations, waging wars, nudity, and the establishment of African independent churches and community schools. They demonstrated their agency by deploying complex and diverse initiatives that questioned conventional norms, and by strategically negotiating with colonial and indigenous authority figures who defined and regulated them. African women's colonial historiography has shown a historical experience that was marked by both opportunities and limitations; as well as the diverse ways they engaged different authorities and power brokers around them and the myriad contradictory policies imposed on them. It is not surprising that 'colonizing [African] women', as Kanogo aptly states, 'drew together the largest number of relentless power brokers' across the continent.[84]

The ambivalent impact of mission and colonial education on African women has also been analyzed. The gender-based formal education domesticated African women and girls and placed them at a disadvantaged position vis-à-vis their male counterparts in the competitive labor market. It also reinforced African male dominance over women and girls. But in its transformative mode, formal education offered women and girls opportunities to navigate geographical, cultural, ideological, and social boundaries which resulted in their acculturation and socio-economic mobility. It transformed African women's identities by creating the pioneer working-class women and professional elite in the continent who were equipped with knowledge of alternative skills, values, and lifestyles to form new alliances and networks for their individual self-esteem and group solidarity. Remarkably, these women successfully negotiated a balance between their family life, employment, and professional growth. Many of them became leaders in their respective communities, professions, organizations, and countries. They also served as role models to subsequent generations of African girls and young women.

With its variegated outcomes, colonialism created new avenues of power and authority as it foreclosed others. Generally, colonialism undermined African women's political power and authority just as it created new avenues and power structures that enabled a tiny minority to serve in the colonial bureaucracies as chiefs, advisers, treasurers, ritual specialists, informants, and agents. It showcased the collective power of African women just as it sharpened their individualism. In numerous instances, African women used the provisions of the customary and colonial laws as interpreted in colonial courts to assert their agency on their own terms, for example over divorce, inheritance, custody rights, choice of liaisons and marriages. African women as historical actors questioned and complicated the colonial and missionary fixed boundaries of male and female spaces, gender roles, public and domestic, morality and immorality, and legality and illegality.

Colonialism created spaces that congregated various kinds of people and conditions that forced them to define and redefine the meanings and boundaries of African cultural norms and practices, customary and European laws, indigenous and formal education, and gender roles and expectations. Attempts to mold an African womanhood in an acceptable fashion (or what were considered to be appropriate gender roles, spaces and identities through mission and colonial education, codified family and marriage laws, the courts, restricted spatial mobility, and limited employment opportunities, as well as alliances between European and indigenous authorities) were met with mixed reactions from both the colonized and the colonizers. They also produced unintended and uncontrollable outcomes that paradoxically enhanced women's upward mobility and undermined it, too. The history of colonialism and African womanhood is characterized by protracted negotiations, reformulations, and contestations of strategies by African women as they dealt with diverse constituencies and conditions that mediated their lives, their households, and their communities. It was a history of African women's versatility, assertiveness, resourcefulness, survival and resilience, resistance and cooperation, collectivism and individualism, hopefulness and disappointments, and of successes and failures.

Notes

1. See, for instance, Gloria Chuku, *Igbo Women and Economic Transformation in Southeastern Nigeria, 1900–1960* (London: Routledge, 2005); Tabitha Kanogo, *African Womanhood in Colonial Kenya, 1900–50* (Oxford, UK: James

Currey, 2005); Jean Allman, Susan Geiger and Nakanyike Musisi, eds., *Women in African Colonial Histories* (Bloomington: Indiana University Press, 2002); Jean Allman and Victoria Tashjian, *"I Will Not Eat Stone": A Women's History of Colonial Asante* (Portsmouth, NH: Heinemann, 2000); and Marc Epprecht, *"This Matter of Women Is Getting Very Bad": Gender, Development and Politics in Colonial Lesotho* (Natal, South Africa: University of Natal Press, 2000).
2. See Corrie Decker, *Mobilizing Zanzibari Women: The Struggle for Respectability and Self-Reliance in Colonial East Africa* (New York: Palgrave Macmillan, 2014); Janice Boddy, *Civilizing Women: British Crusaders in Colonial Sudan* (Princeton, NJ: Princeton University Press, 2007); Brett L. Shadle, *"Girl Cases": Marriage and Colonialism in Gusiiland, Kenya, 1890–1970* (Portsmouth, NH: Heinemann, 2006); Allman, Geiger and Musisi, eds., *Women in African Colonial Histories*; Teresa A. Barnes, *"We Women Worked So Hard": Gender, Urbanization and Social Reproduction in Colonial Harare, Zimbabwe, 1930–1956* (Portsmouth, NH: Heinemann, 1999); and Kathleen Sheldon, ed., *Courtyards, Markets, City Streets: Urban Women in Africa* (Boulder, CO: Westview Press, 1996).
3. See Marijke Steegstra, "Krobo Queen Mothers: Gender, Power, and Contemporary Female Traditional Authority in Ghana," *Africa Today* 55, no. 3 (2009): 105–23; T.C. McCaskie, "The Life and Afterlife of Yaa Asantewaa," *Africa* 77, no. 2 (2007): 151–79; Holly Hanson, "Queen Mothers and Good Government in Buganda: The Loss of Women's Political Power in Nineteenth-Century East Africa," in *Women in African Colonial Histories*, ed. Allman, Geiger and Musisi, 219–36; Robert B. Edgerton, *Warrior Women: The Amazons of Dahomey and the Nature of War* (Boulder, CO: Westview Press, 2000); Edna G. Bay, *Wives of the Leopard: Gender, Politics, and Culture in the Kingdom of Dahomey* (Charlottesville: University of Virginia Press, 1998); Flora Edouwaye Kaplan, ed., *Queens, Queen Mothers, Priestesses, and Power: Case Studies in African Gender* (New York: New York Academy of Sciences, 1997); Emmanuel K. Akyeampong and Pashington Obeng, "Spirituality, Gender and Power in Asante History," *International Journal of African Historical Studies* 28, no. 3 (1995): 481–508; Oladipo Yemitan, *Madame Tinubu: Merchant and King-Maker* (Ibadan, Nigeria: University Press 1987); and Bolanle Awe, "The Iyalode in the Traditional Yoruba Political System," in *Sexual Stratification: A Cross-Cultural View*, ed. Alice Schlegel (New York: Columbia University Press, 1977), 144–60.
4. Emily Lynn Osborn, *Our New Husbands Are Here: Households, Gender, and Politics in a West African State from the Slave Trade to Colonial Rule* (Athens: Ohio University Press, 2011).
5. See Gloria Chuku, "Okwei," in *The Oxford Dictionary of African Biography*, Vol. 5, ed. Emmanuel K. Akyeampong and Henry Louis Gates Jr. (Oxford, UK: Oxford University Press, 2012), 26–28; Gloria Chuku, "Ugbabe, Ahebi," in *Dictionary of African Biography*, Vol. 6, ed. Akyeampong and Louis Jr., 94–96; Gloria Chuku, "Igbo Women and Political Participation in Nigeria, 1800s–2005," *International Journal of African Historical Studies* 42, no. 1 (2009): 81–103; and Felicia Ekejiuba, "Omu Okwei, the Merchant Queen of Ossomari: A Biographical Sketch," *Journal of the Historical Society of Nigeria* 3, 4 (1967): 633–46.

6. Lynda Day, *Gender and Power in Sierra Leone: Women Chiefs of the Last Two Centuries* (New York: Palgrave Macmillan, 2012); Lorelle D. Semley, *Mother Is Gold, Father Is Glass: Gender and Colonialism in a Yoruba Town* (Bloomington, IN: Indiana University Press, 2011); and Epprecht, "*This Matter of Women Is Getting Very Bad.*"
7. Semley, *Mother Is Gold, Father Is Glass*.
8. Day, *Gender and Power in Sierra Leone*; Caroline Bledsoe, "The Political Use of Sande Ideology and Symbolism," *American Ethnologist* 11, no. 3 (1984): 445–72; Carol P. Hoffer, "Madam Yoko: Ruler of the Kpa Mende Confederacy," in *Woman, Culture, and Society*, ed. Michelle Rosaldo and Louise Lamphere (Stanford, CA: Stanford University Press, 1974), 173–87; and Carol P. Hoffer, "Mende and Sherbro Women in High Office," *Canadian Journal of African Studies* 6, no. 2 (1972): 151–64.
9. Marc Epprecht, "Women's 'Conservatism' and the Politics of Gender in Late Colonial Lesotho," *Journal of African History* 36, no. 1 (1995): 39–40.
10. Epprecht, "Women's 'Conservatism' and the Politics of Gender," 34.
11. Epprecht, "*This Matter of Women Is Getting Very Bad*;" Epprecht, "Women's 'Conservatism' and the Politics of Gender," 35, 37–39.
12. See Elizabeth Schmidt, *Mobilizing the Masses: Gender, Ethnicity, and Class in the Nationalist Movement in Guinea, 1939–1958* (Portsmouth, NH: Heinemann, 2005); Tanya Lyons, *Guns and Guerilla Girls: Women in the Zimbabwean Liberation Struggle* (Trenton, NJ: Africa World Press, 2004); Susan Geiger, *TANU Women: Gender and Culture in the Making of Tanganyikan Nationalism, 1955–1965* (Portsmouth, NH: Heinemann, 1997); Cora Ann Presley, *Kikuyu Women, the Mau Mau Rebellion, and Social Change in Kenya* (Boulder, CO: Westview Press, 1992); Amrit Wilson, *The Challenge Road: Women and the Eritrean Revolution* (Trenton, NJ: The Red Sea Press, 1991); Cherryl Walker, *Women and Resistance in South Africa* (New York: Monthly Review Press, 1982); and Stephanie Urdang, *Fighting Two Colonialisms: Women in Guinea-Bissau* (New York: Monthly Review Press, 1979).
13. Linda J. Beck, "Democratization and the Hidden Public: The Impact of Patronage Networks on Senegalese Women," *Comparative Politics* 35, no. 2 (2003): 153.
14. Beck, "Democratization and the Hidden Public;" Hilary Jones, *The Metis of Senegal: Urban Life and Politics in French West Africa* (Bloomington: Indiana University Press, 2013); Solang Bandiaky, "Engendering Exclusion in Senegalese Democratic Decentralization: Subordinating Women through Participatory Natural Resource Management" (PhD diss., Department of Women's and Gender Studies, Clark University, Worcester, Massachusetts, 2008).
15. Jane Turrittin, "Aoua Keita and the Nascent Women's Movement in the French Soudan," *African Studies Review* 36, no. 1 (1993): 59–89.
16. Rachel Jean-Baptiste, *Conjugal Rights: Marriage, Sexuality, and Urban Life in Colonial Libreville, Gabon* (Athens: Ohio University Press, 2014), 95; Rachel Jean-Baptiste, "'These Laws should be Made by Us': Customary Marriage Law, Codification and Political Authority in Twentieth-Century Colonial Gabon," *Journal of African History* 49, no. 2 (2008): 217–40.
17. Meredeth Turshen, "Algerian Women in the Liberation Struggle and the Civil War: From Active Participants to Passive Victims?" *Social Research* 69, no. 3

(2002): 889–911; Daniele Djamila Amrane-Minne and Farida Abu-Haidar, "Women and Politics in Algeria from the War of Independence to Our Day," *Research in African Literatures* 30, no. 3 (1999): 62–77; and Rick Fantasia and Eric L. Hirsch, "Culture in Rebellion: The Appropriation and Transformation of the Veil in the Algerian Revolution," in *Social Movements and Culture*, ed. Hank Johnston and Bert Klandermans (Minneapolis: University of Minnesota Press, 1995), 144–60.
18. Epprecht, "*This Matter of Women Is Getting Very Bad.*"
19. Scott Rosenberg and Richard F. Weisfelder, *Historical Dictionary of Lesotho*, 2nd ed. (Lanham, MD: Scarecrow Press, 2013), 63 and 295.
20. Epprecht, "Women's 'Conservatism' and the Politics of Gender," 49.
21. Ibid., 52.
22. See Chuku, "Igbo Women and Political Participation in Nigeria"; Jonathan T. Reynolds, *The Time of Politics (Zamanin Siyasa): Islam and the Politics of Legitimacy in Northern Nigeria, 1950–1966* (Lanham, MD: University Press of America, 1999); Barbara J. Callaway, "Women and Political Participation in Kano City," *Comparative Politics* 19, no. 4 (1987): 379–93; and Nina Mba, *Nigerian Women Mobilized: Women's Political Activity in Southern Nigeria, 1900–1965* (Berkeley: University of California Press, 1982).
23. See Karen T. Hansen, ed., *African Encounters with Domesticity* (New Brunswick, NJ: Rutgers University Press, 1992).
24. Jones, *The Metis of Senegal*, 96–108; Martin Thomas, *The French Empire between the Wars: Imperialism, Politics and Society* (Manchester, UK: Manchester University Press, 2005), 151–84; and Diane Barthel, "Women's Educational Experience under Colonialism: Towards a Diachronic Model," *Signs* 11, no. 1 (1985): 141.
25. Olatunji Oloruntimehin, "Education for Colonial Dominance in French West Africa from 1900 to Second World War," *Journal of the Historical Society of Nigeria* 7, no. 2 (1974): 354.
26. Phyllis M. Martin, *Catholic Women of Congo-Brazzaville: Mothers and Sisters in Troubled Times* (Bloomington: Indiana University Press, 2009), 75–76; Thomas, *The French Empire between the Wars*, 173–74; Peggy R. Sabatier, "'Elite' Education in French West Africa: The Era of Limits, 1903–1945," *International Journal of African Historical Studies* 11, no. 2 (1978): 247–66; and David E. Gardinier, "Schooling in the States of Equatorial Africa," *Canadian Journal of African Studies* 8, no. 3 (1974): 517–38.
27. Oloruntimehin, "Education for Colonial Dominance in French West Africa," 350.
28. Thomas, *The French Empire between the Wars*, 175.
29. Barthel, "Women's Educational Experience under Colonialism," 142–43.
30. See, for instance, Boddy, *Civilizing Women*; Nancy Rose Hunt, *A Colonial Lexicon of British Ritual, Medicalization, and Mobility in the Congo* (Durham, NC: Duke University Press, 1999)
31. See Jane Turrittin, "Colonial Midwives and Modernizing Childbirth in French West Africa," in *Women in African Colonial Histories*, ed. Allman, Geiger, and Musisi, 71–91; LaRay Denzer, *Women in Government Service in Colonial Nigeria, 1862–1945*, African Studies Center Working Papers in African Studies no. 136 (Boston, MA: Boston University, 1989), 6.

32. Barthel, "Women's Educational Experience," 146–47.
33. Jean-Baptiste, *Conjugal Rights*, 86. In Libreville, the focus of this book, girls accounted for 32% of primary-school enrollments and 19% of junior-high students; figures said to have represented an elevated number of African girls attending school in the whole colony.
34. Out of a total of 1.6 million Congolese school pupils in 1960, 77% and 19% attended Catholic and Protestant institutions, respectively. See Barbara A. Yates, "Church, State and Education in Belgian Africa: Implications for Contemporary Third World Women," in *Women's Education in the Third World: Comparative Perspectives*, ed. Gail P. Kelly and Carolyn M. Elliott (Albany: State University of New York Press, 1982), 127.
35. See Gertrude Mianda, "Colonialism, Education, and Gender Relations in the Belgian Congo: The *Évolué* Case," in *Women in African Colonial Histories*, ed. Allman, Geiger and Musisi, 144–63; Yates, "Church, State and Education in Belgian Africa," 135–45. Mlle. Sophie Kanza, the daughter of the then mayor of Leopoldville, was the first Congolese woman to receive a high-school diploma in 1961 (Yates, p. 127).
36. See Peter K. Tibenderana, "The Beginnings of Girls' Education in the Native Administration Schools in Northern Nigeria, 1930–1945," *Journal of African History* 26, no. 1 (1985): 93–109; Peter K. Tibenderana, "The Emirs and the Spread of Western Education in Northern Nigeria, 1900–1946," *Journal of African History* 24, no. 4 (1983): 519–20, 523–24; Albert Ozigi and Lawrence Ocho, *Education in Northern Nigeria* (London: George Allen and Unwin, 1981), 40–1; C.N. Ubah, "Problems of Christian Missionaries in the Muslim Emirates of Nigeria, 1900–1928," *Journal of African Studies* 3, no. 3 (1976): 362–65; A. Barbs Fafunwa, *History of Education in Nigeria* (London: George Allen and Unwin, 1974); E.A. Ayandele, *The Missionary Impact on Modern Nigeria, 1842–1914* (London: Longman, 1966), 139–52; Sonia F. Graham, *Government and Mission Education in Northern Nigeria, 1900–1919* (Ibadan, Nigeria: Ibadan University Press, 1966), 32–97; L.J. Lewis, *Society, Schools and Progress in Nigeria* (Oxford: Pregamon Press, 1965); S. Phillipson, *Grant-in-aid of Education in Nigeria: A Review with Recommendations* (Lagos, Nigeria: Government Printers, 1948), 6–12; Nigerian National Archives, Kaduna (NNAK), Kadmineduc 4/12/DDN 883/1, A. Booker to Education Officers, Sokoto, 15 April 1940; NNAK, Kadmineduc 4/12/DDN 883/1, A. Booker to Assistant Director of Education, Sokoto, 21 September 1936; NNAK, SOKPROF 3/2/4388, G.J. Lethem to E.J. Hussey, Kaduna, 30 May 1933; NNAK, SNP 17/2/11133/1, SNP to Chief Secretary to the Government, Kaduna 27 July 1933; NNAK, SOKPROF, 3/2/574/1, "Extract from an Account of a Visit to Lagos by the Sultan of Sokoto and the Emir of Gwandu," June 1933; Public Record Office, CO 583/173/3, "Education Policy of Nigeria, 1930"; and Fredrick D. Lugard, *Report on the Amalgamation of Northern and Southern Nigeria, and Administration, 1912–1919* (London: Her Majesty's Stationery, 1920), 63–64.
37. Nigeria, "Nigerian Educational Policy," Being a Summary of *the Memorandum on Educational Policy in Nigeria. Sessional No. 20 of 1947* [Lagos, Nigeria: Government Printer], published in *African Affairs* 47, no. 186 (1948): 52.

38. Tibenderana, "The Beginnings of Girls' Education in the Native Administration Schools," 104–5.
39. Nigeria, "Nigerian Educational Policy," 53.
40. Nigeria, *Annual Digest of Educational Statistics* 2, no. 1 (Lagos, Nigeria: Federal Ministry of Education, 1962), 17.
41. J.F. Ade Ajayi and Tekena N. Tamuno, eds., *The University of Ibadan, 1948–1973: A History of the First Twenty-five Years* (Ibadan, Nigeria: Ibadan University Press, 1973); A. Babs Fafunwa, *A History of Nigerian Higher Education* (Lagos, Nigeria: Macmillan, 1971); and Nigeria, *Annual Digest of Educational Statistics*, 15 and 17.
42. Kanogo, *African Womanhood*, 229–33.
43. The women included Charlotte O. Obasa, Oyinkan Abayomi, Kofoworola Ademola, Funmilayo Ransome-Kuti, Margaret Ekpo, and others. This group of women established women's associations such as Lagos Ladies League, later, the Lagos Women's League, through which they mobilized other women and resources; campaigned for women's issues and concerns such as education, increasing the number of women in the colonial service, equal pay for men and women; and also influenced policies. See Gloria Chuku, "European Victorian Ethos, Igbo Women, and Gender (Re)Construction: An Examination of Policy Implication in Colonial Southeastern Nigeria," in *Negotiating the Public Space: Activism and Domestic Politics*, ed. Sarah Ssali and A. Madanda (Kampala, Uganda: Makerere University, 2006), 120–49; Bolanle Awe, ed., *Nigerian Women in Historical Perspective* (Lagos, Nigeria: Sankore Publishers, 1992); Denzer, *Women in Government Service in Colonial Nigeria*; Kristin Mann, *Marrying Well: Marriage, Status and Social Change among the Educated Elite in Colonial Lagos* (Cambridge, UK: Cambridge University Press, 1985); Fafunwa, *History of Education in Nigeria*; Ayandele, *The Missionary Impact*; Nigerian National Archives, Ibadan (NNAI), COMCOL 1, 498, "Olajumoke Obasa to the Resident of the Colony," August 6, 1926; NNAI, COMCOL 1, 498, "Mrs. Obasa to the Honourable Chief Secretary to Government," February 26, 1924; and NNAI, COMCOL 1, 498, "Lagos Women's League to Hugh Clifford," October 24, 1923.
44. Carole Summers, "'If You Can Educate the Native Women …': Debates over the Schooling and Education of Girls and Women in Southern Rhodesia, 1900–1934," *History of Education Quarterly* 36, no. 4 (1996): 449–71.
45. Deborah Gaitskell, "Housewives, Maids or Mothers: Some Contradictions of Domesticity for Christian Women in Johannesburg, 1903–1939," *Journal of African History* 24, no. 2 (1983): 241–56.
46. See Corrie Decker, "The Elusive Power of Colonial Prey: Sexualizing the Schoolgirl in the Zanzibar Protectorate," *Africa Today* 61, no. 4 (2015): 43–60; Decker, *Mobilizing Zanzibari Women*.
47. Kathleen E. Sheldon, *Pounders of Grain: A History of Women, Work, and Politics in Mozambique* (Portsmouth, NH: Heinemann, 2002), 84 and 89.
48. See, for example, Elizabeth Schmidt, *Peasants, Traders and Wives: Shona Women in the History of Zimbabwe, 1870–1939* (Portsmouth, NH: Heinemann, 1992), 143; Arie J. van der Ploeg, "Education in Colonial Africa: The German Experience," *Comparative Education Review* 21, no. 1 (1977): 99.

49. See Mianda, "Colonialism, Education, and Gender Relations in the Belgian Congo," 148–58; Audrey C. Smock, *Women's Education in Developing Countries: Opportunities and Outcomes* (New York: Praeger Publishers, 1981); Remi Clignet, "Social Change and Sexual Differentiation in the Cameroon and Ivory Coast," *Signs* 3, no. 1 (1977): 244–60; and Remi Clignet and P.J. Foster, *The Fortunate Few: A Study of Secondary Schools and Students in the Ivory Coast* (Evanston, IL: Northwestern University Press, 1966).
50. See Judith Marshall, *Literacy, Power and Democracy in Mozambique: The Governance of Learning from Colonization to the Present* (Boulder, CO: Westview Press, 1993), 72–75; Michael Cross, "The Political Economy of Colonial Education: Mozambique, 1930–1975," *Comparative Education Review* 31, no. 4 (1987): 550–69.
51. See Martin, *Catholic Women of Congo-Brazzaville*, 86.
52. Kanogo, *African Womanhood*, 209–10.
53. See Chuku, *Igbo Women and Economic Transformation*, 83–84; Sheldon, *Pounders of Grain*, 97; Philomena E. Okeke-Ihejirika, *Negotiating Power and Privilege: Igbo Career Women in Contemporary Nigeria* (Athens: Ohio University Press, 2004), 79–102; and Summers, "If You Can Educate the Native Women," 468.
54. Chuku, *Igbo Women and Economic Transformation*, 192–96.
55. Summers, "If You Can Educate the Native Women," 456.
56. Amrane-Minne and Abu-Haidar, "Women and Politics in Algeria," 62.
57. Nigeria, "Nigerian Educational Policy," 53.
58. Decker, "The Elusive Power of Colonial Prey," 48 and 52.
59. Daniel Haag, *The Right to Education: What Kind of Management?* (Paris, France: UNESCO, 1982), 128.
60. Anton Johnston, *Education in Moçambique, 1975–1984* (Stockholm: Swedish International Development Authority, 1984), 21.
61. Sheldon, *Pounders of Grain*, 103.
62. See Emily S. Burrill, *States of Marriage: Gender, Justice, and Rights in Colonial Mali* (Athens: Ohio University Press, 2015); Jean-Baptiste, *Conjugal Rights*; Shadle, "*Girl Cases*;" Schmidt, *Peasants, Traders and Wives*, Chap. 1; Mann, *Marrying Well*.
63. See Margot Lovett, "'She Thinks She's like a Man': Marriage and (De)Constructing Gender Identity in Colonial Buha, Western Tanzania, 1943–1960," *Canadian Journal of African Studies* 30, no. 1 (1996): 52–68; Gisela Geisler, "Moving with Tradition: The Politics of Marriage amongst the Toka of Zambia," *Canadian Journal of African Studies* 26, no. 3 (1992): 437–61.
64. Shadle, "*Girl Cases*;" Kristin Mann, "Women's Rights in Law and Practice: Marriage and Dispute Settlement in Colonial Lagos," in *African Women and the Law: Historical Perspectives*, ed. Margaret Jean Hay and Marcia Wright (Boston, MA: Boston University, 1982), 151–62.
65. Thomas V. McClendon, "Tradition and Domestic Struggle in the Courtroom: Customary Law and the Control of Women in Segregation-Era Natal," *International Journal of African Historical Studies* 28, no. 3 (1995): 527–61.
66. See, for example, Richard Roberts, "Representation, Structure and Agency: Divorce in the French Soudan during the Early Twentieth Century," *Journal of African History* 40, no. 3 (1999): 389–410.

67. Sean Hawkins, "'The Woman in Question': Marriage and Identity in the Colonial Courts of Northern Ghana, 1907–1954," in *Women in African Colonial Histories*, ed. Allman, Geiger and Musisi, 116–43.
68. J. Malcolm Thompson, "Colonial Policy and the Family Life of Black Troops in French West Africa, 1817–1904," *International Journal of African Historical Studies* 23, no. 3 (1990): 450.
69. See Steven Pierce, "Farmers and 'Prostitutes': Twentieth-Century Problems of Female Inheritance in Kano Emirate, Nigeria," *Journal of African History* 44, no. 3 (2003): 463–86.
70. Sheldon, ed., *Courtyards, Markets, City Streets*; Teresa A. Barnes, "The Fight for Control of African Women's Mobility in Colonial Zimbabwe, 1900–1939," *Signs* 17, no. 3 (1992): 586–608; Elizabeth Schmidt, "Negotiated Spaces and Contested Terrain: Men, Women and the Law in Colonial Zimbabwe, 1890–1939," *Journal of Southern African Studies* 16, no. 4 (1990): 622–48; and George Chauncey Jr., "The Locus of Reproduction: Women's Labour in the Zambian Copperbelt, 1927–1953," *Journal of Southern African Studies* 7, no. 2 (1981): 135–64.
71. Epprecht, "Women's 'Conservatism' and the Politics of Gender," 35; Phil L. Bonner, "'Desirable or Undesirable Basotho Women?' Liquor, Prostitution and the Migration of Basotho Women to the Rand, 1920–1945," in *Women and Gender in Southern Africa to 1945*, ed. Cherryl Walker (Cape Town, South Africa: David Philip, 1990), 221–50.
72. Hamilton Sipho Simelane, "The State, Chiefs and the Control of Female Migration in Colonial Swaziland, c. 1930s–1950s," *Journal of African History* 45, no. 1 (2004): 103–24.
73. Barnes, "The Fight for Control of African Women's Mobility in Colonial Zimbabwe;" Chauncey Jr., "The Locus of Reproduction."
74. Barnes, "The Fight for Control of African Women's Mobility in Colonial Zimbabwe," 605–6.
75. See, for instance, Giulia Barrera, "Colonial Affairs: Italian Men and Eritrean Women, and the Construction of Racial Hierarchies in Colonial Eritrea (1885–1941)" (PhD diss., Northwestern University, 2002); Luise White, *The Comforts of Home: Prostitution in Colonial Nairobi* (Chicago: The University of Chicago Press, 1990); and Barnes, "The Fight for Control of African Women's Mobility in Colonial Zimbabwe."
76. See Schmidt, *Peasants, Traders and Wives*, Chap. 6.
77. Helen Callaway, *Gender, Culture and Empire: European Women in Colonial Nigeria* (Urbana: University of Illinois Press, 1987), 48–50. For different dimensions of female sexuality and the complexity of sexual politics in colonial Nigeria, see Saheed Aderinto, *When Sex Threatened the State: Illicit Sexuality, Nationalism, and Politics in Colonial Nigeria, 1900–1958* (Urbana: University of Illinois Press, 2015); Lisa A. Lindsay, "A Tragic Romance, a Nationalist Symbol: The Case of the Murdered White Lover in Nigeria," *Journal of Women's History* 17, no. 2 (2005): 118–41.
78. Thompson, "Colonial Policy and the Family Life," 432–33.
79. See, for instance, Aderinto, *When Sex Threatened the State*; Sheryl A. McCurdy, "Urban Threats: Manyema Women, Low Fertility, and Venereal Diseases in Tanganyika, 1926–1936," in *"Wicked" Women and the Reconfiguration of*

Gender in Africa, ed. Dorothy L. Hodgson and Sheryl A. McCurdy (Portsmouth, NH: Heinemann, 2001), 212–33; Hunt, *A Colonial Lexicon*; and Megan Vaughan, *Curing Their Ills: Colonial Power and African Illness* (Stanford: Stanford University Press, 1991)
80. Thompson, "Colonial Policy and the Family Life," 434.
81. Phyllis M. Martin, *Leisure and Society in Colonial Brazzaville* (Cambridge, UK: Cambridge University Press, 1995), 139–40.
82. Thompson, Ibid., 439.
83. Ibid., 446.
84. Kanogo, *African Womanhood*, 240.

Bibliography

Archival Sources

Nigerian National Archives, Ibadan (NNAI)
COMCOL 1, 498, "Lagos Women's League to Hugh Clifford," October 24, 1923.
COMCOL 1, 498, "Mrs. Obasa to the Honourable Chief Secretary to Government," February 26, 1924.
COMCOL 1, 498, "Olajumoke Obasa to the Resident of the Colony," August 6, 1926.
Nigerian National Archives, Kaduna (NNAK)
Kadmineduc 4/12/DDN 883/1, A. Booker to Assistant Director of Education, Sokoto, 21 September 1936.
Kadmineduc 4/12/DDN 883/1, A. Booker to Education Officers, Sokoto, 15 April 1940.
SNP 17/2/11133/1, SNP to Chief Secretary to the Government, Kaduna 27 July 1933.
SOKPROF, 3/2/574/1, "Extract from an Account of a Visit to Lagos by the Sultan of Sokoto and the Emir of Gwandu," June 1933.
SOKPROF 3/2/4388, G. J. Lethem to E. J. Hussey, Kaduna, 30 May 1933.

United Kingdom

Public Record Office, Kew, London
CO 583/173/3, "Education Policy of Nigeria, 1930."

Government Publications

Lugard, Fredrick D. *Report on the Amalgamation of Northern and Southern Nigeria, and Administration, 1912–1919.* London: Her Majesty's Stationery, 1920.
Nigeria. *Annual Digest of Educational Statistics* 2, no. 1. Lagos, Nigeria: Federal Ministry of Education, 1962.
Phillipson, S. *Grant-in-aid of Education in Nigeria: A Review with Recommendations.* Lagos, Nigeria: Government Printers, 1948.

BOOKS, ARTICLES, AND DISSERTATIONS

Aderinto, Saheed. *When Sex Threatened the State: Illicit Sexuality, Nationalism, and Politics in Colonial Nigeria, 1900–1958*. Urbana: University of Illinois Press, 2015.

Ajayi, J.F. Ade, and Tekena N. Tamuno, eds. *The University of Ibadan, 1948–1973: A History of the First Twenty-five Years*. Ibadan, Nigeria: Ibadan University Press, 1973.

Akyeampong, Emmanuel K., and Pashington Obeng. "Spirituality, Gender and Power in Asante History." *International Journal of African Historical Studies* 28, no. 3 (1995): 481–508.

Allman, Jean, Susan Geiger, and Nakanyike Musisi, eds. *Women in African Colonial Histories*. Bloomington: Indiana University Press, 2002.

Allman, Jean, and Victoria Tashjian. *"I Will Not Eat Stone": A Women's History of Colonial Asante*. Portsmouth, NH: Heinemann, 2000.

Amrane-Minne, Daniele D., and Farida Abu-Haidar. "Women and Politics in Algeria from the War of Independence to Our Day." *Research in African Literatures* 30, no. 3 (1999): 62–77.

Awe, Bolanle, ed. *Nigerian Women in Historical Perspective*. Lagos, Nigeria: Sankore Publishers, 1992.

———. "The Iyalode in the Traditional Yoruba Political System." In *Sexual Stratification: A Cross-Cultural View*, edited by Alice Schlegel, 144–60. New York: Columbia University Press.

Ayandele, E. A. *The Missionary Impact on Modern Nigeria, 1842–1914*. London: Longman, 1966.

Bandiaky, Solang. "Engendering Exclusion in Senegalese Democratic Decentralization: Subordinating Women through Participatory Natural Resource Management." PhD diss., Department of Women's and Gender Studies, Clark University, Worcester, Massachusetts, 2008.

Barnes, Teresa A. "The Fight for Control of African Women's Mobility in Colonial Zimbabwe, 1900–1939." *Signs* 17, no. 3 (1992): 586–608.

———. *"We Women Worked So Hard": Gender, Urbanization and Social Reproduction in Colonial Harare, Zimbabwe, 1930–1956*. Portsmouth, NH: Heinemann, 1999.

Barrera, Giulia. "Colonial Affairs: Italian Men and Eritrean Women, and the Construction of Racial Hierarchies in Colonial Eritrea (1885–1941)." PhD diss., Northwestern University, 2002.

Barthel, Diane. "Women's Educational Experience under Colonialism: Towards a Diachronic Model." *Signs* 11, no. 1 (1985): 137–54.

Bay, Edna G. *Wives of the Leopard: Gender, Politics, and Culture in the Kingdom of Dahomey*. Charlottesville: University of Virginia Press, 1998.

Beck, Linda J. "Democratization and the Hidden Public: The Impact of Patronage Networks on Senegalese Women." *Comparative Politics* 35, no. 2 (2003): 147–69.

Bledsoe, Caroline. "The Political Use of Sande Ideology and Symbolism." *American Ethnologist* 11, no. 3 (1984): 445–72.

Boddy, Janice. *Civilizing Women: British Crusaders in Colonial Sudan*. Princeton, NJ: Princeton University Press, 2007.

Bonner, Phil L. "'Desirable or Undesirable Basotho Women?': Liquor, Prostitution and the Migration of Basotho Women to the Rand, 1920–1945." In *Women and Gender in Southern Africa to 1945*, edited by Cherryl Walker, 221–50. Cape Town, South Africa: David Philip, 1990.

Burrill, Emily S. *States of Marriage: Gender, Justice, and Rights in Colonial Mali*. Athens: Ohio University Press, 2015.

Callaway, Barbara J. "Women and Political Participation in Kano City." *Comparative Politics* 19, no. 4 (1987): 379–93.

Callaway, Helen. *Gender, Culture and Empire: European Women in Colonial Nigeria*. Urbana: University of Illinois Press, 1987.

Chauncey, George, Jr. "The Locus of Reproduction: Women's Labour in the Zambian Copperbelt, 1927–1953." *Journal of Southern African Studies* 7, no. 2 (1981): 135–64.

Chuku, Gloria. *Igbo Women and Economic Transformation in Southeastern Nigeria, 1900–1960*. London: Routledge, 2005.

———. "European Victorian Ethos, Igbo Women, and Gender (Re)Construction: An Examination of Policy Implication in Colonial Southeastern Nigeria." In *Negotiating the Public Space: Activism and Domestic Politics*, edited by Sarah Ssali and A. Madanda, 120–49. Kampala, Uganda: Makerere University, 2006.

———. "Igbo Women and Political Participation in Nigeria, 1800s–2005." *International Journal of African Historical Studies* 42, no. 1 (2009): 81–103.

———. "Okwei." In *The Oxford Dictionary of African Biography*, Vol. 5, edited by Emmanuel K. Akyeampong and Henry Louis Gates Jr., 26–28. Oxford, UK: Oxford University Press, 2012.

———. "Ugbabe, Ahebi." In *Dictionary of African Biography*, Vol. 6, edited by E.K. Akyeampong and H.L. Gates Jr., 94–96. Oxford, UK: Oxford University Press, 2012.

Clignet, Remi. "Social Change and Sexual Differentiation in the Cameroon and Ivory Coast." *Signs* 3, no. 1 (1977): 244–60.

Clignet, Remi, and P.J. Foster. *The Fortunate Few: A Study of Secondary Schools and Students in the Ivory Coast*. Evanston, IL: Northwestern University Press, 1966.

Cross, Michael. "The Political Economy of Colonial Education: Mozambique, 1930–1975." *Comparative Education Review* 31, no. 4 (1987): 550–69.

Day, Lynda. *Gender and Power in Sierra Leone: Women Chiefs of the Last Two Centuries*. New York: Palgrave Macmillan, 2012.

Decker, Corrie. *Mobilizing Zanzibari Women: The Struggle for Respectability and Self-Reliance in Colonial East Africa*. New York: Palgrave Macmillan, 2014.

———. "The Elusive Power of Colonial Prey: Sexualizing the Schoolgirl in the Zanzibar Protectorate." *Africa Today* 61, no. 4 (2015): 43–60.

Denzer, LaRay. *Women in Government Service in Colonial Nigeria, 1862–1945*. Working Papers in African Studies no. 136. Boston, MA: Boston University, 1989.

Edgerton, Robert B. *Warrior Women: The Amazons of Dahomey and the Nature of War*. Boulder, CO: Westview Press, 2000.

Ekejiuba, Felicia. "Omu Okwei, the Merchant Queen of Ossomari: A Biographical Sketch." *Journal of the Historical Society of Nigeria* 3, no. 4 (1967): 633–46.

Epprecht, Marc. "Women's 'Conservatism' and the Politics of Gender in Late Colonial Lesotho." *Journal of African History* 36, no. 1 (1995): 29–56.

———. *"This Matter of Women Is Getting Very Bad": Gender, Development and Politics in Colonial Lesotho*. Natal, South Africa: University of Natal Press, 2000.

Fafunwa, A. Barbs. *A History of Nigerian Higher Education*. Lagos, Nigeria: Macmillan, 1971.

———. *History of Education in Nigeria*. London: George Allen and Unwin, 1974.

Fantasia, Rick, and Eric L. Hirsch. "Culture in Rebellion: The Appropriation and Transformation of the Veil in the Algerian Revolution." In *Social Movements and Culture*, edited by Hank Johnston and Bert Klandermans, 144–60. Minneapolis: University of Minnesota Press, 1995.

Gaitskell, Deborah. "Housewives, Maids or Mothers: Some Contradictions of Domesticity for Christian Women in Johannesburg, 1903–1939." *Journal of African History* 24, no. 2 (1983): 241–56.

Gardinier, David E. "Schooling in the States of Equatorial Africa." *Canadian Journal of African Studies* 8, no. 3 (1974): 517–38.

Geiger, Susan. *TANU Women: Gender and Culture in the Making of Tanganyikan Nationalism, 1955–1965*. Portsmouth, NH: Heinemann, 1997.

Geisler, Gisela. "Moving with Tradition: The Politics of Marriage amongst the Toka of Zambia." *Canadian Journal of African Studies* 26, no. 3 (1992): 437–61.

Graham, Sonia F. *Government and Mission Education in Northern Nigeria, 1900–1919*. Ibadan, Nigeria: Ibadan University Press, 1966.

Haag, Daniel. *The Right to Education: What Kind of Management?* Paris, France: UNESCO, 1982.

Hanson, Holly. "Queen Mothers and Good Government in Buganda: The Loss of Women's Political Power in Nineteenth-Century East Africa." In *Women in African Colonial Histories*, edited by J. Allman, S. Geiger and N. Musisi, 219–36. Bloomington: Indiana University Press, 2002.

Hansen, Karen T., ed. *African Encounters with Domesticity*. New Brunswick, NJ: Rutgers University Press, 1992.

Hawkins, Sean. "'The Woman in Question': Marriage and Identity in the Colonial Courts of Northern Ghana, 1907–1954." In *Women in African Colonial Histories*, edited by J. Allman, S. Geiger and N. Musisi, 116–43. Bloomington: Indiana University Press, 2002.

Hoffer, Carol P. "Mende and Sherbro Women in High Office." *Canadian Journal of African Studies* 6, no. 2 (1972): 151–64.

———. "Madam Yoko: Ruler of the Kpa Mende Confederacy." In *Woman, Culture, and Society*, edited by Michelle Rosaldo and Louise Lamphere, 173–87. Stanford, CA: Stanford University Press, 1974.

Hunt, Nancy R. *A Colonial Lexicon of British Ritual, Medicalization, and Mobility in the Congo*. Durham, NC: Duke University Press, 1999.

Jean-Baptiste, Rachel. "'These Laws should be Made by Us': Customary Marriage Law, Codification and Political Authority in Twentieth-Century Colonial Gabon." *Journal of African History* 49, no. 2 (2008): 217–40.

———. *Conjugal Rights: Marriage, Sexuality, and Urban Life in Colonial Libreville, Gabon*. Athens: Ohio University Press, 2014.

Johnston, Anton. *Education in Moçambique, 1975–1984*. Stockholm: Swedish International Development Authority, 1984.

Jones, Hilary. *The Metis of Senegal: Urban Life and Politics in French West Africa*. Bloomington: Indiana University Press, 2013.

Kanogo, Tabitha. *African Womanhood in Colonial Kenya, 1900–1950*. Oxford, UK: James Currey, 2005.

Kaplan, Flora Edouwaye, ed. *Queens, Queen Mothers, Priestesses, and Power: Case Studies in African Gender*. New York: New York Academy of Sciences, 1997.

Lewis, L.J. *Society, Schools and Progress in Nigeria*. Oxford: Pregamon Press, 1965.

Lindsay, Lisa A. "A Tragic Romance, a Nationalist Symbol: The Case of the Murdered White Lover in Nigeria." *Journal of Women's History* 17, no. 2 (2005): 118–41.

Lovett, Margot. "'She Thinks She's like a Man': Marriage and (De)Constructing Gender Identity in Colonial Buha, Western Tanzania, 1943–1960." *Canadian Journal of African Studies* 30, no. 1 (1996): 52–68.

Lyons, Tanya. *Guns and Guerilla Girls: Women in the Zimbabwean Liberation Struggle.* Trenton, NJ: Africa World Press, 2004.

Mann, Kristin. "Women's Rights in Law and Practice: Marriage and Dispute Settlement in Colonial Lagos." In *African Women and the Law: Historical Perspectives*, edited by Margaret Jean Hay and Marcia Wright, 151–62. Boston, MA: Boston University, 1982.

———. *Marrying Well: Marriage, Status and Social Change Among the Educated Elite in Colonial Lagos.* Cambridge, UK: Cambridge University Press, 1985.

Marijke, Steegstra. "Krobo Queen Mothers: Gender, Power, and Contemporary Female Traditional Authority in Ghana." *Africa Today* 55, no. 3 (2009): 105–23.

Marshall, Judith. *Literacy, Power and Democracy in Mozambique: The Governance of Learning from Colonization to the Present.* Boulder, CO: Westview Press, 1993.

Martin, Phyllis M. *Leisure and Society in Colonial Brazzaville.* Cambridge, UK: Cambridge University Press, 1995.

———. *Catholic Women of Congo-Brazzaville: Mothers and Sisters in Troubled Times.* Bloomington: Indiana University Press, 2009.

Mba, Nina. *Nigerian Women Mobilized: Women's Political Activity in Southern Nigeria, 1900–1965.* Berkeley: University of California Press, 1982.

Mianda, Gertrude. "Colonialism, Education, and Gender Relations in the Belgian Congo: The *Évolué* Case." In *Women in African Colonial Histories*, edited by J. Allman, S. Geiger and N. Musisi, 144–63. Bloomington: Indiana University Press, 2002.

McCaskie, T.C. "The Life and Afterlife of Yaa Asantewaa." *Africa* 77, no. 2 (2007): 151–79.

McClendon, Thomas V. "Tradition and Domestic Struggle in the Courtroom: Customary Law and the Control of Women in Segregation-Era Natal." *International Journal of African Historical Studies* 28, no. 3 (1995): 527–61.

McCurdy, Sheryl A. "Urban Threats: Manyema Women, Low Fertility, and Venereal Diseases in Tanganyika, 1926–1936." In *"Wicked" Women and the Reconfiguration of Gender in Africa*, edited by Dorothy L. Hodgson and Sheryl A. McCurdy, 212–33. Portsmouth, NH: Heinemann, 2001.

Nigeria. "Nigerian Educational Policy." Being a Summary of *the Memorandum on Educational Policy in Nigeria. Sessional No. 20 of 1947* [Lagos, Nigeria: Government Printer], published in *African Affairs* 47, no. 186 (1948): 52–54.

Okeke-Ihejirika, Philomena E. *Negotiating Power and Privilege: Igbo Career Women in Contemporary Nigeria.* Athens: Ohio University Press, 2004.

Oloruntimehin, Olatunji. "Education for Colonial Dominance in French West Africa from 1900 to Second World War." *Journal of the Historical Society of Nigeria* 7, no. 2 (1974): 347–55.

Osborn, Emily L. *Our New Husbands Are Here: Households, Gender, and Politics in a West African State from the Slave Trade to Colonial Rule.* Athens: Ohio University Press, 2011.

Ozigi, Albert, and Lawrence Ocho. *Education in Northern Nigeria*. London: George Allen and Unwin, 1981.

Pierce, Steven. "Farmers and 'Prostitutes': Twentieth-Century Problems of Female Inheritance in Kano Emirate, Nigeria." *Journal of African History* 44, no. 3 (2003): 463–86.

Presley, Cora A. *Kikuyu Women, the Mau Mau Rebellion, and Social Change in Kenya*. Boulder, CO: Westview Press, 1992.

Reynolds, Jonathan T. *The Time of Politics (Zamanin Siyasa): Islam and the Politics of Legitimacy in Northern Nigeria, 1950–1966*. Lanham, MD: University Press of America, 1999.

Roberts, Richard. "Representation, Structure and Agency: Divorce in the French Soudan during the Early Twentieth Century." *Journal of African History* 40, no. 3 (1999): 389–410.

Rosenberg, Scott, and Richard F. Weisfelder. *Historical Dictionary of Lesotho*, 2nd ed. Lanham, MD: Scarecrow Press, 2013.

Sabatier, Peggy R. "'Elite' Education in French West Africa: The Era of Limits, 1903–1945." *International Journal of African Historical Studies* 11, no. 2 (1978): 247–66.

Schmidt, Elizabeth. "Negotiated Spaces and Contested Terrain: Men, Women and the Law in Colonial Zimbabwe, 1890–1939." *Journal of Southern African Studies* 16, no. 4 (1990): 622–48.

———. *Peasants, Traders and Wives: Shona Women in the History of Zimbabwe, 1870–1939*. Portsmouth, NH: Heinemann, 1992.

———. *Mobilizing the Masses: Gender, Ethnicity, and Class in the Nationalist Movement in Guinea, 1939–1958*. Portsmouth, NH: Heinemann, 2005.

Semley, Lorelle D. *Mother Is Gold, Father Is Glass: Gender and Colonialism in a Yoruba Town*. Bloomington, IN: Indiana University Press, 2011.

Shadle, Brett L. *"Girl Cases": Marriage and Colonialism in Gusiiland, Kenya, 1890–1970*. Portsmouth, NH: Heinemann, 2006.

Sheldon, Kathleen E, ed. *Courtyards, Markets, City Streets: Urban Women in Africa*. Boulder, CO: Westview Press, 1996.

———. *Pounders of Grain: A History of Women, Work, and Politics in Mozambique*. Portsmouth, NH: Heinemann, 2002.

Simelane, Hamilton S. "The State, Chiefs and the Control of Female Migration in Colonial Swaziland, c. 1930s–1950s." *Journal of African History* 45, no. 1 (2004): 103–24.

Smock, Audrey C. *Women's Education in Developing Countries: Opportunities and Outcomes*. New York: Praeger Publishers, 1981.

Summers, Carole. "'If You Can Educate the Native Women …': Debates over the Schooling and Education of Girls and Women in Southern Rhodesia, 1900–1934." *History of Education Quarterly* 36, no. 4 (1996): 449–71.

Thomas, Martin. *The French Empire Between the Wars: Imperialism, Politics and Society*. Manchester, UK: Manchester University Press, 2005.

Thompson, J. Malcolm. "Colonial Policy and the Family Life of Black Troops in French West Africa, 1817–1904." *International Journal of African Historical Studies* 23, no. 3 (1990): 423–53.

Tibenderana, Peter K. "The Emirs and the Spread of Western Education in Northern Nigeria, 1900–1946." *Journal of African History* 24, no. 4 (1983): 517–34.

———. "The Beginnings of Girls' Education in the Native Administration Schools in Northern Nigeria, 1930–1945." *Journal of African History* 26, no. 1 (1985): 93–109.

Turrittin, Jane. "Aoua Keita and the Nascent Women's Movement in the French Soudan." *African Studies Review* 36, no. 1 (1993): 59–89.

———. "Colonial Midwives and Modernizing Childbirth in French West Africa." In *Women in African Colonial Histories*, edited by J. Allman, S. Geiger and N. Musisi, 71–91. Bloomington: Indiana University Press, 2002.

Turshen, Meredeth. "Algerian Women in the Liberation Struggle and the Civil War: From Active Participants to Passive Victims?" *Social Research* 69, no. 3 (2002): 889–911.

Ubah, C. N. "Problems of Christian Missionaries in the Muslim Emirates of Nigeria, 1900–1928." *Journal of African Studies* 3, no. 3 (1976): 362–65.

Urdang, Stephanie. *Fighting Two Colonialisms: Women in Guinea-Bissau*. New York: Monthly Review Press, 1979.

van der Ploeg, Arie J. "Education in Colonial Africa: The German Experience." *Comparative Education Review* 21, no. 1 (1977): 91–109.

Vaughan, Megan. *Curing Their Ills: Colonial Power and African Illness*. Stanford: Stanford University Press, 1991.

Walker, Cherryl. *Women and Resistance in South Africa*. New York: Monthly Review Press, 1982.

White, Luise. *The Comforts of Home: Prostitution in Colonial Nairobi*. Chicago: The University of Chicago Press, 1990.

Wilson, Amrit. *The Challenge Road: Women and the Eritrean Revolution*. Trenton, NJ: The Red Sea Press, 1991.

Yates, Barbara A. "Church, State and Education in Belgian Africa: Implications for Contemporary Third World Women." In *Women's Education in the Third World: Comparative Perspectives*, edited by Gail P. Kelly and Carolyn M. Elliott, 127–51. Albany: State University of New York Press, 1982.

Yemitan, Oladipo. *Madame Tinubu: Merchant and King-Maker*. Ibadan, Nigeria: University Press, 1987.

CHAPTER 8

Administration, Economy, and Society in the Portuguese African Empire (1900–1975)

Philip J. Havik

Portugal's Third Empire was governed by three different regimes from the early 1900s to 1974: a monarchy, the First Republic, and the New State (Estado Novo). For most of the modern colonial period until the end of empire (1926–1974), the empire was governed by the New State dictatorship, which emphasized political transitions and ideological rationales for colonial rule. The antecedents of its Third Empire are particularly important for the shaping of myths and mystifications regarding imperial history that have persisted in the postcolonial context.[1] The wake-up call provoked by the British Ultimatum of 1891, when Portugal was in the midst of a deep economic crisis, has figured ever since as a historical marker for the country's colonial renaissance.[2] Following the independence of Brazil in 1822 (at a time when most Latin American territories had shed their colonial ties) and the protracted civil war in Portugal (1822–1833), attentions shifted towards Africa.[3]

However, given that the dream of a 'new Brazil' in Africa would only come to partial fruition after the Second World War, it long remained

The author wishes to acknowledge the support of the Fundação para a Ciência e Tecnologia (FCT), in Lisbon, and thank Malyn Newitt and Miguel Bandeira Jerónimo for their comments.

P.J. Havik (✉)
Universidade Nova de Lisboa (IHMT/UNL), Lisbon, Portugal

© The Author(s) 2018
M.S. Shanguhyia and T. Falola (eds.),
The Palgrave Handbook of African Colonial and Postcolonial History,
https://doi.org/10.1057/978-1-137-59426-6_8

confined to the realm of fiction and fantasy.[4] The 'turning point' of the British Ultimatum was thus largely a political event which propelled Portuguese authorities into action, obliging them to extend Portugal's claim to sovereignty over African territories by military means. Portugal's protracted campaigns to break the resistance of African populations, which preceded and coincided with the First World War in which it participated, set the tone for the country's affirmation of its modern imperial role.[5] The emergence largely unscathed of a neutral Portugal from the Second World War without, however, having made significant investments towards colonial development as Great Britain and France had done (from 1929/1940 and 1946 respectively), also points towards a particular trajectory. The fact that until the 1930s Portugal largely depended on re-exporting (processed) colonial raw materials to wealthier European countries such as Great Britain and France shaped subaltern inter-imperial relations.[6] Finally, Portugal's refusal to decolonize at the time most other European nations were doing so, while linking the destiny of the nation to retaining its control of its African territories, forms another key indicator of Portuguese specificity in empire.[7] The armed struggles which marked the end of empire and its collapse coincided with a change of regime, denoting a distinct historiographical perspective on modern Portuguese colonialism. Thus, the 'shuffling of papers', which in the Portuguese case was to continue for a decade-and-a-half after most African territories had achieved independence, placed the process of decolonization in markedly different international contexts than its European counterparts.

The historiography of Portugal's modern imperial enterprise has largely emphasized four contentious issues[8]: the racial categories guiding colonial administration, forced labor practices, economic (under) development, and armed conflict. In geographical terms, publications have mainly centered on Portugal's continental African colonies such as Angola and Mozambique, owing to their sheer size and economic relevance, relegating other territories such as Guinea, São Tomé and Príncipe, and the Cape Verde Islands to a marginal role. Therefore, the principal emphasis will be put here on the main theatres of empire, without however neglecting the periphery. The geography of empire is significant here, given its dispersal across the continent and insular locations: the lack of territorial unity mirrors the centrifugal nature of imperial rule. The notable lack of territorial cohesion, or imperial dislocation, which contrasts with French and Belgian imperial clusters and the British 'corridor' would however strengthen the need for stressing imperial unity across countless continental and maritime boundaries. At the same time, its global reach would engender narratives on the 'integralist' nature of the Portuguese empire 'from Cabo Verde to Timor'.[9]

In the following sections, the four principal strands identified above will be addressed in three separate sections, which cast a broad perspective upon the historiography of Portugal's Third (African) empire during the period under consideration. Besides including data culled from published sources, this chapter is also based upon archival research and includes data from hitherto unpublished documents.

THE RACIAL DIMENSIONS OF COLONIAL RULE

Portuguese administration in Africa generally adhered to the practice of 'direct rule', borrowing from centralized metropolitan traditions as well as bearing similarities with the French example. Despite formal appearances, in practice colonial rule was characterized by a heterogeneous administrative culture: while direct rule was the custom in rural areas where the bulk of *indígenas* or native African populations lived, in urban centers indirect forms prevailed, with selective forms of representation limited to *civilizados*, i.e. those with Portuguese civil status. In some areas, public administration actually 'shared' control with private concessionaires, whether companies or individual planters. In a highly dispersed and centrifugal empire, forms of governance in continental and insular territories differed: whereas the latter had been settled from the 1500s under a feudal regime, the former emerged under the nation-state erected upon the foundations of the constitutional monarchy in 1833. The slave trade, which provided the bulk of insular populations, enabled *latifúndio* type property (based on slave labor) to dominate in Cabo Verde and São Tomé and Príncipe, where it was well entrenched in the 1870s when trafficking was abolished. The de facto *mise en valeur* of continental areas beyond coastal regions only began in earnest during the end of the monarchy (1910) and the early years of the First Republic. Laws on land concessions severely limited the access of 'natives' to land concessions,[10] while labor and fiscal legislation imposed special regimes for indigenous Africans.[11]

From the 1850s, colonial affairs fell under the auspices of the Ministério da Marinha e Ultramar, transformed into the Ministério das Colónias (Colonial Office) following the proclamation of the Republic in 1911.[12] The establishment of a colonial administration in the continental territories claimed by Portugal at the Berlin Conference followed protracted 'wars of "pacification"' in continental colonies until the early 1920s.[13] From 1914 onwards, a unitary imperial blueprint for colonial administration based on the *indigenato* system (similar to the French *indigénat*) was passed by republican lawmakers. Subsequently, statutes were introduced regulating 'native' civil and penal rights and labor, which further refined already existing racial definitions of colonial populations. These criteria would remain in place until 1961 when, under international pressure, racial *indigenato* laws were abolished. Given that these laws referred to Portugal's continental colonies, insular possessions with a particular emphasis on Cabo Verde, a Creole society, remained largely peripheral to these policy shifts.[14] Owing to their 'civilized' status, Cape Verdeans were to become important subaltern administrators of empire in Portugal's continental African colonies.[15]

Nevertheless, the legal imposition of racial criteria[16] permeated all aspects of colonial rule, i.e. administrative hierarchy and culture, the rights and obligations of settlers and 'natives', and their access to services. However, variations were common, owing to differences in: population density; African political, ethnic and religious institutions; local economic conditions; and the presence of colonial 'elites'. Also, processes of inter-ethnic mixing, miscegenation, and creolization had resulted in hybrid social formations, especially in urban areas.[17] Members of these groups were to give voice to a budding African civil society, publicizing their views in pamphlets and journals while forming local associations, above all following the republican turn in Portugal in 1910.[18]

The question of miscegenation led some foreign observers to hold that 'racial mixing' was actually condoned, and much more common in Portuguese than in British or French colonies.[19] Seasonal, tropical cycles (i.e. the rainy and dry seasons) also created annual disparities in terms of production, consumption, mobility, and revenue generation between *indigena* and *civilizado* populations. Distinctions were also felt between urban and rural areas, where the bulk of African populations resided. In the latter, administration was organized in *circunscrições* (administrative districts) and *postos* (administrative posts), whereas municipalities and districts (*câmaras municipais* and *concelhos*) exercised authority in urban environments. A two-tier system operated with segregated courts, labor relations, educational and health services. African communities were divided into *regedorias* where local ethnic chiefs (*sobas* in Angola and *régulos* in Mozambique and Guinea) appointed by district administrators exercised delegated authority under the *chefes de posto*. Nevertheless, chiefly authority was, with few exceptions, systematically undermined by administrative officials in Angola, Guinea, and Mozambique.[20] Land concession policies allowed considerable scope for individual settler-planters to freely manage their estates, which often included entire 'native' villages. Large company concessions controlling vast estates in the Centre and North of Mozambique and Angola exercised extensive leverage over indigenous communities in terms of labor recruitment and work contracts, mobility, taxation, trade, health, education, and socialization. Reports show that administrative officials often failed to verify the tax levies and labor contracts in these concessions.[21] Similarly, the owners of cocoa plantations, or *roças*, on the islands of São Tomé and Príncipe also formed a small but powerful *latifúndio* elite who, counting on a subservient administration, exercised a notable hegemony over many aspects of insular life.[22]

The transformation of 'natives' into workers, tax payers, and producers relied on the native identification (ID) system, labor 'contracts', hut and poll taxes, and the imposition of export crops. The local bureaucratic apparatus for the registration of tax payers, laborers, and crop producers was generally understaffed and underfunded. As a result, the circulation rate of officials was relatively high compared to British and French regimes. Owing to an inefficient administration and large-scale evasion, the civil register and the emission of ID cards was faulty and full of lacunae, allowing Africans to 'slip through the net'.[23] The emergence of 'bureaucratized' officialdom and its tendency to cut corners was the result of the broad brief of district administrators, acting simultaneously as lawmakers, judges, tax collectors, labor agents, and employers, whilst also appointing ethnic chiefs and being responsible for the maintenance of public order and security in their respective districts.[24]

The reforms introduced with the Reforma Administrativa Ultramarina in 1933 attempted to redeem this situation by depicting them as 'men of action' rather than armchair bureaucrats. Thus, administrators were expected to regularly visit their districts and interact with chiefs they appointed, reorganized in *regedorias*, and above all with local village heads.[25] However, in practice they delegated these tasks to 'their' subaltern *chefes de posto* and locally recruited administrative guards or *cipaios*. The latter served as a key pillar of civil authority in terms of the extraction of labor, taxes, and crops, and the gathering of information.[26] The exercise of administrative authority over natives (*indígenas*) was expressed in terms of twin complementary tasks, i.e. law and order on the one hand and 'protection' and the 'civilizing mission' on the other. The latter function was generally relegated to religious (Catholic) missions charged with proselytization and 'rudimentary' primary education, especially in rural areas, whilst Protestant missions were tolerated.[27]

Besides local administrators, fiscal departments (*Fazenda*) and those responsible for native affairs (*Negócios Indígenas*) exercised their own autonomous authority over African populations. In insular colonies, these responsibilities pertained to the *Curadoria Geral dos Serviçais e Indígenas*, above all with regard to plantation labor. Special central and urban administrative bodies were responsible for relations with settler communities, which were particularly relevant in the case of Angola and Mozambique. The Colonial Act of 1930 consolidated the legal framework based on the distinction between *civilizados*, whose status was similar to that of Portuguese citizens, and *indígenas*.[28] A novel intermediate but unstable category, the *assimilados*, or assimilated Africans, originally proposed by French colonial specialists such as Girault in the late 1800s, had already been introduced in 1926 for Angola and Mozambique, followed by Guinea the year after. Despite claims regarding the progressive transformation of customs and integration of Africans into colonial society, the criteria were applied with great caution while the status initially granted was reversible, thus restricting the potential number of assimilated citizens.[29] By 1950, there were 30,089 (0.08%) assimilated citizens in Mozambique, 4.349 (0.75%) in Angola and 1478 (0.29%) in Guinea.[30] In insular colonies such as Cape Verde and São Tomé, legal distinctions differed: the indigenous statute did not apply to the Creole population of the former (given civilizado status in 1947), while the latter was only extended to the population of São Tomé and Príncipe in 1953.[31]

Subsequent constitutional and legislative reforms in the 1950s (which incorporated the *indigenato* status in the Portuguese constitution of 1954) maintained discriminatory norms based on more subtle distinctions between 'primitive natives' and 'evolving natives' having absorbed some European influences, and 'detribalized natives', i.e. those who assumed a Europeanized lifestyle whilst maintaining some traces of native culture.[32] The latter were viewed with concern, given their unstable social status, thus necessitating their progressive integration into the assimilado category.[33] Nevertheless, these belated attempts at retaining colonies while 'refining' racial distinctions and the criteria for the 'civilizing mission', which were subject to growing criticism from international and anti-colonial quarters, had little impact. Although the *indigenato* laws were formally abolished in 1961 they remained deeply ingrained in colonial culture. The reforms coincided with the beginning of the colonial wars, when nationalist movements took up arms against colonial rule, first in Angola in 1961, and thereafter extending their struggle to Guinea in 1963 and Mozambique in 1964.

Labor, Production, and Taxation

Metropolitan and colonial legislation were to establish the parameters for the recruitment and contracting of 'native' labor from 1878 onwards.[34] Hence the term '*contrato*' (contract) which, while underlining the seemingly voluntary nature of these agreements, was associated with abusive practices, which found expression in the local vernacular.[35] Legal regimes varied between forced, penal, and contract labor, as did the methods of public and private recruitment. Following the introduction of the Native Labor Code in 1899, successive alterations were to refine criteria and alter procedures in 1899, 1914, 1928, and 1954, without however altering its basic racial precepts until 1961. Establishing the 'moral obligation for natives to work', labor legislation effectively imposed formal remunerated employment, created a pliable workforce, and monetized the economy in a modernizing effort based upon the notion of social engineering.[36] The latter also included the introduction of the hut tax in the late 1800s and early 1900s, in Mozambique (1880s), Guinea (1903) and Angola (1906); distinct fiscal systems operated in insular colonies, strongly centered on municipal authorities. Direct native taxes were imposed in continental colonies by means of military 'pacification' campaigns and subsequently transformed into poll and personal tax regimes.[37] Owing to ever changing fiscal criteria, their arbitrary application, the lack of means-testing, the abundant use of fiscal surcharges as stop-gap measures, extraction and evasion became a cat-and-mouse game in which guards and traders doubled as tax collectors.[38] In order to circumvent legislative norms regarding compulsory labor (which in essence was a variable direct tax paid in kind) new direct taxes were introduced from the 1930s.[39] Large-scale ethnic migrations took place in Angola, Guinea, and Mozambique, settling hitherto uncultivated areas while working on short contracts to supplement income. Many sought refuge across the border.[40] Road construction for military and civil purposes, which enabled the penetration of hitherto untapped resources, was largely achieved through coercive schemes.[41] The introduction of cash crops such as cotton, coffee, cocoa, sisal, sugar and peanuts (which also involved compulsory measures in the case of cotton and rice in Mozambique, cotton and coffee in Angola, cocoa in São Tomé and Príncipe and peanuts in Guinea) was meant to provide colonial export-based revenue while being re-exported via the metropole to other European countries.[42]

The extraction of 'native' labor power, taxation and export crops (the pillars of colonial rule) became an integral part of the *esprit de corps* of colonial officialdom. Portuguese labor codes created conditions for a large-scale migrant labor system focused on public works. Private contractors benefited from the cooperation and complacency of administrative authorities. In this respect, they did not essentially differ from similar legislation in other colonial territories.[43] However, the perception of Portugal's weakness as an imperial power was to fuel international pressures following the foundation of the League of Nations in 1919. Previously, abusive labor regimes had been denounced from the late 1800s onwards, for São Tomé and Angola.[44] Large-scale labor migration from Mozambique to the Southern African mines, facilitated by the Natal railway built in the late 1800s, gave rise to the first labor conventions with South Africa and agreements with miners' associations.[45]

Spearheaded by the International Labor Organization (ILO) and missionary societies, international campaigns against compulsory labor in colonial Africa focused above all on the humanitarian dimensions of 'contract' labor and debt bondage.[46] The *Curadoria dos Negócios Indígenas* in continental colonies (called *Curadoria dos Serviçais e Indígenas* in São Tomé and Príncipe) exercised the trusteeship with regard to 'native' employees.[47] However, reports showed that central and district services were not verifying the situation in rural areas with regard to labor recruitment and contracts.[48] Acting as the sole executors of native policies and supervisors of their implementation in rural areas, administrators acting as trustees often rubber stamped 'contract' labor. The penalties imposed on local populations could range from fines to correctional penal labor.[49]

The idea that the Portuguese were 'colonizers by vocation' was severely tested in 1925 with the publication of the caustic report by Edward Ross on labor conditions in Angola, based upon interviews with '*contratados*'.[50] Putting Portuguese governing circles on the defensive, such denunciations were to play a key role in shaping legislation, propaganda, and the 'civilizing mission' in Portuguese colonies.[51] The revised labor code of 1928 and the 1926 and 1929 laws on native rights for Angola, Mozambique, and Guinea incorporated a number of international legal formulae following Portugal's ratification of the League's 1926 convention on slavery. However, by rejecting the convention on forced labor in 1930 (together with France [ratified 1937] and Belgium [ratified 1944]), based on the principle of foreign non-intervention in Portuguese colonial affairs, practices on the ground remained unaltered.[52] Although subsequent reforms essentially perpetuated the legal and political framework, the colonial inspection service would provide an alternative perspective from the mid-1930s onwards, based upon visits and enquiries conducted in loco, which could result in disciplinary action. Inspection reports were to document administrative practice, compliance with legal and procedural standards, and identify problems and correct them whenever possible. Strong criticism of labor conditions in Angola, Guinea, and Mozambique (including forced labor by women and children) and their impact on African populations were expressed with some regularity in inspection reports.[53] As public health became an increasing concern in the 1940s and broad reforms were introduced for the empire as a whole, reports began to emphasize the need for stricter rules for the recruitment, transport, and treatment of laborers in accordance with procedures adopted in other African colonies.[54]

Based upon his experience as a provincial governor and as a probing inspector in Angola and in the 1940s in Mozambique, Henrique Galvão became one of the major critics of Portuguese colonial administration. Galvão's 1947 report before the Committee of Colonial Affairs of the Portuguese National Assembly amounts to a strong indictment of Portuguese rule, above all in Angola, the 'jewel in the Crown' of empire.[55] The report highlighted the administrative incapacity to implement 'native affairs' policies with regard to African labor, taxation, and production, which had in turn provoked a veritable demographic exodus to neighboring colonies while destroying the foundations of the African family.[56] By laying bare the difference between propaganda and practice, it revealed serious contradictions with regard to the implementation of labor, tax, and production policies. It also highlighted the serious lack of human and material resources, of competent officials, and of an effective organization on the ground capable of relating to African populations' conditions and needs.[57] The wide-ranging nature of his statement, and the fact that it was made by a high-ranking figure and MP, enhanced its political significance, which was immediately grasped by the British embassy in Lisbon.[58] Nevertheless, in international forums, some inspector colleagues vehemently denied the 'existence of a generalized system of compulsory labor' in Angola, Mozambique and São Tomé, and Príncipe.[59]

Despite submitting another report commissioned by the then Minister of Colonial Affairs on Mozambique, which arrived at similar conclusions, Galvão's warnings remained unheeded and he became a persona non grata and one of the regime's major critics in exile.[60] Although highly critical of the ad hoc nature of governance, the lack of de facto territorial administrative control, and of reforms in terms of 'native affairs', the supporter-turned-opponent of the New State's methods did reserve praise for a private labor regime. DIAMANG, a private diamond-mining company with mixed Portuguese, Belgian, French, and US capital, operated a large concession in the North East of Angola.[61] Heralded by its administrators and authorities as a showcase of colonial modernity, the inhuman conditions to which workers in the DIAMANG mines in the Lunda region of Angola were subjected were denounced by Gilberto Freyre, the Brazilian proponent of 'lusotropicalism', which was adopted as the New State's official ideology in the 1950s (see below).[62] Simultaneously, other reports by foreign scholars also strongly criticized labor conditions in Southern Mozambique and the absence of the 'racial harmony' that 'lusotropicalism' preached.[63] By the time the complaint by newly independent Ghana was submitted to the ILO in 1961 on Portugal's non-compliance with the Forced Labor Convention (which Portugal had ratified in 1956), nationalist movements in Angola had already taken up arms against Portuguese rule.[64] The Batepá massacre of workers by plantation owners in Saõ Tomé in February 1953, the Pindjiguiti uprising of stevedores in the port of Bissau (Guinea) in August 1959, the Mueda massacre in June 1960 in Mozambique, and the popular revolt in the COTONANG-controlled Cassange area in Northern Angola in January 1961 (generally regarded as the spark that ignited anti-colonial resistance) revealed the increasingly tense labor relations, heavy-handed colonial repression, and authorities' political ineptitude.[65]

Economic Modernization and Armed Conflict

Soon after civil administrations were established in recently occupied African territories in the 1920s, the 1926 military coup in Portugal and the 1929 world crisis served to temper ambitious development plans. The New State regime curbed public investment, the colonial civil service was subjected to rigorous cuts and controls, and new taxes and surcharges were meant to balance the budget as revenues from export crops sharply decreased because of lower world market prices.[66] The reversal of the devolution of colonial autonomy under the first Republic was reinforced by the fiercely nationalist regime's attempt to put in place autarchic economic policies that largely depended on 'closed' circuits between colonies and metropole. In the meantime, new strata of (mostly Portuguese) landed property holders affirmed themselves, whilst large private companies with Portuguese and foreign capital (such as the Sena Sugar Estates, the Companhia de Moçambique, DIAMANG and COTONANG) emerged as important economic actors, producing sugar, coffee, cotton, sisal, cacao, peanuts, rice, maize, rubber, and diamonds. Railway corridors were built linking coastal ports in Mozambique (Beira, Lourenço Marques) and Angola (Lobito, Benguela) to their respective (British and Belgian) hinterlands. At the same time, the economies in insular territories tended to lag behind, owing to the small scale transactions in the trade of raw materials (coal, salt) or processed food (canned fish) in the case of Cape Verde, or cocoa, copra, coconuts, and coffee in São Tomé and Príncipe.[67]

Although metropolitan authorities encouraged European settlement, Portuguese emigration to continental colonies proceeded in a controlled fashion

Table 8.1 Population of Portugal's former African colonies (1926–1970). *Source* Boletim Geral das Colonias, 3, 21, 1927; Celia Reis, 2000; Censo Populacao de, 1950; Provincia Guine, 1959; Anuario Estatistico de Angola, 1933; Anuario Estatistico Mozambique, 1960; AEU (Anuario estatistico Ultramar), 1943, 1954, 1965, 1972

Population	Guinea		Angola		Mozambique		Cabo Verde	S. Tomé	
	Indigenous	Total	Indigenous	Total	Indigenous	Total	Total	Indigenous[a]	Total
1926								20,301	58,907
1927									
1928	384,394	386,425							
1933			2,972,587	3,098,281	3,814,407	3,849,977	150,160		
1940	345,267	351,089	3,646,399	3,738,010	5,030,179	5,085,630	181,286	28,456	60,490
1950	502,457	510,777	4,009,911	4,145,266	5,640,363	5,732,317	148,331	16,768	60,159
1960		519,229		4,830,449		6,578,604	201,549		63,485
1970		487,448		5,673,046		8,233,834	272,072		73,631

Note
[a]Figures for indigenous populations do not include 'serviçais' or contract laborers

until 1945. From then on it was encouraged by the New State regime, albeit in a highly selective fashion, leading to a significant growth of colonial ranks and urban populations through migration from Portugal to Angola and Mozambique.[68] Europeanized African 'elites' emerged in continental cities in Angola (Luanda, Huambo, Benguela, Malanje, Uíge), Mozambique (Lourenço Marques, Beira, Chimoio, Tete), and Guinea (Bissau and Bafatá).[69] Urban development projects also flourished from the late 1940s in a coordinated effort toward infrastructural, architectural, and sanitary modernization.[70] At the same time, the influx of Europeans caused indigenous Africans (whose numbers grew significantly from the 1930s) to be relegated to the urban periphery in terms of housing, jobs, and services.[71] The end of empire between 1950 and 1970 was to witness a large population increase (32% overall) in Portugal's African colonies, signaling a notable African demographic momentum (see Table 8.1).[72]

Tax regimes, land concession policies, agricultural extension, and health services were expected to facilitate European settlement in order to promote exports of cash crops and raw materials to the metropole.[73] At the same time, reformist tendencies became apparent in administrative circles, as some officials adopted paternalist attitudes towards African populations, highlighting discrimination, and advocating reforms.[74] This coincided with a shift in terms of tax revenue from African towards European strata in (growing) settler colonies such as Angola and Mozambique, contrasting with greater burdens being put on the shoulders of Guinean populations.[75] With the aim of 'nationalizing' colonial economies and societies, Portuguese investment in trade, industry, and agriculture was officially promoted. Portuguese conglomerates such as the CUF (Companhia União Fabril) and the 'imperial bank', the Banco Nacional Ultramarino, which issued currency and supervised financial transactions, exercised effective control over colonial economies and imperial trade flows.

A two-pronged policy served to strengthen economic ties between Portugal and Europe, as well as with its empire. This was symbolized by Portugal joining the European Free Trade Association (EFTA) in 1959 and the establishment in 1962 of the Portuguese Economic Space (*Espaço Económico Português* [EEP]), which was meant to further economic integration in the empire. This process of economic internationalization relied on the influx of Europeans, which, although most returned to Europe, succeeded in attracting a significant number of settlers. By 1960, the European presence in Angola and Mozambique had reached over 170,000 and 97,000 respectively, quadrupling compared to 1940, further rising between 60 and 70% until 1970 (see Table 8.1).[76] European settlement coincided with a considerable increase in the prices of export commodities on world markets after 1945, leading to a coffee, peanut, and cotton boom in Angola, Guinea, and Mozambique respectively.[77]

The 1950s were to witness a concerted effort to infuse colonial economies with much needed capital investment in order to modernize their rudimentary infrastructures whilst enhancing Portugal's reputation abroad. The *Planos de Fomento* (Development Plans) introduced from 1953 onwards in metropolitan Portugal and its colonies (I: 1953–1958; II: 1959–1964; *Plano Intercalar*, 1965–1968; III: 1969–1973) signified a change of course towards state-led modernization and private investment[78] but falling short of 'welfare colonialism'. Although partially inspired by broad investment programs introduced in the British and French empires to modernize their economies and increase self-sufficiency,[79] Portuguese programs started out by centering on infrastructural investment rather than promoting social and economic welfare. Social dimensions were only addressed from the mid-1960s as a result of pressures from the international organizations and nationalist liberation movements,[80] with the additional caveat that colonies were expected to fund a large part of the costs with self-generated revenue.[81] Despite the fact that in absolute terms Angola and Mozambique were by far the main beneficiaries of the Plans' investment programs, relatively speaking, Cape Verde (which had just emerged from a severe and deadly famine in 1947[82]) would champion the financial assistance provided between the mid-1950s and mid-1960s. São Tomé and Príncipe would be second to Cape Verde in relative terms, as its cocoa export economy steadily declined (from the 1920s onwards). Prospecting for natural resources in the 1950s was to result in the finding of oil deposits in Angola, while iron ore, manganese, and copper were also mined there, as were bauxite and coal in Mozambique (Fig. 8.1).

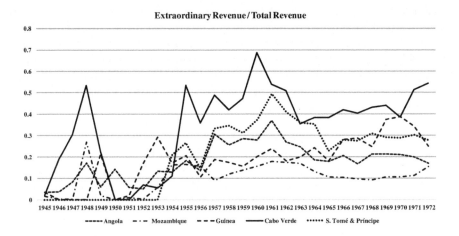

Sources: AIC (Anuário Estatístico Império Colonial), 1949; AEU (Anuário Estatístico do Ultramar), 1951, 1953, 1954, 1955, 1956, 1957, 1960, 1962, 1964, 1966, 1968, 1970, 1972.

Fig. 8.1 Total Revenue (*c.*1949–1972)

Portugal's membership of the United Nations in 1955 coincided with the birth of nationalist movements in its colonies. The UPA/FNLA, MPLA and UNITA in Angola, PAIGC in Guinea and Cape Verde, MLSTP in São Tomé and Príncipe, and FRELIMO in Mozambique shared a common goal but differed in terms of political programs, ideologies, mobilization strategies, and guerilla tactics.[83] A significant number of future nationalist leaders, such as Agostinho Neto, Mário Pinto de Andrade, Holden Roberto, Jonas Savimbi, Eduardo Mondlane, Samora Machel, and Uria Simango had been trained in (Protestant and Catholic) mission schools which often operated with foreign (non-Portuguese) personnel and funding. The armed struggle waged by these movements in Angola, Guinea, and Mozambique against Portuguese rule (1961–1974) led to the stationing of large numbers of Portuguese troops and military personnel and the rapid growth of a security apparatus.[84] In the face of the 'nationalist threat', 'white elites' in the colonies also called for greater autonomy from Lisbon, which initially reacted sympathetically while promoting a program of public investment to allay the concerns of local economic interests.[85] Securitarian considerations and social engineering went hand in hand with the regrouping of Africans in *aldeamentos* or model villages located close to roads, bringing them under military control whilst providing access to basic infrastructures and services. In the 1950s, significant inputs were also directed towards agricultural settlement schemes (*colonatos*) for rural Portuguese families introduced in Angola and Mozambique, providing them with land, tools, seeds, housing, livestock, extension, and health services.[86] Thus, the idealized notion of a rural way of life deeply rooted in the New State's make-up was combined with a push towards implementing economic development, repressive counter-insurgency methods and intensifying Portugal's 'civilizing mission'. Its 'lusotropicalist' ideology, which professed the competence and adaptability of Portuguese colonizers in the tropics, and expounded the virtues of a 'harmonious, multiracial, pluri-continental nation' which included the metropole and 'overseas provinces' was under threat.[87]

Although nationalist movements rapidly debunked this myth and countered colonial rule with armed resistance, the programs of both colonizer and contestants had certain aspects in common, such as a strong emphasis on nation, modernization, and the state's role in it.[88] Whereas Portuguese armed forces took their cue from counter-insurgency strategies developed by the British in Kenya,[89] nationalist forces adopted guerilla tactics and mobilization drives first tested in Asia and Latin America, reinventing them in Africa in territories with a complex ethnic mosaic.[90] Crucially, the wars of liberation illustrated the large-scale mobilization of Africans by both anti-colonial and colonial sides, thus deeply affecting African societies.[91] Owing to overlapping and competing responsibilities, administrative officials (many of whom felt increasingly sidetracked by their military counterparts) protested at the lack of knowledge and incompetence of the Armed Forces in terms of comprehending local traditions.[92] Although the Portuguese economy experienced significant economic growth as a result of industrialization during the 1960s and early 1970s, as would Angola,[93] the lack of monetization, credit facilities, and capital, red tape, and above all armed conflict, were to hamper economic and social development in the colonies. From the mid-1960s onwards, the financial contributions of the colonies to the metropolitan economy were to decrease significantly, being overshadowed by remittances from Portuguese emigrants in Europe.[94]

The pressure from nationalist movements, above all in Guinea and Mozambique, was to provoke an acceleration of reforms in the late 1960s towards developmental programs which included social welfare, for example in terms of health and education.[95] Public health and social services were expanded for African populations, while secondary schools were introduced from the 1950s as well as institutions for higher education in Angola and Mozambique in the 1960s. At the same time, nationalist movements erected new, rudimentary forms of government in their own liberated areas, above all in Guinea and Mozambique, while offering social support and educational and health services to mobilized rural communities. However, as social-engineering efforts intensified, repressive interventions such as the aforementioned *aldeamento* policy would be forcibly applied on a large scale by the Portuguese Armed Forces during the colonial wars in order to exercise control over indigenous populations.[96] The heightened social, political, economic, and racial tensions resulting from armed conflict were to uproot hundreds of thousands of Africans. As they fled to neighboring countries where nationalist movements kept their bases, the regionalization of armed conflict directly involved independent states such as Senegal, Guinea-Conakry, Congo-Brazzaville, Congo/Zaire, Zambia, Rhodesia, Malawi, South Africa, and Tanzania. In the course of the war, Portugal also established strategic military alliances with neighboring countries such as South Africa and Rhodesia in the Alcora Treaty of 1970.[97]

The nationalist diplomatic offensive, internal political tensions, and the broad international condemnation of Portugal's colonial wars were to culminate in the Carnation Revolution in April 1974 which overthrew the New State dictatorship. The subsequent decolonization process would result in the independence of Guinea-Bissau (1974), followed by Mozambique, Cabo Verde, São Tomé, and Príncipe and Angola in 1975.

Conclusion

This chapter has provided a broad view of the policies and practice of administration and its impact upon the economy and society in Portugal's former African colonies over a period of 75 years. The contradictions and discontinuities between policy and practice in empire, and the reactions of African populations to colonial rule have been highlighted, with regard to racial precepts, labor relations, economic development, and violent conflict. It revealed three principal strands for an analysis of the former Portuguese empire in Africa: the (aspiring) imperial nation in overreach, the lack of imperial unity, and the ad hoc nature of colonial rule on the ground. Dominated for the most part by the New State dictatorship, the deep-seated concern with the identification of the Portuguese nation with empire was to increasingly insulate the regime from political change in Africa and beyond. The belated attempt to develop its colonies coincided not only with late industrialization in Portugal and its turn towards Europe, but also with the nationalist challenge in Africa. The sudden but inevitable collapse of empire in the mid-1970s, which was associated with the regime's wars in Africa, set in motion processes of decolonization, long after other colonial nations had shed their respective possessions in Africa. The regime's refusal to negotiate with nationalist movements and embrace the idea of decolonization, and the mounting momentum of nationalist movements' campaigns served to regionalize and internationalize these conflicts during the Cold War. These struggles and the delayed end of empire were to leave a legacy fraught with long-term implications for its deeply divided former colonies, above all in the case of Angola and Mozambique.

Notes

1. Luís Madureira, *Imaginary Geographies in Portuguese and Lusophone-African Literature: Narratives of Discovery and Empire* (New York: Edwin Mellen Press, 2006); and Manuela Ribeiro Sanches, *Portugal não é um país pequeno: contar o império na pós-colonialidade* (Lisbon: Cotovia, 2006).
2. Richard J. Hammond, *Portugal and Africa, 1815–1910: A Study in Uneconomic Imperialism* (Stanford: Stanford University Press, 1966).
3. Valentim Alexandre, "O Império Português (1825–1890): ideologia e economia," *Análise Social* XXXVIII, no. 169 (2005): 959–79.
4. Valentim Alexandre, *Origens do Colonialismo Português Moderno* (Lisbon: Sá da Costa, 1979); and by the same author, "Ideologia, Economia e Política: a questão colonial naimplantação do Estado Novo," *Análise Social* XXVIII, no. 123–24 (1993); and also *Velho Brasil, Novas Áfricas: Portugal e o Império (1808–1975)* (Oporto: Afrontamento, 2000).
5. René Pélissier, *Les Campagnes Coloniales du Portugal, 1841–1941* (Paris: Flammarion, 2004).
6. William Gervase Clarence-Smith, *The Third Portuguese Empire (1825–1975): A Study in Economic Imperialism* (Manchester: Manchester University Press, 1983); and Pedro Lains, "An Account of the Portuguese African Empire, 1885–1975," *Revista de História Económica* 16, no. 1 (1998): 235–63.
7. Omar Ribeiro Thomaz, *Ecos do Atlântico Sul* (Rio de Janeiro: UFRJ/Faperj, 2002); Cláudia Castelo, *"O Modo Português de estar no Mundo": o Luso-tropicalismo e a Ideologia Colonial Portuguesa (1933–1961)* (Oporto, Portugal: Edicões Afrontamento, 1998).
8. The four strands are discussed in Malyn Newitt, *Portugal in Africa: The Last Hundred Years* (London: Longman, 1981), and in a condensed form, by the same author, in "The Late Colonial State in Portuguese Africa," *Itinerário* 23, no. 3–4 (1999): 110–22.
9. Luís Reis Torgal, *Estados Novos, Estado Novo: ensaios de história política e cultural* (Coimbra: Universidade Coimbra, 2009).

10. SEMU, Concessões de Terrenos nas Províncias Ultramarinas. Carta de Lei de 9 de Maio 1901 (Lisbon: Secretária de Estado da Marinha e Ultramar,1901).
11. Barbara Direito, Terra e africanos no pensamento colonial português, c. 1920– c. 1945, *Análise Social* XLIX, no. 213 (4.°) (2014): 768–93.
12. Pedro Tavares de Almeida and Paulo Silveira e Sousa, "Ruling the Empire: The Portuguese Colonial Office (1820s–1926)," *Revista da História das Ideias* 27 (2006): 1–33.
13. Réné Pélissier, *Les Campagnes Coloniales du Portugal*.
14. Sergio Neto, *Colónia Martir, Colónia Modelo: Cabo Verde no pensamento ultramarino português, 1925–1965* (Coimbra: Imprensa da Universidade de Coimbra, 2009).
15. Alexander Keese, "Imperial Actors? Cape Verdean Mentality in the Portuguese Empire Under the Estado Novo, 1926–1974," in *Imperial Migrations: Colonial communities in the Portuguese World*, ed. Eric Morier-Genoud and Michel Cahen (Leiden: Brill, 2013), 129–48.
16. The standard legal formula asserted that '*indígenas*' or natives were "all individuals pertaining to the black race or descended from it, who by their education and customs do not distinguish themselves from the common traits of that race" (Regulamento Geral do Trabalho dos Indígenas, *Diário do Governo*, 262, 25-11-1899).
17. Christoph Kohl, "The Limitations and Ambiguities of Colonialism in Guinea Bissau: Examining the Creole and 'Civilised' Space in Colonial Society," *History in Africa* 43 (2015): 169–203; Wilson Trajano Filho, "The Creole Idea of Nation and Its Predicaments: The Case of Guinea-Bissau," in *The Powerful Presence of the Past: Integration and Conflict Along the Upper Guinea Coast*, ed. Jacqueline Knorr and Wilson Trajano Filho (New York: Berghahn, 2015), 157–84; Gerhard Seibert, "Criouliização em Cabo Verde e São Tomé e Príncipe: divergências históricas e identitárias," *Afro-Ásia* 49 (2014): 41–70; Jacopo Corrado, *The Creole Elite and the Rise of Angolan Proto-Nationalism, 1870–1920* (Amherst: Cambria Press, 2007); and Malyn Newitt, *A History of Mozambique* (London: Hurst, 1997), 127–46.
18. See for exemple the pamphlet *Voz d'Angola Clamando no Deserto* (1901) in Angola, the journals *O Africano* (1906–1918), *O Comércio da Guiné* (1930–1931) in Guinea, *O Brado Africano* (1918–1974) in Mozambique, *Claridade* (1936–1960) in Cape Verde and *A Liberdade* (1919–1923) in São Tomé. After 1926, press freedom was suppressed, only to be challenged from the 1950s by nationalist movements and cultural associations.
19. Visit by French Diplomatic Adviser of the AOF to Portuguese Guinea, *Voyage en Guinée Portugaise*, August 1959; Ministére des Affaires Étrangers (MAE), Paris, Direction Afrique-Levant, Série: GP, Sous Serie: I, Dossier III: Guinée Portugaise, 1953–1959; Report HM Consul Luanda, A.J.S. Pullan, on a tour of southern Angola, 18–28 July 1955; and National Archives, London, FO 371/113878.
20. Newitt, *Portugal in Africa*, 105.
21. Luís Augusto Vieira Fernandes, Relatório da Inspecção aos Serviços Centrais e Provinciais da Colonia de Moçambique, 1940–41; AHU, MU, ISAU.
22. Augusto Nascimento, *Poderes e Quotidiano nas Roças de São Tomé e Príncipe* (Lousã: Tipografia Lousanense, 2002), op cit. 108.

23. Alexander Keese, "Taxation, Evasion and Compulsory Measures in Angola," in *Administration and Taxation in Former Portuguese Africa, 1900–1945*, ed. Philip J. Havik, Alexander Keese, and Maciel Santos (Newcastle upon Tyne: Cambridge Scholars Publishing, 2015), 98–137.
24. Philip J. Havik, "Tchon I Renansa: Colonial Governance, Appointed Chiefs and Political Change in 'Portuguese' Guinea," in *Ethnicity and the Long-Term Experience*, ed. Alexander Keese (Berne: Peter Lang, 2010), 155–90.
25. Decreto-Lei (D-L) 23:229, in *Diário do Govêrno*, 261, 15-11-1933.
26. Maria Conceição Neto, "In Town and Out of Town: A Social History of Huambo (Angola), 1902–1961" (PhD diss., School of Oriental and African Studies (SOAS), UCL/London, 2012), 265–78; and Philip J. Havik, "Direct or Indirect Rule? Reconsidering the Roles of Appointed Chiefs and Native Employees in Portuguese West Africa," *Africana Studia* 15 (2010): 29–56.
27. Susana Goulart Costa, "Portugal and the Building of an Imaginary Empire," in *Religion and Politics in a Global Society: Comparative Perspectives from the Portuguese Speaking World*, ed. Paul C. Manuel, Alynna Lyon, and Clyde Wilcox (Lanham: Lexington Books, 2013), 33–46. In 1940, Portugal and the Vatican signed a concordat and missionary convention, formally recognizing and regulating the key role of Catholic missions in empire.
28. Acto Colonial, D-L 22.465, *Diário do Governo*, 83, 11-4-1930, Carta Orgânica do Imperio Colonial Português, D-L 23.228, *Diário do Governo*, 261, 15-11-1933. The latter was subject to alterations in 1946 (Portaria 11: 380, 11-6-1946).
29. Estatuto Civil, Político e Criminal dos Indígenas, D-L 16.473, *Diário do Governo*, 30, 6-2-1929.
30. Peter K. Mendy, *Colonialismo Português em África: a tradição de resistência na Guiné Bissau (1879–1959)* (Bissau: INEP, 1993), 313.
31. Patrícia Ferraz de Matos, *The Colours of the Empire: Racialised Representations During Portuguese Colonialism* (New York: Berghahn, 2006), 50; and Seibert, "Crioulização," 66.
32. Lei Orgânica do Ultramar Português, D-L 2.066, *Diário do Governo*, 135, 27-6-1953.
33. José Carlos Ney Ferreira and Vasco Soares da Veiga, *Estatuto dos Indígenas das Províncias da Angola, Guiné e Moçambique* (Lisbon: Authors' Edition, 1957).
34. Regulamento para os Contratos de Serviçais e Colonos nas Províncias de África Portuguesa, *Diário do Governo*, 237, 18-11-1878; Regulamento Geral do Trabalho dos Indígenas, *Diário do Governo*, 262, 25-11-1899; Regulamento Geral do Trabalho dos Indígenas nas Colónias Portuguesas, *Diário do Governo*, 1ª série, 187, 14-10-1914; *Código do Trabalho dos Indígenas nas Colónias Portuguesas de África* (Luanda: Colónia de Angola, 1928); and D-L 3966, Estatuto dos Indígenas Portugueses das Províncias da Guine, Angola e Moçambique, *Diário do Governo*, 110, 20-5-1954.
35. On the practice and term *chibalo* used in Mozambique, see Malyn Newitt, *A History of Mozambique* (London: Hurst, 2009); Valdemir Zamparoni, "Colonialism and the Creation of Racial Identities in Lourenço Marques, Mozambique," in *Africa, Brazil and the Construction of Trans-Atlantic Black Identities*, ed. Livio Sansone, Elisée Soumonni, and Boubacar Barry (Trenton, NJ: Africa World Press, 2008), 20–43; Bridget O'Laughlin,

"Proletarianisation, Agency and Changing Rural Livelihoods: Forced Labor and Resistance in Colonial Mozambique," *Journal of Southern African Studies* 28, no. 3 (2002): 511–30; Jeanne Penvenne, *African Workers and Colonial Racism: Mozambican Strategies and Struggles in Lourenço Marques, 1877–1962* (Oxford: James Currey, 1995); and Allen Isaacman, "Coercion, Paternalism and the Labor Process: The Mozambican Cotton Regime, 1938-1961," *Journal of Southern African Studies* 18 (1992): 487–526.

36. Art. 1, Regulamento Geral do Trabalho dos Indígenas, *Diário do Governo*, 262, 25-11-1899.
37. Philip J. Havik, "Colonial Administration, Public Accounts and Fiscal Extraction: Policies and Revenues in Former Portuguese Africa (1900–1960)," *African Economic History* 41 (2013): 162–226; op. cit. 174.
38. Neto, In and Out of Town, 288: "In the search for a way out of *indigenato* constraints, 'natives' used migration, deception, tax evasion and every possibility offered by the system".
39. The *contribuição braçal* (Port: Manual Contribution), a compulsory labor tax, was introduced in Guinea in 1935 and in Mozambique in 1942.
40. Newitt, *Portugal in Africa*, 102–4; and Neto, In and Out of Town, 256–65.
41. Philip J. Havik, "Motorcars and Modernity: Pining for Progress in Portuguese Guinea (1915–1945)," in *The Speed of Change: Motor-Vehicles and People in Africa: 1890–2000*, ed. J.B. Gewald, S. Luning, and K. Walraven (Leiden: Brill, 2009), 48–74; and Neto, In and Out of Town.
42. Clarence-Smith, *The Third Portuguese Empire*, 116–45; and M. Anne Pitcher, *Politics in the Portuguese Empire: The State, Industry and Cotton, 1926–1974* (Oxford: Clarendon Press, 1993).
43. Miguel Bandeira Jerónimo and José Pedro Monteiro, "Internationalism and the Labours of the Portuguese Colonial Empire," *Portuguese Studies* 29, no. 2 (2013): 142–63.
44. Miguel Bandeira Jerónimo, *The 'Civilising Mission' of Portuguese Colonialism, 1870–1930* (Cambridge: Cambridge University, 2015); Catherine Higgs, *Chocolate Islands: Cocoa and Slavery in Colonial Africa* (Athens: Ohio University Press, 2012); Lowell J. Satre, *Chocolate on Trial: Slavery, Politics and the Ethics of Business* (Athens: Ohio University Press, 2005); William Gervase Clarence-Smith, 'Labour Conditions in the Plantations of São Tomé and Príncipe, 1875–1914,' *Slavery and Abolition* 14 (1993): 149–67; and James Duffy, *A Question of Slavery: Labour Policies in Portuguese African and the British Protest, 1850–1920* (Oxford: Oxford University Press, 1967).
45. Newitt, *A History of Mozambique*, 482–516.
46. Daniel R. Maul, "The International Labour Organization and the Struggle Against Forced Labour from 1919 to the Present," *Labor History* 48, no. 4 (2007): 477–500.
47. Jeremy Ball, *Angola's Colossal Lie: Forced Labor on a Sugar Plantation, 1913–1977* (Leiden: Brill, 2015); Eric Allina, *Slavery by Any Other Name: African Life under Company Rule in Colonial Mozambique* (Charlottesville: University of Virginia Press, 2012); and Gerald Bender, *Angola under the Portuguese: The Myth and the Reality* (Berkeley: University of California Press, 1978).
48. António de Almeida, Relatório de Inspecção da Colónia de Moçambique, 1947; AHU, ISAU.

49. Arts. 12 & 13, Estatuto Político, Civil, Criminal dos Indígenas, 1929.
50. Edward A. Ross, *Report on Employment of Native Labor in Portuguese Africa* (New York: Abbott Press, 1925). Similar accusations had already been made and would continue to be voiced by Protestant missionaries, which in part influenced the timing and urgency of Ross's visit.
51. For a detailed analysis of the Ross Report, see Bandeira Jerónimo, *The 'Civilising Mission'*, Chap. 5. The idea of Portugal as a colonizing and civilizing nation by vocation, was reiterated in art. 2 of the Colonial Act of 1930: "It is the organic essence of the Portuguese Nation to engage in the historical function of possessing and colonizing overseas dominions and to civilize the indigenous populations included in them".
52. Report, J. Coutinho, Colonial Ministry, Lisbon, 27-4-1938; AHU, DGAPC, 436-A.
53. Mário Costa, Relatório da Inspecção Administrativa da Colónia da Guiné, 1944–45; AHU, ISAU, Mç. 2245; José N. Nunes de Oliveira, Relatório Inspecção Geral Colonia de Angola, Lisbon, 4-2-1944; AHU, MU, ISAC; and Fernandes, Relatório da Inspecção aos Serviços Centrais e Provinciais, op.cit.
54. Tertuliano Soares, "Acerca dalguns problemas de assistência relativos aos trabalhadores indígenas de África," *África Médica* 8–9 (1944): 165–80. For health reforms, see DL 34–417, Reorganização dos Serviços de Saúde no Império Português, *Diário do Governo*, I, 38, 21-2-1945.
55. Exposição do deputado Henrique Galvão à Comissão de Colónias da Assembleia Nacional em Janeiro de 1947; AHU, ISAU, 1943–1970.
56. Exposição do deputado Henrique Galvão, 10.
57. Ibid., 50–54.
58. Report, Sir Nigel Ronald, British Ambassador, Lisbon, to Foreign Office in London, confidential, 29-4-1949, National Archives London, FO 371/73954.
59. Nunes de Oliveira, Confidential, Report to Minister of Colonies, Inspecção Superior Administrativa Ultramarina (ISAU), Lisbon, 14-2-1953; AHU, ISAU, Angola, Guiné, Moçambique, STP, Timor, 1944–1961.
60. On Henrique Galvão's 1947 report see, Douglas Wheeler, "The Galvão Report on Forced Labour (1947) in Historical Context and Perspective: The Trouble Shooter Who Was in Trouble," *Portuguese Studies Review* 16, no. 1 (2008): 115–52; and Aida Freudenthal and Philip J. Havik, Henrique Galvão: Relatório de 1947 (forthcoming).
61. Todd Cleveland, *Diamonds in the Rough: Corporate Paternalism and African Professionalism on the Mines of Colonial Angola, 1917–1975* (Athens: Ohio University Press/Swallow Press, 2015).
62. Conceição Neto, Ideologias, contradições e mistificações da colonização de Angola no século XX, *Lusotopie* (1997): 327–59; op. cit. 330.
63. Marvin Harris, *Portugal's African "Wards": A First-Hand Report on Labor and Education in Moçambique* (New York: The American Committee on Africa, 1958); James Duffy, *Portuguese Africa* (Cambridge: Harvard University Press, 1959), 317–28.
64. Bandeira Jerónimo and Monteiro, "Internationalism and the *Labours* of the Portuguese Colonial Empire," 155–61.
65. Gerhard Seibert, "Le massacre de Fevrier 1953 á São Tomé: raison d'être du nationalisme santomeen," *Lusotopie* (1997): 173–92; Aida Freudenthal,

"A Baixa de Cassanje: algodão e revolta," *Revista Internacional de Estudos Africanos*, 18–22 (1995–1999): 245–83; Leopoldo Amado, Simbólica de Pindjiguití na cultura libertária da Guiné, *Guineidade*, 21-2-2006, http://guineidade.blogs.sapo.pt/15548.html; Michel Cahen, "The Mueda Case and Maconde Political Etnicity: Some Notes on Work in Progress," *Africana Studia* 2 (1999): 29–46; and Diogo Ramada Curto, Bernardo Pinto da Cruz and Teresa Furtado, *Políticas Coloniais em Tempo de Revoltas—Angola circa 1961* (Oporto: Afrontamento, 2016).

66. Havik, "Colonial Administration," 168/169.
67. Armando Castro, *O Sistema Colonial Português em África* (Lisbon: Caminho, 1980), 222–31, 377–81.
68. Cláudia Castelo, *Passagens para África: o povoamento de Angola e Moçambique com naturais da metrópole (1920–1974)* (Oporto: Afrontamento, 2007).
69. Nuno Domingos and Elsa Peralta, eds., *Cidades e Império: dinâmicas coloniais e reconfigurações pós-coloniais* (Lisbon: Edições 70, 2013). On African elites, see Adriano Moreira, As elites nas províncias portuguesas de indigenato, *Ensaios*, no. 34, Junta de Investigações do Ultramar, 1960, 37–62.
70. Ana C.F. Vaz Milheiro, "O Gabinete de Urbanização Colonial e o traçado das cidades luso-africanas na última fase do período colonial português," *Urbe: Brazilian Journal of Urban Management* 4, no. 2 (2012): 215–32.
71. Neto, In and Out of Town, 256.
72. INE, *Anuário Estatístico de Portugal* (Lisbon: Instituto Nacional de Estatística, 1954; 1972); and *Anuário Estatístico do Ultramar* (Lisbon: Instituto Nacional de Estatística, 1954; 1972).
73. Castelo, *Passagens para África*, 61–98.
74. Keese, *Living with Ambiguity*, 162–75.
75. Havik, "Colonial Administration," 191, 197; and Philip J. Havik, "'Taxing the Natives': Fiscal Administration, Labour and Crop Cultivation in Portuguese Guinea (1900–1945)," in *Administration and Taxation*, ed. Havik, Keese and Santos, 167–227.
76. Castelo, *Passagens para África*, 79, 143.
77. D.A. Abshire and M.A. Samuels, *Portuguese Africa: A Handbook* (London: Praeger, 1969), 255–58, 270–71; and Clarence-Smith, *The Third Portuguese Empire*, 198–99.
78. Miguel Bandeira Jerónimo and António Costa Pinto, "A Modernizing Empire: Politics, Culture and Economy in Portuguese Late Colonialism," in *The Ends of European Colonial Empires: Cases and Comparisons*, ed. M. Bandeira Jerónimo and A. Costa Pinto (Basingstoke: Palgrave-Macmillan, 2015), 51–80.
79. George C. Abbott, "A Re-Examination of the 1929 Colonial Development Act," *The Economic History Review* 24, no. 1 (February, 1971): 68–81; Stephen Constantine, *The Making of British Colonial Development Policy, 1914–1940* (London: Frank Cass, 1984); and Tony Chafer, *The End of Empire in French West Africa: France's Successful Decolonization?* (Oxford: Berg, 2002).
80. Claudia Castelo, "Developing 'Portuguese Africa' in Late Colonialism: Confronting Discourses," in *Developing Africa: Concepts and Practices in Twentieth-Century Colonialism*, ed. Joseph Hodge, Gerald Hodl, and Martina Kopf (Manchester, Manchester University Press, 2014), 63–68.
81. Clarence-Smith, *The Third Portuguese Empire*, 167.

82. António Carreira, *Cabo Verde: aspectos sociais, secas e fomes do século XX* (Lisbon: Ulmeiro, 1984).
83. On the history of these nationalist movements, see Didier Péclard, *Les Incertitudes de la Nation en Angola: aux racines sociales de l'Unita* (Paris: Karthala, 2015); Christian Gefrray, *La Cause des Armes au Mozambique: anthropologie d'une guerre civile* (Paris: Karthala, 1990); José Vicente Lopes, *Cabo Verde: os bastidores da independência* (Praia: Spleen, 2002); Leopoldo Amado, *Guerra Colonial e Guerra de Libertação Nacional, 1950–1974: o caso da Guiné Bissau* (Lisbon: IPAD, 2011); Christine Messiant, *1961: L'Angola colonial, histoire et société. Les prémisses du mouvement nationaliste* (Paris: Karthala, 2006); and Gerhard Seibert, *Comrades, Clients and Cousins. Colonialism, Socialism and Democratization in São Tomé and Príncipe* (Leiden: Brill, 2006).
84. Dalila Mateus, *A PIDE-DGS na Guerra Colonial, 1961–1974* (Lisbon: Terramar, 2004); Sayaka Funada-Classen, *The Origins of War in Mozambique: A History of Unity and Division* (Somerset West: Africans Minds, 2012).
85. Fernando T. Pimenta, *Angola: os Brancos e a Independência* (Oporto: Afrontamento, 2008).
86. The *colonatos* and *aldeamentos*, first proposed in the 1930s, also served to introduce cash crops such as cashew trees, which would become important export crops in a postcolonial context, above all in Mozambique and Guinea-Bissau.
87. With the constitutional reforms of 1951, Lusotropicalist notions were enshrined in the constitution, as well as the Colonial Act, *Diário do Governo*, 117, 11-6-1951; the new Organic Law of Portuguese Overseas Territories was passed in 1953.
88. Rosemary E. Galli, "Amílcar Cabral and Rural Transformation in Guinea Bissau: A Preliminary Critique," *Rural Africana* 25, no. 6 (1986): 55–73.
89. John P. Cann, *Counterinsurgency in Africa: The Portuguese Way of War 1961–74* (Solihull: Helion, 2012).
90. See Patrick Chabal, *Amílcar Cabral: Revolutionary Leadership and People's War* (London: Hurst, 2002), 67–77; and Mustafah Dada, *Warriors at Work: How Guinea Was Really Set Free* (Niwot: University Press of Colorado, 1993).
91. Carlos Matos Gomes, "A africanização na Guerra Colonial e as suas sequelas. Tropas locais—Os vilões nos ventos da História," in *As Guerras de Libertação e os Sonhos Coloniais: alianças secretas, mapas imaginados*, ed. Maria Paula Meneses and Bruno Sena Martins (Coimbra: CES/Almedina, 2013), 123–41.
92. Inquérito Funcionários Administrativos, Guiné e Moçambique, 1972; AHU, MU, ISAU.
93. Nuno Valério and Maria Paula Fontoura, "A evolução económica de Angola durante o segundo período colonial—uma tentativa de síntese," *Análise Social* XXIX, no. 129 (1994): 1193–208.
94. Lains, An Account of the Portuguese African Empire, 255/6. Between 1961 and 1970, an average of 26% of the Portuguese government budget (8% of GNP) went towards military expenditure; 242, 251. In 1970, more than 120,000 Portuguese troops were stationed in Angola, Guinea, and Mozambique. Although metropolitan emigration to the colonies was strongly promoted by the regime in the 1960s, by then the major migratory flux was directed towards Northern Europe.

95. Bandeira Jerónimo and Costa Pinto, "A Modernizing Empire."
96. João Borges Coelho, "Da violência colonial ordenada à ordem pós-colonial violenta Sobre um legado das guerras coloniais nas ex-colónias portuguesas," *Lusotopie* (2003): 175–93.
97. Amélia Neves de Souto, Relações entre Portugal, África do Sul e Rodésia do Sul e o Exercício Alcora: elementos fundamentais na estratégia da condução da guerra—1960-1974, in *As Guerras de Libertação e os sonhos coloniais*, ed. Meneses and Martins, 143–69.

BIBLIOGRAPHY

Abbott, George C. "A Re-Examination of the 1929 Colonial Development Act." *The Economic History Review* 24, no. 1 (February, 1971): 68–81.
Abshire, D.A., and M.A. Samuels, eds. *Portuguese Africa: A Handbook*. London: Praeger, 1969.
Alexandre, Valentim. *Velho Brasil, Novas Áfricas: Portugal e o Império (1808-1975)*. Oporto: Afrontamento, 2000.
———. "O Império Português (1825–1890): ideologia e economia." *Análise Social* XXXVIII, no. 169 (2005): 959–79.
Allina, Eric. *Slavery by Any Other Name: African Life under Company Rule in Colonial Mozambique*. Charlottesville: University of Virginia Press, 2012.
Almeida, Pedro Tavares de, and Paulo Silveira e Sousa. "Ruling the Empire: The Portuguese Colonial Office (1820s–1926)." *Revista da História das Ideias* 27 (2006): 1–33.
Amado, Leopoldo. Simbólica de Pindjiguití na cultura libertária da Guiné, *Guineidade*, 21-2-2006. http://guineidade.blogs.sapo.pt/15548.html.
———. *Guerra Colonial e Guerra de Libertação Nacional, 1950–1974: o caso da Guiné Bissau*. Lisbon: IPAD, 2011.
Arquivo Histórico Ultramarino (AHU), Lisbon, Ministério do Ultramar (MU), Inspecção Superior Administrativo do Ultramar (ISAU) and Inspecção Superior Administrativo das Colónias (ISAC).
Arquivo Histórico Ultramarino (AHU), Lisbon, Ministério do Ultramar (MU), Direcção Geral de Administração Político e Civil (DGAPC).
Ball, Jeremy. *Angola's Colossal Lie: Forced Labor on a Sugar Plantation, 1913–1977*. Leiden: Brill, 2015.
Bender, Gerald. *Angola under the Portuguese: The Myth and the Reality*. Berkeley: University of California Press, 1978.
Cahen, Michel. "The Mueda Case and Maconde Political Etnicity: Some Notes on Work in Progress." *Africana Studia* 2 (1999): 29–46.
Cann, John P. *Counterinsurgency in Africa: The Portuguese Way of War 1961–74*. Solihull: Helion, 2012.
Carreira, António. *Cabo Verde: aspectos sociais, secas e fomes do século XX*. Lisbon: Ulmeiro, 1984.
Castelo, Cláudia. *'O Modo Português de estar no Mundo': o Luso-tropicalismo e a Ideologia Colonial Portuguesa (1933–1961)*. Oporto, Portugal: Edições Afrontamento, 1998.
———. *Passagens para África: o povoamento de Angola e Moçambique com naturais da metrópole (1920–1974)*. Oporto: Afrontamento, 2007.

---. "Developing 'Portuguese Africa' in Late Colonialism: Confronting Discourses." In *Developing Africa: Concepts and Practices in Twentieth-Century Colonialism*, edited by Joseph Hodge, Gerald Hodl, and Martina Kopf, 63–86. Manchester: Manchester University Press, 2014.

Castro, Armando. *O Sistema Colonial Português em África*. Lisbon: Caminho, 1980.

Chabal, Patrick. *Amílcar Cabral: Revolutionary Leadership and People's War*. London: Hurst, 2002.

Chafer, Tony. *The End of Empire in French West Africa: France's Successful Decolonization?* Oxford: Berg, 2002.

Clarence-Smith, William Gervase. *The Third Portuguese Empire (1825–1975): A Study in Economic Imperialism*. Manchester: Manchester University Press, 1983.

---. "Labour Conditions in the Plantations of São Tomé and Príncipe, 1875–1914." *Slavery and Abolition* 14 (1993): 149–67.

Cleveland, Todd. *Diamonds in the Rough: Corporate Paternalism and African Professionalism on the Mines of Colonial Angola, 1917–1975*. Athens: Ohio University Press/Swallow Press, 2015.

Coelho, João Borges. "Da violência colonial ordenada à ordem pós-colonial violenta Sobre um legado das guerras coloniais nas ex-colónias portuguesas." *Lusotopie* (2003): 175–93.

Constantine, Stephen. *The Making of British Colonial Development Policy, 1914–1940*. London: Frank Cass, 1984.

Corrado, Jacopo. *The Creole Elite and the Rise of Angolan Proto-Nationalism, 1870–1920*. Amherst: Cambria Press, 2007.

Costa, Susana Goulart. "Portugal and the Building of an Imaginary Empire." In *Religion and Politics in a Global Society: Comparative Perspectives from the Portuguese Speaking World*, edited by Paul C. Manuel, Alynna Lyon, and Clyde Wilcox, 33–46. Lanham: Lexington Books, 2013.

Curto, Diogo Ramada, Bernardo Pinto da Cruz, and Teresa Furtado. *Políticas Coloniais em Tempo de Revoltas—Angola circa 1961*. Oporto: Afrontamento, 2016.

Dada, Mustafah. *Warriors at Work: How Guinea Was Really Set Free*. Niwot: University Press of Colorado, 1993.

Direito, Bárbara. "Terra e africanos no pensamento colonial português, c. 1920–c. 1945." *Análise Social* XLIX, no. 213 (4.º) (2014): 768–93.

Domingos, Nuno, and Elsa Peralta, eds. *Cidades e Império: dinâmicas coloniais e reconfigurações pós-coloniais*. Lisbon: Edições 70, 2013.

Duffy, James. *Portuguese Africa*. Cambridge: Harvard University Press, 1959.

---. *A Question of Slavery: Labour Policies in Portuguese African and the British Protest, 1850–1920*. Oxford: Oxford University Press, 1967.

Ferreira, José Carlos Ney, and Vasco Soares da Veiga. *Estatuto dos Indígenas das Províncias da Angola, Guiné e Moçambique*. Lisbon: Authors' Edition, 1957.

Freudenthal, Aida. "A Baixa de Cassanje: algodão e revolta." *Revista Internacional de Estudos Africanos* 18–22 (1995–1999): 245–83.

Funada-Classen, Sayaka. *The Origins of War in Mozambique: A History of Unity and Division*. Somerset West: Africans Minds, 2012.

Galli, Rosemary E. "Amílcar Cabral and Rural Transformation in Guinea Bissau: A Preliminary Critique." *Rural Africana* 25, no. 6 (1986): 55–73.

Gefrray, Christian. *La Cause des Armes au Mozambique: anthropologie d'une guerre civile*. Paris: Karthala, 1990.

Gomes, Carlos Matos. "A africanização na Guerra Colonial e as suas sequelas. Tropas locais—Os vilões nos ventos da História." In *As Guerras de Libertação e os sonhos coloniais: alianças secretas, mapas imaginados*, edited by Maria Paula Meneses and Bruno Sena Martins, 123–41. Coimbra: CES/Almedina, 2013.

Hammond, Richard J. *Portugal and Africa, 1815–1910: A Study in Uneconomic Imperialism*. Stanford: Stanford University Press, 1966.

Harris, Marvin. *Portugal's African "Wards": A First-Hand Report on Labor and Education in Moçambique*. New York: The American Committee on Africa, 1958.

Havik, Philip J. "Motorcars and Modernity: Pining for Progress in Portuguese Guinea (1915–1945)." In *The Speed of Change: Motor-Vehicles and People in Africa: 1890–2000*, edited by J.B. Gewald, S. Luning, and K. Walraven, 48–74. Leiden: Brill, 2009.

———. "Tchon I Renansa: Colonial Governance, Appointed Chiefs and Political Change in 'Portuguese' Guinea." In *Ethnicity and the Long Term Experience*, edited by Alexander Keese, 155–90. Berne: Peter Lang, 2010.

———. "Direct or Indirect Rule? Reconsidering the Roles of Appointed Chiefs and Native Employees in Portuguese West Africa." *Africana Studia* 15 (2010): 29–56.

———. "Colonial Administration, Public Accounts and Fiscal Extraction: Policies and Revenues in Former Portuguese Africa (1900–1960)." *African Economic History* 41 (2013): 162–226.

———. "Taxing the Natives: Fiscal Administration, Labour and Crop Cultivation in Portuguese Guinea, 1900–1945." In *Administration and Taxation in Former Portuguese Africa, 1900–1945*, edited by Philip J. Havik, Alexander Keese, and Maciel Santos, 167–227. Newcastle upon Tyne: Cambridge Scholars Publishing, 2015.

Higgs, Catherine. *Chocolate Islands: Cocoa and Slavery in Colonial Africa*. Athens: Ohio University Press, 2012.

INE. *Anuário Estatístico de Portugal*. Lisbon: Instituto Nacional de Estatística, 1954.

———. *Anuário Estatístico do Ultramar*. Lisbon: Instituto Nacional de Estatística, 1954.

———. *Anuário Estatístico de Portugal*. Lisbon: Instituto Nacional de Estatística, 1972.

———. *Anuário Estatístico do Ultramar*. Lisbon: Instituto Nacional de Estatística, 1972.

Isaacman, Allen. "Coercion, Paternalism and the Labor Process: The Mozambican Cotton Regime, 1938–1961." *Journal of Southern African Studies*, 18 (1992): 487–526.

Jerónimo, Miguel Bandeira. *The 'Civilising Mission' of Portuguese Colonialism, 1870–1930)*. Cambridge: Cambridge University, 2015.

Jerónimo, Miguel Bandeira, and António Costa Pinto. "A Modernizing Empire: Politics, Culture and Economy in Portuguese Late Colonialism." In *The Ends of European Colonial Empires: Cases and Comparisons*, edited by M. Bandeira Jerónimo and A. Costa Pinto, 51–80. Basingstoke: Palgrave-Macmillan, 2015.

Jerónimo, Miguel Bandeira, and José Pedro Monteiro. "Internationalism and the Labours of the Portuguese Colonial Empire." *Portuguese Studies* 29, no. 2 (2013): 142–63.

Keese, Alexander. "Imperial Actors? Cape Verdean Mentality in the Portuguese Empire Under the Estado Novo, 1926–1974." In *Imperial Migrations: Colonial Communities in the Portuguese World*, edited by Eric Morier-Genoud and Michel Cahen, 129–48. Leiden: Brill, 2013.

———. "Taxation, Evasion and Compulsory Measures in Angola." In *Administration and Taxation in Former Portuguese Africa, 1900–1945*, edited by Philip J. Havik, Alexander Keese, and Maciel Santos, 98–137. Newcastle upon Tyne: Cambridge Scholars Publishing, 2015.

Kohl, Christoph. "The Limitations and Ambiguities of Colonialism in Guinea Bissau: Examining the Creole and 'Civilised' Space in Colonial Society." *History in Africa* 43 (2015): 169–203.

Lains, Pedro. "An Account of the Portuguese African Empire," 1885–1975. *Revista de História Económica* 16, no. 1 (1998): 235–63.

Lopes, José Vicente. *Cabo Verde: os bastidores da independência*. Praia: Spleen, 2002.

Madureira, Luís. *Imaginary Geographies in Portuguese and Lusophone-African Literature: Narratives of Discovery and Empire*. New York: Edwin Mellen Press, 2006.

Mateus, Dalila. *A PIDE-DGS na Guerra Colonial, 1961–1974.* Lisbon: Terramar, 2004.

Matos, Patrícia Ferraz de. *The Colours of the Empire: Racilaised Represetnations During Portuguese Colonialism*. New York: Berghahn, 2006.

Maul, Daniel R. "The International Labour Organization and the Struggle against Forced Labour from 1919 to the Present." *Labor History* 48, no. 4 (2007): 477–500.

Mendy, Peter K. *Colonialismo Português em África: a tradição de resistência na Guiné Bissau (1879–1959)*. Bissau: INEP, 1993, 313.

Messiant, Christine. *1961: L'Angola colonial, histoire et société. Les prémisses du mouvement nationaliste*. Paris: Karthala, 2006.

Milheiro, Ana C.F. Vaz. "O Gabinete de Urbanização Colonial e o traçado das cidades luso-africanas na última fase do período colonial português." *Urbe: Brazilian Journal of Urban Management* 4, no. 2 (2012): 215–32.

Ministére de Affaires Étrangers (MAE), Direction Afrique-Levant, Guinée Portugaise.

Moreira, Adriano. "As elites nas províncias portuguesas de indigenato." *Ensaios*, no. 34 (Junta de Investigações do Ultramar, 1960): 37–62.

Nascimento, Augusto. *Poderes e Quotidiano nas Roças de São Tomé e Príncipe*. Lousã: Tipografia Lousanense, 2002.

National Archives (NA), London, Foreign Office (FO) Files.

Neto, Maria Conceição. "Ideologias, contradições e mistificações da colonização de Angola no século XX." *Lusotopie* (1997): 327–59.

———. "In Town and Out of Town: A Social History of Huambo, (Angola), 1902–1961." PhD diss., School of Oriental and African Studies (SOAS), UCL/London, 2012.

Neto, Sérgio. *Colónia Martir, Colónia Modelo: Cabo Verde no pensamento ultramarino português, 1925–1965*. Coimbra: Imprensa da Universidade de Coimbra, 2009.

Newitt, Malyn. *Portugal in Africa: The Last Hundred Years*. London: Longman, 1981.

———. *A History of Mozambique*. London: Hurst, 1997.

———. "The Late Colonial State in Portuguese Africa." *Itinerário* 23, nos. 3–4 (1999): 110–22.

O'Laughlin, Bridget. "Proletarianisation, Agency and Changing Rural Livelihoods: Forced Labor and Resistance in Colonial Mozambique." *Journal of Southern African Studies* 28, no. 3 (2002): 511–30.

Péclard, Didier. *Les Incertitudes de la Nation en Angola: aux racines sociales de l'Unita*. Paris: Karthala, 2015.

Pélissier, René. *Les Campagnes Coloniales du Portugal, 1841–1941.* Paris: Flammarion, 2004.
Penvenne, Jeanne. *African Workers and Colonial Racism: Mozambican Strategies and Struggles in Lourenço Marques, 1877–1962.* Oxford: James Currey, 1995.
Pimenta, Fernando T. *Angola: os Brancos e a Independência.* Oporto: Afrontamento, 2008.
Pitcher, M. Anne. *Politics in the Portuguese Empire: The State, Industry and Cotton, 1926–1974.* Oxford: Clarendon Press, 1993.
Ross, Edward A. *Report on Employment of Native Labor in Portuguese Africa.* New York: Abbott Press, 1925.
Sanches, Manuela Ribeiro. *Portugal não é um país pequeno: contar o império na pós-colonialidade.* Lisbon: Cotovia, 2006.
Satre, Lowell J. *Chocolate on Trial: Slavery, Politics and the Ethics of Business.* Athens: Ohio University Press, 2005.
Seibert, Gerhard. "Crioulização em Cabo Verde e São Tomé e Príncipe: divergências históricas e identitárias." *Afro-Ásia* 49 (2014): 41–70.
Seibert, Gerhard. *Comrades, Clients and Cousins. Colonialism, Socialism and Democratization in São Tomé and Príncipe.* Leiden: Brill, 2006.
Seibert, Gerhard. "Le massacre de Fevrier 1953 á São Tomé: raison d'être du nationalisme santomeen." *Lusotopie* (1997): 173–92.
Soares, Tertuliano. "Acerca dalguns problemas de assistência relativos aos trabalhadores indígenas de África." *África Médica* 8–9 (1944): 165–80.
Souto, Amélia Neves de. "Relações entre Portugal, África do Sul e Rodésia do Sul e o Exercício Alcora: elementos fundamentais na estratégia da condução da guerra—1960–1974." In *As Guerras de Libertação e os sonhos coloniais: Alianças secretas, mapas imaginados,* edited by Maria Paula Meneses and Bruno Sena Martins, 143–69. Coimbra: CES/Almedina, 2013.
Thomaz, Omar Ribeiro. *Ecos do Atlântico Sul: representações sobre o terceiro império português.* Rio de Janeiro: UFRJ/Faperj, 2002.
Torgal, Luís Reis. *Estados Novos, Estado Novo: ensaios de história política e cultural.* Coimbra: Universidade Coimbra, 2009.
Trajano Filho, Wilson. "The Creole Idea of Nation and Its Predicaments: The Case of Guinea-Bissau." In *The Powerful Presence of the Past: Integration and Conflict Along the Upper Guinea Coast,* edited by Jacqueline Knorr and Wilson Trajano Filho, 157–84. New York: Berghahn, 2015.
Valério, Nuno, and Maria Paula Fontoura. "A evolução económica de Angola durante o segundo período colonial—uma tentativa de síntese." *Análise Social* XXIX, no. 129 (1994): 1193–208.
Zamparoni, Valdemir. "Colonialism and the Creation of Racial Identities in Lourenço Marques, Mozambique." In *Africa, Brazil and the Construction of Trans-Atlantic Black Identities,* edited by Livio Sansone, Elisée Soumonni, and Boubacar Barry, 20–43. Trenton, NJ: Africa World Press, 2008.

CHAPTER 9

Christian Evangelization and Its Legacy

Andrew E. Barnes

This chapter outlines the evolution of Christian social-welfare practices as first developed in Europe and then pursued in Africa. It has three objectives. The first is to provide some background to the provisioning of European-style social-welfare institutions, such as schools, hospitals, orphanages, etc., during the colonial era in Africa. The chapter will explain how and why Christian missions constructed their strategies for Christianizing Africa based upon the establishment and maintenance of such institutions. Social-welfare institutions were an attribute of a strategy of proselytization which may be labeled evangelization through poor relief. The strategy played a crucial role in the Christianization of Europe, which is why there was so much interest in pursuing it in Africa. The strategy built upon the presentation of Christianity to the 'poor' (that is, individuals and groups viewed by evangelizing Christians as on the margins of society) as a means towards self-improvement and collective empowerment. Christianity was portrayed as having the capacity to make the sick healthy, the poor prosperous, the weak strong, to make all those who embraced its tenets better individuals, better community members, better persons in general. Following the strategy, evangelizing Christians preached conversion as the most important step an individual could take towards solving the problems of the world.

European missionaries were not the only group of Christians who sought to save Africa by means of evangelization through poor relief. They had competition from African Christians with Ethiopianist sympathies. African

---

A.E. Barnes (✉)
School of Historical, Philosophical & Religious Studies,
Arizona State University, Tempe, AZ, USA

© The Author(s) 2018
M.S. Shanguhyia and T. Falola (eds.),
The Palgrave Handbook of African Colonial and Postcolonial History,
https://doi.org/10.1057/978-1-137-59426-6_9

Christians took a number of ideas from across the Atlantic, from people they considered as 'Africans in America'.[1] It was African Americans who first drew attention to the proclamation in the Hebrew Bible that, 'Princes shall come out of Egypt and Ethiopia shall stretch forth her hands unto God' (Psalms 68:31). As Christians of African descent on both sides of the Atlantic understood the passage, it was a prophecy that one day Africans would be the agents of Africa's Christianization. Christians of African descent who accepted the truth of the passage embraced the name Ethiopianists.

A second objective of the chapter is to focus some attention on Ethiopianist movements among African Christians, and the importance of these movements as a first articulation of African-Christian sensibilities. Ethiopianism is a word that, historically, has held a number of different meanings for a number of different groups of people. As used by Christians of African descent in the New World from the 1840s, and Christians of African descent in Africa from the 1880s, Ethiopianism had to do with any notion, any agenda, that promoted African racial uplift through black Christian agency.[2]

More than disagreements over such things as polygamy, bride price, or the worship of traditional deities, the initiatives that African Ethiopianists took to evangelize other Africans, through the use of social-welfare institutions, served as a source of contention between African and European Christians. Before modern secular debates about the economic or social development of Africa began to take place, Christians framed discussions of the 'civilizing' or social transformation of African peoples by reference to ideas of the Christian 'regeneration' of Africa. Christian regeneration in these conversations involved the creation of societies with economies led by Christianized entrepreneurial classes, much in the image of similar classes in European Protestant societies.[3] Both European and African Christians took for granted the fact that this type of society was the outcome of the cultural and social processes that occurred in Christian social-welfare institutions, most importantly schools. For this reason both European and African Christians anticipated leading the Christianization of Africa using such institutions as instruments. Ethiopianists explained their determination to replicate the efforts of missions as justified by European racism, which they felt so permeated missionary thinking that it compromised the integrity of whatever social transformation Europeans hoped to effect via missionary social-welfare institutions. The alternative institutions Ethiopianists hoped to establish would educate fellow Africans in the right ways, towards a commitment to ending European domination of Africa and Africans. Ethiopianist movements failed, in part because they could never find funding to pay for the cost of building and maintaining social-welfare institutions, as well as due to the coming together of colonial governments and European missions to assert European hegemony over all European-styled charity. Still, Ethiopianist movements were among the first fruits of the planting of Christianity in Africa. They represent the first efforts on the part of African believers to reconstruct Christianity as an indigenous faith. They deserve greater recognition for their role in shaping the larger contours of the evolution of Christianity on the continent.[4]

The third and broadest objective of the chapter is to use the discussion of Ethiopianism to prompt a redirection in scholarly research concerned with the history of Christianity in Africa. To employ a dichotomy first formulated by the German sociologist Max Weber, recent studies have contrasted the success of new *charismatic* African-Christian Churches introduced by African prophets and healers with the failure of old *bureaucratic* Churches introduced by European and American missions. Such scholarship has overdrawn the opposition between African and European notions of Christianity to the detriment of the historical understanding of how Africans have experienced Christianity as a lived religion and of how Christianity has grown over time in Africa.

Recent scholarly presentations of the Christianity that missionaries brought with them to Africa have persisted in the modernist/postmodernist debates of the last decades of the twentieth century. The presentations still challenge narratives of the Christianization of Africa that originated in the nineteenth century.[5] In these older narratives, missionaries, as heroic white saviors, brought 'light' to indigenous peoples lost in the cultural darkness outside the pale of European Christian civilization. With due acknowledgement of the missionary literature that popularized such narratives in Europe and America, it is doubtful even the most chauvinistic missionaries, once they were on the ground, long maintained such illusions of who they were and what they were doing. Recent scholarly studies, however, remain committed to demonstrating the falsity of these older narratives, mostly by contrasting the character and nature of Christianity as practiced in Africa today with some construct of the Christianity that arrived with missionaries in the past, the point to these counter-narratives being that whatever light Christianity brought to Africa, Africans discovered themselves.[6]

The problem with these demonstrations is that they beg the question of the institutional legacy of mission Christianity. The counter-narratives support a telling of the story of Christianity in Africa as discontinuous, as illustrating the failure of something European, something extraneous before the triumph of something African, something indigenous. However, there are a number of gaps in the resulting histories. Two are of concern here. First is the gap in the story of African-Christian agency. In the counter-narratives about the new African Christendom, almost all based upon developments in the years since the end of the colonial era, African Christians are depicted as protagonists, capable of and in fact initiating religious and historical change. These same capabilities are not granted to earlier groups of African Christians, those who had to contend with Europeans during precolonial and colonial times. In narratives about Christianity in Africa during these ages, African Christians are usually pictured as victims of racial domination, men and women manipulated into passive subjectivity, sometimes by missionary duplicity, other times by government deceit. In these narratives Ethiopianism is sometimes identified as a symptom of racial domination, yet Ethiopianism is rarely discussed as a solution aimed at addressing racial imbalance.

Materials written by Ethiopianists suggest a different narrative, however, one of racial visionaries convinced that Christianity could serve as a weapon to battle colonial conquest. An adversarial dialectic between African Christians and European Christians emerged during the later decades of the nineteenth century, when the earliest groups of Africans born and raised Christians first began to challenge the ways Europeans preached Christianity. The African side to this adversarial dialectic encompassed a number of initiatives, almost all involving Africans appropriating some attribute of the institutional edifice of European Christianity and attempting to build an African Church based upon it. On the European side, missions endeavored to blunt these initiatives, ultimately cooperating with colonial governments in the characterization and then suppression of Ethiopianism as seditious.

In the histories of Christianity in Africa now being written, scholars rush through the story of Ethiopianism to get to what for them are the more edifying stories of the rise of African Independent Churches (AICs) and Pentecostalism. Yet AICs and Pentecostalist Churches did not come into existence *ex nihilo*. There is a need for more investigation of Ethiopianism as a phenomenon distinct and independent of mission Christianity. Such investigations should make clear both the debt more recent forms of African Christianity owe to Ethiopianism and the critical importance of Ethiopianism as an initial stage in the indigenization of Christianity in Africa.

A point to appreciate is that, when mission Christianity is viewed from the perspective of Ethiopianism, it is possible to see what excited Africans about Christianity in the first place. The second gap in the historical understanding of the evolution of Christianity in Africa is the blank space in the scholarly picture of how African Christianity, as a church experience, relates back to European Christianity. Whatever the cultural baggage the missionaries brought with them, there were some things about Christianity as instituted in churches and congregations that African Christians chose to keep, not discard. Further, whatever these things were, they have remained sufficiently influential that as African-Christian movements have coalesced into Churches, and Churches into denominations, these movements have continued to follow in the footsteps (that is, the same patterns of ecclesiastical growth) as did their Western European predecessors.

The argument below is that evangelization through poor relief provides the link connecting the historical development of Christianity in Africa back to that of Christianity in Europe. Over the centuries, as it evolved in Europe, evangelization through poor relief came to consist of some combination of four elements. The first was a demonstration of Christian charity, from actions as simple as an offer of a free meal to more complex gifts such as the performance of free medical procedures. The second involved an enactment of the religious theater associated with the proffering of Christian salvation to non-believers. The third was the presentation of a program of personal transformation that could supply converts with the self-discipline that could make conversion a life-changing act. The fourth element was the creation of opportunities where new Christians could demonstrate their faith through their actions. In the evangelical strategies they pursued, missionaries introduced various combinations of these elements in Africa, with competing missions fairly guaranteeing that potential converts in any given location would be exposed to all the four elements. Some of the Africans who did convert appropriated these strategies, and reworked and recombined the elements to fit their own capacities and ambitions.

Current scholarship is fixated with the extraordinary ways in which African Christians have taken the message communicated by European missionaries and reconceptualized it in indigenous idioms. But if the question of message is put to the side and focus is trained instead of the question of method, it is possible to see that evangelizing Christians first in Europe, and then in Africa, have followed the same formula in essaying through the social services they provide to demonstrate the capacity of their faith to improve and empower. European missionaries once appeared before African village leaders offering to build medical dispensaries. African prophets still appear before village headmen offering to staff deliverance ministry chapels. Both acts reflect the same approach to evangelization. Missionaries and prophets have staked their promises to make life better on different bodies of knowledge. In their proposals, missionaries place at the disposal of leaders the accumulated expertise of European civilization on dealing with the biology of health and sicknesses. In their proposals, prophets place at the disposal of leaders their own personal knowledge of Christ's capacity to help individuals get to the spiritual malaise at the heart of many physical problems. However, both missionaries and prophets pledge the same social outcome of tighter-knit, more harmonious communities. And the yardstick of success missionaries established centuries ago remains the metric used by present-day prophets. Neither group has assessed its ministry in patients served or healed, or any such secular statistic. Rather, proof that they are doing the Lord's work they have measured in the extent to which they can see themselves as having replicated the efforts of the Apostle Paul in founding new churches, in establishing new congregations of believers.

In sum, evangelizing Christians, from missionaries to Ethiopianists to the leaders of contemporary AICs, all have aspired to spread Christianity by improving the lives of those Africans who embrace the faith. They have attempted this not just through their preaching, but through the social-welfare institutions they have put in place to apply the teachings of the Gospels to everyday life. The discussion below will first survey the development of evangelization through poor relief in medieval and early modern Europe to provide a sense of the Christian world that evolved based upon the approach.

The second topic discussed will be the introduction of the evangelical strategy in Africa by European missionaries. The third topic will actually draw the most attention. The introduction of the strategy in Africa was so successful that groups of African Christians challenged the hegemony missionaries presumed over its use. Ethiopianists may have failed to appropriate evangelization through poor relief from missions, but their efforts need to be viewed as the first in a succession of African attempts aimed at indigenizing the strategy. As suggested in the chapter's conclusion, later forms of African Christianity took their departure from the path Ethiopianists forged. The 'Africanization' of evangelization through poor relief that followed upon the Ethiopianists' defeat is an ongoing process that anthropologists and scholars of religion are still mapping. The chapter's ambition is to illustrate how the pathways being discovered can be traced back through Ethiopianism to European Christianity.

EVANGELIZATION THROUGH POOR RELIEF IN EUROPE

The greatest expression of Christian piety is evangelism, the sharing of the Christian message with those who do not know it. The men who knew Christ, his Apostles, did this. They traveled the ancient Mediterranean world as itinerant preachers, spreading the news about Christ. The stories of their ministries form part of the Christian Bible. Following in the footsteps of the Apostles, living what the European Christian tradition identified as the *vita apostolica*, has remained the ultimate expression of Christian faith. Over time, however, Christian evangelism has taken forms other than itinerant preaching as different peoples have applied the ideal to their contemporary times and contemporary needs.[7]

In the Roman Empire and its successor states, Christianity was first most successfully evangelized through the establishment of monastic communities where believers could go to escape the impurities of the mundane world and ideally, through their devotions, generate sufficient spiritual grace to compensate for the sins of those outside the monastery's walls.[8] Eventually, other forms of evangelism emerged to compete with monasticism. Of these, the one with the greatest historical import was evangelism through poor relief.

Poor relief needs explanation. The term 'the poor' was open-ended; it was used by Christian elites (that is, people with power) to categorize the multiple, typically overlapping, groups of people whom they considered poor (that is, powerless). Poor relief comprised acts of charity, acts out of the 'love' of God, performed by people with power for people without it. These acts might have had ulterior social and political motives, but they were performed in the ritualized, protocol-driven ways of Christian devotion. Thanks to rulers like Constantine, Clovis, and Charlemagne, who declared themselves and all who lived in their territories to be subject to Christ, and, equally importantly, who employed Christian churchmen as state officials, the presumption at the top of European societies was that all the people below were Christians. From the perspective of Christian elites (that is, the churchmen and laymen who exercised some authority in their own right), however, just as Christians were not all equal in power and status, they were also not all equal in faith.[9]

From the Christian elite's point of view, powerless people were deficient not just in political and/or social terms, but also in matters of faith. In addition, the poor's deficiencies deprived the latter of the capacity to save their own souls. The language of Christian faith used in antique and medieval European Christian devotional discourse constructed spirituality on a scale of greater and lesser spiritual perfection. The term meant different things in different ages.[10] However, whatever its meaning, spiritual perfection was something humans strove to attain. Christian elites equated power with volition, and volition with the capacity to strive. A Christian needed power in order to channel the use of power towards spiritual perfection. The poor lacked volition, therefore they had nothing to channel, therefore they lacked the capacity to strive towards spiritual perfection.

In ministering to the needs of the poor, European Christian elites understood themselves to be giving the poor the capacity to strive. Christian elites perceived themselves as standing closer to God, the poor as standing further from God in perfection. They understood poor relief as a challenge to help the poor get closer, if not to God, than at least closer to themselves in spiritual perfection. Their evangelism aimed at disciplining away the deficiencies that made the poor less capable than themselves. In turn, they read the poor's acceptance of the proffered relief as a first act of volition, as a first indication of a poor person's willingness to accept the needed discipline.

The Christian elite's concern to help the Christian poor strive provided the impetus behind the evolution both of social-welfare institutions and the programmatic strategies of social transformation followed in these institutions. To progress towards spiritual perfection, poor souls needed not just to be physically fed and healed, but spiritually mended and fortified. Programs of psychological counseling, social rehabilitation, and the like are not inventions of modern secular society. Their roots go far back into the evangelical strategies pursued in medieval social-welfare institutions. Evangelizing is an act of communication, and communication is a function of using available media to convey ideas. Medieval Christian efforts at social amelioration were not articulated in 12-step programs (that is, systematized curricula presented over some time period, but through the creation and exploitation of visual media and public ritual. The art carved on the outside or painted on the inside of walls of a social-welfare institution, the processions and other rites performed by the clergy who maintained a social-welfare institution, these were the tools of teaching and training. The liturgy (that is, the annual schedule of devotions celebrated by a social-welfare institution) gave this teaching and training whatever programmatic structure it was perceived to have.[11]

The material culture and physical rituals associated with social welfare emphasized how in giving to the poor, elites were demonstrating Christian charity. This much is widely recognized. In focusing on poor relief as it was practiced in Europe as a source of data for the resolution of theoretical debates about the nature of European society, scholars have given insufficient attention to how poor relief also provided medieval European Christians with space and time to act out their own understandings of the stories in the Christian Gospels. It is important to appreciate, however, that in the latters' minds they were successors to the Apostles, aspiring in their turn to achieve the goal of Christian regeneration, the rekindling of the faith that poor Christians were presumed, through their lack of volition, to have lost. Looked at from a religious viewpoint, what stands out about medieval social-welfare institutions is the extent to which they provided venues for the performance of Christian conversion stories, for naïve, but still self-consciously mimetic reenactments of the most inspiring stories of evangelism depicted in the Christian Bible. Christian social-welfare institutions were places where Christians with power displayed their religious convictions by passing on to the powerless the discipline needed to begin the mental and behavioral transformations that stood as thresholds to the pursuit of spiritual perfection.

The would-be evangelists who funded and staffed social-welfare institutions discovered though, probably to their chagrin, that there is no necessary causality between conversion and Christian life. The third element of evangelization through poor relief was the most difficult to realize. Conversion could be a life changing event, but only if in fact a convert changed, and began living life as a Christian. Very often, however, converts fell back into pre-conversion patterns of thought and behavior. The term Christians use for this phenomenon is 'backsliding'. Over the centuries, in response to the failure of poor people to stay true to the promises they made at the moment of conversion, the Christians who ran social-welfare institutions began to think in progressively more programmatic fashion about ways to correct (and, even better, to avert) backsliding. These discussions may be considered the first discourses on the subject of what will be discussed below as the Christian social ethos.[12]

The individuals who converted were known as *conversi* or *donati*.[13] Finding social niches and public opportunities for them to display evangelical volition became problems of success. Social-welfare institutions tended to absorb the most enthusiastic of their converts as lay workers and helpers. Nevertheless, there was not space within the institutions for all who converted. Directing and controlling the enthusiasm of converts outside institutional walls were issues of concern for both clerical and temporal authorities. Worth suggesting is that these concerns were not effectively addressed until the thirteenth century when the Franciscans and Dominicans innovated through the creation of third orders, or tertiaries, which were associations of lay people committed to lives of evangelism but who remained outside the monasteries in secular society. Through these tertiary groups and the devotional associations for which they pioneered a path, it became possible for lay people under clerical supervision to display proof of evangelical volition in public space outside institutional walls.

During the later centuries of the European Middle Ages, what had been originally elite ideas about evangelism through poor relief were popularized across Christian society. Poor relief was organized on a progressively more elaborate institutional basis. Helping the poor was centralized in stone and mortar edifices; that is, almshouses and hospitals. The institutions had what can be recognized as proto-professional staffs, primarily monks and nuns who discovered vocations in helping the poor and developed some expertise in counseling them. These staffs had helpers, typically former participants in the institution's programs.[14]

Opportunities for lay Christians below elite status to demonstrate volition via participation in poor relief also grew through the foundation of devotional associations known as confraternities. Devotional associations augmented social-welfare networks through the creation of new types of institutions such as hostels for poor travelers, and new types of agencies such as collection societies for funds to provide dowries for poor girls. When devotional associations first became common, their memberships were drawn from the upper and middle classes. Towards the end of the Middle Ages, many of these associations opened their doors to Christians from the lower classes. Evangelization through poor relief in many instances became an in-house activity, richer members focusing their proselytizing on poorer members of the association. By the end of the Middle Ages, evangelism through poor relief was a devotional pathway open to Christians of all social ranks. Rich and powerful believers with the wherewithal to establish or fund social-welfare institutions still had many more opportunities to don the persona of an Apostle. Christians of more modest stature could also assume the mantle of an evangelist, if only before the poorer members of the association.[15]

Social-welfare institutions and the evangelical strategies deployed through them were essential attributes of the lived Christian experience that evolved in Europe in the wake of the decline of the monastic ideal. Modern scholars, however, have dismissed medieval social-welfare institutions as having had limited social impact, and lacking this, little historical import. For the most part scholars treat the institutions only as an aspect of a religious sensibility made obsolete by the Protestant and Catholic reform movements of the sixteenth century. Thomas Max Safley traces this reading back to Max Weber's assessment that medieval social-welfare institutions were too preoccupied with irrational sensibilities to be of much use in resolving the problems associated with poor relief. As Weber saw it, the challenge poor relief placed before elites in Europe was how to put the poor to work. The mystical notions of 'brotherly love' that infused Christian social-welfare institutions got in the way of the discovery of systematic processes for turning the poor's potential into productive labor. After centuries of desultory results with allowing Christians to train the poor, the 'loveless realities' of the marketplace finally forced the rationalization and bureaucratization of poor relief that Weber approvingly noted as taking place during his own times. Safley argues that in making this case, Weber performed a neat trick of othering; not really investigating medieval social-welfare institutions but projecting back onto them all the opposite qualities to those he ascribed to modern social welfare.[16] Weber sent scholars off in the wrong direction. Generations of historians, no matter what aspect of poor relief they have investigated, have fallen prey to the 'Weberian trope', as Safely labeled it, of repeating the storyline that from the medieval to the modern centuries, something warm and empathetic but also ineffective gradually wore away to be replaced by something cold and rational but also efficient.

The price tag for the ongoing validation of Weber's characterization of poor relief, Safley suggests, has been a lack of theoretical appreciation of the extent to which something warm and full of pathos (that is, the ideas animating medieval ideas of poor relief) could be and in fact were progressively updated to address the expectations and demands of economic and political elites. To build upon Safley's point, medieval Christians did look at poor relief from the perspective of economic outcomes, but only secondarily, and then from the point of view of how the outcomes validated Christian conversion. Christians never aspired to the transformation of all the poor who came through the doors of their welfare institutions. Rather, their goal was the harvest of those poor souls who, through their actions, gave evidence of God's favor. In their own assessments of the impact of their initiatives, Christians always had in mind some gradient derived from the teachings of Saint Augustine of Hippo. Augustine taught that God chooses only a portion of human souls, an elect, for salvation, leaving the rest, the reprobate, for damnation. Based upon this understanding, in the programs and routines implemented in their social-welfare institutions, Christians sought: firstly to identify the elect among the poor people they served; secondly to help this elect attain self-consciousness of its chosen status. Christians took for granted that 'by their fruits you shall know them', meaning that the onus was on the poor elect to make themselves known through their positive response to the training being offered. Christians invested in the economic success only of the poor who emerged from their institutions. For Christians, the limited social impact of Christian social-welfare institutions condemned by theorists and scholars was actually a measure of success. It demonstrated that Christians had indeed found a way to separate the wheat from the chaff, the elect from the reprobate, the potentially powerful from those eternally damned to poverty.[17]

The practice of evangelization through relief to the poor, the social-welfare institutions it inspired, and the social ethic these institutions sought to inculcate all developed during the European Middle Ages as features of Roman Christianity. All three took an evolutionary step forward as a consequence of the state takeover of Churches during the early modern European centuries. By the seventeenth century, states oversaw and regulated Church life everywhere in Europe, in lands both officially Protestant and officially Catholic. Relief for the poor during the Middle Ages typically had the support of the state, but it did not fall under government oversight. The situation changed during the early modern era when political regimes took control of churches and, through them, of poor relief.[18]

States justified their nationalization of the practice of Christianity by reference to national security. To explain the relationship between state and Church that became the ideal during the era, contemporaries used the expression, '*cuis regio, euis religio*', 'the religion of the ruler is the religion of those under the ruler's rule'. The term communicated a truth recognized by all with some sort of political authority during the time, that faith either supported the political status quo or faith undercut it. 'No bishop, no king', was another contemporary expression that circulated in England after the restoration of the monarchy in 1660. In the previous two decades, civil war, the dissolution of the Church of England, and the execution of a reigning monarch had validated the conventional wisdom that, from the state's perspective, the primary task of religious institutions, the goal towards which they necessarily needed to be dedicated, was maintenance of the political order.[19]

In line with this goal, Churches became departments of the state. Rulers took over all Churches in territories under their sovereignty, and appointed Churchmen committed to advancing the policies of the state Church. Among the responsibilities of these Churchmen was oversight of poor relief. The institutional face of poor relief did not change much over the early modern European centuries. Charity continued to be dispensed from centrally located stone and mortar edifices. The social function of welfare institutions changed, however. The older characterizations of the poor as powerless did not disappear, but these definitions were overlaid with new stereotypes reflecting economic deprivation and displacement. The religious wars, the rise and decline of states, the economic cycles of the period created hundreds of thousands of uprooted people who registered in the minds of the government authorities through whose territories they wandered only as beggars and vagrants; in other words, as at best social nuisances, at worst political threats.[20]

The potential of displaced populations for civil unrest and social rebellion made surveillance and containment primary concerns governments expected social-welfare institutions to address. The state Church, through the social-welfare institutions it maintained, became the triage point for assessing the poor: the threats they posed; the relief they required. The problem of displaced populations, which only increased in magnitude across the early modern European centuries, pushed governments towards policies of incarceration as strategies for containment. Social-welfare institutions became the forerunners of modern prisons. In exchange for the succor they offered, social-welfare institutions required that the poor accept being locked away, if only at night, when they were assumed to pose the greatest threat to law and order. The stone and mortar buildings where charity was dispensed came to be encircled with high stone walls. The walls were for keeping people in.[21]

There was not much space in this world for the idea of evangelization through poor relief that developed during the Middle Ages. But the idea evolved with the times and flourished again. Though states took control of social-welfare institutions, the staffs at these institutions continued to be Church people, for whom helping the poor and saving the latter's souls remained synonymous expressions. Since loyalty to the state was measured by loyalty to the state Church, the Church people running social-welfare institutions drew only praise from governments for developing programs designed to convert the poor simultaneously into good Christians as well as loyal subjects.

The Christians who maintained early modern European social-welfare institutions evolved as intermediaries who used their knowledge and authority to shape the nature of the encounter between Europe's ruling and subject classes. They successfully played both sides against the middle, in this instance convincing both sides that the Christianization going on in Christian-run social-welfare institutions was social progress. Early modern Christians could make such claims because, in contrast to what Weber argued, the educational and behavioral reform programs offered in social-welfare institutions did help equip poor people to fulfill the economic demands of their times. Early modern economies needed proto-industrial laborers, workers ideally with some technological competence trained to toil according to some regimen. Social-welfare institutions, in particular the new charity schools that were founded to educate the children of the poor, endeavored to supply the desired workforce. The institutions passed on to the poor who slept inside their walls life skills that included some basic literacy and numeracy coupled with a rudimentary introduction to the use of selected tools. These were all embedded in a social routine aimed at instilling a disciplined work ethic. The poor who stayed at a social-welfare institution long enough acquired the skills to catch on somewhere in the technology-driven economic world coming into existence as a consequence of transoceanic trade. From the point of view of governments, these people had ceased to be part of the problem and had become instead proof that there existed a solution.[22]

Christians were similarly satisfied with the people leaving their institutions. Conversion is a moment that can take a lifetime and a number of false starts to occur. The Christians who staffed social-welfare centers certainly wanted (but realistically did not expect) most of the individuals passing through their institutions to convert. A far more persistent hope was that poor individuals would come to recognize that whatever other identities they claimed, they were first and foremost sinners. For Christians, conversion, as a spectacle observed was ideally the happy denouement to a personal spiritual drama that could have many acts. However, for this conclusion to be reached, the drama had to begin with some self-consciousness of the sin that permeates every human's life. The clergy and laypeople who ran early modern social-welfare institutions hoped at the least to get the poor to this level of awareness.

The poor who went beyond this level, to actually enquire about how they could be freed from sin, were the prize. For this audience, early modern Christians, much like their medieval predecessors, turned their institutions into theaters where they, as aspiring spiritual directors, staged their own reenactments of conversion stories from the Bible. The performances were open-ended. The early modern centuries were a great age, perhaps the last great age of Augustinianism. Saint Augustine taught that every event is providential. Early modern Christians could proselytize with the confidence that whether or not a conversion drama had a happy ending was up to God, not to them. And one evangelist's failure to help a sinner shed his or her burden might be God's way of giving another evangelist a chance.

From the beginning, European social-welfare institutions were enormously expensive to build and maintain. They were an expression of the faith of the rich and powerful. They only grew to the extent that they did by the end of the Middle Ages through the lavish granting of indulgences by the Roman Church hierarchy, which channeled the pious offerings of prosperous townspeople and well-off peasants into charitable projects. Once the state took over the Church, the state and local governments stepped into supply a good deal of the maintenance cost of social-welfare institutions. Founding and building such institutions, however, involved a separate set of funding issues. Here is where Christians, wealthy individuals acting on their own and Christian communities and associations acting collectively, dictated the contours of the growth of poor relief. Hospitals, schools, and poorhouses came into existence through Christian initiative. In early modern Europe, what was from the Christian perspective a wonderful cycle of development evolved. Church people would find the funding for founding a social-welfare institution, get the institution up and running, and then governments would step in and offer to subsidize operational costs. With the monies they received from government subsidies, Church people would save up and set their sights on the founding of another social-welfare institution.[23] Later in colonial Africa, both governments and missions had this cycle in mind when they negotiated plans for the development of social-welfare institutions.

To use (once again) Weber's terminology, evangelization through poor relief was routinized into the character of European Christianity. It became the process Europeans most readily thought of when they thought of Christian evangelization. By the end of the eighteenth century, the moment when Christian mission expansion to Africa began in earnest, evangelization through poor relief and the institutions through which it was effected had become defining characteristics of European Christianity.

Evangelization Through Poor Relief in Africa

The focus below will be on Protestant missions to Africa.[24] By way of background, is may be noted that the first Christian missions from Europe to Africa began at the end of the fifteenth century. Catholic missionaries under the patronage of the Portuguese monarch set up mission stations, staffed with monks committed to using medieval notions of evangelization through poor relief, in the Kongo kingdom in Central Africa and explored doing something similar in the lands of the emperor of Ethiopia. Catholic mission stations in Central Africa continued to be occupied through the end of the seventeenth century. How much impact the missions had on African religious sensibilities is the subject of ongoing historical investigation. Catholic missions to the continent, albeit to a completely different region, began anew at the end of the eighteenth century, this time under the aegis of the Congregation for the Propagation of the Faith. The mission stations established as part of this push were built along the West African coast. Over the nineteenth century, Catholic missions expanded significantly, several new religious orders emerging with a specific vocation to evangelize people of African descent.[25]

Missions under Protestant sponsorship did not begin until the last years of the eighteenth century. Missionaries from a number of denominations then founded mission stations along the West African coast, most notably in Sierra Leone, where the 'black poor' of England were resettled.[26] Christian conversions in Sierra Leone grew in part through the proselytization of local populations, but in part also through the repatriation to Africa of Africans freed from captivity by the British Naval Squadron. The number of missionaries, the number of mission stations, the number of confessions and denominations represented on Africa's West coast all climbed across the nineteenth century, as did the numbers of African-Christian believers. A second set of mostly Protestant missions began the evangelization of Africa from the southern end of the continent, using European settler towns and communities as their starting points. These missions, led by the great explorer missionary David Livingstone, expanded into the interior of the continent, setting up stations for Africans in proximity to European settlements. In this area as well there came to be a wide range of denominational and confessional mission stations, and a large number of prosperous African-Christian communities came to be associated with these stations.[27]

Christian missionary enterprise in Africa was based upon the strategy of evangelization through poor relief, though this point is hard to discern in the literature produced by missionaries. Missionaries loved the idea of wandering the roadways of Africa, proselytizing in the manner of the original Apostles, and highlighted the moments when they actually did these things in the stories and books they published about their time in Africa. Most missionaries, however, spent the majority of their time tied to mission stations, occupied with the social-welfare institutions they maintained on those stations.

Accepting as accurate the generalization that most missionaries appeared on the scene in African villages and communities as a protected group of outsiders with elite privileges, then it can be said that, initially, Christianity was proselytized in Africa in much the same way it had come to be preached in Europe; that is, from the top down through social-welfare institutions. It can also be argued that Christianity took root in Africa the same way it had in Europe, through the recruitment and empowerment of people with little to no power and authority in existing societies. Lastly, one can postulate that the social dynamics that pushed the Christianization process in European social-welfare institutions were reproduced on mission stations in Africa. Like European customs and practices not sanctioned by state Churches, African customs and practices not sanctioned by missions were condemned as the lures of Satan. Contention over continued performance of such customs and practices was a common occurrence between missionaries and African converts. The disputes that could not be resolved to a convert's satisfaction saw the convert walk away, perhaps to another mission, as the poor in Europe once moved on from one almshouse to another. As for those disputes that could be resolved, these missionaries acknowledged post facto in their writings under the rubric of backsliding. For missionaries, the practice of characterizing negotiations concerning discipline in this manner allowed them to claim the spiritual high ground over the polygamists, beer drinkers and clandestine participants in traditional rites with whom they had been arguing. The reward for the disputants was that they could now rejoin the mission station community.[28]

The strategy worked. Mission stations gave rise to communities of African Christians. Successful stations became hubs for expansion, making use of Christians from these communities as examples of the power of Christian conversion. Looking at evangelization through poor relief from the African perspective, it can be taken as a given that the message the white men were preaching, often half incomprehensibly through translation, did not resonate with every African who heard it. What appealed to the Africans for whom the message did resonate, though, was the Christian social ethos. As introduced by missionaries, this was composed of a number of things, one of the most prominent being a sensibility that viewed social change both as possible and, if the change were in the direction of broader communal engagement in projects aimed at social amelioration, as advancement. Many African peoples shared this sensibility. For a significant number of them Christianity came to be associated with improvement, both on the individual level (the acquisition of intellectual skills and behavioral self-discipline) and on the collective level (the evolution of self-conscious, self-improving communities).

Behind the sensibility were several commonly held assumptions that focused the pursuit of progress on the establishment of Christian social-welfare institutions. One assumption was that an individual assimilated the Christian social ethos through a process distinct from the processes associated with

Christian conversion and/or Christian witness. Christians, both African and European, assumed, based upon the biblical admonition that 'By their fruits you shall know them', that the measure of the assimilation of the Christian social ethos was observable behavioral and attitudinal change. Practicing Christians were expected to behave in certain ways, to think in certain ways. Orthopraxis, that is, acting and thinking according to some established norms of faith, stood as separate from and for the most part posterior to the more dramatic events associated with conversion and witness. Individuals could go through the rituals associated with Christian conversion (that is, baptism and communion), but later 'backslide' in their actions, in this way invalidating for practicing Christians any claim those individuals made of conversion. Similarly, individuals could undergo trials for their faith, enduring ridicule, condemnation and even violent assault, yet later be dismissed by the faithful for leading dissolute lives.

As these qualifications suggest, the Christian social ethos was understood to reflect a state of consciousness achieved only through a continuous disciplining of mental and physical habits. The ethos demanded that individuals learn how to control themselves. African Christians were in broad agreement with European Christians that the best place to learn the desired self-control was a mission school. 'School' is actually a problematic term because it characterized any venue where learning to read the Bible was taught, or where Christian life was talked about in some systematic fashion. As such, schools were everywhere and anywhere missionaries set up shop in Africa. Missions introduced a number of different types of social-welfare institutions to Africa. In the nineteenth century, among others, there were freed slave homes, freed slave villages, and orphanages. All of these types of institutions typically came to maintain some form of school for potential converts.

Beyond these informal, ad hoc introductory programs to Christianity and its tenets, many missions also established formal education institutions where European styled curricula were taught up to the secondary level. At the least, these schools were day schools, where students attended classes five to six days a week. Ideally they were boarding academies, where the students practiced living Christian lives under adult Christian supervision. The intellectual skills to be obtained in such schools were highly prized. The skills were understood to guarantee future employment in some connection with the transoceanic world expanding inward into Africa from the coastal regions. The allure of the skills can be overemphasized, however. For Christians, equally important was the religious persona the schools were understood to inculcate. Mission schools were seen as immersion experiences in Christian identity. It was taken for granted that without some internalization of the Christian social ethos, students would find it impossible to survive at the schools. Students who made it through the course of study at mission schools were thought to have mastered living, thinking, and behaving as Christians. If there was one proof they were asked to give regarding the benefits of

Christianity to Africa, that proof for most African Christians would be the mission school.[29]

To the extent to which there was any collective opposition to mission education in the decades leading up to the colonial era, it came from Europeans living on the continent. For them the issue was race. Mission schools were very good at turning out Christians. Yet, over the course of the nineteenth century, as Europeans came to claim the civilization that evolved in Europe as an expression not of Christian good works but of European racial genius, this outcome came under increasing dispute. For some Europeans, Christian became a synonym for 'civilized', which in turn became a synonym for European. In European discourse all these terms came to be reserved as markers that conveyed racial whiteness. From the perspective of Europeans who thought this way, mission schools were not turning out civilized people; the schools were turning out phony Europeans with pretensions of whiteness. As European states began to conquer African territories this mindset achieved some hegemony among Europeans with power and authority. It also established itself firmly in the heads of the thousands of Europeans who in the last half of the nineteenth century began to take ship from Europe to Africa to seek their fortunes. The latter insisted upon the establishment of social hierarchies in African colonies, with full civil rights and privileges reserved for white people.[30]

Even before the onset of colonialism, African Christians challenged the privileges Europeans sought to reserve for themselves based upon race. African Christians insisted that a positive equation existed between Christianity and civilization, that as Christians they were civilized, therefore they as Christians had a claim to all the rights and privileges from which Europeans were seeking to exclude them. In response to such arguments, European thinkers tied culture more exclusively to race, and insisted that African conversion to Christianity was a form of 'race suicide'.[31] Mission schools came under pressure from Europeans to stop 'denationalizing' Africans, meaning educating Africans to have aspirations beyond the latter's 'nation' or status in a world controlled by Europe. The Christian social ethos measured God's favor by individual initiative and self-improvement, by communities formed and social institutions founded, in sum by aspirations striven for and attained. From the perspective of the thinkers who shaped the colonial European mindset, the Christian social ethos was denationalizing Africans by teaching them to strive for a self-sufficiency that Africans as a race could not be allowed to possess.[32]

African Christians would come to criticize mission schools in one regard. After the reported success of industrial education schools for training freed African peoples in the USA, African Christians petitioned missions to diversify school curricula by augmenting the clerical training that shaped the common offerings in mission schools with more explicitly scientific and technical instruction. Missions rebuffed these entreaties, mostly by dismissing the

Africans who made the entreaties as unrepresentative of African-Christian desires.[33]

The missions' response to the criticisms of mission education leveled by Europeans was more complicated. Missions came to pursue some mixture of two different strategies. Many missions adopted a 'do no evil, see no evil' stance. As the declaration of European suzerainty over African territories picked up steam in the last decades of the nineteenth century, missions tried to distance themselves from any charge of complicity in the emergence of African Christians as the most vocal opponents of the imposition of European rule. The rejection of African requests for curricular diversification in mission schools was one way missions sought to assure imperial governments of their loyalties. Of greater historical consequence, missions began the erection of what would eventually be a two-tiered system of Christian evangelization, where missionaries exercised a fairly exclusive control over all mission social-welfare institutions. This system is discussed in more detail below. In the period under consideration it was anticipated primarily through missions reversing a course of development, most clearly spelled out in the writings of Henry Venn of the Church Missionary Society and most clearly articulated in the career of the African Anglican bishop Samuel Ajayi Crowther, that had advocated placing African Christians in roles of authority over mission churches and mission social-welfare institutions.[34]

With Africans nowhere in sight in the upper echelons of leadership in mission churches, missions could feel justified when, in response to European criticisms, they protested that all they were doing in their schools was training Africans to assist, not lead, in Christian evangelization. Missions could be accused of a bit of disingenuity here. There was an ever expanding market outside churches for the intellectual skills to be gained inside mission schools. More and more missions complained about the allure of Mammon for their students and former students, an acknowledgement of their awareness of that market, and that, with the Church itself no longer viable as a career option, the majority of their students intended to enter it, not the ranks of evangelists. Missions knew that they were not just training Church people. They were also aware that the people they were training were the people leading the charge against colonization. Yet in assuming the stance that they did, missions could treat all such developments as something outside their control and thus not their concern.

Missions tempered this stance of what might be labeled diffidence, or even resistance, with one of cooperation with other Europeans. Missions tried to develop curricula in their schools that kept the striving associated with the Christian social ethic, but limited the goals to which Africans could rightly strive. 'Industrial education' is another term that had multiple meanings to multiple groups of people. The term was used by missionaries to characterize mission school curricula in the late nineteenth century, especially in the parts of Africa settled by the British. It signified an ambition to train Africans to desire a 'square house', instead of a 'round hut', and to seek a job working for Europeans instead of maintaining a farm with 'a few goats and cattle'. 'Industrial' in this context was the adjectival form of 'industriousness', the notion being that mission schools could convince Africans that hard work in subservience to white domination was a Christian way forward.[35]

A counterfactual historical question worth pondering is: What would the Christian evangelization of Africa have looked like if it had not taken place at the same time as the European conquest of the continent? African Christians remembered the earliest generations of missionaries, the ones who came to Africa up through the time of Livingstone, with a good deal of fondness as father figures. Not quite so for the generations of missionaries who came later. From the last decades of the nineteenth century to the end of the colonial era, there was as much suspicion as trust in African characterizations of missionaries and the latter's intentions. There was European racism and African indifference to Christianity long before the closing years of the nineteenth century, yet the coming together at that historical juncture of the modern missionary movement and European imperialism seems to have created critical mass for the synthesis of a set of associations between Christianity and European racism with which Christians, and the historians who write about Christianity in Africa, still struggle.

As the 'Scramble for Africa' took place there was cognitive dissonance if not outright contradiction in the ways that missions sought to reconcile their presence in Africa with the concerns other Europeans had about African Christians. Social-welfare institutions were generating the same social products in Africa as they had in Europe. They were sending out crop after crop of strivers, Christians who wanted to demonstrate their convictions through the transformation of the world around them. Missions wanted this to continue. Yet, to placate white anxieties, missionaries endeavored to temper and/or redirect the enthusiasm that made African Christians want to save Africa for Christ. Their rationalizations here certainly reflected European scientific racism. The Christian social ethos trained Christians to aspire to the role of protagonist in dramas about evangelization. Missionaries convinced themselves, and perhaps some other Europeans that, given the intellectual limitations of the race, Africans could be limited to playing foils to European leads in such dramas.

The 'colonial moment' in Africa, as it has been called, lasted for approximately eighty years, from 1880 to 1960.[36] During this period, European states progressively built up political and economic infrastructures in colonized African territories with the goal of making Africa profitable for Europeans. Governmental institutions that Europeans set up ensured that every African paid his dues to the colonial regime. Railways, motor roads, cities and harbors were constructed, all geared towards the extraction of wealth from Africa and its transport to Europe. African peoples were forced to leave other pursuits to labor in service to the needs of capitalistic development. The pernicious impact of state-supported capitalism on African societies was most obvious in the mining industries that grew up in Southern and Central Africa and then in West Africa, which pulled millions of Africans from their homes to pay taxes to cover the cost of construction of economic infrastructure.

From the 1880s to around 1920, the interactions of three sets of actors shaped the direction in which social-welfare institutions evolved: Christian missionaries, colonial governments, and African Christians. During the period, missionary efforts to Christianize Africa reached their high point. The imposition of colonial rule gave European peoples from across the globe confidence that law and order would prevail sufficiently along the many frontiers in Africa to allow mission stations to be established. The missionaries who set sail for Africa reflected the broad array of understandings of Christianity not just among Protestants, but Catholics as well. There was also, for the first time, a significant number of women missionaries. They came with an explicit dedication to create social-welfare institutions for African women and girls.[37]

The social welfare of Africans was not a primary preoccupation of colonial governments. Certain emerging conditions pushed governments' involvement in social services. First was the needs of African communities and individuals displaced by the various transformations taking place as part of the establishment of colonial rule. Second was the perceived threat of sedition from within the ranks of African Christians. When governments did act, it was mostly to manipulate in desired directions the competition between the ever growing number of missions. Missions that provided what governments deemed as valuable social services got permission to establish stations in choice spots among African peoples identified as open to evangelization. Missions that declined to cooperate with government dictates, or whose African adherents caused concerns, were punished with access to fewer sites typically among African peoples with no displayed interest in Christianity.

Neither missions not governments were looking to alter evangelization through poor relief as the strategy was pursued in Africa at the start of the colonial era. The measures missionaries introduced to tone down the challenges African Christians posed to European domination to some extent did mollify Europeans. And the plenitude of missions, eager for stations, supplied colonial governments with a convenient way to both control missions and to address the social-welfare needs of Africans. Site license for mission stations were granted to missions with the understanding that whatever the status of the evangelical work going on at a station, if the social services being provided at that station did not measure up to government expectations, another mission could be offered a site license in close proximity. Europeans probably would have been content to play this game among themselves ad infinitum had it not been for the intervention of African Christians, who put pressure on both missions and governments to take a very different approach to social welfare.

By the 1880s, the second generations of Christians (individuals who had been born and raised in the faith) were maturing in many places in Africa. These individuals were ready to take leading roles as missionaries and evangelists. Typically, these individuals were literate. They were the producers as well as the consumers of the African newspapers that began to flourish. Through these newspapers, African Christians were exposed to ideas coming from Europe and the New World. African Christians were very conscious of the emerging science of race in Europe and the arguments this science produced justifying the subjugation, perhaps even eradication, of the African race. African Christians perceived the influence of these arguments in the actions of all Europeans, but especially missionaries. In the decades under discussion, there were a number of developments that African Christians could and did read as signs of a missionary willingness to use Christianity to help other Europeans overpower the African race.[38]

Reacting to these perceptions, African Christians with Ethiopianist leanings began to talk among themselves about taking the lead in the regeneration of Africa. Ethiopianists were conscious of Christianity as something over and above the racialized version of the faith then current among Europeans. The challenge for Ethiopianists was to find a way to save the baby while discarding the bathwater, the baby in this context being the ameliorative capacities of the Christian social ethos; the bathwater, missionary racism.

Initially, African Christians turned towards colonial governments. They read in newspapers that in Europe itself, governments were building state school systems, and more broadly state social-welfare systems, with the conscious goal of removing these things from Church control. To Africans reading about such developments, it seemed fair to conclude that governments would want to do the same in the colonies. Such thinking was behind the petitions advanced by Ethiopianists in the 1890s, in Sierra Leone and Nigeria in West Africa, and in Cape Province in South Africa, for European governments to build schools. The schools proposed would be central secondary institutions, set over and above mission-maintained primary-school networks. African Christians envisioned the schools not as replacements for mission schools and the inculcation of the Christian social ethos that took place at mission schools, but as training centers in the higher forms of especially technical knowledge that missionaries refused to share.[39]

Governments turned a cold shoulder to all Ethiopianist petitions for schools. So Ethiopianists looked for ways to sponsor the construction of the schools themselves. Europeans, missionaries as well as others, took for granted that Europe provided the only viable examples of civilized societies. But African Christians looked across the Atlantic to the example of African-American freed people in the USA, and drew inspiration. In the second half of the nineteenth century, African Americans were characterized in the world press as an outstanding illustration of a people who had pulled themselves up by the bootstraps. Freed from slavery but left in poverty in the 1860s, by the

1880s they were presented in newspapers as an emerging capitalist class of landowners and agricultural entrepreneurs. The key to their social transformation was Christianity, to which they had been exposed in what was seen as a definitive demonstration of the effectiveness of evangelism through poor relief. There were a number of successful schools established by missionaries for freed people in the USA. Yet African newspapers focused on two of them. In the decades before 1895, Hampton Institute in Virginia gained its own set of admirers among African Ethiopianists. But after 1895, Tuskegee Institute in Alabama (led its charismatic principal, Booker T. Washington, an alumnus of Hampton) became the model of the kind of social-welfare institution Ethiopianists wanted to copy across Africa.[40]

'Industrial education' as taught at Hampton and Tuskegee today draws mostly condemnation from scholars for its lack of academic rigor and emphasis on manual training, 'working with the hands', as Washington popularized the expression. Yet, in Africa, at the turn of the twentieth century, industrial education as Washington developed it at Tuskegee was viewed with much racial pride. Tuskegee was more than a school; it was the Christian social-welfare institution updated and perfected to the needs of the African race. It was a place where poor black people could not only be mended physically and spiritually, could not only discover the empowering discipline of the Christian social ethos, but also acquire economic skills to make them competitive with whites.[41]

Edward W. Blyden, the most influential Ethiopianist thinker in West Africa, was among Tuskegee's greatest supporters. He praised Washington for discovering a Christian way forward towards an African industrial civilization. He endeavored to build his own version of Tuskegee in Lagos.[42] In South Africa, John Tengo Jabavu, editor of *Imvo Zabantsundu*, the largest and most influential African newspaper, mentioned the school regularly in his newspaper, and conceived a grand plan to build a version of Tuskegee, an Inter-State Native College, in Cape Province.[43]

Both Blyden's and Jabavu's plans for schools like Tuskegee were undermined by funding challenges. All schools are expensive to build and maintain, but perhaps none more that industrial education institutes. Further, once such schools were up and running, they required round after round of what General Armstrong, founder of Hampton, called begging: the constant search for money to support the costs associated with technical training through trial and error learning. Blyden put forward his proposal for a Lagos Literary College and Industrial Training Institute in 1896. The colonial governor of Lagos at that time, Sir Gilbert Carter, offered £2000 to get the school started, with the stipulation that his offer be matched with local contributions. To the chagrin of the proposal's supporters, local contributions were not forthcoming. There were several other initiatives to build an industrial education institute in West Africa, the last of which was a proposal put forward in Ghana in 1918 by a group led by the writer, lawyer and

Pan-Africanist J.E. Casely-Hayford. The group, calling itself the 'Founders of Gold Coast National Schools', solicited contributions of £50 each from 200 'patriotic, educated, well-to-do and influential sons of the soil', in order to build, among other things, industrial education institutes. The group never got the capitalization that it requested.[44]

Ethiopianists elsewhere in Africa had more success in soliciting funding for the establishment of schools on the Tuskegee model, though with tragic outcomes. John Chilembwe was a Malawian who came to the USA in 1897. He spent several years studying at the Virginia Theological College before returning to Malawi in 1900 to found the Providence Industrial Mission (PIM). Chilembwe had the backing of the National Baptist Convention, an African-American Baptist denomination, which helped fund his school and sent two African-American missionaries to help establish it. At its height, about a decade after its foundation, the PIM had approximately 1000 adolescent and 600 adult students. Finding money to maintain his school was a problem for Chilembwe, however. He petitioned the colonial government of Malawi for a visa to return to the USA in pursuit of further funding, but the administration declined his request. In January 1915, Chilembwe led what is considered the first organized rebellion against British colonial rule in Africa. He and his followers were all killed.[45]

John L. Dube was an individual who sometimes shared a stage with Chilembwe in the last years of the nineteenth century when the two young Africans were working the church circuit in the USA, seeking funding to build versions of Tuskegee in their homelands.[46] Dube was the scion of a distinguished African Christian family and one of the first Africans to be ordained in a US seminary. Dube received backing from a number of affluent white American congregations and opened his school, the Zulu Christian Industrial School, better known as Ohlange Industrial Institute, in 1900. Dube initially fared better than Chilembwe. Journalism provided the key. Dube published and edited his own newspaper, *Ilanga lase Natal*, where he regularly made a pitch for funds for his school. Perhaps more important, Dube wrote a number of articles about his school and its needs that appeared in US missionary periodicals. The articles were often rewarded with gifts of money and equipment. Things became more difficult for Dube after he accepted the presidency of the South African Native National Congress, the forerunner to the African National Congress, and focused his energies on the repeal of the South African Native Land Act of 1913. Funds for Ohlange were not forthcoming, no matter how hard he begged. In 1922, Ohlange was taken over by the Natal provincial government with the stipulation that Dube move his newspaper and his family off the premises.[47]

As for Jabavu, his dream of a native college did come true, but his dream of a school like Tuskegee did not. The South African government took over plans for a school for African students and reconceived the plan to fit government and mission needs. The Native College at Fort Hare (later Fort Hare

College) came into existence in 1916. It did not pursue Tuskegee's emphasis on technology and agricultural development. Rather, the college concentrated on clerical training and teacher preparation.[48]

The term 'Ethiopianism' held negative connotations among whites in the regions of Africa where Europeans settled. The term was perceived as representing an ideology of black power derived from the misguided teachings of African Americans. In the mid-1890s, Ethiopianism was identified by whites as the prompt behind the decision of a number of African congregations of denominational mission churches to break away to form their own black denominations. Ethiopianism was brought home to white South Africans as a political threat in 1898 when an American bishop, Henry M. Turner, of the African Methodist Episcopal Church, toured South Africa, preaching about the return of African Americans to Africa. Ethiopianism was presumed to be the motivation behind the Bambatha Rebellion in Natal in 1906– during the course of which Dube was detained and interrogated by the police about his Ethiopianist leanings. Ethiopianism was explicitly indicted by the settler parliament in Malawi as the ideology behind John Chilembwe's failed revolt in 1915.[49]

Chilembwe's Rebellion was perhaps the tipping point in the progression towards colonial states treating Ethiopianism as a form of sedition. Beginning during the First World War, governments began to search for ways to control African vocalizations of opposition to colonialism, in particular Ethiopianism. The search expanded and intensified after the war when newspapers such as *The Crisis*, which communicated the ideas of W.E.B. Du Bois, and *The Negro World*, which conveyed the ideas of Marcus Garvey, began circulating in Africa.[50]

Governments blamed missions for the time and attention administrations wasted in surveilling Christian Africans. Missions made quite obvious their lack of sympathy for all ideas that empowered African Christians to challenge European authority. Colonial governments, however, still traced back to mission school teaching the mistaken impression educated Africans had that they possessed the same rights as British citizens. Once colonial governments had the opportunity after the end of the First World War, they moved to establish control over all missionary activities in their territories. Governments asserted their prerogative to inspect all Christian social-welfare institutions and shut down the ones that, in the opinion of government inspectors, were not adequately provisioned or sufficiently staffed. These actions were deemed necessary in the interest of suppressing political subversion.[51]

Missions protested vehemently against the actions before metropolitan governments. Something of an impasse had developed when Thomas Jesse Jones, education director for the Phelps-Stokes Fund, a US charity, appeared with a compromise solution. Jones volunteered to assemble a team of experts to travel through Africa and assess mission schools from the perspective of how the schools could be reformed to serve the interests of colonial states.

A first tour of schools along the western littoral of Africa from Sierra Leone down to Cape Town was conducted in 1920. Jones wrote the first report of what was called the Phelps-Stokes Education Commission, published in 1921. The Report was considered such a success that funds were found for a second tour of assessment, this time from South Africa up the east coast to Ethiopia. The tour was made in 1924. The second Phelps-Stokes Education Commission Report was published in 1925.[52]

The primary recommendations of both reports emphasized the need of governments and missions to collaborate to provide Africans with high-caliber social-welfare services. Jones lectured missions on the need to suppress the evangelical character of their endeavors, which distracted them from the more important tasks associated with making life better for Africans in Africa. Jones enjoined colonial governments to render every assistance possible to missions that focused their energies explicitly on the development of social-welfare institutions.[53]

Jones's writings on education in Africa, which included but were not limited to the two Phelps-Stokes Education Commission reports, presented a powerful case for the social utility of evangelization through poor relief once the strategy had been stripped of any explicitly Christian agenda. Jones argued that all civilizations were constructed upon four 'simples', by which he meant learned sets of behaviors and attitudes that have to do with health and hygiene; work discipline; family life; and cultural expression. If missionaries in Africa concentrated their energies on the inculcation of the four simples as these things had evolved among Anglo Saxons (the most advanced race on Earth), then Jones predicted that missionaries would truly help save Africa; that is, move Africa from the benighted primitivism in which it found itself towards some future state of civilization.[54]

The above discussion makes it clear that, stripped of the social-scientific dressing and racial posturing, Jones was offering old wine in new bottles. Jones was proposing that missions repeat in Africa what Churches had done in Europe during the early modern European centuries. Jones was convinced and was convincing that Christian social-welfare institutions could work their magic once again and turn Africa's agrarian and pastoral peoples into the kinds of proto-industrial workforces who had made the Industrial Revolution possible in Europe. As for Christian proselytization, Jones argued that Christian missions should admit that they had made a mistake in preaching Christianity to Africans. Christianity as missionaries taught it was an articulation of an evolved European consciousness. Africans, were on the whole a primitive race: Christianity had only confused the few who had ever even grasped it. Jones agreed with other Europeans that African Ethiopianists were the source of much confusion in African colonies, and that missions were impeding the civilizing of Africa through their insistence on creating more and more mission boys. Jones was convinced, however, that missions had a positive, indeed crucial role to play in the development of Africa through the propagation of the four simples in mission social-welfare institutions. So Jones invited missions to stop arguing with African Ethiopianists and start over again. He recommended that missions head as far out into the countryside as possible to establish new mission stations. Here, missionaries should strive to reach Africans uncorrupted by the old evangelism. As for the pursuit of converts which Jones's proposal would take missionaries away from doing, he counseled patience. In the fullness of time, African collective consciousness would evolve to the point where Africans as a group could grasp Christianity. At that point, all the hard work over the generations by missionaries would be rewarded with a harvest.

Across the 1920s, not only did the British Colonial Office get on board with the program that Jones laid out, but the International Missionary Council (IMC), the lobbying agency that came into existence to represent missionary interests before colonial governments, took his proposals as a starting point for future negotiations with governments. A number of US philanthropies also committed to help with funding for promising experiments in new forms of social welfare. The one group of Europeans lukewarm about Jones's ideas were rank-and-file missionaries. The idea that they were supposed to deny their calling and put their lives and health on the line in Africa not to preach, but to provide some social service, did not sit well with many of them. Neither did they buy the idea that they were supposed to just abandon the African Christian communities they and their missionary predecessors had sacrificed so much to help build.

Yet rank-and-file missionaries were attracted to Jones's take on how to deal with African Christians with Ethiopianist proclivities. Based upon his previous experience of dealing with African-American Christians with similar instincts, Jones argued that the best strategy was to marginalize and then ignore them. This approach was illustrated in the solution adopted by colonial governments and missions to what was for them the vexing problem of African-American missionaries in Africa. Both governments and missions were more than willing to trace the source of African Christian restiveness with white authority back to the influence of African Americans and the latter's pernicious ideas. In 1927, at an IMC conference in La Zoute, Belgium, colonial officials and representatives of missions agreed to a set of regulations that effectively denied access to stations in Africa to African-American missions. Individual African-American missionaries could apply to one of the white missionary organizations to serve as missionaries in Africa under that organization's agency. African-American missionaries would need to be vetted first, however. Jones, who helped arrange the conference, offered the Phelps-Stokes Fund as a vetting agency. African-American missionaries did apply to white missionary organizations to go on mission to Africa in the years between the two world wars. Very few were accepted.[55]

In Africa itself, colonial governments eradicated African-Christian social-welfare institutions with at least the missions' passive consent. Starting in the

1920s, governments began to shut down 'bush schools', as village schools maintained by African teacher evangelists were labeled. In those days, the promise of learning to read was a hook that brought people to listen to whatever else an aspiring evangelist had to say. 'Bush school' was a blanket designation that could cover any type of social-welfare institution maintained by an African with the goal of furthering Christian evangelization. Government education ordinances presumed all such institutions to be at best fraudulent operations, at worst nurseries for sedition. Education inspectors closed them all, except those with an explicit affiliation with a mission. Eventually, missions began to protest that governments were applying education ordinances aimed at regulating bush schools too rigorously, at the expense of stifling the evangelical initiatives of missions themselves. But in the beginning the ordinances did the job they were intended to do, which was to asphyxiate any grass-roots efforts on the part of African Christians to assert direction of the Christianization process through copying European strategies of evangelization.[56]

Beyond the suppression of black challenges to the hegemony missions asserted over the provision of Christian charity in Africa, however, there was much in Jones's proposals with which missionaries took exception. Women missionaries, for example, were upset with his ideas on the education of girls, which went against many of the things women missionaries were attempting in the social-welfare institutions they had set up for African women.[57] Initially, missionaries did not see themselves as having many alternatives to going along with government policies derived from Jones's recommendations. Though there were no state Churches in Africa, governments clearly had early modern European precedents in mind in asserting their rights to regulate all activities that might be construed as religious, again with the rationale of maintaining political order. All missions were welcomed, but only to the extent to which they were deemed by government officers as offering to provide some service of value to the state. The filters through which government officers viewed mission petitions for residency permits and site licenses came to be shaped by the recommendations Jones provided in the Phelps-Stokes Education Commission Reports. As such, the petitions had to address in some way one of Jones's four simples. It was during this time that missions became heavily involved in building schools according to yet a third notion of industrial education, this one derived from Jones's understanding of the educational experience offered at Hampton and Tuskegee Institutes in the USA. As Jones depicted them, these schools had perfected a method of teaching African Americans to be technically competent, disciplined in behavior, yet politically subservient. It was also during this time that missions began to invest significant amounts of time, money, and personnel in the development of medical and health services, sending missionaries to be trained as nurses and dispensers, building and staffing hospitals, opening and maintaining leper stations.[58]

Eventually, missions grasped that colonial governments did not have the funds or personnel to do what they threatened to do immediately after the First World War One, which was to build and maintain in African colonies networks of government-maintained social-welfare institutions such as existed in metropolitan countries. The world economic crash of 1929 made the hollowness of the threat even more evident. Growing progressively more aware of their essential role in colonial social welfare, missionaries began to flout government injunctions against using social-welfare institutions as platforms for proselytization. The clandestine nature of much of the proselytization that took place at colonial social-welfare institutions demands acknowledgement. During the period between the two world wars, mission evangelism developed an edge both as a form of resistance and as a form of empowerment. Missionaries traveled to places officially off limits to them to preach, missionaries incorporated Christian devotions into the delivery of nominally secular social services, missionaries cultivated as potential converts patients under their professional care. Missionaries replicated in Africa an evangelical experience that went back to the first decades of Christianity. In medieval and early modern Europe, the Christians running social-welfare institutions essayed to recreate, through stories and play acting, the experiences of the early evangelists who during the Roman era had won converts and built Christian communities in the face of an adversarial political regime. Missionaries in Africa pictured themselves doing something even more dramatic. Out on the frontiers of faith, they were living the same sorts of lives, experiencing the same sorts of dangers and rewards as the first Apostles once did under the Roman empire.[59]

Missionaries broke government rules, but breaking the rules remained a European prerogative. Missionaries, operating out of the social-welfare institutions they established and maintained, remained the protagonists in the stories written about the Christianization of Africa. Colonial government continued to monitor the activities of African Christians, closing down any initiative that appeared too close to what missionaries were doing or too far removed from missionary oversight. As mentioned above, a two-tier system of Christian evangelization came into existence. Control and direction of social-welfare institutions were reserved for European missionaries. African evangelists were tasked with spreading out into the villages, there to identify and recruit potential converts. The most promising of these recruits were sent to social-welfare institutions to learn how to be Christians under European supervision.

Beginning in the 1930s, the discourse among Europeans about colonial development in Africa moved on past Jones's program to a succession of new approaches. The transformations in the delivery of social services prompted by the determination of colonial governments to make Jones's recommendations work, however, remained in place. Jones's appearance on the scene inaugurated the reign of the 'experts'—scholars and scientists with ideas about how to make colonial development profitable for the colonizers that would continue for the rest of the colonial era.[60] Gradually, the new government emphasis had an impact on the nature and character of Christian missions. Progressively, the missionaries who stayed in Africa any significant time possessed some certified expertise, be it in education, medicine or technology. More and more, these people were also preoccupied with providing services based upon their expertise. Missionaries had to accept other new roles as well. Most routinely they became the managerial staff of non-government organizations, 'voluntary agencies', to use the terminology of the colonial era, tasked by governments to maintain the paperwork associated with the supply of some contracted social service. On occasion they also did double duty as local staff for some scholar/researcher sent in by government to test some big new theory about how to make life better for Africans. Proselytizing in the manner of the first Apostles became something missionaries did less and less, and then only in their spare time.

Space developed, both in missionary thought, and the lived Christian experience in Africa, for Africans to take the lead in the spiritual dramas associated with Christian evangelization. In the dramas staged in colonial social-welfare centers from the 1930s onward, however, African Christians continued to play at best, the role of missionary's assistant. These roles did grow, though, both in competence and stature. In the networks of outstations that expanded like spider webs outward from central locations where missionaries resided, African Christians did most of the day-to-day proselytizing. Teacher-training programs and dispensary-training programs granted African evangelists skills they too could brandish to attract potential converts to their stations. Over time, missions were dealing with second and third-generation African-Christian congregations. Many senior evangelists received pastoral training and took upon themselves the ministry of such congregations. Mission Churches in Africa began to look like African Churches run by African peoples for African people. Missionaries continued to reserve the right, however, to admit new members.

In the years leading up to the Second World War, observing the rise of fascism and communism in their home countries, many European Christians became convinced that the Christian age in Europe was over, and that their primary religious obligation was to preserve Christianity by passing it on to non-European peoples. Discussions began about passing the torch from 'older churches' to 'younger churches'.[61] Mission Churches were the younger Churches in these conversations. After the Second World War, European Christians began to pass most of the institutions and activities associated with Church life over to African Christians. Social-welfare institutions, however, because of their various contracts with governments, and because of the absence of Africans trained in the necessary technical competencies, remained under European control.

Conclusion

From one perspective it is possible to say that during the colonial era evangelization through poor relief ceased to operate in Africa for missions as it once had in Europe for Churches. In Europe itself, class had always been the greatest hurdle over which Christian evangelism had had to leap in order to create *communitas*; that is, a sense of shared community. Churches in Europe found ways to use social welfare to transcend class, if only during liminal moments in the private space of devotional chapels. Race was the equivalent obstacle in Africa. But during the era under consideration, due in part to their relationship with the colonial state, missions never discovered ways to use social welfare to transcend race. Social welfare remained something that Europeans did for Africans, not something that Christians did for other Christians. As a result, missionaries did not pass on the torch of evangelizing through European-style social-welfare institutions to African successors in their Churches.

Evangelization through relief to the poor *was* passed on to Africans, however. During the middle of the colonial era, African Christians enthused by the evangelical strategy, but alienated from or suspicious of all things European, began to rethink the use of indigenous practices and rituals for purposes of social amelioration. These Christians did not reject that European knowledge could help to make some aspects of life better. They just insisted that African knowledge could help deal with things European knowledge could not comprehend. New African Churches were founded upon the mandate to apply the power and glory of the Christian god to the everyday struggles of African peoples. The new Churches eschewed the institutional settings used by mission Christians to improve and empower, in part out of choice, in part out of a desire to keep their distance from the colonial state. Rather, in syncretized rituals that appropriated as needed from mission Christian culture as well as indigenous traditions, they introduced new practices aimed at the same ends of individual spiritual renewal and collective social amelioration. These Churches were the seeds of the new African Christendom now flourishing.

Notes

1. For examples of African uses of the construction, see, for West Africa, *Sierra Leone Weekly News*, July 15, 1899; for South Africa, *Imvo Zambantsundu*, January 21, 1887.
2. See Andrew E. Barnes, *Global Christianity and the Black Atlantic: Tuskegee, Colonialism and the Shaping of African Industrial Education* (Waco, TX: Baylor University Press, 2017), 7–31.
3. See Lamin O. Sanneh, *Abolitionists Abroad, American Blacks and the Making of Modern West Africa* (Cambridge, MA: Harvard University Press, 1999), 66–138; Andrew Porter, "'Commerce and Christianity': The Rise and Fall of a Nineteenth-Century Missionary Slogan," *The Historical Journal* 28, no. 3 (September, 1985): 597–621 and *Religion Versus Empire? British Protestant*

Missionaries and Overseas Expansion, 1700–1914 (Manchester: Manchester University Press, 2004); and Brian Stanley, *The Bible and the Flag: Protestant Missions and British Imperialism in the Nineteenth and Twentieth Century* (Leicester: Apollos, 1990).

4. For a discussion of Ethiopianism as a theological/intellectual concept in the New World, see the two books by Wilson Jeremiah Moses, *The Golden Age of Black Nationalism, 1850–1925* (1978); *Afrotopia: The Roots of African American Popular History* (1998). Also worth viewing is James Quirin, "W.E.B. Du Bois, Ethiopianism and Ethiopia, 1890–1955," in *International Journal of Ethiopian Studies* 5, no. 2 (Fall/Winter, 2010–2011). On Ethiopianism in West Africa, see: J. Ayondele Langley, *Pan Africanism and Nationalism in West Africa 1900–1945: A Study in Ideology and Social Class* (1973); Ogbu U. Kalu, "Ethiopianism and the Roots of Modern African Christianity," in *The Cambridge History of Christianity*, Vol. 8, ed. Sheridan Gilley and Brian Stanley. On Ethiopianism in Southern Africa, see: J. Mutero Chirenje, *Ethiopianism and Afro-Americans in Southern Africa, 1883–1916* (1987); and Badra Lahouel, "Ethiopianism and African Nationalism in South Africa before 1937," *Cahiers d'Études Africaines* 26, Cahier 104 (1986): 681–88.

5. These debates crystalized around the work of John and Jean Comoroff. See John and Jean Comaroff, *Of Revelation and Revolution* (Chicago: University of Chicago Press) v. 1. "Christianity, Colonialism, and Consciousness in South Africa" (1991); v. 2. "Dialectics of Modernity on a South African Frontier" (1997). Of the many, many reviews of the Comaroffs' work, most helpful for providing an orientation to their ideas and arguments are: Paul S. Landau, "Review: Hegemony and History in Jean and John L. Comaroff's 'Of Revelation and Revolution,'" *Africa: Journal of the International African Institute* 70, no. 3 (2000): 501–19; Les Switzer, "Review: Christianity, Colonialism and the Postmodern Project in South Africa: The Comaroffs Revisited" *Canadian Journal of African Studies* 32, no. 1 (1998): 181–96; and Andrew Porter, "'Cultural Imperialism' and the Protestant Missionary Enterprise, 1780–1914" *Journal of Imperial and Commonwealth History* 25, no. 3 (1997): 367–91. Of value as an assessment of the impact of the Comoroffs's ideas on the historiography on African Christianity is David Maxwell's, "Writing the History of African Christianity: Reflections of an Editor," *Journal of Religion in Africa*, 36, nos. 3–4 (2006): 379–99.

6. For a sense of the spectrum of discussion of the new African Christianity, see: Allan H. Anderson, *African Reformation: African Initiated Christianity in the 20th Century* (Trenton, NJ: Africa World Press, 2001); Ogbu Kalu, ed., *African Christianity: An African Story* (Trenton, NJ: Africa World Press, 2007); and Philip Jenkins, *The Next Christendom: The Coming Age of Global Christianity* (Oxford, New York: Oxford University Press, 2011). For a review of the subject from the anthropological perspective, see Birgit Meyer, "Christianity in Africa: From African Independent to Pentecostal-Charismatic Churches," *Annual Review of Anthropology* 33 (2004): 447–74. For a sense of the historical investigation of the subject, see Joel E. Tishken, "A Brief History and Typology of the African Reformation," *Nova Religio: The Journal of Alternative and Emergent Religions* 13, no. 1 (August 2009): 4–10.

7. The best guides to the spread of Christianity from the Roman world to Western Europe remain the various works of Peter Brown. See his *The Rise of Western Christendom: Triumph and Diversity, A.D. 200–1000* (New York: Wiley–Blackwell, 2013). See also Richard A. Fletcher, *The Conversion of Europe: From Paganism to Christianity 371–1386 A.D.* (London: Harper Collins, 1977). Older works to consider include Christopher Dawson, *The Formation of Christendom* (New York: Sheed and Ward, 1967).
8. On monasticism in Western Europe, a good starting point is Anne-Marie Halvetius and Michel Kaplan, "Asceticism and Its Institutions," in *The Cambridge History of Christianity, Vol. 3: Early Medieval Christianities, c.600–c.1100*, ed. Thomas F.X. Noble and Julia M.H. Smith (Cambridge: Cambridge University Press, 2008), 275–98. An older, but still useful work is David Knowles, *Christian Monasticism* (New York: McGraw Hill, 1969). Also of value is Jean Leclercq, *The Love of Learning and the Desire for God: A Study of Monastic Culture* (New York: Fordham University Press, 1982). For the evolution of European Christian sensibilities beyond the monastic paradigm, there remains no better guide than Marie-Dominique Chenu, *Nature, Man, and Society in the Twelfth Century: Essays on New Theological Perspective in the Latin West* (Toronto: University of Toronto Press, 1997). A more recent survey with an up-to-date bibliography is provided in G.R. Evans, *The I.B. Tauris History of Monasticism: The Western Tradition* (London, New York: I.B. Taurus, 2016).
9. This definition of the poor is derived from the works of Louis Chatellier, which are focused on a later period, but still have relevance for this discussion. See: Louis Chatellier, *The Europe of the Devout: The Catholic Reformation and the Formation of a New Society* (Cambridge, England, New York: Cambridge University Press, 1989); *The Religion of the Poor: Rural Missions in Europe and the Formation of Modern Catholicism c.1500–c.1800* (Cambridge: New York, Cambridge University Press, 1997). For a discussion from a different perspective that arrives at a similar characterization, see Peter Brown, *Poverty and Leadership in the Later Roman Empire* (The Menahem Stern Jerusalem Lectures) (Hanover and London: University Press of New England, 2002). See also: Michel Mollat, *The Poor in the Middle Ages: An Essay in Social History* (New Haven: Yale University Press, 1986); James William Brodman, *Charity and Religion in Medieval Europe* (Washington, DC: The Catholic University of America Press, 2006); and Adam J. Davis, "The Social and Religious Meanings of Charity in Medieval Europe," *History Compass* 12, no. 12 (2014): 935–50.
10. On notions of spiritual perfection in medieval Europe, see Chenu, 202–69. See also: Herbert Grundmann, *Religious Movements in the Middle Ages: The Historical Links between Heresy, The Mendicant Orders, and The Women's Religious Movement in the Twelfth and Thirteenth Century, with the Historical Foundations of German Mysticism* (Notre Dame, Ind: University of Notre Dame Press, 1995); Lester K. Little, *Religious Poverty and the Profit Economy in Medieval Europe* (Ithaca: Cornell University Press, 1978); and Andre Vauchez, *Sainthood in the Later Middle Ages* (Cambridge: Cambridge University Press, 1988).
11. See: John Henderson, *The Renaissance Hospital: Healing the Body and Healing the Soul* (New Haven: Yale University Press, 2006), especially 113–85; Federico Botana, *The Works of Mercy in Italian Medieval Art* (c.1050–c.1400)

(Turnhout, Belguim: Brepols Publisher, 2011). See also, Brodman, *Charity and Religion*, 245-66.
12. See Lindberg's discussion of medieval charity from the perspective of the Protestant Reformation in Carter Lindberg, *Beyond Charity: Reformation Initiatives for the Poor* (Minneapolis: Fortress Press, 1993), 17-66.
13. See: Henderson, *The Renaissance Hospital*, 186-224; and Brodman, *Charity and Religion*, 178-244.
14. Ibid.
15. See Davis, "Social and Religious Meanings of Charity," 941-44; and Brian S. Pullan, *Rich and Poor in Renaissance Venice: The Social Institutions of a Catholic State to 1620* (Oxford: Blackwell, 1971), 63-98.
16. See Thomas Max Safley's "Introduction," in *The Reformation of Charity: The Secular and the Religious in Early Modern Poor Relief*, ed. Thomas Max Safley (Boston: Leiden, Brill Academic Publishers, Inc, 2003). See also Thomas Max Safley, "Charity and Poor Relief," in *Europe, 1450 to 1789: Encyclopedia of the Early Modern World*, ed. Jonathan Dewald (New York: Charles Scribner's Sons, 2004) Vol. 1, 452-58.
17. See: Brodman, *Charity and Religion*; A.D. Wright, *The Counter-Reformation: Catholic Europe and the Non-Christian World* (New York: St. Martin's Press, 1982), especially 1-39.
18. See: Ute Lotz-Heumann, "Imposing Church Discipline," in *Cambridge History of Christianity Vol. 6: Reform and Expansion 1500-1660*, ed. Ronald Po-chia Hsia (Cambridge: Cambridge University Press, 2007), 244-60; and Catherina Lis and Hugo Soly, "Policing the Early Modern Proletariat 1450-1850," in *Proletarianization and Family History*, ed. David Levine (Orlando: Academic Press, 1984), 163-228.
19. The classic work by Theodore Rabb, and the discussion it provoked, remains the best guide to this point. See Theodore K. Rabb, *The Struggle for Stability in Early Modern Europe* (Oxford: Oxford University Press, 1975). See also J.H. Elliott, "The General Crisis in Retrospect: A Debate Without End," in *The Pattern of the Early Modern Past: From the General Crisis to the Struggle for Stability*, ed. Myron Guttman and Philip Benedict (Newark: University of Delaware Press, 2005), 31-51.
20. In addition to the works of Lindberg and Safley mentioned above, see: Robert Jutte, *Poverty and Deviance in Early Modern Europe* (Cambridge, New York: Cambridge University Press, 1994), and Marco H.D. van Leeuwen, "Logic of Charity: Poor Relief in Preindustrial Europe," *The Journal of Interdisciplinary History* 24, no. 4 (Spring 1994): 589-613.
21. See the various essays published in the edited volume by Safley mentioned above. In addition, see the essays collected and published in: Ole Peter Grell and Andrew Cunningham, eds., *Health Care and Poor Relief in Protestant Europe* (London, New York: Routledge, 1997); Ole Peter Grell and Andrew Cunningham, eds., *Health Care and Poor Relief in Counter-Reformation Europe* (London, New York: Routledge, 1999). See also: Mollat, *The Poor in the Middle Ages*, 251-93; and Brian Pullan, "Catholics, Protestants and the Poor in Early Modern Europe," *Journal of Interdisciplinary History* 35, no. 3 (Winter 2005): 441-56.

22. See: Jean Pierre Gutton, "Enfermement et Charité dans la France de l'Ancien Régime," *Histoire, Economie et Société* 10, no. 3 (1991): 353–58; van Leeuwen, "Logic of Charity," especially 609–13; and Lis and Soly, "Policing the Early Modern Proletariat," 185–213.
23. The best discussion of the costs associated with building and maintaining a social-welfare institution is provided in Henderson, *The Medieval Hospital*, 147–83. On this point, see also Lingberg, *Beyond Charity*, 128–60. On the funding of social-welfare institutions, in addition to the essays collected in Safley, ed., *The Reformation of Charity*, see those collected in: Ole Peter Grell, Andrew Cunningham and Robert Jutte, eds., *Health Care and Poor Relief in 18th and 19th Century Northern Europe* (Burlington, VT: Ashgate, 2002); and Renate Wilson, "Pietist Universal Reform and Care of the Sick and Poor: The Medical Institutions of the Francke Foundations and Their Social Context," in *Institutions of Confinement: Hospitals, Prisons and Asylums in Western Europe and North America, 1500–1950*, ed. Norbert Finzsch and Robert Jutte (Washington, DC: German Historical Institute, Cambridge University Press, 1996), 133–52.
24. While this chapter focuses only on Protestant missions to Africa, for a discussion of Catholic practices from a similar viewpoint, see Andrew E. Barnes, "'On the Necessity of Shaping Men Before Forming Christians': The Institutionalization of Catholicism in Early Modem Europe and Modern Africa," *Historical Reflections/Reflexions Historiques* 16, nos. 2/3 (1989): 217–49. See also Andrew E. Barnes, "Catholic Evangelizing in One Colonial Mission: The Institutional Evolution of Jos Prefecture, Nigeria 1907–1954," *The Catholic Historical Review* LXXXIV, no. 2 (1998): 240–62.
25. On Catholic missions in Africa before the year 1800, see: Bengt Sundkler and Christopher Steed, *A History of the Church in Africa* (New York, Cambridge: Cambridge University Press, 2000), 42–79; Adrian Hastings, *The Church in Africa 1450–1950* (Oxford: Clarendon Press, 1994), 71–129; Irma Taddia, ed., *The Diplomacy of Religion in Africa: The Last Manuscripts of Richard Gray* (Rome: Aracne editrice, 2014); and John K. Thornton, *The Kongolese Saint Anthony: Dona Beatriz Kimpa Vita and the Antonian movement, 1684–1706* (Cambridge, New York: Cambridge University Press, 1998).
26. See: Sanneh, *Abolitionists Abroad*, 22–138; and Stephen J. Braidwood, *Black Poor and White Philanthropists: London's Blacks and the Foundation of the Sierra Leone Settlement 1786–1791* (Liverpool: Liverpool University Press, 1994).
27. For an overview see Sundkler and Steed, *A History of the Church in Africa*, 81–560; and Hastings, *The Church in Africa*, 173–393. See also Elizabeth Isichei, *A History of Christianity in Africa* (London: Society for the Promotion of Christian Knowledge, 1995), 74–208.
28. For discussions of mission education before the advent of European colonial rule, see: Christopher Fyfe, *A History of Sierra Leone* (Oxford: Oxford University Press, 1962); J.F. Ade Ajayi, *Christian Missions in Nigeria, 1841–1891: The Making of a New élite* (Evanston: Northwestern University Press, c.1965), 90–165; E.A. Ayandele, *The Missionary Impact on Modern Nigeria, 1842–1914: A Political and Social Analysis* (London: Longmans, 1966); Norman Etherington, *Preachers, Peasants, and Politics in Southeast Africa, 1835–1880:*

African Christian Communities in Natal, Pondoland, and Zululand (London: Royal Historical Society, 1978), 47–134; Robert W. Strayer, *The Making of Mission Communities in East Africa: Anglicans and Africans in Colonial Kenya, 1875–1935* (London: Heinemann Educational Books, 1978); John P. Ragsdale, *Protestant Mission Education in Zambia, 1880–1954* (Selinsgrove, PA: Susquehanna University Press, London: Associated University Presses, c.1986), 17–55; and J.D.Y. Peel, *Religious Encounter and the Making of the Yoruba* (Bloomington: Indiana University Press, 2003), 123–51.

29. See Andrew E. Barnes, *Making Headway: The Introduction of Western Civilization in Colonial Northern Nigeria* (Rochester: University of Rochester Press, 2009).
30. See: George M. Fredrickson, *White Supremacy: A Comparative Study in American and South African History* (New York, Oxford: Oxford University Press, 1981), 136–282; and Saul Dubow, *Racial Segregation and the Origins of Apartheid in South Africa, 1919–1936* (London: Palgrave Macmillan, 1989), 1–50.
31. See E.D. Morel, *Nigeria, Its Peoples, Its Problems* (London: Frank Cass reprints, 1968), 216.
32. See Barnes, *Making Headway*, 114–22.
33. See Barnes, *Global Christianity*, 98–106, 114–22.
34. The outstanding example here was the Anglican bishop Samuel Ajayi Crowther. See: Ajayi, *Christian Missions in Nigeria*, 206–73; Sanneh, 139–81; and Andrew F. Walls, "The Legacy of Samuel Ajayi Crowther," *International Bulletin of Missionary Research* 16, no. 1 (January 1992): 15–21.
35. James Stewart, "'The Educated Kaffir': Industrial Education: A Sequel," *The Christian Express* (1, September 1880): 3–4, 13–14.
36. The expression comes from the title of a collection of articles reprinted from volume 7 of the *Cambridge History of Africa*. See Andrew. D. Roberts, *The Colonial Moment in Africa: Essays on the Movement of Minds and Materials, 1900–1940* (Cambridge: Cambridge University Press, 1990).
37. See in particular: Jeffrey Cox. *The British Missionary Enterprise since 1700* (New York: Routledge, 2010); Fiona Bowie, Deborah Kirkwood and Shirley Ardener, eds., *Women and Missions: Past and Present. Anthropological and Historical Perceptions* (Providence: Oxford: Berg, 1993).
38. On the development and articulation of European scientific racism, in addition to Fredrickson, *White Supremacy*, see: V.G. Keirnan, *The Lords of Human Kind: European Attitudes to Other Cultures in the Imperial Age* (revised edition) (London: Zed Books, 2015); Douglas Lorimer, *Colour, Class and the Victorians: English Attitudes Toward the Negro in the Mid-Nineteenth Century* (Leicester: Leicester University Press, New York: Holmes and Meier, 1978); Michael Adas, *Machines as the Measure of Man: Science, Technologies and Ideologies of Western Dominance* (Ithaca: Cornell University Press, 1989); Stephan Jay Gould, *The Mismeasure of Man* (New York: Norton, 1996); and Saul Dubow, *A Commonwealth of Knowledge: Science, Sensibility and White South Africa 1820–2000* (Oxford: Oxford University Press, 2006).
39. See Barnes, *Global Christianity*, 7–28.
40. Ibid., 55–80.
41. Ibid., 55–132.

42. Ibid., 88–90.
43. Ibid., 114–22.
44. Ibid., 103.
45. See: George Simeon Mwase, *Strike a Blow and Die; The Classic Story of the Chilembwe Rising* (London: Heinemann, 1975); George Shepperson and Thomas Price, *Independent African: John Chilembwe and the Origins, Setting and Significance of the Nyasaland Native Rising of 1915* (Edinburgh: Edinburgh University Press, 1969); and Patrick Makondesa, *The Church History of Providence Industrial Mission* (Kachere: Kachere Series Publications, 2000).
46. See: Manning Marable, "South African Nationalism in Brooklyn: John L. Dube's Activities in New York State 1887–1899," *Afro-Americans in New York Life and History* 3, no. 1 (1979): 23–30.
47. See Barnes, *Global Christianity*, 130–31.
48. Ibid., 118–20.
49. See the report of the "Nyasaland Native Rising Commission," published in *The Nyasaland Times*, February 10, 1916, 6.
50. Kenneth King, *Pan Africanism and Education: A Study of Race Philanthropy and Education in the Southern States of America and East Africa* (Oxford: Clarendon Press, 1971), 79–94.
51. See: Clive Whitehead, "The Historiography of British Imperial Education Policy, Part II: Africa and the Rest of the Colonial Empire," *History of Education* 34, no. 4 (2005): 441–54; Peter Kallaway, "Education, Health and Social Welfare in the Late Colonial Context: The International Missionary Council and Educational Transition in the Interwar Years with Special Reference to Colonial Africa," *History of Education* 38, no. 2 (2009): 217–46; and Aaron Windel, "British Colonial Education in Africa: Policy and Practice in the Era of Trusteeship," *History Compass* 7, no. 1 (2009): 1–21.
52. African Education Committee, *Education in Africa; A Study of West, South, and Equatorial Africa by the African EducationCommission, Under the Auspices of the Phelps-Stokes Fund and Foreign Mission Societies of North America and Europe; Report Prepared by Thomas Jesse Jones, Chairman of the Commission* (New York: Phelps-Stokes Fund, 1922); African Education Committee, *Education in East Africa; A study of East, Central and South Africa by the Second African Education Commission Under the Auspices of the Phelps-Stokes Fund, In Cooperation with the International Education Board. Report prepared by Thomas Jesse Jones* (New York: Phelps-Stokes Fund, 1925). For the history of the Phelps-Stokes Education Commissions, see King, *Pan-Africanism and Education*; and Edward H. Berman, "Education in Africa and America: A History of the Phelps-Stokes Fund, 1911–1945" (Ed. D. Columbia University, 1970), 89–99.
53. See African Education Committee, *Education in Africa*, 86; and African Education Committee, *Education in East Africa*, 87–88. See also Thomas Jesse Jones, "A Good Word for Missionaries," *Current History* (July 1, 1926): 539–44.
54. See Thomas Jesse Jones, *Four Essentials of Education* (New York: Scribners and Sons, 1926), especially pages, 31–37. See also Stephen Taylor Correia, "'For Their Own Good': An Historical Analysis of the Educational Thought of Thomas Jesse Jones" (PhD diss., Pennsylvania State University, 1993).

55. King, *Pan Africanism and Education*, 91–94.
56. See Barnes, *Making Headway*, 177–89.
57. See Andrew E. Barnes, "'Making Good Wives and Mothers': The African Education Group and Missionary Reactions to the Phelps-Stokes Reports" *Studies in World Christianity* 21, no. 1 (April 2015): 66–85.
58. See Megan Vaughan, *Curing Their Ills: Colonial Power and African Illness* (Cambridge: Polity Press, 1991).
59. See for example Shobona Shankar, *Who Shall Enter Paradise: Christian Origins in Muslim Northern Nigeria, ca 1890–1975* (Athens: Ohio University Press, 2014), 47–115.
60. See: Douglas Rimmer and Anthony Kirk Greene, eds., *The British Intellectual Engagement with Africa in the Twentieth Century* (Houndmills: Macmillan Press, New York: St. Martin's Press, 2000); Joseph M. Hodge, *Triumph of the Experts: Agrarian Doctrines of Development and the Legacies of British Colonialism* (Athens: Ohio University Press, 2007); Helen Tilley, *Africa as a Living Laboratory: Empire, Development and the Problem of Scientific Knowledge, 1870–1950* (Chicago: University of Chicago Press, 2011); and Patrick Harries and David Maxwell, eds., *The Spiritual in the Secular: Missionaries and Knowledge About Africa* (Grand Rapids: W.B. Eerdmans Publishing, 2012).
61. See Godfrey E. Philips, "The Younger Churches Help the Older," *International Review of Missions* 30 (1941): 539–45.

Bibliography

Adas, Michael. *Machines as the Measure of Man: Science, Technologies and Ideologies of Western Dominance*. Ithaca: Cornell University Press, 1989.

Ade Ajayi, J.F. *Christian Missions in Nigeria, 1841–1891: The Making of a New élite*. Evanston: Northwestern University Press, c.1965, 90–165.

African Education Committee. *Education in Africa; A Study of West, South, and Equatorial Africa by the African Education Commission, Under the Auspices of the Phelps-Stokes Fund and Foreign Mission Societies of North America and Europe; Report Prepared by Thomas Jesse Jones, Chairman of the Commission*. New York: Phelps-Stokes Fund, 1922.

———. *Education in East Africa; A Study of East, Central and South Africa by the Second African Education Commission Under the Auspices of the Phelps-Stokes Fund, in Cooperation with the International Education Board. Report prepared by Thomas Jesse Jones*. New York: Phelps-Stokes Fund, 1925.

Anderson, Allan H. *African Reformation: African Initiated Christianity in the 20th Century*. Trenton, NJ: Africa World Press, 2001.

Ayandele, E.A. *The Missionary Impact on Modern Nigeria, 1842–1914: A Political and Social Analysis*. London: Longmans, 1966.

Barnes Andrew E. "'On the Necessity of Shaping Men Before Forming Christians': The Institutionalization of Catholicism in Early Modern Europe and Modern Africa." *Historical Reflections/Reflexions Historiques* 16, nos. 2/3 (1989), 217–49.

———. "Catholic Evangelizing in One Colonial Mission: The Institutional Evolution of Jos Prefecture, Nigeria 1907–1954." *The Catholic Historical Review* LXXXIV, no. 2 (1998), 240–62.

———. *Making Headway: The Introduction of Western Civilization in Colonial Northern Nigeria.* Rochester: University of Rochester Press, 2009.

———. "'Making Good Wives and Mothers': The African Education Group and Missionary Reactions to the Phelps-Stokes Report." *Studies in World Christianity* 21, no. 1 (April 2015), 66–85.

———. *Global Christianity and the Black Atlantic: Tuskegee, Colonialism and the Shaping of African Industrial Education.* Waco, TX: Baylor University Press, 2017, 7–31.

Berman, Edward H. "Education in Africa and America: A History of the Phelps-Stokes Fund, 1911–1945." Ed. D. Columbia University, 1970.

Botana, Federico. *The Works of Mercy in Italian Medieval Art* (c.1050–c.1400). Turnhout, Belguim: Brepols Publisher, 2011.

Bowie, Fiona, Deborah Kirkwood, and Shirley Ardener, eds. *Women and Missions: Past and Present. Anthropological and Historical Perceptions.* Providence: Oxford: Berg, 1993.

Braidwood, Stephen J. *Black Poor and White Philanthropists: London's Blacks and the Foundation of the Sierra Leone Settlement 1786–1791.* Liverpool: Liverpool University Press, 1994.

Brodman, James William. *Charity and Religion in Medieval Europe.* Washington, DC: The Catholic University of America Press, 2006.

Brown, Peter. *Poverty and Leadership in the Later Roman Empire* (The Menahem Stern Jerusalem Lectures). Hanover and London: University Press of New England, 2002.

———. *The Rise of Western Christendom: Triumph and Diversity, A.D. 200–1000.* New York: Wiley–Blackwell, 2013.

Chatellier, Louis. *The Europe of the Devout: The Catholic Reformation and the Formation of a New Society.* Cambridge, England, New York: Cambridge University Press, 1989.

———. *The Religion of the Poor: Rural Missions in Europe and the Formation of Modern Catholicism c.1500–c.1800.* Cambridge, New York: Cambridge University Press, 1997.

Chirenje, J. Mutero. *Ethiopianism and Afro-Americans in Southern Africa, 1883–1916.* Baton Rouge, LA: Louisiana State University Press, 1987.

Comoroff, John and Jean. *Of Revelation and Revolution.* Chicago: University of Chicago Press v. 1. "Christianity, Colonialism, and Consciousness in South Africa." 1991; v. 2. "Dialectics of Modernity on a South African Frontier." 1997.

Correia, Stephen Taylor. "'For Their Own Good': An Historical Analysis of the Educational Thought of Thomas Jesse Jones." PhD diss., Pennsylvania State University, 1993.

Cox, Jeffrey. *The British Missionary Enterprise since 1700.* New York: Routledge, 2010.

Davis, Adam J. "The Social and Religious Meanings of Charity in Medieval Europe." *History Compass* 12, no. 12 (2014): 935–50.

Dawson, Christopher. *The Formation of Christendom.* New York: Sheed and Ward, 1967.

Dubow, Saul. *Racial Segregation and the Origins of Apartheid in South Africa, 1919–1936.* London: Palgrave Macmillan, 1989.

———. *A Commonwealth of Knowledge: Science, Sensibility and White South Africa 1820–2000.* Oxford: Oxford University Press, 2006.

Elliott, J.H. "The General Crisis in Retrospect: A Debate Without End." In *The Pattern of the Early Modern Past: From the General Crisis to the Struggle for Stability*, edited by Myron Guttman and Philip Benedict, 31–51. Newark: University of Delaware Press, 2005.

Etherington, Norman. *Preachers, Peasants, and Politics in Southeast Africa, 1835–1880: African Christian Communities in Natal, Pondoland, and Zululand*. London: Royal Historical Society, 1978, 47–134.

Fletcher, Richard A. *The Conversion of Europe: From Paganism to Christianity 371–1386 AD*. London: Harper Collins, 1977.

Fredrickson, George M. *White Supremacy: A Comparative Study in American and South African History*. New York, Oxford: Oxford University Press, 1981, 136–282.

Fyfe, Christopher. *A History of Sierra Leone*. Oxford: Oxford University Press, 1962.

Gould, Stephan Jay. *The Mismeasure of Man*. New York: Norton, 1996.

Grell, Ole Peter, and Andrew Cunningham, eds. *Health Care and Poor Relief in Protestant Europe*. London, New York: Routledge, 1997.

———. *Health Care and Poor Relief in Counter-Reformation Europe*. London, New York: Routledge, 1999.

———. *Health Care and Poor Relief in 18th and 19th Century Northern Europe*. Burlington, VT: Ashgate, 2002.

Grundmann, Herbert. *Religious Movements in the Middle Ages: The Historical Links between Heresy, The Mendicant Orders, and The Women's Religious Movement in the Twelfth and Thirteenth century, with the Historical Foundations of German Mysticism*. Notre Dame, IN: University of Notre Dame Press, 1995.

Gutton, Jean Pierre. "Enfermement et Charite dans la France de l'Ancien Regime." *Histoire, Economie et Societe* 10, no. 3 (1991).

Halvetius, Anne-Marie and Michel Kaplan. "Asceticism and Its Institutions." In *The Cambridge History of Christianity, Vol. 3: Early Medieval Christianities, c.600–c.1100*, edited by Thomas F.X. Noble and Julia M.H. Smith, 275–98. Cambridge: Cambridge University Press, 2008.

Harries, Patrick and David Maxwell, eds. *The Spiritual in the Secular: Missionaries and Knowledge about Africa*. Grand Rapids: W.B. Eerdmans Publishing, 2012.

Hastings, Adrian. *The Church in Africa 1450–1950*. Oxford: Clarendon Press, 1994, 71–129.

Henderson, John. *The Renaissance Hospital: Healing the Body and Healing the Soul*. New Haven: Yale University Press, 2006.

Hodge, Joseph M. *Triumph of the Experts: Agrarian Doctrines of Development and the Legacies of British Colonialism*. Athens: Ohio University Press, 2007.

Isichei, Elizabeth. *A History of Christianity in Africa*. London: Society for the Promotion of Christian Knowledge, 1995.

Jenkins, Philip. *The Next Christendom: The Coming Age of Global Christianity*. Oxford, New York: Oxford University Press, 2011.

Jones, Thomas Jesse. "A Good Word for Missionaries." *Current History* 20, no. 4 (July 1, 1926): 539–44.

———. *Four Essentials of Education*. New York: Scribners and Sons, 1926.

Jutte, Robert. *Poverty and Deviance in Early Modern Europe*. Cambridge, New York: Cambridge University Press, 1994.

Kallaway, Peter. "Education, Health and Social Welfare in the Late Colonial Context: The International Missionary Council and Educational Transition in the Interwar Years with Special Reference to Colonial Africa." *History of Education* 38, no. 2 (2009): 217–46.

Kalu, Ogbu U. "Ethiopianism and the Roots of Modern African Christianity." In *The Cambridge History of Christianity*, edited by Sheridan Gilley and Brian Stanley, Vol. 8. Cambridge: Cambridge University Press, 2005.

———, ed. *African Christianity: An African Story*. Trenton, NJ: Africa World Press, 2007.

Keirnan, V.G. *The Lords of Human Kind: European Attitudes to Other Cultures in the Imperial Age*. Rev. ed. London: Zed Books, 2015.

King, Kenneth. *Pan Africanism and Education: A Study of Race Philanthropy and Education in the Southern States of America and East Africa*. Oxford: Clarendon Press, 1971.

Knowles, David. *Christian Monasticism*. New York: McGraw Hill, 1969.

Lahouel, Badra. "Ethiopianism and African Nationalism in South Africa Before 1937." *Cahiers d'Études Africaines* 26, Cahier 104 (1986): 681–88.

Landau, Paul S. "Review: Hegemony and History in Jean and John L. Comaroff's 'Of Revelation and Revolution.'" *Africa: Journal of the International African Institute* 70, no. 3 (2000): 501–19.

Langley, J. Ayondele. *Pan Africanism and Nationalism in West Africa 1900–1945: A Study in Ideology and Social Class*. Oxford: Clarendon Press, 1973.

Leclercq, Jean. *The Love of Learning and the Desire for God: A Study of Monastic Culture*. New York: Fordham University Press, 1982.

Lindberg, Carter. *Beyond Charity: Reformation Initiatives for the Poor*. Minneapolis: Fortress Press, 1993.

Lis, Catherina and Hugo Soly. "Policing the Early Modern Proletariat 1450–1850." In *Proletarianization and Family History*, edited by David Levine, 163–228. Orlando: Academic Press, 1984.

Little, Lester K. *Religious Poverty and the Profit Economy in Medieval Europe*. Ithaca: Cornell University Press, 1978.

Lorimer, Douglas. *Colour, Class and the Victorians: English Attitudes Toward the Negro in the Mid-Nineteenth Century*. Leicester: Leicester University Press, New York: Holmes and Meier, 1978.

Lotz-Heumann, Ute. "Imposing Church Discipline." In *Cambridge History of Christianity Vol. 6: Reform and Expansion 1500–1660*, edited by Ronald Po-chia Hsia, 244–60. Cambridge: Cambridge University Press, 2007.

Makondesa, Patrick. *The Church History of Providence Industrial Mission*. Kachere: Kachere Series Publications, 2000.

Marable, Manning. "South African Nationalism in Brooklyn: John L. Dube's Activities in New York State 1887–1899." *Afro-Americans in New York Life and History* 3, no. 1 (1979): 23–30.

Maxwell, David. "Writing the History of African Christianity: Reflections of an Editor." *Journal of Religion in Africa* 36, nos. 3–4 (2006): 379–99.

Meyer, Birgit. "Christianity in Africa: From African Independent to Pentecostal-Charismatic Churches." *Annual Review of Anthropology* 33 (2004): 447–74.

Mollat, Michel. *The Poor in the Middle Ages: An Essay in Social History*. New Haven: Yale University Press, 1986.

Morel, E.D. *Nigeria, Its Peoples, Its Problems*. London: Frank Cass reprints, 1968.
Moses, Wilson Jeremiah. *The Golden Age of Black Nationalism, 1850–1925*. Hamden, CT: Archon Books, 1978.
———. *Afrotopia: The Roots of African American Popular History*. Cambridge: Cambridge University Press, 1998.
Mwase, George Simeon. *Strike a Blow and Die; The Classic Story of the Chilembwe Rising*. London: Heinemann, 1975.
Peel, J.D.Y. *Religious Encounter and the Making of the Yoruba*. Bloomington: Indiana University Press, 2003.
Porter, Andrew. "'Commerce and Christianity': The Rise and Fall of a Nineteenth-Century Missionary Slogan." *The Historical Journal* 28, no. 3 (September 1985): 597–621.
———. "'Cultural Imperialism' and the Protestant Missionary Enterprise, 1780–1914." In *Journal of Imperial and Commonwealth History* 25, no. 3 (1997): 367–91.
———. *Religion Versus Empire? British Protestant Missionaries and Overseas Expansion, 1700–1914*. Manchester: Manchester University Press, 2004.
Pullan, Brian S. *Rich and Poor in Renaissance Venice: The Social Institutions of a Catholic State to 1620*. Oxford: Blackwell, 1971, 63–98.
———. "Catholics, Protestants and the Poor in Early Modern Europe." *Journal of Interdisciplinary History* 35, no. 3 (Winter 2005): 441–56.
Quirin, James. "W.E.B. Du Bois, Ethiopianism and Ethiopia, 1890–1955." *International Journal of Ethiopian Studies* 5, no. 2 (Fall/Winter, 2010–2011).
Rabb, Theodore K. *The Struggle for Stability in Early Modern Europe*. Oxford: Oxford University Press, 1975.
Ragsdale, John P. *Protestant Mission Education in Zambia, 1880–1954*. Selinsgrove, PA: Susquehanna University Press, London: Associated University Presses, c.1986.
Roberts, Andrew. D. *The Colonial Moment in Africa: Essays on the Movement of Minds and Materials, 1900–1940*. Cambridge, Cambridge University Press, 1990.
Rimmer, Douglas, and Anthony Kirk Greene, eds. *The British Intellectual Engagement with Africa in the Twentieth Century*. Houndmills: Macmillan Press, New York: St. Martin's Press, 2000.
Safley, Thomas Max, ed. *The Reformation of Charity: The Secular and the Religious in Early Modern Poor Relief*. Boston, Leiden: Brill Academic Publishers, Inc, 2003).
———. "Charity and Poor Relief." In *Europe, 1450 to 1789: Encyclopedia of the Early Modern World*, edited by Jonathan Dewald, Vol. 1, 452–58. New York: Charles Scribner's Sons, 2004.
Sanneh, Lamin O. *Abolitionists Abroad, American Blacks and the Making of Modern West Africa*. Cambridge, MA: Harvard University Press, 1999.
Shankar, Shobona. *Who Shall Enter Paradise: Christian Origins in Muslim Northern Nigeria, ca 1890–1975*. Athens: Ohio University Press, 2014.
Shepperson, George and Thomas Price. *Independent African: John Chilembwe and the Origins, Setting and Significance of the Nyasaland Native Rising of 1915*. Edinburgh: Edinburgh University Press, 1969.
Stanley, Brian. *The Bible and the Flag: Protestant Missions and British Imperialism in the Nineteenth and Twentieth Century*. Leicester: Apollos, 1990.

Strayer, Robert W. *The Making of Mission Communities in East Africa: Anglicans and Africans in Colonial Kenya, 1875–1935*. London: Heinemann Educational Books, 1978.

Sundkler, Bengt, and Christopher Steed. *A History of the Church in Africa*. New York, Cambridge: Cambridge University Press, 2000.

Switzer, Les. "Review: Christianity, Colonialism and the Postmodern Project in South Africa: The Comaroffs Revisited." *Canadian Journal of African Studies* 32, no. 1 (1998): 181–96.

Taddia, Irma, ed. *The Diplomacy of Religion in Africa: The Last Manuscripts of Richard Gray*. Rome: Aracne editrice, 2014.

Thornton, John K. *The Kongolese Saint Anthony: Dona Beatriz Kimpa Vita and the Antonian movement, 1684–1706*. Cambridge, New York: Cambridge University Press, 1998.

Tilley, Helen. *Africa as a Living Laboratory: Empire, Development and the Problem of Scientific Knowledge, 1870–1950*. Chicago: University of Chicago Press, 2011.

Tishken, Joel E. "A Brief History and Typology of the African Reformation." *Nova Religio: The Journal of Alternative and Emergent Religions* 13, no. 1 (August 2009): 4–10.

van Leeuwen, Marco H.D. "Logic of Charity: Poor Relief in Preindustrial Europe." *The Journal of Interdisciplinary History* 24, no. 4 (Spring 1994): 589–613.

Vauchez, Andre. *Sainthood in the Later Middle Ages*. Cambridge: Cambridge University Press, 1988.

Vaughan, Megan. *Curing Their Ills: Colonial Power and African Illness*. Cambridge: Polity Press, 1991.

Walls, Andrew F. "The Legacy of Samuel Ajayi Crowther." *International Bulletin of Missionary Research* 16, no. 1 (January 1992): 15–21.

Whitehead, Clive. "The Historiography of British Imperial Education Policy, Part II: Africa and the Rest of the Colonial Empire." *History of Education* 34, no. 4 (2005): 441–54.

Wilson, Renate. "Pietist Universal Reform and Care of the Sick and Poor: The Medical Institutions of the Francke Foundations and Their Social Context." In *Institutions of Confinement: Hospitals, Prisons and Asylums in Western Europe and North America, 1500–1950*, edited by Norbert Finzsch and Robert Jutte, 133–52. Washington, DC: German Historical Institute, Cambridge University Press, 1996.

Windel, Aaron. "British Colonial Education in Africa: Policy and Practice in the Era of Trusteeship." *History Compass* 7. no. 1 (2009): 1–21.

Wright, A.D. *The Counter-Reformation: Catholic Europe and the Non-Christian World*. New York: St. Martin's Press, 1982.

CHAPTER 10

Colonial Education

Kelly Duke Bryant

In an essay entitled 'The Education of a British-Protected Child', celebrated writer Chinua Achebe reflected on his experiences as a schoolboy in colonial Nigeria, recounting pleasant memories of his earliest efforts to learn the English language, of his participation in Empire Day festivities in the 1930s, and of reading classics of English literature while a student at Government College Umuahia in the 1940s. Yet, despite his focus on happy stories, Achebe periodically referred to the violence of colonialism, hinted at tensions that emerged between university educators and students, and characterized the education system as flawed due to its association with colonial rule.[1] In his essay, then, Achebe came across as ambivalent about the role played by colonial education in his own life. Such ambivalence is characteristic of the history and legacy of colonial schooling throughout Africa.

The officials and missionaries who operated colonial schools did so with their own goals in mind and offered curricula and experiences that often alienated students or caused them to question their cultures. Once they had become aware of the advantages schools could provide, however, many Africans not only worked to ensure access for themselves or their children, but also attempted to shape the approach, content, and conditions of the

---

I wish to thank the editors and copy-editors of this volume, whose diligent work has helped to make this a stronger chapter. I am also grateful to those who suggested pertinent primary sources and novels: Kathleen Sheldon, Gabeba Baderoon, Claire L. Dehon, Elena Vezzadini, Jennifer Sessions, Robert E. Smith, and Sara Berry.

K.D. Bryant (✉)
Department of History, Rowan University, Glassboro, NJ, USA

© The Author(s) 2018
M.S. Shanguhyia and T. Falola (eds.),
The Palgrave Handbook of African Colonial and Postcolonial History,
https://doi.org/10.1057/978-1-137-59426-6_10

education offered. Yet ultimately, although many Africans actively sought to enroll, engaged in school-related political activity, or derived certain advantages from attendance, some (former) students and scholars came to view colonial education as a mostly negative force. Thus, while African agency played a crucial role in defining colonial education and determining the uses to which it could be put, colonial education left a complicated legacy and occupies an ambivalent position in African history.

This chapter provides an overview of colonial education in Africa, focusing most particularly on the issues of agency and ambivalence and the tensions surrounding them. Though it is grounded in a thorough reading of the secondary literature, this chapter also relies on a variety of primary sources including documents from the colonial archives in Senegal, oral interviews with Senegalese retirees, and, most importantly, a variety of published first-person accounts written by Africans from across the continent who had at least some experience with colonial schooling. Nearly all of these sources represent elite perspectives. Some were written long after their authors completed their schooling and are thus affected by the whims of human memory. Despite the limitations of perspective and memory, however, I think these sources are useful in that they feature Africans speaking for themselves about their experiences with education. These experiences were diverse, and authors' reactions to colonial schools varied widely. So although I cannot make a case that the issues discussed here applied to *all* Africans, I can use these sources to give readers a sense of the range of possibilities. After a brief historiographical section, the chapter provides an overview of the history of colonial schooling, and then examines three issues in some detail: the decision to go (or not to go) to school, politics and protest, and the legacy of colonial schooling. It makes the case that agency and ambivalence were central to all of these processes.

Historical Scholarship and Colonial Schooling

Historians have long shown keen interest in colonial schooling as a way of understanding the techniques of empire, the emergence of new African elites, the impacts of school attendance and literacy, and a whole host of other processes. In the mid-twentieth century, historians tended to focus on educational institutions and policies, tracing the emergence and growth of individual schools or school systems and assessing their impact on African societies. Writing around the time of decolonization or in the decades that followed, many of these scholars made the case that as a tool of missionaries and colonialists, colonial education was essentially disruptive, inadequate, and totally unsuited for African needs. In his study of the history of underdevelopment in Africa, for example, Walter Rodney criticized colonial schools for their limited resources and distribution, their poor quality instruction, and their Eurocentric content. For these reasons and others, Rodney argued, 'colonial schooling was education for subordination, exploitation, the creation of mental confusion, and the development of underdevelopment'.[2] Although she did not condemn colonial education in French West Africa in her encyclopedic study of its history, Denise Bouche made clear that French economic and political interests drove education policy.[3] These and other works effectively established chronologies and evaluated the implications of colonial education policy, but they often paid little attention to African responses or initiatives.[4]

More recent scholarship has built on and added nuance to this earlier work. Some historians have continued in the tradition of institutional histories, but have responded to trends in the historiography of colonial Africa that have privileged African agency and have envisioned colonial institutions as sites of negotiation. For example, in her rich study of the Inanda Seminary, a high school for black South African girls founded in 1869, Meghan Healy-Clancy shows how the school intersected with and contributed to a changing politics of gender in the wider society both before and during apartheid.[5] Others have focused on debates surrounding the classroom learning environment, or have examined its effects on students. Exploring such sources as textbooks, curricula, student writing, and correspondence, scholars have sought to understand how colonialists and Africans alike envisioned colonial education.[6] And still others have traced Africans' active participation in (and influence over) the project of colonial education, or have examined Africans' attempts to take up schooling for their own purposes.[7] In her study of colonial Southern Rhodesia (Zimbabwe), for example, Carol Summers shows how some Africans used colonial education as a way to work out 'dreams, ideals, and creative responses to state power', and she demonstrates that African actions and demands shaped the implementation of colonial education policies on the ground.[8] My own book, which places colonial schooling at the center of local politics in Senegal in the late nineteenth and early twentieth centuries, also fits into this trend.[9] This more recent scholarship recognizes that colonial officials planned to use schools to engender loyalty, reshape African cultures, and train better workers, but it emphasizes the ways that Africans operated creatively within this system as active participants and strategists. Focusing on agency and ambivalence, the present chapter applies many of these insights across empires and regions.

HISTORICAL OVERVIEW

Most of the first sustained efforts at providing Western-style schooling in Africa date to the late eighteenth and early nineteenth centuries and were concentrated in places like Cape Coast (Gold Coast/Ghana), Freetown (Sierra Leone), and Saint-Louis (Senegal); schools arrived even earlier in Cape Town (South Africa). As coastal settlements with long histories of European contact, these towns were focal points for Catholic and Protestant missions, and these organizations played crucial roles in education. In Saint-Louis, for example, the Brothers of Christian Instruction took over struggling secular schools in 1841, at the government's request, and the Sisters of Saint-Joseph of Cluny operated public schools for girls beginning in 1826. Senegal's budget covered at least some of the costs of these schools and its officials had some influence over the education offered. Beginning in 1855, the French administration worked to create a parallel system of secular public schools in Saint-Louis and, later, in other parts of Senegal. In Freetown, the Church Missionary Society (CMS) opened its first schools as the British Crown prepared to take over the colony in 1808, and other mission organizations soon followed suit. Operating with considerable autonomy and some government support, the CMS established Fourah Bay College (West Africa's first university) in 1827, secondary schools for boys and for girls in 1845 and 1849, and a variety of primary schools.[10]

Over the ensuing decades, Western-style schooling expanded in these areas and took root in others, most often through the work of Christian mission societies and, eventually, educated Africans who served as teachers, catechists, and auxiliaries. By the late nineteenth century, mission schools were scattered across the continent, though distribution was uneven since establishing a school often depended on missionaries' ability to obtain land from African rulers and communities, to staff and fund mission stations and schools, and to recruit students. In British colonies and zones of influence, missionaries sometimes looked to British officials for logistical support, but they retained control over their schools. From its base in Saint-Louis, Senegal, the French administration continued to subsidize the Catholic mission organizations that provided public schooling in their expanding West African territory, even as it created secular public schools and allowed independent Protestant and Catholic missions to found private schools. In Central Africa, the French relied even more heavily on the mission organizations that had begun operating schools in the 1840s. Mission societies of a wide variety of denominations and nationalities opened schools in the final decades of the nineteenth century in the Congo, which King Leopold II of Belgium controlled beginning in the 1880s. Similarly, by the late nineteenth century, Protestant and Catholic mission societies based in several countries established schools in both Portuguese and German zones of influence.[11]

As they focused on their expanding African empires in the late nineteenth century and early twentieth centuries, colonial governments began to organize and regulate the patchwork of mission and secular schools that had emerged. The government of the Congo Free State, for example, issued Educational Acts in 1890 and 1892, which regulated primary schooling, created the first government-run schools, and provided subsidies to officially recognized Catholic schools. In 1903, the governor-general of French West Africa issued two education reforms designed to reorganize and centralize public schooling across the federation. Most importantly, the decrees established a single hierarchy with uniform curricula, stated that schooling would be offered for free, and mandated that instruction be secular and given in French. Secularization resulted in the closure of some schools, mostly in Senegal, and in the reduction or elimination of financial support for mission schools everywhere.[12] Significant education reform did not come until the interwar period in most British colonies, where missions continued to operate the large majority of schools. Here, education reform formalized and revised the existing practice of giving grants-in-aid to the missions that ran schools. Now, however, in order to continue receiving aid, mission schools had to acquiesce to state oversight and curricular initiatives. The British also created a small number of state-run schools in various colonies.[13]

In the postwar period, the British and French invested in education as part of their new commitment to economic development and in an effort to placate African nationalists. To an extent, government officials also realized that they needed to prepare African leaders for increasing political autonomy (and perhaps even independence) in the not so distant future. These colonial governments sought to expand schooling at all levels, and many of Africa's oldest universities date from this era. Reforms enacted in 1946 and 1948 adopted metropolitan curricula in the schools of the French colonies, planned for the expansion of schooling from primary through post-secondary grades, and allowed for students to transfer more easily to metropolitan institutions. The British focused especially on literacy campaigns and primary schooling, with varying degrees of success. In the Belgian and Portuguese cases, the state continued to depend heavily on Catholic missions and to focus on primary schooling. Although two universities opened in the Belgian Congo in the 1950s, very few Africans had access to secondary and post-secondary education in this period. Meanwhile, in South Africa, the apartheid state implemented the Bantu Education Act in 1953, which pushed Christian missions out of the business of operating schools for Africans and used schools to promote the ideas of African inferiority and separate development.[14]

Though the focus and intent of education policy varied across time and from place to place, governments and missionaries always intended colonial education to serve their own interests. Yet success in this initiative depended on the active participation of Africans; Africans had to attend in order for schools to have an impact. By showing up or staying home, petitioning, and protesting, Africans had some ability to influence colonial education.

Going to School

Africans' decisions about whether or not, and where, to enroll their children or themselves in school played a significant role in the history of colonial education. Initially, colonial schools faced numerous obstacles in recruiting students, since they seemed to have limited relevance and utility, and since children had other demands on their time. African families generally remained committed to socializing and training children within the family and community, an approach that allowed children to learn by doing and their families to benefit from their labor. In Islamic areas, many children also attended Qur'an schools. However, as the first generations of school leavers were able to obtain new kinds of jobs within the colonial economy, demand for colonial schooling increased. Africans' decisions about school were thus characterized by both ambivalence and agency, and the individual and family strategies that shaped these decisions changed over time.

A large majority of families kept their children away from colonial schools early on, especially in Islamic areas. Despite their best efforts to recruit students, teachers often echoed the frustrations of Isaac Konaré, who worked in a primary school in Kaolack, Senegal, in the 1890s. 'I still have the same number of students', Konaré wrote after months of working to increase enrollment. 'I await the arrival of the Administrator to convince people to send their children to school; they always promise to send their children to classes, but they never keep their word'.[15] The reluctance of African families to send their children (especially their daughters) to school was one reason for low enrollment, which concerned teachers, mission organizations, and colonial officials in this period. And the numbers are striking. In Senegal, a 1910 government report indicated that only 3637 boys and 435 girls attended the colony's schools, many of which had been open for over a decade. This was a small percentage of school-aged children, as evidenced by the government's 1912 estimate that 11,451 children were attending Qur'an schools.[16] Recruitment was thus an important priority in these early years.

Even so, a significant number of Africans ultimately decided to enroll, and they did so for many different reasons. Some, like Susiwe Bengu, a daughter of a Zulu chief, saw the colonial school as a resource they could use in local or familial power struggles. Bengu came to Inanda Seminary in South Africa in August 1892 in an effort to avoid an arranged marriage to a considerably older man. In her testimony to the missionaries who ran the seminary, Bengu explained that she had continually refused to engage with the marriage process, and that she finally 'watched for a chance to get away, and came here to you'.[17] Others, like Samuel Ajayi Crowther, who went on to become an important Anglican missionary and bishop in Nigeria, sought refuge from slavery or other forms of oppression at a mission station and began to attend school. Still others saw the school as an appealing economic pathway in a new colonial world. Amadou Cissé, a twelve-year-old schoolboy from Senegal, for example, noted in a 1906 scholarship request that he had 'a very strong penchant for study, and my biggest dream is to become a teacher'.[18] For many (probably most) Africans, the decision to attend a colonial school was a family matter. Senior relatives decided whether or not to send a child and strategized about whom to send. Sometimes such family decisions happened under pressure from colonial officials, who attempted to use their influence (especially with chiefly families) to help populate colonial schools.[19]

By the 1920s and 1930s, colonial education had become clearly linked to white-collar employment, social mobility, and political or nationalist ambition in much of colonial Africa. As interest in colonial schooling grew among Africans as a result, demand soon outstripped the supply of seats in primary schools. Budgetary and other constraints prevented governments from offering truly mass primary schooling, and they had no interest in making higher levels of education widely available since they feared that this could create an intellectual class, which could challenge the colonial system. Thus, only a tiny minority of students progressed to higher primary or secondary school, while standardized examinations ended the school careers of most. In addition, continued parental opposition kept some children out of school, while others could not attend because their families could not afford the fees that British colonial schools required. Through at least the late 1940s, therefore, colonial schools reached only a small percentage of school-aged children. In Nyasaland in 1935, for example, annual reports estimated that out of a total population of 1,608,023, only 170,617 children attended school, and that all but approximately 30,000 of these went to so-called 'bush schools', in which educated Africans taught others in their community outside the purview of the government.[20] Such statistics notwithstanding, colonial schooling had become a compelling dream, a mark of status, and an important economic resource for some parents and young people.

Memoirs and other sources reveal the excitement and longing with which some African children regarded the colonial school by the 1930s, if not before. Nigerian Nobel laureate Wole Soyinka, for example, wrote about his early fascination with the mission school where his father was headmaster. Before his third birthday, and long before he was officially old enough to register for school, he snuck into a classroom and sat next to his older sister. The teacher indulged him, saying he could come to class when he liked, but that he might not always want to do so. But Soyinka was undeterred. For him, the classroom was an 'inviting playroom', and he told the teacher, '"I shall come everyday"'. Similarly, in a memoir of his early life, renowned Kenyan novelist Ngũgĩ wa Thiong'o suggested that he had so wanted to go to school that he was left speechless when his mother raised the possibility. 'One evening', he wrote, 'my mother asked me: Would you like to go to school? It was in 1947. I can't recall the day or the month. I remember being wordless at first. But the question and the scene were forever engraved in my mind'.[21]

The appeal (indeed, the magic) of colonial education grew out of its clear connection to new economic opportunities, social mobility, and literacy. School leavers, especially those who had earned at least their primary-school certificates, were well placed to obtain low-level employment within the colonial economy, either in private industry or for the colonial administration. A 1924 annual report from a Church Missionary Society school in Kisimu, Kenya, is suggestive of the range of opportunities available to primary-school leavers. Describing the first gathering of the school's 'Old Boys'' club, the school principal observed that some alumni had stayed on at the school to teach, while the 'majority scatter seeking jobs as carpenters, clerks, builders and so forth'. Others had become chiefs.[22] Higher primary-school or secondary-school attendance opened doors to even more desirable jobs. Literate Africans derived regular salaries and, at least sometimes, a sense of importance from such positions, and they could use them to benefit their families and communities as well.[23]

Thus, Africans began to incorporate colonial education into their economic strategies. Sometimes, parents chose a variety of paths for their children in an attempt to ensure future economic stability for the family. Perhaps they sent one child to a colonial school, arranged an apprenticeship for another, and kept another at home. Gender and birth order often influenced such decisions, privileging the education of elder sons. The father of Tom Mboya, for example, strategized about education in this way. In his memoir, Mboya, who in the 1950s became an anti-colonial activist and political figure in Kenya, wrote that his father 'was determined to give me, and as many as possible of his other children, a good education; this was not only because he wanted us to have a better standard of life, but also because education constituted a safe investment against old age'. However, as a laborer on a sisal estate, Mboya's father could not afford equal education for all eight of his children. With support from their father and from scholarships, Tom and at least two of his brothers were able to attend university abroad, while their eldest sister went to school just long enough to achieve literacy.[24]

Colonial schooling itself could bestow prestige on families, especially if their children excelled. Children's conduct, successes, and failures had long reflected back on the families that raised them, and this idea seems to have transferred onto the colonial school. Additionally, families had to have resources to enroll their children in school (to cover the costs of school fees and supplies when necessary, clothing, transport, and the loss of their children's labor) and this too could elevate their status. This dynamic seems to be at work in Camara Laye's remembrances of his childhood in Guinea in the 1930s and early 1940s. Laye, who became a significant Guinean author and politician in his adulthood, suggested that pride in his educational accomplishments had changed the way a family member celebrated him during the public ceremonies leading up to his circumcision. His mother's co-wife joined the dancing while holding 'an exercise-book and a fountain-pen' above her head, instead of the customary hoe. Though uncomfortable with her action, Laye understood that his 'second mother was merely observing an old custom, and doing so with the best will in the world, since the exercise-book and the fountain-pen were the symbols of a profession which, in her eyes, was superior to that of a farmer or a mechanic'.[25]

Although most Africans initially rejected colonial schools and some continued to do so, these examples suggest that by the 1930s, at least some Africans from across the continent had come to value the education they provided.

Attending school became a dream of many young children, a motivation to make financial sacrifice, and a part of the economic strategy of many individuals and families. African parents and children *chose* whether or not to accept colonial education and, despite the ambivalence that still surrounded these decisions, they exercised agency in making them.

Politics and Protest

Once they began to accept the idea of colonial education, Africans also sought to increase access to schooling and to influence both the kind of education they received and the conditions under which they received it. As colonial governments moved toward policies designed to educate Africans in ways deemed most appropriate for their culture, lifestyle, and station in life, Africans called for more schools, and they pushed for a metropolitan-style curriculum. Boarding-school students demanded better food and living conditions at school. As nationalism became more important in the 1940s and 1950s, school strikes and protests reflected tensions in the larger society. By engaging in a politics of petition and protest, young people and their families shaped the process and experience of colonial education in Africa.

By the first decades of the twentieth century, colonial officials and educationists across the continent shared a commitment to so-called 'adapted' education. Adapted education emphasized vocational training and offered only a rudimentary academic one, an approach thought to match the future economic roles Africans would hold and aimed at keeping them grounded in their agricultural societies. For girls, this meant that schooling focused on domestic tasks (cooking, sewing, child-rearing, housework) with the idea that they would become educated wives and mothers and help introduce gradual, appropriate changes to their families and communities. Only a tiny minority of Africans, most believed, should have access to literary education and anything past the primary grades. French officials had begun to lay the groundwork for this approach by privileging agricultural and vocational training in rural schools beginning in the 1890s, and formalizing the practice in the 1903 education reforms for West Africa. Through the first few decades of the twentieth century, officials across French Africa continued to push for vocational and agricultural emphasis in colonial schools. In British colonies, officials embraced this approach following the tours of the Phelps-Stokes Commission in the 1920s, whose reports recommended the US-style industrial education model. These tours also resulted in the creation of Jeanes Schools, which paired agricultural education with community-development projects.[26]

While colonial governments touted adapted education as most useful and relevant to their colonial subjects, many Africans had other ideas. Viewing education as a pathway to white-collar employment and, at least sometimes, as a means of striving for equality with Europeans, they typically valued European-style literary education most highly. Adapted education thus became a flashpoint for debate and negotiation surrounding colonial schooling. In Senegal in 1919, for example, literate elites used the local press to lambast Inspector of Education Georges Hardy, who had worked to channel African students out of the small number of metropolitan-style schools and into schools offering adapted education. One editorial called upon Hardy to leave his post, threatening that if he did not, "'the voice of the people will purely and simply throw you out from French West Africa'".[27] This campaign prompted the Ministry of the Colonies to recall Hardy to France on administrative leave. In this colony, with a long history of French education and where some Africans could exercise citizenship rights, adapted education had little chance of garnering public support.

In British colonies, where primary schools used local vernaculars as languages of instruction and often did not teach English as an academic subject right away, the aversion to adapted education intersected with concerns about language. Realizing that they needed to learn English in order to maximize social mobility and employment opportunities, Africans strongly preferred literary education, and they sometimes made these preferences known. Residents of the village of Umchingwe, Southern Rhodesia, did so in the early 1930s when elders petitioned the government to establish a school and pledged annual financial support. Yet these men could not convince their junior relatives to contribute labor to the school's construction or to attend classes. Hoping to learn English as a pathway to new kinds of jobs, young men were not interested in the industrial education that the government had decided to offer, and the government ultimately withdrew support for the school. In certain areas of Kenya, on the other hand, opposition to colonial education models led Gikuyu people to create their own independent schools, which flourished until the British government banned them in 1952 due to the activities of the Land and Freedom Army.[28] In each of these cases, Africans acted in ways that truly impacted education in the colony.

In addition to demanding schools and seeking specific types of schooling, Africans also shaped colonial education by engaging in student protest. Such protests often aimed at improving living conditions (especially the quantity and quality of food) at boarding schools, and they sometimes took on a distinctly anti-colonial tone. Indeed, Michael O. West characterizes a 1947 strike among students at Dadaya mission school as an important turning point in Southern Rhodesian nationalism. Poor treatment of female students was the immediate catalyst for this strike, which formed part of the political training of strike participant and future nationalist leader Ndabaningi Sithole.[29] Similarly, Carol Summers shows that violence and scandal at King's College in Budo, Uganda in 1942 derived from increasing friction between educated elites, Ganda aristocrats, and colonial officials, and she makes the case that the fallout from this incident had a lingering impact on politics in the colony.[30]

African memoirists sometimes mentioned student protests at the institutions they attended. Ghanaian politician Joseph Appiah, for example, wrote about a days-long student protest that he helped organize in 1936, when he was prefect at Mfantsipim, an elite secondary school outside Cape Coast. Frustrated by a lack of variety in the food and by the patronizing attitude and 'veiled racism' of the principal's wife, who served as school nurse and presided over the dining hall, students threw food, refused to attend class, and marched through the streets of Cape Coast. Negotiations led to an agreement under which the school and its Methodist mission leadership pledged to address these issues, in part through the creation of 'a food committee of students' that would have some influence over the meals served.[31] Appiah also wrote about student reactions to a guest lecture delivered by 'a distinguished representative of the colonial power' who attempted to make the case that colonialism had been beneficial. This did not go over well, and students quickly began shouting so that the speaker could not be heard and left. Appiah viewed this as a successful act of protest that clearly communicated students' nationalism and 'hatred of colonialism'.[32]

The most vociferous resistance took place in South Africa, with the most famous incident being the Soweto uprising of 1976, in which thousands of black students protested against a law that required the use of Afrikaans as a language of instruction. In her memoir of her adult life, Sindiwe Magona, a South African educator and activist, described her experiences with the system of education available to blacks and her reactions to the uprising. Having 'experienced Bantu Education – as a student, as a teacher, as a parent', Magona felt that it was totally inadequate and was an ardent supporter of the students who fought to overturn the system in 1976. She explained their motivations this way: 'Young school-going Africans had had enough of the education given them. Desirous of change, they decided to take to the streets, to let the government know that they were ready for change'.[33]

These examples illustrate some of the ways that Africans engaged with the politics of colonial education. Since colonial schooling succeeded only insofar as children enrolled, attended regularly, and seemed receptive to at least some of what was on offer, this engagement had the potential to profoundly shape education. Indeed, by making demands of the colonial state, Africans affected day-to-day operations, openings and closures of school facilities, the philosophical approach to education, and education policy itself. Though their efforts often did not succeed in producing all desired reforms, they are important in that they demonstrate African choice and strategic action in response to an institution designed to facilitate colonial oppression.

Reflections on Colonial Schooling: Opportunity and Alienation

One of the most resounding critiques of colonial education, lodged in different ways by people ranging from colonial officials to African nationalists, to scholars, was that its content was disconnected from African experiences, and that its methods produced school leavers who felt alienated, uprooted, and distanced from their own culture. Undoubtedly, colonial schooling brought about cultural change in its students, created social distance within families, and allowed school leavers to circumvent existing structures of authority. Yet disruption could produce creative responses, and cultural change did not always lead to alienation. Indeed, as they reflected on the impact of colonial schooling, Africans came to many different conclusions. Taken together, the written and oral sources consulted for this chapter are suggestive of the complicated and ambivalent legacy of colonial education in Africa.

For some Africans who experienced colonial schools, an emphasis on the presumed superiority of European languages and cultures became the defining feature. Indeed, despite his excitement about beginning school as a young boy, Ngũgĩ wa Thiong'o ultimately viewed it much more unfavorably. As a novelist and theorist, Ngũgĩ became a well-known critic of the lingering cultural and linguistic influence of colonialism, and called on African writers to write in their own mother tongues. In an essay on this subject in his 1981 book, *Decolonising the Mind*, Ngũgĩ wrote evocatively of the Gikuyu language world in which he had played, listened to and told stories, worked, and learned as a young boy. After going to a colonial school, he wrote, 'this harmony was broken. The language of my education was no longer the language of my culture'. At school, teachers punished students for speaking Gikuyu, while English 'became the main determinant of a child's progress up the ladder of formal education'.[34] Thus, while he benefited from colonial schools and from his mastery of English in some very clear ways, his overwhelming sentiment was one of loss.[35]

Like Ngũgĩ, Senegalese writer Mariètou Mbaye Biléoma excelled in school but also found it profoundly alienating. As the only girl in her large family to attend the French school, which arrived in her remote village of Gouye only in the final years of colonial rule, her status as a schoolgirl complicated her struggle to feel loved and accepted by her family. The school and the language it taught, Biléoma wrote, 'upset a thousand worlds and a thousand beliefs hidden behind the baobab trees'.[36] Since there was no secondary school in her village, she had to live with relatives and friends in town in order to attend, experiences that further distanced her from her community and that ultimately made her feel her identity was 'torn in two'.[37] Thus, for Biléoma, colonial schooling became an insurmountable divide between herself and her family and community. Though she fully understood Western culture and the French language, ultimately living in Belgium, she felt that she never truly belonged anywhere.

Others focused on the lasting benefits they had received from attending school. For example, Fatima Massaquoi, a Vai aristocrat who attended a US mission school for girls outside Monrovia, Liberia, in the early 1920s, summed up her experiences in this way: 'Well, whatever was the cause of my pleasant stay in Bromley, I am deeply grateful for having been there, and I often find myself observing the moments fleeing away from me, pleading with them to linger, because of their beauty'.[38] Tom Mboya was critical of the patronizing and often racist attitudes of some of the missionaries and teachers he encountered in the schools he attended, but he also recognized that schooling had given him important opportunities and experiences that he used in his later work with trade unions and in politics. School had encouraged him to travel, had allowed him to become a leader of the student body, and had helped him 'become determined to work for my people'.[39] And Joseph Appiah remarked that, decades later, he remained happy with the education he had received at Mfantsipim. The school, he wrote, 'had filled me with some knowledge and therefore some amount of power; it had taught me to stand up nobly for the truth and for what I believed to be right; but above all, Mfantsipim had taught me that the fear of God was, and still is, the beginning of all wisdom'.[40]

Similarly, several retired teachers whom I interviewed in Senegal in 2007 stressed the benefits of the colonial education they had received, and spoke with pride of their work as teachers for the colonial system. Madiké Wade, for example, reflected on the importance of colonial education in preparing him for his roles as a schoolteacher and as an activist in the Rassemblement Démocratique Africaine (RDA) political party in the 1940s. By spending vacation time helping people learn to read and write, he was able to combine teaching with his work for the RDA youth wing. This was significant because, as he put it, literacy was 'one of the factors in liberation'.[41] Wade thus suggested that colonial schooling connected him to his community, which he felt called to serve. Ousman Camara, who completed his training at Senegal's Ecole Normale William Ponty in the 1930s, also characterized his education and teaching job as sources of connection to people. Once he and his peers had obtained jobs from the French administration, Camara said, 'we began to work, to earn a living, to establish a household, to help our parents, to help our brothers'. Their relatives were proud of their successes, he continued, and would tell them 'that truly we had honored them'.[42] Both Wade and Camara seemed to see colonial education as a means of working for other people, and not as a source of alienation.

These examples show that colonial schooling prompted a wide range of responses from Africans. In attempting to convince Africans of the superiority of a foreign culture, language, and history, colonial education had the potential to make them more critical of their own society. In encouraging them to dress, eat, measure time, and behave differently, schools often created cultural differences between students and their families. And in giving them access to new kinds of credentials, opportunities, and networks, colonial education sometimes encouraged young school leavers to challenge social hierarchies that placed elders at the top. On the other hand, schooling prepared Africans to participate in the colonial economy in ways that could benefit their families, their communities, and themselves. It gave them tools with which to criticize colonialism and to push for change. And it trained many of the leaders of anti-colonial movements across the continent. In itself, therefore, colonial education was an ambivalent cultural and political force, and African actors shaped its impacts in important ways.

Conclusion

In the end, educated Africans turned the intent of colonial education (to train loyal subjects and efficient workers for the colonial state) on its head, using the literacy, language, skills, and status they had gained in colonial schools for their own ends. Crucially, educated Africans were well equipped to question, petition, and criticize the colonial state. Able, like Madiké Wade, to use their literacy for the benefit of their people, many became involved with anti-colonial politics, and most of Africa's nationalist leaders were products of colonial schools, as were many in the first generation of public and private leaders in independent Africa. African actors were able to leverage their education against the colonial system that had provided it. At the same time, although it never became mass education, colonial education left behind numerous more troubling legacies, such as uneven infrastructure, Eurocentric curricula, pedagogies that stressed rote learning, and a public perception that literary education was the best route to social mobility.[43] The process of decolonizing this ambivalent educational system would extend well beyond political independence.

Notes

1. Chinua Achebe, "The Education of a British-Protected Child," in *The Education of a British-Protected Child: Essays* (New York: Alfred Knopf, 2009), 3–24, especially 4, 7, 21. Achebe gave an earlier version of this essay as a lecture at Cambridge University in 1993.
2. Walter Rodney, *How Europe Underdeveloped Africa* (Washington, DC: Howard University Press, 1982), 238–61, quotation on 241. See also Jean Suret-Canale, *French Colonialism in Tropical Africa, 1900–1945*, trans. Till Gottheiner (London: C. Hurst, 1971), 371–91; B. Olatunji Oloruntimehin, "Education for Colonial Dominance in French West Africa from 1900 to the Second World War," *Journal of the Historical Society of Nigeria* 7, no. 2 (1974): 347–56; and A. Adu Boahen, "Colonialism in Africa: Its Impact and Significance," in *General History of Africa*, Vol. 7, *Africa under Colonial Domination 1880–1935*, ed. A. Adu Boahen (Paris: UNESCO/London: Heinemann/Berkeley: University of California Press, 1985), 801–2.
3. Denise Bouche, "L'Enseignement dans les territoires français de l'afrique occidentale de 1817 à 1920," (PhD diss., Université de Paris I, 1974). For overviews of the historiography, see Marie-France Lange, "Vers de nouvelles recherches en éducation," *Cahiers d'Études Africaines* 43, no. 169/170 (2003): 7–17; Clive Whitehead, "The Historiography of British Imperial

Education Policy, Part II: Africa and the Rest of the Colonial Empire," *History of Education* 34, no. 4 (2005): 441–54.
4. There are certainly exceptions to this trend. In a 1963 article, for example, J.F. Ade Ajayi explored how Africans helped ensure the literary quality of secondary schooling in colonial Nigeria. See J.F. Ade Ajayi, "The Development of Secondary Grammar School Education in Nigeria," *Journal of the Historical Society of Nigeria* 2, no. 4 (1963): 517–35.
5. Meghan Healy-Clancy, *A World of Their Own: A History of South African Women's Education* (Charlottesville: University of Virginia Press, 2014). See also: Kathleen Sheldon, "'I Studied with the Nuns, Learning to Make Blouses': Gender Ideology and Colonial Education in Mozambique," *International Journal of African Historical Studies* 31, no. 3 (1998): 595–625; Daniel J. Paracka Jr., *The Athens of West Africa: A History of International Education at Fourah Bay College, Freetown, Sierra Leone* (New York: Routledge, 2003); and Terri Ochiagha, *Achebe and Friends at Umuahia: The Making of a Literary Elite* (Suffolk: James Currey, 2015). Narrative histories of schools and education systems have also continued to appear. See, for example: R.J. Zvobgo, *Colonialism and Education in Zimbabwe* (Harare, Zimbabwe: Sapes Books, 1994); Simphiwe A. Hlatshwayo, *Education and Independence: Education in South Africa, 1658–1988* (Westport, CT: Greenwood Press, 2000); and J.C. Ssekamwa and S.M.E. Lugumba, *A History of Education in East Africa*, 2nd ed. (Kampala: Fountain Publishers, 2001).
6. P.S. Zachernuk, "African History and Imperial Culture in Colonial Nigerian Schools," *Africa* 68, no. 4 (1998): 484–505; Gail P. Kelly, "Colonialism, Indigenous Society, and School Practices: French West Africa and Indochina, 1918–1938," in *Education and the Colonial Experience*, ed. Philip G. Altbach and Gail P. Kelly, 2nd rev ed. (New York: Advent Books, Inc., 1991), 9–32; and Gail Paradise Kelly, "Learning to Be Marginal: Schooling in Interwar French West Africa," in *French Colonial Education: Essays on Vietnam and West Africa*, ed. David H. Kelly (New York: AMS Press, Inc., 2000), 189–208.
7. Michael O. West, "Ndabaningi Sithole, Garfield Todd and the Dadaya School Strike of 1947," *Journal of Southern African Studies* 18, no. 2 (1992): 297–316; Carol Summers, "'Subterranean Evil' and 'Tumultuous Riot' in Buganda: Authority and Alienation at King's College, Budo, 1942," *Journal of African History* 47 (2006): 93–113; Sybille Küster, "'Book Learning' versus 'Adapted Education': The Impact of Phelps-Stokesism on Colonial Education Systems in Central Africa in the Interwar Period," *Paedagogica Historica* 43, no. 1 (2007): 79–97; and Mark Hunter, "The Bond of Education: Gender, the Value of Children, and the Making of Umlazi Township in 1960s South Africa," *Journal of African History* 55 (2014): 467–90. For analysis of Muslim efforts to protect their own religious education, see: Louis Brenner, *Controlling Knowledge: Religion, Power, and Schooling in a West African Muslim Society* (Bloomington: Indiana University Press, 2001), chaps. 2–3; Cheikh Anta Babou, *Fighting the Greater Jihad: Amadu Bamba and the Founding of the Muridiyya of Senegal, 1853–1913* (Athens: Ohio University Press, 2007), chap. 7; and Rudolph T. Ware III, *The Walking Qur'an: Islamic Education, Embodied Knowledge, and History in West Africa* (Chapel Hill: University of North Carolina Press, 2014), chap. 4. For an overview of recent research on

colonial education in Africa, see Carol Summers, "Education and Literacy," in *The Oxford Handbook of Modern African History*, ed. John Parker and Richard Reid (Oxford: Oxford University Press, 2013), 319–37.

8. Carol Summers, *Colonial Lessons: Africans' Education in Southern Rhodesia, 1918–1940* (Portsmouth, NH: Heinemann, 2002), 200–1.
9. Kelly M. Duke Bryant, *Education as Politics: Colonial Schooling and Political Debate in Senegal, 1850s–1914* (Madison: University of Wisconsin Press, 2015).
10. Helen Kitchen, ed., *The Educated African: A Country-by-Country Survey of Educational Development in Africa*, compiled by Ruth Sloan Associates (New York: Frederick A. Praeger, Inc., 1962), 326, 387–88; Gladys Harding, "Education in Freetown," in *Freetown: A Symposium*, ed. Christopher Fyfe and Eldred Jones (Freetown: Sierra Leone University Press, 1968), 143–46; Prosser Gifford and Timothy C. Weiskel, "African Education in a Colonial Context: French and British Styles," in *France and Britain in Africa: Imperial Rivalry and Colonial Rule*, ed. Prosser Gifford and Wm. Roger Louis (New Haven, CT: Yale University Press, 1971), 669–73, 678–82; David E. Gardinier, "Schooling in the States of Equatorial Africa," *Canadian Journal of African Studies* 8, no. 3 (1974): 518; C. Magbaily Fyle, *Historical Dictionary of Sierra Leone* (Lanham, Maryland: Scarecrow Press, Inc., 2006), xviii–xix; and Duke Bryant, *Education as Politics*, 14–17.
11. Hanns Vischer, "Native Education in German Africa," *Journal of the Royal African Society* 14, no. 54 (1915): 123–42; Gifford and Weiskell, "African Education in a Colonial Context," 673–74; Oloruntimehin, "Education for Colonial Dominance in French West Africa from 1900 to the Second World War," 350; David E. Gardinier, "The Impact of French Education on Africa, 1817–1960," *Proceedings of the Meeting of the French Colonial Historical Society* 5 (1980): 72; Ungina Ndoma, "Belgian Politics and Linguistic Policy in Congolese Schools, 1885–1914," *Transafrican Journal of History* 13 (1984): 147–48; Bob W. White, "Talk about School: Education and the Colonial Project in French and British Africa (1860–1960)," *Comparative Education* 32, no. 1 (1996): 9–25; and Sheldon, "I Studied with the Nuns, Learning to Make Blouses," 596–98.
12. Gifford and Weiskell, "African Education in a Colonial Context," 674–75; Gardinier, "Impact," 73; Ndoma, "Belgian Politics and Linguistic Policy in Congolese Schools, 1885–1914," 149.
13. Gifford and Weiskell, "African Education in a Colonial Context," 701–3; Andrew E. Barnes, "Western Education in Colonial Africa," in *Africa*, Vol. 3, *Colonial Africa, 1885–1939*, ed. Toyin Falola (Durham, NC: Carolina Academic Press, 2002), 145–47.
14. Kitchen, ed., *The Educated African: A Country-by-Country Survey of Educational Development in Africa*, 131–32, 148–49, 164, 192–201, 236–37, 267–70; Gardinier, "The Impact of French Education on Africa, 1817–1960," 75–76; Boahen, "Colonialism in Africa," 800; Barnes, "Western Education in Colonial Africa," 153–54; Whitehead, "The Historiography of British Imperial Education Policy, Part II," 445–46; Michael Omolewa, "Programmed for Failure?: The Colonial Factor in the Mass Literacy Campaign in Nigeria,

1946–1956," *Paedagogica Historica* 44, no. 1–2 (2008): 107–21; and Summers, "Education and Literacy," 326.
15. I. Konaré to Directeur des Affaires Politiques, December 10, 1893, J30, Archives Nationales du Sénégal (ANS, Dakar, Senegal).
16. Colonie du Sénégal, Statistiques de l'instruction publique, 1910, AOF/X/1, Archives Nationales d'Outre-Mer (ANOM, Aix-en-Provence, France); Tableau général par cercles des écoles maraboutiques du Sénégal, 1912, AOF/X/6, ANOM. The Qur'an school figure likely vastly underestimates actual attendance, since officials had a notoriously difficult time collecting data on these schools that they did not control.
17. Susiwe Bengu, "Testimony of a School Girl," in *Women Writing Africa: The Southern Region*, ed. M.J. Daymond et al. (New York: Feminist Press at the City University of New York, 2003), 134–35.
18. James Frederick Schön and Samuel Crowther, *The Journals of the Rev. James Frederick Schön and Mr. Samuel Crowther* (London: Hatchard and Son, 1842), 384; Cissé Amadou to Gouverneur, August 24, 1906, 1G28, ANS.
19. See, for example, Yves Hazemann, "Un Outil de la conquête coloniale: l'école des Otages de Saint-Louis (1855–1871; 1892–1903)," *Cahiers du C.R.A.* 5 (1987): 135–60.
20. W. Bryant Mumford and B.N. Parker, "Education in British African Dependencies: A Review of the 1935 Annual Reports on Native Education in Nyasaland, N. Rhodesia, Tanganyika, Uganda, Gold Coast, Nigeria and Sierra Leone," *Journal of the Royal African Society* 36, no. 142 (1937): 22.
21. Wole Soyinka, *Aké: The Years of Childhood* (New York: Vintage Books, 1989), 24–25; Ngũgĩ wa Thiong'o, *Dreams in a Time of War: A Childhood Memoir* (New York: Pantheon Books, 2010), 59. For other examples, see: J. Mutuku Nzioki, "Thorns in the Grass: The Story of a Kamba Boy," in *East African Childhood: Three Versions*, ed. Lorene K. Fox (Nairobi: Oxford University Press, 1967), 106; and Lily P. Moya to The Organizer, Non-European Section [Mabel Palmer], February 20, 1949, in *Not Either an Experimental Doll: The Separate Worlds of Three South African Women*, ed. Shula Marks (Bloomington: Indiana University Press, 1987), 60.
22. CMS Kavirondo Annual Report and Maseno Central School Report, 1924. Available through: Adam Matthew, Marlborough, *Empire Online*, accessed June 6, 2016 http://www.empire.amdigital.co.uk.ezproxy.rowan.edu/Documents/Details/CMS Kavirondo Annual Report Masuo Central School.
23. Summers, *Colonial Lessons*, chaps. 3 and 6; Derek R. Peterson, *Creative Writing: Translation, Bookkeeping, and the Work of Imagination in Colonial Kenya* (Portsmouth, NH: Heinemann, 2004); Benjamin N. Lawrance, Emily Lynn Osborn, and Richard Roberts, eds., *Intermediaries, Interpreters, and Clerks: African Employees in the Making of Colonial Africa* (Madison: University of Wisconsin Press, 2006); and Karin Barber, ed., *Africa's Hidden Histories: Everyday Literacy and Making the Self* (Bloomington: Indiana University Press, 2006).
24. Tom Mboya, *Freedom and After* (Boston: Little, Brown and Company, 1963), 6–7, 16–18.
25. Camara Laye, *The African Child*, trans. James Kirkup (Glasgow: Fontana Books, 1954), 97–98. On Laye, see also Eloise A. Brière, "*L'Enfant noir* by

Camara Laye: Strategies in Teaching an African Text," *French Review* 55, no. 6 (1982): 804–10. For additional examples, see: Nafissatou Diallo, *De Tilène au Plateau: une enfance dakaroise* (Dakar: Les Nouvelles Éditions Africaines du Sénégal, 2007), 34–50, 57; and Joseph Appiah, *Joe Appiah: The Autobiography of an African Patriot* (New York: Praeger, 1990), 78.

26. Gifford and Weiskell, "African Education in a Colonial Context," 687–94, 699–703; Oloruntimehin, "Education for Colonial Dominance in French West Africa from 1900 to the Second World War," 349–50, 354–55; Sheldon, "I Studied with the Nuns, Learning to Make Blouses," 614; Tony Chafer, "Teaching Africans to Be French?: France's 'Civilising Mission' and the Establishment of a Public Education System in French West Africa, 1903–1930," *Africa* 56, no. 2 (2001): 190–209; Barnes, "Western Education in Colonial Africa," 147–49; Küster, 79–88; Shoko Yamada, "Educational Borrowing as Negotiation: Re-examining the Influence of the American Black Industrial Education Model on British Colonial Education in Africa," *Comparative Education* 44, no. 1 (2008): 21–37; and Summers, "Education and Literacy," 322–25.

27. *La Démocratie*, February 9, 1919, quoted in Gifford and Weiskell, 692–93.

28. A.E. Afigbo, "The Social Repercussions of Colonial Rule: The New Social Structures," in *General History of Africa*, Vol. 7, *Africa under Colonial Domination 1880–1935*, ed. A. Adu Boahen (Paris: UNESCO/London: Heinemann/Berkeley: University of California Press, 1985), 491; Barnes, "Western Education in Colonial Africa," 147–48; and Summers, *Colonial Lessons*, chap. 2.

29. West, "Ndabaningi Sithole, Garfield Todd and the Dadaya School Strike of 1947".

30. Summers, "'Subterranean Evil'".

31. Appiah, *Joe Appiah: The Autobiography of an African Patriot*, 88–96.

32. Ibid., 40–42.

33. Sindiwe Magona, *Forced to Grow* (New York: Interlink Books, 1998), 149, 158.

34. Ngũgĩ wa Thiong'o, "The Language of African Literature," in *The Post-Colonial Studies Reader*, ed. Bill Ashcroft, Gareth Griffiths, and Helen Tiffin (London: Routledge, 1995), 287–88.

35. Ngũgĩ's ambivalence toward colonial schooling is also apparent in his fiction. Despite the sense of promise in *Weep Not, Child* and *The River Between*, for example, in neither novel does education save the protagonist from tragic downfall or fully heal rifts in the society. Ngũgĩ wa Thiong'o, *Weep Not, Child* (New York: Penguin Books, 2012); and Ngũgĩ wa Thiong'o, *The River Between* (Johannesburg: Heinemann, 1965).

36. Ken Bugul [Mariètou Mbaye Biléoma], *The Abandoned Baobab: The Autobiography of a Senegalese Woman*, trans. Marjolijn de Jager (New York: Lawrence Hill Books, 1991), 98. See also Marilyn Slutzky Zucker, "On Teaching 'The Abandoned Baobab: A Senegalese Woman's Autobiography,'" *Women's Studies Quarterly* 25, no. 3/4 (1997): 127–34. Ken Bugul is a penname, which translates from the Wolof as "the person no one wants." Her experiences in Belgium were even more alienating and destructive, and she ultimately became involved in drugs and prostitution before returning to Senegal. For another

example of alienation, also by a Senegalese woman, see Mariama Bâ, 1943, "My Little Country," in *Women Writing Africa: West Africa and the Sahel*, ed. Esi Sutherland-Addy and Aminata Diaw (New York: Feminist Press at the City University of New York, 2005), 186–88.
37. Bugul, *The Abandoned Baobab*, 123.
38. Fatima Massaquoi, *The Autobiography of an African Princess*, ed. Vivian Seton, Konrad Tuchscherer, and Arthur Abraham (New York: Palgrave Macmillan, 2013), 104.
39. Mboya, *Freedom and After*, 16, 18–20.
40. Appiah, *Joe Appiah: The Autobiography of an African Patriot*, 99.
41. Madiké Wade (retired teacher), interview by Kelly Duke Bryant, Saint-Louis, Senegal, November 28, 2007.
42. Ousman Camara (retired teacher), interview by Kelly Duke Bryant, Saint-Louis, Senegal, November 27, 2007.
43. For analysis of the legacies of colonial schooling in the period immediately following independence, see: Philip Foster, *Education and Social Change in Ghana* (Chicago: The University of Chicago Press, 1965); and David B. Abernethy, *The Political Dilemma of Popular Education: An African Case* (Stanford, CA: Stanford University Press, 1969).

Bibliography

Abernethy, David B. *The Political Dilemma of Popular Education: An African Case*. Stanford, CA: Stanford University Press, 1969.

Achebe, Chinua. "The Education of a British-Protected Child." In *The Education of a British-Protected Child: Essays*, 3–24. New York: Alfred Knopf, 2009.

Afigbo, A.E. "The Social Repercussions of Colonial Rule: The New Social Structures." In *General History of Africa*, Vol. 7, *Africa under Colonial Domination 1880–1935*, edited by A. Adu Boahen, 487–507. Paris: UNESCO/London: Heinemann/Berkeley: University of California Press, 1985.

Ajayi, J.F. Ade. "The Development of Secondary Grammar School Education in Nigeria." *Journal of the Historical Society of Nigeria* 2, no. 4 (1963): 517–35.

Appiah, Joseph. *Joe Appiah: The Autobiography of an African Patriot*. New York: Praeger, 1990.

Babou, Cheikh Anta. *Fighting the Greater Jihad: Amadu Bamba and the Founding of the Muridiyya of Senegal, 1853–1913*. Athens: Ohio University Press, 2007.

Barber, Karin, ed. *Africa's Hidden Histories: Everyday Literacy and Making the Self*. Bloomington: Indiana University Press, 2006.

Barnes, Andrew E. "Western Education in Colonial Africa." In *Africa*, Vol. 3, *Colonial Africa, 1885–1939*, edited by Toyin Falola, 139–56. Durham, NC: Carolina Academic Press, 2002.

Boahen, A. Adu. "Colonialism in Africa: Its Impact and Significance." In *General History of Africa*, Vol. 7, *Africa under Colonial Domination 1880–1935*, edited by A. Adu Boahen, 782–809. Paris: UNESCO/London: Heinemann/Berkeley: University of California Press, 1985.

Bouche, Denise. "L'Enseignement dans les territoires français de l'afrique occidentale de 1817 à 1920." PhD diss., Université de Paris I, 1974.

Brenner, Louis. *Controlling Knowledge: Religion, Power, and Schooling in a West African Muslim Society.* Bloomington: Indiana University Press, 2001.

Brière, Eloise A. "*L'Enfant noir* by Camara Laye: Strategies in Teaching an African Text." *French Review* 55, no. 6 (1982): 804–10.

Bugul, Ken. *The Abandoned Baobab: The Autobiography of a Senegalese Woman.* Translated by Marjolijn de Jager. New York: Lawrence Hill Books, 1991.

Chafer, Tony. "Teaching Africans to Be French?: France's 'Civilising Mission' and the Establishment of a Public Education System in French West Africa, 1903–1930." *Africa* 56, no. 2 (2001): 190–209.

Daymond, M.J., et al., eds. *Women Writing Africa: The Southern Region.* New York: Feminist Press at the City University of New York, 2003.

Diallo, Nafissatou. *De Tilène au Plateau: une enfance dakaroise.* Dakar: Les Nouvelles Éditions Africaines du Sénégal, 2007.

Duke Bryant, Kelly M. *Education as Politics: Colonial Schooling and Political Debate in Senegal, 1850s–1914.* Madison: University of Wisconsin Press, 2015.

Foster, Philip. *Education and Social Change in Ghana.* Chicago: The University of Chicago Press, 1965.

Fyle, C. Magbaily. *Historical Dictionary of Sierra Leone.* Lanham, MD: Scarecrow Press, Inc., 2006.

———. "Schooling in the States of Equatorial Africa." *Canadian Journal of African Studies* 8, no. 3 (1974): 517–38.

Gardinier, David E. "The Impact of French Education on Africa, 1817–1960." *Proceedings of the Meeting of the French Colonial Historical Society* 5 (1980): 70–82.

Gifford, Prosser, and Timothy C. Weiskel. "African Education in a Colonial Context: French and British Styles." In *France and Britain in Africa: Imperial Rivalry and Colonial Rule,* edited by Prosser Gifford and Wm. Roger Louis, 663–711. New Haven, CT: Yale University Press, 1971.

Harding, Gladys. "Education in Freetown." In *Freetown: A Symposium,* edited by Christopher Fyfe and Eldred Jones. Freetown: Sierra Leone University Press, 1968.

Hazemann, Yves. "Un Outil de la conquête coloniale: l'école des Otages de Saint-Louis (1855–1871; 1892–1903)." *Cahiers du C.R.A.* 5 (1987): 135–60.

Healy-Clancy, Meghan. *A World of Their Own: A History of South African Women's Education.* Charlottesville: University of Virginia Press, 2014.

Hlatshwayo, Simphiwe A. *Education and Independence: Education in South Africa, 1658–1988.* Westport, CT: Greenwood Press, 2000.

Hunter, Mark. "The Bond of Education: Gender, the Value of Children, and the Making of Umlazi Township in 1960s South Africa." *Journal of African History* 55 (2014): 467–90.

Kelly, Gail P. "Colonialism, Indigenous Society, and School Practices: French West Africa and Indochina, 1918–1938." In *Education and the Colonial Experience,* edited by Philip G. Altbach and Gail P. Kelly, 2nd rev ed., 9–32. New York: Advent Books, Inc., 1991.

———. "Learning to Be Marginal: Schooling in Interwar French West Africa." In *French Colonial Education: Essays on Vietnam and West Africa,* edited by David H. Kelly, 189–208. New York: AMS Press, Inc., 2000.

Kitchen, Helen, ed. *The Educated African: A Country-by-Country Survey of Educational Development in Africa.* Compiled by Ruth Sloan Associates. New York: Frederick A. Praeger, Inc., 1962.

Küster, Sybille. "'Book Learning' Versus 'Adapted Education': The Impact of Phelps-Stokesism on Colonial Education Systems in Central Africa in the Interwar Period." *Paedagogica Historica* 43, no. 1 (2007): 79–97.

Lange, Marie-France. "Vers de nouvelles recherches en education." *Cahiers d'Études Africaines* 43, no. 169/170 (2003): 7–17.

Lawrance, Benjamin N., Emily Lynn Osborn, and Richard Roberts, eds. *Intermediaries, Interpreters, and Clerks: African Employees in the Making of Colonial Africa*. Madison: University of Wisconsin Press, 2006.

Laye, Camara. *The African Child*. Translated by James Kirkup. Glasgow: Fontana Books, 1954.

Magona, Sindiwe. *Forced to Grow*. New York: Interlink Books, 1998.

Marks, Shula, ed. *Not Either an Experimental Doll: The Separate Worlds of Three South African Women*. Bloomington: Indiana University Press, 1987.

Massaquoi, Fatima. *The Autobiography of an African Princess*, edited by Vivian Seton, Konrad Tuchscherer, and Arthur Abraham. New York: Palgrave Macmillan, 2013.

Mboya, Tom. *Freedom and After*. Boston: Little, Brown and Company, 1963.

Mumford, W. Bryant, and B.N. Parker. "Education in British African Dependencies: A Review of the 1935 Annual Reports on Native Education in Nyasaland, N. Rhodesia, Tanganyika, Uganda, Gold Coast, Nigeria and Sierra Leone." *Journal of the Royal African Society* 36, no. 142 (1937): 17–32.

Ndoma, Ungina. "Belgian Politics and Linguistic Policy in Congolese Schools, 1885–1914." *Transafrican Journal of History* 13 (1984): 146–56.

———. *The River Between*. Johannesburg: Heinemann, 1965.

———. "The Language of African Literature." In *The Post-Colonial Studies Reader*, edited by Bill Ashcroft, Gareth Griffiths, and Helen Tiffin, 285–90. London: Routledge, 1995.

Ngũgĩ wa Thiong'o. *Dreams in a Time of War: A Childhood Memoir*. New York: Pantheon Books, 2010.

———. *Weep Not, Child*. New York: Penguin Books, 2012.

Nzioki, J. Mutuku. "Thorns in the Grass: The Story of a Kamba Boy." In *East African Childhood: Three Versions*, edited by Lorene K. Fox, 77–137. Nairobi: Oxford University Press, 1967.

Ochiagha, Terri. *Achebe and Friends at Umuahia: The Making of a Literary Elite*. Suffolk: James Currey, 2015.

Oloruntimehin, B. Olatunji. "Education for Colonial Dominance in French West Africa from 1900 to the Second World War." *Journal of the Historical Society of Nigeria* 7, no. 2 (1974): 347–56.

Omolewa, Michael. "Programmed for Failure?: The Colonial Factor in the Mass Literacy Campaign in Nigeria, 1946–1956." *Paedagogica Historica* 44, nos. 1–2 (2008): 107–21.

Paracka, Daniel J., Jr. *The Athens of West Africa: A History of International Education at Fourah Bay College, Freetown, Sierra Leone*. New York: Routledge, 2003.

Peterson, Derek R. *Creative Writing: Translation, Bookkeeping, and the Work of Imagination in Colonial Kenya*. Portsmouth, NH: Heinemann, 2004.

Rodney, Walter. *How Europe Underdeveloped Africa*. Washington, DC: Howard University Press, 1982.

Schön, James Frederick, and Samuel Crowther. *The Journals of the Rev. James Frederick Schön and Mr. Samuel Crowther*. London: Hatchard and Son, 1842.

Sénégal et dépendances: Culte, instruction publique, beaux-arts. Fonds Ministériels. Archives Nationales d'Outre-Mer, Aix-en-Provence, France.

Série J: Enseignement jusqu'en 1920. Fonds AOF. Archives Nationales de la République du Sénégal, Dakar, Senegal.
Sheldon, Kathleen. "'I Studied with the Nuns, Learning to Make Blouses': Gender Ideology and Colonial Education in Mozambique." *International Journal of African Historical Studies* 31, no. 3 (1998): 595–625.
Sous-Série 1G: Enseignement. Fonds Sénégal Colonial. Archives Nationales de la République du Sénégal, Dakar, Senegal.
Soyinka, Wole. *Aké: The Years of Childhood.* New York: Vintage Books, 1989.
Ssekamwa, J.C. and S.M.E. Lugumba. *A History of Education in East Africa*, 2nd ed. Kampala: Fountain Publishers, 2001.
Summers, Carol. *Colonial Lessons: Africans' Education in Southern Rhodesia, 1918–1940.* Portsmouth, NH: Heinemann, 2002.
———. "'Subterranean Evil' and 'Tumultuous Riot' in Buganda: Authority and Alienation at King's College, Budo, 1942." *Journal of African History* 47 (2006): 93–113.
———. "Education and Literacy." In *The Oxford Handbook of Modern African History*, edited by John Parker and Richard Reid, 319–37. Oxford: Oxford University Press, 2013.
Suret-Canale, Jean. *French Colonialism in Tropical Africa, 1900–1945.* Translated by Till Gottheiner. London: C. Hurst, 1971.
Sutherland-Addy, Esi, and Aminata Diaw, eds. *Women Writing Africa: West Africa and the Sahel.* New York: Feminist Press at the City University of New York, 2005.
Vischer, Hanns. "Native Education in German Africa." *Journal of the Royal African Society* 14, no. 54 (1915): 123–42.
Ware, Rudolph T., III. *The Walking Qur'an: Islamic Education, Embodied Knowledge, and History in West Africa.* Chapel Hill: University of North Carolina Press, 2014.
West, Michael O. "Ndabaningi Sithole, Garfield Todd and the Dadaya School Strike of 1947." *Journal of Southern African Studies* 18, no. 2 (1992): 297–316.
White, Bob W. "Talk about School: Education and the Colonial Project in French and British Africa (1860–1960)." *Comparative Education* 32, no. 1 (1996): 9–25.
Whitehead, Clive. "The Historiography of British Imperial Education Policy, Part II: Africa and the Rest of the Colonial Empire." *History of Education* 34, no. 4 (2005): 441–54.
Yamada, Shoko. "Educational Borrowing as Negotiation: Re-examining the Influence of the American Black Industrial Education Model on British Colonial Education in Africa." *Comparative Education* 44, no. 1 (2008): 21–37.
Zachernuk, P.S. "African History and Imperial Culture in Colonial Nigerian Schools." *Africa* 68, no. 4 (1998): 484–505.
Zucker, Marilyn Slutzky. "On Teaching 'The Abandoned Baobab: A Senegalese Woman's Autobiography.'" *Women's Studies Quarterly* 25, no. 3/4 (1997): 127–34.
Zvobgo, R.J. *Colonialism and Education in Zimbabwe.* Harare, Zimbabwe: Sapes Books, 1994.

CHAPTER 11

Health and Medicine in Colonial Society

Matthew M. Heaton

This chapter examines the effects of European colonialism in Africa on the health of Africans and the development of medical frameworks for promoting health and combating illness. We will focus on four main themes within the history of health and medicine in colonial Africa. First, we will look at the health consequences of colonial occupation and colonial economies on African subjects. The second section will examine the ways that colonial administrative priorities and racism affected how European medicine was introduced and practiced in African colonies. Following this, we will look at African responses to colonial health policies and medical practices, emphasizing the wide variety of responses overall as well as the ways that issues of health and medicine became key features of anti-colonial resistance in particular. The final section will explain major developments in the expansion of Western biomedical facilities in the post-Second World War era, as nationalist movements pushed for greater autonomy and European administrations began to prepare African colonies for independence.

Through these themes, this chapter will explore specifically the ways that colonialism affected the health of African peoples as well as the ways that European medicine became intertwined with the colonial experience for both colonizer and colonized. This chapter therefore allows us to see issues of health and medicine not just in terms of the spread of germs and the scientific development of medical treatments, but, just as importantly, the limitations of medical science in colonial Africa and the broader dynamics of colonial

M.M. Heaton (✉)
Department of History, Virginia Tech, Blacksburg, VA, USA

© The Author(s) 2018
M.S. Shanguhyia and T. Falola (eds.),
The Palgrave Handbook of African Colonial and Postcolonial History,
https://doi.org/10.1057/978-1-137-59426-6_11

society that affected the ways that people (African and European) thought about the role of health and medicine.

HEALTH CONSEQUENCES OF COLONIAL OCCUPATION

A variety of health-related factors contributed significantly to European powers' ability to colonize most of Africa in the late nineteenth and early twentieth centuries. Innovations in European medical technology combined with advances in military technology to give Europeans the 'tools' needed to conquer African territories. At the same time, many parts of the African continent were experiencing medical and environmental catastrophes that made them vulnerable to European conquest at exactly the time that the Scramble took place. The European conquest of Africa was itself an extremely violent process which killed large numbers of Africans and displaced many more.

Before the mid-1800s, Europeans had referred to tropical Africa as the 'white man's grave' because the likelihood of surviving an extended stay in the region was quite low. For example, 48% of the European soldiers who served between 1819 and 1836 in Sierra Leone lost their lives. Two-thirds of the soldiers in Gold Coast died between 1823 and 1827. Overall, in the early nineteenth century, '77 percent of the white soldiers sent to West Africa perished, 21 percent became invalids, and only 2 percent were ultimately found fit for future service'.[1] The main reason was the lack of immunity that Europeans had to a variety of tropical diseases and the lack of medical knowledge of how to prevent or treat these diseases effectively.

While infectious diseases such as typhoid, yellow fever, and dengue fever contributed to the high death rates of Europeans in tropical Africa, the biggest killer by far was malaria. Efforts to treat malaria medically had existed for a long time. Jesuit missionaries in the 1600s had noticed that peoples of South America staved off malaria with the bark of cinchona trees, and it had been used by Europeans ever since. But several factors prevented its overall effectiveness. Cinchona trees grew only in the Andes, so supply was low, costs high, and the product had often been adulterated or deteriorated by the time it reached European consumers. Its efficacy was also somewhat suspect because it was used for a wide variety of 'fevers', as diagnostic distinctions between malaria, yellow fever, and others were not well known at the time. Finally, the concentrations of the active ingredient in cinchona bark (quinine) were low. It was not until 1820 that two French chemists effectively isolated the quinine alkaloid and began producing it in higher concentrations. Even then, it was another 20 years before Europeans realized that quinine best prevented malaria if it was taken as a preventative *before* exposure rather than as a treatment once fever had set in. Even with all of this knowledge about quinine by the 1840s, Europeans did not understand the cause of malaria. It was not until 1880 that the *plasmodium falciparum* was identified as the agent of malaria in tropical Africa, and it took until 1897 for Ronald Ross to confirm that the anopheles mosquito was the primary vector for the transmission of *falciparum*.[2]

The understanding of how to use quinine effectively to prevent malaria was a game changer for Europeans in tropical Africa. Overall first-year death rates for European soldiers stationed in tropical Africa dropped from 250 to 750 per 1000 before widespread use of quinine to 50 to 100 per 1000 afterwards. This death rate was still relatively high, but made a huge difference in terms of the types of activities that Europeans could undertake in Africa. Whereas Europeans had formerly been confined almost entirely to the African coastline, in the second half of the nineteenth century European exploration into the interior of Africa expanded significantly. And the ability to protect soldiers from malaria meant that military conquest became a much more feasible prospect for European powers that increasingly coveted the resources, markets, and strategic advantages that imperial expansion would bring. Malaria prophylaxis made it possible for Europeans to conquer African territories militarily and, once conquered, inhabit and govern those territories.

At the same time that malaria prophylaxis was contributing to the colonization of Africa by improving European health, the indigenous populations of many parts of the continent were experiencing severe ecological catastrophes. Societies throughout East and Southern Africa experienced a variety of major disruptions to their health and livelihoods in the 1880s and 1890s. Ethiopia experienced drought between 1888 and 1892. The Maasai went through an epidemic of bovine pleuropneumonia in the early 1880s. Shortly thereafter a catastrophic wave of another cattle disease (rinderpest) tore through communities from Somalia to South Africa and then west to Namibia, killing most of the cattle upon which pastoralist peoples relied. It has been estimated that rinderpest killed as much as 95% of all the cattle in East Africa in the 1890s. As if this weren't bad enough, in the 1890s epidemics of smallpox decimated the Maasai and Kikuyu in Kenya and spread throughout much of East and Southern African over the course of several years. Natural disasters and epidemics caused not only significant death and destruction, but also had social consequences as they dislocated people, creating large numbers of environmental refugees seeking means of reconstituting themselves at exactly the time they needed to defend against European invasion.

The European colonization of Africa was a violent process in itself. Conquest frequently involved direct military engagement, often with catastrophic results for Africans. Advances in weaponry in the nineteenth century made Europeans extremely efficient dispensers of death and destruction. Breech-loader rifles and machine guns gave Europeans major advantages in pitched battles, and Europeans were not afraid to use force to subdue resistance. Thus, at the Battle of Omdurman in 1898, British forces were able to kill over 11,000 Sudanese soldiers in the Mahdi's army while losing only 40 of their own men. It is estimated that as much as one third of the population perished in the Maji Maji uprising in Tanzania in 1905–1906, and 75–80% of all Herero of what is now Namibia were killed by German colonizing forces. In the Herero case, not all were killed in battle: to quash all resistance, German forces frequently followed up a battle by poisoning wells in this desert region, inflicting untold suffering that has been classified as genocide. The violence, disruption, and fear that accompanied colonial occupation also convinced many Africans to flee, uprooting people all over the continent and exposing them to inopportune environments, scarcity of food and water, and contributing to the spread of diseases.

The widespread devastation that took place in Africa in the years leading up to and during the Scramble for Africa were therefore highly volatile and dangerous for Africans. Indeed, many historians have concluded that in the wake of European conquest of the continent, it is no exaggeration to say that African peoples were unhealthier than they had ever been. Yet, the onset of colonial rule did not bring about immediate improvements to the health prospects of colonized peoples. Colonial governments employed large numbers of forced laborers, who were often underpaid if they were paid at all, often doing dangerous work such as building railroads. Other forms of wage labor were encouraged through high taxation, which required colonial subjects to work for the government to make money to pay their taxes. Often wage labor was very dangerous as well, as in mining operations in the South African diamond and Nigerian tin industries. Forced and wage labor took workers, mostly men, away from agricultural pursuits, foisting ever more domestic work onto women and children. Cash-cropping initiatives privileged using land and resources to grow inedible or non-nutritious products such as cotton, tobacco, and coffee at the expense of subsistence crops, which were increasingly imported in many rural African settings. The result was that when ecological or economic catastrophes occurred, their impacts were significantly more severe than they would have otherwise been.

Conscription into military duty frequently put African colonial subjects at risk. It is estimated that over 150,000 African soldiers died in the First World War defending the interests of Europeans. Colonial labor patterns also resulted in massive increases in migrant labor, as people had to move from their homes to wherever it was that Europeans wanted them to work, whether it was in wage labor, forced labor, or military service. The massive increases in mobility actually made Africans more susceptible to acquiring and spreading infectious diseases such as tuberculosis, smallpox, sleeping sickness, and influenza. The conditions of migrant and military labor (far from home and lacking familial comforts) also contributed to the increased concentration and spread of venereal diseases in some places.

The most extreme example of the health implications of colonial labor policies might be the outcomes of the infamous 'red rubber' scandal in the Congo Free State, where the government under the rule of Leopold II of Belgium undertook a massive reorientation of the local economy towards the harvesting of wild rubber. People were required to acquire and turn over to authorities large amounts of rubber, the collection of which took up most of their labor time. Those who did not acquire enough rubber or otherwise resisted the appropriation of their labor might be killed, have their families taken hostage, their homes and villages burned, etc. Collecting rubber exposed people to harsh environmental conditions and decreased their nutritional intake, as they had little time to cultivate, tend livestock, or hunt on their own account. Birth rates in the Congo fell dramatically during the horrific reign of terror unleashed in the Congo Free State. An official Belgian commission reported that between the founding of the Congo Free State in 1885 and the end of the First World War in 1918 the population of the Congo had 'been reduced by half'.[3] Although no official census existed at the time, best estimates suggest this means a population decline of between 5 and 10 million.

COLONIAL HEALTH CARE IN PRACTICE

Colonial governments recognized the poor health circumstances of their subjects, but mostly chalked them up to the 'primitive' cultures of presumably inferior African peoples. While there were many dissenters who blamed colonial rule for destabilizing African societies, the general narrative of colonial regimes particularly early on in the colonial encounter was that Africans were naturally diseased, unsanitary people ignorant of basic hygiene and medical practices. This is, of course, not true, but the image of a decrepit African population in need of salvation from moral, humane, knowledgeable Europeans became a basic feature of the 'civilizing mission' of European colonialism. Europeans believed that they were in Africa to save Africans from themselves in many ways, including superior medicine and health care.

However, this paternalistic image of colonial medicine rarely lived up to its own hype. Ultimately colonial government policies regarding health care tended to revolve around three main principles: (1) the prioritization of the health of Europeans over Africans; (2) maintenance of the labor force for purposes of sustaining colonial economies; and (3) reduction of government expenditure on social services such as health care, leaving the bulk of the medical work in colonies to private enterprises, particularly Christian missionaries.

Protection of Europeans from disease, and malaria in particular, was a major concern of colonial administrations in tropical Africa. In the early 1900s, European colonial governments feared that both African tropical environments and African people were major threats to the spreading of tropical diseases. To protect against this problem, many of the colonial urban centers were built on high ground, away from African towns, and strictly segregated. Hill Town, a European enclave in Sierra Leone, for example, was built in the first decade of the twentieth century at 750 feet above sea level, roughly four miles away from the nearby major city of Freetown. Only Europeans were allowed to live there, and Africans were allowed to work there during the day, but had to leave before night. The justification for this state of affairs was partly medical (Europeans believed, however erroneously, that this protected them from dangerous African diseases) but it was also clearly a means of reinforcing notions of racial difference and the power dynamics of colonial society, a reality that was ever more clear as it became apparent that Europeans who lived at Hill Town continued to contract malaria at roughly the same rates as people who lived elsewhere. Many other colonial cities had segregated European quarters, such as French-controlled Algiers and Dakar and Dar es Salaam in German East Africa, for example.[4]

The second major threat to colonial order from the European standpoint was the extent to which infectious diseases threatened African populations and, by extension, the colonial economies that depended upon African labor. Efforts to prevent the spread of infectious diseases often involved isolating infected individuals, curtailing the mobility of people, and sometimes destroying their property. Such measures frequently did little to bring these diseases under control but the social disruption associated with them often did a great deal to incite African opinion against the colonial government and its medical policies. For example, when a plague epidemic hit Senegal in 1914, French authorities instituted a quarantine to protect the European district at Dakar. However, the city so relied on African labor that many thousands of exceptions had to be made to allow Africans to cross the cordon sanitaire for purposes of working in the European district. The French also established isolation camps to contain plague victims. At these camps, plague sufferers, who had been forcibly removed from their homes in central Dakar, were given compulsory vaccinations while their clothes and portable possessions were disinfected. Their homes were usually burned to the ground. After being held in quarantine for ten days, people were then sent to live in new villages on the outskirts of town. Africans were supposed to be compensated for the destruction of their property, but often were not.

Europeans in Senegal, of course, had no restrictions on their own mobility, and their own homes and property were not destroyed to combat plague. While vaccinations were mandatory for Africans, they remained optional for Europeans. The French colonial system in Senegal effectively established plague as an African problem, used it as a justification for further segregation of the colony, and extended a very heavy-handed response that alienated large numbers of African subjects against the colonial regime. In fact, Africans in Dakar vociferously protested against the plague measures of 1914, instituting the colony's first general strike over the government's harsh measures.[5]

The unhealthy conditions that Africans faced in the early years of European occupation had resulted in massive depopulation in many places by the second decade of the twentieth century. By the 1920s, colonial governments recognized that their subject populations were too small to support the labor needs of the colonial economy, and began to develop policies designed to increase birth rates and decrease infant mortality figures. In the Belgian Congo, the colonial government began to subsidize a charitable organization known as *gouttes de lait* (drops of milk) that supplied formula and food for mothers and infants, while simultaneously attempting to persuade Congolese couples to have more children. The milk plan was supposed to help with this process because the Congolese had a cultural belief that couples should abstain from sexual relations during the breastfeeding period, which could last up to three years in Congolese culture. By providing formula and persuading women to wean their children earlier, the spacing of births could be shortened and population increased. The Belgian government and the European women who ran the program placed all the blame for underpopulation on the superstitions of the Congolese rather than on any of the consequences of the rubber economy described above, further reinforcing the paternalist notion of the 'civilizing mission' by emphasizing the 'good' that Europeans were doing and ignoring the negative consequences of the colonial experience.[6] Similar efforts to reform motherhood and child care were undertaken in British East Africa, where colonial authorities were also highly concerned about underpopulation in the interwar years.[7]

Colonial governments did not want to expend the resources necessary to provide health care in African settings along European lines, and, as such, their interventions, while sometimes heavy-handed, were rarely comprehensive or sustained. In British territories, the administrative policy of indirect rule became a justification for not creating and sustaining massive public institutions, including state-funded education, social welfare, and health care. As a result, in Nigeria there were only about 50 doctors in a colony with an estimated population of 16.5 million people in 1920.[8] In many colonies there were small numbers of doctors in private practice, although there were often racialized restrictions on African doctors' ability to practice privately.

Christian missionaries picked up some of the slack in the provision of European-style medicine. Christian missionaries had been active in many parts of Africa since before the Scramble. Indeed, David Livingstone, the famous Scottish explorer of the nineteenth century, was himself a missionary doctor. Medical missions throughout colonial Africa provided much of the European-styled primary care that Africans could access. They also ran vaccination campaigns and leprosaria, providing long-term treatment for people with severe chronic illnesses. However, unlike the colonial state, which frequently claimed to stay out of the business of changing African cultures, missions were very much interested in converting Africans to Christianity, and, in so doing, changing their beliefs and lifestyles significantly. Christian missionaries tended to see the health problems of Africans in terms of their lack of Christian morals, in which physical illness was a representation of African moral failing, very much in keeping with images of Africa as a 'Dark Continent' of 'backward' and child-like people in need of education and salvation.

Mission clinics offered an opportunity not only to heal the body but also to save the soul.

Many Africans healed by missionaries did go on to embrace Christianity, but not all did. Even for those who did not, however, the relationship between medical and spiritual treatment was clear. Historian Megan Vaughan recounted the specific case of a Muslim patient in Uganda in 1902. Despite the fact that he had undergone an operation and was cured in a mission hospital, he was not allowed to go home. The missionaries declared, 'We are keeping him in hospital as we are very anxious to win his soul'. The patient did not agree, however, arguing that he had come 'to the hospital for healing, and didn't see why he should change his religion'.[9] The different goals and ideologies of colonial governments and missionary hospitals meant that European medicine in the colonial context was not by any means homogenous. African responses to European health care were also quite diverse.

African Responses

The majority of Africans living under colonial rule had no access to or experience of either colonial or missionary medicine, and continued to rely on indigenous health practitioners for all of their health needs, as they had always done. Even in settings where missionary medicine or state-run public health measures were instituted, Africans continued to seek medical treatment from indigenous healers for a wide variety of reasons. First, and most significantly, indigenous healers had deep roots in local communities and long track records of providing successful health care in ways that were culturally meaningful to community members. European-styled medical care was new on the scene, did not have the long track record of indigenous healers, and frequently did not have particularly better answers for how to handle local health problems than indigenous healers did. Furthermore, as noted in the examples above, sometimes colonial and missionary health practices were very disruptive to African social structures and often caused problems that were potentially as undesirable as those they professed to be fixing.

This is not to say that Africans rejected colonial and missionary medicine outright, however. Both had positive connotations for many Africans, who appreciated the exotic powers of the outsiders while simultaneously recognizing that that power could have positive or negative impacts. Therefore, in places where African colonial subjects had interactions with state-run health programs or missionary clinics, they were able to incorporate these systems into medical marketplaces that were already pluralistic.

There were sometimes tensions between colonial and missionary medicine on the one hand, and indigenous health systems on the other. Europeans usually saw their own health systems as superior to those of Africans and often intervened to try to marginalize the activities of indigenous healers whom they saw as a threat to their own power or, potentially, to the health of their patients. For example, in South Africa, the European-controlled government passed many laws circumscribing the ways that indigenous healers could legally practice medicine. Indigenous healers were not allowed to sell or dispense any products that were deemed useful in 'European' medicine, even if they were products that indigenous healers had used for a long time. At the same time, indigenous healers who engaged in any form of supernatural processes, particularly witchcraft or anti-witchcraft measures, saw their practices outlawed by colonial authorities in many African colonies. In Nigeria, colonial authorities outlawed the practices of the so-called Soponno cult, which sought to appease the god of smallpox, on the unfounded notion that the cult's activities actually spread smallpox. None of these legal measures ever eliminated the cultural value of indigenous healers to their clienteles, but they did sometimes change the context within which indigenous healers could work and forced some of their activities underground.

The hard line that colonial authorities tried to draw between 'traditional' African practices and 'modern' European ones also fundamentally misunderstood the nature of indigenous African health systems, which had been historically dynamic and incorporative of a wide variety of ideas about how best to promote the health and well-being of individuals and communities. In fact, in many settings even in colonial times, African patients sought out European medicine, seeing it as potentially powerful, but often reinterpreted the meaning of that medicine in local cultural terms that left Europeans flabbergasted. As Luise White has shown:

> Africans chose treatments, tablets and the placement of telescopes because of their own etiologies of disease. Illnesses that were believed to be caused by excessive cold might best be treated by pills that were hot in color, like red or pink. These reinterpretations were debates about the nature of curing itself and reflected divergent ideas about sickness, health, and healing that did not readily conform to the dichotomies between Western and African medicine, both of which changed rapidly in the twentieth century.[10]

Such interconnectedness between medical systems further illustrates the diversity and pluralistic nature of health-care beliefs and practices in colonial Africa: the story is not so much one of the spread of European medicine as the ways that European medicine interacted with preexisting health systems to create new sets of meanings and practices for African patients and healers.

Many Africans also argued that colonial governments had a greater responsibility to provide more and better health care. The colonial system relied heavily on Africans for labor, local 'traditional' administration, and, increasingly, to fill lower-level positions within the colonial administrations and businesses that formed the backbone of the colonial venture. This latter group became known as the 'African middle class' because in order to work within the colonial structures they needed some level of education and enculturation into European languages, beliefs, and preferred skill sets. This African middle class tended to benefit materially more from the colonial system than lower classes, and their lifestyles and beliefs came to incorporate many of the values of the European middle class. Middle-class Africans, who tended to be located in urban areas, near centers of colonial governance and business, became among the harshest critics of colonial administrations, demanding that the government do more to extend to Africans the benefits of 'civilization' that were supposedly a part of the colonial mission. Health care and expansion of medical facilities became one of the realms within which the middle class accused colonial governments of failing their subjects.

Included within this African middle class pushing for greater access to Western medicine and health care were black doctors and other medical professionals whose qualifications made them well suited to make the case that colonial governments could be doing much better. They had undertaken significant education in order to garner the qualifications necessary to participate in the delivery of European-style medicine. As a result, they usually believed very strongly in the value of European-styled medicine (although not necessarily exclusively). Many worked directly for the colonial government, in government hospitals or dispensaries. Others were involved with missionary clinics. They often bought into the rhetoric of the colonial 'civilizing mission', seeing their own professions as examples of the potential for positive development in their home countries and themselves as representatives of the essential capacity of Africans for 'civilization' on European terms. They were therefore in a very good position both to point out the poor quality and quantity of the colonial health-care system and to argue for its expansion and improvement.

African protests against the colonial medical system frequently saw the explicit racism embedded in alien European rule as one of the key causes of the underdevelopment of health care that characterized colonial policy. On the one hand, the minimal resources devoted to expanding health-care services were an indication that African lives were not worth as much to Europeans as their own, despite the fact that colonial government claimed responsibility for African peoples. At the same time, one of the main reasons that there were so few doctors in colonial environments for most of the colonial period was that so little was done to train Africans to provide high-quality medical care. In fact, in many cases, the professional status of medical doctor was jealously guarded as the preserve of the European. The West African Medical Services (WAMS), founded in 1902 to recruit European doctors for service in British West African colonies, did not allow black doctors to become members, thereby leaving them outside professional ranks throughout much of the colonial period.[11] African colonial subjects could become medical doctors in some colonies by overcoming extremely high barriers to entry, but African doctors were usually paid less and had greater restrictions on rights to private practice than Europeans. Many middle-class Africans saw the unwillingness of colonial governments to encourage the growth of a professional class of African medical personnel as one of the key factors perpetuating the underdevelopment of biomedical services in African colonies. It is therefore not surprising that doctors and other medical-service providers were often very active within nationalist movements. Perhaps most famously, Felix Houphouët-Boigny, who became the first president of independent Ivory Coast in 1960, had begun his career as a doctor, only later becoming a politician. The first president of independent Malawi, Hastings Banda, had also been trained as a doctor.

NATIONALISM, DECOLONIZATION, AND HEALTH CARE

Colonial health-care systems limped along as underdeveloped, low-priority institutions throughout the interwar years. In the context of the global depression of the 1930s, resources for major development projects were even less forthcoming than they had been previously. However, the outbreak of the Second World War in 1939 created a new context for the invigoration of colonial health services in Africa. The need for healthy colonial fighting forces resulted in a major influx of military spending on medical care, as well as the training of medical personnel to administer to troops. Many thousands of African colonial subjects fought on behalf of the Allied cause in the Second World War. Much of the fighting took place in the North and East African campaigns, but West African soldiers fought for the British in Burma, and French Equatorial African forces contributed to the Free French cause. Enlisting healthy soldiers and keeping them as healthy as possible during the war therefore required some significant improvement in health-care services in underdeveloped African colonies. Nigeria, for example, served as an important base for airlift operations throughout the war; however, it became clear that troops stationed there were experiencing poor health from a variety of illnesses, malaria most significantly. Over the course of the war, new military hospitals were built at Lagos and Kaduna, with a variety of reception stations around the country. Disinfection of planes became common practice, and by the end of the war Allied forces were using DDT to control mosquitoes. When troops were demobilized in 1945, ex-servicemen's wards were built around Nigeria, with the largest one at Yaba, near Lagos, being converted into an orthopedic hospital.[12] A military psychiatric facility was opened at Lantoro to handle the psychological problems of demobilized Nigerian soldiers on returning home, which became the jumping-off point for the nearby development of Aro Mental Hospital, the first modern psychiatric hospital in Nigeria, in 1954.[13]

After the war ended with Allied victory in 1945, the progressive trajectory of health-care provision in the colonies continued as nationalist movements, noting their own loyalty to the Allied fight for freedom, democracy, and equality, demanded ever more concessions from weakened colonial governments. Improvement in social services, most notably health care and education, both appeased anti-colonial sentiment and helped pave the way for national independence through the Africanization of public-service positions and improvements to human capital necessary for self government. Improvement in health care in the postwar era was therefore not strictly a humanitarian issue; it was also a political one.

The nationalist push for more health care and for a more equitable place for Africans within the health-care system helped to influence the active modernization of health facilities in many African colonies in the 1950s and 1960s. Postwar development plans throughout the British empire provided significant funding for increased medical infrastructure after 1945. In Nigeria, for example, the colonial government instituted a Ten Year Plan in 1945 that allocated £10.4 million for medical and health services. The total number of hospitals operating in Nigeria grew from about 100 in 1945 to over 300 by 1960. About half of this growth was in the realm of government hospitals. Treatment facilities for leprosy and malaria were also created, vaccination campaigns against smallpox were undertaken, and treatment for such epidemic and endemic diseases as yaws, scabies, and trypanosomiasis was expanded. The plan also allocated £8 million to improve water supplies for Nigerian communities, a preventive measure against water-borne diseases and an effort to expand access to a major life necessity.

New hospitals and dispensaries needed to be staffed by qualified doctors, nurses, and attendants. Medical education grew apace with facilities in the postwar years. Again taking Nigeria as an example, as of 1945 there existed only one training hospital in the colony, at Yaba outside Lagos. In 1948, however, the University of Ibadan became the first university in Nigeria and began work on a medical program and the building of a university hospital, which was completed in 1957. Originally, the medical school trained only nurses and aides, with doctors needing to go abroad to complete their medical degrees. However, by the early 1960s, the University of Ibadan had initiated postgraduate studies in medicine, and over the course of the 1960s and 1970s more universities developed medical programs and teaching hospitals. Even for those who did not go to the University of Ibadan, opportunities to study abroad grew in the 1950s, with increasing numbers of Nigerians (and other Africans) matriculating to universities in the United Kingdom, France, the USA, and USSR, among other places. The result was a major increase in the number of doctors practicing in Nigeria in the 1950s. Whereas there had been only about 150 doctors practicing here in 1945, that number had grown to well over 1000 by 1955, most of the increase coming from the entrance of young Nigerians into medical degree programs in the postwar years.[14] A similar story can be told in East Africa, where Makerere University in Uganda had been providing medical training to Africans since the 1920s, but which saw an increase in the size and professionalization of its student body from the 1940s onwards.[15]

International organizations like the newly formed World Health Organization (WHO) also got involved in major projects to eradicate infectious diseases in Africa in the 1950s. From 1955, the WHO was conducting an ambitious, although largely unsuccessful, campaign against malaria in many African countries, and was in the beginning stages of a smallpox eradication program that unfolded in the 1960s and 1970s. The WHO also oversaw a more successful treatment campaign against yaws, and supported a large number of initiatives in African countries against other infectious diseases, as well as in areas such as pediatrics, maternal and child health, mental health, and public-health administration. Bilateral funding for health-care initiatives also came from the USA and grants-in-aid from European countries.

Through these investments and transformations in health-care practices in the postwar context, overall health indicators and medical infrastructure were better for most African countries at the time of independence than they had been at any point during the colonial encounter. According to United Nations data, the median life expectancy for the African continent was 36.2 years between 1950 and 1955, but had risen to 43.0 by 1965. Similar trends occurred in many individual countries. Burkina Faso's average life expectancy rose from 30 to 37 in the same time period, and Cameroon's from 37 to 41, for example.[16] These data are aggregate, however, and it must be recognized that some countries experienced higher growth than others, and some regions and demographics benefited more than others. Improvement in health indicators tended to rise faster in urban areas and among wealthier people than among the poor and rural, who may have seen little improvement over this period. And many of these health indicators have, in fact, slowed or reversed in the period since about 1980, when most African economies collapsed, ushering in a new period of decline.

Conclusion

This examination of health and medicine in colonial society has sought to illustrate the strong connections between health beliefs, medical practice, and the political, economic, and social realities of colonialism in Africa. Colonialism had significant health impacts for African subjects: colonial occupation and colonial economies brought about significantly negative health outcomes for many Africans. European medicine offered some answers to health problems facing Africans, but its relationship with colonial ideologies meant that European medicine, which itself often did not have particularly good solutions to African health problems at the time, remained unavailable to most Africans throughout the colonial period. That medicine which was available was often tailored to meet the goals of European colonial administrations as much as, if not more than, African subjects. The result was that indigenous health systems continued to compete effectively with biomedicine for the trust and care of African patients.

African responses to European medicine varied depending on context: some embraced European medicine where they could get it, if it were seen to offer positive outcomes that could not be achieved through other means. Others resisted European medicine when its proposed procedures or treatments seemed counter-productive to the needs of African patients and/or communities. Still others found great value in the precepts of European medicine but argued that the colonial system did not do enough to extend the benefits to African populations. This response became a key feature of anti-colonial activism that pushed for greater equality between Europeans and Africans in colonial society, ultimately resulting in independence for African countries in the decades after the Second World War. As African colonies moved toward independence, biomedical facilities expanded significantly, but have never achieved the level of saturation in African societies that they have in OECD countries. The colonial legacy in the realm of health and medicine is one of ambivalence and incompletion in which Africans continue to have a variety of options for health care, all of which have benefits and drawbacks, and within which Western biomedicine is frequently seen as only one of many options.

Notes

1. Daniel Headrick, *The Tools of Empire: Technology and European Imperialism in the Nineteenth Century* (Oxford: Oxford University Press, 1991), 62–63.
2. Ibid., 64–65.
3. Adam Hochschild, *King Leopold's Ghost: A Story of Greed, Terror, and Heroism in Colonial Africa* (New York: Houghton Mifflin, 1998), 233.
4. Philip Curtin, "Medical Knowledge and Urban Planning in Tropical Africa," *American Historical Review* 90, no. 3 (1985): 594–613.
5. Myron Echenberg, *Black Death, White Medicine: Bubonic Plague and the Politics of Public Health in Colonial Senegal* (Heinemann: Portsmouth, NH, 2002).
6. Nancy Rose Hunt, "'Le Bébé en Brousse': European Women African Birth Spacing and Colonial Intervention in Breast Feeding in the Belgian Congo," *International Journal of African Historical Studies* 21, no. 3 (1988): 401–32.
7. Lynn Thomas, *Politics of the Womb: Women, Reproduction, and the State in Kenya* (Berkeley: University of California Press, 2003).
8. Ralph Schram, *A History of the Nigerian Health Services* (Ibadan: Ibadan University Press, 1971), 298, 342.
9. Ibid., 62.
10. Luise White, *Speaking with Vampires: Rumor and History in Colonial Africa* (Berkeley: University of California Press, 2000), 99.
11. Ryan Johnson, "The West African Medical Staff and the Administration of Imperial Tropical Medicine, 1902–14," *Journal of Imperial and Commonwealth History*, 38, no. 3 (2010): 419–39.
12. Schram, *History of Nigerian Health Services*, 261.
13. Matthew M. Heaton, *Black Skin, White Coats: Nigerian Psychiatrists, Decolonization, and the Globalization of Psychiatry* (Athens, OH: Ohio University Press, 2013).
14. Schram, *History of the Nigerian Health Services*, 298.

15. John Iliffe, *East African Doctors: A History of the Modern Profession* (Cambridge: Cambridge University Press, 1998).
16. https://data.un.org (accessed 9 October 2014).

Bibliography

Curtin, Philip. "Medical Knowledge and Urban Planning in Tropical Africa." *American Historical Review* 90, no. 3 (1985): 594–613.

Echenberg, Myron. *Black Death, White Medicine: Bubonic Plague and the Politics of Public Health in Colonial Senegal.* Heinemann: Portsmouth, NH, 2002.

Headrick, Daniel. *The Tools of Empire: Technology and European Imperialism in the Nineteenth Century.* Oxford: Oxford University Press, 1991.

Heaton, Matthew M. *Black Skin, White Coats: Nigerian Psychiatrists, Decolonization, and the Globalization of Psychiatry.* Athens, OH: Ohio University Press, 2013.

Hochschild, Adam. *King Leopold's Ghost: A Story of Greed, Terror, and Heroism in Colonial Africa.* New York: Houghton Mifflin, 1998.

Hunt, Nancy Rose. "'Le Bebe en Brousse': European Women African Birth Spacing and Colonial Intervention in Breast Feeding in the Belgian Congo." *International Journal of African Historical Studies* 21, no. 3 (1988): 401–32.

Iliffe, John. *East African Doctors: A History of the Modern Profession.* Cambridge: Cambridge University Press, 1998.

Johnson, Ryan. "The West African Medical Staff and the Administration of Imperial Tropical Medicine, 1902–14." *Journal of Imperial and Commonwealth History* 38, no. 3 (2010): 419–39.

Schram, Ralph. *A History of the Nigerian Health Services.* Ibadan: Ibadan University Press, 1971.

Thomas, Lynn. *Politics of the Womb: Women, Reproduction, and the State in Kenya.* Berkeley: University of California Press, 2003.

White, Luise. *Speaking with Vampires: Rumor and History in Colonial Africa.* Berkeley: University of California Press, 2000.

CHAPTER 12

African Colonial Urban Experience

Uyilawa Usuanlele and Oluwatoyin B. Oduntan

LOCATING THE AFRICAN EXPERIENCE IN HISTORICAL SCHOLARSHIP

The changing shifts and emphases in how scholars narrate the history of urbanization in Africa reflects milieus, historiographical traditions, and methodological tools as they evolve. The earliest accounts equated urbanization in Africa with European presence, and tended to reduce the experience of Africans to their appropriation by and exclusion from colonial cities and modern facilities. Triumphalist accounts in literature, movies, and anthropology promoted the view that European power and ingenuity transformed Africa's massive landscapes into modern cities. That such faulted Eurocentric views continue to dominate the public (and some scholarly) views of urban Africa is well demonstrated by Francis Jaekel's *History of the Nigerian Railway* (1997), in which he declares that Nigeria owes a 'debt of gratitude' to Britain not just for the railways, but for the urbanization it engendered. Similar studies as this racialize urbanization and modern facilities as European natural capacities and, in contrast, promote the image of Africa as tribal and rural.[1]

The UNESCO General History of Africa aimed at combating such racialist prejudices to recover a history that depicts the lived realities and

U. Usuanlele (✉)
History Department, State University of New York (SUNY) Oswego, Oswego, NY, USA

O.B. Oduntan
History Department, Towson University, Towson, MD, USA

experiences of Africans from ancient times to the present. This massive project has received commendations for how it overcame its institutional challenges to produce eight volumes of history written by scholars from around the world; and for its emphasis on an African perspective that highlights African knowledge and agency.[2] In this mold, authors on the *General History* challenged Eurocentric narratives of urbanization by shifting attention away from empire builders and highlighting instead the contributions of African labor in the development of mining cities in South Africa, of merchants on and around the West Atlantic, and Africans who made the Swahili port cities. In Volumes V and VI devoted to precolonial Africa, authors successfully challenge the conceptualization of urbanization that privileged European urbanity as the normative and African urbanization as a preexistent 'Other'.[3] This has promoted recognition for and renewed scholarship in recovering the spatial and cultural geographies of indigenous towns, architectures, palaces, trade routes, markets, cities, etc. across Africa. However, the nationalist framework of the UNESCO model has proved grossly inadequate to overcome the conceptual and methodological claims of colonialism and its epistemological entrenchment of the perspective that modern African cities are new, colonial, 'little Europes'. The idea that African cities are new and different from traditional African forms dominates the chapters even as authors try to push the case that Africans participated in the making of colonial urbanization. It does not help that those Africans mentioned (manual labor recruits, mine workers, harbor hands, *Shabeen queens*) served in subaltern positions. Unwittingly, many accounts reproduce and legitimize Eurocentric notions that modern cities, railways, roads, and urban management are European ways in contrast to African ways. Africans remain cast as interlopers and adopters of European ways in many accounts of colonial urbanization.

The theoretical tools to effectively challenge Eurocentrism and thereby recover the African experience of urbanization during colonial rule began to be available from the 1980s onwards. These tools evolved from the flood of studies that followed Edward Said's *Orientalism* (1978) and later *Culture and Imperialism* (1993), which demonstrated that European knowledge of Africa, as of many parts of the colonized world, and by implication the archive upon which historians rely to recover the African past, was 'invented' to serve imperial purposes. The cultural strategy of imperialism, Said highlights, was to establish difference through premises of posed-opposites between European ways and the ways of the colonized.[4] By appropriating the modern and its claims of science, rationality, etc. as European natural endowments, colonialism rendered African ways as traditional and different from the modern. Thus, African urbanization may only be rendered as a different, inadequate form of the European modern city. By advancing African authenticity, the nationalist school failed to overcome the claims of difference upon which colonial ideology is grounded.

Many historians have adopted new critical tools to attempt the recovery of African urban history. This purpose has been pursued firstly by reevaluating colonial narratives of urbanization in Africa with a recognition of their faults, including their narrowness, propaganda, and as ideological claims to establish and secure colonial power and European dominance. Secondly, several studies delimit the timelines of African urbanization, finding continuities in the histories of cities such as Lagos, Benin, Abeokuta, Kumasi, Timbuktu, Mombasa, Durban, etc., and thereby overcoming the assumption of newness or displacement.[5] They underscore how other processes such as Islamization, Creolization, and hybridization were also at play in the making of modern African urbanization. Furthermore, de-essentializing cities as centers of civilization has led to recognition of varied layers of the urban experience, and for the critical nexuses and influences of comparative rurality (metropolises, small towns, markets, urban, margins, etc.) in the making and sustenance of urban culture.[6] The collection of articles from the 2003 University of Texas Conference on African Urban Studies experiment with these varied strategies with varying degrees of effectiveness. They provide new tools for interrogating old axioms about colonial urbanization and the African experience.[7]

Yet, problems persist, not least in the configuration of the existing library on African urbanization and the knowledge system it has created. Scholars still have a lot to do to push back against *images of Africa*, including in college curriculums, pedagogy, and as projected in the media. The ideas that modern cities were built by Europeans in Africa, that Africans lived in tribal landscapes and were incapable of modern technology and space management continue to dominate some scholarly and media depictions of Africa. The more enduring challenge however remains how to overcoming the stranglehold of European universalizing concepts and imposed categories to fully achieve the production of historical accounts untainted by Eurocentrism. Indeed, despite the strides made to recover African agency, we continue to struggle with the inferiority imposed by marginalization, which automatically renders African roles as poor copies of, and aspirations to, a European referent.

A long chronology of authors has struggled with this dilemma of moving past recognizing alterity, and the 'common cries of anger and anguish among activist African historians and intellectuals sick and tired of being marginalized in the production of scholarly knowledge on and about Africa',[8] to developing frameworks which render more credible histories. As the eminent philosopher Abiodun Jeyifo observes, de-centering is inadequate for Africa if scholars do not go further to 're-center'. He further asserts that, 'there is an absence, a vacuum left from deconstructing or de-territorializing colonization which has not been filled, and without the filling of which old colonial narratives are reinforced as the *only*, even if intensely challenged historical explanation'.[9] The African experience of urbanization during the colonial era still requires a re-centering, a narrative of African agency, of innovation and adaptation, of impositions as well as impacts. Despite many promising discursive experiments, there is yet no consensus on how this might be achieved. Paul Zeleza has suggested a 'double intellectual maneuver' as a strategy for recovering the African past. His preference for a dualistic approach proceeds from a recognition of the promises and limitations of Dipesh Chakrabarty's *Provincializing Europe*, which advances a pluralistic approach to the past; one which reduces European ideas as provincial (and not universal) and narrates how it engages with other 'provinces'. Recognizing the practical inadequacies of *Provincialism* (not least that our scholarly enterprise, including its language, valuation, conceptualization, and chronology all remain tied to the scholarly ethics and standards of the European Enlightenment), Zeleza suggests that Africa should also be conceived of as global to countermand Western universal claims. Other frameworks, including 'multiple modernities', transnationalism, etc. which seek to create space for the histories of colonized peoples also confront the overwhelming universalism of the dominant narrative.[10]

More particularly than the broad issues of African historiography, the main step to recovering the African experience of urbanization must recover the conceptualization of urbanization from its Western universalistic claims. Where Zeleza suggests an excision from the European episteme, and Jeyifo a re-centering of Africa as global, we propose a more reductionist strategy as the way forward for the history of urbanization in Africa. This includes recognizing as a first premise that the grand underpinning of power and dominance is *difference*. It is well recognized that the strength of colonialism was not only its coercive power, but also the legitimization it derived from posing and establishing difference. If difference is the conceptual authority of European universalistic claims, it can be effectively challenged at that crux of its authority. In other words, attempts at rarefying some authentic 'African' forms as a counter-discourse to domination can only reinforce European difference. Africanists need to redefine European claims as human characteristics and not racial ones. This framework does not preclude recognition for the celebrated achievements of the Enlightenment or the Industrial Revolution, or even of colonial conquest and rule; rather they become part of what human beings do. We can thereafter materially explain why Europeans acted in certain ways and how different layers of peoples chose other forms. The history of marginalized peoples, their dynamic science, technology, laws, labor, social order, and in our case urbanization, can be recovered alongside an explanation of the choices they made, and of their marginalization.

The broad outline that follows contextualizes the African urban experience during colonial rule by overcoming difference. It recognizes the multiplicity of African habitations prior to colonial rule. It further reduces colonial rule from its claims of being superhuman to its contextual realities of empire building—a common occurrence in Africa, (and indeed all human history).

Urbanization comes across as how metropolises, cities, towns, and sub-urbans evolved, grew, or modified during an era. In so doing we unlock Africa from alterity to render an account of the lived experience of African peoples.

COLONIZING THE AFRICAN URBAN: THE CONSTRUCTION OF DIFFERENCE

Properly defined, urbanization is a global phenomenon rather than a race-specific or region-configured experience. Scholarly attraction to and concentration on Greek and Roman cities, much of it conducted to find roots that justify *The Rise of the West*, may make the ancient cities of Europe the classical normative. However, recent researches reveal impressive urbanization in virtually all regions of the world.[11] Contrary to the old model which credits the making of cities to the capacity of individual empire builders like Alexander the Great, there is consensus among scholars that urbanization is an ecological and demographic process in which growing populations respond to environmental change to become sedentary in areas where regular supply of food and social needs can be assured.[12] Towns and cities across Africa conform to global patterns of urbanization (growth in population, rise of social classes, centralization of power, mobilization of labor, trans and extra-kinship relationships, etc.) and urban culture.[13]

The earliest European encounters with Africans were stimulated by the reputation African urbanization had acquired in Portugal and across Europe. Embassies exchanged between Portugal and Ethiopia were thought to be correspondences with 'Prester John', the mythical king of a sprawling metropolis popular in medieval Europe,[14] just as the reputation of Mali's Mansa Musa as the richest human in the world was well known. The Portuguese invasion of Ceuta in 1415 required 225 ships, an affirmation that Africa was not lacking in urban centers and complex societies.[15]

Drawn to the attractions of African commerce, Europeans did not settle in wildernesses but near the supply of existing desired markets. Mercantile cities in Europe, on the Indian Ocean, the Atlantic, and across the world were similar in terms of their openness, fluid political systems, and close global interactions and communication to facilitate and sustain production, travel, and commerce. These cities existed on the margins of more rural production centers, usually hidden by middlemen from prying merchants. However, as industrialization induced a favorable shift in European comparative advantage in global trade, it produced a shift in conceptions of urbanization. In Europe, the movement from biological and artisanal modes of production drew a greater percentage of the population to factories in cities, thereby reordering marginality. The ideology of modernity and civilization that followed rendered rural settings, previously the centers of production, as margins of cities—now defined as centers of civilization. Industrialization further consummated growing European conceptions of racial superiority over others and of the superiority of the European city over its rural margins, and over the non-European world. Racial ideology enabled European conquest and colonization, and along with this, the conception of Europe as the normative civilized and modern form of urbanization, and of the colonized world as rural, countryside, 'bush', or aspiring locales.

It is important to note, however, that the rise of European power did not thereby obliterate preexisting social realities. Existing towns and cities continued to thrive, not in any ossified traditional form, but alongside existing patterns of social formation, which were always dynamic, appropriating and localizing new ideas. The needs and outputs of industrial capital energized urbanization globally through increased volume of trade and the fast pace of innovation, new products, and ideas. The social conditions which followed urbanization in Europe, including the rise of a bourgeois class, the influence of labor unions, social and political revolutions, the growth of social leisure (theater, music, and sports), republicanism and suffrages, were not restricted to Europe but were shared variously. Neither did rurality, nobility, and old biological regimes disappear in either Europe or elsewhere. Rather, these ways of life were posed as discursive ideologies in the social and political struggle to define the most acceptable form of society and how it is governed. As Fred Cooper has emphasized severally, historians grant Europeans much more power and capacity than was real when we assume a coherent European identity and power to impose European ways on the colonized world.

The African experience of urbanization during the colonial period did not begin with a jolt or a total newness. As one author has noted, the sun did not fail to rise the day after European conquest. Spatial transformation was slow at best in a few places, and non-existent in many others. Nevertheless, old dynamic forms of urbanization remained, appropriating new ideas and resources (including European ones) and retaining old forms that were sustainable. In all cases, however, the main strategy of colonization was to establish and affirm difference. Accordingly, from the onset of colonial administrations, Europeans set out to define European ways, and to construct and impose opposites as the ways of Africans. They tried to secure European settlements as special and different from Africans settlements. The *colonization* of African urbanity further complicated the experiences of Africans as colonial cities grew.

This is not to deny the profound pace of urbanization that occurred during colonial rule, or to deny its impacts on human settlements and the demography of Africa. As colonial rule became entrenched, complete with functioning secretariats and offices, parastatals and bureaucracy, there occurred a simultaneous decline in the pedigree of existing urban centers in favor of colonial locations. In West Africa, the main driver for the growth of colonial cities was the opportunity they opened to enslaved persons to escape from indigenous slave-holding societies. Thus, Lagos witnessed an ever increasing inflow of escapees, slaves, youths, and women as colonial power began to reach the Yoruba hinterland and fueled political and social instability. Colonial infrastructures such as the railways created employment opportunities that attracted the colonized population to seek their fortunes in colonial cities. Bill Freund reports that one estimate showed that the number of Africans living in urban centers rose from 4.8% in the 1920s (after over two decades of colonial rule) to 14.2% in 1960 at the end of colonial rule in most African countries.[16] Another means by which Africans were attracted to colonial cities and commercial centers was the introduction of colonial regulations and taxes. Forced recruitment of Africans into colonial projects and the imposition of taxes and regulations weakened local economies and forced men into port cities and mining service in East Africa and Southern Africa respectively. This increasing urbanization was propelled largely by diminishing opportunities and the exacerbation of poverty in the rural areas, a condition attested to by John Iliffe's words that urban poverty was the face of rural poverty.[17] By this, Illife meant how the attraction of labor to the mining and agricultural complexes in East and Southern Africa depopulated rural ones. The colonial strategy of defining urbanization as 'unAfrican' was used to justify policies to restrict permanent African residence in colonial cities, and ultimately created conditions of poverty in the rural areas as well as on the margins of colonial cities.

Several shared principles among colonial states guided their policies on urbanization and defined how Africans experienced colonial urbanization. These included the affirmation of racial superiority, financial sufficiency, and economic exploitation, achieving governance at minimal costs, and the protection of European colonial personnel. These principles variously affected the development of urbanization and life and experiences of Africans who inhabited the urban centers. We have established how difference was the main underpinning of colonial rule. To effectively rule, colonial states had to pose European cities as the modern form, distinct from African urbanization. Colonial policies were therefore targeted at clearly mapping European settlements away from natives. Policies in Segregation-Era South Africa denied African residency in Cape colony, first through restrictive legislations and later by denying land ownership for Africans. Before and under apartheid, laws were created to require passes, and at its height to push blacks into homelands. Where European populations were not large enough to sustain a settler colony, and where Europeans settled in preexisting African towns and cities, colonial authorities designated white-only residential areas.

Colonial policies also aimed at the effective exploitation of labor and colonial resources. Colonial states expected their colonies to be at least self-sufficient, capable of supporting colonial administration and serving the needs of the metropolitan economy. The French financial law of 1900, according to Teresa Hayter, 'suppressed subsidies to the colonies and obliged them to subsist on their own budget resources'.[18] The British had a similar policy and the Colonial Office insisted on a policy of adherence to strict financial self-sufficiency without dependence on British taxpayers.[19] The policy of financial self-sufficiency also required the colonies to generate surpluses to invest in the metropole with the colonial power.

Shoestring budgeting influenced urbanization policies in the colonies. The main concern of the financial approving authorities in the colonial administration was a balanced budget with the expenditure on European personnel and welfare prioritized, followed by surpluses for overseas investment. A paltry expenditure was grudgingly approved for the local African personnel and critical infrastructure that could contribute to revenue generation. Expenditure that neither promoted European survival and welfare nor generated revenue was rarely prioritized. The ideology of difference justified the non-provision of public infrastructures and social services to Africans. As such, roads, electricity, postal services, etc. were defined as modern facilities and non-African ways. Public-health facilities were provided only to mitigate the spread of disease to European neighborhoods, because diseases were racialized as African.

Though racial and cultural superiority and difference are rarely stated in colonial policy documents (except the Italian Fascist *Laggi Razziali* of 1938), they are implied in some policy mission statements such as the French *Mission Civilisatrice* (in the colonies) and the unwritten ethos of European racial discrimination and segregation against the colonized. Racial bias was also a major plank in colonial policy that influenced colonial attitudes in their relations with Africans, and manifested too in urban management and development; except that it was masked by other factors such as health concerns and financial incapacity of most Africans to afford some specified building materials in housing codes. The masked racist and cultural superiority claims for segregation similarly morphed with financial self-sufficiency policy to deny Africans access to equal social services and amenities in the urban centers as well as residence.

Colonial administrations aimed to prevent African societies from disintegration through propping up some preexisting African cultural institutions and practices with indirect rule. The system containerized the people in tribes and communal lands, ruled by chiefs (turned autocrats) and armed with customary laws to preserve and guide the communities 'along native lines'.[20] Administering the colonized 'along native lines' was a euphemism for treating Africans differently by denying them services and amenities that could enhance African welfare in their settlements. Though this policy of development 'along native lines' started to be abandoned in British Colonies after the adoption of Colonial Development and Welfare policies of the 1940s, the neglect of African welfare in the urban centers had already prompted the formation of African organizations that not only catered for such welfare but also championed agitation for the dismantling of colonial rule and management of African welfare by Africans.

Organic Cities: Colonial Urbanization and the Limits of Difference

The colonization of Africa was immediately followed by the establishment of administrative centers and development of efficient transport systems that facilitated colonial exploitation of the newly created territories. Though some preexisting urban centers were turned into administrative centers, other factors were at play in the choice of location; natural resource endowment (mines/forest), new transport infrastructural facilities such as roads, railways and harbor/port facilities, as well as health of the Europeans (influenced by limitations of medical knowledge) were particularly important. Apart from the limited number of personnel because of financial policies, only administrative centers could be created, and so not all precolonial urban centers were appropriate. Even some which thrived as administrative/commercial centers in the early colonial period lost their status to nearby, better endowed/resourced or more strategically placed towns. This loss of status was usually followed by neglect. Such was the fate that befell Kilwa Kivinje in Tanzania, a mainland entrepôt town (that succeeded the ancient Island of Kilwa Kisiwani). When a deep harbor was built some 15 miles away during the colonial period, a new town, Kilwa Masoko, was born and made an administrative headquarters, which overshadowed and killed precolonial Kilwa Kivinje.[21] Likewise in Nigeria, Bonny which served as an administrative, commercial, and port town from the precolonial period until the late 1910s was abandoned when a better harbor facility nearby influenced the building of the new town of Port Harcourt, which became the new administrative and commercial center.[22] Similar developments were recorded for Kenya and, according to Otiso, 'Although the arrival of the British initially benefited precolonial or traditional centers it soon destroyed them. After consolidating political power, the colonial administration undermined precolonial centers by developing new centers more suitable to European needs'.[23]

The abandonment and consequent decline of preexisting towns was largely helped by denial of funds to build the necessary infrastructure and amenities needed to grow them. Lacking the new colonial incentives such as infrastructure and social amenities with their multiplier effects of employment and profit-making opportunities, some of the inhabitants relocated in search of better opportunities.

Such precolonial old towns that did not become administrative centers were neglected without the benefit of European planning and services. It was only when European interest got involved that the financial self-sufficiency policy was relaxed. For instance, Siluko in Benin Province (Nigeria) was neither an administrative center nor categorized even as a township (towns were graded in Nigeria under colonial rule), but because it had some resident European traders, it enjoyed government sanitary inspection services in 1922.[24] On the other hand, many similar towns in Benin Province that lacked significant European populations, including some administrative divisional headquarters like Ubiaja (with one or two Europeans) and Auchi, were denied sanitation services until 1938 (and they concentrated on leprosy control work).[25] Even in both old (indigenous) and new (colonial) urban centers, financial parsimony prevailed in areas inhabited by Africans, while no expense was spared in letting the Europeans enjoy particularly good health and comfort where they settled in large numbers. For instance, electric light was introduced to Lagos in 1897, but a survey conducted in 1909 showed that two-thirds of the city did not benefit and streetlights were only available in areas inhabited by Europeans, while Africans bore the brunt of paying for the lights.[26] In Benin City (Nigeria), piped water introduced in 1910 was pumped to individual European homes, while a few public fountains were provided in strategic places for the teaming African residents. When the waterworks malfunctioned in the 1920s, the administration used tanks to ensure steady supply to the European quarters only until completion of a new waterworks in the late 1930s. The administration's attempts to transfer the cost of paying for the waterworks to African residents resulted in the Benin City water rate agitation of 1937–1938.[27] A similar policy was implemented in Dar es Salaam (Tanganyika) with water piped to individual homes of the Europeans and shared public water kiosks provided for non-European residents. The nature of water supply to non-European residents was in accordance with the parsimonious financial policy. This is further attested to by Hilary Hungerford and Sarah Smiley, who have shown that in Dar es Salaam, 'the government chose to instead use cheaper public water points' for African residents because 'British colonial discourse on water supply in Dar es Salaam questioned ... whether the expenses of supplying such water access were justified'.[28] The financial self-sufficiency policy was usually enforced when it concerned catering to the infrastructural and social amenity needs and welfare of African urban dwellers.

European Commercial Interests and the Building and Segregation of New and Old Towns

Even when precolonial towns were made administrative and commercial centers, the colonial administrations were quick to build segregated and cordoned areas as residential quarters for Europeans (officials and non-officials). Various excuses were employed to dislodge the African residents in the areas chosen for European habitation. Home has argued that racism was not absent from pre-nineteenth-century colonial segregation.[29] But the nineteenth and early twentieth centuries were the heyday of social Darwinism and concomitant racism, and their convergence with the exacerbation of segregation of racial residential quarters in the colonies makes it difficult to completely exonerate a racist motive from segregation policy and practice. Similarly, new colonial towns were easily segregated at the point of planning and building. Luanda

(Angola) had from its beginnings in the sixteenth century restricted non-slave Africans' residence, and those Africans who sought to live around the city established themselves in the Musseques (a slum-like conglomeration of huts around the European suburbs.[30] Portuguese prohibition of African residence and consequent segregation was not based on health, but racial and cultural superiority claims which were reinforced with the later fascist policy of 1933. A*ssimilado* (assmimilated Africans) and Portuguese were reserved the best areas, and indigenato (unassimilated Africans) received the worst. What other European colonial powers did later with segregation was not different except that the policies were rationalized citing health/sanitation problems, security, affordability of building materials, and cultural differences.[31] Nevertheless, for the segregated European quarters or town to function, it required the labor and residence of Africans who ministered to the European needs. As a result, such Africans could not be completely eliminated even in apartheid South Africa, where provision was made for the African nanny in the planning of homes in the segregated European towns.[32]

Forging Difference: Patterns of Labor Appropriation in Colonial Urbanization

European colonizers in Africa depended on non-European labor (including unskilled labor), even though they were seemingly reluctant to include it as part and parcel of their lives. As a result, they even imported labor from Asia, partly to meet the shortfall in skilled labor particularly in Eastern and South Africa. The imported Asian laborers joined the preexisting Indian merchants to swell the population of Asian settlers. A few schools were established to train Africans as auxiliary personnel to supplement the Creoles (in Sierra Leone, Angola, and Kenya) who serviced the colonial administration. In the precolonial cities, these skilled auxiliary personnel were either allowed to settle among the colonized natives or sometimes separate quarters were built for them, known as clerks or native quarters. These served as buffers (in addition to the racetracks and golf courses) between the European quarters and the indigenous towns.

Similar African auxiliary personnel quarters were part of the planning of the new towns established by the colonial governments. Such quarters for African workers were not established in every town as Africans were expected to be housed by their employers. However, both the government and many employers did not provide housing for all of their workers.[33] Apart from financial policy (as stated by the Nigerian government committee on housing in 1923, which reported that housing for African staff should not be 'constructed by government out of public funds'[34]), the African laborer was viewed as a 'target worker' and not expected to live permanently in the urban center.[35] The French had established L'office de l' habitat économique (OHE) in 1926 to 'defray the cost of low income housing for qualified families in West Africa'.[36] According to Betts:

the most spectacular construction activity at this time (before end of WWII) was the creation of another African residential quarter, this time at Fann, North of Medina [Senegal], in which 14 buildings were constructed in 1935–1936. In another effort, this to improve Medina, two *cités ourvrières* were erected in 1937–38, one with 47 rooms and the other with 32.[37]

These were for an African population of over 100,000 and so could provide only a few houses to a very insignificant percentage of the African urban residents. Consequently, the worker and his family were not entitled to permanent accommodation and were left to fend for themselves in terms of accommodation. Like the Angolan Africans of old who were excluded from building in Luanda, the Africans had to make do with housing built with materials within their means, without regard for European standards and building codes.

Challenging Difference: The Realities of African Urbanization

Both the old and new urban centers that were turned into administrative, commercial, and transport hubs in the early stages of colonialism attracted Africans in search of opportunities for trade, employment, education, and services. Various factors compelled African migration at the beginning of colonialism, namely the emancipation of slaves, forced labor, environmental crisis, land shortages and congestion of African reservations, low crop prices, and increasingly high taxes that singly and/or combined to orchestrate poverty. In some cases, the colonial governments used propaganda to attract people. In addition to those forced to migrate by changing circumstances, the government also encouraged and persuaded people to migrate to new towns which they were creating. Such persuasion surrounded the building of Port Harcourt (Nigeria), where the government flooded Lagos with posters inviting people to migrate and settle there.[38] In many cases, European colonial officials wanted Africans out of the urban areas as they saw the latter as rural and communitarian. Authorities feared that urbanization would destroy African moral fabric and rural character. As a result, efforts were also made to police and control rural urban migration. Young men were also targeted in crime-control measures to tackle juvenile delinquency and the so-called 'Black Peril' in settler colonies of both East and Southern Africa.[39] Initially, women were the main target of policing and control. Policing women's migrations to towns has been blamed on the patriarchs in the rural areas, who complained about runaway wives and young women's engagement in prostitution and requested their return to their rural homes. The fear of spread of venereal disease by women among workers was another excuse for policing them, which in some cases led to the practice of Bheura. This was the inspection of female genitals before women were allowed entry into some housing facilities in Southern Rhodesia.[40] In addition, Hungwe noted that the women in

Southern African urban centers brewed beer, which competed with the beer halls established by the administration, thereby threatening generation of revenue by the state.

The women who moved to the towns were taking advantage of increased trading opportunities there, especially in foodstuff, educational training, skill acquisition (particularly tailoring), and other services such as hospitality. Colonial governments had no place for African women in their functional operations (except for midwives during the interwar years and secretaries after 1945), and made no provision for their urban needs such as maternity hospitals and family homes. Despite governments' antipathy to women residing in urban settlements, women created a burgeoning informal sector there. They put to good use their trading skills, especially in West Africa, where they formed formidable market-women organizations. Similarly, Asians created bazaars in Central, East, and Southern Africa, while Levantines injected themselves into retail trade in West Africa.[41] These trading opportunities and a booming informal sector created employment in the urban centers and attracted Africans and particularly Asian settlers and a few Levantines. However, the economic slump and later depression of the 1920s brought massive unemployment which continued long into the postwar period. Increasing unemployment created destitution and the associated problems of juvenile delinquency and crime, which became rampant in many urban centers. The unemployment problem was made worse by housing problems and the cost of living.

The colonial government policy towards African housing was virtually laissez faire until the end of the Second World War. In addition, some towns (including a few new ones like Nairobi) were not planned from the beginning before they were built.[42] As a result, land allocation was left to the whims of early administrators and the indigenous African land tenure system. The Africans and Asians capitalized on this laissez-faire policy to put up different kinds of housing in areas assigned to them (called locations and townships in settler colonies) without adhering to any building codes, which was common in French colonies. The housing types ranged from European styles through hybrid ones to African indigenous designs, shacks and huts comingling. In addition, indigenous housing in old towns and huts and houses in neighboring villages near new towns catered for African housing. These African sections of new urban centers and central districts of old towns were either inadequately provided for or lacked basic social amenities, motor vehicle access, and other communication facilities. Some of these places soon degenerated into the sprawling slums which proliferated in many African towns. Even after the war, when the colonial governments started to provide a modicum of housing for some categories of workers, the scarcity of the houses soon resulted in overcrowding. For instance, in the 1930s, 492 people were found to be living in 11 houses constructed for a population of 163, and in spite of seeming improvement it was estimated that 82,000

Africans were living in housing designed for 50,000 in 1947 in Nairobi (Kenya).[43] Population growth quickly outpaced house building, to the extent that accommodation provision in Nairobi for 30,000 people was completed between 1946 and 1957 at a time when the city's population had risen to 52,000.[44]

The consequences of inadequate housing induced overcrowding coupled with chronic shortage of social amenities and communication networks turned the African sections of the urban areas into cesspools of vermin and diseases such as tuberculosis. The episodic plague outbreaks in some African and Asian sections of African towns provided the pretext for (at least attempted) destruction of properties and forced relocations of the inhabitants to new areas. This simultaneously helped to achieve the goal of racial segregation in the towns.[45] Such acts of destruction aimed at redesigning the towns, and high charges for social amenities and welfare singly and or in combination usually galvanized the African inhabitants (locals and/or immigrants) into forming civic associations to protest and agitate for better treatment from the colonial administration. This was usually the only option left to Africans since they were most often excluded from the administration and decision making regarding planning and allocation of funds for the local communities. Even in indigenous urban centers under indirect rule, the European administrative officers maintained monopoly over allocation of resources for development. It was worse in the settler colonies where the European settlers ensured the exclusion of Africans from the administration. Murunga has demonstrated this in the case of Nairobi, where the initial Asian and European participation in the administration was changed with the gradual easing out of the Asians as European settler emigration to the city increased from 1907. There was only perfunctory recognition of an African Advisory Council (window dressing to satisfy the Colonial Office) in 1926.[46] In the non-settler but segregated new town of Port Harcourt,, the cosmopolitan nature not withstanding, ethnic associations soon formed and in 1944 coalesced into the African Community League to wrest the administration of the town from the autocracy of the European Resident before the Local Government Reforms of 1948 assisted leagues gradually to take over administration of the town.[47]

The inadequacy and shortages induced competition in the urban settlements, necessitating the formation of ethnically based associations to assist individuals and communities gain access to resources and opportunities. These ethnic associations adopted self-help in providing some of the amenities the communities lacked, such as schools, dispensaries, town halls, scholarships for children etc. as well as employment and accommodation for new members of the communities and arranging for the repatriation of the destitute and bodies of dead members. Some associations built meeting and club halls, which assisted their recreation activities in addition to organizing indigenous dances, masquerades, and festivals, which further added African flavor, particularly in the new colonial towns. It was only with the Colonial Development and Welfare Act (CDWA) and its community development component in the period after the Second World War that the colonial administrations started providing basic social amenities such as reading rooms, dance halls/clubs, and encouragement of the formation of clubs for boys and girls to depoliticize and engage youth in socially desirable leisure activities such as sport, drama, Art, and so on.

The ethnic associations' agitations provided training grounds for politics and formed the basis of nationalist politics in the urban areas. Some of the ethnic associations transformed into nationalist parties, while some of the earliest political organizations such as the Peoples Union of Lagos emerged from the water-rate agitation, which was an early urban conflict between African residents and the colonial administration. The ethnic associations joined with other civic organizations that emerged from the neglect of the welfare and interests of African residents of urban areas to create the basis of nationalist parties. It was in these colonial urban centers that the independence of African colonies was wrested from the European colonial administrations, which tried to create European islands of urbanization, while Africans in the face of neglect and poverty molded them into their own living spaces.

Conclusion

Urbanization has been a universal development and Africans made their own contributions to the process by building numerous ancient urban centers which dotted various parts of Africa from Jenno-Jenne in the West African interior to the Swahili coastal cities of East Africa and agro-towns of the Tswana in Southern Africa. This chapter has shown that African urbanization predated Arab and European contacts and European colonization, the latter of which resulted in the grafting of European planning on African urbanization which was receptive to new ideas and infrastructure. The European colonial administration in Africa was predicated on financial self-sufficiency and promotion of European health and welfare at the expense of the colonized Africans, who suffered discrimination and neglect in precolonial African urban centers. Though the colonial administrations established some new urban centers that facilitated exploitation and extraction, unofficial African inputs went into creating the sprawling African sections of the towns and even the European sections. This was the case in spite of the European colonial official objective of establishing difference through segregation and neglect. The European sections/quarters remained only negligible islands of European architecture without obliterating the African character of the urban centers. The African urban experience was one of racial discrimination and neglect. It was this negative experience of Africans under colonial administration in the urban centers that orchestrated the formation of the African ethnic associations and nationalist movements that would wrested independence from the colonizers and return urban administration and development to African people.

Notes

1. Francis Jaekel, *The History of the Nigerian Railway*, Vol. 1 (Ibadan: Spectrum Books, 1997).
2. Muryatan Barbosa, "The Construction of the African Perspective: A History of the General History of Africa (UNESCO)," *Revista Brasileira de História*. 32, no. 64 (2012): 14. The General History remains the single, most detailed compendium of African history. See also Paul Zeleza, "The Pasts and Futures of African History: A Generational Inventory," *African History Review* 39, no. 1 (2007): 1–24.
3. See for instance, Jan Vansina, "The Kongo Kingdom and Its Neighbours," 546–83; and B.M. Barkindo, "Kanem Borno: Its Relations with the Mediterranean Sea, Bagirmi and Other States in the Chad Basin," 492–512.
4. For applications of Saidian deconstruction to African history, see V.Y. Mudimbe, *The Invention of Africa* (Bloomington: Indiana University Press, 1988); Achille Mbembe, "The Intimacy of Tyranny," in Mbembe, *On the Postcolony* (Berkeley, CA: University of California Press, 2001); and Paul Tiyambe Zeleza, ed., "Introduction," in *The Study of Africa: Global and Transcontinental Engagements*, Vol. 2, (African Book Collective, 2006), 1–26.
5. Catherine Coquer-Vidrovitch, "The Process of Urbanization in Africa: From the Origins to the Beginning of Independence; An Overview Paper," *African Studies Review* 31, no. 1 (1990): 1–98.
6. See, for instance, David Bell and Mark Jayne, *Small Cities: Urban Experience Beyond the Metropolis* (Abingdon, Oxon: Taylor and Francis, 2006).
7. Steven J. Salm and Toyin Falola, eds., *African Urban Spaces in Historical Perspective* (Rochester: University of Rochester Press, 2005).
8. Paul Tiyambe Zeleza, "The Troubled Encounter between Postcolonialism and African History," *Journal of Canadian Historical Association* 17, no. 2 (2006): 89–129.
9. Transcribed from "Harvard African Studies Workshop Featuring Biodun Jeyifo," accessed November 12, 2015, https://vimeo.com/56034878.
10. Paul Tiyambe Zeleza, "The Troubled Encounter between Postcolonialism and African History," *Journal of Canadian Historical Association* 17, no. 2 (2006): 89–129.
11. Barbara Price, "Cause, Effect and the Anthropological Study of Urbanism," in *Urbanization in the Americas from Its Beginning to the Present*, ed. Richard Schaedel, J. Hardoy, and N. Scott-Kinzer (The Hague: Mouton Publishers, 1978), 52–53.
12. Ancient cities developed around main rivers and ocean coastlines: Euphrates, Yellow River, Niger, Indian Ocean, etc.
13. The Sudanese empires thrived around the Niger, Great Zimbabwe and the Congo on their respective rivers, Egypt, Axum, etc. along the Nile Valley.
14. Andrew Kurt, "The Search for Prester John, a Projected Crusade and the Eroding Prestige of Ethiopian Kings, c.1200–c.1540," *Journal of Medieval History* 39, no. 3 (2013): 297–320.
15. Urban centers speckled the Western Sudan, the East African Swahili region, the Zimbabwe complex, the Nile Valley, etc.
16. Bill Freund, *The African City: A History* (Cambridge: Cambridge University Press, 2007), 65.

17. John Iliffe, *The African Poor: A History* (Cambridge: Cambridge University Press, 1987), 164.
18. Theresa Hayter, *French Aid* (London: Overseas Development Institute, 1966), 23.
19. John M. Carland, *The Colonial Office and Nigeria, 1898–1914* (Stanford, CA: Hoover Institution Press, 1985), 103–4.
20. Mahmood Mamdani, *Citizens and Subjects: Contemporary Africa and the Legacy of Late Colonialism*, Programme on Ethnic and Federal Studies (Ibadan: University of Ibadan, 2002), 50–52.
21. M.G. Vassanji, *And Home was Kariakoo: A Memoir of East Africa* (Penguin Random House, 2015), 75.
22. W. Ogionwo, *The City of Port Harcourt: A Symposium on Its Growth and Development* (Heinemann Educational Books (Nig.) Ltd, 1979), 21.
23. Kefa M. Otiso, "Colonial Urbanization and Urban Management in Kenya," in *African Urban Spaces in Historical Perspective*, ed. Steven J. Salm and Toyin Falola (Rochester: University of Rochester Press, 2005), 78.
24. N.A.I. BP 238/21 D.O. (B.D.) to Resident (B.P.) 1/2/1922.
25. S.A. Shokpeka, "Local Government and Development in Benin Province 1938–1960" (PhD thesis, University of Benin, Benin City, 1990), 191–193.
26. Rina Okonkwo, *Protest Movements in Lagos, 1908–1930* (Enugu: ABIK Publishers, 1998), 13.
27. Phillip Igbafe, *Benin Under British Administration: The Impact of Colonialism on African Kingdom, 1897–1938* (Longman, 1979).
28. Hilary Hungerford and Sarah L. Smiley, "Comparing Colonial Water Supply in British and French Africa," *Journal of Historical Geography* 52 (2016): 77.
29. Robert Home, *Of Planting and Planning: The Making of British Colonial Cities*, 2nd ed. (London: Routledge, 2013), 125.
30. Michael P. Bulfin, "Bursting at the Seams: Water Access and Housing in Luanda," *Ufamahu: A Journal of African Studies* 3, no. 1 (2009): 4–5.
31. Raymond Betts, "The Establishment of Medina in Dakar, Senegal, 1914," *Africa: Journal of the International African Institute* 4, no. 2 (April 1971): 143–144; Maynard Swanson, "The Sanitation Syndrome: Bubonic Plague and Urban Native Policy in the Cape Colony, 1900–1909," *Journal of African History* 18, no. 3 (1977); Giulia Barera, "Mussolini's Colonial Race Laws and State Settler Relations in Africa Orientale Italiana (1935–1941)," *Journal of Modern Italian Studies* 8, no. 3 (2003): 427–428; Allison Hay and Richard Harris, "Shauri ya Sera Kali: The Colonial Regime of Urban Housing in Kenya to 1939," *Urban History* 34, no. 3 (2007): 510; and Sarah Smiley, "The City of Three Colors: Segregation in Colonial Dar es Salaam, 1891–1961," *Historical Geography* 37 (2009): 179.
32. Rebecca Ginsburg, "The View from the Back Step: White Children Learn About Race in Johannesburg Suburban Homes," in *Designing Modern Childhoods: History Space and Material Culture of Children*, ed. Marta Gutman and Nind de Coninck-Smith (New Brunswick, NJ: Rutgers University Press, 2008).
33. Allison Hay and Richard Harris, "'Shauri ya Sera Kali': The Colonial Regime of Urban Housing in Kenya to 1939," *Urban History* 34, no. 3 (2007): 512–516.

34. Quoted in Idyorough "The Development of Formal Social Services Under the Colonial State in Northern Nigeria (1900–1960)" (PhD thesis, University of Jos, Jos), 228.
35. National Archives of Nigeria, Ibadan File CSO 26/1/03571 Vol. II, Information relating to Conditions of Industrial Life and Labour; F.H. Ruxton, Lieutenant General, Southern Nigeria to Mr. H.A. Grimshaw, International Labour Office, Geneva, 25/06/1928, 199–200.
36. Ambe Njoh, "Urban Planning as a Tool of Power and Social Control in Africa," *Planning Perspectives* 24, no. 3 (2009): 305.
37. Raymond F. Betts, "Dakar: Ville IMPERIALE (1857–1960)," in *Colonial Cities: Essays on Urbanism in a Colonial Context*, ed. Robert Ross and Gerard J. Telkamp (Dordrecht: Martinus Nijhoff Publishers, 1985), 204.
38. C.N. Anyanwu, "The Growth of Port Harcourt, 1912–1960," in *The City of Port Harcourt: A Symposium on Its Growth and Development*, ed. W. Ogionwo (Ibadan: Heinemann Educational Books (Nig) Ltd, 1979), 20.
39. Andrew Burton, *African Underclass: Urbanization, Crime and Colonial Order in Dar es Salaam* (London: The British Institute in East Africa, 2005).
40. Chipo Hungwe, "Putting Them in Their Place: "Respectable" and "Unrespectable" Women in Zimbabwe Gender Struggles," *Feminist Africa* 6 (2006): 37.
41. Kalpana Hilaral, "Gujarati Dukawallas in the Indian Ocean Region: A Case Study of Natal (1880–1910)," *Man in India* 94, no. 3 (2014).
42. Godwin R. Murunga, "'Inherently Unhygienic Races': Plague and the Origin of Settler Dominance in Nairobi, 1899–1907," in *African Urban Spaces in Historical Perspective*, ed. Steven J. Salm and Toyin Falola, 106.
43. Iliffe, *The African Poor: A History*, 168.
44. Burton, *African Underclass*, 29–30.
45. Murunga, "'Inherently Unhygienic Races': Plague and the Origin of Settler Dominance in Nairobi, 1899–1907," in *African Urban Spaces in Historical Perspective*, ed. Salm and Falola, 116.
46. Ibid., 112.
47. Anyanwu, "The Growth of Port Harcourt, 1912–1960," in *The City of Port Harcourt: A Symposium on Its Growth and Development*, ed. W. Ogionwo, 32–33.

Bibliography

Anyanwu, C.N. "The Growth of Port Harcourt, 1912–1960." In *The City of Port Harcourt: A Symposium on Its Growth and Development*, edited by W. Ogionwo. Ibadan: Heinemann Educational Books (Nig) Ltd, 1979.
Barbosa, Muryatan. "The Construction of the African Perspective: A History of the General History of Africa (UNESCO)." *Revista Brasileira de História* 32, no. 64 (2012).
Barera, Giulia. "Mussolini's Colonial Race Laws and State Settler Relations in Africa Orientale Italiana (1935–1941)." *Journal of Modern Italian Studies* 8, no. 3 (2003).
Barkindo, B.M. "Kanem Borno: Its Relations with the Mediterranean Sea, Bagirmi and Other States in the Chad Basin."

Bell, David, and Mark Jayne. *Small Cities: Urban Experience Beyond the Metropolis.* Abingdon, Oxon: Taylor and Francis, 2006.
Betts, Raymond. "The Establishment of Medina in Dakar, Senegal, 1914." *Africa: Journal of the International African Institute* 4, no. 2 (April 1971).
Betts, Raymond F. "Dakar: Ville IMPERIALE (1857–1960)." In *Colonial Cities: Essays on Urbanism in a Colonial Context*, edited by Robert Ross and Gerard J. Telkamp. Dordrecht: Martinus Nijhoff Publishers, 1985.
Bulfin, Michael P. "Bursting at the Seams: Water Access and Housing in Luanda." *Ufamahu: A Journal of African Studies* 3, no. 1 (2009).
Burton, Andrew. *African Underclass: Urbanization, Crime and Colonial Order in Dar es Salaam.* London: The British Institute in East Africa, 2005.
Carland, John M. *The Colonial Office and Nigeria, 1898–1914.* Stanford, CA: Hoover Institution Press, 1985.
Coquer-Vidrovitch, Catherine. "The Process of Urbanization in Africa: From the Origins to the Beginning of Independence; An Overview Paper." *African Studies Review* 31, no. 1 (1990).
Freund, Bill. *The African City: A History.* Cambridge: Cambridge University Press, 2007.
Ginsburg, Rebecca. "The View from the Back Step: White Children Learn about Race in Johannesburg Suburban Homes." In *Designing Modern Childhoods: History Space and Material Culture of Children*, edited by Marta Gutman and Nind de Coninck-Smith. New Brunswick, NJ: Rutgers University Press, 2008.
Hay, Allison, and Richard Harris. "'Shauri ya Sera Kali': The Colonial Regime of Urban Housing in Kenya to 1939." *Urban History* 34, no. 3 (2007).
Hayter, Theresa. *French Aid.* London: Overseas Development Institute, 1966.
Hilaral, Kalpana. "Gujarati Dukawallas in the Indian Ocean Region: A Case Study of Natal (1880–1910)." *Man in India* 94, no. 3 (2014).
Home, Robert. *Of Planting and Planning: The Making of British Colonial Cities.* 2nd ed. Routledge, London, 2013.
Hungerford, Hilary, and Sarah L. Smiley. "Comparing Colonial Water Supply in British and French Africa." *Journal of Historical Geography* 52 (2016).
Hungwe, Chipo. "Putting Them in Their Place: "Respectable" and "Unrespectable" Women in Zimbabwe Gender Struggles." *Feminist Africa* 6, (2006).
Igbafe, Phillip. *Benin Under British Administration: The Impact of Colonialism on African Kingdom, 1897–1938.* Longman, 1979.
Iliffe, John. *The African Poor: A History.* Cambridge: Cambridge University Press, 1987.
Jaekel, Francis. *The History of the Nigerian Railway*, Vol. 1. Ibadan: Spectrum Books, 1997.
Kurt, Andrew. "The Search for Prester John, a Projected Crusade and the Eroding Prestige of Ethiopian Kings, c.1200–c.1540." *Journal of Medieval History* 39, no. 3 (2013).
Mamdani, Mahmood. *Citizens and Subjects: Contemporary Africa and the Legacy of Late Colonialism.* Programme on Ethnic and Federal Studies, Ibadan: University of Ibadan, 2002.
Mbembe, Achille. "The Intimacy of Tyranny." In Mbembe, *On the Postcolony.* Berkeley, CA: University of California Press, 2001.
Mudimbe, V.Y. *The Invention of Africa.* Bloomington: Indiana University Press, 1988.

Murunga, Godwin R. "'Inherently Unhygienic Races': Plague and the Origin of Settler Dominance in Nairobi, 1899–1907." In *African Urban Spaces in Historical Perspective*, edited by Steven J. Salm and Toyin Falola. Rochester: University of Rochester Press, 2005.

Njoh, Ambe. "Urban Planning as a Tool of Power and Social Control in Africa." *Planning Perspectives* 24, no. 3 (2009).

Ogionwo, W. *The City of Port Harcourt: A Symposium on Its Growth and Development*. Ibadan: Heinemann Educational Books (Nig.) Ltd, 1979, 21.

Okonkwo, Rina. *Protest Movements in Lagos, 1908–1930*. Enugu: ABIK Publishers, 1998.

Otiso, Kefa M. "Colonial Urbanization and Urban Management in Kenya." In *African Urban Spaces in Historical Perspective*, edited by Steven J. Salm and Toyin Falola. Rochester: University of Rochester Press, 2005.

Price, Barbara. "Cause, Effect and the Anthropological Study of Urbanism." In *Urbanization in the Americas from Its Beginning to the Present*, edited by Richard Schaedel, J. Hardoy, and N. Scott-Kinzer. The Hague: Mouton Publishers, 1978.

Salm, Steven J., and Toyin Falola, eds. *African Urban Spaces in Historical Perspective*. Rochester: University of Rochester Press, 2005.

Shokpeka, S.A. "Local Government and Development in Benin Province 1938–1960." PhD thesis, University of Benin, Benin City, 1990.

Smiley, Sarah. "The City of Three Colors: Segregation in Colonial Dar es Salaam, 1891–1961." *Historical Geography* 37 (2009).

Swanson, Maynard. "The Sanitation Syndrome: Bubonic Plague and Urban Native Policy in the Cape Colony, 1900–1909." *Journal of African History* 18, no. 3 (1977).

Vansina, Jan. "The Kongo Kingdom and Its Neighbours." In *Africa from the Sixteenth to the Eighteenth Century*, edited by Bethwell A. Ogot. Los Angeles: University of California Press, 1992.

Vassanji, M.G. *And Home Was Kariakoo: A Memoir of East Africa*. New York: Penguin Random House, 2015.

Zeleza, Paul. "The Pasts and Futures of African History: A Generational Inventory." *African History Review* 39, no. 1 (2007).

Zeleza, Paul Tiyambe. "The Troubled Encounter between Postcolonialism and African History." *Journal of Canadian Historical Association* 17, no. 2 (2006).

———, ed. "Introduction." In *The Study of Africa: Global and Transcontinental Engagements*, Vol. 2. African Book Collective, 2006.

CHAPTER 13

Africa and the First World War

Meshack Owino

The First World War is remembered almost throughout the African continent with resentment. Indeed, many African soldiers and their families remember the war bitterly, with negative terms and adjectives peppering their conversations about it. In Senegal, veterans of the war and their families often refer to it as '"a very, very bad thing"' or as '"the worst thing I ever saw"'.[1] The main reason for this is that many African soldiers were conscripted to serve in the conflict, and many of these conscripts suffered or lost their lives as a result.[2] The families of these men resented the war because it caused them to lose their loved ones. In fact, many African soldiers and their families equated the war with suffering, toil, and death. Africans in Malawi (Nyasaland) associated the war with *tengatenga*—military labor.[3] Those in East Africa associated it with military-labor units such as the Carrier Corps (Kariokor), and with death.[4] It has been estimated that nearly two million Africans served in the First World War[5] and that almost 200,000 of them perished in it.[6] The death of such a large number of men during and after the war undeniably left many African families grieving and mourning. It has been estimated that, in East Africa alone, nearly one million African servicemen were involved in the war in one way or another, and that about 10% of them lost their lives during it. According to Geoffrey Hodge, 'the total mortality rate' among the men in East Africa 'was well over 100,000'.[7] The overwhelming unpopularity of the First World War in Africa can be discerned from the reaction and behavior of Africans after the outbreak of the Second World War. When the

---

M. Owino (✉)
History Department, Cleveland State University,
Cleveland, OH, USA

© The Author(s) 2018
M.S. Shanguhyia and T. Falola (eds.),
The Palgrave Handbook of African Colonial and Postcolonial History,
https://doi.org/10.1057/978-1-137-59426-6_13

latter broke out and colonial authorities started canvasing for recruits to serve in it, many Africans immediately became apprehensive because they and their family members still remembered how the previous conflict had created many problems such as illness, death, and general suffering among Africans. One colonial official in Kenya reminisced that any time the war was mentioned, people remembered the 'ill-fated Carrier Corps of the First World War and everything connected with it'.[8] When government recruiting agencies in Tanganyika started looking for new recruits to serve in the Second World War, they were shocked to find that memories of illness, injuries, mourning, bereavements, and death during the previous war were still so strong among African families that they 'left a general distrust of military service'.[9] The war was associated with suffering, injuries, and death. Fathers and mothers remembered it for the death of their sons; wives of their husbands; children of their fathers; and communities of their lost future. Many African wars of resistance were in fact organized against conscription into this war. When and how did the First World War begin and spread into Africa? How did Africans get entangled in it? What was the nature of their experience?

THE BEGINNING OF THE FIRST WORLD WAR AND ITS EXPANSION INTO THE AFRICAN CONTINENT

While a full, detailed chronicle of the origin of the First World War is beyond the scope of this chapter, it is necessary to mention the one major factor that contributed to the acceleration of the events that led to the war, and to its expansion into Africa: the assassination of Archduke Ferdinand, the heir to the throne of Austria-Hungary, in Sarajevo, Serbia, on June 28, 1914. Angered by the death of the heir to the throne, Austria-Hungary declared war on Serbia and at the same time started seeking diplomatic and military support from Germany in the event that Russia, the traditional ally of Serbia, came to the aide of Serbia during the quarrel. The dispute between Austria-Hungary and Serbia quickly expanded: Russia came to the aid of Serbia and declared war on Austria-Hungary; and Germany, in retaliation for the Russian declaration of war on Austria-Hungary, in turn declared war on Russia. The war further expanded when Germany declared war on Luxembourg, France, and Belgium. The conflagration soon consumed nearly all of the most powerful nations in Europe at the time that Britain declared war on Germany on August 4, 1914.

Within a short time, the flames of war started flickering over the African continent. The major reason for this was that the nations declaring war and fighting with each other in Europe happened not only to be the most powerful on on earth at the time, but also the most important colonial powers controlling a vast swathe of land in Africa. The British, the French, the Belgians, and the Germans controlled, between them, perhaps more than three-quarters of the colonies in Africa, and certainly the largest and most populous territories.

Thus, when the British, the Germans, the French, and the Belgians and, later on, the Portuguese, declared war on each other in Europe, their conflict quickly expanded into Africa as they rushed to their colonies to draft support.

Thus, following their declaration of the war on the Germans, the British and the French quickly mobilized Africans in their colonies to help them out.[10] The French sent most of their African troops to fight in the trenches overseas in Europe. The British, on the other hand—and to some extent a few French forces in West Africa—decided to mobilize their African troops against the German colonies in Africa, hoping for a quick campaign before focusing their full attention on the campaign in Europe. For a time, everything went according to plan. The fighting in Togo lasted less than one month, coming to an end with the German surrender to the Allied troops on August 25, 1914. The fighting in Namibia lasted a little longer, with the Germans not surrendering until July 1915. The British plans for a quick war in Africa started unraveling in Cameroon, where fighting did not come to an end until April 1916, and completely collapsed in East Africa, where fighting dragged on until the end of the war in 1918. Ultimately, the French deployed 'upwards of 160,000 West African soldiers', known as *tirailleurs*, in the trenches of the European campaign during the war[11] and the British, with the support of their African troops known as *askaris*, fought the longest campaign of the entire war in East Africa.[12]

The campaign in East Africa lasted longer than the British had wanted because, while the plan had been for a short, quick campaign before focusing attention on the European campaign, the Germans, led by General Paul von Lettow-Vorbeck, planned to keep them bogged down in Africa. Thus, when the war broke out, von Lettow-Vorbeck's strategy was to lure the British troops into a long guerrilla campaign that covered many parts of Tanganyika, Mozambique, and Zambia. Indeed, it has been observed by many scholars of the First World War in Africa that the East African Campaign did not come to an end until General Lettow-Vorbeck surrendered to the Allies at Abercon, Northern Rhodesia (Zambia)[13] on November 25, 1918, 'two weeks after the signature of the armistice in Europe'.[14] The war had lasted longer in East Africa than anywhere else on the continent or in any other part of the world, and, consequently, the African participation in it was probably also the longest.

With the exception of a few colonies in Africa belonging to the Portuguese, the Italians, and the Spaniards, Africans in many parts of the continent participated in the war both directly and indirectly from its very outbreak. They participated intensively and extensively in the war. There were many Africans in Senegal, Gambia, Guinea, Niger, Burkina Faso, Côte d'Ivoire, Mali, Togo, Cameroon, Namibia, Tanganyika, Kenya, Mozambique, Zambia, Zimbabwe, the Democratic Republic of Congo, Rwanda, and Burundi who participated in the war as infantrymen on the fronts in Europe and Africa.

There were others who provided manpower and material goods to the European colonial powers involved in the war. Indeed, it has been estimated that nearly 2 million Africans served in the First World War.[15] While some Africans provided food and other material services to the European powers during the war, others provided direct military service as combatants and support troops.

Yet, what is very ironic about the African military service in the First World War in Europe and Africa is that they were actually not supposed to serve. The Europeans, particularly the European colonial powers in Africa, did not want Africans involved for several reasons. First, the Europeans, according to Reigel, believed that the war would be a short one. No one '... expected a long war ... all experts predicted a short conflict, a few months or perhaps a year or so, and of course expected their side to win'.[16] It was consequently felt that there was no need to recruit Africans. The second reason was that European experts believed that the war 'would largely be fought in Europe rather than Africa',[17] making it even more imperative to keep Africans out of it. Otherwise, they might end up travelling to, fighting in, and even living in Europe after the war. The third reason why the Europeans did not want Africans fighting in the war was that it could reduce the status of whites in the eyes of Africans in the African continent. In the words of Stratchan, 'the spectacle of white fighting white would reduce the status of the European' among Africans.[18] 'Blacks would kill whites, and the forfeiture would be white racial supremacy.'[19] According to Reigel, the Europeans perceived the conflict as a 'white man's war'.[20]

The fourth reason why the Europeans did not want Africans fighting in the war was that it would rekindle African military traditions,[21] which, in the end, might jeopardize the very existence of the colonial system in Africa.[22] If Africans were enlisted into the war, it was claimed, their warrior traditions might be 'reawakened' and their knowledge of how to use the new weapons might grow to the detriment of whites and the colonial system in Africa. In the words of Reigel, the Europeans wanted to keep Africans out of the war for 'fear of losing control of their African subjects'.[23] In short, Africans were not supposed to be involved in the First World War.

It was therefore quite ironic that, in spite of the pervasive fear of African participation in the conflict, the European colonial powers began recruiting Africans into their armies almost as soon as it broke out. Immediately the war started and its realities began sinking in, the Europeans abandoned their 'short-lived' plans for keeping Africans out of it.[24] They began recruiting and preparing Africans to fight. Strachan argues that it was the Entente powers that, in spite of their own propaganda warning the Germans against enlisting Africans to fight, started the policy of 'arming the African"[25] for the war. Indeed, once the conflict began in earnest, almost all the European powers, including the Germans, started recruiting a large number of Africans into their armies and deploying them into the war. The French, for example, sent large numbers of West Africans into *tirailleurs Senegalais*, employing well-known and well-connected African leaders such as Blaise Diagne to recruit for them. It is estimated that well over '140,000 West Africans were recruited into the French army and served as combatants on the western front between 1914–1918'.[26] Some scholars believe that the number of Africans who served in the French army during the war was even higher. Nancy Lawler believes that 'upwards of 160,000 West African soldiers, virtually all of them conscripts, fought in the trenches during World War I'.[27] 'The number of African soldiers recruited by the French in French West Africa during the war', according to Strachan 'was something like 200,000 soldiers'.[28] Joe Lunn contends that probably as many as "180,000 Africans [from West Africa] were transported overseas by the French between 1914–1918.[29] Other scholars believe that the French probably sent over 450,000 African soldiers to fight.[30]

The number of African soldiers from West Africa recruited by the British to help them in the war was also not small. According to Stratchan, 'something like 25,000 soldiers' were recruited by the British to serve in the British West African Frontier Force.[31] African soldiers from East and Central Africa were also enlisted by the British to serve in the King's African Rifles (KAR) and their numbers grew from 2319 at the beginning of the war to about 8000 men during the war, and to 35,000 men by the end.[32] Africans in Southern Rhodesia were enlisted into the Rhodesia Native Regiment in 1916 for service in the war. By 1918, the number of Africans in it was '2360 men … less than 1% of the total African male population, and 75% of them originated from outside the colony'.[33] African soldiers were also enlisted by the Germans into the Schuzetruppe for military service in Togo, the Cameroons, Namibia (German South-West Africa), and East Africa during the war. African soldiers also served in the Force Publique of the Belgians in the Congo and in other European armies during the war, notably in that of the Portuguese in East and Central Africa.[34]

There is one important distinction that must be made when discussing the African experience in the First World War. The African servicemen were not homogeneous. While many of them served as infantrymen wielding rifles and fighting on the frontlines (notably deployed by the French in Europe and the British in East Africa), the majority were ordinary military laborers or porters—the African carriers. The African carriers came from all over the continent. Stratchan observes that they originated in 'Eastern Belgian Congo, Rwanda, Uganda, Kenya, German East Africa, Northern Rhodesia, Nyasaland, and the northern areas of Mozambique'.[35] They also came from British West Africa. 'There were 57,500 carriers, twice as many as the number of soldiers, in British West Africa'.[36] A total of 25,000 black South Africans enlisted as laborers in the South African Native Labor Contingent to support British troops in France between September 1916 and January 1918.[37] There were about 260,000 porters serving Belgium's domestic and external needs during the war.[38] There were 30,000 porters recruited by the Portuguese to serve the British needs, and 90,000 to serve their own.[39] The highest number of African carriers serving in the war came from East Africa, because the war lasted longest in that theater, requiring more manpower serving for a longer period than anywhere else. Consequently, many African carriers were variously recruited by the British and the Germans to help them in the war in East Africa. Geoffrey Hodges notes that the number of African carriers from East Africa serving in the war was well over a million.[40]

These carriers constituted the majority of the African men serving in the European armies during the war, and their role in prosecuting the conflict was especially important when one considers that a transport system based on motor vehicles and trains in Africa during the period was almost non-existent.[41] Where motor vehicles and trains were available, their use by the military often turned out to be limited because, according to Reigel, 'trucks, cars, and motorcycles' often got 'stuck in the mud … often teams of draft animals were required to pull trucks out of mud pits'.[42] Where 'draught or pack animals [could be] usable', observes Stratchan, the animals often 'fell prey to the tsetse fly'.[43] The Second Division of the British army in East Africa, was, for example, prevented from moving beyond areas it had conquered by this pest.[44] Moreover, 'tens of thousands of horses, mules, and oxen'[45] were killed by 'animal epidemics spreading out throughout the region'.[46] Worsening the shortage of animals that could be deployed to provide transport to the military were other problems such as 'wild animals … attacking lines of animals harnessed together, such as horse artillery teams'.[47] Faced by all these transport problems and challenges, European powers turned to Africans to serve as porters and laborers in the war, a solution to military transport problems that ultimately became devastating to the health and lives of African carriers. The European powers recruited and relied on large numbers of 'African carriers' to carry supplies to the front, and to evacuate the injured and the dead back to the camps. In all, 'somewhere over 2 million Africans served in the First World War as soldiers and laborers'.[48]

The African soldiers and carriers served in the war with "distinction, dedication, and commitment."[49] They participated in it closely, intimately, and professionally. They were integral to its prosecution in Africa. Indeed, when one thinks about the serious transport problems bedeviling the colonial armies in Africa at this time, it is difficult to imagine how the war would have continued without them. The African carriers were literally the 'feet and hands of the colonial armies'.[50] They were like a 'human chain linking troops to their bases, and without it, they could not move, feed, or fight'.[51] Reigel contends that the carriers were 'the primary method of transport in the military logistics' during the last two years of the war in East Africa.[52] The carriers (those 'beasts of burden' in the African campaigns) literally carried Europeans and their fellow Africans forward and in retreat.[53]

The primary responsibility of the carriers was carrying provisions such as ammunition, food, and other military supplies to the fighting troops on the front lines, and evacuating the injured and the dead. The carriers also carried out many other responsibilities. Reigel provides a very detailed list of the carriers' responsibilities, including: 'armed scouts, headmen, interpreters, guides, cooks, bakers, mounted gun carriers, machine gun carriers, mortar carriers, signal porters, stretcher bearers, stevedores, canoe men (aka boatmen, paddle men), truck drivers, steamer crewmen, road/bridge builders, drain/latrine/trench diggers, hut builders, wood choppers, rail-road gangs, dockworkers, tailors, cobblers, blacksmiths, grooms, sweeps, carpenters, carrier police, and personal servants'.[54] The African carriers also served as personal aides to European soldiers during the war. Stratchan states that 'seven to nine porters' were routinely attached as aides to 'each British officer' in East Africa.[55] Eight porters were attached to each Belgian officer. Four to six porters served as servants and cooks to each German officer in West Africa. When the European soldiers in the German army marched through Portuguese East Africa during the last years of the war, "they were each allowed to have three porters at their disposal."[56] About "two or three porters were attached to British and German officers" in the Cameroons.[57] These African personal aides to European soldiers were among the many African soldiers and carriers who served in the various European armies during the First World War.

The African carriers and soldiers served with courage, élan, dedication, distinction, and professionalism during the war. They readily sacrificed their comfort and lives for the causes for which they were enlisted. Indeed, many of them gave up their lives during military service. They were, in the words of Reigel, 'dedicated and professional'[58] men who ended up paying with their lives for their dedication and professionalism.

The Experience of African Soldiers and Carriers in the First World War

The First World War left a devastating impact on the African landscape. Many African soldiers and carriers lost their lives during the war. As already mentioned, over 2 million Africans served, and, out of that number, more than 200,000 died or were killed in action.[59] There were many factors for this. The first obvious cause was participation in the war itself. Exposure to a war environment brimming with bullets and bombs on the front lines, for four years, could not have ended without African soldiers losing their lives. Many African soldiers died in combat during campaigns in Africa, and, even more were killed on the Western Front in Europe. The number of African soldiers killed during combat grew as the campaigns progressed steadily through Europe and Africa. Analysis reveals that the most African soldiers were killed in Europe. The French army, for example, 'listed almost 30,000 deaths among the 135,000 African troops serving in Europe'.[60] Unfortunately, we will never know the exact number of African carriers killed in the French army because the French, like the Germans, did not leave clear records on the death of their African carriers.[61] Many African soldiers also lost their lives during the campaign in Togo, Namibia (German South-West Africa), Cameroon, and East Africa. It seems that more African soldiers were killed in Cameroon and East Africa than in Togo and Namibia (German South-West Africa) because the war went on for a much longer period in the former territories than in the latter territories. It has been noted that von Lettow-Vorbeck, commander of German forces in East Africa, tried to reduce casualties among his troops by avoiding pitched battles against British troops during the campaign in East Africa;[62] but, still, a considerable number of African soldiers in his army got killed during fighting here. About 1800 African soldiers were killed while serving in the German Schuzetruppe in East Africa during the war,[63] and about 1377 African soldiers were killed on the British side of the campaign during that campaign.[64]

There are scholars who believe that many African soldiers lost their lives on the front lines during the war because of a deliberate policy of the Europeans, especially the French, of using African soldiers as cannon-fodder exposed to greater danger than European soldiers.[65] Admittedly, this view is controversial, but there are scholars who believe that such a policy existed; that African soldiers such as the Senegalese troops in the French army were treated 'as no more than cannon fodder',[66] and were 'systematically employed … as assault troops with the deliberate intention of sacrificing their lives in order to spare French ones'.[67] If such a policy truly existed, then there is no doubt that it contributed to the death of some of the estimated 30,000 French African troops on the Western Front in Europe during the war.[68]

Nevertheless, although many African servicemen died during combat in the war, an analysis of the military casualties reveals that many of them occurred due to non-combat factors. The most serious of these non-combat factors were health problems brought about by exhaustion, exposure to the elements, and diseases. According to Reigel, many 'insects, microorganisms, and the diseases' in the environment caused illness, diseases, and death amongst African soldiers and carriers[69] during the war in East Africa. Reigel estimates that, 'for every combat casualty, there were thirty more due to illness'.[70] Among the most serious of these diseases were malaria and dysentery. Malaria, according to Stratchan, 'was the principal cause of sickness' among soldiers and carriers during the war.[71] Apart from malaria, African soldiers and carriers were also vulnerable to 'cholera, typhoid, dysentery, typhus, guinea worms, and chiggers'.[72] Indeed, Stratchan and Hodges argue that malaria and dysentery were the two most serious problems causing major illnesses and deaths among the African soldiers and carriers in East Africa.[73]

Diseases and other health problems ran riot among African soldiers and carriers for several reasons. To begin with, the recruitment quota system imposed on headmen and chiefs, and the conscription policy that came into effect with it, made many of them so desperate for recruits that they often recruited soldiers and carriers who were not physically fit for military service.[74] Such soldiers and carriers were often very vulnerable to diseases such as malaria and dysentery. The army policy of deploying African carriers and soldiers far away from their homes to reduce desertion from military service during the war also exposed soldiers and carriers to diseases and ill-health. In the words of Stratchan, 'the migration of so many Africans out of their native localities exposed them to fresh infections, and the physical and psychological demands [of the war] lowered their resistance to disease'.[75] Africans from malaria-free regions, for example, became very vulnerable to malaria while serving in areas 'infested with malaria-causing mosquitoes'.[76] The biggest challenge to the African soldiers and carriers in East Africa during the war was, according to Reigel: the environment.[77]

Another reason for the vulnerability of African soldiers and carriers to ill-health was their unfamiliarity with the army food that was often badly cooked. Serving in a new environment far away from home, African soldiers and carriers were often served with new types of food to which they were not accustomed and did not like. To make matters worse, the food was often badly cooked because the cooks did not know how to cook well, did not have enough time to prepare the food adequately, and did not maintain proper sanitary conditions while cooking. The unfamiliar, badly cooked food was also not nutritious enough to keep the soldiers and the carriers healthy. Instead of nourishing the African soldiers and carriers and protecting them from diseases, the often "bland and badly cooked food" left the them suffering from diseases such as "dysentery and beriberi." Soldiers and carriers from Uganda who normally 'subsisted on bananas, sweet potatoes, and beans"[78] at home, for example, 'developed intestinal diseases' when they were made to start eating badly cooked maize meals that they were not used to.[79]

Exhaustion, hunger, and dehydration also contributed to health problems among African soldiers and carriers during the war. Indeed, many African servicemen lost their lives due to dehydration and exhaustion during military service. Reigel observes that large numbers of them often suffered from exhaustion because of fighting and marching over long distances during military service. Many collapsed and died from exhaustion after walking almost non-stop between base camps and the front lines. Others incurred the wrath of the jigger menace after walking bare-footed over long distances in unfamiliar territories.[80] Stratchan observes that as much as '40% of the West African Frontier Force was lame by the end of the Cameroons campaign'.[81] But jiggers were not the only problems causing ailments and deaths among the soldiers and carriers. There were also 'the lions, hippos, and venomous snakes' that were 'frightening enough' but also 'responsible for a few casualties".[82]

Exposure to the elements also contributed to illness, injury, and death among African soldiers and carriers during the war. Poorly built and badly maintained camps left them unprotected from the hot sun, and, sometimes, the unrelenting rainfall, and the cold air, especially at night. In 1915, for example, poorly built, overcrowded, and badly maintained tents serving as barracks led to the creation of 'disease-ridden environments in which mortality rates were often exceptionally high'[83] in Senegal. This problem did not end even after the tents were brought down and permanent barracks constructed in their place. The barracks were often badly maintained and unsanitary. Many soldiers thus continued to lose their lives.

Many African soldiers and carriers who contracted diseases during the war died because of an inadequate supply of proper medicine and lack of trained medical personnel. After contracting diseases or getting injured during military service, many African soldiers and carriers found to their dismay that there was a shortage of medicine and trained health-care personnel to attend to their medical needs, even if they were lucky enough to get to a hospital. Without proper medicine and adequate attention from properly trained health-care personnel, many injured and ill soldiers and carriers needlessly lost their lives to easily curable medical problems.[84] The shortage of medicine and medical personnel was often worsened by overcrowding in hospitals, leading to more people contracting chest problems and other diseases, and dying. All these problems (deployment to unfamiliar territories, bad food, exhaustion, dehydration, exposure to the elements, shortage of medicine, lack of properly trained medical personnel, congestion, among others) contributed to the vulnerability of African troops, especially the carriers, to diseases during the First World War. Most of them lost their lives to diseases during the war. 'Disease, not battle, disabled armies in Africa.'[85]

Thus, although many African soldiers and carriers lost their lives during fighting on the front lines, even more lost their lives to non-combat factors such as diseases malaria, dysentery, beriberi, typhoid, bilharzia, and cholera. For example, while 1377 African soldiers in British service in East Africa were killed in combat, 2923 (more than double that number) died from disease.[86] Similarly, the Allied forces in West Africa 'lost a total of 4600 men through death or wounding in action or through death by disease', in contrast to over 35,000 cases 'admitted to hospital'.[87] Indeed, Stratchan contends that the death rate among the African carriers in East and West Africa was 'about 20%' during the war, which, he observes, was 'similar to that of an army on a so-called major front'.[88] In view of the high casualty rate among African soldiers during the First World War, it should therefore not be very surprising that many Africans viewed the conflict as a 'very bad thing', as 'the worst thing that ever happened'.

The Impact of the First World War on Africa

The First World War had major implications for the African continent. Apart from the large number of Africans who died, the war devastated the economies of many parts of Africa. Young, strong, and energetic men were taken away from their homes to serve, and their farms suffered from a shortage of manpower. Agricultural production in many parts of Africa declined. The combatants' scorched-earth policy (aimed at denying each other provisions) led to the destruction of many African villages and harvests that could not be requisitioned.[89] All these led to cases of famine in many parts of Africa, and the shortage of food was exacerbated by the outbreak of human and livestock diseases leading to even more suffering and death during and after the war. French Equatorial Africa, for example, experienced the worst famine in its history from 1918–1926.[90] East Africa was not spared these calamities either. For example, the 'worst drought and disease epidemic to affect Kenya in the twentieth century'[91] broke out shortly after the end of the war in 1918. The war and the outbreak of these calamities contributed together to the death of many people and their livestock. The population of Belgian Congo 'fell by one-third or one-half'[92] during this period. The colonial state in Kenya 'was forced to import food to meet the distress'[93] following the outbreak of food shortage and famine in Kenya during the same period. Many people therefore suffered during and after the First World War. The conflict also changed the political map of Africa as the German colonies of Togo, Cameroon, Namibia, and Tanganyika changed hands and were governed by other colonial powers. The newly formed League of Nations handed over Togo and Cameroons to the French, Namibia to the Union of South Africa, and Tanganyika to the British. These colonies were supposed to be governed on behalf of the League of Nations. Entrusted with the task of taking care of the former German colonies on behalf of the League of Nation, the British and the French not only consolidated their hold on their African colonies, but also increased their power and influence over many parts of Africa. The war also raised the political consciousness of many Africans. Many Africans started trying to change the political dynamics of their colonies by engaging in politics in their colonies. These Africans formed political associations, trade unions, newspapers, and literary clubs to articulate their grievances against the colonial system and demand redress. Their growing political consciousness forced many colonial powers to recognize the need to implement reforms. The biggest impact of the war, however, was in the experience of African soldiers and carriers. For many of them, it was unforgettably a 'very bad thing', 'the worst thing that ever happened'.

Conclusion

This chapter has examined how the First World War broke out and expanded into Africa. It has focused on the conflict's key campaigns, and the experience of African soldiers and carriers, particularly their suffering and death. The majority of African people remembered the terrible suffering they had endured either on the front lines during the fighting or from related injuries and diseases.

NOTES

1. Joe Lunn, *Memoirs of the Maelstrom: A Senegalese Oral History of the First World War* (Portsmouth, NH: Heinemann, Oxford: James Currey, Cape Town: David Philip, 1999), 215.
2. Geoffrey Hodges, *Kariakor: The Carrier Corps: The Story of the Military Labour Forces in the Conquest of German East Africa, 1914–1918* (Nairobi: University of Nairobi Press, 1997), 19, 150–85.
3. Melvin Page, "The War of Thangata: Nyasaland and The East African Campaign, 1914–1918," in David Birmingham, A.G. Hopkins, R.C.C. Law, and A.D. Roberts, World War I and Africa, *The Journal of African History* 19, no. 1 (1978), 90–97. See also: Melvin E. Page, "Introduction: Black Men in a White Man's War," in *Africa and the First World War* ed. Melvin E. Page (London: The MacMillan Press Ltd., 1987), 8–13.
4. The misery of African veterans of the Carrier Corps was starkly captured by Geoffrey Hodges in his book, *Kariokor: The Carrier Corps*. According to Hodges, African service in the Carrier Corps during the First World War was characterized by suffering and death from negligence, starvation, exhaustion, and diseases.
5. Hew Strachan, *The First World War in Africa* (Oxford: Oxford University Press, 2004), 3.
6. Melvin Page, "The War of Thangata".
7. Geoffrey Hodges, *Kariakor*, 21.
8. S.H. Fazan, "The Pioneers: A Memorandum on Certain Points Outstanding 25 September, 1939" (KNA/PC/NZA/2/3/21, The Pioneers, 1939–1942).
9. Timothy Parsons, *The African Rank-and-File: Social Implications of Colonial Military Service in the King's African Rifles, 1902–1964* (Portsmouth, NH: Heinemann, Oxford: James Currey, Cape Town: David Philip, Nairobi: EAEP, Kampala: Fountain, 1999), 74.
10. Hew Strachan, *The First World War*, 1.
11. Nancy Lawler, *Soldiers of Misfortune: Ivoirien Tirailleurs of World War II* (Athens, OH: Ohio University Press, 1992), 2.
12. Byron Farwell, *The Great War in Africa: 1914–1918* (New York and London: W. W. Norton & Company, July 17, 1989; Charles Miller, *Battle for the Bundu: The First World War i East Africa* (New York: Macmillan Publishing Co., 1974); and Edward Paice, *World War I: The African Front: An Imperial War on the African Continent* (London: Pegasus, 2008).
13. See note 10 above.
14. Ibid.
15. Hew Strachan, The First World War, 3.
16. Corey W. Reigel, *The Last Great Safari: East Africa in World War I* (Lanham, Maryland, Boulder, New York, and London: Rowman and Littlefield, 2015), 18.
17. Hew Stratchan, *The First World War*, 2.
18. Ibid.
19. Ibid.
20. Corey W. Reigel, *The Last Great Safari*, 101.
21. See note 17 above.
22. Ibid.; Corey W. Reigel, *The Last Great Safari*, 102.

23. Corey W. Reigel, *The Last Great Safari*, 102.
24. Ibid., 83–114.
25. Hew Strachan, *The First World War*, 3.
26. Joe Lunn, *Memoirs of a Maelstrom*, 1, 120.
27. Nancy Lawler, *Soldiers of Misfortune*, 2.
28. Hew Strachan, *The First World War*, 4.
29. Joe Lunn, *Memoirs of Maelstrom*, p. 100.
30. C.M. Andrew and A.S. Kanya-Forstner, "France, Africa, and the First World War," in David Birmingham, A.G. Hopkins, R.C.C. Law, and A.D. Roberts, World War I and Africa, *Journal of African History* 19, no. 1 (1978): 16.
31. See note 28 above.
32. Corey W. Reigel, *The Last Great Safari*, 48.
33. See note 28 above.
34. For a general overview of African military experience in the colonial army, see: Timothy Parsons, *The African Rank-and-File*. See also: Michelle Moyd, *Violent Intermediaries: African Soldiers, Conquest, and Everyday Colonialism in German East Africa* (Athens, OH: Ohio University Press, 2014).
35. Hew Strachan, *The First World War*, 5.
36. Ibid.
37. B.P. Willan, "The South African Native Labor Contingent, 1916–1918," in David Birmingham, A.G. Hopkins, R.C.C. Law, and A.D. Roberts, World War I and Africa, *Journal of African History* 19, no. 1 (1978): 61.
38. Hew Strachan, *The First World War*, 6.
39. Ibid.
40. Geoffrey Hodges, *Kariokor*, 15–16.
41. See note 34 above.
42. Corey W. Reigel, *The Last Great Safari*, 28.
43. See note 34 above.
44. See note 41 above.
45. Ibid.
46. Ibid.
47. Ibid.
48. See note 25 above.
49. The best analysis of the dedication, elan, and professionalism of African soldiers and carriers in the war can be gleaned from Melvin E. Page, "Introduction: Black Men in a White Man's War," 9–14.
50. Geoffrey Hodges, *Kariakor*, 3.
51. See note 34 above.
52. Corey W. Reigel, *The Last Great Safari*, ix.
53. Melvin E. Page, "Introduction: Black Men in a White Man's War," 8.
54. Corey W. Reigel, *The Last Great Safari*, 54–55.
55. Hew Strachan, *The First World War*, 8.
56. Ibid.
57. Hew Strachan, The First World War, 5.
58. Corey W. Reigel, *The Last Great Safari*, 50.
59. See note 25 above.
60. Melvin E. Page, "Introduction: Black Men in a White Man's War," 14.
61. Ibid.

62. Corey W. Reigel, *The Last Great Safari*, 26.
63. See note 59 above.
64. Hew Strachan, *The First World War*, 9.
65. Henri Barbusse, "Introduction: Black Men in a White Man's War," quoted in Melvin E. Page, 9.
66. Joe Lunn, *Memoirs of the Maelstrom*, 120.
67. Ibid.
68. Joe Lunn, Memoirs of the Maelstrom, 121.
69. Corey W. Reigel, *The Last Great Safari*, 31.
70. Ibid.
71. See note 63 above.
72. See note 68 above.
73. Hew Strachan, *The First World War*, 7; Hodges, *Kariokor*, 119–30.
74. See note 37 above.
75. Hew Strachan, The First World War, 9.
76. Ibid.
77. Corey W. Reigel, *The Last Great Safari*, 29.
78. See note 37 above.
79. Ibid.
80. See note 68 above.
81. See note 63 above.
82. See note 68 above.
83. Joe Lunn, *Memoirs of the Maelstrom*, 93.
84. Hew Strachan, *The First World War*, 10.
85. Ibid., 8.
86. E. Howard Gorges, *Great War in West Africa* (East Sussex, UK: Naval and Military Press, 2009), 261–62.
87. Hew Strachan, *The First World War*, 8; Gorges, *Great War in West Africa*, 261–62.
88. Ibid., 7.
89. Richard J. Reid, *A History of Modern Africa: 1800 to the Present* (Hoboken, NJ: Wiley-Blackwell, 2009), 192.
90. John Iliffe, *Africans: The History of a Continent* (Cambridge: Cambridge University Press, 1995), 209.
91. Robert Maxon, "The Years of the Revolutionary Advance, 1920–1929," in *A Modern History of Kenya, 1895–1980*, ed. William R. Ochieng (London: Evans Brothers Limited), 72.
92. John Iliffe, *Africans*, 211.
93. Robert Maxon, "The Years of the Revolutionary Advance, 1920–1929," 72.

Bibliography

Andrew, C.M., and A.S. Kanya-Forstner, "France, Africa, and the First World War", in David Birmingham, A.G. Hopkins, R.C.C. Law, and A.D. Roberts, World War I and Africa, *Journal of African History* 19, no. 1 (1978): 11–23.

Farwell, Byron. *The Great War in Africa: 1914–1918*. New York and London: W. W. Norton & Company, 1989.

Gorges, E. Howard. *Great War in West Africa*. East Sussex, UK: Naval and Military Press, 2009.

Hodges, Geoffrey. *Kariakor: The Carrier Corps: The Story of the Military Labour Forces in the Conquest of German East Africa, 1914–1918.* Nairobi: University of Nairobi Press, 1997.

Lunn, Joe. *Memoirs of the Maelstrom: A Senegalese Oral History of the First World War.* Portsmouth, NH: Heinemann, Oxford: James Currey, Cape Town: David Philip, 1999.

Lawler, Nancy. *Soldiers of Misfortune: Ivoirien Tirailleurs of World War II.* Athens, OH: Ohio University Press, 1992.

Miller, Charles. *Battle for the Bundu: The First World War in East Africa.* New York: Macmillan Publishing Co., 1974.

Moyd, Michelle. *Violent Intermediaries: African Soldiers, Conquest, and Everyday Colonialism in German East Africa.* Athens, OH: Ohio University Press, 2014.

Page, Melvin E., "The War of Thangata: Nyasaland and The East African Campaign, 1914–1918," in David Birmingham, A.G. Hopkins, R.C.C. Law, and A.D. Roberts, World War I and Africa, *Journal of African History* 19, no. 1 (1978): 87–100.

Page, Melvin E. "Introduction: Black Men in a White Man's War." In *Africa and the First World War*, edited by Melvin E. Page, 1–27. London: The MacMillan Press Ltd., 1987.

Paice, Edward. *World War I: The African Front: An Imperial War on the African Continent.* London: Pegasus, 2008.

Parsons, Timothy H. *The African Rank-and-File: Social Implications of Colonial Military Service in the King's African Rifles, 1902–1964.* Portsmouth, NH: Heinemann, Oxford: James Currey, Cape Town: David Philip, Nairobi: EAEP, Kampala: Fountain, Heinemann, 1999.

Reid, Richard J. *A History of Modern Africa: 1800 to the Present.* Hoboken, NJ: Wiley-Blackwell, 2009.

Reigel, Corey W. *The Last Great Safari: East Africa in World War I.* Lanham, Maryland, Boulder, New York, and London: Rowman and Littlefield, 2015.

Strachan, Hew. *The First World War in Africa.* Oxford: Oxford University Press, 2004.

Willan, B.P. "The South African Native Labor Contingent, 1916–1918," in David Birmingham, A.G. Hopkins, R.C.C. Law, and A.D. Roberts, World War I and Africa, *Journal of African History* 19, no. 1 (1978): 61–86.

CHAPTER 14

Africa and the Second World War

Meshack Owino

As political and military disputes escalated between various European powers in 1939, the colonial government in Kenya began military preparations for the outbreak of full-scale war. A colonial military unit was, for example, dispatched to the Kenya border with Ethiopia and Italian Somaliland. Circulars were sent to government functionaries in various parts of Kenya to begin identifying potentially hostile German and Italian citizens living in the colony, with the intention of interning them in case war broke out between European powers. Grounds were laid down for the recruitment of African soldiers to participate in the war and for the mobilization of colonial resources to support the government war-effort. As a result of these preparations, close to 100,000 African soldiers from Kenya were recruited and deployed to serve in the war. Such men included Johannes Ochanda Ameny, who abandoned school at Grade 6 and joined the Pioneer Corps on September 2, 1939.[1] They included men like Alfred Juma Bunde, who reportedly tried several times to join the military in Kisumu, Kenya, during the war and was turned away each time because he was too young. Bunde finally succeeded in joining the military when he tried his luck at another recruitment center at Onjiko, a few miles from Kisumu, on November 20, 1939.[2] There were such men all over the African continent who joined the military and served during the Second World War. Such men came from West Africa, North Africa, Southern Africa, East Africa, and Equatorial Africa, and went on to serve not only in their home continent but also in Europe, the Middle East, and the Far

M. Owino (✉)
History Department, Cleveland State University, Cleveland, OH, USA

East. When, how, and why did the war break out, and how did it spread into the African continent? How and why did men like Alfred Juma Bunde and Johannes Ochanda Ameny join the army and serve in the war? What were their experiences of military service? How did the rest of the African population participate in the war? How did the war affect the African continent and its people?

The Outbreak of the Second World War and its Expansion into the African Continent

Officially, the Second World War began with the German invasion of Poland on September 1, 1939. Britain, France, and their allies then issued an ultimatum to Germany to withdraw from Poland or face war. When Germany refused to heed the ultimatum, the British and French declared war on September 3, 1939. Yet, in spite of this war officially breaking out on September 3, 1939, many Africanists and African scholars believe that the war and the events leading to it did not really start on September 1, 1939 but, rather, on October 3, 1935.[3] This was four years before 1939, the official date of the outbreak of the war. It was the day that the Italians under Benito Mussolini unilaterally invaded Ethiopia, got away with it, and created a precedent that eventually emboldened Hitler to lead Germany in its aggressions against its neighbors, beginning with Austria in March 1938, then Czechoslovakia in September 1938 and ultimately Poland in September 1939, sparking off the Second World War.

Africanists and African historians argue that Italy, smarting from many military setbacks suffered at the hands of the Ethiopians during the nineteenth century (that is, during the colonial wars of conquest in Africa), vowed to make amends by one day invading and ruling Ethiopia. The Italian military reverses in Ethiopia included the Battle of Dogali in 1887, which ended with the death of many Italian soldiers at the hands of the Ethiopian army. After this humiliating debacle, the Italians began planning another war against Ethiopia. The opportunity came at the Battle of Amba Alaga in December 1895, which ended without an outright victory for either side. The Italians were therefore still not satisfied and continued looking for that elusive victory against the Ethiopians. In March 1896, they once again went to war with the Ethiopians; a conflict which ended with their rout and utter humiliation at the Battle of Adowa on March 1, 1896. Vandervort estimates that, 'out of the 10,000 Italian men who participated in the war, 289 officers and 4600 soldiers lost their lives'.[4] He observes further that were also '500 ... wounded, and 1500 taken prisoner'[5] during the encounter. The defeated Italians were forced to sign a treaty recognizing Ethiopia as an independent nation, Ethiopia thus carving a proud place for itself in the pages of African history as an independent, powerful nation that was never conquered and colonized by the Europeans. The Italians, on the other hand, felt very humiliated by the Battle of Adowa. They had suffered '50% casualties, far higher than those suffered in any other major battle of the nineteenth century',[6] and vowed to avenge their defeat. Benito Mussolini, who was thirteen years old at the time, swore that 'his 'whole imagination was engaged' by the tragedy of the Adowa so that his 'being labored' for revenge and the restoration of Italian honor'.[7]

After becoming Prime Minister of Italy, and later assuming absolute power in Italy, Benito Mussolini quickly moved to avenge the humiliating military disasters that the Italians had suffered at the hands of the Ethiopians during the nineteenth century. Putting his plans into action, Mussolini sent a strong army of 120,000 to invade Ethiopia on October 3, 1935.[8] The Italians defeated the Ethiopians this time, and they forced Emperor Haile Selassie to flee the Ethiopian capital Addis Ababa on May 2, 1936. The Italians occupied Addis Ababa on May 5, 1936, and officially annexed it to Italy on May 9, 1936.[9] Although the Italians succeeded in ousting the Emperor and were able to occupy and annex Ethiopia to Italy, they never succeeded in forcing Selassie to officially surrender to them. Instead, Selassie went into exile where he embarked on an international diplomatic campaign against the Italian invasion of his country, visiting various nations to raise awareness about Ethiopia's predicament, mobilizing international opinion against the injustice of the unilateral Italian occupation. Three years after the Italian invasion, Germany invaded and annexed Austria to Germany in March 1938 before going on to invade Czechoslovakia in September 1938, and Poland in September 1939. The Italian aggression against the Ethiopians in 1935 cannot be seperated from the German invasion of Austria, Czechoslovakia, and Poland. The road to Addis Ababa, Ethiopia, did not end there. It continued to Warsaw, Poland. It marked the beginning of the Second World War.

Many Africanists and African scholars believe that the Italian invasion of Ethiopia marked the beginning of the Second World War for one major reason. It laid the ground for the subsequent German invasions of Czechoslovakia and Poland. Simply put, it emboldened Germany. When Britain and France and other members of the League of Nations failed to respond robustly to the Italians' unilateral invasion of a country which was not just a sovereign state but also a member of the League of Nations, they created a precedent that ambitious, ruthless world leaders like Hitler could emulate. In the words of Mazrui and Tidy, 'Hitler took heart from the failure of the Western powers to stop Italy's aggression by embarking on a programme of aggression of his own that led inexorably to a new World War'.[10] On September 1, 1939, Hitler ordered the German invasion of Poland. The British and the French finally woke up to the dangers of countries unilaterally invading other countries. Giving the Germans an ultimatum to withdraw from Czechoslovakia and Poland without success, the British and the French subsequently declared war on September 3, 1939.

After the war broke out, it quickly spread into the African continent. The British and French immediately started mobilizing their Africans troops and preparing for war. They feared that the Germans would try to reclaim their former colonies in Africa,[11] and started preparations to stop them. They also feared that, since Italy possessed colonies in Africa, the Italians could use their colonies to jeopardize British and French interests in the continent. Thus, they began preparing their colonies for war against the anticipated German and Italian aggressions. They put the colonies that shared boundaries with the Italian colonies in Africa on a high alert. They arrested German and Italian citizens in their colonies, interviewed them, and interned those deemed a danger. They mobilized British and French citizens in readiness for the war. They also started stationing troops along the border areas with Italian colonies such as Libya, Italian Somaliland, and Ethiopia.

Unlike during the First World War when the colonial powers were not willing or ready to mobilize Africans to fight for them against other colonial powers, this time many of them were ready and prepared to mobilize and deploy African soldiers. When the war broke out, the French, for example, had no hesitation in enlisting African soldiers. 'While the British government entertained doubts about the wisdom of arming large numbers of Africans, the French ... had long ago resolved this issue ....'[12] The French did not dither or debate whether Africans should participate in the war. They began mobilizing African troops as soon as it became apparent to them that war was going to break out in Europe. The British followed suit in mobilizing African soldiers in their African colonies. Only Portugal and Spain did not mobilize African soldiers, and this was largely because they chose to remain neutral (at least at the beginning of the war). The rest began active war preparations and mobilization of African soldiers.

The war came to the notice of the African people when the Allied Powers began appealing for help and started mobilizing African soldiers for military service in 1939. Although many Africans fled their homes to avoid military service once they heard that their colonial governments were looking for recruits, many others expressed what the colonial authorities in Kenya referred to as 'their unanimous and enthusiastic' support for the war by enlisting for military service. Many African men in Ivory Coast enlisted for military service voluntarily while others enlisted under duress.[13] There was no shortage of volunteers in Kenya during the first years of the war.[14]

The men who volunteered did so for different reasons. There were those who enlisted because they truly believed that Hitler was a danger to the world and because they wanted to protect their colonies, themselves, and humanity from him. There were those who perceived themselves as loyal and patriotic to the colonial system.[15] There were those who were motivated by material and financial needs and hoped to earn money to buy livestock for bride price, clothes, blankets, and shoes, or simply wanted to accumulate money to start a business or build a house.[16] Such men saw the war simply as a job, as an opportunity (a hazardous one, admittedly) to make money. There were those who wanted to be employed as village elders and chiefs after the war, like the veterans who had found such employment after the First World War. There were those who joined the war because they thought that it would be thrilling, that the war would give them an opportunity to travel and visit new places, see people, and tour the world. There were those who thought that military service would give them exposure, make them famous, and perhaps even rich. There were those who volunteered because a European man or woman they knew, perhaps a European missionary, a school teacher, or doctor who was friendly to Africans, had told them that their country was under attack from Hitler and that their country needed help. They joined the war to help that European to protect his homeland from Hitler.[17]

There were those who joined military service because that is what 'real men' did. Such men included Alfred Juma Bunde who, for example, tried to join the military several times and was always turned away because he was too young, and only finally succeeded in doing so when he went to a different recruitment center at Onjiko, far away from his home in Kisumu, Kenya. His goal was to prove that he was a man.[18] Another was Johannes Ochanda Ameny, who abandoned school at Grade 6 and joined the army because 'my father told me that that is what real men are doing. I was not scared when I enlisted for military service. My father told me that I would come back from the war alive ... so I was happy when I joined the military'.[19] There were also those who joined military service because they did not want their womenfolk to call them cowards. There were those who joined the army because the government told them that they would be given first preference when looking for jobs after the war. There were those who enlisted for military service after they were promised money and land after the war. There were those who joined military service 'voluntarily' because they were told that if they volunteered they would be allowed to choose the unit they would serve in, such as the King's African Rifles and that, if they did not enlist willingly, they would be conscripted and forced to serve in dangerous labor-intensive units such as the Pioneer Corps, which, they were told, would just be like the Carrier Corps of the First World War. There were those who enlisted because they were promised 'voting rights and, after discharge, entitlement to use the French rather than the 'native' legal system (the *indigénat*)'.[20]

There were those who, technically, can be called 'volunteers', but, in reality, joined the military under pressure when the chiefs in their villages advised that 'each family was required to volunteer a family member to serve in the war'.[21] There were those who were at a marketplace when the chiefs brought in trucks, ordered them to climb aboard, and took them to a recruitment station where they felt they had no choice but to join the army for military service.[22] Thus, many African men enlisted and served in the war for various reasons. As the war escalated and expanded deeper into Africa and the rest of the world during the mid-1940s, many African men were increasingly forced to serve through conscription policies and other unscrupulous methods. From around 1942 to the end of the war, colonial powers largely relied on conscription methods to get Africans to serve in the war.

The African recruits at the beginning of the war were mostly from the French and British colonies in North Africa, West Africa, East Africa, Central Africa, and Southern Africa. The French had the largest number of African soldiers in their service at the beginning of the war. The number of African soldiers in the French *tirailleurs Sénégalais* in West Africa at the beginning of the war was 80,000. The number of West African troops in the French army increased as the French entered deeper into the war. It is estimated that there were about 150,000 West African soldiers in the tirailleurs Sénégalais at the time of the French collapse in 1940.[23] Some scholars believe that as many as 200,000 black African soldiers served in the French army. Many of the French soldiers came from West Africa and Equatorial Africa, while others came from North Africa. By the end of the war, Africans made up almost one-third of the French army.

The British also had a large number of African soldiers in their service during the war. For example, it has been estimated that there were something like 100,000 African soldiers from Kenya serving the British,[24] and 200,000 soldiers from South Africa. Nearly one-third of the soldiers in the South African contingent during the Second World War were black South Africans. It has been estimated that perhaps as many as 320,000 African soldiers from East and Central Africa served the British,[25] and many African soldiers coming from Ghana, Nigeria, and Sierra Leone served in the British West African Frontier Force during the war. Some scholars believe that as many as 370,000 African soldiers served in the British army,[26] while others put the number as high as 700,000.[27] African soldiers also came from Belgian-Congo and participated intensively in the war. Whether they volunteered for it or not, African soldiers saw military service as the war expanded into Africa and beyond.[28]

There were several key moments in the war that had major implications for the African continent and the African soldiers serving. As the war continued, Germany invaded and defeated France in June 1940. Germany's victory split up the French and their government into two camps. One camp was led by the collaborating Vichy Government of Marshall Petain, and another camp, the Free French camp, was led by General Charles de Gaulle. The division in France radiated throughout the French colonies in Africa, reflecting divisions in France itself. Some French colonies in North Africa, West Africa, Eritrea, and Djibouti in the Horn of Africa and Madagascar in the Indian Ocean decided to side with the Vichy Government; but others mostly in Equatorial Africa (notably Chad under the Governor Felix Eboue) decided to throw in their lot with the Free French Government-in-Exile.[29] There was therefore fighting between the French colonies in Africa collaborating with the Vichy administration and those opposed to them. Thus, from June 1940, African soldiers from French Africa served on both sides of the French political and military divide, a situation that no doubt confused many of them.

The most serious moments of the war in Africa began when Italy, after dithering for a while over which side to support, threw its weight behind the Germans and declared war on the British in June 1940. This Italian move expanded the war deeper into the African continent. From August 1940, Italian forces in Africa invaded Egypt, British Somaliland, and northern parts of Kenya. There was fierce fighting between the Italian and British forces in North Africa and the Horn of Africa. War also erupted between the Free French forces and the Vichy-supporting regime in Eritrea. After several months of fighting, the Free French forces conquered Eritrea in March 1941. The British and their allies also defeated the Italian forces in Italian Somaliland, and managed to throw the Italians out of Addis Ababa in May 1941.[30] The Allied victory over the Italians in Ethiopia was significant because it led to Ethiopia reclaiming its independence. After spending almost six years in exile, Haile Selassie came back to his throne as Emperor.

The most intense phase of the war in Africa took place in North Africa. After several months of vicious, back-to-back, inconclusive fighting between the Italian and Allied forces in North Africa, a German military unit known as the Afrika Korps, under the command of General Erwin Rommel, the 'Desert Fox', arrived in North Africa in March 1941 and went on the attack. Fierce fighting broke out in North Africa between the Italian and German forces on the one hand, and the British and French forces, on the other hand. Very many people died during the North African campaign. The West African tirailleurs who fought in North Africa remember the Battle of Bir Hakeim in Libya as 'one of their finest hours'.[31] Kenya African soldiers who participated in the North African Campaign have never forgotten how brutal the campaign in North Africa was. The soldiers especially remember the Battle of Abu Haggag in June 1942, and the Kenyan soldiers involved say that many people perished during it, 'as many as sand'.[32] Other African soldiers remember the fierce fighting that took place between the Allies and the Axis Powers at Tobruk. Fighting in North Africa lasted from 1940 to 1943. African soldiers were also involved in the Allied invasion against the Vichy-collaborating administration in Madagascar in May 1942. After several months of fighting, the Allies took over the island in September, 1942.

The most decisive moment of the North African campaign came at the Battle of El Alamein in October 1942. After many months under sustained fierce attack from the German and Italian forces, the British and their Allies finally managed to repulse the enemy forces and drive them out of Egypt. The momentum decisively swung to the British and French side during the Operation Torch landing, when US forces arrived in North Africa in November 1942 to bolster the British and Free French forces.[33] The Allies were also boosted by the defection of many former Vichy-leaning African colonies to their side. This eclectic Allied force, supported by African soldiers, started scoring victories in battles against the Axis Powers in North Africa. The Allies thus drove the Axis powers from Egypt, Libya, Algeria, and Tunisia by the middle of 1943. They subsequently forced the German and Italian forces to surrender to them on May 13, 1943.

By the middle of 1943, the phase of the war in Africa had largely come to an end. This however did not mean that the African participation in the war also came to an end. Instead, the Allies decided to deploy African troops in campaigns overseas. African soldiers from West Africa were already fighting in the Levant, France, and Italy, and with the end of the North African campaign, many more were sent abroad for service. African troops from British colonies went to fight in the Middle East, Sri Lanka and Burma (Myanmar). They also travelled to Britain. A large number of African soldiers saw service in the Free French army in France until the war came to an end in 1945. In fact, scholars have pointed out that the African troops from West Africa and North Africa participated in the liberation of France itself.[34] These troops fought at St. Elba, Toulon, Marseille among other places, and they were also there on the day Paris was liberated from the Germans and their allies.

The African soldiers' roles and experiences in the Second World War were more varied and complicated than those in the First World War, when they had served as infantry soldiers or as carriers. In the Second World War their roles were more diverse, elaborate, and complicated. They fought not only as infantrymen during the war but also as support troops: drivers, signalers, medics and stretcher-bearers, guides, engineers, chaplains, clerks, teachers, cooks, porters, and entertainers. Their roles in the war were more eclectic and wide-ranging.[35] Their level of training for the war was also more comprehensive and intensive than it had been during the First World War. Many African soldiers remember their military service during the war with something akin to pride. They believed that they served bravely and courageously.[36] Even those who joined as conscripts ended up embracing their roles and regularly boasted about their professionalism. The African soldiers showed off their war medals and military documents attesting to their courage. They proudly talked about fighting in Ethiopia and Somaliland, about how they threw Mussolini out of Ethiopia. They boasted about fighting in Diego Suarez in Madagascar. They proudly recounted their experiences of serving in the East, in the Holy Land, and in Italy, France, and Britain. Many of the African soldiers believed that they were perhaps even more courageous than white soldiers during the war. They asserted that they used to be deployed at the front 'where fighting was fiercest because of our bravery'.[37] The soldiers asserted that war is for 'real men', and that their service during the war proved that they were 'real men'.[38] Those who served in the East, in places such as Burma and Sri Lanka, even claimed that white soldiers used to paint their faces 'black' in order to look like black Africans because the Japanese soldiers were scared of black African soldiers.[39]

While boasting about their bravery and professionalism during the war, the African soldiers were not oblivious to problems in the military. Many believed that these problems were deliberate and caused them unnecessary anguish. The most serious problem concerned racism,[40] which they asserted was a common occurrence.[41] Bildad Kaggia, a veteran of the war who went on to become an influential politician in Kenya, observed that white soldiers were frequently treated as superior to African ones, and that African soldiers often had to demand equality.[42] The soldiers often complained about low pay and the lack of opportunities for promotion. Others complained about bad army rations that often tasted like 'prison food', while others complained about lack of arms during military service. Black South African soldiers, for example, complained about the military policy of denying them the right to bear arms during military service in the war. Kenyan African soldiers in the Pioneer Corps agitated for the right to be issued with arms like other African soldiers. Although some African soldiers did not like army food, others believed that it was good and spoke highly of it. In fact, African soldiers serving in Southeast Asia Command spoke 'very highly of the food … and mention[ed] especially the meat, rice, wheat flour and sweet potatoes'.[43] A Kenyan newspaper observed that African soldiers were given a good army diet consisting of ugali (cooked maize/sorghum meal), vegetables, beef, mixed maize and beans, and sweet potatoes. The newspaper also reported that African troops used to drink tea during the war, which the soldier enjoyed just 'as much as his English brother-in-arms'.[44] The physique of African soldiers also started changing noticeably after getting used to the army diet. In the words of the East African Standard:

> When an East African native comes into the army, he experiences for the first time a scientifically balanced diet … the newly recruited native, rather a fat young man, when he first experiences army food, loses weight for a short while. Then, as he gets used to his new foods, starts to gain weight and eventually over a period of a few weeks becomes more healthy and vigorous than he has been before.[45]

In spite of the fact that many African soldiers such as those from Kenya believed that army diet was 'better than home food', they did not fail to notice that their meals were different and inferior to meals offered to white soldiers during the war. West African soldiers, for example, resented the fact that white soldiers were given wine with their meals, and they were not.[46]

The African soldiers were also aware that they often took their meals in separate mess halls from white soldiers. Many frequently complained about segregation in the military during the war. While acknowledging that medical care during military service was very high, African soldiers were not unaware of the fact that they received treatment at different facilities from white soldiers. Although African soldiers expressed gratitude for the very high medical care they received whenever they fell sick or got injured during the war, they felt that white soldiers got even better medical care than they did during military service. Many also complained about racist white officers who often hurled insults at them, punished them for no reason, or gave them heavy punishments for simple infractions during military service.[47]

African soldiers who were taken prisoner during the war also believed that they were treated badly, especially by the German and Italian prison officers, because of their race. There were also African soldiers who believed that, just as during the First World War, African soldiers were often chosen and deployed to undertake high-risk military operations and participate in fierce, difficult battles because of their race. Their lives were expendable. Indeed, after fighting for so long and putting their lives at risk for the sake of France, West

African soldiers were shocked when they were moved from the front to the back of the French army as it marched into Paris to liberate it from the Axis Powers.[48] After putting their lives on the line for France, they were denied honors and recognition simply because, they believed, they were black.[49]

Many African soldiers also complained about the large number of their compatriots who died during the war. Tens of thousands of African soldiers laid down their lives for the Allied Powers during the war, some in combat, others from disease. Although African soldiers believed that whenever a soldier fell sick or got injured in the course of his duty, he was 'immediately taken to the best army hospital and given the best care by the best doctors',[50] very many of them died. There are no firm figures on the number of African military fatalities, but some scholars believe that the number who died during the fall of France in 1940, for example, was around 24,000 while others put it at around 35,000.[51] There are scholars who believe that the number of East and Central African soldiers who were wounded or killed during the war was probably around 50,000.[52] Scholars estimate that the number of South Africans who perished was 6496, those who were wounded 14,078, and those taken prisoner or missing 14,583.[53] Nevertheless, whether African soldiers experienced problems or not during the war, they almost unanimously remembered their time in it with pride. They regularly talked about their courage, bravery, and professionalism. They always boasted about their loyalty and gallantry, and they talked about how they readily put their lives on the line for their governments.

The African soldiers would not have actively participated in the Second World War without the support of African civilians. Indeed, when examining the experience of the African continent in the Second World War, one must not forget the role of the general African population. While African soldiers enlisted and fought far away from home, African civilians who remained at home participated by producing food and other goods. The African people supported the war in many different ways. One colonial official in Kenya observed that when the war broke out, many Africans in the colony responded to the British call for help by providing monetary contributions 'unanimously and with expressions of very loyal sentiments'.[54] The African civilians also grew food and donated money for various war causes.[55] These Africans supported the war materially. They grew tobacco, cotton, rubber, sisal, cocoa, tea, peanuts, and other cash crops to help raise revenue for the colonial government. They also helped to mine gold, diamonds, copper, tin, and other minerals to boost the economies of their colonies. Furthermore, they remained largely 'peaceful' and tried to avoid agitations during the war, believing that peace, law, and order were necessary to keep their governments focused on the conflict. Thus, Africans contributed to the war both indirectly and directly.

Many scholars have observed and written extensively about the anger and bitterness of the African veterans of the Second World War. They are right.

The anger and disgruntlement of African soldiers who served largely started as the war drew to an end. Although African soldiers had had problems during military service and had even agitated against such problems, their anger, bitterness, and disillusionment grew as the war came to an end. It started as the African soldiers began trooping back home at the end of the war, as they started noticing that their treatment was changing. They began observing that, as the war was coming to an end, their problems were no longer a priority for the colonial governments. The process of demobilization, for example, was often frustratingly slow. Some mutinied and went on the rampage after spending too long in demobilization camps.[56] When they arrived home from overseas, Ivorian soldiers observed that 'no one came to welcome us when we got to Abidjan'.[57] The African soldiers also complained about money. They claimed that they were not given as much money as they expected when they retired from the military after the war.[58] They complained about lack of medical care for the veterans who fell sick as a result of health problems incurred during the war. They complained about the lack of gratuity and pension. As they retired from military service, the African veterans of the war started complaining about abandonment. They started pointing out that they were treated well during military service, when their service was needed, and very badly after the war ended, when their service was no longer needed. Indeed, the biggest complaint by African soldiers who served in the Second World War is that they were forgotten by their governments afterwards.

The Impact of the Second World War on Africa

The Second World War marked the beginning of major social, economic, and political changes for the African people and their continent. Many scholars believe that the war led to the beginning of the decolonization of the African continent, to the end of empire.[59] The war dealt a death knell to colonialism in Africa.[60] In the first place, as early as 1941, it led to the liberation of Ethiopia from Italian occupation and the ascension of Emperor Haile Selassie to power again. As a result of the war, the Italian colonies in Africa were placed under the trusteeship of the United Nations and began their march to independence. The war led to the signing of the Atlantic Charter in 1942, which committed the colonial powers to the ideals of freedom, self-determination, and human rights. These ideas resonated very well with Africans who were suffering under the colonial system.

The colonial powers led by the British and the French suffered politically, economically, and militarily during the war. Their people were exhausted emotionally, mentally, and psychologically. Their economies were devastated. The British owed the US $3 billion after the war. These colonial powers were no longer in a position to continue maintaining their colonies by force. They started becoming aware that they could not maintain their colonies the way they used to do. With the emergence of the USA and the Soviet Union as world powers fighting for world influence and domination, and with the beginning of the Cold War, the colonial powers realized that they needed to placate their colonies with progressive reforms or lose them to the Soviet Union and its communist allies.

The colonial powers also increasingly became aware of their gratitude to Africans for supporting them during the war. Consequently, the colonial powers, the British and the French, in particular, started (admittedly grudgingly) to introduce reforms in their colonies in Africa. The French, led by Charles de Gaulle, promised Africans a 'New Deal' in appreciation for the help they had received from them during the war. Under the terms of the 'New Deal' (signed in Brazzaville, Congo, in 1944), the French started the process of dismantling the hated *corvée* labor system and the indigénat. The French also began granting citizenship rights to Africans, and appointing them to higher political positions in their colonies.[61]

The British started introducing reforms in their colonies even before the end of the war.[62] They set up the Colonial Development and Welfare Fund (CDWF) in 1940 to support development projects in Africa. When the Labor Government of Clement Attlee came to power in Britain after the end of the war, the British committed themselves to even more changes in Africa. They increased funding to the CDWF[63] and started allowing Africans to join the legislative councils in their colonies first as members in the legislative councils and later as ministers in the executive councils. They allowed Africans to form mass political parties to help them channel their grievances and advise their leaders. They introduced agricultural, land, and labor reforms in African colonies. The war changed the attitudes of black Africans and whites to each other. Many whites developed a lot of respect for black Africans as a result of observing and interacting with them during the war. Similarly, black Africans, after interacting with whites at close range for many years during the war, realized that whites were human like them.[64] They realized that whites were not invincible.[65] They started questioning why whites were ruling them, and they started agitating against colonial rule. Their views about the world and the order of things changed. The war expanded their mental horizon. The Allied and Axis propaganda about fighting for human rights and ideals such as freedom and democracy left a 'lasting impression'[66] on the minds of the African people. The Africans started yearning for such ideals.

Many of them were actually bitter with the leaders of their colonies for creating social, economic, and political problems in the colonies. Trade unionists complained about socio-economic problems brought about by the war. Journalists highlighted these problems in the newspapers. African veterans complained that the colonial powers had used them to fight for them during the war and abandoned them afterwards. They complained about money owed to them. They complained about joblessness and the lack of rewards and recognition after the war. They chafed over health problems associated with the war. Many African civilians also complained about suffering during the war.

They said that they had been forced to grow crops, provide food and donate money to support the war effort. Their sons had been taken away from them to serve in the war. The bitterness and anger of African soldiers and civilians led many Africans into movements fighting for the reform of the colonial system. Many African veterans started participating or playing bigger roles in the politics of their colonies before and after independence. They started agitating for change. They started forming movements fighting for economic and political rights in their colonies. Eventually, some of these movements evolved into mass political parties fighting for independence of the African continent.

Indeed, many veterans of the war went on to lead their countries to independence. A good example is Leopold Sedar Senghor of Senegal. The war facilitated the rise of new identities among Africans, based on the colonial states. Instead of defining themselves by ethnic groups, as was common in the past, Africans started defining themselves as, for example, Kenyans, Ugandans, Nigerians, Ghanaians, Sierra Leoneans, etc. In fact, many educated Africans started perceiving themselves as Pan-Africanists, as part of something bigger, larger, and broader, encompassing the whole black race. A new class of Africans started emerging after the war: confident, educated, exposed to the world. The Africans began forming mass political parties and agitating for independence. The Africans started reaching out to Africans in other parts of the African continent and abroad. In 1945, these educated Pan-Africanists organized the 5th Pan Africanist Congress in Manchester. The agenda of the meeting was freedom for the African people.

Conclusion

This chapter has examined the outbreak of the Second World War and how it spread into the African continent. While some scholars contend that the war began with the German invasion of Poland on September 1, 1939, many African specialists believe that the war really began with the Italian invasion of Ethiopia four years earlier, in 1935. The chapter looked at the major campaigns that took place in Africa and outside of Africa where African soldiers were involved during the war. It examined how Africans participated in the war, and how they were in turn affected by their participation. Africans participated actively, intimately, and intensively in the conflict, both directly and indirectly. Although service in the war was very demanding, many African soldiers remember it with pride. In spite of the rigors of the war, African soldiers believe that they served with dignity, honor, and courage. They believe that they suffered greatly during the war, and that many of them sacrificed their lives for their beliefs and their colonies. The chapter has also contended that, although many veterans are proud of their service during the war, the majority of them tend to complain about how they were abandoned by the colonial governments afterwards. They assert that they served loyally and gallantly during the war. They fought on the frontlines. They served both in Africa and abroad. They helped to drive Mussolini out of Ethiopia. They served in Madagascar, North Africa, the Middle East, Burma, Sri Lanka, France, Belgium, and some of them even travelled to Britain. They are very proud of their military service during the war. They blame the colonial government for not attending to their welfare after the war. Feeling betrayed by the governments they loyally served during the war, many African soldiers started agitating against the colonial system and ended up playing a major role in the struggle for independence of their respective colonies.

Notes

1. Johannes Ochanda Ameny joined the Pioneer Corps on September 2, 1939. After the disbandment of the Pioneer Corps, he was transferred to the East African Engineers Corps where he served until August 31, 1945. I interviewed him at Usere Village, Karapul Sub-location, Siaya District, on November 29, 2000.
2. Alfred Juma Bunde, Oral Interview at Kowet Chief's Camp, Nyalgunga Village, Nyalgunga Sub-location, Siaya District, on December 18, 2000.
3. Timothy Parsons, "The Experiences of Ordinary Africans in World War II," in *Africa and World War II*, ed. Judith Byfield, Carolyn Brown, Timothy Parsons, and Ahmad Sikainga (New York: Cambridge University Press, 2015), 3–23.
4. Bruce Vandervort, *Wars of Imperial Conquest in Africa, 1830–1914* (Bloomington and Indianapolis: Indiana University Press, 2009), 163.
5. Ibid., 164.
6. Ibid.
7. Ibid., 165.
8. Ali A. Mazrui and Michael Tidy, *Nationalism and New States in Africa: From About 1935 to the Present* (Nairobi: East African Educational Publishers, 1984), 4.
9. Ibid.
10. Ibid., 7.
11. Richard Osbourne, *World War II in Colonial Africa: The Death Knell of Colonialism* (Indianapolis: Riebel-Roque, 2001), 39, 45.
12. Nancy Lawler, *Soldiers Of Misfortune: Ivoirien Tirailleurs of WW II* (Athens, OH: Ohio University Press, 1992), 19.
13. Ibid., 24–26.
14. Timothy Parsons, *The Rank-and-File: Social Implications of African Military Service in the Kings African Rifles, 1902–1964* (Portsmouth, NH: Heinemann, Oxford: James Currey, Cape Town: David Philip, Nairobi: EAEP, Kampala: Fountain, 1999), 75.
15. O.J.E. Shiroya, *Kenya and World War II* (Nairobi: Kenya Literature Bureau, 1985), 10.
16. Timothy Parsons, *The African Rank-and-File*.
17. R.H. Kakembo, *An African Soldier Speaks* (London: Edinburgh House Press, 1946), 7.
18. Alfred Juma Bunde, Oral Interview, December 18, 2000.
19. Johannes Ochanda Ameny, Oral Interview, November 29, 2000.

20. Nancy Lawler, *Soldiers of Misfortune*, 54.
21. Johannes Ochanda Ameny, interviewed 29th November, 2000.
22. O.J.E. Shiroya, *Kenya and World War II*, 1.
23. Nancy Lawler, *Soldiers of Misfortune*, 29.
24. David E.L. Easterbrook, "Askaris in World War II and their Demobilization with a Special Reference to Machakos District," in *Three Aspects of Crisis in Colonial Kenya*, ed. Myrick Bismarck, David L. Easterbrook, and Jack R. Roelker (Syracuse, NY: Maxwell School of Citizenship and Public Affairs, Syracuse University, 1975), 27–60.
25. Timothy Parsons, *The African Rank-and-File*, 2.
26. Richard J. Reid, *A History of Modern Africa: 1800 to the Present* (Hoboken, NJ: Wiley-Blackwell, 2009), 237.
27. Vincent B. Khapoya, *The African Experience: An Introduction* (New York: Longman, 2010), 161.
28. Moyse-Bartlett, Lt. Col. H., *The Kings' African Rifles: A Study in the Military History of East and Central Africa, 1890–1945* (Aldershot, UK: Gale and Polden Ltd., 1956).
29. Ali A. Mazrui and Michael Tidy, *Nationalism and New States in Africa*.
30. Ibid.
31. Nancy Lawler, *Soldiers of Misfortune*, 155.
32. In a letter, Nuera Omeda, who survived the fighting, wrote that about "40 people died in the same moment … but dead bodies were many as much [sic] as sand" (see: Nyanza Provincial Commissioner to Major ALB. Perkins, Directorate of Pioneers and Labor, letter dated 11th November, 1944, War Casualties, PC/NZA/2/3/97).
33. Ali A. Mazrui and Michael Tidy, *Nationalism and New States in Africa*.
34. Nancy Lawler, *Soldiers of Misfortune*.
35. Timothy H. Parsons, "'Wakamba Warriors were Soldiers of the Queen:' The Evolution of the Kamba as a Martial Race, 1890–1970," *Ethnohisory* 46, no. 4 (1999): 671–701; Timothy H. Parsons, "'Kibra is our Blood:' The Sudanese Military Legacy in Nairobi's Kibera Location, 1902–1968," *The International Journal of African Historical Studies* 30, no. 1 (1997): 87–122; and Timothy H. Parsons, "'Dangerous Education?' The Army as School in Colonial East Africa," *The Journal of Imperial and Commonwealth History* 28, no. 1 (January, 2000): 112–34.
36. O.J.E. Shiroya, *Kenya and World War II*, 27.
37. Nancy Lawler, *Soldiers of Misfortune*, 88.
38. Cpl. Thomas Alfred Oluoch Odawa, Oral Interview on 12 January 2001.
39. Ibid.
40. Ali A. Mazrui and Michael Tidy, *Nationalism and New States in Africa*, 20. See also: Eric T. Jennings, *Free French Africa in World War II: The African Resistance* (New York: Cambridge University Press, 2015), 150–54.
41. O.J.E. Shiroya, *Kenya and World War II*, 31.
42. Ali A. Mazrui and Michael Tidy, *Nationalism and New States in Africa*, 20.
43. "Confidential Extracts from African Mail, May 1945," (African Mail, 1945, KNA, PC/NZA/2/2/89).
44. *East African Standard*, January 19, 1945.
45. Ibid.
46. Nancy Lawler, *Soldiers of Misfortune*, 72.

47. David Killingray, "'The Rod of the Empire:' The Debate over Corporal Punishment in the British African Colonial Forces, 1888–1946," *The Journal of African History* 35, no. 2 (1994): 201–16.
48. Nancy Lawler, *Soldiers of Misfortune*, 180.
49. Eric T. Jennings, *Free French Africa in World War II*, 260–65.
50. Zacharia Ochieng' Adiwa, Oral Interview, Siaya District, 3rd January, 2001.
51. Nancy Lawler, *Soldiers of Misfortune*, 87.
52. Richard Osbourne, *World War II in Colonial Africa*, 395.
53. Ibid., 380.
54. Letter by G.H.C. Boulderson, P.C., Coast Province, to the Information Officer, Nairobi, dated September 16, 1940, quoting Tana River LNC verbatim as providing (Native Authority, 1939–1945, KNA, PC/COAST/2/3/113).
55. David Killingray, "Labour Exploitation for Military Campaigns in British Colonial Africa, 1870–1945," *The Journal of Contemporary History* 24, no. 3 (July, 1989): 483–501; David Johnson, *World War II and the Scramble for Labor in Colonial Zimbabwe, 1939–1948* (Harare: University of Zimbabwe Publications, 2000); David Anderson and David Throup, "Africans and Agricultural Production in Colonial Kenya: The Myth of the War as a Watershed," *The Journal of African History* 26, no. 4 (1985): 327–45; Lonsdale John, "The Depression and the Second World War in the Transformation of Kenya," in *Africa and the Second World War*, ed. David Killingray and Richard Rathbone (New York: St. Martin's, 1986), 97–142; Ian Spencer, "Settler Dominance, Agricultural Production and the Second World War in Kenya," *The Journal of African History* 21, no. 4 (1980): 497–514; and Paul Tiyambe Zeleza, "Kenya and the Second World War," in *A Modern History of Kenya, 1895–1980*, ed. W.R. Ochieng' (London: Evans Brothers Ltd, 1989), 144–72.
56. Myron Echenberg, "'Morts Pour la France:' The African Soldier in France During the Second World War," in World War II and Africa, *The Journal of African History* 26, no. 4 (1985): 363–80; and Myron J. Echenberg, "Tragedy at Thiaroye: The Senegalese Soldier's Uprising of 1944," in *African Labor History*, ed. Peter C.W. Gutkind, Robin Cohen, and Jean Copans (London: Sage, 1978), 109–28.
57. Nancy Lawler, *Soldiers of Misfortune*, 199.
58. Ibid., 195.
59. Michael Crowder, "The Second World War: Prelude to Decolonization in Africa," in *The Cambridge History of Africa, Volume 8, From c.1940 to c.1975*, ed. Michael Crowder (Cambridge: Cambridge University Press, 1984), 8–51.
60. Richard Osbourne, *World War II in Colonial Africa*, 368.
61. Ibid., 315–16, 329–30.
62. Joanna Lewis, *Empire and State-Building: War and Welfare in Kenya, 1925–1952* (Oxford: James Currey, 2000).
63. Richard J. Reid, *A History of Modern Africa*.
64. Frank Furedi, "The Demobilized African Soldier and the Blow to White Prestige," in *Guardians of the Empire: The Armed Forces of the Colonial Powers, c. 1700–1964*, ed. David Killingray and David Omissi (Manchester: Manchester University Press, 1999), 179–97.
65. Vincent B. Khapoya, *The African Experience*, 162.

66. Michael Crowder, "The Second World War: Prelude to Decolonization in Africa."

Bibliography

Anderson, David, and David Throup. "Africans and Agricultural Production in Colonial Kenya: The Myth of the War as a Watershed." *Journal of African History* 26, no. 4 (1985): 327–45.

Crowder, Michael. "The Second World War: Prelude to Decolonization in Africa." In *The Cambridge History of Africa, Volume 8, From c. 1940 to c. 1975*, edited by Michael Crowder, 8–51. Cambridge: Cambridge University Press, 1984.

Easterbrook, David E.L. "Askaris in World War II and Their Demobilization with a Special Reference to Machakos District." In *Three Aspects of Crisis in Colonial Kenya*, edited by Myrick Bismarck, David L. Easterbrook, and Jack R. Roelker. Syracuse, NY: Maxwell School of Citizenship and Public Affairs, Syracuse University, 1975.

Echenberg, Myron J. "Tragedy at Thiaroye: The Senegalese Soldier's Uprising of 1944." In *African Labor History*, edited by Peter C.W. Gutkind, Robin Cohen, and Jean Copans, 109–28. London: Sage, 1978.

Echenberg, Myron. "'Morts Pour la France:' The African Soldier in France during the Second World War, in World War II and Africa." *Journal of African History* 26, no. 4 (1985): 363–80.

Furedi, Frank. "The Demobilized African Soldier and the Blow to White Prestige." In *Guardians of the Empire: The Armed Forces of the Colonial Powers, c. 1700–1964*, edited by David Killingray and David Omissi, 179–97. Manchester: Manchester University Press, 1999.

Jennings, Eric T. *Free French Africa in World War II: The African Resistance*. New York: Cambridge University Press, 2015.

Johnson, David. *World War II and the Scramble for Labor in Colonial Zimbabwe, 1939–1948*. Harare: University of Zimbabwe Publications, 2000.

Kakembo, R.H. *An African Soldier Speaks*. London: Edinburgh House Press, 1946.

Khapoya, Vincent B. *The African Experience: An Introduction*. New York: Longman, 2010.

Killingray, David. "Labour Exploitation for Military Campaigns in British Colonial Africa, 1870–1945." *Journal of Contemporary History* 24, no. 3 (July, 1989): 483–501.

———. "'The Rod of the Empire:' The Debate over Corporal Punishment in the British African Colonial Forces, 1888–1946." *Journal of African History* 35, no. 2 (1994): 201–16.

Lawler, Nancy. *Soldiers Of Misfortune: Ivoirien Tirailleurs of WW II*. Athens, OH: Ohio University Press, 1992.

Lewis, Joanna. *Empire and State-Building: War and Welfare in Kenya, 1925–52*. Oxford: James Currey, 2000.

Lonsdale, John. "The Depression and the Second World War in the Transformation of Kenya." In *Africa and the Second World War*, edited by David Killingray and Richard Rathbone, 97–142. New York: St. Martin's, 1986.

Mazrui, Ali A., and Michael Tidy. *Nationalism and New States in Africa: From about 1935 to the Present*. Nairobi: East African Educational Publishers, 1984.

Moyse-Bartlett, Lt. Col. H. *The Kings' African Rifles: A Study in the Military History of East and Central Africa, 1890–1945*. Aldershot, UK: Gale and Polden Ltd., 1956.

Osbourne, Richard. *World War II in Colonial Africa: The Death Knell of Colonialism.* Indianapolis: Riebel-Roque, 2001.

Parsons, Timothy. *The Rank-and-File: Social Implications of African Military Service in the Kings African Rifles, 1902–1964.* Portsmouth, NH: Heinemann, Oxford: James Currey, Cape Town: David Philip, Nairobi: EAEP, Kampala: Fountain, 1999.

———. "The Experiences of Ordinary Africans in World War II." In *Africa and World War II*, edited by Judith Byfield, Carolyn Brown, Timothy Parsons, and Ahmad Sikainga, 3–23. New York: Cambridge University Press, 2015.

Parsons, Timothy H. "'Kibra is our Blood:' The Sudanese Military Legacy in Nairobi's Kibera Location, 1902–1968." *International Journal of African Historical Studies* 30, no. 1 (1997): 87–122.

———. "'Wakamba Warriors were Soldiers of the Queen:' The Evolution of the Kamba as a Martial Race, 1890–1970." *Ethnohisory* 46, no. 4 (1999): 671–701.

———. "'Dangerous Education?' The Army as School in Colonial East Africa." *Journal of Imperial and Commonwealth History* 28, no. 1 (January, 2000): 112–34.

Reid, Richard J. *A History of Modern Africa: 1800 to the Present*. Hoboken, NJ: Wiley-Blackwell, 2009.

Shiroya, O.J.E. *Kenya and World War II*. Nairobi: Kenya Literature Bureau, 1985.

Spencer, Ian. "Settler dominance, Agricultural Production and the Second World War in Kenya." *Journal of African History* 21, no. 4 (1980): 497–14.

Vandervort, Bruce. *Wars of Imperial Conquest in Africa, 1830–1914*. Bloomington and Indianapolis: Indiana University Press, 2009.

Zeleza, Paul Tiyambe, "Kenya and the Second World War." In *A Modern History of Kenya, 1895–1980*, edited by W.R. Ochieng', 144–72. London: Evans Brothers Ltd., 1989.

CHAPTER 15

Colonialism and African Migrations

Kwabena O. Akurang-Parry and Isaac Indome

Each historical period in world history has experienced human migrations. During the era of European colonialism in Africa, migrations of all types occurred as African initiatives and responses to the colonial conquest itself and the exigencies of the political economy of colonial rule. Some of the major themes slabs that define African migrations in the colonial era are amorphous and complicated colonial policies. These include taxes, military recruitment, and forced labor; economic change characterized by rural-urban migrations; and education, social change, acculturation, and social formations; and abolition of unfree labor and the quest of former slaves and pawns to seek autonomy. In short, the causes of such migrations were often determined by political, economic, social, environmental, and cultural motives. Such motives are conditioned by push or pull factors. The pull factors served as centripetal, indeed, magnetic forces that lured Africans into comparatively comfortable thresholds of the colonial situation. In this regard, in the early colonial period, migration was the result of the movement away from the colonial conquest, while in the late colonial period, voluntary migration was the pull of social change and urbanization. For its part, the push factors were centrifugal dynamisms that sent Africans away from hopeless and bleak vicinities in the early colonial period due to the acidic effects of the colonial conquest and administrative processes. Additionally, the push factors entailed free choices made by Africans to migrate into more furnished urban centers, especially in the post-Second World War epoch.

K.O. Akurang-Parry (✉) · I. Indome
Kwabena Nketia Centre for Africana Studies,
African University College of Communications, Adabraka-Accra, Ghana

This chapter examines the general causes of African migrations during the colonial era, roughly put, between c.1870 and the 1960s. Colonial rule itself, to be sure, was a system of domination and violence that forced Africans to migrate from active centers of colonial oppression: according to Michael Crowder, 'Colonial rule created a new geo-political framework within which Africans had to re-orient their lives'.[1] The differences in the degrees of implementation and enforcement of some colonial policies by the European imperialists and their African political surrogates determined the forms and timing of African migrations. In such situations, African responses and initiatives in resisting colonial policies presented opportunities for migration. Our operational definition of migration in Africa in the colonial period is not necessarily about the conventional designation of movements of large numbers of people from one location to settle down elsewhere. We contextualize migration here to refer to movements of Africans within colonial states and across colonial territories, whether transient or permanent, caused by the colonial conquest, colonial policies, and African responses. Our operational definition covers organized movements of African professionals, such as anti-colonial armies and canoe men, who had to move into specific regions in order to do their work within the colonial situation. It also includes people such as former slaves in flight whose main motivations were determined by migrating from sites of bondage and oppression to coterminous enclaves where freedom could be guaranteed. Also, we theorize the movements of a few political elites, such as journalists, who crossed borders to engage in political actions, even if temporary or episodic, as migrants. In sum, we use migration(s) to mean movements, travels, journeys, exile, mobility, etc. However, our operational definition does not consider the size of the migrating population, or the distance covered in the course of migrating, or the effects of migration.

The period covered in this chapter has been divided into three phases. The first phase is from c.1870 to 1918; that is, the time of the colonial conquest, African responses, the consolidation of colonial rule, and the First World War. The second period from 1919 to 1945 witnessed new forms of cooperative African nationalism from reformism to revolution. The African intelligentsia championed this at a time when local and global forces were melding to shape African responses to colonial rule. The final phase encompasses the epoch-making decolonization between 1945 and the 1960s, indeed, the era of African radical nationalism and the watershed of postcolonial nation building when urban centers became the irresistible theaters of osmotic change and renewal. It should be stressed that these congregated time periods do not mean that particular forms of African migrations had ceased by certain periods. In many cases, causes and forms of migrations intersected periods and either abated or intensified due to colonial policy and consequent African responses. We note that this chapter minimally examines the effects of African migrants on their host societies as well as the ways that such migrations (re)configured colonial rule.

In many ways, human migrations in Africa belong to prehistory and were first undertaken by our ancestors, especially Homo erectus and more ardently Homo sapiens sapiens. Prior to the imposition of European colonial rule, Africans had experienced internal migrations on the continent as well as intercontinental migrations. Overall, human migrations in precolonial Africa, for example, the Bantu Migrations, as well as the peaking phases of migrations that characterized the Atlantic Slave Trade, were far larger and sustained than the scale of migrations in colonial Africa. In the precolonial period, Africans migrated, either voluntarily or forced, into the islands flanking the continent: the Mediterranean, Middle East, the India Ocean, and the Atlantic basin of Europe and the Americas. Thus, during the precolonial epoch, voluntary and forced migrations dispersed Africans across the continent and beyond.[2]

Informal European colonization of Africa started at a slow pace from the late eighteenth century. For its part, the insidious processes of formal colonization materialized in full scale by the early twentieth century. The Berlin Conference of 1884–1885 gave a formal recognition to the ongoing scramble for and partition of Africa among European imperialists. More importantly, the Berlin Act of 1885 offered a macabre bouquet of total colonization of Africa to the European imperialists who effectively occupied their spheres of influence. Thus, the application of the principle of effective occupation, whose pace was accelerated by the Berlin Conference, snuffed out the sovereign existence of Africans.

The Watershed of Migrations in Colonial Africa (c.1870–1918)

This period marked the invasion of Africa by the European imperialists hungry for colonies. For this reason, fierce contestations for power ensued between Africans and the European imperialists. One result was forced migration of Africans under the auspices of their indigenous rulers. In sum, some Africans took to flight as a way of escaping or ingeniously engaging the European invaders. One common form of resistance was migration embarked upon through the initiatives of individuals and groups. For example, from 1882 to 1889, the Fulbe population in the periphery of Saint-Louis dropped from 30,000 to only 10,000. And from 1916 and 1917, the heyday of arbitrary military recruitment and pernicious taxation, more than 12,000 people left the Ivory Coast for the Gold Coast. Also a huge number of migrants migrated from Senegal into the Gambia, Upper Volta into the Gold Coast, and Dahomey into Nigeria. In Southern Africa, more than 50,000 Africans living in the Zambezi Valley migrated into Southern Rhodesia and Nyasaland between 1895 and 1907.[3] Some of these migrants took refuge in inaccessible areas. For example, Bemba dissidents migrated into the interior. In southern Angola, the Gambo rebels took to the rugged Gaerezi Mountains between Mozambique and Southern Rhodesia.[4]

Apart from the flights of individuals and groups, other forms of migrations occurred under the leadership of indigenous African rulers. There are many varying examples. One example is Samori Ture's grand episode of resistance to the French. From 1891 to 1898, Ture the ruler of the Madinka empire fought an epic war, punctuated by skirmishes and scorched-earth battles, against the French. This involved systematic patterns of migrating out of reach in the eastern peripheral sweeps of his empire. In this regard, he expanded the reaches of his empire even as he migrated from the relentless French pursuit. Finally, he reached the frontiers of the British colony of the Gold Coast where the French captured him. As a result, he was sent into exile.[5] Another example is the Oba of Benin, who with some of his sub-chiefs and subjects bravely resisted the British colonial conquest and took to migrations to escape capture from the early 1890s onward. However, the Oba and his subjects were eventually captured and deported to Calabar in 1897.[6] Equally, some East African indigenous rulers and their subjects experienced the same fate of forced migration when they confronted the armies of imperial Europe. For example, The Kabarega of Bunyoro and Mwanga of Buganda, all in Uganda, who tried to defend their independence, were forced to use migrations as instruments of policy.[7] Yet another example is Nana Agyeman Prempeh I, King of Asante, who, together with his family and many other key Asante chiefs and their retinues were all arrested and deported from the Gold Coast in 1896 to Freetown in Sierra Leone and finally to Seychelles Island in 1900.[8] Not to forget that earlier on in the same Gold Coast, the British had deported King Amoako Atta of Akyem Abuakwa and members of the royal family to Lagos between 1880 and 1885 for alleged slave dealing.[9] It is obvious from the above examples that European imperialists adopted a policy of forced migration for Africans they considered 'undesirable elements' during the violent conquering phases of imperialism. In such cases, the mode of migration was indubitably a forced one. It was not as if African rulers and their subjects decided to flee. Rather they were captured and sent into exile. And for the most part, such forced migrations lasted longer than could have been wished by the exile. The push factors involved Africans whose resistances were seen as an affront to the imposition of colonial rule by the imperialists, while the pull factor of migration involved the search for suitable sites in which to confine those who resisted colonial rule.

The migrations of Africans became integral outcomes of the colonial wars and conquest. And here we use the Anglo-Asante War of 1874–1875 as a case study. The war was one of the British efforts to bring the Asante Kingdom under its imperial sway in the nineteenth century. Massive social crises and postwar political anarchy set off migrations from the center of the Asante kingdom to its periphery.[10] In sum, in the aftermath of the war, the weakened Asante kingdom was beset with civil wars, secessionist movements, population displacements, and refugee crises that spilled into the frontier boundary of Asante and the Gold Coast.[11] Additionally, postwar internecine civil wars occurred in Asante, the result of the 1873–1874 war, and involved, for example, Kumasi and Dwaben, Bekwai and Adanse, and Mampong and Nsuta. Such conflagrations spread into the frontiers of Asante and the Gold Coast, consequently, intensified population displacement and generated migrations. For example, the war between Adanse and Bekwai, on June 13, 1886, led to the displacement of '725 Adansi men, women, and children [who] entered ... Akim [Akyem] villages' and on June 16, [1886], 3450 Adansis crossed into Assin.[12] The colonial state put the total number of refugee-migrants who entered parts of the Protectorate in June 1886, at 12,411. The population displacement and refugee crisis affected women and children the most. There is no doubt, as the colonial government suggested, that faced with want and penury, some of the refugees in all probability found themselves in a state of slavery and other forms of dependency.[13]

The process of carving out Africa into colonies by the European imperialists ended up creating artificial boundaries. In some cases, the new boundaries divided preexisting African states and societies into separated colonial enclaves. Such disunions usually stimulated migration, as groups were desirous of uniting with their kin along colonial frontiers. This may be due to the proximate opportunities for economic partnership, for example, usufruct use of land. Also reunion with indigenous authorities that were the custodians of ancestral reverence and rituals caused migrations, even if seasonal ones. Additionally, such separated frontier groups reconnected with their kinsfolk for ritual performance associated with rites of passage and quotidian struggles. For instance, the Sanwi of Ivory Coast were the kin of the Aowi of the Gold Coast, but the French and British imperialisms split them into two in their demarcation of spheres of influence.[14] As a result, there were encompassing waves of Sanwi migrants into the Gold Coast hoping to join their Aowi kin.[15] Similarly, the Ovambo and the Bakongo from Angola as well as the Shona and Chewa from Mozambique migrated across colonial borders to Nyasaland to join their kinsfolk.[16] What the above means is that precolonial migrations that had come to an end by the early nineteenth century leading to the creation of stable sedentary communities were given jolts of instability in the colonial period. This was when boundaries demarcated not only spatiality of existence, but, perhaps more significantly, the hitherto undefined social and cultural boundaries of kinship.

One colonial policy that triggered African migrations which, for the most part, coincided with formal imposition of colonial rule, was abolition ordinances that sought to free domestic slaves and pawns. Absolutely, in the precolonial period, slaves had sought freedom on their own volition by fleeing from their holders. But once abolition was formally put in place by the colonial state, larger numbers of slaves took to flight to secure their freedoms. Such were not forced migrations, but voluntary ones defined by ubiquitous struggles for freedom. While fleeing slaves lacked exact choices of destination. In some cases, they sought refuge in the precincts of Christian mission quarters where efforts were made to convert them to Christianity. Others settled down in freed-slave communities created either by former slaves or established by the colonial state. Yet others found their way to their original homes: this raises questions about the outsider status that has become central to the conceptualization of slaves in precolonial Africa. It is very likely that the majority of former slaves went to communities where the stigma of their former slave status could be concealed and negotiated.[17]

Although, we may never know the exact number of slaves who took advantage of the freedom offered by the colonial abolition ordinances to migrate, it is very likely that the number was huge. This is because servile labor in Africa had considerably expanded in the second half of the nineteenth century due to the growing need for cheap labor to sustain the burgeoning colonial economy. One may hazard that in most cases, such former-slave migrations were not organized. Rather, they were spontaneous and involved groups of slaves or individuals. Also, in a great number of cases, such abolition ordinance-induced slave migrations were episodic and ephemeral, sustained by the vigor or otherwise of colonial policies. Indeed, whether considered from individual or group standpoints, ex-slaves' migrations were revolutionary in the sense that they undermined slave systems in Africa. On the other hand, the processes of their adjustments to freedom in the continuum of autonomy, whether assisted by the colonial state or not, tended to be reformist and hence restorationist. That is to say, a considerable number of them could not effectively adjust to freedom brought about by migrations, but rather found themselves in new forms of bondage and dependency.[18]

The colonial state at times became instrumental in what may be called the controlled migration of former slaves. We know that the British colonial authorities moved former slaves from the Gold Coast to Nigeria and vice versa. Such former slaves were placed in the care of colonial and Christian missionary operatives, both African and European. What is problematic is that we do not know the size of the former slave populations that found themselves in these migratory arrangements. In sum, slave flights and other attendant migratory patterns did not only occur in the late nineteenth century, but also in the early twentieth century. What is obvious is that it was more prevalent in the nineteenth century than during the early twentieth century.[19]

Another push factor of migration in the formative era of colonial rule was the combined colonial policies of taxation, harsh forced-labor regimes, compulsory cultivation of crops, and conscription. These served as the triggering moments of African migrations and cut across all periods. Droves of men, forced by the relentless demands to pay taxes, left their communities to work for low wages in faraway lands to pay colonial taxes at home. As Adu Boahen rightly put it:

This strategy (Africans migrating across colonial boundaries) was particularly popular among the Africans in the French, Belgian, German, and Portuguese colonies, mainly because of rampant forced labor, oppressive direct taxation, compulsory cultivation of crops, and in the case of the French colonies, the *indigent* ... and the use of corporal punishment.[20]

The point here is that the French, Belgians, Germans, and Portuguese were perceived as being extremely harsh in their colonial policies. As a result, a considerable number of Africans under colonial rule migrated into neighboring British colonies, where the demands of colonial rule were seen as better, whether this was real or imagined. In 1910, as many as 14,000 migrated from the district of Misahohe in Togoland to the Gold Coast; and in 1916 and 1917 alone, more than 2000 people migrated from Ivory Coast to Ghana.[21]

Migration for work accounted for a considerable movement of people on the continent in the colonial period. This entailed a number of factors. In many ways people migrated in search of jobs across colonial borders or across economic regions within colonies. Examples are the 'movements of Yoruba traders into the markets of Togo, Gold Coast and Upper Volta, the spread of the Ibo from impoverished or over-populated land to the North of Nigeria as traders and clerks'.[22] Indeed, one official source stipulated that 50,000 Africans living in the Zambezi valley migrated to Southern Rhodesia and Nyasaland between 1895 and 1907.[23] Also, cotton and coffee farmers in Buganda employed migrant workers from northwestern Uganda, Ruanda, and Burundi.[24] African migrants engaged in seasonal work in the cash crop economy. For example, a number of people from Ivory Coast and Burkina Faso worked on cocoa farms in Gold Coast. This was because of the cocoa boom and the need for additional farmhands to meet the supply-and-demand curve.[25]

Again, there was the deliberate colonial practice of population transfer with the objective of securing adequate forced labor to work on projects, be it on cash-crop farming or public infrastructure. This also allowed the colonial state to have more effective ways of controlling the displaced population. Among such was the forced migration or relocation of the Idoo people from their communities along Nzo River to precincts of the new Guiglo-Tai road: this was done to facilitate the forced cultivation of coffee and other cash crops in Ivory Coast.[26] Equally, a variation of forced migration occurred in East Africa where Britain, Italy, and Germany resorted to deliberate policies of destroying normative practices of some pastoral African groups in order to trigger forced migrant labor among them. However couched, it may be that the introduction of the rinderpest disease in East Africa was consciously done, as was suspected by Africans, to wean them off their pastoral economy to take up migrant labor.[27] Whether the conclusions of Africans were true of false, many Basotho people had no option than to migrate to work in the mines of South Africa.[28]

Between 1880 and 1918 saw a wave of African migrations and the First World War. Africans were dragged into the 1914–1918 conflict because the belligerent European imperialists had colonized them. Thus, African states became irrevocably tied to the Europe-driven war. The First World War, dramatized in Africa, compelled a considerable number of Africans to enlist to serve in the imperial forces.[29] It has been estimated that about 211,000 troops were recruited in Francophone Africa and out of this number 163,952 were sent to fight in Europe.[30] In the British territories, things were the same: in Kenya alone, 163,000 Africans left their home to serve the British in the war.[31] Regarding the Allied struggle against the Germans, men from British West Africa fought in East Africa against the Germans. Also Africans from French North Africa and West Africa as well as the South African Native Labor Contingent (SANLC) served in the European theater of the war.[32] But more significantly for our purposes here, the recruitment process itself caused panic and forced migrations from home even if for the short term. For example, compulsory military service had been introduced in French colonies in 1912. As a result, Africans showed their discontent and engaged in overt revolts to the extent that whole communities migrated into inaccessible areas to avoid conscription. For example, from 1915 forward, resistance to military service intensified because Africans realized that no adequate provision had been made for the families of soldiers on the front. As a result, for example, there was a major uprising in the Soudan which spread to Upper Volta, and some areas of Dahomey rose up against the French authorities.[33]

By the outbreak of the First World War, education, diffusion of innovation, and economic change had produced a class of skilled workers who migrated in search of jobs. For example, as massive economic change occurred in West Africa in the early twentieth century, a high demand was placed on Gold Coast laborers in the West African region. As a result, some of them sought employment in other colonial enclaves in the region. One such group was the Gold Coast canoe men who migrated to work on the coast of Dahomey, southern Nigeria, Fernando-Po, and the Congo. It is common knowledge that the colonial state exploited African labor within specific colonies they controlled. But contrary examples abound: in the case of the Gold Coast canoe men, the Gold Coast colonial government assisted them by championing their causes by, for example, ensuring that they had good working conditions overseas. Apart from the colonial state, other formal and bureaucratic institutions supported the overseas employment of the Gold Coast canoe men. These bureaucratic recruiting structures, included contractors or recruiting agents, lawyers, foreign agents, chiefs, Asafo [lineage] groups, and colonial officials. Through the migration of the canoe men, we gain insights into their level of consciousness about and responses to working conditions overseas.[34]

The Confluence of Migrations in Colonial Africa (1918–1939)

This period marked the end of the First World War and presaged the Second World War. Colonial policies that caused African migrations at this time were distinguishable from the previous decades, but worsened in the interwar years and became intense. This was due to the immediate depleting effects of the war on the European imperialists as well as the corrosive outcomes of the Great Depression of the late 1920s and early 1930s. The Great Depression forced the European imperialists to make more demands on colonized Africans. For instance, in the late 1920s and early 1930s, the French embarked upon a policy of compulsory cultivation of cotton in Upper Volta, Mali, and Niger. This led to the forced migration of about 80,000 French colonial subjects, mostly the Mossi and the Dagari in the Upper Volta districts, to Gold Coast.[35] In Kenya in East Africa, the Resident Natives Ordinance of 1918, the Labor Circular of 1919, and the Native Registration Ordinance of 1920, all aimed at making African laborers work on European farms and plantations, caused massive migrations within Kenya.[36] Additionally, in the Belgian Congo, it is on record that by 1935 more than 900,000 peasants were involved in the compulsory production of cotton. In Tanganyika, the British colonial government took over the administration with a mandate by the League of Nations, and passed new labor ordinances that triggered migrations.[37]

Harsh taxation contributed to African migrations in the colonial period. During the interwar years, the inability of the French colonial state to implement the 1935 proposed tax modification policy that would have given Africans comfortable tax relief rates caused migrations from the eastern frontier zone of Ivory Coast into Gold Coast.[38] In many ways, the push factor of migration determined the destination of African migrants who wanted to abandon one sphere of colonial oppression for another perceived as more accommodating. In this regard, the differences in the degree of the implementation of colonial tax policies made some colonies more attractive than others.

In our operational definition of migration, we made mention of ephemeral migrations of African political elites. In fact, between 1918 and 1945 the rise and growth of national consciousness among African social classes caused migrations. Such national consciousness was championed by African educated elites whose activities were not restricted to their own regions or colonial enclaves, but encompassed other areas. Thus, in the 1920s, there emerged in Africa various forms of political organization like the Destour in Tunisia, the White Flag League of the Sudan, the National Congress of British West Africa (Gold Coast, Sierra Leone, Gambia, and Nigeria), the Kikuyu Central Association in Kenya, the Tanganyika African Association, and the African National Congress in South Africa. These interregional associations provided clear evidence of an inexorable political consciousness among groups if not classes of the colonized subject populations and also paved the way for migrations in colonial Africa.[39]

The African educated elites who formed these organizations were obviously frustrated and disappointed by the colonial order. Their ability to mobilize themselves into unions, among other things, resulted from the process of migration and urbanization that gathered momentum in the colonial period as more people migrated into urban centers for employment. Indeed, one colonial labor official remarked in 1933 that 'the degree to which the African is not only travelling, but also observing, is probably not generally recognized; it is, however, easy to hear a camp-fire conversation in the Congo during which conditions in the union, Rhodesia, Tanganyika and Angola are all discussed and commented upon.'[40] In sum, the interregional associations stimulated both labor and politically driven migrations. The activities of the National Congress of British West Africa caused a few of its members to engage in migration even if only temporarily.[41] Through pan-African zeal, some Western-educated Africans crossed colonial borders to practice their anti-colonial sentiments. This happened in Gold Coast where Wallace Johnson and Nnamdi Azikiwe, Sierra Leonean and Nigerian emigrants respectively, openly demanded the overthrow of colonial rule in Gold Coast.[42]

The European imperialists did not stay aloof as the African became politically conscious. In many cases, African leaders were arrested and forced to migrate from their centers of political or religious activities. The arrest on charges of sedition and forced migration to Kismayu of Harry Thuku (leader of Young Kikuyu Association) and of some of his supporters is an example. Again, leaders or founders of politico-religious movements and their followers faced forced migration. Followers of the Kimbanguist and Kitawala Churches, founded by Simon Kimbangu and Tomo Nyirenda respectively in Belgian Congo were exiled into Katanga.[43]

This period also witnessed the outbreak of the Second World War, triggering African migrations. Larger numbers of Africans left their homes to serve in the Second World War than in the First World War. As in the First World War, Britain and France (that had the largest portions of Africa as their spheres of influence) recruited Africans to serve in combatant and non-combatant roles in various theaters of the conflict. For example, African troops fought alongside other troops against Italians in Ethiopia and also against the Japanese in Burma.[44] It is on record, for instance, that no fewer than 87,000 Africans were sent from Tanganyika to serve the British in the Second World War.[45] The magnitude of the war posed threats to Africans, especially during vigorous phases of recruitment that caused them to migrate to inaccessible regions to avoid conscription, its effects, and the camping of troops in newly built barracks.

Crowder wrote that the 'impact of European administration led to change in all spheres of African life ... Colonial occupation grouped peoples into new political units, and facilitated their movement within them, especially towards the new urban centers which were the focus of colonial commerce and administration'.[46] There is no doubt that by the outbreak of the Second World War in 1939, various urban centers had emerged in different parts of the continent. The expansion of urban centers (such as Lagos, Dakar, Nairobi, Kampala, Cairo, Algiers and many others) in the late colonial period was due to a number of factors. First, preexisting urban centers (like Accra and Dakar) that had existed for decades as colonial capitals attracted migrants. This was because both had witnessed rapid infrastructural inputs, such as pipe-borne water, electricity, housing, road networks, and railway terminals.[47] Urban centers serving as administrative and commercial hubs also became the go-to areas because those were where basic services were provided. This resulted in the growth of population and expansion of urban centers. For example, by 1920, almost 200,000 migrants per year migrated from the savanna regions into urban centers of Gold Coast and Nigeria. By 1931, Dakar's population was 54,000; that of Freetown shot up to 44,000, Dar es Salaam rose to 25,000 and Nairobi's hit 48,000.[48] Besides infrastructure and jobs, the colonial urban centers served as cosmopolitan vessels and melting pots that made migrants feel more at home than provincial enclaves where the limitations placed on the individual by family and community were stronger and more constraining.

Additionally, urban centers along the coastal areas and their immediate interior witnessed rapid expansion in Christian missionary and educational activities. The case of Gold Coast is a good example. The area between the Cape Coast in the West and Accra in the East as well as the coterminous regions of Akuapem and Akyem brimmed with many Christian missions and schools. Thus, these regions attracted a large number of people who wanted to soak up Christianity and Western education. Furthermore, urban centers in this period served as pull factors of migration because they were commercial centers of the import-export trade. Traders and merchants were attracted to the urban centers because their professions were given major boosts by urbanization.[49]

Conclusion: The Floodplain of Migrations in Colonial Africa (1945–1960s)

The period between 1945 and the 1960s presaged, but also in many ways birthed, decolonization and also contributed to African migrations. Increasing rural poverty and centralization of facilities in the burgeoning urban centers continued to push the youths in rural areas into the urban centers to look for better opportunities. A considerable number of such rural-urban migrants belonged to those who had completed basic education and needed work. The contradiction between colonial education and consequent social mobility was due to the consideration that farming was not as attractive as the civil or public service. Thus, clerical and other jobs in the urban centers lured the educated youth. In some places such unorganized, but massive migrations of young people in search of jobs led to the creation of slums and an impoverished underclass. More significantly, the youthful migrants in the towns formed literary clubs and ethnic associations that ferried some cosmopolitan zeal to emergent nationalist movements that would have been provincial had they been located in rural enclaves.

The pre-1945 period of harsh taxation regimes and the general need for cash for consumerism called for migrant jobs. This persisted and expanded in the era of decolonization we are looking at here. It has been estimated that there were many migratory workers who crossed colonial frontiers. For example, about 330, 000 from the French territories arrived in Gold Coast and the Gambia; 420,000 temporary immigrants from adjacent colonies found their way into the Union of South Africa; and 440,000 immigrant workers were recorded in the 1948 census of Buganda.[50] Indeed, before 1945, Gold Coast, for example, had already assumed the status of a catchment area for immigrants from Ivory Coast and Upper Volta. This was especially true during the rapidly transformative postwar period.[51]

One unique cause of African migration during this period was the movements of anti-colonial armies in Africa and their consequent population displacement and involuntary migrations. From 1945 to the 1960s was the watershed of decolonization. Africans formed real political parties aimed at regaining their power from the European imperialists. The activities of the various associations, clubs, and political parties among others cut across ethnic lines. For this reason, there were widespread migrations of all forms that contributed to the negotiations for independence. The decolonization of Africa was not always on a silver platter as some of the European colonial oppressors were by no means ready to grant independence. As a result, many colonies in Africa, for example, Guinea-Bissau, Mozambique, Angola, Algeria, and Kenya had to settle their demands for independence through militancy that led to wars and population displacements and migrations.[52]

It is well to note that migrations in colonial Africa became a somewhat mixed blessing, and were in fact one of the unintended effects of colonial rule in Africa. For instance, migrations led to population increase of host regions. And absolutely, while the host-regions benefited from the immigrants, the places of origin of the immigrants sustained losses in human capital:

> ... losses which the French suffered were gains for the British territories where, as in the case of the Dagari, the refugee communities constituted a labor reservoir ... contributing especially to the agricultural and mining industry of Gold Coast. A parallel exodus from Senegal and French Guinea into Gambia contributed to the promotion of groundnut cultivation ... [and] cotton production in the Egbado Division of Abeokuta Province were Yoruba emigrants from Dahomey into Nigeria ...[53]

Thus, as a result of emigration of Africans, the host community, for instance, enjoyed cheap labor. On the contrary, there were other worse effects on the host community: for example, Ngambo, in Zanzibar in East Africa, contained some of the worse features of slums, serious congestion, and inadequate sewage, drainage, and ventilation.[54]

There is no doubt that the colonial period in Africa triggered migrations as the result of colonial policies and African responses. Certainly, the violence of the colonial conquest displaced many who moved away from the localities of instability. But it was the political economy of colonial rule from about 1945 to 1960 that led to more migrations. This is not only because of the exigencies it brought about, but also the incidental or unintended effects of social change, social mobility, and urbanization. These involved making choices to better one's lot by moving away from the constrictions of provincial rural life to cosmopolitan experiences in the melting pot of the urban centers. It is important to note that as colonial rule was consolidated, African responses were tamed. As a result, there was a shift from forced and unplanned migration that had characterized the era of the colonial conquest to one of voluntary migration planned to harvest some of the incidental effects of colonial rule, such as the good and alluring fruits of urbanization. Thus, in the postwar period, due to the expansion of education, urban facilities, and jobs, rural-urban migration took a more forceful shape, and by the time of decolonization and in its aftermath, had become a major design in the political-economy fabric of emergent African states.

Notes

1. Michael Crowder, *West Africa Under Colonial Rule* (London: Hutchinson, 1976), 356.
2. A. Adu Boahen, *African Perspective on Colonialism* (Baltimore: The John Hopkins University Press, 1987), 5.
3. A. Adu Boahen, ed., *Africa Under Colonial Domination 1880–1935, General History of Africa*, VII Abridged Edition (Berkeley: University of California Press, 1990), 69–70 and 89.
4. Ibid., 89.
5. Elizabeth Isichei, *History of West Africa Since 1880* (London: Macmillan Publishing Ltd., 1977), 165.
6. Uyilawa Usuanlele and Victor Osaro Edo, "Migrating Out of Reach: Fugitive Benin Communities in Colonial Nigeria, 1897–1934," in *African Agency and European Colonialism: Latitudes of Negotiation and Containment*, ed. Femi Kolapo and Kwabena Akurang-Parry (Lanham: University Press of America, 2007), 72–74.
7. Boahen, *African Perspective on Colonialism*, 47.
8. Ibid., 46.
9. A. Adu Boahen, *Ghana: Evolution and Change in the Nineteenth and Twentieth Centuries* (London: Longman Group Ltd., 1975), 62.

10. See, for example, Kwabena Akurang-Parry, "Colonial Wars and Local Internecine Wars: Social Crisis and Migrations in the Asante Frontier, 1873–1886," unpublished paper.
11. Ibid.
12. Ibid.
13. Ibid.
14. A.I. Asiwaju, "Migrations as Revolt: The Example of the Ivory Coast and Upper Volta Before 1945," *Journal of African History* 17 (1976): 582.
15. Ibid.
16. Boahen, *African Perspective on Colonialism*, 66.
17. See, for example, Kwabena Akurang-Parry, "The Administration of Abolition Laws, African Responses, and Post-Proclamation Slavery in Colonial Southern Ghana, 1874–1940," *Slavery and Abolition* 19, 2 (1998): 149–66.
18. See, for example, Kwabena Akurang-Parry, "'I Often Shed My Tears About This:' Freed Slave Children, Apprenticeship Policy, and Africa Responses in the Gold Coast (Colonial Ghana), ca.1890–ca.1930," in *Power of Doubt: Essays in Honor of David Henige*, ed. Paul Landau (Madison: Parallel Press, 2011), 147–69.
19. Ibid.
20. See note 16 above.
21. Ibid.
22. Crowder, *West Africa Under Colonial Rule*, 336.
23. See note 16 above.
24. A.D. Roberts, *The Colonial Movement in Africa* (New York, Cambridge University Press, 1990), 225.
25. Ibid.
26. Asiwaju, "Migrations as Revolt," 588.
27. Pule Phoofolo, "Ambiguous Interactions: Basotho-Colonial Relations on the Eve of the Rinderpest Outbreak, 1896," in *African Agency and European Colonialism*, ed. Kolapo and Akurang-Parry, 87–90.
28. Ibid.
29. W.E.F. Ward and W.L. White, *East Africa: A Century of Change 1870–1970* (London: George Allen Unwin Ltd., 1971), 80.
30. Ibid., 259.
31. Ibid., 82–83.
32. Roberts, *The Colonial Movement*, 226.
33. Isichei, *History of West Africa*, 259.
34. See, for example, Robin Law, "Between the Sea and the Lagoons: The Interaction of Maritime and Inland Navigation on the Precolonial Slave Coast," *Cahiers d'Etudes africaines*, 114 (1989): 209; Peter C.W. Gutkind, "The Canoemen of the Gold Coast (Ghana): A Survey and an Exploration in Precolonial African Labor History," *Cahiers d'Edtudes Africaines* 29: 339–76; and Kwabena Akurang-Parry, "'When I Saw Them I Badly Cried What a Bad Treatment': The Employment of Gold Coast Canoemen in West Africa, 1900–1935," unpublished paper.
35. Asiwaju, "Migrations as Revolt," 590.

36. Ward and White, *East Africa*, 112–20. Based on these ordinances, where the distance from African communities to the European farms was not too far, women and children also were encouraged to go to work.
37. Ibid., 163. The 1926 ordinance also affirmed the 1923 one by even extending the period of migration to the working site to twelve months.
38. Asiwaju, "Migrations as Revolt," 585.
39. Robin, Hallett, *Africa Since 1875* (East Lansing: The University of Michigan Press, 2005), 61–62.
40. Roberts, *The Colonial Movement*, 225.
41. Boahen, *Ghana*, 127.
42. Ibid., 143–45. Wallace Johnson had earlier migrated to Lagos in Nigeria where he formed the African Workers' Union of Nigeria in 1931. He later migrated to Gold Coast in 1933 to form the vibrant West African Youth League that used Nnamdi Azikiwe's newspaper, *African Morning Post*, to attack colonial rule.
43. Boahen, *African Perspective on Colonialism*, 88–89. Like other religious movements, the Kimbanguist and the Kitawala Churches were very radical and anti-colonial in character.
44. Ward and White, *East Africa*, 69; and Crowder, *West Africa Under Colonial Rule*, 336–37.
45. Ward and White, *East Africa*, 69.
46. Crowder, *West Africa Under Colonial Rule*, 335.
47. Ibid., 340–42.
48. Boahen, *Africa Under Colonial Domination*, 205.
49. Crowder, *West Africa Under Colonial Rule*, 273–320.
50. D. Houghton Hobart, "Migrant Labor," in *Africa in Transition*, ed. Prudence Smith (London: Max Reinhardt Ltd., 1958), 42.
51. Asiwaju, "Migrations as Revolt," 585–86. The tax reduction policies adopted by the French colonial government from 1945 reduced the African migrations from the Ivory Coast into Gold Coast.
52. Ward and White, *East Africa*, 203.
53. Asiwaju, "Migrations as Revolt," 591.
54. Clayton Anthony, "The General Strike in Zanzibar, 1948," *Journal of African History* 17 (1976): 422.

Bibliography

Akurang-Parry, Kwabena. "Colonial Wars and Local Internecine Wars: Social Crisis and Migrations in the Asante Frontier, 1873–1886," unpublished paper.

———. "When I Saw Them I Badly Cried What a Bad Treatment": The Employment of Gold Coast Canoemen in West Africa, 1900–1935," unpublished paper.

———. "The Administration of Abolition Laws, African Responses, and Post-Proclamation Slavery in Colonial Southern Ghana, 1874–1940." *Slavery and Abolition* 19, no. 2 (1998): 149–66.

———. "'I Often Shed My Tears About This:' Freed Slave Children, Apprenticeship Policy, and Africa Responses in the Gold Coast (Colonial Ghana), ca.1890–ca.1930." In *Power of Doubt: Essays in Honor of David Henige*, edited by Paul Landau, 147–69. Madison: Parallel Press, 2011.

Anthony, Clayton. "The General Strike in Zanzibar, 1948." *Journal of African History* 17, no. 3 (1976): 417–34.

Asiwaju, A.I. "Migrations as Revolt: The Example of the Ivory Coast and Upper Volta Before 1945." *Journal of African History* 17, no. 4 (1976): 577–94.

Boahen, A. Adu. *Ghana: Evolution and Change in the Nineteenth and Twentieth Centuries.* London: Longman Group Ltd., 1975.

———. *African Perspective on Colonialism.* Baltimore: The John Hopkins University Press, 1987.

———, ed. *Africa Under Colonial Domination 1880–1935, General History of Africa,* VII Abridged Edition. Berkeley: University of California Press, 1990.

Crowder, Michael. *West Africa Under Colonial Rule.* London: Hutchinson, 1976.

Gutkind, Peter C.W. "The Canoemen of the Gold Coast (Ghana): A Survey and an Exploration in Precolonial African Labor History." *Cahiers d'Edtudes Africaines* 29, no. 115 (1989): 339–76.

Hallett, Robin. *Africa Since 1875.* East Lansing: The University of Michigan Press, 2005, 61–62.

Hobart, D. Houghton. "Migrant Labor." In *Africa in Transition*, edited by Prudence Smith. London: Max Reinhardt Ltd., 1958.

Isichei, Elizabeth. *History of West Africa Since 1880.* London: Macmillan Publishing Ltd., 1977.

Kolapo, Femi, and Kwabena Akurang-Parry, eds. *African Agency and European Colonialism: Latitudes of Negotiation and Containment.* Lanham: University Press of America, 2007, 72–74.

Law, Robin. "'Between the Sea and the Lagoons': The Interaction of Maritime and Inland Navigation on the Precolonial Slave Coast." *Cahiers d'Etudes africaines*, 114 (1989): 209.

Phoofolo, Pule. "Ambiguous Interactions: Basotho-Colonial Relations on the Eve of the Rinderpest Outbreak, 1896." In *African Agency and European Colonialism: Latitudes of Negotiation and Containment*, edited by Kolapo and Akurang-Parry, 87–90. Lanham: University Press of America, 2007.

Roberts, A.D. *The Colonial Movement in Africa.* New York: Cambridge University Press, 1990.

Usuanlele, Uyilawa, and Victor Osaro Edo. "Migrating Out of Reach: Fugitive Benin Communities in Colonial Nigeria, 1897–1934." In *African Agency and European Colonialism: Latitudes of Negotiation and Containment*, edited by Kolapo and Akurang-Parry, 72–74. Lanham: University Press of America, 2007.

Ward, W.E.F., and W.L. White. *East Africa: A Century of Change 1870–1970.* London: George Allen Unwin Ltd., 1971.

CHAPTER 16

Colonialism and African Childhood

*Temilola Alanamu, Benedict Carton
and Benjamin N. Lawrance*

During the period of European colonial rule over Africa, from the mid-eighteenth until the mid-to-late twentieth centuries, children were central to African social, productive, and cultural life, but often marginal to colonial power. What we know about children's experiences and societal attitudes to and conceptualizations of children is very limited because sources are sparse and children, until very recently, have been relatively ignored by historians. There is still no single history of childhood in colonial Africa, and few readily available sources. In this chapter we discuss shifting ideas and definitions of childhood through the eyes of historical observers and historians, the stages of childhood, and children's activities such as labor, education, pastimes and play.

T. Alanamu (✉)
University of Kent, Rutherford College,
Canterbury, Kent, UK

B. Carton
Department of History and Art History,
George Mason University, Fairfax, VA, USA

B.N. Lawrance
Department of History, The University of Arizona,
Tuscon, AZ, USA

© The Author(s) 2018
M.S. Shanguhyia and T. Falola (eds.),
The Palgrave Handbook of African Colonial and Postcolonial History,
https://doi.org/10.1057/978-1-137-59426-6_16

SHIFTING UNDERSTANDINGS OF CHILDHOOD

What constituted a child in the eighteenth century versus mid-nineteenth century versus twentieth century? Words and their meanings have differed greatly and changed over time and space. No unified definition may be applied for the entirety of the continent or over multiple centuries. The definition of childhood in Africa is a subject of intense scholarly debate, and ideas about it were linked to evolving conceptions of childhood, particularly in Europe and North America, as much as they were to changing attitudes to families, labor, and political power in Africa and beyond.

Although early colonial records are sparse, during the formative stages of European colonization, in places such as the Kongo Kingdom or early South Africa, children were routinely described as dependants, marginal acolytes, property, and subordinates.[1] Erik Hofstee observed that 'any attempt to establish a fixed definition of child or childhood during the … trans-Atlantic slave trade may well be a "fruitless" task'.[2] The most comprehensive resource for studying the early colonial period, the web database *Voyages*, offers 'a cautionary note' with respect to reading much into age definitions.[3] Definitions changed over time and among colonial powers, and colonial officials and Africans employed a host of names and terms to disaggregate children based on perceived age and capacity, many of which filtered into vernacular use. By the time of mature colonial rule in the 1920s and 1930s, European conceptualizations of childhood had begun to filter into colonies in the form of academic and applied schooling, religious indoctrination, the Europeanization of family structure and domestic space, and the widespread use of children as domestic servants.

During the slave trades, across the Sahara and from the West and East coasts of Africa, children were a 'deliberate target' of slave traders. Children were viewed as possessing skills and competencies less accessible to adult slaves, including the powerful dependencies that quickly emerge from the emotional vulnerabilities of childhood. Slave traders realized that children craved security and protection. Slave traders preyed on children's emotional insecurities to entrench the master–slave relationship and refashion it with the paternal dimensions of a pseudo-family. The 'spiriting away' of Ukawsaw Gronniosaw from his Bornu homeland illustrates the naïveté of children; the benefits of vulnerability and malleability convinced a Dutch slave trader to purchase the child.[4] Slave children were highly prized, specifically targeted, and exceptionally valuable investments, at particular moments in time and in discrete geographical and economic contexts.

Ideas about what constituted a child, physically, are tied deeply to European concepts. Children in slave trade records were often identified by height, and four feet four inches was often a standard marker for adolescence or early adulthood. The Royal Africa Company defined children as those who physically appeared to be under 14 years of age according to unstated Eurocentric concepts. Outward signs of puberty or sexual maturity were important. But various standards changed over time. Ships designed specific areas for boys and girls, and with what were considered appropriate measurements: 'five feet by one foot two' for boys, and 'four feet six by one foot' for girls. Children are indicated in records by the lower taxes paid on particular imports and also by the value of insurance paid for cargos. In terms of insuring cargo, three children were occasionally valued as two adults. In Dutch, French, Portuguese, Spanish, German, and English records, different words are used to describe many various types of children, ranging from breast-feeding infants, to infants able to stand by themselves freely, to prepubescent girls, or boys with first whiskers, or children with first adult teeth.[5]

In the nineteenth and early twentieth centuries children become more visible in historical records, such as court records of recaptured slaves "rescued" by the anti-slavery patrols, where they were often identified by an estimated age and height and by physical marks, such as branding. Estimations of age during the illegal phase concentrated on 'sexual maturity as assessed by physical appearance' as the central measure, which for most during this epoch would have 'probably occur[red] in the mid-teens' but may have varied 'according to the diet prevalent in the areas from which Africans were drawn' and 'according to the eye' of the beholder. The bounties paid to officers in the Royal Navy distinguished between adults and children. Slavers and liberators of slaves had conflicting incentives to identify children clearly.[6] Evidence from colonial archives demonstrates how Europeans struggled with how to pay for their colonies, and also sheds light on how children were counted. The clumsiness of British and French colonial legal systems reveals how it became almost impossible to apply laws that specified age as a criterion. Some matters, such as minimum working age, child delinquency, and criminality and legal responsibility, shifted dramatically from the mid-nineteenth to the mid-twentieth centuries. But perhaps nothing was as complex as how to apply direct taxation in the French, Belgian, and Portuguese colonies. A child head tax was applied at various ages—in some colonies at the age of eight, and in others at the age of ten or 16. Students enrolled in schools were often released from taxation.[7]

European colonial powers used the language of childhood to obfuscate. William Cohen noted that French colonizers commonly described Africans as '*peuples enfants*' (infant peoples).[8] In settler colonies it was particularly difficult to discern African children and childhood. In the early 1900s, white supremacists justified their colonial mandate by asserting that they ruled over children. Eugenicists, such as Dudley Kidd, depicted Africans as happy primitives whose development peaked at 'the dawn of puberty ... [when] a degenerative process seems to set in, and the previous efflorescence ... leads to no adequate fruitage later in life'.[9] Such ideas underpinned European rule in Africa. For their part, British authorities in South Africa elaborated why: 'Natives are, in a sense, but children, and should ... be protected from the inherent weaknesses of undeveloped humanity'.[10]

Colonial rule streamlined, simplified, and erased the nuance and complexity of African childhood. Children were captured by the colonial state as laborers, and children became instrumental to the process of capitalist accumulation, particularly in white settler states, such as Kenya, the Rhodesias, and South Africa. Beverly Grier demonstrated how children in colonial Zimbabwe 'struggled to shape the circumstances of their own lives' as they shaped the history of the colony.[11] In Zimbabwe, Kenya, South Africa, and urban settings of other colonies with large European populations, such as Accra, Dakar, Libreville, and Lagos, children grew up in a highly racialized environment and distinctly from European children. The relatively rare memoires of African childhood, such as Thomas Kyei's diaries or Camara Laye's novel, provide important real or fictionalized insight, but few documents exist written by children while they were children.[12] The birth of ever greater numbers of mixed-race children created new 'problems' in the eyes of Europeans, and *métissage* in Francophone territories versus mixed or 'half-cast' identification in Anglophone countries created additional cleavages among children of all ages.[13] The meaning of childhood during the mature colonial period is indeed inseparable from the various forms of colonial power established over the continent. And with its emphasis on cash-crop production, colonization changed labor patterns, agricultural methods, and with it notions of childhood.

Stages of Childhood

Throughout continental Africa during colonial rule, what constituted a child could be indicated by a specific appellation or nomenclature, membership of a social group, such as an age set or age grade, and also various initiation, scarification, and puberty rituals, including male and female genital cutting. Amadé Badini noted that among the Mossi a baby is only consider a child after weaning; prior to weaning it is as if the child is a 'stranger' who might leave at any time.[14] Alma Gottlieb reminds us that the precarious nature of infancy is central to distinctions between infancy and childhood, which speak to the fear that infants may at any time choose to reenter the spirit world.[15] Jacques Sanou's definition of childhood in Burkina Faso expands on this by highlighting ceremonies that usher a child into fully human status and community membership.[16] Indeed, drawing on these and other scholars, Lisa McNee notes, children may be said to constitute a group of people who have been weaned but not yet initiated.[17]

In many African cultures, age was calculated against events rather than by years. Just as slave traders distinguished between suckling infants, crawling children, and toddlers, so African communities too had distinct terminologies reflecting the incremental changes of social, psychological, and physiological growth. But these, and many other culturally specific connotations of children and childhood, may have been lost or abandoned throughout the processes and experiences associated with colonialism; they are certainly difficult to recover today. Practices in the African continent often, however, indicate attitudes to childhood. Child slaves, for example, were often not enchained in compounds, and they performed labor appropriate to their age. To be sure, childhood in Africa did not cease suddenly, but rather it constituted an incremental process whereby one transitioned into youth and then adolescence and then early adulthood, both privately and publicly.

Gerontocracy persisted in many African cultures throughout the colonial period, and it deeply informed conceptions of children and childhood. A patriarch, or 'Big Man', such as the protagonist in John Iliffe's biography of Africa, controlled his wives, children, siblings, and other 'dependents' related by blood and obligation.[18] The 'Big Man' household emerged in equatorial societies, moving westward, eastward, and southward at the start of the first millennium. Big Men and their families used sharp-edged iron tools to clear vegetation for subsistence farming and livestock husbandry; polygyny produced the laboring generations that peopled chiefdoms and, later, states. By the early centuries of the second millennium, this pattern of social reproduction had extended across the continent: in East Africa among Somali and Kikuyu families; in West Africa among Ibo and Yoruba groups; in Central Africa among Gisu and Kongo polities; and in Southern African Bosutswe, Mopedi, and BaSotho settlements.[19]

Understanding children's experiences in colonialism requires attention to the evolving structures of domestic power during the longue durée of European presence. The Big Man's kin depended on unbalanced reciprocity and the work of juniors, particularly children who fulfilled their duties according to senior privilege and gender division. A patriarch drew on the labor of his wives and offspring. Senior wives had rights to the labor of younger wives and their daughters. While this social hierarchy elevated married adults to positions of authority, only certain ranking men and women could earn reverence for directing rituals, negotiating nuptials, and distributing land and livestock. Daughters and sons were socialized to respect elders in return for resources (such as garden plots and cattle bridewealth) to create their own families. Children could gain in status after they met their responsibilities to elders. Individual accumulation fulfilled ambition, but kinship belonging brought security.

Not all children were destined to become powerful patriarchs and senior wives—a situation that triggered different tensions. When disasters such as drought and invasion diminished the birthright of youths, hierarchical respect could be frayed or breached. Generational struggles were exacerbated in the colonial era, as Jean Allman demonstrated in West African Ashanti society.[20] And in late nineteenth-century South Africa, shortly after the rinderpest epizootic killed upwards of 90% of the region's cattle (thus obliterating bridewealth), and colonial rulers imposed a poll tax on single males, Zulu youths rose up against their homestead heads for failing to forestall the ensuing hardship.[21]

Children's lives were deeply shaped by their enrollment in age sets or age grades, which established long-term, peer-based bonds. Initiation ceremonies may be interpreted by focusing on several critical themes. Societal gender division and the gendered realms of power are one important aspect. A second component concerns the transmission of knowledge, cultural practice, and spiritual belief as preparation for marriage, authority, and parenthood. A third aspect is the value of secrecy, consisting of the known, unknown, and rumored or imagined. These are not exclusive themes but rather overlapping and mutually informing. As members of a specially recognized group, some youngsters also taught one another about gender and generational expectations. In Ibo villages, boys of the same age trained together to be married men, and in colonial Kenya mission schools instructed Kikuyu pupils in single-sex grades to model themselves on monogamous Christian husbands and wives.

Rites of passage, honored enactments that brought childhood to a close, took place in the teenage years. During white rule, as it was in the precolonial period, ceremonies required initiates to seek temporary seclusion from the community, where a specialist etched tattoos, removed their teeth and hair, or made body incisions. Male cohorts united in the exuberance of puberty were taught law, war strategy, political tactics, and other masculine realms of knowledge. Initiation was often accompanied by the assigning of a secret name, one known only to the age set. This moniker not only sealed the sacred relationship between the youths, but also established a stealth connection that they carried throughout their adulthood. Some rites of passage for boys (that persist today) focused on the cutting of genitalia, which communicated a message of pain: becoming a man necessitated a sharp, shocking separation from childhood heightening one's awareness of the resilience involved in marriage, procreation, and parenting. Poro ceremonies in Sierra Leone, Liberia, Guinea, and Ivory Coast are routinely referred to as 'bush schools', and in this way they operated as the primary educational institutions for the transmission of male cultural knowledge.[22] Anthropologists have identified circumcision as one of the three most momentous events in male life, along with birth and death. In some cultures, men with intact foreskin may face obstacles to marrying.[23] At times, initiation practices atrophied, as when: British authorities in Kenya outlawed customary incisions of genitalia; Xhosa migrants in squatter settlements outside Cape Town had little space to undergo their coming-of-age operation; precolonial monarchs such as the Zulu founder Shaka replaced boys' circumcision with military service to his royal house.

Girls also underwent genital cutting (often referred to as circumcision), which was performed by senior mothers or lineage heads with designated titles such as *sowei* among the Mende of Sierra Leone. The extent of this observance is unclear but was first noted in the seventeenth century along the Guinea coast, and then in other parts of Africa as colonial rulers fanned out. In some areas, missionaries, colonialists, and modernizing African leaders urged its banning and it declined in the twentieth century. In other parts of Africa, it expanded during colonial rule as gender roles and marital expectations solidified. It is difficult to grasp the emotional life of girls facing the prospect of being forcibly taken into a compound, enclosure, or bush, and mutilated as a necessity for achieving true womanhood, but the pressure to conform is often high. Carol Hoffer MacCormack suggested that the idea that girls are transformed into women through the intervention of secret societies and initiation, rather than leaving matters to nature, provides a rationale for genital operations. Mende women related how the ritual 'made them clean'.[24] Chuck Jedrej interprets an initiate's 'moral transformation' from girl child to woman adult as occurring via three phases (from novice, to virgin, to bride) each marked by public appearances.[25]

Other rites of passage involved less invasive procedures, such as washing limbs with sacred liquid (i.e. the gall of livestock) and coming out ceremonies that signaled, according to Thenjiwe Magwaza, a girl's 'ripeness' for marriage.[26] After initiation, boys and girls maneuvered in a society governed by elder authority that opened to their membership. As children in Africa approached puberty, sexual interest spiked. Various conventions regulated romantic interactions, and while courting could lead to intercourse, this act drew severe reprimand, with fines imposed on the male suitor if premarital pregnancy was the outcome. In societies as diverse as Yoruba, Kongo, Xhosa, and Zulu, if unmarried sexual transgressions occurred (including sexual assault and rape) the girl accused could be harshly ostracized, while her male companion might get a scolding.[27] Patriarchal prerogatives dictated this gender discrimination. In polygynous families, a male elder's vow that a first-time bride retained her virginity often paved the way for her eventual wedding.[28]

Children's Play, Leisure, and Pastimes

Colonialism changed the face of childhood leisure and play and the structure of children's daily routines. With the introduction of colonial mass education in the early twentieth century, the time that many children spent in labor progressively reduced. Tighter labor laws, which sought to exclude children under the age of 16 from economic activities, in an effort to increase school enrollment and enforce European ideals of child rights, also lessened children's work. As children's labor declined, emphasis was placed on filling the void with leisure. Modern emphasis on childhood leisure, play, and pastimes in Africa is largely a product of colonialism. This is not to imply that play was absent from precolonial childhood experiences, and when children did play, usually after they had completed household and economic tasks, their leisurely activities were often left to childhood whims. Play largely took the form of public physical activities such as swimming, wrestling, jumping, and running or more intellectually tasking pastimes involving telling jokes and

Fig. 16.1 Staged stick fight, KwaZulu-Natal, South Africa (*c*.1900). Photo courtesy of Benedict Carton

riddles or listening to adults tell stories and folktales, which often had moral lessons for both children and adults.[29]

Unfettered play affirmed family security. Recreation with peers celebrated the nurturer-mother and warrior-father. Pondo girls, for example, transformed corncobs into dolls, which they toted on their backs, while boys practiced defensive combat skills by tossing sticks at a branch set upright in the ground. In a more elaborate form of recreation, Zulu boys, like their counterparts in neighboring Sotho and Xhosa communities, reinforced peer rankings through stick fighting (Fig. 16.1). In this sport, competitors aspired to be the top warrior-hero (*iqhawe* or *ingqwele*). Losers could face contempt, and to the extent injurious outcomes defined the sport, so too did the imperative of exerting self-discipline (*inkuliso*) during clashes. Winners were praised, not because they inflicted harm, but because they won a bout that heeded the referee's call to cease combat before an opponent suffered damage.[30]

Children, including girls, learned the basics of stick fighting in pastures by fencing with switches employed to guard livestock, a source of tribute. Sifiso

Fig. 16.2 Xhosa women practice their martial arts, Eastern Cape, South Africa (1981). Photo courtesy of Rachel Jewkes

Ndlovu shows that herding, long thought to be a male domain, required female effort. This may be due, Ndlovu argues, to the legacy of 'women's power' and participation in expansionist Zulu campaigns where military service was rewarded with cattle. Indeed, the founder-king Shaka kaSenzangakhona enlisted girls in regiments that raided rivals with vast herds.[31] More generally, colonial and postcolonial ethnographies show that Nguni teenagers, as they aged in chiefdoms from the Cape to Zululand, retained martial traditions associated with stick fighting. Figure 16.2 illustrates this point. It depicts Xhosa women competing in the Transkei south of Shaka's historic territory.

During colonialism, childhood play was crucial to childhood development, and children's time ideally was to be split between schooling and leisure rather than spent exclusively on labor. However, such changes were not experienced by all children and these new ideologies were often the preserve of the indigenous urban middle classes in Africa, themselves products of Western education. Speaking about Egypt and South Africa respectively, Heidi Morrison and Sarah E. Duff argue that children of the poor and working classes did not benefit from extended leisure time because their labor was crucial to the economy of their household and, in Egypt's case, the very survival of the nation.[32] In Egypt, for children of the urban middle class known as *effendiya*, indigenous childrearing methods characterized by work were substituted with education and play. However, children of the peasant class known as the *falaheen*, on whose labor the country depended for its agricultural sustenance, would not benefit from these new pedagogies; instead they would "work and toil".[33]

In the Cape Colony of South Africa, in the late nineteenth and early twentieth centuries, Duff states that religious organizations, but mostly the government, emphasized the crucial need to educate all white children. As racial categories hardened, the government considered universal white education and the continued relegation of black children to manual labor as central to maintaining white supremacy.[34] Nevertheless, many efforts to extend schooling to the white poor, especially the rural white poor, failed because of a combination of a lack of rural infrastructure and the unwillingness of poor families to send their children to school and consequently lose the vital economic contributions children made to the household. It is interesting to note that while the Cape Colony government continued to emphasize universal education for all white children, 'leisure time of children who were black and who were poor was seen as potentially dangerous'.[35] Idleness in poor children, often performed publicly, was considered 'loafing' and 'represent[ed] a threat to the social order'. The absence of productive activity among children of the poor was considered inimical to the colonial state and was thought to ultimately lead to vagrancy and crime. Poor, 'idle' girls were also at risk of falling into prostitution.[36] For the poor, free time was to be spent in organized industrial, manual, and household labor for white boys, black boys, and girls, respectively.

For the children of the middle classes across Africa, leisurely pastimes and play were deemed crucial to childhood development and encouraged. Play was no longer left to the whims of children but was often carefully guided by adults and experts.[37] Organized team sports were introduced to schools and children were recruited into organizations like the Girls Guide and Boys Scouts in the colonies. When established, the Boy Scouts, for example, was initially embraced by the African elites because many of its features incorporated indigenous aspects of childhood socialization such as age grades and practical skills acquisition. Furthermore, Scout leaders made a concerted effort to include African cultural practices such as cultural dances and the use of the indigenous local language in Scouting activities.[38] Writing about the Boy Scouts organization in Nigeria, established in 1915, Adam Paddock states that while colonial education tended to isolate children, the Scouts 'encouraged cultural socialization and … more closely resembled cultural expectations'. He argues, however, that Scouting never gained any real popularity among average and low-income households due to the high cost of membership and uniforms. As a result, Scouting and similar childhood extracurricular organizations became a preserve of the privileged.

The Scouts' affiliation with the African middle class declined during the nationalist struggles of the 1940s and 1950s when the organization's association with the colonial government made it less attractive to locals who sought self-determination.[39] Around this time another trend unfolded in South Africa: the organization was embraced by black elites. As Timothy Parsons shows, Baden-Powell's idea of Scouting 'as an instrument of social discipline to smooth over ... [social] tensions' appealed to disenfranchised communities seeking opportunity for their children. When educated Zulu boys were considered for separate membership in the Pathfinders based on 'tribal' affiliation, a Natal educationalist named Daniel McKenzie Malcolm endorsed their inclusion because it reinforced the aim of divide-and-rule colonialism, which segregated each 'native' in his own reserve. Malcolm hailed his Zulu Scouts for 'understanding the power of tradition ... [and] what it means when a person says this is not done (*akwenziwa lokhu*). There is no law or written rule so strong as this simple phrase and you are going to build this up ... "A Pathfinder is loyal"'.[40]

In settler colonies, such as those in Southern Africa, leisurely pastimes for the white middle classes took on different connotations. In the Cape Colony in the late nineteenth century, leisure time, which was time not spent in education or at church, was crucial for both boys and girls. For girls, activities such as diary keeping were encouraged as they provided opportunities for self-reflection and self-development. Girls were also encouraged to use idle time for self-improvement by attending social events and participating in activities such as 'charity work, piano playing and drawing and exercise, chiefly walking'. These activities served the dual purposes of broadening girls' social circles and providing opportunities to meet future husbands. In essence, it socialized girls from girlhood into respectable middle-class womanhood.[41] Such activities were not encouraged for the white, female, working-class and black contemporaries for whom selfhood was understood differently, being characterized by productive labor which contributed tangibly to the national development.

Middle-class white males also had a substantial amount of free time, which was also used in the development of middle-class masculinity through the pursuit of hobbies like swimming, tennis, and attending concerts and events. Boys were also to widen their social circles by attending tea parties, writing letters to, and going on long walks with, young women. Middle-class boys were often under no obligation to work and only did so when adults were unavailable to perform tasks or to earn extra income in pursuit of hobbies.[42] Therefore, new ideas about childhood in South Africa, which incorporated leisure as a crucial aspect, were the preserve of the middle classes who did not require the financial contribution of their children. Childhood engagement in leisurely pursuits, especially social activities which involved interactions with the opposite sex, was considered a rehearsal of the crucial 'rituals and practices of middle-class adults' which was, in its own way, considered 'productive' and essential to adult middle-class masculinity and femininity.[43]

In Egypt, where the practice of Islam did not encourage extensive interactions between children of the opposite sexes, childhood play among middle-class boys and girls was characterized differently and was aimed at promoting independent thought and action among children. Children's public play was to be discouraged and restricted to allocated rooms and areas where children could play after they had received permission from adults.[44] As local elites were committed to displacing the British notion of the effeminate and backward Egyptian, print culture assumed a prominent role in middle-class children's pastimes. The introduction of children's magazines played a key role in childhood leisure and reading and creative writing was advocated for children of the upper classes. Children were encouraged to send letters, written submissions, and photographs to magazines to express their wants, concerns, and aspirations and to 'assert their unique identity'.[45] Stories in children's magazines were also used to convey messages concerning children's gender roles in societies. Morrison states that in over 200 stories written by the acclaimed early twentieth-century Egyptian children's storywriter Kamil Kilani, 'women were usually portrayed in domestic roles and men as warriors and leaders. There [were] no female heroines and women [were] rarely the main character'.[46]

Through play, middle-class children learned their place in society. Although reading was a new privilege for middle-class females, playtime literature was geared towards teaching girls to perform traditional patriarchal roles and producing home managers and domestic caregivers, while that of boys prepared them for public life. This was also evidenced in the role of Western technology as boys were encouraged to play with the most up-to-date Western gadgets including cameras, clocks, and typewriters, while girls were not.[47] As eloquently put by Morrison, 'learning the home economics of frugality and resourcefulness [was] important for girls; learning how to use a telescope [was] not'.[48]

Children's leisurely pastimes evolved in dynamic ways in colonial Africa. Childhood in precolonial Africa, which was characterized by labor, was to be replaced with education and leisure, two elements considered crucial to proper childhood development. However, these new ideologies of childhood were the preserve of the indigenous middle classes who, unlike their peasant and working-class counterparts, did not require the income from the labor of their children for the survival of the household. Among the middle classes, pastimes developed in disparate ways across Africa. While areas such as Nigeria embraced the hybridity of organizations such as the Boy Scouts that incorporated both Western and indigenous ideas of childhood, childhood among the white middle class in South Africa focused on self-development through social interaction between boys and girls and the pursuit of hobbies. On the contrary, Childhood play in Egypt discouraged interaction between the sexes and was instead characterized by an emphasis on development using print media where ideas of appropriate gender roles were conveyed. Leisure and play, although varied across the continent, were nevertheless crucial to class identity and differentiation in colonial Africa.

CHILD LABOR AND EDUCATION

Children have always been a fundamental component of coerced labor and non-coercive labor systems in continental Africa, but over time, from the slave trade into formal colonial rule, children's roles become more streamlined and their labor specifically targeted. Children's education also transformed rapidly under colonial influence, shifting away from informal or traditional and familial education patterns and Islamic education, toward more European education systems that emphasized religious morality and Eurocentric normative paradigms, such as gendered labor practices, nuclear monogamous families, and patriarchal and hierarchical divisions of responsibility and power.

In precolonial Africa, much of childhood was spent performing some form of work. Childhood labor was near universal and most children were taught work, both household and economic labor, from a very young age. In many cultures, young boys often resided with their mothers until at least the age of seven or eight, and would likely have had to fetch and carry water and assist with home chores, such as keeping the hearth alight, gathering firewood and thatching materials, and tending to chickens, ducks, and goats. Labor, however, often took on gendered dimensions as household labor was often emphasized for girls rather than boys. Morrison writes that girls across Egypt spent much of their childhood doing chores and learning homemaking skills.[49] Caroline Bledsoe also records how Mende girls were drafted into household work (like sweeping) or child-care duties as soon as they were physically capable. Girls learned cooking by observation at home, and instructed their younger sisters in female duties, such as fetching wood and water, making fires, preparing food, thatching huts, making pots, and cultivating crops. Even in areas such as Southern Nigeria, where women have historically participated in rigorous economic activities, girls' labor from an early age involved more household chores than boys' as such tasks were considered to prepare them for marriage, home making, and child rearing.[50]

Labor for both boys and girls nevertheless also involved economic production as soon as children were considered old enough to undertake such tasks. Amongst the Yoruba of southwestern Nigeria, for example, children began to participate in commercial ventures around the age of four when they started to show a measure of independence.[51] Children in precolonial Africa were considered vital to the financial survival of the household. They hawked goods, sold in marketplaces, and participated in marketable craft activities.[52] Children also performed a variety of tasks on family farmsteads and also on farms of extended lineage kinsmen to whom parents may have owed labor. Regardless of the tasks performed (farming, hunting, fishing, salt making, domestic chores, or small-scale trading), young children occupied a tenuous position in a lineage, rivaled in vulnerability only by the most elderly. Throughout Sub-Saharan Africa, boys carrying out collective male tasks took their little brothers along to learn how to build huts and fences, forge metals, carve wood, weave fishing nets, hunt game, drill for battle, and tend livestock. In addition, some African states utilized children to fulfill national obligations. Regents in the nineteenth-century Zulu kingdom enlisted regiments of boys to lug provisions during military campaigns, and recruited girls to weed the gardens of the royal family.

From the early to mid-nineteenth century, children became increasingly vulnerable to enslavement as slavery and labor coercion expanded across the continent with the rise of plantation economies tied to colonial and imperial expansion. Consistent with the widespread socio-economic system in operation, as very junior members of lineages, children were highly susceptible to the operationalization of rights-in-persons, wherein claims on their labor, their future labor capacity, or other valuations made them expendable. As from the trans-Saharan and transoceanic trades, there were highly buoyant shorter and longer-distance trade routes throughout Sub-Saharan Africa, wherein children were increasingly desirable mechanisms facilitating exchange, credit accumulation, or debt obligation. As smaller, lighter, weaker individuals, children were more susceptible to violent seizure, kidnapping, capture in conflict, and subsequent transportation. The paths to enslavement were somewhat narrower for children than for adults. Along with adults, children were captured in warfare and targeted in raids. Children could be separated from kin and family very easily in the context of conflict. Children were enslaved as punishment for witchcraft or as part of a broader 'catastrophe' inflicted against a family group as the result of trial by ordeal. Children were also given as settlements after the conclusion of a palaver, and they could operate as proxies for adult crimes, as Sigismund Koelle's description of his travels among the Vai demonstrates.[53]

Although African children were enslaved by many of the same tactics as adults, various forms of pawnship targeted them. Pawning operated in different ways and was not always directly tied to enslavement. Pawning operated as a 'crucial … way of securing credit' in slave-vending communities and thus functioned as a primary means for enslaving children.[54] Paul Lovejoy and David Richardson argued that 'the use of human pawns to secure goods advanced against the delivery of slaves represented' an 'extension of local credit arrangements to British ship captains enabling them to enforce repayment of debts in compliance with customary law'.[55,56] It may be that the very mechanics of the slave trade rested upon securities afforded by pawns. Elsewhere, however, pawning morphed from being largely a security to a 'vehicle to generate slaves'.[57] Roquinaldo Ferreira notes certain indigenous groups in Portuguese Angola targeted 'disgraced pawns'. Indeed, the habit of converting collateral into slaves was so widespread that the Portuguese introduced additional penalties and punishments.

Formal education for boys, and occasionally for girls, consisted of reading and writing a European language, basic arithmetic, and geography and history, all within the context of a formal program of various branches of (predominantly Christian) teaching. Some schools provided instructional aids and books, and others relied more heavily on teachers to innovate a curriculum. Many European-style schools blended formal education with practical, applied, and 'trade' education. In Christian Missionary Society Service schools throughout Africa, boys and girls swept and scrubbed schoolrooms and dormitories, cleaned tables and cookware, washed clothes, and cleaned shoes. They cleared schoolyards, worked on school farms, and sometimes prepared their own food. Girls learned to weave and spin, and boys to cultivate cash crops, such as tea, coffee, arrowroot, and ginger, teaching what the Protestant Reverend Charles Haensel referred to as 'habits of industry and usefulness'.[58] Many religious schools became pipelines for colonial police, militias, and armies, particularly in Belgian Congo. Secular schooling emerged later in colonial Africa and was more common in Francophone colonies. But regardless of the basis of school, and whereas spelling and reading were important, the moral elevation went hand-in-hand with social indoctrination and the gendered contours of a European education. A universal objective of formal child education across the continent was to create malleable and resilient vessels who could operate and work effectively at the frontier of the colonial enterprise.

Wage work transformed children's lives. Zulu boyhood in South Africa was irrevocably changed by salaried, hourly labor. For most of the nineteenth century, male adolescents enrolled in regiments (*amabutho*) of the Zulu monarchy, which socialized cadets to embrace ideals of patriarchal dignity, *indoda enesithunzi*. In 1879, British imperial invaders destroyed the Zulu kingdom and its military. For the first time, familial homesteads had to meet financial burdens imposed by white rule. As a consequence, they released their boys into colonial service where money could be earned to pay for taxes and provisions. These young jobseekers streamed into cities burgeoning around lucrative mines, where prosperous white employers clamored for household help. Answering the call, migrant Zulu boys worked alongside immigrant European maids. They were known to engage in sexual intimacy, which led to colonial regulations prohibiting contact between white and black servants, Mxolisi Mchunu explains. The *Imperial Colonist*, a lifestyle magazine of settler elites, publicized the racial etiquette for European maids who 'should never ... touch their [black male servants'] hands, or sit in a room where there are [African] boys, or do anything whereby an insolent native may take liberties'.[59] Milestones of Zulu masculinity, once celebrated in regimental anthems (*amahubo*), were now expressed in ambivalent idioms justifying domestic labor: '"*Ngibheke nje, ngizoyindoda ngoba ngangisebenza ezingadini*" (Just look at me, I will be a man because I was once a gardener)'. It was also the norm for male retainers, young and old, to don their 'kitchen suit[s]' (Fig. 16.3). Mchunu describes how they struggled to stomach this tunic

Fig. 16.3 Madam and children: Young Zulu servant in his kitchen suit, Natal, South Africa (c.1900). Illustration courtesy of Benedict Carton

while observing white children in the same outfit playing with the madam. If the Zulu 'house boy' objected to wearing his uniform, he could be fired, 'a choice that would relinquish income to pay taxes, buy food and increase savings for *ilobolo*, (bridewealth, usually in cattle)'.[60]

As plantation economies expanded throughout colonial Africa, more children were drawn into European capitalist economies and away from traditional, childhood laboring experiences. Wiseman Chirwa demonstrated that the employment of children, youth, and women in casual wage labor stemmed from a wider problem of mobilization, compounded by seasonal variability in adult male labor. From the 1930s to the 1950s, colonial planters in Nyasaland (Malawi) could not afford a large and regular wage-labor force, so they therefore relied on cheap categories of casual labor, predominantly that of children and immigrants from Mozambique. Children were easily accessible during the colonial period and the majority of them working on European plantations were drawn from resident tenants and surrounding villages. Labor migration emboldened boys and girls, acquainting them with new cultural possibilities and an economic conduit through which to accumulate their own resources and accelerate their own ascent to seniority. And as Polly Hill, Sara Berry, and others have shown, younger, working sons who bought their own bridewealth did not have to rely on their father's contribution, eroding the generational constraints that prolonged their junior subordination.[61]

Conclusion

At the beginning of the twenty-first century, intriguing issues are being explored by scholars of African childhood. Does girlhood or boyhood end with initiation, or does it linger into late adolescence and a younger adulthood? Is there a liminal stage before marriage and parenthood? Does childhood begin at birth, weaning, or some other phase before pivotal rites of passage? And what role should contemporary law—such as changes to the age of consent, laws on coerced child marriage, or the domestic mandates of the 1989 International Convention of the Rights of the Child—play in these debates? On a continent so vast, one with great diversity and remarkable continuities across time and space, the main intellectual concern is to devise a flexible framework through which to examine variations in children's roles and social development.

Notes

1. John Thornton, *The Kongolese Saint Anthony: Dona Beatriz Kimpa Vita and the Antonian Movement, 1684–1706* (Cambridge: Cambridge University Press); Robert Shell, *Children of Bondage: A Social History of the Slave Society at the Cape of Good Hope, 1652–1838* (Hannover, NH: University Press of New England, 1995).
2. Erik J.W. Hoftsee, "The Great Divide: The Social History of the Middle Passage in the Trans-Atlantic Slave Trade" (PhD diss., Michigan State University, 2001).
3. http://www.slavevoyages.org/voyage/understanding-db/methodology-6.
4. Ukasaw Gronniosaw, *A Narrative of the Most Remarkable Particulars in the Life of James Albert Ukawsaw Gronniosaw, an African Prince, as Related by Himself* (Bath, England, 1792).
5. Benjamin N. Lawrance, *Amistad's Orphans: An Atlantic Story of Children, Slavery, and Smuggling* (New Haven: Yale University Press, 2014), 29.
6. Ibid., 30.
7. Lisa McNee, "The Languages of Childhood: The Discursive Construction of Childhood and Colonial Policy in French West Africa," *African Studies Quarterly* 7, no. 4 (2004): 24.
8. Quotation from François Piétri (1937) in William Cohen, "The Colonized as Child: British and French Colonial Rule," *African Historical Studies* 3, no. 2 (1970): 427.
9. Dudley Kidd, *Savage Childhood: A Study of Kaffir Children* (London: Adam and Charles, Black, 1906), viii.

10. *Colony of Natal Report Native Affairs Commission 1906–7* (Pietermaritzburg, Natal: P. Davis and Sons, 1907), 12.
11. Beverly Grier, *Invisible Hands: Child Labor and the State in Colonial Zimbabwe* (Portsmouth, NH: Heinemann, 2006).
12. Thomas E. Kyei, *Our Days Dwindle: Memories of My Childhood Days in Asante* (Portsmouth, NH: Heinemann, 2001); Camara Laye, *L'Enfant Noir* (Paris: Éditions Plon, 1954).
13. Owen White, *Children of the French Empire: Miscegenation and Colonial Society in French West Africa, 1895–1960* (Oxford, UK: Clarendon Press, 1999); Christopher J. Lee, *Unreasonable Histories: Nativism, Multiracial Lives, and the Genealogical Imagination in British Africa* (Durham: Duke University Press, 2014).
14. Amadé Badini, *Naître et grandir chez les Moosé traditionnels, Découvertes du Burkina* (Paris: Sépia-ADDB, 1994).
15. Alma Gottlieb, "Where Have All the Babies Gone? Toward an Anthropology of Infants (and their Caretakers)," *Anthropological Quarterly* 73, no. 3 (2000): 121–32.
16. Jacques Sanou, "Importance des pratiques traditionnelles de socialisation et d'enculturation de la jeunesse rurale en Haute-Volta. Exemple des jeunes Bobo-fing dans le département des Hauts-Bassins, 1960–1982." Mémoire de Diplôme des Hautes Études Pratiques Sociales, Lyon, 1983.
17. McNee, "*The Languages of Childhood.*"
18. John Iliffe, *Africans: The History of a Continent* (Cambridge: Cambridge University Press, 1995).
19. Paul Landau, *Popular Politics in the History of South Africa, 1400–1948* (Cambridge: Cambridge University Press, 2010); Jan Vansina, *Paths in the Rainforest: Towards a History of Political Tradition in Equatorial Africa* (Madison: University of Wisconsin Press, 1990); and Christopher Ehret, *An African Classical Age: Eastern and Southern Africa in World History, 1000 BC to AD 400* (Charlottesville: University Press of Virginia, 1998).
20. Jean Allman, *Quills of the Porcupine: Asante Nationalism in an Emergent Ghana* (Madison: University of Wisconsin Press, 1993).
21. Benedict Carton, *Blood from Your Children: The Colonial Origins of Generational Conflict in South Africa* (Charlottesville: University Press of Virginia, 2000), 79–86, 91–113.
22. Mark Hanna Watkins, "The West African 'Bush' School," *American Journal of Sociology* 48, no. 6 (1943): 666–75.
23. Marc A. Chevrier, "Note relative aux coutumes des adeptes de la société secrète des Scymos: indigènes fétichistes du littoral de la Guinée," *L'Anthropologie* 27 (1906): 359–76.
24. Carol Hoffer P. MacCormack, "Bundu: Political Implications of Female Solidarity in a Secret Society," in *Being Female: Reproduction, Power, and Change*, ed. Dana Raphael (The Hague: Mouton, 1975), 157.
25. Charles Jedrej, "Cosmology and Symbolism on the Central Guinea Coast," *Anthropos* 81, no. 4/6 (1986): 497–515.
26. Thenjiwe Magwaza, "'So That I Will Be a Marriageable Girl': *Umemulo* in Contemporary Zulu Society," in *Zulu Identities: Being Zulu Past and Present*, ed. Benedict Carton, John Laband, and Jabulani Sithole (New York: Columbia University Press, 2009), 482, 484–85.

27. See Elizabeth Thornberry, "*Ukuthwala*, Forced Marriage, and the Idea of Custom in South Africa's Eastern Cape," in *Marriage by Force? Contestation over Consent and Coercion in Africa*, ed. Annie Bunting, Benjamin N. Lawrance, and Richard L. Roberts (Athens: Ohio University Press, 2016), 137–59.
28. Carton, *Blood from Your Children*, 66–71.
29. Heidi Morrison, *Childhood and Colonial Modernity in Egypt* (London: Palgrave Macmillan, 2015), 65.
30. Benedict Carton and Robert Morrell, "Competitive Combat, Warrior Bodies and Zulu Sport: The Gender Relations of Stick Fighting in South Africa, 1800–1930," in *Beyond C.L.R. James: Shifting Boundaries of Race and Ethnicity in Sport*, ed. John Nauright, Alan Cobley, and David Wiggins (Fayetteville: University of Arkansas Press, 2014), 125–43.
31. Sifiso Ndlovu, "A Reassessment of Women's Power in the Zulu Kingdom," in *Zulu Identities: Being Zulu, Past and Present*, ed. Benedict Carton, John Laband, and Jabulani Sithole (New York: Columbia University Press, 2009), 112–13.
32. Morrison, *Childhood*, 53.
33. Ibid., 81–83.
34. Sarah E. Duff, *Changing Childhoods in the Cape Colony: Dutch Reformed Church Evangelicalism and Colonial Childhood, 1860–1895* (London: Palgrave Macmillan, 2015), 123.
35. Ibid., 75.
36. Ibid., 122.
37. Morrison, *Childhood*, 44.
38. Adam Paddock, "'A World of Good for Our Boys': Boy Scouts in Southern Nigeria, 1934–1951," in *Children and Childhood in Colonial Nigerian Histories*, ed. Saheed Aderinto (New York: Palgrave Macmillan, 2015), 126, 127.
39. Ibid., 135–40.
40. Timothy Parsons, "Undivided Loyalties: Inkatha and the Boy Scout Movement," in *Zulu Identities: Being Zulu, Past and Present* (New York: Columbia University Press, 2009), 345.
41. Duff, *Changing Childhoods*, 61.
42. Ibid., 81–84.
43. Ibid., 81–83.
44. Morrison, *Childhood*, 78.
45. Ibid., 76–77.
46. Ibid., 92.
47. Ibid., 72.
48. Children's camps and camping activities were also incorporated into middle-class playtime activities. Morrison, *Childhood*, 86.
49. Ibid., 2.
50. For more on girlhood and women's labor in Southern Nigeria, see Abosede George, *Making Modern Girls: A History of Girlhood, Labour, and Social Development in Colonial Lagos* (Ohio: Ohio University Press, 2014); Niara Sudarkasa, *Where Women Work: A Study of Yoruba Women in the Marketplace and in the Home* (Ann Arbor: The University of Michigan Press, 1973); and Misty L. Bastian, "Dancing Women and Colonial Men: The Nwaobiala of 1925," in *'Wicked' Women and the Reconfiguration of Gender in Africa*,

ed. Dorothy L. Hodgson and Sheryl A. McCurdy (Portsmouth, NH: Heinemann, 2000), 109–29.
51. There was an identical practice in Egypt where children were introduced to work from a very early age when it was believed they had developed *aql* (reason). Morrison, *Childhood*, 68.
52. Duff, *Changing Childhoods*, 94–96; Bolanle Awe, "Iyalode Efunsetan Aniwura (Owner of Gold)," in *Nigerian Women in Historical Perspective*, ed. Bolanle Awe (Ibadan: Bookcraft, 1992), 55–71; Judith A. Byfield, *The Bluest Hands: A Social and Economic History of Women Dyers in Abeokuta (Nigeria), 1890–1940* (Oxford, UK: James Currey, 2002), 1–42.
53. Sigismund Koelle, *Narrative of an Expedition in the Vy Country of West Africa* (London: Seeleys, 1849).
54. Lovejoy and Richardson, "Trust, Pawnship," 335–36.
55. Lovejoy and Richardson, "Business of Slaving," 67–89.
56. Lovejoy and Falola, *Pawnship in Africa*.
57. Ferreira, *Cross-Cultural*, 79–80.
58. Lawrance, *Amistad's Orphans*, 175.
59. Mxolisi Mchunu, "A Modern Coming of Age: Zulu Manhood, Domestic Work, and the 'Kitchen Suit'," in *Zulu Identities: Being Zulu, Past and Present*, ed. Benedict Carton, John Laband, and Jabulani Sithole (New York: Columbia University Press, 2009), 573–82; Keletso Atkins, "Origins of the AmaWasha: The Zulu Washerman's Guild in Natal, 1850–1910," *The Journal of African History* 27, no. 1 (1986): 41–57; and Luli Callinicos, *Working Life in 1886–1940: Factories, Townships and Popular Culture on the Rand* (Johannesburg: Ravan Press, 1987), 56.
60. Mchunu, "A Modern Coming of Age," 575.
61. Polly Hill, *The Migrant Cocoa-Farmers of Southern Ghana* (Cambridge: Cambridge University Press, 1963); Sara Berry, *Fathers Work for Their Sons: Accumulation, Mobility, and Class Formation in an Extended Yoruba Community* (Berkeley: University of California Press, 1985).

BIBLIOGRAPHY

Aderinto, Saheed. *Children and Childhood in Colonial Nigerian Histories*. New York: Palgrave, 2015.
Aguilar, Mario I., ed. *The Politics of Age and Gerontocracy in Africa: Ethnographies of the Past & Memories of the Present*. Trenton, NJ: African World Press, 1998.
Allman, Jean. *The Quills of the Porcupine: Asante Nationalism in an Emergent Ghana*. Madison: The University of Wisconsin Press, 1993.
Atkins, Keletso. "Origins of the AmaWasha: The Zulu Washerman's Guild in Natal, 1850–1910." *The Journal of African History* 27, no. 1 (1986): 41–57.
Awe, Bolanle. "Iyalode Efunsetan Aniwura (Owner of Gold)." In *Nigerian Women in Historical Perspective*, edited by Bolanle Awe, 55–71. Ibadan: Bookcraft, 1992.
Badini, Amadé. *Naître et grandir chez les Moosé traditionnels, Découvertes du Burkina*. Paris: Sépia-ADDB, 1994.
Bass, Loretta E. *Child Labor in Sub-Saharan Africa*. Boulder, CO: Lynne Rienner, 2004.

Bastian, Misty L. "Dancing Women and Colonial Men: The Nwaobiala of 1925." In *'Wicked' Women and the Reconfiguration of Gender in Africa*, edited by Dorothy L. Hodgson and Sheryl A. McCurdy, 109–29. Portsmouth: Heinemann, 2000.

Baxter, P.T.W., and Uri Almagor, eds. *Age, Generation, and Time: Some Features of East African Age Organization*. New York: St. Martin's, 1978.

Berry, Sara. *Fathers Work for Their Sons: Accumulation, Mobility, and Class Formation in an Extended Yoruba Community*. Berkeley: University of California Press, 1985.

Bledsoe, Caroline, and Barney Cohen, eds. *Social Dynamics of Adolescent Fertility in Sub-Saharan Africa*. Washington, DC: National Academy Press, 1993.

Byfield, Judith A. *The Bluest Hands: A Social and Economic History of Women Dyers in Abeokuta (Nigeria), 1890–1940*. Oxford, UK: James Currey, 2002.

Callinicos, Luli. *Working Life in 1886–1940: Factories, Townships and Popular Culture on the Rand*. Johannesburg: Ravan Press, 1987.

Carton, Benedict. *Blood from Your Children: The Colonial Origins of Generational Conflict in South Africa*. Charlottesville: University Press of Virginia, 2000.

Carton, Benedict, John Laband, and Jabulani Sithole, eds. *Zulu Identities: Being Zulu, Past and Present*. New York: Columbia University Press, 2009.

Chevrier, Marc A. "Note relative aux coutumes des adeptes de la société secrète des Scymos: indigènes fétichistes du littoral de la Guinée." *L'Anthropologie* 27 (1906): 359–76.

Chirwa, Wiseman Chijere. "Child and Youth Labour on the Nyasaland Plantations, 1890–1953." *Journal of Southern African Studies* 19, no. 4 (1993): 662–80.

Cohen, William. "The Colonized as Child: British and French Colonial Rule." *African Historical Studies* 3, no. 2 (1970): 427–31.

Colony of Natal Report Native Affairs Commission 1906–7. Pietermaritzburg, Natal: P. Davis and Sons, 1907.

Decker, Corrie. *Mobilizing Zanzibari Women: The Struggle for Respectability and Self-Reliance in Colonial East Africa*. New York: Palgrave Macmillan, 2014.

———. "The Elusive Power of Colonial Prey: Sexualizing the Schoolgirl in the Zanzibar Protectorate." In *Love & Sex in Islamic Africa*, edited by Elisabeth McMahon and Corrie Decker, special issue, *Africa Today* 61, no. 4 (2015): 43–60.

Duff, Sarah E. *Changing Childhoods in the Cape Colony: Dutch Reformed Church Evangelicalism and Colonial Childhood, 1860–1895*. London: Palgrave Macmillan, 2015.

Ehret, Christopher. *An African Classical Age: Eastern and Southern Africa in World History, 1000 B.C. to A.D. 400*. Charlottesville: University Press of Virginia, 1998.

Ferreira, Roquinaldo. *Cross-Cultural Exchange in the Atlantic World: Angola and Brazil During the Era of the Slave Trade*. New York: Cambridge University Press, 2012.

Forde, Daryll. "Double Descent Among the Yako." In *African Systems of Kinship and Marriage*, edited by A.R. Radcliffe-Brown and Daryll Forde, 285–332, New York: Oxford University Press, 1965.

Gelfand, Michael. *Growing up in Shona Society: From Birth to Marriage*. Gweru, Zimbabwe: Mambo Press, 1979.

George, Abosede. "Within Salvation: Girl Hawkers and the Colonial State in Development Era Lagos." *Journal of Social History* 44, no. 3 (2011): 837–59.

———. *Making Modern Girls: A History of Girlhood, Labor, and Social Development in Colonial Lagos*. New African Histories. Athens: Ohio University Press, 2014.

Gluckman, Max. "Kinship and Marriage Among the Lozi of Northern Rhodesia and Zulu of Natal." In *African Systems of Kinship and Marriage*, edited by A.R. Radcliffe-Brown and Daryll Forde, 166–206, New York: Oxford University Press, 1965.

Gottlieb, Alma. "Where Have All the Babies Gone? Toward an Anthropology of Infants (and Their Caretakers)." *Anthropological Quarterly* 73, no. 3 (2000): 121–32.

Grier, Beverly. "Child Labor and Africanist Scholarship: A Critical Overview." *African Studies Review* 47, no. 2 (2004): 1–25.

———. *Invisible Hands: Child Labor and the State in Colonial Zimbabwe*. Portsmouth, NH: Heinemann, 2006.

Gronniosaw, Ukawsaw. *A Narrative of the Most Remarkable Particulars in the Life of James Albert Ukawsaw Gronniosaw, an African Prince, as Related by Himself*. Bath, UK: Samuel Hazard, 1794.

Guyer, Jane. "Household and Community in African Studies." *African Studies Review* 24, no. 2/3 (1981): 86–137.

Hansen, K.T. "Labor Migration and Urban Child Labor During the Colonial Period in Zambia." In *Demography from Scanty Evidence: Central Africa in the Colonial Period*, edited by B. Fetter, 219–24. Boulder, CO: Lynne Rienner, 1990.

Hill, Polly. *The Migrant Cocoa-Farmers of Southern Ghana: A Study in Rural Capitalism*. Cambridge: Cambridge University Press, 1963.

Hoftsee, Erik J.W. "The Great Divide: The Social History of the Middle Passage in the Trans-Atlantic Slave Trade." PhD diss., Michigan State University, 2001.

Iliffe, John. *Africans: The History of a Continent*. Cambridge: Cambridge University Press, 1995.

Jedrej, Charles. "Cosmology and Symbolism on the Central Guinea Coast." *Anthropos* 81, no. 4/6 (1986): 497–515.

Kidd, Dudley. *Savage Childhood: A Study of Kafir Children*. London: Adam and Charles Black, 1906.

Koelle, Sigismund. "*Narrative of an Expedition in the Vy Country of West Africa.*" London: Seeleys, 1849.

Kuper, Hilda. "Kinship Among the Swazi." In *African Systems of Kinship and Marriage*, edited by A.R. Radcliffe-Brown and Daryll Forde, 86–110. New York: Oxford University Press, 1965.

Kyei Jr., Thomas E. *Our Days Dwindle: Memories of My Childhood Days in Asante*. Portsmouth, NH: Heinemann, 2001.

Landau, Paul. *Popular Politics in the History of South Africa, 1400–1948*. Cambridge: Cambridge University Press, 2010.

Lawrance, Benjamin N. *Amistad's Orphans: An Atlantic Story of Children, Slavery, and Smuggling*. New Haven: Yale University Press, 2014.

Laye, Camara. *L'Enfant Noir*. Paris: Éditions Plon, 1954.

Lee, Christopher J. *Unreasonable Histories: Nativism, Multiracial Lives, and the Genealogical Imagination in British Africa*. Durham: Duke University Press, 2014.

Lovejoy, Paul, and David Richardson. "Trust, Pawnship, and Atlantic History: The Institutional Foundations of the Old Calabar Slave Trade." *American Historical Review* 104, no. 2 (1999): 333–55.

Lovejoy, Paul E., and David Richardson. "The Business of Slaving: Pawnship in West Africa, c. 1600–1810." *Journal of African History* 42, no. 1 (2001): 67–89.

Lovejoy, Paul E., and Toyin Falola, eds. *Pawnship, Slavery, and Colonialism in Africa* (Trenton, NJ: Africa World Press, 2003).
MacCormack, Carol Hoffer P. "Bundu: Political Implications of Female Solidarity in a Secret Society." In *Being Female: Reproduction, Power, and Change*, edited by Dana Raphael, 155–65. The Hague: Mouton, 1975.
McClendon, Thomas. "A Dangerous Doctrine: Twins, Ethnography, and Inheritance in Colonial Africa." *The Journal of Legal Pluralism and Unofficial Law* 29, no. 39 (1997): 121–40.
McKittrick, Meredith. "The 'Burden' of Young Men: Property and Generational Conflict in Namibia, 1880–1945." *African Economic History* 24 (1996): 115–29.
McNee, Lisa. "The Languages of Childhood: The Discursive Construction of Childhood and Colonial Policy in French West Africa." *African Studies Quarterly* 7, no. 4 (2004): 20–32.
Meillassoux, Claude. *Maidens, Meals, and Money*. Cambridge: Cambridge University Press, 1981.
Mchunu, Mxolisi. "A Modern Coming of Age: Zulu Manhood, Domestic Work, and the 'Kitchen Suit'." In *Zulu Identities: Being Zulu Past and Present*, edited by Benedict Carton, John Laband, and Jabulani Sithole, 573–82. New York: Columbia University Press, 2009.
Morrell, Robert. "Of boys and men: masculinity and gender in Southern African studies." *Journal of Southern African Studies* 24, no. 4 (1998): 605–30.
Morrison, Heidi. *Childhood and Colonial Modernity in Egypt*. London: Palgrave Macmillan, 2015.
Nauright, John, Alan Cobley, and David Wiggins, eds. *Beyond C.L.R. James: Shifting Boundaries of Race and Ethnicity in Sport*. Fayetteville: University of Arkansas Press, 2014.
Paddock, Adam. 2015. "'A World of Good for Our Boys': Boy Scouts in Southern Nigeria, 1934–1951." In *Children and Childhood in Colonial Nigerian Histories*, edited by Saheed Aderinto, 123–46. New York: Palgrave Macmillan.
Parsons, Timothy. "Undivided Loyalties: Inkatha and the Boy Scout Movements." In *Zulu Identities: Being Zulu, Past and Present*, edited by Benedict Carton, John Laband, and Jabulani Sithole, 341–52. New York: Columbia University Press, 2009.
Reynolds, Pamela. *Dance Civet Cat: Child Labour in Zambezi*. New York: St. Martin's, 1991.
Richards, A. *Chisungu: A Girls' Initiation Ceremony Among the Bemba of Zambia*. London: Routledge, 1956.
Richards, Paul. *War, Youth, and Resources in Sierra Leone*. Oxford, UK: James Currey, 1996.
Sanou, Jacques. "Importance des pratiques traditionnelles de socialisation et d'enculturation de la jeunesse rurale en Haute-Volta. Exemple des jeunes Bobofing dans le département des Hauts-Bassins, 1960–1982." Mémoire de Diplôme des Hautes Études Pratiques Sociales, Lyon, 1983.
Schapera, Isaac. "Kinship and Marriage Among the Tswana." In *African Systems of Kinship and Marriage*, edited by A.R. Radcliffe-Brown and Daryll Forde, 140–65. New York: Oxford University Press, 1965.
Shell, Robert. *Children of Bondage: A Social History of the Slave Society at the Cape of Good Hope, 1652–1838*. Hannover, NH: University Press of New England, 1994.

Sudarkasa, Niara. *Where Women Work: A Study of Yoruba Women in the Marketplace and in the Home*. Ann Arbor: University of Michigan Press, 1973.

Thomas, Lynn. "'Ngaitana (I Will Circumcise Myself)': The Gender and Generational Politics on the 1956 Ban on Clitoridectomy in Meru, Kenya." *Gender and History* 8 (1996): 338–63.

Thornberry, Elizabeth. "Ukuthwala, Forced Marriage, and the Idea of Custom in South Africa's Eastern Cape." In *Marriage by Force? Contestation over Consent and Coercion in Africa*, edited by Annie Bunting, Benjamin N. Lawrance, and Richard L. Roberts, 137–59. Athens: Ohio University Press, 2016.

Thornton, John. *The Kongolese Saint Anthony: Dona Beatriz Kimpa Vita and the Antonian Movement, 1684–1706*. Cambridge: Cambridge University Press, 1998.

Turner, Victor. "Symbolization and Patterning in the Circumcision Rites of Two Bantu-Speaking Societies." In *Man in Africa*, edited by Mary Douglas and Phyllis Kaberry. New York: Anchor Doubleday, 1971.

Vansina, Jan. *Paths in the Rainforest: Towards a History of Political Tradition in Equatorial Africa*. Madison: University of Wisconsin Press, 1990.

Vaughan, Megan. "Which Family? Problems in the Reconstruction of the History of the Family as an Economic and Cultural Unit." *The Journal of African History* 24, no. 2 (1983): 275–83.

Watkins, Mark Hanna. "The West African 'Bush' School." *American Journal of Sociology* 48, no. 6 (1943): 666–75.

White, Owen. *Children of the French Empire: Miscegenation and Colonial Society in French West Africa, 1895–1960*. Oxford, UK: Clarendon Press, 1999.

Wilson, Monica. *For Men and Elders: Change in the Relations of Generations and of Men and Women among the Nyakusa-Ngonde People, 1875–1971*. New York: Oxford University Press, 1977.

CHAPTER 17

Literature in Colonial Africa

Tanure Ojaide

Literature is a cultural production that often reflects a people's history, experience, sensibility, ontology, belief systems, and realities, among others. In the African tradition, literature and history tend to be closely related with history also associated with politics; hence full knowledge of Africa's history of the colonial period would be incomplete without a comprehensive view of the literature. One can therefore venture to say that history drives the direction of literature in Africa and this is apparently true whether in precolonial, colonial, or postcolonial times. History in its macro state thus incorporates the progress of a people's culture and society, which form the backdrop of African literature. Literature in Africa predates the continent's colonization by the European powers because Africans have always had a literature whether in the form of orality or scripts such as the Egyptian hieroglyphs, the Liberian Vai scripts, and the Nsibidi pictographs of the Ejagham (also called Ekoi) and Efik ethnic groups of southeastern Nigeria and northern Cameroon. The European conquest and subsequent colonization of Africa would add another dimension to the people's literature, which had been mainly oral before, introducing a written component as the products of European schools and administrations.

Before delving into the nature, types, and functions of literature in colonial Africa, it is imperative to explain European justification for the colonization of Africa and the nature of the colonial system as it affected Africans. As Chinua Achebe has described it in *The Education of a British-Protected*

T. Ojaide (✉)
Department of Africana Studies, University of North Carolina, Charlotte, NC, USA

© The Author(s) 2018
M.S. Shanguhyia and T. Falola (eds.),
The Palgrave Handbook of African Colonial and Postcolonial History,
https://doi.org/10.1057/978-1-137-59426-6_17

Child, colonialism involved the total takeover of a people by a small but armed group to dominate their economic and political lives for their own (foreign) benefit. Hegelian and European racist ideas of Africa as 'the other' that was not civilized, not Christian, and a tabula rasa that needed to be civilized fueled the colonial enterprise in Europe. Historians such as Hugh Trevor-Roper and Arnold J. Toynbee saw Africa as consisting of barbarism. The Europeans who needed raw materials from Africa for their industries converged their economic exploitation with philanthropic reasoning of bringing civilization to a part of the world that lacked it in their opinion. The Berlin Conference from November 1894 to February 1895 gave the European imperialists the imprimatur they needed to share Africa among themselves so as to have the legitimacy to loot the continent of its human and natural resources. It is in the context of an armed foreign group taking over other peoples and their lands and running the place for their economic and political benefit that colonialism should be seen. The literature in colonial Africa would inevitably reflect the condition of the colonized people in their 'new' dispensation. The colonial administration affected the state and subjects in social, cultural, psychological, and political ways. Literature, according to Bill Ashcroft, Gareth Griffins, and Helen Tiffin, 'offers one of the most important ways in which these new perceptions are expressed and it is in their writing, and through other arts such as painting, sculpture, music, and dance that the day-to-day realities experienced by colonized people have been most powerfully encoded ...'.[1]

Postcolonial Literature

Literature in colonial Africa involves, but is not limited to, 'postcolonial literature', which is 'writing that has been affected by the imperial process from the moment of colonization to the present day. This is because there is a continuity of preoccupations throughout the historical process initiated by European imperial aggression'.[2] Literature in colonial Africa is synonymous with writing about life shaped by the colonial experience of direct rule and domination by imperialist powers. From most definitions of 'postcolonial literature', literature in colonial Africa is postcolonial. Frantz Fanon (1925–1961), the Martinique-born revolutionary psychiatrist and philosopher, occupies a central place in the discourse of literature in colonial (and postcolonial) Africa. He had personal experience as a psychiatrist treating victims of racism and colonial oppression in Algeria, and he later joined the nationalist Algerian struggle against France.

Fanon maps out three different stages of literature of a colonized people in a paper he presented at the Second Congress of Black Writers and Artists in Rome in 1959. The paper became a chapter, 'On National Culture' in his *The Wretched of the Earth*. Literature in colonial Africa seems to affirm his conceptualization. While I hope to elaborate on this at specific points while discussing aspects of literature in colonial Africa, it is important to note the stages as: first, 'unqualified assimilation', by imitating literary trends of the metropolis; second, the stage of dialectical antithesis to the first stage; and third, a stage of national consciousness of native resistance against colonial domination when the writer becomes 'the mouthpiece of a new reality in action'.[3] Fanon's colonial experience and conceptualization of literature and culture in the colony expose not just the historical dimension of colonialism but also the psychological impact of colonial socio-cultural, economic, and political measures.

Africa in colonial times had many literatures, which included the indigenous oral literatures, Arab literature, Swahili literature influenced by Islam brought by Arab merchants to East Africa, and the 'new' literature that was a byproduct of European takeover of Africa. The objective of European colonization of Africa through its colonial laws and its accompanying missionary proselytizing was to erase African culture, languages, folklore, and art that were denigrated to affirm European superiority over an uncivilized race. However, following Fanon's conceptualization, the literature in colonial Africa would at first imitate European models before trying to affirm itself, and even before independence attempting to decolonize itself. What follows is a summary of the different trends of literature in Africa in colonial times that the context of colonialism made possible. I will also attempt to discuss the function and contribution of the literature to the culture itself, to the effort of dealing with the psychological aspects of colonialism, response to the European encroachment into Africa, and as a tool in the nationalist struggle to gain independence from the colonizers.

ORAL LITERATURE

Literature could be oral or written. Western critics, who once questioned the oral as literature, bearing in mind its connotation of what is written, seemed to have forgotten that early Western literature, such as Homer's *Odyssey* and *Iliad*, was oral before it came to be written down. African oral literature is as old as the African people and still thrives today alongside the 'new' or modern written literature that came with colonization and resulted from the colonialists training Africans in literacy so as to help them in communication and administration. Traditional Africa had no schools as modern Africa has (after interaction with the West). However, there were avenues for teaching young ones about life, society, the environment, and language and literary skills, which the oral tradition brought about. Usually at the end of the day's work, parents and elders gathered their young ones by the fireside to tell them stories. Such sessions were a part of the growing process of young boys and girls, who looked forward to these informal fireside 'schools' with enthusiasm. They not only listened but learnt to tell such stories and sing the songs themselves. The traditional literature was very much integrated into the daily lives of the people as well at different stages of an individual's life. It functioned in the communal society in maintaining a healthy social ethos that bound the people together. It also served moral and ethical purposes and gave the people a sense of belonging to their community. It was (and is) a literature that has its own aesthetics and forms. As would be seen later, oral literature reinforces the written literature and, to some extent, vice versa.

There were different forms of oral literature in precolonial through colonial Africa. They included, but were not limited to, the narrative types of folk tales, epics, myths, legends, and the poetic songs, chants, riddles, and tongue-twisters. Much as there are narratives and songs, there is no clearcut division of genres of fiction, poetry, and drama as in the Western-derived written/modern literature. Oral literature in colonial Africa, as in precolonial and postcolonial Africa, was very integrative in the sense that a good narrative incorporated poetic songs, chants, and when performed became a dramatic experience. Thus, one can say that the literature that the colonialists met in Africa was a multi-media event in the sense that a performance of a folk tale or any other type of traditional narrative (including epics) incorporated songs, the minstrel wearing a mask and/or a special costume and performing to the accompaniment of music. Since this literature was passed down from one generation to another by word of mouth, it relied on memory, which was not always accurate; hence there are many variants of many tales (such as *Sundiata*, the epic of Mali), and many folk tales across sub-Saharan Africa. I have observed many variants of the story of the fastidious girl who wants to marry a complete gentleman or spotless man and, after marrying a stranger who dons such a habit, is rescued to marry someone from her own locality. It is significant to note that there is a close relationship between traditional literature and history in Africa. As the culture is dynamic, so also is the literature that changes according to the prevailing experiences of the people. Proverbs and folk tales adapt to the times in which they are coined or told. Fashion, neologism, modernism, new technology, and other factors affect folk tales, proverbs, and other artistic traditional verbal forms to renew themselves. New variants of folk tales and new proverbs are constantly being born out of contemporary experience. Of great significance is that the oral tradition has become a tool for modern African writers to establish their cultural identity.

Let me mention some specific oral literature traditions that were fully developed and vibrant before and during the European colonization of Africa. There were great epics such as *Sundiata*, *Ozidi*, and *Mwindo*, among many. At the same time, there were oral poetic performance traditions such as the Yoruba *ijala*, the Zulu and Tswana *izibongo*, the Urhobo *udje*, the Ewe *halo*, and a multiplicity of other forms of panegyrics and abuse songs and chants and narratives that reflected the realities, aspirations, and the drama of existence of different groups of people and individuals among them.

The colonial system in its capitalist pursuit of forcing the men to pay so-called 'head tax' and promulgating laws of slander helped to cause the decline of the *udje* oral poetic performance tradition. Christianity also contributed to the demise of *udje* as the sanctity of the god of songs (Uhaghwa), for whom it was performed was vilified as fetish or Satanic. Thus, while there was a vibrant traditional literature before colonialism arrived, the colonial system and its objectives of erasing African culture through its laws and the evangelizing of the accompanying Christian missionaries worked against the thriving of indigenous African literatures in colonial Africa.

Arab/Islamic, Swahili, and Hausa Literatures in Colonial Africa

Before the colonization of Africa towards the end of the nineteenth century, another form of literature, derived from Africa's interaction with the Arab and Muslim world, was flourishing in parts of Africa, especially North Africa, parts of West Africa (particularly the Sokoto caliphate), and the coastal part of East Africa (including Mombasa). Let me begin with the literature of the Swahili coastal people of East Africa. The Indian Ocean trade brought Arabs and Islam to the area especially to Mombasa and Zanzibar. According to Ibrahim Shariff in 'The Function of Dialogue Poetry', 'Poetry is composed more for the ear and not for the eye, for immediate dialogic encounters rather than for solitary reflections, and it is simply the highest art form of a society that attaches exceptional value to refined speech'.[4] This value of speech is comparable to what Chinua Achebe says of the place of the spoken word in Igbo traditional society. There was an increase in the publication of Swahili poetry from the end of the nineteenth century which coincided with the period of colonization of present-day Kenya and Tanzania.

Similarly, in much of Northern Nigeria, especially in the Sokoto caliphate, two types of literature thrived during the British colonial era: Islam-inspired and indigenous Hausa poetic forms and narratives. In the Islamic court of Sokoto, Usman Dan Fodio promoted Islamic literature. His own daughter Nana Asma'u Bint Usman Dan Fodio (1793–1864) is credited with writing many poems in the Islamic and Arab poetic traditions with socio-political themes. This female jihadist had written literature of scholarly and religious depth before the colonial period. Therefore, one can make the point that before European colonization of Africa, indigenous and Arab/Islamic forms of literature thrived and would continue during the colonial period. It is significant that the premium placed on writing in the colonial period would accelerate the growth and spread of Arabic/Muslim and Swahili literatures in Africa. On the other hand, the more indigenous literature in Muslim parts of Africa, as among the Hausa people, was discouraged at the expense of the Islamic one.

THE EARLY WAVE OF WRITTEN OR MODERN LITERATURE IN AFRICA

History, no doubt, greatly influenced literature in Africa in a more compelling manner from colonial times. Modernity, itself a product of history, would diversify literature in Africa by adding new forms of literature, written in European languages, to be a counterpoint to the indigenous oral literature that already existed. The new literature began in an imitative manner as African writers modeled their works on already existing European literary genres.

In order to achieve the colonial mission efficiently, it was necessary for the colonialists (British, French, and Portuguese) to build schools for domestic assistants, interpreters, and junior-cadre administrators in their respective colonial governments, since they could not bring their European kinsfolk for everything. Literacy in the colonial European languages became an enabling factor for the African in getting a job. It was graduates of the different Western schools who had become literate and so knowledgeable of European literature and the Bible who would eventually become writers of the new African literature. Those who graduated from elementary schools had to go to many government colleges and missionary-run secondary schools. At the top were tertiary schools that were linked to metropolitan colonial institutions. For instance, in the Anglophone colonies, many university colleges were established and attached to specific English universities with which they shared the same syllabi and other forms of curricular affiliations. Such colleges include Fourah Bay College in Freetown (Sierra Leone); Legon (Ghana); Ibadan (Nigeria); Makerere (Uganda); and Nairobi (Kenya). Coincidentally, these educational institutions became major centers of literary creativity in colonial and modern Africa. It is noteworthy, for instance, that Chinua Achebe, Christopher Okigbo, Wole Soyinka, J.P. Clark, M.C. Echeruo, and some other writers attended the University College, Ibadan, and Okot p'Bitek attended Makerere. Benedict Wallet Vilakazi attended the University of Witwaterstrand and was the first black man to receive a Ph.D. degree from that university. His doctoral thesis was titled 'Oral and Written Literature in Nguni'.

Most of the instructors were European. It is not surprising therefore to have a strong modernist influence in the Anglophone universities and surrealist and existentialist influence in Francophone institutions bearing in mind the literary trends in Britain and France during the period. The African writers in their writings responded to existing European literatures they were taught in schools, and the Bible. However, before discussing these African writers' works in colonial Africa, it is important also to introduce some European writers, especially on Africa, who foisted on them a responsibility to react to put things right. It was a kind of anxiety of influence.

Europeans Writing on Africa: Conrad, Graham Greene, and Joyce Cary

One cannot have a holistic view of literature in colonial Africa without mentioning some European or Western writers who have created literary works set in Africa or with African characters. Those whose novels have had a lasting impression are Joseph Conrad with his *Heart of Darkness*, Graham Greene with his *The Heart of the Matter*, and Joyce Cary's *Mister Johnson*. In these works, British novelists portray African characters in their narratives from the way they understood Africans during their contact with Africa. Chinua Achebe wrote a lot on Conrad's racist portrayal of Africans in the Congo. The characters are one-dimensional and are not rounded. The same portrayal appears in Cary's *Mister Johnson*. Graham Greene was a British colonial officer in Freetown, Sierra Leone. It is generally believed that his Sierra Leonean experience informed the novel even though his novel was set in South Africa.

Heart of Darkness, a Western classic, was taught in African institutions to Africans who saw its lack of realism and racism and would set out, as Achebe does in *Things Fall Apart*, to give a realistic portrayal of the Africans they lived with and knew very well. Thus, an aspect of the literature in colonial Africa deals with the biased and racist portrayal of Africans by Europeans who visited Africa in colonial times and later used their experiences to write fictional narratives. In fact, Joyce Cary was a colonial administrator in Northern Nigeria and his short story 'Umaru' and novels *Aissa Saved* (1932), *The African Witch* (1936), and *Mister Johnson* (1939) were all informed by his Nigerian experience. Many of the African writers who started to write in colonial times saw it as their responsibility to correct the wrong portrayal of African characters by colonial writers.

Pioneer Poets

All the poets who are described as 'pioneer poets' had their education and their writing careers entirely in colonial times. They came mainly from South Africa, Nigeria, and Ghana. Of the South Africans, D.I.E. Dhlomo, Benedict Wallet Vilikazi, and Mazisi Kunene are the most prominent. It is interesting to note that even in early colonial times before apartheid was formalized in South Africa, there were authors already writing in indigenous languages and calling for African literature to be written in African languages. Benedict W. Vilakazi, in 1939, lamented the fact that South African writers were writing in English and not in African indigenous languages:

> By Bantu drama, I mean a drama written by a Bantu, for the Bantu, in a Bantu language. I do not class English or Afrikaans dramas on Bantu themes, whether these are written by Black people, I do not call them contributions to Bantu

Literature. It is the same with poetry ... I have an unshaken belief in the possibilities of Bantu languages and their literature, provided the Bantu writers themselves can learn to love their languages and use them as vehicles for thought, feeling and will. After all, the belief, resulting in literature, is a demonstration of people's 'self' where they cry: '*Ego sum quod sum*' [I am what I am].[5]

Vilakazi also sees Bantu sensibility as different from what he describes as the Romantic sensibility of South Africans of European stock.[6] Both Vilakazi and Mazisi Kunene wrote in isiZulu. As Dike Okoro wrote of the two Zulu poets:

Vilakazi's poetry shares with readers his love for the natural world of his South African homeland, his closeness to his family, and the deep views he held concerning the role of blacks in South Africa. Conversely, Kunene's poems separate him from Vilakazi in many ways ... His poems in this book share with readers his view of history as a foundational basis for comprehending the history of the black family in the West, and his acknowledgment of pan-Africanism as a vehicle for African diasporic solidarity.[7]

Writing came early, too, to West Africa, and among the 'Pioneer Poets' were Dennis Chukude Osadebay of Nigeria and Kwame Kyeretwie Boakye Danquah, Michael Dei Anang, Gladys Casely-Hayford, and R.E.G. Armattoe of Ghana. Unlike the poets in South Africa, who wrote in isiZulu, the West African pioneer poets wrote in English. They were highly imitative of Victorian poetry and Christian hymns, and their major themes centered on race and Christian virtues. Their poetry generally lacked craft.

One of Dennis Osadebay's major poems was 'Young Africa's Plea', in which the poet demands:

> Don't preserve my customs
> As some fine curios
> To suit some white historian's tastes.
> There's nothing artificial
> That beats the natural way
> In culture and ideals of life.

The speaker of the poem goes on to say that he will 'play with the whiteman's ways' and 'work with the blackman's brains'. There is openness to other ways of life to strengthen his African ways but not to abandon his own. This readiness to combine what is needed in other ways with indigenous ways, the poet believes, will result in a 'sweet rebirth' that should make him a 'better man'. The poet shows courage in trying new ways brought by the European to Africa. There is expression of confidence in the ability to blend the African and European ways that colonialism has brought about. The poet further addresses the colonizing Westerners about the disrespect shown to him and his culture and appeals for them to 'bury their prejudice'. The poem does not make use of imagery to show the poet's displeasure but only ordinary prose. One has to acknowledge, though, the occasional use of rhymes. At the same time, Osadebay thanks 'Sons and daughters of Britannia' for having given Africans hospitals, schools, communications, and Western civilization in another poem titled 'Young Africa's Thanks'. It is for this flirtation with colonial modernity that Tijan M. Sallah and I condemn the pioneer poets:

> Lost to the uncritical voice of the typical pioneer poet were the negative aspects of colonialism, such as the wholesale obliteration of indigenous cultures, the forced labor of 'natives', the siphoning of huge stocks of natural resources, the levying of unfair taxes, and the repression of local freedom.[8]

Négritude

A significant portion of literature in colonial Africa is made up of Négritude poetry which derived from the Pan-Africanist aspirations of Caribbean and African students in France who used their journal, *Presence Africaine*, to affirm their Africanity. Led by Aimé Césaire (Martinique), Léon Damas (Guadeloupe), and Leopold Sedar Senghor (Senegal), these black writers conceived negritude as a form of resistance to European racism and a counter to Western hegemony. They used their writings to invoke their African heritage so as to affirm their humanity. While the three major figures express their 'negritude' differently, Senghor's poetry is important in the discussion of literature in colonial Africa. Despite snide remarks by Wole Soyinka that 'a tiger does not proclaim its tigritude', Senghor's negritude is a crucial response to colonialism in mainly Francophone Africa and the Caribbean, and his poetry influenced such writers as Birago Diop and Bernard Dadie.

In Senghor's poetry there is often a romanticizing of the African past that evokes an Edenic state, which some literary scholars have criticized as too idealized. Poems such as 'Femme Noire' ('Black Woman') and 'In Memoriam' respectively portray the African woman as nurturing and the ancestors as not dead but guiding and protecting the living. His 'New York' sees Black Harlem as sensuous and natural in the music and life that come from it, and different from the artificial and steel-like Manhattan. To the poet, the artificial West needs sensuous Africa to complement it for a fuller life.

It suffices in this discourse on literature in colonial Africa to acknowledge the importance of Négritude poetry during the period as a counterpoint to European claims of cultural superiority. Négritude is to some extent the second stage in Fanon's conceptualization of the literature of colonized peoples, when the writer is free to be the opposite of the trends in the colonial metropolis.

Early Fiction

While poetry occupied a preeminent place in both Anglophone and Francophone colonies, especially from the discussion of 'pioneer poets' and 'Négritude poets', there were writers of fiction in colonial Africa. I will use only three examples here: Guinea's Camara Laye and Nigeria's Amos Tutuola and Cyprian Ekwensi.

Camara Laye's *L'enfant noir* (translated as *The African Child* and *The Dark Child*) was published in 1954 and is seen generally as an autobiographical novel that chronicles the real life of the author from his birthplace of Kouroussa, education in Conakry, to his subsequent departure to France. Though the book won the Prix Charles Veillon, its reception was controversial. Mongo Beti's review finds it pandering to the Western image of Africa. In any case, it presents African culture in its natural setting to the outside world. In 1955, Laye published *Le Regard du Roi (The Radiance of the King)*, which has been described by Kwame Anthony Appiah as 'one of the greatest of the African novels of the colonial period'.[9] Laye would write more after Guinea's independence on October 2, 1958, but these two major novels made a splash in the literature of Africa during the colonial period.

Tutuola was not highly educated and was a clerk whose interest in writing impelled him to tell Yoruba stories in English. *The Palm-wine Drinkard* received good reviews from outside Africa as soon as Faber & Faber brought it out in 1952. While the likes of Dylan Thomas praised the book for its quaintness, African writers and scholars saw the work of an uneducated African and as something Western scholars admired for its 'otherness'. Tutuola tells the story of a palm-wine drinker who goes to the land of the dead to look for his palm-wine tapper, goes through fantastic episodes, and does not succeed in bringing him back. Following the fantasy (magical realism) of *The Palm-wine Drinkard*, Tutuola later wrote *My Life in the Bush of Ghosts* (1954), *Simbi and the Satyr of the Dark Jungle* (1955), and *The Brave African Huntress* (1958) before Nigeria's independence on October 1, 1960.

Another writer of fiction in colonial times was Cyprian Ekwensi, whose pre-independence fictional narratives include *Burning Grass*, *The Passport of Malam Ilia*, and *Jagua Nana*. He moved from narratives set in Northern Nigeria to those set in the city. His novels presented characters in a rather superficial manner in episodic sequences that the public enjoyed. While literary scholars (until Ernest Emenyonu) did not seem to have taken his work seriously, his novels blazed a trail in fictional writing in Nigeria and other parts of Africa.

Early Plays and Theatre

Plays, like poetry and fiction, were being published in colonial Africa. Those of Nigeria's James Ene Henshaw were examples of dramatic writings produced in the later colonial period. *This Is Our Chance: Three Plays* (1956) is perhaps Henshaw's best-known collection of plays. In *The Jewels of the Shrine*, the dramatist presents the young as seeing the old as backward and for that reason tending to ignore their invaluable experience. *A Man of Character* has a protagonist who fights against corruption. *This Is Our Chance* focuses on the conflict between traditional mores and modernity. The simple plot and style of opposing characters standing for indigenous African tradition on the one hand and accepting of the new ways brought by colonialism on the other make his plays popular with audiences. Critics have written about the influence of Bernard Shaw on Henshaw because of his long Introductions. This is not unexpected as his studies in Ireland might have exposed him to the Irish playwright and his propensity towards drama would have drawn him to popular drama of the colonial time.

It is important to mention the 'Traveling Theatre' in parts of Western Nigeria during the colonial period. The major figures of this popular traveling theatre were Hubert Ogunde and Duro Ladipo, who produced plays in Yoruba that reflected the realities of the common people. The 'traveling theatre' would open the way for theatre for mass mobilization for mostly health and political issues during colonial and post-independence periods in Nigeria.

ONITSHA MARKET LITERATURE

Onitsha Market Literature was an integral part of literature in colonial Africa. Flourishing in the large market city of Onitsha in eastern Nigeria, the pamphlets and novellas concerned themselves with a myriad of popular issues of the middle of the twentieth century. The term has become generic for popular writings made up of fictional narratives, plays, tracts on current events, advice, and moral tracts. Many of them also related to city life but with romantic, often sentimental, and often admonitory moralistic tones. In such works, there was glamorization of Western life in the city and the warning against being lost in the city life, which was presented as seductively corrupt. Since common people with little education wrote the works, their readers also had minimal education. The narratives often placed a premium on entertainment; hence the popular appeal to common readers. The plots of narratives were predictable but captivating in the tantalizing stories. In addition to warning against city girls and love, other narratives dealt with guides to making girls fall in love with one and how to become prosperous. Many of the best known of the producers of Onitsha Market Literature are said to have been students, journalists, and even taxi drivers who were not very literate but had a passion for telling their stories and giving advice or teaching how to do things. Some of the writers and their works include Thomas Iguh's *Agnes in the Game of Love* and *Alice in the Romance of Love*; J.O. Nnadozie's *Beware of Harlots and Many Friends, the World is Hard*; and Raja Raphael's *The Right Way to Approach Ladies and Get Them in Love*. Other popular writers include Ogali A. Ogali, O. Olisa, and Felix N. Stephen.

Onitsha Market Literature may not be significant in the growth of African literature as an intellectual discipline, but it occupies an important place in literature in colonial Africa. It generated much interest in reading and provided a medium of entertainment not only in Onitsha but also across much of Nigeria at the time. It also brought a measure of social egalitarianism between the writer and the reader of the same low-education social class. Onitsha Market Literature stands out as different from the later literature in Nigeria and the rest of Africa that became a product of the ivory tower for members of the same position in the universities.

NATIONALIST STRUGGLE AND LITERATURE

Frantz Fanon's third stage of literature in the colonized state appeared during the era of nationalist struggle towards the end of the colonial period. It was more revolutionary than the earlier stage and entailed not only criticizing colonialism but also inspiring Africans and highlighting their culture, history, and personality. I will use two writers and their works before their respective countries' independence as examples of this literature: Cameroon's Mongo Beti and Nigeria's Chinua Achebe.

Mongo Beti (born Alexandre Biyidi Awala and writing under the name Eza Boto) was a major figure in African literature in colonial times. After criticizing Camara Laye's *African Child* in his *Presence Africaine* review, he published a short story titled '*Sans haine sans amour*' ('Without hatred or love') in 1953. Beti published his first novel *Ville cruelle* (*Cruel city*) under the pseudonym of Eza Boto in 1954. He later published the popular *Le pauvre Christ de Bomba* (*The poor Christ of Bomba*) in 1956 and exposed the collaboration between the missionaries and colonial administrators working in Africa. The book was banned in Cameroon because of its biting satire of the foreigners and the manner in which the Cameroonians resisted them. Beti published *Mission Termine* in 1957 and the novel won the Prix Sainte Beuve in 1958. In 1958, he published *Le Roi Miracule*. From Beti's novels written and set in colonial Cameroon, one gets an insight into the impact of colonialism on the colonial subjects. The people's lives were affected culturally, socially, economically, politically, and psychologically. The novelist uses satire as a weapon of native resistance to combat the problems associated with colonialism.

While Beti has a body of work in the colonial period, Nigeria's Chinua Achebe published his classic novel *Things Fall Apart* in 1958. Much has been written about this novel but it suffices in this chapter to make some comments on the inspiration of the book, its purpose, portrayal of colonial Nigeria, and its contribution to African literature. Chinua Achebe in his essay 'The Writer as Teacher' conceives of the author as an educator, and he seems to have set out in *Things Fall Apart* with the purpose of uplifting the self-esteem of Africans whose culture and humanity had been denigrated by colonial policies. At the same time, he wanted to show the foreigners, the colonialists, and the West that Africans had a culture before the European invasion of their land and that Africans through their practices were better organized in many ways than the Europeans who claimed to be superior to them. In other essays, Achebe emphasized that Africans are people and that they are neither angels nor devils; in other words, they have their strengths and weaknesses. Achebe spent much of his writing career responding to the likes of racist Joseph Conrad, Hugh Trevor-Roper, and Hegelian followers who deny Africans their humanity. To Achebe, such racists were wrong in their views of Africa and Africans.

Achebe's *Things Fall Apart* portrayed the insensitivity of the European colonialists who, for one white man killed, wiped out the entire village of Abame. The duplicity of the District Officer who sought dialogue with Okonkwo and his clansmen only to put them in handcuffs and jail tells the sort of people the colonialists were. After Okonkwo hangs himself, the District Officer in his insensitivity only thinks of the book he wants to write and using this tragic event as a part of it. Obierika, who draws his attention to the gravity of what has happened, reprimands him, saying that Okonkwo is one of the greatest men in the clan and that the 'white man' has driven him to take his own life and he would be buried like a dog! Like Mongo Beti, Achebe in his only pre-independence novel gives a graphic portrayal of the socio-cultural, economic, political, and psychological disruption and damage brought by colonialism to Africans.

LATER COLONIAL LITERATURE FROM ZIMBABWE, SOUTH AFRICA, ANGOLA, AND MOZAMBIQUE

The colonial period in Africa varied in length. While the partition of Africa took place in Berlin in 1884/1885, African countries gained independence at different times. Some struggled like Algeria and Kenya to gain independence, while others like Nigeria and Cameroon had independence handed over to them. In any case, after the independence of Ghana and Guinea in 1957 and 1958 respectively, most other African countries became independent between 1960 and 1963. However, peculiarities in Southern Rhodesia and the Lusophone countries of Angola and Mozambique in particular resulted in a longer struggle for independence in a prolonged colonial state. Admitting differences and peculiarities in their respective countries, I will use the example of literature about the struggle against colonialism in Southern Rhodesia.

The liberation struggles created a literature of their own, which can be seen as part of literature in a colonial African state at the late stage of its foreign tutelage. It was a revolutionary literature intended to inspire nationalism in the people and give them the courage to bear the sacrifices that their struggle entailed. While historians speak of three different *chimurengas*, I refer here to the literature, including songs and music, of what has been referred to as the Rhodesian Bush War of 1966–1979—the guerrilla war for black independence of Zimbabwe.

Newspapers, Literary Magazines and Journals in Colonial Africa

One cannot avoid mentioning the role of many newspapers, magazines, and journals in promoting literature in colonial times. Many newspapers in South Africa, Nigeria, and Gold Coast, among others, had newspapers and magazines used as avenues for promoting poetry, short stories, and literary discussions in colonial times. In Nigeria, Chief Ernest Ikoli (1893–1960) started his newspaper career in the early 1920s with the *Lagos Weekly Record* and became the first editor of the *Daily Times* of Nigeria which was launched in June 1926 under the chairmanship of Adeyemo Alakija. Ikoli promoted the publication of creative writing in the paper. *The West African Pilot*, a nationalistic newspaper associated with Nnamdi Azikiwe, also created space for some creative works in colonial times. At the same time there were discussions of literary creations in the same newspapers.

In South Africa, Sol Plaatje was an intellectual and journalist and became the first black South African to write a novel in English. Also in South Africa, the *Drum* magazine was a vehicle for creative works at the time. Many of the journalists working with *Drum* were also writers. It is significant to note that Es'kia Mphalele was the fiction editor from 1955 to 1957 and encouraged the publication of dozens of short stories. Among *Drum* writers who went on to publish their works are: Can Themba, Lewis Nkosi, William 'Bloke' Modisane, Bessie Head, and Richard Rive. *Drum* gave inspiration to much writing about urban life in South Africa in the 1950s.

Of great significance in colonial times in the Francophone areas of Africa is the literary magazine, *Presence Africaine*, based in Paris and edited for a long time by Alioune Diop. It was the medium for the propagation of Négritude, publication of creative works such as short stories and reviews of works of Francophone Africans and those in the diaspora. Newspapers and literary magazines thus played a major part in the dissemination of literary works in colonial Africa.

Conclusion

Literature and history have a symbiotic relationship, especially in colonial Africa. Literature is fueled by historical experiences that it reflects in its peculiar artistic way. To a large extent literature portrays history in a non-conventional way by its portrayal of the implications of social, cultural, economic, political, and psychological consequences of colonialism. It is not surprising that teachers of African colonial history have to use texts such as Mongo Beti's *Poor Christ of Bomba* and Chinua Achebe's *Things Fall Apart* in their courses in African history because of the graphic way that literature projects the details of lives and states that history documents. Literature enhances both the macro and micro modes of history in presenting the colonial state and the characters whose daily life experiences tell the overall consequences of the colonial period.

This chapter has thus given the different but related aspects of the colonial period that political independence has ended in Africa. Literature was active and contributed immensely in exposing the nature of the colonial state and the human beings who were affected by that historical phenomenon. While oral literature existed before the appearance of the modern written literature, the two modes outlived colonialism and thrive side by side today. For better or for worse, the imperial conquest of Africa and its partition to colonies have left indelible marks on the psyche of the people, and the literature of the time gives adequate testimony to the suffering, struggle, and resilience of the African.

NOTES

1. Bill Ashcroft, Gareth Griffins, and Helen Tiffin, *The Empire Writes Back: Theory and Practice in Postcolonial Literatures*, 2nd ed. (London and New York: Routledge, 2002), 1.
2. Frantz Fanon, *The Wretched of the Earth* (New York: Grove Press, 2007), 176–79.
3. Swahili dialogue poetry was popular during the colonial period in Kenya.
4. Ntongela Masilela, *The Cultural Modernity of H.I.E. Dhlomo* (Trenton, NJ: Africa World Press, 2007). 76.
5. Vilakazi saw the Bantu sensibility as different from the European one. Benedict Wallet Vilakazi, "Oral and Written Literature in Nguni." (PhD thesis, University of Witwaterstrand, South Africa, 1946), quoted in Masilela, *The Cultural Modernity*, 75.
6. Dike Okoro compares and contrasts Vilakazi's and Kunene's poetry in *Two Zulu Poets: Mazisi Kunene and Benedict Wallet Villakazi* (Milwaukee, WI: Cissus World Press, 2015), xiv.
7. The Pioneer Poets were not seen as critical of the colonial enterprise as Tanure Ojaide and Tijan M. Sallah observe in their introduction to *The New African Poetry: An Anthology* (Boulder, CO: Lynne Rienner, 1999), 2.
8. https://web.archive.org/web/20070421144243/http://www.nybooks.com/shop/product?usca_p=t&product_id=78. Archived from the original on April 21, 2007. Retrieved Feb 8, 2010.
9. Kwame Anthony Appiah, review of *The Radiance of the King* in the *New York Times Review of Books*, July 15, 2001.

BIBLIOGRAPHY

Achebe, Chinua. *Things Fall Apart*. London: Heinemann, 1958.
———. *The Education of a British-Protected Child*. New York: Alfred A. Knopf, 2009.

Appiah, Kwame Anthony, review of Camara Laye's. *Radiance of the King (New York Times Review of Books)*, July 15, 2001.
Ashcroft, Bill with Gareth Griffins and Helen Tiffin. *The Empire Writes Back: Theory and Practice in Postcolonial Literatures*, 2nd ed. London and New York: Routledge, 2002.
Beti, Mongo. *Mission to Kala*. Translated by Peter Green. London: Heinemann, 1964.
———. *King Lazarus*. Translated by Muller Frederick. London: Heinemann, 1970.
———. *The Poor Christ of Bomba*. Translated by Gerald Moore. London: Heinemann, 1971.
Ekwensi, Cyprian. *When Love Whispers*. Onitsha, Nigeria: Tabansi Press, 1947.
———. *The Leopard's Claw*. London: Thomas Nelson, 1950.
———. *People of the City*. London: Dakers, 1954.
———. *The Passport of Mallam Ilia*. Cambridge: Cambridge University Press, 1960.
———. *The Drummer Boy*. Cambridge and Ibadan: Cambridge University Press, 1960.
Fanon, Frantz. *The Wretched of the Earth*. New York: Grove Press, 2007.
———. *Black Skin, White Masks*. New York: Grove Press, 2008.
Henshaw, James Ene. *This Is Our Chance*. London: University of London Press, 1956.
Iguh, Thomas. *Agnes in the Game of Love*. Onitsha, Nigeria: A. Onwudiwe & Sons.
———. *Alice in the Romance of Love*. Onitsha: Appolos Brothers.
Masilela, Ntongela. *The Cultural Modernity of H.I.E. Dhlomo*. Trenton, NJ: Africa World Press, 2007.
Mazrui, A.M. *Swahili Beyond the Boundaries: Literature, Language, and Identity*. Athens, OH: Ohio University Press, 2007.
Niane, D.T. *Sundiata: An Epic of Old Mali*. Harlow, Essex, UK: Pearson, 2006.
Nnadozie, J.O. *Beware of Harlots and Many Friends, the World is Hard*. Onitsha, Nigeria: J.C. Nnadozie.
Ojaide, Tanure, and Tijan M. Sallah. *The New African Poetry: An Anthology*. Boulder, CO: Lynne Rienner, 1999.
Okoro, Dike. *Two Zulu Poets: Mazisi Kunene & Benedict Wallet Villakazi*. Milwaukee, WI: Cissus World Press, 2015.
Osadebay, Dennis Chukude. *Poems of a Nationalist*. Indianapolis: Realjoy Communications Limited/Indiana University, 2009.
Raphael, Raja. *The Right Way to Approach Ladies and Get Them in Love*. Onitsha, Nigeria: Appolos Bros. Press.
Said, Edward. *Culture and Imperialism*. New York: Vintage, 1994.
Shariff, Ibrahim Noor. "The Function of Dialogue Poetry in Swahili Society." pp. 137–38. Diss., Rutgers University, 1983.
Tutuola, Amos. *The Palm-wine Drinkard*. London: Faber and Faber, 1952.
———. *My Life in the Bush of Ghosts*. London: Faber and Faber, 1954.
———. *Simbi and the Satyr of the Dark Jungle*. London: Faber and Faber, 1955.
———. *The Brave African Huntress*. London: Faber and Faber, 1958.
Vilakazi, Benedict Wallet, "Oral and Written Literature in Nguni." PhD thesis, University of Witwaterstrand, South Africa, 1946.

CHAPTER 18

Art, African Identities, and Colonialism

Sylvester Okwunodu Ogbechie

This chapter reviews the impact of colonialism on African art and identities, especially in the emergent modernity of African artists such as Gerard Sekoto (1913–1993), Ben Enwonwu (1917–1994), Gazbia Sirry (b.1925), Afewerk Tekle (1932–2012), Irma Stern (South Africa 1894–1966), and Iba Ndiaye (1928–2008). The unfolding of colonial rule differed in various regions of Africa and impacted the development of new visual languages for modern African art in these contexts. The artists selected represent these regional differences in their approach to artistic practice and questions of modernist identity. I use their careers to investigate discourses of modern art in the colonial era, and to search out points of convergence in how these discourses unfolded in their national spaces and transnational engagements.

African art has always been modern, and it is now necessary to invent new terminologies and frameworks of interpretation that foreground its responses to changing social conditions. The rigid classification of African art into 'traditional' and modern types has created a schism in the field, which is exacerbated by outdated ideas of indigenous cultural production. Also, analysis of twentieth-century African art marginalizes the impact of pioneer African artists who worked in the colonial period and mainly focuses on postcolonial artists. To understand the role of art in African nationalism and the development of modern and contemporary African identities, we need to pay more attention to how pioneer modern African artists engaged questions of modernity

S.O. Ogbechie (✉)
Department of History of Art and Architecture,
University of California, Santa Barbara, CA, USA

© The Author(s) 2018
M.S. Shanguhyia and T. Falola (eds.),
The Palgrave Handbook of African Colonial and Postcolonial History,
https://doi.org/10.1057/978-1-137-59426-6_18

which, in many instances, shaped the visual languages of postcolonial African art.

The five pioneer artists I discuss developed new visual languages for modern art in various African contexts. I do not intend to write comprehensive biographical histories of these artists; rather I use their careers as reference points to discuss changing forms and discourses of African art under colonialism and the search for unique African identities for the artists involved. Ben Enwonwu was the first modern African artist to gain global fame and he enjoyed immense critical acclaim in Africa, Europe, and the USA. In the colonial culture in which his career originated, and the postcolonial context in which it ended, his affirmation of multiple identities (Igbo, African, Nigerian, Biafran, modern artist, etc.) inserted him into the fractious politics of African nationalism and the continued struggle of African societies against different forms of European imperialism.[1] Afewerk Tekle grew up in Ethiopia during the Italian occupation and initially set out to study engineering in England. He turned instead to fine arts and became celebrated for his paintings on African and Christian themes, and more importantly, his stained-glass artworks. Gazbia Sirry is a notable Egyptian female artist whose works contributed to a feminist consciousness and discussions of 'what it meant to be a modern Egyptian in a world of conflicting and complimentary political, cultural and artistic ideologies'.[2] Iba Ndiaye was a notable pioneer modernist in Senegal, where he co-founded training programs that contributed to one of Africa's most exiting contexts of modern art practice. The South African artist Gerard Sekoto is considered one of the earliest South African modernists and social realists. His work chronicled the traumatic changes imposed on black South Africans by an emergent apartheid system during the 1940s.[3] Sekoto left South African before apartheid was formally introduced, and he lived out his life in exile in France where his resolute identification as an African sustained him. Irma Stern, a white South African complicates our narrative by introducing the divergent history of colonialism in South Africa, which resulted in parallel developments for black and white artists.

These pioneer artists struggled with the meaning of their modern art in the context of colonialism and efforts to define nationalist identities as modern Africans. The analysis that follows evaluates how the colonial context framed their unique responses to modernity, indigenous art traditions, and the global horizons of black cultural subjectivity.

COLONIALISM AND THE POLITICS OF REPRESENTATION

Colonialism defines the imposition of European rule on Africa starting from the late nineteenth century onwards. It is a subset of an ongoing imperialism that asserts Western (white) power and control over African bodies and resources. The colonial period is a key political/social/cultural moment in the history of modern Africa that saw major transformations in all aspects of life. Colonization of Africa also raised for the first time a global consciousness of African identity as being distinctive from, despite being subjugated to, Western imperialism. The effort to define African subjectivity within the confines of colonial rule ultimately led to various forms of anti-colonial and nationalist struggles, which were central to the emergence of new African identities and efforts to define a modern African art in the global context.

European colonization of Africa dates to the Berlin conference of 1884–1885, which oversaw the scramble for and partition of Africa. The push to formally claim colonial spaces assigned to various European powers resulted in wars of colonization which roiled Africa from 1890 to 1910, with Western armies fighting and subjugating many indigenous African kingdoms.[4] Subsequently, European colonizers created new political boundaries that ultimately defined the outlines of modern African nations.

Africa's history predates its colonization by significant margins. In the case of Nigeria, for example, Falola and Heaton note that although 'the borders of modern-day Nigeria were established ... by British colonizers ... the histories of the peoples that make up the polity go back many centuries'.[5] Colonialism in Africa sidelined this history as well as previous engagements with modernity in parts of Africa such as Lagos, Cairo, Freetown, Liberia, Ethiopia and Cape Town during the long nineteenth century. We may thus argue that colonialism produced regressive ideas about African identity that became the focus of nationalist and anti-colonial struggles.[6] Olufemi Taiwo suggests that colonialism preempted an emergent modernity in Africa and it is important to disentangle the supposed links between colonialism and modernism, since many of the central concepts we associate with African modernity either predate or postdate colonialism.[7]

Colonialism reshaped African societies. However, Africans' resistance to colonialism led to nationalist movements through which many African countries achieved independence from 1958 onwards. It is important to stress the global nature of the African resistance to colonization, mainly because the diasporization of Africans due to the transatlantic slave trade and similar practices such as the Indian Ocean and Arabic slave trades had already resulted in the forcible transplantation of millions of Africans from the continent to all parts of the world. Continental and diaspora Africans thus participated in the emergence of the modern world from its inception and contributed in no small measure to the formal and conceptual frameworks of modernity in diverse contexts.

Formal colonial rule in Africa lasted until the 1960s, when many African countries secured political independence, although this happened much later in countries such as Mozambique and Angola (both liberated from Portugal in 1975), Zimbabwe (1980), Namibia (1985) and the Republic of South Africa, which emerged from under apartheid rule in 1994 with its first multiparty elections.⁸ It is notable that European colonial culture in Africa initially intended to produce white settler colonies of the sort found in the Americas, Canada, and Australia, where immigrant whites decimated and largely replaced indigenous populations. Except for the Southern African regions such as South Africa, Namibia, and to a large extent Kenya, where a postcolonial apparatus of non-governmental organizations (NGOs) resulted in a large white population, the attempt failed in most parts of Africa. The transition from colonial rule for many African countries resulted from nationalist anti-colonial struggles which in some cases flared into outright conflict, as in Algeria's bitter war of independence against France. Similar conflicts in Mozambique, Zimbabwe, and Angola also presaged the end of colonial rule.

The definition and parameters of African identity was central to most nationalist movements. In many colonized African countries, indigenous Africans were excluded from the concept of national citizenship, and in South Africa this hardened into apartheid: a formal system of segregation that rendered black Africans estranged in their own country. The question of modern African identity therefore emerges during the colonial period as part of a broad anti-colonial and nationalist movement. Similar struggles occurred among African diaspora blacks who saw their lives reflected in the colonized conditions of blacks in Africa, leading to the development of global strategies to combat colonization. Pan-Africanism was one such platform, in its articulation by W.E.B. Du Bois and political activist Marcus Mosiah Garvey.⁹ The Pan-African Congress Movement was the most notable result of this ideology, starting with the one Du Bois organized in Paris in 1919. This movement built on the momentum generated by the Harlem Renaissance, which offered 'a view of blackness (Africanness ...) that found value and beauty in African culture and history as subjects of art, much in the same way African sculpture and religious rituals had penetrated Cubism and Surrealism'.¹⁰

The ideology of Négritude, conceptualized by Leopold Sedar Senghor of Senegal, Aimé Cesaire of Martinique, and Leon Damas of French Guiana, was arguably the most influential ideology of black subjectivity during the colonial period, and it shaped the works of influential modern African artists such as Ben Enwonwu.¹¹ Négritude can be used as a generic term to describe the various impulses of black consciousness, and the various movements for rehabilitating black African culture in the wake of colonialism. These include: Aimé Cesaire's militant Caribbean variant and Nnamdi Azikiwe's African Renaissance movement (1930–1940s); Kwame Nkrumah's African Personality Campaign (1950–1960s); Amilcar Cabral's Re-Africanization program in Guinea-Bisssau (1960s); and Steve Biko's Black Consciousness movement in South Africa (1970s).¹² All these movements resisted European cultural domination and sought to rediscover and regenerate black African culture. We may add these to appropriations of international cultural styles and movements (such as Surrealism) also adopted by African artists and nationalists in their struggle against Western cultural domination.

Inventing African Traditional Art in Colonial Culture

Colonial culture wrought great transformations in African art, especially in the forms and contents of indigenous artworks. Studies by various Africanists have documented these changes in detail even if their implications are not always thought out. A bias towards identifying all indigenous artworks that emerged from the colonial era as enduring and timeless examples of African culture has led to major errors in identification and classification. This includes the persistent idea that artworks in indigenous cultures emerge from an enduring and timeless past, based on theories couched in functionalist assumptions about the internal coherence of traditional African communities and their symbolic practices. However, the changing aesthetics and iconography of indigenous art resulting from the colonial encounter suggest African art has always been a dynamic context that constantly adapted to new social, political, and environmental conditions.

It is important to stress that most of the African artworks classified in museums as 'precolonial' or 'traditional' art were actually created during the colonial period and were considered examples of an emergent modernity captured in indigenous idioms and visual languages. As John Picton observed, 'most traditional African art in museums today was made, and subsequently taken abroad, during the height of the colonial period – from roughly 1880 to 1960'.[13] In spite of this fact, they are wrongly described in the literature as evidence of pre-colonial African creativity. Alongside this misidentification, the artists who created these works are often seen as exemplars of indigenous creativity. Take, for example, the great Yoruba sculptor Olowe of Ise (1875–1938), who produced many sculptures under royal patronage at the turn of the twentieth century. Roslyn Walker's influential biography of the artist shows Olowe worked almost exclusively for various Yoruba royalty and aristocrats within a sixty-mile radius of his hometown of Ise.[14] However, he came to global attention when a set of his doors for the palace of the Ogoga of Ikere was exhibited at the 1924 British Empire Exhibition in London and was thereafter acquired for the British Museum's collection in 1925. Olowe is credited with creating several important innovations in Yoruba sculpture. He imparted a suggestion of movement to his figures, thus deviating considerably from the hierarchical rigid frontality of classical Yoruba sculpture. He also developed a technique of carving the surface of his doors in very high relief with the figures protruding almost six inches from the surface and considerably animated by the shadows they threw. Based on the evidence of his surviving sculptures, Olowe painted some of his major artworks with an expanded palette of commercial colors and may have helped popularized polychrome sculptures in Yoruba art beyond the traditional practice of coloring sculptures with subdued earth-toned pigments.

Suzanne Blier notes that changing contexts of power, reflected in the subordination of African royal authority to British colonial rule, led local rulers to use visual arts to compensate for their diminished authority.[15] Olowe's artworks contained witty references to the emergent colonial order in the furniture and entourage of the Yoruba kings he depicted. Olowe has been praised for his mastery of classical Yoruba sculptural forms, but there is less commentary on his clear experiments with modernist techniques of representation, including his use of commercial pigments and the high relief his sculptures are known for. For example, an Olowe door from the palace at Ilawe-Ekiti shows a king on a ceremonial outing accompanied by an entourage including porters and his wives (Fig. 18.1). The door is divided into several registers and the figures are carved in high relief, with many of them almost three-dimensional, a technique notable in Olowe's doors but largely absent from comparable Yoruba carvings of that era. Olowe shows the king sitting in an imported folding chair, which was a common item used by colonial officers of that era as they traveled around the country on administrative duties. Also, one register of the door shows the king mounted on a horse whose halter is decorated with beadwork. The complex beadwork found in Yoruba art today includes historical examples that used indigenously produced beads (the city of Ile-Ife was a notable bead-producing center in the first millennium, centuries before the arrival of Europeans in West Africa) but

Fig. 18.1 Olowe of Ise, *Palace Door*. Wood and pigment, 20th Century (copyright Femi Akinsanya African Art Collection)

also modern industrial beads. The adoption of imported industrial beads of uniform sizes significantly expanded bead working in Yoruba culture (and South African Zulu culture, and Native American Navajo and Hopi cultures for that matter). Representations of beadwork in Olowe's art thus speak to the wealth of imagery and technique made possible by the availability of industrially produced beads, which in turn speaks to the impact of an emergent colonial economy.[16]

Olowe's imagery therefore documented both African kings and their European colonizers as they jostled for power and authority within the colonial order. His famous doors (carved c.1910–1914) that were exhibited in London showed the colonial government's subversion of indigenous authority through its representation of porters carrying a European visitor in a palanquin. Olowe's sculptures were brightly painted with imported commercially produced paint, which showed his awareness of new materials and methods and can thus be classed as a response to modernity in Nigerian art. The significant increase in patronage and commissions that Olowe and other Yoruba sculptors of this era enjoyed was in part due to colonial economics and the new forms of wealth it made available to enable innovative practices that the artists themselves considered modern approaches to representation. These artists engaged the emergent modernity of their societies and cast a keen eye on local and foreign elements that impacted their modes of visual representation. They also incorporated representations of European colonizers into their visual landscape to indicate colonial transformations of the social order.[17]

Theorizing African cultural production of the colonial era as evidence of modernity impacts interpretations of modern African art but it does not imply that precolonial Africa lacked indigenous and unique forms of art. It merely recognizes that from 1500 onwards, Africa was embroiled in changes that inextricably linked it to a global context in which mass movements of peoples and ideas, flora and fauna, caused massive changes in all forms of life and visual culture. Colonialism in Africa came at the tail end of five centuries of change, and its impact should be evaluated accordingly. More importantly, colonialism cemented ethnic identities, which in precolonial Africa were often fluid. As Richard Thompson noted, ethnic processes:

> have been relatively recent historical creations of colonialism and imperialism and the subsequent post-colonial period in which primordial communities have become integrated into new and often unstable state structures. Thus, there is little that is 'traditional' or pre-modern about ethnic differences in Africa ... they are part and parcel of a contemporary world and perform critical functions for the combined evolution of that world.[18]

Ethnic identities were not absent in precolonial African culture, but that which we now define as canonical African ethnic identities (such as Amazigh, Yoruba, Omoro, Maasai, Zulu, or Afrikaner for that matter) were concretized during the colonial period.[19]

The encounter between Africa and Europe is documented in the changing forms of African artworks over the centuries, but the transformations caused by colonialism accelerated the pace of change considerably. Thus, while Benin bronze plaques, for example, document the presence and activities of Europeans at the Benin court from 1500 onwards, Benin cultural practices adapted the encounter with Europe into a distinctive Edo cultural matrix that continued to uphold 'traditional' values. We can track such changes in Benin brass casting, which from its inception continually adapted its forms to changing political, social, and symbolic mores. During the colonial period however, changing modes of education and art practice accelerated changes in Edo-Benin art, which now began to show an expanded range of subjects. Benin brasscasters also began to sign their works and individuate themselves from their general identification with the Igun guild that has been responsible for Edo-Benin brass casting for the past seven centuries.

Transformations such as those that occurred in Benin art are relevant to analysis of the changing identities of indigenous African artworks that are often discussed as representative of singular ethnic groups.[20] This is because, to date, studies of indigenous African art have used the idea of ethnic uniqueness to frame questions about the identities of the artists who made these works. For example, the above identification of Olowe of Ise as a 'Yoruba' artist is an overly determined focus on ethnic identity that prevents us from equally seeing him as a modern artist exploring the contours of an emergent global modernity. Ideally, Olowe's encounters with colonial culture and his experiments with modern forms mean we should reclassify him as a modern African artist.

COLONIAL CULTURE AND MODERN AFRICAN ART

Colonialism contributed to the contested modernity of indigenous African art whose forms and meanings were significantly impacted by new techniques and modes of representation. Modern African art was similarly impacted by these changes because it originates in cultural interactions engendered by modernization processes during the colonial period. It consists of those structures of art production and patronage that emerged in Africa with the introduction of European systems of representation, and its implantation was facilitated by colonial encounter.

Many issues complicate any effort to write an overview history of modern art in Africa. Most analysis omits North African countries and South Africa from consideration and locates the emergence of modern African art/identity within the practice of painting linked to the career of Nigerian artist Aina Onabolu (1882–1963). These include publications by Marshall Ward Mount, Jean Kennedy, Kojo Fosu, Ulli Beier, the anthology produced by N'Goné Fall and Jean Loup Pivin, and the influential catalogue produced by Susan Vogel for the *Africa Explores* exhibition.[21] Most of these books aim for comprehensive analysis of modern art in Africa, and analyze the national and cultural identity of African artists through artworks that reflect the complex interactions between local and global notions of modernist aesthetics. However, they neither incorporate the history and impact of photography, despite the fact that it predates all other forms of modern art in Africa, nor seriously engage the divergent development of modern art in North Africa (Egypt especially) and South Africa.

A true history of modern art in Africa should aspire to a multiracial analysis that recognizes that modern art in Egypt predates Onabolu. Tolerant attitudes towards figurative art engendered by new development in publishing and photography meant that questions about modernism were already central to Egyptian art by the turn of the twentieth century, as they were to artists in Nigeria and South Africa, as were questions about the relationship between indigenous cultures (which, in addition to African traditions, included Islam) to modern art and identity. White artists in South Africa were equally engaged with similar questions, as we can see from the work of artists such as Irma Stern (1894–1966).[22] Modern African art therefore signified more than the adoption of different modes of practice; rather it signified a reconfiguration of indigenous systems of symbolic communication. In comparison with extant modes of artistic practice in indigenous African cultural systems (such as in the sculptures of Olowe discussed above), it represented not only a difference in degree but also a difference in kind.

A difference in degree implies contiguous ideas and conceptual structures identified as, for example, 'Impressionism' or 'Classical African art' (Impressionist paintings often look alike, and masks predominate in museum displays of African art). Although regional variations exist in individual types such art, their overall conceptual structures and conventions of representation are usually comparable. A difference in kind however denotes practices whose visual and conceptual structures operate along divergent trajectories. That doesn't mean that the different kinds of objects or concepts in question are mutually exclusive but that they diverge enough that we can ascribe unique characteristics to them.[23] For example, concepts of art and visual representation differed in Portuguese and Edo-Benin cultures but both societies evolved notions of value that invested artworks with unique ritual, aesthetic, political, and other forms of meaning. What differs in each society is how underlying values shape the visual forms and makes their art different. Such differences do not preclude changes in cultural notions of value or the possibility that existing forms can be reconfigured. We may thus juxtapose pre-twentieth-century European art's orientation to Greek ideals of form and representation with other examples such as Islamic art with its non-representational visual structure, or African art with its conceptual paradigms of representation. The visual and architectonic logic of each culture's artworks speak to different modes of cognition and articulation of forms. It is therefore important not to describe them as degenerate imitations of, or regression from, occidental perfection. Instead, we can define their differences as a result of variant approaches to realism, divergences in modes of symbolic communication or differences in the articulation of form.[24]

Mary Nooter contends that the structural form of African artworks lies not only in their materiality as images endowed with physical form; conceptual form is equally important and significant 'absences' comprise an important aspect of African notions of form.²⁵ Indigenous African societies deployed visual and conceptual forms that were radically different from those in European art. In instances where artistic forms share an affinity in the two cultures (sculpture, for example), visual intent and modes of representation differ greatly. In this sense, although modern African artists appropriate indigenous traditions of visual culture, the conceptual focus of their art differs from those found in indigenous art. Because of this, the practice of contemporary African artists cannot be reduced to a continuation or reconfiguration of indigenous traditions. Even when recognizable continuities exist in both practices, there are major differences in the forms and functions of the objects produced, the methods of art training utilized, notions of art and cultural representation deployed, and structures of production and patronage. Indigenous structures of representation in African art survive in the contemporary era where they engage changing social and cultural conditions by a process of continuous reinvention. The interaction between these extant contexts of indigenous representation and those of modern/contemporary African art provides an interesting analytical problematic.

Modern African art was impacted by the global cultural experience of colonialism which engendered a distinct space of practice and a distinctive cadre of practitioners. Pioneer artists in all contexts faced the task of defining new modes of visual representation and notions of artistic identity and subjectivity. Easel painting was the major signifier of this emergent visual tradition, and like many aspects of modernity in Africa it took root mainly among the African intellectual elite. In European art, the development of easel painting as a favored medium of expression was related to the rise of capitalism in a cultural matrix that privileged individual ownership, private property, and inscription of individual identity for both artist and patron. The development of perspective, and the structured visual and conceptual spaces it made possible suggests that the emergence of easel painting in its European and African contexts was not a neutral indicator of simple changes in artistic practice. Rather, it signaled shifts in modes of visual representation expressed by the articulation of new social, cultural, and contextual spaces through images.²⁶ These notable changes apply equally to the emergence of easel painting in African art during the era of colonialism.

As previously stated, European colonialism was a major factor in the constitution of modern Africa. It introduced a new order of governance and new notions of individual and cultural identity. It also brought about new forms of cultural practices in art, music, literature, and modes of social organization. The projection of European modes of visual and conceptual representation onto African colonies, signified by the implantation of modern African art at the turn of the century, did not proceed in a cultural vacuum. Many pioneer modern African artists operated in societies with defined ideas about art and visual culture. During the colonial period, these artists appropriated and reconfigured European aesthetic concepts for use within emergent African contexts of practice. In this sense, modern African art spoke not only to the emergence of new cultural patterns, but also to the critical foundation provided by indigenous aesthetic traditions and modes of (self-) representation.

The principal characteristics of modern African art emerged from the tension between its imported European forms and African concepts of art, which played out against a background of colonialism. Emergent identities therefore often reflected individual struggles against Eurocentric rhetoric and the racial tensions of colonial culture. Pioneer modern African artists were shaped by this struggle; their art and emergent identities were therefore political in the most fundamental sense of the word.

The Pathfinder Protocol: Making Modern African Artists

The pursuit of modernism was also a search for a new African identity in the urban context. The pioneer modern African artists discussed here all operated in cities. The concentration of modern art practices in African cities provides a technique for distinguishing between 'traditional' and modern African arts by associating the former with rural, community-based practices. This created what Sidney Kasfir describes as a distinction between 'the subjectivity of the artist living in the multilayered African city versus one whose world is a rural community somewhere in the African hinterland'.[27]

African cities provided new interactions with global commodities and structures of colonial art education that produced important pioneer artists. However, colonial education by itself did not guarantee new forms of modern art, especially since the objectives of colonial educators did not align with the nationalist orientation of modern African artists. Colonial prescriptions for 'native' education ran counter to the globalizing aspiration of the emergent African intellectual elite, which created an antagonistic relationship between the colonial regimes and African intellectual elites that hastened the rise of a radical politics of emancipation.[28] This idea of radical social change that framed liberation and nationalist movements resulted in calls for political independence. In many parts of Africa, it brought a commensurate interrogation of cultural practices in an effort to reconstitute a sense of indigenous identity disrupted by colonization. The aesthetics of radical politics defines a specific focus on material culture within this process of political transformation. In brief, 'radical politics historically covers individual or collective activities for implementing an ideology challenging the fundamentals of the existing system of politics and governance. Generally, it advocates fundamental changes in the political, legal, and economic structure of the existing authority or state, often, but not necessarily, by extreme means'.[29] In the context of modern African art of the pre-independence period, such calls represented a demand for a new visual language that embodied postcolonial aspirations in different African countries.

Let us be clear, none of these pioneer artists was a flag-waving radical: a true radical politics emerged with the nationalist struggle and continued into the postcolonial era (Frantz Fanon is the most notable purveyor of radical politics in the period of nationalism and liberation movements in Africa). Pioneer modern African artists were acutely aware of the contradictions of their lives as they navigated a colonial culture that often supported their careers while simultaneously marginalizing them. There is also an element of irony in the fact that European languages reign unchallenged in African discourses of cultural identity. The attempt to develop an African literature in African languages, mounted by radical theorists like the Kenyan writer Ngugi wa Thiong'o, was largely unsuccessful. Similarly, modern Africa artists were dependent on European patronage in the colonial context and many of them were trained in some of the best art schools in Europe, often supported by scholarships provided by colonial governments. Ben Enwonwu studied at the Slade School of Art in London, as did Gazbia Sirry and Afewerk Tekle. Iba Ndiaye studied in Paris at the Ecole des Beaux Arts and eventually returned to live out his life there after becoming disillusioned with independent Senegal. Escaping the emergent apartheid regime, Gerard Sekoto left South Africa in 1947, first for London (where he spent three weeks with Enwonwu) but ultimately settling in Paris. Irma Stern studied art in Germany at the Weimar Academy and had her first exhibition in Berlin.

The privileged position of these pioneer modernists in the colonial order and among African intellectual elites constrained the radical potential of their work. Despite these constraints, they invented new visual languages and engaged international discourses of modernity in art. They worried about the meanings of African cultural representation within the matrix of modern art, and their own location within discourses of nationalism and internationalism, achievements now routinely ascribed to postcolonial African artists.[30] In addition, the arbitrary demarcation of modern African art into the colonial and postcolonial periods is often misleading. All the pioneer artists discussed here were also active in the postcolonial period and some lived into the twenty-first century.

Liliane Karnouk, writing about the emergence of modern art in Egypt, points out that:

> The Egyptian artist had to resolve a double dilemma. The first is whether to become an artist in the European, individualistic sense and thus risk losing a connection to the native soil and its traditions, or whether to revive the traditional ethnic arts and risk remaining marginal to the world of international high art.[31]

Other pioneer modern African artists faced a similar dilemma and struggled to escape the limitations of colonially assigned roles in order to define culturally relevant modes of modernist representation. The particulars of their struggle show that regional differences impacted how modern art developed in different colonial contexts.

Differences in the regional characteristics of colonialism in Africa make it difficult to write a comprehensive history of modern art in Africa. The British sphere of colonial control (affecting Enwonwu and Sirry) differed from that of the French (Ndiaye), Italians (Tekle), or Afrikaners (Stern, Sekoto). Iba Ndiaye grew up in the French colony of Senegal, center of France's colonial empire in Africa. For African intellectuals under colonialism, French colonial policy of assimilation provided an impossible ideal since acculturated Black French intellectuals were confronted with their dark skins as a marker of their essential difference.[32] Britain's policy of indirect rule provided enough space for the continued flourishing of a Nigerian intellectual elite with deep transnational links who became active in the anti-colonial struggle. Nigeria also enjoyed a deep history of divergent and important culture, which Ben Enwonwu referenced through his choice of masquerades as a central motif in his art. In Egypt, modern African art developed through a 'deep and complex cultural revolution' that confronted the dilemma of how to 'articulate the existence of several value-systems historically coexisting within this nation on two levels: the Islamic and the Egyptian'.[33] According to Karnouk, modernism in Egypt 'expressed itself in artists' efforts to transform an Egypto-Islamic style into the new "universal" language of international art, while at the same time express[ing] the new self image of Egyptian political reform'.[34]

Afewerk Tekle contended with a similar issue in Ethiopia, whose long and illustrious history (dating to biblical times) includes the honor of being the only African country to defeat its colonial invaders, in 1896 when Emperor Menelik II beat the Italian army at the Battle of Adwa.[35] Ethiopia's important heritage of Coptic Christian art is reflected in a liturgical mode of representation that constitutes a respected canon. It also has an indigenous script which plays a large role in its monastic scriptorium. Tekle, as an Ethiopian modern artist, carved out a career against these important cultural influences and this placed major constraints on his art.

The lives and careers of South African artists Irma Stern and Gerard Sekoto show how white-settler colonialism complicates analysis of the development of modern African art. The history of South Africa dates back to 1910, when the British colonies in the Cape of Good Hope and Natal united with the Boer republics of the Transvaal and Orange Free State to form the Union of South Africa.[36] The resulting state initially comprised Dutch and British settlers and was bolstered by immigration of large numbers of Europeans in the decades after the Second World War, essentially aspiring to build a white homeland for Europeans in South Africa. Despite the obvious problems of amalgamating two groups of whites (British and Dutch settlers, each with their own national agendas), the ensuing Union of South Africa nevertheless inherited an idea of its existence as a nation of white people whose heritage traces back directly to a European ancestry.[37] The assumption that this nation was European rather than African produced a national narrative based on racial exclusivity, which in 1948 evolved into an apartheid regime that marginalized black South Africans and dispossessed them of their lands and resources.[38] The nation constructed around this idea of white supremacy narrated South African history before the coming of the white settlers as *terra nullius* and excluded Africans from citizenship. Isolated by the international community for its apartheid policies, South African art and discourses turned inwards and 'increasingly cut off from major international art events and movements ... remained relatively parochial, conservative and overwhelmingly white'.[39] Additionally, engagement with Western strategies of artistic expression by South African artists were read as derivative by art historians.[40] South Africa's history between 1948 and 1994 is mainly a history of increasingly militant black resistance to the apartheid regime (including an armed struggle), which culminated in a transition to majority rule in 1994. This date, marked by the election of Nelson Mandela (1918–2013) as the first black president of South Africa (he served as president from 1994 to 1999) in the country's first multiracial election, is the true beginning of South Africa's postcolonial era.[41]

The history of South Africa meant that Irma Stern's life and career as a white South African artist unfolded in a context radically different to that of Sekoto. Stern was born in 1894 in the Transvaal to German-Jewish parents. She spent much of her life traveling between Europe and Africa, although more in Africa in her later years. However, she studied in Germany (Weimar Academy, 1913; Levin-Funcke studio, 1914), became associated with German Expressionist painters, and held her first exhibition in Berlin in 1919. She returned to Cape Town and by the 1940s had become an established artist. Irma Stern is considered South Africa's foremost artist in terms of public recognition, and her modernist-style artworks fetch record prices at auction.[42] Her career path shows the intricate links between white South Africans and Europe, and also the complications in defining (white) South African art of this era, which was variously seen as a form of European regional practice.

Gerard Sekoto was also born in the Transvaal in 1913 at Botshabelo, a German Lutheran Mission. According to Chloë Reid, that year was:

> marked by the introduction of the 'Natives Land Act' – the first of the segregation legislations to be passed by the Parliament of South Africa. The series of measures taken by the government to exploit, alienate and degrade non-white South Africans that followed the Land Act drove Gerard Sekoto ... into self-imposed exile [in] Paris where he stayed until his death in 1993.[43]

Sekoto's career was on an upswing before his exile. He won second prize for painting in a competition organized by Fort Hare University College in 1938. Encouraged by this achievement, he moved to Sophiatown to pursue a career as a full-time artist. In 1942, he relocated to Cape Town where he interacted with many white contemporary South African artists. Sekoto's art mostly documented black life at the fringes of the urban metropolis. He exhibited his works in a number of galleries in Cape Town and achieved significant recognition but concerns about achieving his full potential under South Africa's marginalization of blacks ultimately caused him to leave the country.

The racial politics of South Africa illustrate the vast differences in the careers of Stern and Sekoto. Stern trained with modernist artists in Germany and had close links with German Expressionists at a time when European modernists were using African cultural influences to reconfigure all aspects of their art. When she returned to South Africa, her highly individual and modernist style initially proved shocking to Cape Town's conservative public of the 1930s. Stern compounded this shock by her strong interest in portraying black South African peoples. However, her portrayal of black people reads today as rather generic, especially since her interest, like that of her Expressionist antecedents, lay in a fascination with the exotic other. As she once stated:

> it is only through personal contact that one can get a few glimpses into the hidden depths of the primitive and childlike yet rich soul of the native and this soul is what I try to reflect in my pictures of South Africa.[44]

Her statement is deeply invested in the European concept of primitivism and positions her art within a global context of modernist appropriations founded on the unequal power relations of the colonialism that brought African art to the attention of European modern artists.

As a black artist, Sekoto faced a very limited horizon of opportunity, which makes his overall experience, including his exile to Paris, remarkable. As a Christian and the son of a priest/teacher, Sekoto belonged to a new South African black elite.[45] His work reflects what John Peffer defined as a 'struggle for a nonracial aesthetic practice in South Africa within overlapping contexts of the modernist reception of indigenous approaches to art [and] the draconian racial policies' of the emergent apartheid state.[46] Peffer, exploring Seketo's role in the development of 'black modernism', argues that his art presaged the emergence of a non-racial South Africa and depicted his personal exploration of the novelty of urban life. They were also experiments with modernist styles. His audience and principal collectors were white middle-class patrons, critics and artists. Sekoto also interacted with members of the 'New Group', a collective of progressive young South African artists who studied in Europe and in the 1930s opposed the conservative values championed by the institutional South African Society of Artists.[47] According to Peffer, Sekoto 'met with Judith Gluckman and Alexis Preller ... painted alongside Preller ... and learned the rudiments of working in oil in Gluckman's studio'.[48] These interactions were part of what Peffer defined as 'gray areas', sites and locations where black and white South African artists and culture workers mingled.

The New Group artists initiated an engagement with indigenous South African culture in their works, in an effort to get away from an institutional context that promoted academic art based on European classical forms. Peffer notes that 'it is not unusual in the history of modern art for urban artists to search for some (perceived to be) primitive source material to rejuvenate contemporary cosmopolitan culture' as a cursory analysis of the works of European modernists shows. 'But when the sources were actually part of the local culture, in the context of settler colonialism, the stakes for cross cultural inspiration or exchange were that much more profound.'[49]

The appropriation of black art by white artists in mid-twentieth-century South Africa was much criticized since its celebration of indigenous African culture coincided with dispossession of black South Africans who were being forcibly evicted from their lands. Peffer carries out substantive analysis of the implications of this appropriation for efforts to produce a non-racial, inclusive art in South Africa. However, he fails to link his analysis to similar developments in other parts of Africa, where modern African artists challenging colonial prescriptions for cultural production often settled on what Peffer defines as 'two sided-appropriation: of modernist technique from Europe and of indigenous [African] aesthetic forms'. Such comparison allows us to link the experiments of the New Group to those of the famed Zaria Art Group, formed in Nigeria in 1958, and Gazbia Sirry's Group of Modern Art (GMA), formed in Egypt in 1948, through which she 'identified with the intersection of artistic ideology and nationalist political concerns'.[50] Okeke-Agulu notes that Sirry and the GMA 'participated in the discourse of Egyptianness, or what it meant to be modern Egyptian in a world of conflicting political, cultural, and artistic ideologies'.[51] But in another context, he does not link this search for Egyptianness to a comparable project of postcolonial emancipation of the Zaria Art Society, choosing to define the latter's program of Natural Synthesis as a unique and sui generis invention.

Conclusion

According to Stuart Hall, identity is subject to a radical historicization and is constantly in the process of change and transformation.[52] The preceding analysis of the impact of colonialism on African art has shown that the search for a modernist identity is tied to the anti-colonial struggle that ultimately codified into broad independence and liberation movements. It also challenges colonialism's efforts to locate Africa's indigenous art in the pre-colonial period. Olufemi Taiwo suggests colonialism, far from being the source of modernity in Africa, has actually been the main obstacle to its implantation because colonial policy aimed at what he calls 'sociocryonics', or the preservation of archaic social forms, through which it undermined Africans' efforts to fully participate in a global modernism.[53] The usual art historical practice of tracing this search mainly through the works of black artists in Africa undermines its validity. A more inclusive narrative encompassing South Africa and Egypt (among other North African contexts) reveals important points of convergence and establishes a common context of anti-colonial struggle for new nationalist and modernist identities in Africa. Comparative analysis is therefore needed for a complete and more inclusive analysis of modern African art and this should now become the focus of our discourse.

Notes

1. For a comprehensive analysis of Enwonwu's career, see Sylvester Okwunodu Ogbechie, *Ben Enwonwu: The Making of an African Modernist* (Rochester: University of Rochester Press, 2008).
2. Chika Okeke-Agulu, "Politics by Other Means: Two Egyptian Artist, Gazbia Sirry and Ghada Amer," *Meridians: Feminism, Race, Transnationalism* 6, no. 2 (2006): 122.
3. Sekoto's art is chronicled in N.C. Manganyi, *Sekoto: I am an African: A Biography* (Witwatersrand: Wits University Press, 2004).
4. See Bruce Vandervort, *Wars of Imperial Conquest in Africa* (Bloomington: Indiana University Press, 1998).
5. Toyin Falola and Matthew M. Heaton, *A History of Nigeria* (Cambridge: Cambridge University Press, 2008), 1.
6. For analysis of African artists' engagements with modernist discourse, see Elizabeth Harney, *In Senghor's Shadow: Art, Politics and the Avant Garde in Senegal 1960–1995* (Durham: Duke University Press, 2004). Ogbechie, *Ben Enwonwu*; Chika Okeke-Agulu, *Postcolonial Modernism: Art and Decolonization in Twentieth Century Nigeria* (Durham: Duke University Press); John Peffer, *Art and the End of Apartheid* (Minneapolis: University of Minnesota Press, 2009); and Liliane Karnouk, *Modern Egyptian Art 1910–2003* (Cairo: American University in Cairo Press, 2005).
7. Olufemi Taiwo, *How Colonialism Preeempted Modernity in Africa* (Bloomington: Indiana University Press, 2010).
8. South Africa became independent from British rule in 1910 and instituted apartheid in 1948; its transition to a multiracial democracy is considered more relevant to the discourse of colonialism in Africa.
9. For a general definition of Pan-Africanism, see (https://www.britannica.com/topic/Pan-Africanism). Du Bois's assimilationist approach contrasted with Garvey's vision of independence for Africans through a return to Africa. Both views shaped subsequent notions of African identity.
10. Okwui Enwezor, *The Short Century: Independence and Liberation Movements in Africa 1945–1994* (New York: Prestel, 2001), 12.
11. Négritude became a contentious ideology in the postcolonial era. See Sylvester Okwunodu Ogbechie, "Comrades at Arms: The African Avant-Garde at the First World Festival of Negro Arts (Dakar 1966)," in *One Million and Forty-Four Years (and Sixty-Three Days)*, ed. Kathryn Smith (Stellenbosch, SA: SMAC, 2007), 88–103.
12. Gregson Davis, *Aimé Césaire* (Cambridge: Cambridge University Press, 1997); Toyin Falola and Matthew M. Heaton, *A History of Nigeria* (Cambridge: Cambridge University Press, 2008), 136–57; Patrick Chabal, *Amilcar Cabral: Revolutionary Leadership and People's War* (Cambridge: Cambridge University Press, 1983); and Shannen L. Hill, *Biko's Ghost: The Iconography of Black Consciousness* (Minneapolis: University of Minnesota Press, 2015).
13. John Picton, "Art, Identity, and Identification: A Commentary on Yoruba Art Historical Studies," in *The Yoruba Artist: New Historical Perspectives*, ed. Rowland Abiodun et al. (Washington, DC.: Smithsonian Institution Press, 1994), 1–34.

14. Rosslyn Walker, *Olowe of Ise: A Yoruba Sculptor to Kings* (Washington, DC: Smithsonian Institution Press, 1998).
15. Blier, *Royal Arts of Africa: The Majesty of Form* (London: Laurence King, 1998), 39–40.
16. For analysis of colonial economies in Africa, see Peter Duignan and L.H. Gann, eds., *Colonialism in Africa 1870–1960 (Volume 4: The Economics of Colonialism)* (Cambridge: Cambridge University Press, 1975).
17. For a comprehensive overview of representations of Europeans in African art, see Nii Quarcopoome, *Through African Eyes: The European in African Art 1500 to Present* (Detroit: Detroit Institute of Art, 2010).
18. Richard H. Thompson, *Theories of Ethnicity: A Critical Appraisal* (New York: Greenwood Press, 1989), 100.
19. Amazigh peoples of Libya; Yoruba peoples of Nigeria, Republic of Benin, and Brazil; Omoro of Ethiopia; Maasai of Kenya; Zulu and Afrikaners of South Africa.
20. For a critique of how individual artworks stand in for whole ethnic groups in the discourse of African art, see Sidney Kasfir, "One Tribe, One Style? Paradigms in the Historiography of African Art," *History in Africa* 11 (1984): 163–93.
21. Marshall Ward Mount, *African Art: The Years since 1920* (Bloomington: Indiana University Press, 1973); Jean Kennedy, *New Currents, Ancient Rivers: Contemporary African Artists in a Generation of Change* (Washington, DC: Smithsonian Institution Press, 1992); Kojo Fosu, *20th Century Art of Africa* (Zaria: Gaskiya, 1986); Uli Beier, *Contemporary Art in Africa* (New York: Praeger, 1968); N'Goné Fall and Jean Loup Pivin, eds. *An Anthology of African Art: The Twentieth Century* (Paris: Revue Noire, 2002); and Susan Vogel, *Africa Explores: 20th Century African Art* (New York: Center for African Art, 1991).
22. For a comprehensive and multiracial history of South African art, see Mario Pissarra et al., eds., *Visual Century: South African Art in Context* (Johannesburg: University of the Witwatersrand, 2011).
23. Divergence of this kind is also a characteristic of African art where regional or internal representations of an object, such as a Bamana Chiwara mask superstructure, can result in different visual forms.
24. Margaret Hagen, *Varieties of Realism: Geometries of Representational Art* (Cambridge: Cambridge University Press, 1986) investigates different interpretations of perspective in European, Asian and African art.
25. Mary Nooter, ed. *Secrecy: African Art That Conceals and Reveals* (New York: Museum for African Art, 1993).
26. These issues are discussed at length in Bram Kempers, *Painting, Power and Patronage: The Rise of the Professional Artist in the Italian Renaissance* (London: Penguin Books, 1994).
27. Sidney Kasfir, "First Word," *African Arts* 46, no. 1 (Spring 2013): 1.
28. For divergent analysis of the conflicts of colonial education in Nigeria, see Ogbechie, *Ben Enwonwu* (Chap. 1) and Okeke-Agulu, *Postcolonial Modernism* (Chap. 1).
29. "Radical Politics." http://banglapedia.search.com.bd/HT/R_0007.htm.
30. See for example, Enwezor, *The Short Century*, and Chika Okeke-Agulu, *Postcolonial Modernism*.

31. Karnouk, *Modern Egyptian Art*.
32. For the impact of the ideology of assimilation on black intellectuals in the global context of colonialism, see Lilyan Kesteloot, *Black Writers in French: A Literary History of Negritude* (Washington, DC: Howard University Press, 1974).
33. Karnouk, *Modern Egyptian Art*.
34. Ibid.
35. Raymond Jonas, *The Battle of Adwa: African Victory in the Age of Empire* (Cambridge: Harvard University Press, 2011).
36. Peffer, *Art and the End of Apartheid*, xv–xvi.
37. The brief history of South Africa summarized here inevitably glosses over complicated political and social issues, including the presence of immigrants from Asia whose story is an integral aspect of the evolving political landscape of that period. For details of important political and cultural events of this era, see "Timeline" in Pissarra et al., *Visual Century*, Vol. 1, 198–210.
38. For a comprehensive history of apartheid, see David Welsh, *The Rise and Fall of Apartheid* (Charlottesville: University of Virginia Press, 2009).
39. Lize van Robbroeck, "Art in White and Black" in *Visual Century*, Vol. 2 and 3.
40. Partha Mitter, "Interventions: Decentering Modernism: Art History and Avant-Garde Art from the Periphery," *Art Bulletin* 90, no. 4 (2008): 37. Mitter was referring to the history of South Asian artists' adoption of Western strategies of artistic expression, but the statement equally applies to the general reception of modern African art in art history.
41. Sylvester Okwunodu Ogbechie, "Art, Nationalism and Modernist Histories: Writing Art History in Nigeria and South Africa," in *Art/Histories in Cultural Dynamics*, ed. Pauline Bachman et al. (Paderbom: Wilhelm Fink, 2015).
42. *Irma Stern*. South African History Online (accessed October 10, 2016, http://www.sahistory.org.za/people/irma-stern). The biography on this website is taken from Proud, H., ed., *Revisions: Expanding the Narrative of South African Art* (Cape Town: South African History Online and UNISA Press, 2006).
43. Chloë Reid, "The Artist/Sekoto's Life." The Gerard Sekoto Foundation, accessed October 21, 2016, http://www.gerardsekotofoundation.com/artist-overview.htm.
44. Marion Arnold, *Irma Stern: A Feast for the Eyes* (Cape Town: Fernwood Press, 1995).
45. This black middle class was documented in photographs and can be seen in Santu Mofokeng's *Black Photo Album/Look at Me: 1890–1950*, comprising his reworking of nineteenth-century colonial portraits of urban working, middle-class black families.
46. Peffer, *Art and the End of Apartheid*, x.
47. The New Group included Louis Marice, Gregoire Boonzaier, Judith Gluckman, Alexis Preller, Solly Disner, and Walter Batiss.
48. Peffer, *Art and the End of Apartheid*, 3.
49. Ibid.
50. Okeke-Agulu, "Politics by Other Means," 122.
51. Ibid.

52. Stuart Hall, "Introduction: Who Needs Identity," in *Questions of Cultural Identity*, ed. Stuart Hall and Paul du Gay (London: Sage, 1996).
53. Olufemi Taiwo, *How Colonialism Preempted Modernity in Africa* (Bloomington: Indiana University Press, 2010).

Bibliography

Arnold, Marion. *Irma Stern: A Feast for the Eyes*. Cape Town: Fernwood Press, 1995.
Beier, Uli. *Contemporary Art in Africa*. New York: Praeger, 1968.
Blier, Suzanne. *Royal Arts of Africa: The Majesty of Form*. London: Laurence King, 1998.
Chabal, Patrick. *Amilcar Cabral: Revolutionary Leadership and People's War*. Cambridge: Cambridge University Press, 1993.
Davis, Gregson. *Aimé Césaire*. Cambridge: Cambridge University Press, 1997.
Duignan, Peter, and L.H. Gann, eds. *Colonialism in Africa 1870–1960, Volume 4: The Economics of Colonialism*. Cambridge: Cambridge University Press, 1975.
Enwezor, Okwui. *The Short Century: Independence and Liberation Movements in Africa 1945–1994*. New York: Prestel, 2001.
Fall, N'Goné, and Jean Loup Pivin, eds. *An Anthology of African Art: The Twentieth Century*. Paris: Revue Noire, 2002.
Falola, Toyin, and Matthew M. Heaton. *A History of Nigeria*. Cambridge: Cambridge University Press, 2008.
Fosu, Kojo. *20th Century Art of Africa*. Zaria: Gaskiya, 1986.
Hagen, Margaret. *Varieties of Realism: Geometries of Representational Art*. Cambridge: Cambridge University Press, 1986.
Hall, Stuart. "Introduction: Who Needs Identity." In *Questions of Cultural Identity*, edited by Stuart Hall and Paul du Gay. London: Sage, 1996.
Harney, Elizabeth. *In Senghor's Shadow: Art, Politics and the Avant Garde in Senegal 1960–1995*. Durham: Duke University Press, 2004.
Hill, Shannen L. *Biko's Ghost: The Iconography of Black Consciousness*. Minneapolis: University of Minnesota Press, 2015.
Irma Stern. (South African History Online, 2006). (Accessed October 10, http://www.sahistory.org.za/people/irma-stern).
Jonas, Raymond. *The Battle of Adwa: African Victory in the Age of Empire*. Cambridge: Harvard University Press, 2011.
Karnouk, Liliane. *Modern Egyptian Art 1910–2003*. Cairo: American University in Cairo Press, 2005.
Kasfir, Sidney. "One Tribe, One Style? Paradigms in the Historiography of African Art." *History in Africa* 11 (1984): 163–93.
———. "First Word." *African Arts* 46, no. 1 (2013).
Kempers, Bram. *Painting, Power and Patronage: The Rise of the Professional Artist in the Italian Renaissance*. London: Penguin Books, 1994.
Kennedy, Jean. *New Currents, Ancient Rivers: Contemporary African Artists in a Generation of Change*. Washington, DC: Smithsonian Institution Press, 1992.
Kesteloot, Lilyan. *Black Writers in French: A Literary History of Negritude*. Washington, DC: Howard University Press, 1974.
Manganyi, N.C. *Sekoto: I am an African: A Biography*. Witwatersrand: Wits University Press, 2004.

Mitter, Partha. "Interventions: Decentering Modernism: Art History and Avant-Garde Art from the Periphery." *Art Bulletin* 90, no. 4 (2008).
Mofokeng, Santu. *Black Photo Album/Look at Me: 1890–1950.* Göttingen: Steidl, 2013.
Mount, Marshall Ward. *African Art: The Years since 1920.* Bloomington: Indiana University Press, 1973.
Nooter, Mary, ed. *Secrecy: African Art That Conceals and Reveals.* New York: Museum for African Art, 1993.
Ogbechie, Sylvester Okwunodu. "Comrades at Arms: The African Avant-Garde at the First World Festival of Negro Arts (Dakar 1966)." In *One Million and Forty-Four Years (and Sixty-Three Days)*, edited by Kathryn Smith. Stellenbosch, SA: SMAC, 2007.
———. *Ben Enwonwu: The Making of an African Modernist.* Rochester: University of Rochester Press, 2008.
———. "Art, Nationalism and Modernist Histories: Writing Art History in Nigeria and South Africa." In *Art/Histories in Cultural Dynamics*, edited by Pauline Bachman et al. Paderbom: Wilhelm Fink, 2015.
Okeke-Agulu, Chika. "Politics by Other Means: Two Egyptian Artist, Gazbia Sirry and Ghada Amer." *Meridians: Feminism, Race, Transnationalism* 6, no. 2 (2006).
———. *Postcolonial Modernism: Art and Decolonization in Twentieth Century Nigeria.* Durham: Duke University Press, 2015.
Peffer, John. *Art and the End of Apartheid.* Minneapolis: University of Minnesota Press, 2009.
Picton, John. "Art, Identity, and Identification: A Commentary on Yoruba Art Historical Studies." In *The Yoruba Artist: New Historical Perspectives*, edited by Rowland Abiodun et al. Washington, DC: Smithsonian Institution Press, 1994.
Pissarra, Mario, et al. *Visual Century: South African Art in Context.* Johannesburg: University of the Witwatersrand, 2011.
Proud, H., ed. *Revisions: Expanding the Narrative of South African Art.* Cape Town: South African History Online and UNISA Press, 2006.
Quarcopoome, Nii. *Through African Eyes: The European in African Art 1500 to Present.* Detroit: Detroit Institute of Art, 2010.
Reid, Chloë. *The Artist/Sekoto's Life* (The Gerard Sekoto Foundation, 2016). http://www.gerardsekotofoundation.com/artist-overview.htm.
Taiwo, Olufemi. *How Colonialism Preempted Modernity in Africa.* Bloomington: Indiana University Press, 2010.
Thompson, Richard H. *Theories of Ethnicity: A Critical Appraisal.* New York: Greenwood Press, 1989.
Vandervort, Bruce. *Wars of Imperial Conquest in Africa.* Bloomington: Indiana University Press, 1998.
Vogel, Susan. *Africa Explores: 20th Century African Art.* New York: Center for African Art, 1991.
Walker, Rosslyn. *Olowe of Ise: A Yoruba Sculptor to Kings.* Washington, DC: Smithsonian Institution Press, 1998.
Welsh, David. *The Rise and Fall of Apartheid.* Charlottesville: University of Virginia Press, 2009.

CHAPTER 19

Intensification and Attenuation: Colonial Influences on an African Culture

Augustine Agwuele

The study of Africa and its development often engenders two opposing camps: the colonialist\neo-colonialists and the colonialists\misdirected leadership. Nonetheless, the external culture and civilization that were poorly grafted upon Yoruba civilization and customary practices influenced several existing institutions; for example, mode of transport, communications, manufacturing practices, credit institution, development of luxury items, and the modification of paid labor. Colonization either intensified or attenuated the normal (perhaps, natural) course of cultural development in the Yoruba nation. In some instances, existing ideas and tendencies that are more compatible with the introduced colonial systems were rapidly promoted as a result of support; those that were not of immediate concern were arrested in their trajectory. The type of support system that enhanced certain practices and discouraged others was not organic to the Yoruba culture and did not develop in its rightful time. This support system, (e.g. tarred roads, motorized vehicles, formal educational system etc., seen as the benefits of colonialism, but in reality, were structural instruments necessary for colonization) produced a false sense of Europeanization or, if you will, of modernization. In reality, this support system or artifacts of colonialism was without its 'European' socio-cultural bases, and hence a complete misfit.

A. Agwuele (✉)
Department of Anthropology, Texas State University,
San Marcos, TX, USA

A significant number of African scholars, especially those of African descent, often observe, suggest, and forcefully lament the destruction of 'African cultures' by the incursion of Western rule, education, and influence. Modern Africa, contemporary Africa, developing Africa, and different qualifiers to Africa evoked in the discursive context of the contact situation, especially contact due to colonialism, suggest a transformation of the existing order. Germane to the works of many scholars in the humanities and social sciences (especially those with an applied outlook and those who consider political, economic, and social transformation as necessary conditions for achieving a more responsive form of governance, as well as improved quality of life and life chances) is the quest to make sense of the continent with its many complexities. One consideration within this view is the exploration of the probable trajectory of the past relative to the present, a second is the effort to recover the usable values presumed to have been upended by the 400 years of exploitative intrusion, especially from the West. Thus, it is not uncommon for these scholars to cast in oppositional terms the discussions surrounding 'African cultures'.

There is no doubt that colonization, neo-colonization, and imperialism involve a conscious disparagement, denigration, and devaluation of the other; these not only make subjugation conscionable, they elevate it to an ideal, a worthy and benevolent cause in which 'civilized' people were bringing 'light' into the 'heart of darkness'. For example, the so-called white man's burden was an urgent call for redemptive intervention. So were some of the ideals of Levy-Bruhl's work that charged traditional Africa as primitive, preoccupied with supernatural forces, superstition and myth, and incapable of abstract and creative thought.[1] The incursion occasioned, in the case of Africa, the arbitrary partitioning of the landscape and grouping of the effaced people into arbitrary administrative and exploitative units, and, eventually, the interruption to a presumed linearity in the developmental trajectory of the people's history. Observers and scholars alike, all describable as products of the colonial milieu, even when they differ in their level of consciousness and dispositions, are equally divided in the way they view this history of interaction with Westernization. More pertinently, they differ in how they examine different African cultures and evaluate their usefulness. These scholars explore African cultures from opposing sides of the historical divide that now sorts this significant event into precolonial (i.e. traditional culture/society) and postcolonial (modern or Westernized) cultures. From the critical inquirers' camp, there are 'cultural revivalists' championed in part by Gyekye.[2] These scholars are favorably and reverentially disposed towards 'traditional' African cultural institutions, which they presume to have not only been denigrated and suppressed, but forcefully disrupted and upended by the colonialists, who imposed their own values through various socio-cultural and political means. Consequently, holders of this view would like to revive, reclaim, and implement 'traditional' African values, especially in solving perennial problems, most of which are the products of colonialism. This idealization is problematic, as 'traditional' African values remain nebulous, and without a doubt, call up the imagery of exotic practices. I will be arguing, using popular resources, that the deeds and practices of Africans, regardless of the time of existence of the people to whom we attribute them, remain in consonance with universal desires of mankind, especially in the pursuit of life, happiness, and liberty. African peoples employ in these pursuits every available means, without allowing a radical alteration to those cores (values, beliefs, quests, and explanations) indigenous to their formation as peoples, for example Yoruba, Sidama, or Luyia.

Viewing the revivalists as a group of nostalgists are the modernists, among whom a foremost thinker is Paulin Houtoundji. This group advocates a focus on contemporary problems and seeking solutions to them using science and technology. Furthermore, they view as anachronistic the previous political and socio-cultural institutions; this group is affiliated with Western cultural institutions, ideals, and outlooks. They address their concerns to immediate activities of contemporary players and repudiate any presumption to a solidarity[3] of view, or 'the myth of primitive unanimity'.[4]

The discourse around institutions on the continent, including its cultures, remains primarily binary in nature, pitching pre-African (often described as traditional Africa), against contact induced dispositions; that is, modern Africa. Observers are led to either see a truncation to the way of life of the continent, or hegemonic domination of the previously existing (however they may be selectively defined) aspects of the life of the people. Consequently, the emergence of 'new', ways of being, 'strange' ideas, and disciplines that are deployed to engender new power constellations, as well as the different principle in the organization of the society (including the integration through force of Africa into the international market economy), offer an apparent indication of disruption to the ways that such issues were conducted. Furthermore, it suggests not only a severance to the patterns, principles, and philosophies which guided the society at large, but also raises the notion that there were no previously existing ties to international affairs and economy, and where there was some impetus toward the same, it was curtailed. Despite this assumption, wherever one looks, there remain observances, ideologies, and expectations common to the group that challenge the idea of cultural eruption. The challenge to those who not only see the end of 'African traditional cultures' (whatever that means) in the imposition of Western values via colonialism, missionary proselytization, and monetary integration into the Western economy, but also consider it anachronistic and without relevance to the contemporary situation, is to substantiate such claims. In this chapter, I will substantiate the opposing view.

As revealed by the title of this chapter, 'Attenuation and Intensification', my goal is to suggest that there is fundamentally nothing new occasioned into the culture of Yoruba people via European civilization; rather, the new milieu mainly provided another outlet for already existing tendencies. Some of the existing inclinations were formalized and enhanced while others were attenuated. I will buttress this point by drawing from popular resources as well as 'trivial' and 'circumstantial' events. 'When properly articulated, the use of trivialities to study a society avoids the position of arrogance, especially, the estrangement of the isolated thinker who occupies that world of ideals and perfection and is unencumbered by the vicissitudes of ordinary existence.'[5]

In place of the normative historiography that focuses on the study of different past events such as political, economic, social, and intellectual history, it might be informative to evaluate the idea of rupture and continuity by exploring the activities of ordinary Yoruba people and their outlooks from popular sources to see if the propounded discontinuities could be substantiated or if there is only an intensification of existing tendencies as they pursued life in their own particular ways. The social and moral provisions adopted by a society align with, and insure, not only the evolution but the social transformation of its ideas; they assure its economic viability, sustenance, and social provision in terms of justice and protection.

I will explore, in the fashion of Roland Barthes,[6] the denotations in popular accounts or significations of Yoruba culture to extrapolate possible connotations that point to the intensification and in some cases attenuation of existing tendencies. In adopting this approach, I am very conscious of the danger in pursuing a 'single story' or event. Anti-revivalist scholars would no doubt criticize such homogenization of the Yoruba people as part of the myth of an assumed 'primitive unanimity'. At any rate, the approach that I am adopting involves the referencing of singular instances of events and based on such single exemplars I will build a larger case for the pervasiveness of analogous practices. I will suggest that institutions exist primarily to meet individual and group needs and to the extent that those needs are felt met, the institution will continue. Culture fundamentally involves the organization of a people's world, essentially the subjective component in which is expressed the definer of the self, feelings, and, most significantly, the fulcrum of their actions; that is the ideological concept of culture. Seen in this way, culture comes out in language, spirituality, and other observances.

STATEHOOD AND LOYALTY

According to the universal criteria of cultures proposed by Murdock, 'the community and the nuclear family are the social groups that are genuinely universal. They occur in every known human society'.[7] The partitioning of Africa culminated in colonization through which Nigeria became a country that is composed of many states in a federation. Western Nigeria, home to the Yoruba people, consists of six states. Now with statehood (the transition from the existing communal formations), individuals, ranging from government functionaries to citizens are expected to become patriots, whose allegiance is to the state, while maintaining their social and communal ties through which their identities are primarily formed. Loyalty therefore is foremost to the state to which allegiance is pledged. Since at least independence in 1960, every pupil in every school across the nation has pledged allegiance to Nigeria by singing the national anthem every single school day. This daily regimen is designed to foster the spirit of unity and to inculcate in them faithfulness, loyalty, and honesty towards the country, the component states, and the various local government and parastatals that represent the state, and that the people own collectively. A pertinent question however is: Has there been a shift of loyalty to the state?

A casual observation restricted to the Yoruba people, but generalizable across Nigeria (if not the whole continent), indicates that citizenship is local, it is patrilineal, and it cannot be rescinded. The position of every government functionary remains only an outlet to obtain a piece of the national or state resources for his or her own use. The idea for the Yoruba is rooted in the concept of bringing home the fruits (profits) from the farm (*ko ere oko dele*). Traditionally, one goes to farm, and the main farm is always at a distance from the homestead. One therefore sojourns in the farm. This concept of sojourning in the farm is not restricted to actual farming; whatever one's profession, land for the Yoruba is, metaphorically speaking, whatever an individual tills for yield (profession). The gains from such endeavors are expected to be repatriated home, that is back into one's community of birth, homestead, and family. To accumulate wealth abroad is great, but of less significance to the extent that those at home are not beneficiaries of it, or could not vouch that an individual returned with booty from his or her expeditions, because home is our refuge, our resort, and place of succor from sojourn/farmland. (*Ile ni abo simi oko*). This internalized perspective explains why every Yoruba transmigrant has to have a physical presence in their hometown. To appropriate state resources for personal use is not allegiance to the state, nepotism is not allegiance to the state, to offer differential services to clients as a function of their names does not show a transfer of allegiance to the state. Consider the deplorable states of many public infrastructures across Yorubaland, ranging from schools, universities, shopping complexes, roads, and hospitals to name a few. Many citizens comment on their continuous decay and neglect, and no one feels particularly committed to maintain and improve them. Instead, these infrastructures provide continuous opportunities for corruption and theft of public funds. This use of public infrastructures as means of enriching the self or family show that the state remains a foreign concept, poorly grafted onto existing ethnic formations that are more meaningful to the people. Consider a letter to the editor that appears in the *Lagos Times* of 1879. In it, the author decried the waste of public funds when he wrote concerning a public clock that had been erected in the tower of Christ Church, Lagos:

[A]s a matter of favour, an incompetent man, a carpenter, was appointed to attend to the valuable clock for 30s. per month. A Clock, for which the Government has expended an exorbitant amount, to be spoilt by incompetence. This is a sad defect. It is a crying shame that instead of employing a proper man to do the work, it should be left to a novice, who being ignorant and bashful to express his incapacity, keeps it always out of order ....[8]

WRITING AND LITERACY

The disposition of many scholars (such as Appiah, Wiredu and, Hountondji) is that 'literacy' is inevitable to civilization. Thus, where there is apparent lack of a form of writing system recognizable and decipherable by the West or a Western system of writing, their expeditors, missionaries, thinkers, and colonialist affirm for such places and people the absence of civilization and modernization. This devaluation is of course necessary in order to make savages out of a people, thereby justifying the violence on them and the eventual need for redemptive and civilizing missions. The Western-style literacy instituted into the socio-cultural system of the Yoruba people was embraced; there was no way around it, and it was appropriated and put to work in service of an existing outlook. Unlike the case of the Kaluli people,[9] where the introduction of missionary works and Western-type literacy (including a system of writing) has radically altered their culture, ushering in new communicative practices and social stratification, the Yoruba people retained existing stratification, which indeed is fundamental to their societal organization and they have continued to apportion worth and reverence along the lines previously laid down by their worldview. One achieves the good life, however one can, as long as one does not neglect the *Ori* (the spiritual head). As is often the case with imposition, the introduced system is frequently appended poorly to existing institutions and rarely erodes 'traditional' knowledge. As a new means of achieving the good life, there is overt acceptance and immediate implementation of the new system. The consequence is that the existing knowledge (*awo*) regresses in its secrecy and consequently increases in its relevance as it becomes more difficult to access. It also assumes greater mythic status in its efficacy, since the new model fails to address existing problems; rather, it (the new model) expends whatever capital it has at resolving its inherent and created problematics.

The Yoruba society remains largely oral in character (see below Tidbits). People rely more on verbally conveyed information than on written ones and, indeed, there is an absence of a reading culture. Literacy is pervasive; indeed, 60% of Yoruba people are literate. Reading occurs mainly to the extent that it is related to a profession. A lesser form of reading occurs in the consumption of religious materials from one's denomination. Reading for pleasure or for the sake of knowledge is less common. Now, this is not to discountenance the significant amount of reading going on online, especially, social media. Yoruba people, especially the youth, consume an enormous amount of information from diverse social media, including Facebook, Twitter, blogs, Badoo, Meetup, Mylife, and Youtube, Whatsapp, and tabloid sites among many others, using mostly handheld Android-enabled devices. The art and nature of the writings of these sources are akin to the oral mode of dissemination of information that the people are already familiar with. It is fair to suggest that such kinds of reading do not deviate significantly from gossip, jokes, comedic illustrations, and grapevine-type information consumption. Since these electronic resources are easily relatable to the existing style of information sharing, these sites attract heavy, voluntary traffic as opposed to the style of information presentations found in scholarly books.

It might very well be that the village square has given way to the Internet community, that Facebook provides more social information than the town crier, that Yahoo! appears to hold a key to 'making it', and formal classroom instruction has replaced certain intergenerational transfer of information. This creative expressiveness of a common past and shared outlook now remains fossilized in the myths and folklores that appear in books that are cited. It nevertheless remains to be shown that this apparent subsuming of the people's 'existing' mode of disseminating and accessing information into new and citable forms equals an obliteration of them.

Since, I am focusing on popular outlets, especially newspapers that were published shortly before and immediately after the pacification of Yorubaland and the formation of Nigeria, it is important to show how writing in newspapers intensified the existing need to narrate. For instance, *sagesm*, a fundamental means of socializing Yoruba children, continued uninterrupted. Rather than being offered as moonlight tales, as was the case prior to European intrusion, it found an outlet through the written word. On April 20, 1927 there appeared an article in the *Yoruba News Ibadan* that introduced a new column called *Awon Akewi* (Yoruba philosophy). The article, which also praised Mr. Denrele Adetimikan Obasa for his innovativeness and foresight in creating the column, noted in its preamble the absence of a culture of reading when it claimed that many indigenes did not as of then value reading and publishing, but certainly would do so later: '*bi o ti le je pe opolopo ninu awon enia wa ko mo riri iwe-kika ati iwe tite, sibesibe akoko mbo ...*'.[10] Featured also in this newspaper was Mr. Afolabi Johnson, who had a regular column where he waxed didactic in Yoruba, dispensing indigenous wisdom and modes of admonition. His topics ranged from health to social issues such as 'pick pockets', ethics, and morality. Essentially, what we find in the *Yoruba News Ibadan* is a gradual appropriation of the print media for the continuation of existing oratory.

Another example that illustrates the exploitation of this Western mode of documentation (print media), is its use for the dissemination of existing oral historical accounts. For instance, Mr. E.A. Akintan wrote down one of the existing oral narratives on Yoruba history. This was published on June 28, 1947 in the *Lagos Times* under the title 'ITAN YORUBA' (Yoruba History). In it, Mr. Akintan described the origin of Yoruba people as follows:

Nimrod in Mecca – a guard/hunter had 3 children – Oduduwa, Gogobiri (founder of Hausa), King of Kukuwa. There was a religious conflict between Muslims and traditionalists. Nimrod was a traditionalist. Islamists won, and Nimrod fled Mecca; the 2 children went East (iwo-orun) and Oduduwa went west (ila-orun). He settled in a city called Yariba – now Yoruba. After many years he reached ile ife after traveling for adorun ojo. There he met agbon-miregun or Orunmila who taught him divination. Oduduwa and his two sons brought two deities to Ife. This created an abundance of deities in Ife similar to the ones in Egypt. E.g. Opa oranyan. Odududwa's first child is Okonbi, who replaced his father; he had 7 children: Iya oba olowu Abeokuta, Iya Oba Alaketu, Oba bini, Rangun of Ila, Olupopo of popo, Onisabe of Sabe, Oranyan-Alaafin. For this reason, we know that all Yoruba people are descendants of Oduduwa.

Essentially, the tendency to narrate their lives and transfer their wealth of knowledge across generations was enhanced by the use of print media, a Western art. The only difference was that once any version of the stories, that were freely told, appeared in print, it not only had to be cited and attributed to an author, but also became standardized.

In his works, Mudimbe explored the dichotomy between the past, that is the traditional, and the modern, focusing on how African intellectuals could make use of the past to make better the future. In this process of extracting the Usable Past to reconstruct the present and perhaps, create the future, he recognized the existence of experts (that is, intellectual African) who were in a position to perhaps extricate the self from the so-called past in the reconstruction of the moment. As noted by Masolo,[11] this recognition of the intellectual as (a) an individual, (b) an individual who is able to operate cognitively and outside of his own preexisting socialization, and (c) as an individual who would discern, using undefined standards to extract the Usable Past, is quite problematic, Furthermore, Masolo's argument against Mudimbe's estrangement of intellectuals as people who rise above their own traditions by their cognitive practice places him at the center of another Western value; that is, the view that experts are isolated producers and owners of the knowledge which their consumers consume. Western literature, which constructs the other, identifies individuality as a major characteristic of the definition of Western rationality, in contrast to the anonymity and collectiveness which are reputed to be the distinctive characteristics of the other. It might very well be that individuals now take ownership of work by authoring them, yet, when it comes to cultural, indeed, life issues, Africans, in this case, Yoruba, continue to draw from the well of their collective knowledge even when such are printed in books under the name of an individual. Rarely is there a Yoruba person who, despite operating cognitively, functions outside their preexisting socialization.

Traditional and Modern

The various elements invaluable in the social organization and administration of the traditional Yoruba society were so codified as to be easily transmitted, retained, and retold using oral modes of reinforcement in the form of dances, dirges, and ceremonies of sacred nature. All these various means of communicating social values, that were cloaked in memorable and enjoyable celebrations, have now given way to an individuated, in a lot of ways, narcissistic perspective of a single thinker found in a self-contained, nucleated form of transmission that is ill adapted to the socio-cultural and environmental base of Yoruba polity. Much as every Yoruba person seeks to harness the advantage of a nuclear family (which is presumed to save them time and money, grants them some privacy, and absolves them from the various obligations entailed in a communal existence as instituted by the Yoruba nation), it is often the case that the nuclear family lifestyle is impracticable in a lot of ways. For those in Yorubaland, one needs the extended family to accompany one to seek the hand of a woman in marriage. No Yoruba woman would be married off without the involvement of the family. One needs the assistance of one's neighbor in running certain errands, even mundane ones such as charging a phone, grinding pepper, child care, support during times of emergency, a naming ceremony, and many others that modernization has generated but has been unable to resolve. For those in the diaspora, who hover in foreign lands where they are mostly tolerated but rarely accepted, kin, even at large, are the reliable source of information on all things and are resource persons in good and bad times. Imagine giving one's child in marriage in the USA, Germany, Canada, or Great Britain and being the only one wearing *agbada* (flowing gown), or being surrounded exclusively by people of different ethnicities. Imagine losing a loved one and there being no-one to commiserate with one. I will never forget when a prominent Yoruba scholar died in the USA and his European wife decided to cremate his remains and refused to hold a funeral ceremony commensurate to his age and achievement as an illustrious Yoruba son. One of his Yoruba colleagues, and perhaps the foremost historian from Africa, wailed and said with unconstrained surprise, '*o ma sun ni na, mi o mo enikankan ti won sun ni na ri*' (She simply burnt him. I have never known anyone who was burnt.) That the deceased man had ended up in a non-Yoruba way (not interred or entombed) remained not only calamitous, but was an abomination. The inappropriateness of 'two-aloneness' (as a couple or nucleated family is seen) as a way of life for Yoruba people, regardless of times and place and the necessity of the community, has given rise to various ethnic-based associations in the diaspora developing to meet their psychological needs.[12]

What is found intensified in the above narrative is the belief system surrounding the burial rites of a Yoruba man who has accomplished his earthly purpose. According to their ontology and worldview, the Yoruba person is on earth to obtain wealth, have children, and lead a long life.[13] The elderly man who gains all these blessings and dies peacefully is returned to the ancestors through elaborate burial ceremonies that assure his reincarnation. The cremated Yoruba man would have been provided with some elaborate tombstone, possibly with his grave right in from of his homestead. There would have been sculptures describing his life, and perhaps effigies of moments in it. His name and accomplishment would have been inserted in the praise narrative of his lineage (*oriki-ile*). At the very least, he would have had a fullpage obituary in one of the national and local newspapers which have now emerged as outlets for the intensification of the flamboyant life and death of a Yoruba icon; and annually, he would be remembered. The following is a remembrance announcement of a Yoruba death in a newspaper in 1920.

> In Affectionate remembrance of Madam LOUISA GABBIDON (the beloved mother of Mr. J. Omosalewa Thomas, Mrs. Comfort Bailey, and Sarah Salako), who departed this life on the 9th of April, 1915.
> Long we will mourn your loss
> Oh! What a loving mother thou art!
> Upon earth thine equal is rare
> Is this the end of so noble a life?
> Shall thy children without a comforter be?
> Alas mother! alas! alas!!
>
> Good were thy days on earth
> And in heaven the reward is sure
> Beloved thou art among thy children,
> Blessed and beloved also in the Realm above,
> Incessant in well doing she has succeeded
> Doing all she could to improve the world
> Of her body could be said as of old
> Never shall see corruption'[14]

That this Yoruba man was neither entombed nor accorded these rightful rites, as bemoaned by the scholar friend, shows the persistence and continuity of those significant values ordering the life of the people.

YORUBA FILMS

Eegungun is a term used for popular performance, the word employed to describe anything from the décor to their name, to their character and their enactment. For instance, there is Eegun Alarinjo (dancer and entertainer), *Eegun Oje* (performing masquerade), *Eegun Agbeji* (itinerant performer). Each masquerade plays a unique role; the various roles include magical performances, theatrical displays, and political performances. All of these were accepted as legitimate outlets for commentaries and social critique on the king and his chiefs. In addition, there were reverential, commemorative masquerades performed in honor of the ancestors and women. For each *eegungun* performance, there is not only a purpose but also an accompanying storyline. The storyline comes with a complete package, such as a certain pomp and pageantry, a unique character, and exclusive expressions. Included in the popular performance is the mystique which spreads among the people as popular myth. This mysteriousness in theatre is thus sustained and perpetuated and therefore never ceases to dazzle. One popular perception that was spread, and continues, involves the illusion created by the mysterious transformation of an *eegungun* into a lion. The *eegungun* will regain his original nature as long as it did not rain during the performance, otherwise his new form will remain forever unalterable. It is not uncommon to hear even today the murmur within the crowd that the *eegungun* should hurry up before it begins to rain, even if there is no sign of rain. Out of the *eegungun* performances evolved the itinerant performers and entertainers, which morphed into stage plays. When TV stations started in 1960 in Ibadan, the stage theatres turned into sitcoms and, led by Duro Ladipo,[15] the artists began to create films. Sophisticated Yoruba films form a major aspect of the popular Nigerian film industry, Nollywood, and they could be argued to be a continuation of the oral tradition.[16] Significant in the Yoruba films is that their major thematic has not deviated from the preoccupations of the different *eegungun* and traditional itinerant performers. Just as in the olden days, when the performers educated, admonished, and instructed on the various values vital to the Yoruba nation, the Yoruba film industry mainly provides a contemporary illustration to these preexisting tropes. Thus, the Yoruba film industry, in a sense, revolves around the three themes that derived from the Yoruba cosmology and defined the purpose of the earthly journey. These are, riches, longevity, and children. In order to achieve these goals or to assure their continuity when they are attained, the cosmology asks that we reverence the spiritual head (Ori) by keeping watch over it.

Just as in the olden days, when the *eegungun* and their guides received their sustenance and livelihood from the public, contemporary film and TV performers are paid by the consuming public. They are revered as idols and celebrities, just as the *eegungun* and the admiration for them grants them certain recognition which translates into privileges. Essentially, the market square finds an outlet in TV sets, laptops, and various handheld devices. The griot-like nature of instruction finds an outlet in scripts, and rather than it being practiced by a family and transmitted as a family inheritance, there is a democratization of the cast and script writers. The electronic media intensify existing institutions and have not introduced anything new, except for their ability to widely spread the performances (Fig. 19.1).

Fig. 19.1 Masqueraders' family house in Aperin, Ibadan. *Source* The author
Note A banner announces the 2016 festival. Such announcements would have been made by the town-crier. Announcements are not new, the mode is. Having a seal of one's profession is an old practice of the Yoruba people.

Money

For the French philosopher Marcel Mauss,[17] exchange is at the heart of society. While Mauss looked at kinship and solidarity from this perspective, especially the exchange involving individuals in a marital situation, he noted that through gift-giving we understand the many networks that compose the social fabric, including the economic, moral, and religious contexts. My intent here is to note some of the Yoruba's form of exchanges and to point to the underlying self-interest and the interdependence[18] among them. More importantly, I aim to show from citizens' comments that monetary exchange did not come with the Europeans; rather, there were already established systems for the exchange of goods and services based on a local currency. This traditional Yoruba means of exchange was in place when the colonialists came. They also used cowries until the pacification of the Yoruba, when British currency was formally introduced, thereby supplanting the cowries. For instance, according to the *Lagos Times* of October 1878, cowries were still in use in the Yoruba country for stipends and for the passage to and from Ibadan. For instance, Mr. Ambekemo wrote a rejoinder on November 11, 1878; it pertained to a previous letter to the Editor about the so-called 'Christian Parakoyis of Abeokuta', defined as self-constituted, because 'in this our country, by paying large sums of cowries in shape of bribes, one can do what you good people in England would consider almost impossible'. Those expeditors, travelers and merchants who for instance, needed people to move their goods from one city to another (for example, a heavy load transported from Abeokuta to Ibadan) would pay contractors to undertake the journey with them, carrying their luggage. The trip to Ibadan from Abeokuta attracts up to five strings of cowries, the equivalent of £1.5/- (one pound and five shillings). Colonialism did not abrogate monetary exchange, neither did it introduce it; rather, it only introduced a different form of currency and exchange rate. International trade was not new: Yoruba people traded across the border, they were involved in the trans-Sahara trade to the Middle East. Without a doubt, they were integrated into European trade through colonialism, and the values of their commodities were pegged to a different culture and values. Nevertheless, such integration could possibly have evolved organically had there not been any external interventions. What do Yoruba people exchange and how do they make use of exchange? When examined critically, the impetus for their engagement in exchanges has remained unaltered. There were exchanges with the gods, there were exchanges involving pawnship, and there were exchanges in their quest to achieve the good life.

HUMAN SACRIFICE

In 1882, the *Lagos Times* reported on human sacrifice in Yorubaland. The story ran as follows:

> Rev. C. Phillips, native missionary at Ode Ondo, in Ijesha Country, in a sermon spoke to two main concessions exacted from the people: 1. To end human immolation at the death of an influential or consequential persons. (standing in the way of this is the profit to the king to whom a slave is given for each sacrifice that is made). 2. They consented, quite reluctantly, but with conviction based on Christianity to end two main public immolation of human beings that are made periodically between July and August each year to Esu, in order conciliate his much-dreaded anger and cruelty. The second one is to Oramafe, the diviner at Ife, 'who gives to the earth its fatness'. Since yam is the staple food of the people and at the root of their economy, the chief babalawo remains steadfast in arguing against their abolition, against the counsel of some chiefs. According to the report, 'The power of the priesthood in the heathendom here is by no means to be despised. The people are certainly priest-ridden.[19]

While the exchange of currency for food and services is a normal daily and temporal necessity, the most significant form of exchange occurs between humans and the various deities. Born out of their cosmology, which institutes theocratic rulership of their lives, every Yoruba curries the favor of the different deities charged with the delivery of different services to ensure they lead a good life and completely realize their apportioned lots on Earth and that those apportioned goods are secured. These various gods must be palliated through obedience to their wishes, not only so that they continue to perform their duties to the people, but also to avoid their wrath that is bound to be incurred should they consider that there has been a breach in the covenant with the people.[20] This, despite the obvious advantage to the king and to the Babalawo (as suggested in the news report quoted above), is the subtext of the sacrifices made to them on a regular basis. The highest form of reverence that could be shown to the gods included the offering of a human life. Nowadays, there are no overt human sacrifices made to the gods as was the case in the olden days. However, animal sacrifices continue for Muslims, while the traditionalists and the Christians have outsourced this practice, accepting, for instance, the sacrifice of Jesus Christ as adequate. Regardless of the confession, the efficacy of the blood in the social institution is inviolable. At every situation, the Christians plead the blood of Jesus. In this regard, it is particularly important to underscore the persistent worldview guiding physical exertion on earth. According to a slightly deterministic view, the Yoruba people claim that to work while others are playing and to fast while others are feasting would not make one rich or prevent one from becoming fat. (*Kaa sise nijoti gbogbo aye nsere o pe a lowo lowo, ka gbaawe nijo gbogbo aye njeun o nii a ma san ra, ori ni yo ni.*) The spiritual head (Ori) is the provider. Despite this, the Yoruba insist that humans are given legs so that they can work out their own accomplishment. Consequently, to actively supplement belief, through magic, medicine, and sacrifices, does not contravene faith. To not do so would be negligent. This firm understanding, of 'belief and supporting work', informs the various observances infused into whatever received confession the people exhibit. So, Yoruba people engage in extraneous sacrifices to the gods in order to activate all blessings.

In today's world, it is not uncommon to hear complaints against human smuggling, identity theft or impersonation to gain entry to those choice destinations where we presume life would be better for us. Whatever the reason, this practice is not new either. Human cunning and the quest for self-interest remain effective in engineering sources for gain. In the same report of March 1, 1882 was the news from 'Ondo country' about the execution of criminals in place of the existing practice of using them for immolation sacrifices at funerals or selling them off as slaves. Arguably, immolation sacrifices have been attenuated if not abolished due to colonization. This is about the only definite change in the habitual practices of Yoruba people. This, however, does not mean that using humans for ritual purposes has been completely eradicated, despite the capital punishment attached to it. Enslavement continues surreptitiously. Essentially, capitalism is not new to the Yoruba people; neither is circumvention of laws or treaties for gain.

SLAVERY AND PAWNSHIP

According to a letter to the Editor of the *Lagos Times* published February 6, 1882, Libertas, perhaps the penname of the author, decried ongoing slavery in the form of pawnship when he wrote:

> No money interest is paid upon the loan contracted, but the personal labour of the unfortunate pawn till the time the loan is repaid; which is always left open … The pawn receives not a fraction of payment for his toils. Should he die before payment of the loan is made, or should he desert his master, a substitute is to be provided. This wicked slavery is practised under the eye of British law, and that sometimes by persons calling themselves Christians.

Further, the author noted:

> It is sometimes the case that unwary people are decoyed from this place to be sold into slavery in the neighbouring [sic] non-British countries … Slaves bought in and brought from countries beyond British borders and registered as aliens have sometimes been decoyed out of Lagos by those who have registered them as their distant relatives and connections or other friends, and sold off again as the case may be, and there are never wanting those who would help such persons in their wicked transactions.[21]

The author identified as culprits 'young people of intelligence, jurors, as among important owners of slaves'.[22]

There were responses to this assertion. One was a rejoinder written by J. Marshall, the Chief Justice of the Gold Coast Colony. He wrote that 'formerly domestic slavery on the Gold coast was recognized and supported by the Government; but owning, or debt slavery, never was'.[23] It is of no consequence to this discussion whether *de jure* or de facto slavery (either properly or vicariously as pawnship or debt services) was practiced; historians have produced significant works in this area to show the presence of commercial transactions based on the use of pawns.[24] Of importance to me in my pursuit of the trivial and supposedly inconsequential but life-defining practices is the uncovering of a state of mind that informs habitual behaviors. The Yoruba say: *o ni aburo, o so pe o leru, ise wo lo ran eru, t'aburo o je?* (You have younger siblings and you claim that you have no slaves/servants, what services do slaves render that your younger sibling are unable to perform?) The use of relatives in a pseudo-slave position continues despite political speeches and judicial injunctions. Nearly all upper-middle-class and elite Yoruba people, especially (as noted in the 1882 letter) learned individuals, people of consequence, and jurors, are intensifying this practice with increasingly sophisticated and nuanced perspectives that obfuscate the inherent exploitation. The owners of these enslaved or pawned individuals consider themselves to be benevolent, offering socio-economic and academic support for the advancement of the beneficiaries in exchange for minimal domestic services. With a hierarchical and pyramidal spiritual model, which is made up of a retinue of gods and subordinate gods in declining order of power and influence, a hierarchical political order consisting of a king and ranked subordinate chiefs, and a hierarchical family structure with the father at the top and members of the agnatic descent ranked in order of influence based on age and sex, the Yoruba social structure is dominated by the concept of the big man. This spiritual and temporal pyramidal structure that produced the principle for the organization of the Yoruba nation generates the mindset or worldview that culminates in the practice of 'bigmanism',[25] which makes a mockery of philanthropy.

Often the corruption in the government is rooted in the use of state funds to secure the loyalty of a vast number of followers in a patron–client relationship. At each ladder in the hierarchical set-up, the 'big man' employs carrots and sticks and is without sanction except by a higher influence. In 1882, the *Daily News* carried the following news:

> [R]eport concerning the cruelty of Ogundipe, a powerful Abeokuta chief, known to have within the past 12 months preceding the report murdered at least 40 of his slave wives. He is said to take pleasure in compelling his wives to drown their offspring in a river, delights in human sacrifices, and frequently, after decapitating his victims, he has been known to drink their blood as personal offering to his sanguinary deities, he has been known to starve his slaves to death just for personal amusement ...,[26]

While these gory acts have now become attenuated, it is fair to ask if there is law and order in the contemporary Yoruba nation. Presumably, there is no more now than there was when Ibadan was emerging as a military state, nor any more than when Abeokuta was warring against all sides for survival, nor any more than when Kosoko and Dopemu feuded for Lagos, and certainly no more than when Basorun Gaa held sway in Oyo, or the mercilessness of Dahomey when they invaded and destroyed Imeko. Power, position, and influence ruled and continue to do so. As long as you have the means to coerce obedience, your wishes become the standard of etiquette and you remain unassailable. Actually, you are considered valorous. Yoruba people value valor, and modernity has only intensified this social value.

Class and Gerontocracy

Class is endemic in Yoruba social interactions due to a built-in stratification across several social strata. People are primarily stratified by age. More than a week into my research at the National Archive at the University of Ibadan, one of the supervisors suddenly decided to implement a rule that I had never before encountered. It included me providing my name, my address, email and phone number. I complied, but since my Nigerian number was new, I did not have it memorized and could not supply it. He decided that I would not be allowed to use the facility until I had supplied the phone number. According to him, 'we need to know you'. I asked him to produce the written policy that he was now implementing. He said, it is known and he does not need to produce it. I asked for his name. He said, he was Alabi, J.B. I said, 'Alabi, I do not have the phone number and I will take this up above your level'. He was so infuriated, he almost spat fire. He became belligerent, rude, and disruptive, just because I had called him by his name. According to him, 'I am more than you'. It took a while for me to understand the meaning of the utterance and to correlate it with the behavior he exhibited. Just on his conviction that he was older than me, he did not expect me to question him or call him by his name.

Exploring the interaction of Yoruba people on the Internet list-serve USA/African Dialogue, Agwuele[27] in 2012 showed how the ire of participants would be incurred should someone they presume younger than them did not adhere to the traditionally sanctioned mode of address reserved for an elder. Agwuele[28] also documented the manner in which such English terms of address as '*sista, broda, onkul,* and *senior*' are deployed to maintain stratification by age. As a result, someone older is called '*broda* or *sista*' depending on their sex, not because they are related to the younger person who addresses them so, but because social distance has to be maintained at all times. In exchange for this accordance of deference that comes with privileges, the 'senior or older' person is empowered to intervene in the affairs of the younger person and use them as their butler. The younger receives gifts and gets the benefit of the knowledge and experience of the seniors as well as their goodwill. The traditional hierarchy remains pervasive. Individuals are expected to know their position and to keep within their status. Each is expected to offer deference to those above them and trample forcefully on those beneath. The only time that gerontocracy is displaced is when an individual by sheer force of character achieves acclaim in the form of exceptional notoriety, wealth, or success. This form of reciprocal relationship is strongly upheld within the patron–client relationship.

TIDBITS

African Time

At the Society of Arts in 1882, Captain Cameron read out a paper on 'The Gold Fields of West Africa'. He reported concerning his journey: 'As soon as possible we started. The ordinary African delays, of course, occurred'.[29] The said African time is not new, it would seem from this report, and had already become so well known as to merit no definition or explanation. The Captain stated it as a matter of fact. Has anything changed? Watches, to some extent, remain just pieces of jewelry to complement appearance and accentuate attire. The joke is that if you invited a Yoruba to dinner at 6 pm, s/he starts to shower at 6 pm. Although trivial, this stereotypical behavior emerged out of a worldview and frame of mind claiming that *kitakita o dola, ori lo ngbe ni* (regardless of its extent, exertion does not equate success/wealth, only the head grants success[30]). So, time for the Yoruba is a phenomenon. While the West mainly keeps and marks time, the Yoruba person owns time and is not constrained by it. Were Ali Mazrui[31] to offer an opinion on time, he might have said that Africans became complacent about time because they reside in the midst of natural abundance and therefore were not in any way compelled to invent or exert themselves unnecessarily, unlike the Europeans, who are at the mercy of harsh weather and climatic conditions. African time is also intensified by the material consequences of modernity: African infrastructures are inimical to the running of a system, ill grafted to a radically different socio-cultural condition. They have, over time, become so dilapidate, due to lack of maintenance (that is the result of a different consciousness, in addition to other factors already discussed), that even with the best of intentions, time and appointments cannot be kept. A road trip of a hundred kilometers is fraught with so many uncertainties and there are no provisions for emergencies, or even alternate routes. People therefore resort to prayer to accomplish even the most mundane things. This by itself is not new; uncertainties have accompanied Yoruba existence since Oduduwa climbed down an iron chain to found the nation, starting from Ile-Ife.

Fraud

Avarice and greed have always triggered fraud, regardless of the introduction of exact quantification by numbers and measurements. For instance, the January 1, 1878 edition of *African Times* wrote to denounce the practice, which did not fool any one. According to the report, natives were buying 30 yards of fabrics and 2 gallons of oil but were actually receiving 26 yards and 1.5 gallons of spirits due to dubious measuring devices. The Ibadan were particularly concerned about the Egbas and Ijebus, who sold them alcohol containing scarcely 12% spirit (i.e. pretended spirits, of which seven-eighths is water), and they were also keen to get 30 yards of cloth instead of 25 yards. Go through any gas station in Yorubaland: no-one really believes that they are obtaining the same quantity of liters that the pump indicates, despite the fact that the customers added extra tips to the salespeople pumping the gas in order to obtain the advertised price. The women at Gbagi, Dugbe, and Bodija markets have the underside of their pans beaten in just to reduce the volume. Such a pan, known as a *kongo*, is the standard unit of measurements for selling staple foods such as rice, garri, and beans in smaller quantities rather than in bags. Short measures and adulteration continues and intensifies. The government, you ask? They are too busy tinkering with the budget and individual allocations to be bothered with such mundane matters as the worth of 'peanuts'.[32] Remember, statehood has not attenuated filial feelings and loyalty to ethnic origins; hence government is only one of the sources for unlimited funds to maintain the patron-client system.

Gambling: Rondo Rondo

On August 6, 1861, King Dosunmu ceded Lagos to Britain. In 1914, Nigeria was born. By 1921, there were already letters to the Editor of *Lagos Weekly* complaining about the gambling on the streets of Lagos. On April 10, 1920, the writer Veritas described them as itinerant bands, noting the large scale of this business that preyed on people's avarice. Every adult in Ibadan will recollect seeing at one time or another the itinerant magicians and tricksters known as Rondo Rondo. They turn tricks with cards, with a stone or marble hidden under one of their three cups which they shuffle around for unsuspecting clients to choose. Whoever chooses the cup with the stone under it wins double or triple the amount betted. No one ever wins.

The Goal of Earthly Existence

The quest to obtain and secure the good life as instituted by the Yoruba cosmology has always preoccupied the people. It ranges from the time of ascertaining one's destiny immediately after birth to the use of divination to resolve life's problems, and the transposition of such to those received confessions Christianity and Islam. It used to be that through word of mouth the reputations of powerful diviners, healers, and medicine men were broadcast. Making known one's profession not only intensified with the advent of written words; newspaper advertisements are made less transient. Readers can retrieve them and uncover their content in the same way that historians research the documented deeds and quests of the peoples. Being vested in knowing what the future holds for them, it is customary to inquire the content of a new year towards the end of a year. Eight years after the birth of Nigeria, Adam I. Animashaun, an Arabian astrologer, wrote his predictions for the year 1922. According to him:

> Various kinds of winds and sickness will exist in this year.
> Death of kings, chiefs and influential men will be prevalent
> The epidemic of small pox will break out,
> Deaths of children will occur frequently as well as those of old men and women …
> There will be very good crops and plenty of rain
> Cattle sheep and all sorts of Quadrupeds will breed well.
> Pregnant women will experience difficulty before and during child birth ….[33]

Following his predictions for the year, which he claimed would come to pass between January 22 and April, he took out a personal ad touting his qualification as 'Author of Arabic Nigerian Almanack and Proprietor of the Times of Nigeria', reaching out to one of the most fundamental needs of the people:

> If you want to know about your future or that of your relatives what profession suites you what country our fortune lies in whether your [sic] have a long life or not, what day is your lucky day, what wife will best suit you, cause of your ailments and its remedy what is condition of your relatives or friends however far away they may be from you whether pregnant women will easily and safely brin [sic] forth or not and whether the offspring will be male or female whether you will recover from your sickness or not and whether trade commercial partner will be successful or not and a full reading of your life apply to the named astrologer free of charge at his office ....[34]

We merely have the intensification of existing inclinations; nothing is new in all of these developments. While the astrologer appeals to those worldviews of his people pertaining to their earthly goals, pitching his offerings around wealth, procreation, and longevity, the European merchants and their marketers did not fail to exploit the same motif in targeting the Yoruba people with goods by the Europeans in the same newspaper and in the *Yoruba Newspaper*. In both we find ads selling health-related drugs and tonics, for example the Lake Breeze Motor fan that was propelled by burning kerosene was being sold to the elites as a cure for certain ills. Or the blood tonic from Dr. Cassell, who had a remedy for every single ailment. They ranged from tablets which he claimed 'make you strong and healthy, cure all the troubles of weak mean' and also prevented 'malaria fever and dysentery, vital exhaustion, nerve weakness, etc'. There was Phospherine, advertised as the best tonic medicine; Winox wine food, described as 'A delicious wine without drugs and the only tonic giving analyses of content on every bottle; it prevents influenza, fevers, malaria ... nervous weaknesses'. And Hall's Wine which 'banishes weakness and depression', 'makes you strong and always vigorous'. There was Sloan's liniment that kills pain, rheumatism, sciatica neuritis, backache; Veno's lightning cough cure which also cured influenza and catarrh. Dewitt's Pills were billed as 'the world's greatest remedy for rheumatism and backache and disorders of the kidneys and bladder'. Similarly, in the Yoruba newspaper *Eleti-Ofe*, advertisements were made in English and Yoruba. For instance, 'White's Radial Gonkiller', captioned in Yoruba as 'Egbogi Alawotan Atosi' was billed as the cure for Gonorrhoea (sic); Mentholatum was captioned as 'Ipara Awo'gba Arun', and to the Yoruba hunters were marketed American cartridges for 'a no disappointment, western clean kill at any distance' by Nigerian Sporting Goods Depot[35]. Even Christians were not left out: the International Bible Student Association marketed their own literature as follows: 'The outworking of

19 INTENSIFICATION AND ATTENUATION: COLONIAL INFLUENCES ON AN ... 471

the Divine Plan made more interesting than the best novel ever read. God's beneficent designs for all the human family – the overthrow of the Devil and his earthly organization – the deliverance of oppressed mankind into peace, happiness, liberty and life ...'.[36] For those who now reside in the city and perhaps are no longer satisfied with moonlight tales and Elaloro, the traditional mode of entertainment and teasing the brain,[37] the *Lagos Weekly Record*, starting from July 5, 1930, began to include crossword puzzles in their publications.

As trivial, mundane, familiar, or perhaps strange as these stories gleaned from newspapers may seem, especially with respect to the forms of things and manner of events that form the content of the people's existence, when viewed through the prism of culture (that is, an aggregate of learned patterned knowledge that informs attitude towards material and non-material entities as well as conducts), then they begin to take a decidedly remarkable, realistic quality that one can easily relate to but immediately requires theoretical explication. After many years of obtaining other perspectives, interacting with and experiencing the ways of life of the other, I cannot but agree with Hall (1959) that the highly personal things are the most pertinent cultural data. These things are indicators of an emergent frame of mind. Bit by bit, through one seemingly minor and inconsequential act, thought, dos and don'ts that follow one after the other, we build up those categories of importance that we have assigned to set until it is a governing system, carefully fitted to administer the society and guard our ways of life. Thus, the main template in organizing and maintaining Yoruba existence appears to remain intensified even when the people assume differing European garb. Such fundamentals, that is culture, 'a mode in which we are all cast, and [that] controls our daily lives in many unsuspecting ways'[38] is rarely destructible, save for the total annihilation of its owners.

Back in the rusty city of Ibadan, the town of warriors, home to the restless traders, there are many things that are quite obvious: hotels of different sizes, club houses, pipe-borne water, paved roads, taxis, buses, okadas (motorbikes), cocoa house, the tallest building in the city with its elevators, cinemas, swimming pools, and neon lights etc.; all marks of modernity and Westernization. Nevertheless, anyone of experience would immediately see the huge contrast to the Western world in the organization of these things as well as the difference in attitudes that they elicit from the people. Of course, any casual observer will quickly point to those techniques of transport, health, education, certification and accumulation. Is there really anything that is bold, new, defining, and radically transformative in the contacts of cultures of Yoruba and Great Britain? It would seem to me that there remains nothing but the intensification of those positive concerns and the attenuation of those with obvious negative consequences.

These newly introduced cultural artifacts (or elements of modernization), as mentioned above for the city of Ibadan, are mainly other means through which existing tendencies have adapted to newly introduced realities. Since learning, for instance, replaced biological adaptation in humans, the role of instinct has become replaced by culture. Cultural reactions for humans have become as trusted as is the blinking of the eyes for preventive and lubricative purposes. Society has also become so dependent on cultural reaction to existent that its constancies are adjudged inviolable. To illustrate the preceding view, consider Yoruba people's internalized worldview concerning appearance. A certain ill-will is stimulated, that ultimately provokes violence, when an adult Yoruba male wears his hair in an unkempt fashion, that is to say, in dreadlocks.[39] That hairstyle is judged to be a sign of non-conformity to the carefully crafted societal segregation between the forest world, presumed to be infested by nefarious spirits (*igbe*) and the cultivated, orderliness of the city (*ilu*). The city, it is believed, is a place of light and transparency; as such, there is no danger of evil lurking around. Thus, whoever comes across such a dreadlocked person, who personifies the evil from the dark forest world, is duty-bound to exterminate such evil and save their fellow citizens. The violence that is visited upon such a person occurs instinctively, is a cultural instinct. Culture in a lot of ways is indeed the assignment of sets to categories, which once determined mainly unfold in the manner in which the assigned category is treated.[40]

Conclusion

Business attire, that is, a buttoned-up shirt, sport coat, and tie worn with a pair of slacks and black shoes whose heels produce a stepping noise of importance as one approaches an office, did not displace the more regal and respectful flowing gown (*agbada*); rather, business clothes accentuated class (e.g. the class of *akowe*, secretary, that has now morphed into personal assistant). The *akowe* forms the retinue of personnel attending to the personal needs of the rich, who announces their importance by the number of such minions that enhance his/her cult of personality (bigmanism). The business attire, with its brusque salutation, defines the working class, while the chiefs and the *nouveau riche* with their time-consuming gowns continue their ritual of affluence, reflective of certain class, attainment, and position. Elaborate prefatory greetings attend even the briefest casual encounter.

Recycling? We came from nature and to nature we shall return. Out of respect for nature, the Yoruba seek only their place. They carve out of nature a place of abode and places for cultivation, they seem to maintain a careful pact or bargain struck with other earthly inhabitants. Yoruba people do not venture into the forest, and the forest dwellers stay in their territory. To cross the divide between the city and the forest requires strength. A fortified hunter goes into the forest to overcome game for food; if, in the process, he/she falls prey to a stronger creature, that person is mourned but no blame is ever attached to the animal.

A careful balance is maintained at all times. Things obtained from nature are returned to nature. When at dawn you walk through the alleys between the houses, stepping over gutters, or open sewers in Ibadan, you are very mindful, watchful, and attentive. You are mindful not to step into things that will glue to your shoes with smells that trail after you. You are watchful to immediately avert your gaze, especially from crouching figures beneath whom streaks a watery substance. You are attentive and watchful for the creaking noise of windows or gates opening so that you duck quickly; because the later apology, *e maa binu, ito o omo yin ni* (Please pardon, it was only the urine of your children) which is meant as a palliative cannot undo the damage. You are lucky if it fell on your shoes or splashed your trousers. These different examples illustrate the Yoruba simply putting 'out' of the abode those things that they do not need in hope that the wind will blow them back into nature. Other examples include sweeping the front of the compound further away from the main house in hope that the debris will return to earth. This is no different from letting anything out of our hands wherever we may be as a form of recycling. Since (we) Yoruba did not modify anything so radically that we are not decomposable, we rarely pay attention to the lifespan of those things that are now chemically altered, including plastic bags and dead vehicles. The constructed drainage systems are additional spaces for getting rid of refuse and rubbish. To the Yoruba, all these consist of *eyinkunle* (backyard, actually, behind the residence). *Ehikunle* is '*akitan*' (refuse dump), *ehinkunle* is '*igbe*' (forest), ehinkunle is '*ibi igbonse*' (toilet). Coming to our aid in the recycling of waste is a web of animals such as: dogs, cats, rats, and rabbits. Their efforts are augmented by incineration. Finally, whatever is left within the immediate environment/abode, '*iwaju ile*' (front of the compound), is removed by torrential rainfalls.

There appears to be a resurgence of the old ways in popular culture; perhaps we willingly chose to ignore their existence until providence forced their acknowledgment upon us in all we do. The belief in the supernatural is organic and the socialization within them remains uninterrupted. While most households in Ibadan with young children foster Nigerian English upon their school children, and while some pretend to find the Yoruba language limiting, presuming greater opportunity in some creolized foreign tongues, at the most unexpected moments Yoruba sayings, aphorisms, and proverbs spring up, reaching the heart of the Yoruba person. Fresh, as if newly minted, they broadcast the life that has always been there, the life that we have always led, the beliefs that have always guided actions, informed decisions, and given words to prayers that have been uttered ever so silently. They remind us of the taboos that we have observed without acknowledging their source and importance in our interactions, they rekindle those values that have always defined us as Yoruba. At that instance, it becomes clear that we have never departed and our core has remained undiminished. The very self, including culture and ideals, is like treasures of eternal value that are secured in their hiding place while we seek to add to them. The corporate nature of the Yoruba people makes hoarding a lifestyle: we keep what we have, we obtain from others what is of value and we increase, rarely giving up that which we possess.

Notes

1. Lucien Lévy-Bruhl, *Primitive Mentality* [*La mentalité primitive*] (New York, NY: AMS Press, [1922] 1978); Lucien Levy-Bruhl, "How Natives Think," in *African Philosophy: Selected Readings*, ed. Albert Mosley (New York: Prentice Hall, 1995).
2. Gyekye Kwame, *Tradition and Modernity* (New York: Oxford University Press, 1997).
3. Anthony Appiah, *In My Father's House: African in the Philosophy of Culture* (NY: Oxford University Press, 1992), 26.
4. Hountondji Paulin J., *African Philosophy: Myth and Reality*, 2nd ed. (Bloomington and Indianapolis: Indiana University Press, 1996), 60.
5. Augustine Agwuele, *The Symbolism and Communicative Contents of Dreadlocks in Yorubaland* (NY: Palgrave 2016), 23.
6. Roland Bathes, *Mythologies*, trans. Annette Lavers (London: Vintage Press, 1996).
7. George Murdock, *Social Structure* (New York: MacMillan, 1949), 79.
8. Letter to the Editor, *Lagos Times* of April 20, 1879. (Author not named.)
9. Bambi B. Schieffelin, Introducing Kaluli Literacy, in *Regimes of Value*, ed. Paul Kroskrity (Santa Fe, NM: School of American Research, 2000), 293–327.
10. The Yoruba New Ibadan, April 20, 1927 (p. 6).
11. D.A. Masolo, "An Archaeology of African Knowledge: A Discussion of V.Y. Mudimble," *Callaloo* 14, no. 4 (1991): 998–1011.
12. See, for example: Charles Adeyanju, "Yoruba-Nigerians in Toronto: Transnantional Practices and Experiences," in *Yoruba Identity and Power Politics*, ed. Toyin Falola and Ann Genova (Rochester, NY: Rochester University Press, 2006); Akintunde, Oyetade, "The Yoruba Community in London," *African Languages and Cultures* 6, no. 1 (1993): 69–92.
13. For a full discussion see, Ayo Opefeyitimi, "Iwure: Medium of Communicating the Desires of Men to the Gods in Yoruba Land," *Journal of Religion in Africa* 18, no. 17 (1988): 27–41.
14. Published by J.O.T. in the *Lagos Weekly Record* (April 4th, 1920): 8.
15. See Ebun Clark, *Hubert Ogunde: The Making of Nigerian Theatre* (Oxford University Press, 1979).
16. Joel A. Adedeji, "Oral Tradition and the Contemporary Theater in Nigeria," *Research in African Literatures* 1971: 134–49. See also Hutchison, Y. "The Seductive Dance between History and Literature: The Moremi Legend by Historian Samuel Johnson and Playwrights Duro Ladipo and Femi Osofisan," *South African Theatre Journal* 13, no. 1 (1999): 31–47.
17. Marcel Mauss, *The Gift: Forms and Functions of Exchange in Archaic Societies* (London: Cohen and West, 1925 [1954]).
18. See, Edward J. Lawler and Shane R. Thye, "Bringing Emotions into Social Exchange Theory," *Annual Review of Sociology* 25 1999: 217–44.

19. The story, on page 31, was published in the March 1, 1882 issue of the *Lagos Times*.
20. Now classic, Karin Barber's, "How Man Makes God in West Africa: Yoruba Attitude Towards the Orisha," *Africa* 51, no. 3 (1981): 724–45, provides an insightful discussion on the relationship between Yoruba people and their gods.
21. A letter written by Libertas to the Editor, the *Lagos Times*, it was published on February 6, 1882.
22. Ibid.
23. Ibid.
24. See for instance: Paul E. Lovejoy and Toyin Falola eds. *Pawnship, Slavery and Colonialism in Africa*. J. Africa World Press, 2003; and Paul E. Lovejoy and David Richardson. "The Business of Slaving: Pawnship in Western Africa," c. 1600–1810. *Journal of African History* 42 (2001): 67–89.
25. This term derives from Marshall Sahlins. "Poor Man, Rich Man, Chief: Political Types in Melanesia and Polynesia," *Comparative Studies in Society and History* 5, no. 3 (1963): 285–303.
26. *Daily News*, July 1, 1882.
27. Using the exchanges between Yoruba Nigerians on the listserve, the article documents how the traditional mode of interaction that is based on gerontocracy, position, and title, among others has migrated to the virtual space. For a full discussion, see Augustine Agwuele. "From Village Square to Internet Square: Language and Culture at the USA–Africa Dialogue Series," in *Development, Modernism and Modernity in Africa*, ed. Agwuele Augustine (NY: Routledge, 2012), 78–108.
28. Augustine Agwuele, "Popular Culture of Yoruba Kinship Practices," in *Africans and the Politics of Popular Culture*, ed. Toyin Falola and Augustine Agwuele (NY: University of Rochester Press, 2009), 41–63.
29. Captain Cameron, in the *Lagos Times*, August 1, 1882.
30. For a fuller discussion of the concept of *Ori* (head) and earthly success, see Kola Abimbola. *Yoruba Culture: A Philosophical Account* (Birmingham, UK: Iroko Academic Publishers 2005).
31. See for instance Ali Mazrui, *The Africans: A Triple Heritage* (MA: Little Brown & Co, 1986).
32. This word was used by the former director of the Deutsche Bank, Juergen Schneider, to describe the insignificance of the loss of over DM50 million by the bank. It was voted the "Un-wort des Jahres" (non-word of the year) and it is referenced here to illustrate the dissonance between ordinary and rich people in their perceptions.
33. This was republished on page 4 of the Monday edition of the *Times of Nigeria*, May 22, 1922.
34. Ibid.
35. Eleti Ofe, January 12, 1927, p. 10.
36. Ibid., 11.
37. For the explication of *eleloro*, the Yoruba traditional method of instruction, see Michael O. Afolayan, 2012. "*Elaloro*: A Didactic Approach to Yoruba Education," in *Development, Modernism and Modernity in Africa*, ed. Augustine Agwuele (NY: Routledge), 108–20.

38. Edward T. Hall, 1959. *The Silent Language* (Greenwich: Conn. Fawcett Premier Book), 38.
39. See Agwuele, 2016 for a full discussion of treatment of people based on appearance.
40. Hall, *The Silent Language*.

Bibliography

Abimbola, Kola. *Yoruba Culture: A Philosophical Account*. Birmingham, UK: Iroko Academic Publishers, 2005.

Adedeji, oel, A. "Oral Tradition and the Contemporary Theater in Nigeria." *Research in African Literatures* (1971): 134–49.

Adeyanju, C. "Yoruba-Nigerians in Toronto: Transnational Practices and Experiences." In *Yoruba Identity and Power Politics*, edited by Toyin Falola and Ann Genova. Rochester, NY: Rochester University Press, 2006.

Afolayan, Michael O. "Elaloro: A Didactic Approach to Yoruba Education." In *Development, Modernism and Modernity in Africa*, edited by Augustine Agwuele, 108–20. NY: Routledge, 2012.

Agwuele, Augustine. "Popular Culture of Yoruba Kinship Practices." In *Africans and the Politics of Popular Culture*, edited by Toyin Falola and Augustine Agwuele, 41–63. New York: University of Rochester Press, 2009.

———. "From Village Square to Internet Square: Language and Culture at the USA-Africa Dialogue Series." In *Development, Modernism and Modernity in Africa*, edited by Agwuele Augustine, 78–108. NY: Routledge, 2012.

———. *The Symbolism and Communicative Contents of Dreadlocks in Yorubaland*. New York: Palgrave, 2016.

Appiah, Anthony. *In My Father's House: African in the Philosophy of Culture*. NY: Oxford University Press, 1992.

Barber, Karin. "How Man Makes Godin Wes Africa: Yoruba Attitude Towards the Orisha." *Africa* 51, no. 3 (1981): 724–45.

Bathes, Roland. *Mythologies*. Translated by Annette Lavers. London: Vintage Press, 1996.

Ebun, Clark. *Hubert Ogunde: The Making of Nigerian Theatre*. Oxford University Press, 1979.

Gyekye, Kwame. *Tradition and Modernity*. New York: Oxford University Press, 1997.

Hall, Edward T. *The Silent Language*. Greenwich: Conn. Fawcett Premier Book, 1959.

Hountondji, Paulin J. *African Philosophy: Myth and Reality*, 2nd ed. Bloomington and Indianapolis: Indiana University Press, 1996.

Hutchison, Y. The Seductive Dance Between History and Literature: The Moremi Legend by Historian Samuel Johnson and Playwrights Duro Ladipo and Femi Osofisan. *South African Theatre Journal* 13, no. 1 (1999): 31–47.

Lawler, Edward J., and Shane R. Thye. "Bringing Emotions into Social Exchange Theory." *Annual Review of Sociology* 25 (1999): 217–44.

Lévy-Bruhl, Lucien. *Primitive Mentality* [La mentalité primitive]. NY: AMS Press, [1922] 1978.

———. "How Natives Think." In *African Philosophy: Selected Readings*, edited by Albert Mosley. New York: Prentice Hall, 1995.

Lovejoy, Paul E., and David Richardson. "The Business of Slaving: Pawnship in Western Africa," c. 1600–1810. *Journal of African History* 42 (2001): 67–89.

Lovejoy, Paul E., and Toyin Falola eds. *Pawnship, Slavery and Colonialism in Africa*. Africa World Press, 2003.

Masolo, D.A. "An Archaeology of African Knowledge: A Discussion of V.Y. Mudimble." *Callaloo* 14, no. 4 (1991): 998–1011.

Mauss, Marcel. *The Gift: Forms and Functions of Exchange in Archaic Societies*. London: Cohen and West, 1925 [1954].

Mazrui, Ali. *The Africans: A Triple Heritage*. Boston: Little Brown & Co., 1986.

Murdock, George. P. *Social Structure*. New York: MacMillan, 1949.

Opefeyitimi, Ayo. "Iwure: Medium of Communicating the Desires of Men to the Gods in Yoruba Land." *Journal of Religion in Africa* 18, no. 17 (1988): 27–41.

Oyetade, Akintunde. "The Yoruba Community in London." *African Languages and Cultures* 6, no. 1 (1993): 69–92.

Sahlins, Marshall. "Poor Man, Rich Man, Chief: Political Types in Melanesia and Polynesia." *Comparative Studies in Society and History* 5, no. 3 (1963): 285–303.

Schieffelin, Bambi B. "Introducing Kaluli Literacy." In *Regimes of Value*, edited by Paul Kroskrity, 93–327. Santa Fe, NM: School of American Research, 2000.

Wiredu, Kwasi. *Philosophy and an African Culture*. Cambridge: Cambridge University Press, 1980.

CHAPTER 20

Youth and Popular Culture in Colonial Africa

Jamaine M. Abidogun

Youth hold the future for every society. But what informs this future? What do youth see as the trends, issues, and cultural contexts that matter, shape, and form their present and our future? In traditional history, we may look to the major events and standard cultural expectations of the time to find these answers. Yet, in the past 30 years, many historians have moved away from this traditional analysis to embrace new historiographies that share interpretations from other social sciences and humanities. Africa's colonial history is no exception, with newer historiographies assisting in the telling of colonial youth's popular culture. Africa's colonial youth encompasses a daunting range of societies and varied historical contexts. Defining popular culture requires identifying what youth perceived as influential. These influences are described and analyzed from a range of disciplines, including but not limited to cultural studies, anthropology, art, education, and media. Popular culture then and now reflects the changing modes of culture and society, resulting in individual and ultimately institutional changes. This chapter provides some evidence of colonial youth's experiences and their perspectives on changing times.

Identifying colonial youth is the first challenge. What constituted 'youth' in African societies? How did African social constructs intersect or disconnect with European constructs to define colonial youth? Historian Thomas Burgess commented on the problem of how to define African youth:

J.M. Abidogun (✉)
History Department, Missouri State University,
Springfield, MO, USA

© The Author(s) 2018
M.S. Shanguhyia and T. Falola (eds.),
The Palgrave Handbook of African Colonial and Postcolonial History,
https://doi.org/10.1057/978-1-137-59426-6_20

Often invisible to censuses and maps, youth consists of a constantly shifting population moving in and out of locally determined notions of youthfulness. Nor has *generation* in Africa been codified; the absence of any canonized script or normative theoretical guidelines to which scholars may refer has, until now, discouraged both research and debate, particularly among historians.[1]

In the process of defining African youth within African societies and the colonial context, a Pan-African framework was applied to this chapter to track African social structures during the colonial period and to also consider the impact and interaction of Westernized colonial constructs within African youth cultures. It is important when considering the extent of colonial influences to keep in mind that most African colonial youth experienced little to no direct contact with European colonials. Their interaction was most often indirect via the resulting institutional changes. For example, changes due to colonial administration and colonial education more often impacted how these societies defined youth and influences on popular culture. African societies, to provide a very generalized anthropological or sociological construct, often ascribed age grades or age sets that labeled each group, male and female, from birth to adulthood. Age grades remain common reference points today even though the paths that individuals may now follow include many more options in comparison to precolonial or colonial periods. The age grade marked each member within a specific historical period based on their birth era and simultaneously provided a support group that followed the individual from birth to death within the wider society. Prior to colonization, youth were those who were not yet initiated into adulthood. Most societies had initiation rites or transitional time periods for females and males that ushered them into adulthood. These rites or periods might be marked by ceremony and/or physical indicators and involved periods of instruction on the responsibilities of adulthood, marriage, and wider responsibilities to the society. These systems, with all their variations across African civilizations, ensured a division between youth and adult. Bernardo Bernardi's term 'age class systems' indicated these age grade systems also served in part as demarcations of political and labor or class constructions.[2] Often this meant youth's mentoring and training in the societal vocations or responsibilities identified with their specific lineage, gender, and political status. The colonial period introduced European societal structures with new variables that served to complicate who was and was not considered African youth.

Colonial administration complicated these defining markers in at least two ways that cut across all colonial areas with varying degrees of impact. They established and imposed political administrations on top of or in place of African political and state structures. They also imposed formal European education systems that were separate from African social institutions and, as such, effectively separated increasing numbers of youth from indigenous education. Colonial administration created 'heads of households', defined as the oldest male of the household in most cases. Within many African compound systems this meant that unmarried men and women were often labeled as 'dependants', so even if married they might be considered 'dependants' based on lack of individual property. Imposed Western education systems served to lengthen the period one was identified as 'youth', especially as these schools expanded from primary and vocational to secondary and tertiary education over the colonial period. For most of the colonial period, Western education engaged the elite or less than 10% of any colonized population. After the First World War, especially in urban areas and locations with settler communities, youth increasingly were defined by their educational status; that is, those in colonial schools were more readily identified as youth regardless of their age grade, while those who remained within African constructs followed their society's transition process from youth to adult. Thus, colonial administrative organization coupled with the imposition of Western education systems worked to complicate who was considered youth across African societies.

The term 'colonial youth' as applied in this study refers to a cross-section of groups; each group may be cast as youth based solely on African conventional social structures or as historically identified based on colonial identification. It is reasonable to assume that most 'youth' experienced some extent of duality as they shifted back and forth between African-specific and colonial contexts. In reality, many young people often navigated between labels of youth and adult as applied to their day-to-day experiences. These intersections provided evidence of popular culture in transition between and in contrast to Afrocentric and Eurocentric constructs. Their voices ultimately defined popular culture by how they defined themselves, saw their roles, and what trends, issues, and material culture best represented them and their shared experiences.

Presented here are a handful of societies with the goal of extrapolating general trends and differences across the colonial period. By exploring the specifics of each group's popular experience, the chapter provides evidence of how colonial youths viewed their present and impacted Africa's future. Colonial youth groups were selected from a range of colonial contexts to highlight varied experiences based on which African society(ies) and European power(s) engaged as colonized and colonizer across geographical regions. Secondary considerations in selection of youth groups included socio-political and economic dominance of the African society, differences between nominally occupied colonies and European settlements, urban versus rural, and the extent of indigenous versus Western education experience within each group.

Youth groups described in this chapter come from several regions and include many Sub-Saharan African civilizations. Pulling examples from Southern, East, East-Central, and West Africa, it was readily apparent that there were significant differences in experiences based on each society's culture and the extent of interaction with colonial cultures and their social constructs. Southern Africa, cases include the 'Copperbelt Cowboys' of Northern Rhodesia (Zambia), apartheid South African migrant youth and culture formation, and South Africa's Natal Hindu and Muslim Indian youth cultures. East and

East-Central examples come from Tanganyikan and Kenyan youth's use of urban dress and space, and youth differences in urban popular culture based on religion, urban versus rural, and socio-economic contexts. In the West, Gold Coast (Ghana) and colonial Nigerian youth interactions with Western education provided insight into transformations in colonial youth's popular culture that later identified many as part of the national elite. While the examples are predominantly Anglophone, the intersections of multiple African ethno-national groups are significant in looking at these examples. As such, African experience is central. Most ethno-national groups included in this chapter resided within and outside British colonial or settler boundaries; this effectively expanded African influences on youth beyond Anglophone borders. In addition, competing European, Asian, and Middle Eastern influences also informed and further complicated youth perspectives on popular culture.

For the purposes of this chapter, 'colonial' is constructed to include European domination in Africa via political administration of 'effectively occupied' colonies as defined during the Berlin Conference (1884–1885) and European settler areas.[3] The period under consideration covers approximately the 1890s to the 1960s. Each case discussed falls within this colonial timeline. Some settler areas, like Kenya, were clearly colonially administered from Europe as colonial holdings, while Southern Africa settler groups, such as the Afrikaners of Dutch descent and Rhodesian Anglo settlers, remained largely self-governed even while under British political administration. What is common across all cases when looking at colonial youth and popular culture is the imposition of historically European institutions onto or in place of African institutions that positioned them as colonial holdings. For this reason, the political status and extent of colonial presence for each civilization or set of civilizations is described in each case to assess the extent of colonial presence that contributed to the formation of popular culture.

What is popular culture and what aspects of popular culture were considered in this study? While historically the term is first attributed to Johann Gottfried (1784), who simply used it as a marker to delineate the masses or 'popular culture' from 'the culture of the learned',[4] its application in the past thirty years was widely limited to Marxist classist analysis that identified elite control of production as limiting popular culture to mindless consumption to distract the masses from true revolution within a capitalist society. The Weberian view of social status and what Pierre Bourdieu defines as 'cultural capital' are used to distinguish common, 'low' or popular culture from elite or 'high' culture. In the Weberian framework one may belong to one or the other regardless of economic or political class.[5] A Weberian working definition of 'popular culture' provides a broader view that encompasses more than class. In the African colonial context, it more often indicated independence from or appropriation of Western culture. In these cases, colonial youth's expression of popular culture is not solely dependent on class consciousness, although it is likely that youth made connections with these expressions that varied from identification with African political and economic statuses to colonial power alignments or resistance, as well as including fashionable adoption of the foreign as novel.

Bourdieu reinforces the Weberian framework within the colonial construct through what he terms 'cultural capital', defined as cultural aspects that provide access to power and prestige within the dominant society.[6] Youth awareness of Western values as cultural capital is demonstrated as some follow and master Western cultural aspects while others actively resist appropriating colonial European culture. These cultural assets most often included language, religion, Western education, music, and clothing, among other expressive cultural forms. Many youth groups produced and/or endorsed popular culture that rejected all Western cultural forms through exclusive use of indigenous expressive forms. Some others appropriated certain Western aspects and infused them in ways that worked to keep their African culture front and center, while still other youth groups wholeheartedly embraced Western culture as manifested in their popular culture. In comparison, Marxist class analysis proved too narrow a lens for colonial analysis, since it does not take into consideration the imposition of foreign cultural forms or idioms that youth groups engaged in across a continuum that ranged from fully independent of Western influence to complete appropriation of Western culture in the production and promotion of popular culture. For these reasons, the Weberian model provides effective parameters for describing popular culture across Africa's colonial youth.

Neo-colonial, Pan-African, and critical theories frame and inform this chapter. Neo-colonial theory offers a way to historically situate the research. While neo-colonial most often references the postcolonial period, it is important to realize that the process of neo- or internal colonialism begins during the colonial period. Especially as applied to changing youth culture, understanding the imposition of Western administration, education, aesthetic styles, and media allows for a starting point that underlines the forced historical nature of changes in their worldview. Through this framework, the nature of internalization of Western concepts as they replaced indigenous forms of knowing and doing helps identify how youth were impacted to a greater or lesser extent based on the degree of their direct involvement with these institutions. In this way, neo-colonial theory takes into consideration how historically many African youths shifted between Afrocentric and Eurocentric perspectives in their expressions of popular culture.

Pan-African theory positions the historical experience through the eyes of African youth and their cultural perspectives.[7] It supports evaluation based on African ethno-national cultural norms and indigenous knowledge and philosophies, making it possible to track cultural change. As an African counterpoint to Western or European historiographies, it challenges the writer to maintain an African-centered narrative as it seeks to reclaim African youth history by setting it in African contexts and from there describing cultural transformations demonstrated via popular culture. Critical theory works with Pan-African perspectives by emphasizing the necessity to center the subject, colonial youth, as the research focus. This ensures their voices validate the research conclusions. Critical theory assists in identification of Western constructs that the colonized African elite often promoted as status symbols. This critical analysis may be applied directly to Bourdieu's concept of cultural capital. For example, youth's gravitation to Western material forms reflected the development of individualist philosophies that culturally demonstrated their position as caught between African and Western cultures. Critical theory then calls for positioning Africans as agents in their negotiation of what they maintain from their cultures versus what they adopt, reject, or transform from European and other colonial cultures.[8] The following examples of colonial youth and popular culture described within this framework create a picture of cultural transformation as African-centered as each society adopted, rejected, and transformed Western cultural aspects within a continual push-pull interaction that ultimately informed their cultural expressions.

SOUTHERN AFRICA

Southern Africa youth experienced European invasion and advancement as early as 1510 when Francis de Almeida, Viceroy of Portuguese Indies, landed at Table Bay to collect fresh water. While docked there, some of his crew attempted to kidnap two Khoi children and cattle. The Khoikhoi successfully drove the sailors back to their ships, but this only delayed European invasion. First Portuguese then increasingly Dutch and British ships landed at Cape of Good Hope or Table Bay to restock water and meat. Finally, in December 1651, Jan van Riebeeck, an agent for the Dutch East India Company of the Netherlands, established a permanent outpost at the Cape of Good Hope. From that moment forward European advancement into the area dramatically altered the course of African history.[9] By the 1800s most of this area, including South Africa and North and South Rhodesia were European- or European descendent-controlled. Although Europeans were never and are still not the majority, they used European military and economic supports to dominate the region. The examples of colonial youth popular culture reflect both African based experiences and immigrant based experiences within Dutch and British European dominated colonial states. Southern stories of colonial youth popular culture describe at once the triangulation of African civilizations' negotiation of European political and economic domination and long-term cultural interactions and impositions. The final example layers these experiences further with experiences from immigrant Indian cultures and how missionary encounters influenced South African popular culture. The 'Copperbelt Cowboys' of Northern Rhodesia (Zambia) reviews Western cinema's influence on youth culture in the 1940s and 1950s under British colonial rule. The second example highlights cultural, anthropological studies during the 1950s to the end of Apartheid South Africa to examine how popular youth culture was defined and delineated. This piece takes a deconstructive perspective moving these studies by centering their analysis on African experience rather than a Euro- or Western-based colonial analysis. The final Southern Africa example describes Natal Hindu and Muslim Indian youth cultures from the late 1800s to the 1930s through the lens of Indian migration to South Africa and Hindu youth's experience with Muslim missionaries. While all three studies are placed within the context of British-controlled Southern Africa, their experiences vary greatly as each youth group's ethno-national and specific historical positions delineate their unique popular culture.

Northern Rhodesia (Zambia) set in the 1940s and 1950s was nominally under British colonial rule with a significant white colonial settler population in control of administration, education, and labor. Historian Charles Ambler describes the Northern Rhodesian 'Copperbelt Cowboys' colonial context as 'linked with Southern Rhodesia (Zimbabwe) and Nyasaland (Malawi) in a Central African Federation dominated by white settler interests'.[10] Africans were viewed as a colonized labor source and were coerced through colonial taxation and other means to work in British-controlled copper mines. Labor compounds and townships were established to support the mining industry. In the larger townships, local open-air cinemas or 'bioscopes' sprang up beginning in the 1930s and expanded throughout this period. Bioscopes brought in Hollywood films that included westerns, gangster, or private-eye genres, and the occasional Superman film. Under the British and white Rhodesian control, these films were censored, primarily on race-based lines geared to omit sexualized images of white women and to prohibit scenes of organized resistance, such as the oppressed (that is Native American, African, Indian) challenging European or white authority. Rhodesian film venues were segregated spaces throughout the 1960s with white authorities or their colonial African appointees to oversee the African-attended bioscopes. Northern Rhodesian African youth were regularly exposed to disconnected images of cowboys with their gunfights, train robberies, and banditry as well as slick gangsters making wisecracks against local police and political organizations. As Ambler documents, 'it was the working-class male youth with relatively little education who made up the core of film audiences'.[11] While Ambler's only documentation of their African civilization is that they were for the most part Chibemba speakers, he does describe the impact of these Western expressions of popular culture.[12] For these youth, even the most disjointed of storylines due to censorship could not negate the image of men standing up against men.

These youths' adoption of Western aesthetic style demonstrated the impact of Western cinema, while their specific adoption of 'wild west' and 'gangster' themes from these films served as symbolic protest against colonial subjugation. As demonstrated through their popularization of 'posturing' or as a concerned white Rhodesian reported to the Rhodesian Department of Information, 'the idea that to stand and speak to anyone with hands in pockets, lounging, and possibly giving the hat—firmly on the head—an insolent backward tilt is to show a high degree of sophistication'.[13] Youth continued to popularize these cowboy and gangster images through dress, posture, and an internalization of their demonstrated bravado against unfair and seemingly lawless situations that were reflected in these youths' lived realities. Youth, who popularized Western and gangster dress and took on names like 'Jeke' or Jack to represent cowboys or even 'Popeye' to reflect the power and agency of the spinach-eating cartoon sailor, created popular culture that informed their understanding that these movie features embodied both modernity and fashion, but also the call for agency and empowerment in the face of colonial and racial oppression. This popularization of struggle by youth in art and media was replicated throughout Southern Africa.

In another example, anthropologist Heike Becker examined how anthropologists studied popular culture in Southern Africa from the 1950s to the end of apartheid. Becker applied Johannes Fabian's definition of popular culture, a variation on the Weberian definition, as 'contemporary cultural expressions carried by the masses in contrast to both modern elitist and traditional "tribal" culture'.[14] Its archaic minimalist and static idiom of 'traditional "tribal" culture' as opposed to 'social culture' that reflects active and agent-bearing African social cultures draws attention to the often unrecognized and unstudied aspects of the African society(ies) within the colonial context. The previous example demonstrates the danger in this as its author never offered any Chibemba-specific societal structures to contextualize the youth's home culture(s). Becker's analysis compares cultural anthropology and cultural studies as applying seemingly parallel yet divergent roles to popular culture studies. He posits two primary reasons for these societal structures and notes cultural studies' frequent omission of active participants reflected in studies from the 1970s to the 1990s. First, he identifies a focus on neo-Marxist analysis which emphasized the political economy over and above local interpretation or action along with a shift in methodology that distanced the scholar from the field as cultural studies became an academic discipline. The distancing of these new experts, many trained in literary critique, resulted in a focus on analysis and evaluation of social texts presented in various mediums and less on deep or field participant-observer ethnographic methods.[15] Becker sought to correct these participant omissions through a deconstructive perspective that required a shift from primarily Euro-South African focus to an African South African focus to present African colonial youth's home culture as the center of their colonial experience in defining popular culture.

One such African-centered anthropologist and ethnomusicologist was David B. Coplan, who described his work in music and theater as 'Weighed against *apartheid* ... [as] both a record of and a small contribution to the efforts of black South Africans to gain control of their national culture and to use it to regain control of their individual and national lives'.[16] Coplan's study on Lesotho migrant workers' songs in South Africa includes Basotho youth's role in how this 'process of transformation from peasant agro-pastoralism to rural/industrial migrant worker has been accompanied by a dynamic enrichment of existing genres of performance'.[17] The specific oral poetic genre he explored was 'migrant mineworkers' and women's sung poetry, known generically as *difela* (*sefela* singular) *tsa ditsamaya-naha*, "songs of the inveterate travellers".[18] These poetic songs reflect generational changes dating from the 1860s when the first diamond mines at Kimberly were opened to present day Basotho migrant laborers' experiences that stretch across South Africa. These groups were primarily young men and some young women, the majority were unmarried, unlanded, and without cattle, so historically they were viewed as dependants or youth in their natal homes. Wealth of some sort, such as cattle, land, money, is a social expectation for Basotho males to enter full adulthood. Prior to European settlement, cattle were the measure of that wealth. British and Afrikaner colonial presence forced the introduction of a cash economy and politically required the Lesotho kingdom to negotiate with the British to retain its sovereignty. As part of these negotiations the British left Lesotho to administer itself if Lesotho's young men came regularly to work the mines. Some young women also came as cooks, maids, and prostitutes.[19] Their poetic songs documented their changing circumstances and what they held valuable as part of their popular culture.

As these first migrant laborers walked the 200 miles to Kimberly they created *difela tsa ditsamaya-naha* to distract them from the rough conditions. Their words reflected the need to earn cash for cattle to offer as brideprice to enter marriage (manhood), as Lethetsa Malimatle's poem sings in part:

> They want cattle for your brideprice.
> I left home at night ...
> 'Go and drive them at the mines yonder.'[20]

Other poetic verses reflect youths' conversion of Lesotho manhood rites from battle with invaders of Lesotho to battles with the mine bosses or 'cannibals of war' and with the mines or 'the earth' themselves.

> They answered mercifully, the cannibals of war:
> 'This day is your last.'
> I heard, remembering evil times, ...
> It was right out in the unknown wilderness.[21]

Over time, as the train replaced foot and horse, it too became part of these young migrant workers' popularized experience, as in this excerpt by Ngoana Mokhalo:

> The train is a taker and a returner,
> Ours, that of the young men,

> It came running from Rouxville, the white-faced carriage ...
> It galloped like a white-spotted hare.[22]

Coplan explained that Basotho male youth, like the poet above from Mamokhesuoe's village, 'sing of love affairs and faithlessness, not marriage; doubt and danger, not certainty; wage labour, not agriculture; trains and trails, not home and family'.[23] For female youth in the mine compounds or nearby townships, they were often referred to as *matekatse* (literally translated as 'to wander about to odd jobs'). Often viewed as prostitutes by the larger society, these young women in practice were single, working girls who were not married, and as such were not viewed as equal to adult women. Their *sefela* reflected a gendered style. Coplan described its difference from male *difela*: 'women's difela are organised both rhythmically and tonally by the instrumental accompaniment of accordion and drum, and female performers universally decline to sing without such accompaniment'.[24] Many considered these performers of lower social status and some did not equate them to male *difela*. Still their songs, like Nthabiseng Nthako's, a female *sefela* performer, reframed Basotho life to reflect migrant female youths' realities:

> I am a polygamist [I have many men] ...
> I look at them; they look away, yonder ....
> Here they are at Hlotse camp, girls,
> In whose trust do I leave them? ... pray for me.[25]

For South African youth, whether from Lesotho or other Southern African locations, their migrant experiences disconnected and reconnected them to their home lives in new forms and fashions. For male youth, this involved the reimagining of battle as part of male initiation and as cash economy as currency for family life. For female youth, their experience at once reflected new forms of freedom and old forms of potential social retribution on their return home. Basotho migrant youth effectively articulated the colonial experience of exploited labor through their reinvention of Lesotho oral traditions as part of their popular culture.

The final South African example located in Natal colony during the late 1800s highlights immigrant indentured Indians from Calcutta and Madras. Like the Basotho youth, immigrant Indian colonial youth were mostly male and were laborers for British and Euro-settler-controlled ports, fields, and mines. Their experiences were complicated by competing Christian, Hindu, and Muslim missionaries who vied for their conversion.[26] Historian Nile Green's documentation of Natal missionaries included the establishment of Christian missions as early as 1867, and more importantly described the competition of Hindu and Muslim missions which sought to convert Natal's poor young Indian immigrants.[27] One Muslim mission, due to its charismatic leader Ghulam Muhammad, stands out as a cultural shaper of Indian youth culture. While Hindu and Muslim missions were slower to establish themselves in Natal, by the end of the 1800s their presence was a vital part of Natal's religious community. As with many missionary societies, Ghulam Muhammad 'Sufi Sahib' used local language and access to education to entice its followers. For Natal Indians Urdu quickly became the language of Muslim instruction; this served to build bridges across castes, whose divisions certainly worked as a barrier to growing the mission.[28] The adoption of Urdu impacted youth both as a source of religious instruction, but also to build a common community. While Ghulam Muhammad utilized his Arab lineage traced from the Konkani Muslim community on the west coast of India to establish his religious credentials, his origins also provided him support from middle-class Indian merchants who regularly traded at Natal's ports with many Konkani labor and merchant classes also immigrating to Natal. His mission, initially established at Umgeni in Natal's Riverside area, included a mosque, khanaqah, and madrasa, reflecting the Indian diaspora in Southern Africa.

Through the mission's identification markers, which included Urdu as a common language to fashionable Muslim Indian dress, Natal's Indian Muslim youth quickly developed a recognizable popular culture. A popular culture that defined the modern Islam world, as Mahatma Gandhi, himself a recent immigrant to Natal, recorded in the *Indian Opinion* newspaper: '"The progress of Mahomedans" which among its list of ten proposals recommended the same blend of education, independent labour and physical health that also underwrote the ethics of the intellectuals' farmstead at [Gandhi's] Phoenix [Settlement]'.[29] Through the establishments of orphanages and madrasa or schools, Ghulam Muhammad effectively institutionalized generational change for hundreds of Indian Muslim youths as they were provided access to religious and secular instruction and protection from falling through the cracks in South Africa's labor class. Their popular culture reflected these protective strategies as they adopted Bombay clothing styles designed to signify their status as proper Muslims and were provided instruction that cautioned against the use of ganja as an escape from the trials of labor. His mission attracted Hindu and Muslim youths as he incorporated older Indian traditions including the maintenance of *urs* or celebrations of the shrines of blessed or holy men and the celebration of *Muharram* processions in honor of the martyred Husayn. Ghulam Muhammad expanded his brand of modern Muslim Indian culture across South Africa that reflected a unification of South Africa's Indian youth culture.

A clear pattern of marginalizing African culture in Southern African colonial history via youth experience runs through the above described examples. The wide extent and long length of European settlement and the significant immigration of Indian and Arab societies that systematically worked toward the economic and social domination of African cultures is clearly apparent. The cases of Central and West Africa, with comparatively shorter colonial histories, better demonstrated African societies' influence on their colonial youth.

East and East-Central Africa

For the East and East-Central Africa, examples come from colonial policing of Kenyan youth via corporal punishment and the ways that the popular press vied for influence on Kenyan and Tanganyikan youth to shape their religious and social contexts. Paul Ocobock's extensive work on colonial administration's role in policing Kenyan youth provides a broad look at colonial influence on youth as well as specific cases that give insight into youth images of how they defined their roles in colonial society. Kenyan and Tanganyikan youth colonial culture and its shaping are documented via the use of the popular press. Nathaniel Mathews's study described the use of Kenyan Swahili-Arab Muslim newspapers as a venue of modern Islamic reform for youth like that of Natal's Indian youth experience. Maria Suriano's review of a popular monthly press provided details of youth's popular culture expressed through fashion.

As colonial administration of urban space developed, questions about youths and their roles presented themselves. In Kenya's context, colonial administration viewed youth as potential labor and idle youth as a threat to colonial and urban peace. Ocobock's work examined corporal punishment's role as a common demarcation of the generational divide between adults and youth. The colonial experience complicated these experiences for youth as he explained: 'The right to beat a boy, once the exclusive right of African parents and elder kin, increasingly included [colonial] missionaries, schoolteachers, employers, chiefs, and the colonial state. Each of these disciplinarians considered physical violence an appropriate form of punishment for young males'.[30] While his work focused on Kenya, this colonial redistribution of the right to corporal punishment's use to control youth was evident across colonial holdings, as witnessed in schools, churches, and other social contexts. For example, in colonial Nigeria, Toyin Falola recounts his early school experiences, 'Late arrival was punished. 'Kneel down on that hard surface,' ... Even the senior students carried a cane',[31] demonstrating how colonial use of corporal punishment became internalized by African youth. The response of youth formed their popular culture as they negotiated what they viewed as legitimate. As Falola continued, 'The other students were not impressed, and no one vowed to use the humiliation of the latecomers as a valuable lesson'.[32] Like Nigerian youth, Kenyan youth also negotiated its response to colonial authority with some groups adopting its use to identify themselves with power while others actively resisted acknowledging this authority.

In Babcock's case of juvenile vagrants and their dealings with colonial authority, youth popular culture's agency is demonstrated as it negotiated with colonial authority. As early as 1901 in Nairobi, Sub-Commissioner

J.D. Ainsworth arrested twenty male youths for vagrancy and established this practice as policy in 1902 as the Vagrancy Act to continue through to the 1950s. This act along with others was a way to control rural to urban migration and labor supplies for settler farms. Kikuyu male youths were impacted by increased white settlement that took away from their family-based agriculture and left many to look to urban areas for lucrative opportunities. While white settlers vied for their labor, most Kikuyu youths were not inclined to work the fields they saw as rightfully theirs for the profit of these white settlers. Yet these same youths still needed to prepare for their initiation into adulthood that included demonstrating their ability to provide a stable home suitable for marriage and to raise their family. In this way, they found themselves in the city looking for business or employment opportunities.[33] Youths sought to define their life conditions as they swelled the streets of Nairobi.

Looking for autonomy and opportunity, Kikuyu and Kamba male youth, and to a lesser extent female youth, trekked to Nairobi in increasing numbers. They sought Western education in a bid for government jobs or to hire themselves as house helps for the colonial and Kenyan elite; in these pursuits they effectively broadened their choices beyond rural labor. In response, the colonial administration sought to control rural and urban labor by using vagrancy laws that imposed corporal punishment and relocation to rural areas to deter youth from venturing to the city. Although most of these youths set out of their own volition to Nairobi, Kenyan colonial law did not recognize their independence. Obocock documented colonial understanding as, 'the Indian Penal Code, Section 361, boys under the age of fourteen and girls under the age of sixteen enticed away from their families and homes without the consent of their parents and guardians were considered kidnapped'.[34] Vagrancy laws supported this assumption in law as they routinely repatriated Kikuyu and Kamba youth without family ties in Nairobi back to their natal rural villages. By the 1920s. caning and repatriation were routinely enforced for returning vagrant youth. This was in response to what colonial officials viewed as youths' increased ties to organized crime. The combined punishment was an effort to deter youths from continued reentry to the urban area and to reduce crime. Youths' response was consistent from 1902 through to the beginning of the Depression in the 1930s where a slight decrease was noted, but then it steadily rose again from the 1940s forward. They routinely returned to the city despite the calculated risks of short-term imprisonment, caning, and repatriation. Ocobock noted this combined punishment for recidivism increased from approximately 125 cases in 1925 to well over 600 by 1951.[35] Kikuyu's popular youth culture reflected a trend toward urbanization in direct response to the loss of family land. For Kikuyu, this youth culture established a major urbanization trend that is reflected in Kikuyu's dominant numbers in Nairobi society today.[36]

From East African urban centers like Mombasa in Kenya and Dar es Salam in Tanganyika, colonial youth cultural trends developed across East Africa as competing interests weighed into shape them. From popular Muslim reform movements to urban fashions, the press became a vehicle to shape and to reflect youth's popular culture. The Swahili press was a perfect medium for Muslim and Western-educated urban populations to explore new ideas expressed as cultural trends. Mombasa's *al-Islah* (Reform) Swahili Arab newspaper and Tanganyika's *Mambo Leo* (Current Events), a monthly government Swahili magazine, were two examples of media influence on Eastern Africa colonial youth culture.

Similar to Indian youths' experiences in Southern Africa, East Africa's Muslim leaders actively reached out to youth to reinforce Muslim Arabic cultural and religious identities as they faced increasing competition from colonial Christian missions and Western education. One example, reviewed by historian Nathaniel Mathews, was Sheikh al-Amin Mazrui's *al-Islah* newspaper established in 1932, printed in Swahili and Arabic.[37] Its goal was to advocate for cultural and religious change to strengthen the modern image of Muslim identity among East Africans. Since young males were the most likely to attend schools, they made up a significant proportion of *al-Islah*'s readership. The colonial administration supported Muslim and Christian schools and mandated teaching Swahili and English literacy in the schools, so they indirectly contributed to the paper's readership. *Al-Islah*'s articles focused on the return to *shari'a* not just as a legal system, but to include its social aspects.

It was these social aspects that were most likely to catch the imaginations of young people; for example, the popular trend to reinforce Arab origins as a demarcation of social and economic elite status. *Al-Islah* highlighted these Arab Islamic knowledge systems and commercial or economic prominence within the Indian Ocean trade networks that developed over several centuries prior to British colonialism into a uniquely Swahili-Arab culture along the East African coast.[38] Swahili Muslim male youth were most inspired by this rhetoric to refashion their ancestry to match their newfound access to colonial education. This refashioning worked to improve their social status that often translated into economic connections in and outside of Mombasa.

Sheikh al-Amin encouraged these youths to practice their Arabic as a sign of Muslim knowledge by regularly providing Arabic texts in *al-Islah*. In this way, a new generation of up and coming Swahili Arab youth elite could readily demonstrate their reimagined transnational identities.[39] This education via the popular press also served to reinforce Arab-Swahili identities at a time when the British administration had systematically reduced them to 'natives' under British native court structures even as they maintained their status as 'non-natives' for taxation purposes. As Mathews noted, many readers signed their contributions as '"*Mzalia wa Africa*" (native of Africa) or "*Mzalia wa Unguja*" (native of Zanzibar)'.[40] This new generation of Arab-Swahili educated youth transformed into an adult elite who simultaneously claimed African and Arab origins as the true East African leaders despite colonial dictates.

Al-Islah's articles influenced its youthful readers to reinvent and reestablish a transnational Arab-Swahili identity through their popular culture.

In the case of *Mambo Leo*, its pages reached beyond the East Coast to influence East and East-Central African youth. This Swahili language monthly magazine was published under the auspices of the British Tanganyika Department of Social Development. Historian Maria Suriano described its purpose as:

> an educational monthly magazine that began in January 1923 ... to describe British Government efforts: for instance ... Despite its pro-Government orientation, readers throughout the country made use of *Mambo Leo* to voice their complaints and express their opinions on various issues. ... It became a sort of 'forum' of discussion on cultural and social matters ... about the wider Tanganyikan society.[41]

Colonial administrators and Tanganyikan elders alike commented routinely on what youth should aspire to as well as what they observed as the realities of youth culture. Comments ranged from observations about appropriation of Western dress to identify as 'cultured' to concerns about the increase in beer and dance hall goers. For example, a *Mambo Leo* reader, Rashidi Ali Meli, criticized the fad of male youth wearing glasses, even if not needed for sight, as part of Western attire as, 'nowadays I see many youths who love wearing glasses ... for the price of twenty cents without any reason, and if you ask them what does this mean, they would reply that [they] are part of the 'Culture'. But, fellows, is this Culture or ruin? And what is the sense of the word Culture?'.[42] Ali Meli tied these fake glasses to youth adoption of Western slacks, shirt, and tie as a further corruption of Swahili *utamaduni* (culture) and as such identified it as *upotevu* (immoral life, vandalism).

In a similar vein, a concerned reader commented in poetry on female youth dress and connected it to youth participation at beer and dance halls, Chande Ally wrote:

> *Kinamama kwa yakini, Fedhea mwaithamini,*
> *Mwaingia dansini, Kigauni mapajani,*
> *Mtindi Beer kichwani, Mwajiona mpeponi,*
> *Dansi ni ngoma duni, Wajuao kufikiri.*
> For women [dansi] is surely, a valued shame,
> You enter the dancehall, showing-off thigh,
> With alcohol and beer in your head, you feel in paradise,
> Dansi is a worthless music, for those who can think.[43]

The *dansi* style of Western knee-length dresses was equated with the beer and dance halls that youth frequented. Interestingly, Suriano notes that women, especially Muslim women, often shifted between Swahili and Western dress to fit the occasion. A Mrs. R.M. Ngoda 'affirmed in 1950 in a poem against "*nguo gotini* knee-length dresses ... *ni wakati wajioni, zageuza mtu sura* it is nighttime that changes a person's appearance"'.[44] As youth males and females adopted Western dress as part of their popular culture, they also adopted new forms of popular entertainment in beer parlors, dance halls, and cinema. By the 1950s, just like the Rhodesian 'Copperbelt Cowboys' of Southern Africa, some Swahili youth adopted the cinema cowboy dress and style, as the '*uchinjo* or bottle-mouth trousers and the *kilipa* [heavy shoe]' that Suriano noted were accompanied with cowboy-style speech, slouch, and walk. While she disagreed with John Leslie's interpretation of this dress and style as "the revolt of the adolescent, in age and in culture, against the authority of the elders, of the established, of the superior and supercilious' and as 'the safety-valve of the dangerous mob element',[45] the influence of Western cinema clearly shaped youth fashion in their expression of popular culture that transcended African ethnic and colonial boundaries.

Most of youths' Westernized expressions of popular culture were not looked on favorably by older generations. Suriano summarized through cross-validation of mission papers and Swahili readers' contributions to *Mambo Leo* that these elder authorities 'agreed in condemning beer halls and vilabu (African clubs) where people, especially youths, "wasted" time drinking pombe (local beer), while dressed in "indecent" ways"'.[46]

East African colonial youth developed unique and often dual expressions of popular culture that reflected new colonial identities, while refashioning older identities. Whether in negotiating the colonial administration's attempts at controlling their labor or in refashioning older identities of Arab origin, youths demonstrated a tenacity to transform often competing influences into unique expressions of popular culture. In their experiences, the trends of colonial influence are documented. At the same time, they transformed these Western and older Eastern influences to meet their specific cultural contexts.

West Africa

In West Africa, examples of Gold Coast (Ghana) and colonial Nigerian youth interaction with Western education as a vehicle for identity change reimaged youth popular culture. Trade schools and European mission schools in West Africa often worked as business partners and were clearly established by the nineteenth century across Anglophone African colonies. Nkrumah noted that the first successful mission school in Gold Coast was established by the Basel Missionary Society in 1828 outside Accra and in Nigeria; the United Presbyterian Synod of Scotland established a school by 1846 at the Old Calabar River off the Gulf of Benin (present-day Calabar, Nigeria).[47] Interestingly, Eastern schools like Kenya's mission schools were established somewhat later, as George Urch explained: '... it was not until the last quarter of the century that mission work began in earnest. The Berlin Treaty of 1885 provided both freedom to operate and some degree of protection; missionaries soon set up stations in the interior of East Africa'.[48] These Euro-Christian missions effectively established Western education structures that eventually developed into the current national education systems. Mission schools provided the bulk of Western education as late as the 1950s. Edward Berman documented Nigerian and Gold Coast/Ghana mission schools as, 'In 1942, 97% of Nigeria's student population was enrolled in missionary schools ... As recently as 1950, missionary schools accounted for 97% of the total enrollment in Ghanaian schools'.[49] In comparison, Berman described an early appropriation of mission education by the Kikuyu in the Kenyan experience, as he explained:

> In Kenya during the 1920s and 1930s the schools were run almost exclusively by missionaries. The reaction to the demand by the Church of Scotland (CSM) missionaries that all Kikuyu church elders renounce the practice of female circumcision ... [was] Independent schools controlled by the Kikuyu were organized. In 1933 there were 34 schools enrolling 2,518 students; by 1936 these figures had increased to some 50 schools with 5,111 students.[50]

The Kikuyu were unique in their establishment of 'independent' schools to retain the right to ethno-national cultural practices. This shift in control underscored the Africanization of Christianity for youth within these schools. As Berman noted, 'Kikuyu church elders' led the change to Kikuyu-controlled schools, but did not question Christian doctrine. Rather, they made a distinction between Christianity and retention of ethno-national cultural practices.

Effectively, the Christianized curriculum kept the majority of African Muslim ethno-national groups, whether in Ghana, Nigeria, or Kenya, marginalized within the colonial Western education system.[51] The British policy of Indirect Rule sought control over capital in the form of land, labor, and natural resources and claimed minimal interest in forcing religious or cultural change. Education served the Colonial Office's purpose of training colonial labor. It was a marriage of convenience that Christian missions were willing and able to provide this needed education. These missions were a cost saver for the colonial administration; so long as Africans were trained for the colonial labor market, inclusion of Christian coursework was incidental at worst and advantageous at best to assist in assimilating Africans to Western norms.

As the colonial presence grew the Christian missions and the few colonial trade schools could not keep up with the labor needs of the British Colonial Office. Over time, the mission schools were often at odds with the Colonial Office regarding the ideal curriculum (religion-focused versus workforce preparation). In the face of increased business and government offices within the colonies, there was an increased need for English literate white-collar workers. After the First World War, the British Colonial Office took a more direct interest in Anglophone African education policy. This took the form in 1925 of the Advisory Committee on Native Education in the British Tropical

African Dependencies (Advisory Committee). The Advisory Committee's official report back to the Colonial Office resulted in part in the following official policy:

1. The British government reserved the right to direct educational policy and to supervise all educational institutions.
2. Voluntary missionary efforts in the field of education were to be welcomed and encouraged with a program of grants-in-aid.
3. Technical and vocational training should be carried out with the help of government departments.
4. Education should be adapted to local conditions in such a manner as would enable it to conserve all sound elements in local tradition and social organization, while functioning as an instrument of progress and evolution.
5. Religious training and moral instruction should be regarded as fundamental to the development of a sound education.[52]

The policy maintained 'missionary efforts in the field of education' and 'religious training and moral instruction as fundamental' that in turn ensured generations of youth culture that centered itself in Christianity. At the same time, it provided guidelines on including '"sound" elements in local tradition and social organization, while functioning as an instrument of progress and evolution'. This policy point had mixed responses as mission and colonial schools alike were divided on the idea of maintaining African social norms and practices.

They all agreed on the inclusion of a curriculum that 'function[ed] as an instrument of progress and evolution' as this was the 'civilizing mission' writ large in the curriculum. This policy did result in two changes: (a) the addition of African geography and/or history to social studies curriculums; and (b) the establishment of English as the language of education. These provisions created a duality within youth popular culture. This new social studies curriculum downplayed the depth and complexity of their historical, political, and economic heritages and instead focused on African music and the arts to create social cohesion. Sociologist Cati Coe described this cultural display of the African curriculum at Achimota school in Gold Coast:

> Drumming and dancing were the strongest part of its teaching of 'African culture', ... relegated to an extracurricular, albeit compulsory, activity. Most of the senior teachers in the school were European, with little ... knowledge of Gold Coast culture; outside experts had to be brought into teach 'African culture' ... [with more of] a focus on students' appreciation of 'African culture' than on actual competence or knowledge, both in the founding philosophy and the curriculum: the students were expected to respect the traditions of a reified 'ancient' past, but not necessarily participate fully in that realm as competent adults. Ultimately, to incorporate 'African culture' into an anglicized elite

school, the founders and teachers of Achimota had to define 'culture' quite narrowly.[53]

In this manner, youths who were physically separated from access to indigenous education via Western boarding schools began to express their 'African' culture as elements of popular culture in retention of drums in high life music or shifting between Western and African dress with Western dress identified with the 'educated' class.

Regarding language policies, prior to 1925, many Christian mission schools used indigenous languages ('vernaculars') as the language of instruction, especially in learning scripture to help converts better relate to them and therefore more readily embrace Christianity. After 1925 in Gold Coast and Nigeria, African languages of instruction were completely replaced with English. To maintain their effort to enforce 'native education', African language instruction was maintained, but as secondary languages that was dependent on each local area identification of the dominant mother tongues. Interestingly, the emphasis on teaching African language was more prominent in the development of secondary schools, as Michael Omolewa noted: 'October 1922, London University adopted Hausa and Yoruba as "optional special languages" for its university entrance qualifying examinations … the London University Faculty Senate approved the recommendation of the senate-appointed "Board of Studies in Oriental Languages and Literature" that these two languages be adopted as suitable examination subjects'.[54] Such a language policy reinforced the cultural role assigned to African languages while maintaining adherence to English as the language of instruction. Many Western-educated youths defaulted to internalizing Western identities expressed in popular culture to align with their colonial overlords. Others shined in this colonial era and overcame the reductionist view of African language and culture in their work to become Pan-African leaders.

These important curricular changes taught students that their ethnonational knowledge, cultures, and languages were to be marginalized and replaced by Western knowledge, culture, and language. The schools' informal curricula reinforced this formal curriculum as students were indoctrinated in proper Euro-Christian norms and practices; that is. appropriate dress, food and table etiquette, courting, Western medicine, vocational skills, recognition of British and Christian holidays, and of course loyalty to the Crown. In comparison, due to Arab-Swahili and Kikuyu efforts, Kenya's schools established English as the language of instruction, but Swahili was retained as a secondary language of instruction. In Northern Nigeria, as on the East Coast, Islam was retained for religious instruction in Muslim-dominant areas. This aligned with British Indirect Rule and ensured youth and adult cooperation within the colonial administration from African Muslim societies.

The impact of Western education combined with non-indigenous religious instruction on youth culture cannot be overstated. It resulted in what Falola described as 'a mess'. He demonstrated youths' awareness of religious and political influences and their results during his educational experience in Ibadan, Nigeria in the 1950s, writing:

> Before the mess, there was a clean body, not pure but clean. In my day, the anthem of cults that circulated in schools, one that we all sang, was about the retention of the cultures of old.
>
> We shall perform our rites
> We will obey our customs
> No religion can forbid us
> Not at all
> From performing our rites.[55]

His experience as a secondary student in Yorubaland during the last years of British rule in Nigeria references youths' awareness of the new political and religious structure that was imposed upon the old political and religious structure. He explained that 'the mess' developed later, 'As they strengthened their faith, Christians and Muslims slowly but surely eroded the cultural foundations of the city, creating a mess that the visitor can see today'.[56] Through this experience, youth gradually adopted Christianity or Islam and English to identify as a new elite. While initially Western-educated youth continued to combine ethno-national cultural practices with Christian or Muslim practice, later generations, especially youths who were second or third-generation Western-educated, steadily shift away from involvement with ethno-national cultural practices and adopted an increased use of English or Swahili language in social venues. The song above indicates this initial duality reflected in early Western-educated youth culture simultaneously acknowledging African culture while promoting Westernized cultural expectations. Youth selectively adopted, rejected, or transformed Western cultural expectations that ultimately became foundational elements in the establishment and maintenance of West African nation-states.

Conclusion

While the examples are at first glance predominantly Anglophone, the intersections of multiple African ethno-national groups are significant in looking at these examples. In Southern Africa, the early existence of Indian Ocean trade from the East and comparatively early Euro-settler groups of Dutch/Afrikaner and later French and British set in motion complex cultural, political, and economic relations across Southern African ethno-nations. During the more traditional colonial era of the 1800s to mid-1900s, many Southern African ethno-nations once again reorganized these relationships in partial response to the *Mfecane* (Zulu, 'crushing') or *Difaqane* (Basotho, 'forced migration') from the early 1800s to 1820–1830s followed by the Boer

(Dutch/Afrikaner) Great Trek or migration into these same areas in response to British control. This forced geographical disbursement of ethno-nations due initially to Kwa-Zulu invasions and later Afrikaner advancements into ethno-national territories triggered colonial involvement across the region to better regulate colonial investments and control labor. By the close of the 1800s, the colonial presence stretched across Southern Africa. This colonial presence, whether internal from Euro-settler classes or external from British, Dutch, Portuguese, or German administrations, interacted with every African ethno-nation to consolidate power and profit. In East and East Central Africa these colonial administrations and newer Euro-settler groups competed with older Arab-Swahili and Indian connections and cultural constructs that served to further complicate youth experience and perspectives on popular culture. In West Africa, as a result of the centuries-old trans-Saharan trade, Africanized Muslim Hausa and Fulani ethno-nations dominated the northern corridor, while African Traditional empires, such as the Ashanti and the Yoruba, controlled the core West and maintained much of their cultural influence across colonial holdings. These varied colonial contexts surprisingly presented a fairly globalized colonial youth experience.

The two most prominent trends in colonial youth popular culture appeared to be in adoption of Western clothing and in endorsement of Western education as an expression of elite identity. Whether Euro-settlers were present in large numbers or not did not seem to change youths' adoption of Western clothing or wanting to be identified as Western-educated. The examples provided above are only complicated to the extent that the Muslim or Koranic education was already available in these areas. As evidence indicated in Arab-Swahili and Hausa Fulani communities, the colonial administrations were successful in combining Muslim instruction with Western education. Colonial youth, Muslim, Christian, or Traditional, embraced the new Western dress and, as Bourdieu explains, used this newfound 'educated' status as cultural capital.

The most readily evident difference was in relation to access to Western influences. Rural African youth groups tended not to follow Westernized dress trends. This difference set these youths up as 'bush' or 'uneducated' in the view of urban, more Westernized youth. As Suriano explained in the Tanganyikan case:

> Clothes worn by ... urban residents, who called themselves ... *waungwana* (gentlemen), and those worn by newcomers from rural areas, scornfully referred to as *washenzi* (barbarians, savages). Although the identities of most of the urban dwellers were inextricably woven together with the rural ones, in the 1920s and 1930s many urban Africans (both Christian and Muslim) increasingly expressed their conscious sense of belonging to the cities.[57]

This difference played out across African regions, colonial administrations, and ethno-nations as Western culture increasingly became cultural capital that could be negotiated into opportunity. Whether that opportunity was a colonial job or social status, youth routinely expressed popular culture through Westernized dress, incorporation of Western instruments in their music, and Westernized dance. It was not surprising that this rural-urban split sharpened over time as urban, Western-educated youth became the Westerneducated adult elite and new generations of youth took on increasingly dual senses of African-Western popular culture.

Further Research

One glaring absence in most of the work presented in this chapter is the lack of representation of individual African ethno-nations' or societies' cultural contexts within the historical or anthropological work of the authors. There appears almost a universal assumption that colonialism somehow came with a homogenizing impact on African civilizations—at once making them a bland mix vested in different colored robes and accompanying drums. There is much more work to do to document how and in what ways individual ethnonational youths lived these colonial experiences.

Much of what is documented in these pages comes from the popular press and colonial archives. Too little of it comes from the inner workings and negotiations of these youths. Many questions are left unanswered. What were their mindsets, their attitudes toward this Westernization? How did they view the trans-national Muslim image of the day? How did they negotiate between ethno-national-specific cultural custom and process and Western-imposed practices? Most importantly, to what extent did they internalize Westernized popular culture versus using it as negotiable currency within the colonial context?

Colonial youth included a wide range of voices and contexts. Burgess summarized the historical context of colonial youth as:

> Colonial rule, Christianity, capitalism, urbanization, nationalism, and independence infinitely complicated relations between youth and elders. If gerontocratic discourse affirmed that youth was a liminal stage between childhood and adulthood, and between dependence and autonomy, the category came in the colonial period to exist in a very general sense somewhere between village and town, 'tradition' and modernity.[58]

While Suriano provided a summary of the significance of material culture as expressed in popular culture:

> By arguing that material culture is intertwined with processes of social change, and that people in Africa have been imagining alternatives in their own lives in spite of colonial domination, ... [by exploring] the relationship between popular culture and the changing identities of Tanganyikan urban youths by focusing on

fashion. The meaning of clothing has implications for our understanding of the relationship between 'tradition' and 'modernity' ... as well as for our knowledge of rural-urban, generational and gender relations. Moreover, the focus on clothing can contribute to grasp local strategies of resiliency and broader processes by which African actors forged translocal connections and created 'translocalities' that increasingly sustained new ways of 'being-in-the-world'.[59]

As the definition of African youth became more Westernized and its length expanded under colonialism as it gradually included the rubric of Western education through to secondary school, colonial youths sought to make sense of their experience. Popular culture, whether expressed via dress, as in Suriano's example, or through music, popular press, language use, or new entertainment venues, demonstrated colonial youths' incorporation of colonial, Western culture to negotiate their newfound status as colonial laborers to Western-educated colonial elite.

These cultural expressions did not negate African ethno-national cultures, but served to negotiate the colonial realities of their period. With more research on the retentions of Afrocentric popular culture on the continent, the ethno-national specificity of these cultural negotiations may be documented. While many diasporic academics document Afrocentric or Pan-African cultural 'retentions' or 'survivals', especially in Atlantic or American studies, not enough of this work is readily available within the African continent. African youth culture, in particular, is a newer field that has much left to explore within the colonial period. While the examples provided in this chapter only document the surface, they do provide the preliminary groundwork to go further and seek the necessary historical, personal sources to complete the historical description of ethno-national differences and changes in expressions of youth popular cultures that emerged during this period.

NOTES

1. Emphasis is mine. Thomas Burgess, "Introduction to Youth and Citizenship in East Africa," *Africa Today* 51, no. 3 (Spring 2005): viii.
2. For a full discussion on African age grades, implications of class, and political hierarchy, see Bernando Bernardi, *Age Class Systems: Social Institutions and Politics Based on Age* (Cambridge: Cambridge University Press, 1985).
3. See Berlin Conference (1884–1884) overview in Kevin Shillington, History of Africa, 3rd ed. (London: Palgrave Macmillan, 2012), 313–34.
4. Johann Gottfried Herder, *Ideen zur Philosophie der Geschichte der Menschheit* (Riga and Leipzig: Hartknoch, 1784), as cited in Holt N. Parker, "Toward a Definition of Popular Culture," *History and Theory* 50, no. 2 (May 2011): 148.
5. For a full and insightful discussion on the history and defining of popular culture, see Holt N. Parker, "Toward a definition of Popular Culture," *History and Theory* 50, no. 2 (May 2011): 147–70.

6. For a full discussion of cultural capital, see Pierre Bourdieu, *Language and Symbolic Power*, ed. John B. Thompson, trans. Gina Raymond and Matthew Adamson (Cambridge, MA: Harvard University Press, 1991).
7. See: Kwame Nkrumah, *Consciencism: Philosophy and Ideology for Decolonisation and Development with Particular Reference to the African Revolution* (London: Heinemann, 1964); Imanuel Geiss, *The Pan-African Movement: A History of Pan-Africanism in America, Europe, and Africa* (New York: Africana Pub. Co., 1974); Peter O. Esedebe, *Pan-Africanism: The Idea and Movement* (Washington, DC: Howard University Press, 1982); and Hakim Adi and Marika Sherwood, *Pan-African History: Political Figures from Africa and the Diaspora Since 1787* (New York: Routledge, 2003).
8. Critical theory also Critical Radical theory as described in Henry Giroux, *Theory and Resistance in Education* (London: Bergin & Garvey, 2001).
9. "Colonial History of Cape Town: The Dutch Settlement" from South African History Online, www.sahistory.org.za, accessed November 10, 2016, http://www.sahistory.org.za/article/dutch-settlement.
10. Charles Ambler, "Popular Films and Colonial Audiences: The Movies in Northern Rhodesia," *The American Historical Review* 106, no. 1 (Febuary 2001): 82.
11. Ibid., 95. For a detailed account of Rhodesian mining town life during the 1930–1950s period, see Hortense Powdermaker, *Copper Town: Changing Africa: The Human Situation on the Rhodesian Copperbelt* (New York: Harper and Row, 1962).
12. This part of Ambler's study is problematic as he never states whether Chibembe is their ethno-national language or whether it is the lingua franca of the mining compound or townships with multiple ethno-nations engaged in these experiences. For this reason, the study may overgeneralize African viewpoints in the interviews and reports as no African societal structural information is provided other than a generalized expectation of respect for elders and a conservative view of male and female public image and interactions.
13. R.J. Allanson to Director, Department of Information, Lusaka, North Rhodesia, January 27, 1956, NAZ, Sec. 2/1125, no. 19, as cited in Ambler, 93.
14. Johannes Fabian, "Popular Culture in Africa: Findings and Conjectures," *Africa* 48, no. 4 (1978): 315.
15. Heike Becker, "Anthropology and the Study of Popular Culture: A Perspective from the Southern Tip of Africa," *Research in African Literatures* 43, no. 4 (Winter 2012): 19.
16. David B. Coplan, *In Township Tonight! Three Centuries of South African Black City Music and Theatre*, 2nd ed. (Johannesburg and Chicago: Jacana Media and University of Chicago Press, 2007), 1, as cited in Becker, 25.
17. David B. Coplan, "'I've Worked Longer Than I've Lived': Lesotho Migrants' Songs as Maps of Experience," *Journal of Ethnic and Migration Studies* 32, no. 2 (March 2006): 224.
18. Ibid., 225.
19. For a fuller discussion on Lesotho and South Africa migrant labor history see: Tshidiso Maloka, "Khomo Lia Oela: Canteens, Brothels and Labour Migrancy in Colonial Lesotho, 1900–40," *The Journal of African History* 38, no. 1 (1997): 101–22; and Samuel N.A. Mensah and Vannie Naidoo, "Migration

Shocks: Integrating Lesotho's Retrenched Migrant Miners," *International Migration Review* 45, no. 4 (Winter 2011): 1017–42.
20. Coplan, "'I've Worked Longer Than I've Lived': Lesotho Migrants' Songs as Maps of Experience," 227.
21. Ibid., 231.
22. Ibid., 228.
23. Ibid.
24. Ibid., 235.
25. Ibid., 237.
26. Nile Green, "Islam for the Indentured Indian: A Muslim Missionary in Colonial South Africa," *Bulletin of the School of Oriental and African Studies* 71, no. 3 (2008): 529–53.
27. Ibid., 530.
28. Ibid., 531–32.
29. Gandhi, *Indian Opinion*, 4 June 1910, 187, as cited in Green, 540.
30. Paul Ocobock, "Spare the Rod, Spoil the Colony: Corporal Punishment, Colonial Violence, and Generational Authority in Kenya, 1897–1952," *The International Journal of African Historical Studies* 45, no. 1 (2012): 31.
31. Toyin Falola, *A Mouth Sweeter Than Salt: An African Memoir* (Ann Harbor, MI: University of Michigan 2004), 143.
32. Ibid.
33. Paul Ocobock, "'Joy Rides for Juvenile': Vagrant Youth and Colonial Control in Nairobi, Kenya, 1901–52," *Social History* 31, no. 1 (February 2006): 42.
34. Ibid., 45.
35. Ibid., 48.
36. Minorities at Risk, "Assessment for Kikuyu in Kenya," College Park, MD: Center for International Development and Conflict Management, 2006, accessed December 20, 2016 at http://www.mar.umd.edu/assessment.asp?groupId=50103.
37. Nathaniel Mathews, "Imagining Arab Communities: Colonialism, Islamic Reform, and Arab Identity in Mombasa, Kenya, 1897–1933," *Islamic Africa* 4, no. 2 (Fall 2013): 135–63.
38. Ibid., 138–39.
39. Ibid., 141.
40. Ibid., 145.
41. Maria Suriano, "Clothing and the Changing Identities of Tanganyikan Urban Youths, 1920s–1950s," *Journal of African Cultural Studies* 29, no. 1 (June 2008): 97.
42. Rashidi Ali Meli, "Letter to the Editor," *Mambo Leo* (1932), 6b as cited in Suriano, 99.
43. Chande Ally, "Poem. Dansi ni ngoma duni, wajuao kufikiri," *Mambo Leo* (1953), 4 as cited in Suriano, 106.
44. R.M. Ngoda, "Poem. Nguo gotini, tunachelea hasara," *Mambo Leo* (1950), 4 verse 4 as cited in Suriano, 106.
45. John A.K. Leslie, *A Survey of Dar es Salaam*, London: Oxford University Press, 1963, 112 as cited in Suriano, 104.
46. Suriano, "Clothing and the Changing Identities of Tanganyikan Urban Youths, 1920s–1950s," 98.

47. Kwame Nkrumah, "Education and Nationalism in Africa," *Educational Outlook* 18, no. 1 (November 1943): 33–34.
48. George E. Urch, "Education and Colonialism in Kenya," *History of Education Quarterly* 11, no. 3 (Autumn 1971): 250.
49. Edward H. Berman, "African Responses to Christian Mission Education," *African Studies Review* 17, no. 3 (December 1974): 527.
50. Ibid., 531.
51. The exceptions were Arab and Asian (Indian) Muslims in British-controlled Kenya, where as early as 1909 separate schools were recommended for them. Unlike African Muslims they were classified as citizens with representation on the Governor's Legislative Council. See: T. Walter Wallbank, "British Colonial Policy and Native Education in Kenya," *The Journal of Negro Education* 7, no. 4 (October 1938): 521–32; Hassan Ndzovu, "Muslims and Party Politics and Electoral Campaigns in Kenya," working paper No. 09-001, Institute for the Study of Islamic Thought in Africa: Working Paper Series (March 2009), 1–13; and Alwiya Alwy and Susanne Schech, "Ethnic Inequalities in Education in Kenya," *International Education Journal* 5, no. 2 (2004): 266–74.
52. Great Britain, Colonial Office, Advisory Committee on Native Education in the British Tropical African Dependencies, *Educational Policy in British Tropical Africa*, Cmd. 2347 (London: H.M.S.O., 1925), 2, as cited in Urch, 259–60.
53. Cati Coe, "Educating an African Leadership: Achimota and the Teaching of African Culture in the Gold Coast," *Africa Today* 49, no. 3 (Autumn 2002): 24.
54. Michael Omolewa, "Educating the 'Native': A Study of the Education Adaptation Strategy in British Colonial Africa, 1910–1936," *The Journal of African American History* 91, no. 3 (Summer 2006): 272.
55. Falola, "A Mouth Sweeter Than Salt," 230.
56. Ibid.
57. Suriano, "Clothing and the Changing Identities of Tanganyikan Urban Youths, 1920s–1950s," 98–99.
58. Burgess, xi.
59. Suriano, "Clothing and the Changing Identities of Tanganyikan Urban Youths, 1920s–1950s," 97.

Bibliography

Adi, Hakim, and Marika Sherwood. *Pan-African History: Political Figures from Africa and the Diaspora Since 1787.* New York: Routledge, 2003.

Alwy, Alwiya, and Susanne Schech, "Ethnic Inequalities in Education in Kenya." *International Education Journal* 5, no. 2 (2004): 266–74.

Ambler, Charles. "Popular Films and Colonial Audiences: The Movies in Northern Rhodesia." *The American Historical Review* 106, no. 1 (February 2001): 81–105.

Becker, Heike. "Anthropology and the Study of Popular Culture: A Perspective from the Southern Tip of Africa." *Research in African Literatures* 43, no. 4 (Winter 2012): 17–37.

Berman, Edward H. "African Responses to Christian Mission Education." *African Studies Review* 17, no. 3 (December 1974): 527–40.

Bernardi, Bernardo. *Age Class Systems: Social Institutions and Politics Based on Age.* Cambridge: Cambridge University Press, 1985.

Bourdieu, Pierre. *Language and Symbolic Power.* Edited and introduced by John B. Thompson. Translation by Gina Raymond and Matthew Adamson. Cambridge, MA: Harvard University Press, 1991.

Burgess, Thomas. "Introduction to Youth and Citizenship in East Africa." *Africa Today* 51, no. 3 (Spring 2005): vii–xxiv.

Coe, Cati. "Educating an African Leadership: Achimota and the Teaching of African Culture in the Gold Coast." *Africa Today* 49, no. 3 (Autumn 2002): 23–44.

Coplan, David B. "'I've Worked Longer Than I've Lived': Lesotho Migrants' Songs as Maps of Experience." *Journal of Ethnic and Migration Studies* 32, no. 2 (March 2006): 223–41.

Coplan, David B. *In Township Tonight! Three Centuries of South African Black City Music and Theatre*, 2nd ed. Johannesburg and Chicago: Jacana Media and University of Chicago Press, 2007.

Esedebe, Peter O. *Pan-Africanism: The Idea and Movement.* Washington, DC: Howard University Press, 1982.

Fabian, Johannes. "Popular Culture in Africa: Findings and Conjectures." *Africa* 48, no. 4 (1978): 315–34.

Falola, Toyin. *A Mouth Sweeter Than Salt: An African Memoir.* Ann Harbor, MI: University of Michigan, 2004.

Geiss, Imanuel. *The Pan-African Movement: A History of Pan-Africanism in America, Europe, and Africa.* New York: Africana Pub. Co., 1974.

Giroux, Henry. *Theory and Resistance in Education.* London: Bergin & Garvey, 2001.

Green, Nile. "Islam for the Indentured Indian: A Muslim Missionary in Colonial South Africa." *Bulletin of the School of Oriental and African Studies* 71, no. 3 (2008): 529–53.

Herder, Johann Gottfried. *Ideen zur Philosophie der Geschichte der Menschheit.* Riga and Leipzig: Hartknoch, 1784.

Leslie, John A.K. *A Survey of Dar es Salaam.* London: Oxford University Press, 1963.

Maloka, Tshidiso. "Khomo Lia Oela: Canteens, Brothels and Labour Migrancy in Colonial Lesotho, 1900–40." *The Journal of African History* 38, no. 1 (1997): 101–22.

Mathews, Nathaniel. "Imagining Arab Communities: Colonialism, Islamic Reform, and Arab Identity in Mombasa, Kenya, 1897–1933." *Islamic Africa* 4, no. 2 (Fall 2013): 135–63.

Mensah, Samuel N.A., and Vannie Naidoo. "Migration Shocks: Integrating Lesotho's Retrenched Migrant Miners." *International Migration Review* 45, no. 4 (Winter 2011): 1017–42.

Minorities at Risk. "Assessment for Kikuyu in Kenya." College Park, MD: Center for International Development and Conflict Management (CIDCM), 2006. Accessed December 20, 2016. http://www.mar.umd.edu/assessment.asp?groupId=50103.

Ndzovu, Hassan. "Muslims and Party Politics and Electoral Campaigns in Kenya." Working Paper No. 09-001, Institute for the Study of Islamic Thought in Africa: Working Paper Series (March 2009): 113.

Nkrumah, Kwame. "Education and Nationalism in Africa." *Educational Outlook* 18, no. 1 (November 1943): 32–40.

Nkrumah, Kwame. *Consciencism: Philosophy and Ideology for Decolonisation and Development with Particular Reference to the African Revolution.* London: Heinemann, 1964.

Ocobock, Paul. "'Joy Rides for Juvenile': Vagrant Youth and Colonial Control in Nairobi, Kenya, 1901–52." *Social History* 31, no. 1 (February 2006): 39–59.

Ocobock, Paul. "Spare the Rod, Spoil the Colony: Corporal Punishment, Colonial Violence, and Generational Authority in Kenya, 1897–1952." *The International Journal of African Historical Studies* 45, no. 1 (2012): 29–56.

Omolewa, Micheal. "Educating the 'Native': A Study of the Education Adaptation Strategy in British Colonial Africa, 1910–1936." *The Journal of African American History* 91, no. 3 (Summer 2006): 267–87.

Parker, Holt N. "Toward a Definition of Popular Culture." *History and Theory* 50, no. 2 (May 2011): 147–70.

Powdermaker, Hortense. *Coer Town: Changing Africa: The Human Situation on the Rhodesian Coerbelt*. New York: Harper and Row, 1962.

Shillington, Kevin. *History of Africa*, 3rd ed. London: Palgrave Macmillan, 2012.

South Africa History Online. "Colonial History of Cape Town: The Dutch Settlement." South African History Online. www.sahistory.org.za. Accessed November 10, 2016. http://www.sahistory.org.za/article/dutch-settlement.

Suriano, Maria. "Clothing and the Changing Identities of Tanganyikan Urban Youths, 1920s–1950s." *Journal of African Cultural Studies* 29, no. 1 (June 2008): 95–115.

Urch, George E. "Education and Colonialism in Kenya." *History of Education Quarterly* 11, no. 3 (Autumn 1971): 249–64.

Wallbank, T. Walter. "British Colonial Policy and Native Education in Kenya." *The Journal of Negro Education* 7, no. 4 (October 1938): 521–32.

CHAPTER 21

The Horn of Africa and the Black Anticolonial Imaginary (1896–1915)

Fikru Negash Gebrekidan

In 2002, historian Gebru Tareke wrote a laudatory review of the second edition of Bahru Zewde's *History of Modern Ethiopia*, describing it as 'the best introduction to contemporary Ethiopian history'. One of the main points upon which Tareke begged to differ, however, was Zewde's treatment of the Battle of Adwa as a Pan-African watershed. 'The legacy of the Battle of Adwa is overdone', he rebutted. 'There is little evidence, if any, to show that it had any direct and immediate bearing on the rest of Africa or on the Africans of the diaspora unless history is read backwards'.[1]

Tareke's statement is reminiscent of Africanists who came of age at the height of area studies, when the nation-state was still the primary unit of historical analysis. Augmenting the mainstream literature on the first Italo-Ethiopian war with African American and Caribbean contemporary accounts, this chapter affirms the global significance of the Battle of Adwa. In the process, it raises critical questions that historians have so far ignored. Why was Adwa not little more than a fleeting moment in history? What distinguished it from the few other anticolonial victories before it: the 1879 Battle of Isandlwana, or the 1885 Mahdist triumph over Charles Gordon of Khartoum? The chapter locates the answer in the Pan-African career of Benito Sylvain, the Haitian national whose preoccupation with Ethiopia is discussed in great detail for the first time. Sylvain's travel to the Horn of Africa in 1897, the

F.N. Gebrekidan (✉)
History Department, St. Thomas University, Fredericton, NB, Canada

© The Author(s) 2018
M.S. Shanguhyia and T. Falola (eds.),
The Palgrave Handbook of African Colonial and Postcolonial History,
https://doi.org/10.1057/978-1-137-59426-6_21

first of its kind by a diaspora black, transformed the global extent of Ethiopia's military exploits. It not only popularized Ethiopia's image abroad as a symbol of anticolonial resistance, it added a new ingredient to the Black Atlantic discourse on hybridity and modernism. By the early twentieth century, the Horn of Africa had moved into the center stage of black history, its past mythologized and celebrated in W.E.B. Du Bois's Afrocentric classic *The Negro*.

Adwa and the International Media

Unlike the highly sensational antifascist protests of 1935 and 1936, the media coverage of Adwa did not spark instant mass reactions. Still, Adwa was a milestone in the history of black nationalism. In fact, long before modern-day historians, it was Du Bois who, in 1915, referred to the event of 1896 'as one of the most decisive battles in world history'.[2] His assessment was not exaggerated. The war and its aftermath were extensively reported in leading US and European newspapers, including those catering to African American readers. Among the latter, in particular, such reports were of double significance. First was the psychological role of Adwa to arguments of racial vindication. Second was the geohistorical awareness of the Horn of Africa that the coverage of Adwa promoted: the transnational convergence of the Black Atlantic with the Red Sea-Indian Ocean littoral.

Since the late eighteenth century, diaspora Africans had identified with ancient Ethiopia, whose exaltations were to be found scattered in scriptural verses and the Western classics. Yet, the Horn of Africa remained the least familiar region of Africa in black diaspora thought. Few knew that the name Abyssinia, the toponym outsiders had adopted since the seventeenth century, referred to the Nile Valley state that was once part of greater Ethiopia. Physical distance and absence of direct contact accounted for much of the mystification. Eastern Africa did not produce the likes of Martin Delany and Robert Campbell, Pan-Africanists who spearheaded the famous Niger Valley expedition of 1859. It lacked the evangelical appeal of Western and Southern Africa, where most of the nineteenth century missionary work in Africa was concentrated. Nor did it measure up to the unique history of Liberia and Sierra Leone, home to thousands of ex-slave repatriates, that made West Africa an intimate partner of the Atlantic world.[3]

It is against this backdrop that the 1896 Italo-Ethiopian War became a turning point in global African consciousness. What characterized the relationship between Italy and Ethiopia in the early 1890s was the steady erosion of mutual trust. This was after Italy had declared Ethiopia a colonial protectorate, a fact that Emperor Menelik II was to learn by accident, by manipulating the phrasing of a diplomatic document that the two countries had signed in 1889: the Wichale Treaty of Friendship and Commerce.[4] The tension escalated into a diplomatic imbroglio, and from then into open military preparations. Armed confrontations that began in December 1895, with Menelik having declared a national mobilization in September, would conclude on March 1, 1896, following a day-long battle near the market town of Adwa. Defying every prediction, Ethiopians would emerge decisively victorious, safeguarding their national independence and puncturing the myth of European racial superiority.[5]

For Italy, Adwa was a historic rout, a national blemish that Benito Mussolini would try to expunge in the 1930s. Italy's casualties of 70%, against Ethiopia's 20%, were unprecedented in the annals of modern colonial warfare. They consisted of 15,000 dead, 1400 wounded, and 1900 captured. Of the five generals, two died in action, one was wounded and captured, and only two managed to straggle back to Eritrea.[6] In Rome, spontaneous mass protests would force Prime Minister Francesco Crispi and his cabinet to resign, the first time an African event was directly responsible for regime change in Europe.[7]

Ethiopia found itself catapulted into the outside world by the international media. On March 4, for example, the *New York Times* published two lengthy features on different aspects of the Italo-Ethiopian War. In the first, a dispatch from Rome offered a detailed account of the actual battle. It put the number of Italian deaths at 3000, a very conservative estimate. Oreste Baratieri, the top commander who was rumored to have committed suicide, was said to have been found alive, while two other generals were reported wounded and another one was missing.[8] The second article traced causes of the war to Italy's growing colonial ambitions in the Horn of Africa, which was obstructed by the politics of inter-European rivalry that made it possible for France to arm the Ethiopian side. It also listed the names of Ethiopian commanders, or *Rases*, together with the size and strength of their fighting units, including Empress Taytu's force of 15,000.[9]

In all, the name Abyssinia appeared in several dozen stories in the *New York Times* in the month of March alone. They included headings such as 'Italy is Awe Struck' (March 5), 'Abyssinian Reverses Provoke Paroxysms of Rage in Rome' (March 6), 'Women Against Expeditions' (March 8), 'Kassala is Evacuated' (March 10), 'Magnanimity of King Menelik' (March 14), 'Russia and Abyssinia' (March 17), 'Partition of Africa' (March 22), and 'A Personal View of Menelik' (March 22). The last was a tongue-in-cheek piece about a French commercial explorer fresh from Africa, who was joined for dinner by some 40 New York socialites, so as 'to hear him say how Menelik looked and Menelik talked'.[10]

Even as knowledge about East Africa improved with fresh insights of history and geography, most of that went hand-in-hand with the prevailing order of white supremacy. According to historian Raymond Jonas, the North American media simply evaded the paradox of Adwa by adopting the myth of Ethiopian racial exceptionalism. The *Atlanta Constitution* reported news of the Italo-Ethiopian war with a few factual errors, including the placement of Ethiopia in South Africa. The conservative Southern paper understood, as a matter of fact, that it owed its readers some explanation for the unusual turn of events. Under the heading of 'The Abyssinian Race Question', its physiognomic analysis established that Ethiopians were 'of Phoenician origin', a conclusion supported by drawn images of Menelik with the likeness of Tsar Nicholas II. Editorials of similar content appeared in several papers, among them the *Chicago Tribune* and the *New York World*, in which Abyssinians were identified as dark-skinned Caucasians. The message was clear. Since Abyssinians belonged to a more intelligent, civilized, non-African pedigree, the threat of an actual African military specter was no more real after the war than it was before it.[11]

The whitening of Horn of Africans, which initially began as a tactic of accommodation by social Darwinists and colonial apologists, would periodically spill over to the black press. In the 1930s, in the years leading up to the second Italo-Ethiopian war, it would revive the volatile question of 'blood kinship', on which many African Americans wanted to predicate their stands with the beleaguered country.[12] What the racial controversy confirmed to most black readers was, however, the arbitrariness of modern race science, a hypocrisy made all the more obvious by the fact that racial boundaries shifted back and forth in accordance with European dictates. The one-drop rule, on which basis Americans of mixed backgrounds were denied citizenship rights, was now used to confer the status of fictive whitehood to the militarily victorious swarthy Ethiopians. Part of the African American struggle for equality and justice was to expose and challenge this self-serving notion of whiteness, and it was in this context that the news from Adwa was seen through the prism of racial vindication.[13]

According to James Quirin, who sampled African American newspaper coverage of the first Italo-Ethiopian war in a brief but illuminating essay, in the scattered references to Adwa was the universal picture of race pride. This was not surprising. In May 1896, only two months after the Battle of Adwa, the US Supreme Court had issued its verdict on *Plessy v. Ferguson*, recognizing as constitutional the 'separate but equal' racial doctrine. On the rise in the 1890s was also the physical persecution of African Americans, with about a hundred lynchings reported every year.[14] Against this background of despair, many detected a providential sign in the extraordinary news from Africa. They saw in it the negation of Darwinian logic, or so-called scientific racism, on which ground American racial totalitarianism had been justified.[15]

The vindicationist tone ranged from reflective to celebratory. 'They hit 'em hard in Abyssinia' and 'The partitioning of Africa will soon cease to be a midsummer's night dream', declared the *Indianapolis Freeman* on March 14.[16] 'Who said an African would not or could not fight', rejoined the *Cleveland Gazette* on the same day, adding: 'King Menelek is proving himself more than a match for civilization's trained and skilled warriors, with all their improved machinery of war. More power to him!'[17]

In its issue of March 28, the *Cleveland Gazette* published the most detailed account of the war so far. Contributed by a certain G. Weippiert, the 1500-word essay provided an encyclopedic outline of Ethiopian history: Axum's embrace of Christianity in the fourth century, the religious wars of the sixteenth century, and the recent military engagements with Italy and Mahdist Sudan. Having described Adwa as the 'Italian Waterloo', the column concluded with a cautionary note on domestic politics: 'One lesson which the American people can learn from the present crisis is that the colonizing and annexation fever is not only a source of danger, but a menace to the stability of home government'.[18]

Similar articles appeared in Georgia's *Savannah Tribune*, another black weekly. 'The Abyssinians have shown themselves equal to any emergency', its editorial of March 21 read. 'They have given the Italians a severe flogging and if England persists in interfering she will be taught a serious lesson'. At stake was more than a military honor, moreover. Italian defeat epitomized the bankruptcy of the 'civilizing mission' along with its self-serving, lofty moral claims. 'The Abyssinians are defending their homes and native land; they are perfectly right in expelling foreign aggressions', the weekly further sympathized. 'This overbearing spirit exercised by European nations over African nations should be stopped. It is cruel, unworthy of Christian nations and unjust'.[19]

Not all commentaries were as favorable. Without international correspondents of their own, fledgling black newspapers covered Africa using syndicated columns and dispatches. The practice, among other things, posed the risk of recycling mainstream media prejudices. At least in two instances, according to Quirin, images of Ethiopian savagery were invoked. In one paper, Taytu was singled out and blamed for influencing her husband into waging a bloody and atavistic type of warfare.[20] In another paper, Ethiopians were relegated into a racial no-man's land that defied classification. 'The Copts, who are the ruling race of the country, are descendants of the ancient Egyptians, their blood being mingled with that of the Greeks, Arabs, and Nubians', was the take by G. Weippiert, the contributor of the lengthy essay in the *Cleveland Gazette*. Taken as a whole, however, the black media adopted a strongly partisan position.[21] The majority of the newspaper articles celebrated Adwa as a genuinely African military victory. In Ethiopia's continued independence they saw a beacon of hope and freedom, a reminder that racial domination was neither divinely sanctioned nor scientifically defendable.

Finally, in the new geohistorical knowledge about the Horn of Africa, made possible by media's extensive coverage of the Battle of Adwa, was the disruption of the historic Black Atlantic. The insular flow of ideas and cultural innovations between West Africa, North America, the Caribbean, and the European metropoles was flung open for possibilities from the Red Sea and the Indian Ocean world. Evidence of this new transnational interaction at the global level was the Pan-African career of Benito Sylvain of Haiti.

Reminiscent of the pioneering work by Martin Delany and Robert Campbell in West Africa, Sylvain would spend many years of his life trying to build a diplomatic bridge between Ethiopia and Haiti. Charismatic and dashing, he would serve as Ethiopia's de facto roving ambassador internationally, keeping the Battle of Adwa fresh in public memory and reinforcing the image of Menelik as an icon of anticolonial resistance.

BLACK ATLANTIC MEETS HORN OF AFRICA

Marie-Joseph Benoit Dartagnan Sylvain was born in Port-de-Paix, Haiti, on March 21, 1868.[22]

His father, Michel Sylvain, belonged to the urban establishment, best remembered as the first person to run a theatre in Port-au-Prince.[23] His older brother, Georges, who went on to serve as Haitian ambassador to France in the 1910s, was a leading literary figure and an outspoken patriot. Benito (Benoit was dropped at infancy) grew up sharing similar academic aspirations, at least until his idealistic visions got the better of him in the aftermath of the Italo-Ethiopian war. Establishment of bilateral ties between the independent countries of Haiti and Ethiopia would become the raison d'être of the adult Benito Sylvain, making him the first Occidental black to travel to East Africa. As it turned out, it would take another half century for the diplomatic relations to become real. What Sylvain's historic visit to East Africa accomplished was, instead, a new chapter in the transoceanic narrative: the immersion of Ethiopia in the global Pan-African discourse.[24]

For over a millennium, East African seafarers had tapped into the Monsoon winds, while the importance of the West African seaports had surpassed the inland caravan trade by the sixteenth century. Because the Atlantic and the Indian Ocean systems were oriented in opposite directions, divergence characterized the experience of the vast African world in the East and that of its counterpart in the West. The former stood outside the cultural and intellectual dialectics taking place between West Africa, the Americas, and Western Europe, for which Paul Gilroy coined the phrase 'Black Atlantic'. It is against this background that Sylvain's arrival in East Africa was to become transformational. African transnationalism would henceforth take on a truly global dimension, thanks to the representation of East Africa in the Afro-Atlantic fusion.

Having studied in a Port-au-Prince Catholic seminary since 1874, or the age of six, in 1887 Sylvain qualified for an advanced high-school diploma from the Stanislas College of Paris. Two years later materialized Sylvain's first real job as a secretary in the Haitian legation in London, a post he soon abandoned in pursuit of a journalistic career. For representing Haiti at the 1890 antislavery conference in Brussels and for his journalistic work in general, in 1893 the Haitian government conferred on Sylvain an honorary naval title: ensign of the vessel. Here was indeed a renaissance man on the rise. In 1894 alone, the year Sylvain completed his law degree, he founded and headed two associations: Circle of Fraternal Union (a Haitian student organization), and the Committee of Oriental and African Society of Ethnologists of Paris.[25]

Eclectic as these interests seemed, Sylvain's true sentiment lay in his role as editor of *La Fraternité*. This was the journal he introduced in 1889, its mission boldly announced in its provocative subtitle: Organ for the Defense of Haitian Interest and the Black Race. The paper, which he directed for the next seven years, with subventions from the Haitian government and the abolitionist Victor Schoelcher, would remain an important platform for the discussion of contemporary race and race-related issues. In conjunction with the 1896 Italo-Ethiopian war, *Fraternité* was the main factor behind Sylvain's initiation into the politics of Pan-Africanism.

Sylvain did not fight in Ethiopia, as claimed in the obituary of his famous niece: the folklorist Suzanne Comhaire Sylvain.[26] To the contrary, Benito Sylvain learned about the 1896 Ethiopian victory at Adwa from the European papers. The last time European soldiers had suffered a serious defeat in Africa was in January 1885, when Sudanese nationalists, or Mahdists, overran General Charles Gordon's Anglo-Egyptian garrison in Khartoum. The year 1896 was, therefore, the first time in recent memory that an African nation and its fighting prowess made news in Europe. *La Liberté*, for example, extolled that 'all European countries will be obliged to make a place for this new brother who steps forth ready to play, in the Dark Continent, the role of Japan in the Far East'.[27] Across the channel, likewise, the *Times* of London adopted a favorable tone, reversing earlier portraits of Ethiopians as a 'barbarous foe'.[28] Among educated Haitians in Europe, the news must have struck an even more poignant tone: it was reminiscent of the laurels of Haiti's own victory over the invading forces of Napoleon almost a hundred years prior. For Sylvain, in particular, homage to the court of Menelik, the Toussaint Louverture of Africa, would become a life-defining moment. He would spend the next several years traveling back and forth between Ethiopia, Europe, and the Americas promoting his brand of Pan-Africanism, or what may be characterized as a one-man's South–South diplomacy.

Despite the construction of the Suez Canal decades earlier, in 1897 Ethiopia was still an expensive and difficult country to reach. The 500 miles from the Djibouti coast to its capital, Addis Ababa, passed through an inhospitable desert landscape and mountainous terrains, and could be traversed only on foot or animal back. According to biographer Antoine Bervin, Sylvain's critical question of how to pay for his ambitious scheme was resolved by a certain Amir Johannes Salim, an acquaintance he struck in the Latin quarter of Marseille. The Amir, the son of an Ethiopian mother and an Arab father, and who apparently grew up in Ethiopia, agreed to finance the journalist's prohibitive undertaking. Besides money, he furnished Sylvain with three Amharic letters of introduction, which he was to present to the Ethiopian sovereign and other officials along the way. 'What interests does he have in the success of my voyage?' Sylvain was to wonder by the seemingly providential encounter. Artifacts such as the Ethiopian national costume, palace curios, and a richly bound Book of Psalms was what Salim asked in exchange, which is to say his largesse was not as altruistic as Sylvain had assumed.[29]

Sylvain disembarked at the port of Djibouti sometime in the month of February of 1897. For a first-time arrival on the extremely hot and arid East African coast, his observations were relatively impersonal and scientific. There was no port facility in Djibouti, so passengers had to be rowed ashore by Somali fishermen. The town, whose major buildings were the governor's residence, the jail, and the post office, was home to about 1500 locals, 20 French servicemen, and just as many Greek merchants, plus countless goats, camels, and donkeys. Somalis and Dankalis made up the local inhabitants, but Ethiopian interpreters and caravan escorts also came and went freely. Because of its heat, Djibouti earned the reputation as 'the antechamber to hell'; but Sylvain, anticipating the cooler climes of the highlands, thought of it as 'the antechamber to purgatory'.[30]

It took six days for Sylvain's small caravan of eleven men, four mules, and two camels to reach the walled city of Harar, better known in France for its association with the romantic poet Arthur Rimbaud. In Harar, a 20-day wait followed before Ras Makonnen, the 45-year-old governor, returned home from an official trip to Addis Ababa. Sylvain's subsequent interview with the statesman, Menelik's younger cousin, could not have gone more smoothly. 'The great Ethiopian chief fixed on me his expressive eyes and looked at me attentively ... and said, in a grave voice, these unforgettable words, which my interpreter translated with a visible emotion', Sylvain recorded in his diary: "Since your first visit, you have inspired my sympathy. I trust you. It is God that sent you to us for the good of this country and all the men of our race. You may leave for Addis Ababa; I will make the necessary arrangements for you to receive the hospitality of the Emperor and the Empress."[31]

Sylvain left for the capital two days after the audience with the Ras, grateful for his generous provisions of fresh escorts and pack animals. Covering as many as 30 miles a day, his men would reach the outskirts of Addis Ababa on April 8, ten days after they had left Harar. The next day they entered the city, with food rations doubled for men and beasts to lift their spirits, and egged on by the sound of a trumpet. 'Where is he rushing to? Asked the populace, alerted by the call of the bugle', Bervin wrote, summarizing Sylvain's diary and his upbeat mood. 'And his men replied: "He goes to Addis Ababa; he comes from afar, from very far off beyond the seas, to see our Emperor Menelik!" And all these brave people, who are so proud of their beloved sovereign, from whom we can obtain everything by invoking his venerated name, were well pleased by this story and implored the blessings of Heaven on his travels, and offered him advice and gifts.'[32]

Until Bervin's work, the only source of information about Sylvain's historic meeting with Menelik had come from the controversial passage in

Robert P. Skinner's book of 1906. Since the late 1890s, Skinner had been serving as the US consul-general in the Mediterranean city of Marseille, and it was his lobbying that had convinced President Theodore Roosevelt of the value of establishing political and commercial presence in the Red Sea hinterlands. In 1903, Skinner himself would head the historic diplomatic mission to Ethiopia, and three years later he would publish his travel accounts as *Abyssinia of To-Day*. The passage in question, which some scholars have cited as proof of Ethiopian xenophobia, or even racism, was based on hearsay Skinner picked up while in Addis Ababa, more likely from the foreign legations. According to the story, Sylvain had taken all the trouble to come to Ethiopia with an ambitious program of race amelioration, only to discover that the Ethiopians saw themselves differently. "The negro should be uplifted," Menelik was said to have responded firmly. "But in coming to me to take the leadership, you are knocking at the wrong door, so to speak. You know, I am not a negro at all: I am a Caucasian."[33]

In fairness to the US emissary, the passage had positive things to say of the West Indian. Just a few lines below was the portrait of Sylvain as well-educated and socially refined. Skinner's agenda was more complex, however. His insistence on an Ethiopian phenotype, as in the chapter entitled 'The Caucasians of Cush', aimed at defending Roosevelt's decision of sending a costly diplomatic mission to the Horn of Africa, a region of which US Americans knew very little.[34] By reenacting the fictive whitehood of post-Adwa Ethiopia, the consul-general thus hoped to assuage post-bellum racial concerns. After all, as one historian commented, the racial jargons in which Menelik seemed to feel so much at home sounded more American than Ethiopian.[35]

Sylvain Meets Menelik

To the Ethiopian court chronicler, used to the coming and going of career diplomats and eccentric men of means, Sylvain's humble private mission no doubt aroused little interest. Still, in the palace calendar for April 10, 1897, the name of the West Indian was entered next to the names of other foreign visitors received by the emperor that day: Count Le Gonidec, Prince de Lucinge, and Ensign Benito Sylvain of the Haitian Navy.[36]

Against such dearth of sources on the Ethiopian side, Sylvain's diary notes need to be understood in their intellectual and psychological context. The writings constitute a travel genre, of course, but not of the classic Euro-American type. Sylvain, who sees himself as civilized by virtue of a French education, has his Haitian background to fall back on during the rough and tumble of his African sojourns. His travel observations, therefore, comprise the dualistic perspective of an outside insider. In some pages, he deprecates the lifestyle of the lowland pastoralists as savage and primitive. In others, he eagerly and uncritically embraces the high culture of the Christian highlands, which he believes is at the same level of sophistication as that of diaspora blacks and can serve as an agent of social transformation. As shown in the paragraphs below, what Sylvain's notes about his meeting with Menelik reveal is a conflicted Pan-African worldview, a tension reminiscent of the Du Boisian notion of double consciousness.

On the morning of April 10, at eleven o'clock, the Haitian presented himself at the Ethiopian palace, attired in a sharp navy uniform with white gloves and carrying a sword. The sight of an overseas black person in a European military uniform must have been startling. For Taytu, indifferent to protocol, impetuously stepped closer, studied the stranger critically, and exclaimed to the nearby interpreter: 'He is definitely a man of our race!'[37] For his part, Sylvain saw in the queen's body language natural intelligence, shrewdness of character and dominance, traits that made her the most uncompromising patriot in the eyes of Europeans. Her opulent physique spoke of her untoiling life as a noble woman. And her light complexion, at least by local standards, must have reminded Sylvain that in Ethiopia, as in Haiti and the rest of the Caribbean, society paid attention to shades of pigmentation, light skin commanding more social value than dark skin. Taytu was regal but not attractive, however. Sylvain found her natural beauty compromised by hydropsy, better known as edema, a potentially debilitating medical condition characterized by a swelling of the skin tissues due to excessive water retention.[38]

Menelik, Taytu's third husband according to Sylvain, exuded a more affable personality. In his mid-50s, the king remained physically active, starting his day at five in the morning with a stroll in the palace garden, and spending much of the day consulting with local and foreign dignitaries. He was an iconoclast in his own ways, but with the virtues and vitality of a great monarch. Sylvain described him in superlatives as one of the greatest men alive, in league with the Pope, the German Kaiser, and the Russian Tsar. Having grown up since the age of six in a strictly disciplinarian boarding seminary, it was as if Sylvain had finally discovered the paternal figure he had longed for as a child. In one passage, Sylvain wrote how he was welcomed with spontaneous cordiality by the great African sovereign. In another, he felt a dream-come-true in seeing with his own eyes the illustrious *Negus*, the moral exemplar of all humanity.[39]

Indeed, the exchange between Menelik and Sylvain could not have been more different from what was imagined by Skinner. Notorious for asking practical questions, Menelik used occasions like this to gauge the world's opinion about himself and his empire. On the issue of territorial integrity, he elicited Sylvain's consent that Ethiopia's encirclement by the colonial powers of Italy, Britain, and France posed the country's most serious existential threat. On his part, responding to a question about the slave trade, Menelik reminded his guest that he had already promulgated two imperial edicts banning the practice, and that he hoped that domestic slavery would die as a consequence. Sylvain remarked that ending slavery would not only deprive Europeans of the pretext for their anti-Ethiopian propaganda, but it would also transform the mixed feelings that blacks in the Americas had for their ancestral land.[40]

Then the discussion drifted to Sylvain's vision of 'African regeneration'. Even countries like Egypt and Ethiopia, with a long history of 'civilization', were often disparaged in popular opinion because of unfavorable European coverage, Sylvain explained. The solution, as the West Indian saw it, was for blacks in Africa and the Americas to set aside petty differences and unite in a common cause of racial solidarity. This was not about a racial backlash. Rather, it was about uplifting oneself to the level of Europeans, with Western blacks playing the 'civilizing' role. More specifically, it was up to the elites of Haiti, Ethiopia, and North American blacks to join hands in working for collective social transformation. The concept was elitist, even avidly Eurocentric, by present-day standards. However, it was also prescient in its own right, as it foreshadowed the South–South dialogues of the late twentieth and early twenty-first centuries. The palace audience ended with Menelik having decorated Sylvain with the Cross of Solomon and appointed him an aide-de-camp, his liaison to the Pan-African world at large.[41]

Thus opened the first chapter of Ethiopian-American relations, whose rise and fall over a century has since fascinated many a historian. Sylvain would visit Ethiopia a few more times. Menelik would hire as his personal physician a French-speaking West Indian doctor, Joseph Vitalien of Guadeloupe. He would personally welcome a certain Daniel R. Alexander, the ex-slave Missourian who married and settled in the outskirts of Addis Ababa. In the mid-1930s, just before the threat of Italian invasion forced foreigners like Alexander out of Ethiopia, the number of black repatriates in the country would number close to a hundred, most of them colonial nationals from the English-speaking Caribbean islands.[42]

Second Visit

Sylvain's documented second voyage to Ethiopia took place in 1903.[43] This was the year that the Western hemisphere was represented in the court of Menelik by two other guests. African American William Henry Ellis, a wealthy New York stockbroker, made his call in November, presenting himself as a savvy business prospector.[44] In his footsteps followed the aforementioned Skinner, the US consul-general in Marseille, to whose memoir has already been traced the distorted interpretation of the 1897 event. Having concluded with Menelik the draft of the first diplomatic treaty between Ethiopia and USA, Skinner and his entourage left for the coast shortly after celebrating Christmas with the European legations, just days before the arrival of the Haitian mission in the capital.[45]

By 1901, a railway service between Djibouti and Ethiopia's eastern town of Diredawa, about 30 miles northwest of Harar, had shortened by half the several-week journey into the Ethiopian heartlands. Still, it was not unusual for travelers to run into one another during the latter half of the leg, and that was how Skinner and Sylvain met. Rumors in the capital, to which Skinner himself had fallen prey, were that Sylvain had come and gone several years ago feeling misunderstood, told in no uncertain terms that Ethiopia was the wrong place for his political cause. Fortunately, Skinner's description of the 1903 Haitian mission relied on his own observation. The somber image the consul-general drew of the West Indian envoy, following their brief encounter in person, belied the caricaturist portrait of the legations. If anything, it showed a man conscious of protocol, purpose-driven, and proudly wearing the badge of honor placed on him by host Menelik more than six years earlier.

According to Skinner's account, his escort of two dozen marine guards and sailors had barely left the highlands when it crossed paths with that of Sylvain's much smaller group, moving in the opposite direction. The meeting took place serendipitously at a resting stop where both parties had pitched their camps. Only by chance did the Americans take notice of the white tent with a foreign flag, out of which came a messenger who produced a card bearing the name of Sylvain and his personal credentials. 'Within a few moments Commandant Benito Sylvain arrived in person, in full uniform, varnished Wellington boots, spurs, white breeches, sword, and the Order of the Cross of Solomon upon his breast', Skinner wrote. 'Mr. Sylvain said that he was going to Addis-Ababa to present a letter from his Government to the Emperor. He intimated that he might remain there, to establish a permanent Legation', Skinner added. 'He was a most polite young man, speaking French that was a pleasure to hear, and I have no doubt whatever that he is persona grata at the capital quite as much as he was in the American camp'.[46]

Indeed, the Sylvain of 1903 was a worldly figure, well connected to a burgeoning group of Pan-African activists on both sides of the Atlantic. At the 1900 race conference in London, Sylvain had skillfully exploited his aide-de-camp soubriquet, giving the impression that he was either from Ethiopia or had direct access to its government. The completion of his doctor of law degree the next year, based on research he undertook on the plight of indigenes in the French colonies, further enhanced his intellectual standing. At home, it was time that the Haitian elite took notice of one of its own. In April 1903, President Pierre Nord Alexis finally recognized Sylvain's achievements by elevating him to the rank of commandant. It was at the peak of this social and intellectual potential, when opportunities were there for the picking, that the 35-year-old pioneer chose to return to East Africa.[47]

This time, Sylvain arrived in Ethiopia bearing a message of friendship and goodwill from the Haitian president. The timing was deliberate, as it coincided with the celebration of Haitian independence from France exactly a hundred years before. On the morning of December 31, 1903, fifteen soldiers, with what must have been a crash course on Haitian history by their drill master, climbed the highest summit of Addis Ababa where they raised the Haitian flag. Firing volleys, they shouted 'long live Haiti, long live the American Ethiopia' and gave salutes to the Caribbean bicolor. The group then proceeded to the imperial palace expecting a reception, only to learn that the emperor had left the previous night for his estate in the countryside. Thus was the token commemoration in Ethiopia on the eve of the centennial anniversary of Haitian independence day. It did not have the spectacular ending that Sylvain had hoped. But the commotion on the summit was dramatic enough to have attracted the attention of the locals, some of whom joined in the merrymaking by firing their guns into the air.[48]

Sylvain's 1903 mission focused on establishing formal bilateral ties between the two independent countries. This was an important distinction, as African American and West Indian travelers in West and Central Africa were mostly interested in business ventures, religious work, or migration. Thanks to that effort, Haiti became the first country to exchange diplomatic overtures with Ethiopia outside the governments of Europe and the USA. 'We congratulate Your Excellency on your election to the presidency of the Republic of Haiti, the independence of which has been dear to us, ever since we came to know of its history', read Ethiopia's reply to Nord Alexis. Although it bore Sylvain's editorial fingerprints, the letter was dictated to an interpreter by Ras Makonnen, Menelik's de facto foreign minister. The text mentioned the need for Haiti and Ethiopia to 'establish good rapports', as well as to work together for mutual benefits and for the benefit of the African race. 'If men are separated by great maritime and terrestrial distances, common aspirations towards the Good can and do bring them closer', it concluded.[49]

The letter, dated May 23, 1904, stayed undelivered for several years, a delay Bervin attributed to indifference, even jealousy, within the Haitian bureaucracy. Sylvain's own speech as he finally deposited the document on March 21, 1907, gave credit to that sentiment. 'The reward from the physical and mental exertions that I have had, that nobody here has yet heard', it said, 'is the patriotic satisfaction of putting in your hands the reply of His Majesty Menelik II to the letter Your Excellency addressed to him on the occasion of the centennial anniversary'. The series of obstacles leading to the exchange of diplomatic messages between the two governments were unprecedented in ordinary international relations, Sylvain continued. But so was the historic significance of that exchange, in which the two standard-bearers of the 'black race' felt united by a common sense of duty for the first time. As he finished the speech, Sylvain handed to President Alexis the grand cross he was given by Menelik exactly ten years earlier. It was a symbolic gesture in which the vision of a man and his years of relentless toil were being entrusted to the government, although the latter would have neither the resources nor the passion to pursue them.[50]

According to Bervin, Sylvain made his fourth and final voyage to Ethiopia in 1906, although nothing is said of its significance or what it sought to achieve. News worthy of international coverage that year was the passing away of Ras Makonnen, Menelik's right-hand man and potential successor. The 54-year-old governor died of a sudden illness, probably of typhus, on March 21, 1906, leaving behind two sons: the 14-year-old Tefari (future Emperor Haile Selassie) and his much older half-brother Yilma. A seasoned statesman at home and abroad, Makonnen's death was a major blow to the government, and it is possible that Sylvain's last trip to Ethiopia was motivated by the desire to express his condolences in person.[51]

At any rate, by now Ethiopia had lost much of its allure for the Haitian ideologue. Since his audience with Pope Pius X in Rome in June 1905, Sylvain had gravitated toward a sympathetic understanding of the Church as the handmaiden of African colonialism.[52] His new organization, Work for the Social Rehabilitation of Blacks (WSRB) hoped to thrive financially as a proponent of the civilizing mission. Unfortunately, the decision to move WSRB to French-speaking Catholic Canada, where untapped resources were anticipated, would turn out to be a great miscalculation. In fact, it would mark the anticlimactic end of a long and colorful Pan-African career. The extent of racism in Montreal was such that, after a year of struggle, Sylvain was forced to close WSRB and move back to Haiti to try his luck in mainstream politics.[53]

In Port-au-Prince, Sylvain was quickly promoted to the rank of adjutant general in the navy and then to the chamber of deputies, making him head of the senate committee overseeing the work of the army. His success was short-lived. Caught between the interests of US banks and land concessionaires on the one hand, and that of the rural insurgents on the other, Haiti would revert to another round of civil war, ousting no fewer than five presidents between 1911 and 1915. In November 1914, after Sylvain wrote to the press denouncing the landing of US and German forces on the island to protect European interests, the government downgraded him as head of a non-existent department of agriculture. A broken man, the Pan-Africanist died on January 3, 1915, a few months short of his 47th birthday.[54] His only son, René, a soldier in the French army, fell in the line of duty in February 1916 during an infantry charge against German forces. A newspaper obituary described him as being 20 years old.[55]

Ethiopia in Haiti

One of the earlier, possibly the earliest, references to Sylvain's trip to Africa in the Haitian newspapers was the brief article in *Le Nouvelliste* in its issue of July 31, 1900. The article announced Sylvain's return to France after nine months of absence in Abyssinia. Other than the mention of the meeting between Sylvain and Menelik, the article provided no additional factual information. Sylvain's historic sojourn in the Horn of Africa, which took place in 1897, did not become public knowledge until three years later. The reasons were not difficult to fathom. First, *Nouvelliste*, the oldest Haitian newspaper, did not start publishing until 1898. Second, typical media coverage of Africa did not go past the Atlantic shores, and even then a vast gap of information existed.[56]

Ironically, it was an unlikely event in 1902 that resulted in a lengthier piece about Ethiopia by the Haitian newspaper. In July of that year, Ethiopia was among the world governments that the British foreign office had invited to the coronation of Edward VII. Because of his relative familiarity with Europe from his visit to Italy in 1890, Ras Makonnen represented his country at the royal pomp and ceremony. Accompanied by his mission-educated translator, Gebru Desta (later Kentiba Gebru), Makonnen used the occasion to travel through France, Germany, and Turkey. While in London he made the acquaintance of William Henry Ellis, the New York stockbroker who would visit his country the next year as a business prospector. In France, he used his old contact Sylvain, to recruit Joseph Vitalien, a medical doctor from the Caribbean island of Guadeloupe, to help him start the first modern hospital in Harar.[57]

Because of the special attention Makonnen drew as the only black guest at the Court of St. James, the Haitian newspaper not only came to know of the African representation but seemed to be critical of it. On August 22, *Nouvelliste* published a rather facetious piece on the Ras, a commentary about the Ethiopian's supposed lack of 'etiquette'. Indifferent to protocol, Makonnen was said to have been seen greedily perusing the collection of Ethiopian manuscripts at the national library of France, which the paper interpreted as proof of the man's lack of social refinement. How a casual incident became newsworthy, in which Makonnen's behavior was dubbed as 'vulgar' by the Editor, was not clear, although sentiments of national rivalry could not be ruled out. In fact, it was not until the arrival of *Le Matin* in 1907, as the commercial competitor to *Nouvelliste*, that Ethiopia began to appear favorably to Haitian readers.[58]

In *Matin*, Menelik was addressed more formally, and the words emperor and its Amharic equivalent *negus* were often used interchangeably, as were the names Abyssinia and Ethiopia. Most of all, the king's ever deteriorating health condition remained of particular interest. On October 19, 1908, *Matin* included a short dispatch from Paris, which announced that the rumors about Menelik's demise were unsubstantiated. The story was repeated on January 30 based on the latest dispatch from London, only to be modified a few days later, with reports indicating that the king was seriously ill but not dead. Implicated was Taytu, who supposedly poisoned her husband out of sheer lust for power, an allegation that brought Sylvain into the fray. On April 13, 1910, Sylvain, now a deputy in the senate, wrote to *Matin* denouncing the negative media coverage. Taytu, even more than Menelik, he argued, was the one who had spared her country from the fate of colonialism, hence why she was a target of retaliation by the pro-European press, including *Nouvelliste*. To give the op-ed more weight, Sylvain signed the letter with his military title as Colonel Benito Sylvain, honorary aide-de-camp to Emperor Menelik.[59]

In 1913, *Matin* published two detailed articles on Ethiopia. The first was the June 26 summary of the previous day's senate debate, in which the paper paid particular attention to exchanges between Deputy Sylvain and Foreign Minister Morel Bonamy. During the question-and-answer session, Sylvain had asked the minister if the government of Ethiopia was informed of the election of Michel Oreste as the new president of Haiti. On learning that nothing of that nature had been tried, Sylvain reminded his colleague that he, Bonamy, and President Alexis were among those who had supported the 1903 historic mission to East Africa. Since the governments of Ethiopia and Haiti had since been in de facto recognition of each other, a fact made evident by the correspondence between Menelik and Alexis, it was only proper that Bonamy and his Ethiopian counterparts kept each other abreast of contemporary developments; so advised Sylvain.[60]

The second editorial, 'Emperor Menelik: Is He Dead or Alive?', appeared on November 26, coincidentally just weeks before the actual demise of the monarch. Digressing from the original question for lack of evidence, the article directed its attention to the topic of the press in Ethiopia. *Le Courrier D'Ethiopie* had just found a niche in the expatriate community of Addis Ababa as the city's only foreign-language weekly. *Matin* introduced the serial as the first newspaper in the whole country, unaware of the Amharic *Aimro* that had preceded it by more than a decade. To support its claim, *Matin* reproduced the promotional section that had appeared in the August issue of *Courrier*. To business competitors, accessing a copy of the overseas African paper no doubt demonstrated *Matin's* growing international network. To casual readers, the story of *Courrier D'Ethiopie* must have served an equally compelling lesson. Haiti had at least two well-established daily papers, *Matin* and *Nouvelliste*; while Ethiopia, with many times the size of Haiti's population, could count on just an expatriate-driven weekly publication.[61]

SYLVAIN AND ETHIOPIA IN NORTH AMERICA

A reference to Sylvain's African odyssey appeared in the North American media as early as October 1898.[62] By 1899, Sylvain's name had made it into the correspondence between Booker T. Washington and Henry Sylvester Williams, a British-trained Trinidadian barrister. As founder and president of the African Association in Britain, Williams was in communication with the prominent US educator on the upcoming Pan-African conference that his organization was to host in London. 'Our plans (sic) for the Pan African Conference is maturing gradually. Have had a very favorable response from Mr. Benito Sylvain', he wrote to Washington.[63] 'You will be pleased to learn that M. Benito Sylvain of Abyssinia will be present', he added in a follow-up letter.[64]

Sylvain and Washington were not strangers to one another. A detailed account of the Pan-African conference, which took place at the Westminster Town Hall from July 23 to July 25, 1900, was published in Sylvain's 1901 doctoral dissertation: *Du Sort des Indigènes dans les Colonies d'Exploitation*. According to that account, translated into English by the historian Tony Martin, Sylvain and Washington had crossed paths as early as 1897. 'In the month of December 1897, returning from Haiti after our first voyage to Abyssinia, we came in contact with Professor Booker T. Washington', Sylvain was to remember. Washington put Sylvain in touch with Williams and other kindred spirits in Britain, a day's trip from Paris by land and sea: 'and we decided to join an African Association which had just been formed in London through the zealous efforts of a clergyman, the Rev. Joseph Mason, and a young student, Henry Sylvester Williams, originally from Trinidad'.[65]

Despite having been consulted at the preparatory stage, Washington did not attend the Westminster gathering, typical of someone known for his aversion to protest politics. Among the 33 delegates who participated, in addition to Williams, were W.E.B. Du Bois, Anna Julia Cooper, and Bishop Alexander Walters, all from the USA. F.R. Johnson, an ex-attorney general, attended on behalf of the Republic of Liberia, while the governments of Haiti and Ethiopia were represented by Sylvain. Colonial delegates came from Gold Coast, Lagos, Sierra Leone, Canada, Jamaica, and some of the smaller Caribbean islands, as well as from Cuba. Influential Britons, including Members of Parliament and the Bishop of London, joined, and the *Times* of London gave the event positive coverage.[66]

The conference concluded with what few then suspected would be the occasion's most remarkable oration: Du Bois's 'Address to the Nations of the World'. In a passage wrongly traced to his 1903 masterpiece *Souls of Black Folk*, the 32-year-old scholar made the century's most prophetic observation on North–South relations: 'The problem of the twentieth century is the problem of the color-line'. The most critical question of the new era, he continued, was 'the question as to how far differences of race (which show themselves chiefly in the color of the skin and the texture of the hair) will hereafter be made the basis of denying to over half the world the right of sharing to their utmost ability the opportunities and privileges of modern civilization'.[67] The Atlanta University professor pointed out the pervasive nature of racial exploitation internationally, against which a collective and conscientious struggle had to be waged. 'Let the nations of the World respect the integrity and independence of the free Negro States of Abyssinia, Liberia, Haiti, and the rest', Du Bois pleaded, 'and let the inhabitants of these States, the independent tribes of Africa, the Negroes of the West Indies and America, and the Black subjects of all nations take courage, strive ceaselessly, and fight bravely, that they may prove to the world their incontestable right to be counted among the great brotherhood of mankind'.[68]

In its deliberation, the conference recommended the establishment of a Pan-African Association under which the various international activities were to be centrally coordinated. The Association would meet every two years: in a city in the USA by 1902, and in Haiti by 1904, so as to coincide with the country's centennial commemoration of its national independence. Finally, 'a memorial would be addressed to the Emperor Menelik and to the Presidents of the Republics of Haiti and Liberia, proclaiming them Grand Protectors of the Pan-African Association'. With whatever diplomatic resources the three governments had in their reach, the message envisaged, they would intervene 'against the policy of extermination and degradation which prevails in Europe in regard to Black and colored people'.[69]

Constraining factors faced by the Pan-African Association, as it tried to live up to its ambitious mandates, are outside the scope of this chapter. In the immediate aftermath, North American newspapers praised the Westminster conference as an important milestone. On August 18, the *Appeal* of St. Paul, Minnesota, described the three-day event as the first time that international black activists had been able to come together and speak with one voice about their aspirations for equality and freedom.[70] A few days later, the *Colored American* of Washington, D.C., applauded the conference as 'a great success'. The latter's detailed account contained, among other things, a comprehensive list of personalities involved, daily activities, and receptions. Bishop Walters, pastor of the African Methodist Episcopal Church of New York, merited a particular acknowledgement for his presiding role, as did his assistant Sylvain, identified by his Ethiopian military title.[71]

The New York Times, North America's leading daily, said nothing about the historic meeting. In an unrelated incident, however, it too was to draw attention to the man who was now Menelik's de facto roving ambassador. On his way to Haiti in December 1901, Sylvain had disembarked at the New York port for a four-day stay in the city. His arrival on the French liner *La Gascogne*, bedecked colorfully, caught the attention of custom officials, resulting in an extended interrogation. 'A picturesque young officer, in a profusely gold-braided military suit, wearing two swords at his side and carrying another in his hand, was down on the passenger list as M. Benito Sylvain', the article read. 'When asked the reason for all of the gold lace and swords, he, with a decided French accent, told his questioner that he was a naval officer in the navy of Abyssinia, and also an aide de camp to King Menelek of that country'. In exaggeratedly poor English, the article reconstructed the dialogue between the 'Abyssinian' passenger and the custom inspector, with the former insisting that he be shown respect as a subject of King Menelek, and the latter retorting rudely: 'Who's Menelek? He don't count over here'.[72]

There was no mention of what Sylvain planned to do during his four-day layover in New York, although it would have been uncharacteristic of him if his schedule had not included a call on acquaintances, even a confab with the very Bishop Walters himself. That would not have been the first time the West Indian had tried to insert himself in the African American political landscape. As mentioned, he and Washington had crossed paths in 1897. In fact, just two months prior to his last transit through New York, Sylvain had cabled the Tuskegee Wizard, congratulating him on his dinner invitation from the White House, the first time a black leader had been accorded that honor.[73] If Washington, a practical man, thought of Sylvain as little more than a peripatetic ideologue, he at least appreciated his broader transoceanic perspective. In April 1904, as Congress discussed the ratification of Skinner's diplomatic treaty with Ethiopia, Washington would try to have an African American official fill the new position that might open within the State Department's overseas desk. 'I have talked with the President several times with a view of getting him to send a colored man to represent this country since Abyssinia is practically a Negro nation', he wrote to one Mr. Anderson.[74] The lobby did not succeed. In the same year, however, Washington was able to send three Tuskegee graduates to nearby eastern Sudan, then under British administration, to serve as technical advisors in a cotton-growing agricultural scheme.[75]

The last time Sylvain was in touch with the African American community was in 1908. During his short domicile in Montreal, Canada, he was able to appear at several US venues, including at New York City's Bethel Church on West 25th Street.[76] An individual Sylvain sought to meet in person during the lecture tours, but was able only to write to, was his old London acquaintance: Du Bois. 'I am very glad to have gotten the little note from you and to know that you are well', the New Englander scribbled back in January 1908, adding: 'I should like very much to hear of your work in Ethiopia and to see if there is a chance for our co-operation'.[77] In the follow-up letter, Sylvain explained briefly about his book project on 'Abyssinia, which will surely have some echo everywhere', before apologizing for his poor English and moving on to a topic of mutual interest. 'I received and read with the greatest satisfaction the litterature (sic) concerning the Niagara Movement that you have sent me', he continued. 'Our aim is the same: the complete emancipation of our Race, by exercising with dignity all the rights and prerogatives granted and warranted to white people'.[78]

The correspondence seems to have progressed no further. Du Bois was perhaps put off by a sentence in Sylvain's last missive about his hope for an African American college graduate wife, a subject the professor deemed rather too personal and inappropriate. Or, perhaps, instinct told him, and rightly so, that Sylvain was also in touch with his ideological archrival Washington.[79] Decades later, however, Du Bois would credit the West Indian for his ambassadorial role in introducing Ethiopia to the outside world. 'I remember the stiff, young officer who came with credentials from Menelik of Abyssinia', Du Bois wrote in *Darkwater*, his first autobiographical work, in 1920.[80] 'As early as 1900', he later added in a correspondence with an Ethiopian official, 'a Pan-African Conference met in London, and there was present a young

Haitian who had been in Abyssinia and brought us some information concerning the country'.[81]

Whether at the London conference, in the newspaper articles, or in the personal communications sampled above, there was a common thread. The insertion of Sylvain into the Ethiopian body politic helped write a new counter-discourse. The deracination of Ethiopia, a byproduct of post-Adwa racial anthropology, was subtly reversed. Thus began the incorporation of Ethiopian symbolism into the anticolonial imaginary. Because of his extensive network and wide travels, Sylvain epitomized the era's consummate global activist, becoming the true progenitor of modern Pan-Africanism in the eyes of some. And Menelik, whom Sylvain continued to represent abroad, grew into a larger-than-life figure, an anticolonial icon that a generation of black internationalists revered and looked up to.

Laudatory praises about Ethiopian war heroes in the black press long after the Battle of Adwa were, indeed, a testament to the country's evolving folkloric stature. In its issue of December 1900, the *Colored American Magazine* published a five-page biographical profile of Menelik. 'And to-day, his empire is recognized as a first-class power all over the world', was its compliment to the African sovereign.[82] In 1909, Ras Makonnen was called the 'Napoleon of Africa' by the *New York Age*, as well as being compared with Toussaint Louverture of Haiti. 'It was through his strategy and valor that the Italians were routed, and Abyssinia, that great Negro African kingdom, has remained free and independent', read the paper's overdue tributes to deceased Makonnen.[83]

Menelik's death in December 1913 was seen as the closing of an era by the *Chicago Defender*, prompting another flattering eulogy. 'King Menelik of Abyssinia, who recently died, was indeed a great man. Even though the country over which he ruled was comparatively small, his fame was worldwide.' The paper described Menelik as 'primitive in his own ways' for turning his back to modernity, but still concluded that he was a just and brave leader. 'His army of wild tribesmen have defeated some of the best disciplined and equipped soldiers of the old world ... Although he ruled with an iron will, he ruled justly; and many of the more civilized countries might well pattern after Abyssinia.'[84]

Finally, as Robert Hill has argued, the black anticolonial imaginary appropriated a more subtle trope in the tradition of *Ethiopis vagantes*. In the USA, Europe, the West Indies, and even among Africans had emerged a group of 'wandering Ethiopians', who either identified themselves as Ethiopians or claimed ancestral roots in Ethiopia.[85] Some of them were impostors of royalty, with copycat stories of a stranded traveler desirous of help. One of them was so credible that his story appeared in the *New York Times* of December 22, 1907. That was the story of Prince Ludwig Menelik, globe-trotting nephew of the African emperor, who became the unfortunate victim of theft while traveling through Europe.[86] Little did the paper suspect foul play. In 1904, Prince Thomas Mackarooroo had his cover of Zulu nobility blown by

London police and was deported back to Jamaica as a certain Charles Isaac Brown, only to reappear a few years later as Prince Ludwig Menelik of Abyssinia. In explaining Brown's new avatar, Menelik, Hill writes: 'Emperor Menelik II's status as the culture hero of the black world, following the stunning military victory of Ethiopia at the Battle of Adwa in 1896, had grown by leaps and bounds in the preceding years'.[87] Hill could have added that Sylvain was the catalyst behind that transformation. After all, no one performed the role of 'wandering Ethiopians' better than Sylvain of Haiti, Menelik's legendary ambassador to the Pan-African communities abroad.

Conclusion

Once distant and obscure to blacks in the Western hemisphere, by the early twentieth century the Horn of Africa had become an important trope in the modern anticolonial imaginary. The catalyst was the 1896 Ethiopian victory over Italy at the Battle of Adwa. Contemporary social Darwinists reinvented the post-Adwa state as a non-African sociopolitical entity. Diaspora blacks, by contrast, read in the Ethiopian victory the very theme of racial vindication that their newspapers and religious institutions had relentlessly promoted. Thanks to the role of Benito Sylvain, Ethiopia and Emperor Menelik had become household names in Pan-African circles, and bilateral diplomatic ties between Addis Ababa and Port-au-Prince even seemed a possibility.

Whatever ambivalence lingered on the 'Abyssinian race question', Du Bois tried addressing it in his 1915 Afrocentric classic *The Negro*. Du Bois described Menelik as 'a shrewd man of predominantly Negro blood' and his wife Taytu as 'a full-blooded Negress'. However crude the professor's language, his logic was clear. The Red Sea and the Nile Valley lay at the crossroads of cultures where populations from Africa and Asia met and mixed. According to the conventional definition of blackness, therefore, the people of the Horn of Africa were as Negroid as diaspora blacks.[88]

This extended into the classical past as well. Ancient Egypt, one of the earliest complex societies and home to many impressive innovations, was not African just by geography, but its progenitors were Ethiopians native to the vast region of the upper Nile. 'Pre-dynastic Egypt was settled by Negroes from Ethiopia', Du Bois posited. 'They were of varied type: the broad-nose, wooly-haired type, to which the word "Negro" is sometimes confined; the black curly-haired, sharper feature type, which must be considered an equally Negroid variation'.[89]

Du Bois himself treated race as a social construct, or 'a philosophic speculation', as he dubbed it. 'It is of no more importance now to know how many human races there are than to know how many angels can dance on the point of a needle', was his witty comment on the subject.[90] Yet, this was the era of scientific racism, and some level of race thinking was necessary to prove that the black past was no less impressive than the past of other peoples. Du Bois's

Nilocentric outline of history, from Ethiopia's ancient conquest of Egypt to its recent defeat of Italy at the Battle of Adwa, was meant to do that. It was a timely perspective that transcended the spatial and temporal constraints of the Black Atlantic. From the back-to-Africa homilies of Marcus Garvey to the prose and poetry of the Harlem artists, henceforth the Horn of Africa would play a critical role in popularizing the theme of resurgent Africa. Thus was the long-term significance of Emperor Menelik's defiant spirit at Adwa, which the Haitian Sylvain promoted internationally, and which was to inform profoundly the early history of the modern Pan-African movement.

NOTES

1. Gebru Tareke, review of *History of Modern Ethiopia 1855–1991*, 2nd ed., by Bahru Zewde, *International Journal of African Historical Studies* 35, no. 2/3 (2002): 587–90.
2. W.E.B. Du Bois, *The Negro* (Oxford and New York: Oxford University Press, 1970), 26.
3. For a discussion of classical Ethiopia and its place in black thought, or what Scott calls the "Ethiopian Tradition," see William R. Scott's *Sons of Sheba's Race: African–Americans and the Italo-Ethiopian War, 1935–1941* (Bloomington: Indiana University Press, 1993), chap. 1. For a comprehensive account of the history of African American sojourn in Africa, including missionary travels and repatriations, see James Campbell's *Middle Passages: African American Journeys to Africa, 1787–2005* (New York: Penguin, 2006).
4. The most controversial clause of the Wichale Treaty, also spelt as Wuchale or Ucciali, was Article 17. The Amharic version, which was the original draft, gave the Ethiopian government the option to negotiate with other sovereign powers through the Italian government: "His Majesty, the King of Kings of Ethiopia, *may, if he so desires,* avail himself of the Italian government for any negotiations he may enter into with other Powers and Governments." The Italian translation, which was distributed to the various European governments and which implied Ethiopia's protectorate status, stated that Ethiopia's diplomatic dealings with foreign powers were to be conducted through the Italian government: "His Majesty, the King of Kings of Ethiopia, *consents to avail himself* of the government of his Majesty the King of Italy *for all negotiations* in affairs which he may have with other Powers or Governments." (Italics added by the author for emphasis). For a comparative analysis of the Amharic and Italian versions of the treaty, see Paulos Milkias's "Battle of Adwa: Historic Victory of Ethiopia over European Colonialism," in *Battle of Adwa: Reflection on Ethiopian Victory Against European Colonialism*, ed. Paulos Milkias and Getachew Metaferia (New York: Algora, 2005), 43–50.
5. For a detailed account of the battle, see Raymond Jonas's *Battle of Adwa: African Victory in the Age of Empire* (Cambridge: Harvard University Press, 2011), chaps. 9–13.
6. Milkias and Metaferia, *Battle of Adwa*, 71, 128.
7. "Italy Like Pandemonium: Abyssinian Reverses Provoke Paroxysms of Rage in Rome," *New York Times*, March 6, 1896.

8. "Italy's Terrible Defeat," *New York Times*, March 4, 1896.
9. Article 2: no title. *New York Times*, March 4, 1896.
10. "A Personal View of Menelek: Impressions of Commercial Traveler Who Talked with Him in His Imperial Camp Last Month," *New York Times*, March 22, 1896.
11. Jonas, *Adwa*, 269.
12. For an insightful discussion on the Ethiopian race debate in the 1930s, a carry-over from the 1890s, see the chapter entitled "Black or White: The Hamitic Controversy," in Scott's *Sons of Sheba's Race*, 191–207.
13. Scott, *Sons of Sheba's Race*, 21 and 32.
14. Darlene Clark Hine, *African–American Odyssey*, combined volumes (Upper Saddle River, NJ: Pearson Education, 2003), 320.
15. James Quirin, "African–American Perceptions of the Battle of Adwa, 1896–1914," in *Proceedings of the XVth International Conference of Ethiopian Studies*, ed. Siegbert Uhlig (Wiesbaden: Harrassowitz, 2006), 344–48.
16. Quoted in Quirin, "African–American Perceptions," 346.
17. *Cleveland Gazette*, March 14, 1896.
18. Ibid., March 28, 1896.
19. Quoted in Quirin, "African–American Perceptions," 345.
20. Quirin, "African–American Perceptions," 346.
21. *Cleveland Gazette*, March 28, 1896.
22. Key texts in constructing this section have been travel diaries and other primary sources found in Antoine Bervin's biography of Benito Sylvain. Although a treasure trove to Horn of Africa specialists, the documents have been inaccessible to non-French readers and therefore hardly explored. For those who might be interested in these sources but may not have the language skill, effort has been made to integrate a few copious excerpts without altering the flow or the pace of the narrative. The author would like to thank his erudite bilingual student assistant, Denis Boulet of St. Thomas University, for translating into English relevant sections from Bervin's biography as well as the various articles from *Le Matin* and *Le Nouvelliste*. This chapter would have taken a totally different course without his help.
23. Emmanuelle Sibeud, "Comment Peut-on être Noir? Le Parcours d'un Intellectual Haïtien à la Fin du XIXe Siècle," *Cromohs* 10 (2005): 2.
24. Antoine Bervin, *Benito Sylvain: Apôtre du Relèvement Social des Noirs* (Port-au-Prince: La Phalange, 1969), 25. Also Sibeud, "Comment Peut-on être Noir?" 1–2.
25. Sibeud, "Comment Peut-on être Noir?" 2.
26. Daniel J. Crowley, "Suzanne Comhaire Sylvain: 1898–1975," *Obituaries* (1978): 700–1.
27. David Levering Lewis, *The Race to Fashoda: European Colonialism and African Resistance in the Scramble for Africa* (New York: Weidenfeld and Nicolson, 1987), 121.
28. Richard Pankhurst, "British Reactions to the Battle of Adwa: As Illustrated in the *Times of London* for 1896," in Milkias and Metaferia *Battle of Adwa*, 218.
29. Bervin, *Benito Sylvain*, 27.
30. Ibid., 32–34.
31. Ibid., 42–43.

32. Ibid., 45–46.
33. Robert P. Skinner, *Abyssinia of To-Day: An Account of the First Mission Sent by the American Government to the Court of the King of Kings, 1903–1904* (New York: Longman, 1906), 131.
34. Skinner, *Abyssinia*, 178–84.
35. Jonas, *Adwa*, 283.
36. Chris Prouty, *Empress Taytu and Emperor Menelik II: Ethiopia 1883–1910* (Trenton, NJ: Red Sea Press, 1986), 192.
37. Bervin, *Benito Sylvain*, 46.
38. Bervin, *Benito Sylvain*, 49–50. According to Chris Prouty, Taytu's biographer, the medical condition got more serious as the queen grew older, and surgery was discussed as a solution at some point. See Prouty, *Empress Taytu*, 277.
39. Bervin, *Benito Sylvain*, 47.
40. Ibid., 54–55.
41. Ibid., 55–56.
42. Jerrold Robins, "The Americans in Ethiopia," *Mercury* 29 (May–August 1933): 63–69. On Daniel Alexander, see "Rogers Found Four Americans in Abyssinia," *Afro-American* December 20, 1930; "Former Missourian Describes Menelik," *Pittsburgh Courier* February 8, 1936; and "Abroad for Thirty Years, Speaks Eleven Languages," *Afro-American* December 30, 1939.
43. According to Bervin, Sylvain made his second trip to Ethiopia in December 1903. However, in a letter to the Provisionary Government of Haiti, in October 1902, Sylvain writes about having returned from his third voyage to Ethiopia in July 1902 (87). Similarly, during his audience with Menelik in December 1903, Sylvain reminds the emperor that the last time they saw each other was two years earlier (68). Chances are Sylvain made more than the four trips (possibly six) acknowledged in the biography. In a couple of instances, Sylvain might not have proceeded farther than Harar, the abode of Ras Makonnen, just a day's train ride from Djibouti after 1901. Yet, Bervin seems to have counted only those involving a visit to Menelik's palace in the capital, hence the discrepancy.
44. The Texan William Henry Ellis, also known as Guillaume Enriques Ellesio, claimed a dual identity both as an African American and a Mexican national. Having risen to a great financial success in New York City as a business associate of Henry Hotchkiss, the famous gun manufacturer, Ellis was perhaps the richest black American of his time. On January 1, 1904, the *New York Times* published an article by Ellis about his Ethiopian expedition, "Tales of King Menelik," which was mostly a make-believe story of primal Africa. For a comprehensive biography on Ellis, see Karl Jacoby's, *The Strange Career of William Henry Ellis: The Texas Slave Who Became a Millionaire* (New York: W.W. Norton, 2016).
45. Skinner, *Abyssinia*, 73–82.
46. Ibid., 131–32.
47. Sylvain's role at the London conference, sometimes referred to as the First Pan-African Congress, is best captured in Tony Martin's, *Pan-African Connection: From Slavery to Marcus Garvey and Beyond* (Dover, MA: Majority Press, 1984), chap. 13. Scattered references to Sylvain's participation are also found in Marika Sherwood's *Origins of Pan-Africanism: Henry Sylvester Williams*

and the African Diaspora (New York: Routledge, 2010). For Sylvain's promotion to the rank of commandant in 1903, see the chronological timetable in Bervin's, *Benito Sylvain*, 156.
48. Bervin, *Benito Sylvain*, 69–71.
49. Ibid., 144–45.
50. Ibid., 145–46.
51. For obituary, see "Makonnen Dead," *New York Times*, March 24, 1906.
52. Bervin, *Benito Sylvain*, 100–3.
53. For Sylvain in Canada, see Bervin's *Benito Sylvain*, 127–40.
54. Bervin, *Benito Sylvain*, 148–49.
55. "Décoré et Porté à l'Ordre du Jour," *Le Matin*, February 15, 1916.
56. "Benito Sylvain," *Le Nouvelliste*, July 31, 1900.
57. For Makonnen's 1902 trip to Europe, where he was to meet with the African American Ellis, see Dawit Gebru Desta, *Kentiba Gebru Desta Ye Ethiopia Kiris* (Addis Ababa: self-published, 1993), 199–200. Also see Karl Jacoby's *Strange Career of William Ellis*, 146–47. Makonnen's recruitment of Dr. Joseph Vitalien, in 1902, is mentioned in Chris Prouty's *Empress Taytu*, 283. More likely, the contact between Makonnen and Vitalien was initiated by Sylvain. In one of his letters to the Haitian government, Sylvain mentions having met with Makonnen in Paris and of having run a special errand on his behalf. See Bervin's *Benito Sylvain*, 87.
58. "Le Ras Makonen," *Le Nouvelliste*, August 22, 1902.
59. Benito Sylvain, "Respect à la Femme! l'Impératrice d'Ethiopie et la Presse Européenne," *Le Matin*, April 13, 1910.
60. "La Chambre," *Le Matin*, June 26, 1913.
61. "L'Empereur Ménélik: Est-Il Mort ou Vivant?" *Le Matin*, November 26, 1913.
62. On October 2, 1898, a Californian newspaper included a dispatch from Paris about a social event at which Sylvain was a guest speaker. The occasion was inspired by the hundredth birthday of the now-deceased Jules Michelet, the celebrated French historian. Madam Michelet's father had served as the personal secretary of Toussaint Louverture in the 1790s, and Sylvain's presence was meant to symbolize that connection. Sylvain spoke representing his newly established organization: The Black Youth of Paris. The newspaper described him as "a Negro naval officer and aide-de-camp to the Abyssinian Emperor Menelik." See *Sacramento Record-Union*, October 2, 1898.
63. Louis R. Harlan, ed., *Booker T. Washington Papers* (Urbana and Chicago: University of Illinois Press, 1989), Vol. 5, 158.
64. Harlan, *BTW Papers*, Vol. 5, 569.
65. Quoted in Tony Martin, *Pan-African Connection*, 207.
66. Martin, *Pan-African Connection*, 207.
67. W.E.B. Du Bois, *ABC of Color* (New York: International Publishers, 1969), 20.
68. Du Bois, *ABC of Color*, 23.
69. Martin, *Pan-African Connection*, 207–8.
70. "Pan-African Conference," *Appeal*, August 18, 1900.
71. "Pan-African Conference," *Colored American*, August 25, 1900.

72. "King Menelek's Agent Was Forced to Wait," *New York Times*, December 2, 1901.
73. Harlan, *BTW Papers*, Vol. 6, 261.
74. Harlan, *BTW Papers*, Vol. 7, 486.
75. Harlan, *BTW Papers*, Vol. 7, 403–4, 520; and Vol. 8, 153–54, 288–89.
76. Letter from Benito Sylvain to W.E.B. Du Bois: May 23, 1908. W.E.B. Du Bois Papers (MS 312). Special Collections and University Archives, University of Massachusetts Amherst Libraries.
77. Letter from Du Bois to Sylvain: January 24, 1907 (more likely 1908). Du Bois Papers (MS 312). Special Collections and University Archives, University of Massachusetts Amherst Libraries.
78. Letter from Sylvain to Du Bois: June 24, 1908. Du Bois Papers (MS 312). Special Collections and University Archives, University of Massachusetts Amherst Libraries.
79. In May 1908, the same month Sylvain was in communication with Du Bois, he wrote to Washington inquiring about a teaching post at Tuskegee University, to which Washington responded negatively. See W. Manning Marable, "Booker T. Washington and African Nationalism," *Phylon* 35, no. 4 (1974): 399–400.
80. W.E.B. Du Bois, *Darkwater: Voices from Within the Veil* (New York: Harcourt, 1920), 193.
81. Memorandum to His Excellency Kentiba Gebrou and Mr. Malaku E. Bayen, Representing His Majesty Ras Tafari, King of Ethiopia: August 14, 1930. Du Bois Papers (MS 312). Special Collections and University Archives, University of Massachusetts Amherst Libraries.
82. S.E.F.C.C. Hamedoe, "Menelik, Emperor of Abyssinia: A Direct Descendant of Solomon the Great and the Queen of Sheba," *Colored American Magazine* 2, no. 2 (December 1900): 149–54.
83. Quoted in Quirin, "African–American Perceptions," 346–47.
84. "King Menelik," *Chicago Defender*, January 3, 1914.
85. Robert A. Hill, "King Menelik's Nephew: Prince Thomas Mackarooroo, aka Prince Ludwig Menelek of Abyssinia," *Small Axe* 26 (June 2008): 16.
86. "African Prince on Hunt for Capital: Nephew of Menelek Has 150,000 Abyssinian Acres He Wishes to Sell," *New York Times*, December 22, 1907.
87. Hill, "King Menelik's Nephew," 28.
88. Du Bois, *Negro*, 26.
89. Du Bois, *Negro*, 18.
90. Du Bois, *Negro*, 16.

Bibliography

Contemporary newspapers

Afro-American. Baltimore, MD.
Chicago Defender. Chicago, IL.
Cleveland Gazette. Cleveland, OH.
Le Matin. Porte-au-Prince, Haiti.
Le Nouvelliste. Port-au-Prince, Haiti.

New York Times. New York City, NY.
Pittsburgh Courier. Pittsburgh, PA.
Savannah Tribune. Savannah, GA.

DIGITAL ARCHIVES

W.E.B. Du Bois Papers. MS 312. Special Collections and University Archives, University of Massachusetts Amherst Libraries. http://credo.library.umass.edu/.

PUBLISHED SOURCES

Berkeley, George. *The Campaign of Adwa and the Rise of Menelik.* New York: Negro University Press, 1969.
Bervin, Antoine. *Benito Sylvain: Apôtre du Relèvement Social des Noirs.* Port-au-Prince: La Phalange, 1969.
Campbell, Horace. *Rasta and Resistance: From Marcus Garvey to Walter Rodney.* Lawrenceville, NJ: Africa World Press, 1987.
Campbell, James T. *Middle Passages: African American Journeys to Africa, 1787–2005.* New York: Penguin, 2006.
Desta, Dawit Gebru. *Kentiba Gebru Desta Ye Ethiopia Kiris.* Addis Ababa: Self-published, 1993.
Du Bois, W.E.B. *Darkwater: Voices from Within the Veil.* New York: Harcourt, 1920.
———. *ABC of Color.* New York: International Publishers, 1969.
———. *The Negro.* Oxford and New York: Oxford University Press, 1970.
Gebrekidan, Fikru Negash. *Bond Without Blood: A History of Ethiopian and New World Black Relations, 1896–1991.* Trenton: Africa World Press, 2005.
———. "Ethiopia in Black Studies: From W.E.B. Du Bois to Henry Louis Gates Jr." *Northeast African Studies* 15, no. 1 (2015): 1–34.
Gilroy, Paul. *The Black Atlantic: Modernity and Double Consciousness.* London: Verso, 1993.
Hamedoe, S.E.F.C.C. "Menelik, Emperor of Abyssinia: A Direct Descendant of Solomon the Great and the Queen of Sheba." *Colored American Magazine* 2, no. 2 (December 1900): 149–54.
Harris, Joseph E. *African–American Reactions to War in Ethiopia, 1936–1941.* Baton Rouge: Louisiana State University Press, 1994.
Hill, Robert A. "King Menelik's Nephew: Prince Thomas Mackarooroo, aka Prince Ludwig Menelek of Abyssinia." *Small Axe* 26 (June 2008): 15–44.
Jacoby, Karl. *The Strange Career of William Henry Ellis: The Texas Slave Who Became a Millionaire.* New York: W.W. Norton, 2016.
Jonas, Raymond. *Battle of Adwa: African Victory in the Age of Empire.* Cambridge: Harvard University Press, 2011.
Marable, W. Manning. "Booker T. Washington and African Nationalism." *Phylon* 35, no. 4 (1974): 398–406.
Marcus, Harold G. "The Black Men Who Turned White: European Attitudes Toward Ethiopians, 1855–1900." *Archiv Orientalni* 39 (1979): 159–66.
———. *A History of Ethiopia.* Berkeley: University of California Press, 1994.
———. *The Life and Times of Menelik II: Ethiopia 1844–1913.* 2nd ed. Lawrenceville, NJ: Red Sea Press, 1994.

Martin, Tony. *Pan-African Connection: From Slavery to Marcus Garvey and Beyond.* Dover, MA: Majority Press, 1984.

Milkias, Paulos, and Getachew Metaferia, eds. *Battle of Adwa: Reflection on Ethiopian Victory Against European Colonialism.* New York: Algora, 2005.

Prouty, Chris. *Empress Taytu and Emperor Menelik II: Ethiopia 1883–1910.* Trenton, NJ: Red Sea Press, 1986.

Quirin, James. "African–American Perceptions of the Battle of Adwa, 1896–1914." Siegbert Uhlig, ed., *Proceedings of the XVth International Conference of Ethiopian Studies.* Wiesbaden: Harrassowitz, 2006.

Robins, Jerrold. "The Americans in Ethiopia." *Mercury* 29 (May–August 1933): 63–69.

Scott, William R. *Sons of Sheba's Race: African–Americans and the Italo-Ethiopian War, 1935–1941.* Bloomington: Indiana University Press, 1993.

Sherwood, Marika. *Origins of Pan-Africanism: Henry Sylvester Williams and the African Diaspora.* New York: Routledge, 2010.

Sibeud, Emmanuelle. "Comment Peut-on être Noir? Le Parcours d'un Intellectual Haïtien à la Fin du XIXe Siècle." *Cromohs* 10 (2005): 1–8.

Skinner, Robert P. *Abyssinia of To-Day: An Account of the First Mission Sent by the American Government to the Court of the King of Kings, 1903–1904.* New York: Longman, 1906.

Washington, Booker T., Harlan R. Louis, and Raymond W. Smock. *Booker T. Washington Papers.* 14 volumes. Urbana and Chicago: University of Illinois Press, 1989.

Zewde, Bahru. *A History of Modern Ethiopia 1855–1991.* Oxford: James Currey, 2002.

CHAPTER 22

Colonial Africa and the West

Enocent Msindo

To understand Africa's postcolonial condition and its relationship with the West we need to first appreciate historical linkages between the two.[1] Africa's relationship with Western countries, particularly European countries, emerged mainly as a result of colonization and the systems that colonizers established. Colonization happened at a specific era in Western history. By 1800, mercantile capitalism had firmly established itself in Europe and had extended its tentacles across the globe. Mercantile capitalism was strengthened by the profits of the slave trade and aggressive industrialization, leading to social and political changes in Europe. The evolution of efficient shipping technology and the invention of lethal military technology were also important factors. The rapid expansion of mercantile commerce, post-slave trade, which period is glibly referred to as the era of legitimate commerce (which it was not); the rise of new Western forms of aggressive nationalisms spurring and themselves further spurred by aggressive unifications (for instance Germany, Italy, France, and others), and the birth of certain philosophies, especially social Darwinism, all heightened appetites for adventure, impelled notions of Western grandeur and also dictated changing ideas towards modes of business between Europe and the rest of the world.

Colonization became one preferred approach to create and safeguard new markets for the industrial revolution in Europe, to accelerate the extraction of cheap raw materials, and to reproduce cultures of perpetual dependency by delegitimizing African indigenous innovation and knowledge systems

E. Msindo (✉)
Department of History, Rhodes University,
Grahamstown, South Africa

© The Author(s) 2018
M.S. Shanguhyia and T. Falola (eds.),
The Palgrave Handbook of African Colonial and Postcolonial History,
https://doi.org/10.1057/978-1-137-59426-6_22

through incorporating Africans into a lasting regime of cheap labor.[2] This helps us to understand why colonialism became primarily an extractive enterprise which depended on the establishment of certain political and economic systems which continued to shape and further undermine African economies after Independence, exacerbating Africa's dependency on former colonizers. Even in this era of Chinese economic dominance, African countries' links with former colonizers have remained strong. In this chapter, we examine how the colonial system worked and how it was closely tied to Western politics, how it fed into the Western economic system and how it created conditions that dictated Africa's future. Without radical economic decolonization, the African story remains one of abject misery.

Legacies of the Colonial Economy

Colonialism was a complete package that thrived by integrating Africa to the Western economic system on unequal terms. This happened through a combination of processes. First, African judicial and political structures were destroyed and replaced by European structures that facilitated the extraction of resources through monopoly capitalist entities. In settler colonies, colonial officials undermined preexisting African political and economic systems. They also passed a raft of laws that impacted on Africans' productive capacity. These included discriminatory land laws; laws controlling the prices of agricultural goods such as the 1934 Maize Control Act in colonial Zimbabwe, and laws controlling labor mobilization in the colonies.

In protectorates and indirect rule colonies, colonial power was exercised through salaried despotic monarchies (mainly kings and chiefs) and through a few African educated elites who served in the civil service. Where centralized polities did not exist, such as in Eastern Nigeria, new warrant chiefs were invented to make the system work.[3] In the Great Lakes region of Central Africa, where there were established monarchies, divide and rule was used to facilitate colonial resource extraction. The institution of kingship was transformed as kings became key in mobilizing forced labor from weaker ethnic groups for colonial projects such as railway and road construction and cash-crop agriculture. In Rwanda and Burundi, Tutsi kings and chiefs, who were 'Nilotes', were given unwieldy powers over the mainly Hutu 'Bantu' subjects. This cemented the Hamitic myth. In Uganda, the Baganda monarchy, headed by the *kabaka* (king) was retained, this time under a new colonial mandate. Unsurprisingly, when the nationalist movement rose in the late 1950s in the Great Lakes region, it was strongly anti-monarchy as the latter was associated with the evils of indirect-rule colonialism. In Uganda, the king's residence was attacked in 1966, the king forced into exile in Britain, and his residency turned into one of President Milton Obote's military barracks. The institution of kingship was legally abolished in 1967.

In Rwanda and Burundi, Tutsi regimes that had been in power during Belgian colonial rule were violently overthrown between 1959 and 1962 and replaced by majoritarian Hutu leaders. Consequently, huge Tutsi populations trekked into parts of Central and Eastern Africa such as Zaire (now the Democratic Republic of Congo), Uganda, Tanzania, and elsewhere. In many ways, this refugee crisis situation explains many challenges that we have in Central Africa today such as: the perpetual refugee crisis in the region; the 1994 Rwanda genocide; the crisis in Zaire that ended Mobutu's reign, himself a Western Cold War ally; the perpetuation of ethnic politics in the region; the rise of new political heavyweights in the region, namely Yoweri Museveni and Paul Kagame (both key Western allies in the region)[4] at a time when Nyerere's influence was in decline following his retirement from politics in 1985; the failure of democratic transitions in the entire Great Lakes region; the rise of insurgencies and the collapse of traditional social structures. Scholarship has demonstrated that the West has been the key beneficiary of the disorder in the Great Lakes region. Since the short-lived reign of Patrice Lumumba, Western multinational corporations, allied with local and international criminal networks, have continued to foment disorder and loot the economy during times of civil war in the Congo.[5] In addition to Mobutu's use of mainly Hutu refugees against his fellow citizens since the Rwanda genocide, Western food, financial aid, and other interventions have continued to fuel the refugee crisis and violence in the region as perpetrators use human hostages as shields.[6]

The second point is that under colonial rule, industrial production in Africa focused on extracting raw materials mainly through mining and (cash-crop) agriculture, both of which produced raw materials for the colonizers' countries from where they were processed into finished goods.[7] These finished products were then imported from the metropolitan countries into Africa and elsewhere, usually by companies wholly owned by citizens of those colonizing countries. Invariably, these firms repatriated most of their profits to their parent countries. The capitalist system was an organized cyclical system. Consequently, there was no deliberate attempt to invest in the manufacturing sector as doing so would severely compromise the colonial project by creating possibilities for colonies to become more competitive and self-sufficient, which would make them more difficult to govern and possibly become more self-reliant, should they gain political independence.

Moreover, any attempt to develop processing industries in colonies required either a massive immigration of skilled white personnel to the colonies or heavy financial investment in setting up tertiary education institutions for Africans so that they would get the skills required to run new industries. Neither of these possibilities was inherently desirable to the colonizers as this would directly undermine the colonial project for no apparent gain. In settler colonies such as Rhodesia (now Zimbabwe), massive immigration campaigns were started to attract new white settlers between the 1950s and 1970s, but such campaigns were not successful as this did not bring in the much needed capital investment and the skilled persons envisaged by the Rhodesian government.[8] The few immigrants who came into Africa after 1945 did not set up new competitive manufacturing industries but served mainly in the agricultural and mining sectors. Elsewhere, in the 1950s, white settlers were already leaving Africa mainly due to the end of colonial rule in different African countries. Some were leaving their colonies for other African settler colonies which still appeared to be intact. For instance, some left the Belgian Congo for Southern Rhodesia following the collapse of Belgian rule; the same applied to whites from Kenya after the Mau-Mau insurgency.

The cyclical nature of the capitalist system that we described above is a very pertinent factor in understanding African economic history. It helps us to understand why Africa is still dominated by huge multinational corporations, which are listed on stock exchanges of their parent countries, such as Anglo-American, BHP Billiton, Shell and others. None of these corporations focused on manufacturing in Africa as their model was and is still based on extracting it raw, shipping it out, processing it abroad, then selling it worldwide, including to the original source. This was Africa's first impediment. When African countries received their independence, the new states had to maintain close ties with established Western corporations and Western governments because these were the only known and available economic avenues for Africa to access the outside world with its raw materials. Any diplomatic relationships were handled with care as feared to upset this status quo. Those who tried to delink from the West by adopting socialist principles immediately faced thAfricae wrath of the West; Congo, Mozambique, Somalia, Angola, and a few others are examples. Those who became pro-capitalist, like Ivory Coast, yet with an Afro-centric economic model were not spared either. They held on for a few years, but by the mid-1970s they were also in trouble and highly indebted.

The third challenge for Africa was that at independence, most Africans were not yet trained and skilled enough to initiate and run their own industries. At independence, in Congo only a handful had a university degree, and these were mainly African priests. This was the situation in many other African countries at independence, except in parts of West Africa, where missionary education predated colonialism and an educated elite class emerged much earlier. Moreover, the education system that was established in many post-colonial African countries did little to solve Africa's economic conundrum as the education system reproduced the colonial education model of producing workers to serve in established entities as opposed to training entrepreneurs.

In Africa, the relationship between capitalism and colonialism dictated that capital be invested in those colonies where there was more likelihood of extracting more raw materials, particularly in mineral-rich areas. By 1938, more than half of Britain's £1222 million investment to Africa went to South Africa (£555 million) and Southern Rhodesia (£102 million) as colonial

Zimbabwe was then known. These two were the mineral-rich settler colonies of Southern Africa. This made South Africa and Zimbabwe economically stronger than their regional neighbors, and they were used as springboards by the British to control neighboring colonies which were under indirect rule.[9] The story was the same for other settler colonies that were strategically scattered in different African regions. Before the Mau Mau insurgency and its ultimate independence, Kenya dominated Tanzania, Uganda, and the Island of Zanzibar. This history of strong colonial investment and the corresponding huge white-settler populations in these colonies increased these colonies' dependence on Western economic models and heightened their vulnerability to Western corporations' disinvestment. Zimbabwe is currently struggling to revive its economy following the closure of mainly foreign-owned firms, most of which were owned by the descendants of British settlers. South Africa is also beginning to experience an economic downturn following similar Western capital flight and the speculative tendencies of its international investors.

We alluded above to the relationship between colonialism and resource extraction. Each African colony was a specialized economic unit that produced a narrow range of products, particularly certain minerals or cash crops that were required in metropolitan countries for their industrial, military, and food necessities. By creasing a situation in which Africans produced what they could not consume (raw materials) and consumed what they did not produce (finished products), colonial economies entrenched Africa's cycles of dependency which had started during the slave trade era.[10] This narrow economic structure had serious ramifications for Africa's food security after independence, particularly in the light of Africa's postwar population boom, and also for Africa's overall balance of trade. For instance, in South Africa (where the major economic venture was mining), huge urban centers emerged with the Africans evicted from certain areas into reserves. Consequently, by the 1930s, their food security situation and their tradable products had drastically declined to almost 50% below their 1885 levels because of declining production in the dry areas into which they had been driven. Inhabitants of South Africa's Ciskei and Transkei regions were so impoverished that they became nothing more than reservoirs of cheap colonial labor for the mines.[11] The historical connection between these poor areas and mine labor has continued to this day as the majority of miners working in the platinum mines of the North West province come from these areas. Post-apartheid South Africa currently contends with this huge and vulnerable rural populace whose plight will not change because they have been submersed into a permanent social and economic crisis.

Furthermore, the narrowness of the colonial economy, which remained so after independence, meant that in the event of a fall in prices of certain products, many African countries had no fall-back plan. This happened to Ivory Coast of Houphouet-Boigny in 1988, then a producer of about 40% of world cocoa. When the price of cocoa declined by 50%, the Ivorian economy collapsed, also worsening the Ivorian food security situation as the country did not have sufficient foreign currency to import food.[12] Zambia, which relied on copper, also suffered when copper prices fell drastically in the 1970s.

Colonial cash-crop specialization was a deliberate economic choice to turn colonies into specialized economic zones so as to connect Africa to the global capitalist economy. Certain African colonies were better known for growing certain cash crops. Cotton was mainly produced in Mozambique and Uganda, rubber in Liberia and Belgian Congo, coffee in Kenya and Uganda, cocoa in Ivory Coast and Ghana, palm oil in Nigeria, groundnuts in Senegal and Gambia, and many others. Between a quarter and a third of all cultivated land in Africa was dedicated to cash-crop agriculture.[13] Before the rise of African nationalism in Africa, mainly after 1945, African peasants who were drawn into this parasitic colonial economy could not successfully challenge the system because of increasing colonial violence. Colonial cash-crop cultivation during the colonial era thrived because of the use of violence including physical force, the rejection of African indigenous agrarian knowledge systems, the evictions of villagers from their land, price-fixing by the state-controlled marketing boards, and an introduction of a dual-tiered pricing model whereby products from European farmers fetched higher prices than from those of Africans.[14] In the 1940s, efforts by African peasants to create alternative markets for their products were thwarted by colonial regimes which tightly controlled the marketing boards so as to undermine peasants' economic competitiveness.[15]

Post-independence African governments inherited the above parasitic character of the colonial state. They did not perform well as they either failed or were unwilling to move beyond the limits of the colonial economy as moving away entailed creating a completely new and different relationship with the West. Peasants remained at the center of the state's developmental goals, perhaps because the peasants were viewed as softer targets to manipulate than the burgeoning urban populace which was politically virulent because of their trade union movements, their access to information, and their being politically outside 'tribal' structures where they had been controlled through despotic chiefs and headmen. In post-independent Africa, peasants had the dual role of producing food for the rapidly expanding urban population and at the same time producing cash crops that helped boost the export sector.

In Tanzania and Ethiopia, peasants were moved from their original villages into resettlements where they were forced to farm under close supervision from government development agents. This undermined their own agency. The same socialist experiment was adopted in Mozambique. In other countries, peasants were forced to work on chiefs' farms at the expense of their own farms; were forced to pay back government loans by being beaten up or sprayed with fertilizer or insecticides (Senegal); or were threatened that their farms would be seized if they disobeyed (Ghana) or were not productive enough (Ivory Coast).[16] Post-independence peasants never got to control the marketing of their produce as this role continued to be managed by state-controlled marketing boards, which fixed producer prices of their cash and food crops so as to compete on international markets. Declining profits, coupled with the rise in input costs, especially in the 1970s and 1980s, drove many African peasants out of business, leading to what Brycesson termed the problem of Africa's 'vanishing peasantry'.[17] The ultimate result of the collapse of the peasant agricultural sector is the food crisis which drives Western non-governmental organizations into Africa with their associated hidden agendas.

And finally, colonies were sustained through a system of gate keeping, which thrived on the capacity of the colonial officials to force colonial subjects to pay taxes that sustained administrative costs. A raft of taxes such as hut tax, poll tax, cattle tax and many others were introduced. The introduction of taxes was multipronged. First, to meet the tax obligations, Africans had to participate in the colonial cash economy by accepting cheap labor. Cheap labor was necessary for company profit maximization. Second, taxes were symbolic, a kind of vulgarization of the precolonial tribute system, to make a political statement. The third and most important factor is that colonial taxes played a huge part in sustaining the small colonial economies. Metropolitan countries wanted to spend as little as possible on service delivery in the colonies, particularly on African education and health, and also on their increasing administrative costs. By 1934, a sizeable amount of revenue in most African colonies came from taxes from Africans which exceeded taxes from non-Africans. Table 22.1, which demonstrates the tax revenues in 1934, is instructive.

Historian Basil Davidson argued that, in general, taxes that were levied from Africans increased during the Great Depression of the 1930s when living conditions were harder than before.[18] Reliance on taxes to pay most of the administrative costs was due to the fact that colonial economies were not diversified enough. To prevent a total collapse of such colonies, colonial officials instituted a gate-keeping system, which relied on levying taxes and charges on certain services provided to its citizens.[19] This system was also followed by the post-independent state, except that the latter abolished some of the repugnant taxes, like hut-tax. The gate-keeper system impedes innovation and popular participation in the state's economic development. This is

Table 22.1 Tax revenues in 1934. *Source* B. Davidson, *Modern Africa*, p. 55

Country	Currency	Tax from Africans	Tax from non-Africans	% of annual budget revenue
Nyasaland	£ Sterling	129,562	18,970	43.0
Kenya	£ Sterling	544,480	116,495	32.5
Nigeria	£ Sterling	775,010	32,633	18.5
French Equatorial Africa	French francs	37,298,300	1,185,000	57.0
Belgian Congo	Belgian francs	80,709,434	19,764,683	28.8

so because gate keeping thrives primarily on coercion and patronage whereby the big men (usually senior politicians) have a chain of small men (their lower-level administrators, governors, and others) who pay homage to them and do the errands for the big men to stay in power and also to get richer. These small men are in turn rewarded for their services in some way, either by promotion or by being given certain powers to abuse state resources knowing full well that they have protection from above. We will finish this discussion by briefly analyzing the impact of the post-1945 developments on post-independent Africa.

Postwar Transitions

The situation facing colonies after 1945 varied. Some colonies suffered economic stagnation as a result of the economic slowdown after the war. In some parts of Africa, however, particularly in some British and French colonies, the period saw a measure of economic development triggered by attempts by British and French governments to promote colonial capital projects and limited infrastructural development in colonies under the assumption that this investment would boost chances of the metropolitan countries' recovery from their postwar recession.[20] New capital projects such as hydroelectric power generation, mechanization of agriculture, capacitation and development of some industries were undertaken in a few colonies. However, it is a gross exaggeration to assume, as Fieldhouse does, that these initiatives '... stimulated an unprecedented expansion of African economies which was still under way when the colonies received their independence' and that '... the African economies, far from being "underdeveloped", were well equipped for sustained development, provided that they maintained the sensible policies previously imposed on them by the colonial authorities'.[21] The allocated funds for most of these projects were insufficient to meet the overall developmental needs. Marxist theorists, whom Fieldhouse is critical of, help us to understand why this investment was minimal. A key argument by Giovanni Arrighi (quoting Oskar Lange) in his discussion of the duality of the center (Western countries) and the periphery (African countries) is useful, notwithstanding its flaws. He rightly argues that there was no interest in making African economies competitive as this threatened Western economic monopoly. With the development of large capitalist monopolies in the leading capitalist countries, the capitalists of those countries lost interest in developmental investment in the less developed countries because such investment threatened their established monopolistic positions.[22]

In British colonial Africa, settler colonies also engaged immigration experts to help them attract new, white, skilled immigrants to bring in human and financial capital to boost industry. This effort reaped very limited results because Africa competed with the new world (New Zealand and Australia, for example) for immigrants.[23] Moreover, the waves of protests that led to the first phases of decolonization in the 1950s scared away prospective immigrants and new investors, who preferred safer investment havens elsewhere. Protests and anticolonial movements also added to the financial, military, and administrative costs of sustaining colonies. For these reasons, the envisioned grand projects of the period (which are usually termed 'the second colonial occupation' in Africa) were unsuccessful.[24] These initiatives did not provide foundations for a dynamic, sustainable and strong African economy. As Frederick Cooper argued, African '... economies remained externally oriented and the state's economic power remained concentrated at the gate between inside and outside'.[25] Undiversified and unindustrialized economies remained, and these were entrenched by the entrance, after 1945, of bigger multinational corporations, mainly backed by the USA, whose economy was strengthening relative to other Western countries that had been severely battered by the war.[26] These new corporations added to already existing European capitalist monopolies, some of which were established in the nineteenth century, years before the Scramble for Africa. The US corporations were however more technologically advanced and engaged in some basic, low-cost, integrated manufacturing industries (such as Unilever's turn into soap making and cooking oils in West Africa), which did not require highly skilled labor. They also injected high-capital investments, mainly in perceived stable African states such as South Africa (and Brazil) where settler colonialism was still entrenched.[27] American multinational corporations grew mainly due to their government's expenditure in research and development, which multiplied fivefold between 1948 and 1966, further strengthening the relationship between technology, state policy, and resource extraction. By the 1960s, their market share in Africa had overtaken most British and French corporations'.[28]

Also relevant to the developmental colonial states' initiatives after the war were the colonial officials' attempts to control agriculture in African communities. In Kenya and in colonial Zimbabwe, new land laws were passed to deal with soil erosion and to enforce new farming practices. Technical experts were deployed to rural areas to teach Africans 'modern' ways of farming, usually by using force, such as the violence meted out to Africans when the 1951 Native Land Husbandry Act was implemented in Zimbabwe. These top-down approaches, emerging from Western notions about land use and the Green revolution, ignored indigenous knowledge systems in Africa. This led to peasant discontent and the eventual rise of African nationalism in rural areas. Europe was not prepared for this political ferment in Africa, which happened when the West was financially stretched due to the Second World War.

Another notable development in the colonies was the postwar advances in medicine, especially the availability of anti-malarial drugs. This made it possible for new areas to be developed for human settlement. In apartheid South Africa, this accelerated the movement of African people into Bantustans, which were usually dry, inhospitable, and far from major transport networks. Colonial Zimbabwe also experienced new waves of evictions to previously uninhabited areas as colonial officials alienated land in anticipation of the arrival of many white immigrants. Medical advance also led to a general reduction in population mortality rates, which led to rapid population growth. Attempts to open up new districts for human settlement and to increase agricultural production proved costly as investment in social services and public infrastructure was required. Invariably, many new resettlements remained inaccessible from major road and railway networks. Rising population also called for increasing the economic and human capital costs of 'native' administration. The rising cost of colonial administration and infrastructure meant that new models of running the colonies should have been imagined. There was a need for the colonizers to plough back some of their profits into colonial development, which they were not prepared to do. Evidently, traditional colonial rule was facing a crisis. In the absence of meaningful, direct financial support from the metropoles, settler colonies were no longer going concerns. There was also a brewing political crisis.

In African communities, the rise of politically active, educated elites sharpened critiques of colonial power, especially through their writings and broadcasts. Educated Africans were not many, but were usually resolute and were generally respected by their African compatriots. Intellectuals like Jomo Kenyatta, Tom Mboya, Kwame Nkrumah, Julius Nyerere, Nelson Mandela, Nnamdi Azikiwe, Leopold Senghor, Ndabaningi Sithole and others were using their connections to global emancipatory and socialist movements to influence and radicalize political thought in Africa. It is not a coincidence that most African protest movements of the late 1940s and 1950s happened at a time similar movements were happening globally: the August Revolution of 1945 that created the Republic of Vietnam; the Workers Party of Korea's revolution that led to the birth of the Democratic People's Republic of Korea in 1948; the Chinese Communist peasant victory of 1949; and the Cuban revolution (1953–1959).[29]

African nationalism grew partly as a result of local conditions within African states that were further radicalized by the philosophies and revolutionary ideas of African intellectuals of the time, one of which was Pan-Africanism, championed in Africa by Kwame Nkrumah of Ghana. Nkrumah's radical writings were inciting Africans to unite and overthrow colonialism as a precondition for economic change. He stressed:

> ... the only solution to the colonial problem is the complete eradication of the entire economic system of colonialism, by colonial peoples, through their gaining political independence. Political freedom will open the way for the attainment of economic and social improvement and advancement.[30]

True to Nkrumah's thoughts, Sudan gained independence in 1956 and Ghana in 1957 after Nkrumah raised radical youths and women protesters. Many other colonies followed suit until the last African state (South Africa) was liberated in 1994. By the 1970s, more than three-quarters of Africa had become politically independent.

A number of factors led to decolonization. One was the change in official thinking about the economics and politics of empire, especially in postwar Britain which was now under the Labour Party. Another was the heavy cost of suppressing political movements in Africa, as Britain realized in Kenya. A third crucial factor was the anti-colonialism pressure from the US government, which was a rising global economic giant after 1945. The USA preferred a new economic model in the former colonies whereby multinational corporations would take advantage of the structural economic setting provided by the colonial governments to create a new neo-colonial relationship between Africa and the West. For it to thrive, neo-colonialism did not require formal political empires, but only a manipulative and exploitative economic and political relationship with African governments. A fourth factor was crisis in certain European countries that led them to decolonize. For instance, Portugal (which was poor and badly governed) ousted its dictator Salazar. He was replaced by a new government which feared the embarrassment of continuing to fight a losing battle against African nationalist movements. This led to abrupt decolonization in Portuguese Africa. As for France, French colonies collapsed following the embarrassing defeat in Algeria, which happened after protracted efforts by the French to repress anticolonial demonstrations in their West African colonies after 1945.

Conclusion

In conclusion, a few key points stand out clearly in this chapter. First, since the colonial era, the relationship between Africa and the West has been unequal, as it had been characterized by systematic extraction of African resources by Western corporations without corresponding development of local manufacturing industry. The colonial economy was what economic historian A.G. Hopkins, influenced by Dudley Seers's writings, termed an open economy.[31] It exhibited the following characteristics that we identified above. First, it exported a very limited range of primary products and imported a wide range of largely consumer goods in return. Second, foreign interests dominated the major sectors of that economy. Third, corporations exercised strong influence on its economic policies, which were consequently developed in their favor. In other words, the colonial state acted as a legitimizing instrument for corporate looting by international corporations. Trade restrictions, for instance, were kept at a bare minimum for the benefit of the corporations. Fifth, metropolitan powers expected the colonies to be self-sustaining financially, and put in as little money as possible for the running of the colonies. This was why the biggest share of the budgets of most of the colonies was covered by taxes from the colonized and peasant mono-cropping agriculture. This also explains Africa's weak public infrastructure at independence.

And lastly, in an open economy, the monetary system is an appendage of the colonizing country, as the system was designed to increase ties with the West. Monetary policy was controlled from abroad, with exchange controls manipulated to stem capital leakage from the colonizing country.[32] For the colonies, this situation created an environment of dependency which post-independence Africa is still struggling to deal with. In essence, dependency theorists like André Gunder Frank and others were correct as their argument is backed by overwhelming evidence from every African country that experienced colonialism. The legacy of colonialism on African economies, which in turn dictated Africa's relationship with the West, must not be underestimated, neither should other factors that we will explore below.

The postwar European economic situation paved the way for the entrance into the African economy and dominance of US multinational corporations (oligopolies). This was backed by the USA's increased public spending on research and development and technology as well as its aggressive economic policies. The USA's domination started when Europe's major colonialists were weighed down, not only by the postwar economic downturn but also by the rising economic costs of sustaining formal empires. The US neo-colonial approach later became an important vector in Africa's postcolonial politics as African leaders tried to renegotiate their positions after independence. At the time of dependence, many African states experienced a generally similar trend; namely, the immediate capital flight of many small-scale but skilled enterprises and an inflow of big conglomerates that specialized in raw material extraction and agro-based industries. This trend meant that the colonial pattern of capital investment for export purposes never changed after independence, but was further entrenched. Other than mining, multinational corporations also focused on processing primary products for export purposes, or on import substitution by developing light industries that processed soap, cooking oil, textiles, beverages, footwear, and others. These products were profitable because they were daily human necessities with high turnovers. But, heavy manufacturing industries remained either non-existent or were export-oriented, and this continued to stall Africa's industrialization.[33]

Finally, at the time of independence, Africa inherited a number of impediments. The majority of its African citizens were uneducated. Tertiary education was rare and the few universities that were there were still very new. Africans with degrees constituted a very tiny minority. In 1960, only 16% of adult Africans were literate. In British settler colonies, a racialized dual education system existed, with Africans exposed to a system that did not help them to develop into highly skilled workers. In colonies under indirect rule, some Africans never got any access to education. In Portuguese Africa, the education situation was a lot worse than in other colonies. In French colonial Africa, the assimilationist education system sought to integrate Africans to French culture so that the most educated Africans became (in theory) the most brainwashed supporters of the French Union. In practice, reactions to

French assimilation produced militant anti-colonialists like Leopold Senghor. At independence, the same, semi-literate Africans were expected to take over political power, serve in the public service, create policies to run the economy, and at the same time negotiate the murky waters of the Cold War era which complicated Africa's international relations. In terms of infrastructure, most areas were inaccessible because of poor road networks, most of which were gravel roads. Electricity generation was below the required capacity to industrialize Africa. The agricultural sector had been compromised by the colonial regimes which had focused on cash crops. Moreover, land redistribution was a burden that African countries faced after independence, with no clear clue on how this could be done without upsetting the inflow of foreign direct investments.

Economically, African families were generally poor as their earnings during colonialism were not competitive enough to encourage meaningful investment which would have created a basis for Afro-capitalism. There was severe racial economic inequality that makes it futile to argue about the economic performance of colonial Africa versus postcolonial Africa in the manner that Fieldhouse (cited above) tried to do. Because of Africans' widespread poverty (not to say that no Africans could empower themselves), most initiatives to empower black Africans would require efforts from the African governments themselves. This did not happen in most cases, and where it did, it was usually marred by systemic challenges such as the politics of citizenship, as was the case with the Ivorian cocoa agriculture which triggered the politics of autochthony versus foreigners, and also instances of corruption and nepotism elsewhere.[34]

Efforts to ensure broad-based economic empowerment were also hampered by financial sustainability challenges. As we stated in this chapter, manufacturing was weak as companies continued extracting, also threatening to pull out whenever governments tried to do anything that was not in their favor. Consequently, the tax that was levied from the big corporations remained relatively low, to the extent that most of their profits did not help develop the former colonies. Meanwhile, the new African governments faced a bloated civil service that increased public debt. They had to relapse into the colonial mode characterized by gate keeping and living off rural peasants' agricultural production. These were some of the economic constraints facing Africa at independence. Independent African governments tried to deal with these in various ways.

Notes

1. This work is based on the research supported in part by the National Research Foundation of South Africa (Grant Number 90985). Any errors or omissions, however unintended, are entirely mine.
2. Kwame Nkrumah, *Towards Colonial Freedom: Africa in the Struggle against World Imperialism* (London: Heinemann, 1962), 10.

3. A.E. Afigbo, *The Warrant Chief System: Indirect Rule in Southern Nigeria, 1891–1929* (London: Longman, 1972).
4. J. Fisher and D.M. Anderson, "Authoritarianism and the Securitization of Development in Africa," *International Affairs* 91, no. 1 (2015): 131–51.
5. D. Renton, D. Seddon and L. Zeilig, *The Congo: Plunder and Resistance* (London: ZED Books, 2007), 173; T. Turner, *The Congo Wars: Conflict, Myth and Reality* (London: ZED Books, 2007), 31–33.
6. Renton et al., *The Congo: Plunder and Resistance*, 176; J. Murison, "The Politics of Refugees and Internally Displaced Persons in the Congo War," in *The African Stakes of the Congo War*, ed. J.F. Clark (New York: Palgrave Macmillan, 2002), 225–37.
7. D.K. Fieldhouse, *Black Africa 1945–1980: Economic Decolonization and Arrested Development* (London: Allen and Unwin, 1986), 4.
8. E. Msindo, "Winning Hearts and Minds': Crisis and Propaganda in Colonial Zimbabwe, 1962–1970," *Journal of Southern African Studies* 35, no. 3 (2009): 663–81.
9. A.A. Mazrui, *The African Condition* (London: Heinemann, 1980), 73, 79.
10. For this common cliché, see C. Legum, *Africa Since Independence* (Bloomington: Indiana University Press, 1999), 48.
11. C. Bundy, *The Rise and Fall of the South African Peasantry*, 2nd ed. (Cape Town: David Philip, 1988), 221–28.
12. D. Benjamin and A. Deaton, "Household Welfare and the Pricing of Cocoa and Coffee in Cote d'Ivoire: Lessons from the Living Standards Surveys," *The World Bank Economic Review* 1, no. 3 (1993), 293–318.
13. Mazrui, *The African Condition*, 78.
14. D. Acemoglu and J.A. Robinson, "Why is Africa Poor," *Economic History of Developing Regions* 25, no. 1 (2010), 21–50. See also T.O. Ranger, *Peasant Consciousness and the Guerrilla War: A Comparative Study* (London: James Currey, 1985).
15. B. Davidson, *Modern Africa: A Social and Political History*, 2nd ed. (Longman: London, 1989), 18–19; F. Cooper, *Africa Since 1940: The Past of the Present* (Cambridge: Cambridge University Press, 2002), 21–24; and K. Nkrumah, *Towards Colonial Freedom*, 18.
16. J.-F. Bayart, *The State in Africa: The Politics of the Belly* (Cambridge: Polity Press, 2009), 60–65.
17. D.F. Brycesson, "Sub-Saharan Africa's Vanishing Peasantry and the Specter of a Global Food Crisis," in *Monthly Review*, 62, no. 3, 2009, online at http://monthlyreview.org/2009/07/01/sub-saharan-africas-vanishing-peasantries-and-the-specter-of-a-global-food-crisis/ accessed 14 March 2016.
18. B. Davidson, *Modern Africa*, 55.
19. Cooper, *Africa Since 1940*, 5.
20. Fieldhouse, *Black Africa*, 6–13, 33.
21. Ibid., 30.
22. Giovanni Arrighi, "International Corporations, Labor Aristocracies, and Economic Development in Tropical Africa," in *Essays on the Political Economy of Africa* ed. G. Arrighi and J.S. Saul (New York: Monthly Review Press, 1973), 106.
23. Msindo, "Winning Hearts and Minds," 663–81.

24. J. Alexander, J. McGregor and T. Ranger, *Violence and Memory: One Hundred Years in the 'Dark Forests' of Matabeleland* (Oxford: James Currey, 2000), 67.
25. F. Cooper, *Africa Since 1940*, 5. In other words, the colonial state was a gatekeeper state.
26. Immanuel Wallerstein, "Globalization or the Age of Transition? A Long-Term View of the Trajectory of the World System," *International Sociology* 15, no. 2 (2000): 251–67.
27. A. Seidman and N.S. Makgetla, *Outposts of Monopoly Capitalism: Southern Africa in the Changing Global Economy* (London: ZED Press, 1980), 9.
28. Seidman and Makgetla, *Outposts of Monopoly Capitalism*, 7–10, 17–21.
29. André Gunder Frank, "The Underdevelopment of Development," (University of Antiqua: draft paper, 1996).
30. Nkrumah, *Towards Colonial Freedom*, 20.
31. A.G. Hopkins, *An Economic History of West Africa* (London: Longman, 1973), 168.
32. Hopkins, *An Economic History*, 168–70.
33. Arrighi, *Essays on the Political Economy*, 109–12.
34. See generally: S. Dorman, D. Harmett and P. Nugent, *Making Nations, Creating Strangers: States and Citizenship in Africa* (Leiden: Brill, 2007); Bayart, *The State in Africa*, chap. 2.

Bibliography

Acemoglu, D., and J.A. Robinson. "Why is Africa Poor." *Economic History of Developing Regions* 25, no. 1 (2010): 21–50.

Afigbo, A.E. *The Warrant Chief System: Indirect Rule in Southern Nigeria, 1891–1929*. London: Longman, 1972.

Alexander, J., J. McGregor, and T.O. Ranger. *Violence and Memory: One Hundred Years in the 'Dark Forests' of Matabeleland*. Oxford: James Currey, 2000.

Arrighi, G., and J.S. Saul. *Essays on the Political Economy of Africa*. New York: Monthly Review Press, 1973.

Bayart, J.-F. *The State in Africa: The Politics of the Belly*. Cambridge: Polity Press, 2009.

Benjamin, D., and A. Deaton. "Household Welfare and the Pricing of Cocoa and Coffee in Cote d'Ivoire: Lessons from the Living Standards Surveys." *The World Bank Economic Review* 1, no. 3 (1993): 293–318.

Brycesson, D.F. "Sub-Saharan Africa's Vanishing Peasantry and the Specter of a Global Food Crisis." *Monthly Review* 62, no. 3 (2009).

Bundy, C. *The Rise and Fall of the South African Peasantry*, 2nd ed. Cape Town: David Philip, 1988.

Cooper, F. *Africa Since 1940: The Past of the Present*. Cambridge: Cambridge University Press, 2002.

Davidson, B. *Modern Africa: A Social and Political History*, 2nd ed. Longman: London, 1989.

Dorman, S., D. Harmett, and P. Nugent. *Making Nations, Creating Strangers: States and Citizenship in Africa*. Leiden: Brill, 2007.

Fieldhouse, D.K. *Black Africa 1945–1980: Economic Decolonization and Arrested Development*. London: Allen and Unwin, 1986.

Fisher J. and D.M. Anderson. "Authoritarianism and the Securitization of Development in Africa." *International Affairs* 91, no. 1 (2015): 131–51.

Frank, A.G. "The Underdevelopment of Development." University of Antiqua: Draft paper, 1996.

Hopkins, A.G. *An Economic History of West Africa*. London: Longman, 1973.

Legum, C. *Africa Since Independence*. Bloomington: Indiana University Press, 1999.

Mazrui, A.A. *The African Condition*. London: Heinemann, 1980.

Msindo, E. "'Winning Hearts and Minds': Crisis and Propaganda in Colonial Zimbabwe, 1962–1970." *Journal of Southern African Studies* 35, no. 3 (2009): 663–81.

Murison, J. "The Politics of Refugees and Internally Displaced Persons in the Congo War." In *The African Stakes of the Congo War*, edited by J.F. Clark, 225–37. New York: Palgrave Macmillan, 2002.

Nkrumah, K. *Towards Colonial Freedom: Africa in the Struggle Against World Imperialism*. London: Heinemann, 1962.

Ranger, T.O. *Peasant Consciousness and the Guerrilla War: A Comparative Study*. London: James Currey, 1985.

Renton, D., D. Seddon, and L. Zeilig. *The Congo: Plunder and Resistance*. London: ZED Books, 2007.

Seidman, A., and N.S. Makgetla. *Outposts of Monopoly Capitalism: Southern Africa in the Changing Global Economy*. London: ZED Press, 1980.

Turner, T. *The Congo Wars: Conflict, Myth and Reality*. London: ZED Books, 2007.

Wallerstein, I. "Globalization or the Age of Transition? A Long-Term View of the Trajectory of the World System." *International Sociology* 15, no. 2 (2000): 251–67.

CHAPTER 23

International Law, Colonialism, and the African

Ibrahim J. Gassama

INTRODUCTION

In this chapter, I examine the enduring and evolving role of received law and all its manifestations in the lives of Africans during both the colonial era and the present day. I argue that international law not only facilitated imperialism and colonialism, it remains at the core of what Africans received from imperialism and colonial rule. Africans are still subjects of this alien species of law, introduced by Western conquerors and colonizers, and they remain in many ways unable to fully escape its tragic hold on their lives. In short, international law occupies a predominant role today in organizing African realities and in justifying the complex web of persistent and violent exploitative relationships that order the place of ordinary Africans within the present even more alienating globalized world order.

Law played an essential role in the European conquest and exploitation of Africa. The most important characteristic of any legal system is sanctioned regularity.[1] It is in this sense that law defined, elaborated, and sanctified the common interests of the antagonistic European sovereignties that preyed upon Africa economically, socially, culturally, and otherwise over the course of

---

I dedicate this chapter to the memory of my dearest friend and longtime collaborator, Professor Louise Hope Lewis (1962–2016). I am grateful for the insights and comments of colleagues Professors Antony Anghie, A. B. Assensoh, Michael Fakhri, and Michelle McKlinley. I am also grateful for the research assistance provided by Marissa Martinez and Colin R. Saint-Evens.

I.J. Gassama (✉)
Frank Nash Professor of Law, University of Oregon, Eugene, OR, USA

© The Author(s) 2018
M.S. Shanguhyia and T. Falola (eds.),
The Palgrave Handbook of African Colonial and Postcolonial History,
https://doi.org/10.1057/978-1-137-59426-6_23

several centuries. Law therefore emerged in concert with violence to develop efficient colonial systems for the subjugation and exploitation of Africa, a process which began in earnest during the Scramble for Africa in the late 1880s.[2] Law was an integral part of the systems before, during, and after the initial incursions, just as it was during the transatlantic slave trade. Specifically, law allowed European powers, great and small, to eventually establish jurisdiction over specific portions of African territory and its people, and it legitimized their exercise of power within such domains

This perspective is consistent with the following observation by Walter Benjamin about the relationship between law and violence:

> All violence as a means is either lawmaking or law preserving. If it lays claim to neither of these predicates, it forfeits all validity. It follows, however, that all violence as a means, even in the most favorable case, is implicated in the problematic nature of law itself ... When the consciousness of the latent presence of violence in a legal institution disappears, the institution falls into decay.[3]

The Europeans needed law to validate both the violence they unleashed on the unsuspecting people and the ideology behind the violence, even as the law itself needed the violence (or the consciousness of its latent presence) to sustain its efficacy and legitimacy. In this way, international law was both the child and the nurturer of European colonial violence. As will be shown shortly, this intimate relationship between international law and violence has continued well into the postcolonial era.

Joseph Conrad (1857–1924) noted that:

> The conquest of the earth, which mostly means the taking it away from those who have a different complexion or slightly flatter noses than ourselves, is not a pretty thing when you look into it too much. What redeems it is the idea only ... and an unselfish belief in the idea-something you can set up, and bow down before, and offer a sacrifice to ....[4]

Conrad was a percipient witness to events in Africa during the period when fully fledged imperialism transitioned into bureaucratic colonialism. He understood well that ideas were important to create the foundations for violence and rapacity as well as to facilitate enduring systems of domination. Conrad's *Heart of Darkness* captured the particular sensibilities of the Christian/capitalist civilizing missions undergirding imperialism and colonialism in Africa. As he elaborated, even ideas as high-minded or 'unselfish' as those of bringing Christ or civilization to 'savages' needed discipline and an operational system. This is where law, specifically international law, came into service for Europeans; to flesh out the ideas and bridge the gap between a legitimacy that had once been conferred solely by divine grace and that which would subsequently emanate from secular sovereign commands.

Law in general protects and enhances the utility of violence, insofar as it sanctions and regularizes it. So it did during the colonial era.

International law thus sanctioned colonialism, the extension of European sovereign jurisdiction to Africa. Colonialism was the direct outgrowth of the processes of sanctioning and regularizing the subjugation and plunder of the continent or, as Conrad termed it, the 'taking it away'. Colonialism became the end game that resolved various conflicting efforts by private parties to gain commercial advantages throughout Africa. The processes of colonialism were sustained and elevated by law, at least in their most enduring and efficient manifestations. Without international law, a law accepted by diverse European parties, investment in colonialism would not have been as valuable, and imperialism would have remained locked and hobbled by its rougher unsophisticated edges. In turn, by extending European sovereign jurisdiction over particular portions of the continent, colonial rule was able to deploy international law internally to facilitate a more efficient subjugation of the population, the erasure of their organized communal identities, and the extraction of wealth from subject entities to the benefit of interests sanctioned by occupying powers. Colonial rule as such was sustained by a mutual acceptance among imperial powers that the rules and processes of the law that they were evolving benefited them more in the long run than unbridled competition or violent conflicts. In this sense, law was indelibly superior to the alternative of conquest purely by force of arms. Law did not completely replace the latter of course, since law, like force, was fundamentally an instrument of the conquest. However, law provided an organized system to better ensure that the fruits of conquests were recognized by others similarly situated.

Law made European violence more acceptable and efficient in Africa, reducing the number of occasions that would give rise to intractable inter-European conflicts. This was also the essential aim of the Berlin Conference, and this heritage persists today. It is critical to emphasize here that law in Africa during the partitioning era spoke primarily to the mutuality of interests among competing European powers. It was only much later that the law came to play a dominant role in prescribing the relationship between the European subjugators, be they public or private, and the local African authorities and subjects. When it did, it was largely to confirm the subjugation of the latter, and to inscribe the terms of European dominion in perpetuity.

It is also important to acknowledge at this juncture that the political independence that African states have attained in the postcolonial era has not fundamentally changed the fact that these countries emerged from colonial domination essentially as creatures of international law, with their agencies and capacities for self-determination severely constrained in both the domestic and international spheres. The postcolonial reality of the African state today is that while formal imperialism and direct colonial rule have ended, the imperial project accomplished two important objectives that have endured: (1) It buried its core principles deep within the institutional structures and processes of each emerging African state; (2) It developed new systems that are just as exploitative and efficient at privileging the interests of the former colonial powers as the explicitly imperial systems that preceded them.[5]

The passionate embrace by postcolonial African leaders of this received law and its embedded legal principles (principles such as national sovereignty, self-determination, or *uti possidetis juris*) testify to the success of the first objective. In support of the second objective, note how the United Nations and the Bretton Woods institutions have consolidated and managed the postcolonial world order in much the same manner as those efforts that were initiated by the Berlin Conference. The ideas, principles, structures, and aims of these post-Second World War institutions are fundamentally indistinct from those of the earlier colonial era.

In the next section, I examine the foundational role that international law played in the acquisition and control of African territory, the destruction of African political communities, and the cultivated dissonance that permeates the politics of the continent to this day. The main point here is that international law greatly facilitated the European 'idea' or enterprise in Africa. This idea first manifested itself as a civilizing mission but it quickly morphed into something 'not pretty': wholesale plunder. Force of arms and the codification of the law of conquests were essential means in operationalizing the idea.

In the third section, I examine how international law dictated both the course of the struggle for African independence and the present course of the emerging nations of Africa. In addition, I illustrate how contemporary African societies are managed by domestic and international elites who quite comfortably embrace the contours established by this alien legal order, as well as the nature and methods of violence it justifies. As a result, Africans remain unable to conceive of or reconstruct an alternative and authentically African worldview. The war on memory that international law has in effect facilitated has thus achieved considerable success. As time passes, Africans find it increasingly difficult to disentangle the forces that continue to oppress them or to remember a time when subjugation and dependency were not the essence of their reality.

International Law and the Conquest of African Territories and People

Joseph Conrad was unequivocal about the ulterior motives of Western European seizure of territory in Africa at the end of the nineteenth century. 'They grabbed what they could get for the sake of what was to be got', he asserted, and concluded that 'It was just robbery with violence, aggravated murder on a great scale, and men going at it blind – as it is very proper for those who tackle a darkness'.[6] Scholars of international law have noticed the legacy of this imperialism on international law. For instance, some of them have perceived 'the construction and universalization of international law' as having been pertinent to the imperial expansion that led to subordination of non-European peoples and societies to European domination.[7]

The Peace of Westphalia in 1648 is often crudely anointed as the starting point of international law. This is wildly inaccurate. Actually, that particular moment marked a series of agreements among various European powers that ended decades of brutal warfare among them. The main outcome of Westphalia was a degree of communal recognition of the sovereign independence of fragments of the Holy Roman Empire that had successfully resisted efforts at imperial reconsolidation. The acceptance of this primitive concept of national sovereign independence in Western Europe would of course face numerous tests over the coming centuries, but it could be claimed that, from this point forward, the basic idea of sovereign independence was accepted as legitimate and supported by law, as opposed to being mere diktat. Yet, this story of the origin of international law does not properly incorporate the essential roles played by the processes of European migration and conquests of territories and peoples outside the European continent, especially in Africa and what would later become the Americas. Seen through that lens, the Westphalian accomplishment was to broaden the embrace of secular or positivist principles that justified and sanctioned the right of European powers to conquer and exploit diverse native peoples in Africa and the Americas. Those principles had actually been in operation for more than a century before the Peace of Westphalia.

The narrow Westphalian account of the origins of international law also presents the discipline as a progressive advance over a more barbarous period of European history. As such, international law is extolled as the source of a new era of peace and progress, the enduring solution to conflicts amongst Europeans with different political, cultural, social, or economic interests and perspectives. In this vein, the scholarship of the Dutch jurist, Hugo Grotius (generally regarded as the 'father' of international law) has been front and center.[8] It is important to note that Grotius made significant contributions towards the subjugation and exploitation of non-European peoples by developing modern rationales for just wars and freedom of navigation and trade.[9] It is more accurate to understand that international law developed and expanded during this period to serve as a vehicle for a more legitimate and enduring resolution of conflicts between the burgeoning numbers of fundamentally equal European sovereign states. In this sense, international law differed from *Jus Gentium*.

It is also more accurate to recognize that long before the supposed Westphalian founding of international law in 1648, European powers were actually deploying international law of a sort to defend their titles to 'discovered' territories in Africa and the 'New World'. How else should we interpret the various papal bulls that purported to grant and defend titles to new territories claimed by the Portuguese and the Spanish?[10] True, papal bulls were not international law documents of the positivist variety, but they were essential precursors in terms of doctrine and processes. These documents granted title and established jurisdiction, albeit subject to the authority of the Pope. As Grovogui has argued:

> [M]edieval Christianity and papal interpretations of the Scriptures have defined the modern international order, including its hierarchical systems and various forms of unequal subjectivities (or sovereignties). These hierarchies and subjectivities in turn have delineated the realm of international law from the Renaissance, through the Enlightenment, and to the present.[11]

The earliest papal bull, for example, *Romanus Pontifex*, issued by Pope Nicholas V in 1455, purported to give Portugal, under King Afonso V, title to its discoveries in Africa.[12] However, Spain convinced Pope Alexander VI to issue a series of bulls in 1493, titled *Inter Caetera Divinae*, which sought to resolve disputes between Spain and Portugal over the new territories they had invaded and wished to exploit without interference from other European powers.[13]

These papal bulls were legal documents of an international character that sanctioned wars of conquests as just, granted titles to European sovereigns, and established jurisdiction over foreign territories and peoples. Among other principles and rules created by these papal dispensations was an imaginary line (established by *Inter Caetera*) that divided Portuguese and Spanish possessions and jurisdictions. It is in this sense that international law was itself a product of conflicts within and outside Europe; and importantly, also a product of European imperialism and colonialism. Indeed, Portugal and Spain successfully negotiated an amendment to the papal orders that moved the line of demarcation issued by Pope Alexander 270 leagues to the West of the Cape Verde Islands.[14] This very early form of international dispute resolution, employing a third party mediator or arbiter (albeit one still deeply attached to divine grace and natural law perspectives) also established the overarching justification for international law's legitimacy: the civilizing mission. For the Pope and European despots of that age, the civilizing mission was centered on the spread of Christianity among 'non-rational infidels,'[15] the supposedly barbarous peoples in the new lands outside Europe. The freedom and right to navigate and trade came as important justifications shortly after the religious imperative, to further mask naked desire and greed.

Over time, the rationales for intervention in the lives of non-European peoples have been presented under various guises, but they remain fundamentally inseparable from these early justifications. In a sense, the primary contribution of the Peace of Westphalia was to free even more Europeans to participate in the pillage of non-European territories and the subjugation of their inhabitants. The competition and conflicts among many European powers henceforth would be mediated to significant degrees by international law. The possibilities of plunder in Africa and the Americas increased, with international law becoming an essential and dynamic participant.

Not only does international law's development as an essential vehicle for interstate relations owe a lot to European imperialism in Africa and the Americas (initiated more than a century before the treaties of Westphalia), but it was also aided by the subsequent commercial and colonial policies and practices that would mature a few centuries later. As Anghie has asserted, 'colonialism was central to the constitution of international law in that many of its basic doctrines of international law – including, most importantly, sovereignty doctrine – were forged out of the attempt to create a legal system that could account for relations between the Europeans and non-European worlds in the colonial confrontation'.[16] The widespread acceptance of international law was thus aided greatly by its value as a vehicle for conquest, domination, and rapacious exploitation of weaker peoples before and during the colonial era.

International law played a critical role in the consolidation of European interests in Africa. Pakenham has noted that:

> [I]n 1880 most of the continent was still ruled by its inhabitants and was barely explored. Yet by 1902, five European powers (Britain, France, Germany, Belgium and Italy) had grabbed almost all of its ten million square miles, awarding themselves thirty new colonies and protectorates ....[17]

International law worked intimately alongside brute force to ensure the success of this crude epochal process of continental consolidation and partitioning. Conrad noted about the European conquerors that their mission was actually 'aggravated murder on a great scale', and that 'they grabbed what they could get for the sake of what was to be got'. Hence, the value of the idea and methods of civilization. The justificatory mechanism of the civilizing mission and the methods of international law allowed for the Europeans to see themselves as purveyors of light who found darkness only in the continent and amongst their victims.

Of course, Pakenham's notion of rule by inhabitants prior to the institution of direct colonial rule was substantially inaccurate. Well before the Scramble for Africa, the authority and processes of indigenous rule or self-determination had been systematically undermined by European interests, whether private, public, or some combination of the two. It was not a huge leap from the seemingly benign interests of anti-slavery crusaders, Christian missionaries, adventurers, investors, and traders, to an open embrace of empire. The thinly obscured arrogance of missionaries like David Livingstone, who pleaded for Africa to be saved from the evils of the slave trade, easily gave way to the rapacity of conquerors like Belgium's Leopold II and England's Cecil Rhodes.[18] These robber barons, arriving in the wake of the missionaries, understood the value of the sanctioning mechanism of law as creator of enduring wealth. Treaties and other forms of legally binding agreements gave them concessions they could exploit in due course and sanctioned their right to subjugate and exploit, and even destroy, native inhabitants to the exclusion of others. When their assorted ventures, aimed at securing long-term access and profits, came under unmanageable threat, primarily from other Europeans, they demanded the full imprimatur of state support. Some have disputed the eagerness of European powers to take on this burden in defense of private or quasi-private interests, but the facts are that once it became clear that the pre-Scramble period of imperial exploitation was no longer tenable, the race was on, and European powers stepped in swiftly and greedily to expand and defend their respective spheres of influence.

This essential point was captured succinctly by Chapter VI of the General Act of the Berlin Conference on West Africa. That article demanded that any European power that took 'possession of a tract of land on the coasts of the African continent outside of its present possessions' including those that established a protectorate on the continent, should notify other powers of such moves, so as to enable them to 'make good any claims of their own'. The signatory powers to the Berlin Act were also encouraged to establish an authority in their newly acquired regions to protect their existing rights to those regions, but allow freedom of international trade and transit through those regions.[19]

International law occupied a central place in this process right from the start. The fact that Europeans were deploying a legal system that had developed organically out of centuries of European struggles, and that the system was foreign to the indigenous inhabitants of these conquered territories, was of no consequence to the alien invaders. Indeed, the law was not actually speaking to the indigenous inhabitants. They were not its subjects, for they were 'savages' or, at best, abject wards at the mercy of international sensibilities. Again, Conrad captured the spirit of this naked enterprise in all its suffocating racist splendor when he noted '… and of course, as long as there was a piece of paper written over in accordance with some farcical law or other made down the river, it didn't enter anybody's head to trouble how they [the subjugated people] would live'.[20]

The law was effectively directed at creating a scheme by which Europeans could communicate with each other about the division of spoils, in a language more efficient than naked force alone.[21] This was clearly one of Bismarck's goals as he convened the conference in 1884, and it was broadly accepted by all the participants in the adoption of this 'constitution of dispossession'. It of course did not trouble these plenipotentiaries to consider the perspectives of the land's inhabitants. After Berlin, Africans again found themselves completely shut out of global processes mediated by law. They were (and remain) bound to a scheme of ordered subjugation and exploitation that they had no role in developing and that has offered them no possibilities of escape. Their options were to submit or die. Even today, one must appreciate the audacity and hubris of Europeans racing to extract these concessions from diverse African communities or convening international gatherings like the Berlin Conference to discuss the fate of the African continent without any hint of their absurd nature. Then again, not much has changed since then. The essential lesson from the confirmation of colonial rule in Africa, which the Berlin Conference signified, is that desires or interests developed entirely within the European psyche dictated the future of Africans. It matters little whether these circumstances came about because of the inevitable progression of imperialism, a desire to protect European bondholders and other investors, a need to access raw materials in Africa, the necessity to develop new markets for the products of the European working class, an extension of European nationalism or politics, or simply by casual accident. Whatever the governing factors, the end result was that Africans found themselves swiftly imported into a European world order in which law worked assiduously to consolidate and secure gains achieved by deceit or the force of arms. The Maxim machine gun could not have achieved by itself what it did in concert with the law. This lesson has been learned only too well by African leaders. As such, Africans remain fully conscious of 'the latent presence of violence' in law and institutions.[22]

INTERNATIONAL LAW AND THE STRUGGLE TO END COLONIALISM

Some have posed the old question of whether the postcolonial world can deploy for its own purposes the law which had enabled its suppression in the first place?[23] Once transported into the realm of European colonial rule, Africans found themselves unable to achieve any measure of extrication without recourse to the tools laid out by colonial masters. This was true to some degree even regarding armed liberation struggles, but it was even more so in the case of the political mass-mobilization struggles of a less convulsive nature. These efforts at liberation effectively proceeded within confines defined or permitted by international law. The language, the means, and the processes of change were all supplied by international law. Undoubtedly, international law was not static, and it was itself challenged and influenced by the anti-colonial struggles of subjugated peoples. Still, efforts against colonialism generally succeeded only when they came to embrace foundational aspects of the global order mediated by international law. In sum, newly independent African states were not allowed into the global order until they made substantial and lasting compromises with the scheme developed by the masters in the course of their subjugation.

The employment of international law to manage Africa's place in the developing global order expanded and deepened after the Berlin Conference. Again, it was events, practices, and policies emanating from Europe that drove the process and, again, Africans were not consulted. The First and Second World Wars were seminal events. The defeat of Germany during the First World War removed it as a major player in Africa and, more importantly, introduced the Western world's newest empire, the USA, into the old politics of Europe. US involvement in Europe helped to transform Manifest Destiny into the American Century. President Woodrow Wilson projected and promoted a nuanced belief in world peace through law, and saw, in the plight of some oppressed people, fertile ground for the spread of the US democratic vision.[24] Wilson had the great gift of not being burdened too much by irony. At home, he was an unadorned racist who promoted policies that pulled back the meager human-rights gains African Americans had made over the decades after the American Civil War. He was also ideologically and morally unconstrained by lessons from the US' own record of violence and rapacity against weaker peoples as well as its burgeoning empire in the Americas and Asia.

With soaring language and unyielding commitment, Wilson promoted a vision of international law in the service of world peace through legal order. He spoke in opposition to the growth of European empires and in defense of the rights to self-governance of certain oppressed minorities. He sponsored the League of Nations and a Permanent Court of International Justice. Neither institution lasted long, but both served to sow the ground for the global embrace of a sanitized version of international law as the proper vehicle for resolving international disputes. The principle of self-determination of peoples also gained ground as the preeminent normative yardstick for the legitimate exercise of governmental power. Wilson supported the League of Nations' Mandate System that offered opportunities for former colonies of Germany and the Ottoman Empire to gain some measure of self-determination, even though he did not challenge the legitimacy of other instances of ongoing European colonial rule in Africa.[25] Regardless, Wilson's profession of faith in international law helped to infect much of the world with an idealism that worked over time to erode the legitimacy of colonial power exercised without the support of an international law that had come to accept self-determination as a core principle.

Wilsonian idealism floundered in the face of post-First World War skepticism and a general turn to realism. The failure of the US Congress to go along with Wilson's internationalist plans doomed the institutions and processes he championed. It took another global conflagration, the Second World War, emanating from Europe, to revive these ideas and give impetus to the African struggle for independence from direct colonial rule. At the conclusion of the war, the victors, under US leadership, doubled down on Wilson's ideas and promoted a revitalized and totally ahistorical rendition of international law as an almost secular religion and the primary vehicle to unite humanity. Arguably, this approach functioned substantially to consolidate and extend their dominance, albeit under changing circumstances. African anti-colonial activists, like others around the world, took advantage of what they perceived as openings and pressed their case for freedom from European colonial rule. When political rhetoric and non-violent mass mobilization failed to achieve their aims, some turned to armed struggle.

Two consequences of the Second World War aided the efforts of the independence movements. First, while Germany and its allies were again the major losers of this conflict, the victorious nations in Europe were also devastated and even more dependent on the USA. Second, the Soviet Union with its socialist and internationalist ideology also emerged as a serious competitor to Western interests on a global scale. In short, European colonial powers became trapped between the soaring rhetoric of US idealism, now reconstituted with even more vigor by President Franklin D. Roosevelt, and the threats posed by an evangelical strain of socialism coming from the Soviet Union, soon to be joined by China under communist rule. However, it is crucial in appreciating the anti-colonialist struggles of that era to recognize that their leaders were operating largely on the reconstructed terrain of colonial masters. The openings they saw were actually invitations of a sort. Thus, even when they achieved victory they found that they had largely negotiated terms of their surrender within the broader dynamically reconstituting global architecture.

Post-Second World War international law developments supplied national independence movements with principles and guidelines to support and constrain their struggles. Three developments in particular came to define the contours of African anti-colonial liberation struggles and the paths to admission of new states into the postwar global order: the centrality of the concept of self-determination; the promotion of sovereign equality of nation-states with defined and inherited territorial boundaries; and subordination to the supervisory authority of postwar international political and economic security institutions. In this manner, international law became, in essence, the constitutional law for newly independent states of Africa. Further, the embrace of these ideas and principles by independence movements also served to coopt their struggles and trap them even more securely within the world order that had been created in the process of subjugating and exploiting them.

The principle of the self-determination of peoples became a central tenet of African independence struggles. It had gained prominence after the First World War and became sanctified in the major international agreements of the post-Second World War period. The United Nations Charter affirms it as one of the organization's foundational principles. The first article of the two principal binding human rights agreements states that, 'All peoples have the right to self-determination. By virtue of that right they freely determine their political status and freely pursue their economic, social and cultural development'.[26] The right to self-determination is considered by many today to be the foundation of all human rights. However, as Grovogui has argued, this right, 'like other rights claimed by the colonized, derives from particular conceptions of community and politics that are specific to western culture'.[27] He further notes the 'endless quest for material well-being and a reliance on violence to achieve political ends' that are characteristic of this culture.[28] In embracing this particular organizing principle of freedom, African leaders in essence endorsed both the violent alchemy that created the entities of colonialism they were seeking to liberate and also a future that would put them on an endless path of violence as they sought material well-being within these entities. Self-determination applied in the context of sovereign equality of states isolated, indeed imprisoned, the various African communities that had been violently forged by alien interests. Crucially, veneration of this ideal denied Africans other possibilities.

Of course there was opposition to this ideal, such as was seen in places like Katanga, Biafra, Eritrea, or South Sudan; and not all of it operating from principled grounds. Still, such dissenting voices found very little legal or material support that could have enabled a more critical understanding of the consequences of an uncritical embrace of self-determination along the lines defined by international law. It is instructive that no independent African regime has hesitated to defend its colonial inheritance by resorting to the domestic and international privileges and powers derived from international law and the monopoly on violence it conferred on the state. Indeed, without a hint of irony, African rulers have not only insisted upon a limited and self-serving understanding of the principle of self-determination, they have often advocated an unconstrained right to the monopoly of force within their inherited boundaries. They have also sought to exclude external criticism or concern about treatment of their fellow citizens by citing international law's claimed protection of matters within their internal jurisdiction. This has been the case even when such expressions of concern or criticism have emanated from other Africans.

When European powers had carved out their territories in Africa, they had given little weight to historical or existing relationships while squeezing together diverse nationalities within newly created borders. These borders were essentially crudely drawn lines on maps that essentially defined domains of convenience. In almost every instance when political independence was achieved, national liberation movements embraced these externally constructed entities as legitimate and enduring sovereign political subdivisions. Ethiopia's struggle against Italian aggression and colonialism was a case in point. When the post-First World War Wilsonian renovation of international law failed and Italy decided to revive its imperial legacy in Africa, a deposed Emperor Haile Selassie escaped to Britain to continue Ethiopian nationalist resistance from the soil of a nation that Italy was merely trying to imitate in Africa. The Emperor's well-received plea on behalf of the right to self-determination of all small nations obscured the reality of European colonialism in Africa and the foundational illegitimacy of all colonial boundaries, including his own. Ironically, his claims were received positively not only by European audiences who identified in his stance a defense of progressive aspects of colonialism, but also by Pan-African activists worldwide who uncritically adopted him as a symbol of African resistance to imperial rule. In effect, activists and even revolutionaries committed themselves to going forward with a reality that had been created through violent subjugation, instead of challenging the past. They embraced the legitimacy and privileges that had been conferred by conquest.

The Emperor and ruling elites in Ethiopia and elsewhere in Africa benefited from an international law that offered the right to self-determination and governance to those who accepted uncritically the territorial boundaries and other obligations inherited from an imperial era. This bargain has held in general over time. In exchange for gaining international legitimacy for their postcolonial regimes, Africa's postcolonial rulers (the elites who have mastered the rules and processes of international affairs) have essentially confirmed the logic of imperial and colonial domination. They sustain the processes that led to the creation of their territories and boundaries and the global order that was created to sustain neo-colonial privileges. The long suppressed interests and concerns of unprivileged or minority communities locked within these exalted boundaries have not found favor in a world constructed out of the imperialist imagination. Tragically, nationalist rulers continue to suppress challenges from within their countries to the boundaries of their artificial entities by employing ideas and means developed and perfected in the course of the imperial processes. After a while, and unsurprisingly, ordinary Africans could hardly perceive a substantive difference in the course of their lives.

In his study of the Mandate System, Anghie argued that 'the transfer of sovereignty to non-European peoples ... was simultaneous with, and indeed inseparable from, the creation of new systems of subordination and control administered by international institutions'.[29] The same holds true with even greater force for the newly independent African states of the post-Second World War era. Even as Africans were extracting their freedoms from old colonialism, newly created multilateral institutions were being perfected to maintain the status quo.

At the end of the Second World War, victorious nations under the leadership of the USA became even more committed to developing international institutions to supervise the new world order. The institutions were permeated with law and legalisms, with built-in escape hatches such as weighted voting and veto rights only for the most powerful, as well as alluring traps such as state and government recognition, economic and security assistance, and educational and technological exchanges, for all those that accepted the rules of the new order. Three principal institutions were created in 1945 during the first wave of institution building: the United Nations, the World Bank, and the International Monetary Fund. A global trade organization was delayed until the 1990s, although the General Agreement on Tariffs and Trade (GATT) essentially carried out that function in the interim years.

The United Nations was created, 'determined to save succeeding generations from the scourge of war, which twice in our lifetime has brought untold sorrow to mankind'.[30] Its most powerful organ was its Security Council, with veto powers granted to a select group of influential states over the most crucial aspects of UN work. The World Bank and the International Monetary Fund were established to supervise the global economy, but they were operated through a system of unequal voting powers that essentially preserved the status quo. Over time, even more institutions were created with varying degrees of supervisory powers over global affairs.

Embrace of international institutions by leaders of newly independent African states was effectively a prerequisite to admission to the club of nations. These new leaders perhaps saw membership in the postwar institutions as either unavoidable or necessary to bring about change. With membership came incentives, mostly in terms of access to capital, technology, and trade. As is now well documented, the terms of these incentives and assistance quickly proved onerous. African and other Third-World leaders would of course denounce, ad nauseam, their subordinate status within the postwar order, but most were merely calling for a rearrangement of the deckchairs of this *Titanic*. The web of multilateral arrangements proved too complex and manipulation or extrication quickly became impractical. Acquiescence proved the easier course. The effective result, even to the present day, is that the interests of African and other weaker states remain generally subordinate to the interests of those who had invaded, subjugated, and exploited them in the colonial era.[31]

Thus, the end of the Second World War helped to spur the struggle for national liberation in Africa as Wilson's heirs in the USA moved to more aggressively and comprehensively center international law as the legitimate medium of interstate relations. One result was that the nation-state emerged as the hegemonic vehicle for capturing and advancing popular aspirations. The principle of self-determination emerged as the organizing principle of national liberation, even as it confirmed the logic and end-products of colonialism. Another result was the development of a network of international political and economic institutions with extraordinary powers over weaker nation-states. Leaders of African liberation from colonial rule embraced all of these results even as they challenged marginal aspects. Africa is still plagued by these foundational legacies.

Conclusion

International law was essential to the success of colonialism in Africa. It legitimized the use of enormous and often unconstrained violence in the service of rapacity and subjugation. It provided a roadmap for successful colonization and made the process far more efficient by creating and affirming the rules that diverse competing European interests could use to protect their African interests. International law became an important companion to the civilizing mission by filling in the details for what could otherwise have been an unorganized and uncivilized plunder. In essence, international law helped to operationalize, systematize, and legitimize the idea of civilizing 'savage' people with violence and linked the idea to the subjugation of these people and the extraction of their labor and wealth for the benefit of the civilizers. Moreover, by supplying the principles, rules, and processes of decolonization, international law helped to ensure that even the end of colonialism would not result in a meaningful challenge to Western hegemony. African liberation leaders came to embrace these principles, rules, and processes. They became invested in them as they later gained control of the signal creation of international law, the nation-state, and have subsequently defended them, thus tragically reaffirming the logic and consequences of colonialism and international law.

NOTES

1. As Joyner puts it, "Generally speaking, international legal rules function to preserve order. That is, international law embodies a system of sanctioned regularity, a certain order in itself, which conveys expectations to the members of international society. International legal rules provide for the regularity of activities that can be discerned, forecast, and anticipated within the international community. Through international law, the attempt is made to regulate behavior to ensure harmony and to maintain international society's values and institutions." Christopher C. Joyner, *International Law in the 21st Century: Rules for Global Governance* (New York: Rowan & Littlefield, 2005), 293.
2. The "Scramble for Africa," also known as the "Partition of Africa," was the term that the European Powers used at their meeting in Berlin, Germany, where spheres of colonial influence were determined at the 1884 conference. It marked the carving and annexation of African countries according to colonial interests. See: Thomas Pakenham, *The Scramble for Africa* (New York: Random House, 1991); M.E. Chamberlain, *The Scramble for Africa* (London: Longmans, 1974); and S.E. Crowe, *The Berlin West African Conference 1884–1885* (New York: Longmans, 1942). See also Siba Grovogui, *Sovereigns, Quasi Sovereigns, and Africans* (Minneapolis: Univ. of Minn. Press, 1996).
3. Walter Benjamin, *Reflections* (New York: Schocken Books, 1986), 287.
4. Joseph Conrad, *Heart of Darkness and Selections from the Congo Diary* (New York: The Modern Library, 1999).
5. See: René Dumont, *False Start in Africa* (London: Andre Deutsch, 1966); Walter Rodney, *How Europe Underdeveloped Africa* (Washington, DC: Howard U. Press, 1974).
6. Conrad, *Heart of Darkness*.
7. Makau Mutua, "What Is TWAIL?," *American Society of International Law Proceedings* 94 (2000): 49.
8. For an excellent evaluation of Grotius's contributions, see Henry Richardson III, *The Origins of African-American Interests in International Law* (Durham: Carolina Academic Press, 2008), 87–101.
9. Grotius published two seminal international law texts: *Mare Liberum* ("The Freedom of the Seas"), first published in 1609 and *De Jure Belli ac Pacis* ("On the Law of War and Peace"), published in 1625.
10. Grovogui, *Sovereigns, Quasi Sovereigns, and Africans*, 19–20.
11. Ibid., 16.
12. See Robin Blackburn, *The Making of New World Slavery: From the Baroque to the Modern 1492–1800* (London: Verso, 1997).

13. Grovogui, *Sovereigns, Quasi Sovereigns, and Africans*, 19–20.
14. Ibid.
15. Ibid.
16. Antony Anghie, *Imperialism, Sovereignty and the Making of International Law* (Cambridge: CUP, 2007), 3.
17. Pakenham, inside cover.
18. Ibid., generally.
19. General Act of the Berlin Conference on West Africa, 26 Feb. 1885, Chapter VI, Articles 35 and 36.
20. Conrad, *Heart of Darkness*, 42.
21. For example, the conference unanimously approved a resolution that required "that each nation should notify the other of its plans for colonization, and at the same time outline the territories within which it proposed to operate." Maurice N. Hennessy, *Congo* (London: Frederick A. Praeger Publishers, 1961).
22. See John L. Comaroff and Jean Comaroff, eds. *Law and Disorder in the Postcolony: An Introduction*, in *Law and Disorder in the Postcolony* (Chicago: Univ. of Chicago Press, 2006).
23. Anghie, *Imperialism, Sovereignty and the Making of International Law*, 8.
24. See generally Erez Manela, *The Wilsonian Moment: Self-Determination and the International Origins of Anticolonial Nationalism* (Oxford: OUP, 2007).
25. Anghie, *Imperialism, Sovereignty and the Making of International Law*, 136–44.
26. See International Covenant on Economic, Social and Cultural Rights, 993 U.N.T.S. 3, 1966 U.N.J.Y.B. 170, and International Covenant on Civil and Political Rights, 999 U.N.T.S. 171, 1966 U.N.J.Y.B. 193.
27. Grovogui, *Sovereigns, Quasi Sovereigns, and Africans*, 4.
28. Ibid.
29. Anghie, *Imperialism, Sovereignty and the Making of International Law*, 179.
30. See Preamble, Charter of the United Nations, 1 U.N.T.S. XVI, 1976 Y.B.U.N. 1043.
31. As Grovogui puts it, "only the rights sanctioned by the former colonialists were accorded to the colonized, regardless of the needs and demands of the latter. That the will of the colonial powers was so central to the implementation of self-determination was not considered an aberration in international law." Grovogui, *Sovereigns, Quasi Sovereigns, and Africans*, 6.

Bibliography

Antony Anghie. *Imperialism, Sovereignty and the Making of International Law*. Cambridge: CUP, 2007.
Benjamin, Walter. *Critique of Violence*. New York: Schocken Books, 1986.
Blackburn, Robin. *The Making of New World Slavery: From the Baroque to the Modern 1492–1800*. London: Verso, 1997.
Chamberlain, M.E. *The Scramble for Africa*. London: Longmans, 1974.
Charter of the United Nations, Preamble. 1 U.N.T.S. XVI, 1976 Y.B.U.N. 1043.

Comaroff, John L., and Jean Comaroff, eds. *Law and Disorder in the Postcolony: An Introduction, in Law and Disorder in the Postcolony*. Chicago: Univ. of Chicago Press, 2006.

Conrad, Joseph. *Heart of Darkness and Selections from the Congo Diary*. New York: The Modern Library, 1999.

Crowe, S.E. *The Berlin West African Conference 1884–1885*. New York: Longmans, 1942.

Dumont, Rene. *False Start in Africa*. London: Andre Deutsch, 1966.

General Act of the Berlin Conference on West Africa. 1885.

Grotius, Hugo. *Mare Liberum* (The Free Seas; from chapter 12 of *De Indis*). Leiden, 1609.

———. *De Jure Belli ac Pacis* [On the Law of War and Peace]. Paris, 1625 2nd ed. Amsterdam 1631.

Grovogui, Siba. *Sovereigns, Quasi Sovereigns, and Africans*. Minneapolis: Univ. of Minn. Press, 1996.

Hennessy, Maurice N. *Congo*. London: Frederick A. Praeger Publishers, 1961.

International Covenant on Civil and Political Rights. 999 U.N.T.S. 171, 1966 U.N.J.Y.B. 193.

International Covenant on Economic, Social and Cultural Rights. 993 U.N.T.S. 3, 1966 U.N.J.Y.B. 170.

Joyner, Cristopher C. *International Law in the 21st Century: Rules for Global Governance*. New York: Rowan & Littlefield, 2005, 293.

Manela, Erez. *The Wilsonian Moment: Self-Determination and the International Origins of Anticolonial Nationalism*. Oxford: OUP, 2007.

Mutua, Makau. What Is TWAIL? *American Society of International Law Proceedings* 94 (2000): 49.

Pakenham, Thomas. *The Scramble for Africa*. New York: Random House, 1991.

Richardson, Henry III. *The Origins of African-American Interests in International Law*. Durham: Carolina Academic Press, 2008.

Rodney, Walter. *How Europe Underdeveloped Africa*. Washington, DC: Howard U. Press, 1974.

CHAPTER 24

Colonialism and Development in Africa

Ruth Rempel

'Development' is a term with many meanings. Positive change is one of its non-biological ones. While this can be an evolutionary process, development history focuses on intentional change.[1] Jan Nederveen Pieterse defines development as 'organized intervention in collective affairs according to a standard of improvement'.[2] As Kenneth Dadzie put it: 'Development is the unfolding of people's individual and social imagination in defining goals and inventing ways to approach them'.[3] Development history involves following what social actors say about their goals for collective improvement, as well as the means they use to achieve it.[4] Looking at how resources are allocated is an important way to identify actors' means as well as their development goals, both overt and latent.

Some scholars argue that development was invented in 1949, pointing to US President Truman's second inaugural address as its birth announcement.[5] The Point Four Program (1950–1954), which Truman's speech initiated, was the practical embodiment of this new idea. However, this interpretation is undercut by both contemporary and recent analyses.[6] More importantly for African development history, the continent received only six percent of the Point Four funds; the bulk of the money went to Asia. Roughly, half the Africa funds went to one country, Egypt, and the next largest amount was transferred to Britain, France and Portugal for use in their 'Dependent Territories'.[7] This followed a pattern already established with the Marshall Plan (1948–1952), in which US allies were allowed to finance development

R. Rempel (✉)
International Development Studies, Menno Simons College,
Canadian Mennonite University, Winnipeg, MB, Canada

in their empires with transferred funds.[8] As this suggests, European imperial governments were a crucial external source of development ideas and practices in the continent. As the experiences of Liberia and Ethiopia will show, the US approach to development in independent African countries was not a coherent 'project'. In addition, an exclusive focus on these external actors obscures the development initiatives undertaken by African actors in the nineteenth and early twentieth centuries, as well as the crucial role of African agency in reshaping European and US development initiatives. This chapter can only sketch a part of this rich, emerging field of history.

Modernization and Development in Nineteenth-Century Africa

Modernization interested historians and political scientists who studied pre-colonial African states in the 1960s and 1970s. They looked at African empires as well as states like Buganda and Asante.[9] Some took up the argument that modernization—by which they meant the adoption of European technology and institutions as part of a conscious program of social change—was widespread in nineteenth-century Africa, and that this process was frustrated rather than accelerated by European imperialism.[10] Nineteenth-century Africans did not necessarily use terms like 'modernization' and 'development', but Pieterse's definition suggests that the initiatives of various African states and non-state actors could be reexamined with development in mind.[11] Some of their 'organized intervention' was an explicit response to or tool of imperialism; all of it was part of the social landscape that empire-builders had to take into account by the end of the nineteenth century.

Some African developmental interventions have been researched, though few have so far been interpreted as development history. A notable exception was Bahru Zewde's collective biography of two generations of Ethiopian intellectuals who called for developmental changes in conjunction with, and occasionally at odds with the Ethiopian emperors of their day.[12] Education was a central part of their initiatives, together with administrative modernization. These changes would give substance to the political independence defended at the Battle of Adowa (1896), and encourage social justice, especially improvements for peasants and slaves. To the extent these intellectuals considered the condition of conquered peoples like the Oromo, they expressed sentiments and suggested solutions similar to those of contemporary Europeans writing about European empires.[13] Zewde's study built on national histories, which described initiatives by Emperor Menelik II (ruled 1889–1913) and several of his predecessors to change as well as expand the Abyssinian empire. They sought to centralize the state, build enabling infrastructure and institutions, acquire key European technologies, promote crafts and manufactures, and expand agricultural production.[14] This has been analyzed as defensive modernization, a response to European imperialism, though defense of the empire against European encroachment was only one reason for change.[15] Programs of change like these were also not the reflexive response of isolated peoples to an external threat. Nineteenth-century African reformers looked to and learned from the Meiji regime's transformation of Japan, for example, and the Nizam-ı Cedid (new order) in Ottoman Turkey.[16]

Another developmental intervention that interested both historians and development scholars was that of Muhammad Ali, the Ottoman viceroy in Egypt (ruled 1805–1848). A regime-commissioned account of his initiatives placed them in—and against—the convention of *islah* (reform), a guiding concept for intentional change.[17] Creation of an effective military was at the heart of Muhammad Ali's program, but he believed this required social transformation. He initiated improvements in education, changes to government structure, new irrigation and transport infrastructure, state monopolies in crop marketing, a land survey, and redistribution of land in aid of increased commodity production and taxation.[18] Rapid industrialization was another element in his program. It included agricultural processing, production of textiles and consumer goods, and weapons manufacturing. State-owned factories, manipulation of internal markets for labor and raw materials, and protectionist trade policies were all used to support these industries.[19] Effective autonomy from the Ottoman Empire, even independence from it, was the ultimate goal. In this context, imperialism was an important way to express Egypt's power and status.[20] Muhammad Ali's 1820 invasion of Sudan provided resources, as well as conscripts for Egypt's reformed army. Improving the welfare of Sudan's peoples by opening up the region and administering it in a mutually beneficial way were among the justifications for the conquest.[21] Among Muhammed Ali's successors, Ismail Pasha (ruled 1863–1879) was also known for his modernization efforts, which focused on civilian rather than military institutions.[22]

The Eastern Congo settlements established by traders from the Sultanate of Zanzibar were another kind of developmental intervention.[23] Traders like Hamed bin Muhammed el Murjebi, better known as Tippu Tip, were consciously transforming the places in which they operated. Tippu Tip and his competitors initiated three linked changes. First, through training and example, the region's people were to be weaned away from their alleged 'barbarous' practices—paganism, cannibalism, and nakedness—and introduced to *ustaarabu* (civilization), as this was understood along the Swahili-speaking coast. The aim was 'conversion' in the broad sense used by Valentin Mudimbe to describe European imperial intentions in Africa.[24] Second, peace and order were to be imposed in the region. Tippu Tip said of Maniema: 'In this country there are no hereditary chiefs'; rather, outsiders came and offered goods to those who 'own the land' and the people accepted these new leaders.[25] This legitimized control by Zanzibari traders who—despite their own escalating violence—presented themselves as an improvement on the conflict-ridden rule of existing leaders. Third, agriculture in the region was reoriented. In major settlements like Nyangwe and Kassongo, it increasingly involved plantations and enslaved labor.[26] New crops like rice, maize, and citrus fruits were also introduced. In villages along emerging caravan routes, production was regularized so villagers could provision passing traders. As inhabitants often responded by withdrawing from areas through which the Zanzibaris were advancing, they had to be forcibly returned to their villages and made to resume cultivation.

Modernity, reform, and civilization were not static; neither were the 'traditional' institutions they sought to supplant. All were tools for a variety of individuals and groups seeking betterment, or at least security, whether in empires or other kinds of state.[27] As the three examples above suggest, developmental initiatives were not desired by all involved in them. Sanction and violence were needed to ensure the participation of the unwilling, often people with less power. This was true to an even greater extent for the developmental initiatives of European imperialists, on which the remainder of this chapter will focus.

EUROPEAN 'HIGH' IMPERIALISM AND DEVELOPMENT

The decades between 1870 and 1914 were an era of 'high' or 'new' imperialism.[28] Africa was a focal point for this, with several European states making claims in the continent. Non-state actors, such as chartered companies and Christian missions, expanded in counterpoint.

Gareth Austin argued that the relation between land and indigenous labor envisioned by the imperialists was a determining factor in development history.[29] He distinguished three main types of colony: settler-elite, concession, and peasant colonies.[30] In the first, European settlers were present in larger numbers, though always still a minority. Crucially, they were given rights to the best land, and the colony's indigenes were forced to work for them. Africa had a few settler-elite colonies—Algeria, Kenya, Southern Rhodesia (Zimbabwe), South Africa, and South West Africa (Namibia)—created by France, Britain, and Germany. Italians also settled in numbers in Libya and Eritrea.

In concession colonies, European companies were granted rights to tracts of land in which they could extract resources, typically rubber, ivory, timber, or minerals; concessions were also the contractual basis for plantations and some infrastructure projects. This delegated the cost of developing a colony to private investors. Concession companies were granted special privileges, some involving control of inhabitants' labor, and they were ill regulated, with violence and extreme exploitation the tragically common result.[31] Concessions were granted in many parts of the continent, but colonies dominated by them were concentrated in equatorial Africa, with King Leopold II's Congo Free State the infamous exemplar. By the 1920s, many of the concessions had been wound down, and after 1930, the remainder were subject to the Forced

Labour Convention of the International Labour Organization (ILO). Portugal's African colonies were a hybrid of the settler-elite and concession types, and endured to the early 1970s.

This chapter focuses on what Austin called peasant colonies, which were home to more than half of Africans. In them, most of the land remained in indigenous hands, and indigenous authorities were important adjuncts to colonial administration. Agriculture was taxed, and colonial officials sought to change crops and farming methods.[32] Most of the agriculturalists were peasants (or smallholders), but there were usually a few settlers and indigenous farmers operating on a larger scale as well. The chapter also focuses on British and French colonies since they covered almost three-quarters of the continent by 1920, the height of these two empires. While the French ruled a somewhat larger area, at nearly 12 million square kilometers, the British ruled about 60 million Africans, almost twice as many as the French.[33] British and French development policies also served as a model for those of other European imperial powers.

Development was one of the justifications offered for the Scramble for Africa. This social interventionism was a distinguishing mark of 'high' imperialism.[34] However, European colonial claims had to be realized on the ground before the changes Europeans envisioned could be initiated. Conquests and treaties were followed by ad hoc initiatives that brought as much inadvertent as intentional change. As Frederick Cooper commented, European rule was distinguished by trespass more than transformation in the decades following the 1884–1885 Berlin Conference.[35]

CIVILIZATION AND DEVELOPMENT IN FRENCH WEST AFRICA

The extension of French control in West Africa between the 1850s and 1900 occurred largely by military conquest. By 1895, *mission civilisatrice* (civilizing mission) had become the official ideology of the Third Republic's empire. As Alice Conklin documented, its initial emphases were transformative. African societies, once conquered, would undergo 'constructive exploitation' directed by the French state. Slavery would be replaced by free labor, the oppressive feudal rule of kings and chiefs by rational administration, while French education and medicine, together with railroads and printing presses would end African isolation and ignorance. This revolutionary and racist program was widely accepted in French policy circles, as was the assumption that it would benefit both Africans and the French.[36] Funds for this transformation were limited, though, and the new colonies were expected to be self-financing.[37] Railways were a priority, as the French believed the changes they desired would follow from increased trade and communication. They were financed by head (poll) taxes, compulsory labor, and loans contracted in France. Health was another early policy focus, though it received much less funding.[38]

Colonial administration was established gradually after conquest brought more peoples under French rule. As Emily Osborn shows, in the early years of French rule, African soldiers, translators, and clerks were the face of the colonial state in West Africa, and they reinterpreted French demands and initiatives. This accentuated local variation in the implementation of colonial policy, as did the manipulation, inertia, and withdrawal with which elites and commoners responded to the new French administration.[39] The African interpreters Osborn discusses appropriated some of the spoils of French occupation, and encouraged a partial reshuffling of social and political hierarchies, but did not advance an alternative to either precolonial or French development programs.

Indirect Rule and Development in British Uganda

Uganda was declared a British protectorate in 1894. Since 1886, it had been part of a British sphere in East Africa, negotiated with the Germans and the Sultan of Zanzibar. Mimicking the trade-based sultanate, both European powers used chartered companies to establish themselves in the region. The inability of the Imperial British East Africa Company (IBEAC) to administer effectively the area assigned to it led the British government to step into prevent loss of territory to regional rivals.[40]

Like many parts of the African interior, Uganda posed a challenge for its new rulers. The nearest port was 1200 kilometers away and the British did not consider mainstays of regional trade—salt, bark cloth, fish, and slaves—tradable. The minerals, ivory and rubber they did value were not abundant in Uganda.[41] Generating revenue to recover the costs of pacification and of building a railway to the coast became a British preoccupation. They instituted taxes in the early 1900s, with a head tax and import duties generating most of the protectorate's revenue.[42] They also sought to increase the protectorate's profitability through cash-crop production. Officials believed that if they provided security and infrastructure, then British businesses would invest and economic advancement would follow. However, tropical development proved more complex, and British investors narrowly interested in mining and commerce.[43] Consequently, after 1900, colonial administrators played an active role in supporting and enforcing cotton cultivation.[44] It spread rapidly among peasants in the protectorate's East and South as the least disruptive way of satisfying British demands.[45] However, as Grace Carswell's research on Kigezi showed, where farmers had other ways to earn money for taxes they resisted growing designated cash crops.[46] The administration quickly became dependent on taxing cotton, which supplied 90% of its revenue by 1920.[47]

In the protectorate's early years, the chiefs and generals of existing states, especially Buganda, were essential to the expansion and administration of the minimally resourced British administration. The practices of the Buganda kingdom consequently influenced the creation of what was effectively an 'indigenous civil service'. This was an early version of Indirect Rule, the policy that Frederick Lugard, the IBEAC's Ugandan administrator, was later to articulate. In it the legitimacy and capacity of 'native authorities'—stereotypically a chief and his advisory council—were harnessed by the new British administration. These authorities were expected to maintain order among their traditional subjects, communicate British requirements to them, and enforce these when necessary.[48]

While Uganda was not envisioned as a settler colony like neighboring Kenya, the establishment of plantations by a few European settlers and by resident Indians after 1911 was a welcome development in the eyes of many British officials. Some Baganda, Basoga and Bagisu chiefs also used their control over land and labor to establish large personal cash-crop farms.[49] However, all these producers needed labor and land, which interfered with peasant agriculture. Labor shortages were especially severe because of the pacification wars, famine, and epidemics in the preceding decades. When these shortages were compounded by falling export prices after 1920, most of the European-owned plantations went out of business. Peasant production was more resilient because African farmers could fall back on subsistence crops, and because most had to continue to grow some cash crops to pay their taxes.[50]

INSTITUTIONS FOR DEVELOPMENT: EDUCATION AND MISSIONS

Economists became increasingly interested in the role of institutions in development after the mid-1980s.[51] Many concluded that British colonial institutions were more beneficial for development than those of other European powers. As Ewout Frankema observes, education lies at the heart of this supposed difference, but the economic literature examines neither the context for education in Britain's African colonies nor the significant differences between them. Frankema also argues that the uneven distribution of schools in British-ruled Africa—and the subsequent large variation in literacy rates—was more strongly influenced by African agency than by imperial policy.[52]

In the early years of British rule, education and health care were left to private actors, primarily Christian missions, who supplemented indigenous services. Teaching and medicine were aids to the missions' goals of religious conversion and social progress; the degree to which they intended their work to be a contribution to or a corrective for colonialism varied. Even when colonial administrations became more actively interested in education after the mid-1920s, missions still played an important role. In Uganda, the Church Missionary Society, the Church of England's mission organization, provided about half of the roughly 100,000 primary-school spaces in the late 1920s. Three Catholic missions—only one of them British—provided the remainder. Mission schools ranged from village ones with a single teacher and large multi-grade classes to King's College Budo, Gayaza High School and St Mary's College Kisubi, the boarding schools that educated the elite of Uganda's kingdoms. The vast majority of teachers in mission schools were regional converts, not Europeans, as was also the case for service providers in clinics and churches. Indeed, the Africanization of missions was essential to their expansion, even after medical advances improved the tropical life expectancy of Europeans. Further, the money and in-kind resources used to build and run schools came mostly from converts and from colonial taxpayers, not from the metropole. This varied by colony, though. In Uganda, the colonial administration covered 20–30% of the cost of mission schools; in the wealthier Gold Coast, it was about two thirds of the cost, while in impoverished Nyasaland it was less than eight percent.[53]

The British were more open to the operation of missions than were other imperial powers. The French tolerated Catholic mission schools in prescribed roles and locations. Generally, they were more active in French Equatorial Africa than in the West African colonies, and more active in the early nineteenth century—and thus in coastal regions—than at the end of the century. Legislation passed between 1902 and 1905 directed the secularization of church-run schools, forcing administrators in France's colonies to involve themselves with education. However, state investment in education was low.[54]

THE EMERGENCE OF DEVELOPMENTAL IMPERIALISM IN FRENCH SUDAN AND BRITISH UGANDA

The economic crisis between the two World Wars was a significant period in African development history. Although generally treated as a single event—a Great Depression lasting for a decade after 1929—there were in fact three interwar economic contractions: a short recession in the early 1920s, a more severe one from 1929 through the mid-1930s, and then a faltering of the economic recovery in 1937.[55] Trade transmitted the global recession to Africa, since the continent was not deeply integrated into international financial markets.[56] Production for trade and taxation of trade thus became central issues for Africans and their European administrators. War and recession caused the European colonial powers to rethink their position in Africa. They systematized the ad hoc development measures they had previously relied on, and introduced new ones.

French rule underwent important changes earlier, during the First World War. Shortages of money and personnel prompted significant colonial public-service cuts, affecting health and education more than general administration.[57] Wartime desperation also prompted the imposition of conscription in France's African colonies, and greater use of forced labor. These became flashpoints for opposition to French rule; they also drew French attention to the problem of labor scarcity, and to the deplorable condition of their West African subjects.[58] A new policy of association emerged in response. Traditional elites and institutions were reinterpreted: they were now useful, not inherently oppressive. Under French tutelage, chiefs and other elites would help govern and civilize their peoples. Marital Merlin, the Governor General of French West Africa, argued that this differed from Britain's policy of Indirect Rule because it better protected the rights of the African masses vis-à-vis their indigenous leaders. However, the bigger difference lay in the concessions eventually made to French-educated Africans, who demanded a political role and rights.[59]

These policies were accompanied by a shift in thinking about imperial trade. A strategy of systematic economic development known as *mise en valeur* (literally, value creation) received new attention after 1919.[60] The term had been used since the early 1890s, but interest in it intensified among officials and politicians who saw that the empire had not provided resources France needed during or after the war. Minister of Colonies Albert Sarraut formalized the strategy in *La mise en valeur des colonies françaises* (1923).[61] It involved comprehensive modernization based on state investment in colonial infrastructure and commerce. This would increase trade within the empire and better the condition of France's African subjects, since economic improvement would bring social progress in its train.[62] This was linked to a race-based regeneration policy known as *faire du noir* (literally making black), to increase the African birth rate while reducing illness and hunger.[63] However, state capacity in both Dakar and Paris was limited and, since the latter was not willing to give up the principle of self-financing colonies, the strategy was only partially implemented.[64]

An irrigation scheme in French Sudan (Mali) was a *mise en valeur* project that did proceed. The colony was envisioned from the first as a supplier of cotton to France, though peasants who already grew cotton would need to increase production and grow varieties preferred by French manufacturers. However, even after a rail link to Senegal and ginning equipment were in place, French merchants were reluctant to involve themselves and French manufacturers were unwilling to compete with the higher prices offered by the region's artisanal weavers.[65] Large-scale, irrigated cotton production would sidestep the perennial problem of peasant colonies—managing peasants. A private consortium proposed a system of dams and canals in 1918, promising investors it would create an El Dorado on the Niger River.[66] Two years later, engineer Émile Bélime carried out a state-sponsored survey, proposing a grand irrigation project that was incorporated into Sarraut's plans. However, the limited public funding this project initially received came from West African taxpayers rather than France. The forced labor of civilians and military conscripts was another essential contribution.[67] While its size was distinctive, the project's focus and methods were consistent with those of other agricultural development projects in the continent, both British and French.[68]

Cotton production was the project's primary goal. It would make the empire self-sufficient in this increasingly expensive commodity; it would also rescue land from the encroaching Sahara. The proposal was modified in 1924 to include rice production, which would end famine in the region and support *faire du noir*.[69] Work began in 1925; it accelerated in 1931 when a scaled-down version of the project was approved for a French colonial loan. The *Office du Niger* was created to administer the project, an agency with powers so vast that it was effectively a state within the state of French West Africa.[70] The project was also an exemplar of France's *colonisation indigène* (native colonization) policy, which sought to address labor and African welfare problems identified after the First World War. It involved resettling African farmers in areas that the French considered best suited for agriculture. European agricultural methods, such as ox ploughs and new crop rotations, would also help these farmers become more productive.[71]

While the project experienced technical challenges, its persistent failure to meet its goals stemmed from labor scarcity.[72] There were few volunteers so 'settlers' were recruited by force, some from neighboring districts and some from Upper Volta (Burkina Faso). French officials described the *Office* as a project of 'independent peasant production under European supervision', but the agricultural regimen was strict enough to suggest plantation life. It illustrated the increasingly illiberal orientation of French policy in the 1930s.[73] Many of the project's involuntary participants, nicknamed *tubabu jonw* (slaves of the white man), fled. Those who stayed cultivated additional land outside the *Office* and sold their crops in local markets rather than through its official marketing channel, actions that undermined the project. French administrators who believed that indigenous 'settlers' would change their farming methods and undergo a social transformation—accepting private property in land and living in nuclear families—were frustrated.[74]

Global recession prompted additional changes in French policy. France's trade policies in Africa had been more protectionist than British ones from the outset, relying on tariffs and preferential treatment to structure trade within the empire.[75] This protectionism intensified during the 1930s, and by mid-decade France's African colonies were an important market for its most recession-affected industries.[76] However, dependence on trade taxes in France's West African colonies meant that their revenues fell significantly during the interwar recessions.[77] The higher taxes imposed as a result impoverished those who remained on the land and tried to increase their cashcrop production. It also drove many off the land, pushing them to seek urban employment, though opportunities were limited.[78] Although the West African administration received larger transfers from France to counter-balance tax shortfalls, this aid did little to improve well-being in the colonies.[79]

The postwar recessions' effects were also a rude shock to the British colonial establishment, which assumed that imperialism brought different, but mutual benefits to the metropole and its subjects. The decline in African well-being triggered by the trade crisis was revealed in a series of reports. As in French-ruled Africa, it was magnified by colonial budget cuts, which affected health, education, and agricultural services.[80] For peasants under British rule, particularly the indebted, this was a time of great difficulty.[81] Landless people, such as migrant agricultural workers, faced a sharp drop in wages or lay-offs.[82] While negative effects dominated, some producers evaded new exactions and pressures to increase export production, or even found opportunities in the misfortunes of their region.[83]

Prior to the recessions, British policy had been reactive, rather than a tool for a deliberate, consistent development vision.[84] In 1918, Uganda's governor Robert Coryndon complained of the lack of a long-range plan for the protectorate. As was the case in France, war and recession heightened consciousness of Britain's dependence on raw materials and prompted efforts to create supplies of them within the empire.[85] In response, British officials systematized their strategy for agricultural development: indigenous farmers would grow the cash crops most needed by British industry, and their earnings would allow them to purchase its products. The British favored a diversity of crops, though, fearing the consequences of over-reliance on one commodity.[86]

The interwar years were pivotal ones in Uganda. Cash-crop production increased, though it was coffee rather than cotton production that grew most rapidly, both arabica in Bugisu and robusta in Buganda.[87] While the British promoted arabica production, the expansion of robusta was the result of farmer initiative. It was in part a rural protest against low cotton prices, and in part a recognition by Baganda peasants and chiefs that once the bushes were established, coffee gave a higher return with less labor than other cash crops. Land and tribute laws passed by Buganda's *Lukiiko* (legislature) in 1928 provided peasants with security of tenure that made a perennial crop like coffee attractive.[88] Nevertheless, the incomes of Ugandans grew more slowly than did their export crop production, and income was not equitably distributed. Reported one observer: 'A few wealthy chiefs and landowners could now live in brick houses, wear smart European suits and ride in motorcars, but as far as the mass of the people were concerned the improvement in the standards of living had not been particularly impressive'.[89]

Coffee production had other, unanticipated effects. It tied peasants into broader markets, whose functioning affected their livelihoods. As Stephen Bunker found, increased coffee production in Bugisu during the 1930s made peasants there more sensitive to prices, but also 'to questions of taxes, the condition of warehouses, roads, and bridges, and the procedures followed at the buying stations. They were also increasingly concerned with the availability of education and medical attention in the rural areas'.[90] Both indigenous leaders and British administrators had to consider these concerns.

Cashcrop production also created tension along other lines. Although coffee required less labor than cotton, hulling the beans made a significant demand on women's time, one that was resisted since decisions about coffee and the income from it were generally the province of men.[91] In Buganda, this tension was relieved by hiring migrant workers from the North and East of the protectorate, as well as neighboring Ruanda-Urundi.[92] This fueled a growing differential between the wealth and influence of coffee-growing regions and other parts of the protectorate.[93]

Already during the First World War, cashcrop production allowed Uganda's administration to be self-financing.[94] Export taxes were raised further in 1919, with the justification that this would generate funds for development. However, the per capita revenue raised was relatively low and, before the demise of the European plantation sector, it received a disproportionate benefit from the resultant development spending.[95] This included transport and communication infrastructure, though the salaries and pensions of British officials and security also consumed significant amounts. Spending on health and education for Ugandans increased too, but less than the increases in other sectors.[96]

In 1932, Britain abandoned decades of relatively free trade for protectionism. The Uganda protectorate's administration also started to intervene in the purchase of cash crops during the 1930s. Its initial concern was to stave off farmer protest over their treatment by traders, most of them resident Asians. It also wanted to ensure coffee quality, and find a price that incentivized growers but did not upset the European-run export firms. While focused on domestic issues, this action was consistent with the colonial powers' broader concern during the interwar recessions—stabilizing international commodity markets.[97]

THE LEAGUE OF NATIONS AND DEVELOPMENT

The interwar years were also important ones in the emerging intergovernmental sphere. The League of Nations and the ILO, both created in 1919, were important elements. As Rachel Crowdy of the League's Secretariat commented, peace was the organization's primary task but it would be achieved 'by working for social welfare', not only by negotiating treaties. The League addressed social problems like working conditions, human trafficking, and disease.[98] Collecting information was an important part of this, both via investigative reporting and improving data collection by states.[99] The 1930 Commission of Inquiry into forced labor in Liberia was an example of the former.[100] Work like this built on an existing tradition of international humanitarian involvement in Africa, particularly for the abolition of slavery. Some of the work was novel, though, like the decade-long study of nutrition jointly undertaken by the League's Health Organization, the International Institute of Agriculture, and the ILO. It created international nutrition standards, sponsored nutrition surveys in selected countries, and collected information about member countries' nutrition policies. All this information was assembled, analyzed, and disseminated in conferences and publications. This initiative had a galvanizing effect on British colonial policy.[101] As Christopher Wrigley said with respect to Uganda:

> during the 1930s a silent revolution, discernible both in London and in Entebbe, in intellectual as well as in political and administrative circles, was taking place in the values of Colonial Government. The intellectual revolution

can perhaps be pin-pointed to 1936, when the International African Institute turned aside from the study of tribal institutions and how to preserve them and devoted a whole issue of its journal to the problem of nutrition.[102]

Susan Pedersen argues that the League's work on issues like labor and nutrition had lasting effects on development ideas and institutions, though her primary focus is the impact of the mandate system.[103] The colonies seized from the Germans and Ottomans during the First World War became Mandated Territories to be administered in trust, not additions to the empires of the victors. Half of the League Mandates were in Africa.[104] The League of Nations Covenant instituted the Mandates and also required its signatories to 'secure the just treatment of the native inhabitants' elsewhere in their empires, setting norms for imperial rule that included the welfare of subject peoples.[105] The Permanent Mandates Commission and the League's Mandates Section were tools (novel ones) for trying to hold imperial governments accountable. The norms they used were based on British policies and practices, particularly in Egypt, or at least Britain's 'best intentions'.[106] The philosophy behind this was Indirect Rule, and Pedersen documents the role that Frederick Lugard's *Dual Mandate in British Tropical Africa* (1922) played in articulating global norms of welfare and development under colonial rule, reinforced by his membership in the Mandates Commission between 1922 and 1936.[107]

All this did not mean that Mandate Territories were better governed in practice. Rather, Pedersen argues that the mandate system's impact lay in 'internationalization', the process by which an issue was transposed from a national (and imperial) political sphere into an international one. The creation of an intergovernmental civil service was part of this. The League's staff were not simply tools of the imperial powers who dominated the organization. Some sought a degree of autonomy from their home governments and a progressive interpretation of their mandate.[108] A network of lobbyists, philanthropists, and experts grew around the League, which both shaped and amplified its actions. The League's internationalization built the skills and credibility of people who petitioned for their rights under Mandates as well. Metropolitan policymakers and politicians were changed too, as they had to incorporate extranational interests into their work.[109] They were also forced to acknowledge—though not necessarily to change—the racism inherent in trusteeship, the idea that underpinned developmental imperialism.[110]

LIBERIA: INTERWAR DEVELOPMENT VIA CORPORATE ALTRUISM

Entrepreneurs were also among the agents of colonialism, though as of the First World War Africa hosted only six percent of global investment. During the interwar years, foreign direct investment in the continent grew and, more importantly, its focus shifted. Prior to 1914, only South Africa and Egypt attracted much investment; after 1919, investment in other African countries grew more rapidly.[111] These investments were small by global standards, but investors like Lever Brothers in the Belgian Congo, Imperial Tobacco in Nyasaland (Malawi), Schneider et Cie in Morocco, or Firestone in Liberia had significant development impacts.[112]

US investment in Africa increased during the interwar years, though it remained much less significant than British investment.[113] The Firestone Tire and Rubber Company's concession in Liberia was a prominent example, one that paved the way for subsequent US investments.[114] Liberia in the early 1920s was in desperate financial straits. Its leaders, descendants of the black Americans who founded the republic of Liberia, maintained economic ties with the USA, but US isolationist policies meant this relationship generated little aid.[115] The traditional fix, international borrowing, was not an option since Liberia's finances were already under creditor supervision.[116] The need of the Liberian government coincided with the interests of US tire companies, the world's largest users of rubber. They wanted affordable supplies because after 1910 the Brazilian government and the British, acting for several South-East Asian colonies, raised the international price of rubber by controlling exports.[117]

Between 1924 and 1926, Firestone representatives signed a set of agreements with the Liberian government. The Firestone Plantation Company, a wholly owned subsidiary, received a 99-year lease to a million acres of Liberian land.[118] The agreements included a clause that bound the Liberian government to take a substantial loan from Firestone. Harvey Firestone insisted on this to give his company leverage over the government.[119] The five million dollar loan was opposed by many Liberians, but its defenders believed the loss of sovereignty it represented was the lesser of two evils; the greater evil being a lack of engagement by the USA at a time when Liberia needed protection from British and French encroachment.[120] They also hoped that the infrastructure Firestone agreed to build would stimulate the country's stagnant economy.[121]

Firestone did not use all its leased land, but even so it established the world's largest rubber plantation, with a second smaller plantation nearby. Daily production decisions were made in Ohio and communicated by radio.[122] The plantations were largely self-sufficient, having built roads, hydroelectric stations, latex processing factories, and an airfield. Labor was covered in Firestone's agreement with Liberia's government, which used the annual hut tax that inhabitants of the interior had been compelled to pay since 1910, and force, to supply thousands of plantation workers.[123] As the country's only large employer, Firestone was an important means by which cash for taxes could be earned. By the early 1930s, the Company switched to dealing directly with chiefs, paying them a stipend for each worker they supplied.[124]

Firestone's involvement in Liberia was intentionally developmental. As with nineteenth-century model industrial projects, the paternalistic vision of the company's head was crucial. For Harvey Firestone, the Liberian plantations were more than a business investment. He was, as a former State Department official observed, also 'very interested in the idea of establishing schools, hospitals, agricultural training schools, and so forth for the development of the aborigines'. Firestone was attracted by the idea of 'doing welfare work' on a grand scale. Where peers like Henry Ford were building model towns, he would be 'developing a model nation'.[125] This was little compensation, though, for those displaced by the government's appropriation of land for the Firestone concession or forced to work for Firestone.

As with the plantation, the development Firestone initiated was considerably less grandiose than his initial plans. He had two hospitals built, funded medical, ethnographic, and linguistic research, and made some investment in schools and agricultural training.[126] The scope for development spending by external actors was great, since the Liberian government focused its development spending on infrastructure, mostly in the coastal region. By comparison, the government of British-ruled Sierra Leone, with a similar population, spent twenty times as much on education, health, and agriculture.[127] In this context, Nigerian nationalist Nnamdi Azikiwe called Firestone's efforts 'unavoidable expedient altruism'.[128]

Firestone's involvement in Liberia preceded the idea of a business-led 'American Century' of global development—and President Truman's speech—by several decades.[129] Firestone's development activities in Liberia, like those in interwar British and French African colonies, were ad hoc and limited. US officials assisted the negotiations between Firestone and Liberia, but the concession-based development that followed was not a 'project' of the US government. Its involvement in Liberia was sporadic, frustrating both Firestone and members of the Americo-Liberian ruling elite.[130]

The Second World War and Imperial Development Policy

Second World War battles were fought in East and North Africa, but the war effort affected the entire continent.[131] African soldiers and laborers, both conscripts and volunteers, played important roles. So did farmers: the demand for food and industrial crops intensified, as did the demand for rubber and timber. The mining sector was also deeply affected, as African miners and mines were crucial to meeting the wartime demand for coal, iron, and copper, as well as specialty metals like molybdenum.[132] Given existing labor shortages, quotas and compulsion often substituted for higher prices and wages as Vichy, Free French, and British administrators sought to meet the high expectations of their metropolitan leaders and those of regional military commanders. Privation, discrimination, and abuse met with predictable reactions from the Africans subjected to them: protest, mutiny, desertion, smuggling, and migration.

After the war, veterans were among those making new demands, which African nationalists sought to harness.[133] British and French colonial administrations tried to manage specific demands as well as broader pressures for political, economic, and social change, though in different ways. The French admitted qualified Africans to citizenship and a reimagined metropolitan political process; the British made openings in local government and cooperatives.[134] The war brought less obvious changes as well. It accelerated urbanization, and young women and men in cities experienced new freedoms. African traders lost ground to the European firms favored in managed wartime trade, and European settlers took advantage of discriminatory wartime incentives to advance their interests at the expense of indigenous farmers and laborers.[135] Multinational corporations were more involved in Africa at the war's end, having played an important role in meeting resource demands. They benefited from wartime technological developments as well, and a congenial postwar policy climate.[136] African economies were, overall, more monetized and more strongly oriented toward commodity exports by the war's end, though peasant agriculture and pastoralism were still the basis for most Africans' livelihoods. Last, but far from least, state intervention in the economy was normalized in both the metropole and colonies, and new tools created to facilitate it.

There were also important development policy changes during the war. Britain's parliament passed a Colonial Development and Welfare Act in 1940. It was a product of events and ideas from the preceding few years, but was overtaken by the outbreak of war in 1939. The senior Colonial Office officials pushing this policy change argued, successfully, that attention to the welfare of colonial subjects was more necessary than ever to prevent the war effort from being undermined by unrest and low productivity.[137] While the war limited the Act's implementation, its principles informed the 1945 and 1950 Acts of the same name. These included the transfer of metropolitan resources to the colonies through a Colonial Development and Welfare Fund, and their use to promote social development, not just economic growth. Allocations were made on advice from a committee of experts, who also vetted the ten-year development plans each colony was required to submit under the Act. Disputes within the Colonial Economic Advisory Committee revealed the conflicting impulses behind the new policy, with progressives like the St Lucian economist W. Arthur Lewis arguing for rapid economic growth based on agricultural change and industry, substantial investment in a few designated colonies, and a central role for the colonial state in economic development. Colonial officials on the Committee wanted less disruptive change. They feared that deliberately uneven allocation of development funds would cause an uproar in the colonial service, while encouraging large-scale farming would provoke unrest among rural peasants. More fundamentally, they believed the state should leave plenty of room for private actors in planning and implementing development projects.[138]

In the late 1930s, political instability precluded a parallel process of policy reform for French colonial development. The Brazzaville Conference of 1944, attended by Free French officials and senior French administrators in Africa, was a point where principles for long-term policy could again be articulated. These included support for planning and a strong state role in the economy. The welfare of the indigenous population was identified as a policy priority.[139] As Frederick Cooper argued, the Second World War created an opening for change in the French empire, one that Africans seized.[140] For example, in 1946, striking workers in Dakar rallied for coverage under the metropolitan labor code with the slogan '*à travail égal, salaire égal*' (equal work, equal salary).[141] Reforms initiated in 1946 also included the abolition of forced labor, which inspired peasants. As Monica van Beusekom documented, this change meant the French managers of the *Office du Niger* had to take indigenous farmers' views into much greater account.[142]

French reformist thinking was reflected in the 1946 *Plan de modernisation et d'équipement* which guided postwar reconstruction. It included a ten-year plan with a wide remit for the French African territories, one modeled on the 1940 British Act. While this differed from the ad hoc and short-term policy processes of the preceding years, the *Plan's* greater novelty was the significant growth in publicly funded transfers, both grants and loans that were to finance change in every aspect of life in French-ruled Africa.[143] The *Fonds d'investissement pour le développement économique et social* (FIDES), established in 1938, would channel annual allocations from the metropolitan budget for a range of development initiatives in French colonies. The Fund was managed by the *Caisse centrale de* la France *d'outre-mer* (CCOM), which was also empowered to make concessional loans for modernizing projects.[144] Although these were the main channels for aid to the colonies, they were not the only ones. This complexity is an ongoing characteristic of the French development aid system.[145] The changes laid the foundation for a dramatic expansion of development aid transfers within the French empire.[146] However, Patrick Manning has calculated that the metropolitan government continued to receive more in taxes from its African colonies than it spent in them.[147]

Postwar Trade Policy: Entrenching Commodity Specialization

African development was also fundamentally affected by the substantial debts that Allied European governments owed to the USA by 1945. Dollars to repay those debts and to finance reconstruction were desperately scarce. This not only jeopardized Europe's postwar recovery, it caused US officials to fear another recession if their country's wartime levels of production and export fell. Trade was consequently key to postwar planning. Europe's colonies were expected to contribute in two ways. First, they would provide a market for metropolitan products, substituting for markets in Eastern Europe lost in the intensifying Cold War. This meant that the colonies' purchasing power had to be increased via economic development. The colonies' second role was to earn dollars for the metropole by exporting raw materials to the USA, or save dollars by producing substitutes for US goods the empire would otherwise have imported.[148] The main dollar-saving goods produced in Africa were sugar, tobacco, coffee, cotton, and copper, entrenching African colonies as the source of these commodities for France, Britain, and Portugal.[149] A new version of the Atlantic triangular trade was institutionalized: European countries traded manufactures to their African colonies and purchased their raw materials, and the colonies traded their raw materials to the USA. The dollars earned returned to Europe to sustain a flow of debt repayment to the USA and the import of essential US goods by Europe.

Britain used two mechanisms created before the war to structure this trade. One was dollar pooling, whereby colonies deposited the dollars their exports earned in a central account in London from which the British government could borrow. South Africa and several West African colonies were net contributors in the postwar years, but the main depositors were Asian.[150] Marketing boards were the other mechanism. They came to play so crucial a role in subsequent African development that a colonial official called their introduction a 'silent revolution'.[151]

Marketing boards had their genesis when the British government made cocoa purchasing in West Africa a state monopoly in 1939. This was in response to a strike by growers in the Gold Coast (Ghana), protesting against their treatment by European trading companies. When war broke out the monopoly also helped officials match exports with available shipping.[152] An expanded West African Produce Control Board was made responsible for marketing palm oil and oilseeds in 1941. In Uganda, a temporary state marketing structure for coffee and cotton were set up at the beginning of the war; they were made permanent after the war's end.[153] At that point, territorial marketing boards for specific cash crops also replaced the central one in West Africa. By the early 1950s, these boards had been set up throughout Britain's African colonies.[154] They ended up controlling between 66 and 100% of the colonies' main exports. After the war, they were ostensibly a mechanism for price stabilization and forced savings for colonial investment. However, in the eyes of officials their main purpose was solving Britain's postwar financial problems, since the boards paid growers less than the world price for their crops.[155]

After the war, France, like Britain, saw trade with its colonies as essential to its recovery. As in Britain, the institutions that structured France's postwar trade were established in the 1930s.[156] To reinvigorate trade with its African colonies France intensified its menu of quotas and duties, and added price-support funds to compensate for some of the trade deficit its colonies were forced to run. This *surprix* (surcharge) system kept the prices of

African exports artificially high in the French market to enable its colonies to purchase even more overpriced French manufactures. France also invested substantial public funds in colonial export production and infrastructure to increase imperial trade.[157] Like marketing boards, the *surprix* system was precedent setting, as elements of it were subsequently adopted by the European Economic Community.[158]

Uganda's Post-Second World War Development

The disarray of international markets in aftermath of the Second World War, which prompted fears of economic crisis like the one that had followed the peace of 1919, convinced colonial officials—and African nationalists—that continuing state management of the economy was a necessity. The corollary of the state's dominant role in economic development was the need for it to direct the voluntary organizations that grew in number and prominence after the war. These included faith-based self-help and charity organizations, trade unions and occupational associations, cooperatives, secular service organizations, recreational-interest clubs, ethnic and hometown associations, as well as international non-governmental organizations.[159]

Spending under the 1940 Colonial Development and Welfare Act had been limited by wartime shortages of cash and staff. After the war, the Colonial Office was anxious that the Act be seen as more than just an empty gesture, so its Development Fund was increased and officials were urged to disburse more of it.[160] Colonies were required to submit a multi-year development plan to access the Fund but, as had been the case since the start of British rule, most of the resources invested in development came from taxation—particularly via the marketing boards—rather than British aid or loans. Uganda made only modest requests for money under the Act, and used them to finance roads, hospitals, and a radio broadcast network.[161]

Official development intervention intensified in Uganda with the 1945 iteration of the Act, guided by a ten-year development plan. Nevertheless, the ideas on which the Worthington Plan was based remained largely those of the 1930s. Cash-crop exports were still the mainspring of development, and state-directed modernization would improve agricultural production. Substantial investment in education and health waited on the increased revenue that achievement of agricultural goals would bring.[162] Faith-based and other volunteer organizations continued to be an important supplement to the administration's social development efforts, and they were growing in number and membership. The National Council of Social Service was established in 1954 to coordinate the work of the relevant government ministries and the protectorate's main private welfare organizations.[163] As agriculture could not provide an adequate living for the growing rural population, an expansion of mining and industry was also called for, and the Uganda Development Corporation was established in 1952 to support this diversification.[164]

Light industry supplying consumer goods was encouraged, as such goods might otherwise be imported from non-British sources and require scarce dollars.[165]

Coffee production expanded significantly after the war, and it outstripped cotton as the protectorate's main export. The British government's financial needs were one reason for this, but not the main one; international coffee price increases in the early 1950s were more important.[166] Ugandan peasants responded to them by planting more coffee. Production of robusta rose fourfold between 1946 and independence in 1962, while production of arabica rose almost threefold.[167] Cooperatives were an additional factor. Ugandan farmers saw them as a way to increase their power vis-à-vis crop buyers, and to improve the price they received by ensuring better initial processing of their crops. After significant rural protest, cooperatives were legalized in 1946.[168] Grudging acceptance turned to official encouragement after 1952, when it was hoped cooperatives would channel rural political energies. Rapid growth in cooperative membership followed this policy change.[169] In the final decade of British rule, cooperatives became powerful institutions. Beyond their economic roles, they gave leadership experience to many who became politicians and civil servants at independence.[170]

Ugandan growers also used cooperatives to help pressure the Coffee Board to pass on a greater share of the high world price. Even though the full increase was not transferred to them, it did put more cash in the hands of many peasants. The resulting wealth was concentrated in Buganda, providing an average per capita income almost twice the national level. This exacerbated regional inequality and added to tension around the special status of the kingdom within the protectorate.[171] The coffee price boom was also associated with rapid growth in government spending, from £8 to £22 million between 1950 and 1955. The spending was concentrated in the south-central districts of the country, though, reinforcing the inequality of cash-crop wealth and continuing a pattern of uneven access to public services dating back to the early years of the protectorate.[172] Some of the administration's new income was invested in infrastructure—the hydroelectric dam at Jinja and expansion of the railway network, for example—as well as in schools, clinics, and roads.[173] This led to rapid increases in school enrollment and an estimated literacy rate of 40% in 1961, though with significant regional differences as well as much higher rates for boys.[174]

Government spending continued to grow even after the price boom ended in the mid-1950s, though at a slower rate. By the early 1960s, falling coffee prices and potential budget deficits, together with political tensions, were casting a shadow over the prospect of independence.[175] Added to concerns about the ability of coffee exports to finance Uganda's independent development were commitments made as part of the new International Coffee Agreement. France, Portugal, and Britain joined it on behalf of their African colonies, agreeing to export quotas to raise and stabilize the world price for coffee.[176]

The Transition from Colonial to Post-Colonial Development

Colonial development policy changes in the 1940s were not intended as preparation for decolonization, though some who advocated for them hoped for this. The reforms were intended to revitalize the British and French empires. Wartime promises of change were remembered by Africans, though, and became part of the demand for improvements made by many, including nationalist leaders. Although nationalists began calling for more change than colonial officials were willing to grant, the two groups found common ground in some elements of postwar development policy.

Economic planning was one such area. It emerged as a policy tool in the interwar recessions. Worldwide fascination with it grew in the 1930s, spurred by the Soviet Union's rapid industrialization and the Tennessee Valley Authority's modernization project.[177] Planning became an essential state function during the Second World War as governments sought to maximize production, minimize civilian consumption, and manage military supply. This required systematic economic measurement and forecasting, as well as the capacity to coordinate activity in multiple sectors. After the war, planning addressed two important problems: states' international status, and their citizens' expectation of employment and improved welfare.[178] The route to both was economic growth, which planning promised to deliver. Planning also encouraged unity, by drawing private firms and trade unions into state-led action to achieve economic growth.[179] In France, elements of the Catholic Church were also advocates of planning, and of specific types of development as a moral project as well as a progressive economic one.[180]

Early development economists, notably W. Arthur Lewis and Paul Rosenstein-Rodan, argued strongly for planning in colonial economies too. They saw planning as the best way to address the particular problems of poor countries. African nationalists embraced these ideas, as evidenced by their response to Lewis's 1949 study for the Fabian Society, *The Principles of Economic Planning*.[181] Planning for state-led economic growth appealed to them for some of the same reasons it attracted metropolitan politicians and bureaucrats. To begin with, it guaranteed them significant roles.[182] More importantly, they believed rapid and effective modernization required action on a scale that only states could achieve.[183]

The British Colonial Office, where Lewis was a consultant during and after the war, embraced planning though not some of Lewis's other ideas. Planning would allow development interventions 'on a scale quite unknown in the past', in the words of one secretary of state for the colonies.[184] The International Bank for Reconstruction and Development (IBRD), where Rosenstein-Rodan worked, also adopted planning as the basis for more effective postwar reconstruction lending. The IBRD initially showed little interest in colonial economies, but by the late 1950s, planning had become the prerequisite for development lending to newly independent countries.[185]

It was routine for colonial administrations in Africa to issue a territorial development plan after 1945, as did countries that had already gained independence.[186] However, as Lewis observed, these varied in content and format.[187] Toyin Falola's book on planning in colonial Nigeria remains the only in-depth study of this crucial element of African development history. As he documented, the plans that guided Nigeria's imperial development were aggregations of projects chosen from the wish lists submitted by provincial and district officials, with some commercial initiatives thrown in. It was not specified how these would combine to generate economic growth and improved welfare.[188] By the 1940s, Nigeria's colonial administration had come to see aid from Britain as a means of balancing its budget while still undertaking some public works. Planning was a means of accessing that aid, not a tool for directing economic change. The plethora of planning committees it created encouraged competition for funds between regions, rather than prioritization of projects within them. The capacity to implement projects, or to find the local resources required to match metropolitan grants were not considered when these committees drafted proposals. Development success was measured by the amount of funding obtained more than by change in the welfare of Nigerians.[189] These were unfortunate precedents for development planning after independence.

Official development assistance was another area of emerging consensus. In 1955, the World Council of Churches sought expert advice on their efforts to assist people in newly independent and soon-to-be independent countries. They received the wisdom of the day: development required resources that were far beyond the means of charities. Big transfers of money, expertise, and technology from governments were needed. The idea of an aid target for already industrialized countries emerged from the Council's discussion of this advice, and was forwarded to the offices of all representatives to the United Nations in 1958.[190] This target—one percent of the national income of industrialized countries to be transferred annually to developing countries in the form of aid and investment—was adopted by the UN General Assembly in 1960, and a version of it was included in the first Development Decade document.[191] Many African nationalists agreed that large-scale transfers were needed for development; they also supported the implicit assumption of moral obligation for them on part of countries that had already industrialized, especially those which had used African labor and resources to do so. Some, however, cautioned that relying on external aid would foster dependence on its donors.[192]

France was the only donor that met the UN aid target.[193] Its aid institutions were those established after the war, such as FIDES, as were the objects of its aid. The West African Federation received the largest share of FIDES funds, and almost two-thirds of that was spent on transport infrastructure in the first five years of the 1946 *Plan*, with production and social development receiving equal shares of the remainder.[194] This spending disproportionately benefited urban areas, though. Adjustments were made in 1952 for the second half of the *Plan*. Production was emphasized, a response to both French opponents of aid and a deteriorating international economic climate. This shifted development spending toward mining, export processing, and economic infrastructure. Unfortunately, the neglect of rural areas and agriculture continued. French contributions to the *Plan* were also cut, with private investors and West African taxpayers expected to fill the gap. As falling commodity prices made public funds even scarcer in West Africa than in the metropole and French investors did not follow the lead of public money, much of the Federation's postwar development spending was financed with CCOM loans.[195]

The West African colonies faced a growing financial crisis in the 1950s. Many, especially inland colonies like French Sudan were running substantial deficits. The rapidly rising cost of French personnel and imported goods under the *surprix* system consumed the lion's share of public funds. It was a financial strain simply to operate and maintain the infrastructure built with FIDES money and to repay the CCOM loans.[196] Another dynamic that the 1952 reforms did not address was the unevenness of development spending within the colonies. While the French colonial administration was centralized, in practice it gave individual administrators, both governors and district administrators, substantial power. This resulted in considerable variation in development spending between districts.[197]

If the primary goal of postwar French aid was maximizing dollar-saving imperial trade, the advent of decolonization brought other issues to the fore. The spread of communism and of US influence were concerns that predated the war, but intensified after it.[198] So did the desire to demonstrate France was a world power, and to display the value of its culture. A sphere of influence in Africa was essential to achieve these goals, and aid an important tool for maintaining it.[199] Francophone African nationalists were also united in stressing the need for ongoing aid from France.[200] Unsurprisingly, the volume of French aid rose after the late 1950s. It took the form of technical assistance—especially teachers, support for investment, and coverage for the budget deficits of former colonies. Cooperation became the catchword for French aid, and its colonial-era channels were renamed, but French aid institutions remained largely intact; so did their focus on Africa.[201]

Increases in aid required initiatives in which it could be deployed. Grand projects intended to reengineer entire social and physical environments excited both late colonial development planners and their nationalist successors.[202] They sent concrete messages to a range of audiences about the state's power. Ideally, these projects flowed from a coherent national plan; in practice, a collection of projects was often the core around which development plans were crafted.[203] Practically, big projects were seen as the best way to allocate scarce funds in vast regions with immense needs; they also lowered administrative costs.[204] Theoretically, it was suggested that certain industries or initiatives stood out for their dynamism, and concentrating resources on them would create a *pôle de croissance* (growth pole) that would spark broader change.[205]

In Africa's dry regions, many of these grand projects involved water.[206] The *Office du Niger* remained an exemplar and, as French involvement in postwar African development intensified, it remained a centerpiece project despite its critics. Between 1945 and 1959, it received 30% of the aid given to French Sudan.[207] At independence, Mali's government adopted the *Office du Niger* with relatively few changes, despite its desire to establish a more autonomous development policy. Ownership of the *Office* was formally transferred from France in 1962, two years after independence. The Malian government reorganized and reduced the *Office's* staff, and curtailed a few of its quasi-sovereign powers, but they also increased the scale of its irrigation works and retained its comprehensive mandate and top-down approach.[208] Rice rather than cotton had already become the project's focus under French administration. After independence, the *Office's* goal was reformulated: it would ensure national food security, particularly the urban food supply. Although less than one percent of Mali's population farmed under the project, it received one-third of the government's rural development budget in the years after independence.[209]

In sum, the duration of European imperial rule in Africa varied from centuries in some coastal entrepôts to decades in remote inland areas. The era of effective rule throughout the continent was between sixty and seventy years. This was short in comparison to European rule in the Americas and Asia, but sharp nonetheless. In calling it a trespass, Frederick Cooper characterized it well.[210] Shoe-string administrations, desperation triggered by global war and recession, and the depth of European racism vis-à-vis Africans all played a role in this. Despite the rhetoric of imperialists, there were few resources and little time for transformation. The institutions they bequeathed were more effective at extraction and coercion than the promotion of well-being. Nevertheless, development became one of the catchwords of the twentieth century in Africa. It was far more than a neo-colonial ploy. It was a core demand of peoples seeking independence from empire and from an international system conditioned by empire; it was indeed a right.[211] It was both a reason for independence (genuine development could only occur with an indigenized state and economy) and a reason for continued sacrifices afterward. A slogan of the Tanganyika African National Union, *uhuru na kazi* (freedom and work), captured this perfectly.[212]

The Early Cold War and US Aid to Africa

The emerging discipline of development economics prescribed aid when 'there is reasonable assurance that it will be effectively used' to support investment for self-sustaining economic growth.[213] However, the distribution of aid was governed by multiple and sometimes conflicting rationales in the 1950s, and economic theory was often an after-the-fact justification. One rationale for aid was the purchase of political influence and economic access, making it a tool for the exercise of neo-imperial power. This element of aid was heightened when an intensification of the Cold War coincided with a growing interest in development in the late 1950s.[214] A modest but well-publicized Soviet diplomatic and aid offensive to win hearts and minds in the developing world and the end of the Korean War commodity boom, which renewed doubts about trade-financed development, spurred a new interest in development aid among US officials. As one explained, the main 'appeal of Soviet communism to underdeveloped areas is to hold out promises of better food and rising living standards for the common masses'. Aid-funded development programs, 'which visibly produce higher living standards' would 'build confidence in the possibilities [of life] under free institutions'.[215]

Events in the Middle East—such as Egypt's 1952 change of government—led US officials to reevaluate their country's position in this crucial region.[216] Military bases were central to US security in the 1950s, and Ethiopia's province of Eritrea contained a prize: the Italian-built Qaqnaw (or Kagnew) base.[217] Aid was understood by the Americans to be the price for its use. The Department of Defense would have given the emperor rent for it in 'solid gold Cadillacs' if that was what he wanted.[218] For the emperor, aid was an important resource for maintaining his and Ethiopia's position.

Haile Selassie's wartime diplomatic overtures to the United States had already yielded a lend-lease agreement in 1943 and a US technical assistance mission in 1944. Ethiopia joined the Point Four Program late, in 1952.[219] Ethiopia's Point Four agreement emphasized agriculture, but included education, health, and administrative capacity building.[220] These projects, like the entire program, were the product of conflicting development ideas. Some were ideas that had circulated among Ethiopian intellectuals for decades already. Education and technology were central to their hopes for an indigenous modernity, and the emperor supported education as well.[221] This was a point of overlap with Point Four. However, Haile Selassie also had a longstanding preoccupation with security. As journalist James Morris observed, to provide security for the throne 'schools have actually been closed down to save money for guns'.[222]

The ideas put forward by the Emperor and his ministers, refracted through the 1944 US mission's report, were not adopted wholesale for the Point Four Program. The USA was an interventionist donor, insisting that it identify aid priorities and oversee use of its aid. It also required institutional changes to support its aid projects, such as reform of the tax system, and of trade and investment regulations.[223] However, US officials did not have as unified an approach to development as this suggests. Many in the Technical Cooperation Administration that ran the Point Four Program favored a small-scale, bottom-up approach to development.[224] Together with key officials at the new State Department Bureau of Near Eastern, South Asian, and African Affairs, they saw land reform as a foundation for agricultural modernization and the rural republicanism they believed was responsible for US democracy.[225] Others in these departments thought rural productivity more important. The Point Four Program's first administrator, for example, dreamed that Ethiopia would become a breadbasket for the Middle East through mechanized farming.[226] Productivity's supporters preferred large-scale development initiatives, since they doubted the productive capacity of smallholders and they feared the destabilizing effects of substantial land reform. In the end, they hoped successful elite-driven modernization in agriculture would be crowned by democracy, but did not think political change should be a short-term goal of US aid.[227] As this suggests, development was a negotiation between the interests of diverse internal and external actors. Neither in Ethiopia nor in the USA was there a single development 'project'.

THE OTHER TWENTIETH-CENTURY DEVELOPMENT 'PROJECT'

When Asian and African countries started to become independent after the Second World War their leaders and those of already independent Latin American countries shared a sense of urgency about the problems they faced.[228] During the United Nations' first session in 1946, Lebanon proposed that the UN provide expert advice on development to member countries. In presenting this resolution Lebanon's ambassador, Charles Habib Malik, noted the grossly unequal development of the UN's member countries and classified them into four groups: 'developed, non-self governing, trusteeship territories, and sovereign but underdeveloped countries'.[229] This preceded President Truman's Point Four speech, with its supposed invention of development, by more than two years. Malik, like Truman after him, assumed that development could be used to classify countries, but the vision of change associated with Malik's speech was different. As Thandika Mkandawire argues, there were two strands to the postwar development 'project'. The first, which has received relatively little scholarly attention, was an emancipatory one that involved 'catching up' by underdeveloped and not yet independent countries.[230] It was articulated in the United Nations, and in regional gatherings such as the 1955 Bandung conference.

In 1946, the Americans and victorious European powers were preoccupied with employment, international economic stability, and reconstruction. The new UN, for them, was a forum for these issues. UN member countries that identified with what Alfred Sauvy called the *Tiers Monde* (Third World) saw things differently. They repeatedly and forcefully directed attention to their concerns: anti-imperialism and development.[231] They pressured the Secretary General to appoint experts to study the latter problem. Trygve Lie appointed a five-person expert panel with, remarkably for the times, only one member from an industrialized country.[232] Their 1951 report, *Measures for the*

Economic Development of Underdeveloped Countries, became the UN's template for development. W. Arthur Lewis was its lead author.[233]

The 1951 report's model remained the dominant one at the start of the first UN Development Decade in 1961, accepted by most economists and national leaders. Poverty was a trap, they believed, and countries could escape it into self-sustaining economic growth with a 'big push'. Planning and a massive increase in investment were the essential tools for this.[234] Since capital was scarce in poor countries, investment by government would be crucial. External aid could amplify the 'push' and initiate it more quickly. Development was understood to be economic growth; other desired changes would follow automatically from it. Growth required structural transformation of the economy, especially industrialization, though not all development enthusiasts put the same degree of emphasis on industry.[235] The Third Worldist and Trumanesque strands of development intersected in African countries when an emerging cadre of international development workers, both official and volunteer, facilitated changes called for in the 1951 model.[236]

Additional elements of the Third Worldist development 'project' were articulated at the 1955 Bandung conference, attended by delegates from 29 Asian and African countries.[237] These included non-interference, peaceful co-existence, and mutual benefit. They were drawn from the five principles (*panchsheel*) in a 1954 treaty between India and China.[238] These principles situated development in a different kind of international relations than those underlying the Trumanesque strand. Over the next two decades, plans for a New International Economic Order built on and reinforced this difference.

What were the African contributions to Third Worldist development? Individually, Algeria's government provided leadership in organizations like the Non-Aligned Movement and the Group of 77.[239] Collectively, African governments contributed through the weight of their vote in the General Assembly. The UN was a critical arena in which newly independent African countries exercised their sovereignty, and the UN Africa Group was a large and effective voting bloc on issues of continental consensus: decolonization and anti-racism, development, and strengthening the role of the UN.[240]

African countries also brought development ideas to the UN system. An early example was the interdependence of economic and social development, which was first enshrined in the 1958 mandate of the UN Economic Commission for Africa (UNECA).[241] Later that year, five of the African countries that had fought for the UNECA and its distinctive mandate proposed the linkage be incorporated into the UN's model of development. They called for the addition of social development measures that would increase productivity, 'minimize social disorganization resulting from economic and technological change as well as from rapid urbanization', and 'promote equitable distribution of national incomes'.[242] Florence Wilson Addison, a member of the Ghanaian delegation who spoke to this proposal, identified education as an essential part of these social development measures. This was a consistent priority for African countries, and their growing vote in the UN drew institutional resources for education and training to the continent.[243] The proposal also embodied other recurring themes in African development: the beliefs that technology and policies for economic growth could be adopted without jeopardizing social stability, and that inequality threatened social harmony. While none of these ideas was uniquely African, this combination was an African emphasis within the Third Worldist 'project'.

The UNECA was also a pioneer in the area of women and development. Starting in the early 1960s, some of the Commission's workshops, conferences, and publications identified women's roles in and concerns about national development. This effort paralleled those of African women's organizations that held national, regional, and continental meetings in the early 1960s. They articulated a desire for involvement in national development that grew out of the active role women played in the independence struggles of many African countries. At the 1975 UN conference on women in Mexico City, these initiatives were identified as a model for other regions. Margaret Snyder and Mary Tadesse argue that historians of the women's movement have ignored these African initiatives.[244] Newly independent African governments, though, showed they were in no hurry to embrace these pioneering ideas.

Notes

1. Robert Chambers, *Ideas for Development* (London: Earthscan, 2005), 184–86; and Michael Cowen and Robert Shenton, "The Invention of Development," in *Power of Development*, ed. Jonathan Crush (London: Routledge, 1995), 28.
2. Jan Nederveen Pieterse, *Development Theory: Deconstructions/Reconstructions* (Los Angeles: Sage Publications, 2001), 3.
3. K.K.S. Dadzie, "Economic Development," *Scientific American*, 243, no. 3 (1980): 64. Amartya Sen and others subsequently built on this kind of agency-focused definition of development. See: Amartya Sen, *Development as Freedom* (New York: Anchor Books, 1999); Martha Nussbaum, *Creating Capabilities: The Human Development Approach* (Cambridge, MA: Harvard University Press, 2011); and Khadija Haq and Richard Ponzio, eds., *Pioneering the Human Development Revolution: An Intellectual Biography of Mahbub ul Haq* (Oxford: Oxford University Press, 2008).
4. Denis Goulet, *Development Ethics: A Guide to Theory and Practice* (New York: Apex Press & Zed Books, 1995), 38–40; and Chambers, *Ideas for Development*, 184–86.
5. For example, Gilbert Rist, *The History of Development: From Western Origins to Global Faith*, trans. Patrick Camiller, 2nd ed. (London: Zed Books, 2006); and Philip McMichael, *Development and Social Change: A Global Perspective*, 3rd ed. (Thousand Oaks, CA: Pine Forge Press, 2004).
6. For example, Jahangir Amuzegar, "Point Four: Performance and Prospect," *Political Science Quarterly* 73, no. 4 (1958): 530–46; Tarun Bose, "The

Point Four Programme: A Critical Study," *International Studies* 7, no. 1 (1965): 66–97; and Stephen Macekura, "The Point Four Program and U.S. International Development Policy," *Political Science Quarterly* 128, no. 1 (2013): 127–60.
7. Jonathan Bingham, *Shirt-Sleeve Diplomacy: Point 4 in Action* (1953; reprint, Freeport, NY: Books for Libraries Press, 1970), 245, 255–56. Egypt was one of four African countries that received Point Four aid directly; the others were Ethiopia, Liberia, and Libya.
8. Robert Wood, *From Marshall Plan to Debt Crisis: Foreign Aid and Development Choices in the World Economy* (Berkeley and Los Angeles: University of California Press, 1986), 43, 55–56.
9. These included studies like David Apter's "The Role of Traditionalism in the Political Modernization of Ghana and Uganda," *World Politics* 13, no. 1 (1960): 45–46; and *The Political Kingdom in Buganda: A Study of Bureaucratic Nationalism* (Princeton: Princeton University Press, 1967). They also included analyses of prominent individuals like Emmanuel Akyeampong's "Christianity, Modernity and the Weight of Tradition in the Life of *Asantehene* Agyeman Prempeh I, c. 1888–1931," *Africa* 69, no. 2 (1999): 279–311.
10. For example, Agneta Pallinder-Law, "Aborted Modernization in West Africa? The Case of Abeokuta," *Journal of African History* 15, no. 1 (1974): 65–82.
11. See, for example, J.D.Y. Peel, "*Olaju*: A Yoruba Concept of Development," *Journal of Development Studies* 14, no. 2 (1978): 139–65; and Philip Zachernuk, "The Lagos Intelligentsia and the Idea of Progress, ca. 1860–1960," in *Yoruba Historiography*, ed. Toyin Falola (Madison: University of Wisconsin, 1991), 147–65.
12. Bahru Zewde, *Pioneers of Change in Ethiopia: The Reformist Intellectuals of the Early Twentieth Century* (Oxford: James Currey et al., 2002).
13. Zewde, *Pioneers of Change*, 130–35.
14. Bahru Zewde, *A History of Modern Ethiopia, 1855–1974* (London: James Currey et al., 1991); and Richard Pankhurst, *The Ethiopians: A History* (Oxford: Blackwell, 2001).
15. For a general discussion of this phenomenon see Philip Curtin, *The World and the West: The European Challenge and the Overseas Response in the Age of Empire* (Cambridge: Cambridge University Press, 2000), 128–55.
16. See, for example, Christopher Clapham, "Ethiopian Development: The Politics of Emulation," *Commonwealth & Comparative Politics* 44, no. 1 (2006): 137–50; and Bettina Dennerlein, "South-South Linkages and Social Change: Moroccan Perspectives on Army Reform in the Muslim Mediterranean in the Nineteenth Century," *Comparative Studies in South Asia, Africa and the Middle East* 27, no. 1 (2007): 52–61.
17. Dyala Hamzah, "Nineteenth-Century Egypt as Dynastic Locus of Universality: The History of Muhammad 'Ali by Khalil Ibn Ahmad Al-Rajabi," *Comparative Studies of South Asia, Africa and the Middle East* 27, no. 1 (2007): 62–82. There has been much recent research on Islamic reform movements in the continent; see, for example, Sean Hanretta, *Islam and Social Change in French West Africa: History of an Emanicpatory Community* (Cambridge: Cambridge University Press, 2009).

18. P.J. Vatikiotis, *The History of Modern Egypt: From Muhammad Ali to Mubarak*, 4th ed. (Baltimore: Johns Hopkins University Press, 1991), 49–69; and Anouar Abdel-Malek, "The Renaissance of Egypt, 1805–81," in *General History of Africa*, Vol. VI *Africa in the Nineteenth Century Until the 1880s*, ed. J.F. Ade Ajayi (Paris: UNESCO et al., 1989), 325–55.
19. Laura Panza and Jeffrey Williamson, "Did Muhammad Ali Foster Industrialization in Early Nineteenth-Century Egypt?," *Economic History Review* 68, no. 1 (2015): 81–83.
20. G.N. Sanderson, "The European Partition of Africa: Origins and Dynamics," *Cambridge History of Africa*, Vol. 6 *c. 1870–c. 1905*, ed. R. Oliver and G.N. Sanderson (Cambridge: Cambridge University Press, 1985), 107.
21. Hassan Ibrahim and Bethwell Ogot, "The Sudan in the Nineteenth Century," in *General History of Africa*, Vol. VI *Africa in the Nineteenth Century*, 358.
22. For an overview see P.J. Vatikiotis, *History of Modern Egypt*, 70–89.
23. This late nineteenth century process is described in greater detail in Ruth Rempel, "Trade and Transformation: Participation in the Ivory Trade in Late 19th-Century East and Central Africa," *Canadian Journal of Development Studies* 19, no. 3 (1998): 537–42.
24. Melvin Page, "The Manyema Hordes of Tippu Tip: A Case Study in Social Stratification and the Slave Trade in Eastern Africa," *International Journal of African Historical Studies* 7, no. 1 (1974): 76; Melvin Page, "Tippu Tip and the Arab 'Defense' of the East African Slave Trade," *Etudes d'Histoire africaine* (Lubumbashi) 4 (1974): 105–17; and V.Y. Mudimbe, *The Invention of Africa: Gnosis, Philosophy, and the Order of Knowledge* (Bloomington: Indiana University Press et al., 1988), 44–64. See also Jonathon Glassman, "Slower Than a Massacre: The Multiple Sources of Racial Thought in Colonial Africa," *American Historical Review* 109, no. 3 (2004): 720–54.
25. Hamed bin Muhammed el Murjebi, *Maisha ya Hamed bin Muhammed el Murjebi yaani Tippu Tip*, trans. and ed. W.H. Whitely (Nairobi, East African Literature Bureau, 1974), Sect. 87.
26. François Renault, "The Structures of the Slave Trade in Central Africa in the 19th Century," in *The Economics of the Indian Ocean Slave Trade*, ed. W.G. Clarence-Smith (London: Frank Cass, 1989), 153.
27. Frederick Cooper, "Modernity," in *Colonialism in Question: Theory, Knowledge, History* (Berkeley and Los Angeles: University of California Press, 2005), 146–47. Sara Berry made a similar argument in *No Condition is Permanent: The Social Dynamics of Agrarian Change in Sub-Saharan Africa* (University of Wisconsin Press, 1993), 13–35.
28. For an overview see Michael Adas, "'High' Imperialism and the 'New' History," in *Islamic and European Expansion: The Forging of a Global Order*, ed. Michael Adas (Philadelphia: Temple University Press), 311–44.
29. Gareth Austin, "The Economics of Colonialism in Africa," in *The Oxford Handbook of Africa and Economics*, Vol. 1 *Context and Concepts*, ed. Célestin Monga and Justin Yifu Lin (Oxford: Oxford University Press, 2015), 525.
30. Colonial is used here as a synonym for imperial. The formal relation of European imperial powers to African polities varied, however. At the height of empire in the early 1920s this included a distinction between colonies and protectorates, and the situation was further complicated by the

Condominium Agreement through which Britain jointly ruled Egypt's Sudanese empire and the creation of Trust Territories after the First World War.
31. See Cyrus Veeser, "A Forgotten Instrument of Global Capitalism? International Concessions, 1870–1930," *International History Review* 35, no. 5 (2013): 1136–55.
32. On the creation of these colonies and of peasantization in them see Moses Ochonu, "African Colonial Economies: State Control, Peasant Maneuvers, and Unintended Outcomes," *History Compass* 11, no. 1 (2013): 1–13.
33. S. Herbert Frankel, *Capital Investment in Africa: Its Course and Effects* (London: Oxford University Press, 1938), 334, 349; William Hailey, *An African Survey: A Study of Problems Arising in Africa South of the Sahara* (London: Oxford University Press, 1938), 108; Edgar Sydenstricker, "Population Statistics of Foreign Countries," *Journal of the American Statistical Association* 20, no. 149 (1925): 87; and Melvin McKnight, "Water and the Course of Empire in North Africa," *Quarterly Journal of Economics* 43, no. 1 (1928): 44–93. The population figures referred to are for 1923–1925.
34. For example, Henry Stanley, "The Story of the Development of Africa," *Century Illustrated Magazine* N.S. 29, no. 4 (1896): 500–9; and Frederick Cooper and Ann Stoler, "Introduction: Tensions of Empire: Colonial Control and Visions of Rule," *American Ethnologist* 16, no. 4 (1989): 617. For a comparative view see Kenneth Pomeranz, "Empire and 'Civilizing' Missions, Past & Present," *Daedalus* 134, no. 2 (2005): 34–45.
35. Frederick Cooper, "Conflict and Connection: Rethinking Colonial African History," *American Historical Review* 99, no. 5 (1994): 1529.
36. Alice Conklin, *A Mission to Civilize: The Republican Idea of Empire in France and West Africa, 1895–1930* (Stanford: Stanford University Press, 1997), 8, 11, 13, 18.
37. For example, Virginia Thompson and Richard Adloff, *French West Africa* (Stanford: Stanford University Press, 1957), 269.
38. Conklin, *Mission to Civilize*, 39, 43–45.
39. Emily Lynn Osborn, "'Circle of Iron': African Colonial Employees and the Interpretation of Colonial Rule in French West Africa," *Journal of African History* 44, no. 1 (2003): 29–50.
40. See P.L. McDermott, *British East Africa, or I.B.E.A.: A History of the Formation and Work of the Imperial British East Africa Company* (London: Chapman and Hall, 1895); and John Galbraith, *Mackinnon and East Africa, 1878–1895: A Study in the 'New' Imperialism* (Cambridge: Cambridge University Press, 1972).
41. Christopher Wrigley, *Crops and Wealth in Uganda* (Kampala: East African Institute of Social Research, 1959), 13; and Richard Reid, *Political Power in Pre-Colonial Buganda: Economy, Society and Warfare in the Nineteenth Century* (Oxford: James Currey et al., 2002), 136–41.
42. Wrigley, *Crops and Wealth in Uganda*, 71; and Christopher Youé, "Peasants, Planters and Cotton Capitalists: The 'Dual Economy' in Colonial Uganda," *Canadian Journal of African Studies* 12, no. 2 (1978): 182.
43. Michael Havinden and David Meredith, *Colonialism and Development: Britain and Its Tropical Colonies, 1850–1960* (London: Routledge, 1993), 91.

44. Crawford Young, Neal Sherman and Tim Rose, *Cooperatives and Development: Agricultural Politics in Ghana and Uganda* (Madison: University of Wisconsin Press, 1981), 34.
45. Thomas Taylor, "The Establishment of a European Plantation Sector Within the Emerging Colonial Economy of Uganda, 1902–1919," *International Journal of African Historical Studies* 19, no. 1 (1986): 51; and Holly Hanson, *Landed Obligation: The Practice of Power in Buganda* (Portsmouth, NH: Heinemann, 2003), 169–70.
46. Grace Carswell, "Food Crops as Cash Crops: The Case of Colonial Kigezi, Uganda," *Journal of Agrarian Change* 3, no. 4 (2003): 521–51.
47. Thomas Taylor, "The Struggle for Economic Control of Uganda, 1919–1922: Formulation of an Economic Policy," *International Journal of African Historical Studies* 11, no. 1 (1978): 7.
48. William Hailey, "Some Problems Dealt with in the 'African Survey'," *International Affairs* 18, no. 2 (1939): 195–97; and William Hailey, "A Turning Point in Colonial Rule," *International Affairs* 28, no. 2 (1952): 178.
49. Taylor, "*Establishment of a European Plantation Sector*," 35, 46–47; and Stephen Bunker, *Peasants Against the State: The Politics of Market Control in Bugisu, Uganda, 1900–1983* (Urbana: University of Illinois Press, 1987), 20.
50. Wrigley, *Crops and Wealth in Uganda*, 37–39, 44; Youé, "Peasants, Planters and Cotton Capitalists," 174–75; and Peter Robertshaw et al., "Famine, Climate and Crisis in Western Uganda," *Developments in Paleoenvironmental Research* 6 (2004): 543–44.
51. For a survey see Oliver Williamson, "The New Institutional Economics: Taking Stock, Looking Ahead," *Journal of Economic Literature* 38, no. 3 (2000): 595–613.
52. Ewout Frankema, "The Origins of Formal Education in Sub-Saharan Africa: Was British Rule More Benign?" *European Review of Economic History* 16, no. 4 (2012): 335–55. One exception noted by Frankema was the restricted access of Christian missions to areas where administrators feared they would cause costly destabilization of existing Islamic institutions.
53. Frankema, "Origins of Formal Education," 340–43.
54. Frankema, "Origins of Formal Education," 338, 347; Elise Huillery, "History Matters: The Long-Term Impact of Colonial Public Investments in French West Africa," *American Economic Journal: Applied Economics* 1, no. 2 (2009): 185–88; and Ana Isabel Madeira, "Portuguese, French and British Discourses on Colonial Education: Church–State Relations, School Expansion and Missionary Competition in Africa, 1890–1930," *Paedagogica Historica* 41, nos. 1–2 (2005): 31–60.
55. Ian Brown, "Introduction," in *The Economies of Africa and Asia in the Inter-War Depression*, ed. Ian Brown (London: Routledge, 1989), 2–3.
56. Catherine Coquery-Vidrovitch, "Economic Changes in Africa in the World Context," in *General History of Africa*, Vol. VIII *Africa Since 1935*, ed. Ali A. Mazrui (Paris: UNESCO et al., 1993), 286.
57. Conklin, *Mission to Civilize*, 147.
58. Ibid., 66–67, 142–47.
59. Conklin, *Mission to Civilize*, 174–75, 187–95. See also Cooper, "Conflict and Connection," 1531.

60. C.M. Andrew and A.S. Kanya-Forstner, "France, Africa, and the First World War," *Journal of African History* 19, no. 1 (1978): 17–20.
61. Conklin, *Mission to Civilize*, 41.
62. Martin Thomas, "Albert Sarraut, French Colonial Development, and the Communist Threat, 1919–1930," *Journal of Modern History* 77, no. 4 (2005): 923.
63. See Alice Conklin, "Faire Naître *v.* Faire du Noir: Race Regeneration in France and French West Africa, 1895–1940," in *Promoting the Colonial Idea: Propaganda and Visions of Empire in France*, ed. Tony Chafer and Amanda Sackur (Houndmills: Palgrave Macmillan, 2001), 143–55.
64. Frederick Cooper, "Modernizing Bureaucrats, Backward Africans, and the Development Concept," in *International Development and the Social Sciences: Essays on the History and Politics of Knowledge*, ed. Frederick Cooper and Randall Packard (Berkeley and Los Angeles: University of California Press), 65.
65. Richard Roberts, *Two Worlds of Cotton: Colonialism and the Regional Economy in the French Soudan, 1800–1946* (Stanford: Stanford University Press, 1996), 76, 80–98.
66. Conklin, *Mission to Civilize*, 224; and François Molle and Philippe Floch, "The 'Desert Bloom' Syndrome: Irrigation Development, Politics, and Ideology in the Northeast of Thailand" (Chiang Mai, Thailand: Institut de Recherche pour le Développement and the International Water Management Institute, 2008), 4.
67. Jean Filipovich, "Destined to Fail: Forced Settlement at the *Office Du Niger*, 1926–45," *Journal of African History* 42, no. 2 (2001): 239; and Myron Echenberg and Jean Filipovich, "African Military Labour and the Building of the *Office Du Niger* Installations, 1925–50," *Journal of African History* 27, no. 3 (1986): 537.
68. Thompson and Adloff, *French West Africa*, 269; and Monica van Beusekom, "*Colonisation Indigène*: French Rural Development Ideology at the *Office Du Niger*, 1920–1940," *International Journal of African Historical Studies* 30, no. 2 (1997): 299–323.
69. Conklin, *Mission to Civilize*, 224–25; Monica van Beusekom, "Disjunctures in Theory and Practice: Making Sense of Change in Agricultural Development at the *Office du Niger*, 1920–60," *Journal of African History* 41, no. 1 (2000): 81; and Monica van Beusekom, *Negotiating Development: African Farmers and Colonial Experts at the Office Du Niger, 1920–1960* (Portsmouth: Heinemann et al., 2002), 2–3, 7.
70. Jon Moris, "Irrigation as a Privileged Solution in African Development," *Development Policy Review* 5, no. 2 (1987): 108; van Beusekom, "*Colonisation Indigène*," 317; and van Beusekom, "Disjunctures in Theory and Practice," 81–82.
71. van Beusekom, "*Colonisation Indigène*," 302–3. As Maurits Ertsen observed, colonial irrigation schemes in Africa tried to control and change farmers to a much greater extent than comparable projects in Asian colonies; see "Controlling the Farmer: Colonial and Post-Colonial Irrigation Interventions in Africa," *Journal for Transdisciplinary Research in Southern Africa* 4, no. 1 (2008): 212.

72. John de Wilde, *Experiences with Agricultural Development in Tropical Africa*, Vol. 2: *The Case Studies* (Baltimore: Johns Hopkins University Press for the IBRD, 1967), 287–88; and Filipovich, "Destined to Fail," 240.
73. Conklin, *Mission to Civilize*, 250.
74. van Beusekom, "*Colonisation Indigène*," 318–19; and van Beusekom, "Disjunctures in Theory," 83–84.
75. Virginia Thompson and Richard Adloff, "French Economic Policy in Tropical Africa," in *Colonialism in Africa 1870–1960*, ed. Peter Duignan and L.H. Gann (Cambridge: Cambridge University Press, 1975), 144.
76. Coquery-Vidrovitch, "Economic Changes in Africa," 286.
77. Dependence on trade taxes grew after a spate of administrative reforms in 1904. The repayment of loans for West African infrastructure and development projects was an additional draw on tax revenue. See Conklin, *Mission to Civilize*, 47; and Thompson and Adloff, *French West Africa*, 269.
78. Susan Martin, "The Long Depression: West African Export Producers and the World Economy, 1914–45," in *Economies of Africa and Asia in the Inter-War Depression*, 81.
79. Thompson and Adloff, "French Economic Policy in Tropical Africa," 135.
80. Stephen Constantine, *The Making of British Colonial Development Policy, 1914–1940* (London: Frank Cass, 1984), 228–31.
81. Martin, "The Long Depression," 85.
82. Michael Crowder, "Africa Under British and Belgian Domination, 1935–45," in *General History of Africa*, Vol. VIII Africa *since 1935*, 89.
83. See, for example, Moses Ochonu, *Colonial Meltdown: Northern Nigeria in the Great Depression* (Athens, OH: Ohio University Press, 2009); together with David Anderson and David Throup, "The Agrarian Economy of Central Province, Kenya, 1918 to 1939," and Wolfgang Döpcke, "'Magomo's Maize': State and Peasants During the Depression in Colonial Zimbabwe," both in *Economies of Africa and Asia in the Inter-War Depression*, 8–28, 29–58, respectively.
84. Taylor, "Establishment of a European Plantation Sector," 37; and Havinden and Meredith, *Colonialism and Development*, 148–49.
85. Youé, "Peasants, Planters and Cotton Capitalists," 169, 177.
86. Youé, "Peasants, Planters and Cotton Capitalists," 182; and Benoit Daviron, "Mobilizing Labour in African Agriculture: The Role of the International Colonial Institute in the Elaboration of a Standard of Colonial Administration, 1895–1930," *Journal of Global History* 5, no. 3 (2010): 492.
87. Asiimwe Godfrey, *The Impact of Post-Colonial Policy Shifts in Coffee Marketing at the Local Level in Uganda: A Case Study of Mukono District, 1962–1998* (Maastricht: Shaker Publishing, 2002), 31–32.
88. Wrigley, *Crops and Wealth in Uganda*, 60–61; B.D. Bowles, "Economic Anti-Colonialism and British Reaction in Uganda, 1936–1955," *Canadian Journal of African Studies* 9, no. 1 (1975): 53; Young et al., *Cooperatives and Development*, 38; and Hanson, *Landed Obligation*, 237–38.
89. Christopher Wrigley, "Buganda: An Outline Economic History," *Economic History Review* N.S. 10, no. 1 (1957): 57.
90. Bunker, *Peasants against the State*, 46.
91. Carswell, "Food Crops as Cash Crops," 534.

92. Nakanyiki Musisi, "The Environment, Gender, and the Development of Unequal Relations in Buganda: A Historical Perspective," *Canadian Woman Studies* 13, no. 3 (1993): 57–58.
93. For example Wrigley, *Crops and Wealth in Uganda*, 58.
94. Young et al., *Cooperatives and Development*, 35.
95. Taylor, "The Struggle for Economic Control of Uganda," 7–8; and Ewout Frankema, "Raising Revenue in the British Empire, 1870–1940: How 'Extractive' Were Colonial Taxes?" *Journal of Global History* 5, no. 3 (2010): 453–54.
96. Ewout Frankema, "Colonial Taxation and Government Spending in British Africa, 1880–1940: Maximizing Revenue or Minimizing Effort?" *Explorations in Economic History* 48, no. 1 (2011): 139, 147–48.
97. Young et al., *Cooperatives and Development*, 39; Bunker, *Peasants Against the State*, 42; and Godfrey, *Impact of Post-Colonial Policy*, 38. On market stabilization see Gerald Meier, "The Formative Period," in *Pioneers in Development*, ed. Gerald Meier and Dudley Seers (New York: Oxford University Press for the World Bank, 1984), 6.
98. Rachel Crowdy, "The League of Nations: Its Social and Humanitarian Work," *American Journal of Nursing* 28, no. 4 (1928): 350.
99. See, for example, Lucien March, "International Statistics and the League of Nations," *Quarterly Publications of the American Statistical Association* 17, no. 133 (1921): 629–35.
100. A contemporary account can be found in W.E. Du Bois, "Liberia, the League and the United States," *Foreign Affairs* 11, no. 4 (1933): 682–95.
101. John Boyd Orr, "Foreword," *Africa* 9, no. 2 (1936): 146. This introduced a special issue of the International African Institute journal titled "Problems of the African Native Diet."
102. Wrigley, *Crops and Wealth in Uganda*, 63.
103. Susan Pedersen, *The Guardians: The League of Nations and the Crisis of Empire* (Oxford: Oxford University Press, 2015), 9.
104. Pedersen, *The Guardians*, xviii. The African territories also contained about 60% of the people governed under the mandate system.
105. Covenant of the League of Nations, Article 23.
106. Michael Callahan, "'Mandated Territories Are Not Colonies': Britain, France, and Africa in the 1930s," in *Imperialism on Trial: International Oversight of Colonial Rule in Historical Perspective*, ed. R.M. Douglas et al. (Lanham: Lexington Books, 2006), 6; and Pedersen, *The Guardians*, 34.
107. Pedersen, *The Guardians*, 107–11, 131–34.
108. Pedersen, *The Guardians*, 46–48. For a similar dynamic at the ILO see Daniel Roger Maul, "The International Labour Organization and the Struggle against Forced Labour from 1919 to the Present," *Labor History* 48, no. 4 (2007): 478.
109. Pedersen, *The Guardians*, 4–5, 7, 11, 93–94. For examples of impact on policy-makers and politicians see Constantine, *Making of British Colonial Development Policy*, 229–33; and Conklin, *Mission to Civilize*, 228, 235.
110. Callahan, "'Mandated Territories Are Not Colonies'," 5–6. On trusteeship as a central theme in development see Michael Cowen and Robert Shenton, *Doctrines of Development* (London: Routledge, 1996).

111. Frankel, *Capital Investment in Africa*, 151; Charles Issawi, *An Economic History of the Middle East and North Africa* (New York: Columbia University Press, 1982), 73; Mira Wilkins, "Comparative Hosts," *Business History* 36, no. 1 (1994): 20–21; and John Dunning and Sarianna Lundan, *Multinational Enterprises and the Global Economy*, 2nd ed. (Cheltenham: Edward Elgar, 2008), 175.
112. For example, see Frankel, *Capital Investment in Africa*, 299, 301; K. Dike Nworah, "The Politics of Lever's West African Concessions, 1907–1913," *International Journal of African Historical Studies* 5, no. 2 (1972): 248–64; Mira Wilkins, "European and North American Multinationals, 1970–1914: Comparisons and Contrasts," in *Transnational Corporations: A Historical Perspective*, ed. Geoffrey Jones (London: Routledge for the United Nations, 1993), 41; and Tony Woods, "'Why Not Persuade Them to Grow Tobacco?': Planters, Tenants, and the Political Economy of Central Malawi, 1920–1940," *African Economic History*, no. 21 (1993): 131–50.
113. Frankel, *Capital Investment in Africa*, 151; and Michael Twomey, *A Century of Foreign Investment in the Third World* (Abingdon: Routledge, 2000), 44, 47–48. British firms accounted for most of the foreign investment stock in the continent both before and after the First World War.
114. See, for example, Rudolph Grimes, "Liberia and Foreign Investments," *Columbia Journal of International Affairs* 4, no. 2 (1950): 65–67.
115. Robert Miller and Peter Carter, "The Modern Dual Economy—A Cost-Benefit Analysis of Liberia," *Journal of Modern African Studies* 10, no. 1 (1972): 114.
116. Cuthbert Christy, "Liberia in 1930," *Geographical Journal* 77, no. 6 (1931): 526; and Jacob Pereira-Lunghu, "Trends in Deficits in the Liberian Economy from 1912 to 1990: Implications for Fiscal Policy in Post-Civil War Liberia," *Liberian Studies Journal* 20, no. 2 (1995): 209.
117. Fiona Gordon-Ashworth, *International Commodity Control: A Contemporary History and Appraisal* (London: Croon Helm, 1984), 192–94.
118. Christy, "Liberia in 1930," 526–27; and J.H. Mower, "The Republic of Liberia," *Journal of Negro History* 32, no. 3 (1947): 279.
119. Frank Chalk, "The Anatomy of an Investment: Firestone's 1927 Loan to Liberia," *Canadian Journal of African Studies* 1, no. 1 (1967): 22.
120. Baron De Lynden, "The Liberian Centenary," *African Affairs* 46, no. 185 (1947): 210; and Chalk, "Anatomy of an Investment," 25.
121. R.J. Harrison Church, "The Firestone Rubber Plantation in Liberia," *Geography* 54 (1969): 431.
122. Louis Wells, "The Multinational Business Enterprise: What Kind of International Organization?" *International Organization* 25, no. 3 (1971): 457.
123. Mower, "Republic of Liberia," 290–91; and Augustine Konneh, "The Hut Tax in Liberia: The High Costs of Integration," *Journal of the Georgia Association of Historians* 17 (December 1996): 41–42.
124. Christy, "Liberia in 1930," 527.
125. Sidney De La Rue (1924) as quoted in Chalk, "Anatomy of an Investment," 21.
126. Mower, "Republic of Liberia," 296–97; Adell Patton, "Liberia and Containment Policy Against Colonial Take-Over: Public Health and Sanitation

Reform, 1912–1953," *Liberian Studies Journal* 30, no. 2 (2005): 42; and Twomey, *A Century of Foreign Investment*, 84. Firestone's initial investment in Liberia was around US$3 million, and it spent at least US$360,000 on development projects and research.

127. De Lynden, "Liberian Centenary," 210; and Mower, "Republic of Liberia," 300.
128. B. Nnamdi Azikiwe, "In Defense of Liberia," *Journal of Negro History* 17, no. 1 (1932): 31.
129. Rodney Carlisle, "The 'American Century' Implemented: Stettinius and the Liberian Flag of Convenience," *Business History Review* 54, no. 2 (1980): 175–91.
130. For the role of American officials see Stephen Krasner, *Defending the National Interest: Raw Materials Investments and U.S. Foreign Policy* (Princeton: Princeton University Press, 1978), 98, 104–5.
131. See Judith Byfield et al., eds., *Africa and World War II* (Cambridge: Cambridge University Press, 2015) for a recent overview.
132. Raymond Dumett, "Africa's Strategic Minerals During World War II," in *Imperialism, Economic Development and Social Change in West Africa* (Durham, NC: Carolina Academic Press, 2013), 493–521. Although oil and natural gas had been found at a few sites in Africa, the big discoveries that led to commercial exploitation did not occur until the 1950s; see Jonathan Baker, "Oil and African Development," *Journal of Modern African Studies* 15, no. 2 (1977): 175.
133. Judith Byfield, "Producing for the War," in *Africa and World War II*, 40–41.
134. Ahmad Alawad Sikainga, "Conclusion: Consequences of the War," in *Africa in World War II*, 507.
135. Byfield, "Producing for the War," 35–39.
136. For example, Dumett, "Africa's Strategic Minerals," 514. It is worth noting that Africa still hosted a relatively small share of global multinational activity. For an overview of multinational enterprises in this period see Dunning and Lundan, *Multinational Enterprises and the Global Economy*, 172–89.
137. Constantine, *Making of British Colonial Development Policy*, 227–66 offers a detailed account of the policy process.
138. Robert Tignor, *W. Arthur Lewis and the Birth of Development Economics* (Princeton: Princeton University Press, 2006), 56–65.
139. Thompson and Adloff, *French West Africa*, 251; Hubert Deschamps, "France in Black Africa and Madagascar Between 1920 and 1945," in *Colonialism in Africa 1870–1960*, 233–35.
140. Frederick Cooper, *Citizenship Between Empire and Nation* (Princeton: Princeton University Press, 2014), 7–8; see also Conklin, *Mission to Civilize*, 254–55.
141. Frederick Cooper, "From Free Labor to Family Allowances: Labor and African Society in Colonial Discourse," *American Ethnologist* 16, no. 4 (1989): 753–54.
142. Monica van Beusekom and Dorothy Hodgson, "Lessons Learned? Development Experiences in the Late Colonial Period," *Journal of African History* 41, no. 1 (2000): 29–33; and van Beusekom, *Negotiating Development*, 118–46.

143. Edgar Beigel, "France Moves Toward National Planning," *Political Science Quarterly* 62, no. 3 (1947): 381–97; Thompson and Adloff, *French West Africa*, 252–53, 270; and Deschamps, "France in Black Africa," 231–32.
144. Thompson and Adloff, *French West Africa*, 253, 270; and David Fieldhouse, *The West and the Third World* (Oxford: Blackwell, 1999), 84, 88.
145. See, for example, Carol Lancaster, *Foreign Aid: Diplomacy, Development, Domestic Politics* (Chicago: University of Chicago Press, 2007), 143.
146. Twomey, *Century of Foreign Investment*, 48; and Gérard Bossuat, "French Development Aid and Co-Operation under De Gaulle," *Contemporary European History* 12, no. 4 (2003): 441.
147. Patrick Manning, *Francophone Sub-Saharan Africa*, 2nd ed. (1998) as cited in Gareth Austin, "African Economic Development and Colonial Legacies," *International Development Policy/Revue Internationale de Politique de Développement* 1 (2010): para. 17, doi:10.4000/poldev.78.
148. Wood, *From Marshall Plan to Debt Crisis*, 40–41.
149. United Nations Department of Economic and Social Affairs, *Review of Economic Activity in Africa, 1950–1954* (New York: United Nations, 1955), 73.
150. Wood, *From Marshall Plan to Debt Crisis*, 54.
151. C.Y. Carstairs (1943) as quoted in David Meredith, "State Controlled Marketing and Economic 'Development': The Case of West African Produce During the Second World War," *Economic History Review* 39, no. 1 (1986): 77. While the French government allowed private firms to conduct the empire's commodity trade during and after the war, the governments of newly independent French colonies chose to establish national marketing boards; see Fieldhouse, *Black Africa*, 19.
152. Peter Bauer, "Origins of the Statutory Export Monopolies of British West Africa," *Business History Review* 28, no. 3 (1954): 199–200; and Fieldhouse, *The West and the Third World*, 95.
153. Godfrey, *Impact of Post-Colonial Policy Shifts*, 43–44; and J.J. Oloya, "Marketing Boards and Post-War Economic Development Policy in Uganda, 1945–1962," *Indian Journal of Agricultural Economics* 23 (1968): 51.
154. Bauer, "Origins of the Statutory Export Monopolies," 197; Meredith, "State Controlled Marketing," 84, 88–89; and Gavin Williams, "Marketing Without and With Marketing Boards: The Origins of State Marketing Boards in Nigeria," *Review of African Political Economy* 12, no. 34 (1985): 5.
155. Woods, *From Marshall Plan to Debt Crisis*, 54; and Meredith, "State Controlled Marketing," 78.
156. Fieldhouse, *The West and the Third World*, 99.
157. Thompson and Adloff, "French Economic Policy," 144–45; and Fieldhouse, *Black Africa*, 13, 15–16.
158. See Louis Sicking, "A Colonial Echo: France and the Colonial Dimension of the European Economic Community," *French Colonial History* 5 (2004): 207–28.
159. Most of the research on this subject is national in scope, or focused on a single organization like Timothy Parsons, *Race, Resistance and the Boy Scout Movement in British Colonial Africa* (Athens, OH: Ohio University Press, 2004). Continental surveys like Wogu Ananaba, *The Trade Union Movement*

in Africa: Promise and Performance (New York: St. Martin's Press, 1979) and Aili Mari Tripp et al., *African Women's Movements: Transforming Political Landscapes* (Cambridge: Cambridge University Press, 2008) do not give much space to the colonial period. For an overview of postwar growth see Kjell Skjelsbaek, "The Growth of International Nongovernmental Organization in the Twentieth Century," *International Organization* 25, no. 3 (1971): 420–42.

160. Havinden and Meredith, *Colonialism and Development*, 223–27.
161. Ralph Clark with Tom Soper and Peter Williams, *Aid in Uganda: Programmes and Policies* (London: Overseas Development Institute, 1966), 26–29; and Havinden and Meredith, *Colonialism and Development*, 254–55.
162. Wrigley, *Crops and Wealth in Uganda*, 63, 68; Clark et al., *Aid in Uganda*, 24–25; and Havinden and Meredith, *Colonialism and Development*, 223.
163. Kathleen Heasman, "Women and Community Development in Kenya and Uganda," *Community Development Journal* 1, no. 4 (1966): 16; see also Hilda Mary Tadria, "Uganda Women's Organizations: Their Contribution Towards Raising Uganda's Standard of Living," *Africa Spectrum* 8, no. 2 (1973): 217–26.
164. Wrigley, *Crops and Wealth in Uganda*, 68; A.B. Adimola, "Uganda: The Newest 'Independent'," *African Affairs* 62, no. 249 (1963): 327; and Garth Glentworth and Mulozi Wozei, "The Role of Public Corporations in National Development: Case Studies of the Uganda Development Corporation and the Uganda Electricity Board," *African Review* 1, no. 3 (1972): 54–90.
165. Keith Ede, "An Analysis of Regional Inequality in Uganda," *Tijdschrift voor economische en sociale geografie* 72, no. 5 (1981): 300; and Young et al., *Cooperatives and Development*, 44–45.
166. Richard Bilder, "The International Coffee Agreement: A Case History in Negotiation," *Law and Contemporary Problems* 28, no. 2 (1963): 334; and Gordon-Ashworth, *International Commodity Control*, 210–12.
167. Young et al., *Cooperatives and Development*, 46; and Bunker, *Peasants Against the State*, 44, 259.
168. Young et al., *Cooperatives and Development*, 48, 58; Wrigley, *Crops and Wealth in Uganda*, 80; and Bunker, *Peasants Against the State*, 53.
169. Young et al., *Cooperatives and Development*, 57, 59–60.
170. Oloya, "Marketing Boards," 51; and Young et al., *Cooperatives and Development*, 60–61.
171. Edward Manson et al., *The Economic Development of Uganda* (Baltimore: Johns Hopkins University Press for the IBRD, 1962), 442; Wrigley, "Buganda," 75, 79; and Joseph Mubiru, "Uganda: Nationalism Unresolved," *Africa Today* 8, no. 7 (1961): 8.
172. Young et al., *Cooperatives and Development*, 44–45; and Ede, "Analysis of Regional Inequality in Uganda," 301.
173. Joseph Haring et al., "Marketing Boards and Price Funds in Uganda, 1950–1960," *Journal of Agricultural Economics* 20, no. 3 (1969): 351; and Adimola, "Uganda," 328.
174. UN Economic Commission for Africa, *A Survey of Economic Conditions in Africa, 1960–1964* (New York: United Nations, 1968), 171; Manson et al., *Economic Development of Uganda*, 346; and Robert Byrd, "Characteristics of

Candidates for Election in a Country Approaching Independence: The Case of Uganda," *Midwest Journal of Political Science* 7, no. 1 (1963): 10.
175. Wrigley, *Crops and Wealth in Uganda*, 73; Patrick Wall and Brian Macdona, "News Out of Africa," *African Affairs* 59, no. 236 (1960): 222; and Adimola, "Uganda," 332.
176. Bart Fisher, *The International Coffee Agreement: A Study in Coffee Diplomacy* (New York: Praeger Publishers, 1972), 23, 25; and Gordon-Ashworth, *International Commodity Control*, 212.
177. For example Tignor, *W. Arthur Lewis*, 58–59. The global impact of the TVA is explored in David Ekbladh, "Meeting the Challenge from Totalitarianism: The Tennessee Valley Authority as a Global Model for Liberal Development, 1933–1945," *International History Review* 32, no. 1 (2010): 47–67.
178. Postwar planning by the French government, especially the 1946 Monnet Plan, was particularly influential. See Irwin Wall, "Jean Monnet, the United States and the French Economic Plan," in *Jean Monnet: The Path to European Unity*, ed. Douglas Brinkley and Clifford Hackett (New York: Palgrave Macmillan, 1991), 86–87; and Astrid Ringe, "Background to Neddy: Economic Planning in the 1960s," *Contemporary British History* 12, no. 1 (1998): 82–83.
179. See Frances Lynch, "Resolving the Paradox of the Monnet Plan: National and International Planning in French Reconstruction," *Economic History Review* 37, no. 2 (1984): 229–43; and Jim Tomlinson, "Managing the Economy, Managing the People, Britain c. 1931–70," *Economic History Review* 58, no. 3 (2005): 555–85.
180. French Catholic thought on planning is discussed in Giuliana Chamedes, "The Catholic Origins of Economic Development After World War II," *French Politics, Culture and Society* 33, no. 2 (2015): 55–75.
181. Tignor, *W. Arthur Lewis*, 28–29.
182. This parallels the argument Benedict Anderson made with respect to education, print, and nationalists in *Imagined Communities: Reflections on the Origin and Spread of Nationalism*, rev. ed. (London: Verso, 1991). See also Immanuel Wallerstein, "Elites in French-Speaking West Africa: The Social Basis of Ideas," *Journal of Modern African Studies* 3, no. 1 (1965): 1–33; and Toyin Falola, *Nationalism and African Intellectuals* (Rochester: University of Rochester Press, 2001), 107–8.
183. Cooper, "Modernity," 146.
184. Oliver Stanley (1943) as quoted in Tignor, *W. Arthur Lewis*, 59.
185. Olav Stokke, *The UN and Development: From Aid to Cooperation* (Bloomington: Indiana University Press, 2009), 93; and Henry Bloch, "Regional Development Financing," *International Organization* 22, no. 1 (1968): 185. See also Transcript of interview with Paul Rosenstein-Rodan, 14 August 1961, Oral History Program, World Bank Group Archives, http://oralhistory.worldbank.org/person/rosenstein-rodan-paul-n.
186. The work of India's national Planning Commission, set up in 1950, was particularly influential; see Jagdish Bhagwati, "Comment," in *Pioneers in Development*, 199–200.
187. W. Arthur Lewis, *Development Planning: The Essentials of Economic Policy* (London: George Allen & Unwin, 1966; reprint, Routledge, 2003), 1.

188. Toyin Falola, *Development Planning and Decolonization in Nigeria* (Gainsville: University Press of Florida, 1996), 27, 31, 65; and Charlotte Neisser, "Community Development and Mass Education in British Nigeria," *Economic Development and Cultural Change* 3, no. 4 (1955): 358.
189. Falola, *Development Planning and Decolonization*, 66, 68, 120, 159.
190. David Lumsdaine, *Moral Vision in International Politics: The Foreign Aid Regime, 1949–1989* (Princeton: Princeton University Press, 1993), 247; Michael Clemens and Todd Moss, "Ghost of 0.7%: Origins and Relevance of the International Aid Target" (Working Paper 68 Washington, DC: Center for Global Development, 2005), 4; and Stokke, *The UN and Development*, 643. The World Council of Churches was an umbrella body that spoke for mainline churches in 44 countries.
191. Helmut Führer, "The Story of Official Development Assistance: A History of the Development Assistance Committee and the Development Co-Operation Directorate in Dates, Names and Figures," Organisation for Economic Co-operation and Development, Paris, 1994, pp. 7 and 13, OCDE/GD(94)67, http://www.oecd.org/dac/1896816.pdf.
192. See for example, Wallerstein, "Elites in French-Speaking West Africa," 27.
193. The complexity of France's development aid system results in differing estimates of French Official Development Assistance (ODA) in relation to national income. Bossuat estimates French ODA/GNP at 2.03% in 1956 and 2.15% in 1960. The OECD provides standardized figures for 1960 onward, at which point it calculates French ODA/GNI at 1.35%. In both datasets, French development aid was double the level suggested by the World Council of Churches and, despite a steady decline in this ratio, continued to exceed that target until the mid- or late 1960s. See Bossuat, "French Development Aid," 440; and OECD Query Wizard for International Development Statistics, https://stats.oecd.org/qwids/.
194. Thompson and Adloff, *French West Africa*, 255, 270; Fieldhouse, *The West and the Third World*, 88.
195. Thompson and Adloff, *French West Africa*, 255, 257–59, 272, 287.
196. Ibid., 259–60, 286–87.
197. Deschamps, "France in Black Africa," 235, 237; and Huillery, "History Matters."
198. Fieldhouse, *Black Africa*, 13; and Thomas, "Albert Sarraut."
199. John James Quinn and David Simon, "*Plus ça change* ...: The Allocation of French ODA to Africa During and after the Cold War," *International Interactions* 32, no. 3 (2006): 299–301; and Lancaster, *Foreign Aid*, 146.
200. Thomas Hodgkin, "Pressure for Self-Rule in French Black Africa," *Africa Report*, Special Report 2 (January 1957): 4–5. Hodgkin was reporting on the Bamako conference of the *Rassemblement Démocratique Africain* in September 1956.
201. Anton Andereggen, *France's Relationship with Subsaharan Africa* (Westport: Praeger Publishers, 1994), 122; and Bossuat, "French Development Aid," 431, 433, 444–45, 448–89.
202. Fieldhouse, *Black Africa*, 13.
203. Transcript of interview with Paul Rosenstein-Rodan, 6–8.

204. Tignor, *W. Arthur Lewis*, 63–64; and Anne Krueger, Constantine Michalopoulos, Vernon Ruttan et al., *Aid and Development* (Baltimore: Johns Hopkins University Press, 1989), 127–28.
205. Mamadou Dia, *The African Nations and World Solidarity*, trans. Mercer Cook (New York: Frederick A. Praeger, 1961), 96–97, 110, 125. See also José Lasuen, "On Growth Poles," *Urban Studies* 6, no. 2 (1969): 137–61. The influence of French economists like François Perroux and Gérard Destanne de Bernis on African development policy before and after independence needs further research.
206. Moris, "Irrigation as a Privileged Solution;" and Ertsen, "Controlling the Farmer."
207. Thompson and Adloff, *French West Africa*, 370; and van Beusekom, "*Colonisation Indigène*," 320–21.
208. de Wilde, *Experiences with Agricultural Development*, 249, 251.
209. Djibril Aw and Geert Diemer, *Making a Large Irrigation Scheme Work: A Case Study from Mali* (Washington, DC: IBRD, 2005), 6, 12; and Sander Zwart and Lucie Leclert, "A Remote Sensing-Based Irrigation Performance Assessment: A Case Study of the *Office Du Niger* in Mali," *Irrigation Science* 28, no. 5 (2010): 373.
210. Cooper, "Conflict and Connection," 1529.
211. Paul Tiyambe Zeleza, "The Struggle for Human Rights in Africa," *Canadian Journal of African Studies* 41, no. 3 (2007): 487–88. As Zeleza notes, the concept of a right to development originated with Senegalese jurist Kéba Mbaye.
212. See, for example, William Edgett Smith, *We Must Run While They Walk: A Portrait of Africa's Julius Nyerere* (New York: Random House, 1971), 5, 100–1, 284.
213. Paul Rosenstein-Rodan, "International Aid for Underdeveloped Countries," *Review of Economics and Statistics* 43, no. 2 (1961): 107.
214. Nick Cullather, "The Third Race," *Diplomatic History* 33, no. 3 (2009): 507–12.
215. Omar Pancoast, "The 'Point Four' Policy," *Bulletin of the Atomic Scientists* 10, no. 3 (1954): 87.
216. Sidney Warren, "The Background of Our Aid Program," *Current History* 33, no. 193 (1957): 136; and McVety, "Pursuing Progress," 395–98.
217. Zewde, *History of Modern Ethiopia*, 183. Eritrea was a former Italian colony that federated with Ethiopia in 1952.
218. Jeffrey Lefebvre, "Donor Dependency and American Arms Transfers to the Horn of Africa: The F-5 Legacy," *Journal of Modern African Studies* 25, no. 3 (1987): 471.
219. Bingham, *Shirt-Sleeve Diplomacy*, 245; Zewde, *History of Modern Ethiopia*, 184; and Amanda McVety, "Pursuing Progress: Point Four in Ethiopia," *Diplomatic History* 32, no. 3 (2008): 371, 383, 401.
220. On the Point Four Program generally see Rollin Atwood, "The United States Point Four Program – a Bilateral Approach," *Annals of the American Academy of Political and Social Science* 323 (1959): 35. On Ethiopia's program see Bingham, *Shirt-Sleeve Diplomacy*, 252; and McVety, "Pursuing Progress," 383, 389–90.

221. Zewde, *Pioneers of Change*, 27–34, 138.
222. Zewde, *History of Modern Ethiopia*, 129–37, 208; and James Morris, *The Road to Huddersfield: A Journey to Five Continents* (New York: Pantheon Books, 1963), 106.
223. Atwood, "The United States Point Four Program;" and Paul Streeten, *Aid to Africa: A Policy Outline for the 1970s* (New York: Praeger Publishers for the United Nations, 1972), 28.
224. McVety, "Pursuing Progress," 385.
225. Nathan Citino, "The Ottoman Legacy in Cold War Modernization," *International Journal of Middle East Studies* 40, no. 4 (2008): 583.
226. Bingham, *Shirt-Sleeve Diplomacy*, 80.
227. Citino, "The Ottoman Legacy," 579–80, 584–85.
228. Gerald Meier, "The Formative Period," 5.
229. Charles Malik (1946), as quoted in Digambar Bhouraskar, *United Nations Development Aid: A Study in History and Politics* (New Delhi: Academic Foundation, 2007), 24. The resolution, 52(I), was passed by the General Assembly on December 14, 1946.
230. Thandika Mkandawire, "Running While Others Walk: Knowledge and the Challenge of Africa's Development," *Africa Development* 36, no. 2 (2011): 6–7.
231. Nassau Adams, *Worlds Apart: The North-South Divide and the International System* (London: Zed Books, 1993), 51–53. For a discussion of the Third World's changing meanings see Marcin Wojciech Solarz, "'Third World': The 60th Anniversary of a Concept that Changed History," *Third World Quarterly* 33, no. 9 (2012): 1561–73. For an example of action against imperialism, see Ernest Gross, "The South West Africa Case: What Happened?" *Foreign Affairs* 45, no. 1 (1966): 36–48.
232. John Toye and Richard Toye, "Arthur Lewis and the United Nations," Paper presented at "The Lewis Model After Fifty Years" conference, Manchester University, 6–7 July 2004, https://johntoyedotnet.files.wordpress.com/2012/02/arthur-lewis2004.pdf. As Amy Staples documents, the UN's international civil service played an important role in institutionalizing development; see *The Birth of Development: How the World Bank, Food and Agriculture Organization, and World Health Organization Changed the World, 1945–1965* (Kent, OH: Kent State University Press, 2006).
233. For example, John Toye and Richard Toye, *The UN and Global Political Economy: Trade, Finance, and Development* (Bloomington: Indiana University Press, 2004), 102–6. See also W. Arthur Lewis, "United Nations Primer for Development: Comment," *Quarterly Journal of Economics* 67, no. 2 (1953): 267–75.
234. Tony Killick, "Trends in Development Economics and Their Relevance to Africa," *Journal of Modern African Studies* 18, no. 3 (1980): 368; and Richard Jolly et al., *UN Contributions to Development Thinking and Practice* (Blooomington: Indiana University Press, 2004), 50–54.
235. See, for example, Tignor, *W. Arthur Lewis*, 176–77 on differences between Lewis and Kwame Nkrumah, whose government he was advising.

236. The term Third Worldist is borrowed from Robert Malley, "The Third Worldist Moment," *Current History* 98, no. 631 (1999): 359–69.
237. See, for example, Christopher Lee, ed., *Making a World After Empire: The Bandung Moment and Its Political Afterlives* (Athens, OH: Ohio University Press, 2010).
238. Craig Murphy, *The Emergence of the NIEO Ideology* (Boulder: Westview Press, 1984), 37, 46, 95.
239. Carol Geldart and Peter Lyon, "The Group of 77: A Perspective View," *International Affairs* 57, no. 1 (1980/1981): 94; Robert Mortimer, "Global Economy and African Foreign Policy: The Algerian Model," *African Studies Review* 27, no. 1 (1984): 6; and Robert Mortimer, *The Third World Coalition in International Politics*, 2nd ed. (Boulder: Westview Press, 1984), 49.
240. Hayward Alker, "Dimensions of Conflict in the General Assembly," *American Political Science Review* 58, no. 3 (1964): 650; plus Adekeye Adebajo, "Ending Global Apartheid: Africa and the United Nations," and James Jonah, "The Security Council, the General Assembly, the Economic and Social Council, and the Secretariat," both in *From Global Apartheid to Global Village: Africa and the United Nations*, ed. Adekeye Adebajo (Scottsville: University of KwaZulu-Natal Press, 2009), 3–4, 72–73, respectively.
241. Adebayo Adedeji, "The ECA: Forging a Future for Africa," in *Unity and Diversity in Development Ideas: Perspectives from the UN Regional Commissions*, ed. Yves Berthelot (Bloomington: Indiana University Press, 2004), 235–36. See also Frederick Arkhurst, *African Diplomacy: The UN Experience* (Bloomington, IN: AuthorHouse, 2010), Chap. 2.
242. United Nations General Assembly, Third Committee, Thirteenth Session, Agenda Item 12, "Report of the Economic and Social Council: Formulation of Social Policies Related to Economic Development," A/C.3/L.666, 3 October 1954. The five countries were Ethiopia, Ghana, Morocco, Tunisia, and the United Arab Republic; they were joined by Indonesia. Subsequent revisions of this motion had additional sponsors.
243. H.E. Caustin, "United Nations Technical Assistance in an African Setting," *African Affairs* 66, no. 263 (1967): 113–26; and Stokke, *The UN and Development*, 138. The comments of Ms. Addison can be found in the official record of the UN General Assembly, Thirteenth Session, Third Committee, 6 October 1958, Agenda Item 12. I am indebted to the staff of the UN's Dag Hammarskjöld Library for copies of this and the drafts of the A/C.3/L.666 resolution discussed at this meeting.
244. Margaret Snyder and Mary Tadesse, *African Women and Development: A History* (London: Zed Books, 1995), 32–33.

Bibliography

Adams, Nassau. *Worlds Apart: The North-South Divide and the International System*. London: Zed Books, 1993.

Adas, Michael. "'High' Imperialism and the 'New' History." In *Islamic and European Expansion: The Forging of a Global Order*, edited by Michael Adas for the American Historical Association, 311–44. Philadelphia: Temple University Press.

Adebajo, Adekeye, ed. *From Global Apartheid to Global Village: Africa and the United Nations*. Scottsville: University of KwaZulu-Natal Press, 2009.

Adedeji, Adebayo. "The ECA: Forging a Future for Africa." In *Unity and Diversity in Development Ideas: Perspectives from the UN Regional Commissions*, edited by Yves Berthelot, 233–306. Bloomington: Indiana University Press, 2004.

Ajayi, J.F. Ade, ed. *UNESCO General History of Africa*, Vol. VI *Africa in the Nineteenth Century*. Paris: UNESCO, Heinemann & University of California Press, 1989.

Akyeampong, Emmanuel. "Christianity, Modernity and the Weight of Tradition in the Life of *Asantehene* Agyeman Prempeh I, C. 1888–1931." *Africa* 69, no. 2 (1999): 279–311.

Andereggen, Anton. *France's Relationship with Subsaharan Africa*. Westport: Praeger Publishers, 1994.

Andrew, C.M., and A.S. Kanya-Forstner. "France, Africa, and the First World War." *Journal of African History* 19, no. 1 (1978): 11–23.

Apter, David. "The Role of Traditionalism in the Political Modernization of Ghana and Uganda." *World Politics* 13, no. 1 (1960): 45–68.

———. *The Political Kingdom in Buganda: A Study of Bureaucratic Nationalism*. Princeton: Princeton University Press, 1967.

Austin, Gareth. "African Economic Development and Colonial Legacies." *International Development Policy/Revue Internationale de Politique de Développement* 1 (2010): 11–32.

———. "The Economics of Colonialism in Africa." In *The Oxford Handbook of Africa and Economics*, edited by Célestin Monga and Justin Yifu Lin, 522–35. Oxford: Oxford University Press, 2015.

Berry, Sara. *No Condition Is Permanent: The Social Dynamics of Agrarian Change in Sub-Saharan Africa*. Madison: University of Wisconsin Press, 1993.

Bhouraskar, Digambar. *United Nations Development Aid: A Study in History and Politics*. New Delhi: Academic Foundation, 2007.

Bossuat, Gérard. "French Development Aid and Co-Operation Under De Gaulle." *Contemporary European History* 12, no. 4 (2003): 431–56.

Bowles, B.D. "Economic Anti-Colonialism and British Reaction in Uganda, 1936–1955." *Canadian Journal of African Studies* 9, no. 1 (1975): 51–60.

Brown, Ian, ed. *The Economies of Africa and Asia in the Inter-War Depression*. London: Routledge, 1989.

Bunker, Stephen. *Peasants Against the State: The Politics of Market Control in Bugisu, Uganda, 1900–1983*. Urbana: University of Illinois Press, 1987.

Byfield, Judith, Carolyn Brown, Timothy Parsons, and Ahmad Alawad Sikainga, eds. *Africa and World War II*. Cambridge: Cambridge University Press, 2015.

Callahan, Michael. "'Mandated Territories Are Not Colonies': Britain, France, and Africa in the 1930s." In *Imperialism on Trial: International Oversight of Colonial Rule in Historical Perspective*, edited by R.M. Douglas, Michael Callahan and Elizabeth Bishop, 1–20. Lanham: Lexington Books, 2006.

Carlisle, Rodney. "The 'American Century' Implemented: Stettinius and the Liberian Flag of Convenience." *Business History Review* 54, no. 2 (1980): 175–91.

Carswell, Grace. "Food Crops as Cash Crops: The Case of Colonial Kigezi, Uganda." *Journal of Agrarian Change* 3, no. 4 (2003): 521–51.

Chalk, Frank. "The Anatomy of an Investment: Firestone's 1927 Loan to Liberia." *Canadian Journal of African Studies* 1, no. 1 (1967): 12–32.

Chamedes, Giuliana. "The Catholic Origins of Economic Development After World War II." *French Politics, Culture & Society* 33, no. 2 (2015): 55–75.

Citino, Nathan. "The Ottoman Legacy in Cold War Modernization." *International Journal of Middle East Studies* 40, no. 4 (2008): 579–97.

Clapham, Christopher. "Ethiopian Development: The Politics of Emulation." *Commonwealth & Comparative Politics* 44, no. 1 (2006): 137–50.

Clemens, Michael, and Todd Moss. "Ghost of 0.7%: Origins and Relevance of the International Aid Target." Working Paper 68, Center for Global Development, Washington, DC, 2005.

Conklin, Alice. *A Mission to Civilize: The Republican Idea of Empire in France and West Africa, 1895–1930*. Stanford: Stanford University Press, 1997.

———. "Faire Naître v. Faire Du Noir: Race Regeneration in France and French West Africa, 1895–1940." In *Promoting the Colonial Idea: Propaganda and Visions of Empire in France*, edited by Tony Chafer and Amanda Sackur, 143–55. Houndmills: Palgrave Macmillan, 2001.

Constantine, Stephen. *The Making of British Colonial Development Policy, 1914–1940*. London: Frank Cass, 1984.

Cooper, Frederick. "From Free Labor to Family Allowances: Labor and African Society in Colonial Discourse." *American Ethnologist* 16, no. 4 (1989): 745–65.

———. "Conflict and Connection: Rethinking Colonial African History." *American Historical Review* 99, no. 5 (1994): 1516–45.

———. "Modernizing Bureaucrats, Backward Africans, and the Development Concept." In *International Development and the Social Sciences: Essays on the History and Politics of Knowledge*, edited by Frederick Cooper and Randall Packard, 64–92. Berkeley and Los Angeles: University of California Press, 1997.

———. *Colonialism in Question: Theory, Knowledge, History*. Berkeley and Los Angeles: University of California Press, 2005.

———. *Citizenship Between Empire and Nation: Remaking France and French Africa, 1945–1960*. Princeton: Princeton University Press, 2014.

Cooper, Frederick, and Ann Stoler. "Introduction Tensions of Empire: Colonial Control and Visions of Rule." *American Ethnologist* 16, no. 4 (1989): 609–21.

Cowen, Michael, and Robert Shenton. *Doctrines of Development*. London: Routledge, 1996.

Cullather, Nick. "The Third Race." *Diplomatic History* 33, no. 3 (2009): 507–12.

Curtin, Philip. *The World and the West: The European Challenge and the Overseas Response in the Age of Empire*. Cambridge: Cambridge University Press, 2000.

Daviron, Benoit. "Mobilizing Labour in African Agriculture: The Role of the International Colonial Institute in the Elaboration of a Standard of Colonial Administration, 1895–1930." *Journal of Global History* 5, no. 3 (2010): 479–501.

Dumett, Raymond. "Africa's Strategic Minerals During World War II." In *Imperialism, Economic Development and Social Change in West Africa*, 493–521. Durham, NC: Carolina Academic Press, 2013.

Dunning, John, and Sarianna Lundan. *Multinational Enterprises and the Global Economy*. 2nd ed. Cheltenham: Edward Elgar, 2008.

Echenberg, Myron, and Jean Filipovich. "African Military Labour and the Building of the *Office Du Niger* Installations, 1925–50." *Journal of African History* 27, no. 3 (1986): 533–51.

Ede, Keith. "An Analysis of Regional Inequality in Uganda." *Tijdschrift voor economische en sociale geografie* 72, no. 5 (1981): 296–303.

Ekbladh, David. "Meeting the Challenge from Totalitarianism: The Tennessee Valley Authority as a Global Model for Liberal Development, 1933–1945." *International History Review* 32, no. 1 (2010): 47–67.

Ertsen, Maurits. "Controlling the Farmer: Colonial and Post-Colonial Irrigation Interventions in Africa." *Journal for Transdisciplinary Research in Southern Africa* 4, no. 1 (2008).

Falola, Toyin. *Development Planning and Decolonization in Nigeria*. Gainsville: University Press of Florida, 1996.

———. *Nationalism and African Intellectuals*. Rochester: University of Rochester Press, 2001.

Fieldhouse, David K. *The West and the Third World*. Oxford: Blackwell, 1999.

Filipovich, Jean. "Destined to Fail: Forced Settlement at the Office Du Niger, 1926–45." *Journal of African History* 42, no. 2 (2001): 239–60.

Fisher, Bart. *The International Coffee Agreement: A Study in Coffee Diplomacy*. New York: Praeger Publishers, 1972.

Frankema, Ewout. "Raising Revenue in the British Empire, 1870–1940: How 'Extractive' Were Colonial Taxes?" *Journal of Global History* 5, no. 3 (2010): 447–77.

———. "Colonial Taxation and Government Spending in British Africa, 1880–1940: Maximizing Revenue or Minimizing Effort?" *Explorations in Economic History* 48, no. 1 (2011): 136–49.

———. "The Origins of Formal Education in Sub-Saharan Africa: Was British Rule More Benign?" *European Review of Economic History* 16, no. 4 (2012): 335–55.

Gann, L.H., and Peter Duignan, eds. *Colonialism in Africa 1870–1960*. Cambridge: Cambridge University Press, 1970.

Glassman, Jonathon. "Slower Than a Massacre: The Multiple Sources of Racial Thought in Colonial Africa." *American Historical Review* 109, no. 3 (2004): 720–54.

Glentworth, Garth, and Mulozi Wozei. "The Role of Public Corporations in National Development: Case Studies of the Uganda Development Corporation and the Uganda Electricity Board." *African Review* 1, no. 3 (1972): 54–90.

Godfrey, Asiimwe. *The Impact of Post-Colonial Policy Shifts in Coffee Marketing at the Local Level in Uganda: A Case Study of Mukono District, 1962–1998*. Maastricht: Shaker Publishing, 2002.

Gordon-Ashworth, Fiona. *International Commodity Control: A Contemporary History and Appraisal*. London: Croon Helm, 1984.

Hanretta, Sean. *Islam and Social Change in French West Africa: History of an Emancipatory Community*. Cambridge: Cambridge University Press, 2009.

Hanson, Holly. *Landed Obligation: The Practice of Power in Buganda*. Portsmouth, NH: Heinemann, 2003.

Havinden, Michael, and David Meredith. *Colonialism and Development: Britain and Its Tropical Colonies, 1850–1960*. London: Routledge, 1993.

Huillery, Elise. "History Matters: The Long-Term Impact of Colonial Public Investments in French West Africa." *American Economic Journal: Applied Economics* 1, no. 2 (2009): 176–215.

Issawi, Charles. *An Economic History of the Middle East and North Africa.* New York: Columbia University Press, 1982.

Jolly, Richard, Louis Emmerij, Dharam Ghai, and Frédérick Lapeyre. *UN Contributions to Development Thinking and Practice.* Blooomington: Indiana University Press, 2004.

Killick, Tony. "Trends in Development Economics and Their Relevance to Africa." *Journal of Modern African Studies* 18, no. 3 (1980): 367–86.

Krueger, Anne, Constantine Michalopoulos, Vernon Ruttan et al. *Aid and Development.* Baltimore: Johns Hopkins University Press, 1989.

Lee, Christopher, ed. *Making a World After Empire: The Bandung Moment and Its Political Afterlives.* Athens, OH: Ohio University Press, 2010.

Lumsdaine, David Halloran. *Moral Vision in International Politics: The Foreign Aid Regime, 1949–1989.* Princeton: Princeton University Press, 1993.

Macekura, Stephen. "The Point Four Program and U.S. International Development Policy." *Political Science Quarterly* 128, no. 1 (2013): 127–60.

Madeira, Ana Isabel. "Portuguese, French and British Discourses on Colonial Education: Church-State Relations, School Expansion and Missionary Competition in Africa, 1890–1930." *Paedagogica Historica* 41, nos. 1–2 (2005): 31–60.

Maul, Daniel Roger. "The International Labour Organization and the Struggle Against Forced Labour from 1919 to the Present." *Labor History* 48, no. 4 (2007): 477–500.

Mazrui, Ali A., ed. *UNESCO General History of Africa,* Vol. VIII *Africa Since 1935.* Paris: UNESCO, 1993.

McMichael, Philip. *Development and Social Change: A Global Perspective.* 3rd ed. Thousand Oaks, CA: Pine Forge Press/Sage, 2004.

McVety, Amanda Kay. "Pursuing Progress: Point Four in Ethiopia." *Diplomatic History* 32, no. 3 (2008): 371–403.

Meier, Gerald, and Dudley Seers, eds. *Pioneers in Development.* Washington, DC: Oxford University Press for the World Bank, 1984.

Meredith, David. "State Controlled Marketing and Economic 'Development': The Case of West African Produce During the Second World War." *Economic History Review* 39, no. 1 (1986): 77–91.

Mkandawire, Thandika. "Running While Others Walk: Knowledge and the Challenge of Africa's Development." *Africa Development* 36, no. 2 (2011): 1–36.

Moris, Jon. "Irrigation as a Privileged Solution in African Development." *Development Policy Review* 5, no. 2 (1987): 99–123.

Mortimer, Robert. "Global Economy and African Foreign Policy: The Algerian Model." *African Studies Review* 27, no. 1 (1984): 1–22.

———. *The Third World Coalition in International Politics.* 2nd ed. Boulder: Westview Press, 1984.

Mudimbe, V.Y. *The Invention of Africa: Gnosis, Philosophy, and the Order of Knowledge.* Bloomington: Indiana University Press, 1988.

Murphy, Craig. *The Emergence of the NIEO Ideology.* Boulder: Westview Press, 1984.

Musisi, Nakanyiki. "The Environment, Gender, and the Development of Unequal Relations in Buganda: A Historical Perspective." *Canadian Woman Studies* 13, no. 3 (1993): 54–59.

Nederveen Pieterse, Jan. *Development Theory: Deconstructions/Reconstructions.* Los Angeles: Sage, 2001.

Nworah, K. Dike. "The Politics of Lever's West African Concessions, 1907–1913." *International Journal of African Historical Studies* 5, no. 2 (1972): 248–64.

Ochonu, Moses. *Colonial Meltdown: Northern Nigeria in the Great Depression.* Athens, OH: Ohio University Press, 2009.

———. "African Colonial Economies: State Control, Peasant Maneuvers, and Unintended Outcomes." *History Compass* 11, no. 1 (2013): 1–13.

Oloya, J.J. "Marketing Boards and Post-War Economic Development Policy in Uganda, 1945–1962." *Indian Journal of Agricultural Economics* 23 (1968): 50–8.

Osborn, Emily Lynn. "'Circle of Iron': African Colonial Employees and the Interpretation of Colonial Rule in French West Africa." *Journal of African History* 44, no. 1 (2003): 29–50.

Pallinder-Law, Agneta. "Aborted Modernization in West Africa? The Case of Abeokuta." *Journal of African History* 15, no. 1 (1974): 65–82.

Pankhurst, Richard. *The Ethiopians: A History.* Oxford: Blackwell, 2001.

Panza, Laura, and Jeffrey Williamson. "Did Muhammad Ali Foster Industrialization in Early Nineteenth-Century Egypt?" *Economic History Review* 68, no. 1 (2015): 79–100.

Patton, Adell. "Liberia and Containment Policy Against Colonial Take-Over: Public Health and Sanitation Reform, 1912–1953." *Liberian Studies Journal* 30, no. 2 (2005): 40–65.

Pedersen, Susan. *The Guardians: The League of Nations and the Crisis of Empire.* Oxford: Oxford University Press, 2015.

Peel, J.D.Y. "*Olaju*: A Yoruba Concept of Development." *Journal of Development Studies* 14, no. 2 (1978): 139–65.

Pereira-Lunghu, Jacob. "Trends in Deficits in the Liberian Economy from 1912 to 1990: Implications for Fiscal Policy in Post-Civil War Liberia." *Liberian Studies Journal* 20, no. 2 (1995): 207–31.

Pomeranz, Kenneth. "Empire & 'Civilizing' Missions, Past & Present." *Daedalus* 134, no. 2 (2005): 34–45.

Quinn, John James, and David Simon. "*Plus ça change,* …: The Allocation of French ODA to Africa During and After the Cold War." *International Interactions* 32, no. 3 (2006): 295–318.

Reid, Richard. *Political Power in Pre-Colonial Buganda: Economy, Society & Warfare in the Nineteenth Century.* Oxford: James Currey et al., 2002.

Rempel, Ruth. "Trade and Transformation: Participation in the Ivory Trade in Late 19th-Century East and Central Africa." *Canadian Journal of African Studies* 19, no. 3 (1998): 37–42.

Renault, François. "The Structures of the Slave Trade in Central Africa in the 19th Century." In *The Economics of the Indian Ocean Slave Trade in the Nineteenth Century*, edited by W.G. Clarence-Smith, 146–65. London: Frank Cass, 1989.

Rist, Gilbert. *The History of Development: From Western Origins to Global Faith.* 2nd ed. Translated by Patrick Camiller. London: Zed Books, 2006.

Roberts, Richard. *Two Worlds of Cotton: Colonialism and the Regional Economy in the French Soudan, 1800–1946*. Stanford: Stanford University Press, 1996.

Rosenstein-Rodan, Paul. "International Aid for Underdeveloped Countries." *Review of Economics and Statistics* 43, no. 2 (1961): 107–38.

Sicking, Louis. "A Colonial Echo: France and the Colonial Dimension of the European Economic Community." *French Colonial History* 5 (2004): 207–28.

Skjelsbaek, Kjell. "The Growth of International Nongovernmental Organization in the Twentieth Century," *International Organization* 25, no. 3 (1971): 420–42.

Snyder, Margaret, and Mary Tadesse. *African Women and Development: A History*. London: Zed Books, 1995.

Staples, Amy. *The Birth of Development: How the World Bank, Food and Agriculture Organization, and World Health Organization Changed the World, 1945–1965*. Kent, OH: Kent State University Press, 2006.

Stokke, Olav. *The UN and Development: From Aid to Cooperation*. Bloomington: Indiana University Press, 2009.

Streeten, Paul. *Aid to Africa: A Policy Outline for the 1970s*. New York: Praeger Publishers for the United Nations, 1972.

Taylor, Thomas. "The Struggle for Economic Control of Uganda, 1919–1922: Formulation of an Economic Policy." *International Journal of African Historical Studies* 11, no. 1 (1978): 1–31.

———. "The Establishment of a European Plantation Sector Within the Emerging Colonial Economy of Uganda, 1902–1919." *International Journal of African Historical Studies* 19, no. 1 (1986): 35–58.

Thomas, Martin. "Albert Sarraut, French Colonial Development, and the Communist Threat, 1919–1930." *Journal of Modern History* 77, no. 4 (2005): 917–55.

Thompson, Virginia, and Richard Adloff. *French West Africa*. Stanford: Stanford University Press, 1957.

Tignor, Robert. *W. Arthur Lewis and the Birth of Development Economics*. Princeton: Princeton University Press, 2006.

Twomey, Michael. *A Century of Foreign Investment in the Third World*. Abingdon: Routledge, 2000.

van Beusekom, Monica. "Colonisation Indigène: French Rural Development Ideology at the Office Du Niger, 1920–1940." *International Journal of African Historical Studies* 30, no. 2 (1997): 299–323.

———. "Disjunctures in Theory and Practice: Making Sense of Change in Agricultural Development at the Office Du Niger, 1920–60." *Journal of African History* 41, no. 1 (2000): 79–99.

———. *Negotiating Development: African Farmers and Colonial Experts at the Office Du Niger, 1920–1960*. Portsmouth: Heinemann, James Currey, and David Philip, 2002.

van Beusekom, Monica, and Dorothy Hodgson. "Lessons Learned? Development Experiences in the Late Colonial Period." *Journal of African History* 41, no. 1 (2000): 29–33.

Vatikiotis, Panayiotis. *The History of Modern Egypt: From Muhammad Ali to Mubarak*. 4th ed. Baltimore: Johns Hopkins University Press, 1991.

Veeser, Cyrus. "A Forgotten Instrument of Global Capitalism? International Concessions, 1870–1930." *International History Review* 35, no. 5 (2013): 1136–55.

Wallerstein, Immanuel. "Elites in French-Speaking West Africa: The Social Basis of Ideas." *Journal of Modern African Studies* 3, no. 1 (1965): 1–33.

Williams, Gavin. "Marketing Without and With Marketing Boards: The Origins of State Marketing Boards in Nigeria." *Review of African Political Economy* 12, no. 34 (1985): 4–15.

Williamson, Oliver. "The New Institutional Economics: Taking Stock, Looking Ahead." *Journal of Economic Literature* 38, no. 3 (2000): 595–613.

Wood, Robert. *From Marshall Plan to Debt Crisis: Foreign Aid and Development Choices in the World Economy.* Berkeley: University of California Press, 1986.

Woods, Tony. "'Why Not Persuade Them to Grow Tobacco?': Planters, Tenants, and the Political Economy of Central Malawi, 1920–1940." *African Economic History*, no. 21 (1993): 131–50.

Youé, Christopher. "Peasants, Planters and Cotton Capitalists: The 'Dual Economy' in Colonial Uganda." *Canadian Journal of African Studies* 12, no. 2 (1978): 163–84.

Young, Crawford, Neal Sherman, and Tim Rose. *Cooperatives and Development: Agricultural Politics in Ghana and Uganda.* Madison: University of Wisconsin Press, 1981.

Zeleza, Paul Tiyambe. "The Struggle for Human Rights in Africa." *Canadian Journal of African Studies* 41, no. 3 (2007): 474–506.

Zewde, Bahru. *A History of Modern Ethiopia, 1855–1974.* London: James Currey, Ohio University Press, and Addis Ababa University Press, 1991.

———. *Pioneers of Change in Ethiopia: The Reformist Intellectuals of the Early Twentieth Century.* Oxford: James Currey, Ohio University Press, and Addis Ababa University, 2002.

CHAPTER 25

Nationalism and African Intellectuals

Toyin Falola and Chukwuemeka Agbo

Thomas Hodgkin has identified three distinct themes that illustrate the trajectory of scholarship on Africa's interaction with the West.[1] The first of these themes, which characterized the first phase of the intercontinental relation, focused on 'the competition for colonial possession as a factor tending to promote, or intensify, conflict between the major European Powers. The practical question which absorbed them was how to limit or remove the rivalries between imperial and would be imperial Powers, as an evident contributory cause of international wars'.[2] The second theme was developed during the interwar years. Scholars at this time were concerned with 'the problem of the social ends to be sought, and the administrative methods to be used, by the colonial powers in the territories which they controlled'.[3] The third theme shifts attention from an exclusive discussion of the superpowers to a shared attention involving them (European overlords) on the one hand and their African subjects on the other hand. In our generation, Hodgkin writes:

> the colonial problem means, principally, the problem of the relationship between Europe and its outpost communities in Africa, on the one hand, and the indigenous African societies on the other. Put crudely, it means what adjustments, compromises, surrenders, must the European colonial Powers (and their settlers) make in the face of the claims of African nationalism?[4]

T. Falola (✉) · C. Agbo
Department of History, The University of Texas,
Austin, TX, USA

© The Author(s) 2018
M.S. Shanguhyia and T. Falola (eds.),
The Palgrave Handbook of African Colonial and Postcolonial History,
https://doi.org/10.1057/978-1-137-59426-6_25

It is on the individuals who pushed for these drastic changes in Africa's relations with Europeans, their efforts, and activities towards securing greater freedom and eventually independence for Africa in the nineteenth and twentieth centuries, that this chapter reflects.

This chapter is about nationalism (the 'consciousness on the part of individuals or groups, of membership in a nation, or of a desire to forward the strength, liberty, or prosperity of a nation'[5]), a persistent theme in African history since the nineteenth century. According to Hodgkin, historiography on nationalism in Africa falls into three categories or eras: the era of political explosions, the emergence of new sovereign states, and the era of interdependence among African states.[6] The question that has dominated intellectual thinking in Africa in the last 200 years has been constant: against the background of Western incursion, how can Africa uplift itself? This is an intellectual confrontation with a modern world where continuity and change go hand in hand, compete and clash, reinforce and complement one another. Change, continuity with the past, and adaptation to new circumstances have all been part of the challenges that intellectuals have confronted as they make sense of modernity and reflect on what they perceive as their alienation in a world increasingly dominated by European values. As with the intelligentsia in other lands, Africans are not merely trying to understand the process of change and continuity, but they also have to experience the reality and insert themselves into the very process and society that they are analyzing.

This chapter examines the intersection between nationalism and African intellectuals in the quest by African elites to address issues of tradition, change, politics, and ultimately power. It discusses efforts by African elites to reshape or reconstruct a new image for Africa. Although it focuses on one class of elites, this chapter does not suggest that Africa has always had only one class of elites. In fact, if the Europeans obtained power from a traditional elite during the nineteenth century, they handed it over to a new educated elite in the twentieth century. Modern elites proved to be interested also in power by challenging traditional authority at virtually all levels of government. They successfully positioned themselves as the only ones who could reflect effectively on the profound changes that characterized the various periods and who had the means to bring them about.

This chapter, however, is not about power politics, but how nationalism has shaped the production of knowledge and influenced politics in Africa since the nineteenth century. It is about the relationship between African intelligentsia and the Europeans (missionaries and colonial apparatus) and subsequent state formations; the contradictions manifested within Pan-Africanism and nationalism; and the relation of academic institutions and intellectual production to the state during the nationalist period and beyond.

Africa has always had its intellectuals. This chapter focuses on those who emerged during the nineteenth and twentieth centuries. The representatives of the previous intellectual traditions also remain, but they are often marginalized by the modern educated elite that control power. In this chapter, this earlier class of intellectuals is referred to as traditional elites. They consist of priests, kings, chiefs, and merchants who generated knowledge and exercised considerable power and authority. Their knowledge was usually oral and constituted the foundation of politics, it could be esoteric, and there were specialists who handled the interpretation of complex religious ideas. An indigenous education system, informal and varied, existed partly to reproduce the traditional intellectuals and socialize everybody into the community. Diviners, griots, and priest contributed to the development of society by using their specialized knowledge to interpret reality, produce relevant histories for leaders, mediate in conflicts, and even predict the future.

Another important class of intellectuals that has developed in Africa is the Islamic intelligentsia. This school of thought was based on Islam and a formal Islamic education system. Prior to the founding of Islam by Mohammed in the seventh century, writing had, of course, been invented, and schools had been in existence in various parts of the world. For example, the monasteries, the Alexandria museum and library in Egypt had existed since the third century BCE. This early intellectual tradition continued to develop and be built upon in the Middle East, Europe, Asia, and North Africa. The spread of Islam into Africa meant the introduction of a formal Islamic educational system in North, West, and East Africa. Islamic education was quickly developed at various levels of education—elementary, secondary, and university. The first Islamic university in Africa was located at Karawiyyin, founded in 859 CE in the old city of Fez. From here, Islamic professors spread the Maliki code of law, religious brotherhoods, and other cultural ideas to the Maghreb and West Africa. Al-Azhar University in Cairo became prominent in the tenth century CE.

The spread of Islam went hand in hand with the spread of the Arabic language, thereby creating an intelligentsia who relied on writing. Like the traditional intelligentsia, Islam was oral, thus retaining an aspect of culture well established in the African continent. For instance, Swahili poetry reveals an oral tradition rich in history and culture. Similarly, the Fulani and Hausa of West Africa established a rich Islamic-cum-oral tradition. A literate intelligentsia relied on the radicalism supplied by Islam to develop a vision of society in different parts of Africa. For instance, during the nineteenth and twentieth centuries, Islam became a tool to fight imperialism by resorting to radicalism and tradition, both already tested in previous years in reforming society.

The Rise of Modern Elites

As important as the above intellectual traditions were, they did not create the modern intellectual tradition. A number of factors were responsible for the rise of modern elites in Africa. Modern intellectuals owe their origins to the spread of Western formal education, which began in some parts of Africa in the sixteenth century. European contact with Africa was first initiated by the Portuguese. The British, Danes, French, Dutch, and Germans joined later. As the slave trade became more lucrative, more and more Europeans went to Africa. They established trading stations along the coast in St. Louis and Goree in Senegal, Elmina, Accra, and Cape Coast in Gold Coast, Benin in the area of modern Nigeria, and the Kingdom of the Congo. In these places, rudimentary elementary schools sprang up. They were meant to introduce a handful of Africans to basic accounting as well as reading and writing European languages. A small scheme to produce teachers was also started by sending Africans to Europe for further education.

Writing about the Yoruba of Western Nigeria, Falola observes that:

> changes in the nineteenth century were rapid, chaotic, and reformist ... Also during the nineteenth century, the circumstances that produced the new intelligentsia began to unfold with the abolition of the slave trade, the return of liberated slaves to the Yoruba homeland, evangelization by foreign missions, the British annexation of Lagos, and the subsequent imposition of colonial rule ... The acceptance of Christianity and Western education since the mid-nineteenth century rapidly transformed the Yoruba and created an educated elite that has played a leadership role in tropical Africa.[7]

Members of this class of Yoruba modern elite were quick to employ nationalism in their relations with the Europeans.

Falola further observes:

> Chronicles began in the nineteenth century, as a cultural project by a new intelligentsia interested in presenting to the European world a rich and different heritage. This intelligentsia was connected with the church. It believed in 'legitimate' commerce and the recently inaugurated process of Westernization, as long as it did not rob Africans of political and economic power. The defining characteristics of this elite were Western education and claims to the knowledge of (and connection with) Western culture. The elite constituted the labor pool for the emerging government sector, the consumers for imported items, readers of available books, and the chroniclers of the age ... In a country where the majority were unable to read and write, literacy especially in English, was a source of power. They could communicate with foreign merchants and officers and at the same time serve as the representatives of the extra-literate traditional elite.[8]

The production of a Western educated elite in Africa was a slow process, but the pace accelerated in the twentieth century as Africans insisted on change. A second important factor in the rise of modern elites in Africa was the activities of Christian missionaries. In establishing elementary schools, the missionaries offered the basis for producing literate people. Euro-African relations in the nineteenth century called for the use of more literate Africans in commercial houses, churches, and government establishments. The African elite had to respond to the changing nature of Euro-African relations. The abolition of slavery led to trade in raw materials and later colonial conquest. The 'success' of Western education can be dated to the nineteenth century, when missionaries started arriving in large numbers. More and more Africans were receptive to conversion and secular education. Some governments, such as those of Egypt, and many individuals, notably liberated slaves, demanded education for Africans. The provision of Western education enabled the missionaries to propagate Christianity, campaign against the slave trade, and create a new, Western-oriented African intelligentsia. They used education to convert Africans to Christianity and assimilate them to a new way of thinking. The missionaries and colonial powers both understood the relevance of Western education, and they tried to balance its provision with perceived need and the awareness of its power as a social agency. Higher education was completely neglected, as there was no need to produce education at that level. Only a few secondary schools were provided, and by and large, the education of Africans was restricted to the elementary level. The self-interest of the missionaries made them front runners in the provision of education. As long as education was the handmaid of evangelization, they were ready to work for it.

Both for Africans and the colonizers, education was necessary for survival. For the colonizers, the system could not function without an elite, or at the very minimum, a group of people who could read or write. While a number of European administrators learned and used African languages, many others had to depend on interpreters to serve as intermediaries. Thus, the first major job of educated Africans was to mediate in all sorts of relations: to present the Bible on behalf of the white missionaries, to relay instructions on behalf of European administrators, and to negotiate trade deals. As important as these roles were, the elites extended this to become also the mediators of history and culture. They presented European value to Africans, either as critics or as modernizers. Yet on the other hand, they presented Africa to the Europeans. Intellectual works by Edward Wilmot Blyden and others show that these elites regarded this mediation as important to themselves and to the continent.

The colonizers and representatives of European firms also needed educated Africans as workers. The missionaries required native agents, mainly schoolteachers and priests. The firms needed clerks, cashiers, and others to facilitate the import–export trade. The government required clerks, tax collectors, police, soldiers, and many others to serve in different agencies. Where the colonial officers depended on local chiefs, as in the case of the British system of 'indirect rule', the number of educated Africans required was small indeed. In other colonial systems, a selfish calculation was made that training Africans for positions that Europeans could occupy was in effect creating a revolution that would destroy the system. The number of Africans required was dependent on the nature of the colonial economy and politics, the extent to which a colonial government was willing to depend on European migrants and settlers, and the extent of exploitation or modernization underway. As new occupations became necessary, including nursing, teaching, law, and medicine, the system also needed qualified Africans to fill them. Nevertheless, the colonial government deliberately created an educational system that would make Africans subordinate to Europeans.[9]

For Africans, Western education was also necessary. We have made mention of the mediation role of the elite, which was an exercise of power. Indeed, the voice of mediation was a source of great power for the court interpreters who profited from closeness to the judiciary, for the officers in the police and army who served as agents of coercion, and for the highly educated who were negotiating old and new cultures. Education was an agency of social change, indeed the most potent agency of change. Africans who wanted to join in the new sectors needed the knowledge of a European language and education.

Piecemeal measures never satisfied Africans, who understood the game the missionaries and colonial governments were playing with them. Having realized that education brought many advantages, notably mobility and social status, the African beneficiaries of Western education in the nineteenth century wanted to retain their privileges, to consolidate their power, to educate their offspring, and to use education to transform the continent. Wherever a mission had established a school, the community ensured that education survived and expanded.

Africans also exerted pressure on the missionaries and government to create secondary schools and universities. If education was confined to the elementary level, Africans could only work as subordinates to white superiors in all establishments. Creating an alliance with a Christian missionary turned out to be the easiest way for Africans to ensure the creation of new secondary schools, as in the case of Southern Nigeria where the Church Missionary Society (CMS) and the Baptist and the Roman Catholic Churches established secondary schools.[10] Those Africans who received higher education and held positions of power (for example, as school principals) used their influence to persuade communities and congregations to contribute money to start new schools, which a mission or government could then acquire or subsidize. This was the case in a number of southwestern Nigerian towns in the first two decades of the twentieth century, when six new secondary schools were created. In Ghana, the elite raised money from traditional leaders and businessmen to start new schools in Accra and Cape Coast.[11]

In order to obtain schoolteachers, pressure was also directed at creating teacher-training colleges. While a number were established in different parts of the continent, so acute was the shortage of teachers that this became a factor in the expansion and creation of secondary schools. In South Africa, the Churches began to make an important impact from the 1840s onward; following the London Missionary Society's leadership, the Methodists and the Paris Evangelical Mission took an interest in teacher-training colleges, and settlers, and the extent of exploitation or modernization underway. As new occupations became necessary, including nursing, teaching, law, and medicine, the system also needed qualified Africans to fill them. Nevertheless, the colonial government deliberately created an educational system that would make Africans subordinate to Europeans.[9]

For Africans, Western education was also necessary. We have made mention of the mediation role of the elite, which was an exercise of power. Indeed, the voice of mediation was a source of great power for the court interpreters who profited from closeness to the judiciary, for the officers in the police and army who served as agents of coercion, and for the highly educated who were negotiating old and new cultures. Education was an agency of social change, indeed the most potent agency of change. Africans who wanted to join in the new sectors needed the knowledge of a European language and education.

Piecemeal measures never satisfied Africans, who understood the game the missionaries and colonial governments were playing with them. Having realized that education brought many advantages, notably mobility and social status, the African beneficiaries of Western education in the nineteenth century wanted to retain their privileges, to consolidate their power, to educate their offspring, and to use education to transform the continent. Wherever a mission had established a school, the community ensured that education survived and expanded.

Africans also exerted pressure on the missionaries and government to create secondary schools and universities. If education was confined to the elementary level, Africans could only work as subordinates to white superiors in all establishments. Creating an alliance with a Christian missionary turned out to be the easiest way for Africans to ensure the creation of new secondary schools, as in the case of Southern Nigeria where the Church Missionary Society (CMS) and the Baptist and the Roman Catholic Churches established secondary schools.[10] Those Africans who received higher education and held positions of power (for example, as school principals) used their influence to persuade communities and congregations to contribute money to start new schools, which a mission or government could then acquire or subsidize. This was the case in a number of southwestern Nigerian towns in the first two decades of the twentieth century, when six new secondary schools were created. In Ghana, the elite raised money from traditional leaders and businessmen to start new schools in Accra and Cape Coast.[11]

In order to obtain schoolteachers, pressure was also directed at creating teacher-training colleges. While a number were established in different parts of the continent, so acute was the shortage of teachers that this became a factor in the expansion and creation of secondary schools. In South Africa, the Churches began to make an important impact from the 1840s onward; following the London Missionary Society's leadership, the Methodists and the Paris Evangelical Mission took an interest in teacher-training colleges, respond to the changing nature of Euro-African relations. The abolition of slavery led to trade in raw materials and later colonial conquest. The 'success' of Western education can be dated to the nineteenth century, when missionaries started arriving in large numbers. More and more Africans were receptive to conversion and secular education. Some governments, such as those of Egypt, and many individuals, notably liberated slaves, demanded education for Africans. The provision of Western education enabled the missionaries to propagate Christianity, campaign against the slave trade, and create a new, Western-oriented African intelligentsia. They used education to convert Africans to Christianity and assimilate them to a new way of thinking. The missionaries and colonial powers both understood the relevance of Western education, and they tried to balance its provision with perceived need and the awareness of its power as a social agency. Higher education was completely neglected, as there was no need to produce education at that level. Only a few secondary schools were provided, and by and large, the education of Africans was restricted to the elementary level. The self-interest of the missionaries made them front runners in the provision of education. As long as education was the handmaid of evangelization, they were ready to work for it.

Both for Africans and the colonizers, education was necessary for survival. For the colonizers, the system could not function without an elite, or at the very minimum, a group of people who could read or write. While a number of European administrators learned and used African languages, many others had to depend on interpreters to serve as intermediaries. Thus, the first major job of educated Africans was to mediate in all sorts of relations: to present the Bible on behalf of the white missionaries, to relay instructions on behalf of European administrators, and to negotiate trade deals. As important as these roles were, the elites extended this to become also the mediators of history and culture. They presented European value to Africans, either as critics or as modernizers. Yet on the other hand, they presented Africa to the Europeans. Intellectual works by Edward Wilmot Blyden and others show that these elites regarded this mediation as important to themselves and to the continent.

The colonizers and representatives of European firms also needed educated Africans as workers. The missionaries required native agents, mainly schoolteachers and priests. The firms needed clerks, cashiers, and others to facilitate the import–export trade. The government required clerks, tax collectors, police, soldiers, and many others to serve in different agencies. Where the colonial officers depended on local chiefs, as in the case of the British system of 'indirect rule', the number of educated Africans required was small indeed. In other colonial systems, a selfish calculation was made that training Africans for positions that Europeans could occupy was in effect creating a revolution that would destroy the system. The number of Africans required was dependent on the nature of the colonial economy and politics, the extent to which a colonial government was willing to depend on European migrants

236. The term Third Worldist is borrowed from Robert Malley, "The Third Worldist Moment," *Current History* 98, no. 631 (1999): 359–69.
237. See, for example, Christopher Lee, ed., *Making a World After Empire: The Bandung Moment and Its Political Afterlives* (Athens, OH: Ohio University Press, 2010).
238. Craig Murphy, *The Emergence of the NIEO Ideology* (Boulder: Westview Press, 1984), 37, 46, 95.
239. Carol Geldart and Peter Lyon, "The Group of 77: A Perspective View," *International Affairs* 57, no. 1 (1980/1981): 94; Robert Mortimer, "Global Economy and African Foreign Policy: The Algerian Model," *African Studies Review* 27, no. 1 (1984): 6; and Robert Mortimer, *The Third World Coalition in International Politics*, 2nd ed. (Boulder: Westview Press, 1984), 49.
240. Hayward Alker, "Dimensions of Conflict in the General Assembly," *American Political Science Review* 58, no. 3 (1964): 650; plus Adekeye Adebajo, "Ending Global Apartheid: Africa and the United Nations," and James Jonah, "The Security Council, the General Assembly, the Economic and Social Council, and the Secretariat," both in *From Global Apartheid to Global Village: Africa and the United Nations*, ed. Adekeye Adebajo (Scottsville: University of KwaZulu-Natal Press, 2009), 3–4, 72–73, respectively.
241. Adebayo Adedeji, "The ECA: Forging a Future for Africa," in *Unity and Diversity in Development Ideas: Perspectives from the UN Regional Commissions*, ed. Yves Berthelot (Bloomington: Indiana University Press, 2004), 235–36. See also Frederick Arkhurst, *African Diplomacy: The UN Experience* (Bloomington, IN: AuthorHouse, 2010), Chap. 2.
242. United Nations General Assembly, Third Committee, Thirteenth Session, Agenda Item 12, "Report of the Economic and Social Council: Formulation of Social Policies Related to Economic Development," A/C.3/L.666, 3 October 1954. The five countries were Ethiopia, Ghana, Morocco, Tunisia, and the United Arab Republic; they were joined by Indonesia. Subsequent revisions of this motion had additional sponsors.
243. H.E. Caustin, "United Nations Technical Assistance in an African Setting," *African Affairs* 66, no. 263 (1967): 113–26; and Stokke, *The UN and Development*, 138. The comments of Ms. Addison can be found in the official record of the UN General Assembly, Thirteenth Session, Third Committee, 6 October 1958, Agenda Item 12. I am indebted to the staff of the UN's Dag Hammarskjöld Library for copies of this and the drafts of the A/C.3/L.666 resolution discussed at this meeting.
244. Margaret Snyder and Mary Tadesse, *African Women and Development: A History* (London: Zed Books, 1995), 32–33.

Bibliography

Adams, Nassau. *Worlds Apart: The North-South Divide and the International System*. London: Zed Books, 1993.

Adas, Michael. "'High' Imperialism and the 'New' History." In *Islamic and European Expansion: The Forging of a Global Order*, edited by Michael Adas for the American Historical Association, 311–44. Philadelphia: Temple University Press.

221. Zewde, *Pioneers of Change*, 27–34, 138.
222. Zewde, *History of Modern Ethiopia*, 129–37, 208; and James Morris, *The Road to Huddersfield: A Journey to Five Continents* (New York: Pantheon Books, 1963), 106.
223. Atwood, "The United States Point Four Program;" and Paul Streeten, *Aid to Africa: A Policy Outline for the 1970s* (New York: Praeger Publishers for the United Nations, 1972), 28.
224. McVety, "Pursuing Progress," 385.
225. Nathan Citino, "The Ottoman Legacy in Cold War Modernization," *International Journal of Middle East Studies* 40, no. 4 (2008): 583.
226. Bingham, *Shirt-Sleeve Diplomacy*, 80.
227. Citino, "The Ottoman Legacy," 579–80, 584–85.
228. Gerald Meier, "The Formative Period," 5.
229. Charles Malik (1946), as quoted in Digambar Bhouraskar, *United Nations Development Aid: A Study in History and Politics* (New Delhi: Academic Foundation, 2007), 24. The resolution, 52(I), was passed by the General Assembly on December 14, 1946.
230. Thandika Mkandawire, "Running While Others Walk: Knowledge and the Challenge of Africa's Development," *Africa Development* 36, no. 2 (2011): 6–7.
231. Nassau Adams, *Worlds Apart: The North-South Divide and the International System* (London: Zed Books, 1993), 51–53. For a discussion of the Third World's changing meanings see Marcin Wojciech Solarz, "'Third World': The 60th Anniversary of a Concept that Changed History," *Third World Quarterly* 33, no. 9 (2012): 1561–73. For an example of action against imperialism, see Ernest Gross, "The South West Africa Case: What Happened?" *Foreign Affairs* 45, no. 1 (1966): 36–48.
232. John Toye and Richard Toye, "Arthur Lewis and the United Nations," Paper presented at "The Lewis Model After Fifty Years" conference, Manchester University, 6–7 July 2004, https://johntoyedotnet.files.wordpress.com/2012/02/arthur-lewis2004.pdf. As Amy Staples documents, the UN's international civil service played an important role in institutionalizing development; see *The Birth of Development: How the World Bank, Food and Agriculture Organization, and World Health Organization Changed the World, 1945–1965* (Kent, OH: Kent State University Press, 2006).
233. For example, John Toye and Richard Toye, *The UN and Global Political Economy: Trade, Finance, and Development* (Bloomington: Indiana University Press, 2004), 102–6. See also W. Arthur Lewis, "United Nations Primer for Development: Comment," *Quarterly Journal of Economics* 67, no. 2 (1953): 267–75.
234. Tony Killick, "Trends in Development Economics and Their Relevance to Africa," *Journal of Modern African Studies* 18, no. 3 (1980): 368; and Richard Jolly et al., *UN Contributions to Development Thinking and Practice* (Blooomington: Indiana University Press, 2004), 50–54.
235. See, for example, Tignor, *W. Arthur Lewis*, 176–77 on differences between Lewis and Kwame Nkrumah, whose government he was advising.

Africa. They participate in local and global cultures; their perspectives are drawn from local, national, continental, and international issues; they were originally resented by the Europeans but later acquired power from them; they constitute essentially a public-sector elite, that is, they are not primarily 'an economic bourgeoisie', which means that they have had to seek relevance and power in government and the apparatus of state.

The third agent in the rise of modern elites in Africa was improvement in communication. The development of printing presses, newspaper houses, and broadcasting revolutionized communication systems in Africa. Hodgkin has shown that communication increased interdependence which enabled Africans to:

> [s]peak and listen to one another and to the outside world in a way that has never previously been possible. The development of a nationalist Press, which seeks to stimulate political awareness and activity among the literate and barely literate mass rather than to inform a small elite, has been of special importance. African controlled journals like the *West African Pilot* in Nigeria and *Afrique Noire* in French West Africa, have been powerful instruments for the diffusion of the new outlook. Mass education projects, particularly in British Africa, have widened the circle of the literate. Through broadcasting and films, as well as through newspapers, Africans even in the remoter small towns and villages, are able to learn about Apartheid in the Union of South Africa, Indian independence, the conflict in Korea and Viet-Nam [sic], the hydrogen bomb. In Nigeria especially there has been a post-war spate of pamphlet literature, comparable with English pamphleteering in the 1640s, dealing with every kind of current topic, from polygamy to educational reform. Anti-colonial ideas imported, partly through returning students, from a variety of sources—the American gospel of free enterprise, the Marxist theory of the self-destructive character of imperialism, the Moslem Brotherhood's rejection of Western culture, the Gandhist concept of passive resistance—circulate widely in contemporary Africa.[14]

Highlighting the importance of communication to West African nationalism, Falola writes as follows:

> the educated elites in their respective countries had conceived the value of networks that used education as a cement. Books circulated, ideas traveled within the region, and newspapers carried information far and wide. Key figures also moved around to give lectures and for purposes of business and political dialogue.[15]

Lastly, the rise of new 'African political leadership' was also instrumental to the emergence of modern elites in Africa. Many countries in all regions of Africa witnessed this revolution. Writing about this political phenomenon in Africa in 1957 (a period in African history that witnessed the emergence of many of these leaders), Hodgkin notes that such men as Kwame Nkrumah of Ghana, Nnamdi Azikiwe and Obafemi Awolowo of Nigeria, Leopold secondary schools, and agricultural and industrial schools. As Fourah Bay College acquired fame in West Africa, so did the Lovedale Institution, established in 1841 by the Scottish Presbyterian Mission in South Africa. The objective of Lovedale was to train students in a variety of occupations (industrial, evangelical, teaching, and so on). It offered courses in carpentry, masonry, printing, and bookbinding.[12] Its academic offerings were equally diverse and rigorous. Lovedale provided the model and inspiration for the establishment of other secondary schools in South and East Africa after 1870.

The next phase in the pursuit of Western education by Africans came in the form of study abroad. Those who had enjoyed the opportunity of a secondary-school education or who had such a school in their area sought to establish an institution of higher education or travel abroad for further education. In British West Africa, a few students went to Fourah Bay College, which was upgraded to a university in 1876. However, as theology dominated the training there, those seeking education in law, medicine, accountancy, and other fields had to seek opportunities in Europe. Others went to the USA; these included such men as Kwame Nkrumah of Gold Coast (later Ghana) and Nnamdi Azikiwe of Nigeria. Slow to be accepted as possessing the same credentials as those trained in Europe, the graduates of US universities became strong advocates of the American system of higher education. The combination of academic, vocational, and technical training, as in Tuskegee Institute, was highly recommended for producing a new elite that would be able to think and invent.[13]

The extent of opportunities for higher education turned it into a desirable aim for many Africans. Those who managed to obtain college diplomas were able to obtain good jobs. Among them were the évolués, who were committed to French culture and were encouraged to travel to France for more education. A number of Africans (notably from Togo, Cameroon, and Dahomey) traveled on their own to France for secondary and higher education, and many of them developed anticolonial ideas and supported the emerging idea of Pan-Africanism. A number of others resisted what they perceived as the imposition of French culture, and they began to call for the study of African culture and customs.

For most of the period under consideration, the number of these elites was small, thereby constituting them as a minority. But this elite had always been a powerful minority, so successful that it inherited power from the Europeans and has continued to generate ideas, in spite of the domination of politics by the military. The intellectuals have always invested in the notion of progress—the genuine hope that Africa would develop and that they would be the agency of the transformation. The notion of progress has intermeshed with that of nationalism: most demands in the nineteenth and twentieth centuries have been couched in the language of nationalism. The intellectuals have constructed or accepted not only the ideas of the nation-state, but also those of ethnicity, and even the larger project of continental identity for

Sedar-Senghor of Senegal, Felix Houphouët-Boigny of Ivory Coast, to mention but a few, emerged with a new kind of power. Hodgkin further notes of these individuals:

> They differ profoundly both from the traditional chiefly leadership and from the past generation of lawyer-politicians. They combine, perhaps, some of the qualities of both, in that they enjoy the kind of reverence which the chief, as the intermediary between God and man, and symbol of his people's unity and continuity through time, enjoys in traditional African society; but also the new kind of authority attaching to those who have mastered the European's political techniques, and know how to use them to press African claims. These leaders have the advantage of being at home in both worlds—the world of the ancestors, the dance and the market, and the world of parliamentary debate and the struggle for state power. Thus they can command popular loyalties and win votes at elections no less effectively than party leaders in Western Europe … Judged simply on their political ability, these men do not compare unfavorably with Western European statesmen. A few of them—M. Senghor, for example—are intellectually well above the normal British or French Cabinet Minister Standard. It is not unreasonable that they should expect to be treated—as indeed they are beginning to be treated—on terms of equality by the political leaders of Europe, Asia, and America.[16]

The above factors empowered Africa's modern elites to confront their European visitors and demand freedom, equality, and respect for Africa, its political, economic, social, and cultural institutions and infrastructure.

Modern Elites and African Nationalism in the Nineteenth and Twentieth Centuries

African nationalism developed in three different ways, from cultural nationalism to political nationalism and finally territorial nationalism. A foremost figure in African nationalism is Edward Wilmot Blyden (1832–1912), a notable thinker. Blyden's front-line activism earned him recognition as *The Father of Cultural Nationalism*.[17] His great ideas and numerous opportunities to deliver speeches in different countries and to diverse audiences would pave the way for him to become more famous than his contemporaries. He was a strong advocate of self-pride and self-assertion for Africans. His antecedents lay in slavery, as his ancestors were taken from West Africa, but he himself was born in the West Indies (St Thomas). Denied the opportunity to study in the USA because of racism, he migrated to Liberia in 1851 where he went to school. His skills were reflected in his leadership of the *Liberia Herald* in the 1850s. He became a teacher in his alma mater and its principal in 1858. In the same year, he became an ordained minister of the Presbytery of West Africa. In 1861, he traveled to the USA to seek African Americans who would return to Liberia. A year later, he became a professor of Latin and Greek in the new Liberia College. He was teacher, preacher, scholar, and diplomat. He held ambassadorial appointments (1877–1878, 1892), was the president of the Liberia College (1880–1884), failed in his bid for the presidency of Liberia in 1885, and relocated to Freetown where he became interested in Islam and lived until his death.

He condemned racism and asked Africans to be proud of their race. 'I would rather be a member of this race', he maintained, 'than a Greek in the time of Alexander, a Roman in the Augustus period, or an Anglo-Saxon in the nineteenth century'.[18] He was of the opinion that Africa did not need to seek universalism but an African identity. 'An African nationality is the great desire of my soul. I believe nationality to be an ordinance of nature and no people can rise to an influential position among nations without a distinct and efficient nationality. Cosmopolitanism never effected anything and never will.'[19] He advocated Pan-Africanism, the concept of the 'African personality', and a slogan, 'Africa for Africans'. He observed:

> It is sad to think that there are some Africans, especially among those who have enjoyed the advantages of foreign training, who are so blind to the radical facts of humanity as to say, 'Let us do away with the sentiment of Race. Let us do away with our African personality and be if possible in another Race' ... Preach this doctrine as much as you like, no one will do it, for no one can do it, for when you have done away with your personality, you have done away with yourself ... the duty of every man, of every race, is to contend for its individuality—to keep and develop it ... Therefore, honour and love your Race ... If you are not yourself, if you surrender your personality, you have nothing left to give the world.[20]

Blyden's activism was not limited to theories; he reduced his intellectual liberation agenda to practice. His first step in this direction was the study of local history and cultures, from the 'uncontaminated Africans' who knew the songs, traditions, and history of 'the wonderful and mysterious events of their tribal and national life'.[21] He was of the opinion that only Africans can uplift their race in Africa, thus he encouraged educated African elites to return to Africa. He rejected the prevailing European notion that races could be organized in a pyramid on the basis of achievement, ability, and civilization, with the white man at the top. If the white man had constructed this pyramid and placed himself on top, another race could do the same, using a different set of criteria. For Blyden, each race excelled in certain things and lagged behind in others. Rather than regard races as competitive, he saw them as complementary, equal but different. If Africans were looking for a race to emulate, Blyden warned them against the white race.

Another notable figure of Blyden's time was Surgeon-Major James Africanus Beale Horton (1835–1883), the first black to be commissioned into the British army, a prolific author, and radical intellectual.[22] Horton was the son of a liberated slave. He had the vision of a free, united Africa. As early as 1859, he remarked in his doctoral thesis that the Krumen, Yoruba, and Igbo would, through intermarriage, produce the leading race for Africa. He saw theories of racial inferiority as misleading. While not denying differences in stage of civilization between blacks and whites, he attributed this not to race but to 'external circumstances'. He dismissed negative views that found Africa incapable and argued that the black race would take its place in the history of the civilized world. He compared African history with that of Europe and saw hope on the horizon:

> 'Rome was not built in a day'; the proudest kingdom in Europe was once in a state of barbarism perhaps worse than now exists among the people inhabiting the West Coast of Africa; and it is an incontrovertible axiom that what has been done can again be done. If Europe, therefore, has been raised to her present pitch of civilization by progressive advancement, Africa too, with a guarantee of the civilization of the north, will rise into equal importance.[23]

He advocated policies for change: Africans must liberate themselves from the notion of inferiority; they must seek political independence, self-government that would enable them to govern themselves in a more orderly and progressive manner; they must all unite. He was of the view that whatever inadequacies were to be found in Africa would be corrected by education.[24]

An elite network emerged during the nineteenth century, one that was sustained for over a hundred years, until it was redefined by 'territorial nationalism', which privileged the emerging nation-state. In West Africa, Freetown was the leading center of intellectual production for a while. The Krio of Sierra Leone essentially comprised liberated African slaves from West Africa, primarily Yoruba, Nova Scotians from Canada, and Maroons from Jamaica. They were predisposed to new thinking about the Self and Africa as a result of the conditions of slavery, their loss of connection to their original homeland, their contact with other cultures, their suffering, and their weak linkages with other African groups in Sierra Leone. Their intellectualism appears to have been primarily focused on how to combine European and African cultures. In this activity the Krio were defining themselves as a new ethnic and cultural group, in the process becoming maligned by other groups as neither African nor European.[25] The Krio contributed to the spread of Western education and culture in West Africa and acted as agents of modernization and instigators of nationalism. From 1839 onward, the Krio began to disperse to other parts of West Africa, notably Southern Nigeria.

In Nigeria, the Krio and other liberated slaves who returned to Nigeria from Sierra Leone and elsewhere after 1840 were known as the Saro.[26] They cherished education, and many served as native agents of missionaries in converting fellow Africans. Based mainly in Abeokuta and Lagos, the most successful among them took to the new occupations of medicine, law, trade, and the clergy, and many distinguished themselves as missionaries and traders. Many regarded themselves as mediators between the indigenous population and Europeans. Ethiopianism took deep root among a number of them; they established independent Churches and demanded a number of reforms. Of the prominent intellectuals who emerged, J.A. Otonba Payne was a pioneer historian, writing short accounts of the Yoruba and attempting to provide chronicles of annual events.[27] There was also J.O. George, another famous antiquarian.[28]

In Gold Coast (Ghana), the elite behaved more like its Nigerian counterpart rather than like the Krio of Sierra Leone. John Mensah Sarbah (1864–1910) founded the first cultural organization, the Mfatsi Amanbuhu Feku (Fanti National Society), which was interested in the collection and compilation of indigenous history and culture. While this intention was initially shared by a few of Sarbah's colleagues, the emphasis was not sustained,[29] although Sarbah himself wrote two important books.[30] The organization was subsequently transformed into the country's first political party, the Gold Coast ARPS, which established a newsletter and encouraged its members to take an interest in indigenous laws and customs. The members of the ARPS sought Western education, but not at the expense of their cultures, and they were part of a new vanguard telling the world that Africans were great achievers. Some of the members also adopted African names, wore African clothing, and encouraged the use of the Fante language. As with their Yoruba counterparts, significant authors emerged among them, including Sarbah, J.E. Casley Hayford, and S.R.B. Attoh Ahuma.[31] These authors and others also worked within the ARPS to criticize British policies.

In French West Africa, Senegal took the lead in receiving ideas from France, generating fresh ones in the communes with their assimilated elite, and transmitting many of these ideas to other French colonies. The Senegal Socialist Party was established in the 1920s and participated in the French Popular Front, a regime that promoted the formation of trade unions in Africa. A few Africans succeeded in becoming prominent in French politics, and a number of French socialists also went to Africa, spreading the ideas of Jaures and Lenin. Arguably, the most sustained idea was that of Négritude, in part an outcome of the French policy of assimilation. In the hands of Senghor, a learned man, poet, and politician, Négritude reached a level of great refinement and profound romanticism. Senghor did not object to Western education or the understanding of other cultures, but the essence of black spirituality was to be maintained. Africa's contribution to civilization was profound, argued Senghor, and aspects of its civilization survived until the present, in intuitive reason and passion.[32] Négritude accused imperialism of attempting to destroy African values and culture.

The sites of intellectual production have been diverse and the genres multiple. If the intellectuals presented so far in this chapter became prominent through their connections with state power or as university academics, there have been many others whose career paths and ambitions have been different. One path has been the writing of town histories in the fashion of chronicles. The transition from oral histories to written histories can be seen as one of the major intellectual achievements of the last one hundred years or so. If academic historians were later to work for the integration and acceptance of oral traditions into history writing, their predecessors successfully turned the tradition into their major source of writing outstanding town and national histories. The writers were many, but among the famous were Sir Apollo Kagwa of Uganda, Carl Reindorf of Ghana, Samuel Johnson, Jacob Ehgharevba, and Akiga Sai of Nigeria, Hampate Ba of Mali, and Boubou Hama of Niger.[33] These writers resorted to oral testimonies, mainly transmitted spoken words and eyewitness accounts. The testimonies were transmitted from one generation to another in the context of the culture of each society. The majority of African societies preserved their historical traditions and customs in this manner.

By writing historical texts, the authors were making a profound contribution to knowledge; they were converting oral traditions to written forms, a process that preserved the traditions and made them available to a wider audience. Writing at a time when the impact of colonialism was still minimal, they were able to observe the producers and cultures of the events they were describing and the traditions they were using. They contributed to the creation of written sources that a later generation has relied upon for the construction of historical knowledge. If the bulk of the writings on Africa by Africans have concentrated on the nineteenth and twentieth centuries, one reason is the abundance of written materials. Writers like Samuel Johnson and Carl Reindorf provided the materials that have made possible subsequent historical reconstruction by academic historians. As Africans, they provided an alternative way of looking at a variety of institutions and events in contrast to the way in which European sources had presented them. Thus, in a way, the writings are insiders' accounts. To take one example, if European writers had presented missionary enterprises and imperialism in a glorious light, some African writers offered a contrary opinion or emphasized the African side of the encounter. Indeed, some of the works of this era have become the 'authentic voices' of Africans.[34]

The years before the Second World War witnessed a consolidation of the intellectual movement started by Blyden. African elites of this generation were more activists than intellectuals, thus pushing the frontier of nationalism to a higher level. Their intellectual focus was no different from Blyden's: how to retain African culture, how to borrow from Western civilization without destroying African culture, and how to blend imported with local cultures. To use the dictum of Senghor, Africans should assimilate, but not be assimilated. They theorized about cultural reforms. Not all the writers sought a distinction between politics and knowledge, as they combined to defend their continent and its people, to reveal the heritage of Africa, and to demonstrate their own ability to think. This class of elites refocused nationalism to a set of ideas and power. There must be educational opportunities and jobs for all qualified members of the educated elite. Some among them, including J.G. Campbell, regarded the nineteenth-century abolitionist phase as the ideal, the time when educated Africans such as Bishop Crowther occupied leading positions in the ministry. Africans must be invested with power, sharing it with Europeans. They were the leaders of their people, not followers to be treated like political inferiors. The Europeans must include them in the administration, not all Africans, to be sure, but the best minds among them. If a bridge were to be built to reach the masses, the elites must be the architects, as they understood Africans in a way Europeans could not. Beside J.G. Campbell, Mojola Agbebi and Kobina Sekyi were also outstanding.

During the later years of the twentieth century a group of African elites who eventually entered the nationalist movements as territorial advocates emerged. These men led their different countries to independence starting from the end of the first half of the twentieth century, and to a greater extent during the 1960s. As the system became more repressive and antagonistic toward the elite, the intelligentsia became more critical of the system, rejecting the moderate ideas propounded by people like Casely Hayford. In the 1930s, men such as J.B. Danquah of Gold Coast and Herbert Macaulay of Nigeria were asking for more. From the late 1930s onward, a radical moment descended on the continent, with unanimity that freedom meant the transfer of power and the dismantling of the empire. Shouts of 'immediate self-government' by men such as Nnamdi Azikiwe of Nigeria and Kwame Nkrumah of Ghana filled the air.

Kwame Nkrumah was born on September 18, 1909, in the Western Region of Gold Coast. He attended a Catholic elementary school and later the Government Teachers Training College in Gold Coast. From 1931 to 1934, he served as a schoolteacher, and became exposed to the Pan-Africanist ideas of Marcus Garvey and W.E.B. Du Bois. In 1935, he traveled to the USA for higher education, attending Lincoln University, a black college. While a college student, he was a member of the African Students Association, took a keen interest in black culture, and studied some of the papers in the Schomburg Collection of the African Diaspora in 1936. His advanced degree focused on the 'Philosophy of Imperialism' and the indigenous philosophy of the Akan people of Ghana. By the time Nkrumah returned from his study abroad, he had developed anti-racist ideas. Like his contemporaries, he began to write, work within associations, join protest movements, and develop long-lasting and productive associations with such notable Pan-Africanists as W.E.B. Du Bois and George Padmore.[35] He developed a keen interest in African cultures, partly in order to demonstrate that there was nothing inferior about them. He lambasted the colonialist debasement of African culture:

> [Africans] were trained to be inferior copies of Englishmen, caricatures to be laughed at with our pretensions to British gentility, our grammatical faultiness and distorted standards betraying us at every turn. We were denied the knowledge of our African past and informed that we had no present. What future

could there be for us? We were taught to regard our culture and traditions as barbarous and primitive. Our text-books were English text-books, telling us about English history, English geography, English customs, English ideas, English weather.[36]

His style was radical, combative, and often polemical. He declared in 1945 that:

[o]nly the united movement of the colonial people, determined to assert its right to independence, can impel any colonial power to lay down its 'whiteman's burden', which rests heavily on the shoulders of the so-called 'backward' peoples, who have been subjected, humiliated, robbed, and degraded to the level of cattle.[37]

Nkrumah's strategy was to mobilize peasants and workers to capture power in order to create a better society. The people could take to non-violent protest, as advocated by Mahatma Gandhi, and African intellectuals must support all anti-colonial struggles. His theories were tested in Gold Coast where he led the nationalist movement to independence.[38] He was originally invited in 1947 to join the United Gold Coast Convention (UGCC), led by J.B. Danquah, with key members drawn from the professional middle class. By 1948, it was clear that Nkrumah's strategy did not conform to that of the party. In November of the same year, he founded the Convention People's Party (CPP). The CPP used the media to radicalize anti-colonial nationalism. In 1951, CPP won the majority of seats in the new assembly, and Nkrumah became the first prime minister. Further agitation for independence led to a new constitution in 1954, internal self-government, and the transfer of ministerial responsibility to Africans. In 1956, the CPP won the elections yet again, and Ghana became independent a year later.

In Nigeria, Nnamdi Azikiwe was equally prominent, with a remarkable political career and prolific writing talents.[39] Born in 1904, he had direct exposure to the colonial bureaucracy and to colonial changes. His father worked as a clerk for the government and lived with his son in an emerging, heterogeneous Nigerian city. Azikiwe himself worked for the government, complained about the slowness of career mobility, and, in 1925, traveled to the USA for further education. He was influenced by the Pan-Africanist ideas of Marcus Garvey and George Padmore. From the 1930s onward, he became a radical anti-colonial fighter. His philosophy and works incorporate virtually all the major strands in African political thought: Pan-Africanism, nationalism, the nation-state, ethnicity, democracy, development, and military rule. He was a learned man as well as a notable activist. Like his contemporaries, he called for colonial disengagement and blamed many of Africa's woes on the Europeans.

He was persuaded by the ideas of leading African–American thinkers such as W.E.B. Du Bois and Leo Hansberry. He returned to West Africa in 1934, where he emerged as a leading nationalist. He established his newspaper in Nigeria, the *West African Pilot*, in 1937. In a politically astute manner, he turned his media into an extension of his personal politics and a vehicle to express anti-British propaganda, beginning to mobilize the people. At the same time, he was enunciating a political philosophy: that Africans must wrest control from Europeans, unite, overcome all divisive politics, and solve the problem of the 'colonial mentality', that is, the feeling that everything European was superior.[40] Azikiwe was not just a writer but a front-line activist. When he joined the Nigerian Youth Movement in 1938, he invigorated it with his zeal and energy. Not long afterward, Nigerian politics abandoned Pan-Africanism and also moved away from the nationalist vision of a united Nigeria in favor of regionalism. Azikiwe had to fight with an emerging member of the Yoruba elite, Obafemi Awolowo (1909–1987), who was equally interested in power. Awolowo chose the path of federalism and nationalism, and his strategy of building an ethnic-based political party may be interpreted as undercutting Pan-Africanism. Also a prolific writer, journalist, and businessman, Awolowo's own strategy was that the regions of Nigeria should develop in a federal system.[41]

In 1942, Azikiwe, teamed with others to establish the National Council of Nigeria and the Cameroons (NCNC), which later became the National Council of Nigerian Citizens. For a while, the NCNC still projected a national image, but the pressure of regionalism eventually turned it into an Eastern regional party. While consolidating his power in the East, Azikiwe continued to work with others to press for European disengagement. He never achieved what he wanted the most, the leadership of Nigeria, but he was abundantly rewarded as the first indigenous premier of Eastern Nigeria and later the governor-general (and later ceremonial president) of independent Nigeria.[42]

Conclusion

Although this chapter focuses on modern elites, pre-nineteenth century African societies had each had their own elites, classified here as traditional elites. These had been equally important in the production of knowledge in the continent. The major strengths of their works include: their ability to study Africans from the African point of view, thereby challenging the biased nature of early European records on the continent, the documentation of Africa's oral tradition, thus setting the stage for academic historians to reconstruct town and national histories by relying on these records as their primary sources. Also important is the fact that traditional elites provided alternative ways of studying Africa.

As was the case with the infrastructures instituted by Europeans to exploit Africa, the same exploitative measures were extended by the Europeans in the development of Western education in Africa. Africans were considered important only for positions that would keep them in perpetual subordination to the Europeans. But with the gains of Western education, modern African elites, beginning from the nineteenth century, continuously challenged European dominance in their own land. With the nationalist ideas gained through their studies at home and abroad, African elites engaged in continuous activism, demanding greater freedom for Africa. They employed their educated minds and used various media in their push for African freedom: the mass media, propaganda, demonstrations/mass action, formation of pressure groups, some of which were later transformed into political parties, and, very importantly, writing. With these weapons, nationalist activities in Africa touched on the cultural, political, and territorial integrity of Africa.

The fact that the elites were small in number constituted them into subaltern groups. Yet, they were able to break through this limitation and speak up. Contrary to the logic that subaltern groups cannot speak for themselves, the success of these elites thus questions the idea that defines subalternity in terms of numbers. Their success show that armed with necessary weapons and ideas, any group, no matter how small, can confront its challenges, overcome its limitations, overthrow its task masters, and establish its freedom.

Notes

1. In 2001, Toyin Falola published a detailed analysis of this topic. Certain aspects of this chapter emanate from that study. See Toyin Falola, *Nationalism and African Intellectuals* (New York: University of Rochester Press, 2001).
2. Thomas Hodgkin, *Nationalism in Colonial Africa* (New York University Press, 1957), 9. Also refer to J.A. Hobson, *Imperialism: A Study* (London: G. Allen Unwin Ltd. 1938); and Norman Angell, *The Great Illusion* (London: Heinemann, 1935).
3. Thomas Hodgkin, *Nationalism in Colonial Africa*, 9; Frederick Lugard, *The Dual Mandate in Tropical Africa* (Edinburgh: William Blackwood and Sons, 1922); and Margery Perham, *Native Administration in Nigeria* (London: Oxford University Press, 1937).
4. Thomas Hodgkin, *Nationalism in Colonial Africa*, 10; Paul Henry, "The European Heritage," in *Africa Today*, ed. Grove Haines (Baltimore: John Hopkins Press, 1955).
5. Royal Institute of International Affairs, *Nationalism: A Report by a Study Group of Members of the Royal Institute of International Affairs* (London: Oxford University Press, 1939).
6. Thomas Hodgkin, *Nationalism in Colonial Africa*, 10-13.
7. Toyin Falola, *Yoruba Gurus: Indigenous Production of Knowledge in Africa* (Trenton, New Jersey: Africa World Press, 1999), 2.
8. Ibid., 3-4.
9. See for instance, Okechukwu Ikejiani, ed., *Nigerian Education* (Lagos: Longman, 1964).
10. J.F. Ade Ajayi, *Christian Missions in Nigeria, 1841-1891: The Making of a New Elite* (London: Longman, 1965).

11. David Kimble, *A Political History of Ghana: The Rise of Gold Coast Nationalism, 1850-1928* (Oxford: Clarendon Press, 1963), 84–87.
12. C.P. Groves, *The Planting of Christianity in Africa, Vol. 2.* (London: Lutterworth Press, 1955), 136.
13. See for instance, J.F. Ade Ajayi, "The American Factor in the Development of Higher Education in Africa," *James Coleman Memorial Paper Series*, no. 1 (Los Angeles: 1988).
14. Hodgkin, *Nationalism in Colonial Africa*, 13. See also, The United Nations, Special Study on Educational Conditions in Non-Self-Governing Territories (1954), Chap. 6.
15. Toyin Falola, *Nationalism and African Intellectuals*, 64.
16. Hodgkin, *Nationalism in Colonial Africa*, 14–15. For more insights on the emergence of new political leadership in Africa see; Philip Garigue, "Changing Political Leadership in West Africa," *Africa: Journal of the International African Institute* XXXIV, no. 3 (1954): 220–32.
17. The book, which was completed in 1889, appeared in book format in 1895, without a major publisher; perhaps the publication was paid for by the author after the Basel Mission had shown little or no interest. A second edition was later published by the Basel Mission in Switzerland. A reprint was undertaken by Ghana Universities Press in 1966. Ray Jenkins has observed that the second edition contains a number of additions not found in the first, although he does not dismiss the value of either edition. Jenkins, "Impeachable Source? On the Use of the Second Edition of Reindorf's History as a Primary Source for the Study of Ghanaian History," Part I, *History in Africa*, 4 (1977): 123–47; Part II, 5 (1978): 81–100.
18. *West Africa*, March 8, 1930. Cited in Kimble, *Political History*, 521.
19. See for instance, Carl Reindorf, ed., *Remembering the Rev. Carl Reindorf* (Accra: self-published, n.d.).
20. C.C. Reindorf, *History of the Gold Coast and Asante* (Basel: Basel Mission, 1895), 4–5.
21. Ibid., x.
22. An important study on this figure has been carried out by Toyin Falola, *Pioneer, Patriot, and Patriarch: Samuel Johnson and the Yoruba People* (Madison: African Studies program, University of Wisconsin-Madison, 1993).
23. Samuel Johnson, *The History of the Yoruba from the Earliest Times to the Beginning of the British Protectorate*, ed. O. Johnson (Lagos: CMS, 1921), vii.
24. Ibid., 642.
25. Akintola Wyse and C. Magbaily Fyle, "Kriodom: A Maligned Club," *Journal of the Historical Society of Sierra Leone* 3, nos. 1 and 2 (1969), 37–44; Akintola Wyse, *The Krio of Sierra Leone: An Interpretive History* (London: C. Hurst, 1989).
26. See: Jean Herskovits Kopytoff, *A Preface to Modern Nigeria: The "Sierra Leonaians" in Yoruba, 1830-1890* (Madison, University of Wisconsin Press, 1965); Kristin Mann, *Marrying Well: Marriage, Status, and Social Change among the Educated Elite in Colonial Lagos* (Cambridge: Cambridge University Press, 1985); and Mac Dixon-Flye, *A Saro Community in the Niger Delta, 1912-1984: The Potts Johnson of Port Harcourt and Their Heirs* (Rochester, New York: University of Rochester Press, 1999).

27. See J.A. Otonba Payne, *Historical Notices of the Yoruba People, Table of Principal Events in Yoruba History* (Lagos: self, 1893).
28. *Historical Notes on the Yoruba Country and Its Tribes* (Lagos: self, 1895).
29. David Kimble, *A Political History of Ghana: The Rise of Gold Coast Nationalism, 1850–1928* (Oxford: Clarendon Press, 1963), 517–20.
30. Johnson Mensah Sarbah, *Fanti Customary Laws* (1897; reprint ed., London: Frank Cass, 1968); and *Fanti National Constituion...* (1906; reprint ed., London: Frank Cass, 1968).
31. Attoh Ahuma, *Memoirs of West African Celebrities* (Liverpool: D. Marples, 1905).
32. Leopold Senghor, "What is Negritude?" *West Africa*, no. 4 (1961): 1211.
33. See, for instance, Akiga Sai, *Akiga's Story: The Tiv Tribe as Seen by One of Its Members* (Oxford: Oxford University Press, 1939); Jacob Egharevba, *A Short History of Benin* (Lagos: CMS Bookshop, 1963). A number of interpretive essays have been written on these chronicles, especially in the journal *History in Africa*.
34. See, for example, Samuel Johnson, *The History of the Yoruba*. Details on Samuel Johnson could also be found in Michel R. Doortmont, "Recapturing the Past: Samuel Johnson and the Construction of Yoruba History" (Ph.D. thesis, Erasmus University, Rotterdam, 1994). Also important is, Carl Reindorf, *History of the Gold Coast and Asante*.
35. For more details on Nkrumah's life and activism, see Kwame Nkrumah, *The Auto-Biography of Kwame Nkrumah* (New York: International Publishers, 1971); and Kwame Arhin, ed., *The Life and Work of Kwame Nkrumah* (Trenton, NJ: Africa World Press, 1993).
36. Kwame Nkrumah, *Africa Must Unite* (London: Heinemann, 1963, reprint, New York: International Publishers, 1973), 49.
37. Kwame Nkrumah, *Towards Colonial Freedom* (London: Panaf Books, 1962).
38. See, for instance, David Birmingham, *Kwame Nkrumah: The Father of African Nationalism* (Athens: Ohio University Press, 1990); and Arhin, ed., *The Life and Work of Kwame Nkrumah*.
39. Examples include: Nnamdi Azikiwe, *Zik: A Selection from the Speeches of Nnamdi Azikiwe* (Cambridge: Cambridge University press, 1961). His career has generated a great deal of literature, usually adulatory by his followers and admirers. See, for instance, Agbafor Igwe, *Zik: The Philosopher of Our Time* (Enugu: Fourth Dimension, 1992); M.S.O. Olisa and O.M. Ikejiani-Clark, eds., *Azikiwe and the African Revolution* (Onitsha: Africana FEP Publishers, 1989).
40. Nnmadi Azikiwe, *Renascent Africa* (New York: Negro University Press, 1937; reprint ed., London: Frank Cass, 1966). See also his essay, "In Defense of Liberia," *Journal of Negro History*, no. 17 (1952): 30–50.
41. On Awolowo, see, for instance, *Awo: The Autobiography of Chief Obafemi Awolowo* (Cambridge: Cambridge University Press, 1960); and Francis Ishola, Ogunmodede, *Chief Obafemi Awolowo's Socio-Political Philosophy: A Critical Interpretation* (Rome: Pontifica Universitas, 1986).
42. For Nnamdi Azikiwe's political career, see, K.A.B. Jones-Quartey, *A Life of Azikiwe* (Baltimore: Penguin Books, 1965).

Bibliography

Ahuma, Attoh. *Memoirs of West African Celebrities*. Liverpool: D. Marples, 1905.
Ajayi, J.F. Ade. *Christian Missions in Nigeria, 1841–1891: The Making of a New Elite*. London: Longman, 1965.
———. "The American Factor in the Development of Higher Education in Africa." *James Coleman Memorial Paper Series*, no. 1 (Los Angeles: 1988): 19–23.
Arhin, Kwame, ed. *The Life and Work of Kwame Nkrumah*. Trenton, NJ: Africa World Press, 1993.
Awolowo, Obafemi. *Awo: The Autobiography of Chief Obafemi Awolowo*. Cambridge: Cambridge University Press, 1960.
Azikiwe, Nnamdi. *Renascent Africa*. New York: Negro University Press, 1937.
———. "In Defense of Liberia." *Journal of Negro History*, no. 17 (1952): 30–50.
———. *Zik: A Selection from the Speeches of Nnamdi Azikiwe*. Cambridge: Cambridge University Press, 1961.
Birmingham, David. *Kwame Nkrumah: The Father of African Nationalism*. Athens: Ohio University Press, 1990.
Dixon-Flye, Mac *A Saro Community in the Niger Delta, 1912–1984: The Potts Johnson of Port Harcourt and Their Heirs*. Rochester, NY: University of Rochester Press, 1999.
Doortmont, Michel R. "Recapturing the Past: Samuel Johnson and the Construction of Yoruba History." Ph.D. thesis, Erasmus University, Rotterdam, 1994.
Egharevba, Jacob. *A Short History of Benin*. Lagos: CMS Bookshop, 1963.
Falola, Toyin. *Pioneer, Patriot, and Patriarch: Samuel Johnson and the Yoruba People*. Madison: African Studies program, University of Wisconsin-Madison, 1993.
———. *Yoruba Gurus: Indigenous Production of Knowledge in Africa*. Trenton, NJ: Africa World Press, 1999.
———. *Nationalism and African Intellectuals*. New York: University of Rochester Press, 2001.
Garrigue, Philip, "Changing Political Leadership in West Africa." *Africa: Journal of the International African Institute* XXXIV, no. 3 (1954): 220–32.
Groves, C.P. *The Planting of Christianity in Africa, Vol. 2*. London: Lutterworth Press, 1955.
Henry, Paul. "The European Heritage." In *Africa Today*, ed. Grove Haines. Baltimore: John Hopkins Press, 1955.
Hobson, J.A. *Imperialism: A Study*. London: G. Allen Unwin Ltd. 1938.
Hodgkin, Thomas. *Nationalism in Colonial Africa*. New York University Press, 1957.
Igwe, Agbafor. *Zik: The Philosopher of Our Time*. Enugu: Fourth Dimension, 1992.
Ikejiani, Okechukwu, ed. *Nigerian Education*. Lagos: Longman, 1964.
Johnson, Samuel. *The History of the Yoruba from the Earliest Times to the Beginning of the British Protectorate*. Lagos: CMS, 1921.
Jones-Quartey, K.A.B. *A Life of Azikiwe*. Baltimore: Penguin Books, 1965.
Kimble, David. *A Political History of Ghana: The Rise of Gold Coast Nationalism, 1850–1928*. Oxford: Clarendon Press, 1963.
Kopytoff, Herskovits Jean. *A Preface to Modern Nigeria: The "Sierra Leonaians" in Yoruba, 1830–1890*. Madison: University of Wisconsin Press, 1965.
Lugard, Frederick. *The Dual Mandate in Tropical Africa*. Edinburgh: William Blackwood and Sons, 1922.

Mann, Kristin. *Marrying Well: Marriage, Status, and Social Change among the Educated Elite in Colonial Lagos.* Cambridge: Cambridge University Press, 1985.

Nkrumah, Kwame. *Towards Colonial Freedom.* London: Panaf Books, 1962.

———. *Africa Must Unite.* London: Heinemann, 1963.

———. *The Auto-Biography of Kwame Nkrumah.* New York: International Publishers, 1971.

Ogunmodede, Francis Ishola. *Chief Obafemi Awolowo's Socio-Political Philosophy: A Critical Interpretation.* Rome: Pontifica Universitas, 1986.

Olisa, M.S.O., and Ikejiani-Clark, O.M., eds. *Azikiwe and the African Revolution.* Onitsha: Africana FEP Publishers, 1989.

Payne, Otonba J.A. *Historical Notices of the Yoruba People, Table of Principal Events in Yoruba History.* Lagos: self, 1893.

———. *Historical Notes on the Yoruba Country and Its Tribes.* Lagos: self, 1895.

Perham, Margery. *Native Administration in Nigeria.* London: Oxford University Press, 1937.

Reindorf Carl. *History of the Gold Coast and Asante.* Basel: Basel Mission, 1895.

———. "History as a Primary Source for the Study of Ghanaian History." Part I, *History in Africa* 4 (1977): 123–47; Part II, 5 (1978): 81–100.

———, ed. *Remembering the Rev. Carl Reindorf.* Accra: self-published, n.d.

Royal Institute of International Affairs. *Nationalism: A Report by a Study Group of Members of the* Royal Institute of International Affairs. London: Oxford University Press, 1939.

Sai, Akiga. *Akiga's Story: The Tiv Tribe as Seen by One of Its Members.* Oxford: Oxford University Press, 1939.

Sarbah, Johnson Mensah. *Fanti Customary Laws* London: Frank Cass, 1968.

———. *Fanti National Constitution.* 1906. reprint ed., London: Frank Cass, 1968.

Senghor, Leopold. "What is Negritude?" *West Africa*, no. 4 (1961): 1211.

United Nations. Special Study on Educational Conditions in Non-Self-Governing Territories, (1954), Chap. 6.

Wyse, Akintola, and Fyle, Magbaily C. "Kriodom: A Maligned Club." *Journal of the Historical Society of Sierra Leone* 3, nos. 1 and 2 (1969): 37–44.

———. *The Krio of Sierra Leone: An Interpretive History.* London: C. Hurst, 1989.

CHAPTER 26

Decolonization Histories

Robert M. Maxon

'Decolonization' is a term used to denote the process by which colonial territories became independent states. In Africa it was a historical course that stretched over several decades in the twentieth century and involved multiple actors and factors.[1] The different time frames as well as the varied factors involved in decolonization mean that while there were similarities that marked the path to independent status for African states, many differences characterized this transition. These reflected regional variations and differing policies and approaches of the colonial powers. Even neighboring colonies controlled by the same European ruler experienced the decolonization process at varied speeds that were the result of different sets of variables. One narrative or interpretation does not fit all cases. Thus, the term 'decolonization histories' is appropriate for this discussion.

In general, scholars recognize three sets of factors or forces at work that influenced the process of African decolonization and produced varying decolonization histories. These were African, metropolitan, and international.[2] All were significant in varying degrees, and they often influenced each other. Of these, the African factors will be most closely examined in this chapter, as what happened in Africa, as well as the colonial rulers' perception of why, proved most influential.

Also important to consider are the varied paths to the creation of independent states that characterized decolonization histories. One was a handover of power to an elite within the African dependency that was unrepresentative of the populace at large with the transition characterized by the absence of democratic elections and universal human rights. A second path

R.M. Maxon (✉)
History Department, West Virginia University, Morgantown, WV, USA

© The Author(s) 2018
M.S. Shanguhyia and T. Falola (eds.),
The Palgrave Handbook of African Colonial and Postcolonial History,
https://doi.org/10.1057/978-1-137-59426-6_26

was the emergence of an independent state based upon a negotiated settlement between the colonial power and African leaders validated by universal-suffrage elections and democratic constitutions. The third path involved wars of liberation where independence was wrung from the colonial power or unrepresentative minority by guerilla conflicts lasting longer than a decade followed by the dominance of a single political movement or party usually associated with the victorious insurgent force.

Overall, decolonization histories were marked by similarities though the outcome for each colony was unique, reflecting local realities. There thus has been, and continues to be, a division of opinion among scholars in the assessment of African decolonization. The relative weights to be given to African, metropolitan, and international factors remain open to differing views. The brief summary that follows seeks to illustrate this through a regional and chronological account.

Forces/Factors

Despite disagreement on the relative significance of the three sets of forces, there is a good deal of agreement as to what they actually were. Among the metropolitan are normally counted the weakened military and economic status of the European colonial powers that were the result of the Second World War. These made it hard for them to hold on to African colonies after 1945. Wartime propaganda which had focused on opposition to authoritarian rule and racism had an impact on the populace in the metropoles and colonies in undermining support for colonial rule. Also influential on the people, particularly in Britain and France, was the need to rebuild shattered economies as well as increase spending in support of improvements in welfare (e.g. education, health care, and housing). The means of financing these postwar economic and social necessities came to constitute a significant reason for the European colonial powers to adopt a strategy of 'developmentalist empire' after the war that had such a huge impact in speeding the end of empire in Africa itself.[3]

Among international forces, on the other hand, scholars have counted the changing international balance of power after the Second World War. Britain and France (to say nothing of Belgium and Portugal) were no longer great powers. The superpowers after the war, the USA and the Soviet Union, were both, at least in theory, anti-imperialist. The independence of Asian colonies of European powers, such as India, Pakistan, and Indonesia in the 1940s, proved important international examples for the African colonies. The newly formed United Nations also provided an international focus for pressure for decolonization, particularly from the newly independent countries mentioned above, and through the actions of that body's Trusteeship Council.

Examined more broadly, a critical international factor was the changed process of globalization after the war. As A.G. Hopkins noted, changes in the world economy reduced the value of colonial forms of integration. A changed economic environment now favored an Africa consisting of independent states rather than a continent of dependent territories.[4] Britain, France, Belgium, and even Portugal actually speeded up African decolonization in their attempts to exploit this postwar globalization.

The most important set of forces/factors, however, were African. The opposition to colonial rule within the various colonial territories (including technically independent South Africa) was clearly most critical. This was provoked by varied reasons and took different forms, but the emergence of discontent with colonial rule and its eventual rejection by large segments of the population brought an end to European colonial rule in Africa.[5] Among the most fundamental causes for this situation was the rebounding of the Second World War and Cold War propaganda that emphasized democracy and human rights. In Africa, as in Britain and France, 'the propagation and implementation of principles of human and civil rights undercut systems of domination' based on racial and cultural superiority.[6] Increasing numbers of Africans, starting with the educated elite, questioned why such ideals were not applied in the colonies. This was most obvious to the many African men who had fought in the armies of the imperial power during the war. They had fought side by side with European soldiers, but returned to Africa as second-class citizens. Moreover, opposition to colonial policies emerged in Africa from the earliest days of colonial control, and continued into the era of decolonization. These included opposition to the brutality and discrimination practiced by most colonial states, economic exploitation, taxation without representation, and lack of economic opportunity. Such causes of anti-colonial activities continued into the period of decolonization, and they were enhanced by the post-Second World War policies of the colonial powers framed to promote economic and social development in their African colonies.

This initiative, often termed the 'second colonial occupation of Africa', reflected the ideal of developmentalist empire. The European powers had done relatively little to develop their colonies economically and socially (e.g. schools, hospitals, health clinics, urban housing) prior to 1945, but thereafter development was to be spurred for the metropolitan reasons noted above as well as to exploit African resources more efficiently. The economic expansion that characterized most African colonies during the war demonstrated potential opportunities for further growth, especially in the areas of agricultural and mineral exports. The fact that colonial rule was under attack in Africa and other parts of the world was another reason for pushing the strategy of developmentalist empire. A particularly important reason was one often overlooked in accounts of decolonization that emphasize metropolitan and international factors: this was the growing demand among Africans for an expansion of formal education, greater influence within an expanding economy, and an increased voice in the administration of the political entity within which they lived. There can be little doubt that it was the political, economic, and social changes in Africa before, during, and after the war that had 'the greatest impact on the process that led to the end of colonial rule in Africa'.[7]

As the process worked itself out, what was involved was nothing less than the failure of the colonial state all over Africa. The irony here was that these colonial states sought ambitiously to intrude much more extensively than ever before in the lives of Africa's peoples.[8] The attempts to enhance economic and social change led to pressure on peasants, traders, and workers that hit women disproportionately and provoked massive resistance. Likewise, the expansion of formal education so as to facilitate economic expansion produced an ever greater desire among the African population for such education which colonial states found it impossible to meet. The developmentalist push brought forth another fundamental contradiction in putting less emphasis on political change. This led to even greater pressure for expanding African political and administrative participation within the colonial state. In the end, the inability of the colonial states to meet the economic, social, and political demands of their populations led to political independence as the outcome.

Timing

Decolonization in Africa was a twentieth-century phenomenon, and whereas the majority of independent states achieved that status after the Second World War, some colonies gained political independence earlier. The Union of South Africa moved from British colony to self-rule in 1910 with full independence the result of the 1931 Statute of Westminster. Egypt, while not officially a colony, became independent of British rule in 1922. Libya gained independence from Italy in 1951 under the auspices of the United Nations, with a monarchy in control. These early examples of decolonization fit the first path to independence noted above in that they gained political independence without full participation of the majority of the population in the political process.

The independence of most African colonies, on the other hand, fell within the period 1955–1968. Most gained political independence as a result of a negotiated settlement with the colonial power. Nevertheless, exceptions to this path may be noted in the experience of Morocco (handover to an unrepresentative elite), and Sudan (government not representative of the population).

The final period of African decolonization stretched from 1974 to 1994. The time frame included the independence of Zimbabwe, Namibia, Eritrea, and Portugal's colonies in Africa. Very significant in this period was transformation of South Africa from a republic ruled by the white minority to a democratic state. This period is notable in that all these states moved to independence as a result, at least in part, of wars of liberation.

SOURCES OF DISCONTENT IN AFRICA

For the period of decolonization after the Second World War, experience in Africa was characterized by opportunities and obstacles. The opportunities mainly resulted from the globalization that impacted Africa during this time. The war had brought some prosperity after a decade of depression marked by a lack of export markets and unemployment. The opportunities to build on this after 1945 reflected a favorable market for African produce and minerals. This was the case for agricultural producers in Africa as well as those seeking employment in industries (such as railways and docks) that depended on agricultural and mineral exports. Employment opportunities expanded for those with professional training, notably teachers. This era also witnessed a substantial upsurge in commerce within the colonies that attracted ever greater African interest. The postwar emphasis on human rights seemed to open the way for greater African participation within the government of the colonial states. The developmentalist approach was an important means that the colonial rulers utilized to take advantage of these opportunities.

As the first two postwar decades unfolded, however, far too many obstacles emerged to restrict and block the opportunities that Africans and their colonial rulers sought to exploit.

Peasants who wished to expand production and sale for market met many problems. These included new priorities and regulations as to which crops to grow and how. The agents of the colonial states, whether expatriate officers or chiefs, met growing opposition to, among other things, crop preferences, cultivation techniques, and soil conservation measures. African workers also encountered numerous obstacles. They were faced by poor working and living conditions and low wages. These had produced labor unrest and strikes before and after the war as in Gold Coast, Nigeria, Kenya, Tanganyika, and in French West Africa where in 1947–1948 the railway system was shut down for months.[9] The system of migrant labor, so common over many parts of colonial Africa, came under stress nearing breakdown. Developmentalist colonialism sought to meet these difficulties in the path of development by coercion, encouraging trade unionism that focused on welfare of workers, and what was termed 'labor stabilization' through the emergence of an urban working class not migrant workers.[10] These measures proved far from effective in both the eyes of colonial officials and subjects. In addition, African traders struggled during the war and its aftermath, for example with the absence of consumer goods. They likewise found obstacles in a developmentalism that placed limits on competition in terms of trading licenses and assistance to aspiring traders.[11]

Perhaps the most important obstacle of all was the 'colonial mentality' that characterized so many of the European civil servants, both administrative and technical, who made up the leadership of the colonial states. Despite the influence of war and postwar ideology, they viewed Africans as 'different' from Europeans in terms of intelligence and culture. Although the prevailing postwar ideology held that difference would, with time, be overcome, leaders of the colonial states and the colonial ministries in Europe believed that this would take many decades. In the meantime, paternalistic thinking held sway that since Africans were not 'ready' to be scientific farmers, productive workers, profitable traders, responsible civil servants, and political leaders, the colonial rulers must call the shots.[12] Such views were enhanced in those colonies where there were numbers of European farmers and wage workers as these groups demanded that the postwar period should mean continued precedence for their interests.

As can be deduced from the above, the key groups in Africa that were impacted by the opportunities and obstacles described were peasants, wage laborers, traders, and the educated elite. These groups often faced different sets of circumstances or challenges, but a majority within each came ultimately to the same conclusion: colonial rule must end.

Peasants all over colonial Africa faced the obstacles noted above and more. Peasant households sought to maximize production of food crops and commodities, but they were faced with widening state restrictions. This situation produced growing discontent that led to significant rural unrest as peasants balked at following the dictates of developmentalism. Wage laborers likewise found obstacles in their way. The attempt to stabilize African workers and create an urban working class encountered many difficulties. Wages continued to be low and did not keep pace with the cost of living in most African cities. Most cities grew rapidly after the war, and the market and the colonial state could not keep pace with the demand for housing, transport, and access to utilities such as water and electricity. Another discontented and influential group in African colonies after the war was traders. This definition included individuals and households ranging from itinerant traders, retail merchants, artisans, produce buyers, wholesalers, to those involved in transport.

The reasons for each group's discontent with the colonial state were varied. African traders in West and East Africa were unhappy with the competition they faced from so called 'foreign' merchants (Syrian and Lebanese in West Africa, and Asian in East Africa). They claimed the colonial state did little to improve opportunities for entering varied forms of commerce and placed other obstacles in the path of African traders such as lack of access to credit, state control of the market, and overregulation. Just as with peasants, the second colonial occupation served to heighten unhappiness among traders.

The last of the groups discontented with state obstacles was the educated elite. These individuals were distinguished by their formal schooling, including university and professional education. Members of this group were initially fewer in number than those described above due to the lack of educational facilities at the high-school level and above in most African colonies. After the war, numbers of schools expanded, but the elite found obstacles in the way of their gaining greater access to education, to civil service jobs, and participation in governance. The group was also greatly impacted by the pervasive racial segregation that characterized most African colonies. The usual answer to demands for greater participation in governance, for example, was that the elite were too small in numbers to be important and that the real representatives of the African population in the colonies were the state-appointed chiefs.

Discontent with the obstacles placed in each group's way found many voices and forms. Those voicing displeasure included local political organizations, trade unions, elite political parties, reform movements focusing on a single issue (e.g. forced soil conservation), and religious movements. As to forms of protest, these included worker stoppages and strikes, protest marches, letters and petitions addressing specific grievances, agitation using African-owned newspapers, and passive resistance (e.g. organized refusal to pay taxes or obey regulations). These escalated further to involve violence in the form of urban or rural riots and armed insurgencies (e.g. the Mau Mau revolt/war in Kenya). The latter produced colonial state violence that further inflamed discontent.

Experience

The different forms of discontent involving the varied groups combined with the colonial powers' perceptions of it to shape the trajectory of Africa's decolonization histories. This produced a changing environment in which neither the colonizer nor the colonized succeeded in calling all the shots or determining the outcome. Protests of varied sorts burst forth in many parts of Africa in the 1940s. Initially, not all sought the creation of an independent state as one of the desired changes. This was true for the leaders of the political parties that emerged in the postwar period, including those that came to adopt a nationalist focus in appealing to varied groups within the colony to support the goal of ending colonial rule. It was also true for the rulers of Britain and France, who recognized the need for political change after the war but thought they could move such changes along lines they thought beneficial. For the rulers of Belgium and Portugal, on the other hand, there was no thought of independence for the African territories they controlled in 1945. These points will be illustrated by the following summary.

The start of what proved to be a relatively rapid process of change from colony to nation-state emerged first in West Africa within the British and French colonies there. Most colonies in this region attained independence between 1957 and 1960. In this transformation, Gold Coast led the way. Here a combination of urban protest and rural unrest led to the emergence of mass nationalism that caused the scuttling of British plans for gradual economic and political development. The years 1947 to 1951 were crucial. Rapid urban growth, including the return of former soldiers. heightened problems with employment, a lack of consumer goods, and housing as the cost of living soared causing urban unrest and strikes; all contributed. In rural areas, a huge wave of discontent resulted from the colonial state's attempts to cope with swollen-shoot disease in cocoa trees. The discontent led to boycotts supported by farmers, workers, traders, and members of the elite, and to the Accra riots of February 1948 that spread to other towns. Eventually, the Convention People's Party (CPP) led by Kwame Nkrumah took the lead in welding together support from the four groups for Nkrumah's goals of self-government now and 'seek ye first the political kingdom'. According to this formula, political independence would be the way to effectively deal with the issues that caused discontent among all groups. The educated elite were to lead the people of the colony to a promised land where Africans, not the colonial rulers, would make the political, economic, and social policy decisions. By 1951, the majority of the voting public backed the CPP; self-government was granted by Britain.

This pattern of political independence, achieved in 1957 as the new state of Ghana, characterized other British colonies in Africa. Faced with a nationalist movement backed by a majority in elections, the British rulers opted to negotiate with, and cede power to, the elite leadership of a nationalist party rather than continue repressive policies, such as those used against the CPP (e.g. arrest of leaders and banning newspapers). From the start of the 1940s, if not earlier, British goals for decolonization in Africa included: insuring the loyalty of the new ruling class to Britain, protecting British material interests in the colony (trade, investment, and access to natural resources), supporting Britain's strategic interests, and standing with Britain internationally in a divided postwar world.[13] Whereas British leaders claimed that their goals had been met in Ghana and elsewhere in British-ruled Africa, in reality the imperial power accommodated itself to African conditions. Decisions were based on the philosophy that it was better to move too fast rather than too slowly so as to sustain satisfactory relations with successor states.

While British rule in other colonies gave way before movements reflecting support for nationalist parties. Ghana's experience illustrated another issue that marked Africa's decolonization histories. This was that the process of protest was characterized by rival nationalisms that reflected regional, religious, and ethnic differences in competing political parties. This was an era, for example, of 'ethnic patriotism' in many colonies.[14] A division of the nationalist movement emerged in Nigeria, Kenya, Uganda, and Angola, to note just a few.

The decolonization experience of the French colonies, on the other hand, witnessed many of the same forces at work in producing discontent, protest, and eventual independence. Here the key period was similarly the postwar years down to 1960. Like the British, the French colonial rulers sought economic development after the war through improved productive techniques, infrastructure, and the conditions of labor. Like the experience in British colonies also, the best laid plans were not fulfilled as the colonial rulers had hoped. Trade-union resistance marked by strikes during the 1946–1948 period pushed the reform movement in new directions, and the agricultural improvement sought through the second colonial occupation did not succeed as hoped, producing new forms of resistance.[15]

Nevertheless, major difference marked the political arena where, unlike in the British experience, politicians participated in metropolitan politics as well as West African ones. A voice in the French legislature was important for events in the 1950s, but African factors turned French colonies away from continued association with France. Politicians aspiring to influence had to build a support base in Africa. For example, Leopold Senghor in Senegal and Felix Houphouët-Boigny in Ivory Coast formed political parties that gained support in urban and rural areas as they took advantage of discontent among farmers, workers, traders, and the elite.

Events in French-ruled Africa thus helped lead to the decolonization of French West and Equatorial Africa by 1960, but here, too, the process proved different to that envisioned by colonial rulers and the ruled. In 1950, it was unclear whether these territories would emerge from the decolonization process as nation-states or as a self-governing units within a federation that was part of a wider French union of territories. The latter seemed to have won out as the French instituted a new policy through the *loi-cadre* (foundation law) of 1956 with gave each territory in French Africa its own government to control a budget and internal administration while France was responsible for defense and foreign affairs.

The final push for decolonization came about because of these forces as well as changes in France. The establishment of the Fifth Republic in 1958, the result of African factors in the form of the Algerian war of liberation, proved influential. French president Charles de Gaulle offered a new relationship with France's territories in Sub-Saharan Africa. In the 1958 referendum, all dependencies but one chose autonomy within the French Union. Only Guinea, led by Sékou Touré, rejected that option and chose immediate independence from France. Within two years, however, the other territories in West and Equatorial Africa became separate nation-states following relatively brief negotiations with the French government. Numerous factors were responsible for this outcome, but African experiences and decisions were decisive.

Another decolonization history of this era associated with a negotiated independence was that of the Belgian Congo. Here the experience deviated from that of British or French West Africa. Dissent and discontent with European domination in the Congo took a variety of forms during the prewar and postwar periods in a dependency characterized by paternalistic colonialism. This had emphasized economic progress and social welfare over politics, and unlike other European colonial territories, the educated elite was extremely small in numbers. This, combined with Belgian policy that only allowed local political organizations in 1954, meant that national political parties did not emerge in the Congo. Not surprisingly, the local associations reflected regional and ethnic differences that later characterized decolonization politics. As the 1950s came to an end, moreover, religious, ethnic, and economic grievances surged and tension heightened, particularly among the urban population of the capital Leopoldville, and in the copper-mining region of Katanga (later Shaba) province. These African factors produced a crucial response from Belgium. Faced in 1959 by riots in the capital, the Belgian government quickly conceded independence to the Congo with minimal preparation for a smooth transfer of power. This decolonization initiative produced. weak government, division, and civil war.

A second stage in African decolonization marked the period 1961–1968. The focus during this period was largely on the eastern and central portions of the continent. The British territories of Kenya, Tanganyika, Uganda, Zanzibar, Nyasaland, and Northern Rhodesia achieved independence during 1961–1964. These territories were viewed by British policymakers as being distinctly different from the West African empire. British rule had begun later in East and Central Africa, and there were significant racial minorities resident there. The latter comprised European farmers in Kenya, Southern Rhodesia, and Tanganyika, Arabs as the ruling minority and plantation owners on Zanzibar, and Asian (people who had come from British India) traders in the East African dependencies. These proved particularly significant so far as British calculations of the future were concerned. These groups wielded economic influence out of proportion to their population size. After the Second World War, Britain applied a policy that became known as multiracialism. It was to provide a means for sharing political power among members of racially defined groups.

This multiracialism implied that independence could be granted when there was 'proper provision' for all 'the main communities' that had made their homes in British East and Central Africa. The policy also meant that Britain had a responsibility to move the African populations more rapidly along 'on the path of political, social and economic progress'.[16] These goals and the policy itself proved impossible to achieve as multiracialism was rejected by the African majority as well as the Europeans. The policy was meant, for example, to protect the economic and political dominance as well as social influence of Kenya's and Southern Rhodesia's European settler community, but it never drew enthusiastic support from the latter.

Opposition to the official policy was one constant reason for the rise of anti-colonial movements and the eventual emergence of mass nationalism, but it was far from the only factor. The legacy of earlier discontent continued to be felt after the Second World War in terms of labor unrest, peasant opposition to the state's market and agricultural policies, religious dissidence, and opposition to colonial land and labor policies that disadvantaged Africans. Just as in other parts of British-ruled Africa, peasants, workers, traders, and the educated elite were increasingly discontented with postwar conditions, including the developmentalist initiatives, in the rural and urban areas.

The most important manifestation of this unhappiness took the form of the Mau Mau revolt/war in Kenya between 1952 and 1956. The British suppressed the armed resistance, but metropolitan policymakers realized that reforms were needed to sustain colonial rule in Kenya and the other East and Central African colonies. While those fighting the British forces for land and freedom were largely drawn from among the landless, poor, and modestly educated people of central Kenya, the discontent underlying the revolt/war exemplified African unhappiness with their lack of voice in politics and administration, little chance for education, the absence of economic and social equality, and the difficulties African farmers and traders faced in gaining access to high-value cash crops, markets, and credit.

In seeking to address the discontent associated with Mau Mau, the British rulers' reform agenda actually speeded the end of colonial rule in Kenya and other East African territories, especially Tanganyika. The rural and urban reforms pushed so vigorously by the colonial state in Tanganyika provoked resistance leading to massive support for the nationalist political party, the Tanganyika African National Union (TANU). Such was the level of support for TANU, that by mid-1959 Tanganyika's last governor, Sir Richard Turnbull, admitted that he was not confident his administration could for much longer rule the colony without facing another major rebellion in East Africa. Faced with this assessment of an important African factor, the British government decided to accede to TANU's demands, agreeing to independence in December 1961.

With this decision, the independence of Uganda (1962), Kenya (1963), and Zanzibar (1963) could not be far behind. In Kenya, for example, attempts by the colonial state to control nationalist dissent (banning nationwide African political parties and manipulating elections) failed in that by the early 1960s resistance to colonial rule had escalated to such an extent in western Kenya as to threaten British control itself. Unlike in Tanganyika's decolonization, divisive forces marked that of Uganda (ethnic, regional, and religious), Kenya (ethnic), and Zanzibar (racial), and presented problems for negotiators. Nevertheless, this final process was characterized by the haste with which British rule was formally ended with no solution to problems that British rule had created (e.g. the Lost Counties in Uganda).

The British Central Africa decolonization experience, on the other hand, was in some ways similar to that of East Africa. Just as there, the multiracial policy faced huge difficulties as a result of opposition from those who were meant to benefit from it. Europeans in Southern Rhodesia had enjoyed internal self-government since 1923 with an all-white legislature and cabinet. They refused to share power with the African majority after the war. In addition, the centerpiece for Britain's implementing the multiracial ideal, the

Central African Federation (officially Federation of Rhodesia and Nyasaland) spurred nationalist opposition.

The federation was established in 1953 linking the three territories (which retained their own territorial administrations) in a federal government (led by a prime minister) and close economic collaboration, but it was imposed in the face of African opposition. The existence of the federation, and African dislike of it, became the most critical factor which drove resistance in the form of mass nationalism. Most of the promised economic benefits of federation went to Southern Rhodesia. However, federation was not the only significant African factor as rural and urban discontent surged to the surface in all three territories as a result of issues such as land shortage, wages and working conditions, discrimination in employment and marketing, and a demand for greater education.

By the end of the 1950s, nationalist political parties had emerged in all three territories with an end of the federation topping the list of demands. In Nyasaland the opposition reached such proportions as to convince the governor to declare a state of emergency in 1959. This involved attempts to suppress the nationalist party by banning it and arresting its leaders, and the Northern Rhodesia administration also banned the largest nationalist party and arrested the party leader. The year 1959 also witnessed similar action by the minority government in Southern Rhodesia. The state actions did not have the desired effect of slowing discontent. The conduct of the Nyasaland emergency drew criticism in Britain and, according to many students of British decolonization, caused the government of Harold Macmillan to move quickly to decolonize in East as well as Central Africa.[17] An important element of the latter was the agreement to dissolve the federation in 1963. Nyasaland reached independence as Malawi and Northern Rhodesia as Zambia in 1964. Decolonization at this time was not the fate of Southern Rhodesia, however; the unwillingness of the ruling white minority meant that a negotiated settlement was not possible.

Instead, decolonization in Southern Rhodesia came about as a result of a war of liberation. This experience placed the British dependency in a category of decolonization histories similar to the Portuguese African territories, Algeria, Eritrea, Namibia, and South Africa. With the exception of Algeria, the histories of the wars of liberation fell in the post-1965 period.

A popular, but simplistic, explanation for this decolonization scenario recognized the strength of many of the forces and factors that produced hostility to colonial rule in those parts of Africa that experienced the rise of nationalism. In the end, however, no agreement on such a transfer proved possible as the colonial powers, such as Portugal, or the minority rulers, such as in Southern Rhodesia (Rhodesia after 1965), refused to give way and grant independence to a successor state in which the majority of the population would have the most powerful voice. The failure to achieve a negotiated decolonization, therefore, led to a war of liberation as the only means to alter a situation marked by growing frustration among the majority of the territory's population.

Wars of liberation reflected this pattern, but they also involved other factors. For example, most, starting with the Algerian conflict, involved Cold War rivalry and shifting support by the Western and Eastern blocs. In most cases, moreover, wars of liberation were not confined territorially to the colonial entity itself, but spilled over into neighboring states. Metropolitan factors were influential here as changes in the system of governance in France and Portugal proved significant in ending the wars in Africa with decolonization.

Yet with wars of liberation also we may see the critical importance of African factors in the decolonization histories. An important one was the division among the liberation forces that grew out of competing political movements seeking an end to foreign or minority domination. This division had important ramifications as far as the wars in Rhodesia (independent as Zimbabwe) and Angola were concerned. Rival armies sought to liberate those territories and establish majority rule.

As in any war, victory in a military sense is important, but these were guerilla conflicts. Victory for the liberation forces often constituted maintaining a presence in the territory and inflicting damage on the enemy. Even more important, it meant winning support of the hearts and minds of the territorial population and maintaining it as the conflict dragged on for years. This African factor was critical for the ultimate success of most wars of liberation. Also significant was the takeover of a portion of the disputed territory by the liberation forces so as to initiate an alternative government that could provide security and services for the people under their rule, as in Mozambique. Weariness with the conflict and its impact among the population backing the rebels as well as the government in each territory was a local force that played a part in ending wars of liberation with decolonization.

South Africa's democratic transformation illustrates these factors and more. It is generally agreed that armed struggle was not, by itself, the key factor. Rather, a combination of changing international pressures together with internal discontent and hostility to the apartheid system, particularly in urban areas, forced the ruling whites to negotiate a transfer of power. Growing trade-union influence and youth discontent with educational and economic opportunities meant that the government was ultimately unable to paper over the contradictions emerging in the system constructed to protect and maintain white supremacy.

One other point may be made with regard to wars of liberation. This was their association with large movements of people. The process of decolonization in any historical era, of course, involved the departure or 'going home' of the colonial rulers.[18] In the twentieth-century African cases, however, movement of peoples constituted more than this. The wars themselves caused movements of refugees. The aftermath of wars provoked an exodus not just of colonial rulers, but of people from the metropole who had come to settle and work in the dependent territory. This was most obvious in the departure of thousands of French from Algeria and Portuguese from Angola and Mozambique that accompanied the transfer of power to a successor regime.[19] This chapter raises this issue as one of many where research will likely provide new insights as to Africa's decolonization histories that occurred over differing time periods and involved regional and other differences. It offers several examples to illustrate the importance of African factors in the process. Though one narrative will not be likely to suffice, decolonization histories offer continued opportunities for significant research contributions to modern African history.

Notes

1. For an overview, see Toyin Falola, *Africa Volume 4: The End of Colonial Rule: Nationalism and Decolonization* (Durham, NC: Carolina Academic Press, 2002).
2. Robert Tignor, *Capitalism and Nationalism at the End of Empire* (Princeton: Princeton University Press, 1998), 5.
3. Frederick Cooper, *Africa Since 1940* (New York: Cambridge University Press, 2002), 74.
4. A.G. Hopkins, "Rethinking Decolonization," *Past and Present* 200 (2008): 215–16.
5. Eritrea gained independence from another African country, Ethiopia.
6. Hopkins, "Rethinking Decolonization," 216.
7. Cheikh Anta Babou, "Decolonization of National Liberation: Debating the End of British Colonial Rule in Africa," *The Annals of the American Academy of Political and Social Science* 642 (2010): 44.
8. Cooper, *Africa Since 1940*, 4.
9. Ibid., 30–32.
10. Ibid., 34.
11. Robert Maxon, *Going Their Separate Ways: Agrarian Transformation in Kenya, 1930–1950* (London: Associated University Presses, 2003), 115–16.
12. Cooper, *Africa Since 1940*, 37.
13. Robert Maxon, *Britain and Kenya's Constitutions, 1950–1960* (Amherst, NY: Cambria Press, 2011), 22–23.
14. Derek Peterson, *Ethnic Patriotism and the East African Revival: A History of Dissent, c. 1935–1972* (New York, Cambridge University Press, 2012), 23–25.
15. Cooper, *Africa Since 1940*, 41–44.
16. Maxon, *Britain and Kenya's Constitutions*, 34–35.
17. Wm. Roger Louis, "The Dissolution of the British Empire," in *The Oxford History of the British Empire Volume IV The Twentieth Century*, ed. Judith M. Brown and Wm. Roger Louis (Oxford: Oxford University Press, 2001), 353.
18. Anthony Kirk-Greene, "Decolonization: The Ultimate Diaspora," *Journal of Contemporary History* 36 (2001): 133–35.
19. Pamila Gupta, "Decolonization and (Dis)possession in Lusophone Africa," in *Mobility Makes States: Migration and Power in Africa*, ed. Darshan Vigneswaran and Joel Quirk (Philadelphia: University of Pennsylvania Press, 2015), 169–70.

BIBLIOGRAPHY

Babou, Cheikh Anta. "Decolonization of National Liberation: Debating the End of British Colonial Rule in Africa." *The Annals of the American Academy of Political and Social Science* 642 (2010): 41–54.

Cooper, Frederick. *Africa Since 1940*. New York: Cambridge University Press, 2002.

Falola, Toyin. *Africa Volume 4: The End of Colonial Rule: Nationalism and Decolonization*. Durham, NC: Carolina Academic Press, 2002.

Gupta, Pamila. "Decolonization and (Dis)possession in Lusophone Africa." In *Mobility Makes States: Migration and Power in Africa*, edited by Darshan Vigneswaran and Joel Quirk, 169–93. Philadelphia: University of Pennsylvania Press, 2015.

Hopkins, A.G. "Rethinking Decolonization." *Past and Present* 200 (2008): 211–47.

Kirk-Greene, Anthony. "Decolonization: The Ultimate Diaspora." *Journal of Contemporary History* 36 (2001): 133–51.

Louis, Wm. Roger. "The Dissolution of the British Empire." In *The Oxford History of the British Empire Volume IV The Twentieth Century*, edited by Judith M. Brown and Wm. Roger Louis, 329–56. Oxford: Oxford University Press, 2001.

Maxon, Robert. *Britain and Kenya's Constitutions, 1950–1960*. Amherst, NY: Cambria Press, 2011.

———. *Going Their Separate Ways: Agrarian Transformation in Kenya, 1930–1950*. London: Associated University Presses, 2003.

Peterson, Derek. *Ethnic Patriotism and the East African Revival: A History of Dissent, c. 1935–1972*. New York, Cambridge University Press, 2012.

Tignor, Robert. *Capitalism and Nationalism at the End of Empire*. Princeton: Princeton University Press, 1998.

Printed by Printforce, United Kingdom